THE
CAMBRIDGE
MODERN HISTORY

VOL. XIII

LONDON
Cambridge University Press
FETTER LANE

NEW YORK · TORONTO
BOMBAY · CALCUTTA · MADRAS
Macmillan

TOKYO
Maruzen Company Ltd

THE
CAMBRIDGE
MODERN HISTORY

PLANNED BY

LORD ACTON

EDITED BY

SIR A. W. WARD

SIR G. W. PROTHERO

AND

SIR STANLEY LEATHES, K.C.B.

VOLUME XIII

GENEALOGICAL TABLES AND LISTS

AND

GENERAL INDEX

NEW YORK: THE MACMILLAN COMPANY

CAMBRIDGE, ENGLAND: AT THE UNIVERSITY PRESS

1934

First Edition, 1911
Reprinted   1931
Cheap edition, 1934

PRINTED IN GREAT BRITAIN

PREFACE TO THE FIRST EDITION

THIS Volume contains a series of *Genealogical Tables and Lists*, the purpose and character of which are described in some preliminary remarks prefixed to this section, and a *General Index* to the twelve preceding Volumes, arranged on principles stated in a brief explanatory note.

The *Genealogical Tables and Lists* have been mainly prepared by Miss Alice D. Greenwood, Somerville College, Oxford; valuable help has also been given by Mr H. G. Aldis, M.A., Peterhouse, Secretary of the University Library. The *General Index* has been compiled by Miss Alice M. Cooke, M.A., formerly of the Acton Department of the University Library, Cambridge, now Lecturer in History at the University of Leeds, with the assistance of Miss Greenwood and Mrs Quiggin. We desire to acknowledge with cordial thanks the aid thus received in bringing our work to its completion.

A. W. W.
G. W. P.
S. L.

CAMBRIDGE
July, 1911

CONTENTS

I

GENEALOGICAL TABLES AND LISTS

PRELIMINARY REMARKS.

THE series of *Tables and Lists* here supplied consists, in the first instance, of *Genealogical Tables* of the sovereign families of European and certain other countries, together with *Lists* of elected potentates, within the period treated in *The Cambridge Modern History*. To these are added *Genealogical Tables* of certain noble houses, with *Lists* of chief ministers of great States, and of governors of important dependencies and colonies, within the same period. Finally, *Lists* are given of English (and British) Parliaments and of Imperial Diets, together with one or two lists of a special kind adverted to below.

These *Tables and Lists* are primarily intended as aids in the use of *The Cambridge Modern History*; and no pretence is made that every one of them is complete in itself. It is, however, hoped that they will be found to supply the information likely to be required by a large proportion of students of modern history, and that no personage of any historical importance has been passed by in the table or list where his or her name ought to find a place. The *Tables and Lists* should throughout be used in conjunction with the *General Index*.

Among the *Genealogical Tables* are included those of various families which were prominent in European Succession questions, or took a leading part in the civil and religious wars of the sixteenth and seventeenth centuries. Room has been found for *Tables* of certain other families of which various members are not easily identifiable in the usual books of reference. Thus, several notable Irish clans are given. On the other hand, it has not been thought necessary to include *Tables* of wellknown houses in the English and the Scottish nobility, which may be traced without difficulty in peerages or other handbooks. The Howard, Douglas, and Campbell families have, however, been exceptionally introduced, in order to draw attention to their political alliances; and, on much the same grounds, certain of the great ministerial families of the sixteenth and eighteenth centuries have been included. The Reding *Table*, which has been placed by the side of that of the De Retz family for the sake of convenience only, is intended to show a connexion not usually noticed.

As to order of sequence, the *Tables* and *Lists* have, so far as possible, been arranged under the heads of the countries to which they severally relate, beginning in each division with the British Empire. Here, the governors of the more important colonies only are given, the lists beginning ordinarily from the date when representative or responsible ministerial government was first set on foot in the several colonies.

In the case of the German *Genealogical Tables* selection has not been easy, owing to the large number of sovereign families; so far as possible, preference has been given to those of which prominent members are mentioned in the *History*. The Spanish *Tables* likewise required much compression, owing to exigencies of space. The identification of individuals is peculiarly difficult here, occasionally in consequence of a form of Spanish pride, which showed itself in the systematic suppression, in family genealogies, of members of the family who had "disgraced" it. Spanish titles usually descended to daughters as well as to sons; and records often only date from the creation of the Grandees of Spain onwards.

An enumeration of the works used in the compilation of the *Genealogical Tables* and for certain of the *Lists* would be in some respects misleading, but it may be of service to the student to direct his attention, among more recent publications, to A. Cohn's revised edition of T. G. Voigtel's *Stammtafeln der Geschichte der europäischen Staaten*, of which unfortunately only Vol. I (*Germany and the Netherlands*) has appeared (Brunswick, 1871); to Fernández de Bethencourt's *Historia genealogica y heraldica de la Monarquía Española* (Vols. I–VIII, Madrid, 1897–1910, *in progress*); to Burgos' *Blazon de España* (Madrid, 1853–60); and to P. Litta's *Famiglie Celebri Italiane* (Milan, 1819 sqq., *in progress*). J. Hübner's venerable *Genealogische Tabellen*, 4 vols. (1733–66) with Supplements (Copenhagen, 1822–4), have been put largely under contribution, together with Koch's *Tables Généalogiques des Maisons souveraines de l'Europe* (Strassburg, 1780), especially useful for Italy and France, and L. Moréri's *Grand Dictionnaire historique*, particularly in the Spanish edition, 8 vols., Paris, 1753.

The list of *English Parliaments* has been compiled from the *data* in the *Journals* of the two Houses (which often supplement each other), the *Statutes of the Realm*, and the *Calendars of State Papers*, compared with C. H. Parry's *The Parliaments and Councils of England* (1839) and other authorities.

The *List of Congresses and Conferences* has been confined mainly to formal gatherings of plenipotentiaries of the chief European States, or of particular States negotiating with one another as to terms of peace and other objects of common interest; but a few meetings between sovereigns

mentioned in the earlier portions of this *History*, and a few meetings of representatives of particular opinions or interests in recent times, have been exceptionally included.

The *List of Leagues and Alliances* is essentially a selected list. It might, of course, have been extended almost indefinitely in many periods of Modern History between the fifteenth and the twentieth century; the guiding consideration has in each case been the relative historical importance of the league or alliance mentioned, and its consequent mention in this work. Confederations of States formed on the basis of a written constitution have been consistently omitted.

No List of General Councils has been inserted, the number of Councils acknowledged as such by the Western Church at large from the fifteenth century onwards being so small that an enumeration of them seemed unnecessary. On the other hand, a *List of Secularised Bishoprics* seemed desirable, in view of the difficulty in following the main territorial changes involved. It has not however proved possible to include the large list of Abbots and Abbesses of princely rank; the dates of the secularisation of their dominions may easily be ascertained from C. Wolff's *Die unmittelbaren Theile des ehemaligen römisch-deutschen Kaiserreiches, etc.* (Berlin, 1873), or from other sources.

The *Lists of Congresses and Conferences* and of *Leagues and Alliances* are expressly intended to be selections only; from the former, Religious Colloquies have been excluded.

Finally, the *List of Universities* has been restricted to Universities proper; single Faculties as well as University Colleges, Academies, and similar institutions providing higher instruction being, for want of space, excluded. The list does not include Universities founded before 1450. Among the Universities of the United States of America, those are enumerated which report to the United States Bureau of Education and are included in its lists. Some of the more important Academies and Societies founded for the advance of learning and research are mentioned in Chapter XXIII of Vol. v of this *History*.

Titles borne and offices held by persons mentioned in the *Tables* or *Lists* have been inserted only in so far as they seemed necessary for the purpose of identification. Fuller descriptions will often be found in the *General Index*, or in the *Indexes* of particular volumes.

The spelling of names conforms so far as possible to the rules adopted in the compilation of the *General Index*, in view of the precedents set by the *History* itself. Christian names are Anglicised or left in their foreign form as in the *Index* and the *History*, and foreign surnames are spelt as they are spelt there. Titles are given in English where English

equivalents exist; in the case of French titles, they are given in French (*Duc*, etc.) from the French Revolution onwards, when they ceased to be territorial and became honorific only.

In the *Genealogical Tables*,

Black type is used for crowned heads, Emperors and Kings—but not for those incidentally mentioned (*e.g.* as married) in *Tables* of other Houses.

SMALL CAPITALS are used for succession of minor territorial potentates, as Electors, Archdukes, etc., and for titles of a branch line in the table, in brackets, *e.g.* [WEIMAR].

Explanatory indications (of various kinds) are given in *italics*.

Dates of accession are given only when necessary to avoid confusion— date of death alone is given when succession went from father to son, or from brother to brother, or is obvious without a date of accession.

A reference to another table (*see e.g. Table* 100) signifies that a line not shown in the *Table* containing the reference continues in the *Table* referred to; or that there is some other special reason for the reference.

In the *Tables* and *Lists* use has been made of the following

ABBREVIATIONS AND SYMBOLS.

abd.	for abdicated	s.	for son
Abp.	,, Archbishop	Sec.	,, Secretary
Adm.	,, Administrator	*s.p.*	,, *sine prole* (*i.e.* *legitima*),
Archd.	,, Archduke		only inserted when some
Archdss.	,, Archduchess		importance attaches to
b.	,, born		the fact
Bp.	,, Bishop	Visct.	,, Viscount
C. Ctss.	,, Count, Countess	wid. wdr.	,, widow, widower
Capt.	,, Captain	(1)(2)(3)	if placed next to the name
Card.	,, Cardinal		of a person, signifies the
Col.	,, Colonel		ordinal among his or her
Cons.	,, Consort		marriages of that noted
cr.	,, created		in the table (e.g. Henry
D. Dss.	,, Duke, Duchess		VIII(6)=(3)Cath. Parr).
dau.	,, daughter		If placed above a name,
dep.	,, deposed		(1) (2) indicates child of
div.	,, divorced		first or second marriage
Dow.	,, Dowager	*1, 2* (ital.)	above name indicates order
E. Ctss.	,, Earl, Countess		of birth (used where this
El.	,, Elector		is altered in the order of
Emp.	,, Emperor		printing, for the sake of
Empss.	,, Empress		convenience)
ex.	,, executed	=	for married
G. D.	,, Grand Duke	†	,, died
Gen.	,, General	≡	,, 4 generations (and so with
Gov.	,, Governor		other numbers)
K.	,, King	⋮	,, lapse of several genera-
Lgr.	,, Landgrave		tions, not specified
Lieut.	,, Lieutenant	↓	,, descendants not here shown
Lt.-Gen.	,, Lieutenant-General	∼	,, illegitimate
Lt.-Gov.	,, Lieutenant-Governor	( )	enclosing title, signifies, in
M.	,, Marquis or Margrave		the *Tables*, that this was
morg.	,, morganatic		acquired after marriage;
Mss.	,, Marchioness		enclosing a lower title, it
murd.	,, murdered		means that this is the
P. Pss.	,, Prince, Princess		title generally used; in
Pal.	,, Palatine		the *Lists*, that the date
Pres.	,, President		of its acquisition was
Q.	,, Queen		after that of appoint-
ren.	,, renounced claim		ment to the office in
rest.	,, restored		question

GENEALOGICAL TABLES AND LISTS.

Part I. Genealogical Tables of Ruling and Noble Houses.

A. *The British Empire.*

Table 1 Houses of Tudor in England and of Stewart in Scotland. (The Tudor and the Stewart Succession.)
,, 2 House of Stewart.
,, 3 The English Succession, 1714.
,, 4 Hanover line.
,, 5 Saxe-Coburg and -Gotha line.
,, 6 Grey, Seymour and Dudley.
,, 7 Howard and Dacre.
,, 8 Devereux (Essex) and Sidney.
,, 9 Cecil and Bacon.
,, 10 Cromwell.
,, 11 Churchill, Spencer, Cavendish, Walpole, Townshend, and Pelham.
,, 12 Stanhope, Pitt, and Grenville.
,, 13 Granville and Russell.
,, 14 Fox and Lennox.
,, 15 Douglas and Hamilton. (Principal branches in the sixteenth century.)
,, 16 Campbell (Argyll and Breadalbane). (To the latter part of the eighteenth century.)
,, 17 Earls of Desmond and Kildare (Fitzgerald).
,, 18 Butler (Ormond, Ossory, and Mountgarret).
,, 19 O'Neill (Tyrone).
,, 20 O'Donnell (Tyrconnel).
,, 21 O'Brien (Thomond and Inchiquin).

B. *France.*

Table 22 House of Valois (1) to Charles VIII.
,, 23   ,,   (2) from Louis XII.
,, 24 House of Bourbon and Bourbon-Orleans.
,, 25 Bourbon and Montpensier.
,, 26 Bourbon (Condé and Vendôme)
,, 27 Montmorency and Coligny.
,, 28 Bouillon.
,, 29 Guise and Longueville.
,, 30 De Retz.
,, 30 A Reding.
,, 31 House of Bonaparte.

C. *The Empire and Austria.*

Table 32   House of Habsburg to Charles VI.
,,   33   Habsburg-Lorraine line.   (The Austrian Succession.)
,,   34   Lorraine.
,,   35   Electors of Brandenburg.
,,   36   Prussia.
,,   37   Brandenburg-Baireuth (Culmbach) and Brandenburg-Ansbach.
,,   38   The Succession to Jülich, Cleves and Berg.
,,   39   The House of Wittelsbach in the Palatinate and Bavaria.
,,   40   Bavaria (1).   House of Wittelsbach from 1460.
,,   41   ,,   (2).
,,   42   The Palatinate (1) old line.
,,   43   ,,   (2) Simmern line.
,,   44   ,,   (3) Zweibrücken line.
,,   45   ,,   (4) Neuburg line.
,,   46   ,,   (5) Sulzbach line.
,,   47   ,,   (6) Birkenfeld line and Kings of Bavaria.
,,   48   Saxony.   House of Wettin: earlier Ernestine line in Gotha, Weimar, and Altenburg.
,,   49   Electors and Kings of Saxony.   House of Wettin, Albertine line.
,,   50   Saxony.   Later Ernestine lines in Gotha, Coburg, and Altenburg (Hildburghausen).
,,   51   Saxony.   Later Ernestine lines in Weimar-Eisenach and Meiningen.
,,   52   Brunswick and Brunswick-Lüneburg (to George II).
,,   53   Brunswick-Wolfenbüttel.
,,   54   Kings of Hanover (from George III).
,,   55   Landgraves, Electors and Grand Dukes of Hesse and Princes of Battenberg.
,,   56   Margraves and Grand Dukes of Baden.   House of Zähringen.
,,   57   Dukes and Kings of Würtemberg and Dukes of Teck.
,,   58   Anhalt.
,,   59   The Schleswig-Holstein Succession.
,,   60   Dukes of Holstein-Gottorp and Grand Dukes of Oldenburg.
,,   61   Mecklenburg.
,,   62   Dukes of Pomerania (from 1478).
,,   62 A   Later Counts of Mansfeld (of Eisleben).

D. *The Netherlands.*

Table 63   Burgundy and Brabant.
,,   64   Orange-Nassau; Stadholders of Holland and Zeeland etc.
,,   65   Nassau-Dillenburg, Nassau-Siegen; Kings of Holland; Stadholders of (West) Friesland; Grand Dukes of Luxemburg
,,   66   Belgium.   House of Coburg.

E. *Italy.*

Table 67   Savoy.
,,   68   Visconti and Sforza in Milan (showing the French claim to Milan).
,,   69   Florence and Tuscany: House of Medici.
,,   70   Dukes of Parma: Farnese line.
,,   71   Naples: lines of Aragon and Anjou and the French claim.
,,   72   Naples (two Sicilies) and Parma: Bourbon lines.
,,   73   Grand Dukes of Tuscany and Modena.
,,   74   Ferrara and Modena: House of Este.

E. *Italy* (contd.).

Table 75 Dukes of Mantua: House of Gonzaga from 1478.
„ 76 Cibò and Chigi.
„ 77 Borgia.
„ 78 Dukes of Urbino: Montefeltro and della Rovere.
„ 79 Aldobrandini, Borghese, and Pamfili.

F. *Spain.*

Table 80 Houses of Castile and Aragon to Philip III.
„ 81 The family of Charles V.
„ 82 The Spanish Succession.
„ 83 House of Bourbon.
„ 84 Kings of Navarre.
„ 85 Toledo (Alva), Figueroa, and Henriquez.
„ 86 Zuñiga (Ayamonte, Miranda, Monterey) and Sandoval.
„ 87 Velasco, Mendoza, and Guzman (Medina Sidonia and Olivares).

G. *Portugal and Brazil.*

Table 88 Kings of Portugal from John I to John IV.
„ 89 House of Braganza

H. *Sweden and Norway.*

Table 90 Houses of Vasa and Holstein-Gottorp.
„ 91 House of Bernadotte.
„ 92 King of Norway.

I. *Denmark.*

Table 93 Kings of Denmark, Norway and Sweden. (House of Oldenburg I.)
„ 94 Kings of Denmark and Norway. (House of Oldenburg II.)

J. *Poland, Hungary and Transylvania.*

Table 95 Houses of Jagello and Zapólya.
„ 96 Báthory.
„ 97 Bethlen and Apaffy. (a) Bethlen of Iktàr, (b) Apaffy.
„ 98 Rákóczy and Zrínyi.
„ 99 Czartoryski.

K. *Russia.*

Table 100 Tsars in Russia from 1462.
„ 101 House of Romanoff.

L. *Turkey and the Balkan States.*

Table 102 The Ottoman Sultans from 1451.
„ 103 Greece.
„ 104 Montenegro.
„ 105 Servia. (a) House of Karageorgevich, (b) House of Obrenovich.
„ 106 Roumania.
„ 107 Bulgaria.

M. *The East.*

Table 108 Egypt. (a) Grand Vezirs of the family of Kiuprili, (b) Khedives of the family of Mohammad 'Alí (Mehemet Ali).
„ 109 Persia. Sháhs of the Kájár Dynasty.
„ 110 Moghul Emperors of India.
„ 111 (a) Manchu-Tartar Emperors of China, Ta Ch'ing Dynasty, (b) Recent Emperors of Japan.
„ 112 Japan. Shōguns of the Tokugawa Dynasty from 1603.

PART II.   LISTS OF SPIRITUAL PRINCES, ELECTED SOVEREIGNS, ETC.

Table 113   The Popes from 1447.
„   114   Electors of Cologne from 1463.
„   115   „   Mainz from 1434.
„   116   „   Trier from 1439.
„   117   Archbishops of Canterbury from 1454.
„   118   Archbishops of York from 1480.
„   119   Bishops and Archbishops of Paris from 1473.
„   120   Generals of the Order of Jesus.
„   121   Elected Kings of Poland.
„   122   Doges of Venice from 1414.
„   123   Presidents of the United States of America.
„   124   „   French Republic.
„   125   Presidents of Mexico.
„   126   „   Brazil.
„   127   Lords Lieutenant, Lords Deputy, and Lords Justices of Ireland
            from 1485.
„   128   Governors-General of India and other Indian Governors.
„   129   Governors and Acting Governors (1656–1904) of Jamaica.
„   130   „   of North American Colonies before 1776.
„   131   „   and Governors-General of the Dominion of Canada.
„   132   „   „   „   of Australia and New Zealand.
„   133   „   and Commissioners of South Africa.
„   134   Consuls-General, etc., of Egypt and the Sudan.
„   135   Governors of the Spanish Netherlands and Governors of the
            Austrian Netherlands.
„   136   Palatines of Hungary and Princes of Transylvania.
„   137   Spanish Governors of Milan.
„   138   Viceroys of Naples and Sicily.
„   139   Chief Ministers in Great Britain (England) from 1485.
„   140   „   France from Henry IV.
„   141   „   the Empire and Austria from Charles V to
                            1871.
„   142   „   Prussia to 1871.
„   143   Chancellors of the German Empire.
„   144   Chief Ministers in the Kingdom of Italy.
„   145   „   Spain from Philip III to 1873.

PART III.   LISTS OF PARLIAMENTS, GENERAL COUNCILS, ETC.

Table 146   List of Secularised Bishoprics (with dates of secularisation and
            new sovereigns).
„   147   „   English Parliaments (1485 to the Septennial Act).
„   148   „   Imperial Diets (selection only).
„   149   „   Congresses and Conferences (selection only).
„   150   „   Leagues and Alliances (selection only).
„   151   „   Universities founded from 1450.

TABLE 1

HOUSES OF TUDOR IN ENGLAND AND
OF STEWART IN SCOTLAND

GENEALOGIES

BRITISH EMPIRE

THE TUDOR AND THE STEWART SUCCESSION

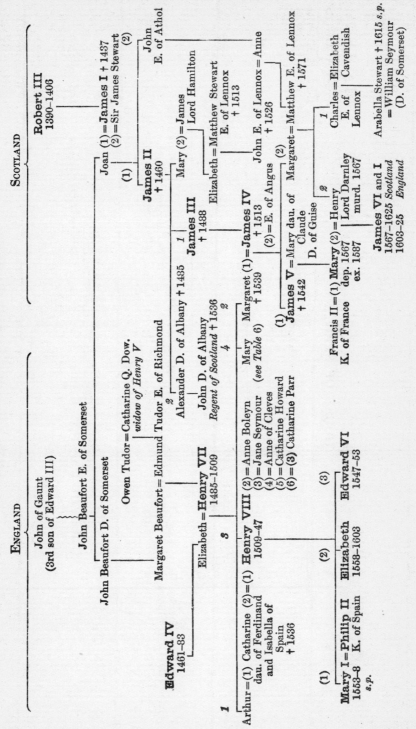

TABLE 2

GENEALOGIES
BRITISH EMPIRE

HOUSE OF STEWART

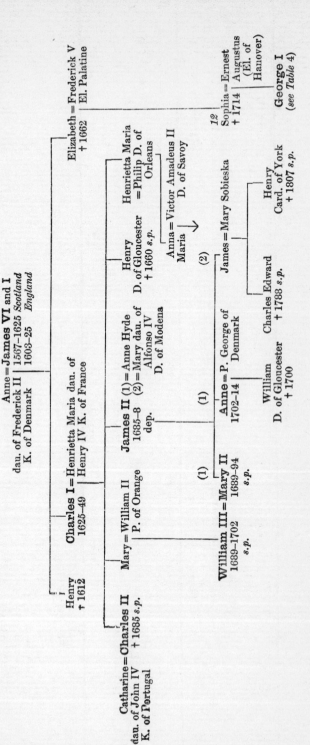

TABLE 3

GENEALOGIES

BRITISH EMPIRE

THE ENGLISH SUCCESSION, 1714

(Possible claimants by descent at the date of Queen Anne's death are in small capitals)

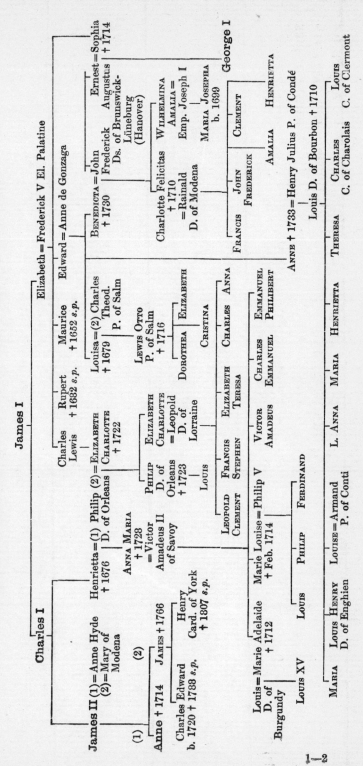

TABLE 4
GENEALOGIES
BRITISH EMPIRE

HANOVER LINE

George I 1714–27 = Sophia Dorothea of Brunswick-Lüneburg (Celle)

George II = Caroline of Brandenburg-Ansbach
† 1760

Augusta = Frederick Lewis P. of Wales † 1751 | Anne = William IV P. of Orange (see Table 65) | Emily | Caroline | William D. of Cumberland † 1765 s.p. | Mary = Frederick II Lgr. of Hesse-Cassel (see Table 55) | Louisa = Frederick V K. of Denmark

Charles Wm. = Augusta Ferd. D. of Brunswick | George III = Charlotte of Mecklenburg-Strelitz † 1820 | Edward Augustus D. of York † 1767 s.p. | William Henry D. of Gloucester | Henry Frederick D. of Cumberland † 1790 s.p. | Caroline = Christian VII Matilda (see Table 94)

Caroline = George IV † 1821 † 1830 | Frederick D. of York † 1827 | William IV † 1837 = Adelaide of Saxe-Meiningen | Charlotte = (2) Frederick I K. of Würtemberg | Edward D. of Kent | Ernest D. of Cumberland K. of Hanover 1837 † 1851 (see Table 54) | Adolphus D. of Cambridge † 1850 = Augusta of Hesse-Cassel

Charlotte = Leopold of Saxe-Coburg-Gotha (K. of the Belgians) † 1817 s.p. (see Table 66) | Victoria (2) = Edward D. of Kent | Victoria = Albert of Saxe-Coburg-Gotha (see Table 60) † 1901

George D. of Cambridge † 1904 | Augusta | Mary = Francis D. of Teck

Adolphus D. of Teck | Victoria Mary = George V

William Frederick D. of Gloucester † 1834 s.p. | Mary = William

TABLE 5

GENEALOGIES

BRITISH EMPIRE

SAXE-COBURG AND -GOTHA LINE

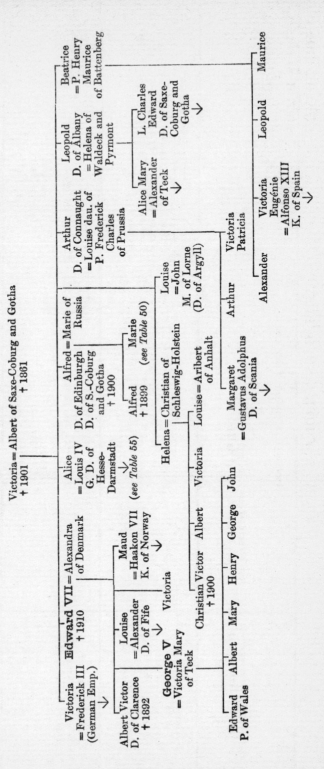

TABLE 6

GENEALOGIES

BRITISH EMPIRE

(Small capitals indicate Tudor descent)

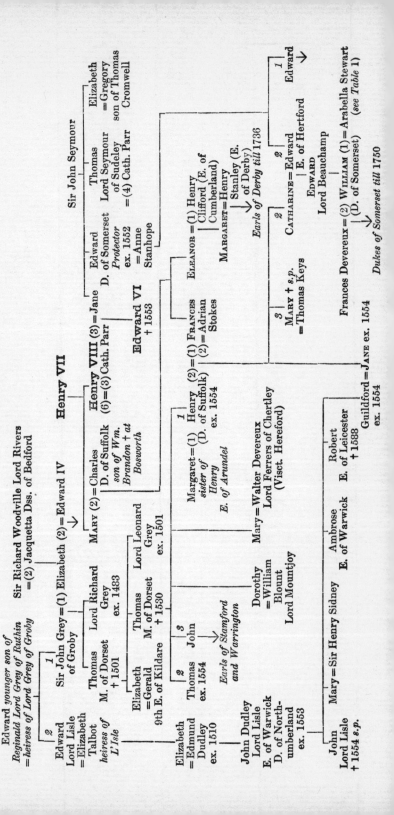

GREY, SEYMOUR AND DUDLEY

TABLE 7

GENEALOGIES

BRITISH EMPIRE

HOWARD AND DACRE

John Howard (*son of Sir Robert Howard and Margaret heiress of Mowbray of Norfolk*)
D. of Norfolk † 1485 *at Bosworth*

Thomas E. of Surrey 2nd D. of Norfolk (*commander at Flodden*)

Thomas (1) = Anne dau. of
3rd D. of   Edward IV
Norfolk (2) = Elizabeth Stafford
† 1554   dau. of Edward
         D. of Buckingham

Sir Edward
† 1513 *at*
Brest
Lord High
Admiral

Edmund

Sir
Thomas

William
Lord Howard of Effingham

Charles E. of Nottingham
(*commander against Armada*)

Muriel
(1) = John Grey
     2nd Visct. Lisle
(2) = Sir Thos. Knyvet

Elizabeth
= Sir Thomas Boleyn
E. of Wiltshire and
Ormond † 1539

Catharine = (5) **Henry VIII**
† 1542   1509–47
         (2) = Anne
            ex. 1536

Mary = William
       Carey

George
Lord Rochford
ex. 1536

Elizabeth
1558–1603

Catharine = Sir Francis
        Knollys

Henry Carey
Lord Hunsdon
† 1596

Mary = Sir
     Edward
     Hoby

Robert
E. of
Monmouth
† 1639

George = Elizabeth
Governor of Spencer of
I. of Wight   Althorpe
    Earls of Berkeley

George
† 1569 *s.p.*

Anne   Mary   Elizabeth

Frances (1) = Robert E. of Essex
      (2) = R. Carr E. of Somerset

Henry = Frances
E. of Surrey   Vere
ex. 1547

Thomas
Visct. Howard
of Bindon

Mary
= Henry Fitzroy
   D. of Richmond

Henry
E. of Northampton
K.G. † 1614

William
Lord Dacre
of Gilsland
† 1563

Leonard
† 1573

Magdalen
= (2) Anthony Browne
    Visct. Montagu

Mary = (1) Thomas 4th D. (2) = Margaret heiress
        of Norfolk   of Audley of
        † 1572   Walden

           (3) = (2) Elizabeth (1) = Thomas
               Lelburne   Lord Dacre
                       of Gilsland
                       † 1566

Mary = (1) = Philip
Fitzalan   † 1589
heiress of
Arundel   Anne = Philip
           Dacre † 1589

*Earls of
Arundel
and Dukes
of Norfolk*

Thomas (1) = Mary Dacre
Lord Howard (2) = Catharine
de Walden   Knevet
E. of Suffolk   widow of
           Richard Rich

William
= Elizabeth
   Dacre
Earls of Carlisle

Edward

Sir Robert

Theophilus
Earls of Suffolk

TABLE 8

GENEALOGIES

BRITISH EMPIRE

DEVEREUX (ESSEX) AND SIDNEY

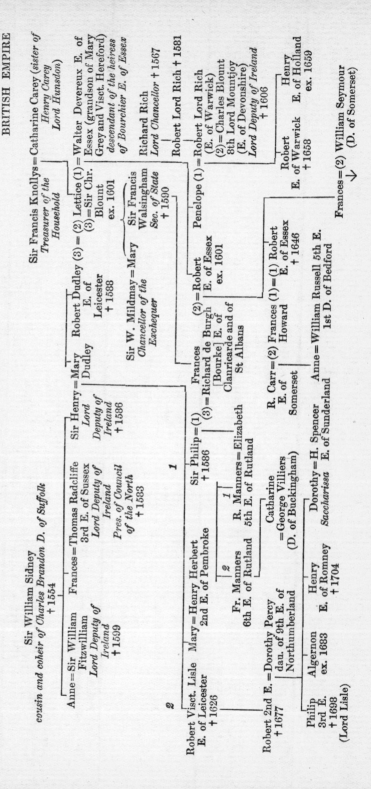

TABLE 9

GENEALOGIES

BRITISH EMPIRE

CECIL AND BACON

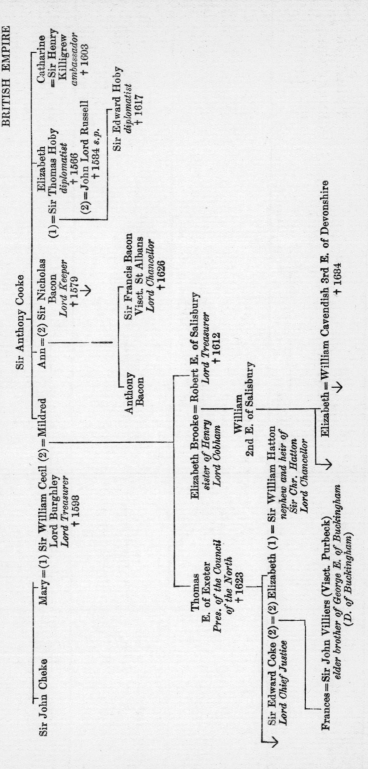

TABLE 10
GENEALOGIES
BRITISH EMPIRE

CROMWELL

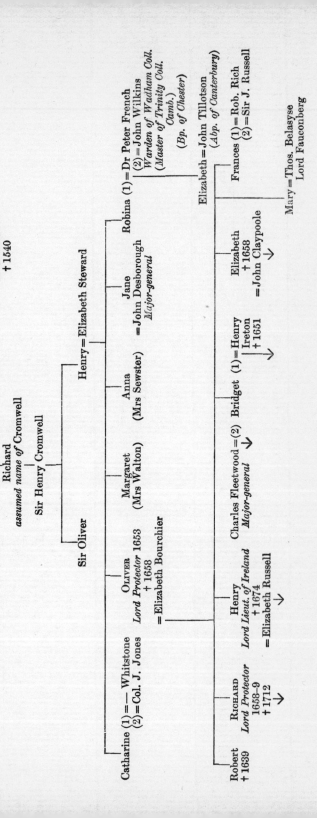

Morgan Williams = Catharine | Thomas Cromwell, E. of Essex † 1540

Richard (assumed name of Cromwell)

Sir Henry Cromwell

Henry = Elizabeth Steward

Sir Oliver

— Margaret (Mrs Walton)
— Anna (Mrs Sewster)
— Jane = John Desborough, Major-general
— Robina (1) = Dr Peter French
  (2) = John Wilkins, Warden of Wadham Coll. (Master of Trinity Coll. Camb.) (Bp. of Chester)
— Elizabeth = John Tillotson (Abp. of Canterbury)

OLIVER, Lord Protector 1653 † 1658 = Elizabeth Bourchier

— Catharine (1) = — Whitstone
  (2) = Col. J. Jones
— Henry, Lord Lieut. of Ireland † 1674 = Elizabeth Russell
— Bridget (1) = Henry Ireton † 1651
  (2) = Charles Fleetwood, Major-general
— Elizabeth † 1658 = John Claypoole
— Frances (1) = Rob. Rich
  (2) = Sir J. Russell
— Mary = Thos. Belasyse, Lord Fauconberg

RICHARD, Lord Protector 1658–9 † 1712

Robert † 1639

TABLE 11

GENEALOGIES

BRITISH EMPIRE

CHURCHILL, SPENCER, CAVENDISH, WALPOLE, TOWNSHEND AND PELHAM

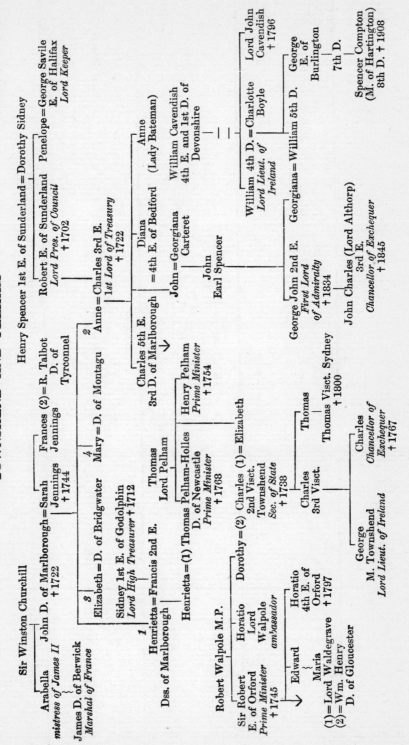

TABLE 12

GENEALOGIES

BRITISH EMPIRE

STANHOPE, PITT AND GRENVILLE

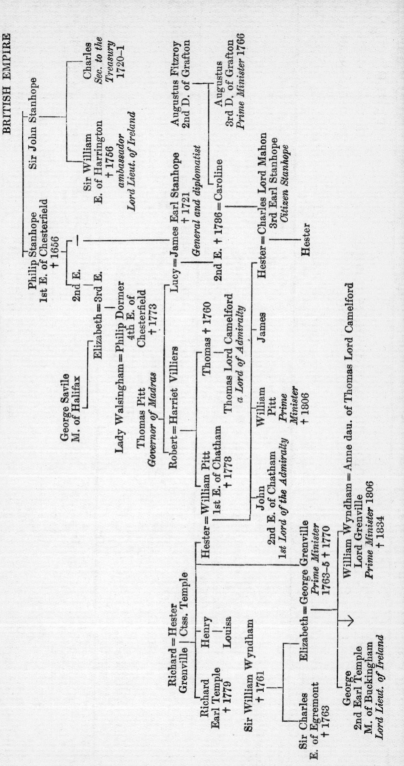

TABLE 13

GENEALOGIES
BRITISH EMPIRE

GRANVILLE AND RUSSELL

Sir Bevil Granville (*grandson of Admiral Sir Richard Grenville*) † 1643 *at Lansdowne*

Bernard

Sir John Granville E. of Bath † 1701

Charles
E. of Bath
† 1701

John
cr. Lord Granville
of Potheridge † 1707

Sir William = Jane
Leveson-Gower

Grace = George
Ctss.   Lord
Granville   Carteret

Sir Bevil
*Governor of
Barbados*

George = (2) Mary (1) = Thomas
Lord   Thynne
Lansdowne
*Granville
the polite*

Catharine Manners = John Lord Gower
dau. of 1st D. of Rutland

Evelyn Pierpont
D. of Kingston

Lady Mary Wortley
Montagu

Evelyn = John
Earl
Gower
† 1754

John Lord Carteret
E. Granville † 1763

William = Sophia
E. of Shelburne
M. of Lansdowne

Louisa = Thomas
2nd Visct.
Weymouth

Georgiana
= John
Spencer

Thomas
3rd Visct. Weymouth

William Russell
5th E. 1st D. of Bedford

William
Lord Russell
ex. 1683
= Rachel Wriothesley

Mary = John E. of Bute

Wriothesley
2nd D. of Bedford

Rachel = William Cavendish
2nd D. of Devonshire

John (2) = Gertrude
4th D. of Bedford
Sec. of State
† 1771

Mary = Rev. Sir Richard Wrottesley
dean of Worcester

Elizabeth = (2) Augustus
3rd D. of Grafton

Granville E. Gower (2) = Lady Louisa Egerton
M. of Stafford   (3) = Lady Susan Stewart

Francis Lord Tavistock = Elizabeth
Keppel

John
6th D. of Bedford

George
D. of Sutherland
*ambassador
Postmaster-Gen.*

Granville
1st Earl Granville
ambassador
† 1846

Charles = Caroline
4th D. of
Marlborough

Francis 5th D. of Bedford
† 1802

John
Earl Russell
Prime Minister † 1878

Granville George
2nd Earl Granville
Foreign Sec.
† 1891

George William

Francis 7th D.

Odo (Lord Ampthill) = Lady Theresa Villiers
ambassador † 1884   dau. of E. of Clarendon *Foreign Sec.*

TABLE 14

GENEALOGIES

BRITISH EMPIRE

FOX AND LENNOX

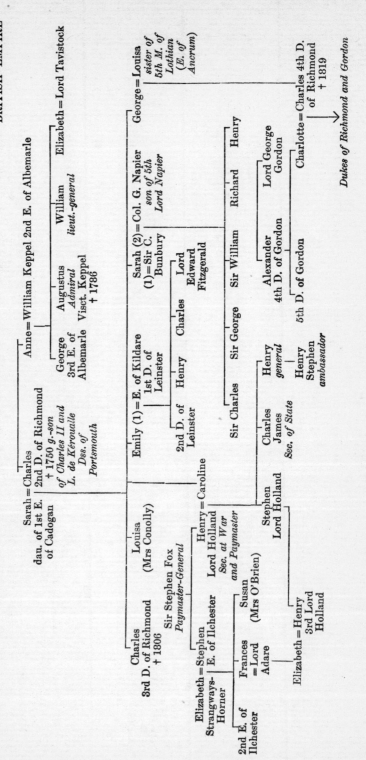

TABLE 15

GENEALOGIES
BRITISH EMPIRE

DOUGLAS AND HAMILTON

(PRINCIPAL BRANCHES IN SIXTEENTH CENTURY)

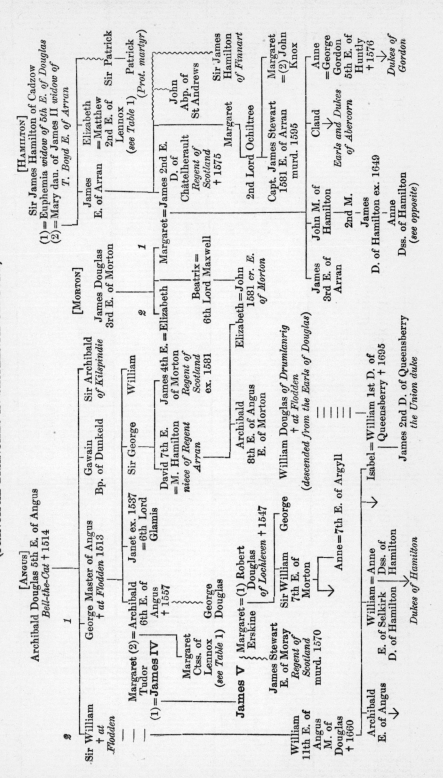

TABLE 16

GENEALOGIES
BRITISH EMPIRE

CAMPBELL (ARGYLL AND BREADALBANE)
(TO THE LATTER PART OF EIGHTEENTH CENTURY)

Colin Campbell 1st E. of Argyll = Isabel coheir of John Stewart lord of Lorne
High Chancellor of Scotland etc. † 1493

Elizabeth Stewart = Archibald 2nd E. † *at Flodden 1513*
dau. of 1st E. of Lennox |

Colin 3rd E. † 1530

James Stewart = (1) Agnes Keith dau. of
E. of Moray   William E. Marischal
Regent of Scotland
murd. 1570

James 2nd E. of Moray = Elizabeth
murd. 1692

Helen Hamilton = (1) Archibald 4th E. (2) = Margaret
dau. of 1st E. of Arran   Graham

Margaret = James Stewart
           Lord Doune

Archibald 5th E. (1) = Jane illeg. dau.
                       of James V

Colin = (2) Agnes widow of
6th E.   the Regent Moray

Anne Cornwallis = (2) Archibald 7th E. (1) = Anne Douglas dau. of
                       † 1638   Wm. E. of Morton

James E. of Irvine   Archibald 8th E.
† 1645   M. of Argyll ex. 1661

Alexander Lindsay = (1) Anne (2) = (2) Archibald 9th E. (1) = Mary dau. of
(E. of Balcarres)   Mackenzie   ex. 1685   E. of Moray
† 1659

John of Mamore

Mary = (2) John Campbell of *Glenorchy*
           1st E. of Breadalbane

Lord Glenorchy = Henrietta Villiers
(2nd E.)

John
3rd E. of Breadalbane
† 1782

Primrose = (3) Simon Fraser
               Lord Lovat
               ex. 1747

Anne = R. Maitland
       E. of Lauderdale

Col. John = Mary
Campbell   Bellenden
4th D.

Archibald 10th E.
and 1st D. of Argyll
† 1703

Anne = James Stuart
       2nd E. of Bute

Archibald
(Lord Islay)
3rd D. † 1761

John 3rd E. of Bute
Prime Minister 1761–3

later Dukes of Argyll

John
2nd D. and
D. of Greenwich
† 1743

Mary = Visct. Coke

4 daus.

TABLE 17
GENEALOGIES
BRITISH EMPIRE

EARLS OF DESMOND AND KILDARE (FITZGERALD)

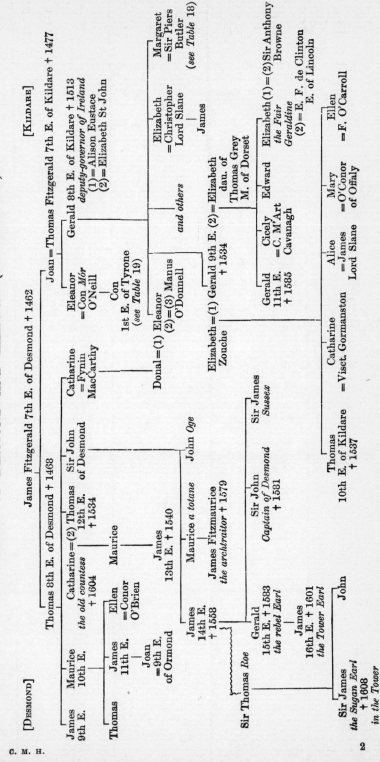

C. M. H.

2

TABLE 18
GENEALOGIES
BRITISH EMPIRE

BUTLER (ORMOND, OSSORY AND MOUNTGARRET)

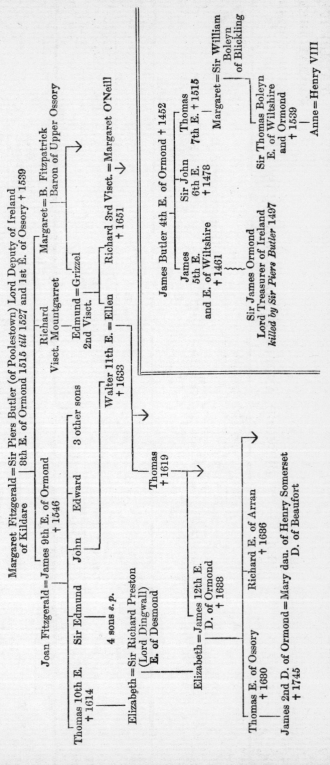

James Butler 4th E. of Ormond † 1452

James 5th E. and E. of Wiltshire † 1461 — Sir John 6th E. † 1478 — Thomas 7th E. † 1515 — Margaret = Sir William Boleyn of Blickling

Sir James Ormond Lord Treasurer of Ireland *killed by Sir Piers Butler 1497*

Sir Thomas Boleyn E. of Wiltshire and Ormond † 1539

Anne = Henry VIII

Margaret Fitzgerald = Sir Piers Butler (of Poolestown) Lord Deputy of Ireland 8th E. of Ormond 1515 *till* 1527 and 1st E. of Ossory † 1539

Richard Visct. Mountgarret — Margaret = B. Fitzpatrick Baron of Upper Ossory

Edmund = Grizzel 2nd Visct.

Richard 3rd Visct. = Margaret O'Neill † 1651

Joan Fitzgerald = James 9th E. of Ormond † 1546

Thomas 10th E. † 1614 — Sir Edmund — John — Edward — 3 other sons

4 sons *s.p.*

Walter 11th E. = Ellen † 1633

Elizabeth = Sir Richard Preston (Lord Dingwall) E. of Desmond

Thomas † 1619

Elizabeth = James 12th E. D. of Ormond † 1688

Richard E. of Arran † 1686

Thomas E. of Ossory † 1680

James 2nd D. of Ormond = Mary dau. of Henry Somerset D. of Beaufort † 1745

TABLE 19

GENEALOGIES

BRITISH EMPIRE

O'NEILL (TYRONE)

Owen O'Neill † 1456

Henry

Hugh
lord of the Fews

Sir Phelim † 1653

[O'NEILL OF CLANDEBOY]

Brian
Faghartach
† 1548

Phelim
Bacagh
† 1533

[MACDONNELL]

Sadhbh
=John MacDonnell
of Antrim

Con *Mór* = Eleanor Fitzgerald
† 1493

Con = Mary
E. of Tyrone

Shane
† 1567

Sir Brian † 1574

Hugh   Henry   Con

James
(*killed by
Shane*)
=(1) Agnes
Campbell
dau. of 3rd
E. of Argyll

Angus   Alexander
(*killed Shane*)

Sorley
Boy

Sir James
† 1601

Randal
E. of
Antrim

Randal
2nd E. of
Antrim
† 1683

Art *Oge* † 1502

Judith = Manus O'Donnell

Niall Conallagh
† 1545

Sir Turlough Luineach
=(2) Agnes Campbell

Cormac † 1595

Sir Art † 1600

Ferdoragh
(Matthew)

Mary = Sorley *Boy*
MacDonnell

Art
MacBaron

Owen
Roe
† 1649

Con

Sir Cormac
MacBaron

Art *Oge*

Hugh
† *c.* 1660

dau. = Hugh
Roe O'Donnell

Brian

dau. of =(4) Hugh (2) = Joan dau.
Sir Hugh   2nd E.   of Hugh
Maginnis   of Tyrone   O'Donnell
            † 1616

Hugh
Baron of
Dungannon
† 1608

Alice = Randal Macdonnell
(1st E. of Antrim)

Con

Brian
† 1617

John
El Conde di Tirone
† 1641

TABLE 20

GENEALOGIES

BRITISH EMPIRE

O'DONNELL (TYRCONNEL)

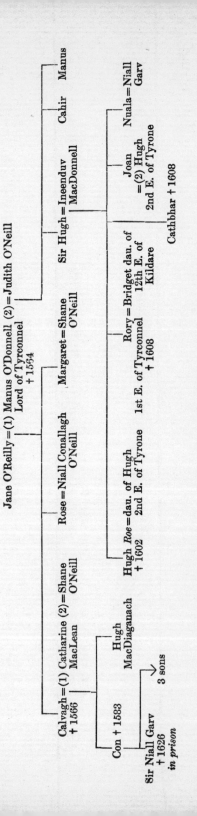

Jane O'Reilly = (1) Manus O'Donnell (2) = Judith O'Neill
Lord of Tyrconnel
† 1554

Calvagh = (1) Catharine (2) = Shane O'Neill
† 1566   MacLean

Rose = Niall Conallagh O'Neill

Margaret = Shane O'Neill

Sir Hugh = Ineenduv MacDonnell

Cahir   Manus

Con † 1583

Hugh MacDiagranach

3 sons

Sir Niall Garv † 1626 in prison

Hugh Roe = dau. of Hugh 2nd E. of Tyrone
† 1602

Rory = Bridget dau. of 12th E. of Kildare
1st E. of Tyrconnel
† 1608

Joan = (2) Hugh 2nd E. of Tyrone

Nuala = Niall Garv

Cathbhar † 1608

TABLE 21

GENEALOGIES

BRITISH EMPIRE

O'BRIEN (THOMOND AND INCHIQUIN)

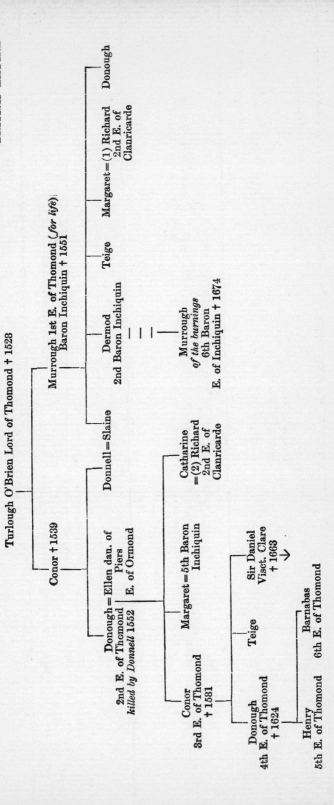

TABLE 22
GENEALOGIES
FRANCE

HOUSE OF VALOIS (1)

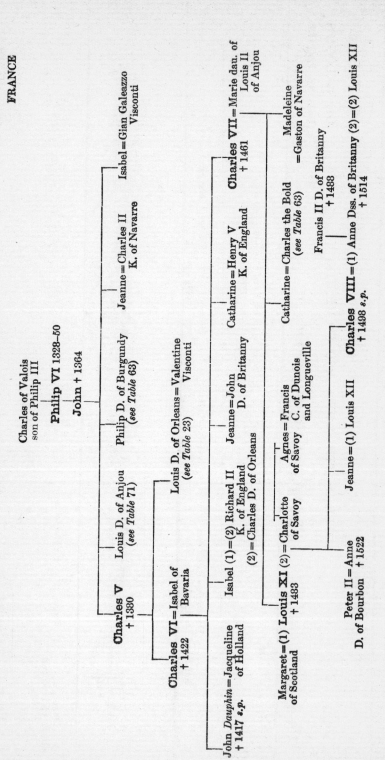

Charles of Valois
son of Philip III

Philip VI 1328-50

John † 1364

Philip D. of Burgundy
(*see Table* 63)

Louis D. of Orleans = Valentine
(*see Table* 23)   Visconti

Isabel = Gian Galeazzo
   Visconti

Jeanne = Charles II
   K. of Navarre

Charles V
† 1380

Louis D. of Anjou
(*see Table* 71)

Charles VI = Isabel of
† 1422   Bavaria

John *Dauphin* = Jacqueline
† 1417 *s.p.*   of Holland

Isabel (1) = (2) Richard II
   K. of England
   (2) = Charles D. of Orleans

Jeanne = John
   D. of Britanny

Catharine = Henry V
   K. of England

Charles VII = Marie dau. of
† 1461   Louis II
     of Anjou

Margaret = (1) **Louis XI** (2) = Charlotte
of Scotland   † 1483   of Savoy

Agnes = Francis
of Savoy   C. of Dunois
    and Longueville

Catharine = Charles the Bold
    (*see Table* 63)

Madeleine
= Gaston of Navarre

Francis II D. of Britanny
† 1488

Peter II = Anne
D. of Bourbon † 1522

Jeanne = (1) Louis XII

Charles VIII = (1) Anne Dss. of Britanny (2) = (2) Louis XII
† 1498 *s.p.*   † 1514

TABLE 23

GENEALOGIES

FRANCE

HOUSE OF VALOIS (2)

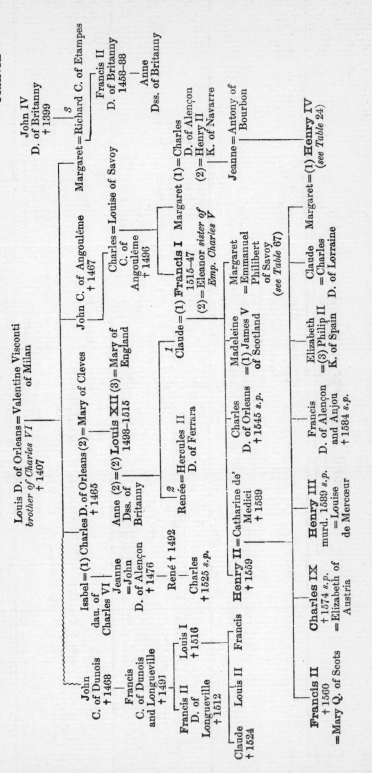

TABLE 24
GENEALOGIES
FRANCE

HOUSE OF BOURBON AND BOURBON-ORLEANS

Marie de' Medici = (2) **Henry IV** (1) = Margaret dau. of Henry II
1589–1610 murd.

Louis XIII = Anne *of Austria* dau. of Philip III K. of Spain
† 1643

Gaston = Marie *heiress of Montpensier* D. of Orleans † 1660
Anne Marie Louise *la Grande Mademoiselle*

Elizabeth = Philip IV K. of Spain
Christina = Victor Amadeus I D. of Savoy
Henrietta Maria = Charles I K. of England

Elizabeth Charlotte = (2) Philip (1) = Henrietta Maria
of the Palatinate   D. of Orleans

Maria Theresa = **Louis XIV**
of Spain   † 1715

Philip D. of Orleans Regent † 1723 = Elizabeth Charlotte = Leopold Joseph D. of Lorraine

Maria Louisa = Charles II of Spain

Anna Maria = Victor Amadeus II (K. of Sardinia)
Marie Adelaide = D. of Burgundy

Louis Dauphin = Maria Anna of Bavaria
† 1711

Charles = Marie D. of Berri Louise

Charlotte = Francis III D. of Modena Louis † 1752

Louis Elizabeth = Louis of Spain

Louis Philippe † 1785

Louis D. of = Marie Adelaide Burgundy of Savoy
† 1712

Philip D. of Anjou (Philip V K. of Spain)

Louis Dauphin (2) = Maria Josepha of Saxony
† 1765

Louis Philippe *Égalité* ex. 1793

Louis XV = Marie Leszczynska
† 1774

Marie Louise = Philip D. of Parma

Elizabeth ex. 1794

Louis Philippe = Marie Amélie dau. of Ferdinand K. of Naples
1830–48 † 1850

Louis D. of = Marie Adelaide Burgundy of Savoy
† 1712

Marie = **Louis XVI** ex. 1793

Louis XVIII 1814–24 C. of Provence

Charles X 1824–30 †1836 C. of Artois = Maria Theresa of Sardinia

Charles = Caroline D. de Berri of Naples murd. 1820

Ferdinand D. d'Orléans † 1842

Louise = Leopold I K. of the Belgians

Louis D. de Nemours † 1896

François P. de Joinville † 1900

Henri D. d'Aumale † 1897

Antoine D. de Montpensier † 1890

Louis Dauphin

Marie = Louis Thérèse D. d'Angoulême † 1844 *s.p.*

Antoinette of Austria ex. 1793

Henry D. de Bordeaux [C. de Chambord] † 1883 *s.p.*

Louis Philippe C. de Paris

Robert D. de Chartres

Philippe D. d'Orléans

Marie Amélie = Charles K. of Portugal

TABLE 25

GENEALOGIES

FRANCE

BOURBON AND MONTPENSIER

John D. of Bourbon ✝ 1434 = (3) Mary heiress of John D. of Berri
fourth in descent from Robert son
of St Louis and Beatrix heiress of Bourbon

Charles D. of Bourbon = Agnes dau. of John D. of Burgundy

Louis C. of Montpensier

John II
✝ 1488
s.p.

Charles
Card. de Bourbon
Abp. of Clermont
✝ 1488

Peter II = Anne
de Beaujeu dau. of Louis XI

Louis
Abp. of Liége

Gilbert C. of Montpensier = Clara di Gouzaga
Viceroy of Naples

le bâtard de Bourbon
Admiral of France

Susanna = Charles
D. of Bourbon
Constable of France
✝ 1527

Francis
✝ 1515
at Marignano

Louise = Louis de Bourbon
(see Table 26)

Louis
D. of Montpensier
✝ 1582

Francis
D. of Montpensier
✝ 1592

Charlotte
= (3) William
P. of Orange
the Silent

Henry
D. of Montpensier
✝ 1608

Gaston = Marie
D. of Orleans

Anne Marie Louise
la Grande Mademoiselle
✝ 1693

TABLE 26
GENEALOGIES
FRANCE

BOURBON (CONDÉ AND VENDÔME)

fifth in descent from Robert son of St Louis and Beatrix heiress of Bourbon

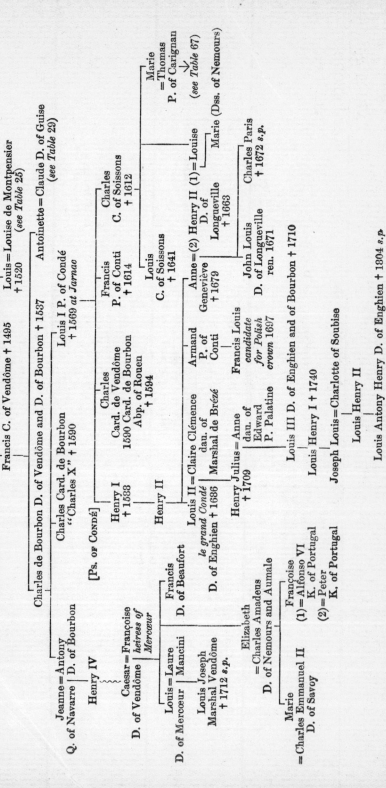

TABLE 27

GENEALOGIES
FRANCE

MONTMORENCY AND COLIGNY

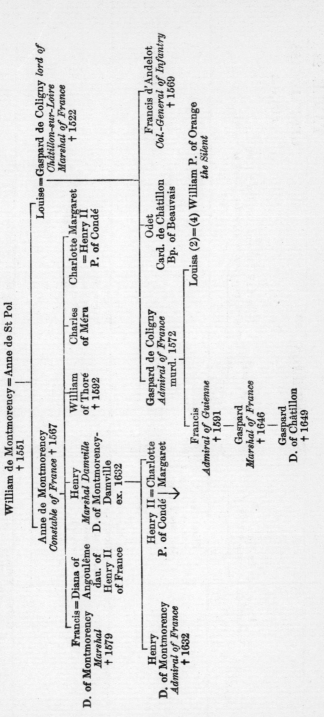

William de Montmorency=Anne de St Pol
† 1551

Anne de Montmorency
Constable of France † 1567

Louise=Gaspard de Coligny lord of
Châtillon-sur-Loire
Marshal of France
† 1522

Francis=Diana of
Angoulême
dau. of
Henry II
of France

D. of Montmorency
Marshal
† 1579

Henry
Marshal Damville
D. of Montmorency-
Damville
ex. 1632

William
of Thoré
† 1592

Charles
of Méru

Charlotte Margaret
= Henry II
P. of Condé

Henry
D. of Montmorency
Admiral of France
† 1632

Henry II=Charlotte
P. of Condé Margaret

Gaspard de Coligny
Admiral of France
murd. 1572

Odet
Card. de Châtillon
Bp. of Beauvais

Francis d'Andelot
Col.-General of Infantry
† 1569

Francis
Admiral of Guienne
† 1591

Louisa (2)=(4) William P. of Orange
the Silent

Gaspard
Marshal of France
† 1646

Gaspard
D. of Châtillon
† 1649

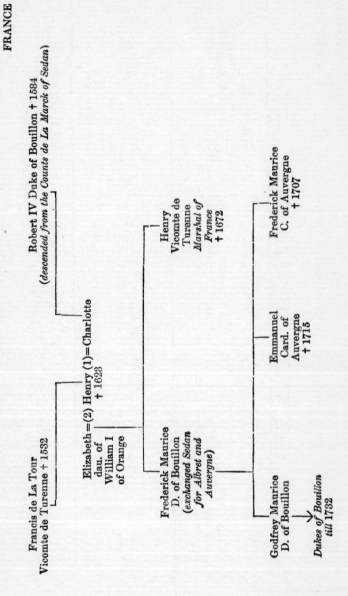

TABLE 28

GENEALOGIES

FRANCE

BOUILLON

Robert IV Duke of Bouillon ✝ 1584
(*descended from the Counts de La March of Sedan*)

Francis de La Tour
Vicomte de Turenne ✝ 1532

Elizabeth = (2) Henry (1) = Charlotte
dau. of   ✝ 1623
William I
of Orange

Frederick Maurice
D. of Bouillon
(*exchanged Sedan
for Albret and
Auvergne*)

Henry
Vicomte de
Turenne
*Marshal of
France*
✝ 1672

Emmanuel
Card. of Auvergne
✝ 1715

Frederick Maurice
C. of Auvergne
✝ 1707

Godfrey Maurice
D. of Bouillon

*Dukes of Bouillon
till 1732*

TABLE 29

GENEALOGIES

FRANCE

GUISE AND LONGUEVILLE

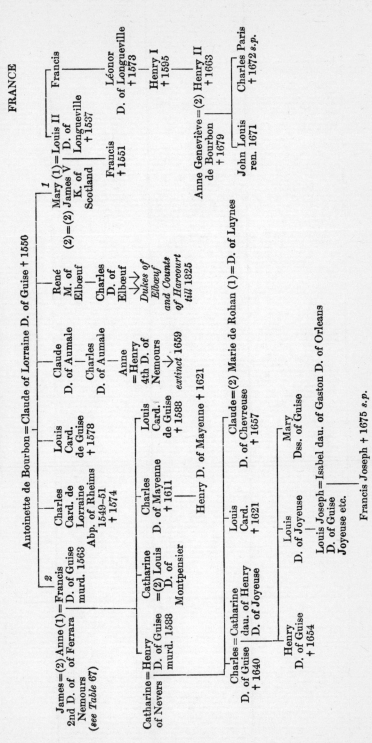

TABLE 30

GENEALOGIES

FRANCE

DE RETZ

Antonio de Gondi = Catharine dame du Perron
banker at Lyons   governess to the
royal Maître d'hôtel   Enfants de France
† 1560

Pierre
Bp. of Paris 1532–1616
Card. (1587)

John Francis
Card. Abp. of Paris
1622

Philip
C. of Joigny

J. Fr. Paul Card. de Retz
Coadjutor of Paris 1643 Abp. 1654
† 1679

Catharine de Clermont = Albert
widow of the   Marshal
C. of Retz   D. of Retz
† 1603

Henry
Coadjutor and Bp. of Paris 1598–1622
Card. de Retz (1618)

Charles = Antonia of Longueville
M. of Belle-Isle
† 1596

Henry D. of Retz

Margaret = Louis de Cossé
D. of Brissac

TABLE 30 A

REDING

Theodore Antonio Reding
Spanish lieut.-col.

Rudolf
Captain of the Swiss Guard of Louis XVI
† 1792

Aloys
Landammann of Schwyz

Nazar
Spanish Marshal
Governor of Balearic Is.

Theodore
Marshal and Grandee
of Spain

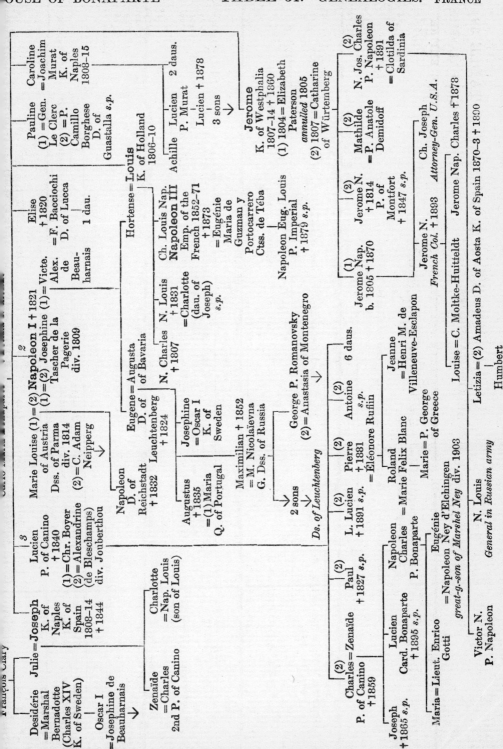

TABLE 32

GENEALOGIES

THE EMPIRE

HOUSE OF HABSBURG

Ernest D. of Styria Carinthia and Carniola † 1424

Frederick III = Eleonora dau. of Edward K. of Portugal
Emp. 1440–93

Bianca Maria Sforza = (2) Maximilian (1) = Mary dau. of Charles the Bold
Emp. 1493–1519   D. of Burgundy

Philip = Joanna of Aragon
† 1506   (see Table 80)

Margaret (1) = John P. of Asturias
(2) = Philibert of Savoy
Governess of the Netherlands

Charles V Emp. 1519 abd. 1556
(see Table 81)

Ferdinand I = Anne dau. of Ladislas K. of Bohemia and Hungary
Emp. 1556–64

Mary = Maximilian II   Ferdinand   Andrew
K. of Hungary   C. of Tyrol † 1595
and Bohemia
Emp. 1564–76

Matthias = Anne

Anne
= (4) Philip II   Rudolf II   Ernest Governor of   Elizabeth
K. of Spain   Emp.   the Netherlands   = Charles IX
1576–1612   † 1595   of France

Mary = William   Joanna = Francis   Anne = Albert III
D. of Jülich   G. D. of   of Bavaria
and Cleves   Tuscany

Charles = Sibylla of Jülich
M. of Burgau   (see Table 38)

Matthias   Maximilian   Albert Card.
Emp. 1612–19   G. M. of Teutonic   Governor of the Netherlands
= Anne of Tyrol   Order   (see Table 80)

Mary = Charles
D. of
Austria
Styria, etc.

Margaret = Philip III   Leopold = Claudia
K. of   Bp. of Strassburg   of Tuscany
Spain   Passau etc.
C. of Tyrol

Ferdinand Charles C. of Tyrol = Anne

Mary Magdalen   Anne
= Cosimo II   = Sigismund III
D. of Tuscany   K. of Poland

Mary = Sigismund
Bathory
P. of
Transylvania

Maria Anna = Ferdinand II   Eleonora
of Bavaria   Emp. 1619–37   (2) = Charles
D. of Lorraine

Maria Anna   Maria Anna Josepha
= Philip IV   = John William of
K. of Spain   Neuburg

Maria Theresa = (1) Leopold I (2) = Claudia Felicitas
of Spain   Emp.   (3) = Eleonora Magdalena of Neuburg
1658–1705

Ferdinand III = Mary
Emp. 1637–57

Ferdinand
K. of the
Romans
† 1654 s.p.

Maria Anna
(see Table 33)

Maximilian II = Maria Antonia
of Bavaria

(1)   (3)   (3)
Joseph I   Charles VI Emp. 1711–40
Emp. 1705–11   (see Table 33)

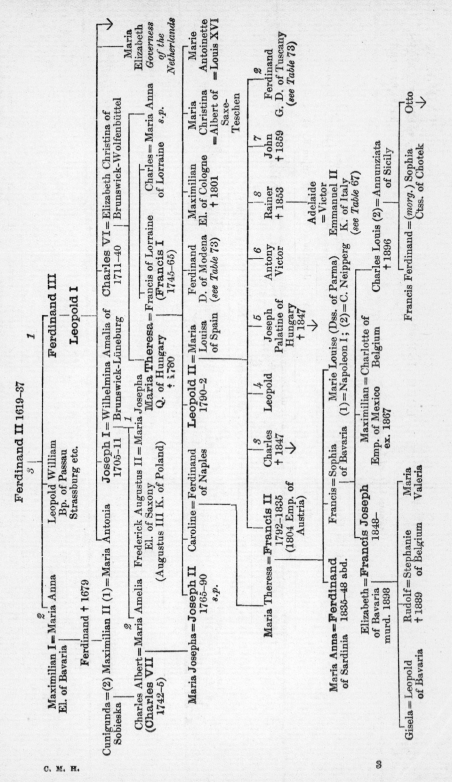

HABSBURG-LORRAINE LINE

THE AUSTRIAN SUCCESSION

TABLE 34
GENEALOGIES
THE EMPIRE

LORRAINE

CHARLES I D. of Lorraine † 1430

Isabella = René I of Anjou K. of Naples † 1480

Yolande = FREDERICK C. of Vaudémont
(3rd in male descent from John 14th D. of Lorraine)

Margaret = Henry VI K. of England

John of Calabria

Joanna = Charles of Anjou K. of Naples

RENÉ II † 1508

ANTONY † 1544

Claude D. of Guise (see Table 29)

John Card. of Lorraine Abp. of Lyons etc. † 1550

Louis C. of Vaudémont † 1527

Francis † 1525 at Pavia

Nicholas C. of Vaudémont

FRANCIS † 1545

Anne = Philip C. of Aerschot

Henry C. of Chaligny

Charles Card. de Vaudémont † 1587

Louise = Henry III K. of France

Claudia = CHARLES II dau. of † 1608
Henry II
K. of France

Philip D. of Mercœur † 1602

Françoise = Caesar D. of Vendôme

Francis C. of Chaligny
↓
Counts of Chaligny

FRANCIS = Christina heiress of C. of C. Paul of Salm
Vaudémont † 1632

Christina = Ferdinand I D. of Tuscany

4 daus.

HENRY † 1624

Charles Card. Bp. of Strasburg Bp. of Metz † 1599

CHARLES III † 1675

NICHOLAS FRANCIS = Claudia (see opposite) Card. Bp. of Toul † 1670

Claudia = Nicholas Francis (see opposite)

Charles Henry P. of Vaudémont † 1723

CHARLES IV or V LEOPOLD = Eleonora of † 1690
Austria

Charles Bp. of Osnabrück † 1715

Elizabeth = LEOPOLD JOSEPH † 1729

Charles = Maria Anna of Austria

Elizabeth = Charles Emmanuel III Theresa D. of Savoy

Charlotte of Orleans

Maria Theresa = FRANCIS STEPHEN
of Austria (Emp. FRANCIS I)
Q. of Hungary ↓ exchanged Lorraine
(see Table 33) for Tuscany

TABLE 55

GENEALOGIES
THE EMPIRE

ELECTORS OF BRANDENBURG

FREDERICK 1st El. of Brandenburg † 1440

John *Alchymista*

Dorothea
(*see Table 93*)

FREDERICK II
abd. 1470

Margaret

Margaret of Baden =(1) ALBERT ACHILLES † 1486 (2)= Anne of Saxony

(1)

(2)

Margaret of Saxony = JOHN CICERO † 1499

Sigismund † 1495
M. of Baireuth

Frederick
M. of Culmbach

Sibylla
= William III
D. of Jülich

JOACHIM I † 1535

Albert Card. Abp. of Mainz

Anna

Ursula

John M. of Cüstrin

Magdalen of Saxony = JOACHIM II † 1571

Margaret
(1) = George
D. of Pomerania
(2) = John II
P. of Anhalt

Catharine

JOHN GEORGE † 1598 (1) = Sophia of Liegnitz
(2) = Sabina of Ansbach
(3) = Elizabeth of Anhalt

Magdalen
= Lewis
the Younger
Lgr. of Hesse-
Darmstadt

Joachim
Ernest
M. of
Ansbach
(*see
Table 37*)

Agnes
= Philip
Julius
D. of
Pomerania

Elizabeth
Sophia
= (1) Janus I
D. of
Radzivil
= (2) Julius
Henry
D. of
Lauenburg

Dorothea
Sophia
= John
Christian
D. of
Liegnitz

Sigismund
*Governor
of Cleves*

and
11 *others*

Erdmutha
= Joachim
Frederick
D. of
Pomerania

Anna Maria
= Barnim XII
D. of Pomerania

Sophia
= Christian I
El. of Saxony

Christian
M. of
Baireuth (*see Table 37*)

John George
M. of Jägerndorf † 1624

Christian William
Abp. of Magdeburg

Catharine = Bethlen Gabor
P. of Transylvania

Eleonora = Gustavus
Adolphus
K. of Sweden

JOACHIM
FREDERICK
(1) = Catharine
of Cüstrin
(2) = Eleonora
of Prussia

Albert Frederick
D. of Prussia
(*see Table 37*)

Ernest

Anne = JOHN SIGISMUND
† 1619

GEORGE WILLIAM = Elizabeth Charlotte
† 1640   of the Palatinate

FREDERICK WILLIAM (1) = Louisa Henrietta dau. of Henry Frederick P. of Orange
the Great Elector

Dorothea = (2) FREDERICK WILLIAM (1)
of Holstein-
Glücksburg

FREDERICK III
(**Frederick I** K. of Prussia)
(*see Table 36*)

Philip
M. of Schwedt

(*extinct* 1788)

3—2

TABLE 36

GENEALOGIES

THE EMPIRE

PRUSSIA

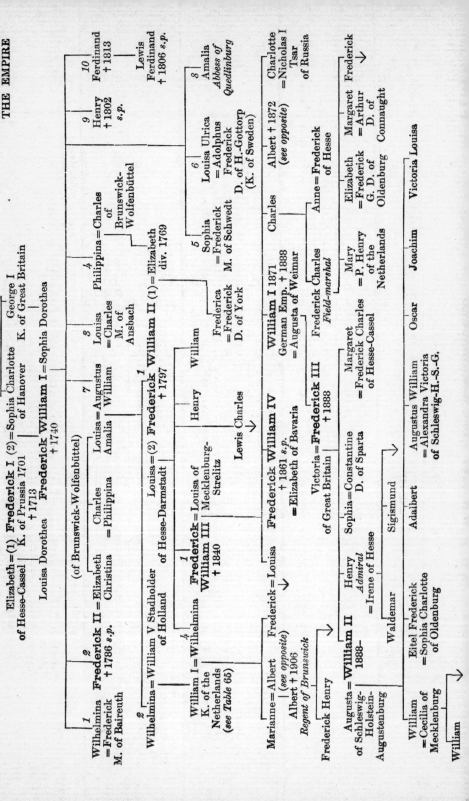

TABLE 37

BRANDENBURG-BAIREUTH (CULMBACH) AND BRANDENBURG-ANSBACH GENEALOGIES
THE EMPIRE

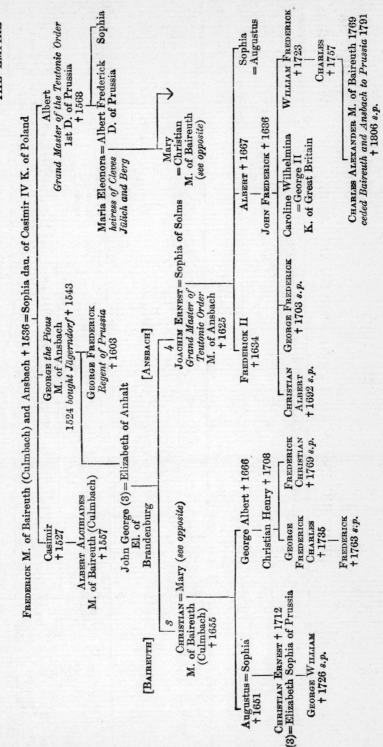

FREDERICK M. of Baireuth (Culmbach) and Ansbach † 1536 = Sophia dau. of Casimir IV K. of Poland

Albert
Grand Master of the Teutonic Order
1st D. of Prussia † 1568

Maria Eleonora = Albert Frederick
heiress of Cleves D. of Prussia
Jülich and Berg

Sophia

Mary
= Christian
M. of Baireuth
(*see opposite*)

Casimir † 1527

GEORGE the Pious
M. of Ansbach
1524 *bought Jägerndorf* † 1543

GEORGE FREDERICK
Regent of Prussia
† 1603

ALBERT ALCIBIADES
M. of Baireuth (Culmbach)
† 1557

John George (3) = Elizabeth of Anhalt
El. of Brandenburg

[ANSBACH]

JOACHIM ERNEST = Sophia of Solms
Grand Master of
Teutonic Order
M. of Ansbach
† 1625

FREDERICK II
† 1634

GEORGE FREDERICK
† 1703 *s.p.*

CHRISTIAN ALBERT
† 1692 *s.p.*

ALBERT † 1667

JOHN FREDERICK † 1686

Sophia
= Augustus

Caroline Wilhelmina
= George II
K. of Great Britain

WILLIAM FREDERICK
† 1723

CHARLES
† 1757

CHARLES ALEXANDER M. of Baireuth 1769
ceded Baireuth and Ansbach to Prussia 1791
† 1806 *s.p.*

[BAIREUTH]

CHRISTIAN = Mary (*see opposite*)
M. of Baireuth
(Culmbach)
† 1655

George Albert † 1666

Christian Henry † 1708

FREDERICK CHRISTIAN
† 1769 *s.p.*

GEORGE FREDERICK CHARLES
† 1735

FREDERICK
† 1763 *s.p.*

Augustus = Sophia
† 1651

CHRISTIAN ERNEST † 1712
(3) = Elizabeth Sophia of Prussia

GEORGE WILLIAM
† 1726 *s.p.*

TABLE 38

GENEALOGIES

THE EMPIRE

THE SUCCESSION TO JÜLICH, CLEVES AND BERG

(Claimants on the death of John William are in small capitals)

John I D. of Cleves C. of Mark
† 1481

Engelbert
C. of Nevers † 1506

Charles I

Francis I
D. of Nevers † 1561

Henrietta † 1601
= Louis di Gonzaga

Francis II † 1562

CHARLES II † 1637

[NEVERS]

John II † 1521
D. of Cleves
C. of Mark

William IV
D. of Jülich and Berg
C. of Ravensberg

Mary = John III † 1539
1521 Cleves and Mark
1524 Jülich Berg and
Ravensberg
1528 Ravenstein

Philip = Anne
C. of Waldeck-
Eisenburg

Anne = Henry VIII
K. of
England

Sibylla = John Frederick
of Saxony

Sibylla (1) = Philip
M. of Baden-Baden
(2) = CHARLES OF HABSBURG
M. of Burgau
† 1618

Magdalen = John I
C. Palatine of
Zweibrücken
† 1604

JOHN II

Magdalen = JOHN GEORGE I
Sibylla
El. of
Saxony

Eleonora = Joachim
Frederick
El. of
Brandenburg

William V
D. of Jülich Cleves and Berg
Gelders 1538–43
† 1592

Maria = Albert Frederick
Eleonora
D. of Prussia

Anna = Philip Lewis
C. Palatine of Neuburg † 1614

WOLFGANG WILLIAM

Sophia = William
D. of Courland

John William
D. of Jülich Cleves and Berg
Bp. of Münster † 1609 *s.p.*
(1) = Jacobaea of Baden
(2) = Antonia of Lorraine

Mary = Christian
M. of Baireuth
(Culmbach)

Anne = JOHN SIGISMUND
El. of
Brandenburg

TABLE 39

GENEALOGIES

THE EMPIRE

THE HOUSE OF WITTELSBACH IN THE PALATINATE AND BAVARIA

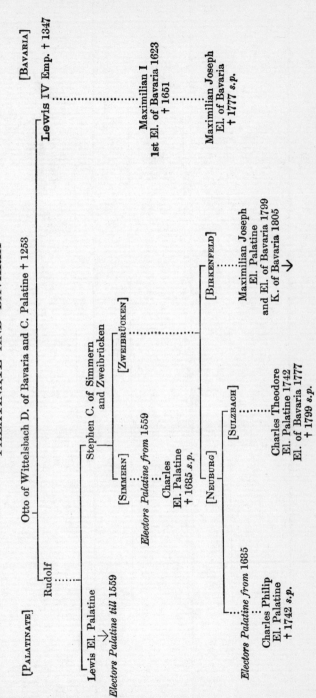

TABLE 40
GENEALOGIES
THE EMPIRE

BAVARIA. HOUSE OF WITTELSBACH FROM 1460 (1)

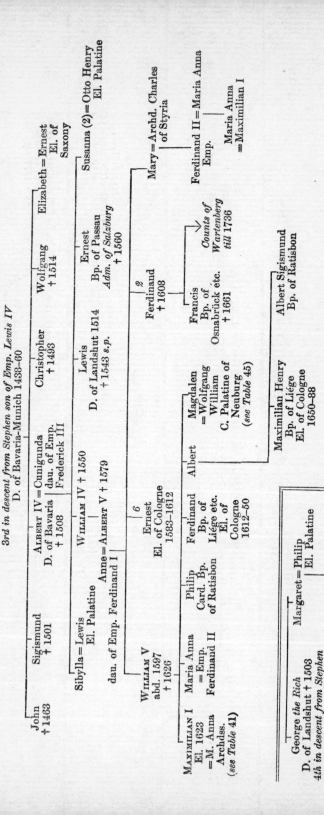

ALBERT III
3rd in descent from Stephen son of Emp. Lewis IV
D. of Bavaria-Munich 1438–60

John † 1463

Sigismund † 1501

ALBERT IV = Cunigunda dau. of Emp. Frederick III
D. of Bavaria † 1508

Christopher † 1493

Wolfgang † 1514

Elizabeth = Ernest El. of Saxony

WILLIAM IV † 1550

Lewis D. of Landshut 1514 † 1543 s.p.

Ernest Bp. of Passau Adm. of Salzburg † 1560

Susanna (2) = Otto Henry El. Palatine

Sibylla = Lewis El. Palatine

Anne = ALBERT V † 1579

Mary = Archd. Charles of Styria

WILLIAM V abd. 1597 † 1626

Ernest El. of Cologne 1583–1612

Ferdinand † 1608

Ferdinand II = Maria Anna Emp.

Maria Anna = Maximilian I

MAXIMILIAN I † 1623 = M. Anna Archdss. (see Table 41)

Maria Anna = Emp. Ferdinand II

Philip Card. Bp. of Ratisbon

Ferdinand Bp. of Liége etc. El. of Cologne 1612–50

Albert

Magdalen = Wolfgang William C. Palatine of Neuburg (see Table 45)

Francis Bp. of Osnabrück etc. † 1661

Counts of Wartenberg till 1736

Maximilian Henry Bp. of Liége El. of Cologne 1650–88

Albert Sigismund Bp. of Ratisbon

George the Rich D. of Landshut † 1503 4th in descent from Stephen son of Emp. Lewis IV

Margaret = Philip El. Palatine

Elizabeth = Rupert (see Table 42)

TABLE 41
GENEALOGIES
THE EMPIRE

BAVARIA (2)

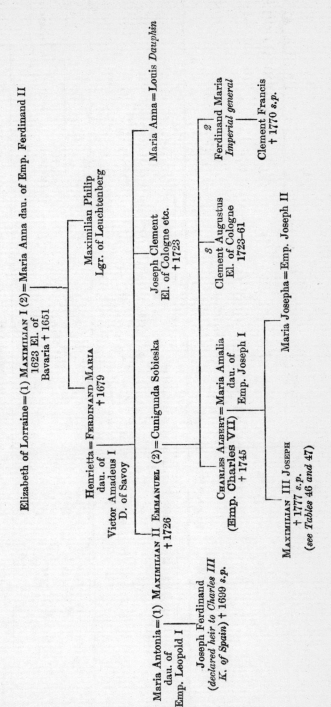

TABLE 42
GENEALOGIES
THE EMPIRE

THE PALATINATE (1) OLD LINE

(Electors Palatine are in small capitals)

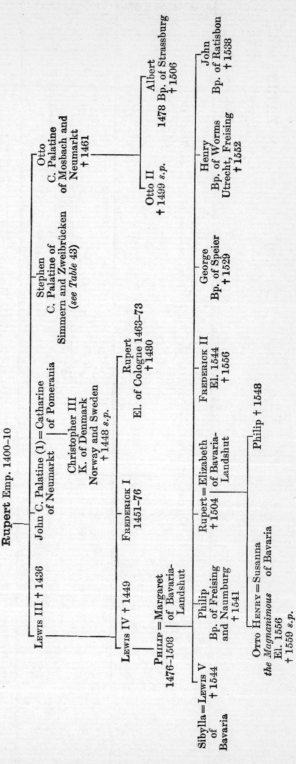

Rupert Emp. 1400–10

Lewis III † 1436   John C. Palatine of Neumarkt = Catharine of Pomerania   Stephen C. Palatine of Simmern and Zweibrücken *(see Table 43)*   Otto C. Palatine of Mosbach and Neumarkt † 1461

Christopher III K. of Denmark Norway and Sweden † 1448 *s.p.*

Otto II † 1499 *s.p.*   Albert 1478 Bp. of Strassburg † 1506

Lewis IV † 1449   Frederick I 1451–76   Rupert El. of Cologne 1463–73 † 1480

Philip = Margaret of Bavaria-Landshut 1476–1508

Rupert = Elizabeth of Bavaria-Landshut † 1504   Philip Bp. of Freising and Naumburg † 1541   George Bp. of Speier † 1529   Frederick II El. 1544 † 1556   Henry Bp. of Worms Utrecht, Freising † 1552   John Bp. of Ratisbon † 1538

Sibylla = Lewis V of † 1544 Bavaria   Otto Henry = Susanna *the Magnanimous* of Bavaria El. 1556 † 1559 *s.p.*   Philip † 1548

TABLE 43

GENEALOGIES
THE EMPIRE

THE PALATINATE (2) SIMMERN LINE

(Electors Palatine are in small capitals)

Stephen C. Palatine of Simmern = Anna heiress of *Veldenz and Sponheim*
and Zweibrücken *(see Table 42)*

Frederick = Margaret of Gelders

Rupert
Bp. of Ratisbon 1492–1507

Lewis
C. Palatine of Zweibrücken
(see Table 44)

Johanna of Nassau-Saarbrück = John I † 1509

John II = Beatrice of Baden
† 1557

George
1559 Simmern
† 1569 *s.p.*

Richard
1569 Simmern
† 1621 *s.p.*

Sabina = Lamoral
C. of Egmont

Helene = Philip
C. of Hanau

FREDERICK III = Maria
1559–76   of Brandenburg-
             Culmbach

John Casimir
1583 *Regent*
† 1592

Christopher
† 1574

Elizabeth = (1) LEWIS VI (2) = Anna dau. of Edzard II
            † 1583   of East Friesland

FREDERICK IV = Louisa Juliana dau. of
† 1610   William I of Orange

Louisa = John C. Palatine
Juliana   of Zweibrücken
          Regent 1610–14

Elizabeth = George William
Charlotte   El. of Brandenburg
            C. Palatine of Simmern

Anna Maria = Charles IX K. of Sweden

Catharine

Elizabeth = FREDERICK V
of England 1619 K. of Bohemia
            1623 dep. † 1632

Maurice
† 1652

Louise
Hollandina
abbess of
Maubuisson

Edward
† 1663
(see Table 3)

Henrietta
= Sigismund of
Transylvania

Philip
† 1655

Sophia
= Ernest
Augustus
(El. of
Hanover)
(see Table 3)

Lewis
1632 *Regent*

Philip
1649

Maurice
Henry
† 1674

Lewis
1655

Henry
Frederick
† 1629

Charlotte = CHARLES
of Hesse- LEWIS
Cassel   † 1680

Elizabeth
abbess of
Herford

Rupert
† 1682

Elizabeth Charlotte = Philip
(see Table 3)   D. of Orleans

CHARLES
† 1685 *s.p.*

TABLE 44

GENEALOGIES

THE EMPIRE

THE PALATINATE (3) ZWEIBRÜCKEN LINE

Lewis C. Palatine of Zweibrücken and Veldenz 1459–89 (*see Table 43*)

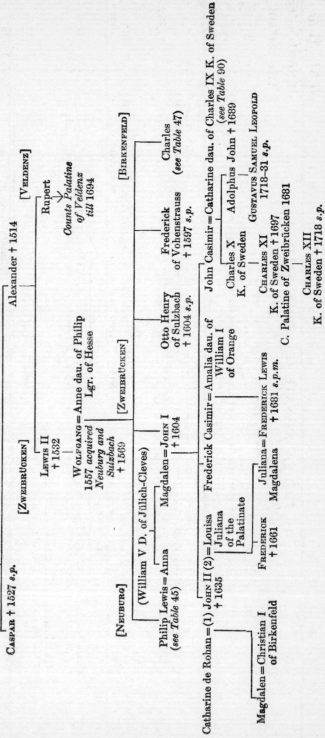

TABLE 45

GENEALOGIES

THE EMPIRE

THE PALATINATE (4) NEUBURG LINE

Philip Lewis = Anna dau. of William V D. of Jülich-Cleves
1569 D. of Neuburg
(see Table 44)

[NEUBURG]   [SULZBACH]

Magdalen = (1) Wolfgang William † 1653
of Bavaria

Augustus (see Table 46)

John Frederick of Hilpoltstein † 1644 s.p.

Philip William (2) = Elizabeth Amalia dau. of George II
1685 El. Palatine   Lgr. of Hesse-Darmstadt
† 1690

Eleonora Magdalen = Emp. Leopold I

John William † 1716 s.p.
(1) = Anna Maria Josepha of Austria
(2) = Maria Anna Louisa of Tuscany

Lewis Antony Coadjutor of Mainz † 1694

Charles Philip † 1742
(1) = Louisa Charlotte widow of M. Lewis of Brandenburg

Alexander Bp. of Augsburg † 1737

Francis Lewis Bp. of Breslau 1683 of Worms 1694 El. of Trier 1716 of Mainz 1729 † 1732

Maria Sophia = Peter K. of Portugal

Maria Anna = Charles II K. of Spain

Philip Wm.

Ferdinand Maria = Maria Anna of Bavaria † 1733

Joseph Charles Emmanuel = Elizabeth Augusta Maria of Sulzbach (see Table 46)

TABLE 46
GENEALOGIES
THE EMPIRE

THE PALATINATE (5) SULZBACH LINE

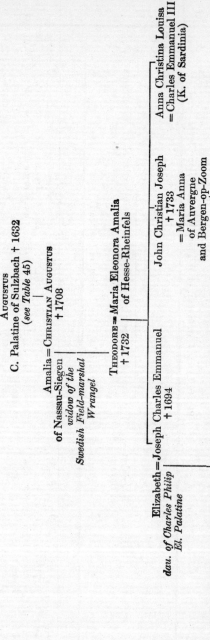

TABLE 47

GENEALOGIES
THE EMPIRE

THE PALATINATE (6) BIRKENFELD LINE AND KINGS OF BAVARIA

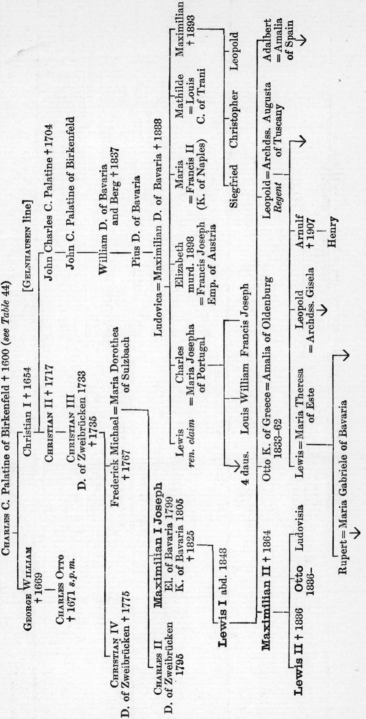

CHARLES C. Palatine of Birkenfeld † 1600 (*see Table 44*)

TABLE 48
GENEALOGIES
THE EMPIRE

SAXONY. HOUSE OF WETTIN: EARLIER ERNESTINE LINE IN GOTHA, WEIMAR AND ALTENBURG

FREDERICK I El. of Saxony † 1428 *representative of the Margraves of Meissen and Landgraves of Thuringia*

FREDERICK II † 1464

Albert of Meissen
(*see Table 49*)

ERNEST = Elizabeth of Bavaria
† 1486

FREDERICK III *the Wise* El.
† 1525

Albert
El. of Mainz
† 1584

Ernest
Abp. of Magdeburg
† 1513

JOHN El.
† 1532

JOHN ERNEST
D. of Coburg † 1553

Sibylla of Cleves = JOHN FREDERICK I El.
(*deprived of electorate 1547*)
† 1554

[WEIMAR]

JOHN WILLIAM † 1573

[GOTHA]

JOHN FREDERICK II † 1594

JOHN ERNEST
of Eisenach
† 1638 *s.p.*

John Philip

[ALTENBURG]
FREDERICK WILLIAM I † 1602

JOHN † 1605

(*line extinct 1672*)

[WEIMAR]

JOHN CASIMIR
of Coburg
† 1633 *s.p.*

JOHN ERNEST
† 1626

[EISENACH]
WILLIAM
† 1662

Elizabeth Sophia = Ernest
[GOTHA]

John Frederick
† 1628

ERNEST = Elizabeth Sophia
the Pious   *heiress of*
† 1679   *Saxe-Altenburg*

BERNARD
† 1678
(*Jena line till 1690*)

Bernard
D. of Franconia
*general in the
Thirty Years' War*
† 1639

JOHN ERNEST II
† 1683
(*see Table 51*)

ADOLPHUS WILLIAM
† 1662

JOHN GEORGE † 1686
(*Eisenach line till 1741*)

ALBERT
of Coburg
† 1699 *s.p.*

BERNARD
of Meiningen
(*see Table 51*)

HENRY
of Römhild
† 1710 *s.p.*

CHRISTIAN
of Eisenberg
† 1707 *s.p.m.*

ERNEST
of Hildburghausen
(*see Table 50*)

[SAALFELD]
JOHN ERNEST
of Saalfeld
† 1679
(*see Table 50*)

FREDERICK
(*see Table 50*)

Albert D. of Meissen and Friesland, *Gov. of the Netherlands* † 1500 (*see Table 48*)

Philip of Hesse

George † 1539 s.p.m.

Henry † 1541

Frederick *Grand Master of the Teutonic Order in Prussia* † 1511

Agnes=MAURICE El. 1547-53

Emily=(3) George M. of Ansbach

AUGUSTUS=Anna of Denmark † 1586

William I of Orange (2)=Anna

CHRISTIAN I † 1591

John Casimir=Elizabeth
C. Palatine of Simmern

CHRISTIAN II † 1611

JOHN GEORGE I † 1656=Magdalen Sibylla of Prussia

Augustus *Adm. of Magdeburg*

Christian † 1691 *Adm. of Merseburg*

Maurice D. of Saxe-Zeitz

JOHN GEORGE II = Magdalen Sibylla dau. of Christian M. of Baireuth † 1680

Christian II

Henry † 1738

JOHN GEORGE III † 1691 = Anna Sophia of Denmark

Maurice William † 1731

FREDERICK AUGUSTUS I elected K. of Poland (Augustus II) 1697 † 1733

JOHN GEORGE IV † 1694 s.p.

Maurice William † 1718

Frederick Henry † 1713

Maurice C. de Saxe *Marshal of France*

Archdss. Maria Josepha=FREDERICK AUGUSTUS II (AUGUSTUS III of Poland) † 1763

Maria Antonia=FREDERICK CHRISTIAN † 1763 dau. of Emp. Charles VII

Xavier † 1806

Charles D. of Courland † 1796

Albert Casimir=Archdss. D. of Teschen † 1822 Maria Christina

Antony † 1836

Clement El. and Abp. of Trier † 1812

Maximilian=Caroline of Parma

Maria Amalia=Charles III of Spain

Maria Anna=Max. Joseph of Bavaria

Maria Josepha=*dauphin* Louis son of Louis XV

FREDERICK AUGUSTUS III
K. Frederick Augustus I 1806-27

Frederick Augustus II † 1854

Albert=Caroline dau. of † 1902 P. Gustavus Vasa

John=Amalia of Bavaria † 1873

George = Maria Anna of Portugal † 1904

Archdss. Louisa=Frederick Augustus III div. 1903

Frederick Christian

John George

Maximilian *priest*

George

Ernest Henry

TABLE 50

SAXONY. LATER ERNESTINE LINES IN GOTHA, COBURG AND ALTENBURG (HILDBURGHAUSEN)

GENEALOGIES
THE EMPIRE

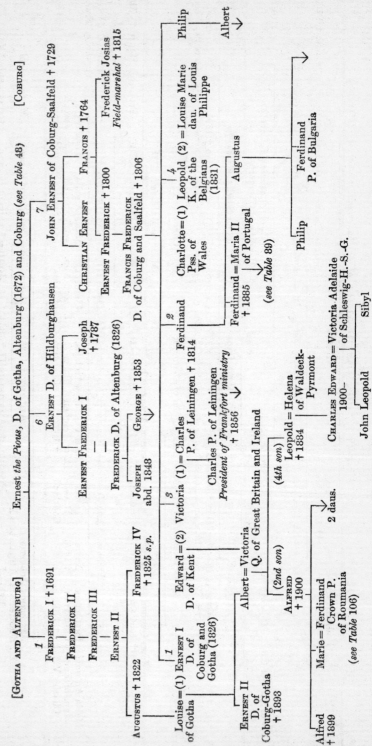

TABLE 51

GENEALOGIES
THE EMPIRE

SAXONY. LATER ERNESTINE LINES IN WEIMAR-EISENACH AND MEININGEN

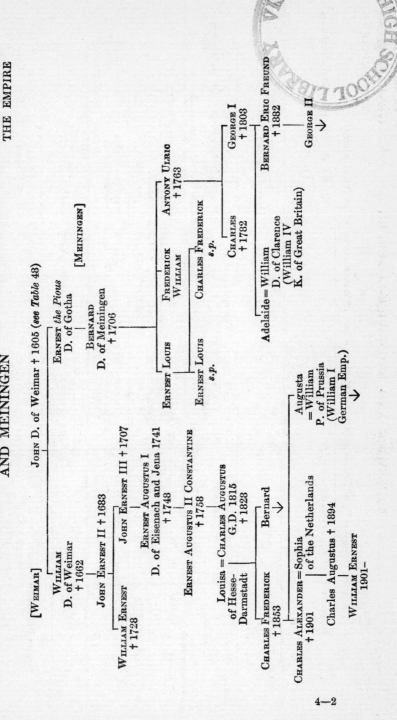

TABLE 52

GENEALOGIES

THE EMPIRE

BRUNSWICK AND BRUNSWICK-LÜNEBURG

Magnus Torquatus D. of Brunswick † 1373 = Catharine dau. of Waldemar 1st El. of Brandenburg

BERNARD D. of Brunswick-Lüneburg

HENRY D. of Brunswick-Wolfenbüttel

HENRY abd. 1521

HENRY JULIUS † 1613

Otto D. of Harburg
(line extinct 1642)

ERNEST of Celle

Francis of Giffhorn

FREDERICK ULRIC † 1634

Sophia = Ernest Casimir of Nassau-Dietz

Christian Bp. of Halberstadt † 1626

Francis Otto † 1559 s.p.

Henry C. of Dannenberg (resigned)

WILLIAM † 1592 (Brunswick-Lüneburg and Celle)

Dorothy Hedwig = Rudolf of Anhalt-Zerbst

Julius Ernest D. of Dannenberg † 1636

Sophia = (3) AUGUSTUS (2) = Dorothea of D. of Brunswick-
Mecklenburg Wolfenbüttel 1635 (see Table 53)

Dorothea = Augustus (see opposite)

ERNEST † 1611

CHRISTIAN † 1633

AUGUSTUS † 1636

FREDERICK † 1648

GEORGE = Anne of Hesse-Darmstadt
P. of Harburg † 1641

7 daus.

CHRISTIAN LEWIS † 1665
= (1) Dorothea of Holstein-Glücksburg

GEORGE WILLIAM D. of Celle † 1705
= Eleonora d'Olbreuse

JOHN = Benedicta FREDERICK Pss. † 1679 Palatine

ERNEST AUGUSTUS = Sophia 1692 El. of Hanover Pss. † 1698 Palatine † 1714

Sophia Amelia = Frederick III K. of Denmark

Charlotte = Rainald Felicitas D. of Modena

Wilhelmina = Emp. Joseph I

Sophia Dorothea = GEORGE LEWIS George I K. of Great Britain and Ireland † 1727 (see Table 4)

Frederick Augustus † 1691

Maximilian William † 1726

Sophia Charlotte = Frederick I K. of Prussia

Ernest Augustus Bp. of Osnabrück D. of York † 1728

GEORGE AUGUSTUS
George II K. of Great Britain and Ireland
↓ (see Table 4)

Sophia Dorothea = Frederick William I K. of Prussia

TABLE 53
GENEALOGIES
THE EMPIRE

BRUNSWICK-WOLFENBÜTTEL

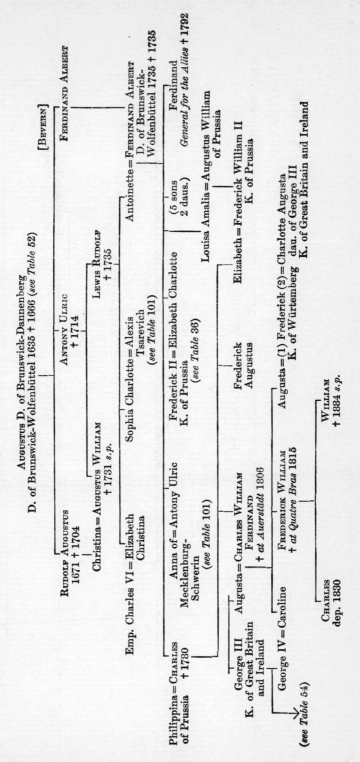

Augustus D. of Brunswick-Dannenberg
D. of Brunswick-Wolfenbüttel 1635 † 1666 (see Table 52)

Rudolf Augustus 1671 † 1704

Antony Ulric † 1714

Lewis Rudolf † 1735

[Bevern]

Ferdinand Albert

Christina = Augustus William † 1731 s.p.

Sophia Charlotte = Alexis Tsarevich (see Table 101)

Antoinette = Ferdinand Albert D. of Brunswick-Wolfenbüttel 1735 † 1735

Emp. Charles VI = Elizabeth Christina

Frederick II = Elizabeth Charlotte K. of Prussia (see Table 36)

Ferdinand General for the Allies † 1792

(5 sons 2 daus.)

Philippina = Charles K. of Prussia of Great Britain † 1780

Anna of = Antony Ulric Mecklenburg-Schwerin (see Table 101)

Frederick Augustus

Louisa Amalia = Augustus William of Prussia

Elizabeth = Frederick William II K. of Prussia

George III K. of Great Britain and Ireland

Augusta = Charles William Ferdinand † at Auerstädt 1806

Frederick William † at Quatre Bras 1815

Augusta = (1) Frederick (2) = Charlotte Augusta K. of Würtemberg dau. of George III K. of Great Britain and Ireland

George IV = Caroline

Charles dep. 1830

William † 1884 s.p.

(see Table 54)

TABLE 54

GENEALOGIES

THE EMPIRE

KINGS OF HANOVER

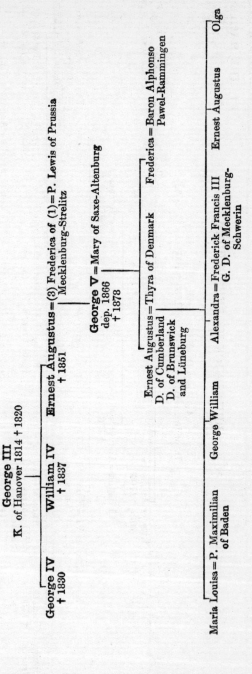

George III
K. of Hanover 1814 † 1820

George IV † 1830 — **William IV** † 1837 — **Ernest Augustus** † 1851 = (3) Frederica of (1) = P. Lewis of Prussia
Mecklenburg-Strelitz

George V = Mary of Saxe-Altenburg
dep. 1866 † 1878

Ernest Augustus = Thyra of Denmark
D. of Cumberland
D. of Brunswick
and Lüneburg

Frederica = Baron Alphonso
Pawel-Rammingen

Maria Louisa = P. Maximilian of Baden

George William

Alexandra = Frederick Francis III
G. D. of Mecklenburg-Schwerin

Ernest Augustus

Olga

AND PRINCES OF BATTENBERG

Philip the Magnanimous (1) = Christina of Saxony
Lgr. of Hesse † 1567 *9th in descent from Henry I D. of Brabant* † 1235   (2) = (*morg.*) Margaret von der Saal

[Landgraves of Hesse-Cassel]   *Counts of Dietz*   [Hesse-Darmstadt]

Sabina = **William IV**   Anne   Lewis III   Philip   **George the Pious**   [Homburg]
dau. of Christopher   † 1592   of Marburg   of Rheinfels
D. of Würtemberg

Maurice abd. 1627   Lewis V † 1626   George II † 1661   Wm. Christopher   Frederick   [Homburg]

Frederick II

William V = Amalia Elizabeth of Hanau-   Ernest   Lewis VI   Frederick   George Christian
† 1637   Münzenberg † 1651   of Hesse-   † 1829   Lewis
(*Regent till* 1650)   Rheinfels   = Elizabeth   † 1839
grand-dau. of   of Gt. Britain
William I of Orange

Hedwig Sophia = **William VI**   Philip   Lewis VII   Frederick † 1829   Frederick † 1661
dau. of Geo. Wm.   † 1663   † at   Ernest Lewis   = Elizabeth
El. of Brandenburg   Latter 1626   of Gt. Britain

[Philippsthal]   Lewis VIII   Lewis IX † 1790

William VII   Charles   Philip   Elizabeth = (1) Frederick III   Lewis X
† 1670   † 1730   † 1721   El. of Brandenburg   **G. D. of Hesse** 1806
(Lewis I)
† 1830

Frederick I   Charles   **William VIII**   Lewis   Lewis II
1720 K. of Sweden † 1751   † 1702   *Regent from* 1730   —
(*see Table* 90)   † 1760   —

Lewis
defender of Gaeta
† 1816

Frederick II (1) = Mary dau. of George II K. of Gt. Britain and Ireland   Lewis III   Charles   Alexander
† 1785   (2) = Philippina dau. of Fredk. Wm. M. of Brandenburg-Schwedt   † 1877   = (*morg.*) Ctss. von Hanke
(Pss. of Battenberg)

Frederick   Lewis = Victoria   Alexander   Henry   Francis
of Rumpenheim   P. of Battenberg   P. of Bulgaria   † 1896   Joseph
British Admiral   1879–86   = Beatrice   = Anna of
of Gt. Britain   Montenegro

William (IX) I = Wilhelmina   Charles   Augusta   Alice = P. Andrew   (*see Table* 5)
1803 Elector   of Denmark   *Regent of Schleswig-*   = Adolphus   of Greece
† 1821   *Holstein* (1767) † 1836   D. of Cambridge

William II abd. 1831   William = Charlotte of   Lewis IV = Alice of   George
Denmark   † 1892   Gt. Britain

Frederick William I   Frederick (1) = Alexandra   Andrew
abd. 1866 † 1875   † 1884   dau. of Tsar Nicholas I
ren. claim   (2) = Anne dau. of
P. Charles of Prussia

Louise   Victoria   Elizabeth   Ernest Lewis   (Alix)
= **Christian IX**   = Louis   = G. D. Sergius   1892 —   Alexandra Féodorovna
K. of Denmark   P. of Battenberg   of Russia   →   = Nicholas II Tsar of Russia
(*see Table* 94)   →

Frederick   Alexander   Frederick = Margaret
William   Charles   of Prussia
† 1888   →

TABLE 56

GENEALOGIES

THE EMPIRE

MARGRAVES AND GRAND DUKES OF BADEN. HOUSE OF ZÄHRINGEN

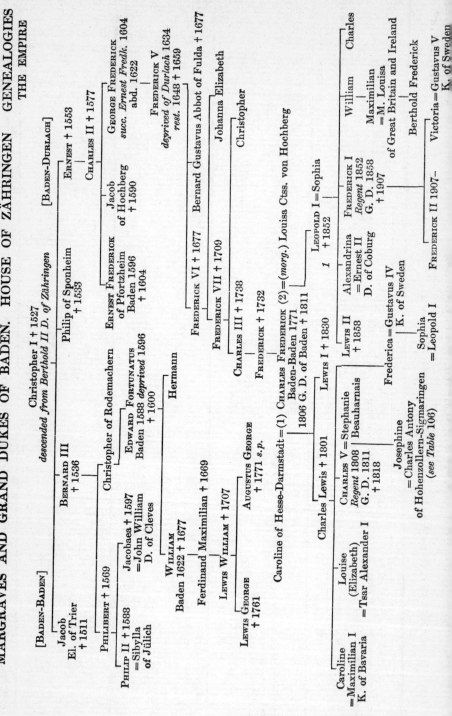

Lewis
C. of Würtemberg

Eberhard I
1493 D. of Würtemberg
† 1496

Ulric V † 1480
of Stuttgart and Mömpelgard

Eberhard II
1493 D. of Würtemberg † 1504 s.p.

Henry
of Mömpelgard

Ulric VI
dep. 1519 rest. 1534 † 1550
Christopher † 1568
Lewis † 1593

George

Frederick I † 1608

[Würtemberg-oels]

Magnus
† 1622

[Mömpelgard]

John Frederick
† 1628

Julius Frederick

[Stuttgart]

Eberhard III
† 1674

Lewis Frederick

Frederick
of Neustadt

Ulric
of Neuburg
† 1671

William Lewis † 1677

Frederick Charles

Ferdinand William
Danish general
† 1701

Eberhard Lewis † 1733

Charles Alexander † 1737

Charles Eugene
† 1793

Lewis Eugene
† 1795

Frederick Eugene
† 1797

Charlotte = (2) Frederick II (1) = Augusta of
of Gt. Britain   K. Frederick I   Brunswick
                  1806 † 1816

Lewis (2) = Henrietta of
             Nassau-Weilburg

Eugene
† 1822

William
† 1830

Alexander
† 1833

Ferdinand
Governor of Mainz
† 1834

Catharine = (2) William I
of Russia   † 1864
Pauline = (3)
dau. of Lewis
D. of
Würtemberg

Catharine = Jerome Napoleon
             K. of Westphalia

Paul
= (morg.) Ctss. Rhedey

Alexander

Charlotte = Grand D. Michael
             of Russia

Frederick = Catharine

William II

Alexander
Francis D. of Teck
† 1900
= Mary of Cambridge

Alexander

Philip

Albert

Adolphus D. of Teck
= Margaret Grosvenor
→

Victoria Mary
= George V
K. of Gt. Britain
and Ireland

Francis
† 1910

Alexander
= Alice of
Albany

(2)
Sophia = William III
K. of the
Netherlands

(3)
Catharine
= Frederick

(3)
Charles = Olga
† 1891   Nicolaïevna
         of Russia

TABLE 58
GENEALOGIES
THE EMPIRE

ANHALT

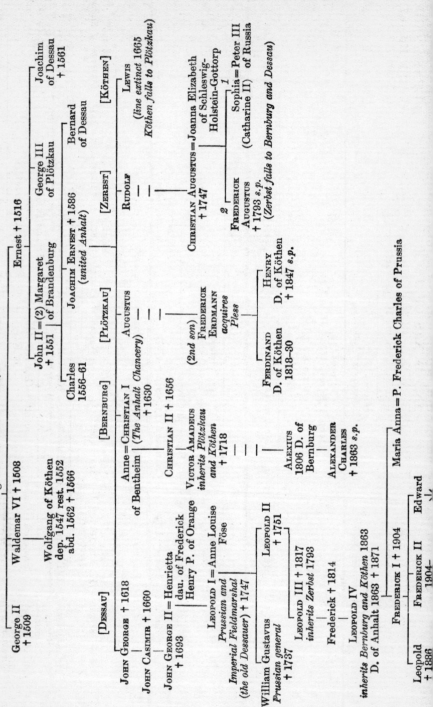

George I P. of Anhalt † 1474

Ernest † 1516

Waldemar VI † 1508

John II = (2) Margaret † 1551 of Brandenburg

George III of Plötzkau

Joachim of Dessau † 1561

Wolfgang of Köthen dep. 1547 rest. 1552 abd. 1562 † 1566

Charles 1556–61

Joachim Ernest † 1586 (united Anhalt)

Bernard of Dessau

[Dessau]

[Bernburg] Anne = Christian I (The Anhalt Chancery) of Bentheim † 1630

[Plötzkau] Augustus

[Zerbst] Rudolf

[Köthen] Lewis (line extinct 1665 Köthen falls to Plötzkau)

George II † 1609

John George † 1618

Christian II † 1656

Frederick Erdmann acquires Pless (2nd son)

Christian Augustus = Joanna Elizabeth † 1747 of Schleswig-Holstein-Gottorp

John Casimir † 1660

John George II = Henrietta dau. of Frederick † 1693 Henry P. of Orange

Victor Amadeus inherits Plötzkau and Köthen † 1718

Ferdinand D. of Köthen 1818–30

Henry D. of Köthen † 1847 s.p.

Frederick Augustus † 1793 s.p. (Zerbst falls to Bernburg and Dessau)

Sophia = Peter III (Catharine II) of Russia

Leopold I = Anne Louise Föse Prussian and Imperial Fieldmarshal (the old Dessauer) † 1747

Alexius 1806 D. of Bernburg

Alexander Charles † 1863 s.p.

William Gustavus Prussian general † 1737

Leopold II † 1751

Leopold III † 1817 inherits Zerbst 1793

Frederick † 1814

Leopold IV inherits Bernburg and Köthen 1863 D. of Anhalt 1863 † 1871

Maria Anna = P. Frederick Charles of Prussia

Frederick I † 1904

Leopold † 1886

Frederick II 1904–

Edward

TABLE 59

GENEALOGIES
THE EMPIRE

SCHLESWIG-HOLSTEIN SUCCESSION

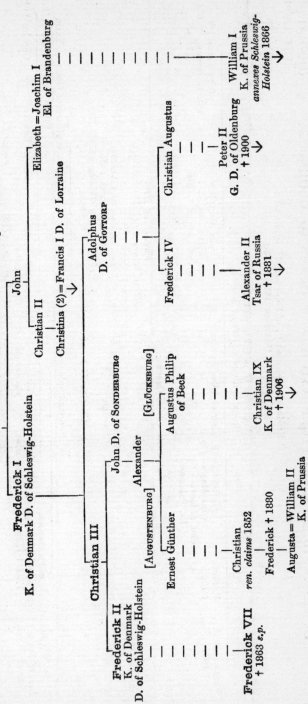

TABLE 60

GENEALOGIES

THE EMPIRE

DUKES OF HOLSTEIN-GOTTORP AND GRAND DUKES OF OLDENBURG

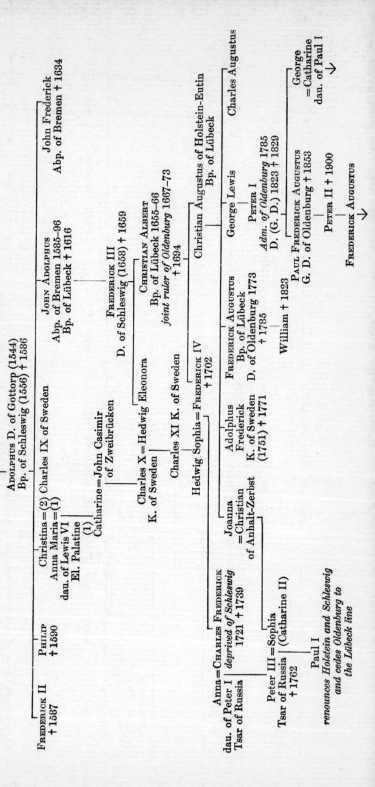

HENRY IV = Dorothea of Brandenburg

D. of Mecklenburg-Schwerin and Güstrow † 1477

MAGNUS II = Sophia of Pomerania
† 1503

HENRY V = Ursula
D. of Schwerin of Brandenburg
† 1552

Magnus
Bp. of Schwerin † 1550

[SCHWERIN]

Sophia = John El. of Saxony

ALBERT VII = Anna dau. of Joachim I El. of Brandenburg
D. of Güstrow † 1547

JOHN ALBERT I = Sophia
D. of Güstrow dau. of Albert
and Schwerin D. of Prussia
† 1576

ULRIC III
Bp. of Schwerin and
D. of Güstrow and Schwerin
† 1603

CHARLES I
D. of Güstrow and Schwerin
† 1610

Christopher = Elizabeth
D. of Gadebusch of Sweden
and Ratzeburg

JOHN VII D. of Schwerin † 1592

[STRELITZ]

ADOLPHUS FREDERICK I dep. 1628 rest. 1632 † 1658

Margaret Elizabeth
(1) = of Anhalt-Bernburg
JOHN ALBERT II (3) = Eleonora Maria of
D. of Güstrow Anhalt-Bernburg
dep. 1628 rest. 1632
† 1636

GUSTAVUS ADOLPHUS D. of Güstrow
† 1695 s.p.

ADOLPHUS FREDERICK II

Frederick D. of Grabow
† 1688

Caroline
= Christian
Lewis II

Charles Lewis
Frederick

CHRISTIAN LEWIS I † 1692

ADOLPHUS
FREDERICK III
† 1752

Adolphus

George
Augustus

Ernest

FREDERICK WILLIAM
† 1713

CHARLES
LEWIS II † 1756
= Caroline

Lewis

ADOLPHUS
FREDERICK IV
† 1794

CHARLES II
G. D. 1815
† 1816

Sophia
Charlotte
= George III
K. of
Great Britain

Sophia
Charlotte
Ernest Augustus (K. of Hanover)

Frederica
(1) = P. Lewis
of Prussia
(3) = Ernest Augustus (K. of Hanover)

Alexandra
= Fredk.
Francis III

CHARLES LEOPOLD
dep. 1728 † 1746
(2) = Catharine Ivanovna
of Russia

FREDERICK † 1785

FREDERICK FRANCIS I
G. D. 1815 † 1837

Sophia
= Frederick V
K. of Denmark

Louisa
= Frederick
William III
K. of Prussia

GEORGE
† 1860

Caroline
= Frederick VII
K. of Denmark

FREDERICK = Elizabeth
1904– of Anhalt

Adolphus
Frederick

Antony Ulric = Elizabeth (Anna)
of Brunswick-
Wolfenbüttel
† 1775

Helena of Russia = (1) Frederick Lewis (2) = Augusta Caroline
dau. of Charles Augustus
G. D. of Weimar

PAUL FREDERICK
† 1842
(1)

FREDERICK = Augusta dau. of Adolphus
WILLIAM D. of Cambridge

Jutta (Militza)
= P. Danilo
of Montenegro

Ferdinand = Helena
(2)
D. of Orleans

Augustina = (1) FREDERICK FRANCIS II (3) = Marie of Schwarzburg-Rudolstadt
of Reuss-Schleiz-Köstritz † 1883

Henry = Wilhelmina Q. of Holland

John Albert
Regent of Brunswick

Cecilia = William German P. Imperial

Augustina = (1) Frederick Lewis (2)
Paul Frederick

FREDERICK FRANCIS III
† 1897
= Alexandra

FREDERICK FRANCIS IV 1897–

Alexandrina = Christian Crown P. of Denmark

TABLE 62
GENEALOGIES
THE EMPIRE

DUKES OF POMERANIA FROM 1478

Eric II † 1474

Bogislav X = Margaret | Sophia = Magnus II
D. of all Pomerania 1478 | dau. of Frederick II | D. of Mecklenburg
† 1523 | El. of Brandenburg

[WOLGAST]   [STETTIN]

George I D. of Wolgast (2) = (1) Margaret dau. of
† 1531   Joachim El. of Brandenburg

Barnim XI
D. of Stettin 1532-69
† 1573

Philip I
D. of Wolgast
† 1560

John Frederick
Bp. of Cammin 1556-74
D. of Stettin 1569
† 1600
= Erdmutha
dau. of John George
El. of Brandenburg

Bogislav XIII
D. of Stettin
† 1606

Ernest Lewis
D. of Wolgast
† 1592

Barnim XII
D. of Stettin
† 1603
= Anna Maria
dau. of John George
El. of Brandenburg

Casimir IX
Bp. of Cammin
1574-1602

Francis
Bp. of Cammin
s.p.

Philip II
† 1618 s.p.

Bogislav XIV
D. of all Pomerania 1625
† 1637 s.p.

Agnes = Philip Julius
dau. of John George   D. of Wolgast
El. of Brandenburg   † 1625 s.p.

George III
† 1617

Ulric
Bp. of Cammin
† 1622

Anna = Ernest D. of Croy

Ernest Bogislav
D. of Croy
Bp. of Cammin
resigned Pomerania to Brandenburg 1650
† 1684

TABLE 62 A
GENEALOGIES
THE EMPIRE

LATER COUNTS OF MANSFELD (OF EISLEBEN)

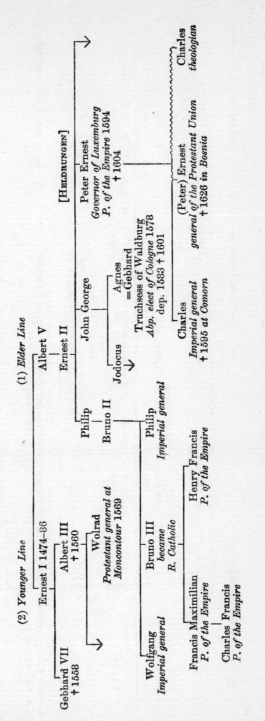

(1) Elder Line

[HELDRUNGEN]

Albert V
Ernest II
Philip — Bruno II
John George
Jodocus
Agnes = Gebhard, Truchsess of Waldburg, Abp. elect of Cologne 1578, dep. 1583 † 1601
Peter Ernest, Governor of Luxemburg, P. of the Empire 1594 † 1604
Philip, Imperial general
Charles, Imperial general † 1595 at Comorn
(Peter) Ernest, general of the Protestant Union † 1626 in Bosnia
Charles, theologian

(2) Younger Line

Ernest I 1474–86
Gebhard VII † 1558
Albert III † 1560
Wolrad, Protestant general at Moncontour 1569
Bruno III, became R. Catholic
Henry Francis, P. of the Empire
Wolfgang, Imperial general
Francis Maximilian, P. of the Empire
Charles Francis, P. of the Empire

TABLE 63
GENEALOGIES
THE NETHERLANDS

BURGUNDY AND BRABANT

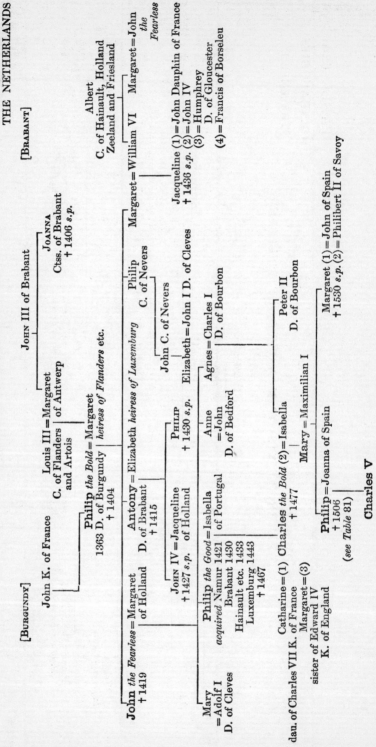

TABLE 64

GENEALOGIES

THE NETHERLANDS

ORANGE-NASSAU; STADHOLDERS OF HOLLAND AND ZEELAND ETC.

John C. of Nassau † 1475

Engelbert † 1504

William = Juliana of Stolberg

C. of Dillenburg

John † 1516

John de Chalons
P. of Orange

Philibert
P. of Orange
† 1530

Claude = Henry
of Breda

René
P. of Orange
† 1544 s.p.

William I the Silent (1) Anne of Egmont = (2) Anne of Saxony = (3) Charlotte de Bourbon = (4) Louisa de Coligny
P. of Orange
Stadholder of Holland and Zeeland etc.
† 1584

John
C. of Dillenburg
(see Table 65)

Lewis † 1574

Adolphus † 1568

Henry † 1575

6 daus.

Frederick = Amalia of Solms
Henry
† 1647

Isabella = Henry
D. of Bouillon

Henry Marshal Turenne

Amalia = Frederick Casimir of Zweibrücken

Louisa Juliana = Frederick IV El. Palatine

Frederick V El. Palatine

Anna
(see Table 65)

Lewis of Lecke

(d'Auverquerque)

(1) Philip William
P. of Orange
† 1618

(2) Maurice
† 1625

Albertina = William Frederick of Nassau-Dietz
Agnes

Henrietta Amalia = Henry Casimir (see Table 65)

Henrietta = John George II
Catharine | of Anhalt-Dessau

Leopold
the old Dessauer
(see Table 58)

Louisa = Frederick William
Henrietta El. of Brandenburg

Mary = William II † 1650

Charles I K. of England

James II

Mary = William III
King of England and Scotland
† 1702 s.p.

TABLE 65

NASSAU-DILLENBURG, NASSAU-SIEGEN; KINGS OF HOLLAND; STADHOLDERS OF (WEST) FRIESLAND; GRAND DUKES OF LUXEMBURG

GENEALOGIES
THE NETHERLANDS

Johannette=(3) John C. of Nassau-Dillenburg (1) =Elizabeth dau. of George Lgr. of Leuchtenberg
of Sayn-Wittgenstein   9th in descent (Ottonian line)   (2) =Cunigunda dau. of Frederick III El. Palatine
                              from Henry II C. of Nassau † 1247

[NASSAU-SIEGEN]   [NASSAU-DILLENBURG]   [NASSAU-DIETZ]   [NASSAU-HADAMAR]

WILLIAM LEWIS
Stadholder of
Friesland
† 1620 s.p.
=Anne
dau. of
William I
of Orange

John
† 1623

John Maurice
Governor-
General of Dutch
W. Indies
P. of the Empire
† 1679

Philip
† 1595

George
† 1623

Lewis Henry
† 1662

George Lewis
† 1656

Henry
† 1701

Lewis Günther
† 1604 s.p.

HENRY
CASIMIR I
† 1640

ERNEST CASIMIR
† 1632

WILLIAM FREDERICK
† 1664
=Albertina Agnes
dau. of F.ederick Henry

HENRY CASIMIR II † 1696

John Lewis
† 1653

Maurice Henry
† 1679

Francis
Alexander
† 1711 s.p.m.

Amelia
=William
C. of Solms

11 daus.

[LUXEMBURG]

John
Francis
† 1699

William
Hyacinth
† 1743

William
† 1724 s.p.

Christian
† 1739 s.p.

JOHN WILLIAM FRISO † 1711
(declared heir by William III)

Anne=WILLIAM IV
dau. of George II   Hereditary Stadholder
K. of England   of the Netherlands 1748
† 1751

WILLIAM V dep. 1802
† 1806

Sophia Hedwig
=Charles Leopold
D. of Mecklenburg-
Schwerin

George William of Nassau-Weilburg
18th in descent (Walramian line)
from Henry II C. of Nassau

ADOLPHUS
G. D. of
Luxemburg 1890
† 1905

Nicholas
=(morg.)
→

Helen
=G. Victor
P. of Waldeck

Frederick Wm. II K. of Prussia   Wilhelmina=WILLIAM I K. of the Netherlands 1815
                                                      Holland only 1830
                                                      abd. 1840 † 1843

Frederick=Louisa of Prussia

WILLIAM
G. D. 1905–

Hilda
=Frederick II
G. D. of Baden

Maria=Hermann
P. of Wied

Frederick
P. of Waldeck
and Pyrmont

Sophia
=Oscar II
K. of Sweden

Frederick William III

Frederica=WILLIAM II
                † 1849

Louisa

Marianne=Albert
           ↓ of Prussia
(see Table 36)

Louisa.
=Charles XV K. of Sweden

6 daus.

Wilhelmina=William
                P. of Wied

Elizabeth=Charles
           K. of Roumania

Albert

Anna=WILLIAM II
        † 1849
of Russia

Sophia dau. of William I K. of Würtemberg=(1) WILLIAM III (2) =Emma of Waldeck
                                                          † 1890

Wilhelmina=Henry D. of Mecklenburg (P. of the Netherlands)
                        1890–

William Nicholas
P. of Orange † 1879

Alexander
P. of Orange † 1884

TABLE 66

GENEALOGIES

THE NETHERLANDS

BELGIUM. HOUSE OF COBURG

Leopold I
P. of Saxe-Coburg-Gotha (*see Table 50*)
elected K. of the Belgians 1831 † 1865
= Louisa dau. of Louis-Philippe K. of the French

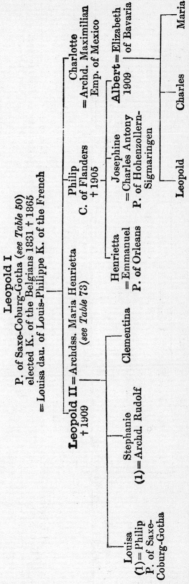

Leopold II = Archdss. Maria Henrietta
† 1909   (*see Table 73*)

Louisa
(1) = Philip
P. of Saxe-
Coburg-Gotha

Stephanie
(1) = Archd. Rudolf

Clementina

Henrietta
= Emmanuel
P. of Orleans

Philip
C. of Flanders
† 1905

Josephine
= Charles Antony
P. of Hohenzollern-
Sigmaringen

Charlotte
= Archd. Maximilian
Emp. of Mexico

Albert = Elizabeth
1909   of Bavaria

Leopold   Charles   Maria

TABLE 67

GENEALOGIES

ITALY

SAVOY

COUNTS OF SAVOY

AMADEUS VIII = Mary dau. of Philip the Bold D. of Burgundy

first D. of Savoy 1416–1434 abd. 1434 *Pope Felix V* 1440–9 † 1451

Louis = Anne de Lusignan (*titular heiress of Cyprus and Jerusalem*) † 1465

AMADEUS IX † 1472 = Yolande dau. of Charles VII K. of France

Louis = Charlotte de Lusignan

Philip II *de Bresse* (*the landless*) † 1497 (1) = Margaret of Bourbon (2) = Claudia de Penthièvre

Charlotte = Louis XI K. of France

Bona = Galeazzo Maria D. of Milan

Agnes = Francis C. of Longueville

Louis I

[NEMOURS]

Philip = Charlotte D. of Nemours † 1533

PHILIBERT † 1482

CHARLES I † 1490

CHARLES II † 1496 *s.p.*

PHILIBERT II *the Fair* † 1504 (2) = Margaret dau. of Maximilian I

CHARLES III † 1553 = Beatrix of Portugal

Louisa = Charles C. of Angoulême

Francis I K. of France

EMMANUEL PHILIBERT *Ironhead* † 1580 = Margaret dau. of Francis I K. of France

James 2nd D. † 1585

Margaret

Henry 4th D.

Réné C. of Tende grand seneschal of France † 1525 at Pavia

CHARLES EMMANUEL I *the Great* † 1630 [CARIGNANO] = Catharine dau. of Philip II K. of Spain

Charles Emmanuel 3rd D. † 1595

Louis 5th D.

Charles Amadeus 6th D.

Henry 7th D. *s.p.*

M. Giovanna = Charles Emmanuel II

Thomas Francis = Marie de Bourbon P. of Carignano *heiress of Soissons*

M. Francesca (*see Table 89*)

Eugene = Olympia C. of Soissons Mancini

Philibert P. of Oneglia *in Spanish service*

VICTOR AMADEUS I † 1637 = Christina dau. of Henry IV K. of France

Maurice Card.

Emmanuel Philibert

Eugene Francois *Imperial gen.* † 1736 *s.p.*

Eugene C. of Soissons

Cs. of Soissons to 1734

FRANCIS HYACINTH † 1638

CHARLES EMMANUEL II † 1675

Margaret *Regent of Portugal* = Francis IV D. of Mantua

V. Amadeus Louis Victor

Eugenio P. of Carignano † 1888

Marie (Pss. de Lamballe) murd. 1792

Anna Maria = VICTOR AMADEUS II K. of Sicily 1713 K. of Sardinia 1720 abd. 1730 † 1732 = dau. of Orleans

Mary Adelaide = Louis D. of Burgundy

Philip V = Louisa Maria K. of Spain

Eugene Joseph

Eugenio P. of Carignano † 1888

V. Amadeus Charles Emmanuel

CHARLES ALBERT 1831–49 = Theresa of Tuscany [CARIGNANO]

CHARLES EMMANUEL III K. of Sardinia 1730–73 = Marie Antoinette of Spain

VICTOR EMMANUEL II K. of Italy 1861 † 1878 = Adelaide of Austria

Ferdinand

VICTOR AMADEUS III † 1796

Margaret = HUMBERT I murd. 1900

Clotilda = P. Napoleon

Maria = Luis K. of Portugal

CHARLES EMMANUEL IV abd. 1802 † 1819

CHARLES FELIX 1821–31 *s.p.*

Maurice † 1799

VICTOR EMMANUEL III 1900– = Helen of Montenegro

Letizia = (2) Amadeus (1) = M. dal Pozzo 1870–3 † 1890 ↓ K. of Spain

VICTOR EMMANUEL I

TABLE 68

GENEALOGIES
ITALY

MILAN

[VISCONTI]

[SFORZA]

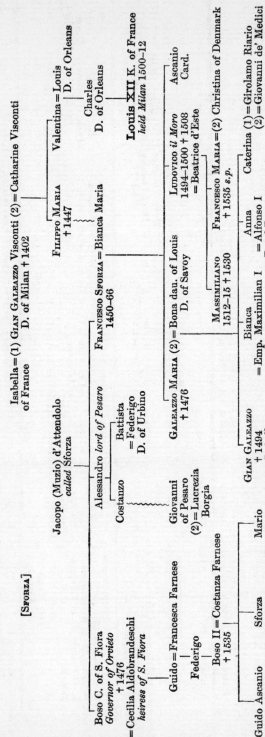

Isabella = (1) GIAN GALEAZZO Visconti (2) = Catharine Visconti
of France   D. of Milan † 1402

Valentina = Louis
   D. of Orleans

Charles
D. of Orleans

FILIPPO MARIA † 1447

FRANCESCO SFORZA = Bianca Maria
1450–66

Louis XII K. of France
held Milan 1500–12

Ludovico il Moro
1494–1500 † 1508
= Beatrice d'Este

Ascanio
Card.

FRANCESCO MARIA = (2) Christina of Denmark
† 1535 s.p.

Jacopo (Muzio) d'Attendolo
called Sforza

Alessandro lord of Pesaro

Battista
= Federigo
D. of Urbino

Costanzo

Giovanni
of Pesaro
(2) = Lucrezia
Borgia

GALEAZZO MARIA (2) = Bona dau. of Louis
† 1476   D. of Savoy

MASSIMILIANO
1512–15 † 1530

Bianca
= Emp. Maximilian I

Anna
= Alfonso I
D. of Ferrara

Caterina (1) = Girolamo Riario
(2) = Giovanni de' Medici

Bona = Sigismund I K. of Poland

GIAN GALEAZZO
† 1494
= Isabella
of Naples

Francesco † 1521 s.p.

Cs. of S. Fiora
to 1833

Boso C. of S. Fiora
Governor of Orvieto
† 1476
= Cecilia Aldobrandeschi
heiress of S. Fiora

Guido = Francesca Farnese

Federigo

Boso II = Costanza Farnese
† 1535

Mario
French general
† 1611

Sforza
papal and
imperial general
† 1605

Guido Ascanio
Card. † 1564

Sforza Pallavicini
Card.
historian of the
Council of Trent

TABLE 69

GENEALOGIES

ITALY

FLORENCE AND TUSCANY: HOUSE OF MEDICI

Giovanni (d'Averardo) de' Medici † 1429

Lorenzo † 1440

Pier Francesco

Cosimo *Pater Patriae* † 1464

Piero = Lucrezia Tornabuoni
† 1469

Lorenzo = Clarice Orsini
the Magnificent † 1492

Giuliano murd. 1478

Giuliano = Semiramide Appiani
† 1503

Lorenzo = Semiramide Appiani
† 1503

Giovanni = (2) Caterina Sforza
† 1498

Giovanni = Maria Salviati
delle Bande Nere

Pier Francesco
= Maria Soderini

Laodomia
= Francesco Salviati

Giuliano
† 1588

Lorenzino *murderer of Alessandro*
† 1548

Laodomia
(2) = Pietro Strozzi

Cosimo I (1) = Eleonora de Toledo 1537
(2) = Camilla Martelli

D. of Florence 1537
G. D. of Tuscany 1569
† 1574

Maddelena = Fr. Cibò

Contessina = Pietro Ridolfi

Niccolò Card.

Giuliano D. of Nemours † 1516

Ippolito Card. murd. 1535

Giulio **Clement VII** † 1534

Antonio de' Medici
2nd cousin of Giovanni (d'Averardo)

Octavian *last Gonfalonier* † 1546

Alessandro **Leo XI** † 1605

Pietro † 1503
= Alfonsina Orsini

Lucrezia = Jacopo Salviati

Giovanni **Leo X** † 1521

Maria

Giovanni Card.

Clarice = Filippo Strozzi

Lorenzo = Madeleine de la Tour d'Auvergne
Lorenzo D. of Urbino

Pietro Strozzi

ALESSANDRO D. of Florence 1531
murd. 1537
= (1) Margaret of Austria

Caterina = Henry II K. of France
(see Table 23)

Garzia † 1562

Giovanni Card. † 1562

FERDINAND I † 1609
= Christina of Lorraine

Francis † 1587
= Bianca Capella

Joanna = (1) Francis † 1587
Archdss. (2) = Bianca Capella

Maria = Henry IV K. of France
(see Table 24)

Piero † 1604
= Eleonora de Toledo murd. 1576

Isabella murd. 1576
= Paolo Giordano Orsini

Virginia
= Caesar D. of Modena

Lucrezia
= Alfonso II D. of Ferrara

Claudia (1) = Federigo D. of Urbino
(2) = Leopold C. of Tyrol

Cosimo II = M. Magdalen *sister of Emp. Ferdinand II*
† 1621

Ferdinand Charles = Anna

Eleonora = Vincent I D. of Mantua

Emp. Leopold I (2) = Claudia

FERDINAND II † 1670

Leopold Card. † 1675

Emp. Leopold I (2) = Claudia

Margaret = Odoardo D. of Parma

Cosimo III † 1723
= Margaret dau. of Gaston D. of Orleans

Francis Maria Card. † 1711

Anna = (2) John William El. Palatine

TABLE 70

GENEALOGIES

ITALY

DUKES OF PARMA: FARNESE LINE

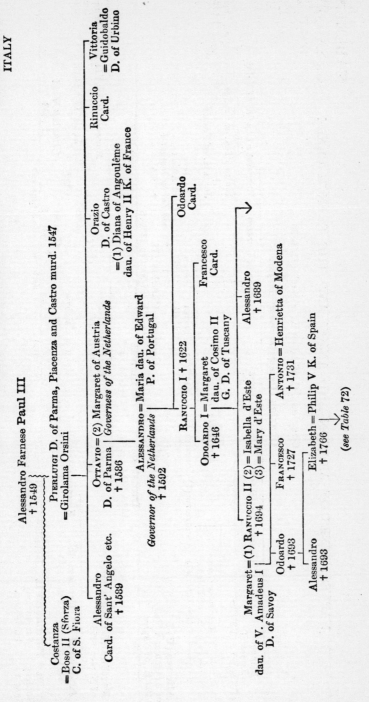

Alessandro Farnese **Paul III** † 1549

Costanza
=Boso II (Sforza)
C. of S. Fiora

Pierluigi D. of Parma, Piacenza and Castro murd. 1547
=Girolama Orsini

Alessandro
Card. of Sant' Angelo etc.
† 1689

Ottavio = (2) Margaret of Austria
D. of Parma   *Governess of the Netherlands*
† 1586

Orazio
D. of Castro
=(1) Diana of Angoulême
dau. of Henry II K. of France

Rinuccio
Card.

Vittoria
=Guidobaldo
D. of Urbino

Alessandro = Maria dau. of Edward
P. of Portugal
Governor of the Netherlands
† 1592

Ranuccio I † 1622

Odoardo
Card.

Odoardo I = Margaret
† 1646   dau. of Cosimo II
G. D. of Tuscany

Francesco
Card.

Alessandro
† 1689

Margaret=(1) Ranuccio II (2) =Isabella d'Este
dau. of V. Amadeus I † 1694 (3) =Mary d'Este
D. of Savoy

Odoardo
† 1693

Francesco
† 1727

Antonio=Henrietta of Modena
† 1731

Alessandro
† 1693

Elizabeth = Philip V K. of Spain
† 1766

(see Table 72)

TABLE 71

GENEALOGIES

ITALY

NAPLES: LINES OF ARAGON AND ANJOU AND THE FRENCH CLAIM

Charles I C. of Anjou K. of Naples 1266–85

Charles II = Mary heiress of Hungary

Blanche = James II K. of Aragon and Sicily

Charles Martel

Robert 1309–43

John of Durazzo

Margaret = Charles of Valois

Lewis the Great K. of Poland (see Table 95)

Mary = Charles of Valois †1328

Mary = Charles of Valois †1328

Philip VI K. of France

Mary = Charles †1328

Andrew = (1) **Joanna I** 1343–82 s.p. adopted Louis D. of Anjou

Charles †1348

Mary (1) = Charles †1348

Lewis †1362

John K. of France

Louis 2 **D. of Anjou** †1385 adopted by Joanna I

Margaret = **Charles III** K. of Naples 1382–6

Ladislas 1386–1414 s.p.

Joanna II 1414–35 s.p.*

Louis II †1417

Louis III †1434 s.p.

Réné †1480 (see Table 34)

John of Calabria †1470

Charles C. of Mayenne †1472

Charles †1481 s.p. declared Louis XI his heir

Mary = Charles VII K. of France

Louis XI †1483

Charles VIII †1498

Eleanor = Hercules I D. of Ferrara

Nicholas †1473 s.p.

Alfonso (V) I K. of Aragon and Sicily 1435 K. of Naples †1458

Ferdinand I (Ferrante) K. of Naples 1458–94

Alfonso II 1494–5

Frederick 1496–1501

Ferdinand II (Ferrantino) 1495–6 s.p.

Isabella = Gian Galeazzo D. of Milan

Sanchia = Godfrey Borgia

* Adopted (a) Alfonso V, (b) Louis III, (c) Réné

ITALY

NAPLES (TWO SICILIES) AND PARMA: BOURBON LINES

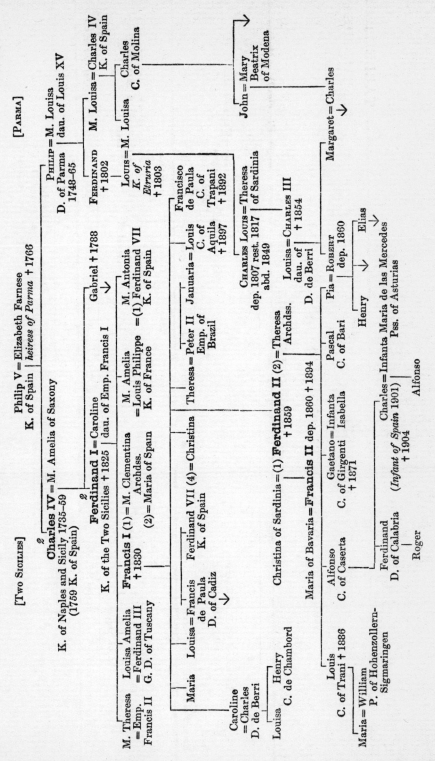

TABLE 73

GENEALOGIES

ITALY

GRAND DUKES OF TUSCANY AND MODENA

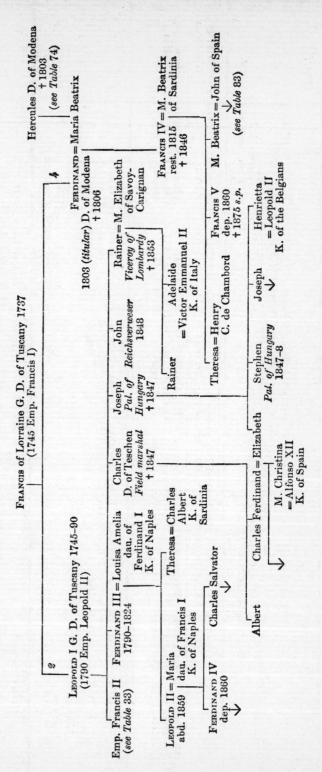

Francis of Lorraine G. D. of Tuscany 1737
(1745 Emp. Francis I)

Hercules D. of Modena
† 1803
(see Table 74)

Ferdinand = Maria Beatrix

1803 (titular) D. of Modena
† 1806

Leopold I G. D. of Tuscany 1745–90
(1790 Emp. Leopold II)

Emp. Francis II (see Table 33)

Ferdinand III = Louisa Amelia dau. of Ferdinand I K. of Naples
1790–1824

Charles D. of Teschen Field marshal † 1847

Joseph Pal. of Hungary † 1847

Rainer = M. Elizabeth of Savoy-Carignan Viceroy of Lombardy † 1853

John Reichsverweser 1848

Francis IV = M. Beatrix of Sardinia
rest. 1815 † 1846

Leopold II = Maria dau. of Francis I K. of Naples
abd. 1859

Theresa = Charles Albert K. of Sardinia

Rainer

Adelaide = Victor Emmanuel II K. of Italy

Theresa = Henry C. de Chambord

Stephen Pal. of Hungary 1847–8

Francis V dep. 1860 † 1875 s.p.

Henrietta = Leopold II K. of the Belgians

M. Beatrix = John of Spain
(see Table 83)

Ferdinand IV dep. 1860

Charles Salvator

Charles Ferdinand = Elizabeth

Joseph

Albert

M. Christina = Alfonso XII K. of Spain

Marquises of Este, lords of Ferrara, Modena and Reggio

Nicholas III † 1441

[FERRARA AND MODENA]

[ESTE]

[MODENA]

Lionel M. of Este † 1450

Borso M. of Este 1452 D. of Modena D. of Ferrara 1470 † 1471

HERCULES I = Eleanor of Naples D. of Ferrara and Modena † 1505

Sigismund M. of St Martin

Lucrezia = Alberic de Malaspina

Hercules = Angela Sforza † 1617

Sigismund II *Spanish Viceroy of Sicily* † 1579

Ferdinand † 1540

Hippolyto Card. Abp. of Milan † 1520

Beatrice = Ludovico Sforza *Moro*

Alfonso M. of Montecchio *French general* † 1587

Isabella = Francesco II D. of Mantua

ALFONSO I (1) = Anna Sforza (2) = (3) Lucrezia Borgia † 1534

Hippolyto Card. Abp. of Milan † 1572

Francesco M. of Massa-Lombarda *imperial and French general*

CAESAR = Virginia de' Medici D. of Modena and Reggio † 1628

Alessandro Card. Bp. of Ferrara † 1624

Philip *minister in Savoy* † 1592 = Maria nat. dau. of Emmanuel Philibert D. of Savoy

HERCULES II = Renée of France † 1558

Anna (1) = Francis D. of Guise (2) = James D. of Nemours M. of Villars

Ludovico Card. Abp. of Ferrara † 1586

Lucrezia = Fr. Maria II D. of Urbino

Leonora

Marfisa = Alfonso

Borso *general of Milan* † 1657

Ludovico *imperial general*

Sigismund M. of Lanzo

Charles Philibert M. of St Martin *grandee of Spain* † 1607 s.p.

Philip Francis *Governor of Saluzzo etc.* † 1628

Charles Emmanuel *grandee of Spain envoy to England and Vienna* M. of Borgomainero † 1695

ALFONSO II † 1597 s.p. (1) = Lucrezia de' Medici (2) = Barbara dau. of Emp. Ferdinand I (3) = Margaret di Gonzaga

Alfonso

FRANCESCO I † 1658

ALFONSO III abd. 1629 = Isabel of Savoy

Rinaldo Card. † 1672

Charles Philibert M. of St Martin *grandee of Spain* † 1607 s.p.

Philip Francis M. of St Martin and of Lanzo † 1653 = Margaret nat. dau. of Charles Emmanuel I

Charles Philibert *captain-gen. of Milan*

ALFONSO IV † 1662

Obizzo Bp. of Modena

RINALDO = Charlotte Felicitas of Brunswick-Lüneburg (see Table 3) † 1737

FRANCESCO II † 1694

Mary Beatrice = James II K. of England

FRANCESCO III † 1780 = Charlotte of Orleans

HERCULES III dep. 1797 † 1803

Maria Beatrice = Archd. Ferdinand 3rd son of Emp. Francis I † 1829

DUKES OF MANTUA: HOUSE OF GONZAGA FROM 1478

TABLE 75

GENEALOGIES

ITALY

GIAN FRANCESCO DI GONZAGA *first M. of Mantua* (1432) †1444

LUDOVICO III = Barbara dau. of John *Alchymista* of Brandenburg †1478 — Carlo *condottiere* †1456

FEDERIGO I †1484

Barbara = Eberhard of Würtemberg

Gian Francesco of Sabionetta

Ludovico Bp. of Mantua †1511

Francesco Card. Bp. of Mantua

Rudolfo → Ds. of Castiglione till 1692 line extinct 1819

Susanna

Ludovico *French general*

GIAN FRANCESCO II †1519 = Isabella d'Este

Elizabeth = Guidobaldo D. of Urbino

Clara = Gilbert C. of Montpensier (see Table 25)

Giovanni M. of Vescovado *imperial gen.* †1525

Luigi *Spanish and papal gen.*

Ds. of Bozzolo till 1703 →

Sigismund Card. Bp. of Mantua †1614

Sigismund *imperial gen.* †1530

Vespasian *Spanish envoy and viceroy* †1591

Julia = Vespasian Colonna D. of Traietto

Margaret = FEDERIGO II †1540 *heiress of Montferrat* D. of Mantua 1530 M. of Montferrat 1536

Ercole Card. Regent †1563

(Ferrante) C. of Guastalla *Viceroy of Sicily* †1557

Eleonora = Francesco Maria D. of Urbino

FRANCIS III †1550

WILLIAM †1587 = Eleanor dau. of Emp. Ferdinand I

Isabella = Francesco d'Avalos M. of Pescara

Louis = Henrietta *French general* dau. of Francis D. of Nevers D. of Nevers †1595

Camilla = Caesar I *sister of* †1575 *St. Charles Borromeo*

Ottavio *Spanish general*

Eleonora = (2) VINCENT I †1612 de' Medici

Anne = Ferdinand C. of Tyrol †1595

Margaret = (3) Alfonso II D. of Ferrara

Charles II D. of Nevers †1637 *claimed Mantua* (1627)

Maria = Henry D. of Maine

Catharine = Henry I D. of Longueville

Ferrante II D. of Guastalla †1632 *claimed Mantua in 1627*

Margaret = Henry D. of Lorraine

FRANCIS IV †1612

FERDINAND †1626

VINCENT II †1627

Eleonora = Emp. Ferdinand II

Maria = Charles †1631 †1630

Mary = Casimir K. of Poland

Anne †1684 = Edward P. Palatine (see Table 3)

Ferrante III †1679

Caesar II

Vincent *Viceroy of Sicily* 1677

Andrew

Nicolea = Charles III of Lorraine

Claudia = Nicolas Francis of Lorraine

CHARLES (IV) D. of Mantua and Montferrat †1665

Eleonora = K. Ferdinand III

Eleonora (1) = Michael K. of Poland (2) = Charles Leopold

Anna Isabella = Ferdinand Charles

Vincent D. of Guastalla Sabionetta and Bozzolo †1714 → line extinct 1746 (Guastalla annexed to Parma)

Charles Leopold †1690

FERDINAND CHARLES = Anna Isabella D. of Mantua and Montferrat dep. 1706 †1708 s.p. (Mantua annexed by Austria and Montferrat by Savoy)

TABLE 76
GENEALOGIES
ITALY

CIBÒ.   CHIGI

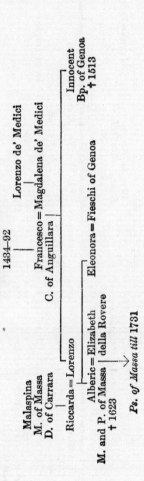

CIBÒ

Giovanni Battista Cibò
Innocent VIII
1484–92

Lorenzo de' Medici

Francesco = Magdalena de' Medici
C. of Anguillara

Malaspina
M. of Massa
D. of Carrara

Riccarda = Lorenzo

Eleonora = Fieschi of Genoa

Innocent
Bp. of Genoa
† 1613

Alberic = Elizabeth
M. and P. of Massa │ della Rovere
† 1623

Ps. of Massa till 1731

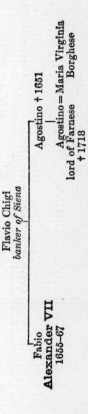

CHIGI

Flavio Chigi
banker of Siena

Fabio
Alexander VII
1655–67

Agostino † 1651

Agostino = Maria Virginia
lord of Farnese   Borghese
† 1718

TABLE 77
GENEALOGIES
ITALY

BORGIA

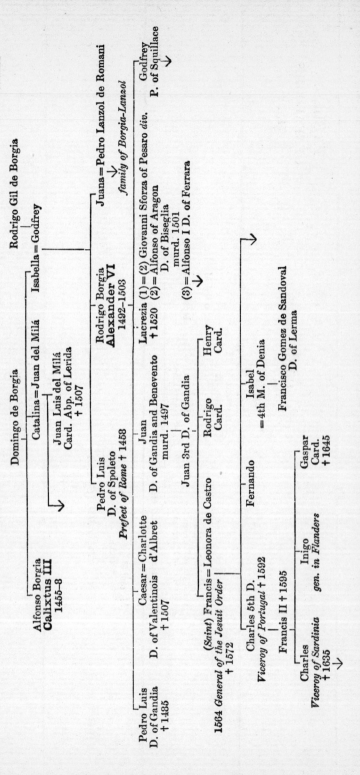

TABLE 78

GENEALOGIES

ITALY

DUKES OF URBINO: MONTEFELTRO AND DELLA ROVERE

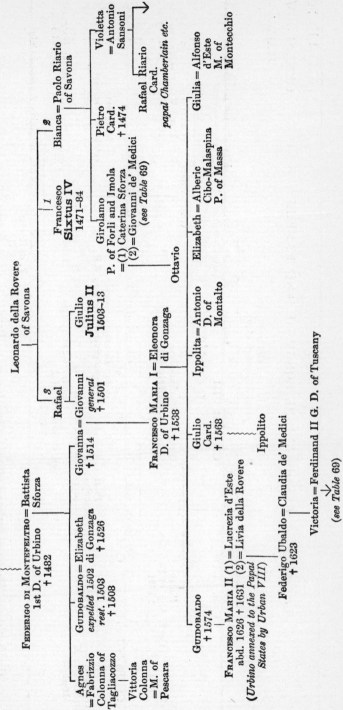

Guido Antonio 8th C. of Montefeltro

FEDERIGO DI MONTEFELTRO = Battista
1st D. of Urbino   Sforza
† 1482

Leonardo della Rovere
of Savona

1 Francesco
Sixtus IV
1471–84

2 Bianca = Paolo Riario
of Savona

3 Rafael

Agnes
= Fabrizzio
Colonna of
Tagliacozzo

Vittoria
Colonna
= M. of
Pescara

GUIDOBALDO = Elizabeth
expelled 1502 di Gonzaga
rest. 1503   † 1526
† 1508

Giovanna = Giovanni
† 1514   general
† 1501

Giulio
Julius II
1503–13

Girolamo
P. of Forli and Imola
= (1) Caterina Sforza
(2) = Giovanni de' Medici
(see Table 69)

Pietro
Card.
† 1474

Violetta
= Antonio
Sansoni

Rafael Riario
Card.
papal Chamberlain etc.

Ottavio

FRANCESCO MARIA I = Eleonora
D. of Urbino   di Gonzaga
† 1538

Giulio
Card.
† 1568

Ippolito

Ippolita = Antonio
D. of
Montalto

Elizabeth = Alberic
Cibo-Malaspina
P. of Massa

Giulia = Alfonso
d'Este
M. of
Montecchio

GUIDOBALDO
† 1574

FRANCESCO MARIA II (1) = Lucrezia d'Este
abd. 1626 † 1631 (2) = Livia della Rovere
(Urbino annexed to the Papal
States by Urban VIII)

Federigo Ubaldo = Claudia de' Medici
† 1623

Victoria = Ferdinand II G. D. of Tuscany
(see Table 69)

TABLE 79

GENEALOGIES

ITALY

ALDOBRANDINI, BORGHESE AND PAMFILI

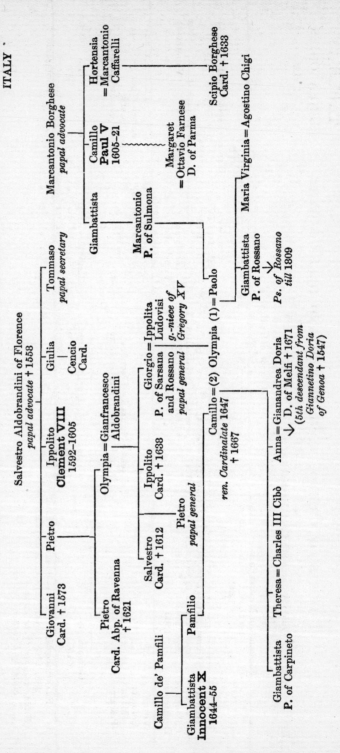

TABLE 80

GENEALOGIES
SPAIN

HOUSES OF CASTILE AND ARAGON TO PHILIP III

[CASTILE]

[ARAGON AND SICILY]

Eleanor=(1) **John I** (2)=Beatrix
dau. of Peter IV   dau. of Ferdinand K. of Portugal
K. of Aragon

Ferdinand I
elected K. of Aragon and Sicily 1412
† 1416

Henry III=Catharine
† 1406   dau. of John of Gaunt

Alfonso V
† 1458

Ferdinand
K. of Naples
(*see Table 71*)

Joanna=(2) **John II** (1)=Blanche Q. of Navarre
Henriquez   K. of Aragon,
Sicily and
Navarre
† 1479

Blanche
=Henry IV
K. of Castile

Eleanor
Q. of Navarre
(*see Table 84*)

Joanna=Ferdinand K. of Naples

John II=(1) Maria
† 1454 (2) Isabella of
Portugal

Isabella=(1) **Ferdinand II** (2)=Germaine
† 1504   *the Catholic*   de Foix
† 1516

Henry IV=Blanche
† 1474   of Aragon

1

Alfonso=(1) Isabella (2)=Emmanuel (2)=Mary
of Portugal   K. of Portugal
(*see Table 88*)

4

John=Margaret
† 1497

2

(*see Table 32*)

Isabella=**Charles I**
(Emp. Charles V)
abd. 1556

Philip I=**Joanna**
† 1506   † 1555
(*see Table 81*)

3

Catharine (1) = Arthur P. of Wales
† 1558
(2) = Henry VIII
K. of England

5

Maria=(1) **Philip II** (2)=Mary Q. of England † 1558
of Portugal   1580 K. of (3)=Elizabeth of France † 1568
† 1545   Portugal (4)=Anne dau. of Emp. Maximilian II
(3) † 1598   † 1580

Isabella Clara Eugenia=Archd. Albert
† 1633

(1)

Carlos
† 1568

(3)

Catharine=Charles Emmanuel I
D. of Savoy

(4)

Philip III
† 1621

TABLE 81

GENEALOGIES

SPAIN

THE FAMILY OF CHARLES V

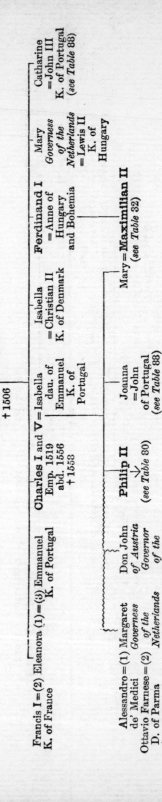

Philip = Joanna
of Austria | of Aragon
the Fair | † 1555
† 1506

Francis I = Eleanora (1)=(3) Emmanuel
K. of France | K. of Portugal

Charles I and V = Isabella
Emp. 1519 | dau. of
abd. 1556 | Emmanuel
† 1558 | K. of Portugal

Ferdinand I
= Anne of
Hungary
and Bohemia

Mary
Governess
of the
Netherlands
= Lewis II
K. of
Hungary

Catharine
= John III
K. of Portugal
(see Table 88)

Isabella
= Christian II
K. of Denmark

Mary = Maximilian II
(see Table 32)

Philip II
(see Table 80)

Joanna
= John
of Portugal
(see Table 88)

Don John
of Austria
Governor
of the
Netherlands
† 1578

Margaret
Governess
of the
Netherlands
† 1586

Alessandro = (1) Margaret
de' Medici
Ottavio Farnese = (2)
D. of Parma
(see Table 70)

TABLE 82

GENEALOGIES

SPAIN

THE SPANISH SUCCESSION

(Claimants in small capitals)

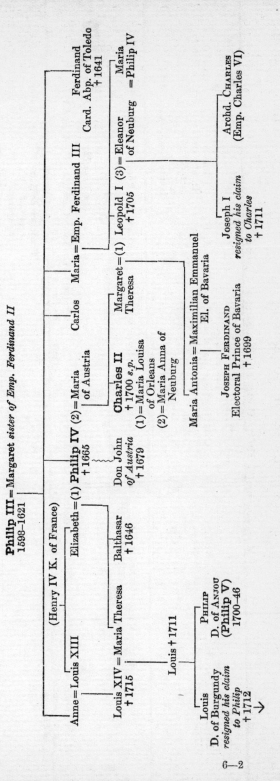

TABLE 83

GENEALOGIES

SPAIN

HOUSE OF BOURBON

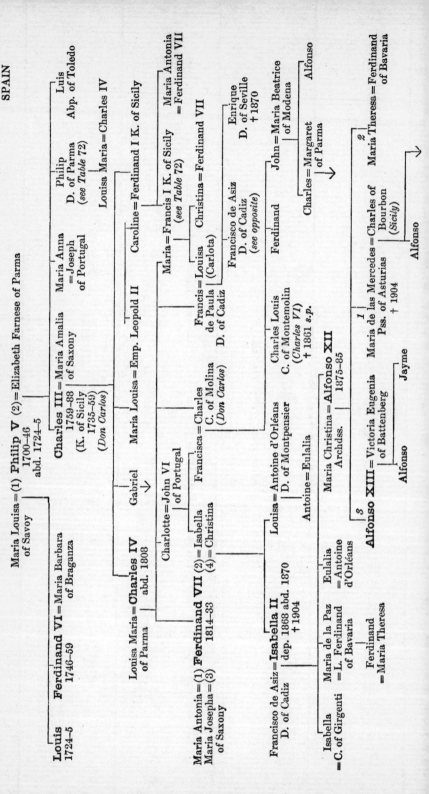

TABLE 84
GENEALOGIES
SPAIN

NAVARRE

Charles III
K. of Navarre † 1425

Martin I (2)=(1) Blanche (2)=(1) John II K. of Aragon and Sicily
K. of Sicily   *heiress of*   K. of Navarre 1425-79
† 1409 *s.p.*   *Navarre*
         † 1441

Charles
† 1461 *s.p.*

Eleanor=Gaston IV de Foix † 1472
† 1479

Gaston=Madeleine
† 1470 dau. of Charles VII
      K. of France

John=Mary *sister of*
    Louis XII
    K. of France

Margaret=Francis II
       D. of Britanny

Gaston † 1512
at Ravenna

Germaine (1)=(2) Ferdinand II
         K. of Spain

Francis Phoebus
1479-83 *s.p.*

Catharine=John d'Albret
1483-1614   † 1516

Charlotte
=Caesar Borgia

Margaret=Henry II
      † 1555

sister of Francis I K. of France

Jeanne=Antony of Bourbon
† 1572   † 1562

Henry III
(Henry IV K. of France)
(*Navarre united with France*)

Catharine=Henry
      D. of Lorraine

TABLE 85
GENEALOGIES
SPAIN

TOLEDO (ALVA), FIGUEROA, AND HENRIQUEZ

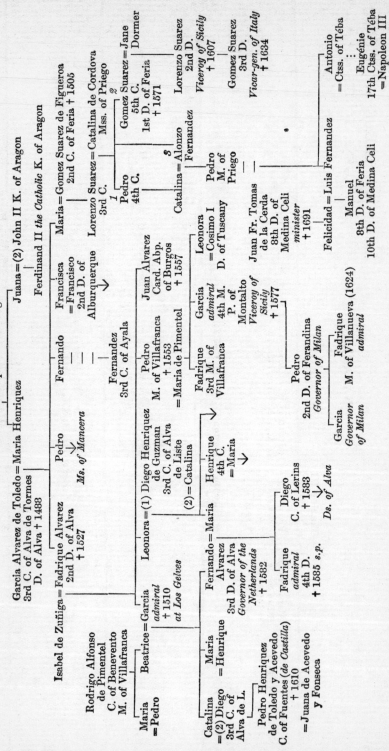

ZUÑIGA (AYAMONTE, MIRANDA, MONTEREY) AND SANDOVAL

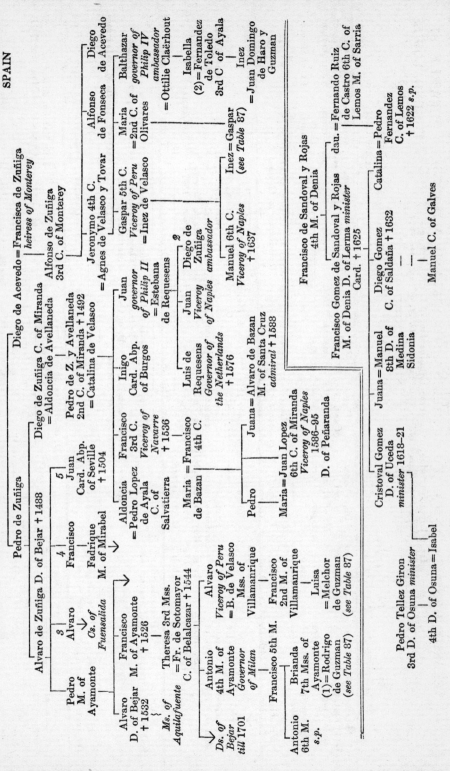

TABLE 87
GENEALOGIES
SPAIN

VELASCO, MENDOZA AND GUZMAN (MEDINA SIDONIA AND OLIVARES)

Inigo Lopez Hurtado de Mendoza = Catalina dau. of Lor. Suarez de Figueroa G. M. of Santiago
M. of Santillana † 1458

Diego D. of Infantado

Pero Gonzalez Card. of Spain Abp. of Seville and Toledo † 1495

Inigo C. of Tendilla

Lorenzo C. of Coruña

Maria = Pedro Fernandez de Velasco Constable of Castile 2nd C. of Haro

Mencia = (1) Beltran de la Cueva 1st D. of Alburquerque † 1492

Francisco 2nd D.

Inigo 2nd D.

Diego 3rd D. † 1531

Inigo 4th D.

Francisco 10th D. † s.p.

Diego C. of Melito

Inigo Lopez 2nd C.

Diego Card. Abp. of Seville † 1502

Inigo Lopez M. of Mondéjar Capt.-gen. of Granada † 1515

Luis Viceroy of Navarre

Diego D. of Francavilla

Inigo Viceroy of Naples 1579

Pedro Gonzalez Bp. of Salamanca historian † 1574

P. Fernandez D. of Frias Constable † 1512

Inigo 2nd D. of Frias 4th C. of Haro Constable † 1528

Isabel = Juan Clarus de Guzman D. of Medina Sidonia

Maria = (3) 1st D. of Alburquerque

Cs. of Siruela

Pedro 11th D. of Alburquerque

José Maria 14th D. † 1811 s.p.

[GUZMAN]

Pedro 3rd D. 5th C.

Juan 5th D. Gov. of Milan ambassador to England

I. Melchior 7th D. Governor † 1696

Joseph 8th D. minister † 1713

Francisco admiral of Aragon

Inigo ambassador to Venice

Diego ambassador to England (poet) † 1575

Francisco

Anne = Ruy Gomez da Silva P. of Eboli D. of Pastrana
Anne (Pss. of Eboli)

Alfonso = Juana Ximenes niece of Francisco Ximenes de Cisneros Card. Abp. of Seville † 1517

Pedro C. of Olivares † 1562

Leonora = D. Velasquez Davila

Juan Alfonso 6th D. of Medina Sidonia ambassador

Leonora = Pedro Giron D. of Osuna

Henrique 2nd C. Viceroy of Naples = Maria de Acevedo Zuñiga

Diego V. Davila M. of Leganés

Juan Clarus

Anne = Alfonso Perez 7th D. admiral of the Armada † 1615

Gaspar Philip = Inez D. of Medina de las Torres the Count-Duke † 1645

Gaspar 3rd C. of Olivares

Manuel = Leonora 6th C. of Monterey

Francisca = D. Lopez de Haro 4th M. of Carpio

Luis Mendez de la Paz

Juan Domingo = Inez 7th C. of Monterey † 1716 heiress of Monterey and Ayala

M. of Eliche and Carpio

Rodrigo 2nd D. of Pastrana

Diego da Silva D. of Francavilla

Rodrigo = (1) Brianda de Zuñiga 7th Mss. of Ayamonte
(M. of Ayamonte) ex. 1641

Maria = (1) Ramiro Nuñez F. de Guzman M. of Toral
(2) = Anna Caraffa Pss. of Stigliano

Gaspar D. of Montoro Governor of

Maria Dss. of M. de las Torres

Alfonso Manuel (or Juan M. Domingo) 8th D.

Luisa = Juan D. of Braganza (John IV K. of Portugal)

Melchor M. of Villamanrique † 1639

Gaspar 9th D. of Medina Sidonia

TABLE 88

KINGS OF PORTUGAL FROM JOHN I TO JOHN IV

GENEALOGIES

PORTUGAL AND BRAZIL

TABLE 89

GENEALOGIES

PORTUGAL AND BRAZIL

HOUSE OF BRAGANZA

John IV = Luisa Maria de Guzman
1640–56
(see Table 88)

Catharine = Charles II K. of England

Alfonso VI dep. 1667 †1683

Peter II (2) 1667–1706 = (1) M. Françoise (2) of Savoy-Nemours

John V †1750 = Maria Antonia dau. of Emp. Leopold I

Joseph †1777 = Maria Anna of Spain

Ferdinand VI K. of Spain = Maria Barbara

Maria Benedetta

Maria I = Peter III †1816 †1786

Joseph Francis = Maria Benedetta †1788 s.p.

Carlota Joaquina = John VI of Spain 1816–26

Isabella = (2) Ferdinand VII K. of Spain

Charles = Francisca C. of Molina (see Table 83)

Peter IV (I) = Leopoldina of Austria (Dom Pedro) abd. 1826 Emp. of Brazil 1826–31 †1834

Miguel (K. of Portugal 1828–34) †1866

Augustus = (1) Maria II (2) da Gloria †1853 = Ferdinand of Saxe-Coburg
Beauharnais

Peter II = Theresa of Naples Emp. of Brazil dep. 1889 †1891

Leopoldina = Augustus of Saxe-Coburg

Louis = Januaria C. of Aquila

Francisca = Francis P. de Joinville

Miguel D. of Braganza

Miguel   Francisco

6 daus.

Isabella

Antonia = Leopold of Hohenzollern-Sigmaringen (see Table 106)

Alfonso Henrique D. of Oporto

Peter V †1861 s.p.

Fernando

João

Luis I †1889 = Maria Pia of Italy

Carlos = Amélie of Orleans murd. 1908

Manuel
1889–11 dm...

Luis Felipe D. of Braganza murd. 1908

HOUSES OF VASA AND HOLSTEIN-GOTTORP

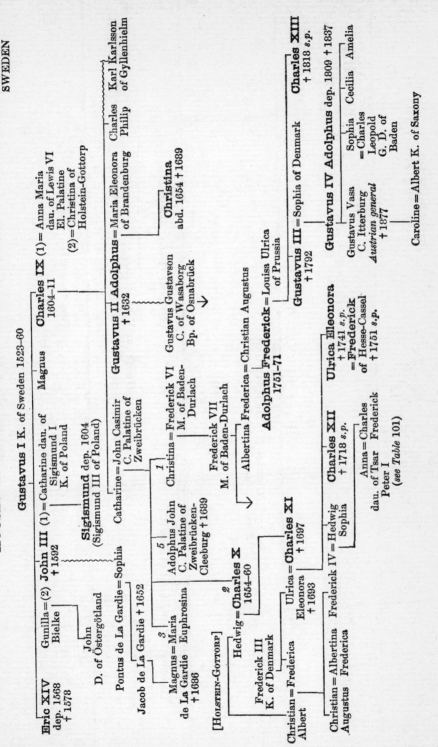

TABLE 91

GENEALOGIES

SWEDEN

HOUSE OF BERNADOTTE

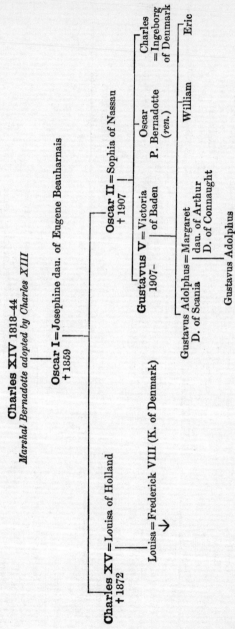

Charles XIV 1818–44
Marshal Bernadotte adopted by Charles XIII

Oscar I=Josephine dau. of Eugene Beauharnais
† 1859

Oscar II=Sophia of Nassau
† 1907

Charles XV=Louisa of Holland
† 1872

Louisa=Frederick VIII (K. of Denmark)
→

Gustavus V=Victoria
1907– of Baden

Oscar
P. Bernadotte
(*ren.*)

Charles
=Ingeborg
of Denmark

Gustavus Adolphus=Margaret
D. of Scania dau. of Arthur
D. of Connaught

William

Eric

Gustavus Adolphus

TABLE 92

GENEALOGIES

NORWAY

KING OF NORWAY

Louisa = Frederick VIII
of Sweden | K. of Denmark
      | 2
(Charles) **Haakon VII** = Maud dau. of Edward VII
elected K. of Norway 1905 | K. of Great Britain and Ireland
             Olaf

TABLE 93
GENEALOGIES
DENMARK

KINGS OF DENMARK, NORWAY AND SWEDEN.
(HOUSE OF OLDENBURG I)

Waldemar III K. of Denmark 1340–75
(fourth in descent from Waldemar II the Victorious)

[MECKLENBURG]

1

Albert
K. of Sweden 1363–89

2

Margaret = Hakon
Q. of Denmark † 1412 | K. of Norway † 1380

Ingeborg = Henry

Mary = Wratislav of Pomerania

Olaf VI
K. of Denmark,
Norway and
Sweden
† 1387

Catharine = John D. of Bavaria

[OLDENBURG]

Eric = Philippa
dep. 1439 | dau. of Henry IV
K. of England

[SCHLESWIG-HOLSTEIN]

Hedwig = Theodoric
C. of Oldenburg

1

Christian I = (2) Dorothea (1) = Christopher III 1439–48
K. of Denmark and Norway | dau. of
1448–81 ; and Sweden 1457–64 | John Alchymista
D. of Schleswig-Holstein 1460 | of Brandenburg

Adolphus VIII
D. of Schleswig
and Holstein
† 1459

2

Gerard
C. of Oldenburg
↓
(male line extinct 1681)

Margaret = James III K. of Scotland

John
K. of Denmark, Norway
and Sweden † 1513

Frederick I (1) = Anna of Brandenburg
K. of Denmark (2) = Sophia of Pomerania
and Norway
1523–33

[HOLSTEIN-GOTTORP]

Elizabeth = Joachim I
El. of Brandenburg

John
of Hadersleben

Dorothea
= Albert
D. of Prussia

Adolphus
of Gottorp
(see Table 60)

Isabella = Christian II
sister of Emp. Charles V | dep. 1523 † 1559

Christian III
† 1559

[SONDERBURG]

Christina
(1) = Fr. Maria Sforza D. of Milan
(2) = Francis I D. of Lorraine
(see Table 34)

John
† 1532

Dorothea
= Frederick II
El. Palatine

Frederick II
(see Table 94)

Anna
= Augustus
El. of Saxony

Magnus
K. of Livonia 1570
† 1583

John

[AUGUSTENBURG]   [GLÜCKSBURG]

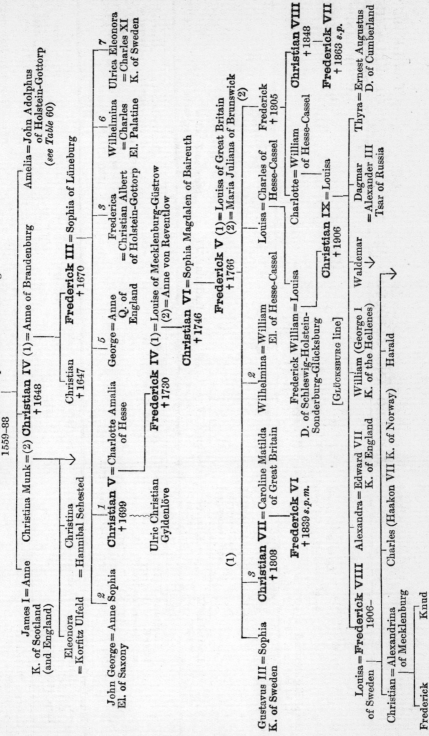

TABLE 95

GENEALOGIES

HUNGARY AND POLAND

JAGELLO AND ZAPÓLYA

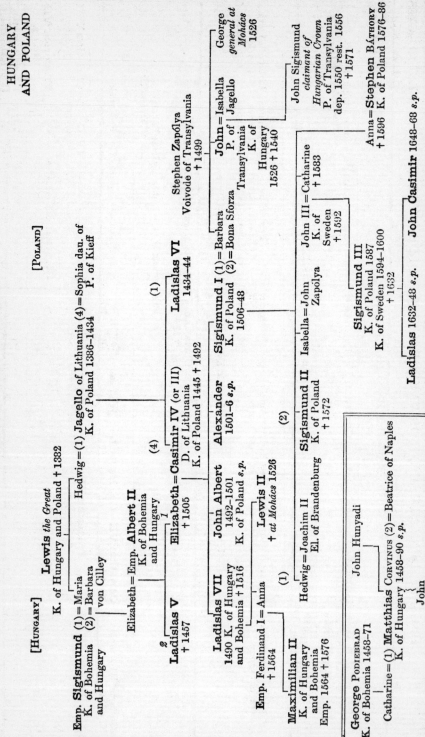

TABLE 96

GENEALOGIES

POLAND, HUNGARY AND TRANSYLVANIA

BÁTHORY

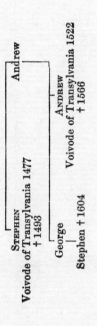

ECZED LINE

STEPHEN Voivode of Transylvania 1477 † 1493

Andrew

George

ANDREW Voivode of Transylvania 1522 † 1566

Stephen † 1604

SOMLYÓ LINE

STEPHEN BÁTHORY Palatine of Hungary combatant at Mohács 1526 † 1531

Stephen = Anne Jagello P. of Transylvania 1572–6 K. of Poland 1576–86

CHRISTOPHER = Christina Radziwill P. of Transylvania 1576 † 1581

Andrew C. of Szatmár

ANDREW Card. P. of Transylvania 1598–9 † 1599

Stephen † 1601

GABRIEL P. of Transylvania 1608 murd. 1613

Andrew

Sophia = GEORGE RÁKÓCZY II P. of Transylvania 1648–60

SIGISMUND P. of Transylvania 1581–98 dep. 1598 rest. 1601–2 † 1613 *in captivity*

TABLE 97

GENEALOGIES
TRANSYLVANIA

BETHLEN AND APAFFY

(A) BETHLEN OF IKTÀR

Gregor (Gergely)
† 1567

Farkas (Lupus, Wolfgang) † 1590
= Drusiana Lásár

STEPHEN
P. of Transylvania 1629
† 1648

Drusiana = Francis Rhedey
claimed Transylvania 1658–61
† 1667

Stephen
† 1633

CATHARINE = GÁBOR (Gabriel)
of Brandenburg   P. of Transylvania
Pss. of Transylvania   1613–29
1629–30

(B) APAFFY

George Apaffy
High Steward to John Zapólya Anti-K. of Hungary † 1540

Nicholas

Francis
Chief Chamberlain to Gabriel Báthory

George † 1655
Councillor to Gabriel Bethlen

Stephen

Balthasar

MICHAEL I = Anna Bornenisza
P. of Transylvania
1663–90

George
Chief Chamberlain
to George Rákóczy I
† 1655

MICHAEL II = Catharine Bethlen
P. of Transylvania 1690–1   † 1725
† 1713 s.p.

TABLE 98

GENEALOGIES

TRANSYLVANIA

RÁKÓCZY AND ZRÍNYI

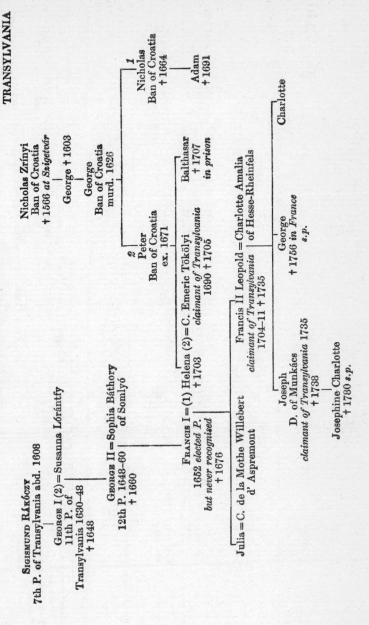

TABLE 99
GENEALOGIES
POLAND

CZARTORYSKI

P. Michael Czartoryski

Casimir = Isabella (Sophia) dau. of Andreas Ratzibor-Morsztyn and Miss Gordon
P. Palatine of Wilna

Augustus = Pani Sienowska
P. Palatine
† 1782

Elizabeth
= P. Stanislaus
Lubomirski

Adam Casimir = Isabella
P. General   Flemming
† 1823

Michael
P. Chancellor
† 1773

Antoinette = (1) Geo. Detlev Flemming (2) = Constantia
Gd. Treasurer
of Lithuania

Isabella = Adam Casimir

Constantia = P. Stanislaus Čoilek Poniatowski

4
Stanislaus
Augustus
last K. of
Poland

Michael
last Primate
of Poland

Maria Anna
= (1) D. Lewis Frederick
of Würtemberg div. 1792

Adam
† 1831
at Pulawy

Sophia
= Stanislaus
Zamoiski

Constantine Adam Alexander (1) = Pss. Angelica Radziwill
† 1860   (2) = Maria Dzierzonowska

Adam Constantine = Pss. Augusta Radziwill

Adam George = Anna Sapieha
Adviser of Alexander I
President of Polish Senate
1831 † 1861

Witold
† 1865

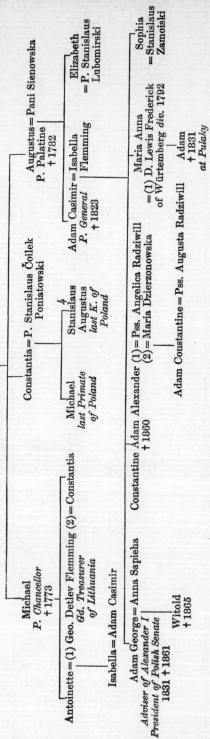

TABLE 100

GENEALOGIES

RUSSIA

TSARS IN RUSSIA FROM 1462

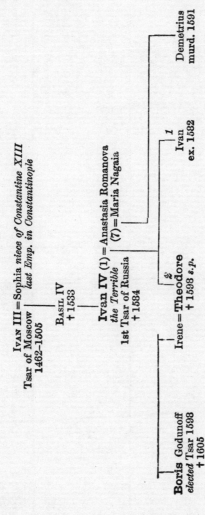

IVAN III = Sophia *niece of Constantine XIII*
Tsar of Moscow   *last Emp. in Constantinople*
1462–1505

BASIL IV
† 1533

Ivan IV (1) = Anastasia Romanova
the Terrible   (7) = Maria Nagaia
1st Tsar of Russia
† 1584

2
Irene = **Theodore**
† 1598 *s.p.*

1
Ivan
ex. 1582

Demetrius
murd. 1591

Boris Godunoff
elected Tsar 1598
† 1605

Theodore

TABLE 101
GENEALOGIES
RUSSIA

HOUSE OF ROMANOFF

Anastasia
= Ivan IV

Nicetas Romanoff

Theodore = Marta the Nun
(Philaret)
Patriarch 1619 † 1633

Michael *elected* Tsar 1613 † 1645

Alexis (2) = Natalia Naruishkin
† 1676

Peter I (1) = Eudoxia Lupokhin
the Great (2) = Martha Skavronska
† 1725   Catharine I 1725–7

Maria Milaslovski = (1)

Martha

Sophia
Regent 1682–9

Theodore
† 1682 *s.p.*

Ivan V
dep. 1689 † 1696

Anna = Frederick
1730–40 *s.p.* D. of Courland

(2)

Anna = Charles Frederick
† 1728 of Holstein-Gottorp

Elizabeth
1741–62

Charles Leopold = Catharine
D. of Mecklenburg-Schwerin

(1)

Alexis = Charlotte
ex. 1718 of Brunswick-
Wolfenbüttel

Peter III = Catharine II (Sophia)
dep. and † 1762 of Anhalt-Zerbst 1762–96 murd.

Antony Ulric = Anna *Leopoldovna*
of Brunswick-
Wolfenbüttel

Natalia
† 1728

Peter II
1727–30

Sophia Dorothea = **Paul** 1796–1801 murd.
of Würtemberg

Ivan VI
1740–1 dep.

Alexandra = Archd. Joseph

Anna = William II
K. of Holland

Nicholas I = Charlotte
† 1855   of Prussia

Constantine
ren. claim 1822
† 1831

Catharine
(1) = P. George
of Oldenburg
(2) = William
K. of Würtemberg

Constantine
Gov. of Poland

Olga
= Charles
K. of
Würtemberg

Michael

Nicholas

Alexander I
† 1825 *s.p.*
= (Louisa) Elizabeth
of Baden

Alexander II
murd. 1881
= Marie
of Hesse-Darmstadt

Marie
= Alfred
D. of
Edinburgh

Sergius
murd. 1905

Paul

Constantine

Nicholas

Nicholas
= Anastasia
of Montenegro

Peter
= Militza
of Montenegro

Vladimir   Alexis

Alexander III
† 1894

Marie (Dagmar) =
of Denmark

Michael = Charlotte (Helena)
of Würtemberg

Olga = George
K. of Greece

Nicholas II = Alexandra
(Alix) of Hesse

TABLE 102

GENEALOGIES

TURKEY

THE OTTOMAN SULTANS FROM 1451

Mohammad II 1451–81

Jem

Bayezid II † 1512

Selím I † 1520

Sulaymán I = Roxolana
(the Magnificent) † 1566 |
dau. = Rustem Vezír

Selím II † 1574

Murád III (Amurath) † 1595

Mohammad III † 1603

Ahmad I † 1617

Mustafa I 1617–8 1622–3

Osmán II (Othman) † 1622

Murád IV (Amurath) † 1640

Ibrahim dep. 1648

Mohammad IV dep. 1687

Sulaymán II (Solyman) † 1691

Ahmad II † 1695

Mustafa II dep. 1703

Ahmad III dep. 1730

Mahmúd I 1730–54

Osmán III (Othman) 1754–7

Mustafa III 1757–74

Abd-ul-Hamíd I 1774–89

Selím dep. 1807

Mustafa IV dep. 1808

Mahmúd II 1808–39

Abd-ul-Mejíd † 1861

Abd-ul-Azíz 1861–76

Murád V dep. 1876

Abd-ul-Hamíd II dep. 1909

Mohammad V (Reshíd Efendi) 1909—

Yúsuf Izzedin heir presumptive 1909

TABLE 103
GENEALOGIES
BALKAN STATES

GREECE

(a) Otho K. of Greece 1833–62 (see Table 47)

(b) HOUSE OF SCHLESWIG-HOLSTEIN-SONDERBURG-GLÜCKSBURG

George elected K. of Greece 1863 = Olga of Russia
(William son of Christian IX K. of Denmark)
(see Table 94)

- Constantine = Sophia of Prussia
  - George
  - Alexander
  - Paul
- George, High Commissioner of the Powers in Crete
- Nicholas = Helena Vladimirovna of Russia
- Maria = George Michailovich G. D. of Russia
- Andrew = Alice of Battenberg
- Christopher

TABLE 104
GENEALOGIES
BALKAN STATES

MONTENEGRO

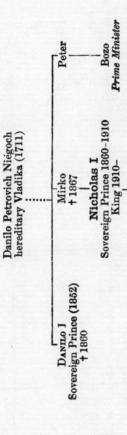

Danilo Petrovich Niégoch hereditary Vladika (1711)

DANILO I Sovereign Prince (1852) † 1860 — Mirko † 1867

Nicholas I Sovereign Prince 1860-1910 King 1910–

Zorka = Peter I K. of Servia

Militza = Peter Nicolaïevich G. D. of Russia

Anastasia = Nicholas Nicolaïevich G. D. of Russia

Danilo = Militza (Jutta) of Mecklenburg

Helena = Victor Emmanuel III K. of Italy

Peter

Bozo *Prime Minister*

Anna = P. Francis Joseph of Battenberg

Mirke = Natalie Constantinovich

TABLE 105

GENEALOGIES

BALKAN STATES

SERVIA

(a) HOUSE OF KARAGEORGEVICH

George Petrovich (Kara George)
Hospodar of Servia 1804–13 murd. 1817

Alexander I Karageorgevich
elected P. 1842
abd. 1859 † 1885

Peter I = Zorka of Montenegro
1903–

George   Alexander   Helena

Arsen

Paul

(b) HOUSE OF OBRENOVICH

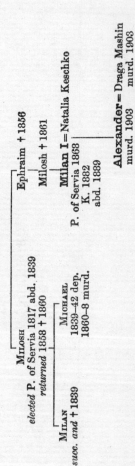

Milosh
elected P. of Servia 1817 abd. 1839
returned 1858 † 1860

Michael
1839–42 dep.
1860–8 murd.

Milan
succ. and † 1839

Ephraim † 1856

Milosh † 1861

Milan I = Natalia Keschko
P. of Servia 1868
K. 1882
abd. 1889

Alexander = Draga Mashin
murd. 1903   murd. 1903

TABLE 106

GENEALOGIES

BALKAN STATES

ROUMANIA

HOUSE OF HOHENZOLLERN-SIGMARINGEN

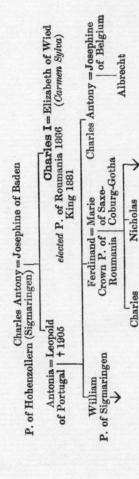

Charles Antony = Josephine of Baden
P. of Hohenzollern (Sigmaringen)

Antonia = Leopold of Portugal † 1905

William
P. of Sigmaringen

Charles I = Elizabeth of Wied
elected P. of Roumania 1866   (*Carmen Sylva*)
King 1881

Ferdinand = Marie
Crown P. of | of Saxe-
Roumania | Coburg-Gotha

Charles

Nicholas

Charles Antony = Josephine
of Belgium

Albrecht

TABLE 107

GENEALOGIES

BALKAN STATES

BULGARIA

(a)

Alexander
P. of Hesse-Darmstadt

ALEXANDER P. of Battenberg (C. of Hartenau)
P. of Bulgaria 1879 abd. 1886 † 1894

(b) HOUSE OF COBURG

Augustus = Clementina dau. of Louis Philippe K. of France
P. of Coburg

Ferdinand I of Saxe-Coburg and Gotha (see *Table* 51)
elected P. of Bulgaria 1887
King 1909
= Marie Louise of Bourbon (Parma)

Boris   Cyril

TABLE 108
GENEALOGIES
TURKEY AND EGYPT

(A) GRAND VEZIRS OF THE FAMILY OF KIUPRILI

Mohammad Kiuprili
Vezir 1656–61
- Kiuprili-záda Ahmad *Vezir* 1661–76
- Kiuprili-záda Mustafá *Vezir* 1689–91

Hasan
- Husayn Kiuprili *Vezir* 1697–1702
- Nu'mán Pasha Kiuprili *Vezir* 1710–11

(B) KHEDIVES OF THE FAMILY OF MOHAMMAD 'ALÍ (MEHEMET ALI)

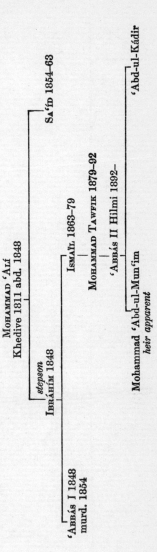

Mohammad 'Alí
Khedive 1811 abd. 1848
- *stepson* Ibráhím 1848
  - 'Abbás I 1848 murd. 1854
- Ismaïl 1863–79
  - Mohammad Tawfik 1879–92
    - 'Abbás II Hilmi 1892–
    - Mohammad 'Abd-ul-Mun'im *heir apparent*
- Sa'íd 1854–63
- 'Abd-ul-Kádir

TABLE 109
GENEALOGIES
PERSIA

SHÁHS OF THE KÁJÁR DYNASTY

Fath-'Alí † 1726

Mohammad Hasan
Gov. of Mázandarán 1747–57

Husayn-Kuli

Fath-'Alí 1797–1835

'Alí
(and numerous other children)

Aghá Mohammad 1794
ruler of all Persia 1796
† 1797

'Abbás † 1833

Mohammad 1835–48

Náșir-ed-dín 1848–96 murd.

Muẓaffar-ed-dín 1896–1907

Ná'ib-us-Salțana

Sálár-ud-Dawla

Shu'á'-us-Salțana

Żill-us-Sulțán

Mohammad 'Alí 1907–9 dep.

Hasan Mirzá
(Crown Prince)

Sulțán Ahmad
1909–

TABLE 110

GENEALOGIES

THE EAST

MOGHUL EMPERORS OF INDIA

Bábar † 1530

Humáyun † 1556 — Kámrán

Akbar † 1605 — Mirza Hakim

Jehángir (Selim) = Nur Jehán — Asof Khan
† 1627

Khusru

Parwiz

Shah Jehán dep. 1658 — Shahryar

Dára

Shah Shujah

Aurungzeb — Morád
1658–1707

Bulaki

Azim Shah

Akbar

Kam Bakhsh
† 1709

Bahádur Shah † 1711
(Shah Alam)

Azim-ush-Shah

Jehán Shah

Jehándar Shah 1712

Farrukhsiyar
1712–19

Mohammad Shah 1719–48

Alamgir II
1754–9

Ahmed Shah dep. 1754

Shah Álam II
1759–1806

Akbar Shah
1806–37

Bahádur Shah
last Moghul
1837–58 dep. † 1862

TABLE 111
GENEALOGIES
CHINA AND JAPAN

(A) MANCHU-TARTAR EMPERORS OF CHINA, TA CH'ING DYNASTY

("Year-titles" by which the Emperors are generally known)

Shun Chih 1644–62

K'ang Hsi 1662–1723

Yung Chêng † 1736

Ch'ien Lung abd. 1796

Chia Ch'ing † 1821

Tao Kwang † 1850

Kung
president of the
Tsungli-Yamên 1861–84
† 1898

Ch'un
† 1891

17th son
|
(adopted) Ch'ing
president of the Tsungli-Yamên 1884

4th son
Ch'un Regent *since 1908*

Kwang Hsü
1875–1908

Hsüan T'ung 1908–1912 *dep.*

4th son
Hsien Fêng † 1861
= Tz'ŭ An Empss. † 1881
secondary wife Tz'ŭ Hsi Empss.
† 1908

T'ung Chih
† 1875

(B) RECENT EMPERORS OF JAPAN

Sakuramachi (Akhito) 1736 abd. 1746 † 1750
115th Mikado, descended from Jinmu Tennō, first Mikado

Momozono (Tohohito) 1747–62

Go Sakuramachi (Toshiko)
1763 abd. 1770 † 1813

Go Momozono (Fanahito) 1771 † 1779

Kōkaku (Tomohito) 1780 abd. 1817 † 1841

Ninkō (Ayahito) 1817 † 1846

Kōmei (Osahito) 1847 † 1867

TABLE 112

GENEALOGIES

JAPAN

SHŌGUNS OF THE TOKUGAWA DYNASTY FROM 1603

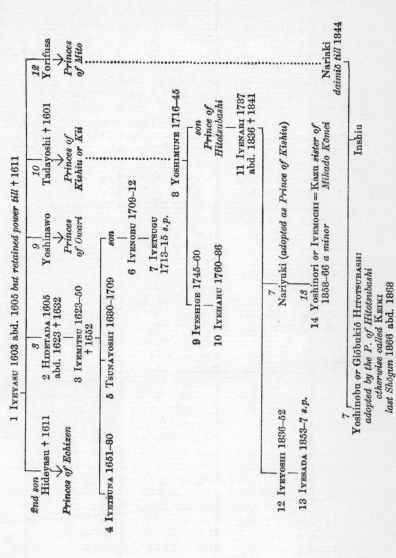

TABLE 113

THE POPES FROM 1447

1447 Mar.—1455 Mar.	Nicholas V (Thomas of Sarzana).
1455 Ap.—1458 Aug.	Calixtus III (Alfonso Borgia).
1458 Aug.—1464 Aug.	Pius II (Aeneas Sylvius Piccolomini).
1464 Aug.—1471 July	Paul II (Pietro Barbo).
1471 Aug.—1484 Aug.	Sixtus IV (Francesco della Rovere).
1484 Aug.—1492 July	Innocent VIII (Giambattista Cibò).
1492 Aug.—1503 Aug.	Alexander VI (Rodrigo Borgia).
1503 Sept.—Oct.	Pius III (Francesco Todeschini (Piccolomini)).
1503 Nov.—1513 Feb.	Julius II (Giulio della Rovere).
1513 Mar.—1521 Dec.	Leo X (Giovanni de' Medici).
1522 Jan.—1523 Sept.	Adrian VI (Adrian Boyers (of Utrecht)).
1523 Nov.—1534 Sept.	Clement VII (Giulio de' Medici).
1534 Oct.—1549 Nov.	Paul III (Alessandro Farnese).
1550 Feb.—1555 Mar.	Julius III (Giovanni Maria del Monte).
1555 Ap.	Marcellus II (Marcello Cervini).
1555 May—1559 Aug.	Paul IV (Giovanni Pietro Caraffa).
1559 Dec.—1565 Dec.	Pius IV (Gian-Angelo de' Medici).
1566 Jan.—1572 May	Pius V (Michele Ghislieri).
1572 May—1585 Ap.	Gregory XIII (Ugo Buoncompagno).
1585 Ap.—1590 Aug.	Sixtus V (Felix Peretti (Card. Montalto)).
1590 Sept.	Urban VII (Giambattista Castagna).
1590 Dec.—1591 Oct.	Gregory XIV (Niccolò Sfondrato).
1591 Oct.—Dec.	Innocent IX (Gian-Antonio Facchinetto).
1592 Jan.—1605 Mar.	Clement VIII (Ippolito Aldobrandini).
1605 Ap.	Leo XI (Alessandro Ottavio de' Medici).
1605 May—1621 Jan.	Paul V (Camillo Borghese).
1621 Feb.—1623 July	Gregory XV (Alessandro Ludovisi).
1623 Aug.—1644 July	Urban VIII (Maffeo Barberini).
1644 Sept.—1655 Jan.	Innocent X (Giambattista Pamfili).
1655 Ap.—1667 May	Alexander VII (Fabio Chigi).
1667 June—1669 Dec.	Clement IX (Giulio Rospigliosi).
1670 Ap.—1676 July	Clement X (Giambattista Altieri).
1676 Sept.—1689 Aug.	Innocent XI (Benedetto Odescalchi).
1689 Oct.—1691 Feb.	Alexander VIII (Pietro Ottobuoni).
1691 July—1700 Sept.	Innocent XII (Antonio Pignatelli).
1700 Nov.—1721 Mar.	Clement XI (Gianfrancesco Albano).
1721 May—1724 Mar.	Innocent XIII (Michelangelo Conti).
1724 May—1730 Feb.	Benedict XIII (Pietro Francesco Orsini).
1730 July—1740 Feb.	Clement XII (Lorenzo Corsini).
1740 Aug.—1758 May	Benedict XIV (Prosper Lambertini).
1758 July—1769 Feb.	Clement XIII (Carlo Rezzonico).
1769 May—1774 Sept.	Clement XIV (Giovanni V. Antonio Ganganelli).
1775 Feb.—1799 Aug.	Pius VI (Giovan-Angelo Braschi).
1800 Mar.—1823 Aug.	Pius VII (Gregorio Bernabò Chiaramonte).
1823 Sept.—1829 Feb.	Leo XII (Annibale della Genga).
1829 Mar.—1830 Nov.	Pius VIII (Francesco Xavier Castiglione).
1831 Feb.—1846 June	Gregory XVI (Mauro Capellari).
1846 June—1878 Feb.	Pius IX (Count Giovanni Maria Mastaï-Ferretti).
1878 Feb.—1903 July	Leo XIII (Joachim Pecci).
1903 Aug.	Pius X (Giuseppe Sarto).

TABLE 114

ELECTORS OF COLOGNE FROM 1463

Date of
election

1463   Rupert C. Palatine (48th Abp.).

1480   Hermann IV, *son of* Lewis I Lgr. of Hesse.

1508   Philip II C. von Daun-Oberstein.

1515   Hermann V C. von Wied, *dep. by* Paul III 1546, *abd.* 1547.

1546   Adolphus III C. von Schauenburg.

1556   Antony C. von Schauenburg.

1558   Gebhard I C. von Mansfeld.

1562   Frederick IV C. von Wied, *abd.* 1567.

1567   Salentin C. von Isenburg, *abd.* 1577.

1577   Gebhard II Truchsess von Waldburg, *married* 1583, *dep. by* Gregory XIII.

1583   Ernest, *son of* Albert V D. of Bavaria.

1612   Ferdinand, *son of* William V D. of Bavaria (Coadjutor from 1595).

1650   Maximilian Henry, *son of* Albert VI D. of Bavaria.

1688   Joseph Clement, *son of* Ferdinand Maria El. of Bavaria.

1723   Clement Augustus, *son of* Maximilian II El. of Bavaria.

1761   Maximilian Frederick C. von Königseck-Rothenfels.

1784   Maximilian, *son of* Emp. Francis I (Coadjutor from 1780).

1801   Antony Victor, *son of* Emp. Leopold II. *Renounced election.*

TABLE 115

ELECTORS OF MAINZ FROM 1434

1434   Dietrich C. of Erbach (54th Abp.).

1459   Diether C. of Isenburg, *dep.* 1461, *abd.* 1463.

1461   Adolphus II C. of Nassau.

1475   Diether *rest.*

1482   D. Albert of Saxony (*son of* El. Ernest of Saxony; Coadjutor from 1479).

1484   Berthold C. of Henneberg.

1504   Jacob Frhr. von Liebenstein.

1508   Uriel von Gemmingen.

1514   M. Albert of Brandenburg, Abp. of Magdeburg.

1545   Sebastian von Heusenstamm.

1555   Daniel Brendel von Homburg.

1582   Wolfgang von Dalberg.

1601   John Adam von Bicken.

1604   John Schweikhard von Kronberg.

1626   George Frederick von Greiffenklau zu Vollraths.

1629   Anselm Casimir Wambold von Umstadt.

1647   John Philip von Schönborn, Bp. of Würzburg and Worms.

1673   Lothar Frederick von Metternich, Bp. of Speier and Worms (Coadjutor from 1670).

1675   Damian Hartard von der Leyen, Bp. of Worms.

1679   Charles Henry C. von Metternich (Coadjutor from 1670).

1679   Anselm Francis von Ingelheim.

1695   Lothar Francis von Schönborn, Bp. of Bamberg (Coadjutor from 1694).

1729   Francis Lewis C. Palatine of Neuburg, Bp. of Breslau and Worms, *translated from* Trier (Coadjutor from 1710).

1732   Philip Charles Frhr. von Eltz.

1743   John Frederick Charles C. von Ostein, Bp. of Worms 1756.

1763   Emmerich Joseph Frhr. von Breitbach-Büresheim, Bp. of Worms 1768.

1774   Frederick Charles Joseph Frhr. von Erthal, Bp. of Worms.

1802–3 Charles Theodore Frhr. von Dalberg (Coadjutor from 1787), Chancellor of the Empire 1803–6; Abp. of Ratisbon 1805–17; Primas of the *Rheinbund* 1806–13; G. D. of Frankfort 1810–13; † 1817.

TABLE 116

ELECTORS OF TRIER FROM 1439

Date of
election

1439	James I von Sirk.
1456	John II of Baden.
1503	James II M. of Baden.
1511	Richard von Greiffenklau zu Vollraths.
1531	John III von Metzenhausen.
1540	John IV von Hagen.
1547	John V C. von Isenburg.
1556	John VI von der Leyen.
1567	James III von Eltz.
1581	John VII von Schönenberg.
1600	Lothar von Metternich.
1623	Philip Christopher von Sötern.
1652	Charles Caspar von der Leyen (Coadjutor from 1650).
1676	John Hugo Frhr. von Orsbeck (Coadjutor from 1672).
1711	Charles Joseph D. of Lorraine.
1716	Francis Lewis C. Palatine of Neuburg, *translated to* Mainz 1729.
1729	Francis George C. von Schönborn.
1756	John Philip Frhr. von Walderdorf.
1768	Clement Wenceslaus, *son of* Frederick Augustus II of Saxony (Augustus III of Poland), *abd.* 1802.

TABLE 117

ARCHBISHOPS OF CANTERBURY FROM 1454

1454–86	Thomas Bourchier (Bp. of Ely) (65th Abp.).
1486–1500	John Morton (Bp. of Ely) (Card. 1493).
1500–3	Henry Dean (Bp. of Salisbury).
1503–32	William Warham (Bp. of London).
1533–56	Thomas Cranmer (Archdeacon of Taunton).
1556–8	Reginald Pole (Card. 1536).
1559–75	Matthew Parker (Dean of Lincoln).
1576–83	Edmund Grindal (Abp. of York).
1583–1604	John Whitgift (Bp. of Worcester).
1604–10	Richard Bancroft (Bp. of London).
1611–33	George Abbot (Bp. of London).
1633–45	William Laud (Bp. of London) (*ex.* 1645).
1645–60	*See vacant.*
1660–3	William Juxon (Bp. of London).
1663–77	Gilbert Sheldon (Bp. of London).
1678–91	William Sancroft (Archdeacon of Canterbury).
1691–4	John Tillotson (Dean of Canterbury).
1694–1715	Thomas Tenison (Bp. of Lincoln).
1716–37	William Wake (Bp. of Lincoln).
1737–47	John Potter (Bp. of Oxford).
1747–57	Thomas Herring (Abp. of York).
1757–8	Matthew Hutton (Abp. of York).
1758–68	Thomas Secker (Bp. of Oxford).
1768–83	Frederick Cornwallis (Bp. of Lichfield and Coventry and Dean of St Paul's).
1783–1805	John Moore (Bp. of Bangor).
1805–28	Charles Manners-Sutton (Bp. of Norwich and Dean of Windsor).
1828–48	William Howley (Bp. of London).
1848–62	John Bird Sumner (Bp. of Chester).
1862–8	Charles Thomas Longley (Abp. of York).
1868–82	Archibald Campbell Tait (Bp. of London).
1882–96	Edward White Benson (Bp. of Truro).
1896–1903	Frederick Temple (Bp. of London).
1903	Randall Thomas Davidson (Bp. of Winchester).

TABLE 118

ARCHBISHOPS OF YORK FROM 1480

1480–1500	Thomas Rotherham (53rd Abp.).
1501	Thomas Savage.
1508	Christopher Bainbridge.
1514	Thomas Wolsey.
1531	Edward Lee.
1545	Robert Holgate, *deprived* 1554.
1555	Nicholas Heath, *deprived* 1559.
1561	Thomas Young.
1570	Edmund Grindal.
1576	Edwin Sandys.
1589	John Piers.
1595	Matthew Hutton.
1606	Tobias Matthew.
1628	George Monteigne.
1628	Samuel Harsnett.
1632	Richard Neile.
1641	John Williams, † 1650.
1650–60	*See vacant.*
1660	Accepted Frewen.
1664	Richard Sterne.
1683	John Dolben.
1688	Thomas Lamplugh.
1691	John Sharp.
1714	Sir William Dawes Bart.
1724	Lancelot Blackburne.
1743	Thomas Herring.
1747	Matthew Hutton.
1757	John Gilbert.
1761	Robert Hay Drummond.
1777	William Markham.
1807	Edward Harcourt.
1847	Thomas Musgrave.
1860	Charles Thomas Longley.
1862	William Thomson.
1891	William Connor Magee.
1891	William Dalrymple Maclagan, *res.* 1908.
1908	Cosmo Gordon Lang.

TABLE 119

BISHOPS AND ARCHBISHOPS OF PARIS FROM 1473

BISHOPS

Date of
succession

1473   Louis de Beaumont de la Forêt.
1492   Jean-Simon de Champigny.
1503   Étienne de Poncher.
1519   François de Poncher.
1532   Jean du Bellay, Card.
1551   Eustache du Bellay.
1564   Guillaume Viole.
1568   Pierre de Gondi, Card., *resigned* 1598, † 1616.
1598   Henri de Gondi, Card. de Retz.

ARCHBISHOPS

1622   Jean-François de Gondi, Card.
1654   Jean-François-Paul de Gondi, Card. de Retz, *resigned* 1662, † 1679.
1662   Pierre de Marca.
1664   Harduin de Péréfixe de Beaumont.
1671   François de Harlai de Champvallon.
1695   Louis-Antoine de Noailles, Card.
1729   Charles-Gaspar-Guillaume de Vintimille du Luc.
1746   Jacques-Bonne-Gigault de Bellefonds.
1746   Christophe-Beaumont de Répaire.
1781   Antoine-L.-L. Leclerc de Juigné.
1802   Jean-Baptiste du Belloy, Card.
1817   Alexandre-Angélique de Talleyrand Périgord, Card.
1821   Hyacinthe-Louis C. de Quelen.
1840   Denis d'Affre, *murd.* 1848.
1848   Marie-Dominique-Auguste Sibour.
1857   François-N.-M. Morlot, Card.
1863   Georges Darboy.
1871   Joseph-Hippolyte Guibert, Card.
1886   François-Marie-Benjamin Richard, Card.
1908   Leo Augustus Amette, Card.

TABLE 120

GENERALS OF THE ORDER OF JESUS

1. St Ignatius Loyola (Iñigo Lopez de Recalde), † 1556, canonised 1622, founded the Order 1534 (authorised by Paul III 1540).
2. 1556   Father James Laynez.
3. 1565   St Francis Borgia.
4. 1572   Father Everard Mercurian.
5. 1581   ,,   Claud Aquaviva.
6. 1615   ,,   Mutio Vitelleschi.
7. 1645   ,,   Vincent Caraffa.
8. 1649   ,,   Francis Piccolomini.
9. 1651   ,,   Alexander Gottifredi.
10. 1652   ,,   Goswin Nickel.
11. 1664   ,,   John Paul Oliva.
12. 1681   ,,   Charles de Noyella.
13. 1687   ,,   Thyrsis Gonzales de Santalla.
14. 1706   ,,   Michael Angelo Tamburini.
15. 1730   ,,   Francis Retz.
16. 1750   ,,   Ignatius Visconti.
17. 1755   ,,   Louis Centurione.
18. 1758   ,,   Lorenzo Ricci († 1775).

    1775–1802   *Vacancy.*   { Stanislaus Czerniewicz / Gabriel Lienkiewicz / Francis Xavier Kareu }   Vicars-general.

19. 1802   Father Gabriel Gruber.
20. 1805   ,,   Thaddeus Brzozowski.
21. 1820   ,,   Louis Fortis.
22. 1829   ,,   John Roothaan.
23. 1853   ,,   Peter-John Beckx, *retired* 1884.
24. 1887   ,,   Antony Anderledy.
25. 1892   ,,   Louis Martin.
26. 1906   ,,   Francis Xavier Wernz.

[The Order was expelled from France 1594, readmitted 1603, expelled 1764; expelled from Venice 1606, Bohemia 1618, Naples 1622, the Indies 1623, Portugal 1759, Spain 1767, readmitted 1818, Russia 1817. It was dissolved by Clement XIV 1773, restored by Pius VII 1814.]

TABLE 121

ELECTED KINGS OF POLAND

1574 Henry of Valois (Henry III K. of France).

1575 Stephen Báthory, † 1586 *s.p.*

1587 Sigismund III (K. of Sweden), † 1632.

1632 Ladislaus VII, *son of* Sigismund III, † 1648.

1648 John Casimir V, *son of* Sigismund III, *abd.* 1668.

1669 Michael Korybut Wisniowiecki, † 1673.

1674 John III Sobieski, † 1696.

1697 Augustus II (El. Frederick Augustus I of Saxony), *dep.* 1704.

1704 Stanislaus Leszczynski, *dep.* 1709.

1709 Augustus II, *rest.*, † 1733.

1733 Stanislaus Leszczynski, *rest.*

1734 Augustus III (El. Frederick Augustus II) *son of* Augustus II,
      † 1763.

1764 Stanislaus Augustus Poniatowski, *abd.* 1795.

[First Partition of Poland 1772 ; Second Partition 1793 ; Third Partition 1795.]

TABLE 122

DOGES OF VENICE FROM 1414

Date of election		Date of election	
1414	Tommaso Mocenigo (64th Doge).	1618	Nicolò Donato.
1423	Francesco Foscarini.	1618	Antonio Priuli.
1457	Pasquale Malipiero.	1623	Francesco Contarini.
1462	Cristofero Moro.	1624	Giovanni Cornaro.
1471	Nicolò Tron.	1630	Nicolò Contarini.
1472	Nicolò Marcello.	1631	Francesco Erizzo.
1474	Pietro Mocenigo.	1646	Francesco Molin.
1476	Andrea Vendramin.	1655	Carlo Contarini.
1478	Giovanni Mocenigo.	1656	Francesco Cornaro.
1485	Marco Barbarigo.	1656	Bertucci Valier.
1486	Agostino Barbarigo.	1658	Giovanni Pesaro.
1501	Leonardo Loredano.	1659	Domenico Contarini.
1521	Antonio Grimani.	1675	Nicolò Sagredo.
1523	Andrea Gritti.	1676	Alvise Contarini.
1539	Pietro Lando.	1684	Marcantonio Giustinian.
1545	Francesco Donato.	1688	Francesco Morosini.
1553	Antonio Trevisan.	1694	Silvestro Valier.
1554	Francesco Venier.	1700	Alvise Mocenigo II.
1556	Lorenzo Priuli.	1709	Giovanni Corner.
1559	Girolamo Priuli.	1722	Alvise Mocenigo III.
1567	Pietro Loredano.	1732	Carlo Ruzzini.
1570	Alvise Mocenigo I.	1735	Alvise Pisani.
1577	Sebastiano Venier.	1741	Pietro Grimani.
1578	Nicolò da Ponte.	1752	Francesco Loredano.
1585	Pasquale Cicogna.	1762	Marco Foscarini.
1595	Marin Grimani.	1763	Alvise Mocenigo IV.
1606	Leonardo Donato.	1779	Paolo Renier.
1612	Marcantonio Memmo.	1789	Ludovico Manin (*dep.* 1797).
1615	Giovanni Bembo.		(*Venice annexed by Austria.*)

TABLE 123

PRESIDENTS OF THE UNITED STATES OF AMERICA

(Elected for a term of four years)

	Elected	Elected for second term of office
George Washington	1789	1793
John Adams	1797	
Thomas Jefferson	1801	1805
James Madison	1809	1813
James Monroe	1817	1821
John Quincy Adams	1825	
Andrew Jackson	1829	1833
Martin Van Buren	1837	
William Henry Harrison	1841 († April 1841)	
John Tyler	1841	
James Knox Polk	1845	
Zachary Taylor	1849 († 1850)	
Millard Fillmore	1850	
Franklin Pierce	1853	
James Buchanan	1857	
Abraham Lincoln	1861	1865 (*murd.* 1865)
Andrew Johnson	1865	
Ulysses Simpson Grant	1869	1873
Rutherford Birchard Hayes	1877	
James Abram Garfield	1881 (*murd.* 1881)	
Chester Alan Arthur	1881	
Stephen Grover Cleveland	1885	
Benjamin Harrison	1889	
Stephen Grover Cleveland	1893	
William McKinley	1897	1901 (*murd.* 1901)
Theodore Roosevelt	1901	1905
William Howard Taft	1909	

TABLE 124

PRESIDENTS OF THE FRENCH REPUBLIC

(Elected for a term of seven years)

Date of election

August	1871	Marie-Joseph-Louis-Adolphe Thiers.
May	1873	Marie-Edmé-Patrice-Maurice de Macmahon, D. of Magenta, Marshal of France, *resigned*.
January	1879	François-Paul-Jules Grévy, *re-elected* 1886, *resigned*.
December	1887	Marie-François-Sadi Carnot, *murd*.
June	1894	Jean-Paul-Pierre Casimir-Périer, *resigned*.
January	1895	François-Félix Faure, *died*.
February	1899	Émile Loubet.
January	1906	Armand Fallières.

TABLE 125

PRESIDENTS OF MEXICO

(The dates are those of election)

[1821 Independence declared; Augustin Iturbidi Generalissimo; 1822 declared himself Emperor and deposed; 1823 dictatorship of Guerrero, Bravo, and Negretti.]

Gen. G. Victoria, 1824.
Gen. Guerrero, 1827, Dictator 1829–30.
Gen. Anastasio Bustamente, 1830–2.
Gen. Pedraza, 1832.
Gen. Antonio Lopez de Santa Anna, 1835.
José J. Caro, 1836.
Gen. A. Bustamente, 1837–40.
Gen. Farias, 1840.
Gen. de Santa Anna, President 1840; Dictator 1841–4.
Gen. José Joaquin Herrera, *ad int.* 1844; President 1845.
Gen. Paredes, 1845–6.
Gen. Sales, *ad int.* 1846–7.
Gen. de Santa Anna, 1847–8.
Gen. Herrera, 1848–51.
Gen. Mariano Arista, 1851.
M. J. Ceballos, 1852.
Gen. de Santa Anna, Dictator 1853–5.
Gen. Ignacio Comonfort, *ad int.* 1855–8.
Gen. Felix Zuloago, *ad int.* 1858.
Gen. Miguel Miramon, 1859.
Gen. Benito Juárez, 1861 (with dictatorial powers).

Maximilian Archd. of Austria, *Emp.* 1864, *ex.* 1867.

Gen. Benito Juárez, 1867.
Sebastian Lerdo de Tejarda, 1872.
Porfirio Díaz, 1877–80.
Manuel Gonzales, 1880–4.
Porfirio Díaz, 1885–1911.

TABLE 126

BRAZIL

1822 Pedro I, *King*. *Emp.* 1825, *abd.* 1831.
1831 Brazilian Declaration of Independence.
  ,,   Pedro II, *dep.* 1889.
1889 Republic proclaimed.

PRESIDENTS (*elected in March, assume office in December*).

1889 Gen. Manoel Deodoro da Fonseca, *res.* 1891.

    [1891 *Constitution adopted.*]

1891 Floriano Peixoto (*Vice-president*).
1894 Dr Prudente de Moraes Barros.
1898 Dr Campos Salles.
1902 Rodriguez Alves.
1906 Dr Affonso Penna († June, 1909).
1909 (June) Dr Milo Peçanha (*Vice-president*).
1910 Marshal Hermes da Fonseca.

TABLE 127

LORDS LIEUTENANT, LORDS DEPUTY AND LORDS JUSTICES OF IRELAND FROM 1485

(All Lords Lieutenant and Deputy are given, but not dates of renewal of office when consecutive. Temporary deputies of Lords Deputy are not given. Some Justices holding office for very brief periods are omitted.)

	Lords Lieutenant	Lords Deputy	Lords Justices
1485	Jasper (Tudor) D. of Bedford	Gerald (Fitzgerald) 8th E. of Kildare	
1492		Walter FitzSimons Abp. of Dublin	
1493		Rob. (Preston) Lord Gormanstown	
,,		William Preston	
1494	P. Henry D. of York	Sir Edward Poynings	
1495			Hy. Deane Bp. of Bangor
1496–1513		E. of Kildare	
1498	P. Henry		
1503			Abp. FitzSimons
1513–20		Gerald 9th E. of Kildare	
1515			Wm. (Preston) Lord Gormanstown
1520	Thomas (Howard) E. of Surrey		
1522		Piers (Butler) E. of Ormond (Ossory)	
1524		E. of Kildare	
1527		Rich. (Nugent) Lord Delvin	
1528			Piers (Butler) E. of Ossory
1529	Henry Fitzroy E. of Richmond		
1530		Sir William Skeffington	
1532		E. of Kildare	
1535		Lord Leonard Grey	
1540			William (Brereton) Lord Leighlin

TABLE 127 (*continued*)_b

	Lords Lieutenant	Lords Deputy	Lords Justices
1540–7		Sir Anthony St Leger	
1547			Sir Wm. Brabazon
1548			Sir Edw. Bellingham
1549			Sir Francis Bryant *and* Sir Wm. Brabazon
1550		Sir A. St Leger	
1551		Sir James Croft	
1552			Sir Thomas Cusacke *and* Sir Gerald Aylmer
1553–6		Sir A. St Leger	
1556–60		Thos. (Ratcliffe) Lord Fitzwalter (E. of Sussex)	
1557–9			Sir Henry Sidney *acting Deputy during Sussex' absence*
1559–71			Sir Wm. Fitzwilliam *5 times between* 1559 *and* 1571
1560–2	E. of Sussex		
1561		Sir Wm. Fitzwilliam	
1564			Sir Nicholas Arnold
1565–7		Sir Henry Sidney	
1568–71		,, ,,	
1572–5		Sir Wm. Fitzwilliam	
1575–8		Sir Henry Sidney	
1578			Sir Wm. Drury
1579			Sir Wm. Pelham
1580		Arthur Lord Grey de Wilton	Adam Loftus Abp. of Dublin *and* Sir Hy. Wallop
1584		Sir John Perrott	
1588		Sir Wm. Fitzwilliam	
1594		Sir Wm. Russell	
1597		Thomas Lord Burgh	Sir Thomas Norris (*died*)
1597			{Abp. Loftus, Sir Rob. Gardiner *and* E. of Ormond}
1599	Robert (Devereux) E. of Essex		Abp. Loftus *and* Sir Geo. Carey
1600		Charles (Blount) Lord Mountjoy	
1603	Lord Mountjoy (E. of Devonshire)	Sir Geo. Carey	
1604–16		Sir Arthur Chichester	
1613			R. Wingfield (Visct. Powerscourt) *and* Thos. Jones Abp. of Dublin

TABLE 127 (*continued*)_c

	Lords Lieutenant	Lords Deputy	Lords Justices
1615			Abp. Jones *and* Sir John Denham
1616		Sir Oliver St John	
1622–9		Henry (Carey) Visct. Falkland	
1623			Adam (Loftus) Visct. Ely *and* Visct. Powerscourt
1629			Visct. Ely *and* Rich. (Boyle) E. of Cork
1633–9		Thomas Visct. Wentworth (E. of Strafford)	
1636			Visct. Ely *and* Chr. Wandesford
1639			Robert Lord Dillon *and* Chr. Wandesford
1640	E. of Strafford	Chr. Wandesford	Lord Dillon *and* Sir Wm. Parsons
1641	Robert (Sidney) E. of Leicester *absentee*		
1643			Sir J. Borlace *and* Sir Hy. Tichborne
1644	James (Butler) M. (D.) of Ormond		
1647	Philip (Sidney) Lord Lisle *for Parliament*		
1648	M. of Ormond *for the King*		
1649	Oliver Cromwell		
1650		M. of Clanricarde *for Ormond* Henry Ireton *for Cromwell*	
1651		Major-Gen. Lambert	
1653		*Commissioners for Parliament*	{ Major-Gen. Fleetwood Lieut.-Gen. Edmund Ludlow *and others*
1655		,,	Henry Cromwell *and others*
1657–60	Henry Cromwell		
1659		,,	{ Edmund Ludlow Major Bury *and others*
1660		*Commissioners for the Army*	{ R. Boyle (E. of Orrery) Sir C. Coote Major Bury *and others*

TABLE 127 (*continued*)ₔ

	Lords Lieutenant	Lords Deputy	Lords Justices
1660	George (Monck) D. of Albemarle *absentee*	John Lord Robarts *absentee*	E. of Orrery *and others*
1662	James (Butler) 1st D. of Ormond		
1664		Thomas E. of Ossory	
1665	D. of Ormond		
1668		E. of Ossory	
1669	John Lord Robarts (E. of Radnor)		
1670	John Lord Berkeley of Stratton		
1671			Michael Boyle Abp. of Dublin *and* Arthur (Forbes) Visct. (E. of) Granard
1672–5 and 1676	Arthur (Capel) E. of Essex		
1675			Abp. Boyle *and* E. of Granard
1677–85	D. of Ormond		
1682		Rich. (Butler) E. of Arran	
1684			Abp. Boyle *and* E. of Granard
1685	Henry (Hyde) E. of Clarendon		
1686–9	Rich. (Talbot) E. of Tyrconnel		
1687			Sir Alex. Fitton *and* Wm. (Burke) E. of Clanricarde
1689	[K. JAMES II *in person*]		
1690	[K. WILLIAM III *in person*]		Henry (Sidney) Visct. Sidney Sir Chas. Porter *and* Thos. Coningsby
1692	Visct. Sidney		
1693–5			Henry (Capel) Lord Capel *and others*
1695		Lord Capel	
1696			Sir C. Porter *and others*
1697			Henry (de Massue de Ruvigny, M. de Ruvigny), E. of Galway *and others*
1699			{ Narcissus Marsh Abp. of Dublin E. of Galway *and others*
1701	Lawrence (Hyde) E. of Rochester		
1702			Abp. Marsh *and others*
1702	(*Access. of Q. Anne*)	(*No more Lords Deputy appointed*)	Hugh (Montgomery) E. of Mountalexander *and others*

9—2

TABLE 127 (*continued*).

Lords Lieutenant	Lords Justices
1703–7 James (Butler) 2nd D. of Ormond	Sir Richard Cox *and others*
1707 Thomas (Herbert) E. of Pembroke	Abp. Marsh of Armagh *and* Sir R. Cox
1709 Thomas (Wharton) E. of Wharton	R. Freeman *and* R. Ingoldsby
1710–13 D. of Ormond	
1711, 1712, 1714	Sir Constantine Phipps *and others*
1713 Charles (Talbot) D. of Shrewsbury	
1714	Abp. Lindsay of Armagh, John Vesey Abp. of Tuam, *and* Sir C. Phipps
(*Accession of George I*)	
1714 Charles (Spencer) E. of Sunderland *absentee*	Wm. King Abp. of Dublin, Abp. Vesey, *and* E. of Kildare
1715	Charles (Fitzroy) D. of Grafton *and* E. of Galway
1716 Charles (Townshend) Visct. Townshend *absentee*	
1717–9	Abp. King, E. of Middleton, Speaker Conolly *and* Lord Brodrick (*thrice*)
1719 Charles (Paulet) D. of Bolton	
1721 D. of Grafton	
1722	Abp. King, Visct. Shannon, *and* Speaker Conolly
1723–4	E. of Middleton, Speaker Conolly, *and* Visct. Shannon
1724–31 John (Granville) Lord Carteret (E. Granville)	
1726–9	Hugh Boulter Abp. of Armagh, Lord Chancellor West, *and* Speaker Conolly
1731 Lionel (Sackville) D. of Dorset	
1732–9	Abp. Boulter, Thos. Lord Wyndham *and others, usually* Speaker Boyle *and* Robert Jocelyn (Lord Newport)
1737 Wm. (Cavendish) 3rd D. of Devonshire	
1740	Abp. Boulter *and others*
1742–6	John Hoadly Abp. of Armagh *and others*
1745 Philip (Stanhope) E. of Chesterfield	
1747–64	George Stone Abp. of Armagh *and others; usually* Lord Chancellor Newport *and* Speaker Boyle *or* Lord Bessborough
1747 William (Stanhope) E. of Harrington	
1751 D. of Dorset	
1755 William (Cavendish) M. of Hartington (D. of Devonshire)	
1757 John (Russell) D. of Bedford	
1761 George (Dunk) E. of Halifax	
1763 Hugh (Smithson) E. of Northumberland	

TABLE 127 (*continued*),

Lords Lieutenant	*Lords Justices*
1764 Thomas (Thynne) Visct. Weymouth *absentee*	
1765 Francis (Seymour) E. of Hertford	Lord Chancellor Bowes *and* Speaker Ponsonby
1766 Wm. Geo. (Hervey) E. of Bristol *absentee*	
1767 George (Townshend) Lord Townshend	
1772 Simon (Harcourt) Earl Harcourt	
1777 John (Hobart) E. of Buckinghamshire	
1780 Fredk. (Howard) E. of Carlisle	
1782 Wm. (Bentinck) D. of Portland	
,, George (Grenville) Earl Temple (M. of Buckingham)	
1783 Robert (Henley) E. of Northington	
1784 Charles (Manners) D. of Rutland	
1787 M. of Buckingham	Richard Robinson Abp. of Armagh, Lord Chancellor Lifford *and others*
1789	Lord Chancellor Fitzgibbon *and* Speaker John Foster (Lord Oriel)
1790 John (Fane) E. of Westmorland	
1795 William (Fitzwilliam) Earl Fitzwilliam	Fitzgibbon *and* Foster
,, John (Jeffreys) Earl Camden	
1798 Charles (Cornwallis) M. Cornwallis	

[*After the Union of Great Britain and Ireland Lords Justices are of less importance, the Lord Lieutenant being resident.*]

    1801   Philip (Yorke) E. of Hardwicke.
    1805   Edward (Clive) E. of Powis *absentee*.
    1806   John (Russell) D. of Bedford.
    1807   Charles (Lennox) D. of Richmond.
    1813   Charles Visct. (E.) Whitworth.
    1817   Charles (Talbot) E. Talbot.
    1821   [Aug.—Sept. GEORGE IV *in person.*]
     ,,   Richard (Wellesley) Marquis Wellesley.
    1828   Henry (Paget) (E. of Uxbridge) M. of Anglesey.
    1829   Hugh (Percy) D. of Northumberland.
    1830   M. of Anglesey.
    1833   M. Wellesley.
    1834   Thomas (Baillie) E. of Haddington.
    1835   Henry (Phipps) E. of Mulgrave (M. of Normanby).
    1839   Hugh (Fortescue) Visct. Ebrington (Earl Fortescue).
    1841   Thomas Philip (de Grey) E. de Grey.
    1844   William (Holmes-A'Court) Lord Heytesbury.
    1846   John (Ponsonby) E. of Bessborough.
    1847   George (Villiers) E. of Clarendon.
    1852   Archibald (Montgomerie) E. of Eglinton.

TABLE 127 (*continued*)₀

Lords Lieutenant

1853   Edward Granville (Eliot) E. of St Germans.

1855   George (Howard) E. of Carlisle.

1858   E. of Eglinton.

1859   E. of Carlisle.

1864   John Lord Wodehouse (E. of Kimberley).

1866   James (Hamilton) M. of (D. of) Abercorn.

1868   John (Spencer) Earl Spencer.

1874   James (Hamilton) D. of Abercorn.

1876   John (Churchill) D. of Marlborough.

1880   Francis (Cowper) Earl Cowper.

1882   Earl Spencer.

1885   H. Howard Molyneux (Herbert) E. of Carnarvon.

1886   John (Campbell Hamilton-Gordon) E. of Aberdeen.

  ,,   Charles (Vane-Tempest-Stewart) E. of Londonderry.

1889   Laurence (Dundas) E. of (M. of) Zetland.

1892   Robert O. A. (Crewe-Milnes) Lord Houghton (E. of Crewe).

1895   George (Cadogan) Earl Cadogan.

1902   William (Ward) E. of Dudley.

1905   E. of Aberdeen.

TABLE 128

INDIA

[Until 1862 the dates given are those of assumption of government and of retirement; after 1862, of appointment. Deputies pro tem. are omitted.]

GOVERNORS OF BENGAL

1765   Robert Lord Clive.
1767   Henry Verelst.
1769   John Cartier.

GOVERNORS-GENERAL OF BENGAL AND OF INDIA 1773-1858

Governors-General of Bengal with supreme authority

1773-85   Warren Hastings.
1785-6   (Sir) John Macpherson.
1786-93   Charles E. (M.) Cornwallis.
1793-8   Sir John Shore (Lord Teignmouth).
1798-1805   Richard E. of Mornington (M. of Wellesley).
1805   Charles M. Cornwallis.
1805-7   Sir George Hilaro Barlow.
1807-13   George Lord (E. of) Minto.
1813-23   Francis E. of Moira (M. of Hastings).
1823-8   William Lord (E. of) Amherst.
1828-35   Lord Wm. Cavendish-Bentinck.

[1833 the Governors-General of Bengal become Governors-General of India.]

1835-6   Sir Charles Theophilus (Lord) Metcalfe.
1836-42   George (Eden) Lord (E. of) Auckland.
1842-4   Edward (Law) Lord (E. of) Ellenborough.
1844-8   Sir Henry (Visct.) Hardinge.
1848-56   James (Ramsay) E. (M.) of Dalhousie.
1856-62   Charles Visct. Canning.

[1858 the Governors-General become Viceroys and Governors-General.]

VICEROYS

1858   Visct. Canning *as above.*
1862   James (Bruce) E. of Elgin and Kincardine.
1863   Sir John Lawrence (Lord Lawrence).
1868   Richard (Bourke) E. of Mayo.
1872   Thomas Geo. (Baring) Lord (E. of) Northbrook.
1876   Edward (Bulwer-Lytton) Lord (E. of) Lytton.
1880   George (Robinson) M. of Ripon.
1884   Frederick (Temple Hamilton-Blackwood) E. of Dufferin (M. of Dufferin and Ava).
1888   Henry (Petty-Fitzmaurice) M. of Lansdowne.
1893   V. Alexander (Bruce) E. of Elgin and Kincardine.
1898   George (Curzon) Lord Curzon of Kedleston.
1905   Gilbert (Elliot) E. of Minto.
1910   Charles (Hardinge) Lord Hardinge of Penshurst.

TABLE 129

JAMAICA

[In this and the subsequent colonial lists the dates, before the 19th century, are usually those of assumption of office; the dates of appointments are often several months earlier. The Deputy-Governors, Lieutenant-Governors and Presidents of the Council holding office during the intervals between Governorships are not included in this list.]

GOVERNORS AND ACTING GOVERNORS 1656–1904

1656	Colonel Edward D'Oyley.
1661–4	Thomas Hickman (Windsor) Lord Windsor *absentee*.
1662–4	Sir Charles Littleton *or* Lyttelton *Acting Governor*.
1664	Sir Thomas Modyford.
1674–8	Sir John Vaughan, *styled* Lord Vaughan (Earl of Carbery).
1678–81	Charles (Howard) E. of Carlisle.
1682	Sir Thomas Lynch.
1684	Sir Philip Howard.
1687–8	Christopher (Monck) D. of Albemarle *Governor-General*.
1690–2	William (O'Brien) 2nd E. of Inchiquin.
1701	Major-Gen. William Selwyn.
1702	Charles (Mordaunt) E. of Peterborough *absentee*.
	Major-Gen. Thomas Handasyde *Acting Governor*.
1711	Lord Archibald Hamilton.
1714	Peter Heywood.
1716	Thomas Pitt *absentee*.
1718	Sir Nicholas Lawes.
1722–6	Henry (Bentinck) D. of Portland.
1727	Major-Gen. Robert Hunter.
1735	Henry Cunninghame.
1738–52	Edward Trelawney.
1752	Vice-Admiral (Sir) Charles Knowles.
1758	Brigadier-Gen. George Haldane.
1762	Wm. Henry Lyttelton (Lord Westcote).
1767	Capt. Sir Wm. Trelawney, R.N.
1773	Capt. Sir Basil Keith, R.N.
1777	Lt.-Gen. John Dalling.
1782	Major-Gen. Archibald Campbell.
1790	Thomas (Howard) E. of Effingham.
1794–1801	Alexander (Lindsay) 6th E. of Balcarres.
1801	Lt.-Gen. Sir George Nugent.
1806	Sir Eyre Coote.
1808	William (Montagu) D. of Manchester.
1809	Lt.-Gen. Edward Morrison.
1829	Somerset (Lowry-Corry) 2nd E. of Belmore.
1832	Sir Constantine Henry (Phipps) E. of Mulgrave (M. of Normanby).
1834	Horne Peter (Browne) M. of Sligo.
1836	Major-Gen. Sir Lionel Smith.
1839	Sir Charles Theophilus Metcalfe.

TABLE 129 (*continued*)_b

1842   James (Bruce) 8th E. of Elgin (12th E. of Kincardine).
1847   Sir Charles Edward Grey.
1853   Sir Henry Barkly.
1857   (Sir) Charles Henry Darling.
1864   Edward John Eyre, *superseded Jan.* 1866.
1866   Lt.-Gen. Sir Henry Storks *temporary Gov., Jan.* 1866.

[1866 *Constitution abrogated, Jamaica becomes a Crown Colony.*]

1866   Sir John Peter Grant.
1874   Sir William Grey.
1877   Sir Anthony Musgrave ; *Acting Governor* Edward Newton 1878–80.
1883   Gen. Sir Henry Wylie Norman.
1889   Sir Henry Arthur Blake.
1898   Sir Augustus Hemming.
1904   Sir Alexander Swettenham *Capt.-Gen. and Gov.-in-chief.*
1907   Sir Sydney Haldane Olivier

TABLE 130

NORTH AMERICAN COLONIES BEFORE 1776

(1) VIRGINIA

[1606–25 *governed under the Virginia Company. Company's Charter surrendered* 1625.]

GOVERNORS AND LT.-GOVERNORS UNDER THE CROWN

1625	Sir John Harvey *sent prisoner to England* 1639, *but restored.*
1641	Sir William Berkeley *for the King.*
	Col. Digges *for Parliament.*
	Mr Bennet and Mr Matthews *for Oliver Cromwell.*
1660	Sir W. Berkeley *restored.*
1677	John Lord Culpeper *appointed Governor for life* 1677; *visited colony* 1680 *and* 1682; *deprived* 1683.
1683	Francis Lord Howard of Effingham.
1690–4	Sir Francis Nicholson *Lt.-gov.*
1692–8	Sir Edmund Andros.
1698–1704	Sir Francis Nicholson *Lt.-gov.*
1704	George (Hamilton) 1st E. of Orkney *absentee.*
	Edward Notte *Lt.-gov.*
	Brigadier-Gen. R. Hunter *Lt.-gov.*
1710	Alexander Spotswood *Lt.-gov.*
1723	Hugh Drysdale *Lt.-gov.*
1726	(Sir) Wm. Gooch *Lt.-gov.*
1737	William Anne (Keppel) 2nd E. of Albemarle.
1751–8	Robert Dinwiddie *Lt.-gov.*
1756	John (Campbell) 4th E. of Loudoun.
1759	Jeffrey (Lord) Amherst.
1768	Norborne (Berkeley) Lord Bottetourt.
1770	John (Murray) 4th E. of Dunmore.

(2) GOVERNORS OF NEW ENGLAND

[Massachusetts Bay *also* 1641–80 New Hampshire.]

[1643 *Confederation formed by Massachusetts Bay, Plymouth, Connecticut, and New Haven.*]

Elected by the colonists annually under the authority of the Massachusetts Bay Company.

1630–5	John Winthrop.
1636	Sir Harry Vane *the younger.*
1637–40	John Winthrop.
	Thomas Dudley *Deputy.*
1641	Richard Bellingham.
1642	John Winthrop.
1644	John Endicott.
1645	Thomas Dudley *Deputy.*
1646–9	John Winthrop († 1649).
	(John Winthrop *the younger Assist. or Lt.-gov.* 1634–5, 1640, 1645–9.)
1651–3	John Endicott.

TABLE 130 (*continued*)_b

GOVERNORS OF NEW ENGLAND (*continued*)

1653–65 John Endicott († 1665).
   (John Winthrop *the younger Gov. of* Connecticut 1660–76.)
1665–71 Richard Bellingham († 1671).
 1672 John Leveret.
 1676 Simon Bradstreet.
   [*Charter revoked* 1684.]
 1685 Joseph Dudley *Gov. of* New England, *temporarily pres. of provisional Council.*

Governors of Massachusetts Bay and New Hampshire 1685–1740

 1686–9 Sir Edmund Andros *Governor of* Massachusetts,
     Plymouth, New Hampshire and Maine.
      Joseph Dudley *Lt.-gov.*
  1691 Sir William Phipps († 1691) *also Gov. of* Maine.
  1695   William Stoughton *Lt.-gov.*
  1699 Richard (Coote) E. of Bellomont, *also Gov. of* Maine.
      W. Stoughton *Lt.-gov.*
  1702 Joseph Dudley.
  1715 Col. Elisha Burgess.
      Wm. Taylor *Lt.-gov.*
  1716 Col. Samuel Shute.
      Jeremiah Dummer *Lt.-gov.*
  1728 William Burnett († 1729).
  1729 Andrew Belcher.

Governors of Massachusetts Bay

  1741 William Shirley.
  1757 Thomas Pownall.
  1759 (Sir) Francis Barnard.
  1770 Thomas Hutchinson.
  1774 Gen. Thomas Gage.

Governors of New Hampshire

  1740 Benning Wentworth.
  1776 John Wentworth.

(3) GOVERNORS OF NEW YORK

[1664–88 *Lieutenant governors under James D. of York (James II);
Governors from* 1688.]

 1664 Richard Nicolls.
 1668 Francis Lovelace.
 1674 Edmund Andros, *recalled* 1680.
 1682 —— Brockhurst.
 1683 Thomas Dongan.
 1688 Sir Edmund Andros *Governor, and of* the Jerseys, *dep.* 1689.
    Francis Nicholson *Lt.-gov.*

TABLE 130 (*continued*)_c

GOVERNORS OF NEW YORK (*continued*)

[1689 Jacob Leisler *assumed government*.]
1691 Col. Henry Sloughter († 1692).
1692 Benjamin Fletcher.
1696   Col. W. Sloughter *Lt.-gov.*
    Col. Joseph Dudley *Lt.-gov.*
1698 Richard (Coote) E. of Bellomont († 1701).
1701 Edward (Hyde) Visct. Cornbury (E. of Clarendon).
1708 John Lord Lovelace († 1709).
    Col. Ingoldsby *Lt.-gov.*
1710 Col. Robert Hunter.
1720 William Burnett.
1728 John Montgomery.
1732 William Cosby.
1736 Major-Gen. Richard Tyrel.
    George Clarke *Lt.-gov.*
1741 George Cleriton.
1753 Sir Danvers Osborne.
1755 Sir Charles Hardy.
1761   Robert Monkton *Lt.-gov.*
1765 Sir Henry Moore.
1769 John (Murray) 4th E. of Dunmore.
1770   William Tryon *Lt.-gov.*
1779   James Robertson *Lt.-gov.*

GOVERNORS OF NEW JERSEY

[*East and West New Jersey united to form a royal colony, 1702.
1702–36 ruled by Governors of New York.*]

1736 Lewis Morris († 1746).
1747 Andrew Belcher.
1758 (Sir) Francis Bernard.
1759 Thomas Boon.
1761 Josiah Hardy.
1762 William Franklin.

(4) GOVERNORS OF CAROLINA

[*1663–1728 governed under the Carolina Company. Company's Charter surrendered
1728 (except by Earl Grenville proprietor of one-eighth share).*]

GOVERNORS UNDER THE CROWN

1728 Francis Nicholson.
1729 Robert Johnson.

GOVERNORS OF SOUTH CAROLINA

1730 Robert Johnson.
1735 Thomas Broughton.
1736 Charles Craven.
1739 James Glen.

TABLE 130 (*continued*)_d

GOVERNORS OF SOUTH CAROLINA (*continued*)

1755   Wm. Henry Lyttelton (Lord Westcote).

1759   Thomas Pownall.

1761   Thomas Boon.

1766   Lord Charles Greville Montagu.

1777   Capt. Lord W. Campbell, R.N.

GOVERNORS OF NORTH CAROLINA

1730   George Barrington.

1733   Gabriel Jonson.

1743   Arthur Dobbs.

1765   William Tryon.

1770   Josias Martin.

(5) GOVERNORS OF GEORGIA

1734   James Oglethorpe.

1745   John Reynolds.

1758   Henry Ellis.

1761   Sir James Wright.

(6) GOVERNORS OF MARYLAND

[*Till* 1691 *under the proprietors, the Lords Baltimore, with the approval of the Crown.*]

1637   Leonard Calvert *Lt.-gov.*

1647   Thomas Green *Lt.-gov.*

1649   William Stone *Lt.-gov.*

1658   Jonah Fendale.

1660   Philip Calvert.

1662   Charles Calvert (3rd Lord Baltimore).

1678   Thomas Notley *Lt.-gov.*

1681   Charles Calvert (3rd Lord Baltimore).

[1691 *Maryland declared a royal province.*]

GOVERNORS UNDER THE CROWN 1692–1714

1692   Lionel Copley.

1694   Francis Nicolson *or* Nicholson.

1699   Nathaniel Blakiston.

1703   Thomas Finch *President.*

1704   John Seymour *Governor.*

       Edward Lloyd *President.*

1714   John Hart *Governor.*

GOVERNORS UNDER LORD BALTIMORE AS PROPRIETARY 1720–76

1720   Charles Calvert.

1727   Benedict Leonard Calvert.

1733   Charles (Calvert) 5th Lord Baltimore.

1737   Samuel Ogle *Governor.*

1742   Thomas Bladen *Governor.*

1747   S. Ogle.

1751   Benjamin Tasker *President.*

1753   Horatio Sharp *Governor.*

1769   (Sir) Robert Eden.

TABLE 130 (*continued*).

(7) PROPRIETORS, GOVERNORS, ETC. OF PENNSYLVANIA

1682	William Penn *Proprietor.*
1684	Thomas Lloyd *President of Council.*
1688	John Blackwell *Lt.-gov.*
1690–3	*Government by President and Council.*
1693	Ben. Fletcher *Governor.*
,,	William Markham *Lt.-gov.*
1699	William Penn *Proprietor and Governor.*
1701	Andrew Hamilton *Lt.-gov.*
1703	*Government by President and Council.*
1704	John Evans *Lt.-gov.*
1709	Charles Godkin *Lt.-gov.*
1717	Sir Wm. Keith *Lt.-gov.*
1726	Patrick Gordon *Lt.-gov.*
1736	Theo. Thomas *Lt.-gov.*
1747	Anthony Palmer *President.*
1748	James Hamilton *Lt.-gov.*
1754	Robert Hunter Morris *Lt.-gov.*
1756	William Denny *Lt.-gov.*
1759	James Hamilton *Lt.-gov.*
1763–70	John Penn *Lt.-gov.*
1771	James Hamilton *President.*
1771–7	Richard Penn *Lt.-gov.*

TABLE 131

CANADA

GOVERNORS AND GOVERNORS-GENERAL

1763–6   Lt.-Gen. James Murray *Governor of* Canada (*Governor of* Quebec 1760).
1767–70   Major-Gen. Guy Carleton (Lord Dorchester), *Governor of* Quebec (*Acting Governor*).
1770–5   *President* Hector C. Cramahé (*Acting Governor*).
1775–8   Sir Guy Carleton (Lord Dorchester) *Governor-general.*
1778–85   Lt.-Gen. Sir Frederick Haldimand *Governor, Commander-in-chief.*
1786–96   Guy (Carleton) Lord Dorchester *Governor-general.*
[1791–3 *Lt.-Gov.* Major-Gen. Alured Clarke *Governor of* Upper Canada (Ontario) *and* Lower Canada (Quebec).]

GOVERNORS-GENERAL OF UPPER AND LOWER CANADA

1796–9   Gen. Robert Prescott.
1799   Sir Robert Shore Milnes.
1807   Gen. Sir James Henry Craig.
1811   Gen. Sir George Prevost.
1814   Major-Gen. Sir Gordon Drummond.
1816   Gen. Sir John C. Sherbrooke (*Governor of* Nova Scotia 1812–6).
1818   Charles (Lennox) D. of Richmond.
1819   George (Ramsay) E. of Dalhousie (*Governor of* Nova Scotia *from* 1816) *Captain-general and Governor-in-chief.*
1828   Lt.-Gen. Sir James Kempt *Governor-general* (*Governor of* Nova Scotia 1820–8).
[Lt.-Gen. Sir John Colborne *Lieutenant-Governor of* Upper Canada 1828–35.]
1830   Gen. Lord Aylmer.
1836   Archibald (Acheson) E. of Gosford.

GOVERNORS-GENERAL OF THE NORTH AMERICAN PROVINCES

1838   John George (Lambton) E. of Durham *High Commissioner and Governor-general.*
1839   Charles Edward Poulett Thomson (Visct. Sydenham).
1841   Sir Charles Bagot.
1843   Sir Charles Theophilus (Lord) Metcalfe.
1846   Charles Murray (Cathcart) 2nd E. of Cathcart *and Commander-in-chief.*
1847   James E. of Elgin and Kincardine.
1854   Sir Edmund Walker Head.
1861   Charles Stanley (Monck) Visct. Monck.

TABLE 131 (*continued*)_b

GOVERNORS-GENERAL OF THE DOMINION OF CANADA

1867   Visct. Monck.

1869   Sir John Young (Lord Lisgar).

1872   Frederick (Temple Hamilton-Blackwood) E. of Dufferin (M. of Dufferin and Ava).

1878   John (Campbell) M. of Lorne (D. of Argyll).

1883   Henry Charles Keith (Petty-Fitzmaurice) M. of Lansdowne.

1888   Frederick Arthur Lord Stanley of Preston.

1893   John Campbell (Hamilton-Gordon) E. of Aberdeen.

1898   Gilbert (Elliot) E. of Minto.

1904   Albert Henry George (Grey) Earl Grey.

1911   Arthur D. of Connaught.

PRIME MINISTERS.

Sir John Macdonald, 1867–73.

Alexander Mackenzie, 1873–8.

Sir John Macdonald, 1878–91.

Sir John Joseph Caldwell Abbott, 1891–2.

Sir John Sparrow David Thompson, 1892–4.

Sir Mackenzie Bowell, 1894–6.

Sir Charles Tupper, 1896.

Sir Wilfrid Laurier, 1896.

Robert Laird Borden, 1911.

TABLE 132

AUSTRALIA AND NEW ZEALAND

(1) GOVERNORS-GENERAL OF THE COMMONWEALTH (*established* 1901)

1901 John Adrian Louis (Hope) E. of Hopetoun (M. of Linlithgow).
1902 Hallam (Tennyson) Lord Tennyson.
1904 Henry Stafford (Northcote) Lord Northcote.
1908 William H. (Ward) E. of Dudley.
1911 Thomas (Denman) Lord Denman.

PRIME MINISTERS.

Sir Edmund Barton, 1901–3.
Alfred Deakin, 1903–4.
George Houstoun Reid, 1904–5.
Alfred Deakin, 1905–8.
Andrew Fisher, 1908.

(2) GOVERNORS OF NEW SOUTH WALES FROM 1855

[1788–92 Capt. Arthur Phillip *first Governor*.]
1855 Sir William Thomas Denison.
1861 Sir John Young (Lord Lisgar).
1868 Somerset (Lowry-Corry) 4th Earl of Belmore.
1872 Sir Hercules George Robert Robinson.
1885 Charles Robert (Wynn-Carrington) Lord (E. of) Carrington.
1891 Sir Robert Duff.
1895 Henry (Brand) Visct. Hampden.
1899 William (Lygon) Earl Beauchamp.
1902 Admiral Sir Harry Rawson.
1909 Frederic John Napier (Thesiger) Lord Chelmsford.

(3) GOVERNORS OF VICTORIA FROM 1851

[*Victoria created a separate colony in July, 1851; responsible government established* 1854.]

1851 Charles Joseph La Trobe *Lt.-gov.*
1854 Capt. Sir Charles Hotham *Lt.-gov.*, 1855 *Governor.*
1856 Sir Henry Barkly.
1864 Sir Charles Henry Darling.
1866 Sir John Henry Thomas Manners-Sutton (Visct. Canterbury).
1873 Sir George Ferguson Bowen.
1879 George Augustus Constantine (Phipps) 2nd M. of Normanby.
1884 Sir Henry Brougham Loch.
1889 John Adrian Louis (Hope) 7th E. of Hopetoun.
1895 Thomas Lord Brassey.
1901 Sir George Sydenham Clarke.
1904 Sir Reginald Talbot.
1908 Sir Thomas David Gibson Carmichael.

TABLE 132 (*continued*)ₐ

(4) GOVERNORS OF QUEENSLAND FROM 1859

1859   Sir George Ferguson Bowen.
1868   Col. Samuel Wensley Blackall.
1871   George A. C. (Phipps) 2nd M. of Normanby.
1875   William Wellington Cairns.
1877   Sir Arthur Edward Kennedy.
1883   Sir Anthony Musgrave.
1889   Gen. Sir Henry Wylie Norman.
1896   Charles W. A. N. (Cochrane-Baillie) Lord Lamington.
1901   Sir Samuel Walker Griffith.
1902   Major-Gen. Sir Herbert Charles Chermside.
1905   Frederic J. N. (Thesiger) Lord Chelmsford.
1909   Sir William McGregor.

(5) GOVERNORS OF SOUTH AUSTRALIA FROM 1855

1855   Sir Richard Graves MacDonnell.
1862   Sir Dominick Daly.
1869   Sir James Fergusson.
1873   Sir Anthony Musgrave.
1877   Sir William W. Cairns.
   Sir William Francis Drummond Jervois.
1883   Sir William Cleaver Francis Robinson.
1889   Algernon H. T. (Keith-Falconer) E. of Kintore.
1895   Sir Thomas Fowell Buxton.
1899   Hallam (Tennyson) Lord Tennyson.
1903   Sir George Ruthven Le Hunte.
1908   Admiral Sir Day Hort Bosanquet.

[Sir Samuel James Way *Administrator* 9 times, 1877–1902.]

(6) GOVERNORS OF WESTERN AUSTRALIA FROM 1869

[1829–69 *governed by Lt.-governors under the Colonial Office.*]
(*The dates in this list are those of appointment.*)

1869   Frederick Aloysius Weld.
1874   W. C. F. Robinson.
1877   Major-Gen. Sir Harry St George Ord.
1880   Sir W. C. F. Robinson.
1883   Sir Frederick Napier Broome.
1890   Sir W. C. F. Robinson.
1895   Col. Sir Gerard Smith.
1901   Sir Arthur Lawley.
1903   Admiral Sir Frederick George Denham Bedford.
1909   Sir Gerald Strickland.

TABLE 132 *(continued)*

(7) GOVERNORS OF NEW ZEALAND FROM 1840

1840	Capt. W. Hobson.
1843	Capt. Robert Fitzroy.
1845	Sir George Grey.
1855	Col. Sir Thomas Gore Browne.
1861	Sir George Grey.
1868	Sir George Ferguson Bowen.
1873	Sir James Fergusson.
1874	George A. C. (Phipps) 2nd M. of Normanby.
1879	Sir Hercules G. R. Robinson.
1880	Sir Arthur Hamilton Gordon.
1883	Lieut.-Gen. Sir W. F. D. Jervois.
1889	William Hillier (Onslow) 4th E. of Onslow, *res.* 1891.
1892	David (Boyle) 7th E. of Glasgow.
1897	Uchter John Mark (Knox) 5th E. of Ranfurly.
1904	William Lee (Plunket) 5th Lord Plunket, *Gov. and Commander-in-chief.*
1910	John Poynder (Dickson-Poynder), Lord Islington.

(8) GOVERNORS OF TASMANIA FROM 1855

1855	Sir Henry Edward Fox Young.
1861	Col. Sir T. Gore Browne.
1869	Sir Charles Du Cane.
1875	Frederick A. Weld.
1881	Maj. Sir George Cumine Strahan.
1886	Sir Robert George Crookshank Hamilton.
1893	Jenico W. J. (Preston) 14th Visct. Gormanston.
1900	Sir Arthur Havelock.
1904	Sir Gerald Strickland.
1909	Major-Gen. Sir Harry Barron.

TABLE 133

SOUTH AFRICA

(Deputy or Acting Governors omitted.)

(1) GOVERNORS OF CAPE COLONY 1795—1906

1795   Gen. James Henry Craig.
1797   George (Macartney) Earl Macartney.
1799   Sir George Yonge.
1803   Jan Willem Jansens *(under the Batavian Republic)*.
1806   Sir David Baird.
1807   Du Pré (Alexander) E. of Caledon.
1811   Sir John Francis Cradock.
1814   Lord Charles Henry Somerset.
1828   Hon. Sir Galbraith Lowry Cole.
1834   Sir Benjamin D'Urban.
1838   Sir Geo. Thos. Napier.
1843   Sir Peregrine Maitland.
1847   Maj.-Gen. Sir Henry Pottinger.
          Lieut.-Gen. Sir Henry George Wakelyn Smith.
1852   Lieut.-Gen. George Cathcart.
1854   Sir George Grey, *recalled 1859, restored 1860*.
1861   Sir Philip Edmond Wodehouse.
1870   Sir Henry Barkly.
1877   Sir Henry Bartle Edward Frere.
1881   Sir Hercules G. R. Robinson (Lord Rosmead).
1889   Sir Henry Brougham Loch.
1895   Sir Hercules Robinson.
1897   Sir Alfred Milner (Visct. Milner).
1901–10   Sir Walter Francis Hely-Hutchinson.

(2) LIEUTENANT-GOVERNORS AND GOVERNORS OF NATAL

[Natal was erected into a separate colony in 1856.]

LIEUTENANT-GOVERNORS

1856   John Scott.
1864   John Maclean.
1867   Robert William Keate.
1872   Anthony Musgrave.
1873   Sir Benjamin Chilley Campbell Pine.
1875   Sir Henry Ernest Gascoyne Bulwer.

TABLE 133 (*continued*) b

NATAL (*continued*)

Governors

1879 Gen. Sir Garnet Joseph Wolseley (Visct. Wolseley).
1880 Maj.-Gen. Sir George Pomeroy Colley.
1882 Sir Henry E. G. Bulwer.
1886 Sir Arthur Elibank Havelock.
1889 Lieut.-Col. Sir Charles Mitchell.
1893 Sir Walter Francis Hely-Hutchinson.
1901 Sir Henry Edward McCallum.
1907-9 Sir Matthew Nathan.

(3) SOUTH AFRICA, HIGH COMMISSIONERS

1900 Visct. Milner.
1905-10 Wm. Waldegrave (Palmer) 2nd E. of Selborne.

(4) SOUTH AFRICAN CONFEDERATION

Governor-General

1910 Herbert (Gladstone) Visct. Gladstone.

TABLE 134

EGYPT AND THE SUDAN

I. AGENTS AND CONSULS-GENERAL IN EGYPT

1883   Evelyn (Baring) Visct. (E. of) Cromer.
1907   Sir Eldon Gorst.
1911   Horatio Herbert (Kitchener) Visct. Kitchener of Khartum.

II. GOVERNORS-GENERAL OF THE SUDAN PROVINCES AND SIRDARS OF THE EGYPTIAN ARMY

1896   Sir Horatio Herbert Kitchener Visct. Kitchener.
1899   Sir Francis Reginald Wingate.

TABLE 135

THE NETHERLANDS

GOVERNORS OF THE NETHERLANDS

1477	C. Adolphus of Cleves-Ravenstein.
1485–6	C. Engelbert II of Nassau-Breda.
1486–94	Albert D. of Saxony.
1506–7	William of Croy M. of Aerschot.
1507–30	Margaret of Austria, Dss. of Savoy.
1531–55	Mary of Austria, Q. of Hungary.
1555–9	Emmanuel Philibert, D. of Savoy.
1559–67	Margaret of Austria, Dss. of Parma.
1567–73	Fernando Alvarez de Toledo, D. of Alva.
1573–6	Luis de Requesens y Zuñiga.
1576–8	Don John *of Austria*.
1578	Alexander Farnese, D. of Parma.

GOVERNORS OF THE SOUTHERN (SPANISH) NETHERLANDS

1581–92	Alexander Farnese, D. of Parma.
1592–4	C. Peter Ernest of Mansfeld.
1594–5	Archd. Ernest of Austria.
1595–6	Pedro Henriquez de Acevedo, C. of Fuentes.
1596–1633	Archd. Albert of Austria († 1621) *and* Clara Isabella Eugenia, Infanta (*dau. of Philip II*, † 1633).
1633–4	Ferdinand, Card. Infant.
1641–4	Francisco de Mello, M. of Terceira.
1644–7	Emmanuel de Moura Cortereal, M. of Castel Rodrigo.
1647–56	Archd. Leopold William of Austria.
1656–9	Don Juan *of Austria*.
1659–64	Louis de Benavides Carillo, M. of Fromiata.
1664–8	Francisco de Moura Cortereal, M. of Castel Rodrigo.
1668–70	Iñigo Fernandez de Velasco, D. of Feria.
1670–5	Juan Domingo de Zuñiga y Fonseca.
1675–7	Carlos de Gurrea, D. of Villahermosa.
1678–82	P. Alexander Farnese.
1682–5	Otto Henry, M. of Caretto.
1685–92	Fr. Antonio de Agurto, M. of Castagna.
1692–1706	Maximilian II, El. of Bavaria (*deputy* 1701–4, M. of Bedmar).

[1706–14 *the Southern Netherlands under joint rule of England and the Allies.*]

GOVERNORS OF THE AUSTRIAN NETHERLANDS

1716–24	P. Eugene Francis of Savoy.
1724–41	Archdss. Maria Elizabeth (*dau. of Leopold I*).
1741–4	C. Frederick Augustus von Harrach-Rohran.
1744–80	Archdss. Maria Anna (*dau. of Charles VI*, † 1744) *and* Prince Charles Alexander of Lorraine.
1781–93	Archdss. Maria Christina (*dau. of Francis I*) *and* Albert, D. of Saxe-Teschen.
1793–4	Archd. Charles Lewis.

TABLE 136

HUNGARY AND TRANSYLVANIA

PALATINES (FROM MATTHIAS CORVINUS)

1458–81　Michael Orságh of Guth.

1482–4　*Vacancy.* Urban Dóczy, Bp. of Erlau, *Commissioner.*

[*Palatines elected from 1485 for life by the Diet; Commissioners appointed by the Sovereign.*]

1485–7　Emeric Zapólya.

1488–91　*Vacancy.* Bp. Dóczy, *Commissioner.*

1492–9　Stephen Zapólya.

1500–3　Peter Gereb of Wyngarth.

1504–19　Emeric Perényi.

1519–25　Stephen Báthory, *dep.*

1525–6　Stephen Verbóczy.

1526–33　*Vacancy.* *Rivals* ⎰ Stephen Báthory, 1526 († 1531), *for Ferdinand I.*
Michael Kesserew, 1526–9, *and*
John Bánffy, 1530–2, *for John Zapólya.*

1534　Alexius Thurso, *Judex Curiae, Commissioner.*

1535–53　*Vacancy.*

1554–62　Thomas Nádasdy.

1562–1608　*Vacancy.* Alexius Thurso and several ecclesiastics, *Commissioners.*

1608–9　Stephen Illesházy.

1609–16　George Thurso.

1617–21　Sigismund Forgacs.

1622–5　Stanislaus Thurso.

1625–45　C. Nicholas Esterházy.

1646–8　C. John Draskovich.

1649–55　Paul Pálffy.

1655–67　Francis Vesselényi of Hadad.

1668–80　*Vacancy.*

1681–1713　C. Paul Esterházy.

1714–32　C. Nicholas Pálffy.

1732–41　*Vacancy.* Francis D. of Lorraine, *Regent.*

1741–51　C. John Pálffy.

1751–61　C. Ludwig Ernest Batthyány.

1762–89　*Vacancy.*

1790–5　Archd. Leopold.

1796–1847　Archd. Joseph.

1847–8　Archd. Stephen (*son of Archd. Joseph*), † 1867.

[*Office of Palatine abolished* 1867.]

TABLE 136 (*continued*)_b

PRINCES OF TRANSYLVANIA

1526–40   John I Zapólya (Anti-K. of Hungary).
1540–71   John II Sigismund Zapólya.
1571–5   Stephen I Báthory (K. of Poland, 1576).
1576–81   Christopher Báthory, *Regent.*
1581–98   Sigismund II Báthory.
1598–9   Andrew Báthory.
1600–4   Emp. Rudolf II.
                Rival, Sigismund Báthory, 1601–2.
                Claimant, Mozes Székhely, 1603.
                Imperial Deputy, George Básta, 1602–4.
1604–6   Stephen II Boczcai.
1607–8   Sigismund III Rákóczy, *abd.*
1608–13   Gabriel Báthory, *murd.*
1613–29   Gabriel Bethlen (Bethlen Gábor).
1629   Catharine of Brandenburg.
                Rival, Stephen Bethlen.
1630–48   George I Rákóczy.
1648–60   George II Rákóczy.
                1658–61, *Claimants,* Francis Rhedey,
                                        Achatius Barczai.
1661–3   John Kemenyi.
1663–90   Michael I Apaffy.
1690–1   Michael II Apaffy.
                Claimant, Emeric Tökölyi
1691   Emp. Leopold I, *recognised* 1694.

[*Transylvania was united to Hungary until* 1526, *independent* 1526–1691, *dependent on Austria* 1691–1713, *created a grand duchy* 1764.]

TABLE 137

GOVERNORS OF MILAN

(IMPERIAL, SPANISH AND AUSTRIAN)

(Some Governors who were in office for quite short periods are omitted.)

1538–46	Alfonso d'Avalos, M. del Vasto.
1546–55	Ferrante Gonzaga, P. of Molfetta.
1555–6	Fernando Alvarez de Toledo, D. of Alva.
1556–8	Card. Cristofero Madruzzo.
1558–60	Gonzalo Fernandez de Córdoba, D. of Sessa.
1560–3	Francisco Fernando d'Avalos, M. of Pescara.
1563–4	Gonzalo Fernandez de Córdoba, D. of Sessa.
1564–71	Gabriel de la Cueva, D. of Alburquerque.
1572–3	Luis de Requesens.
1573–80	Antonio de Guzmán, M. of Ayamonte.
1580–3	Sancho de Guevara y Padilla.
1583–92	Carlos de Aragona, P. of Castelvetrano.
1592–5	Fernando de Velasco.
1595–1600	Pedro de Padilla.
1600–10	Pedro Henriquez de Acevedo, C. of Fuentes.
1610–12	Fernando de Velasco.
1612–14	Juan de Mendoza, M. de la Hinyosa.
1614–16	Sancho de Luna.
1616–18	Pedro Alvarez de Toledo, M. of Francavila.
1618–25	Gomez Suarez de Figueroa y Córdoba, D. of Feria.
1625–9	Gonzalez Fernandez de Córdoba.
1629–30	Ambrogio, M. of Spinola.
1630–1	Alvaro de Bazán, M. of Santa Cruz.
1631–3	Gomez Suarez de Figueroa y Córdoba, D. of Feria.
1633–4	Card. Fernando, Infant of Spain.
1634–5	Card. Gil Albornoz.
1635–41	Diego Felipe de Guzmán, M. of Leganés.
1641–3	Juan de Velasco, C. of Sirvela.
1643–6	Antonio Sancho Davila, M. of Velada.
1646–7	Bernardino Fernando de Velasco, C. of Haro.
1647–8	Iñigo Fernando de Velasco, C. of Haro.
1648–56	Louis de Benavides, M. of Caracena.
1656–60	Alonzo Perez de Vivero, C. of Fuensaldagna.
1660–2	Francesco Gaetani, D. of Sermoneta.
1662–8	Louis de Guzmán Ponce de Leon.
1668–70	Paolo Spinola, M. of los Balbases.
1670–4	Gaspar Tellez Girón, D. of Osuna.
1674–8	Claude Lamoral, P. of Ligne.
1678–86	Juan T. Henriquez de Cabrera, C. of Melgar.

TABLE 137 *(continued)*

1686–91   Antonio Lopez de Ayala Velasco y Cardeñas, C. of Fuensalida.
1691–8   Diego Felipe de Guzmán, M. of Leganés.
1698–1706   P. Charles Henry of Lorraine-Vaudémont.
1706–17   P. Eugene of Savoy.
1717–9   P. Maximilian Charles of Loewenstein.
1719–25   C. Girolamo Colloredo.
1725–36   C. Wirich Philip von Daun.
1736–43   C. Otto Ferdinand von Traun.
1743–5   P. George Christian von Lobkowitz.
1745–7   Gian Luca Pellavicini.
1747–50   C. Ferdinand Bonaventura von Harrach.
1750–4   Gian Luca Pellavicini.

Plenipotentiaries

1754–71	Francesco III, D. of Modena.	1754–8	C. Beltrame Cristiani.
		1758–82	C. Charles Firmian.
1771–96	Archd. Ferdinand of Austria.	1782–92	C. Joseph Wilczek.

TABLE 138

VICEROYS OF NAPLES AND SICILY

A. SPANISH VICEROYS OF NAPLES 1504–1734

[*Naples, with Sicily, united to the Crown of Spain from* 1503 *till* 1713 (1707); 1714 *transferred to Austria; from* 1735 *to* 1860, *with Sicily, as kingdom of the Two Sicilies, under Spanish* (*Bourbon*) *younger line* (*but from* 1806 *to* 1815 *Naples under French rule*); 1860 *became part of kingdom of Italy.*]

(*Temporary Governors for short periods omitted.*)

1504–7	Gonsalvo de Córdoba.
1507–9	Juan de Aragona, C. of Repacorsa.
1509–22	Ramón de Cardona.
1522–4	Charles de Lannoy.
1524–6	Andrea Caraffa, C. of S. Severina.
1527–9	Hugo de Moncada.
1529–30	Philibert, P. of Orange.
1530–2	Pompeo Colonna.
1532–53	Pedro de Toledo, M. of Villafranca.
1553–5	Card. Pedro Pacheco de Villena.
1555	Bernardino de Mendoza.
1555–8	Fernando Alvarez de Toledo, D. of Alva.
1558	Juan Manriquez de Lara.
„	Card. Bartolomé de la Cueva d'Alburquerque.
1558–71	Perefan de la Ribera, D. of Alcalà.
1571–5	Antonio Perrenot, Card. de Granvelle.
1575–9	Iñigo Lopez Hurtado de Mendoza, M. of Mondéjar.
1579–82	Juan de Zuñiga, P. of Pietrapersa.
1582–6	Pedro Girón, D. of Osuna.
1586–95	Juan de Zuñiga, C. of Miranda.
1595–9	Enrique de Guzmán.
1599–1603	Fernando Ruiz de Castro, C. of Lemos.
1603–10	Juan Alfonso Pimentel d'Errera, C. of Benevento.
1610–6	Pedro Fernandez de Castro, C. of Lemos.
1616–20	Pedro Girón, D. of Osuna.
1620–2	Card. Antonio Zapata.
1622–9	Antonio Alvarez de Toledo, D. of Alva.
1629–31	Fernando de Ribera, D. of Alcalà.
1631–7	Manuel de Guzmán, C. of Monterey.
1637–44	Ramiro de Guzmán, D. of Medina de las Torres.
1644–6	Juan Alfonso Henriquez.
1646–8	Rodrigo Ponce de Leon, D. of Arcos.
1648	Don Juan *of Austria*.
1648–53	Iñigo Velez de Guevara, C. of Oñate.
1653–9	Garcia de Avellaneda y Haro, C. of Castrillo.
1659–64	Gaspar de Bracamonte, C. of Peñaranda.

TABLE 138 (*continued*)

1664–5   Card. Pasquale of Aragon.
1665–71   Pedro Antonio de Aragona.
1672–5   Antonio Alvarez, M. of Astorga.
1675–83   Fernando Joaquin Fajardo, M. of Los Veles.
1683–7   Gaspar de Haro, M. del Carpio.
1687–95   Francisco Benavides, C. of Santisteban.
1695–1702 Luis de la Cerda, D. of Medina Celi.
1702–7   Juan Manuel Fernandez Pacheco de Acuña, D. of Escalona and
          M. of Villena.

Imperial Viceroys

1707   C. George Adam von Martinitz.
1707–8   Wirich Philip Lorenz, C. Daun, P. of Thiano.
1708–10   Card. Vincenzo Grimani.
1710–3   Carlo Borromeo, C. of Arona.
1713–9   W. P. L., C. Daun, P. of Thiano.
1719   C. John Wenzel Gallas.
1719–21   Wolfgang Hannibal von Schrattenbach, Abp. of Olmütz.
1721–2   Marcantonio, P. Borghese.
1722–8   Card. Michael Frederick von Althann.
1728–33   C. Aloys Thomas Raymond Harrach.
1733–4   Giulio de' Visconti.

B. SPANISH VICEROYS OF SICILY FROM 1507

[*Sicily* 1409 *united with the Crown of Aragon* (1512 *of Spain*); 1713 *transferred, as kingdom, to Savoy;* 1720 *to Austria.*]

(*Temporary Governors for short periods omitted.*)

1507–9   Ramón de Cardona.
1509–16   Ugo de Moncada.
1517–34   Ettore Pignatelli, C. of Monteleon.
1535–46   Ferdinando de Gonzaga, D. of Guastalla.
1547–57   Juan de Vega.
1557–65   Juan de la Cerda, D. of Medina Celi.
1565–7   Garcia de Toledo.
1566–7   Carlos de Aragona, D. of Terranova.
1568–71   Francisco Fernando d'Avalos, M. of Pescara.
1571–7   Carlos de Aragona, P. of Castelvetrano, *Presidente del regno.*
1577–84   Marcantonio Colonna, D. of Tagliacozzo.
1585–91   Diego Henriquez de Guzmán, C. of Alva de Liste.
1592–5   Henrique de Guzmán, C. of Olivares.
1595–8   Giovanni Ventimiglia, M. of Gerace, *Presidente del regno.*
1598–1601 Bernardino de Cardines, D. of Macqueda.
1602–6   Lorenzo Suarez de Figueroa, D. of Feria.

TABLE 138 (*continued*),

1607–10	Juan Fernandez Pacheco, M. of Villena and D. of Escalona.
1611–16	Pedro Girón, D. of Osuna.
1616–22	Francisco de Lemos, C. of Castro.
1622–4	Emmanuel Philibert of Savoy, P. of Oneglia.
1625–7	Antonio Pimentel, M. of Tavora.
1627–32	Francisco Fernandez de la Cueva, D. of Alburquerque.
1632–5	Fernando de Ribera, D. of Alcalà, *Luogotenente and Cap.-gen.*
1635–9	Luis de Moncada, P. of Paterno and D. of Montalto, *Presidente del regno.*
1639–41	Francisco de Mello de Braganza, C. of Assumar.
1641–4	Alfonso Henriquez de Caprera, C. of Modica.
1644–7	Pedro Fajardo de Zuñiga y Requesens, M. of Los Veles.
1649–51	Don Juan *of Austria.*
1651–5	Rodrigo de Mendoza Roxas y Sandoval, D. of Infantado.
1655–6	Juan Tellez Girón, D. of Osuna.
1657–60	Pietro Rubeo, Abp. of Palermo, *Presidente del regno.*
1660–3	Fernando de Ayala, C. of Ayala.
1663–7	Francesco Gaetano Romano, D. of Sermoneta.
1667–70	Francisco Fernandez de la Cueva, D. of Alburquerque.
1670–4	Claude Lamoral, P. of Ligne.
1674–6	Fadrique de Toledo, M. of Villafranca.
1676	Angelo de Guzmán, M. of Castel Rodrigo.
1677–8	Card. Luis Fernandez de Portocarrero, Abp. of Toledo.
1678	Vincenzo da Gonzaga, P. of the Empire.
1679–87	Francisco Bonavides, C. of San Stefano.
1687–96	Juan Francisco Pacheco, D. of Uçeda.
1696–1701	Pedro Colón, D. of Veragua.
1701–2	Juan Manuel Fernandez Pacheco de Acuña, D. of Escalona and M. of Villena.
1702–5	Card. Francisco del Giudice.
1705–7	Isidor de la Cueva y Benavides, M. of Bedmar.
1707–13	Carlo Spinola, M. of Los Balbases.

VICEROYS OF VICTOR AMADEUS II, D. OF SAVOY, K. OF SICILY

1714–8	C. Annibale Maffei.
1718	Giovanni Francesco di Bette, M. of Lede.

AUSTRIAN VICEROYS

1720–2	Niccolò Pignatella, D. of Monteleon.
1722–8	Fra Joaquin Fernandez Portocarrero, M. of Almenara.
1728–34	Cristóbal Fernando de Córdoba, C. of Sagasta.

TABLE 139

CHIEF MINISTERS IN ENGLAND (FROM HENRY VII)

Sovereigns

Henry VII
1485–1509

Card. Morton (Abp. of Canterbury), Lord Chancellor 1487–1500.

Richard Fox, Bp. of Winchester, Sec. of State and Lord Privy Seal 1485–1516.

Henry VIII
1509–47

Thomas E. of Surrey (1514 D. of Norfolk), Lord High Treasurer 1501–22.

Card. Wolsey, Abp. of York, Lord Chancellor 1515–29.

Sir Thomas More, Lord Chancellor 1529–32.

Thomas Cromwell, E. of Essex, Sec. of State 1534, Vicar-General 1535, Lord Privy Seal 1536–40.

Sir Thomas Wriothesley (E. of Southampton), Lord Chancellor 1544–7.

Edward VI
1547–53

Edward Seymour, D. of Somerset, *Protector* 1547–9.

John Dudley, D. of Northumberland, 1550–3.

Mary I
1553–8

Stephen Gardiner, Bp. of Winchester, Lord Chancellor 1553–6.

William Lord Paget, Lord Privy Seal 1556–8.

Elizabeth
1558–1603

Sir William Cecil, Lord Burghley, Sec. of State 1558, Lord High Treasurer 1572–98.

Sir Robert Cecil, Sec. of State 1596–1603.

James I
1603–25

Sir Robert Cecil, E. of Salisbury, Secretary 1603–8, Lord High Treasurer 1608–12.

George Villiers, D. of Buckingham, Master of the Horse 1616, Lord High Admiral 1619.

Charles I
1625–49

D. of Buckingham, 1625–8.

Sir Thomas Wentworth, E. of Strafford, Pres. of the Council of the North 1628–33, Lord Deputy of Ireland 1633–41.

[Commonwealth 1649]
[Protectorate 1653–9

John Bradshaw, Pres. of the Council of State 1649–53.

Oliver Cromwell,
Protector 1653–8.
Richard Cromwell,
Protector 1658–9]

John Thurloe, Sec. of the Council of State 1653–60.

Charles II
1660–85

Edward Hyde, E. of Clarendon, Lord Chancellor 1660–7.

(*"The Cabal"*) Henry Bennet, E. of Arlington, Sec. of State 1667–73.

Sir Thomas Osborne, E. of Danby, Lord High Treasurer 1673–8.

Robert Spencer, E. of Sunderland, Sec. of State 1679–81 and 1683–5.

James II
1685–8

E. of Sunderland, Sec. of State and Lord Pres. of the Council 1685–8.

William III
1689–1702
and
Mary II
1689–94

Thomas Osborne, E. of Carmarthen (Danby) (1694 D. of Leeds), Lord Pres. of the Council 1690–5.

(*"The Junto"*) Charles Montagu, E. of Halifax, First Lord of the Treasury 1697–1700.

Sidney Godolphin, Lord Godolphin, Lord High Treasurer 1700–2.

TABLE 139 (*continued*)_b

Sovereigns

Anne
1702–14

E. of Godolphin, Lord High Treasurer 1702–10.

Robert Harley, E. of Oxford, Chancellor of the Exchequer 1710, Lord High Treasurer 1711–4.

Henry St John, Visct. Bolingbroke, Sec. of State 1710–4.

George I
1714–27

James Stanhope, E. Stanhope, Sec. of State 1714 and 1718–21, First Lord of the Treasury and Chancellor of the Exchequer 1717–8.

Charles Townshend, Visct. Townshend, Sec. of State 1714–7, 1721–30.

Sir Robert Walpole, First Lord of the Treasury and Chancellor of the Exchequer 1721–7.

George II
1727–60

The same 1727–42.

John Lord Carteret (E. Granville), Sec. of State 1742–3.

Henry Pelham, First Lord of the Treasury and Chancellor of the Exchequer 1743–53.

Thomas Pelham, D. of Newcastle, First Lord of the Treasury 1754–6.

William Cavendish, D. of Devonshire, First Lord of the Treasury 1756–7.

William Pitt, Sec. of State.

D. of Newcastle, First Lord of the Treasury 1756–61.

William Pitt, Sec. of State.

(*Henceforth the Prime Minister is almost invariably First Lord of the Treasury.*)

George III
1760–1820

John Stewart, E. of Bute, First Lord of the Treasury 1762–3.

George Grenville, First Lord and Chancellor of the Exchequer 1763–5.

Charles Wentworth-Watson, M. of Rockingham, 1766.

Augustus Fitzroy, D. of Grafton, 1766–9.

William Pitt, E. of Chatham, Lord Privy Seal.

Frederick Lord North (E. of Guildford), 1770–82.

M. of Rockingham, 1782.

William Petty, E. of Shelburne (M. of Lansdowne), 1782–3.

William Bentinck, D. of Portland, 1783.

(*Coalition Ministry*) Lord North and Charles James Fox, Secretaries of State.

William Pitt, First Lord and Chancellor of the Exchequer 1783–1801.

Henry Addington (Visct. Sidmouth), First Lord and Chancellor of the Exchequer 1801–4.

William Pitt, First Lord and Chancellor of the Exchequer 1804–6.

(*"All the Talents"*) William Lord Grenville, 1806–7.

Charles James Fox, Foreign Secretary 1806.

D. of Portland, 1807–9.

Spencer Perceval, First Lord and Chancellor of the Exchequer 1809–12.

Robert Banks Jenkinson, E. of Liverpool, First Lord and Chancellor of the Exchequer, 1812–20.

TABLE 139 (*continued*).

Sovereigns

George IV
1820–30

William IV
1830–7

Victoria
1837–1901

Edward VII
1901–10

George V
1910

E. of Liverpool, 1820–7.

George Canning, First Lord and Chancellor of the Exchequer 1827.

Frederick John Robinson, Visct. Goderich (E. of Ripon), 1827.

Arthur Wellesley, D. of Wellington, 1827–30.

Charles Grey (Lord Howick), Earl Grey, 1830–4.

William Lamb, Visct. Melbourne, 1834.

Sir Robert Peel, First Lord and Chancellor of the Exchequer 1834–5.

Visct. Melbourne, 1835–7.

The same, 1837–41.

Sir Robert Peel, 1841–6.

Lord John Russell (Earl Russell), 1846–52.

Edward Stanley, E. of Derby, 1852.

George Hamilton-Gordon, E. of Aberdeen, 1852–5.

Henry J. Temple, Visct. Palmerston, 1855–8.

E. of Derby, 1858–9.

Visct. Palmerston, 1859–65.

Earl Russell, 1865–6.

E. of Derby, 1866–8.

Benjamin Disraeli, 1868.

William Ewart Gladstone, 1868–74 (Chancellor of the Exchequer 1873).

Benjamin Disraeli (E. of Beaconsfield from 1876), 1874–80.

W. E. Gladstone, First Lord 1880–5, and Chancellor of the Exchequer 1880–2.

Robert A. T. G. Cecil, M. of Salisbury, Foreign Sec. 1885–6.

W. E. Gladstone, First Lord and Privy Seal 1886.

M. of Salisbury, First Lord 1886–7; Foreign Sec. 1887–92.

W. E. Gladstone, First Lord and Privy Seal 1892–4.

Archibald Philip Primrose, E. of Rosebery, First Lord and Lord Pres. of Council 1894–5.

M. of Salisbury, Foreign Sec. 1895–1900.

The same, Privy Seal 1900–2.

Arthur James Balfour, 1902–5.

Sir Henry Campbell-Bannerman, Prime Minister 1905–8.

Herbert Henry Asquith, Prime Minister 1908–10.

The same.

TABLE 140

CHIEF MINISTERS IN FRANCE (FROM HENRY IV)

Sovereigns	
Henry IV 1589–1610	Maximilien de Bethune (Rosny), D. of Sully, 1597–1610.
Louis XIII 1610–43	[*Regent*, 1610–4, Q. Marie (de' Medici)] Concini, Marshal d'Ancre, 1610–7.
	Charles d'Albert, C. (D.) of Luynes, 1617–21.
	Armand-Jean du Plessis, D. of Richelieu, Card., 1624–43.
Louis XIV 1643–1715	[*Regent*, 1643–52, Q. Anne (of Austria)] Jules Mazarin, 1643–52.
	Jules Mazarin, Card. (First Minister), 1652–9.
	Jean-Baptiste Colbert (Comptroller-general), 1661–83.
	Franç.-Michel le Tellier, M. of Louvois (Minister of War 1666), 1671–91.
Louis XV 1715–74	[*Regent*, 1715–23, Philip, D. of Orleans] Card. Dubois, 1718–23.
	Louis Henry, D. of Bourbon (First Minister), 1724–6.
	André-Hercule Fleury, Bp. of Fréjus, Card., 1726–43.
	Abbé F.-J. de Pierre de Bernis, C. of Lyon (Card.), 1756–8.
	Étienne-François, D. of Choiseul, 1758–70.
	(*"The Triumvirate"*) Armand Vignerot-Duplessis-Richelieu, D. d'Aiguillon, 1770–4.
Louis XVI 1774–92 *dep.* 1793 *ex.*	Anne-Robert-Jacques Turgot, M. de l'Aulne, 1774–6.
	Jacques Necker, 1776–8.
	Charles-Alexandre de Calonne, 1783–6.
	Loménie de Brienne, Card., 1787.
	J. Necker, 1788–90.
	C. Honoré-Gabriel Riquetti de Mirabeau, 1791.
[**First Republic** 1792–1804 The *Consulate* 1799–1802 Bonaparte *First Consul for Life* 1802–4]	The Directory, 1794–9.
Napoleon I 1799 (Emp. 1804) –1814	Charles-Maurice Talleyrand C. de Périgord, P. of Benevento (Foreign Minister), 1799–1807.
	Fouché, D. of Otranto (Minister of Police), 1804–10.
	Maret, D. of Bassano (Foreign Minister), 1811–14.
	Savary, D. of Rovigo (Minister of Police), 1810–14.
Louis XVIII 1814–24	Talleyrand (First Minister), 1815.
	Armand-E.-S.-S. du Plessis, D. de Richelieu (First Minister), 1815–21.
	C. Jean-Baptiste-G.-M.-S.-J. de Villèle (First Minister), 1821–4.

TABLE 140 (*continued*)ₕ

Sovereigns

Charles X
1824–30

Louis-Philippe
1830–48

C. de Villèle, 1824–7.

Jean-Baptiste-S.-Gaye, Vic. de Martignac (First Minister), 1828–9.

Auguste-J.-A.-M.-B., P. de Polignac, 1829.

Jacques Laffitte, 1830–1.

Casimir Périer, 1831–2.

("*Les Doctrinaires*") Marshal Soult, 1832–6.

M.-J.-Louis-Adolphe Thiers, 1836.

François-Pierre-Guillaume Guizot, 1836–7.

Louis-Matthieu, C. Molé, 1837–9.

A. Thiers, 1839–40.

F.-P.-G. Guizot, 1840–8.

Second Republic
1848–52

Provisional Government:

    President: Jacques-Charles Dupont (de l'Eure).

    Foreign Minister: Alphonse de Lamartine (February–June).

    Minister of War: General L.-C. Cavaignac (May—June).

National Assembly:

    Head of Executive: General Cavaignac (June—December).

Presidency of Prince Louis-Napoleon:

    Camille-Hyacinthe-Odilon Barrot, 1848–9.

    Eugène Rouher, 1849–51.

Napoleon III
Emp. 1852–70

Charles-Auguste-Louis-Joseph, D. de Morny, President of the Legislative Assembly, 1851–65.

Eugène Rouher (1855–9) (First Minister), 1863–9.

O.-Émile Ollivier (First Minister), Jan.—Aug. 1870.

Third Republic
1870

*Government of
National Defence*
1870–1

Gen. Trochu (President); Jules Favre (Foreign Affairs); Léon Gambetta (Minister for the Interior).

A. Thiers, *Chief of
Executive Power*,
Feb.—Aug. 1871
(*For list of Presidents
see Table* 124)

J. Favre (Foreign Affairs) Feb.—July 1871.

C. Charles de Remusat (Foreign Affairs) July 1871—May 1873.

Jacques-Victor-Albert Duc de Broglie, 1873.

Louis-Joseph Buffet, 1875.

Jules-Armand-Stanislas Dufaure, 1876.

Jules Simon, 1876.

Duc de Broglie, 1877.

(Gen. Rochebouet, 1877.)

J.-A.-S. Dufaure, 1877.

William Hugh Waddington, 1879.

Charles-Louis de S. de Freycinet, 1879.

Jules Ferry, 1880.

Léon Gambetta, 1881.

C.-L. de S. de Freycinet, 1882.

C.-J.-E. Duclerc, 1882.

TABLE 140 (*continued*)

Third Republic
(*continued*)

Armand Fallières, 1883.

Jules Ferry, 1883.

Eugène-Henri Brisson, 1885.

C.-L. de S. de Freycinet, 1885.

René Goblet, 1886.

Maurice Rouvier, 1887.

Pierre-Emmanuel Tirard, 1887.

Charles-Thomas Floquet, 1888.

P.-E. Tirard, 1889.

C.-L. de S. de Freycinet, 1890.

Émile Loubet, 1892.

Alexandre-Félix-Joseph Ribot, 1892.

Charles-Alexandre Dupuy, 1893.

Jean-Paul-Pierre Casimir-Périer, 1893.

C.-A. Dupuy, 1894.

A.-F.-J. Ribot, 1895.

Léon-Victor-Auguste Bourgeois, 1895.

Félix-Jules Méline, 1896.

E.-H. Brisson, 1898.

Pierre-Marie-René Waldeck-Rousseau, 1899.

Justin-Louis-Émile Combes, 1902.

Jean-Maire-Ferdinand Sarrien, 1905.

Georges-Benjamin-Eugène Clemenceau, 1906.

Aristide Briand, 1909.

Joseph Caillaux, 1911.

TABLE 141

CHIEF MINISTERS IN THE EMPIRE AND AUSTRIA
(FROM CHARLES V TO 1871)

Emperors

Charles V 1519–56	Arborio de Gattinara, 1519–30, Chancellor. Nicolas Perrenot, Sieur de Granvelle, 1530–50, Sec. of State. Card. Antonio Perrenot de Granvelle, 1550–8.
Matthias 1612–19	Card. Melchior Klesl, 1611–18, Director of Privy Council.
Ferdinand II 1619–37	P. Hans Ulrich von Eggenberg, 1615–34, Obersthofmeister and Director of Privy Council.
Ferdinand III 1637–57	C. Max von Trautmannsdorf, 1634–50, President of Privy Council (Obersthofmeister from 1628). P. Johann Weikhard von Auersperg, 1650–7.
Leopold I 1658–1705	P. Wenzel Eusebius von Lobkowitz, 1669–74, President of Privy Council. C. Theodor von Strattman, 1683–93, Hofkanzler. C. Ferdinand Bonay von Harrach, 1698–1706, Obersthofmeister and President of Conference of State.
Joseph I 1705–11	C. Johann Wenzel Wratislaw, 1705–12, Bohemian Chancellor and Member of Conference of State.
Charles VI 1711–40	Frhr. Joseph Christian von Bartenstein, 1727–53, Secretary of State.
Francis I 1745–65	P. Wenzel Anton von Kaunitz, 1753–92, Hof- and Staatskanzler.
[Maria Theresa Q. of Hungary 1740–80]	*The same.*
Joseph II 1765–90	*The same.*
Leopold II 1790–2	*The same.*
Francis II 1792–1804	C. John Philip Cobenzl, 1792–3, Hof- and Staatskanzler (*from* 1793 for Italy only). Frhr. John Amadeus Francis Maria von Thugut, 1793–1800, Director of State Chancery.
Emperors of Austria **Francis** 1804–35	C. John Ludwig Joseph Cobenzl, 1800–5, Director of State Chancery. C. John Philip Charles Stadion, 1805–9, Hof- and Staatskanzler.
Ferdinand 1835–48	Clement Wenzel Lothar, P. Metternich, Minister of Imperial House and of Foreign Affairs 1809–21, Haus-, Hof- and Staatskanzler 1821–43. C. Franz Kolowrat-Liebsteinsky, Minister of State 1826–40.

Francis Joseph
 1848
	B. Francis von Pillersdorff, Minister-President 1848.
	 P. Felix von Schwarzenberg, Minister-President 1848–52.
	     Alexander Bach, Minister of Interior 1849–59.
	     Anton von Schmerling, Minister of Interior 1860–5.
	 C. Belcredi, Minister-President and Minister of the Interior (1865–7).
	 P. Carlos Auersperg, Minister-President (1868–70).
	 C. Friedrich Ferdinand von Beust, Minister of Foreign Affairs 1866, Reichskanzler 1867–71.

(*Austro-Hungarian Dual Government begins with the Ausgleich of 1871.*)

TABLE 142

CHIEF MINISTERS IN PRUSSIA (TO 1871)

Sovereigns	
Frederick I (1688) 1701–13	[Eberhard Christoph Balthazar von Danckelmann, President and First Minister 1695–7.] John Casimir von Kolb, C. von Wartenburg, Ober-kammerherr 1697–1711.
Frederick William I 1713–40	Heinrich Rüdiger von Ilgen, Minister of State (Foreign Affairs) 1711–25. Friedrich Wilhelm von Grumbkow, Minister of State 1713, Chief of General Supreme Directory 1723–39.
Frederick II 1740–86	C. Charles William Fink von Finkenstein, Minister of State 1747, Cabinet Minister 1749–1800. C. Ewald Friedrich von Hertzberg, Minister of State and Cabinet 1763–91.
Frederick William II 1786–97	John Rudolf von Bischoffswerder, 1786–8, Adjutant 1786, Adjutant-Gen. 1789.
Frederick William III 1797–1840	C. Christian August Heinrich Kurt von Haugwitz, Cabinet Minister 1792–1806. Frhr. Heinrich Friedrich Karl vom Stein, 1807–8. Frhr. Karl August von Hardenberg, Minister of State 1804–6, Chancellor of State 1810–22.
Frederick William IV 1840–61	C. Adolf Heinrich von Arnim-Boitzenburg, President of Ministry 1848. Ludolf Camphausen, President of Ministry 1848. David Justus Hansemann, Minister of Finance 1848. Rudolf von Auerswald, President of Ministry, June–Sept. 1850, Minister without portfolio, 1858–1862. C. Frederick William von Brandenburg, 1848–50. General Joseph von Radowitz, Minister for Foreign Affairs 1850. Otto Theodor von Manteuffel, Minister for Foreign Affairs 1850, President of Ministry 1850–8.
Regency of Prince of Prussia (*William I*) 1858–61	P. Anton of Hohenzollern, 1858–62. P. Adolf von Hohenlohe-Ingelfingen, President of Ministry, March-Oct. 1862. C. Maximilian von Schwerin-Putzar, Minister of Interior 1859–62.
William I 1861–88 (German Emp. 1871)	P. Otto von Bismarck, 1862–90.

TABLE 143

CHANCELLORS OF THE GERMAN EMPIRE

Emperors

William I   P. Otto von Bismarck, 1871–88.

Frederick III *The same*, 1888.

William II   *The same*, 1888–90.

C. George Leo von Caprivi, 1890–4.

P. Chlodwig von Hohenlohe-Schillingsfürst, 1894–1900.

P. Bernhard von Bülow, 1900–8.

Theobald von Bethmann-Hollweg, 1909.

TABLE 144

CHIEF MINISTERS IN THE KINGDOM OF ITALY

Sovereigns
Victor Emmanuel II
1862 (1849)–78

C. Camillo Benso di Cavour, 1852–9 and 1860–1.
[Sicily, Depretis Dictator, Crispi Sec. of State 1859-60.]

Presidents of the Council of Ministers.

B. Bettino Ricasoli, 1861–2.
Urbano Rattazzi, 1862.
Marco Minghetti, 1863–4.
M. Alfonso La Marmora, 1864–6.
B. B. Ricasoli, 1866–7.
U. Rattazzi, 1867.
Gen. Federigo Luigi Menabrea, 1867–9.
    Quintino Sella, 1861–73 (Finance).
    Giovanni Lanza, 1869–73 (Interior).
M. Emilio Visconti-Venosta, 1869–73.
M. Minghetti, 1873–6.
Agostino Depretis, 1876–8.
    B. Giovanni Nicotera, 1876–7 (Interior).

Humbert I
1878–1900

Francesco Crispi, 1878 Jan.–March.
M. Cairoli, 1878 March–Dec.
A. Depretis, 1878–87.
F. Crispi, 1887–91.
M. di Rudini, 1891–2.
Giovanni Giolitti, 1892–3.
F. Crispi, 1893–6.
M. di Rudini, 1896–8.
Gen. Luigi Pelloux, 1898–1900.
    M. Visconti-Venosta (Foreign Affairs), 1899–1901.

Victor Emmanuel III
1900

Giuseppe Saracco, 1900–2.
Giuseppe Zanardelli, 1902–3.
G. Giolitti, 1903–6.
B. Sonnino, 1906.
G. Giolitti, 1906–10.
Luigi Luzzatti, 1910–11.
G. Giolitti, 1911–.

TABLE 145

CHIEF MINISTERS IN SPAIN (FROM PHILIP III TO 1873)

Sovereigns

Philip III
1598–1621

Francisco Gomez de Sandoval, D. of Lerma, 1598–1618.
Cristoval Gomez de Sandoval, D. of Uçeda, 1619–21.

Philip IV
1621–65

Gaspar Philip de Guzmán, C. of Olivares (*"the Count-Duke"*), 1621–43.
Luis de Haro, D. of Carpio, 1643–61.

Charles II
1665–1700
[*Regent 1665–75,*
Queen Maria Anna]

Father Niethard (Card.), 1665–8.
Fernando de Valenzuela, 1668–75.
Don Juan *of Austria*, 1676–9.
Juan Franc. Tomas de la Cerda, D. of Medina Celi, 1680–5.
Emmanuel Joaquin de Toledo, C. of Oropesa, 1685–91.
The C. of Melgar, D. of Sessa, D. of Infantado, C. of Monterey, Card. Portocarrero successively, 1691–1700.

Philip V
1700–46

Card. Portocarrero, 1700–4.
       Pss. Orsini Camarera mayor, 1700–14.
Card. del Giudice, 1714.
Card. Giulio Alberoni, 1715–9.
Jan Willem Ripperdà, 1725–6.
José de Patiño, 1726–36.
de la Quadra, M. of Villarias, 1736–40.
José Campillo, 1740–3.
Zeno Somo de Villa, M. of Enseñada, 1743–6.

Ferdinand VI
1746–59

M. of Enseñada   } 1746–54.
José de Carvajal y Lancaster}

Charles III
1759–88

Francisco Borgia, M. of Squillace, 1760–6.
Pedro Abarea y Bolea, C. of Aranda, 1766–73.
José Guttierez de Solarzano, M. of Grimaldo (Foreign Minister), 1773–6.
José Moñino, M. of Florida Blanca, 1776–88.

Charles IV
1788–1808

M. of Florida Blanca, 1788–92.
C. of Aranda, 1792.
Manuel de Godoy, P. of the Peace, 1792–1808.

Ferdinand VII
1814 (1808)–33

José Leon y Pizarro, 1816–8.

Isabella II
1833–68 *dep.*
Regent 1833–40,
Q. Cristina.
Regent 1841–3,
Gen. Espartero.
1868 *Interregnum*
Regent, Gen. Franc.
Serrano Dominguez,
D. of La Torre

Gen. Boldomero Espartero, 1837–40.
Ramón Maria Narváez, D. of Valencia, 1844–5; 1847–51; 1856–7; 1863; 1865–8.
Enrique O'Donnell, C. de La Bisbal, 1856; 1858–63; 1864–5.

Amadeus (of Aosta)
1870–3 *abd.*

Gen. Juan Prim, M. of Los Castillejos, 1870.
Gen. Serrano, 1871 (Jan.–July).
Ruiz Zorrilla, 1871 (July–Dec.).
Práxedes Mateo Sagasta, 1871–2.
Adm. Topete, 1872 (May–June).
R. Zorrilla, 1872–3.

TABLE 146

SECULARISED BISHOPRICS

[*Principal dates of secularisation:*

        Peace of Westphalia, 1648.
        Peace of Lunéville, 1801.
        Reichsdeputationsrecess, 1802.
        Reichsdeputationshauptschluss, 1803.
        Peace of Pressburg, 1805.
        Dissolution of the Holy Roman Empire, 1806.
        Peace of Tilsit, 1807.
        Peace of Paris, 1814.
        Peace of Vienna, 1815.
        Treaty of Prague, 1866.]

Bishoprics of :

Augsburg.   1803 annexed to Bavaria.

Bamberg.   1803 annexed to Bavaria.
    After introduction of Reformation at B. (1529) Bishops reside at Prunstrut.

Basel.   1792 see declared itself a Republic.   1793 annexed by French Republic.
    1803 territory on right bank of Rhine ceded by France to Baden.   1814
    territory on left bank assigned to Switzerland.

Brandenburg.   Lutheran 1539; territory divided between Elector and local
    nobility.

Bremen (Bremen-Hamburg) (Archbprc.).   Lutheran from 1558.   Duchy of
    Bremen ceded to Sweden 1648 ; 1715 (confirmed, 1719) sold by Denmark
    to Hanover ; 1866 annexed to Prussia.

Cologne (Archbprc.).   1801 territory on left bank of Rhine annexed to France,
    1815 to Prussia.   On right bank of Rhine divided between :

        (*a*)   Wied-Runkel (annexed 1806 to Nassau, 1815 to Prussia).
        (*b*)   Nassau-Usingen (annexed 1815 to Prussia).
        (*c*)   Hesse-Darmstadt (annexed 1815 to Prussia).
        (*d*)   Aremberg (annexed 1815 to Prussia).

Constance.   1803 annexed to Baden.   Its dependency Conzenberg in 1803
    a fief of the Empire, 1806 annexed to Würtemberg.

Eichstedt.   1803 created a principality for Archd. Ferdinand (as compensation
    for Tuscany).   1805–6 annexed to Bavaria.

Freisingen.   1803 annexed to Bavaria.

Halberstadt.   1486–1566 united with Magdeburg: 1648 annexed to Branden-
    burg: 1807 to kingdom of Westphalia ; 1815 to Prussia.

Havelberg.   1548 practically annexed to Brandenburg.

Hildesheim.   1803 annexed to Prussia: 1807 to Westphalia : 1813 to Hanover :
    1866 to Prussia.

Liége.   1801 annexed by France: 1815 transferred to Netherlands as princi-
    pality of Liége.

Lübeck.   1803 annexed to Oldenburg: 1842 to Holstein (in exchange).

Magdeburg (Archbprc.).   After 1566 administered by temporal princes of
    Brandenburg or Saxony.   1648 annexed to Brandenburg on death of
    D. Augustus of Saxony (took effect 1680).

TABLE 146 (*continued*)_b

Bishoprics of:

Mainz (Archbprc.). 1801 territory on left bank of Rhine annexed to France: later, divided between Hesse-Darmstadt and Rhenish Prussia.

1803 the remainder (in exchange for compensatory dominions) ceded by the Imperial Chancellor and divided amongst: Hesse-Cassel, Hesse-Darmstadt, Nassau-Usingen, Leiningen, Löwenstein-Wertheim, Salm-Reifferscheid-Bedbur, and Prussia, which in 1866 acquired the shares assigned to Hesse-Cassel and Nassau-Usingen, and a portion of that of Hesse-Darmstadt.

Meissen. Protestant from 1580. Merged in the Meissen Circle and united with Saxony.

Merseburg. Protestant from 1561. Administered by Christian, 3rd son of John George I, El. of Saxony. Saxon principality, united with the Electorate 1738. Ceded to Prussia 1815.

Metz. 1648 formally ceded to France. Secularised in French Revolution. 1871 part of territory ceded to Germany.

Minden. 1648 annexed to Brandenburg: 1807 to Westphalia; 1810 to the French Empire; 1813 to Prussia.

Münster. 1719–1803 united with Archbprc. of Cologne; 1803, and again 1813, to Prussia.

Naumburg-Zeitz. Protestant from 1564. 1652 Saxon principality for Maurice, 4th son of John George I. 1718 united with Electorate. 1815 greater part ceded to Prussia.

Osnabrück. From 1648 the Bishop was alternately Roman Catholic and Protestant; the latter always of the House of Brunswick-Lüneburg. 1803 annexed to Hanover: 1806 to Prussia: 1807 to Westphalia: 1810 to the French Empire: 1814 to Hanover: 1866 to Prussia.

Paderborn. 1802 annexed to Prussia: confirmed 1803.

Passau. 1803 Western and lesser portion annexed to Bavaria, Eastern and larger to Electorate of Salzburg, for the Grand Duke of Tuscany. 1805 the whole to Bavaria.

Ratisbon. 1803 secularised and transferred as principality of Ratisbon to the Prince Primas. 1810 transferred to Bavaria.

Ratzeburg. Lutheranised by Bp. Christopher (II) of Mecklenburg († 1592), afterwards administered by Mecklenburg. 1648 annexed to Mecklenburg.

Salzburg (Archbprc.). 1802 assigned to Grand Duke Ferdinand of Tuscany (except Mühldorf, annexed to Bavaria). 1805 ceded to Austria in exchange for Würzburg. 1809 annexed to Bavaria. 1814 reverts to Austria except portion on left bank of Salza, remaining to Bavaria.

Schwerin. Lutheranised 1530 and from that date administered by princes of Mecklenburg (Schwerin). Annexed to Mecklenburg-Schwerin 1648 as compensation for Wismar.

Speier. 1801 territory on left bank of Rhine (the lesser portion) annexed to France: 1814 to Bavaria.

1803 territory on right bank (the larger portion) annexed to Baden. 1789 outlying dependencies annexed by France, included in Alsace: 1815 part of these ceded to Bavaria. 1871 the remainder annexed by the German Empire (incl. in Elsass-Lothringen).

TABLE 146 (*continued*)₀

Bishoprics of:

Strassburg. 1803 territory on right bank of Rhine annexed to Baden (principality of Ettenheim). 1789 territory on left bank (under French sovereignty since 1648) incorporated in Departments of Lower and Upper Alsace. 1871 annexed by German Empire.

Toul. 1648 formally ceded to France. Secularised in French Revolution.

Trent (Archbprc.) and Brixen. From 1511 reckoned as territorially belonging to Tyrol. 1803 annexed to Austria, as compensation for Ortenau, and incorporated with Tyrol.

Trier (Archbprc.). 1794 territory on left bank of the Rhine annexed to France: 1803 to Prussia, except St Wendel, ceded to Coburg till 1834. 1803 territory on right bank annexed to Nassau-Weilburg: 1815 to Prussia, with certain exceptions. 1866 the whole annexed to Prussia.

Verden. 1648 secularised and ceded to Sweden. 1719 sold by Denmark to Hanover.

Verdun. 1648 formally ceded to France. Secularised in French Revolution.

Worms. 1705 district of Reithausen annexed to the Palatinate. 1801 territory on left bank of the Rhine annexed to France: 1814–5 divided between Bavaria and Hesse. 1803 territory on right bank of the Rhine annexed to Hesse-Darmstadt.

Würzburg. (1) 1803 major part annexed to Bavaria in compensation for lost Rhine provinces, as a hereditary principality: 1805 ceded to Grand Duke Ferdinand of Tuscany as compensation for Salzburg. 1815 restored to Bavaria: 1866 small portion in north ceded by Bavaria to Prussia.

(2) 1803 minor part divided between (1) P. of Hohenlohe-Bartenstein: 1806 transferred to Würtemberg with the rest of Hohenlohe; (2) P. of Leiningen; 1806 transferred to Baden; (3) principality of Aschaffenburg (1810 part of grand duchy of Frankfort): 1814 transferred to Bavaria with Aschaffenburg; (4) Würtemberg; (5) Ansbach-Baireuth (Prussian principalities of): 1806 ceded to Bavaria, 1810 to grand duchy of Würzburg, 1814 to Bavaria and Würtemberg.

Fulda. (Abbey declared exempt bishopric 1752.) 1803–6 ceded in compensation to Nassau-Orange. 1809 to grand duchy of Frankfort. 1810 Herbstein ceded to Hesse-Darmstadt. 1815 the rest to Prussia, but divided between: (1) Prussia, (2) Electoral Hesse (1866 annexed by Prussia), (3) Saxe-Weimar-Eisenach, and (4) Bavaria.

TABLE 147

ENGLISH PARLIAMENTS, 1485—1722

[The first date is in each case that for which the Parliament was summoned. Ordinary adjournments, and the very short prorogations of Tudor Parliaments equivalent to adjournments, are not given. Unless otherwise stated the Parliaments sat at Westminster. The dates have been verified from Statutes of the Realm, Journals of House of Lords and House of Commons and Calendars of State Papers. The year dates are N.S.]

Henry VII (Aug. 22, 1485–April 21, 1509)

No. of Parliament	Regnal year	Date of meeting	Sessions	Notes
I	1st	Nov. 7, 1485	Not known	
II	3rd	Nov. 9, 1487	,,	
III	4th and 5th	Jan. 13, 1489	(1) Jan. 13—Feb. 23	
			(2) Oct. 14—Dec. 4	
			(3) Jan. 25—Feb. 27, 1490	
IV	7th	Oct. 17, 1491	Dissolved March 5, 1492	
V	11th	Oct. 14, 1495	Not known	
VI	12th	Jan. 16, 1497	,,	
VII	19th	Jan. 25, 1504	,,	

[A Great Council, with representatives from the chief towns, held in Oct. 1496 is sometimes incorrectly reckoned as a Parliament.]

TABLE 147 (*continued*)b

Henry VIII (April 22, 1509—Jan. 28, 1547)

No. of Parliament	Regnal year	Date of meeting	Sessions	Notes
I	1st	Jan. 21, 1510	Jan. 21—Feb. 23	
II	3rd	Feb. 4, 1512	(1) Feb. 4—Mar. 30 (2) Nov. 4—Dec. 20	
III	5th	Jan. 23, 1514	Jan. 23—Mar. 4	Called for Jan. 1513 but prorogued continuously until Jan. 23, 1514
IV	6th and 7th	Feb. 5, 1515	(1) Feb. 5—Ap. 5 (2) Nov. 12—Dec. 22	
V	14th and 15th	Ap. 15, 1523	Ap. 15—Aug. 13	Met at Blackfriars and moved to Westminster (July 31), adjourned May 21—June 10 5 prorogations
VI	21st to 27th	Nov. 3, 1529	(1) Nov. 3—Dec. 17 (2) Jan. 16, 1531—Mar. 30 (3) Jan. 15, 1532—May (?) (4) Feb. 4, 1533—July 9? [*or* May 15?] (5) Jan. 15, 1534—Mar. 30 (6) Nov. 3—Dec. 18 (7) Feb. 4, 1536—Ap. 4	Adjourned Mar. 31—Ap. 10
VII	28th	June 8, 1536	June 8—July 18	
VIII	31st and 32nd	Ap. 28, 1539	(1) Ap. 28—June 28 (2) Ap. 12, 1540—July 24	
IX	33rd, 34th and 35th	Jan. 16, 1542	(1) Jan. 16—Ap. 1 (2) Jan. 22, 1543—May 12 (3) Jan. 14, 1544—Mar. 29	Adjourned May 11—25
X	37th and 38th	Nov. 23, 1545	(1) Nov. 23, 1545—Dec. 24 (2) Jan. 14, 1547—Jan. 31	Dissolved by commission Prorogued to Nov. 4, 1546, and again to Jan. 14, 1547 Dissolved by Chancellor

TABLE 147 (*continued*).

Edward VI (Jan. 28, 1547—July 6, 1553)

No. of Parliament	Regnal year	Date of meeting	Sessions	Notes
I	1st to 6th	Nov. 4, 1547	(1) Nov. 4—Dec. 24	Prorogued to Ap. 20, 1548, then to Oct. 15
			(2) Nov. 24, 1548—Mar. 14, 1549	
			(3) Nov. 4, 1549—Feb. 1, 1550	
			(4) Jan. 23, 1552—Ap. 15	
II	7th	Mar. 1, 1553	March 1—31	

Mary I (July 6, 1553—July 24, 1554, or Nov. 17, 1558)

No. of Parliament	Regnal year	Date of meeting	Sessions	Notes
I	1st	Oct. 5, 1553	Oct. 5—Dec. 5	
II	1st	Ap. 2, 1554	Ap. 2—May 5	Summoned to meet at Oxford but adjourned to Westminster before assembled

Philip and Mary I (July 24, 1554—Nov. 17, 1558)

No. of Parliament	Regnal year	Date of meeting	Sessions	Notes
I *or* III	1st and 2nd	Nov. 12, 1554	Nov. 12—Jan. 16, 1555	
II *or* IV	2nd and 3rd	Oct. 21, 1555	Oct. 21—Dec. 9	
III *or* V	4th and 5th	Jan. 20, 1558	(1) Jan. 20—Mar. 7	Expired
			(2) Nov. 5—17	

Elizabeth (Nov. 17, 1558—Mar. 24, 1603)

No. of Parliament	Regnal year	Date of meeting	Sessions	Notes
I	1st	Jan. 23, 1559	Jan. 23—May 8	
II	5th, 8th and 9th	Jan. 11, 1563	(1) Jan. 11—Ap. 10	
			(2) Sept. 30, 1566—Jan. 2, 1567	
III	13th	Ap. 2, 1571	Ap. 2—May 29	
IV	14th, 18th, 22nd and 25th	May 8, 1572	(1) May 8—June 30	
			(2) Feb. 8, 1576—Mar. 15	(24 prorogations)
			(3) Jan. 16, 1580—Mar. 18	(18 prorogations)
			(4) Ap. 19, 1583, *and dissolved*	

TABLE 147 (*continued*)ᵃ

Elizabeth (*continued*)

No. of Parliament	Regnal year	Date of meeting	Sessions	Notes
V	27th	Nov. 23, 1584	(1) Nov. 23—Dec. 21 (2) Feb. 4, 1585—Mar. 29	Dissolved during prorogation, Sept. 14, 1586
VI	28th and 29th	Oct. 29, 1586	(1) Oct. 29—Dec. 2 (2) Feb. 15, 1587—Mar. 23	Summoned for Oct. 15, prorogued to 29th
VII	31st	Feb. 4, 1589	Feb. 4—Mar. 29	Summoned for Nov. 12, 1588, prorogued to Feb. 4, 1589
VIII	35th	Feb. 19, 1593	Feb. 19—Ap. 10	
IX	39th and 40th	Oct. 24, 1597	Oct. 24—Feb. 9, 1598	
X	43rd and 44th	Oct. 27, 1601	Oct. 27—Dec. 19	

James I (Mar. 24, 1603—Mar. 27, 1625)

No. of Parliament	Regnal year	Date of meeting	Sessions	Notes
I	1st to 8th	Mar. 19, 1604	(1) Mar. 19—July 7 (2) Nov. 5, 1605—May 27, 1606 (3) Nov. 18, 1606—July 4, 1607 (4) Feb. 9, 1610—July 23 (5) Oct. 16—Dec. 6	Adjourned Dec. 18—Feb. 10, and prorogued Adjourned Feb. 9—14 Prorogued to Feb. 9, 1611 and then dissolved
II	12th	Ap. 5, 1614	Ap. 5—June 7	"The Addled Parliament"
III	18th and 19th	Jan. (16)30,1621	(1) Jan. 30—Nov. 14 (2) Nov. 20—Dec. 18	Prorogued Jan. 16—30 Prorogued to Feb. 8, 1622 and then dissolved
IV	21st and 22nd	Feb.(12)19,1624	Feb. 19—May 29	Prorogued till Feb. 2, 1625 and subsequently, but expired Mar 27, 1625

TABLE 147 (continued)e

Charles I (Mar. 27, 1625—Jan. 30, 1649)

No. of Parliament	Regnal year	Date of meeting	Sessions	Notes
I	1st	May 17, 1625	(1) June 18—July 11 (2) Aug. 1—12	 At Oxford
II	1st and 2nd	Feb. 6, 1626	Feb. 6—June 15	
III	3rd and 4th	Mar. 17, 1628	(1) Mar. 17—June 26 (2) Jan. 1629—Mar. **2**	
IV	16th	Ap. 13, 1640	Ap. 13—May 5	Adjourned till Mar. 10, then dissolved "The Short Parliament"
V	16th to 24th	Nov. 3, 1640	(a) sat almost continuously till Dec. 6, 1648	"The Long Parliament" Recess Sept. 8, 1641, till Oct. 20 Dec. 6, 1648, many members expelled ("Pride's purge")
			(b) unexpelled members ("the Rump") continue to sit until Ap. 20, 1653, expelled (c) reassembles May 7, 1659, till Oct. 13, expelled (d) reassembles Dec. 26 till Mar. **16**, 1660, dissolves itself	From Feb. 6, 1649, House of Commons only
		[Jan. 22, 1644 at Oxford]	(1) Jan. 22—Ap. 11	Greater part of House of Lords, about one-third of House of Commons: "the Oxford Parliament"
			(2) Oct. 8?—Mar. 10, 1645	Adjourned to Oct. 10, but did not meet again]

Commonwealth (May 19, 1649—Dec. 16, 1653)

		[July 4, 1653]	Assembly of Nominees ("Barebones' Parliament") declares itself a Parliament (July 6), House of Commons only Dec. 12, resigns its powers to Lord-Gen. Oliver Cromwell]	

TABLE 147 (*continued*)

Oliver Cromwell, Protector (Dec. 16, 1653—Sept. 3, 1658)

No. of Parliament	Regnal year	Date of meeting	Sessions	Notes
I		[Sept. 3, 1654	Sept. 3—Jan. 22, 1655	House of Commons only]
II		[Sept. 17, 1656	(1) Sept. 17—?	1656–7 House of Commons only, nearly 100 excluded
			(2) Jan. 20, 1658—Feb. 4	House of Lords also]

Richard Cromwell, Protector (Sept. 4, 1658—May, 1659)

| | | [Jan. 27, 1659 | Jan. 27—Ap. 22] | |

[*Convention (summoned by the dissolving Long Parliament, March 16, 1660) met Ap. 25, 1660 ; see below.*]

Charles II (Jan. 30, 1649 [*or May 29, 1660*]—Feb. 6, 1685)

No. of Parliament	Regnal year	Date of meeting	Sessions	Notes
I	12th	Ap. 25, 1660	Ap. 25—Dec. 29	The Convention
II	13th to 30th	May 8, 1661	(1) May 8—May 19, 1662	"The Long Parliament of the Restoration," "Cavaliers" or "Pensioners' Parliament"
			(2) Feb. 18, 1663—July 27	
			(3) Mar. 16, 1664—May 17	
			(4) Nov. 24—Mar. 2, 1665	
			(5) Oct. 9, 1665—Oct. 31	*At Oxford*
			(6) Sept. 18, 1666—Feb. 8, 1667	
			(7) Oct. 10, 1667—Dec. 10, 1669	Adjourned by command (*a*) Dec. 19, 1667—Feb. 10, 1663, (*b*) May 9—Aug. 11, (*c*) by proclamation to Mar. 1, 1669, (*d*) to Oct. 19

TABLE 147 (continued)

Charles II (continued)

No. of Parliament	Regnal year	Date of meeting	Sessions	Notes
			(8) Feb. 14, 1670—Ap. 22, 1671	Adjourned by command Ap. 6—Oct. 24, 1670, then prorogued for a year and subsequently
			(9) Feb. 4, 1673—Mar. 20	Adjourned and prorogued
			(10) Oct. 27—Nov. 4	
			(11) Jan. 7, 1674—Feb. 24	
			(12) Ap. 13, 1675—June 9	
			(13) Oct. 13—Nov. 16	
			(14) Feb. 15, 1677—May 13, 1678	Adjourned by command Ap. 16—May 21, 1677, May 28, 1677—Jan. 1678
			(15) May 23, 1678—July 13	Prorogued to Feb. 4 but dissolved by proclamation Jan. 24, 1679
			(16) Oct. 21, 1678—Dec. 30	
III	31st	Mar. 6, 1679	Mar. 6—May 27	Prorogued but dissolved July 12
IV	32nd	Oct. 21, 1680	Oct. 21—Jan. 10, 1681	Summoned for Oct. 17, 1679, but prorogued continuously until Oct. 1680
V	33rd	Mar. 21, 1681	Mar. 21—28	At Oxford

James II (Feb. 6, 1685—Dec. 11, 1688)

No. of Parliament	Regnal year	Date of meeting	Sessions	Notes
I	1st to 3rd	May 19, 1685	(a) May 19—July 2	Adjourned by command July 2—Nov. 9. Prorogued continually till dissolved by proclamation July 2, 1687
			(b) Nov. 9—20	

[Convention of Estates Jan. 22, 1689; see below.]

12—2

TABLE 147 (continued)ₕ

{William III (Feb. 13, 1689—Mar. 8, 1702)
{Mary II (Feb. 13, 1689—Dec. 27, 1694)

No. of Parliament	Regnal year	Date of meeting	Sessions	Notes
I	1st W. and M.	Jan. 22, 1689	(1) Jan. 22—Aug. 20, 1689	Convention becomes Parliament Feb. 13
			(2) Oct. 23—Jan. 27, 1690	Dissolved Feb. 6, 1690 by proclamation summoning next parliament*.
II	2nd W. and M. to 7th W.	Mar. 20, 1690	(1) Mar. 20—May 23	
			(2) Oct. 2—Jan. 5, 1691	
			(3) Oct. 22—Feb. 24, 1692	
			(4) Nov. 4—Mar. 14, 1693	
			(5) Nov. 7—Ap. 25, 1694	
			(6) Nov. 12—May 3, 1695	Dissolved by proclamation Oct. 11, 1695
III	7th to 10th W.	Nov. 22, 1695	(1) Nov. 22—Ap. 27, 1696	
			(2) Oct. 20—Ap. 16, 1697	
			(3) Dec. 3—July 5, 1698	Dissolved July 7
IV	10th to 12th	(Aug. 24) Dec. 6, 1698	(1) Dec. 6—May 4, 1699	Summoned for Aug. 24 but prorogued by writ several times until Dec. 6
			(2) Nov. 16—Ap. 11, 1700	Dissolved Dec. 19, 1700
V	12th and 13th W.	Feb. (6) 11, 1701	Feb. 11—June 24	Dissolved Nov. 11, 1701
VI	14th W. and 1 Anne	Dec. 30, 1701	Dec. 30—May 25, 1702	Dissolved by proclamation July 2, 1702

* This now becomes the custom.

Anne (Mar. 8, 1702—Aug. 1, 1714)

No. of Parliament	Regnal year	Date of meeting	Sessions	Notes
I	1st to 4th	Oct. 20, 1702	(1) Oct. 20—Feb. 27, 1703	
			(2) Nov. 9—Ap. 3, 1704	
			(3) Oct. 24—Mar. 14, 1705	Dissolved Ap. 5, 1705

TABLE 147 (continued)_k

Anne (continued)

No. of Parliament	Regnal year	Date of meeting	Sessions	Notes
II	4th to 6th	Oct. 25, 1705	(1) Oct. 25—Mar. 19, 1706 (2) Dec. 3—Ap. 8, 1707 (3) Ap. 14—24, 1707 (4) Ap. 30, 1707	Prorogued. Directed by proclamation to assemble Oct. 23 (with Scottish members) as 1st Par. of Gt. Britain. *Reckoned as a new Parliament*
		1st Par. of Gt. Britain		
III	6th and 7th	Oct. 23, 1707	Oct. 23—Ap. 1, 1708	Dissolved Ap. 15
IV	7th to 9th	(July 8) Nov. 16, 1708	(1) Nov. 16—Ap. 21, 1709 (2) Nov. 15—Ap. 5, 1710	Dissolved by proclamation Sept. 21, 1710
V	9th to 12th	Nov. 25, 1710	(1) Nov. 25—June 12, 1711 (2) Dec. 7—June 21, 1712 (3) Ap. 9—July 16, 1713	Adjourned by command to July 8, then prorogued 12 times Dissolved Aug. 8
VI	12th and 13th	(Nov. 12) Feb. 16, 1714	(1) Feb. 16—July 9, 1714 (2) Aug. 1, 1714	Prorogued to Aug. 10 but met Aug. 1 Prorogued Aug. 25, by K. George I, to Sept. 23, then further and dissolved Jan. 5, 1715

George I (Aug. 1, 1714—June 12, 1727)

No. of Parliament	Regnal year	Date of meeting	Sessions	Notes
I	1st to 8th	Mar. 17, 1715	(1) Mar. 17—June 26, 1716	Sept. 21, 1715, adjourned at King's request 5 times successively till Jan. 9, 1716 *Septennial Act passed 1716*
			(2) Feb. 20, 1717—July 15 (3) Nov. 21—Mar. 21, 1718 (4) Nov. 11—Ap. 18, 1719 (5) Nov. 23—June 11, 1720 (6) Dec. 8—Aug. 10, 1721 (7) Oct. 19—Mar. 10, 1722	

[*Septennial Act henceforth regulates duration of Parliaments.*]

TABLE 148

IMPERIAL DIETS

(Dates of assembly, from 1485; *meetings of Electors* (Kurfürstentage) *are not enumerated.)*

1485	Frankfort.	1543	Nürnberg.
1489	Frankfort.	1544	Speier.
1491	Nürnberg.	1545	Worms (removed to Ratisbon).
1495	Worms.	1547	Augsburg.
1496	Lindau (removed to Worms).	1555	Augsburg.
1500	Augsburg.	1556	Ratisbon.
1501	Nürnberg.	1559	Augsburg.
1505	Cologne.	1570	Speier.
1507	Constance.	1576	Ratisbon.
1510	Augsburg.	1582	Augsburg.
1512	Trier (removed to Cologne).	1594	Ratisbon.
1518	Augsburg.	1597	Ratisbon.
1521	Worms.	1603	Ratisbon.
1523	Nürnberg.	1608	Ratisbon.
1526	Speier.	1613	Ratisbon.
1529	Speier.	1623	Ratisbon.
1530	Augsburg.	1640	Ratisbon.
1532	Ratisbon.	1653	Ratisbon.
1541	Ratisbon.	From 1663	Diet permanently in session at Ratisbon.
1542	Speier.		
1542	Nürnberg.		(1806 Dissolution of Empire.)

TABLE 149

CONGRESSES AND CONFERENCES
(SELECTION ONLY)

(Dates of opening only are given.)

1520   Field of the Cloth of Gold (Henry VIII and Francis I).
1530   Conference of Bologna (Charles V and Clement VII).
1532   Second Conference of Bologna (Charles V and Clement VII).
1552   Conferences of Linz and Passau.
1562   Conference of St Germain.
1565   Conference of Bayonne.
1594   Conference of Heilbronn.
1600   Conferences of Bergen-op-Zoom and Boulogne.
1609   Conference of the Hague.
1633   Convention of Heilbronn.
1634   Conventions of Frankfort and Worms.
1645   Congress of Westphalia.
1650   Congress of Nürnberg.
1677   Congress of Nymegen.
1697   Congress of Ryswyk.
1710   Conference of Gertruydenberg.
1712   Congress of Utrecht.
1713   Conference of Rastatt.
1714   Congress of Baden.
1724   Congress of Cambrai.
1728   Congress of Soissons.
1748   Congress of Aix-la-Chapelle.
1762   Conferences at Fontainebleau and Hubertusburg.
1790   Congress of Reichenbach.
1791   Conference of Pillnitz.
1794   Congress of St Petersburg.
1797   Congress of Rastatt.
1800   Conference of Lunéville.
1801   Conference of Amiens.
1807   Conference of Tilsit.
1808   Congress of Erfurt.
1814   Conference of Châtillon-sur-Seine.
        Conference at Paris.
        Congress of Vienna.
        Conference of Ghent.
1815   Conference at Paris.
1818   Conference of Aix-la-Chapelle.
1819   Conference of Vienna.
1820   Conference of Troppau.
1821   Conference of Laibach.
1822   Preliminary Conference at Vienna.
        Congress of Verona.

TABLE 149 (*continued*)_b

1824   Conference of St Petersburg.
1827   Conferences of London.
1849   Conference at Berlin.
1850   Conference of Dresden.
       Conference of London.
1856   Conference of Paris.
1871   Conference of London.
1878   Conference of Berlin.
1882   Conference at Tōkiō.
1886   Conference at Tōkiō.
1887   First British Colonial Conference.
1889   Conference at Berlin (Samoa question).
       First Panamerican Conference at Washington
1899   First Peace Conference at the Hague.
       Conference at Washington (Alaska Boundary).
1900   Socialist Congress at Paris.
1905   Conference of Algeciras.
1907   Imperial British Colonial Conference.
       Second Peace Conference at the Hague.
1908   International Naval Conference at London.

TABLE 150

LEAGUES AND ALLIANCES
(SELECTION ONLY)

1487 Swabian League founded (renewed 1512).
1495 League of the Pope, the Emperor, Spain, Milan, and Venice against France.
1496 *Magnus Intercursus.*   (England and the Netherlands.)
1503 League of Cambrai.
1511 The Holy League.
1512 Alliance of Scotland with France, and of Maximilian I with Julius II.
1514 Alliance of Henry VIII and Louis XII.
1516 French Concordat with the Papacy.
1521 Alliance of Bruges (Henry VIII, Charles V, and Leo X).
1522 Alliance of Windsor (Henry VIII and Charles V).
1524 Catholic Alliance of Ratisbon.
1526 League of Cognac.
      Alliance of Torgau.
1531 League of Schmalkalden.
1533 League of Halle.
1536 Alliance of France and the Porte.
1538 League of Nürnberg.
1546 Alliance of Charles V and Paul III.
1547 League of Princes (against Charles V).
1548 Alliance of Scotland and France.
1551 Habsburg Family Compact.
1553 League of Heidelberg.
1558 Landsberg League.
1571 Triple Alliance (the Pope, Spain, and Venice) against the Turks.
1576 French Catholic League formed.
1577 Union of Brussels.
1578 League between Savoy and Swiss Catholic Cantons.
1579 League of Arras and Union of Utrecht.
1596 Alliance of England, France, and United Provinces.
1607 Franco-Venetian Alliance with the Grisons.
1608 Union of Ahausen.
      Pressburg Alliance.
1609 German Catholic League.
1610 Alliance of Brosolo (France and Savoy against Milan).
1614 League of French Princes.
1633 Alliance of Heilbronn.
1656 Alliance of England and France against Spain.
1658 Confederation of the Rhine.
1661 Defensive alliance of England and Brandenburg.
1666 Quadruple Alliance (United Provinces, Denmark, Brandenburg, and Brunswick-Lüneburg).

TABLE 150 (*continued*)ₕ

1668	Triple Alliance (England, United Provinces, and Sweden) against France.
1670	Secret Alliance between Louis XIV and Charles II.
1683	The Hague Alliance.
1684	The Holy League (the Emperor, Poland, and Venice) against the Turks.
1685	Alliance of Brandenburg and the United Provinces.
1686	Alliance of Brandenburg and the Emperor.
	Augsburg Alliance.
1689	First Grand Alliance.
1699	Alliance of Denmark, Poland, and Russia against Sweden.
1701	Second Grand Alliance.
1707	"Perpetual" Alliance of Sweden and Prussia.
1709	Alliance of Denmark, Poland, and Russia against Sweden.
1715	Alliance of Great Britain, Russia, Denmark, and Prussia against Sweden.
1717	Triple Alliance (France, Great Britain, and United Provinces).
1718	Quadruple Alliance (the same and the Emperor).
1725	First Vienna Alliance (Spain, the Emperor, and the Empire; 1726 joined by Russia).
	Alliance of Hanover (Great Britain, France and Prussia; 1726 joined by United Provinces; 1727 joined by Sweden and Denmark).
1733	First Bourbon Family Compact.
1743	Alliance of Fontainebleau (Second Bourbon Family Compact).
1744	Secret Alliance between Prussia and France.
	Union of Frankfort.
1745	Alliance of Austria and Russia.
1746	Alliance of France and Sardinia.
	Alliance of Denmark and France.
1756	Convention of Westminster.
	Defensive Alliance of Versailles (second Treaty 1757).
1761	Third Bourbon Family Compact.
1767	Confederation of Radom.
1768	Confederation of Bar.
1773	Alliance of France and Sweden.
1778	Alliance of France with the American Colonies; 1779 joined by Spain; 1780 by Holland.
1780	First Armed Neutrality.
	Alliance of Austria and Russia against the Porte.
1785	The *Fürstenbund*.
1788	Triple Alliance (Great Britain, United Provinces, and Prussia).
1790	Alliance of Prussia with the Porte, and with Poland.
1792	First Coalition (Prussia and Austria; 1793 joined by Great Britain, Holland, Spain, and the Italian States).
1799	Second Coalition (Great Britain, Austria, Russia, Naples, and the Porte).
1800	Second Armed Neutrality.
1803	Swiss Act of Mediation.
1805	Third Coalition (Great Britain, Austria, and Russia).
1806	Confederation of the Rhine.
1807	Fourth Coalition (Great Britain, Prussia, and Russia).
1812	Secret Alliance between Russia and Sweden.

TABLE 150 (*continued*)_c

1813   Alliance between Russia and Prussia.

1814   Quadruple Alliance of Chaumont.
Congress of Vienna.

1815   Defensive Triple Alliance of Great Britain, Austria, and France.
Alliance of the Eight Powers.
The Holy Alliance.
Renewal of Quadruple Alliance of Chaumont.

1818   Renewal of Quadruple Alliance of Chaumont.

1833   Secret Alliance of Austria, Prussia, and Russia.

1845   The *Sonderbund*.

1849   The *Dreikönigsbündniss* (Prussia, Saxony, Hanover) and Union.

1850   The Germanic Confederation revived.

1851   Secret Alliance between Austria and Prussia.

1854   Alliance of Great Britain and France (1855 joined by Sardinia).

1863   Alliance of South American States against Spain.

1866   Alliance of Italy and Prussia.

1872   The *Dreikaiserbund* (1884 renewed).

1876   Alliance between Servia and Bulgaria.

1879   Secret Defensive Alliance between Germany and Austria.

1882   Triple Alliance (Germany, Austria, and Italy ; renewed quinquennially since).

1895   Alliance between France and Russia.

1902   Alliance between Great Britain and Japan (1905 amplified).

TABLE 151

UNIVERSITIES FOUNDED FROM 1450

(The dates are where possible those of foundation. Dates enclosed in ( ) are those of second foundation. The names of universities which have ceased to exist or to hold rank of universities are enclosed in [ ].)

I. EUROPE

GREAT BRITAIN AND IRELAND.
Glasgow 1450.
Aberdeen 1495.
Edinburgh 1582.
Dublin (Trinity College) 1591.
Durham 1831.
London 1836 (1900).
Manchester, Victoria U., 1880 (1903).
[Ireland, Royal U. of, 1880.]
Wales, U. of, 1893.
Birmingham 1900.
Liverpool 1903.
Leeds 1904.
Sheffield 1905.
Belfast, Queen's U. of, 1909.
Bristol 1909.
Ireland, National U. of, 1910.

AUSTRIA-HUNGARY.
Pressburg 1467.
Clausenburg 1580.
[Olmütz 1581.]
Graz 1585 (1817).
[Salzburg 1623.]
Budapest 1635 (1769).
Innsbruck 1677 (1826).
Lemberg 1784 (1817).
Agram 1874.
Czernowiz 1875.

BELGIUM.
Ghent 1816.
Liége 1817.
Brussels 1834.
[Malines 1834.]

BULGARIA.
Sofia 1888.

DENMARK.
Copenhagen 1479 (1539 and 1788).

FRANCE.
Nantes 1463.
[Bourges 1464.]
[Rheims 1547.]
[Douai 1562.]
[Besançon 1564.]
Dijon 1722.
[Imperial University 1808 (University of France).]
Lyon 1808.
Rennes 1808.
[Free Catholic Faculties 1875.]
Aix-en-Provence 1896.
Clermont-Ferrand 1896.
Lille 1896.
Marseilles 1896.
Nancy 1896.

GERMANY.
[Trier 1450.]
Greifswald 1456.
Freiburg-i.-B. 1457.
[Ingolstadt 1472.]
[Mainz 1477.]
Tübingen 1477.
[Wittenberg 1502.]
Marburg 1527 (1650).
Königsberg 1544.
[Dillingen 1549.]
Jena 1557.
Braunsberg 1564 (1818).
[Helmstedt 1576.]
[Neustadt (Palatinate) 1578.]
Giessen 1607.
[Paderborn 1614.]
[Molsheim 1618.]
[Rinteln 1621.]
Strassburg 1621 (1872).
[Altorf 1623.]

TABLE 151 (*continued*)$_b$

GERMANY (*continued*).
   Kiel 1665.
   [Lingen 1685.]
   Halle 1693.
   Breslau 1702.
   Göttingen 1733.
   [Fulda 1734.]
   Erlangen 1742.
   Münster 1780 (1902).
   [Stuttgart 1791.]
   [Landshut 1802.]
   Berlin 1810.
   [Ellwangen 1812.]
   Bonn 1818.
   Munich 1826.

GREECE.
   [Corfu 1824.]
   Athens 1837.

ITALY.
   Macerata 1540.
   Messina 1548.
   Parma 1549.
   [Milan 1565.]
   Sassari 1620 (1763).
   [Mantua 1625.]
   Urbino 1671.
   Camerino 1727.
   Cagliari 1764.
   Genoa 1812.

THE NETHERLANDS.
   Leyden 1575.
   [Franeker 1585.]
   Utrecht 1636.
   Groningen 1815.
   Amsterdam 1877.

NORWAY.
   Christiania 1811.

PORTUGAL.
   Coimbra (1537) (1772).

ROUMANIA.
   Jassy 1860.
   Bucharest 1864.

RUSSIA.
   Warsaw 1576 (1864).
   [Wilna 1576.]
   Kieff 1588 (1833).
   Dorpat 1632.
   [Abo 1640.]
   St Petersburg 1728 (1819).
   Moscow 1755 (1804).
   Kazan 1804.
   Kharkoff 1804.
   Helsingfors 1827.
   Odessa 1865.
   Tomsk 1879.

SERVIA.
   Belgrade (1864).

SPAIN.
   [Siguenza 1472.]
   Toledo 1474.
   Zaragossa 1474.
   [Alcalà 1499.]
   Seville 1504.
   Granada 1531.
   San Jago di Compostella 1532.
   [Osuña 1548.]
   [Gandia 1549.]
   [Osma 1550.]
   [Orihuela 1552.]
   Oviedo 1580.
   Barcelona 1596.
   [Pamplona 1680.]
   [Cervera 1717.]
   Madrid 1836.

SWEDEN.
   Upsala 1477.
   Lund 1666.
   Stockholm 1878.
   Göteborg 1887.

SWITZERLAND.
   Basel 1460.
   Zürich 1521 (1833).
   [Lausanne 1537.]
   Bern 1834.
   Geneva 1873.
   Fribourg 1889.

TURKEY.
   Constantinople 1900.

TABLE 151 (*continued*)_c

II. ASIA

INDIA.

 Bombay 1857.
 Calcutta 1857.
 Madras 1857.
 Lahore (Punjaub U.) 1882.
 Allahabad 1887.
 [Alighur.]

ANNAM.

 Hanoi 1907.

CHINA.

 Peking 1867.
 Shansi (Imperial U.) 1902.
 Hongkong 1910.

JAPAN.

 Tōkiō 1868.
 Kyōto 1897.

PHILIPPINE ISLANDS.

 Manila 1611.

SYRIA.

 Beirut 1875.

(See also RUSSIA.)

III. AFRICA

EGYPT.

 Cairo 1908.

SOUTH AFRICA.

 Cape Town 1873.

IV. NORTH AMERICA

DOMINION OF CANADA

Quebec 1678.
Windsor (U. of King's College) 1788.
Halifax (Dalhousie U.) 1818.
Montreal (McGill U.) 1821.
Toronto 1827 (1906).

Kingston (Queen's U.) 1840.
Montreal (U. Laval) 1852 (1878).
Lennoxville (U. of Bishop's College) 1853.
Winnipeg (U of Manitoba) 1877.

UNITED STATES OF AMERICA

The localities are in ( ).

ALABAMA.

 Southern U. (Greensboro) 1856.
 Alabama (Tuscaloosa) 1885.

ARIZONA.

 Arizona (Tucson) 1885.

ARKANSAS.

 Arkansas (Fayetteville) 1871.

CALIFORNIA.

 The Pacific (San Jose) 1852.
 California (Berkeley) 1869.
 Southern California (Los Angeles) 1880.
 Leland Stanford Junior 1885.

COLORADO.

 Colorado (Boulder) 1861.
 Denver (University Park) 1864.
 Westminster 1907.

COLUMBIA.

 Georgetown (Washington) opened 1789.
 George Washington (Washington) 1821.
 Howard (Washington) opened 1867.
 Catholic U. of America (Washington) 1887.

CONNECTICUT.

 Yale (New Haven) 1701.
 Wesleyan (Middletown) opened 1831.

FLORIDA.

 Florida (Gainesville) opened 1884.
 John B. Stetson (De Land) 1887.

TABLE 151 (*continued*)*d*

UNITED STATES OF AMERICA (*continued*)

GEORGIA.
Georgia (Athens) 1785.
Mercer (Macon) 1838.
Atlanta 1867.
Clark (South Atlanta) 1877.

IDAHO.
Idaho (Moscow) 1889.

ILLINOIS.
Northwestern (Evanston) 1851.
Illinois (Urbana) 1867.
Chicago, opened 1892.
James Millikin (Decatur) 1901.

INDIANA.
Vincennes 1806.
Indiana (Bloomington) 1828.
De Pauw (Greencastle) opened 1837.
Notre Dame 1844.
Taylor (Upland) 1846.
Valparaiso 1907.

IOWA.
Iowa Wesleyan (Mount Pleasant) opened 1844.
State U. of Iowa (Iowa City) 1847.
Central U. of Iowa (Pella) 1853.
Upper Iowa (Fayette) 1856.
Drake University (Des Moines) 1881.

KANSAS.
Baker (Baldwin) 1858.
Kansas (Lawrence) 1864.
Ottawa 1865.
Highland 1867.
Kansas City 1895.

KENTUCKY.
Central U. of Kentucky (Danville) 1819.
Transylvania (Lexington) opened 1836.
Louisville 1837.
State U. (Lexington) 1865.

LOUISIANA.
Tulane U. of Louisiana (New Orleans) 1845.
Leland (New Orleans) 1870.
Louisiana State U. (Baton Rouge) 1877.

MAINE.
Maine (Orono) 1865.

MARYLAND.
Johns Hopkins (Baltimore) 1867.

MASSACHUSETTS.
Harvard (Cambridge) 1650.
Boston 1869.
Clark (Worcester) 1887.

MICHIGAN.
Michigan (Ann Arbor) 1837.

MINNESOTA.
Minnesota (Minneapolis) 1851.
Hamline (St Paul) 1854.
St John's (Collegeville) 1857.

MISSISSIPPI.
Mississippi 1844.
Rust (Holly Springs) 1872.

MISSOURI.
St Louis 1832.
Missouri (Columbia) 1839.
Christian (Canton) 1853.
Washington (St Louis) 1853.

MONTANA.
Montana (Missoula) 1893.

NEBRASKA.
Nebraska (Lincoln) 1869.
Nebraska Wesleyan (University Place) 1886.
Cotner (Bethany) opened 1889.

NEVADA.
Nevada (Reno) opened 1886.

NEW JERSEY.
Princeton 1746.

NEW MEXICO.
New Mexico (Albuquerque) 1889.

NEW YORK.
Union (Schenectady) 1795.
Columbia (New York) 1810.
Colgate (Hamilton) opened 1819.
New York U. 1831 (1893).
Buffalo, 1845.

TABLE 151 (*continued*).

UNITED STATES OF AMERICA (*continued*)

NEW YORK (*continued*).
Fordham (New York) 1846.
Rochester 1850.
St Lawrence (Canton) 1856.
Alfred (Alfred) 1857.
Cornell (Ithaca) 1865.
Syracuse 1871.
Niagara 1883.

NORTH CAROLINA.
North Carolina (Chapel Hill) 1793.
Shaw (Raleigh) 1875.

NORTH DAKOTA.
N. Dakota (University) 1883.

OHIO.
Ohio (Athens) 1804.
Miami (Oxford) 1809.
Denison (Granville) 1832.
Ohio Wesleyan (Delaware) 1844.
Ottobein (Westerville) 1849.
Capital (Columbus) 1850.
Heidelberg (Tiffin) 1851.
Baldwin (Berea) 1854.
Wilberforce 1856.
Wooster 1866.
Ohio State (Columbus) 1870.
Cincinnati, opened 1874.
Western Reserve (Cleveland) 1882.

OKLAHOMA.
Oklahoma (Norman) 1892.
Epworth (Oklahoma) 1903.

OREGON.
Willamette (Salem) 1853.
Pacific (Forest Grove) 1854.
Oregon (Eugene) opened 1876.

PENNSYLVANIA.
Pennsylvania (Philadelphia) 1755.
Pittsburg 1819.
Lafayette (Easton) 1826.
Bucknell (Lewisburg) 1846.
Lincoln, opened 1854.
Lehigh (South Bethlehem) 1866.
Temple (Philadelphia) 1888.
Susquehanna (Selinsgrove) 1894.

RHODE ISLAND.
Brown (Providence) opened 1764.

SOUTH CAROLINA.
South Carolina (Columbia) 1801.
Furman (Greenville) 1850.
Claflin (Orangeburg) 1869.
Allen (Columbia) opened 1881.

SOUTH DAKOTA.
South Dakota (Vermilion) 1862.
Dakota Wesleyan (Mitchell) 1883.

TENNESSEE.
Tennessee (Knoxville) 1794.
Nashville 1826.
Cumberland (Lebanon) 1843.
U. of the South (Sewanee) 1858.
Walden (Nashville) 1866.
Chattanooga, opened 1867.
Fisk (Nashville) 1867.
Vanderbilt (Nashville) 1872.
Lincoln Memorial (Cumberland Gap) 1897.

TEXAS.
Baylor (Waco) 1845.
St Mary's (Galveston) 1856.
Trinity (Waxahachie) 1871.
Fort Worth 1881.
Texas (Austin) opened 1883.

UTAH.
Utah (Salt Lake City) opened 1850.

VERMONT.
Vermont (Burlington) 1791.

VIRGINIA.
Washington and Lee (Lexington) 1782.
University of Virginia (Charlottesville) 1825.
Virginia Union (Richmond) 1896.

WASHINGTON.
George Washington (Seattle) 1859.
Puget Sound (Tacoma) opened 1903.

TABLE 151 (*continued*)ƒ

UNITED STATES OF AMERICA (*continued*)

WEST VIRGINIA.
    West Virginia (Morgantown) 1868.
WISCONSIN.
    Wisconsin (Madison) 1838.
    Northwestern U. (Watertown) 1867.

WYOMING.
    Wyoming (Laramie) 1886.

V. SOUTH AMERICA AND WEST INDIES

SOUTH AMERICA.

ARGENTINE REPUBLIC.
    Cordoba 1613.
    Buenos Aires 1821.
    La Plata 1905.

CHILI.
    U. of Chili (Santiago) 1743.

COLOMBIA.
    National U. (Bogotá) 1867.

ECUADOR.
    Central U. of Ecuador (Quito) 1787
    (1895).

PARAGUAY.
    National U. (Asuncion) 1890.

SOUTH AMERICA (*continued*).

PERU.
    U. of St Mark (Lima) 1553.

URUGUAY.
    Montevideo 1876.

VENEZUELA.
    Central U. of Venezuela (Caracas)
    1721.

CENTRAL AMERICA.

SALVADOR.
    San Salvador.

WEST INDIES.

CUBA.
    Havana 1728.

VI. AUSTRALASIA

COMMONWEALTH OF AUSTRALIA.

NEW SOUTH WALES.
    Sydney 1850.

VICTORIA.
    Melbourne 1853.

NEW ZEALAND 1870.

COMMONWEALTH OF AUSTRALIA (*continued*).

SOUTH AUSTRALIA.
    Adelaide 1872.

TASMANIA.
    Hobart (U. of Tasmania) 1890.

II
GENERAL INDEX

EXPLANATORY NOTE

Kings, queens, queens-consort, royal princes and princesses, archdukes, arch-duchesses, popes and cardinals, are to be found as a rule under their Christian names (or, in the last instance, surnames). Grand-dukes, dukes, electors and other territorial princes of lesser rank are to be found under the names of their States. Bishops of the British Isles appear under their ordinary surnames, those of other countries (unless they are cardinals or, in rare cases, specially mentioned by name only in the text, and in one or two instances of obscure Polish bishoprics) under their sees. Noblemen are under their highest or best-known titles. Exceptions have been made where a strict following of rule would seem pedantic, as in the case of the Cromwells or of Colbert, of Napoleon I's marshals and others, and in the case also of a few men whose titles do not appear in the book. These have been put under their well-known names.

The principle of arrangement of long headings under a single name (in different forms) "Anna, Anne," "Maria, Marie," has been that of the alphabetical order of the countries to which the name is attached. Thus a queen of France would precede a queen of Spain of the same name. When a second name follows the first that has been taken as the alphabetical guide.

For compound names of persons the ordinary rules have been followed. Where in the text a name is preceded by a preposition the order is here reversed; for example, Gallars, Nicholas de; where a name is made up of a preposition and article, the article precedes, the preposition follows; for example, La Motte Fouqué, F. H. K. de; where the preposition and article have formed a compound, as in Du Bellay, Della Casa, the compound precedes. But occasional allowance has been made on this point for family usage, and here, as elsewhere throughout the Index, cross-references have been carefully added where doubt might arise.

Compound names of places have been treated as one word, as for example, La Hogue, St Domingo, Port Arthur, Cape Passaro, with the single exception of those beginning with Fort, which it seemed possible to group under Fort.

In the case of the Greater States it has not been found possible to give more than the main references from which their continuous history may be drawn. For the slighter references the Indexes of the individual volumes must be consulted.

To the names of persons and places a number of Subject Headings have been added. In general comprehensive headings, such as Religion, Church, Catholics, Protestants, have been avoided. More limited sections of such subjects, however, as for instance, Toleration, Calvinists, Lutherans, and even Huguenots, have been included.

GENERAL INDEX

Aachen, Charles V crowned at (1520), II 42, 139, 417; Catholicism in, III 156, 163; ecclesiastical troubles in, 705–8, 712, 715, 718; Protestants in, IV 10; decay of, 420; VI 689; Gustavus III at, 783; capitulates (1793), VIII 265; spinning mills near, X 754

—— Peace of (1668), V 39, 153 sq., 200, 373, 443, 650; (1748), VI 117, 243, 249 sq., 273, 319, 331 sq., 363; Frederick the Great and, 398; and America, 411; and India, 537 sq.; Charles III and, 597; 608; and Corsica, 609; 622; 640; 642

—— Congress of (1818), VII 367 sq., IX 666, 761, X 12, 14 sqq., 56, 69, 353; and Baden, 362; 364; XII 729

Aalborg, siege and capture of (1534), II 615; capture of Danish horse at, IV 102; port of, VI 737

Aar river, Charles of Lorraine at, VI 247

Aarau, Treaty of, VI 611, 613

Aargau, added to Swiss confederation (1415), II 306; IX 427; subject to Bern, VI 613, IX 600 sq., 670; XI 236; 240; joins the *Siebnerkonkordat*, 242; 244; and the Articles of Baden, 246; suppression of monasteries in, 246 sq., 248; 251; industries of, 259

Aarhuus, port of, VI 737

—— Ove Bilde, Bishop of, II 616

Aasen, Ivar, Norwegian philologist, XI 701

Abancourt, Charles-X.-J.-Franqueville de, French Minister of War, VIII 406

Abaya, Lake, discovered, XII 813

Abaza, Russian Minister of Finance, XII 309; 312

Abbás I, Viceroy of Egypt, XII 429 sq.

—— II, Viceroy of Egypt, XII 454

—— II, Shah of Persia, VI 518; 527

—— Pasha, X 550

Abbeville, ethnological discoveries at, XII 772

Abbot, Charles. *See* Colchester, Lord

—— George, Archbishop of Canterbury, III 560; appeal of Commons to, IV 260

Abbott, James, in Afghánistán, XII 800

Abd-el-Aziz, Sultan of Morocco, XII 132 sq.

Abd-el-Kader, Algerian chief, X 503 sqq.

Abd-el-Kader, Egyptian Pasha, XII 441

Abd-ul-Aziz, Sultan of Turkey, accession of, XI 636; 637; 639; XII 381; 383; death of, 385; 430; and Ismail, Viceroy of Egypt, 432; 439

Abd-ul-Hamid I, Sultan of Turkey, death of, VIII 326; IX 388

—— II, Sultan of Turkey, XI 637; XII 14; 33; accession of, 385; 386 sq.; and Eastern Rumelia, 408; 416; and the Armenian massacres, 417 sq.; and Crete, 419; and the war with Greece, 420 sq.; and Macedonian reform, 425 sq.; deposed, 428; and Egyptian affairs, 435 sqq., 445

Abd-ul-Kerim, Ottoman commander, XII 388

Abdullah, Pasha of Acre, X 549

Abdulla Jan, son of Sher Ali, XII 460; 465; death of, 469

Abd-ul-Mejid, Sultan of Turkey, X 562; XI 18; reforms by, 275 sq.; 314; 316; and the Treaty of Paris, 323 sq.; death of, 636

Abdulmelek, Emperor of Morocco, III 597

Abdurrahman Khan, Amir of Afghánistán, XII 34 sq.; 459; 467; 469; becomes Amir, 471 sq.; 475; and the frontier question, 478; and Lord Dufferin, *ib.*; relations of, with Great Britain, 482 sq.; death of, 483; 488; 490

Abdy Bey, Turkish Court jester, X 556

Abel, Karl von, Bavarian statesman, XI 61

Abell, Thomas, trial and execution of, II 443 sq.

Abenaki, The, VII 95, 101

Abensberg, battle of (1809), IX 349

Abercrombie, James, VII 126, 132

Abercromby, Sir Ralph, VIII 617; Commander-in-Chief in Ireland, IX 701; in the West Indies, 749

Aberdeen, Episcopal clergy of, and the penal laws, V 290; Jacobites at, VI 98, 103, 116

—— George Hamilton-Gordon, 4th Earl of, VII 391, 671; and the Greek Question, X 200, 203; and the agreement with France (1830), 482 sq.; Colonial Secretary, 667; XI 2; and the Scottish Church, 6 sq.; 10; foreign policy of,

16 sq.; 21; 31; 33; forms a coalition ministry (1852), 309 sq.; 312; and the question of war with Russia, 315 sq.; resigns, 320; character of, *ib.*; 346; 379; and the Spanish marriages, 554; xii 683

Aberdeenshire, elections in, vi 93; 98

Abeshr (Wadai), explorers at, xii 811

Abhorrers, English party (1679), v 226

Abjuration, Act of, at the Hague (1581), iii 254

Åbo, surrender of (1563), iv 162; taken by Charles IX (1597), 172; free school of, founded by Gustavus Adolphus, 187; vi 314; Peace of, 761, 782

—— Michael Agricola, Ordinary (and Bishop) of, ii 629

—— Skytte, Bishop of, ii 628

Abomey, explorers at, xii 807

Abonyi, Louis, Hungarian novelist, xi 430

Aborigines Protection Society, xi 788; and the Congo State, xii 663

Aboukir, French fleet at (1798), viii 604, 625; Turkish defeat at (1799), 614 sq., 674; Mehemet Ali at, x 547; rebel army at, xii 437

About, Edmond, French writer, xi 526

Abraham, Plains of, vii 139 sqq.

Abrantes, Lippe's army at, vi 369; Wellesley's army at, ix 451

Abrial, André-Joseph, Comte, Minister of Justice (1801), ix 9

Abruzzi, Luigi (of Savoy-Aosta), Duke of the, Polar expedition of, xii 795, 815

Abruzzo, peasant movement in, xi 536; 542

Abu Hamed, taken by Egyptian troops, xii 448

Abyat, crypto-Socinian leader in Poland, iii 80 sq.

Abyssinia, the war in (1868), xi 752 sq.; xii 3; the Italian campaign in, 240 sq.; 343; war in (1875), 440; the Mahdi and, 444; 449; 659; Italy and, 664; 805; explorers in, 806, 813; 811

Academies, Humanistic teaching and, i 553 sq.; in Florence, the Platonic, 559 sq.; in Rome, 560; in Naples, *ib.*; in Venice, Aldo's, the *Neacademia*, 561, 563; in various Italian towns, *ib.*; of the *Elevati*, ii 384; the Modenese, 386 sq.; the Platonic, of Florence, 702; under Cosimo de' Medici, iii 394; spread of, 469 sq.; *Akademia Jagiellonska*, 77; *Académie française* constituted, iv 156; followed by others, v 741; Colbert and five new French, 15; *Académie des Sciences*, 715, 741; *Académie des Inscriptions*, and historical research in the eighteenth century, xii 817, 829; decline of literary, in Italy, v 118; scientific in general, 739 sqq.; English scientific, 740; Austrian scientific, 741; Prussian, of 1696 and 1700, 670; of Elector Frederick III, 741; Russian, of

Theodore III, 519; of Peter the Great, 547, 741

Acadia, Anglo-French struggle for, iv 747; assigned to England (1631), v 442; Acadians driven from, vi 337; disputed governorship of, vii 23; 72; ceded to England (1656), 75; restored to France (1667), 89; ceded to England (1713), 95, 109; history of, 110 sqq.; transferred to Britain (1763), x 685. *See also* Nova Scotia

Acapulco, trade of, with Manila, x 255

Acarnania, insurrection in, xi 279

Acciaiuoli, Donato, translation of L. Bruni's *History of Florence* by, iii 471

—— Franco. *See* Athens, Duke of

Accialli, Treaty of, xii 240

Accoramboni, Vittoria, iii 427 sqq.

Achaltsik, acquired by Russia (1829), x 444, xi 274

Achard, Charles François, attempts to manufacture sugar from beetroot, ix 377

Aché, de, French naval officer, vi 547 sq.

—— French royalist, tries to effect a rising in Normandy, ix 136

Achin, English East India Company and, iv 731; Dutch war with, xii 243 sqq., 669; 248

Achmet Aga of Dospad, xii 384

A'Court, Sir William. *See* Heytesbury

Acqs (or Dax), François de Noailles, Bishop of, ambassador to England (1556), ii 544 sqq., 548; iii 265; ambassador to the Porte, 137

Acqua Felice, Sixtus V and, iii 441

Acquaviva, Father Claudio, fifth Jesuit General, iii 448, 766

Acqui, Austrian retreat to (1796), viii 566 sq.

Acre, besieged (1190), v 630, (1799), viii 610 sqq., (1831), x 549; Sultan's messengers killed at, ix 385; 387; captured by Ibrahim Pasha (1832), x 549; offered to Mehemet Ali, 553, 560, 565 sq., 569, 571; the *divan meshura* at, 559; surrender of (1840), 571

Acs, Hungarian camp at, xi 210

Act of Grace, English, of May, 1690, v 260

Act of Mediation, Swiss (1803), xi 236 sqq.

Act of Neutralisation, Swiss (1815), xi 238 sq.

Act of Resumption, of all grants of Irish forfeited estates (Ap. 1700), v 323

Act of Seclusion (Dutch), Cromwell and, v 141 sqq.; reception of, in the Union, 143 sq.; rescinded, 148

Act of Security, Scottish (1703-4), v 298

Act of Settlement, English (1701), v 275, 277; repeal of two clauses of, 464; and the Electress Sophia, vi 8 sqq.: of Ireland (1662), v 302 sq.; repealed by the Irish Parliament (1689), 310

Act of the Six Articles (1539), ii 450; results of, 466 sq.; failure of, 477

Act of Succession (1534), II 442, (1536), 445
Act of Supremacy, Henry VIII's (1534),
II 442, Elizabeth's (1559), 567 sqq.;
first results of, III 284; in later action,
340 sqq., 349
Act of Uniformity (1549), II 485, (1552),
507 sq., Elizabeth's (1559), 569; first
results of, III 284; enforcement of, 340
sqq.; of 1662, character and results of,
v 98 sqq.; 329 sqq.
Act of Union, between England and Scot-
land, VI 90 sqq., Chap. III *passim*
Act of Union, of Great Britain and Ireland,
IX 702 sqq., Chap. XXII *passim*
"Act of Union and Security," of Gusta-
vus III of Sweden, VI 781
Acta Augustana, by Martin Luther, II 133
Actium, sea-fight off (1538), III 114
Acto Addicional, Portuguese, of Saldanha,
XI 573
Acton, John Emerich Edward Dalberg-
Acton, Lord, v 2; 253; 616; 617; VI 85;
XII 766; 841; 848
—— Sir John Francis Edward, Prime
Minister of Naples, VIII 650 sq., 778
Aculhuaquê ("Strong men"), Mexicans,
I 38
Acuña, Alonzo Osorio de. *See* Zamora,
Bishop of
—— Diego Sarmiento de. *See* Gondomar
Adair, Sir Robert, British ambassador, IX
309; 389; x 542
Adalbert, St, v 629
Adam, Edmond, Parisian official, XI 113
Adami, Adam, Bishop. *See* Hildesheim
Adams, Charles Francis, American Minis-
ter in London, VII 399, 610, 640; XI
336 sq.; XII 21
—— Henry, historian, XII 841
—— John, President of the United States
(1797–1801), VI 461; VII 146, 151, 154,
164, 189, 232; elected Vice-President,
315 sqq.; elected President, 320 sqq., 324,
372, 730; and Spanish America, x 280
—— John Couch, astronomer, XII 768
—— John Quincy, President of the United
States (1825–9), VII 350, 363, 365 sq., 371,
373 sq., 378 sq.
—— Samuel, American statesman, VII
146, 159 sqq., 173, 182, 189, 197, 730
—— Thomas, major, defeats Mír Kasim,
VI 561; 562
—— William, and Japanese trade, IV 740
Adana, occupied by the Egyptian army
(1832), x 550; 553 sq.
Adasheff, Alexis, favourite of Ivan the
Terrible, v 489
Adda, Count de, papal Nuncio in England,
v 235
Addington, Henry. *See* Sidmouth, 1st
Viscount
Addison, Joseph, French influence on, v
70; 122; 133; 271; *Cato*, 474; 476 sqq.;
succeeded as Secretary by Craggs, VI 30;
x 696; 699

Adelaide, capital of South Australia, XI 792
sq.; 798; industries of, XII 623; 624; the
federation question at, 631; University
of, founded, 627
Adelaïde, Madame (Princess Eugène-Louise-
Adelaïde of Orleans), sister of Louis-
Philippe, x 479; 484
Adelantado (admiral), of Castile. *See*
Padilla, Martin de
Adeler, Kort, Norwegian admiral, v 561
Adelfi, secret society, in Lecce, x 111
Adelmann, Bernhard, von Adelmannsfel-
den, German reformer, II 138
Aden, attacked by Turkish fleet, III 117
Aderklau, Archduke Charles attacks the
French at (1809), IX 353
Adet, Pierre-Auguste, French Minister to
the United States, VII 320
Adige river, French army on, v 402; VI
153; crossed by the allies (1735), 154;
Austrian retreat towards (1800), IX 68; 69
Adil Khan, ruler of Goa, I 31
Adlerberg, Count Vladimir, XI 614
Adlersparre, George, Count, Swedish gen-
eral, forces abdication of Gustavus IV,
IX 323
Admiralty, Courts of, in the American
colonies, contested jurisdiction of, and
the War of Independence, VII 184 sqq.
See also Navies
Admiralty Colleges of Holland, Zeeland
and the North Quarter, III 621
Adolphus Frederick, King of Sweden, VI
354; 741 sq.; 761 sqq.; death of, 766
—— John, Prince, brother of Charles X
of Sweden, IV 587; 590; v 563
Adorno, Botta, Austrian general, Regent in
Tuscany, VI 601; 608
Adowah, battle of, XII 219, 241, 447, 664
Adrian IV (Nicholas Breakspeare), Pope,
Northern mission of, II 601; and the
donation of Ireland, III 582, 585
—— VI (Adrian Boyers of Utrecht), Pope,
the fall of Rhodes and, I 94; Spanish
regent, 368, 372 sqq., 457; at Louvain
University, 436, 674; Church reform and,
678; Erasmus and, 682; failure of, 691;
election of, II 20, 44, 378, 418; reign and
character of, 19 sqq.; reasons for failure
of, 27; reforming policy of, 32, 170 sqq.,
378, 400, 641; Bavaria and, 169; Gustavus Vasa and, 623; III 186; v 635
—— Patriarch of Russia, v 530
Adriani, Giovanni Battista, III 394
Adriano de Corneto. *See* Castellesi, Cardinal
—— Mateo, Melanchthon and, II 402
Adrianople, Mohammad IV in, v 353;
Turkish army at, 359; Tökölyi at, 364,
366; x 556; Peace of (1713), v 607;
Treaty of (1829), x 98, 200, 202 sq., 444,
481, 545, XI 274, 281, and Moldo-
Wallachia, 281 sq., and Servia, 284;
Russian occupation of, XII 389; 390 sq.;
426

Adriatic Sea, VI 241; Venice and, 605; British evacuation of places on, IX 77; tribute from the islands of, X 172; Greek piracy in, 186; Neapolitan fleet in, XI 85; 366

Adwalton Moor, Fairfaxes defeated at, IV 313

Adullamites, faction of the, XI 339

Advancement of Learning, Bacon's, III 377

Aegean Sea, Venetians lose their islands in, III 115-6; tribute from the islands of, X 172; Greek piracy in, 186

Aegidius of Viterbo, I 648; II 8, 28; at Fifth Lateran Council, 30 sqq.

Aegina, surrendered by Venice to the Turks, III 116

Aegineta, Petrus (Greek professor at Florence), II 16

Aehrenthal, Baron Aloys L. B., Austrian statesman, XII 211

Aeneas Sylvius. *See* Pius II, Pope

Aerschot, Philip de Croy, Prince of Chimay, Duke of, III 190, 194, 214, 226, 232, 244, 245, 248, 250

Aerssens, Francis van (Franz van Aerssen), lord of Sommelsdijk, III 649, 651, 655; councillor of Frederick Henry, IV 690; appeals to Richelieu for help, 691; negotiations of, in England, 701

Æsop, Russian translation of, V 529

Assens, victory of Christian III over Lübeck at, II 230, 615

Affane, ford of, III 594

Affonso V, King of Portugal, the Guinea trade and, I 16; schemes of exploration and, 19, 21

Affre, Denis-Auguste. *See* Paris, Archbishops of

Affry, Louis-Auguste-Augustin, Comte de, lieutenant-general, French envoy at the Hague, VI 343

—— Louis-Auguste-Philippe, Comte de (son of above), appointed Landammann of the Swiss Confederation, IX 423

Afghan Boundary Commission, XII 477 sq.

Afghánistán, the Emperor Bábar in, VI 508 sq.; 510 sqq.; 517; Shah Jehán in, 518; insurrection in, 521; 524; physical features of, 526 sqq.; and Oudh, IX 721; British mission to, 732; history of (1815-69), Vol. XI, Chap. XXVI; Russia and, 632; affairs in (1863-1907), XII, Chap. XVI *passim*; 4; British war with, 34, 36 sq.; 56; 161; Russia and, 343; political mission to, 800

Afíz, Pasha of Nissa, IX 387

Africa, exploration of, I 13 sqq., 17, 20; English and Dutch in, V 108, 149, 179; Brandenburg colony in, 647; European settlements in, 691 sqq.; VI 151; colonisation of, 184; the slave trade in, 186 sqq.; the European Powers in, 187 sqq.; Moslem States of, IX 385; and the slave trade, X 19; XII 3 sq.; British progress in, 47; 94; the French in, 128 sqq., 159; German colonisation in, 160 sq., 167,

172; Italy and, 219, 240; the Portuguese in, 270; the colonisation and partition of, 657 sqq.; exploration in, 805 sqq.

Africa, Central, opening up of, XII 255 sq.; 635

—— South, English and Dutch in (1850-70), Vol. XI, Chap. XXVII (3); British rule in, 761; Union of, XII 2; 39; Chinese labour in, 54; British emigration to, 63; 603; affairs in (1871-1910), 635 sqq.; England and, 658; 734

—— West, the West Indies and, IV 759; XII 658 sq.

African Association, VI 188, XII 805 sq.

—— Company, Swedish (1647), IV 759; English (1618), 759; English (1631), 759; French (West) (1626), 759; VI 173. *See also* Royal African Company, British East and South African Companies, etc.

—— Society (German), XII 658

—— Trading Company (Brandenburg), V 647

Africander Bond, in South Africa, XII 638

Afridis, The, attack British posts, XII 488

Afrosina, Tsarevich Alexis' mistress, V 539 sq.

Aftonblad, Swedish journal, XI 685

Afzal, son of Dost Mohammad, XII 459

—— Khan, general of the Bijapur army, VI 521

Agadem, explorers in, XII 807

Agades, explorers in, XII 810

Agassiz, Louis, naturalist, XI 260

Agen, Republican attack on, XI 137

—— Matteo Bandello, Bishop of, II 15; the novels of, III 368, 467 sq.

Agénois, peasants' rising in, III 664

Agnadello, Venetian defeat at (1509), I 132, 246

Agnew, Patrick Alexander Vans, British official in India, XI 740

Agordat, Italian success at, XII 240

Agostini, Agostino de (Wolsey's physician), II 434

Agoult, Antoine-Jean, Vicomte de, VIII 156

Agra, William Hawkins at, IV 741; English factory at, 742; captured by Bábar, VI 509; 511; Emperor Shah Jehán proclaimed at, 517; 519 sq.; 523 sqq.; Sindhia seizes, IX 718; 719, 725; British capture of, 726; presidency of, XI 731; 738; relief of (1857), 747

—— and Oudh, United Provinces of, XII 495

Agram, revolutionary movement at, XI 156; Croato-Slavonic Diet at, 179 sq.; disturbances at, XII 198, 209

Agrarian revolution, in England. *See* England

"Agreement of the People," IV 345; 353; V 327 sq.

Agricola, Georgius. *See* Bauer, George

—— Johann, Lutheran theologian, II 201, 264

—— Michael. *See* Åbo

Agricola, Rudolf (Roelof Huysmann), I 436, 569, 572, 634
—— Stephen, Lutheran theologian at the Conference of Marburg, II 207
Aguesseau, Henri-François de, Chancellor of France, VI 129 sqq.; 162; IX 165; 167 sq.
Aguila, Don Juan del, Spanish general in Ireland, III 532
Aguinaldo, Emilio, Filipino leader, VII 679; XII 530 sq.
Ahalya Bái, IX 727
Aharlow, forest of, III 595
Ahlden, Sophia Dorothea at, VI 8
Ahmad I, Sultan, III 700
—— II, Sultan, V 369
—— III, Sultan, V 604 sqq.
—— Pasha, III 123; murdered, 124
—— Pasha, Turkish admiral, X 562
—— Shah Abdali, Afghan ruler, VI 524
—— Vefyk Effendi, Turkish ambassador in Paris, XI 636
Ahmadábád, English factory at, IV 742; captured, VI 576
Ahmadnagar, kingdom of, VI 512; 515; Khan Jehán in, 517; 518; 523; Wellesley captures, IX 726
Aidzu clan and *daimiōs*, Vol. XI, Chap. XXVIII (2), *passim*
Aigues Mortes, conference of Charles V and Francis I at (1538), II 73, 98, 235, 288, III 115
Aiguillon, Emmanuel-Armand de Vignerot-Duplessis-Richelieu, Duke of, VI 595; Governor of Britanny, 356; Minister of Foreign Affairs, 357 sq.; VIII 82
—— Armand de Vignerot-Duplessis-Richelieu, Duke of (son of above, d. 1800), VIII 179; 692; 715
Aigun, Treaty of, XI 273, 632, XII 796
Aikin, John, physician, VIII 764 sq.
Ailly, Pierre de, Cardinal, doctrine of Conciliar authority of, I 623; at Constance, II 281
Aïnali Kavak, Treaty of, VI 709, XI 282
Ain-Sefra, French boundary at, XII 129
Airds Moss, Covenanters defeated at, V 287
Aire, ceded to France, V 39, 45; captured by the Allies (1710), 429
—— river, pollution of, XI 1
Aislabie, John, statesman, VI 41; 180 sq.
Aisne river, French army at, XI 596; 597
Aitchison, Sir Charles Umpherston, and the Indian Civil Service, XII 480
Aix, the plague at, VI 128; Fouché retires to, IX 140; *Parlement* of, III 6, 415–6, 662, IV 610 sq., V 4; VIII 47; and Mirabeau, 150; Terrorists lynched at, 387
—— Albert Genebrard, Archbishop of, I 615
—— Gilbert Genebrard, Archbishop of, I 615
—— Jean-de-Dieu-R. de Cucé de Boisgelin, Archbishop of, VIII 24, 179
Aix-la-Chapelle. *See* Aachen

Aix Roads, Willaumez anchors in, IX 238
Ajaccio, French fleet off, IX 220
Ajmir, Sir Thomas Roe at, VI 515; 519
Akashi, *daimiō* of, XI 832
Akbar Khan, son of Dost Mohammad, XI 733; 735
—— Shah, Moghul Emperor, VI 511 sq.; character of, 513 sqq.
Akhalzik, Pasha of, IX 385
Akkerman, Russian capture of, VI 673; Treaty of (1826), X 192 sq.; repudiated by the Sultan, 198; XI 282
Ak Mechet, captured by Russia, XI 273
Akrotiri, Christian insurgents in, XII 420
Aksakoff, Ivan, Russian journalist, XI 625 sq.; XII 298; 300; 309; 311
Aksu, travellers at, XII 799; 802
Alabama, Spanish claims in, VII 315, 323; migration into, 359; enters the Union, 359, 413; and the Tariff, 377; secedes (1860), 446; joins the Confederacy, 453, 603; cut off from Confederate centre, 522; threatened by Grant, 528; emancipation in, 595; representation of, 632; becomes Democratic, 642
Alabama incident, VII 565 sq., 636; XI 336 sq., 776; XII 20 sq., 27 sq., 717, 720
Alagón, Duke of, X 208
Alain le Grand, Lord of Albret. *See* Albret
Alais, Louis de Valois, Comte de. *See* Angoulême
Alam, Shah, and Indian politics, IX 717 sqq.
Alamanni, Luigi, III 55, 459, 468; *Giron il Cortese*, 469; exile of, 470
Alamo, massacre of the (1836), VII 392
Åland Isles, Conference at, VI 28; 34; 36; seized by Russia (1808), IX 323
Alanio, Pedro, Spanish revolutionary, XII 267
Alary, Abbé, and the *Club de l'Entresol*, VIII 15
Alaska, boundary dispute of, VII 371, XII 617, 722; purchased by the United States, VII 637, 666, XII 344; XI 632 sq.; 776; XII 814
Alatau mountains, XII 793; exploration in, 799
Alava, incorporated in Castile, I 235
—— Don Francis de, III 16 sq., 210
Alba, Duke of. *See* Alva
—— de Tormes, del Parque defeated at, IX 455, 456; Spanish force placed at, 473
Albani, Alessandro, Cardinal, VI 587; 595
—— Giovanni Francesco. *See* Clement XI, Pope
—— Jean François, Cardinal, VIII 637
—— Joseph, Cardinal, Papal Secretary of State, X 154 sq.
Albania, Scanderbeg and, I 70, 71; Venice fights the Turks in, 80; suggested occupation of, by France, IX 308; Ali Pasha in, 386, (1814), X 176, 177; revolts in, 549, 560, XI 279; Italian

and Austrian rivalry in, XII 242; 381;
the Treaty of Berlin and, 396, 398;
425; 428
Albanian League, XII 401; 403
Albanians, and Montenegro, XII 401 sq.;
415 sq.; 425
Albany (U.S.A.), conquest of (1664), VII
39 sq.; fortified, 42; charter granted to,
43; 44 sq.; federation meeting at (1754),
VI 412; operations round (1756), VII 126;
railway from Boston to, 694
—— Western Australia, XI 790 sq.
—— Alexander Stewart, Duke of, I 484
—— John Stewart, Duke of (son of
Alexander), I 484, 488; advances on
Naples (1524), II 50; in Scotland, 419
sq., 422 sq.; returns to France, 426,
453 sq.
Albemarle, The, VII 563 sq.
Albemarle, Arnold Joost van Keppel, 1st
Earl of, V 257
—— George Keppel, 3rd Earl of, VI
369; 426
—— George Monck, Duke of, at Nantwich,
IV 321; 443; victory of, off Scheveningen,
476; 480 sq.; soldier and seaman, 485;
subdues Scotland, 436, 510 sq.; in Ulster,
531; 532; declares for a free Parlia-
ment, 538; 540; 545 sqq.; marches into
England, 548 sq.; and the Restoration,
550–9; V 93; 100; and the marriage of
Charles II, 105; 106; in naval campaign
of 1666, 183 sqq.; 190; death of, 191;
280; VI 795 sq.; VII 34
—— William Anne Keppel, 2nd Earl of,
VI 333
Alber, Matthäus, of Reutlingen, reformer,
II 160; Zwingli and, 332
Albericus Gentilis, III 767
Alberoni, Giulio, Cardinal, Spanish statesman, VI 25; 29; and Great Britain, 30 sq.;
and Sicily, 32; 33 sqq.; and the Jacobites, 104; and England, 122 sq.; and
the Regent Orleans, 123; reforms by, *ib.*;
foreign policy of, 124; fall of, 125; 126;
134; 136; 138; and Ripperdá, 139, 142
sq.; 157; Elisabeth Farnese and, 166;
586 sq.
Albert I, King of the Belgians, XII 256
—— II (of Habsburg), Emperor, reforms
of, in the Empire, I 294; 687; II 198;
V 623
—— King of Poland. *See* John Albert
—— I (of Mecklenburg), King of Sweden,
defeated at Falköping (1393), II 600; 601
—— Archduke, Archbishop of Toledo
(later sovereign of the Netherlands),
Governor of Lisbon, III 318, 519; in
Italy, 527; marriage of, 630; Governor
of Netherlands, 522 sqq., 634; efforts of,
for peace, 534, 628, 639; and the war,
535, 629; at battle of the Dunes, 635 sq.;
takes Calais, 670; fails to relieve Amiens,
522, 672 sq.; attacks France, 679, 686 sq.;
and Jülich, 689 sq., 730, 732; and

Emperor Rudolf, 720, 735; death of,
655; IV 77; career of, III 699; and the
Imperial throne, IV 1; 11; 13; Henry IV
and, 624
Albert IV, Duke of Bavaria-Munich. *See*
Bavaria
—— of Brandenburg, Duke of Prussia.
See Prussia
—— Prince, of Saxe-Coburg-Gotha, and
Prince Consort of Queen Victoria, married
to her, X 681; XI 33; 163; and Napoleon
III, 308; 338; and William I of Prussia,
406; and the Spanish marriages, 553;
death of, 336
—— Edward Nyanza Lake, XII 810; 812
—— Nyanza Lake, discovery of, XII 439,
662; 809; 812
—— Alexandre-Martin, French politician,
XI 101; 103; 105; 107
Alberta, district of, XI 776; ranching in,
XII 610; 615
Alberti, Aristotile (Ridolfo Fioravanti), V
482
—— Leo Battista, architect and painter,
I 559; II 702; III 458
Albertini, Francesco, Italian scholar, I 549
Albigny, C. E. Philibert de Simiane, seigneur
de, Governor of Savoy, and the escalade
of Geneva, III 420 sq.; death of, 686
Albitte, Antoine-Louis, Commissioner of
the Convention, VIII 561
Albizzi, Giovanna, I 176
—— Luca, supporter of Savonarola, I 169
Albornoz, Gil Álvarez Carillo, Cardinal, I
237, 663
Albrecht, Archduke of Austria, XI 153 sq.; 216
—— C., professor at Göttingen, X 379
—— Wilhelm Eduard, German jurist, XI
162
Albret, Alain le Grand de, Sieur d'Albret
and Count of Dreux, I 393 sqq., 397
—— Catherine, Queen of Navarre. *See*
Navarre
—— Charlotte de, marriage of, to Cesare
Borgia, I 120
—— Henri and Jean de, Kings of Navarre.
See Navarre
—— Jeanne de, Queen of Navarre. *See*
Navarre
Albuera, battle of (1811), IX 467
Albufera, Duke of. *See* Suchet
Albuquerque, Aranda winters at, VI 359
Alburquerque (Albuquerque), Affonso de,
crusading schemes of, I 11; capture of
Goa by, 31; ideals of, IV 728; V 695
—— Antonio de, Governor of the Rio,
V 679
—— José Maria de la Cueva, 14th Duke
of, defence of Cadiz by, IX 456
—— Matthias de, IV 707
Alcabala, Spanish tax, II 99; under
Philip III, IV 627
Alcalá, University of, founded by Ximenes,
I 355, 380, 622, 651, II 400
—— Alfonso de, Spanish scholar, II 400

Alcañiz, Suchet repulsed at, IX 454

Alcantara, Order of, I 11

Alcasabah, The, III 105

Alcazar-Kebir, battle of (1578), III 499, 597

Alciati, Andrea, Calvin and, II 352; III 58

—— Giovanni Paolo, Italian reformer, II 393

Alcolea, battle of, XI 569

Alcott, Amos Bronson, transcendentalist, VII 739

Alcoy, outrages at, XII 267

—— Federico Roncali, Count of, Spanish Minister, XI 559

Alcuin, and the schools of Charles the Great, I 535

Aldan, river, XII 794

Aldea de Ponte, fight at (1811), IX 468

Alderney, naval works at, XI 333

Alderson, Dr John, of Norwich, VIII 764 sq.

Aldini, Antonio, Count, IX 84

Aldobrandini, Pietro, Cardinal, III 419; and Clement VIII, IV 667; friendly towards France, 668

—— Silvestro, IV 666

—— papal nuncio in Spain (1724), VI 137

Aldringer, Johann, Count, Austrian Field-Marshal, IV 72; Mantua taken by, 115; at Erfurt, 205; Tilly reinforced by, 208; 210; at Leipzig, 219; 231; Feria and, 234; protection of Bavaria and, 238; Emperor and, 239 sqq.; at Ratisbon, 244

Aldrovandus, Ulysses (Ulisse Aldrovandi of Bologna), naturalist, V 736; 738

Aldus Manutius, Venetian printer, V 508

Aleander, Girolamo, Cardinal, Rector of University of Paris, I 575; the Reformation and, 678; 686, 690; at the Diet of Worms (1521), II 139 sqq., 240; church reform and, 379; 383, 643

Aleardi, Aleardo, Italian poet, XI 546 sq.; 549

Aleko Pasha. *See* Vogorides, Alexander

Aleksinats, battle at, XII 386

Alembert, Jean-Baptiste le Rond de, Encyclopaedist, VI 698; 825; VIII 26

Alemtejo, awarded to Godoy, IX 302; the Duke of Terceira in, X 333

Alençon, Frotté surrenders at, IX 14

—— Charles, Duke of, at Pavia, II 51

—— Francis of Valois, Duke of. *See* Anjou, Francis of Valois, Duke of

—— Margaret, Duchess of. *See* Margaret, Queen of Navarre

Aleppo, trade of, I 32; Turkish victory at (1516), 91; winter-quarters of Prussian Army at, III 121; Ibrahim Pasha enters (1832), X 550; 553; revolt in (1834), 559

Aleria, John Andreas de Bossi, Bishop of, I 558

Alesius (Alexander Aless), Scottish divine, II 555

Alessandria, fall of (1499), I 121; claimed by Francis I, III 110; 400; French garrison at, V 415; VI 160; siege of, 161, 245, 608; fortress of, VIII 554; occupied by the French (1796), 567; surrenders (1799), 659; IX 61–2; retreat of Austrians to, 63; revolt at (1821), X 116; fortress of, XI 366 sq.; 371

Alet, canonry at, V 85

—— Nicolas Pavillon, Bishop of, V 84 sq.

Alexander III (Roland Bandinelli), Pope, II 422

—— IV (Rinaldo Conti), Pope, the Augustinian Eremites and, II 114

—— V (Pietro Philargi), Pope, I 268

—— VI (Rodrigo Borgia), Pope, I 105; elected, 225; question of deposition of, 110; Savonarola and, 149, 177 sqq.; allied with Naples, 227 sq.; treats with Charles VIII, 231; the Orsini and, 223; allied with France, 124, 236–9; Church reform and, 620; nepotism of, 234; extravagant and splendid, 667; methods of raising money used by, 669, 670, 672; a pluralist, 659; death and character of, 126, 195, 241, II 1 sq.; 400; the Spanish Inquisition and, 650; prohibited books and, 687; Bull of, in regard to the New World, IV 728; 744

—— VII (Fabio Chigi), Pope, papal nuncio at Münster, IV 402, 688; Charles X and, 582; V 76; 84

—— VIII (Pietro Ottobuoni), Pope, V 58

—— I, King of Poland, I 345

—— I, Tsar of Russia, VI 681; 696; VIII 785 sq.; IX 35; 49, 50, 93; reconciled with England in Treaty of St Petersburg, 73; champions the King of Sardinia, 79; 236; relations of, with France, 245; 249; with Austria, 248; 249; threatens the Prussian Government, 250; 255; welcomed at Potsdam, 256; Napoleon and, 259; at Austerlitz, 261; relations of, with Prussia, 266; 272, 280–2, 287; with France, 269; 270–2, 283; with Turkey, 281; and the negotiations of Tilsit, 291 sqq., 295, 297 sq.; consequent relations of, with Britain and Turkey, 304 sqq.; 307; hesitates to complete the Tilsit agreement, 308–13; and Finland, 314; Napoleon's communications to, 315; policy of balance of, 317; at Erfurt, 318 sqq., 325; 337; power of, in Baltic lands, 340; 341; resists overtures of Prussia and Austria, 344; declares war against Great Britain (1807), 366–7; yields to Napoleon, 374; 375; offends Napoleon, 379; hesitating attack of, on Turkey, 388 sq., 485; character and policy of, 483–6, 670; refuses to treat with Napoleon, 497; allies himself with Prussia, 507, 512 sq.; at Dresden, 523, 527; at Leipzig, 535 sq.; at Frankfort, 542 sq.; 546; and the Conference of Châtillon, 548, 550; enters Paris, 555; and Talleyrand, 556; considers

Napoleon's terms, 558 sq.; at the Congress of Vienna, 580 sq., 653 sqq., 670 sq.; and the slave-trade, 614, x 19; and the Holy Alliance, IX 664 sq., x 9 sq.; and the Treaty of Tilsit, 3; and the Quadruple Alliance (1815), 7; character and policy of, 8 sq.; and the Treaty of Paris, 11; at Aix-la-Chapelle, 14–20; and Austria's German policy, 22 sq.; change of opinions of, 23, 25, 27, 364 sq., 438 sq.; at Troppau, 27–30, 438; and the Turkish Question, 32; influenced by Metternich, 34; and Spanish affairs, 35, 211, 222 sqq.; hostile to France, 45; and the Duc de Richelieu, 47; 50; favours the evacuation of France by the Allies, 56; 69; 74; and Cardinal Consalvi, 141; and the Treaty of Bucharest, 169; and the disputes with the Porte, 175; and the Ionian Islands, 177; 179; and the execution of Gregorios, 183; 199; and the Eastern Question, 187 sqq.; at Czernovitz, 187; and the St Petersburg Conference, 188; 349; influence of, upon the King of Prussia, 352; and Stourdza's pamphlet, 364; and the Germanic Federal constitution, 368; 370; wars of, prior to 1815, 413; the military colonies of, 415 sq.; and the navy, 417; and Jeremy Bentham, 418; and the Senate, *ib.*; and the Committee of Ministers, 419; and provincial administration, 420; and the prisons, 422; and the Church, 424; dismisses Galitzin, 425; and the abolition of serfdom, 428; and the secret societies, 432, 439; and Finland, 434 sq.; and the imperial family, 436; and the succession to the throne, 437; schemes of (1815–19), 437 sq.; and Poland, 445 sq., 448; enters Warsaw, 446; signs the Polish Constitution, *ib.*; Concordat of, with Pius VII (1818), 449; at the Diets at Warsaw, 450 sqq., 455 sq.; and the Polish bishops, 452; and Polish secret societies, 453 sq.; 458; and the Lithuanian provinces, 459, 464; and the Republic of Cracow, 460; death of (1825), 190, 439; and Bern, XI 236; 262; 264 sq.; 268; 664; and Charles XIV of Sweden, 681 sqq.; XII 729

Alexander II, Tsar of Russia, x 436; at Warsaw, 458; visits England (1839), 558; and the Crimean War, XI 323, 373; and Austria, 402; and the King of Prussia, 434; and the Austro-Prussian War, 456; attempts on the life of, 484, 626, 630; character of, 613; and the emancipation of the serfs, 614; and the railway system, 619; and local government, 620; and law reform, 622 sq.; and national education, 624; and the Press, 625; 627; Asiatic policy of, 632; foreign policy of, 633 sq.; and the Black Sea, 633 sq.; and the poet Odyniec, 658; and France, XII 97; 138; at Berlin, 139, 141; and

Germany, 142 sqq.; domestic policy of, 294 sqq.; 304; and the Liberal demonstrations, 306; plots against, 308; assassination of, 310 sq.; 314; 317; and Finland, 334; and Servia, 386; and the war with Turkey, 388 sq.; and the Congress of Berlin, 394; 398; 404; arbitrates between Japan and Peru, 555

Alexander III, Tsar of Russia, XII 98; and Germany, 162; 291; 311; character of, 312; 313; 315 sq.; policy of, 322; 324; and Finland, 334; and the Jews, 340; foreign policy of, 341; and Bulgaria, 406, 409; and the Armenians, 416

—— King of Servia, XII 411 sqq.

—— Prince of Bulgaria, XII 163; 341; rule of, 404 sqq.; abdicates, 408 sq.

—— Prince, of the Netherlands, XII 244 sq.

—— Karageorgevich, Prince of Servia, XII 413

—— Grand Duke. *See* Alexander I, Tsar of Russia

—— Blasius, IV 38; leader among the Grisons *Prädikanten*, 52; capture of, 55

—— Sir William. *See* Stirling, Earl of

—— Lord (son of E. of Stirling), settles in Nova Scotia, VII 75

—— of Aphrodisia, commentator on Aristotle, II 702

—— the Great, Asiatic conquests of, VI 506

—— of Hales, and the conception of the Treasury of merits, II 124 sq.

Alexandra, Queen of Great Britain, XI 338; XII 409

—— Grand Duchess of Russia, IX 36–8, 41

—— Feodorovna (Princess Charlotte of Prussia), Tsarina, consort of Nicholas I, x 436

Alexandre, Charles-Louis, Revolutionary leader, VIII 228

Alexandretta, Turkish fleet at, x 550

Alexandria, captured (1798), VIII 599; battle outside (1801), 617; surrenders, 617 sq.; IX 53; Nelson at, 220; British expedition to (1807), 235, 368; force from Bombay in, 734; Mehemet Ali at, x 551 sq., 569; Turkish fleet at, 562, 567; 565; Sir Charles Napier at (1840), 571; 572; bombardment of, XII 40, 436 sq.; 430; British occupation of, 438; 455

—— (Virginia), attacked (1814), VII 344; Federal troops at (1861), 464

Alexandroff, Ivan IV at, v 491

Alexandrovsk, fortress of, XI 273; mine laid at, XII 308

Alexéyeff, Erghenyi Ivanovich, Admiral, Russian Viceroy, XII 346; 376; 521; in the Russo-Japanese War, 582 sq., 587, 596

Alexis Romanoff, Tsar of Russia, the Cossacks and, IV 580; 581; in the Baltic Provinces, 582 sq.; 584; Charles X and, 586–8; feud between Poland and, 591;

position of, v 343 sq.; 503; the reign of, 504 sq.; and the Patriarch Nikon, 506 sq.; and ecclesiastical reforms, 508 sq.; 514; the Code of, 515; 516; character of, 516 sq.; 518; laws of, xi 264

Alexis, Crown Prince of Russia, xii 346
—— Tsarevich, son of Peter the Great, v 536 sqq.; death of, 542; 547
—— Wilibald. *See* Häring, Wilhelm

Alexius III, Emperor of the East, i 255

Alfieri, Giuseppina, Marchioness, xi 392
—— Count Vittorio, poet, vi 824; viii 778 sq.; ix 86; x 106; xi 549
—— di Sostegno, Cesare, Marquis, Piedmontese Minister of Education, xi 75; 79; and Italian Federation, 90; 92; retires, 93

Alfonso V of Aragon, King of Naples, i 105, 560
—— II, King of Naples, i 105, 110, 114, 231
—— VI, King of Portugal, v 34; 105
—— XII, King of Spain, xi 569 sqq.; xii 257 sq.; 260; proclaimed, 262; reign of, 263
—— XIII, King of Spain, xii 257; birth of, 264; marriage of, 266
—— II of Ferrara. *See* Ferrara, Dukes of

Alfred, Prince, Duke of Edinburgh. *See* Saxe-Coburg-Gotha, Duke of

Algarve, awarded to Godoy, ix 302

Algeciras, naval actions at (1801), ix 54; Freemasons of, x 215
—— Conference, xii 55, 98, 133, 242, 456

Algeria, France and, x 98 sq., 502 sqq., 545, xii 95, 128 sq., 132, 658; the Queen of Madagascar deported to, 131

Algiers, Charles V and the pirates of, ii 68 sq., 75 sq., 242; Charles V retires from, iii 112; 398, 399; Spanish expedition to, 420, 435; pirates of, 438; Spanish and Italian expedition to, 541; Blake at, iv 483; French fleet sent to, v 53; Spain and, vi 374, 381; Venice and, 606; Denmark and, 745; expedition to (1816), ix 662; France and, xi 35; transportations to, 139 sq., 304

Algoa bay, Livingstone at, xii 808

Algonquins, i 34; origin of name, 44; vii 75 sq.

Aliaga, Father, and Uceda, iv 629; bribed, 632

Ali Alta, Russian advance on, xi 630

Alicante, v 376; capture of (1709), 426

Alidosi, Francesco, Cardinal, i 136; 249 sq.

Aligre, Étienne-François de, President of the *Parlement* (1787), viii 106 sq.

Alikhánoff, General, in Georgia, xii 363

Alima river, exploration on, xii 812

Ali Masjid, British mission at, xii 469 sq.

Ali Murad, Chief of Khairpur, xi 737

Ali, Pasha of Drama, x 181; 185

Ali Pasha of Janina, ix 269; makes himself independent in Albania, 386; x 172 sq.; the successes of, 176; claims Parga, 177;

deposed by the Sultan, *ib.*; death of, 178; 181; 547

Ali Pasha, Grand Vezir of Turkey, dies (1565), iii 125
—— Grand Vezir, superseded (1710), v 604

Alison, Sir Archibald, *History of Europe*, xii 837

Ali Verdi Khan, Nawáb of Bengal, vi 551

Aliwal (Punjab), battle of, xi 739
—— North (S. Africa), Treaty of, xi 787

Alkmaar, assault on, iii 236; and the Act of Seclusion, v 143; Convention concluded at (1799), viii 662; Duke of York capitulates at (1799), ix 41

Allaci, Leone, papal commissary, iv 82

Allahábád, vi 524; 563; ceded to the Marathas, 568; 569; xi 748; proclamation at, 749

Allardin, Reformed minister at Emden, v 757

Alle river, and the campaign of 1807, ix 285, 287, 290

Alleghany mountains, and the Civil War, vii 470

Allègre, Ives de, French general in Italy, i 117, 122 sq., 126, 129, 137

Allemand, Comte Zacharie Jacques-Théodore, replaces Missiessy, ix 225; fails to effect a junction with Villeneuve, 227; returns to Rochefort, 234; sails for Toulon, 237; replaces Willaumez, 238; replaces Ganteaume, 239

Allemane, French socialist, xii 124 sq.

Allen, John, Archbishop of Dublin, murdered, ii 442
—— Samuel, governor of New Hampshire, vii 31
—— Sir Thomas, naval commander, v 108; 180; 186; 190
—— William, Cardinal, iii 285–9, 290, 350–1, 358, 436, 449
—— William, Quaker, visits Russian prisons, x 422
—— William O'Meara, Fenian, xii 65

Allenstein, French army at, ix 285

Allerheim, French victory at, iv 390

Allgemeine Zeitung, xi 719

Allier, rising in, xi 137

Allion, de, French *chargé d'affaires* in Russia, vi 315

Allix, Jules, French politician, xi 502

All-Polish Review, xii 339

All Saints' Bay. *See* Bahia

Allstedt, success of Münzer's preaching at, ii 186

Alma, battle of the, xi 317, 319, 364

Almada, captured by the Duke of Terceira (1833), x 334

Almanza, battle of (1707), v 419

Almaraz, Cuesta's position near, ix 450, 452; seized by Wellesley (1809), 453 sq.

Almeida, siege of, vi 369; ix 303; garrisoned by Junot, 440; taken by Masséna (1810), 459; 462; besieged by Wellington (1811), 465; surrendered, 466; 468; 476

Almeida, Don Francisco de, first Viceroy of Portuguese India, i 31, v 695

Almenara, victory of Starhemberg at (1710), v 428

Almonacid, Venegas beaten at (1809), ix 454, 455

Almoster, victory of Saldanha at (1834), x 336

Alopa, Laurentius Francisci de, Italian printer, i 562

Alost, negotiations at (1482), i 445; seized by Spanish mutineers (1576), iii 244 sq.; Archbishop Gebhard's victory at, 708

Alpujarras, Morisco fastnesses in the, iii 494

Alquier, Charles-Jean-Marie, French envoy at Rome, ix 195; press to be controlled by, 196

Alsace. *See* Elsass

Alsen, island of, taken by Charles X, iv 432; xi 161; captured by the Prussians (1864), 442

Alsh, Loch, men-of-war in, vi 105

Altai mountains, xii 793 sq.; exploration in, 798 sq.

Altamira, Rafael, Spanish historian, xii 842

Alt-Breisach, ceded by France, v 436, 454

Altemps, Marc de (Count Marcus Sitticus von Hohenems), Cardinal, Bishop of Constance, at Council of Trent, ii 676, 682

Altenburg, peace negotiations opened at (1809), ix 359; Schwarzenberg at, 533; revolutionary movement at, xi 150

Altenkirchen, Jourdan repulsed at, viii 497

Altenstein, Karl von Stein zum, ix 332; Prussian statesman, x 351; educational system of, 355; 370; 372; 382

Althan, Count, vi 37

Althorp, Viscount. *See* Spencer, 3rd Earl

Althusius, A. Johann, of Herborn, iii 765; the *Politics*, 767 sq.

Altieri, Baldassare, the Italian Reformers and, ii 383

Altmark, truce of (1629), iv 115, 187, 193, 578

Alton, victory of Waller at, iv 315

— Richard Alton, Count de, Austrian general, vi 651 sq.; viii 320, 328

Altona, Congress at (1687), v 579; Swedish sack of (1713), 609; 612; 756; port of, vi 737; 745; death of the Duke of Brunswick at, ix 278; smuggling at, 378

Altoona (Pennsylvania), Convention at (1862), vii 593

Altoviti, Antonio, Cardinal, Archbishop of Florence, and Cosimo I, iii 390

Altranstädt, Charles XII at, v 417, 597; Peace of (1706), 595, 597

Altyn Tagh mountains, discovery of, xii 799

Alula, Ras, xii 240

Aluté, Empress of China, xii 501 sq.

Alva, Fadrique de Toledo, 2nd Duke of (d. 1527), i 480

Alva, Fernando Alvarez de Toledo, 3rd Duke of, defends Perpignan, ii 76; Paul IV and, 91 sq.; 250, 261; 409; invades papal territory, 545; defeats Guise, 547; iii 7 sqq., 132, 174, 190 sqq., 208, 213 sqq., 271 sqq.; 297, 302, 404, 410, 476 sqq.; recalled to lead Spanish army into Portugal, 500, 514 sqq., 705

Alvarez de Castro, Mariano, Spanish general, Gerona held by, ix 454

Alvear, Supreme Director of the Argentine Provinces, x 301

Alvensleben, Count Philip Charles von, Prussian Minister, viii 288

— Konstantin von, Prussian general, xi 586; 590 sq.

Alvensleben-Erxleben, Count Albert von, Prussian statesman, xi 157 sq.; 192; 199; at the Dresden Conference, 233; mission of, to St Petersburg, 434

Alverstone, Richard Everard Webster, Lord, Lord Chief Justice of England, xii 617

Alviano, Bartolommeo de (Venetian general), i 131 sq., 197

Alvintzy, Baron Joseph von Barberek, Austrian Field-marshal, viii 435, 579 sq.

Alvite, Spanish success at, vi 369

Alxinger, Johann Baptist von, Austrian poet, viii 776

Amadeo I, King of Spain (Duke of Aosta), xi 570 sqq.; xii 257; 259 sq.

Amadis of Gaul, Spanish romance, i 381

Amalia, Queen of Greece, xi 279

— Prussian Princess, vi 281

— von Solms, Princess of Orange. *See* Orange

Amalfi, Costanza d'Avalos, Duchess of, ii 390

Amanvilliers, French army corps at, xi 592; 593

Amar, J.-P.-André, French politician, viii 350, 385

Amaral, General, Governor of Macao, xii 507

Amarante, Count of, x 316

Amari, Michele, Italian historian, xi 548; xii 842

Amasia, Treaty at (1555), between Turks and Persians, iii 122; Morier at, xii 800

Amat, Cardinal-Legate at Ravenna, x 156

Amazon river, trade on, iv 709; Portugal and, v 448, 679; Jesuits on, 683, vi 386; 389 sq.; unexplored regions on, xii 814

Ambala, British forces at, xi 738

Amberg, Christian of Anhalt at, iii 717; French troops in, vi 232; Jourdan repulsed at (1796), viii 497

Amberger Händel, iii 713

Ambleteuse (Newhaven), captured by the French (1549), ii 493

Amboina, Dutch trade at, iii 638, 644; "massacre" at, iv 87, 713, 738 sqq., 755, v 138, 697, vii 22; taken by the

Dutch (1605), IV 733, 735; agreement of June 1619 and, 737; forts in, 742; capture of (1796), VIII 484, IX 750, (1810), 240

Amboise, Tumult of (1560), II 297, 576 sq., III 265; Edict of (1563), II 584, III 5

—— Charles de, Seigneur de Chaumont, I 123, 129, 135 sq.

—— Georges de, Cardinal of Rouen, I 123, 129, 245, 388, 415

Ambras, Castle of, Cardinal Klesl at the, IV 22

Ambriz, slavery abolished at, XI 575

Ambrogini, Angelo. *See* Politian

Ambrosius, St, writings of, revised by Sixtus V, III 426, 445

Ambur, battle of, VI 539

Amegial, battle of (1663), V 34, 105

Amelia, Princess, of Great Britain, death of, IX 689

Amelot de Chaillou, Jean-Jacques, French statesman, VI 109 sq.; 156; 159; 239

Amelot, Sebastien-Michel, French Minister of the Household, VIII 87 sq.

America (*General mention: see also Central, North, South and the various States, especially the United States and Canada*), Colombo and the discovery of, I 21–4, 518; the Cabots and, 34–5; Magalhaēs and, 36; exploration of, by Verazzano, *ib.*, 43; influence of discovery of, 43, 47 sq., 56, 62, 65, 518, VII 1; treasure sent from, I 43, 46, 518; Cartier explores, 44; Huguenot settlements in, 48 sqq.; English in, 50 sqq., 56; Montaigne and, 58 sqq., 63; Catholic Church in, 60 sqq.; Bacon and, 63 sqq.; European capitalists and, 518; partition of, IV 747; the European Powers in, VI 61 sqq., 69; Wesley in, 82, 86; Whitefield in, 83 sq.; 157; colonisation in, 183 sqq., 189; 340; 344; Spanish successes in, 377; 383; British policy in, 432 sq., 436; 491; Ireland and the war in, 495; the Jesuits in, 590 sq.; influence of, on the French Revolution, VIII 1 sq., 727 sq.; French possessions in, 80; British trade with, IX 71; cotton imported from, 125; the Irish in, XII 70; the Clan-na-Gael in, 75 sqq.; Parnell in, 77; Swedish emigration to, 279

—— Central, and the United States, VII 649, 656; XII 1, 6; the Republics of, Chap. XXI

—— North, English colonisation in, IV 747 sq., V 685 sq., (1607–1700), Vol. VII, Chap. I, (1700–63), Chap. II; French in, V 57, 438, 442, 648 sq., VI 172, 299, 327, 331, Vol. VII, Chap. III; English and Dutch in, IV 749, V 108; conflict of French and English in, VI 332, 410 sqq., Vol. VII, Chap. IV; Pitt's policy in, VI 414 sq.; withdrawal of France from, 422; quarrel of the English colonies of, with Great Britain, VI 438 sq., 446 sq., Vol. VII,

Chap. V; independence of, declared, VI 448, VII 174, 208; legal relations between Great Britain and, Chap. VI; War of Independence in, Chap. VII; and France, VIII 73, 77, 91 sqq.; constitution of the United States of (1776–89), Chap. VIII; trade with, X 759 sqq.; emigration to, 762, XII 63, 168; XI 16; trade of, with Bremen, 54; French exiles in, 140; Confederate States of, 248; Russian policy in, 632; British North America, 765, 770 sq.; XII 2; historical study in, 841. *See also* United States, Canada

America, South, English schemes of colonisation in, IV 754 sq.; V 107; Portuguese in, 372, 674 sqq.; Spanish colonisation in, 680 sqq.; 693; the South Sea Company and, VI 177 sq., 181; 374; 471; trade of, VII 327; Republics of, and the United States, 366 sqq., 649; XII 1, 6

—— (Spanish), bullion from, III 481; Spanish trade with, 492, 496; possessions of Philip of Spain in, 500; Spanish exports to, 512; slave-trade to, V 403, 445, 455; illicit trade with, VI 64 sq.; 158; South Sea Company and, 177 sq.; 343; 351; Jesuits expelled from, 372; 475; under Spanish rule, Vol. X, Chap. VIII *passim*; establishment of independence in, Chap. IX *passim*, 31, 34, 38; 19; and the Congress of Verona, 33 sq.; 186; and Great Britain, 212; revolutionary agents from, 213; and the United States, *ib.*; foreign trade with, 586, 761

Amersfoort, Oldenbarneveldt born at (1547), III 624; captured by de Berg (1629), IV 693

Amherst, Jeffrey Amherst, Lord, Field-marshal, VI 426; VII 97, 132 sqq.; expedition of, to Montreal, 137, 139, 141 sqq.

—— of Arracan, William Pitt Amherst, Baron Amherst of Montreal, Earl, retires from Sicily, IX 383; Governor-General of India, XI 727; 729; embassy of, to Peking, 803

Amicable Grant, English (1525), II 425, abandoned, *ib.*

Amidas, Captain Philip, in Virginia, VII 3

Amiens, taken and lost by Spaniards, III 522; fall of, 629; submission of, to Henry IV, 663, 666; taken by Spaniards, 671–2; taken by Henry IV, 673; Biron at, 679; XI 601; 603; German occupation of, 606; 607; 610

—— Treaties at, between Francis I and Henry VIII (1527), II 428; Peace of (1802), V 444, VI 549, IX 18, 19, 76 sqq., 90 sq., 187, 269, 321; rupture of, 28, 122, 124, 244, 270, 752; and trade, 90, 242, 363; and Switzerland, 101; and Turkey, 386; and Malta, 604, 752; and Ireland, 706

—— François Lefèvre de Caumartin, Bishop of, V 756

Amiens, Jean-Pierre de Gallien de Chalons, Bishop of, x 85

Amigues, Jules, French journalist, xii 94

Amio, Domenico de, executes statue of Leo X, ii 13

Amir Khan, founder of the Tonk State, xi 725 sq.

Ammirato, Scipione (the younger), Florentine historian, i 200; iii 394; 457

Amnesty Association, in Ireland, xii 73

Amoravieta, Convention concluded at, xii 260

Amouroux, Charles, French politician, xi 502

Amoy, capture of, xi 809

Ampère, Jean-Jacques, x 101

Ampfing, retreat of Grenier from, ix 67

Ampringen, Caspar von, Governor of Hungary, v 352 sq.; 357

Ampthill, Odo W. L. Russell, Lord (Lord Odo Russell), xii 28; 97; 139

Ampudia, Pedro de, Mexican general, vii 394, 396

Amsdorf, Nicholas. *See* Naumburg, Bishop of

Amsterdam, commercial rise of, i 459; iii 250; Separatist congregations formed at, 346; corn trade in, 620, 631; East India trade with, 632–3, 640 sqq.; interests of, iv 466 sq.; threatened by de Berg, 693; difficulties of Frederick Henry with, 694, 699, 724; Chamber of, 709; Academy founded at, 717; 718 sqq.; Spinoza born at, 722; William II and, 725 sq.; v 43; peace party in, 164 sq.; 199; Bank of, 266 sqq., vi 169, x 746; v 270; 420; Peter the Great in, 525, 612; Russian printing at, 529; Treaty of (1717), 613, vi 28; and the American Congress, 448 sq.; flight of Independents to (1593), vii 12; Republicans in, viii 287; surrenders (1787), 323; French troops in (1795), 436; French ambassador in, ix 371; Napoleon and, 416, 417; risings in (1813), x 517; assembly of notables at, 518; discontent in, 533; and European finance, 728, 742 sq.; 745; and the Eastern trade, 761; socialism in, xii 248; 249

Amu Daria river, Russian expedition to, v 544

Amundsen, Roald, makes the North-West passage, xii 815

Amur, Russian advances in, xi 272 sq.

—— river, Chinese drowned in, xii 521; Japanese force on, 600; 792; 794 sqq.

Amurath III, Sultan, iii 91 sqq.; truce between Stephen Báthory and, 101; mission of William Harborne to the Court of, iv 729

Amyot, Jacques, Bishop of Auxerre. *See* Auxerre

Anabaptists, and their relation to the other Reformers, i 686; in the Netherlands, ii 103; rise of, in Germany, 165 sqq.;

the movement of, at Münster, 222 sqq.; Swiss, and Zwingli, 319; a radical rather than doctrinal movement, 323 sq.; and Lutheranism and Calvinism, 715; theocratic ideas of, iii 740 sq., 755 sq.; English, v 100; 326

Anadyr river, xii 794

Anagni, captured by Colonna (1526), ii 53

Anahuac, the Indians of, x 260 sq.

Anapa, acquired by Russia, x 202, 444, xi 274

Anastasia Romanova, Tsaritsa, v 495

Anastro, Gaspar, iii 255

Anatolia, Ibrahim Pasha in (1833), x 553; Reshid Pasha in, 559 sq.

Anatolian railway, The, xii 170

Ancel, Guillaume, French ambassador in Germany, iii 671

Anchialos, Greek quarter in, destroyed, xii 426

Ancillon, Johann Peter Friedrich, Prussian Minister, x 350 sq.; 376

Anckarström, Jakob Johan, assassinates Gustavus III, vi 784

Anckarsvärd, Baron, Swedish politician, xi 685

Ancón, Peace of, xii 679

Ancona, death of Pius II at, i 79; trade with, iii 131, 393, 438, vi 606; French garrison in, viii 573, 633, 636; Napoleon at, 595; surrenders (1799), 663; despatches captured at, ix 40; capitulation of (1798), 41; 63; restored to the Pope, 189; occupied by Saint-Cyr, 193; seizure of Papal revenues in, 195; 203; March of, annexed by Napoleon (1808), 400; occupied by Austrians, x 150; occupied by French troops (1832), 155 sq., 488; troops withdrawn (1838), 506; xi 71; capitulates (1860), 389

Ancrum Moor, victory of Scots at (1545), ii 460

Andalusia, Isabella in (1477), i 354; exposed to Barbarossa's attacks, iii 110; Moors expelled from, 494; Philip's troops ready in, 500; the Duke of Medina Sidonia and, iv 652 sq.; evacuated by French, v 416; colonisation of, vi 383; ix 430; 431; Spanish army in, 435, 437 sq., 450; Napoleon's projected invasion of, 447; occupied by French (1809–10), 456; Soult in, 457, 469; re-occupied by Spanish, 473; French evacuate (1812), 475; revolt of troops in, x 220; French in (1823), 228, (1810), 285; xi 557; harsh measures in, 566; brigandage in, xii 259; 261; 267

Andaman Islands, Lord Mayo assassinated in, xii 463

Andelot, François de. *See* D'Andelot

Andermatt, Swiss general, ix 100

Andernach, captured by French, viii 437

Andersen, Hans Christian, xi 699

—— Jens. *See* Odense, Bishops of

Anderson, Robert, defends Fort Sumter (1860–1), VII 446 sq., 450; 461 sqq.; 545
—— William, British officer in India, XI 740
Andes, Bolívar crosses the, X 294
Andigné, Chouan leader, IX 2; 3, 13
Andkhui, travellers at, XII 800 sq.
Andō, Japanese statesman, XI 844
Andover, James II at, V 247
Andrada, José Bonifacio de, and the independence of Brazil, X 314 sq.; 317 sq.; guardian of Pedro II, 325
—— Martin Francisco de, Brazilian statesman, X 315; 317 sq.
Andrade, Gomez Freire de, Portuguese general, X 312
Andral, Gabriel, physician to the Court of Naples, IX 571
Andrássy, Count Julius, Hungarian statesman, XI 214; 400; and Bismarck, XII 144; and Hungary, 183 sq.; 188 sq.; Minister of Foreign Affairs, 190 sq.; and the Austro-German alliance, 192; 383; at the Congress of Berlin, 394, 396
—— Count Julius, the younger, XII 205 sqq.; 210
André, John, VII 217, 226
—— de Puyraveau, French deputy, X 476; 491
Andrea, Girolamo di, Cardinal, XI 392
—— Frà, of Ferrara, Lutheran, II 380
Andreae, Jacob, III 704
—— Laurentius (Lars Andersson), II 624, 628
Andrée, Salomon August, Polar expedition of, XII 795
Andrelini, Fausto, and the *Julius Exclusus*, II 9
Andréossi, Comte Antoine-François de, in Egypt, VIII 616; ambassador to London, IX 102; 244
Andrew, Archduke, III 535
Andrewes, Lancelot, Bishop of Winchester, and religious controversy, IV 268
Andriani, General, defends Sagunto, IX 470
Andrieux, François-Guillaume-Jean-Stanislas, IX 153
Andros, Colonel Sir Edmund, colonial governor, VII 28 sqq., 42 sqq., 47, 64
Andrusovo, Treaty of (1667), V 505
Andujar, Dupont retreats to (1808), IX 437
Anethan, Baron Jules Joseph de, Belgian statesman, XI 674; XII 250
Angelico, Frà, I 168, 647
Angennes, Claude de, Bishop of Le Mans. *See* Le Mans
Angermannus, Abraham, Archbishop of Upsala. *See* Upsala
Angers, seized by Huguenots, III 41; gift to Mary de' Medici of, IV 126; feudal courts in, VIII 49; cavalry school at, 446; d'Hédouville at, IX 3
Anghera, Peter Martyr of, historian, the *Decades*, I 53; 248, 379

Angiolillo, Michael, murders Cánovas, XII 268
Anglesey, Sir Henry William Paget, Marquis of (Earl of Uxbridge), General, brilliant feat of, at Benavente, IX 445; charge of, at Genappe, 630; Viceroy of Ireland, X 648; 650 sq.; and reforms in Ireland, 657; 663
Angola, taken by the Dutch, IV 752; Brandenburg trade with, V 647; Portuguese in, XI 575, XII 3, 657, 663, 808; 811
Angostura, Bolívar captures, X 293 sq.
Angoulême, negotiations between Louis XIII and Queen-Mother at, IV 126
—— Charles d'Orléans, Count of (d. 1496), I 393
—— Charles d'Orléans, Duke of, II 70, 72
—— Charles de Valois (bastard son of Charles IX, King of France, Comte d'Auvergne, 1591–1619), Duke of, plots against Henry IV, III 672, 679 sq.; heads an embassy to Saxony (1620), IV 34
—— Diana of. *See* Montmorency
—— Francis, Count of. *See* Francis I, King of France
—— Louis de Valois, Comte d'Alais, Duke of, IV 611; 614; Mercoeur and, 618
—— Louis-Antoine de Bourbon, Duc de, proclaimed Prince Regent at Bordeaux, IX 481; in Bordeaux, 555; and the Ministry of Louis XVIII, 566; 568; at Nîmes, 617; enters Spain with a French army (1823), X 36; 46; in Spain, 80, 228, 230; return of, 80
—— Louise of Savoy, Duchess of, II 46, 52, 59, 97, 123, 423
—— Marie-Thérèse-Charlotte, Duchesse de, welcome of, in Paris, IX 562; suspicions against, 572; at Bordeaux, 617; X 62
—— Bastard of, Grand Prior of Malta (son of Henry II), III 19
—— Ant. Charles Cousseau, Bishop of, XI 473
Angra, garrison of, X 323 sq.; English mercenaries at, 327
—— Pequeña, acquired by Germany, XII 41; 160 sq.
Angria, admiral of the Maratha fleet, VI 531
Angrogne (Piedmont), Conference of Waldenses at (1532), II 289
Anguilla, colonised by the English, V 687
Anguillara, sale of, to Virginio Orsini, I 110; recovered by Alexander VI, 233
—— Giovanni Andrea della, the *Metamorphoses*, III 471
Angus, Archibald Douglas, 6th Earl of, marriage of, with Margaret Tudor, I 485; II 453 sqq., 560
—— William Douglas, 10th Earl of, III 551
Anhalt, sufferings of the principality of, IV 418
—— House of, III 704, 712, 715, 725; Gustavus Adolphus and, IV 207; V 618

Anhalt-Bernburg, revolutionary movement in, xi 150
—— extinction of House of, x 343
—— Alexander Karl, Duke of, xi 150
—— Alexius, Duke of, x 373
—— Anne, Princess of (Countess Anne of Bentheim), iii 717
—— Prince Christian I of, iii 712, 717, 719; negotiations of, 721–6; 730–2, 734; diplomatic efforts of, iv 1; the guiding spirit of the Palatine clique, 12; 16 sqq.; and the Elector Palatine, 29, 33; with Mansfeld, 64; and the battle of Prague, 65 sq.; 68; the "Chancery" of, 3, 69 sq.; end of political importance of, 71
—— Prince Christian, the younger, iv 65 sq.
Anhalt-Dessau, and the Germanic Confederation, x 344
—— John George I, Duke of, iii 717
—— Leopold, Duke of, x 373
—— Leopold IV, Duke of, xi 150
—— Prince Leopold of, vi 206 sq.; 210; 213; 215 sq.; 244
—— Prince Moritz of, vi 262; 268; 284; 286; 289
Anhalt-Köthen, revolutionary movement in, xi 150
—— extinction of House of, x 343
—— Ferdinand, Duke of, and the Prussian tariff treaty, x 372 sq.
—— Wolfgang, Prince of, ii 196, 205, 215
Anhalt-Zerbst, Prince Christian August of, vi 657
—— Princess Elizabeth of, vi 316; 657 sqq.
—— Princess Sophia Augusta Frederica of. *See* Catharine II, Tsarina
Anhausen, Protestant Union founded at (1608), iii 725
Anholt, island of, seized (1809), ix 236
—— Johann Jakob, Freiherr von, *afterwards* Count of, Tilly's lieutenant, iv 79, 85; 162
Anhui, disturbances in, xii 517
Aniello, Tommaso (Masaniello), heads insurrection in Naples, iv 657 sq.; death of, *ib.*
Anjala, vi 778; 780; confederation of, 782
Anjou, annexed to the French Crown, i 396; the League in, iii 663; customs of, v 13; scarcity in, vi 162
—— House of, i 396
—— Charles, Count of, King of Sicily, iii 464 sq.
—— Francis of Valois, Duke of Alençon, Duke of, and the marriage with Queen Elizabeth, iii 17 sq., 238; and the Netherlands, 249, 252 sq.; inaugurated Duke of Brabant, 254–8, 501 sq.; 669; death of, 288, 617
—— Gaston-Jean-Baptiste, Duke of. *See* Orleans
—— Henry of Valois, Duke of. *See* Henry III, King of France

Anjou, Louis I, Duke of, i 108
—— Louis III, Duke of, i 108
—— Philip, Duke of. *See* Philip V, King of Spain
—— René, Duke of, King of Naples, etc., i 108, 396
Anna, Anne, St, the cult of, in Germany, ii 107, 114
Anna, Anne:—
—— Empress, consort of Matthias, iv 1; death of, 25
—— (of Hungary and Bohemia), Empress, consort of Ferdinand I, i 318; ii 198
—— Queen of Great Britain and Ireland, party government under, Vol. v, Chap. xv; 63; 211; marriage of, 230; 247; 262; and the Act of Settlement, 275; and the Union, 297 sqq.; and the peace negotiations, 417, 430; and Marlborough, 428; 429; 441; 451; illness and death of, 459 sq., 610; vi 6; and the succession, 8, 10 sqq.; illness of, 15; death of, 17 sq., and the Scottish peers, 93; and the Union; 96; 97; 815 sq.
—— (Boleyn), Queen of England, second consort of Henry VIII, marriage of, ii 67; 429 sqq., 439 sqq.; trial and execution of, 445
—— (of Cleves), Queen of England, fourth consort of Henry VIII, ii 237, 239, 450 sq.
—— (of Denmark), Queen of England, consort of James I, iii 551; estranged from the Protestant faith, iv 89
—— (of Austria), Queen of France (Infanta), consort of Louis XIII, iii 538; 547, 684; marriage of, iv 119; Richelieu Grand Almoner to, 123; relations of Châteauneuf with, 142; former adherents of, 596; Mazarin and, 597, 608 sq., 702; Anne di Gonzaga and, 610; affronted by Condé, 612; 614 sq., Regency of, 593, 659; the marriage of Louis XIV and, 660; v 72; 376 sq.
—— Duchess of Britanny, Queen of France, consort of Charles VIII and Louis XII, Maximilian and, i 302, 395, 450; Charles VIII marries, 111, 450, 467; Louis XII and, 483; Henry VII and, 466; death of, 483
—— Queen of Holland, consort of William II, xi 664
—— (de Candale), Queen of Hungary, consort of Wladislav II, i 336
—— (Korolewna), Queen of Poland, iii 87–9, 97; crowned with Stephen Báthory (1576), 99
—— (of Styria), Queen of Poland, consort of Sigismund III, iii 699, 714
—— Tsarina of Russia, v 556 sq.; vi 195; and Poland, 196 sq.; reign of, 301 sqq.; 312 sq.; 665; 672; 760; death of, 228, 309
—— Tsaritsa of Russia, consort of Vladimir, v 483

Anna, Anne, *contd.*:—
—— (of Austria), Queen of Spain, fourth consort of Philip II, marriage of, III 175, 177; intercession of, 227 sq.; death of, 490, 500, 699
—— Duchess of Bavaria, VI 229
—— de Beaujeu. *See* Bourbon
—— Feodorovna (of Coburg), consort of the Tsarevich Constantine, X 436
—— Grand Duchess of Russia, Napoleon the suitor of, IX 486
—— Leopoldovna. *See* Brunswick-Wolfenbüttel, Princess of
—— (of Egmont), first wife of William of Orange. *See* Orange
—— (of Saxony), second wife of William of Orange. *See* Orange
—— Petrovna *or* Tsesarevna. *See* Holstein-Gottorp, Anne, Duchess of
Annam, China and, XI 802; affairs in (1787–1902), XII 523 sqq.; France and, 4, 131 sq.; 536
Annapolis (Maryland), Convention at (1786), VII 244, 312, 314
—— (Nova Scotia), settlement at, VII 71 sq., 111; destroyed (1613), 72; 75; recovered, 89; taken by Sidgwick (1654), 111; destroyed (1704), 112
—— Basin, Nova Scotia, American fishing vessel seized in, VII 659
Annebaut, Claude de, baron de Retz, admiral and marshal of France (d. 1552), II 78, 97, 460; Venetian mission of, III 115; dismissed by Seigniory, 116
Annecy, Charles Emmanuel at, III 420; added to France, IX 564, 576
Annenkoff, Michael, Russian general, XI 629; and the Samarkand railway, XII 343
Annesley Bay, expedition to, XI 753
Annone, capture of, by French (1499), I 121
Annunzio, Gabriele di, XII 13
Anrep, von, Russian politician, XII 376
Ansbach, re-united to Baireuth, V 622; margravate of, VI 633; 704; principality of, reverts to Prussia (1792), VIII 530; proposed cession of, to Austria, 534; French army marches through, IX 255, 256; cession of, to Bavaria, 262, 264, 265, 267, 656
—— Margraves, etc. of. *See* Brandenburg-Ansbach
Anselme, Jacques-B.-M. de, French general, VIII 437
—— Provençal adventurer, III 408
Anson, George Anson, 1st Viscount, VI 75; 248; 250; First Lord of the Admiralty, 419; 424; death of, 427; X 273
—— George, General, in India, XI 746
Anstett, Baron Hans P., Russian diplomatist at the Congress of Vienna, IX 586
Anstruther, Sir Robert, IV 89
Antananarivo, French troops at, XII 130
Antarctic, expeditions to the, XII 815

Antella, Lamberto della, betrays Medicean conspiracy, I 175
Antibes, the Young Pretender at, VI 110; 150; 159 sq.
Anticosti, placed under Newfoundland government, X 685
Anti-Erasmistas, in Spain, II 401
Antietam, battle of (1862), VII 481 sqq., 591
Anti-Eugeniani, secret society, in Milan, X 111
Antigua captured by the French, V 110; 687; VI 454; cotton-growing in, XII 654
Anti-Jacobin, The, X 580, 700
Antilles, British successes in, VI 421; French colonial expedition to, IX 80; Missiessy sails for, 221; administration of, X 248; Spanish trade with, 275
Anti-Martinists, III 344
Anti-Masons, VII 379
Antiparos surrendered by Venice to Turks, III 116
Antivari, captured by Montenegrins, XII 390; 392; Treaty of Berlin and, 396 sq.; 414
—— bay of, XII 427 sq.
Antoine, François-P.-N., member of the Directory of Insurrection, VIII 232
Antologia, Italian review, X 128
Antonelle, Pierre-Antoine, Marquis de, VIII 504
Antonelli, Count, XII 240
—— Giacomo, Cardinal, papal Secretary of State, X 156; XI 93; Napoleon III and, 128; 378; 389; 392; character of, 705; 709; 712; and the dogma of Infallibility, 722
Antonino (St). *See* Florence, Archbishops of
Antonio, Don, of Portugal, III 34; English expedition for, 317 sq.; vicissitudes of, 500 sq., 511
Antonius, Lutheran preacher in Norway, II 618
Antonovich, Ivan, claimant to the Russian throne, VI 660; 680
Antony (Antoine) of Bourbon (King-consort of Navarre). *See* Bourbon
—— King of Saxony, X 374
Antraigues, Emmanuel-Louis-Henri de Launay, Comte de, VIII 509; 511
Antrim, English Colony in, III 601; the Steelboys in, VI 491
—— Alexander Macdonnell, 3rd Earl of, V 307
—— Randal MacDonnell, 2nd Earl and 1st Marquis of, taken prisoner in Ulster, IV 316; promises to attack Argyll, 520; army and, 522; transports Irish troops into Scotland, 527
Antung, XII 511; Boxers at, 519; 583 sq.
Antwerp, commercial rise and importance of, I 429, 459, 507 sqq.; Anjou's attempt on, III 35; Calvinists in, 206; Iconoclastic riot in, 208; William of Orange at, 211; Act of amnesty at, 227; "Spanish

Fury" at, 245–6, 498; Spaniards expelled from, 248; States General at, 249; Thanksgiving service at (1582), 255; "French Fury" at, 256; remains faithful to William of Orange, 257–8; Philip II at, 480; bullion landed at, 493; crowning of Anjou as Duke of Brabant at, 502; threatened by Maurice of Nassau, 538; Peace negotiations transferred to, 540; truce signed at (1609), 558, 642; taken by Parma, 618–9; trade of, 630, 640; v 199; 407; 457; surrenders to Marlborough (1706), 416; conference at (1713), 458 sq.; siege of, vi 246; 247; 641; and the navigation of the Scheldt, 642; 644 sqq.; disturbances in, 651; defences of, viii 281; seminary at, closed, 327; 418; Council of Allies at (1793), 429; Pichegru captures (1794), 436; port improvements at, ix 120; and the Walcheren expedition, 358; prosperity of, x 522, 533; Prince of Orange at (1830), 535, 537; plots at, 539; siege of (1832), 543; 759; the *Regulation* of, xi 672; port of, *ib.*; 674

Anwar-ud-din, Nawáb of the Carnatic, vi 539

Ányos, Paul, Hungarian poet, xi 422

Anzengruber, Ludwig, Austrian novelist and dramatist, xi 412; 415; 420

Anzino, Canon, xii 216

Aosta, occupied by Lanneo (1800), ix 60
—— Duke of. *See* Amadeo I, King of Spain

Aoust, Eustache de, French commander, viii 439

Apa Sahib, Marátha chief, xi 725

Apaffy, Michael, Prince of Transylvania. *See* Transylvania

Apia, German aggression at (1885), vii 662

Apocrypha, early printed editions of the, i 613

Apodaca, Juan Ruiz de, Viceroy of Mexico, x 304

Apolda, Davout marches on, ix 276; Bernadotte at, 277

Apologia of William of Orange, iii 191, 251, 253, 254

Apologie for Poetrie, Sir P. Sidney's, iii 366, 372

Apologists, Greek (Athenagoras, Justin Martyr, Tatian, Theophilus, Clement of Alexandria, Eusebius of Cesarea, Irenaeus, Origen), early printed editions of, i 615–6
—— Latin (Lactantius, Arnobius, Minucius Felix), early printed editions of, i 617

Aportanus, Georgius. *See* Dare, Jurien van der

Apostolato popolare, x 106

Apostolic Fathers (Barnabas, Clement, Ignatius, Polycarp, etc.), early printed copies of, i 614–5

Apostolicum Pascendi, Bull of Clement XIII, vi 593

Appenzell, joins the Swiss confederacy (1513), i 308; Canton of, xi 244; 248; 250 sq.

Appleby, Jacobite force at, vi 101

Appomattox, surrender of Lee at (1865), vii 452, 541 sq.; capture of provisions at, 540

Apponyi, Count Albert, xii 204 sq.; 209
—— Anton Rudolf, Count, at Rome, x 139; at Paris, 495
—— Count George, xi 152

Aprakin, Stephen, Count, Field-marshal, Russian Commander-in-chief, vi 264; 266; 277; 322

Apraksin, Fedor Matveievitch, Russian admiral, v 601 sq.; 613

Apsley, Lord. *See* Bathurst, 2nd Earl

Apu-Capac-Incas, "headchiefs" of the Peruvians, i 45

Apukhtin, Curator of Education in Poland, xii 336

Apulia, Barbarossa descends upon, iii 112; grazing rights on the *tavoliere* of, ix 406

Apulian aqueduct, xii 238

Aquaviva, Cardinal, Spanish protector at the Vatican, vi 110

Aquednok (Rhode Island), settlement of, vii 20, 23 sq.

Aquila, Alvaro de la Quadra, Bishop of, Spanish ambassador in England, ii 563, 582 sq.; iii 265, 480, 590

Aquileia, patriarchate of, vi 606; regained by Austria, ix 660
—— Niccolò Donato, Archbishop of, i 657

Aquinas, St Thomas, influence of, in the Netherlands, i 627; ii 125, 127; influence of, iii 740, 749; his *Summa*, 766; xi 718

Aquisgran, Treaty of, vi 363; 366

Aquitaine, Charles, Duke of Normandy and Berry, Duke of, brother of Louis XI, i 389 sq., 393

Arabi, Ahmad, Pasha, xii 40; 240; War Minister in Egypt, 436 sqq.; 441

Arabia, importance of, in trade, i 28; the Ottomans conquer, 91; Wahabites masters of, ix 385; their successes in, 387; British India and, xi 753; Turkey and, xii 4

Arabian Sea, pirates in, vi 531

Arabs (Spanish), translations of, iii 546

Arad, fortress of, xi 184; Hungarian Government at, 210 sqq.; military executions ("the Arad Martyrs") at, 214

Arago, Étienne, French politician, xi 99
—— François-Jean-Dominique, ix 133; x 499; xi 26; 102; Minister of Marine, 104; 118; 124; xii 782
—— François-Victor-Emmanuel, French politician, xi 600

Aragon, constitution of, i 350 sq., 353; claim of, on Naples, iii 465; Cortes of, 485, 513–4; conflict with Philip II, 488, 496, 516–7; Inquisition in, 488, 514; judicial system of, 513 sqq.; flight of Perez to, 515; Parliament of, iv 643;

Los Velez in, 648; Philip IV and, 650, 652 sq., 654, 658; v 419; invaded by the Allies (1710), 428; vi 136; disaffection in, 145; canal of, 383; insurrection in (1808), ix 436, 438; French operations in, 447, 454, 457; Carlist forces in (1837), x 239 sq.; clerical influence in, xii 258

Arakan, xi 727; ceded to Great Britain, 728; 729; lost by Burma, xii 479

Arakcheieff, Count Alexei A., Russian general and statesman, ix 35; 49, 50; Minister for War, 314; influence of, in Russia, 483; 484, 487; x 416; supports Archbishop Seraphim, 425; oppressive rule of, 427; 428; 437

Aral, Sea of, Russian expedition to, v 544; xi 273

Arana, José. *See* Baena, Duke of

Aranda, Synod of (1473), i 651

—— Pedro Abarca y Bolea, Count of, Spanish statesman, vi 351; 369; 371 sqq.; and peace negotiations, 380; 382; 592; viii 782; xii 691

Arande, Michel de, preacher of Meaux, ii 282 sqq.

Aranjuez, the Spanish Court at, v 376, 391, vi 166; Treaty of, 363; 371; 383; League of, 608; revolution of (1808), ix 430-1; absolutist demonstrations in, x 224; Queen Isabel at, xi 556

Arany, John, Hungarian poet, xi 428 sqq.

Araujo de Lima, Pedro, Regent of Brazil, x 325

Arbitration, extended use of, xii 12; and the United States Civil War, 21 sq. *See also* Law, International

Arboga, Articles of, iv 161-9; Estates meet at, 172

Arbroath, Argyll at, vi 103 sq.

Arbués, Peter, Spanish Inquisitor, xi 715

Arbuthnot, John, English writer, v 70

—— Marriot, Admiral, vi 453

Arcadia, insurrection in, xi 279

Arcadia, Sidney's, iii 371

Archangel, Dutch factory at, iii 632; v 531; leather exports from, 534; Orthodox mission in province of, x 422

"Archdukes, the" (Archduke Albert of Austria and the Infanta Isabel Clara Eugenia), iii 536-40, 685. *See* Albert, Archduke

Archdukes (the five sons of Maximilian II), iii 698; family compact of (1606), 720

Archenholz, Johann Wilhelm von, German historian, viii 773

Archimedes, v 707 sq.

Archinard, occupies Timbuktu, xii 129

Archivio Storico, founded, xii 842

Arcimboldo, Giovanni Angelo. *See* Milan, Archbishop of

Arcis-sur-Aube, battle of (1814), ix 552

Arco, Duke of, vi 166

Arcola, fighting at (1796), viii 579 sq.

Arçon, Chevalier Jean-Claude-Eléonore le Michaud de, vi 379 sq.

Arcos, revolt at (1820), x 216

—— D. Rodrigo Ponz de Léon, Duke of, Viceroy of Naples, iv 656; flight of, 657

Arcot, seized by Clive, vi 541; 543; 576

—— Nawábs of. *See* Mohammad Ali and Azím-ud-daulah

Arctic Ocean, and the North-East passage, xii 792 sqq.

Arcueil, Huguenots at, iii 4

Ardagh, Sir John Charles, xii 722

Ardahan, Russia and, xii 392, 398

Ardee, James II retires to, v 313

Ardennes, separation of, from France, ix 664; agriculture in, x 750

Ardoch, Jacobite force at, vi 100

Ardres, fall of, iii 670

Ardschel, Island of, iii 109

Areizaga, Spanish general, ordered to march on Madrid, ix 455; troops of, flee to Murcia, 456

Arellano, Cristóbal de, Spanish reformer, ii 406

Aremberg, Count Jan van Ligne of, iii 9, 194, 211, 223, 536

—— William of. *See* La Marck, William de

Aréna, Barthélemy, Jacobin, arrested, ix 17

Arenales, Juan Antonio Alvarez de, x 293

Areniti, Constantin, military adviser of Maximilian I, i 133

Areopagus, London Literary Club, iii 369

Aresen, Jon. *See* Holum, Bishop of

Aretin, J. A. von, ix 595

Aretino, Cristoforo, ii 16

—— Pietro, ii 17, 28, iii 459, 468

Arezzo, rebellion of (1510), i 193 sq.

—— Gentile di, Italian scholar, ii 16

Argall, Sir Samuel, deputy governor of Virginia, vii 110

Argaum (Argáon), victory of Wellesley at, ix 440, 726

Argenson, Count Marc-Pierre de Voyer de, Minister of War, vi 334; 338; 348

—— Marc-René de Voyer de, Chancellor of France (d. 1721), vi 129; x 45; 61; 65; and the plots of 1820-2, 68, 76; 485; 491

—— René-Louis de Voyer de Paulmy, Marquis of, minister and economist (d. 1757), Foreign Minister, vi 110; 113; 160 sq.; 243 sqq.; fall of, 247; 329; and Benedict XIV, 591; viii 9, 12; his career and principles, 16, 19, 21, 27; x 770

Argenteau. *See* Mercy-Argenteau, F. C.

Argentine Republic, independence of, x 287, 293, 301; war of, with Brazil (1825-8), 301, 325; affairs in (1833-1904), xii 680 sqq.; 672; and Paraguay, 674; Brazil and, 676; 679; development of, 690; 692; foreign capital in, 694; 701; boundary arbitration by, 722, 727; 734

Argos, French occupation of, xi 277

Argüelles, Augustin, x 218; 222; appointed guardian to Queen Isabel, 242

Argyll, Archibald Campbell, 3rd Duke of (Earl of Islay), vi 99

—— Archibald Campbell, 4th Earl of, ii 457

—— Archibald Campbell, 5th Earl of, the Scotch Covenant supported by, ii 558, 573; iii 270-1, 273, 550

—— Archibald Campbell, 8th Earl, later Marquis, of, Presbyterianism and, iv 339; 347; at the General Assembly at Glasgow, 500; "Plotters" and, 505; Cromwell and, 350, 508; crowns Charles II at Scone, 510; 520; execution of, v 282

—— Archibald Campbell, 9th Earl of, v 229; 232; and the Scottish Test Act, 287; execution of, 289

—— George Douglas Campbell, 8th Duke of, xii 23; resigns office, 39; 746

—— John Campbell, 2nd Duke and 11th Earl of, v 298; 476; vi 96; and the Earl of Mar's rising, 99 sq., 102

Argyropoulos, Johannes, Greek professor at Florence, i 543; ii 16

Ariosto, Alfonso, iii 462

—— Ludovico, ii 11, 15; 28; iii 457-62, 466; *Orlando Furioso*, ii 19; iii 469, 471

Arista, Mariano, Mexican general, vii 395

Aristophanes, Hungarian translation of, xi 429

Aristotle, Gemistos Plethon and the study of, ii 701; Pomponazzi and the study of, 702 sqq.; influence of, iii 740, 745, v 707 sq.; 712; 736; xii 704

Arisugawa, Prince, Japanese Minister, xi 834; 857

Arizona, ceded to the United States (1848), vii 397

Arkansas, enters the Union (1836), vii 413, 421; and secession, 453-581, 603; in the Civil War, 462; emancipation in, 595, 598; new government set up in, 625; becomes Democratic, 642; population of, 695, 711

Arklow, Parnell at, xii 83

Arkwright, Sir Richard, vii 374; x 735

Arlanges, General de, in Algeria, x 504

Arles, clamours for Papal protectorate, iii 416; the plague at, vi 128; and the States General, viii 125; the "White Terror" at, 387

Arleux, fort at, taken by Marlborough, v 431

Arlington, Henry Bennet, Earl of, v 100; 113; 152 sq.; 198; and the Triple Alliance, 200; signs the Treaty of Dover, 204; 205; created Earl, 207; 208 sq.; and the Test Act, 210; and the Prince of Orange, 213 sq.; grants in Virginia made to, vii 9

Armada, The Spanish, *see* Vol. iii, Chap. ix; Sixtus V and, 436; equipment, despatch and catastrophe of, 505 sqq.; v 326

Armagh, Bagenal's defeat at, iii 530; Cathedral of, garrisoned, 590; victory of Tyrone near (1598), 607; plantation of, 614; resists English allotment, 615; the Oakboys' rising near, vi 490; Catholics in, x 644

Armagnac, Jacques de, Duke of Nemours. *See* Nemours

—— Jean V, Count of, treachery and death of, i 396 sq., 415

—— Louis de, Duke of Nemours. *See* Nemours

Armagon, fort at, iv 742

Armed Neutrality, the first (1780), vi 449, 460, ix 42 sqq.; the second (1800), 46 sqq.

Armella, Nicole, French mystic, v 762

Armellini, Carlo, Triumvir in Rome, xi 94

Armenia, the Elector Palatine and, v 660; geographical situation of, vi 528; Russia and, x 545; xii 10; 37

Armenians, xii 342; 393; the Treaty of Berlin and, 398 sq.; 415 sqq.

Arménonville, Joseph-J.-B. Fleurian de, French Keeper of the Seals, vi 162

Armenteros, Tomas, secretary of Margaret of Parma, iii 195-6, 198, 206, 207

Armfelt, Baron Gustaf Maurice von, Swedish statesman, vi 778; plot of, ix 38; 46; 487; Governor-General of Finland, x 433, 435

—— Baron Karl Gustaf von, Swedish general, v 609

Armies, their conditions, organisation etc., 16th century barbarities of, iii 105, 111; use of Spanish military treatises for, 548; Austrian, in 1809, ix 346 sq.; in 1813, 522; Egyptian, reform in, xii 447 sq.; English, under Henry VIII, ii 473; the Army Plot (1641), iv 288-9, 291; in 1642, 302 sqq.; Cromwell's Ironsides, 312; reform of, and the Self-denying Ordinance, 325 sqq.; the New Model in the field, 329 sqq.; political and military action of, during the years 1645-9, *see* Chap. xi *passim*, 336-55; Cromwell's Major-Generals, 441 sq.; 542 sqq.; question of a standing army, v 113; Wellington's, of 1815, ix 622; Act of Gladstone's first Ministry and following Acts, xii 25 sq.; attempts at reform during the last few years, 59 sq.; Indian, Lord Curzon's reforms in, 493; European in general, burden of, 7 sq.; Flemish, under Philip the Good and Charles the Bold, i 432; under Mary of Burgundy, 439; French, early misrule and reform in, under Charles VII and his successors, i 411 sqq.; in the earlier 16th century, ii 96 sq.; under Henry IV, iii 691 sq.; under Louvois, v 18 sq.; under Louis XV, vi 269; Choiseul's reforms in, 348 sq.; under Louis XVI, viii 51 sq.; and the constitution of 1791, 207; at the opening of the wars of the Revolution, 401 sqq.; reorganisation of, 432 sq.; change of spirit

in (*c.* 1795), 445 sq.; the Law of Conscription, 518 sq.; Conscription under the First Empire, IX 114 sqq.; strength of, in 1808–9, 345; the Grand Army of 1812, 488 sq., 498, 506; in 1813, 508, 522; Napoleon's, in 1815, 618 sq.; reorganised (1832), X 487; under Louis Napoleon, XI 291; in 1870, XI 580 sqq.; since 1870, XII 96 sq.; Italian, of recent years, 233 sq.; Japanese (1904), 578; the Ottoman, constitution of, I 98 sqq.; under Solyman the Magnificent, III 126 sq.; Prussian, organised by the Great Elector, V 642 sq., by Frederick I, 669; under Frederick William I, VI 213 sqq.; remodelling of the (from 1807), IX 331 sqq.; in 1813, 510; Blücher's, of 1815, 623; in 1870, XI 579; Russian, the *Strieltzy*, and Peter the Great; V 523 sqq.; in 1812, IX 489 sq., in 1813, 509, 522; in and after the revolutionary wars, X 415 sqq.; military colonies, 415 sq.; under Alexander II, XI 623 sq.; reorganised (1874), XII 295; (1904) East of Lake Baikal, 577 sq.; Savoyard, under Emmanuel Philibert, III 411; of the Spanish Indies, X 256 sq.; the Spanish, in recent years, XII 258 sqq.; Swedish, under Gustavus Adolphus, IV 193 sq.; after his death, 228 sqq.; organisation of, under Charles XI, V 578; reformed in the late 19th century, XII 276 sq.

Arminius, Jacobus (Jakob Herman), and the doctrine of predestination, II 717; III 646–7; IV 717

Arnau, Austrian position at, VI 706

Arnauld, Angélique, Abbess of Port-Royal, V 83
—— Antoine, Pascal and, IV 795; Cartesianism and, V 73; 83 sq.; exile and death of, 89

Arnauts, in Servia, XII 416

Arndt, Ernst Moritz, IX 328; 335, 589; X 352; 365; 403 sq.; XI 49; 164; 168; 199; XII 818
—— Johann, theologian, V 758 sq.

Arneth, Reichsritter Alfred von, XII 825; 829

Arni, Clive at, VI 541; 577

Arnim, *or* Arnheim, Hans Georg von, IV 101; in Pomerania, 104, 106; besieges Stralsund, 107 sq.; 109; 187; sent to the Polish frontier, 192; in Saxony, 204; 206; in Bohemia, 209; 211; 213; 215 sq.; 219; commands Saxon forces in Silesia, 221; commands Brandenburg troops, 225; Wallenstein and, 231, 234 sqq., 240 sq.; Silesian scheme of, 236; march of, towards the Oder, 237; 243; victory of, at Liegnitz, 244; 247; negotiations at Pirna and, 252
—— Count Harry, German ambassador in Paris, XII 140; 149
—— Heinrich Alexander, Baron von, Prussian Foreign Minister, XI 159

Arnim, Ludwig Achim von, German Romanticist, X 401 sqq.; goes to Berlin, 404; 405 sqq.; XII 818; 822

Arnim-Boitzenburg, Count Adolf Heinrich von, XI 157 sqq.

Arnim-Heinrichsdorf, Count Heinrich Friedrich von, Prussian Foreign Minister, XI 200

Arnold of Brescia, and Zurich, II 311
—— Benedict, American general, VII 170 sq., 215, 226, 230
—— Gottfried, historian, V 760 sqq.
—— Matthew, the poems of, XI 354 sq.; 365
—— Dr Thomas, and convict colonies, XI 794; XII 835
—— water-miller in the Neumark, VI 714

Arnold-Forster, Hugh Oakeley, and army reform, XII 59

Arnoldi, Wilhelm, Bishop of Trier. *See* Trier

Aron, Peter, Prince of Moldavia, I 83

Arques, battle of (1589), III 48, 658, 660

Arquien, Henri de Lagrange, Marquis de, V 356; 360
—— Mary de. *See* Mary d'Arquien, Queen of Poland

Arrabbiati, I 169 sq., 174

Arran, James Hamilton, 2nd Earl of. *See* Châtelherault, Duke of
—— James Hamilton, 3rd Earl of, II 557, 559; proposed as husband to Queen Elizabeth, 574 sq., 580
—— Captain James Stewart, Earl of (*cr.* 1581), III 550

Arras, Peace of (1482), I 229, 391, 395, 399, 445; Treaty of (1435), 389, 418, 423, II 36; Treaty of (1579), III 251; attempted surprise of (1596), 671; Condé defeated before, IV 619; the "Terror" at, VIII 372; fortress of, XI 607
—— Bishop of. *See* Granvelle, Cardinal

Arrazola, Lorenzo, Spanish statesman, XI 566

Arrêt de Mérindol (1540), against the Waldenses, II 289

Arrhenius, Svante, Swedish scientist, XII 280

Arrighi, Jean-Toussaint, French general, the duchy of Padua granted to, IX 111

Arrow, The (*lorcha*), incident of, XI 325, 815

Ars, Louis de, French general, I 125, 127

Arsilli, Francesco, the *De Poetis Urbanis*, II 15

Art and architecture, English, of late years, XII 64; European, in general, in the latest age, 13 sq.; French, in the 15th century, I 414 sq.; under the First Empire, IX 133 sqq.; painting, sculpture and music of the Restoration, X 103; in the 19th century, XI 528; German, Maximilian I and, I 326 sq.; in Holland, revival of Dutch painting in recent years, XII 249 sq.; Italian, in general, effects of the French invasions (from 1494) on, I

143; and the Italian Renaissance, II 14 sqq., 27 sq.; after the French Revolution, x 129 sq.; in the Netherlands, under the Burgundian Dukes, I 432 sq.; in Spain, in the early 16th century, 382 sq.; under Philip IV, IV 662 sqq.; in Tuscany, under Cosimo de' Medici, III 394; in Rome, especially under Sixtus V, 438 sqq.; Venetian, I 284 sq.; in the United States, VII 748 sq.

Arta, bridge of, XII 403

Arta-Volo, frontier of Greece, x 202, 204

Artevelde, Jacques van, I 426

Arthur, Chester Alan, President of the United States, VII 650, 652

Articles of Religion, The Forty-Two, II 508; the Thirty-Nine, 587 sq.; the Marburg, 209

Artico, Filippo, Bishop of Asti. *See* Asti

Articuli cleri, III 563

Artigas, José, x 300

Artista, El, Spanish periodical, x 241

Artois, ceded by France (1493) to Burgundy, I 229, 392, 395, 451, 454; claim of Francis I to, II 72 sq.; march on, 76; France renounces claim to (1529), 102; French designs on, III 16, 34; Catholics in, 251; raids into, 666, 671; loss of greater part of, to Spain, IV 620, 660 sqq.; Estates of, v 4; VIII 39; agricultural population in, 61

—— Charles-Philippe, Comte de. *See* Charles X, King of France

Arundel, Henry Fitz-Alan, 12th Earl of, II 497 sqq., 505, 525; and Philip II, III 281

—— of Wardour, Henry Arundel, 3rd Baron, v 202; 204; 220

—— and Surrey, Thomas Howard, 2nd Earl of, confinement and release of, IV 264 sq.; at Vienna, 276

—— Thomas, Archbishop of Canterbury, II 464

Aruwhimi river, exploration on, XII 812

Asan, XII 510; Japanese occupation of, 511

Asben, explorers at, XII 810

Asbjörnsen, Peter Christian, Norwegian writer, XI 701

Aschaffenburg, taken by the Swedes, IV 208; "Pragmatic Army" at, VI 238; Jourdan repulsed at, VIII 497; granted to Dalberg, IX 414; acquisition of, by Bavaria, 658

Ascham, Roger, and classical studies at Cambridge, I 580; and John Frederick of Saxony, II 275

Aschersleben, castle of, v 618

Ascoli, Trojano Marulli, Duke of, x 112

Asél, Anton, Spanish Reformer, II 408

Aselli, Gaspar, anatomist, v 727

Asényeff, Russian journalist, XII 298

Ashbourne, Edward Gibson, Lord, Lord Chancellor of Ireland, XII 83

Ashburnham, John Ashburnham, 2nd Earl of, VI 428

Ashburton, river, gold discovered on, XII 619

—— Alexander Baring, Lord, and the Webster-Ashburton Treaty (1842), VII 391 sq.; x 355; 615

—— John Dunning, Lord, as Solicitor-general, VI 439; 442; 455; 459

Ashinoff, Cossack adventurer, XII 343

Ashley, Anthony, Lord. *See* Shaftesbury

Ashta, fight at, XI 726

Asia, Russian policy in, v 544 sq.; a market for English products, IX 363; Russian advances in, XI 272 sqq., 630, 632; European influence in, XII 4; Russia and England in, 94; French colonisation in, 159; bubonic plague in, 486 sq.; modern exploration in, 792 sqq.

—— Central, rivalry of Great Britain and Russia in (1833), x 556, 558, XII 343; 373

—— Eastern, Germany and, XII 160

—— Minor, insurrection in, III 701; Turkey and, XII 4; Germany and, 10; the Russo-Turkish War in, 389; the Treaty of Berlin and, 398; 416; massacres in, 417; 418; archaeological research in, 774

Asiatic Company of Denmark, VI 738

Asiento, secured for French traders, v 403; England and, 445; 455; 684; VI 25; the English South Sea Company and, 64 sqq.; 157; 178; 181; 363

Asiu, explorers at, XII 810

Aske, Robert, rebellion of (1536), II 446 sq.; 468

Askew, Anne, II 466 sq.

Asparros, André de Foix de, invades Navarre and Castile (1521), I 378

Aspern, battle of (1809), IX 345 sq., 350 sqq.; results of, 352; 353; 401

Aspre, Constantin de, Baron, Austrian general, IX 353; XI 95

Aspromonte, Garibaldi wounded at, XI 534; 535

Asquith, Herbert Henry, Home Secretary (afterwards Prime Minister), XII 49; 750

Assab bay, Italian occupation of, XII 664

Assada Association, IV 731; 746

Assam, XI 727; ceded to Britain, 728; united to Eastern Bengal, XII 495; caravan route to, 793; 796

Assaye, victory of Wellesley at (1803), IX 440; 726

Assche, Marlborough at, v 420

Asseirceira, the Miguelists defeated at (1834), x 336

Assembly of Notables (1527), II 57, 284; (1558), 93; at Fontainebleau (1560), 298. *See also* Council of Notables

Assiette, Col de, Belleisle's march by, VI 245; 362

Assiniboia, district of, XI 776

Assiout, travellers at, XII 805

Assuan, dam of, XII 446; James Bruce at 805

Assyria, researches in, XII 845 sq.

Asti, claimed by Francis I, III 110, claimed by Spain, 400, disorder in, 401, evacuation of, 407; Peace of (1615), IV 129; VI 161; French defeat at, 245

—— Filippo Artico, Bishop of, XI 369

Astley, Sir Jacob (Baron Astley), IV 304; at Naseby, 330; at Stow-on-the-Wold, 335

Aston, Sir Arthur, in Drogheda, IV 533

—— Sir Richard, Irish Chief Justice, VI 490

Astorga, Baird reaches, IX 443; the Emperor at, 445; 448; fall of (1810), 458

Astoria, port of, VII 364

Astrabad, ceded to Russia, V 545

Astrakhan, annexed to Russia, V 479; 494; revolt at (1705), 531; 544; system of recruiting in, X 415

Astronomy, history of. *See* Science

Astruc, Jean, studies of, on the Pentateuch, XII 816

Asturias, arrival in London of deputies from, IX 440; Liberalism in, X 214; revolt in (1820), 216; Riego banished to, 221; the Junta of, 282, 303

—— Prince of the. *See* Ferdinand VII, King of Spain

Asunción, government of, X 246; 269

Atacama, XII 678; frontier dispute in, 679

Atahualpa, Head-chief of the Inca people, X 299

Atalaya, Spanish periodical, X 207

Atbara river, sources of, XII 805

Ath, restored to Spain, V 45, 63; captured by Marlborough (1706), 416

Athabasca, district of, XI 776

Athenry, Cathedral Church of, III 593

Athens, surrendered to the Turks (1457), I 74, 285; captured by the Venetians (1687), V 365; civil war in, XI 642; XII 403; demonstrations at, 408; rising at, 420; 421 sq.

—— Franco Acciaiuoli, Duke of, I 74

Athlone, besieged (1690), V 315, (1691), 317 sq.

—— Godert de Ginkel, 1st Earl of, in Ireland, V 316 sqq.; takes Limerick, 319

Atholl, John Murray, 1st Duke of, VI 92

—— John Stewart, 4th Earl of, III 270, 272, 279

Athos, Mount, V 507 sq.

Atkins, Sir Jonathan, Governor of Barbados, V 690

Atlanta, Sherman's campaign against, VII 514, 521; captured (1864), 522, 523, 526, 579; 551

Atlantic Monthly, VII 746

Atlantic Ocean, submarine telegraph under, XI 346

Atlas, Mount, XII 805

Atouguia, Count of, executed, VI 386

Atrek river, Russia and, XII 343

Atterbury, Francis, Bishop of Rochester, VI 44

Attrition, doctrine of, in later Middle Ages, II 126; distinguished from contrition, 126

Attwood, Thomas, and the Birmingham Political Union, X 612, 615; in Parliament, 656; 675; and the Chartist movement, 683

Atuntse, caravan route to, XII, 793; 796

Auber, Daniel-François-Esprit, X 103

Aubert-Dubayet, J.-B.-Annibal, Minister of War, VIII 490

Aubigné, Theodore-Agrippa de, III 62, 64; V 20

Aubigny, Esmé Stewart, Seigneur de. *See* Lennox

—— Stuart de, French general (1494), I 113, 123 sq., 155

Aubray, Sieur de, leader of the *Politiques*, III 70

Aubry, Émile, French politician, XI 492

—— François, member of the National Convention, VIII 442, 512

Aubusson, Pierre de, Grand Master of the Knights of St John, I 84, 86

Auch, Republican attack on, XI 137

Auchmuty, Sir Samuel, at Buenos Ayres, IX 753

Auchterarder, Jacobite force at, VI 100; 102

Auchy, member of the Extraordinary Junta for Tuscany, IX 399; 419

Auckland, capital of New Zealand, XI 793 sq.; province of, 796

—— George Eden, 1st Earl of, Governor-General of India, XI 731 sqq.; 743

—— William Eden, 1st Baron, VI 471; VIII 284, 287 sq.; British Minister at the Hague, 294, 301; 429; and Ireland, IX 699; 702

Audéoud, and the conquest of Dahomey, XII 129

Audijos, leader of the rising in Gascony, V 9

Audley, Edmund, Bishop of Salisbury, books collected by, I 597

—— Thomas, succeeds More as Chancellor, II 438

Auerbach, Berthold, German novelist, XI 418; 420

Auersperg, Prince Adolf von, XII 188 sq.; 192; 194

—— Count Anton Alexander von (" Anastasius Grün "), XI 173; 413

—— Prince Carlos von, XII 185 sq.

—— Prince Johann Weichard von, Austrian statesman, V 349; 352

Auerstädt, Prussian army at, IX 275; battle of (1806), 276 sqq., 326; Scharnhorst at, 332

Auerswald, Alfred von, Prussian statesman, XI 159

—— Hans Adolf Erdmann von, Prussian general, XI 169

—— Rudolf von, Prussian Minister-President, XI 166, 191

Aufklärung, in Switzerland, VI 625; penetrates Poland, 671; in Russia, under Catharine II, 686 sqq.; Frederick the Great and, Chap. XX *passim*; the Rosicrucians and, 726 sq.; in Germany, VIII 772 sqq.

Augereau, Pierre-François-Charles, Duc de Castiglione, Marshal of France, VIII 440, 444, and the *coup d'état* (1797), 508 sq., 512, 591; in Italy, 564, 566 sqq., 574 sq., 578; IX 66; 89, 252; marches from Brittany, 253; sent to Tyrol, 256; surrender of Jellachich to, 258; in Swabia, 258; 262; commands the 7th corps, 275; at Thorn, 281; 284; at Eylau, 286; 287; captures the fortress of Hostalrich, 457; superseded by Macdonald, 464; on the Council of War, 565

Aughrim, battle of (1691), V 261, 318

Augier, Guillaume-Victor-Émile, French dramatist, XI 516 sq.; 548

Augila, Hornemann at, XII 806

Augsburg, decline of, I 507; Lutheranism adopted by, II 233 sq.; Zwinglianism at, 216; the *Interim* in, 264, 266; submits to Charles V (1547), 258; Luther at, 133; Catholics in, III 158, IV 12, 77; saved by Werth, 391; Treaty of Ulm and, *ib.*; Swedish army in, 214; and the Peace of Westphalia, 413; commercial state of, 420; Bavaria and, V 52; 408; 410; Alliance (1686), 35, 52 sq., 235, 654; proposed Congress at, VI 343; occupation of, by the French, IX 64; Napoleon reaches, 255; annexed by Bavaria, 262, 269

—— Diets of (1500), I 308, (1510), 319, (1518), II 40, 133, (1525), 191, 196, (1530), 25, 211, 213, (1547), 84, 262 sq., (1555), 276, 672, (1559), III 163, (1566), 172 sq., (1582), 706; Recess of (1530), 214, (1555), 277; Confession of (1530), 211 sqq., III 141, 163, 174, 180, 210, 740, IV 68, 111, 200, 412; Religious Peace of (1555), II 89, 277 sq., III 140 sqq., 162 sqq., 714, 718, 723 sqq., 754, IV 3, 109, 410, 676, V 627

—— Henry von Knorringen, Bishop of (d. 1646), III 723; IV 110

—— Otto Truchsess of Waldburg, Cardinal-Bishop of, at the Diet of Augsburg (1555), II 276; III 161; 707

Augusta (Georgia), settlement of, 62; occupied by the British (1778), VII 219, abandoned, *ib.*

—— Maria Louisa, Princess of Weimar, German Empress, consort of William I, in 1848, XI 159; XII 149

—— Princess of Bavaria, wife of Eugène Beauharnais, IX 265

—— Princess of Wales, VI 417; 423; 434

—— Victoria, Empress of Germany, XII 165

Augustenburg, Christian, Duke of, XI 226 sq.; 696

Augustenburg, Prince Christian Augustus of. *See* Schleswig-Holstein-Augustenburg

—— Frederick, Duke of, claims on Schleswig-Holstein of, XI 437 sqq.; 477; Prussia and Austria and, 444 sqq.; 448 sq.

Augustine, St, Rule of, II 114; Calvin's relation to, 365; and the Teutonic Renaissance, 712 sq.; the Jansenists and, V 82; 755

Augustinian Eremites, Order of, II 106; history of, 114; University of Wittenberg and, 117; 131; and the Reform movement, 161

Augustinus Triumphus. *See* Triumphus

Augustov, Polish province, X 449; 470

Augustus II, King of Poland (Frederick Augustus I, Elector of Saxony), V 369; King of Poland, 370 sq., 417; 438; and Peter the Great, 526; 555; and Denmark, 580 sq.; and Patkul, 586, 595; joins the league against Sweden (1699), 580, 587; and the great Northern War, 587 sqq.; Charles XII and, 589, 592; deposed, 593; treaty of, with Sweden (1706), 595; and the Emperor Joseph, 596; and the second anti-Swedish league (1709), 602; 603 sq.; 606 sq.; 660; and Frederick I of Prussia, 666; 743; VI 35 sq.; 151; 156; crowned, 191; and Lithuania, 192; 193 sq.; 198; and the Pragmatic Sanction, 202; 239; 303; 665; death of, 166

—— III, King of Poland (Frederick Augustus II, Elector of Saxony), VI 193; 195 sqq.; marriage of, 201; and the Austrian Succession, 228 sq., 231 sq.; 242; and the Convention of Hanover, 244; Frederick the Great and, 251, 254 sq., 266; 303; 310; 346; 665 sq.; 703; and the Peace of Teschen, 707; death of, 200, 353, 628; VIII 522

Aulard, François-V.-Alphonse, historian, XII 833 sq.

Aulic Council. *See* Reichshofrath

Aulich, Louis, Hungarian general, XI 214

Aulick, Commodore, mission of, to Japan, XI 824

Aulnay-Charnisé, Charles de Menou, Sieur de, VII 110 sq.

Aumale, Henry IV in danger of capture at, III 51

—— Caroline, Duchesse de, XI 553

—— Charles of Lorraine, Duke of (son of Claude II), III 46 sq.; 663; 669

—— Claude II of Lorraine, Duke of, II 273; III 5, 12, 19

—— Henri-Eugène-Philippe-Louis d'Orléans, Duc de, XI 33; 505; 553; XII 105; 107; 834

Aumont, Jean de, Marshal of France, III 47

Aungier, Gerald, in India, V 698

Aunis, customs of the, V 13

Aurangábád, Málik Ambar at, VI 515; Wellesley captures (1803), IX 726

Auras, Russian troops at, VI 294; 299

Auratus (Jean Dorat). *See* Dorat

Aurès, revolt of, XII 129

Aurispa, Giovanni, Italian humanist, I 550

Aurungzeb, Moghul Emperor, V 697 sqq.; VI 518 sqq.; and the Marathas, 521 sq.; death of, 523; 532

Ausserrhoden, VI 625

Aussig, Charles of Lorraine at, VI 244; 257

Austen, Jane, novelist, VI 833; XI 360

Austerlitz, battle of (1805), IX 117, 260 sqq.; campaign of, 396; effect of the news of, on Pitt, 684

Austin, John, jurist, IX 160 sq.; X 598

Australasia, development of (1815–70), Vol. XI, Chap. XXVII (4); self-government in, 761; emigration to, XII 63; and Chinese immigration, 508; development of, 618 sqq.; 734 sq.; 805

Australia, trade of, with California, VII 402; colonial empire in, IX 735 sqq.; the wool trade with, X 751, 759 sq.; British policy in, XI 16; 310; 760; Constitutional Act (1850) of, 763; XII 2; and imperial defence, 47; 57; 94; and Germany, 160 sq.; development and progress of, 603 sqq., 618 sqq.; federation of, 631 sqq.; and naval defence, 649, 651; 650; and New Guinea, 666; and the Pacific Islands, 667 sq.; labour legislation in, 751; social movements in, 753, 755, 763

— South, XI 792; a Crown colony, 794; population of, 796, 799; 797 sq.; development and progress of, XII 619 sqq., 624 sqq., 629, 631

— Western, origin of, XI 791; convicts sent to, 795; 797 sq.; population of, 799; development and progress of, XII 619 sqq.; and immigration, 626; 630 sq.; 634; aboriginal population of, 624, 629

Australian Agricultural Company, XI 790

Austria

I   x   Hungary and the Sclavonic kingdoms, *passim*, *(chiefly)* 329–44
        See also here Maximilian I, Emperor-Elect

II   ii   Habsburg and Valois (i), 36–65
    iii   Habsburg and Valois (ii), 66–103
        See also Germany

III   v   The Empire under Ferdinand I and Maximilian II, *passim*, 140–81
    xxi   The Empire under Rudolf II, *passim*, 696–735
        For Austrian relations with Turkey, *see also* iv The Height of the Ottoman Power, *passim*, 104–39

IV   i   The Outbreak of the Thirty Years' War, *passim*, 1–34
    ii   The Valtelline (1603–39), *passim*, 35–63

Austria, *contd.*

IV   iii   The Protestant Collapse (1620–30), *passim*, 64–117
    iv   Richelieu, *passim*, 129, 138, 141 sqq.
    vi   Gustavus Adolphus, *passim*, 190–222
    vii   Wallenstein and Bernard of Weimar (1632–5), *passim*, 223–55
    xiii   The later years of the Thirty Years' War (1635–48), *passim*, 364–94
    xiv   The Peace of Westphalia, *passim*, 395–433
    xxiii   Papal policy (1590–1648), *passim*, 673 sq., 676 sqq.

V   xii   Austria, Poland and Turkey, 338–71
    xiii   The Treaties of Partition and the Spanish Succession, *passim*, 372–400
    xiv   The War of the Spanish Succession and the Peace of Utrecht, *passim*, 401–59

VI   viii   The War of the Austrian Succession, 201–50
    ix   The Seven Years' War, 251–300
    xi   The reversal of alliances and the Family Compact, *passim*, 329–60
    xvi   Italy and the Papacy, *passim*, 586–610
    xviii   Joseph II, 626–56
    xx   Frederick the Great and his successors, *passim*, 702–34

VIII   xi   The European Powers and the Eastern Question, *passim*, 306–37
    xiv   The General War [of the French Revolution], *passim*, 398–446
    xvii   The extinction of Poland (1788–97), *passim*, 521–52
    xxi   The Second Coalition [against the French Revolution], *passim*, 633–64
    xxv   p. 776

IX   iii   The pacification of Europe (1799–1802), *passim*, 55–80
    iv   France and her tributaries (1801–3), *passim*, 81–106
    ix   The Third Coalition, I (1805–6), *passim*, 244–64
    x   The Third Coalition, II (1806–7), *passim*, 265–93
    xi   The Napoleonic Empire at its height (1807–9), *passim*, 294–340
    xii   The War of 1809, 341–60
    xiv   The French dependencies, *passim*, 390–427
    xvii   The War of Liberation (1813–4), 506–54
    xix   The Congress of Vienna, I (1814–5), 576–615

Austria, *contd.*
IX   xxi   The Congress of Vienna, II (1815), 646–71
X   i   The Congresses (1815–22), *passim*, 1–39
     iv   Italy, *passim*, 104–30
     v   The Papacy and the Catholic Church, *passim*, 131–68
     vi   Greece and the Balkan Peninsula, *passim*, 169–204
     xi   The Germanic Federation (1815–40), *passim*, 340–82
     xvii   Mehemet Ali, *passim*, 545–72
XI   iii   Liberalism and Nationality in Germany and Austria (1840–8), 43–64
     iv   Italy in Revolution (1846–9), *passim*, 65–95
     vi   The Revolution and the Reaction in Germany and Austria, I (1848–9), 142–201
     vii   The Revolution and the Reaction in Germany and Austria, II, 202–33
     xiv   Cavour and the Kingdom of Italy (1849–61), *passim*, 366–92
     xv   Austria, Prussia, and the Germanic Confederation
         (1) Reaction and Reorganisation (1852–62), 393–410
         (2) German Literature (1840–70), 411–20
         (3) The National Spirit in Hungarian Literature (1686–1900), 421–31
     xvi   Bismarck and German Unity, *passim*, 432–66
     xix   The completion of Italian Unity, *passim*, 529–49
     xxv   Rome and the Vatican Council, *passim*, 703–23
XII   vii   Austria-Hungary, 174–212
     xiv   The Ottoman Empire and the Balkan Peninsula, *passim*, 381–423

Austria, House of. *See* Habsburg

—— Leopold III, Duke of, I 264, 342

Austro-Hungarian Bank, XII 191; 203

Austruweel, rout of Calvinists at (1567), III 211–2

Auteil, de, French officer in India, VI 541

Auteuil, *idéologues* at, IX 21, 24

Autichamp, Charles de Beaumont, Count de, IX 2; 14

Autos-de-fé, at Seville and Valladolid, II 404, 407 sq.; at Palma, Majorca, 1691, V 375

Autre Église, and battle of Ramillies, V 415 sq.

Autun, revolt of (1595), III 667

Auvergne, III 418

—— Charles de Valois, Count of. *See* Angoulême

Auxerre, Napoleon at, IX 574

—— Jacques Amyot, Bishop of, III 56

Ava, XI 727; British Resident at, 729; 742

Avalos, Costanza de. *See* Amalfi

Avanti, Italian socialist journal, XII 225; 231 sq.

Avaux, Claude de Mesmes, Count of, agent of Richelieu at Stuhmsdorf, IV 365; French plenipotentiary in Germany, 373; negotiations at Hamburg between Salvius and, 377; 397; proposal of, in 1641, 398; at Münster, 402 sq.; at the Hague, 602

—— Jean-Antoine de Mesmes, Count of, French ambassador at the Hague, V 165 sq., 244, 397; in Ireland, 307 sq., 312, 314; 417; in Sweden, 566, 585

Aveiro, Duke of, executed, VI 386

Avellain, Admiral, visits Toulon, XII 98

Avellaneda, Bernardino de, III 322

Avellino, revolt at (1820), X 112

Avenir, Le, founded by Lamennais, X 163; 164

—— *national, Le,* French journal, XI 487

Aventinus, Johannes, Bavarian historian, II 202

Aversa, capitulation of the French at (1528), II 59

—— Carlo Caraffa, Bishop of, nuncio to Emperor Ferdinand II, IV 73, 83; zeal of, 111

—— Giovanni Bernardino di, Italian reformer, II 391

Averysborough, Slocum attacked at (1865), VII 530

Avesnes, acquired by France, V 33

Avignon, Charles IX at, III 7, Henry III at, 25; city of, V 449; the Old Pretender at, VI 27, 104; 128; 594; restored to the Papacy, 595; revolutionary disorder in, VIII 217 sq.; united to France, 217; Marseillais routed at, 348; Napoleon at, 352; the "White Terror" in, 387; compensation demanded for loss of, IX 182; Pius VII banished to, 196; added to France, 564; retained by France, 576; claim of Papacy to, 661; Pius VII and, X 144

Avila, Juan de, Spanish reformer, II 409

—— Juan Alvarez de, Spanish admiral, III 639

—— Sancho de, III 215, 239, 245, 520

Avogadro, Americo, Conte di Quaregna, man of science, XII 769 sq.

Avonmore, Barry Yelverton, 1st Viscount, as Irish Attorney-general, VI 502

Avranches, captured by Montpensier, III 51

—— Jean Bochard, Bishop of, I 637

Avvakum, Russian ecclesiastic, V 509; 524

Awa, *daimiō* of, XI 834; 836; 846; 850; 864

Awans, political faction in Liége, I 422

Axarquia, battle of the (1483), I 358

Axiake. *See* Ochakoff

Axim, taken by the Dutch (1642), IV 759

Ayacucho, battle of, 295 sq., (1824), X 307, XII 689

Ayala, Pedro de (Bishop of Catania), Spanish ambassador in England, I 471

Ayamonte, Rodrigo de Guzman, C. of Saltes, Marquis of, treason and execution of, IV 652 sq.

Aylmer, John, Bishop of London, III 343

Aymara-Quichua (Peruvians), I 38, 45

Ayr, and the Treaty of Union, V 299

Ayrshire, recusants in, V 283 sq.; 285

Ayrton, Acton Smee, First Commissioner of Works, XII 29

Ayscue, Sir George, Admiral, West Indian Islands subdued by, IV 466; 468; 470; in the Downs, 471; defeated by Ruyter off Plymouth, 472; 477

Ayub Khan, XII 37; defeated at Kandahar, 475

Ayuthia, capital of Siam, XII 534 sq.

Azarea, José Nicolas de, Spanish ambassador, IX 77

Azeff, Russian police agent, XII 350; 376

Azeglio, Massimo Taparelli, Marquis de, the *Ricordi*, X 108–9, XI 547; other publications of, X 127; 156; 167 sq.; XI 65; the *Casi di Romagna*, 66 sq., 69, 73; expelled from Florence, 69; 70; the *Lutti di Lombardia*, 80, 546; 84; Minister for Foreign Affairs, 367 sqq.; separates from Cavour, 370 sq.; Ministry of, 371; 373; 529; 548

Azim, son of Dost Mohammad, XII 459

Azim-ud-daulah, Nawáb of Arcot (or the Carnatic), accession of, IX 724

Azím-ul-Umará, at Haidarábád, IX 721; 722

Azoff, conquered by Peter the Great, V 370; 371, 521 sq.; 503; 520; ceded to Russia, 527; 531; 545; 603 sq.; abandoned by Russia, 606; 677; VI 305 sqq.; acquired by Russia, 674

—— Sea of, Russian fleet in, V 527, 605; XI 322

Azores Islands, discovery of, I 12; projects to colonise, 10, 15, 19; Lord Thomas Howard sent to, III 319; Spanish squadron at, 531; Dutch squadron at, 539; British convoys captured at, VI 377; Miguelists in (1828), X 323; Villa Flôr in, 326; Dom Pedro in, 327

Aztecâ ("crane-people"), Mexican tribe, I 39

Baahus, Treaty of Roeskilde and, IV 586

Bábar, Zahirruddin Mahmud, Moghul Emperor, VI 507; career of, 508 sqq.; death of, 510; 514; 524

Babeau, A., on social conditions in France, VIII 63 sq.

Baber, Colborne, in China, XII 797

Babeuf, François-Noël, French communist, VIII 34, 503 sq., 790

Babington, Antony, arrest of, III 291 sq.

Babylonish Captivity, Luther's, III 738

Bacciochi, Élise. *See* Bonaparte, Élise

Bacelli, Alfredo, Italian statesman, XI 228

Bach, Alexander von, Austrian statesman, XI 153; 155; 171; and the Austrian Constitution, 174; Minister of Justice, 176,

190; 179; and Hungary, 181, 183, 398 sq.; 185; resigns, 186; 187; policy of, 215 sq.; Minister of the Interior, 216, 398; 217; 401; dismissed, 403; XII 176; 178 sqq.; 192

Bacher, French President in the Grand Duchy of Frankfort, IX 414

"Back-lane Parliament," of Myles Keon and Wolfe Tone, X 628

Bac-le pass, French troops attacked in, XII 131

Baco de la Chapelle, Mayor of Nantes, VIII 341

Bacon, Anthony, III 335

—— Sir Francis (Viscount St Albans and Baron Verulam), influence of New World discovery on, I 62 sq.; 205; II 691, 706; III 329 sq.; and Essex, 335 sq.; and Puritanism, 347; 553; 557; and Coke, 564 sqq.; fall of, 571–2; 737; 748; and Ireland, IV 513; his *Novum Organum*, V 716, 724 sq.; VI 793; 803

—— Nathaniel, Virginian settler, VII 9

—— Sir Nicholas, becomes Chancellor, II 565, 568; III 280

—— Roger, I 18, 585; works of, 587, 590

Badagry, explorers at, XII 807 sq.

Badajoz, death of Anne of Austria at, III 500; V 416; 456; royal wedding at, VI 166; Treaty of (1801), IX 72, 75, 605; Victor advances on, 449 sq.; army of La Romana at, 460; surrenders to Soult (1811), 462; 463; besieged by Wellington (1811), 466; siege of, abandoned, 467 sq.; captured by Wellington (1812), 471 sq.

Badakshán, province of, VI 518; Russia and, XII 461; 801

Baden, margravate of, invaded by the French, V 57; 418; receives bishopric of Constance, IX 94; the Church in, 201; joins France, 253; 262; Grand Duchy of, 581; and the Congress of Vienna, 649, 651; succession of, and the Allied Powers, X 19; 22; 31; relations of the Papacy with, 148 sq.; and German unity, 342 sq.; and the Germanic Confederation, 344; and Bavaria, 346, 359, 361 sq.; 358; the political position of, 361; Constitution of (1818), 362; 363; and the Carlsbad meeting, 366; and the *Triasidee*, 369; and customs reform, 372; constitutional concessions in, 375; and the press laws, 377; 380; and the Protestant Churches, 382; revolutionary movement in, XI 60 sqq., 144 sq., 152, 192, 218; and the *Vorparlament*, 163; insurrection in, 221; and Prussia, 228; the "Articles" of, 246; 259; and the Schleswig-Holstein question, 438; and the Austro-Prussian war, 457; and the North German Confederation, 460 sq., 464 sq.; and the Franco-German War, 464; and the Papacy, 708; legal code of, XII 150

Baden, House of, III 704; religious attitude of, 159; an original member of the Protestant Union, 725
—— Margraves of:—Charles II, III 150, 164; Christopher I (and of Hochberg), excluded from the Swabian League, I 321; Philibert, at Moncontour, III 12 sq.; Philip I, humane policy of, II 191
—— Charles Frederick, Grand Duke of, x 361
—— Charles (Louis Frederick), Grand Duke of, marries Josephine's niece, IX 265, x 361; and the Congress of Vienna, IX 582; 610 sq.; x 145 sq.; 362
—— Frederick I, Grand Duke of, XI 397; 406
—— Leopold I, Grand Duke of, x 375; XI 60; 145; 218 sq.
—— Frederica Dorothea of, marries Gustavus IV Adolphus of Sweden, IX 38
—— Louisa Caroline (Countess von Hochberg), Grand Duchess of, x 361
—— (in Aargau), Federal Swiss Diet at (1523), II 320; (1528), 329; Disputation at (1526), 325 sq.; Peace of (1714), v 436, 450, 454 sq., VI 614
Baden-Baden, margravate of, IV 84; Catholicism of House of, III 710
—— Edward Fortunatus, margrave of, IV 79
—— Lewis William, margrave of, v 61; 341; 366; commander of the Imperial Army, 368; 369; and the Spanish Succession, 401; Rhine campaign of (1702), 406; at Stolhofen, 407; 408; joins Marlborough, 409; besieges Ingolstadt, 410; 414; 416; 437; 452; death of, 418; VI 191
—— Philip, margrave of, III 716; his wife Sibylla, *ib.*
—— Jacobæa of. *See* Jülich-Cleves
Baden-Durlach, margravate of, IV 66; 84; re-instatement of House of, at Peace of Westphalia, 409
—— Ernest Frederick, margrave of, at Heilbronn, III 714
—— George Frederick, margrave of, IV 1; 67; 79; defeated by Tilly at Wimpfen, 80
—— Prince of (son of Prince Christopher of), VI 289 sq.
Baden-Hochberg, Jacob III, margrave of, III 710
Badeni, Count Kasimir Felix, Austrian statesman, XII 197; administration of, 200 sqq.
Badenoch, Jacobites at, VI 103, 117
Bader, Augustin, German sectary, II 224
Badia, Tommaso, church reform and, II 379, 643 sq.
Badius Ascensius (Bade of Asche), the Brethren of the Common Life and, I 435
Badli Sarai, fight at, XI 746
Badoer, Alberto, ambassador to Sixtus V, III 445

Badoer, Alvisi, sent to Constantinople, as ambassador of peace, III 116
Baduel, Claude, Protestant Rector of Nismes University, II 292
Baeda, ecclesiastical historian, I 535
Baena, Isabel de, Spanish Reformer, II 406 sq.
—— José Arana, Duke of, XI 560
Bärenklau, Johann Leopold, Baron zu Schönreith, Austrian Field-marshal, VI 233; 236
Bärsch, Georg B., one of the founders of the *Tugendbund* (1808), IX 328
Bärwalde, Treaty of (1631), IV 141, 198 sq., 210, 220; 226; 249; 251
Baffin bay, explorers at, XII 814
—— William, navigator, XII 814
Bagchaserai. *See* Bakchi-serai
Bage, Robert, novelist, VI 836
Bagenal, Sir Henry, in Ireland, III 604; defeated at Armagh, 530, 607
Bagge, Jakob, Danes defeated by, IV 163
Baggesen, Jens Immanuel, Danish poet, VIII 788; XI 697
Baghdad, Turkish army at, III 112; becomes Ottoman fortress, 113; Russia and, x 545; XII 170; caravan route to, 793
—— Pasha of, IX 385
Baghirmi, XII 130; Barth in, 810
Baglione, Giampaolo, of Perugia, I 194; submission of, to Julius II, 128; 134; 136; II 14
Bagni, Papal nuncio, in Paris, IV 680
Bagno, Marchese di, commands papal troops, IV 57 sq.
Bagnolo, Peace of (1484), between Venice, Milan and Naples, I 287
Bagot, Sir Charles, x 32; 37; at the Conference of St Petersburg, 189; Governor General of Canada, XI 767
Bagration, Peter Ivanovitch, Prince, IX 257; 260; at Friedland, 290; and the war with Turkey, 485; and the invasion of 1812, 489 sqq.
Bagyidaw, King of Ava, XI 727 sq.
Bahádur, King of Guzerat, VI 510
—— Shah, Moghul Emperor, VI 523; 531
Bahamas, the, landing of Colombo on, I 23; piracy in, v 691; VI 184; 380; relinquished by Spain, 464; government of, XII 657
Bahawalpur, Nawáb of, XI 736
Bahia (San Salvador), the Dutch and, IV 703 sq.; retaken by the Spaniards, 705, 706; Oquendo at, 707, 708; 750, 752 sq.; growth of importance of, v 676; 677; VI 184; 389 sq.; Portuguese troops in, x 312, 314 sq.; blockade of (1823), 316
—— dos Vaqueiros (Mossel Bay) discovered by Diaz, I 17
Bahr-el-Gazal, XII 130; taken by the Mahdi, 442; 449; France and, 660; 661; exploration in, 811 sqq.
Baif, Jean Antoine de, III 54 sq.

Baikal, Lake, xii 344; and the Russo-Japanese War, 577 sq.; 794

Baikie, William, African traveller, xii 810

Bailleul, ceded to France, v 45

—— Jacques-Charles, member of the *Corps Législatif*, viii 510 sq., 515, 517

Bailli de Litta, Prior of the Russian branch of the Order of St John, viii 648

Baillie, Robert, iv 317; 324

—— William, Lieutenant-colonel, defeat of, vi 576, ix 714

Bailly, Antoine, French Inspector-general of Finance, viii 74

—— Jean-Sylvain, viii 101; elected to the States General, 131 sq., 153, 155, 157; Mayor of Paris, 165, 167 sqq., 200; resigns, 225; guillotined, 357

Bainbridge, Cardinal Christopher, death of, i 483

Bairactar, Pasha of Rustchuk, ix 388

Bairam Khan, Moghul general, vi 512

Baird, Sir David, General, viii 617; lands at Corunna, ix 443; joins Moore, 445; at Kosseir, 734; expedition of, to Cape Colony, 752; xi 778

Baireuth, and Ansbach, v 622; margravate of, vi 633; Frederick the Great and, 704; principality of, reverts to Prussia (1792), viii 530; proposed cession of, to Austria, 534; the boundary of, ix 262, 266; French troops enter, 273; Soult at, 274; lost to Prussia (1815), 656

—— Margraves, etc. of. *See* Brandenburg-Baireuth

Baius, Michael, professor at Louvain, v 82

Baji Rao I, Peshwa, vi 531 sq.

—— II, Peshwa of Poona, xi 725 sq.; 747

Bajza, Joseph, Hungarian writer, xi 426

Bakchi-serai, Treaty of (1680), v 506; vi 305; captured by the Cossacks, 306

Bakel, French outpost at, xii 129

Baker, Sir Samuel White, in Africa, xii 439; 809

—— Valentine (Baker Pasha), in Egypt, xii 440 sq.

—— Major, at Dromore, v 307

Bakewell, Robert, agriculturist, x 731

Bakkerzeel, Jan de Casembroot, lord of, secretary to Egmont, iii 216

Bakócz, Thomas, Primate of Hungary, i 336 sq.

Baku, ceded to Russia, v 545; evacuated by Russia, vi 304; labour agitation in, xii 332; 342

Bakunin, Michael, Russian revolutionary, xi 219; 504; escapes from Siberia, 629; 630; xii 294; 296; *Statecraft and Anarchy*, 303; at Geneva, *ib.*; 307; 758

Balaban, Turkish general defeated by Scanderbeg, i 71

Balagny, Jean de Montluc, Sieur de, Marshal of France, holds Cambray, iii 47, 669; ambassador to Poland, 85

Balaguer, captured by Starhemberg, v 426

Bala Hissar, xi 733; occupation of, 735

Balaklava, battle of, xi 319 sq., 364

Balashoff, Russian Minister of Police, ix 487

Balassi, Valentine, Hungarian poet, xi 422

Balbini, Niccolò, Italian Minister at Geneva, ii 387

Balbo, Conte Cesare, Italian patriot, ii 35; ix 399; opinion of, on Italian priests, 401; x 109; 115; writings of, 167; 168; xi 65 sqq.; 70; 73; Piedmontese Minister, 80; 371; 547

—— Lorenzo, Spanish scholar at Alcalá, ii 400

Baldiron, Imperialist commander, iv 41; 48; and the Engadine, 54 sq.; flight of, 56

Baldissera, Antonio, Italian general, xii 241

Baldo, Monte, Prince Eugene crosses, v 402

Baldwin I, King of Jerusalem, grants privileges to Venetians, i 254

—— Abraham, Georgian deputy, vii 246

Bale, John, Bishop of Ossory, the Bibliography of, i 611; ii 19

Balearic Islands, prisoners sent to, xi 556, 568

Balfour, Arthur James, Secretary for Scotland, xii 45; Secretary for Ireland, 46, 48, 85 sq.; 52; Ministry of, 54; and the Education Act, 57; and the War Office, 59; 90; 594

—— Gerald William, Secretary for Ireland, xii 87

—— Sir James, Act of Revocation and, iv 490; Traquair and, 503

—— Sir William, dismissal of, iv 297

Balkan Peninsula, 1812–33, Vol. x, Chap. vi, *passim*; evacuated by Russia, xi 402; Chap. xxii (2); 1870–1909, Vol. xii, Chap. xiv; 6; 9 sqq.; 37; 57; Austria and, 211; 212; Italy and, 242; 341; the Powers and, 728

Balkh, province of, vi 518; caravan route through, xii 793; 800

Ball, Sir J. Alexander, naval captain at Naples, viii 658

Ballanche, Pierre-Simon, x 101

Ballarat, gold in, xi 796; 798

Ballard, John, and the Babington conspiracy, iii 291

Ballenstädt, House of, v 618. *See* Brandenburg

Ballesteros, Francisco, Spanish general, disgraced, ix 475; x 217; 227 sq.; 231

Ballinamuck, French force surrenders at, viii 476

Ballot, African explorer, xii 129

Ball's Bluff, engagement at (1861), vii 469

Ballybay, Catholic demonstration at, x 647 sq.

Ballycastle, battle at (1565), iii 591

Ballymore, captured by Ginkel, v 317

Ballyneety, Sarsfield at, v 316

Balmaceda, José Manuel, President of Chile, xii 677 sq.

Balmerino, Arthur Elphinstone, 6th Baron, Jacobite, vi 114; 117
—— John Elphinstone, 2nd Baron, trial of, iv 493 sq.
Balmont, K. D., Russian poet, xii 333
Baltaji Mehemet, Grand Vezir, v 604 sqq.
Balta Liman, Convention of, xi 284
Baltasar Carlos, Infante, Isabel of Bourbon and, iv 649 sq., 654; 658; death of, 659; 664
Baltic Convention, The, xii 290 sq.
—— Powers (1780–1801), Vol. ix, Chap. ii, section 1, *passim*; 295 sq. *See also* Russia, Sweden, Denmark, Prussia
—— Sea, struggle for supremacy in, ii 228; corn and timber trade in, iii 631; Imperial schemes as to, iv 193; United Provinces and, v 146 sq.; Russia and, 343, 494, 520; Poland and, 344; Peter the Great and, 526, 528; English fleet in (1715–26), 551, 611, vi 24, 37, 59, 207; Sweden and, v 562 sq., 607; 615; 634; 638; trade in, vi 24, 28; 35; 57; Russia and, 304, 694, 733; non-intervention in, by England, 408 sq.; 754; British trade with, vii 1, 4; British operations in (1800–1), ix 51 sq.; results of control of, by Napoleon, 241 sq.; British fleet in (1854), xi 317; 346; Germany and, xii 171; 348
Baltimore, expedition against (1814) (later abandoned), vii 344, 352; Union Manufacturing Co. of Maryland organised at, 353; emigration from, 359; Lincoln in, 449; fighting in (1861), 453 sq., 464, 469; Republican Convention at (1864), 599; railway from the Ohio to, 694
—— (Co. Cork), Spanish ships at, iii 532
—— Benedict Calvert, 4th Baron, vii 34
—— Cecilius Calvert, 2nd Baron, vii 31, 33
—— Charles Calvert, 3rd Baron, vii 34
—— George Calvert, 1st Baron, founds Maryland, iv 747; patent of, 748; vii 31, 52, 74
Baltimore, U.S.S., affair of the, vii 666
Baltinglas, James Eustace, 3rd Viscount, iii 598
Baltringen, beginning of the Peasants' War at, ii 179
Baltzer, Johann Baptista, philosopher, xi 712
Baluchistan, the Emperor Humáyun in, vi 511; xi 731; 736; 753; xii 458; 485; 491
Balue, Cardinal Jean de La, Minister of Louis XI, i 403, 415
Balzac, Honoré de, vi 833; x 102; 516; xi 427; 509; 516; novels of, 521 sq.
—— Jean-Louis-Guez, Seigneur de, iii 72; Member of French Academy, iv 156; v 70
Bamberg, see of, iii 709, vi 704; Bavaria insists on restoration of, iv 210; captured by Horn, 213; Maximilian I at, ix 253; 273

Bamberg, Johann Georg Fuchs von Darnheim, Bishop of, and Gustavus Adolphus, iv 207
Bamian, Moorcroft at, xii 800
Bancroft, George, xii 680; *History of the United States*, 841
—— Richard, Archbishop of Canterbury, iii 60, 343, 554, 563 sq.
Banda Islands, spices of, iv 734; Anglo-Dutch struggle in, 735; agreement of June 1619 and, 737; 738; captured by the English, viii 484, ix 750; restored to the Dutch (1814), 755
—— Neira, the Dutch and, iv 735 sq.; 742; captured (1810), ix 240
—— Oriental (Uruguay), Portugal and, v 456, 680; x 281; 286; independence of, 300 sq.; forms the *Provincia Cisplatina*, 316; xii 674; 680; Anglo-French action in, 681; 690
Bandello, Matteo, Bishop of Agen. *See* Agen
Bandiera, Attilio and Emilio, x 122 sq.; xi 65, 67
Bandon, Tyrone and O'Donnell at, iii 608
Bandula, Burmese general, xi 727 sq.
Banér, Gustaf, flight and death of, iv 172 sq.
—— Johann, Swedish Field-Marshal, iv 185; occupies Magdeburg, 207; holds Bavaria, 216 sq.; in Silesia, 247; ordered to invade Bohemia, 252; at Magdeburg, 255; German War and, 366 sqq.; at Eisenach, 372; falls back upon Torgau, 373; on the Oder, 374; 378; 379; 383; death of, 385; 390; Oxenstierna and, 569
—— Sten, flight and death of, iv 172 sq.
Bánffy, Baron, Hungarian statesman, xii 199; 203 sq.
Banfy, George, iii 98
Bangkok, British envoy at, xii 535; 536
Bangweolo, Lake, xii 663; Livingstone at, 809
Bankaert, Adrian van, Dutch naval commander, v 195 sq.
Bankes, Sir John, and the ship-money case, iv 283
Bankhem, Jan van, and the murder of the de Witts, v 159
Banks' Peninsula, purchased by a French company, xi 793
Banks, the Bank of England, established, v 266 sqq.; vi 45; action of (1793–7), ix 675 sq.; xi 5, 537; Banks of Amsterdam, Genoa, and Venice, v 266, 268, 270; the *Caisse d'Escompte*, viii 86, 96 sq., 694 sq.; Bank of France, created, ix 27; x 746; the Land Bank of Poland, 455 sq.; Continental, in general, 746 sq.; the Banca Romana and politics, xii 218; the Russian Peasants' Bank, 317 sq.; Russian Gentry Bank, 318; Hong Kong and Shanghai Banking Corporation, 513. *See also* Coinage and Currency, etc.
—— Sir Joseph, and New South Wales, ix 736; xii 805 sq.

Banks, Nathaniel Prentiss, American general, VII 477, 503, 506, 514; the Red River expedition (1864) under, 520

Bantam, Dutch trade at, III 638; James Lancaster at, IV 731; Edmund Scott at, 734; 735; English and Dutch ships before, 736; English factory re-established at, 740, V 697

Bantry Bay, French fleet in, VIII 476 sq., IX 700

Baour-Lormian, Pierre-M.-F.-L., French poet, VI 830; X 88

Bar, Duke of Lorraine does homage for, IV 142; recovery of Condé's fortresses in, 613 sq.; Treaty of Pyrenees and, 620; ceded to France, V 33; VI 155; Confederation of, 355, 668, 673, 730

Barailh, Admiral de, VI 110

Baraillon, Jean-François, French politician, VIII 678

Barajas, Francisco Zapata de Cisneros, Count of, III 518

Barante, Aimable-Guillaume-Prosper Brugière, Baron de, X 48; 51; and the *Doctrinaires*, 52–5; created a peer, 58; 67; resigns office, 68; action of, in the Chamber of Peers, 81; opposes the " law of sacrilege," 87; 502; XII 830

Baratieri, General, Governor of Erythrea, XII 240 sq.

Barbaczy, Joseph, commander of Skekler hussars, VIII 655 sq.

Barbados, Dutch forbidden to trade in, IV 470; settlement of, 756; constitution of, 757; V 110; de Ruyter at, 179; 284; 286 sq. ; English government in, 689 sq., VI 186; 454; colonists from, in Carolina, VII 34, 36; English colony in, 78; 87; slaves in, 102; Nelson in, IX 224; government in, 750, X 587; missionaries attacked in, 658; XI 757; negroes in, XII 653; 654; 656; government of, 657

Barbantane-Pujet, Paul-F.-H.-B., Marquis de, French commander, VIII 439

Barbara, Queen of Poland, consort of Sigismund III. *See* Radzivil

—— of Braganza, Queen of Spain, consort of Ferdinand VI, VI 166; 361 sqq.; death of, 366

Barbaresques. *See* Barbary pirates

Barbaro, Ermalao, humanist, I 657, 681

—— Marco Antonio, III 137 sq.

Barbarossa I (Horush), II 68

—— II (Khair Eddin), II 68 sqq., 75 sqq., 390; III 105, 109; seizes Tunis, 110, driven from it by Charles V, 111; exploits of, 112 sq.; gains victory near Actium (1538), 114; takes islands from Venice, 116 sq.; 119; death of (1546), 120

Barbaroux, Charles-J.-M., VIII 231, 249 sq., 260, 357

Barbary, Móriscos deported to, III 543; French Consul established in, 694; French trade with, VI 173; 350

Barbary pirates, Spanish attacks on (1505–10), I 365 sq.; expeditions against, II 68 sq., 75 sq.; and Italy, III 391, 399, 410; defeated by Fajardo, 540 sq.; V 179; X 19 sq.

Barbauld, Mrs (Anna Letitia Aikin), VIII 764

Barbé-Marbois, François de, Count and Marquis of, French *chargé d'affaires* in America, VI 462; VIII 488, 507; IX 9; 116, 117; X 47; 49

Barberet, French labour politician, XII 94

Barberini, enrichment of the, by Urban VIII, IV 684; and the quarrel with Parma, 685 sqq.

—— Cardinal Maffeo. *See* Urban VIII

Barbès, Armand, French socialist, X 511; XI 104 sq.; 108 sq.

Barbesieux, French commander against Naples, II 59

Barbier, Edmond-Jean-François, diarist, VIII 9, 12

Barbin, Claude, French statesman, Ministry of, IV 122 sqq.

Barbo, Pietro. *See* Paul II, Pope

Barbon, Nicolas, *Discourse of Trade*, X 770

Barbosa, Arias, Portuguese Hellenist, I 379, 578

Barcelona, Treaty of (1529), II 25, 203; Charles V sets sail from (1535), III 111; embarkation of Duke and Duchess of Savoy at, 513; captured (1651), IV 618; Philip IV and Olivares at, 647; revolt of, 648 sq.; 652; entry of La Motte into, 653; capitulation of (1652), 661; V 61; taken by the French (1696), 62; 413; by Peterborough (1705), 416; 432; siege of (1713), 446; VI 29; 31 sq.; Navarro's squadron at, 236; trade of, VII 327; British squadron at, IX 46; Duhesme seizes (1808), 430; French forces at, 435, 436, 439; Gouvion Saint-Cyr at, 448; *Carbonaro* agent sent to, X 213; revolts in (1820), 216, 223, (1840), 241 sq., XI 560; XII 260; socialism in, 268

—— (Venezuela), Bolívar's flight to, X 289

Barcelonnette, capture of, III 416

Barclay, Robert Heriot, British naval commander, VII 340

—— de Tolly, Michel, Prince, and the invasion of 1812, IX 489 sqq.; at Bautzen, 518; 519; replaces Wittgenstein, 520; at Leipzig, 535; 538

Barcoo river, exploration of, XI 795; 798

Barcsay, Abraham, Hungarian writer, XI 422

Barczai, Achatius, Prince of Transylvania. *See* Transylvania

Bard, fortress of, IX 60

Bardeleben, Karl Alexander von, one of the founders of the *Tugendbund* (1808), IX 328

Bardo, Treaty of, XII 129, 239

Bareilly, revolt at, XI 746

Barendsz. *See* Barents

Barentin, Charles-L.-F. de Paule de, Keeper of the Seals, VIII 145, 156

Barents, William, Dutch explorer, III 632, XII 795

Barère de Vieuzac, Bertrand, French politician, VIII 153, 249 ; at the King's trial, 258, 262 ; on the *Comité de Salut Public*, 269, 274, 343, 347, 362, 364 sq. ; and the fall of Robespierre, 369, 375 ; charges brought against, 380, 384

Barham, Admiral Sir Charles Middleton, 1st Baron, appointed First Lord of the Admiralty, IX 224

Bari, the Viceroy Visconti at, VI 153 ; and the Apulian aqueduct, XII 238

—— Duke of (Ludovico il Moro). *See* Milan, Dukes of

Bariatinskii, Prince, IX 35

Barileff, Russian naval commander, XI 843 sq.

Barillon, Paul, Marquis de Branges, French ambassador in England, V 219 ; 222 ; 227 ; and James II, 231 sq., 235, 247

Baring, the financial house of, X 743 ; XI 10, XII 48

—— Alexander. *See* Ashburton, Lord

—— Sir Evelyn. *See* Cromer, Earl

—— Sir Francis Thornhill, Lord Northbrook, XI 3

—— Walter, reports on the Bulgarian massacres, XII 384

Barkul, Russian traveller at, XII 799 ; 802

Barlaam, Bernard, Greek scholar and ambassador to Italy, I 540

Barlaeus, Caspar, IV 717

Barlaymont, Baron Charles, *afterwards* Count of, adviser of Granvelle, III 188, 191, 194 ; 198 ; taunts the *Gueux*, 203 sq. ; 214 ; alienated by Alva, 216 sq., 226, 245

Bar-le-Duc, meeting of Francis I and Philip of Hesse at (1534), II 220 ; the Old Pretender at, VI 96, 98

Barlow, Captain Arthur, in Virginia, VII 3

—— Sir George Hilaro, in India, IX 730–1

—— William, consecrates Parker, II 571 sq.

Barnabites, Order of the, founded, II 648

Barnabotti, Venetian party, I 282

Barnard, Sir Henry William, Lieutenant-General, at Delhi, XI 746

Barnave, Antoine-P.-J.-M., member of the National Assembly, VIII 174, 182, 186 sqq., 200 sq., 213 ; and the Court, 216 ; executed (1793), 357

"Barnburners," The, VII 399

Barnes, Dr Robert, executed, II 451

—— Thomas, editor of *The Times*, X 667

Barnet, Curtis, Commodore, in the East Indies, VI 535

Barneveldt, Johan van Olden. *See* Oldenbarneveldt

Barnwell, Robert Woodward, Confederate Senator, VII 605

Baro river, Marchand on, XII 813

Baroche, Pierre-Jules, French Minister of the Interior, XI 131 sqq. ; 294

Báróczy, Alexander, Hungarian writer, XI 422

Baroda, captured by Wellesley, IX 726 ; State of, XI 727

—— Malhar Rao, Gaekwar of, deposed, XII 462

Barodet, Désiré, French politician, XII 107

Baron, Pierre, of Cambridge, Protestant refugee, II 597

Baronets, Order of, creation of the, III 571

Baronius, Cardinal Caesar, ecclesiastical historian, I 568, 609 ; the *Annales Ecclesiastici* of, III 444 ; XII 816

Baross, G. de, Hungarian Minister, XII 198

Barrackpur, mutiny at, XI 729

Barradas, *or* Baradat, François de, Seigneur de Damery, favourite of Louis XIII, driven from Court, IV 131

Barras, Count Louis de, French naval officer, VI 453

—— Paul-F.-J.-Nicolas de, VIII 249, 349, 352 ; and the fall of Robespierre, 366, 369 ; 378 ; and the insurrection of Vendémiaire, 396 ; member of the Directory, 489 sqq., 494, 496, 503 ; and the Babeuf conspiracy, 504 sq. ; 507, 563 sq., 669 sq. ; and Brumaire, 675 sqq., 679

Barrault, seized by Lesdiguières, III 417

Barraux, fort at, III 417

Barré, Isaac, Colonel, VI 425 ; 432 ; pensioned, 459

Barrier Fortresses, the, Joseph II razes, VIII 277, 281

—— Treaties (1709–15), V 424, 439 sq., 448, 456 sqq. ; VI 13, 23, 470 ; from 1715 to 1782, 640 sqq.

Barrington, Jonah, and the Union with Ireland, IX 703

—— William Wildman Barrington, 2nd Viscount, VI 406 ; 424 sq. ; 427 ; 450 ; VII 142

—— Samuel, Admiral, VI 451

Barron, James, American commodore, VII 329 sq.

Barrot, Camille-Hyacinthe-Odilon, X 507 sqq. ; XI 30 ; 32 ; and Thiers, 36 sq., 40 ; 42 ; 96 ; and the Revolution (1848), 99 sq., 102 ; 108 ; and the Republican constitution, 115 sq. ; appointed Premier, 118 ; 119 ; and Pius IX, 121 ; 126 ; declines office, 128 sq. ; Louis-Napoleon and, 133

—— Ferdinand, French statesman, XI 127 ; 129

Barrow, Henry, III 343, 345

Barruel, industrial experiments of, IX 376

Barry, Garret, in Munster, IV 525

Bar-sur-Aube, indecisive battle at (1814), IX 545 ; Oudinot defeated at, 550

Bart, Jean, French seaman, V 59 ; 162

Bartenstein, Convention of (1807), IX 287, 289, 296

Bartenstein, Baron Johann Christoph von, Austrian statesman, vi 204; 626

Barth, Heinrich, in Africa, xii 810 sqq.

Barthélemy, François, Marquis de, and the Peace of Basel, viii 381, 383, 441; Director, 506; arrested (1797), 509 sqq.; transported, 512; ambassador to Switzerland, 639, 781; x 58

—— St Hilaire, Jules, French politician, xi 118

Barthels, Jean Theodore, Belgian journalist, x 532

Bartholdi, Friedrich Christian von, Brandenburg Minister at Vienna, v 664

Bartolucci, Vincent, x 138

Bartolus (Bartolus Severus de Alphanis, d. 1355), iii 749

Barton, Andrew, taken at sea by Lord Thomas Howard (1511), i 479

—— Elizabeth (the Holy Maid of Kent), trial and execution of, ii 441

Barwell, Richard, member of the Indian Council, vi 571 sq.

Baryatinski, Russian Field-Marshal, xii 139

Barzizza, Gasparino da. *See* Gasparino

Baschi, Perron de, French envoy to Rome, i 110

Basedow, Johann Berend, German educational reformer, viii 772

Basel, Council of (1431–49), i 293, 385, 599, 623, 655, 668; Peace of (1499), 307; joins Swiss Confederacy (1501), 308; Greek books at, 599; the Reformation at, ii 328, 355; Evangelic Diet of (1530), 335; Conference of Swiss Reformers at, 339; Calvin and Erasmus at, 355; offer of, for Saluzzo, iii 408; Compactates of, 703; vi 615; 623; 625; Treaty of (1795), viii 289, 381, 383, 386, 413, 422, 441, 551; ix 249, 592, 608; bishopric of, 96, 104, 601; and the Swiss Confederation, 105; manufactures of, 425; xi 234; reaction in, 238; insurrections in, 241 sq.; division of, 245 sq.; 248; silk-weaving in, 259; 491; Nihilist Congress at, 629; Labour Legislation Union at, xii 747

—— Christopher von Uttenheim, Bishop of, ii 324

—— Eugène Lachat, Bishop of, xi 258

Baselga, Gaspar, Swiss Catholic leader, iv 44

Bashkirs, rising of, vi 681

Bashmakóff, and Poland, xii 378

Basil II, Emperor of the East, v 483

—— Tsar (Vasili Shuïski). *See* Vasili IV

Basilicata, condition of the, xii 236 sqq.

Basing House, attempt of Waller to capture, iv 315; Charles I and, 324; taken by Cromwell, 333

Basque provinces, in the Middle Ages, i 352; occupied by the Carlists, x 235, 239; emigration from, to Spanish America, 276; xii 258; Carlist forces in, 260

—— Roads, Willaumez anchors in the, ix 238

Bass, George, explorations of, ix 740

Bassano, Hughes-Bernard Maret, Duc de, ix 10; receives the duchy of Bassano, 111; 141, 145; disaffection of, 572; becomes Secretary of State, 616; x 494

Bassein (India), Treaty of (1802), ix 725, 727

—— (Burma), capture of, xi 742

Bassermann, Friedrich Daniel, Baden politician, xi 61 sqq.; 145; 198; at the Gotha meeting, 221

Basseville, Nicolas-Jean-Hugon de, Secretary of the French legation, viii 581, 778

Bassewitz, Henning Friedrich von, Holstein Minister, v 609

—— Colonel Adolphus Frederick von, Hanoverian envoy at Stockholm, vi 36

Bassi, Antonietta, Countess Pasolini, xi 72

—— Matteo de', founder of the Capuchins, ii 647

Bassignano, Sardinians defeated at, vi 243

Basso, Protestant preacher in Tirano, death of, iv 49

Bassompierre, Baron François de, Marquis d'Harouel, Marshal of France, embassy of, to Madrid, iv 50, 53; *dix-sept seigneurs* and, 156; ambassador in England, 266

Bastia, captured by a British squadron, viii 458

Bastide, Jules, French politician, xi 99; 118; 124

Bastille, fall of the, viii 164, 167, 191, 715, 755

Bastogi, Count Pietro, Italian statesman, xi 538

Bastwick, John, punishment of, iv 280; release of, 291

Basutoland, xi 783; annexed to Cape Colony, 787; government of, xii 645

Basutos, and the Boers, xi 782; 783 sqq.; and the Orange Free State, 787

Batak, massacre at, xii 384

Batang, travellers at, xii 796 sq., 803 sq.

Batarnay, Ymbert de, i 403

Batavia, capital of the Dutch East Indies, iv 710 sqq.; foundation of, 736; power of the Dutch at, 738; 740

Batavian Republic, existence of, recognised by Holland, ix 78; 208; changes effected by Bonaparte in, 88 sqq.; Napoleon's dealings with, 416–7. *See also* Holland

Batbie, Anselme-Polycarpe, French politician, xii 108

Bate, John, his case, iii 557, 748

Batenburg, Dutch commander, relieves Haarlem, iii 236

Bates, Edward, vii 445; Attorney-general, 450

—— William, Presbyterian divine, vi 803

Bath, John Bourchier, 4th Baron Fitzwarine, 2nd Earl of, supporter of Mary, ii 514

Bath, Sir John Grenville, 1st Earl of (2nd cr.), Monck and, IV 555 sq.; 558
—— William Pulteney, Earl of, VI 47; 66; 71; enters the Cabinet, 73; 74; 84
—— Thomas Thynne, 1st Marquis of (Viscount Weymouth), VI 376; 424; 439; resigns, 443; 447; 450
Báthory (or Bátori), Andrew, Cardinal, III 103
—— Christopher, III 97
—— Gabriel, Prince of Transylvania. *See* Transylvania
—— Sophia, V 352
—— Stephen, *Judex Curiae* of Hungary (1491), I 339
—— Stephen, King of Poland. *See* Stephen Báthory
Bathurst, XI 790; discovery of gold at, 795
—— Henry Bathurst, 2nd Earl, Lord Chancellor, VI 443; 450
—— Henry Bathurst, 3rd Earl, VII 363 sq.
—— Richard, President of Trinity College, Oxford, VI 791
Batiffol, Pierre, French scholar, XII 848
Baton Rouge, arsenal at, VII 492
Bátori. *See* Báthory
Battaglia, Francesco, Venetian senator, VIII 585
Battambang, ceded to France, XII 536
Batten, Sir William, admiral, succeeded by Rainborow, IV 347; with the fleet, 350
Battenberg, Prince Alexander of, XII 341
Batthyány, Balthasar, Minister of Matthias Corvinus, I 343
—— Count Casimir, XI 212 sq.; at Widdin, 215
—— Count Karl Joseph von, Austrian general, VI 241 sq.
—— Count Ludwig, XI 155 sq.; 172; 180 sqq.; forms a new Ministry, 183; 184; arrest of, 203; 205; execution of, 214
Batuecas, Ostolaza imprisoned at, X 209
Batum, XII 33; ceded to Russia, 342, 398; 392 sq.; 399
Baturin, destruction of (1708), V 600
Batz, Baron Jean de, VIII 261
Batzlow, Prussian army at, VI 281
Bau, Danish victory at, XI 161, 695
Baudelaire, Charles-Pierre, French poet, XI 511; 513 sq.
Baudin, Jean-B.-A.-V., French politician, XI 136; 488
—— des Ardennes, Pierre-Charles-Louis, member of the Legislative Assembly, VIII 386, 394
—— Nicolas, French captain, in Australia, IX 738-9
Baudissin, W. H. von, Swedish Field-marshal, IV 220
Baudoin, French admiral, IX 239
Baudot, Marc-Antoine, member of the National Convention, VIII 427 sq.
Bauer, George (Georgius Agricola), V 738

Bauernfeld, Eduard von, Austrian dramatic poet, XI 414 sqq.
Bauhin, Jean, naturalist, V 734
Baumann, Governor of Posen, X 464
Baumbach, Moritz von, Hesse-Cassel Minister, XI 232
Baumgartner, Hieronymus, III 159
Baune, Eugène, French politician, XI 136
Baur, Ferdinand Christian von, historian, X 382; XII 847
Bausch, Johann Lorenz, and the *Academia naturae curiosorum*, V 741
Bautzen, Prussian retreat near, VI 290; battle of (1813), IX 519
Bava-Beccaris, General, XII 220
Bavaria, and the Reformation, II 169; papal concessions to, *ib.*; persecution of Lutherans in, 202; supports Charles V (1545), 251; religious attitude of, III 159 sqq., 173, 702; Treaty of Bärwalde and, IV 198; 208; policy of, 211; Tilly driven into, 213; 214; Gustavus Adolphus in, 215; Banér in, 216; 219; sufferings of, during the war, 417 sq.; cloth of, 421; campaigns in (1646-8), 391 sqq., 597; alliance of, with France, V 42, 47, 404; 407; and the Spanish Netherlands, 447; 451; and the Pragmatic Sanction, VI 202 sq.; and the War of the Austrian Succession, 299 sqq.; 275; Austria and, 630 sq., 633; projected exchange of, 644 sqq., VIII 277, 281 sqq., 310, 312 sqq., 533 sqq., 543; VI 677; Frederick the Great and, 703 sq.; 707; Austro-Russian designs on (1795), VIII 441, 549; 634; French revolutionary ideas in, 776; Moreau marches into, IX 64; French acquisitions in, 68; 78; and the Imperial Recess of 1803, 94; reform of the Church in, 201; 202; joins France, 253; 262; receives Ansbach, 267; arrangements for invasion of, 346; crux of the war of 1809, 347; proposals of Metternich to, 507; treaty with (1813), 533; territorial changes in, 591; 592, 597; and the Congress of Vienna, 609 sqq.; and the Federal Act, 650; ambition of, 658; disputes of, with Austria, discussed by the Allied Powers, X 19; 22; 32; ecclesiastical affairs in, 146 sq.; and German unity, 342 sq.; and the Germanic Confederation, 343 sq.; disputes of, with Austria and Baden, 346, 361 sq.; Montgelas' rule in, 359; Constitution of (1818), 359 sq.; 363; and the Carlsbad meeting, 366; and the Vienna Conference (1819), 368; and the *Triasidee*, 369; 370; Liberal measures by Ludwig I, 371 sq.; and the customs treaties, 372 sq., 378 sq.; 374; 380; banking in, 746; 751; industries in, 753 sq.; XI 60 sq.; the revolutionary movement in, 146; 167; and the Frankfort Constitution, 218; and the Berlin Conference, 220; 222 sq.; and the Hesse-Cassel crisis, 229; 408; and the Austro-Prussian War, 457; and the Zollverein,

462; and the North German Confederation, 460 sq., 464 sq.; and the German Empire, 465 sq.; and the Franco-German War, 464; and the Austro-German alliance, XII 145; 148; 747; Riezler's history of, 829

Bavaria, Dukes of:—
—— Albert V, II 681; III 159–61, 172, 180
—— Maximilian I, afterwards Elector. *See under* Electors
—— William IV, II 172, 221, 224, 232; and the League of Nürnberg, 235, 264
—— William V, III 706; 709 sq.

Bavaria, Electors of :—
—— Charles Albert. *See* Charles VII, Emperor
—— Charles Theodore, VI 647; 703; 707; VIII 281, 312, IX 40
—— Ferdinand Maria, and the Imperial succession, IV 426, 430, V 41, 47
—— Maximilian I, III 573; 687 sq.; 709; 718 sqq.; a possible candidate for the Imperial throne, IV 1; Jesuit influence upon, 5; and the Catholic League, 12; and the Imperial succession, 17; 22; 27; and Ferdinand II's policy, 32; and the Protestant Union, 33; empowered to occupy Upper Austria, 34; at Linz, 64; 65 sq.; 68; 69; counsels of, 73; 75; renounces hold upon Upper Austria, 76; 77; conquers the Upper Palatinate, 78; 81; Tilly and, 82; 83; Elector, 84; 88; 92; 93; 96; 100; 108; claims of, 109; Spiritual Electors and, 110; self-confidence of, 111; 112; supports Elector of Saxony, 113; head of the Moderate Party, 114; rift between Ferdinand II and, 115; 116; scheme of Richelieu concerning, 129; 135; 141; orders Tilly to besiege Magdeburg, 199; 203; on right bank of Danube, 208; Richelieu and, 210; 213; at Donauwörth, 214; palace at Munich of, 215; with Wallenstein, 216; in Bohemia, 227; Emperor and, 231; 232; 237; correspondence between Richelieu and, 238; 246; peace negotiations and, 252; 254; and the Imperial succession, 373; 376; and the truce of Ulm, 391; and France, 392; at Salzburg, 393; 398; 401; Sablé and, 402; retains Upper Palatinate, 409; French campaigns in Bavaria and, 597; Mazarin and, 602; 673; 677; Ferdinand II and, 679; at Ratisbon, 680; Urban VIII and, 683
—— Maximilian Emanuel, V 52 sq.; 359; 366 sq.; commander of the Imperial army, 368; marriage of, 377; and the Spanish Succession, 384, 386, 388; alliance of, with France, 404, 406 sqq.; at Donauwörth, 409; at Blenheim, 410; 411; restoration of, 436; 438; 447; 450; 452; and the Peace of Baden, 455
—— Maximilian (III) Joseph, VI 241 sq.; 630 sq.; 703; 707

Bavaria, Electors of, *contd.* :—
—— Maximilian Joseph. *See* Maximilian I, King of Bavaria

Bavaria, Anna of Austria, Duchess of, consort of Albert V, III 159
—— Ernest of, Archbishop of Cologne. *See* Cologne
—— Ferdinand of, III 708
—— Joseph Ferdinand, Electoral Prince of, and the Spanish Succession, V 377, 382, 384 sq.; death of, 385; 386 sqq.; 659; 664
—— Lewis, Crown Prince of, at Vienna, IX 582
—— Maria Antonia, Electress of, V 52; 377

Bavaria-Landshut, George the Rich, Duke of, I 315
—— Ludwig, Duke of (d. 1543), II 172, 251

Bavaria-Munich, Albert IV, Duke of, I 295 sqq., 299
—— Albert and Wolfgang, Dukes of, the Landshut succession and, I 315

Bavarian Academy, Historical Commission of, XII 827

Baxter, Richard, New Model army and, IV 329; V 96; at the Savoy Conference, 97; 100; 201; imprisoned, 231; 238; and Cromwell, 328; 329 sq.; 332; and James II, 335; VI 799; *Holy Commonwealth* of, 801; 807

Bay Islands, XII 685; ceded to Honduras, 686

Bay of Islands, mission at, XI 793

Bayane, Alphonse Hubert de Latier, Comte de, Cardinal, Papal plenipotentiary at Paris, IX 195

Bayard, Pierre de Terrail, Seigneur de, I 133, 412, 481; II 43; death of (1524), 48
—— Thomas Francis, VII 653; Secretary of State, 662

Bayard-Chamberlain Treaty (1888), VII 659

Bayazid, demanded by Russia, XII 392; retained by Porte, 398
—— I, Ottoman Sultan, war of, with Venice, I 259, 278
—— II, Ottoman Sultan, I 82, 85–90, 114, 224, 229
—— younger son of Solyman II, III 124

Bayer, Chancellor to John Frederick of Saxony, II 211
—— Joseph, Hungarian officer, XI 214

Bayeux, surrenders to Henry IV (1589), III 48

Bayham, riot at (1525), II 434

Bayle, Pierre, pupil of Chouet, IV 791; VIII 4; *Dictionary*, 5; 32

Baylen, capitulation of Dupont at (1808), IX 137; 315 sqq., 326, 437 sqq., 565
—— Francis Xavier de Castaños, Duke of. *See* Castaños

Bayol, African explorer, XII 129

Bayonne, Conference at (1565), III 7, 8,

20, 271, 282, 489; French force at, IX
301 sqq.; 304; Napoleon at, 313; 316;
322; constitution issued by Joseph from,
406; Murat summoned to, 410; Dupont's
army at, 430; Ferdinand VII abdicates
at, 432; 433; Joseph Napoleon, proclaimed King at (1808), 434; Soult and
Wellington at (1813), 480 sqq.; Narváez
at, XI 559; harbour of, XII 102

Bayonne, Jean de Moustiers de Froissac,
Bishop of, II 270

Baza, capture of (1489), I 358

Bazaine, François-Achille, Marshal of
France, XI 479; leaves Mexico, 484;
496; 498; 583; 586 sq.; takes over the
command, 588; conduct of the war by,
589 sqq.; capitulates at Metz, 603 sq.;
611

Bazard, Amand, X 485

Bazeilles, fight at, XI 598

Bazire, Claude, VIII 249, 340, 363

Beachy Head, battle of (1690), V 59, 258,
261, 263, 315

Beaconsfield, Benjamin Disraeli, 1st Earl
of, X 669; the novels of, 724, XI 357;
11; and Protection, 20; Chancellor of
the Exchequer, 21, 328; 309 sq.; 330;
and the Reform Bill of 1867, 341 sq.;
rivalry of, with Gladstone, 342 sq.; and
Irish Disestablishment, 344; resigns,
345 sq.; and Portugal, 574; and the
Suez Canal, 638, XII 433; XI 757; XII 14;
resigns, 23; refuses office, 29; Ministry
of (1874-80), 30 sqq.; and Gladstone,
30; created Earl, 33; resigns, 36; 37 sq.;
40; 46; 72; and Irish education, 75;
and the Berlin Congress, 142, 394, 399;
383; and the Russo-Turkish War, 389;
and Greece, 402; and Cyprus, 415; and
Lord Mayo, 458, 463; and Afghánistán,
465 sq.; 468; 472; 474; 774

Beales, Edmond, political agitation of,
XI 340

Beard, John, and the East India Company,
V 700

Béarn, offered to Henry of Navarre, III
510; Perez escapes to, 516; restoration
of the Catholic religion in, 668, 681;
restoration of ecclesiastical property in,
IV 125; Louis XIII and, 126 sq.; persecution of Protestants in, V 24; and the
Provincial Assemblies, VIII 111; and the
States General, 128

Beattie, James, poet, VI 830

Beauchamp, Edward Seymour, Lord, III
361, 534

—— Joseph, mission of, to Constantinople, VIII 608

Beaufort (N. Carolina), captured (1862),
VII 552

—— (S. Carolina), British detachment at,
VII 219

—— François de Vendôme, Duke of, and
les Importants, IV 596; escape of, from
Vincennes, 609; joins rebels, 611 sq.;

made Governor of Paris, 617; kills
Nemours, ib.; Admiral (1666), V 182
sq., 187

Beaufort, Henry, Cardinal, II 531

—— Louis de, historian, XII 817

Beaugency, Peace of (1485), I 393; Condé
at, III 2; de Coligny at, 5; French
troops at, XI 605 sq.

Beauharnais, Alexandre, Vicomte de, VIII
179, 339; commands the army of the
Rhine, 424; IX 107

—— Augustus, Duke of Leuchtenberg.
See Leuchtenberg

—— Eugène de, Duke of Leuchtenberg,
Prince of Eichstädt, in Egypt, VIII 606, 616;
IX 107; 195; Napoleon's Arch-Chancellor
of State, 110; 139; Viceroy of the Italian
Kingdom, 247; 355; 394; wedding of,
265; Napoleon's advice to, 395; rule of,
396 sq.; advised by Napoleon to annex
March of Ancona, 400; and the Russian
campaign, 488 sqq.; replaces Murat at
Posen, 511; forced to evacuate Posen,
512; reaches Frankfort, 513-4; at Nedlitz,
515; and the French throne, 555; at
Congress of Vienna, 583; X 338

—— Hortense de, IX 107; 139

—— Joséphine de (née Tascher de la
Pagerie). See Joséphine, Empress of
France

—— Stéphanie, marries Hereditary Prince
of Baden, IX 265, X 361

Beaujeu. See Bourbon

Beaujolais, The, customs of, V 13

—— Mademoiselle de, VI 126; 139 sq.

Beaujon, Nicolas, farmer-general, VIII 71

Beaulieu, Baron Jean-Pierre de, Austrian
commander, VIII 420, 435; in Italy, 558,
565 sqq., 572

Beaulieu-Marconnay, Baron Karl von,
Oldenburg Minister, XI 151

Beaumarchais, Pierre-Augustin Caron de,
French dramatist, VI 359, 823; VII 210;
VIII 725

Beaumont, engagement at, XI 596

—— C. de, Archbishop of Paris. See
Paris

—— Francis, dramatist, III 381; IV 760

—— Sir Lewis, Arctic expedition of, XII
815

—— Mme de, IX 24

Beaune, revolt of (1595), III 667

—— la Rolande, German victory at, XI
604 sq.

—— Florimond de, V 711

—— Jacques de. See Semblançay

Beauregard, Pierre-Gustave Toutant, Confederate general, VII 465 sq.; at Richmond,
478; evacuates Corinth, 499; succeeded
by Bragg, 506; in Tennessee, 524; and
peace negotiations, 542; 565

—— Sylvain Costa de, X 114

Beausse, de, in Madagascar, V 703

Beauvais, Auguste Potier, Bishop of, and
Mazarin, IV 596

Beauvais de Préaux, Charles-Nicolas, French deputy, VIII 247

Beaver Dam, American force captured at (1813), VII 341

Bebel, Ferdinand August, Socialist politician, XII 153

—— Heinrich, German humanist, II 152

Beccadelli, Antonio (Panormita), his *Hermaphroditus*, II 3; III 470

Beccaria, Cesare Bonesana, Marquis di, Italian economist, VI 602; 687; VIII 13, 743 sq., 748 sqq., 777; IX 169

Beccatello, Lodovico, II 398

Becher, Johann Joachim, chemist, V 731

Bechtold, Baron Philipp, Hungarian general, XI 182

Bechuana tribes, and the Boers, XI 782

Bechuanaland, XI 761; 789; XII 3; annexed to the Cape, 638

Beck, Baron John de, General, in Flanders, IV 598; death of, 599

—— Baron Wladimir von, Austrian statesman, XII 203; Ministry of, 207 sq.; fall of, 209; 210

Beckenried, Catholic League of (1524), II 325

Becker, Nicolaus, German poet, XI 49; 412

Beckerath, Hermann von, German Liberal leader, XI 53; 58; 166; 199; at the Gotha meeting, 221

Beckford, William, X 698; 709; 716

Becquerel, Henri, physicist, XII 789

Beda, Noel, doctor of the Sorbonne, II 285

Bedchamber Plot, The, X 678

Bedeau, Marie-Alphonse, French general, XI 100; 104; 113; imprisoned, 136

Bedford, Francis Russell, 2nd Earl of, II 567; III 280

—— Francis Russell, 5th Duke of, VIII 760

—— John Russell, 1st Earl of, II 475; 495, 499, 517

—— John Russell, 4th Duke of, VI 424 sqq.; at Paris, 346, 428; 430; and the Regency Act, 434; 439; 489

—— John Russell, 6th Duke of, becomes Lord-Lieutenant of Ireland, IX 707

—— Gunning, Governor of Delaware, VII 246, 261

Bedingfield, Sir Henry, supporter of Queen Mary, custodian of Princess Elizabeth, II 514, 529, 535

Bedloe, William, and Titus Oates, V 222; 334

Bedmar, Alonso de la Cueva, Marquis of, cooperates with Osuna against Venice, IV 632 sq.; and the Spanish plot against Venice, 671

Bednore, taken by Tipu Sultan, VI 469

Beele, Sloet van de, Governor-General of the Dutch East Indies, XI 668

Beeli, George, Swiss Catholic leader, IV 44

Beer, Adolf, historian, XII 829

Beernaert, Auguste, Belgian statesman, XII 251; 253

Beets, Nicolaes, Dutch writer, XI 676

Beg, Jakub, ruler of Kashgar, XI 632

"Beggars of the Sea." *See Gueux de Mer*

Behar, VI 556; Clive and, 564; famine in, XII 464

Béhic, Armand, French Minister of Public Works, XI 476

Behlol, Sultan, founds his dynasty, VI 508

Behmaru hills, British defeat at, XI 733

Behn, Aphra, V 129; 136

Behr, Johann August Heinrich von, Saxon Minister, XI 220

Behring, Vitus, rediscovers Behring Strait, XII 794

—— Sea, the sealing question in, VII 666; XII 617; arbitration, 720 sq.

—— Strait, XII 794; explorers in, 814 sq.

Beilan, pass of, Ibrahim defeats Hussein at (1832), X 550

Beilul, Italian occupation of, XII 240

Beira (Mozambique), railway from, to Salisbury, XII 639

—— (Portugal), Masséna's advance through, IX 460

Beirout, bombarded (1840), X 569, 571

Beja, occupied by Mollelos, X 333

Bek, Anthony, Bishop of Durham, I 301

Bekbulatovich, Simeon, of Kazan, V 492; 497

Bekk, Johann Baptist, Baden statesman, XI 61

Bekker, Immanuel, writings of, XII 821

Bekos, Russian force at, X 553

Belasi, Johann Jacob Kuen von, Archbishop of Salzburg. *See* Salzburg

Belcher, Jonathan, Governor of Massachusetts, VII 65

Belchite, Suchet's victory at (1809), IX 454

Belcredi, Count Richard, Austrian Minister of State, XII 183 sq.

Beldenak (Jens Andersen). *See* Odense, Bishops of

Belem, flight of Portuguese royal family from, IX 304

Belemzada, Portuguese plot, X 338

Belfast, taken by Schomberg (1689), V 312; volunteer defence corps in, VI 496; Society of United Irishmen at, IX 694; volunteers of, 695; prosperity of, 708; Queen's College, XII 29, 71 sq.

Belfort, revolt in, IV 43 sq.; military arrests at, X 76; rising at, 492; French force at, XI 582, 584; 594; siege of, 604, 606, 608 sq.; 612; the Peace of Frankfort and, XII 95

Belgiojoso, Christina, Princess of, XI 85

—— Count, VI 651

Belgium. (*See also* Netherlands, seventeen provinces of the, Spanish and Austrian, and Kingdom of the.) France and, V 58; the Grand Alliance (1701) and, 398; and the Barrier Treaty, 424; VI 237; 273; Dutch garrisons in, 640 sq.; plans of Joseph II as to, VIII 277, 281, 293, 317 sq.; rebellion in (1787), 318 sqq., (1789),

327 sqq.; Republic of, vi 653, viii 331 sq.; mission of Dumouriez to, 224; Leopold II and, vi 655 sq., viii 335 sq.; invaded and occupied by the French (1792), 415 sqq.; evacuated by the French (1793), 421; incorporated into the French Republic (1795), 496 sq.; conscription in, 519; influence of the French Revolution in, 786 sq.; ceded to France, ix 69; French troops in, 208; proposal to unite with Holland, 259; Napoleon resolves not to cede, 549; French driven out of, 550; campaign of 1815 in, 622 sqq.; the stumbling-block of Europe, 653; incorporated with Holland in the Kingdom of the Netherlands, 605 sq., 654 sq.; 668, 670; Vol. x, Chap. xvi *passim*; 39; and Rhenish Prussia, 381; revolt (1830) in, 480; France and, 482 sqq.; Casimir Périer and, 487 sq.; 489; French intervention in, 490; independence of, 505 sq.; industries in, 744, 753 sq., 755 sqq.; roads, canals, and railways in, 744 sqq.; joint-stock companies in, 747; the common lands of, 749; the customs tariff in, 752; 762

Belgium, modern kingdom of (1839-70), Vol. xi, Chap. xxiii (2); 9; 28; the Jesuits in, 67; the *Risquons Tout* in, 106; French exiles in, 140; 308; 447; France and, 462; Napoleon III and, 483, 496; neutrality of, 577 sq.; literature in, 676; and China, 819; affairs in (1870-1909), xii 250 sqq.; 3; 11; Great Britain and, 28; and Japan, 544; 621; 658; and the Congo State, 662 sq.; and the partition of Africa, 665; local government in, 734; factory legislation in, 747; social movements in, 755, 762 sq.; 842

Belgrade, siege of (1456) by the Turks, i 69; capture of (1521) by the Turks, 93, 337, ii 151; Solyman II at, iii 107, 118, 125; Turkish army at, 122; taken by the Emperor (1688), v 56, 368; recaptured by the Turks (1690), 61, 369; 346; 359; Kara Mustafa at, 363 sq.; 367, 370; vi 29; 32; 198; 203; captured by Laudon, 648, viii 292, 326; Peace of (1739), vi 308, 674; viii 324; Janissaries at, ix 387; evacuated by the Turks, xi 634; 647; xii 386; 392; 407; 412; revolution in, 413

Belgrano, and the revolution in Buenos Ayres, x 278

Beliardi, Abbé, Agent-general in Spain, vi 351

Belin, Jean-François de Faudoas, Comte de, Governor of Paris, iii 662

Belize, the United States and, xii 685
—— river, the English on, v 687

Bell, Dr Andrew, and elementary education, ix 692
—— Archibald, Lieutenant, in Australia, xi 791
—— John, American politician, vii 439 sq., 445

Bell, Mark, travels of, in Asia, xii 802

Bell, The, Russian journal. *See Kolokol*

Bellamy, French political agent, vii 321

Bellarmin, Roberto, Cardinal, Jesuit theologian, i 611; controversies of, iii 744, 749, 752; on the State, 757-9; iv 4; and ultramontanism v 75; vi 805

Bellasis, John Bellasis, 1st Lord, v 220

Bellay. *See Du Bellay*

Belleau, Remy, iii 55

Belleek, battle at, iii 604

Bellefonds, Bernardin Gigault, Marquis de, Marshal of France, v 59

Bellegarde, Comte Henri de, General, ix 65; 68, 347, 349
—— Roger de Saint Lary de, Marshal of France, Governor of Saluzzo, iii 408
—— Roger de Saint Lary et de Termes, Duke of, iii 47

Belle Isle, French fleet at, v 183; vi 426; ceded to France, 428; Portuguese vessels at, x 326 sq.

Belleisle, Charles-L.-A. Fouquet, Duke of, Marshal of France, vi 230 sqq.; retreats from Prague, 236; 239; in Italy, 245; 339; 362

Bellenden, Sir William, dismissed, v 284

Bellew, Sir Edward, x 634

Belliard, Count Augustin Daniel, French general, viii 603, 614, 617 sq.

Bellin, Christian von, iv 89 sq.

Bellings, Sir Richard, v 204

Bellini, Gentile, paints the portrait of Mohammad II, i 85; 284
—— Laurentio, anatomist, v 729
—— Vincenzo, the music of, x 129 sq.

Bellinzona, given to the Swiss by Louis XII, ii 308

Bello, Francesco, "the Blind Man of Ferrara," iii 461

Bellomont, Richard Coote, Earl of, Governor of Massachusetts, and of New York, vii 64

Belloy, Pierre-Laurent-Buyrette de, French writer, vi 831

Belluno, Austrian occupation of, xi 86
—— Claude Perrin, *alias* Victor, Duc de. *See Victor*

Belmont (Cape Colony), Boers defeated at, xii 642
—— (on the Mississippi), indecisive engagement at (1861), vii 494

Belmonte, Prince of, arrested (July 19, 1811), ix 383; resigns office, 384

Beloch, Julius, historian, xii 845

Below, Frau von, vi 217

Belturbet, captured by Col. Wolseley (1689), v 313

Bem, Joseph, Polish exile and Hungarian general, at the defence of Vienna, xi 188; in Transylvania, 204 sqq.; 209; defeat of, at Temesvár, 211; 213; at Widdin, 215

Bembo, Pietro, Cardinal, Bishop of Bergamo, Italian Latinist, i 56, 545, 560,

564; II 16–20, 30, 118; the Oratory of Divine Love and, 379; III 458 sqq.

Benares, Warren Hastings and, VI 578 sqq., 582, 584

Benavente, Paget defeats the French at (1808), IX 445

Benbow, John, Admiral, X 272

Benburb, victory of Owen O'Neill at, IV 530

Benckendorff, General Count Alexander von, and the Russian secret societies, X 439; 443; chief of Russian Secret Police, XI 263

Bender, Russian capture of, VI 673

Bendereff, Bulgarian Minister of War, XII 408

Bendigo, gold in, XI 796

Benecke, Georg Friedrich, XII 823

Benedek, Field-Marshal Ludwig von, XI 46; 452 sq.

Benedetti, Francesco, the *Cola di Rienzo,* X 125

—— Count Vincent, French diplomatist, XI 313; 388; and Bismarck, 454; 457; and the King of Prussia, 463, 578; 483; 495; Minister at Turin, 531; 577

Benedetto, Frà, and Savonarola, I 188

—— of Mantua, the *Beneficio della morte di Cristo,* II 389

Benedict, St, I 534

—— XIII (Pietro Francesco Orsini), Pope, VI 140; 587; 589

—— XIV (Prospero Lambertini), Pope, VI 228; Concordat of, with Spain, 365; 384; and the Jesuits, 386, 592; 589 sq.; and France, 591; 601; XI 706

Benedictines, guardians of books in the Middle Ages, I 534; literary enterprise of, 592; at Oxford and Cambridge, 643 sq.; Spanish, 651. *See also* Religious Orders, St Maur, etc.

Benedictus Deus, the Bull (1564), confirms decrees of the Council of Trent, II 686

Benedix, Roderich, German dramatist, XI 414 sqq.

Benevento, trade of, III 438; VI 594; restored to the Papacy, 595; occupied by Naples, VIII 650; declared to belong to the Church, IX 189; granted to Talleyrand, 194; 268; no longer held by Talleyrand, 584; claimed by Naples, X 132; rising in, 150

—— Giovanni Della Casa, Archbishop of, II 384; III 466; 474

Benevolences, under James I (1614), III 561, 574; asked for by Charles I (1626), IV 265

Bénézech, Pierre, Minister of the Interior under Directory, VIII 490, 508

Benfeld, Swedes at, IV 381

Benfield, Paul, servant of East India Company, VI 576

Bengal, English settlements on the coast of, IV 742; the Dutch in, V 695, 697; 698; defeat of the English in, 699; French

factory in, 703; 704 sq.; Vol. VI, Chap XV *passim*; 429; government of, 445; 464; Permanent Settlement of (1793), IX 711 sqq., 732; 722; 728; XI 727; Dalhousie and, 744; 751; military system of, 752 sq.; famine in, XII 464; Tenancy Act in, 480; partition of, 494 sqq.

Bengal, Náwab Názim of, legal rights of, IX 711

Benguela, Cameron at, XII 810

Benivieni, Girolamo, poet, II 702

Benjamin, Judah Philip, Confederate Secretary of State, VII 578, 604

Bennet, Henry, Earl of Arlington. *See* Arlington

Bennett, C., and photography, XII 783

—— Richard, and O'Connell, X 630

Bennigsen, Comte Levin Auguste Théophile de, Russian general, IX 49; 50, 251, 259, 261; occupies Warsaw, 283–4; commander-in-chief, 285; retreats to Königsberg, 286; at Friedland, 290; desires peace, 291; at Tilsit, 297; and the invasion of 1812, 489 sqq.; in Bohemia, 531; 533, 537; at Leipzig, 538

—— Count Alexander Levin von, XI 148

—— Rudolf von, Hanoverian statesman, XI 407; XII 146; 151

Bennington, victory of Starke at (1777), VII 215

Benoit, French socialist, XII 123

Benon, captured by La Noue, III 27

Bentham, Jeremy, VI 814; 821; VIII 748, 755, 769; *Treatise on Legislation,* IX 175; and Parliamentary reform, 688; influence of, X 4; and the American republics, 38; 229; and the Tsar, 418; 585; achievements and political views of, 594 sqq.; and parliamentary reform, 602; 609; 661; and James Mill, 778; and Robert Owen, 780; and William Thompson, *ib.*; XI 756 sq.; colonial views of, 765 sq.; XII 734

Bentinck, William, Earl of Portland. *See* Portland

—— Lord George, attacks Sir Robert Peel, XI 11; 15; death of, 20

—— Lord William Cavendish, British commander in Sicily, IX 383; insists on removal of Queen of Naples, 384; supersedes Murray, 479; 599; in India, 731; Governor-General of India, XI 724; 729 sqq.

Bentivegna, Francesco, Baron, XI 380

Bentivoglio, Giovanni, I 112, 123; Julius II and, 128, 245

Bentley, Richard, English scholar, I 582; V 125; and the *Epistles of Phalaris,* XII 816

Bentonville, Slocum attacked at (1865), VII 530

Benue river, XII 130; 659 sq.; explorers on, 807 sq., 810 sq.

Benvenuti, Cardinal, taken prisoner, X 155

Beobachter, Oesterrischischer, x 357; 365
—— *Stuttgart,* suppressed, x 369
Béranger, Pierre-Jean de, x 88; and the fall of Molé, 510; xi 24
Berar, cession of, xi 743
—— Rájah of, hostility of, ix 722; 726; xi 725 sqq.
Berard (Berardus Bonjoannes, Bishop of Camerino), nuncio in Poland, iii 81–2
Bérard, Auguste-Simon-Louis, French politician, x 477 sq.
Beraun Valley, Belleisle in, vi 236
Berber, taken by the Mahdi, xii 442; 443; 448; travellers at, 805 sq.
Berbers, of Africa, iii 682
Berbice, Dutch colony of, iv 709; occupation of (1796), ix 750, 753, 755; ceded to Great Britain (1814), x 520; xi 667
—— river, the Dutch on, vi 186
Berchet, Giovanni, x 124; 126
Berchtold, Count Frederick, xi 654
Berdáyeff, Russian Liberal, xii 333
Berenger, Réné, French politician, xii 107
Beresford, Lord George, and the Waterford election, x 644
—— John, dismissal of, ix 698 sqq.
—— William Carr Beresford, Viscount (general), sent to reorganise the Portuguese army, ix 448; with Wellesley, 451; marches into Spanish Estremadura, 462–3; Wellington joins, 466; at Albuera, 467; 468; marches on Bordeaux, 481; in Buenos Ayres, 753, x 281; in Portugal, 312
Berezina river, Charles XII crosses, v 598; Napoleon's crossing of, ix 501 sqq.
Berezoff, Menshikoff banished to, v 554; iron-works at, xi 618; founded by Cossacks, xii 794
Berezowski, attempts to assassinate the Tsar, xi 484
Berg, secured by Neuburg at the Treaty of Cleves, iv 409; duchy of, v 350; 627 sq.; 643; vi 226; 231; grand duchy of, granted to Murat, ix 267, 409–10; and the Central Administration, 587; cession of, to Prussia, 592, 657; regiment of, 623
—— Duke of (1423), invested with Gelders, i 424
—— William IV, Duke of. *See* Jülich-Berg
—— Grand Duke of. *See* Murat
—— *See also* Jülich-Cleves-Berg
—— Kristen, Danish politician, xii 292
Bergaigne, Joseph de, Archbishop of Cambray. *See* Cambray
Bergamo, acquired by Venice, i 280; democratic revolt at, viii 584 sq.
—— Nicholas Lippomano, Bishop of, ii 30
—— Vittorio Soranzo, Bishop of, Italian reformer, ii 390, 398
Bergasse, Nicolas, member of the National Assembly, viii 173, 178, 183
Bergedorf, meeting of Hanse Towns at, iv 92

Bergen, spoliation of the Church at, ii 618; naval battle off (1665), v 110; 182; port of, vi 737
—— Olaf Thorkildssön, Bishop of, ii 618
—— Gebel Pederssön, Bishop-elect of, ii 620
Bergen-op-Zoom, Conference at (1600), iii 534; Twelve Years' Truce signed at (1609), 540; besieged by Spinola, 655, iv 81; taken by the French (1747), vi 248, 331; Pichegru captures, viii 436; fight at (1799), 662; occupied by Napoleon (1810), ix 370
—— Jan van Glimes, Marquis of, iii 194–5, 201, 205, 207, 227–8
Bergenroth, Gustav Adolf, and Ranke, xii 827
Berger, Jean-Jacques, Prefect of the Seine, xi 119; 303
—— Johann Nepomuk, Austrian statesman, xii 187
—— *See* Lund, Archbishops of
Bergerac, Treaty of (1577), iii 32
Bergeyek, Count, Spanish diplomatist, v 420
Bergh *or* Berg, Herman, Count van den (son of Count William), iii 626
—— Henry, Count van den (son of Count William), at Hertogenbosch, iv 693
—— William (IV), Count van den, iii 217, 222, 257
Berghausen, Austria and, vi 633
Berghen, Marquis of. *See* Bergen-op-Zoom
Bergün, importance of, iv 41; Synod at (1618), 46 sq.
Bergues, Sieur de, Imperial envoy to England, i 477
Beringskjold, Magnus, Colonel, vi 749; 751
Berkeley, George, Bishop of Cloyne, vi 40; 54 sq.; 77 sqq.; 806; vii 58
—— George Cranfield, British vice-admiral, vii 329 sqq.
—— Sir Robert, judge, iv 283; committed to custody, 287
—— Sir William (d. 1677), Governor of Virginia, vii 8 sq.; 34, 59
—— Sir William (d. 1666), vice-admiral, v 184
—— of Stratton, John, 1st Baron, Lord-Lieutenant of Ireland, v 305
—— of Stratton, John, 3rd Baron, proprietary of New Jersey, vii 41, 47
Berks, Bavarian Minister of the Interior, xi 146
Berkshire, Parliament and, iv 549
Berleburg, Count Casimir von, v 761
Berlichingen, Götz von, the Peasants' Rising and, ii 182 sq., 187 sq.; deserts the peasants, 189
Berlier, Comte Théophile, member of the National Convention, viii 386; ix 151; 163

Berlin, German Calvinists in, **iv** 5; 199; Gustavus Adolphus and George William at, 200; march of Gustavus Adolphus upon, 203; Saxon and Imperialist troops in, 367; Cartesian philosophy in, 786; **v** 594; 618; foundation of, 620; 625; 639; 645; French colony at, 646, 670; 669; **vi** 217 sq.; Government departments at, 222; Russian Company in, 224; 240; 244; 253; 265; 267 sq.; 287 sq.; 292 sq.; occupied by Russian and Austrian troops, 296, 326; 297 sq.; 316; 327; Nivernais at, 334; 713; 718; factories in, 719; *Reichsbank* at, 721; Kolychéff despatched to, **ix** 36; negotiations between France and Russia centred in, 41; anti-French feeling at Court of, 249; 250; Treaty of Paris ratified at, 266; British Minister recalled from, *ib.*; popular excitement in, 272; Napoleon marches on, 274, 277; French enter (1806), 279; Davout at, 278; Napoleon at, 281; Fichte at, 325; University established at, 327 sq.; Stein at, 329; *Militärische Gesellschaft* at, 332; return of King and Queen to (1809), 334, 336; Schill departs from, 357; Turkish embassy in, 386; Grenier at, 512; Frederick William leaves, *ib.*; Tettenborn in, 514; guarded by Bülow, 518; Oudinot marches on, 520, 523, 525; retreats from, 526; importance of, **x** 349; 353; relations between Rome and, 381; literary circle in, 404; secret societies in, 453; industrial undertakings in, 732, 744, 754, 757 sq.; the open plough-fields of, 749; *Gewerbeinstitut* at, 752; **xi** 52; 54; insurrection in, 151; the revolutionary movement in, 156 sqq.; the "March Days" in, 157 sqq.; 188; the "National Assembly" at, 192 sq.; disturbance in, 218; and the Hesse-Cassel crisis, 229 sq.; 450; **xii** 12; Tsar Alexander II in, 97; meeting of the Emperors at, 139; 150; African Conference at, 659; University of, 820; 821; 824
—— Peace of (1742), **vi** 235, 240, (1850), **xi** 225; Alliance of (1788), **vi** 709; Decree (1806), **vii** 330 sq., 333, 353, **ix** 283, 361, 364 sq., 378; Convention of (1833), **x** 39, 376; Conference of (1849), **xi** 220, (1866), 458, (1880), **xii** 402 sq.; (1884–5), 3, 130, 256, 662 sq.; (1889), **vii** 663; Congress (1878), **xii** 33; 98; 124 sq.; 153; Italy and, 158, 239; 192; the Armenians and, 416; and Russia, 341 sq.; 394 sqq.; 408; 414; 428; 468 sq.; Treaty of, 37; 305
—— Academy, **v** 670, **xi** 49, **xii** 823, 843
Berlinghieri, Commander of the Order of St John, at the Congress of Vienna, **ix** 604
Bermuda Hundred, Grant and Butler at, **vii** 520
Bermudas, The, settlement of, **iv** 756; failure of Berkeley's scheme in, **vi** 54 sq.; 184;

Somers and Gates wrecked on, **vii** 5; 552; government of, **xii** 657
Bermudez, confessor of Philip V, **vi** 137; 145
Bern, **ii** 325, 328; the Reformation in, 327 sq.; aggression of, **iii** 405 sqq.; and the Spanish alliance, **iv** 45; *Bund* appeals for help to, 50; 52; and Erlach, 375; and Neuchâtel, **v** 449; **vi** 613 sqq.; 619; 622; and Austria, 623; the patriciate of, 624; 625; French occupation of (1798), **viii** 596 sq., 782; plundered, **ix** 96; *coups d'état* at (1800–1), 97 sqq.; Federalists at, 100; and the Swiss Confederation, 105; Napoleon confiscates stores of merchandise at, 373; and the Congress of Vienna, 600–1; 671; **xi** 234; government of, 235; 236 sq.; reaction in, 238; 240; joins the *Siebnerkonkordat*, 242; University of, 241; 246 sq.; Federal Diet at, 248, 250; 249; 253; constituted the capital, 254; 259
Bernadotte, the House of, **xi** 677
—— General, Jean-Baptiste-Jules. *See* Charles (XIV) John, King of Sweden
Bernaldez, André, Spanish historian, **i** 381
Bernard, Aristide-Martin (Martin-Bernard), French politician, **x** 511; **xi** 104; 126; 132
—— Sir Francis, colonial governor, **vii** 152 sq.
—— Nathaniel, imprisonment of, **iv** 279
—— Simon, trial of, **xi** 328 sq.
—— of Chartres, medieval Latinist, **i** 536
—— of Weimar. *See* Saxe-Weimar, Duke Bernard of
Bernardine army (Bernardines), **iv** 382 sqq.
Bernardino, St, of Feltre, **i** 147, 167, 647
—— St, of Siena, **i** 144, 151, 163, 186, 189
Bernardo, Antonio di, Medicean partisan, hanged (1494), **i** 168
—— Secretary to Cosimo I, **iii** 388
Bernburg. *See* Anhalt-Bernburg
Berners, Sir John Bourchier, Lord, **iii** 365
Bernetti, Tommaso, Cardinal, papal secretary of State, **x** 154; 155; 156
Berni, Francesco, the *Orlando Innamorato*, **ii** 395; **iii** 457 sqq.
Bernier, Abbé Étienne-Alexandre-Jean-Baptiste-Marie, Vendean leader, **viii** 382; **ix** 14; 182, 184, 188
—— François, French historian, **vi** 520; 523; 525
Bernis, François-Joachim de Pierre de, Cardinal, French statesman, **vi** 254; at Venice, 335; 337 sq.; fall of, 341 sq.; 400; and the Bull *Unigenitus*, 591; created Cardinal, 594; 595; writings of, 827
Bernoulli, Daniel, **xi** 260
—— Jacob (James), **v** 718; **xi** 260
—— Johann, **v** 718; **xi** 260
Bernstorff, Count Albert, Prussian Foreign Minister, **xi** 407

Bernstorff, Andreas Gottlieb von, Hanoverian statesman, vi 4; 10; 13 sqq.; 20; influence of, in England, 22; and the war with Sweden, 26; 35; 39

—— Count Andreas Peter von, Danish statesman, vi 741; 753; dismissal of, 754; administration of, 755 sqq.; viii 279 sq., 788; ix 43 sq.

—— Christian Günther, Count, at the Congress of Vienna, ix 586; at the Conference of Aix-la-Chapelle, x 14; 366; Metternich and, 372; succeeded by Ancillon, 376

—— Joachim Frederick, Count, at the Congress of Vienna, ix 586

—— Johann Hartwig Ernst, Count von, Danish statesman, vi 735; 740 sqq.; fall of, 746; 749; 751; 753; 755

Beroaldo, Filippo, the younger (Beroaldus), Tacitus' *Annals* edited by, i 566, ii 8, 15; 16

Berovich, Georgi, Governor of Crete, xii 419

Berquin, Louis de, French reformer, ii 283 sq., 346

Berre, surrender of, iii 418

Berrugete, Alonso de, Spanish sculptor, i 382

Berry, Huguenot levy on, iii 30; Condé Governor of, iv 608, 614; customs of, v 13; provincial assembly at, viii 91

—— Caroline de Bourbon, Duchess of, x 286; 288 sq.; imprisonment of, 490; 495; 499

—— Charles, Duke of (grandson of Louis XIV), death of, v 30 sq., 441; 393

—— Charles-Ferdinand d'Artois, Duc de, and the Ministry of Louis XVIII, ix 566; 568; assassination of, x 23, 63, 71, 438

—— Lieutenant, American explorer, xii 795

Berryer, Pierre-Antoine, x 508 sq.; xi 109; 133; 136; 475

Berstett, Baron W. L. L. R. von, Baden minister, x 362; 372

Bert, Paul, French politician, xii 105; 114

Bertaut, Jean, Bishop of Séez. *See* Séez

Bertendona, Martin de, iii 307

Bertheaume Bay, French fleet in, ix 223

Berthelier, Philibert, of Geneva, ii 362

Berthereau, French jurist, ix 166

Berthier, Louis-Alexandre, Prince of Wagram and Neuchâtel, Marshal of France, viii 564, 568 sq., 616, 637 sqq., 674, and Brumaire, 679, 683; ix 1; 10, 59, 107; Napoleon's Vice-Constable, 110; 136; Grand Huntsman, 111; receives Neuchâtel, *ib.*; Prince of Wagram, 112; Prince of Neuchâtel, 267; Napoleon's instructions to, 273; 347–8; rumoured project of Napoleon concerning, 425; Chief of the Staff, 489; refuses to join Napoleon, 621

—— de Sauvigny, Louis-Bénigne-François, murdered, viii 168

Berthold of Mainz. *See* Mainz

Berthollet, Comte Claude-Louis, French chemist, viii 606, 616, 674

Bertin, Henri-L.-J.-B., French Controller-general, vi 356

—— de Vaux, Louis-François, x 91

Bertoldi, Giuseppe, poet, xi 545

Berton, Jean-Baptiste, French general, x 76

Bertrand, Comte Henri-Gratien, French general, viii 602, 606; at Memel, ix 287; 520; at Dennewitz, 529; 530; at Wartenburg, 531; 532; at Lindenau, 535; despatched to Saale, 537; taken prisoner, 540; at St Helena, 757; 761; 769

—— de Molleville, Antoine-François, Marquis de, viii 89, 112, 148, 216; policy of, 222

Bertz, Secretary of Margaret of Parma, iii 213

Bérulle, Pierre, Cardinal, French statesman, and Mary de' Medici, iv 137; founds the Oratory, 156; v 78

Berwick, Treaty of (1560), ii 576, (1639), iv 284, 502 sq., 520

—— James Fitzjames, Duke of, Marshal of France, v 262; 315; 405; in Spain, 416, 419, 446; 421 sq.; Marlborough and, 461; vi 14 sq.; 34; 97 sq.; 102

Berzelius, Baron Jöns Jacob, Swedish chemist, xi 686

Berzsenyi, Daniel, Hungarian poet, xi 424

Besançon, *Parlement* of, v 4, viii 47, 95, 745; v 48; xi 601 sq.; French troops at, 604, 609; 610

Besborodko, Alexander, Russian statesman, vi 678; 682; 697; 783

Beseler, Wilhelm Hartwig, Schleswig political leader, xi 161

Besenval, Baron Pierre-Victor de, viii 163

Beshir, Emir, chief of the Lebanon, x 550; xi 276

Besika Bay, British fleet at, xii 387, 390

Beslay, Charles, French politician, xi 502

Bessarabia, vi 674; annexed to Russia, x 413, xi 485; 323; 633; the Treaty of Paris and, 643; Russia and, xii 305, 339; 354; 392 sq.; the Treaty of Berlin and, 397

Bessarion, John, Cardinal, i 80, 284; the Platonists and, ii 4; 16; v 482

Bessborough, Brabazon Ponsonby, 1st Earl of, vi 431; 489

—— John William Ponsonby (Lord Duncannon), 4th Earl of, x 603; 610; 655; 669

Bessenyei, George, Hungarian writer, xi 421 sq., 431

Bessey, Antoine de, raises Swiss troops for Charles VIII, i 112, 117, 122

Bessières, Jean-Baptiste, Duke of Istria, French marshal, viii 616; ix 111; 351; crosses the Bidassoa, 430; troops of, 435; 436; and Masséna, 465–6; and the Russian campaign, 488; 497

Bessières, Jorje, x 221; in Spain, 223, 227, 230

Bestuzheff, Alexander ("Marlinski"), x 427; 431

—— Alexis, Grand Chancellor of Russia, vi 252; 313 sqq.; fall of, 322; 340; Catharine II and, 660, 663; 679

—— Michael Petrovich, Russian diplomatist, v 551; Minister at Stockholm, vi 309; 315; at Paris, 322 sqq.

—— Count Peter, vi 301

Bestuzheff-Riumin, Michael, x 442 sq.; 454

Bethlen Gabor, Prince of Transylvania. *See* Transylvania

Bethmann-Hollweg, Moritz August von, German politician, xi 192; 396

—— Theobald von, Chancellor of the German Empire, xii 166

Bethmont, Eugène, French Minister of Commerce, xi 104

Béthune, occupied by French, iv 598; 599; captured by the Allies (1710), v 429

—— Maximilien-Alpin, Marquis of, French envoy in Poland, v 354; 356; 566

Beton, David, Cardinal, Archbishop of St Andrews, ii 449, 456, 457 sq.; murdered, 461 sq., 555 sq., iii 262; and the English alliance, 261

—— James, Archbishop of St Andrews, ii 453 sq.; iii 270, 274, 288

Betterton, Thomas, actor, v 130

Betzki, Count, vi 692

Beuckelssen (Bockelsohn), Jan. *See* John of Leyden

Beuermann, Moriz von, African explorer, xii 811

Beugnot, Jacques-Claude, Comte, appointed Imperial Commissioner in the Duchy of Berg, ix 410; government of, 411; 560; ordinance signed by, 569; x 44; and the Doctrinaires, 52; 55; 63

Beulé, Charles-Ernest, French politician, xii 108

Beuningen, Conrad van, v 145; Dutch ambassador at Paris, 152 sq.; in England, 154, 217; and de Witt, 154, 156; 164

Beurnonville, Pierre de Ruel, Marquis de, French Minister of War, viii 263, 269, 415, 417, 421; 679 sq.

Beust, Count Ferdinand Friedrich von, xi 142; Saxon Minister of Foreign Affairs, 149; 219; at the Confederation conferences, 220, 232; 397; 408; 496; and the Vatican Council, 721; and Hungary, xii 182 sqq.; 186 sqq.; and Prussia, 191; fall of, 192; 402

Bevan, Edwyn Robert, historian, xii 845

Beverley, Robert, vii 60

Bevern. *See* Brunswick-Bevern

Beverningh, Hieronymus van, Dutch envoy to England, v 141 sqq.; resigns, 154; 160; 164 sq.

Bevilacqua press, The, iii 412

Beyle, Marie-Henri (Stendhal), x 101 sq.; xi 520

Beyme, K. F. von, Prussian statesman and jurist, ix 264; unpopularity of, 272; 282; x 349; 351; 366

Beza, Theodore, Berquin and, ii 284; intercedes against persecution, 293; 298; at Poissy, 302–3; 350; meets Calvin, 352; 363; at Geneva, 373; 581; epigram on Rabelais by, 711; 717 sq.; iii 5, 743, 755

Bezborodko, Count Alexander Alexandrowich, ix 35

Béziers, Cardinal Consalvi at, x 133; Republican attack on, xi 137

Bezobrazoff, Russian speculator in Korea, xii 576

Bezuidenhout, Frederick, xi 779

—— Jan, xi 779

Bhamo, British mission at, xii 500; 793; 796

Bharatpur, xi 727; capture of, 729

—— Rájah of, treaty with, ix 728

Bhonsla, and Indian politics, ix 717; 725, 726

Bhopal, xi 725; the East India Company and, 726

Bhotans, The, Formosan tribe, xii 556

Bhutan, military operations in, xi 752

Biala, Bennigsen at, ix 285

Bialystok, annexed to Russia (1807), ix 293, 337, x 413; incorporated in province of Grodno (1842), 420; 427; Russian administration of, 459; 469

Biána, battle at, vi 509

Biarritz, Napoleon and Bismarck at, xi 447, 479

Biban (the Iron Gates), occupied by the French, x 504

Bibbiena, Cardinal (Bernardo di Dovizi), ii 8; *La Calandria*, 11; 15 sq.

—— Piero da, iii 388

Biberach, engagement at (1800), ix 58

Bibesco, George, Hospodar of Wallachia, xi 283

Bibikoff, Dmitri Gavrilovich, Russian Minister of the Interior, xi 614

—— Russian general, puts down Pugacheff's rising (1773–5), vi 680; 687

Bible, The, medieval knowledge of, early commentaries, translations, etc., i 585 sqq.; printed in the original (the Complutensian Polyglot, Roman edition of the Septuagint, etc.), 602 sqq., 639 sq.; versions of, Latin, *ib.*; vernacular, *ib.*; general survey of Latin and vernacular, 639 sqq.; German, French, Italian, etc., *ib.*; English, 640 sqq.; dissemination of, 684 sqq.; the *Biblia Hebraica* of Sebastian Munster, ii 355. Versions of: German (by Luther), 164; French (by Lefèvre d'Etaples and by Jean de Rély), 283; Italian (by Brucioli), 383; Slavonic, 395; Spanish, 402, 406, 411; English (authorised), 453, 464 sqq.; English, various, 464 sq.; Danish, 617; Icelandic, 621; Swedish, 624; *The Bishops' Bible,*

III 377; Sixtus V's, published by Clement VIII (1592), 445; the *Berleburg Bible*, v 761. *See also* New Testament

Bibliography, classical, Vol. i, Chap. xvi *passim*; Christian, Chap. xvii *passim*, especially 610 sqq.; *but see also* Libraries, Bible, etc.

Bibliotheca Palatina, given by Maximilian to Pope Gregory XV, iv 83. *See also* Libraries

Bibliothecae Patrum, early (printed) editions of the, i 617 sq.

Bibliothèque Catholique, Royalist journal, x 72

Bichat, Marie-François-Xavier, ix 133

Bicker, Andries, iv 726

—— Cornelis, uncle of the wife of John de Witt, iv 726; v 145

—— Wendela, wife of John de Witt, v 144

Bicocca, battle of the (1522), ii 45

Bidassoa river, Junot crosses, ix 303; Dupont ordered to cross, 430; lines of, 480

Biddle, John, Unitarian, persecuted by Parliament, iv 454; v 327

Biegeleben, Freiherr Ludwig Maximilian von, Austrian Privy Councillor, xi 444

Biel, ceded to Bern, ix 601

—— Gabriel, last of medieval schoolmen, i 637; at Erfurt, ii 111

Bielany, secret society founded at, x 453

Bielaya Krinitza, bishopric at, xi 266

Bielefeld, taxation in, vi 221

Bielinski, Count Peter, x 457

—— Vissarion, Russian writer, xi 614, 649

Bielke, Gunilla, marries John III of Sweden, iv 167

—— Hogenskild, beheaded, iv 174

—— Nils, Swedish statesman, v 573

—— Steno, Swedish diplomatist, iv 373

—— Ture, imprisonment of, iv 169; flight of, to Denmark, 172; beheaded, 173

Bielopolye, Austria and, xii 396

Bielowice, Charles XII at, v 592

Bielski, Bogdan Jakowlewitsch, candidate for Russian crown, v 497

—— Marcin, Polish chronicler, iii 88

Bienerth, Baron Richard von, Austrian statesman, xii 209

Bienhoa, ceded to France, xii 524

Bienvenu Martin, Jean-Baptiste, French Minister of Public Worship, xii 122

Bienville, Céleron de, explores Ohio, vii 119

—— Jean Baptiste Lemoine (*or* Le Moyne), Sieur de, vii 88

Biez. *See* Du Biez

Biffen, Rowland, agricultural scientist, xii 777

Big Bethel, Federal defeat at (1861), vii 464

Big Black River, Confederates driven from (1863), vii 504

Biggar, Joseph Gillis, Irish politician, xii 74

Bigge, John Thomas, mission of, to Australia, xi 789 sq.

Bigi, Medicean party in Florence, i 157, 175

Bigne, Marguerin de La, editor of *Bibliotheca Veterum Patrum*, i 618 sq.

Bignon, Louis-Pierre-Édouard, x 91

Bigod, Sir Francis, in the Pilgrimage of Grace, ii 447

Bigot, Charles, French writer, xii 94

—— François, *Intendant* of New France, vii 95, 143

—— de Préameneu, Felix-Julien-Jean, viii 213, 742; Minister of Public Worship, ix 136; 150

Bihé, Cameron at, xii 810

Bijapur, war of, with Aurungzeb, v 698; besieged by Shah Jehán, vi 517 sq.; 519 sqq.; surrenders to Aurungzeb, 522

Bilad Ghana. *See* Guinea

Bilbao, captured by the French, viii 441; besieged (1835), x 235, (1836), 238, (1874), xii 262

Bilbassoff, B. von, Russian historian, xii 842

Bilde, Marshal Anders, reconquers Bremen and Verden, iv 584; mortally wounded at Frederiksodde, 585

—— Éske, *Kirkebryder*, ii 618

—— Ove. *See* Aarhuus, Bishop of

Bilderdyck, William, Dutch poet, viii 788; xi 675

Bilderling, Russian general, in the Russo-Japanese War, xii 591, 593, 597 sq.

Bilders, Albert, Dutch painter, xii 249

Bilek, Montenegro and, xii 392

Bill of Rights, character of the, v 251 sq., 277

Bill, Dr William, Dean of Westminster, ii 565

Billaud-Varennes, Jean-Nicolas, viii 234, 239, 246 sq., 339; on the *Comité de Salut Public*, 344, 349 sqq., 358 sq., 362; and the fall of Robespierre, 364 sqq., 369; 374 sq., 377; charges against, 380, 384; deported, 385

Billault, Auguste-Adolphe-Marie, French statesman, xi 294; 297; 477

Billicanus, German Reformer, ii 160

Billick, Eberhard, Catholic divine, ii 251

Billingsley, Captain, iv 290

Billioray, Alfred-Édouard, French politician, xi 502

Billot, Jean-Baptiste, French Minister of War, xii 96

Bilma, British explorers at, xii 807

Biloxi, fort at, vii 88, 362

Bilsen, Marlborough at, v 415

Binch, restored to Spain, v 45

Binder, Baron, Austrian diplomatist, at the Congress of Vienna, ix 583

Binger, Louis, African explorer, xii 129; 812

Bingham, Sir Richard, President of Con-
naught, III 604
Binnenhof, The (at the Hague), Remon-
strants imprisoned in, III 652; Olden-
barneveldt sentenced in, 654
Biondo. See Blondus
Bir, Ottoman army at (1839), x 561
Birago, René de, *afterwards* Cardinal,
Chancellor of France, III 19, 27, 33
Biran, Maine de, IX 133
Birch, John, Colonel, v 216
—— British Resident at Perak, XII 532
Biren, Ernst Johann, Duke of Courland,
Grand Chamberlain of Russia, VI 301;
proclaimed Regent, 309; 312 sq.; 665 sq.
Birkenfeld, Christian, Count Palatine of,
victory of, in the Palatinate, IV 229;
defeats Charles of Lorraine, 230
Birmingham, parliamentary representation
of, x 601 sq.; 613; Political Union, 612,
615, 683; the metal trades in, 737;
bombs made in, XI 327; XII 44; University of, 763
—— League, and the Education Act,
XII 25
Birney, James Gillespie, abolitionist, VII
387 sq., 390, 393
Biron, Baron Armand de Gontaut of,
Marshal of France, III 14, 20 sq., 33,
40, 44; 47; 334; 658; 661; 679; death
of, 52
—— Armand-Louis de Gontaut, Duc de
Lauzun and Duc de, VIII 339, 346; executed (1793), 357; commands the Army
of the Rhine (1792), 407, 413; and the
war with Sardinia, 437
—— Charles de Gontaut, Duke of, III
667; 672 sq.; 677; conspiracy and
execution of, 679 sq.; 683
Birse, Peter the Great and Augustus II at,
v 590
Bisamberg, Archduke Charles on, IX 350
Biscay, occupied by Marshal Moncey, IX
430; Blake's advance into, 442; Liberal
discontent in, XII 260; 263; 268
—— Bay of, VI 248; 344; Admiral Keppel
in, 450
Bischoff, Mount, tin discovered at, XII 619
Bischoffswerder, Johann Rudolph von,
Adjutant-General of Frederick William II
of Prussia, VI 726; VIII 529 sq.
Biseglia, Alfonso de, third husband of
Lucrezia Borgia, I 236, 239
Biserta, French expedition against, VI 350
Bishops' Bible, The, III 377
Bishops' Book, The, or *The Institution of
a Christian Man*, II 448
Bishops' Wars, The First and Second (1639-
40), IV 501 sqq.
Bismarck archipelago, XII 668
—— Herbert, Prince von, mission of, to
England, XII 161
Bismarck-Schönhausen, Otto Eduard Leo-
pold, Prince von, VII 661 sqq.; Ministry
of (1862-71), Vol. XI, Chap. XVI; 58; 160;

192; and German Unity, 220, 223, 408,
577; and the Hesse-Cassel crisis, 231;
305; and the Schleswig-Holstein question,
338; 394; 396; and Austria, 402 sq.;
406; 410 sq.; at Biarritz, 447, 479; and
the Luxemburg question, 483; policy of,
towards France, 494 sq., 576 sqq.; and
the peace negotiations with France, 497
sqq., 600, 611 sq.; and the alliance with
Italy, 539 sq.; and the Spanish succession, 571; and army reform, 579; and
the Vatican Council, 719; and the German
Empire, Vol. XII, Chap. VI *passim*; 8 sq.;
14 sq.; 28; and France, 95, 97 sq., 107,
114; and Tunis, 239; and the Triple
Alliance, 240; and the Caroline Islands
dispute, 264; 275; at the Congress of
Berlin, 394; and the Armenian question,
416; and Egyptian affairs, 435; and
colonisation, 528, 658; and colonisation
in Africa, 658; 828; 844
Bissolati-Bergamaschi, Leonida, editor of
l'Avanti, XII 231
Bisticci, Vespasiano da. See Vespasiano
Bitonto, Spanish victory at, VI 153
Bitsch, VIII 407, defences of, 423; occupied
by the Prussians (1793), 425
Bitzius, Albert ("Jeremias Gotthelf"),
Swiss writer, XI 261; 417 sq.
Biveroni, Jakob, IV 36
Biville, Cadoudal lands at, IX 29; Savary
at, 30
Bixio, Jacques-Alexandre, French deputy,
XI 113; 118
Bizen, Japanese noble, XI 850
Bjerregaard, Henrik Anker, Norwegian
poet, XI 700
Björnson, Björnstjerne, Norwegian novelist
and dramatist, XI 701 sq.; XII 281
Blacas, Pierre-Louis-Jean-Casimir, Duc de,
and the Ministry of Louis XVIII, IX 565;
advice of, 574; x 44 sq.; mission of, to
Rome, 143
Black, David, preacher, III 551
—— James Robert, and the Working
Man's Association, x 682
—— Death, effects of, I 426, 500
—— Forest, distress of peasantry of, I
299; French army in, v 406 sqq.; IX
57 sq., 253
—— Sea, Poland and, III 73; Russian
designs on, v 370, 494, 526, 603, VI 304,
630, 633 sq., 648; Russian expedition to
(1770), 673; Treaty of Kutchuk-Kainardji
and, 674; 676, 695; Russian claims on,
x 170, 173, 175; Russia commands (1829),
202, 546 sq., XI 274; Russian fleet in
(1833), x 555; British and French fleets
in, XI 316, 572; the Powers and, 321 sq.;
neutralisation of, 323 sq.; 577; abroga-
tion of the Treaty of Paris clauses, 611,
614, 633 sq., 639; the Powers and, XII
28; Russia and, 298, 382; 388; 395; 398
Blackburn, riots at, XI 2
Blackburne, Robert, *Auctarium*, VI 791

Blackford, burning of, VI 102
Blackfriars, the trial of the Divorce question at, II 431
Blackheath, fight at (1497), I 469
Blackmore, Richard D., novelist, XI 359
Blackness Castle, VI 92
Blackstone, Sir William, judge, VI 811
Blackwater, fort at the, III 605–7
Blackwell, Elizabeth, medical practitioner, XII 763
—— George, III 353
Blackwood's Magazine, XI 362
Blaçons, Henri-F.-L. d'Armand de Forest, Marquis de, deputy of the National Assembly, VIII 156
Bladensburg, British victory at (1814), VII 344
Blagaj, Turks repulsed at, I 73
Blagoveschensk, founded, XI 273; and the Boxer movement, XII 521
Blaine, James Gillespie, Republican Speaker, VII 644 sq.; Secretary of State, 649, 652 sq., 660, 664 sqq.; XII 699
Blainville, Marquis of, French ambassador, Charles I demands recall of, IV 263
Blair Castle, siege of, VI 116
—— Francis Preston, and peace negotiations, VII 535 sq.
—— James, in Virginia, VII 59
—— Montgomery, Postmaster-General, VII 450, 592
—— Robert, poet, VI 828
Blake, Joachim, Spanish general, commands Spanish army in Galicia, IX 438; advances into Biscay, 442; defeated by Marshal Lefebvre, 443; sent to Valencia, 448; defeated before Saragossa, 454; aids Beresford, 466; regiments of, give way, 467; at Seville, 468; raises siege of Sagunto, 470
—— Robert, admiral and general, at Taunton, IV 328 sq.; victory of, off the Kentish Knock, 436, 473; captures the Spanish Plate fleet (1656), 440; one of the "generals at sea," 460; off the coast of Ireland, 463; off Portugal, 464; and Rupert, 464 sqq.; Tromp and, 471; in the North Sea, 472; defeated off Dungeness, 474; victorious off Portland, 475; 477 sqq.; tactics of, 480; expedition of, to the Mediterranean, 482 sq.; victory and death of, off Santa Cruz, 484 sq., 440, 660; V 105; 139; 372
—— William, poet, VI 824
Blakiston, Thomas, surveys the Yang-tsze-kiang, XII 796
Blanc, Louis, X 485; 499; 509; 573; XI 24 sq.; 39; 97; and the Revolution of 1848, 99, 101, 103 sq.; and the Lamartine Ministry, 105 sq.; and the elections, 107; 109 sqq.; 114; edits the *Rappel*, XII 94; 106; 758; 833
Blanchard, French officer, commander of the guard of the Councils, VIII 677

Blanco, Cape, V 691; France and, XII 660; 806
—— Guzmán, President of Venezuela, XII 673; 687
—— y Arenas, Ramon, Marquis de Peña Plata, Governor-General of Cuba, VII 675
Blandford, Marquis of. *See* Marlborough
Blandrata, Giorgio, Italian doctor and sectary, II 393; leader of Polish Unitarians, 637; III 80; 94 sq.
Blankenfeld, fight at (1813), IX 526
Blanqui, Louis-Auguste, French revolutionary, X 511; XI 104 sq.; 107; 109; 290; 474; editor of *Candide*, 486; attempts to establish a Republic, 496; 497 sq.
Blarer, Ambrose, Zwinglian Reformer, II 161, 216, 234; driven into exile, 265, 328
Blasco Ibañez, Vicente, Spanish novelist, XII 257; 269
Blaser, Anselmo, Spanish general, XI 560
Blasere, Dutch councillor, III 216
Blasi, di, advocate of Palermo, VIII 556
Blavet, Spanish raids from, III 321; seizure of, by Spain, 521; surrender of, by Spain, 523; Spanish evacuation of, 674–5; captured by Huguenots, IV 130
Blaxland, Gregory, Australian explorer, XI 790 sq.
Bleddin, fight at (1813), IX 531–2
Bleking, Treaty of Roeskilde and, IV 586
Bléneau, victory of Condé at, IV 616
Blenheim, battle of (1704), V 410 sq., 463, 668
Bles, Dutch painter, XII 249
Blicher, Steen Steensen, Danish writer, XI 698
Bligh, William, Governor of New South Wales, IX 739
Blignières, Minister in Egypt, XII 434
Blindheim, French army crosses the Danube near, IV 64
Blittersdorff, Baron Friedrich Landolin Karl von, Baden Minister, XI 145
Bloemfontein, British garrison at, XI 783; 784; XII 641 sq.; Union convention at, 646
Blois, Treaties of (1504–5), I 127, (1572), III 283 sq.; Coligny at, 17; States General at, 31; Duke of Guise murdered at (1588), 415; Richelieu and the Queen-Mother at, IV 124 sqq.; residence of Madame de Staël near, IX 131
—— William de, Lord of Treslong, III 229–30
Blok, Petrus Johannes, Dutch historian, XII 842
Blomberg, Barbara, III 18
Blomfield, Charles James, Bishop of London, X 660; 673; 679
Blommers, Bernardus J., Dutch painter, XII 249
Blondus (Flavio Biondo), works of, I 547
Blood river, Zulus defeated at, XI 782

Blood, Sir Bindon, general, XII 488
"Bloody Angle," at Spotsylvania, VII 518
"Bloody Assizes," of Judge Jeffreys, V
232
"Bloody Diet" (1547), III 147
Blount, Charles, Earl of Devonshire and
8th Baron Mountjoy. *See* Mountjoy
Bludoff, Count Demetri, XI 614
Blücher, Gebhard Lebrecht, Prince von,
Prussian Field-Marshal, surrender of Lübeck by, IX 280; 328; commands in
Silesia, 514; occupies Dresden, 515; at
Gross-Görschen, 517; 518; at Bautzen,
519; in Silesia, 523 sq.; on the middle
Elbe, 530; decisive action of, 531; 532
sq.; at Möckern, 536–7; at Leipzig, 538;
542–3; advance of, 544; 545–7; retreat
of, 548; crosses the Marne, 550; at Laon,
551; defeats Marmont, 552; illness of,
553; army of, 623; and the Belgian
campaign, 625; at Ligny, 627 sqq.; decision of, 631; at Waterloo, 632 sqq.;
marches on Paris, 643; X 349
Blum, Robert, German politician, XI 59;
149; vice-president of the *Vorparlament*,
163; 165; 168; at the defence of Vienna,
188; execution of, 189
Blumenthal, Leonard von, Prussian general,
XI 456
Board of Trade, the English, constituted
with permanent staff, V 264. *See also*
Trade and Industry
Boavista (Cape Verde Islands), discovered,
I 15
Bobadilla, Nicholas, Jesuit, II 652, 656
Bobovac, captured by the Turks, I 73
Bóbrikoff, General, Governor-general of
Finland, XII 335; 377
Bóbrinsky, Count V., Zemstvo President,
XII 315; 333; 372; at the Prague Con-
gress, 378
Bobrúisk, mutiny at, XII 362
Bocage. *See* Du Bocage
Boccaccio, Giovanni di Certaldo, I 541, 549;
III 368, 468
Bochard, Jean, Bishop of Avranches. *See*
Avranches
Bocher, Joan, execution of, II 501, 538
Bocskai, Stephen, Prince of Transylvania,
King of Hungary. *See* Stephen Bocskai
Bodelschwingh, Ernst von, Prussian
Minister of the Interior, XI 56; 58;
157 sq.
Boden, fortresses at, XII 277
Bodenstein, Andrew, of Carlstadt. *See*
Carlstadt
Bodin, Jean, III 62, 747–9, 753–4, 762–3;
VI 786; 803
Bodkin, Christopher, Archbishop of Tuam,
III 593
Bodley, Sir Thomas, III 44; 710; V 747
Bodmer, Johann Jakob, Swiss writer, VI
625; X 384 sqq.
Boeblingen, defeat of Peasants' Rising at
(1525), II 189

Böckh, August, historian, XII 820 sqq.;
824; 844
Böcklin, Arnold, painter, XI 261
Bödtcher, Ludvig Adolph, Danish poet, XI
699
Böheim, Hans, German sectary, I 674 sq.
Böhl de Faber, J. N., X 210
Böhler, Peter, Moravian preacher, VI 82
Boehme, Jakob, II 690, 714 sq.; IV 425;
V 758 sqq.
Böhmer, Johann Friedrich, German his-
torian, XII 823
Boer Wars (1880–1), XII 39, 245, 637,
(1899–1900), *ib.* 31, 53 sqq., 57, 59,
247, 641 sqq.
Börne, Ludwig, X 375, 410 sq.
Boers, in South Africa, VI 189; Vol. XI,
Chap. XXVII (3) *passim*; XII 3; 35; and
the Sand River Convention, 41; the
German Emperor and, 171 sq.; 636 sqq.
Boetius (Anicius Manlius Torquatus Severi-
nus), influence of, I 534
Bötticher, Karl Heinrich von, Prussian
Minister, XII 155
Bötzow on the Havel. *See* Oranienburg
Bogaers, Adrianus, Dutch poet, XI 676
Bogatzky, Karl Heinrich von, V 762
Bogbinder. *See* Metzenheim, Hans
Bogdanóvich, Russian revolutionary, XII 310
Bogerman, Joannes, III 653
Bogle, George, visits Tibet, XII 798
Bogolyépoff, Russian official, XII 315
Bogolyúboff, Russian revolutionary, XII 305
Bogomils, Greek sect in Bosnia, I 71
Bogosloff district, industrial depression in,
XI 618
Bogotá, government of, X 285, 288, 290;
captured by Bolívar (1815), 290, (1819),
294; 296
Bogue forts, capture of, XI 815
Bohemia, under George Podiebrad, I 293,
331; internal decay of, 329; acquired by
the Habsburgs, 329 sq., 340; comparison
of, with Hungary, 330 sq., 341 sqq.;
religious troubles in, 331, 338, 340;
geographical and political structure of,
331, 334; class wars in, 338; disputed
claims to the crown of, II 198 sq.; constitutional liberties of, destroyed by
Ferdinand I, 262; King of, not included in *Reichsdeputationstage*, III 143;
under Ferdinand I, 147–8; religious
questions in, 147, 180, 703, 719; revolution
in (1618), 569; Frederick V driven out of,
569; German appointments in, 696;
Estates of, 721 sqq., 726 sq.; Anhalt's
intrigues in, 725; the crown of, ceded to
Matthias (1611), 734; and the opening of
the Thirty Years' War, Vol. IV, Chap. I
passim; and the War in 1620–3, 64–84;
Habsburg dominion in, 206; Saxons in,
209; 212; debt of, to Wallenstein, 213;
215; 219; Wallenstein and, 232 sqq.;
242 sqq.; Banér and, 252; Swedish
troops in, 370, 392; peace proclaimed in,

394; part of, held by Sweden at the close of the War, 403; effects of War upon, 417 sq., 421; 634; 640; subdued by the Emperor, 641; and the Habsburgs, v 339; 351; Brandenburg and, 621, 624; and the War of the Austrian Succession, vi 210, 231 sqq., 240, 242 sq., 250; Frederick the Great and, 251; 254; the Seven Years' War in, 255 sqq.; Prussian evacuation of, 262; 275; 277; Prussian army again in (1758), 279; 289; 291; Austrian army in, 294; 317; Joseph II in, 626 sq.; Frederick II in, 632; 638; and the War of the Bavarian Succession, 704 sqq.; Austrian defence in (1790), viii 293; influence of the French Revolution in, 777; ix 41; Austrian and Russian troops in, 257; 346; army of Allies in, 523, 529, 531; the Liberal movement in, xi 45 sq.; and the National Assembly, 164, 170; the national party in, 171; 173; 176 sqq.; 216; Austrian troops in (1850), 230; 399; 402; the Austro-Prussian War in, 452; 563; literature in, 653 sqq.; xii 11; and Hungary, 177; 181; political claims of, 186; 187 sq.; 194 sq.; success of the Young Čechs in, 196; 200; Germans and Čechs in, 201; 209; historical research in, 842

Bohemian Brethren, probable origin of, ii 160; expulsion of, 635 sq.; in Poland, 636, iii 75; 79; in Bohemia itself, 147; 180; under Rudolf II, 703

Boialva, Masséna takes the road through, ix 461

Boiardo, Matteo Maria (Count of Scandiano), iii 458; the *Orlando Innamorato*, 459–61

Boiars, in the early Muscovite State, v 484 sqq., 488 sqq., 501; the shaving of, by Peter the Great, 524

Boigne, Benoît le Borne, Comte de, and Sindhia, ix 718; 720

Boileau-Despréaux, Nicolas, v 65; 67; 70; vi 822; 829; x 384; xi 508

Boinvilliers, Eloi-Ernest Forestier de, French politician, xi 127

Boisdauphin, Marshal de, iv 121

Boisdeffre, Raoul-F.-C. Le Mouton de, French Chief of the Staff, xii 120

Boisgelin, J.-de-Dieu-R. de Cucé de. *See* Aix, Archbishop of

Boisguillebert, Pierre le Pesant, Sieur de, v 8; 29

Boishardi, Charles de, *Chouan* leader, viii 379

Boislisle, Arthur Michel de, xii 834

Boisot, Charles, Governor of Zeeland, iii 242

—— Louis, admiral, relieves Leyden, iii 239–40; death of, 244

Boisselot, Major-General, at the defence of Limerick, v 316

Boisserée, Johann Sulpice, and medieval art, xii 818

Boissise, French envoy to the Protestant Union, iii 689

Boissy d'Anglas, Comte François-Antoine de, viii 249, 339 sq., 380 sqq.; on the Committee of XI, 386, 388; proposals of, for a new Constitution, 392; 488, 506

Bokhara, Russia and, v 544; xi 631; absorbed by Russia, xii 460; 461; 491; caravan route through, 793; travellers at, 800 sq.; 803

Bolan Pass, British troops in, xi 732

Boldù, Venetian envoy in Savoy, iii 409

Boleyn, Anne. *See* Anne (Boleyn), Queen of England

—— George. *See* Rochford, Viscount

—— Sir Thomas. *See* Wiltshire, Earl of

Bolingbroke, Henry St John, 1st Viscount, v 70; 271; 337; 430; and the Peace of Utrecht, 434, 440, 446, 450; 461; and party government, 463; Secretary at War, 464; 465 sq.; 469; Secretary of State, 470; 471; and the Stewart cause, 472 sq.; 473; and the Schism Act, 474 sq.; and the fall of Oxford, 475; 476; and Russia, 608; and the succession, vi 11 sq.; 14 sqq.; dismissed, 18; 42 sq.; 71 sq.; 77; 89; and the Old Pretender, 96 sq.; 98; 394; 817 sqq.; viii 15

Bolívar y Ponte, Simon, in Venezuela, x 288 sqq., 293 sq.; personal characteristics of, 289; in New Granada, 290, 294; 291; and the Republic of Colombia, 294, 296; in Peru, 294 sqq.; and the Republic of Bolivia, 296; returns to Colombia, *ib.*; death of, *ib.*; estimate of, 297; policy of consolidation of, 298; 300; 302; 306; xii 673; 680; 696

Bolivia, native insurrection in (1780–3), x 267; revolution in (1809), 284, 286; 294; Upper Peru forms Republic of, 296 sq.; xii 672; Chili and, 677; 678 sq.; 690; 696

Bologna, taken by Julius II (1506), i 128, 245; surrenders to France (1511), 249, 479; compact of Charles V and Clement VII at (1530), 567, 578; coronation of Charles V at, ii 25, 60 sq., 143; Council of Trent transferred to, 26, 81, 263 sq., 669 sq.; 84; threatened by the Farnesi, 86; Concordat of, between Francis I and Leo X (1516), 32, 281; Conference of, between Charles V and Clement VII (1530), 60, 63; (1532–3), 25, 67, 439; execution of Giovanni Pepoli at, iii 431; University of, 447, ix 86, x 137; botanic gardens at, v 734; Jacobin plot at, viii 556; Legation of, held by the French (1796), 573; 583, 588; Veronese prefect sent to, ix 394; academy of art created at, 396; *Carbonari* meeting at (1819), x 21; *Raggi* in, 111; revolt at (1830), 120, 154; rebellion at (1831), 155; xi 71; Neapolitan troops at, 85; 89; and union with Piedmont, 386; Austrians

driven from, 384; socialist congress at, xii 231; 235

Bolotnikoff, Ivan, Russian revolutionist, v 500

Bolsec, Jérome Hermes, ii 364, 375, 717

Bolton, petitions for peace from, ix 369; conditions of labour in, xii 730 sq., 744, 765

—— Charles Paulet, 2nd Duke of. *See* Winchester, 7th Marquis of

—— Charles Paulet, 3rd Duke of, vi 70

—— Thomas Orde, Lord, chief Secretary for Ireland, vi 503 sq.

Boltwood, Bertram Borden, and radioactivity, xii 790

Boma, Governor-General of the Congo at, xii 662; 663

Bombasius, Greek scholar, teaches Greek to Zwingli, ii 308

Bombay, ceded to England, v 105, 107; 698; vi 445; 529; and the decline of the Moghul empire, 531; 534; 537; 582; Lord Mornington and, ix 722; expedition from, 734; xi 724; Presidency of, 727; High Court of, 751; military system of, 752; frontier of, xii 485; bubonic plague in, 487; 496 sq.

Bombelli, Raffaelle, mathematician, v 710

Bomfim, José Luis Travassos Valdes, Count of, Portuguese statesman, x 339

Bompard, J. B. F., French commodore, viii 476

Bon, Louis-André, French general, viii 599, 601 sqq., 608, 611; killed, 613

Bon Sens, Le, French journal, x 499

Bona, garrisoned by Charles V, iii 111; burnt by Tuscan squadron, 399

Bona Sforza, Queen consort of Sigismund I of Poland, iii 76 sq.

Bonald, Louis-Gabriel-Ambroise, Vicomte de, ix 133; x 43; 47; 94; political theories of, 161; 162

Bonaparte, Caroline. *See* Murat

—— Élise, Grand Duchess of Tuscany, receives Lucca, ix 247; 267, 398, 603; question of indemnity for, 652

—— Jerome, King of Westphalia, ix 53; 107; marriage of, 193; 265; in Silesia, 281; at Dresden, 279; kingdom of Westphalia formed for, 293; government of, in Westphalia, 356–7, 356; forced to retreat from Dresden, 357; Pius VII refuses to sanction the divorce of, 401; appointed King of Westphalia, 411; 413; connives at contraband trade, 474; military mishap of, 490; at Montmartre, 553; xi 119; 293; 385

—— Joseph, King of Spain, vii 366; viii 636 sq., 675; ix 66; 76, 103, 107; Grand Elector of the Empire, 110; King of Naples and Sicily, 111; Regency of France vested in, 147; plenipotentiary for the Concordat, 184; King of Naples, 194; declines kingship of Italy, 247; 267, 270, 271, 315, 324; efforts of, to gain Sicily, 381; crown of Italy offered to, 394; King of Naples, 403; character of, 404; caution to, 405; ordered to exchange Naples for Spain, 406; proclaimed King of Spain, 434; evacuates Madrid, 438; 441; unable to reinforce Victor, 450; Soult's letter to, 453; defeats Venegas at Almonacid, 454; defeats Areizaga, 455; at Madrid, 472; retreat of the army of, 473; at Valencia, 474; retreat of, 477; recalled to France, 478; at Montmartre, 553; x 210; 282 sq.; 285

Bonaparte, Louis, ix 107; Napoleon's Constable, 110; 139; declines kingship of Italy, 247; King of Holland, 267; at Wesel, 274; 278; Holland assigned to (1806), 369; 370; 416; flight of, 371; crown of Italy offered to, 394; letter of Napoleon to, 407; expulsion of, 417; and the crown of Spain, 432; and Napoleon, 758

—— Lucien, viii 673 sqq., 680 sqq.; becomes Minister of the Interior, ix 9; 63, 72, 107; discarded by Napoleon, 267; suggested as President of the Chamber (1815), 620; xi 119

—— Marie-Pauline, wife of Prince Camillo Borghese, ix 110; receives Guastalla, 111; 267, 421

—— Mathilde, Princess, xi 293

—— Napoleon. *See* Napoleon I

—— Napoleon-Charles, death of (1806), ix 139

—— Napoleon-J.-C.-P. (Prince Napoleon), xi 293; 376; at Turin, 381; 386; 484

—— Pierre, Prince, xi 491 sq.

Bonaventura, Saint, and Indulgences, ii 125, 127; works of, printed, iii 445

Boncerf, Pierre-François, writer, viii 87, 714, 744

Bonchamps, Charles-M.-Artus de, Vendean leader, viii 266, 354

—— Christian de, African traveller, xii 813

Bonde, Gustaf, Swedish statesman, v 565 sq.; 575

Bonetti, Cardinal Michael, iii 20

Bonfadio, Jacopo, Italian Reformer, ii 390

Bongars, Jacques, iii 63, 671, 687

Boniface VIII (Benedetto Gaetani), Pope, ii 31, 127; iii 737

—— IX (Pietro Tomacelli), Pope, i 237; introduces sale of offices, 670

—— St, and Fulda, i 534

Bonifacio, Straits of, xi 346

Bonin, Eduard von, Prussian general, xi 224

Bonivard, François de, Abbot of St Victor, ii 362

Bonjean, Louis, French lawyer, xi 505

Bonn, raid on Electoral Palace at, iii 707; surrender of (1584), 708; taken by Schenck (1587), 712; retaken by Spaniards (1588), *ib.*; taken by the Germans (1689), v 57, 661; captured by William of Orange (1673), 161; captured by Marlborough

(1703), 407; University of, x 355, 381, xi 143; Niebuhr at, xii 820

Bonnac, French ambassador in Switzerland, vi 615 sq.

Bonne Anse, the Young Pretender sails from, vi 111

Bonner, Edmund, Bishop of London, ii 440, 467, 481, 484 sq.; imprisonment of, under Somerset, 486, 497; deprivation of (1550), 501; restoration (1553), 521, 533, 538; dispute of, with Horne, 586; iii 344

Bonnet, French general, ix 351

Bonnier, Colonel, occupies Timbuktu, xii 129

Bonnier-d'Arco, Ange-E.-L.-A., plenipotentiary at Rastatt, viii 641 sq., 655

Bonnivet, Guillaume Gouffier de, French admiral, i 490; occupies Fuenterrabia (1521), ii 44; advances on Italy (1523), 47 sq., 97

Bonny-sur-Loire, rising at, xi 137

Bonstetten, Charles-Victor de (Swiss philosopher), ix 427

Bontekoe, Willem, conquers Formosa, iv 711

Bonticus, Hugo, iii 237

Bonvalot, Gabriel, traveller, xii 803

Bonzi, Pietro, Cardinal, Archbishop of Narbonne, v 85

Book of Canons, Charles I's (1635), iv 494 sqq.

—— of Common Prayer. *See* Prayer Book

Book of Discipline, Knox's (1560), ii 593; (Second) (1581), iii 550

—— *of Martyrs,* Foxe's, ii 538

"Books of Rank," in the early Muscovite State, v 485 sq.

Boomplatz, battle of, xi 783

Booth, Sir George, *afterwards* 1st Baron Delamere, rising of, iv 540; 545; defeat and imprisonment of, 541; 544; released, 552

—— John Wilkes, vii 545 sqq.

—— Imperialist colonel, in Livonia, iv 383

Boothby, Sir Brooke, writer, viii 758

Bopp, Franz, philologer, xii 822; 845

Bordeaux, Protestants massacred near, iii 30; Montaigne at, 65, 66, 69; the League in, 661; Jesuits in, 664; the Fronde in, iv 613 sqq.; results of, 621; *Parlement* of, 610 sq., v 4, viii 47; in 1787-90, 60; reaction in (1793), 340; trade of, 486; inhabitants of, declared *émigrés,* 502; Beresford marches on, ix 481; xi 31; 113; 499; National Assembly at, 500, 611 sq., xii 91; the Pact of, 92, 102

—— Henri-Charles-Ferdinand, Duc de, x 68

—— Champion de Cicé, Archbishop of, viii 156, 178; Keeper of the Seals, 186, 727

Bordeaux, Henri d'Escoubleau de Sourdis, Archbishop of, v 755

Bordeaux-Neufville, Antoine de, v 106

Bordesholm, Treaty of (1522), ii 607

Borelli, Giovanni Alfonso, physicist, v 727 sq.; 731; 733 sq.; 740

Borgesius, Hendrik Goeman, Dutch Minister of the Interior, xii 247 sq.

Borghese, Camillo, Duc de Guastalla, ix 110; Governor-General beyond the Alps, 397

—— Scipio, Cardinal, and Fra Paolo Sarpi, iv 671

Borghesi, Bartolommeo, Count, archaeologist, xii 842 sq.

Borgia, Cesare, Cardinal of Valencia, Duke of Valentinois, i 114, 124, 231, 234, 672; character of, 235; relations of, with France, 123, 126, 191 sq., 194, 236; made Duke of Valentinois, 120, 236; policy of, 193; Romagna and, 193, 238-9; capture of Imola and Forlì by, 123, 192, 238; capture of Urbino by, 194, 240; conspiracy against, 195; Machiavelli and, 195, 237, 240, 242; fall of, 126, 128, 195, 242, 245; prisoner in Spain, 128; death of, 126, 196, 242; ii 1

—— Gasparo, Cardinal, Archbishop of Seville and Toledo, and the Catalan revolt, iv 648; protests against papal policy, 680

—— Lucrezia, i 227, 234, 236, 239

—— Rodrigo. *See* Alexander VI, Pope

Borgö, Act of Guarantee issued at (1809), ix 314; Diet at (1809), x 433

Borgo, Count Pozzo di. *See* Pozzo di Borgo

Borgoforte, Austrian force at, vi 153; 154

Borgomainero, Charles Emmanuel d'Este, Marquis of, Spanish ambassador at Vienna, v 358; 364

Boris, Prince, of Bulgaria, xii 342; 410 sq.

—— Godunoff, Tsar, Regent of Russia, v 495 sq.; elected Tsar, 497; death of, 498; 516; 522; 524

Borissoff, French retreat to, ix 501; 502

Borkelo, the Bishop of Münster and, v 150 sq.

Borku, explorer at, xii 811

Borlase, Sir John, appointed Lord Justice, iv 521

Bormida, plain of the, ix 62; 63

Bormio, early history of, iv 35 sqq.; 41; the Grisons and, 50 sqq.; only the Catholic faith permitted in, 58; Jenatsch despatched to, 61; Fernamond defeated at, 62; sovereignty of the Grisons in, 63; Austria gains, ix 660

Borne, Prussian advance on, vi 275

Bornemann, Wilhelm, Prussian politician, xi 159

Borneo, Dutch trade in, iv 711; Dutch and English in, xii 669

Bornholm, victory of Danes over Lübeck near (1535), ii 230, 615; Danes defeated

off (1563), IV 163; 561; captured by Wrangel, 572; Treaty of Roeskilde and, 586; Swedes expelled from, 588; restored to Denmark, 591

Bornhöved, Danish defeat at (1226), V 620

Bornier, Philippe, IX 165

Borodino, battle of (1812), IX 495 sqq.

Borough, William, Vice-Admiral, III 306

Borovsk, Napoleon's retreat by, IX 499

Borromean League, founded (1586), II 341

Borromeo, Saints Carlo and Federigo. *See* Milan, Archbishops of

Borselen, Jan Willem van, Dutch painter, XII 249

Borsieri, Pietro, X 119

Borstell, retreat of, before Eugene Beau-harnais, IX 515; at Dennewitz, 530

Borston Well, Prjevalsky at, XII 798; 802

Bosanquet, Charles, Ricardo's controversy with, X 772

Bosboom, Johannes, Dutch painter, XII 249

Boscawen, Edward, Admiral, VI 333; 342a sqq. (in Vol. XIII); 537 sq.; VII 133

Bosch, Johannes van den, Governor-General of the Dutch East Indies, XI 667

Boselli, Paolo, Italian statesman, XII 227

Bosi, Carlo Alberto, poet, XI 545

Bosio, Antonio, work of, on the Catacombs, I 610

Bosna valley, fighting in, XII 400

Bosnia, dissensions in, I 71 sq.; conquered by the Turks, 72 sqq.; sends reinforcements to Solyman II, III 107; V 366; Prince Eugene in, 370; VI 648; 675; suggested occupation of, by France, IX 308; 312; unrest in, X 549, XI 533; XII 3; 9; rising in, 32; 172; annexed by Austria, 175 sq., 192, 211 sq., 378, 427 sq.; 198; Austrian rule in, 199 sq.; 382 sq.; 385 sqq.; Austria and, 389, 394; 390; the Treaty of San Stefano and, 392; the Treaty of Berlin and, 396, 399; 400

Bosporus, The, passage of, VI 673 sq.; Russian rights in, X 170, 203, 444; Russian squadron in (1833), 552 sq., 558; Great Britain and, 562; closed to war-ships, 564, 572; the Sultan's rights in, XI 634

Bosse, Pieter Philip van, Dutch statesman, XI 667

—— Prussian official, XII 155

Bossu, *or* Bossut, Maximilian de Hennin, lord of, General of the States, III 250

—— Count, Spanish admiral, III 236–7

Bossuet, Jacques-Bénigne. *See* Meaux, Bishop of

Boston (Mass.), settlement of, VII 16; Quakers at, 25; ship-building at, 56; literature in, 60; disaffection in, 146, 149, 151 sqq.; and the tea riot, VI 446 sq., VII 158 sqq.; evacuated by the British (1776), 171; and writs of assistance, 177 sqq.; legislation in, 187; 268; merchants of, 310 sq., 319; 321; action of the

Shannon and the *Chesapeake* off, 342; communication with, 351, 694; imports of, 355; emigration from, 359; woollen manufacturers at, 376; Anti-Slavery Society in, 387; orators of, 743 sq.

Boston Bay, settlements in, VII 16, 18, 21

—— Athenaeum, The, VII 744

"Boston Massacre, The," VII 153 sq.

Boston, John, monk of Bury, *Catalogus Scriptorum*, I 592, 611

Boström, Erik Gustaf, Swedish statesman, XII 277

Boswell, Sir William, advice given to English traders by, IV 749

Bosworth, battle of (1485), I 463 sq.

Botany, history of. *See* Science

—— Bay, convicts at, IX 737

Both, Governor-General Pieter, Dutch trade with Japan and, IV 712

Botha, Louis, Boer general, XII 643

Bothmer, Count Johann (Hans) Caspar von, Hanoverian envoy in London, V 476, VI 12 sqq., 16, in London, 17 sqq.; death of, 13

Bothnia, East, peasant risings in, IV 172

—— Gulf of, V 610; Russian fleet in, VI 779

Bothniensis, Nicolaus, at the *Upsala Möte*, II 632

Bothvid. *See* Strengnaes, Bishop of

Bothwell Bridge, battle of (1679), V 225, 285 sq.

—— James Hepburn, 4th Earl of, II 575, 595; III 268; 270 sqq.; 529

Bott, mutineer at Cadiz, VIII 630

Botta, Carlo G. G., Italian historian, XII 842

—— Paul-Émile, Assyriologist, XII 845

—— Marquis de, Austrian ambassador in Russia, VI 315 sqq.

Botticella, Alessandro, scholar, II 16

Botticelli, Alessandro Filipepi, Florentine painter, I 147

Bottot, Secretary to Barras, VIII 679

Bou Amena, revolt of, XII 129

Bouchain, taken by the French (1676), V 44, (1712), 434; 45; captured by Marlborough (1711), 431

Bouché-Leclercq, Auguste, historian, XII 845

Boucher, Jean, *Sermons de la simulée Conversion*, III 764; the *De Justa Abdicatione Henrici Tertii, ib.*

—— de Perthes, Jacques, archaeologist, XII 850

—— Saint-Sauveur, Antoine, Paris deputy to the National Convention, VIII 247

Bouches de Meuse, department of, IX 417

Bouchotte, J.-B.-Noël, French Minister of War, VIII 339, 343, 362, 424, 429 sq.

Bouet-Willaumez, Comte Louis-Édouard, French vice-admiral, XI 582

Boufflers, Louis-François de Boufflers, Duke of, Marshal of France, V 405 sq.; 421; 425 sq.

Bougainville, Louis-Antoine de, VII 126, 137, 139 sqq., 143

Bouillé, François-C.-A., Marquis of, Governor of the Antilles, VI 451; 453; commands the Army of the East, VIII 192, 403 sq.

Bouillon, duchy of, returned to Bishop of Liége, II 94; and Luxemburg, IX 655; separation of, from France, 664; added to the Netherlands (1815), X 524

—— Frédéric-Maurice de La Tour d'Auvergne, Duke of, rallies to the Crown (1652), IV 610; joins rebels, 611; withdraws to Bordeaux, 613; at court, 616; death of, 618

—— Henri de La Tour d'Auvergne, Duke of (1614), IV 119 sq.; marches to Poitou, 121; 122; gains of, 124; 126; conspiracies of, 150 sq.

—— Henri de La Tour d'Auvergne, Vicomte de Turenne, Duke of, III 22; 27; 35; 50; acquires Bouillon (1591), 665; 418, 669 sqq.; 711; quarrels with Henry IV, 722

—— Henri-Robert, Duke of, III 25

Boulainvilliers, Comte Henri de, VIII 14, 16

Boulanger, Georges-Ernest-Jean-Marie, French Minister of War, XII 96; 112; 162

Boulay, French army corps at, XI 586

—— de la Meurthe, Antoine-J.-C.-J., Comte de, VIII 509 sq.; 515; 517; 677; 686; IX 151

Boulogne, siege and capture of, by Henry VIII (1544), II 78, 245, 459; French siege of (1549), 460, 493; given up to France by Warwick (1550), 86, 268, 499; projected seizure of, III 42; conference at (1600), 534, 536; Elizabeth claims, 670; Napoleon's projected invasion of England and, IX 28, 212–5, 237, 244, 252; British attack on flotilla at, 215–6; French army moved from, 234; Italian troops in manoeuvres at, 396

Boulogneberg, evacuated by the English (1549), II 493

Boulonnais, The, V 4; rising in, 9

Boulter, Hugh, Archbishop of Armagh, VI 486 sq.; death of, 488

Boulton, Matthew, mechanician, VIII 765; X 734

Bounty Act, English (1689), V 264; extended, VI 49

Bouquet, Henry, Swiss officer in the English service, VII 97, 136

Bourbaki, Charles-Denis-Sauter, French general, XI 257; 607 sq.; retreats into Switzerland, 609; 610 sq.

Bourbon, Île de (Réunion), and the Revolution, VIII 194; reduced (1810), IX 240, 731–2, 754; 390

—— House of, IX 70; French clergy work for return of the, 206; 315, 331; restoration of the, 555 sqq.

—— Anne of Beaujeu, Duchess of, I 109, 393, 397; Regent of France, 445; II 37; the Duchy of Bourbon and, 46

Bourbon, Antony, Duke of, King-consort of Navarre, joins the Reformers, II 295; vacillation of, 297 sqq., 303; 567; death of, III 6

—— Charles, Cardinal de, Archbishop of Rouen, III 30 sqq., 45–6; proclaimed Charles X, 48; dies (1590), 49; 415; 451 sqq.; 660

—— Charles II, Cardinal de, 1590 (the younger), *previously* Cardinal de Vendôme, Archbishop of Rouen, III 49; 52

—— Charles, Count of Montpensier and Duke of, Constable of France, II 24, 46 sq., 49 sqq., 53 sqq., 421, 423

—— Charlotte de, 3rd wife of William of Orange. *See* Orange

—— Henry de, of Navarre. *See* Henry IV of France

—— Jean II, Duke of, I 393

—— Juan de, XII 258; 260

—— Louis, Bastard of, sent to occupy the Somme towns, I 438

—— Louis of, Bishop of Liége. *See* Liége

—— Louis-Henri I, Duke of, VI 134; 138; 140; fall of, 143 sq.; 146; 163

—— Louis-Henri II, Duke of, emigrates (1789), VIII 165

—— Peter, Duke of, Regent of France, I 115 sq., 394

—— Susanne, Duchess of, II 46

Bourbonnais, The, customs of, V 13

Bourbotte, Pierre, member of the Convention, VIII 388

Bourboulon, French Minister in China, XI 817 sq.

Bourcet, Pierre-Joseph, French engineer, Napoleon's indebtedness to, VIII 578

Bourdaloue, le père Louis, Jesuit, oratory of, II 373; V 65; as a preacher, 80

Bourdeilles, Pierre de, Abbé de Brantôme. *See* Brantôme

Bourdelot, Queen Christina's French physician, IV 576

Bourdon de la Crosnière, Léonard J. J., deputy to the National Convention, VIII 234, 366, 385

—— de l'Oise, François-Louis, deputy to the National Convention, VIII 361, 366, 512

Bourg, fortification of, III 410; siege of (1600), 418, 677

—— St Pierre, IX 59–60

—— Anne du. *See* Du Bourg

—— Antoine du. *See* Du Bourg

Bourges, Council of (1438), I 386, 671; Andrea Alciati at, III 58; Pragmatic Sanction of, 659; submits to Henry IV, 662; abdication of Don Carlos at, XI 553; arsenal of, 607; 608 sq.

—— Renaud de Beaume, Archbishop of, III 45, 52

—— J.-M. Cliquet de Fontenay, Archbishop of, X 85

Bourget (*or* Le Bourget), abandoned by the French, XI 498; 607

Bourgoing, conferences at, III 417

Bourignon, Antoinette de, pietist, V 762

Bourke, John, commands army in Connaught, IV 525; Galway Castle capitulates to, 526

—— Sir Richard, Governor of New South Wales, XI 792

Bourlamaque, Chevalier de, French lieutenant, VII 126, 135, 143

Bourmont, Louis-Auguste-Victor, Comte de Chaisne de, Marshal of France, IX 2; 14, 17; X 97; in Portugal, 335; 486; 488

Bourne, Gilbert, Bishop of Bath, II 531

—— Rear-Admiral John, appointment of, IV 478; Government and, 540

—— Major Nehemiah, Richard Cromwell's fall and, IV 450 sq.

—— William Sturges-, X 660

Bournonville, Count, Imperial commander, V 651

Bourquin, French commander, defeat of, IX 726

Bourré, Jean, Minister of Louis XI, I 403, 409

Bourrée, Frédéric-Albert, French Minister at Peking, XII 525

Bourrienne, L.-A. Fauvelet de, French diplomatist, VIII 616, 683; Minister at Hamburg, IX 378; advice of, 574

Bouteville, François de Montmorency, Seigneur de, IV 155

Bouthillier, family of, Richelieu and, IV 123; 154; Mazarin and, 593, 596. *See also* Chavigny

—— Claude Le, Sieur de Fouilletourte, member of Council, IV 593; driven from Council by *les Importants*, 596

—— Léon Le. *See* Chavigny

Boutmy, Émile, and French educational reform, XII 114

Bouvet, François-Joseph, Baron, French admiral, VIII 474 sq.

Bouvines, captured by the French (1554), II 89; restored to Liége (1559), 94

Bover, Peter Turner, naval lieutenant, VIII 478

Boves, Tomás, X 289 sq.; 293

Bovey Tracey, Parliamentary victory at, IV 334

Bovillus, Carolus, French philosopher, I 415

Bowdich, Thomas, mission of, to Kumassi, XII 807

Bower, Hamilton, in Tibet, XII 803

Bowes, Sir Robert, II 446; invasion of Teviotdale by (1542), 455

Bowling Green (Kentucky), Buckner at (1861), VII 462 sq., 493 sq.; evacuated, 559

Bowring, Sir John, X 755; Governor of Hongkong, XI 325; 815; 831; mission of, to Siam, XII 535

Bowyer, Ludowic, punishment of, IV 279

Boxall, John, II 501

Boxer movement, The, XII 517 sqq.; 575

Boyacá, victory of Bolívar at (1819), X 294

Boycott, Captain Charles Cunningham, XII 38; 78

Boyen, Hermann von, Prussian Adjutant-general, IX 332; XI 456

—— L. H. L. von, Prussian Minister, X 365 sq.; XI 49; 56

Boyle, Henry. *See* Shannon, Earl of

—— Robert, physicist, V 715; 722; 728; and modern chemistry, 730 sq.; 732

—— Roger, Earl of Orrery. *See* Orrery

Boyne, battle of the (1690), V 58, 261, 314

Boyneburg, John Christian von, policy of, IV 431

Boyve, French socialist, XII 124

Bozius, Franciscus (of Gubbio), III 744; 757

Brabant, acquired by Philip of Burgundy (1430), I 419; devastated by Van Rossem, II 76; influence of William of Orange in, III 248; Maurice of Nassau's army threatens, 519; Parma conquers, 618; North, raided (1590), 626; freed from Spaniards, 629; Spanish influence in, 630; V 153; Marlborough in, 416; 426; VI 248; and the Barrier Treaty, 640; frontiers of, 645 sq.; Estates of, 650 sqq.; discontent in (1787–8), VIII 317 sq., 320, 327 sq.; rebels in, 329; agriculture in, X 731, 750; XI 670; anti-French feeling in, 673

—— Anthony, Duke of, I 418, 421

—— John II, Duke of, I 419

—— Philip, Duke of, I 419

Bracamonte, Gasparo de, at Münster, IV 401

Bracciano, Castle of, III 428–9

Bracton, Henry, III 748

Braddock, Edward, Commander-in-chief in North America, VI 333; 413; VII 123 sqq.

Bradford, and the yarn trade, X 736

—— John, Protestant martyr, II 161, 521, 538 sqq.

—— William, Governor of New Plymouth, VII 12, 14

Bradlaugh, Charles, and the parliamentary oath, XII 37 sq.

Bradleigh, Sir Thomas, III 284

Bradley, Humphry, engineer, I 526

—— James, astronomer royal, V 721

Bradock Down, Royalist victory of, IV 308

Bradshaw, John, at trial of Charles I, IV 355; elected President of the Council, 434

Bradstreet, John, American major-general, VII 135

—— Simon, Commissioner of the New England Confederation, VII 23

Braemar, Earl of Mar in, VI 98

Bragadin, Venetian envoy to Spain, VI 137

Braganza, captured by the Spaniards, VI 369; base of Wellington's operations, IX 476

Braganza, House of, the colonies and, IV 714; IX 315; 428
—— Duke of. *See* John IV, King of Portugal
Bragg, Braxton, Confederate general, VII 506 sqq.; evacuates Chattanooga, 509; 511; defeated at Chattanooga, 513
Bragge-Bathurst, Charles, pamphlet of, IX 682
Brahe, Ebba, and Gustavus Adolphus, IV 178
—— Magnus, Count, XI 685
—— Per, Swedish statesman, Oxenstierna and, IV 569; defends the Swedish peninsula, 584; 590; V 564 sq.; 568
—— Tycho, III 697; claim of, to distinction, IV 562; V 709; 713
Brailoff, Russian capture of (1770), VI 673, (1809), IX 485
Braithwaite, General, defeated by Tipu, VI 577
Bramah, Joseph, and the planing-machine, X 734
Bramahof, French troops in, VI 235
Bramante, Donato Lazzari (of Urbino), II 5, 12 sqq.; III 439, 444
Bramhall, John, Archbishop of Armagh, IV 520; V 321
Brand, Henry B. W. *See* Hampden, Viscount
Brandan, St, Irish missionary, I 19, 50
Brandaris, destroyed by the English (1666), V 187
Brandeis, Banér's success near, IV 379; Prussian force at, VI 257 sq.
—— German trader in Samoa, VII 662
Brandenburg (for later history of Brandenburg-Prussia *see also* Prussia), virtual defection of, from Protestant Union, IV 12; 83; 85; 92; 95; representatives of, at Brunswick, 96; inroads into, 100 sq.; 103; Pomeranian succession secured to, 104; Gustavus Adolphus and, 191 sqq.; compensation suggested for, 218; 219; invaded by Wallenstein, 237; secures Cleves, Mark, and Ravensburg, 409; jealous of Sweden, 416; Thirty Years' War in, 418; agricultural conditions in, 419; native industries in, 421; disputes between Sweden and, 426; and Charles X, 427; and Great Poland, 428; Sweden and, 429; Mazarin supported by, 430; allied with Austria, 431; and Peace of Oliva, 433; Estates of, 254; Oxenstierna and, 255; VI 34; taxation in, 221; cloth manufacture in, 224 sq.; 269; 277; 279; 288; and Poland, 664 sq., 667, VIII 522; levy on, IX 307; Prussian National Assembly at, XI 193; 198; growth and development of, to 1640, Vol. v, Chap. xx; under Electors Frederick William and Frederick III (1640–1713), Chap. xxi; 25; and France, 33, 38; and United Provinces, 37, 157, 161, 164, 166; 39 sq.; and Sweden, 45; 55; 414; 568; 586

Brandenburg, the Mark, VI 265 sq.; Russian army in, 277, 282, 287 sqq., 291 sq.; 295, 716; the Kurmark of, V 618, VI 716, 718; the Middle Mark of, V 618; the New Mark of, 618, 621, 624, 632, 634; Russian army in, VI 279 sq., 287, 296; the Northern Mark of, V 617 sq., 620; the Old Mark of, 618 sq., 621, 625, IX 656; the Vormark (Priegnitz) of, V 618; the Ukermark of, 618, 620; Swedish army in, VI 280, 296
Brandenburg, House of, IX 592
—— Electors of :—
—— Albert Achilles, I 81; 297; V 624 sq.
—— Frederick I, I 297; V 622 sq.
—— Frederick II, I 297; V 620; 623 sq.; 634
—— Frederick III. *See* Frederick I, King of Prussia
—— Frederick William (the "Great Elector"), succeeds, IV 384; Ferdinand III and, 393; futile mediation of, in the Thirty Years' War, 396; 401; 404; Swedish "satisfaction" and, 407; 412; "Jülich War" and, 426; Charles X and, 427 sq.; allied with Austria and Poland, 429; negotiates with France, 430; 431; *Rheinbund* and, 432; Charles X and, 580 sq.; John Casimir of Poland and, 583; Treaty of Wehlau and, 585 sq.; invades Jutland, 588; Treaty of Oliva and, 433, 590; and the persecution of French Protestants, V 22, 25; and Louis XIV, 41 sq., 47; and United Provinces, 37, 42; and Emperor Leopold I, 43; at Colmar, 44; at Fehrbellin, *ib.*; treaty of, with Sweden, 45; and William of Orange, 52, 107, 244; and the Dutch war with England, 109; joins Quadruple Alliance, *ib.*; and the Swedish-Dutch War, 146; 344; and Emperor Leopold, 353, 359, 671; 354; and Sweden, 563, 568 sqq.; 617; youth and accession of, 639 sq.; foreign policy of, 640 sq.; marriage of, 641; administrative reforms by, 642; and the army, 642 sq.; and the Empire, 643; and the duchy of Prussia, 643 sq.; and the Rhenish duchies, 645; encourages immigration and industries, 645 sq.; colonial and naval policy of, 646 sq., 691; religious toleration by, 647 sqq.; and the Bishop of Münster, 649; and England, 649 sq., 653; and France, 649 sq.; and the war with Sweden, 651 sq.; and the treaties of Nymegen and St Germain, 652; and the Emperor Leopold, 652 sqq.; alliance of, with France, 653; with the United Provinces, 654; and the expedition of William of Orange, 655; second marriage of, *ib.*; death of, 54, 655; successive wills of, 656; character of, *ib.*; significance of this rule, 657; 660 sq.; 743; VI 4; postal system of, 205; 206; 208; 213; and the nobility, 217; 221; 227; 664

Brandenburg, Electors of, *contd.* :—
—— George William, III 722; IV 17; 25;
68; 88; mission to Copenhagen from, 89;
concludes treaty with Christian IV, 90;
92; 97; allies himself with Bethlen Gabor,
91, 100; declares for Emperor, 100 sq. ;
104; and the Edict of Restitution, 111,
114, 117; 184; ruler of East Prussia, 185;
policy of, 186; compensated in West
Prussia, 187; policy of, 194; Gustavus
and, 197 sq.; delivers Spandau to Gustavus, 200; at Berlin, *ib.*; 202; 204;
John George and, 211; Oxenstierna and,
224; 225; Heilbronn Alliance and, 226;
peace negotiations with, 233; 235; Arnim
and, 236; Wallenstein and, 237; 244;
Peace of Prague and, 254 sq.; desire of,
for settlement, 366 sq.; lays claim to
Pomerania, 373; concludes treaty with
Poland (1638), 378; death of, 384; v 637
sq.; 640 sqq.
—— Joachim I, I 316; at the Diet of
Nürnberg, II 170; 195, 198; attitude of,
to Lutheranism, 201, 215, 220; death of,
237; v 624 sqq.
—— Joachim II, becomes Lutheran, II
237; 238 sq., 241 sq., 251; persuades
Philip of Hesse to surrender, 261; the
Interim and, 264; III 152 sq.; 168; 176;
v 624; 626 sq.; 636
—— Joachim Frederick, administrator
of Magdeburg, III 153, 706, 710, 714
sqq.; 722 sqq.; IV 22; v 627 sq.;
636
—— John Cicero, v 624
—— John George, III 704 sqq.; 711 sq.;
v 624; 627; 636
—— John Sigismund, Duke of Prussia,
claim of, to Jülich-Cleves, III 642, 687
sq., 716, 729; and the Protestant Union,
725; and Maurice of Nassau, 733; adopts
Calvinism, 723, IV 3, 10; and the Imperial
succession, 17; and the Elector Pala-
tine, 25, 27 sqq., 33; v 627 sq.; 636 sq.;
743
—— Sigismund. *See* Sigismund, Emperor
Brandenburg, Albert the Bear, Margrave
of, v 618 sq.; 624
—— Albert II, Margrave of, v 620
—— Albert of Brandenburg-Ansbach, 1st
Duke of Prussia. *See* Prussia
—— Albrecht (Albert) of, Archbishop
Elector of Mainz. *See* Mainz
—— Anna, Electress of, consort of John
Sigismund, III 716
—— Charles Emil, Electoral Prince of,
v 651
—— Christian William of, Administrator
of Magdeburg and Bishop of Halberstadt,
IV 91; 94; supports Gustavus Adolphus,
195; captured at Magdeburg, 202; Peace
of Prague and, 253
—— Dorothea (of Holstein-Glücksburg),
Electress of, v 655 sq.; 658

Brandenburg, Elizabeth of Denmark, Elec-
tress of, II 202
—— Elizabeth Charlotte, Electress of,
Princess Palatine, consort of George
William, III 722, IV 17; 25
—— Margrave Ernest of, III 730
—— Count Friedrich Wilhelm, Prussian
Prime Minister, XI 193, 218; and the
Hesse-Cassel question, 229; death of,
230
—— Margrave George of. *See* Branden-
burg-Ansbach
—— Margrave John George of, Prince of
Jägerndorf, under the ban (1620), IV 68;
71; 75; v 653
—— Louisa Dorothea Sophia, daughter
of Elector Frederick III, Princess of, v
661
—— Louisa Henrietta (of Orange), Elec-
tress of, consort of Frederick William I,
v 622 *n.*, 641; 655 sq.; 668
—— Matthias von Jagow, Bishop of, II
237
—— Otto II, Margrave of, v 620
—— Waldemar, the False, claiming to be
Margrave of, v 621
—— Waldemar the Great, Margrave of,
v 620; 631
—— *See also* Charles IV, Emperor; John
of Luxemburg; Moravia, Jodocus of
Brandenburg-Ansbach, House of, Protestant, III 704, 724 sq.
—— Albert, Margrave of. *See* Prussia
—— George, Margrave of (Prince of
Jägerndorf, *the Pious*), I 337; and the
Peasants' Rising, II 191; the Protest
signed by, 205; and Schmalkaldic League,
215; condemned by *Kammergericht*, 221;
and Jägerndorf, v 625 sq.; 635
—— George Frederick, Margrave of, III
714; 716; death of (1603), 722; v
636
—— Joachim Ernest, Margrave of, III
725; 732; 735; IV 1; advises Frederick V
to accept Bohemian throne, 29; 67;
agrees to abandon Frederick, 69; in
touch with him, 80
Brandenburg-Ansbach and Baireuth, Sophia
(of Poland), Margravine of, v 635
Brandenburg - Baireuth (and Culmbach),
Margrave Casimir of, I 312; adopts
Lutheranism, II 169, 195; the Peasants'
Rising and, 188, 190
—— Charles Ernest, Margrave of, v 418
—— Christian, Margrave of (*earlier* M. of
Culmbach), III 725
—— John (the Alchemist), Margrave of,
v 623
—— Margravine Wilhelmina of, VI 19;
210; 253
Brandenburg-Cüstrin, John *or* Hans, Mar-
grave of, and the Schmalkaldic League,
II 238; won over by Charles V, 251, 253;
opposition to the *Interim* by, 264, 270
refuses to join Henry II, 271; v 626

Brandenburg-Culmbach (Baireuth), Albert Alcibiades, Margrave of, allied with Charles V, II 87, 252 sq., 273 sq.; 259; allied with Francis I, 270 sq., 273; wins battle at Pommersfelden, 275; defeated by Maurice of Saxony, *ib.*; III 151
—— Margrave Casimir of, I 312
—— Christian, Margrave of (*afterwards* M. of Baireuth), III 725
Brandenburg-Schwedt, Margrave Charles of, VI 280; 288
Brandes, Georg, Danish critic, XI 700; XII 292
Brandis, Christian August, German scholar, XII 822
Brandolini, Raffaelle, lecturer at Rome, II 17
Brandon, Charles. *See* Suffolk, Duke of
—— Duke of. *See* Hamilton, 4th Duke of
Brandt, Carsten, German shipmaster, in Russia, V 520
—— Enevold, Count, Christian VII and, VI 745 sq.; 749; execution of, 750; 751
Brandywine, battle on the (1777), VII 213
Branković, George, despot of Servia, I 69
Brant, Sebastian, *The Ship of Fools*, I 637 sq., 676, 683, II 280
Brantôme, Pierre de Bourdeilles, Abbé de, III 65
Braschi, Giovanni Angelo. *See* Pius VI
Braschi-Onesti, Romuald, Cardinal, X 133
Brask, John. *See* Linkoeping, Bishops of
Braun, Alexander Karl Hermann, Saxon statesman, XI 149
Braunau (Upper Austria), VI 236; fall of, 238; Kutusoff at, IX 255; occupied by French troops, 269; French evacuation of, 309
—— (Bohemia), Protestant action in, IV 14 sq., 19; Abbot of, banished, 21
Bravo, Luis González. *See* González
—— Murillo, Juan, Spanish statesman, XI 557 sqq.; resignation of, 559; 563
Braxfield, Robert Macqueen, Lord, Scottish judge, VIII 770
Bray, John Francis, economic theories of, X 782
—— Sir Reginald, Minister of Henry VII, I 477
Braye, fight at (1814), IX 547
Brazil, discovery of, by Pinzon, I 34; race inhabiting, 38, 59; Durand's colony in, 48 sq.; mines of, III 499; Dutch trade with, 633; expedition of West India Company to (1623), IV 703; Spanish fleet on coast of, 705; extension of Dutch dominion in, 708; revolt of Portuguese in (1645), 709; Portugal, United Provinces and, 714; Admiral Witte de With and, 726; Dutch West India Company in, 750 sqq.; lost by the Dutch (1654), 753 sqq.; 759; Portugal and, V 107, 146; Dutch abandon claim to, 148, 675 sq.; slave labour in, 676 sq.; 677; discovery of gold in, 678 sq.; in the seventeenth and eighteenth centuries, Vol. VI, Chapter XII (3); progress

of, 184; 187; independence of, 189; 351; 384; Jesuits expelled from, 387; French ships off, IX 234; withdrawal of Portuguese fleet to, 236; Prince Regent of Portugal sails for, 304; 321; 363; and the Congress of Vienna, 584; incorporation of, with Portugal, 669; and Portugal, Vol. X, Chap. x *passim*; 212; contraband trade in, 257; trade and industries in, 586, 761; Republic established in, XII 270; 672; affairs in (1840–95), 674 sqq.; and Uruguay, 680; 681; and Argentina, 682; 690 sq.; 693; boundary disputes of, 655, 722; arbitration treaties by, 727
Brazil Company (Portuguese), V 675
—— Don John of. *See* John, Don, of Brazil, Prince Regent of Portugal
Brazos Is., captured (1863), VII 552
Brazza, Count Pietro Savorgnan de, African explorer, XII 130; 256; 658; 812
Bréa, Jean-Baptiste-Fidèle, French general, XI 113
Breadalbane, John Campbell, 1st Earl of, VI 98
—— John Campbell, 3rd Earl of, VI 435
Bréard, Jean-Jacques, member of the *Comité de Salut Public*, VIII 269, 375
Brearly, David, New Jersey deputy at the Constitutional Convention, VII 246, 252
Brechin, Jacobite rising at, VI 98
Breckinridge, John Cabell, Confederate general, VII 439 sq., 445; at Chattanooga, 513; Secretary of War, 542
Breda, conference at (1575), III 241, patriotism at, 248; siege of, 578; capture of (1590), 626; captured by Spinola (1624), 656, (1625), IV 88, 258, 642, 691; Frederick Henry captures, 698, 699; 755; Charles II of England at, V 148; Declaration of, 92; 94; 99; allied forces at, VI 246; Belgian exiles at, VIII 328; captured by the French (1793), 419, (1794), 436; taken by Napoleon (1810), IX 370
—— Treaty of (1667), IV 740, V 37, 112 sq., 151, 154, 187, 189, 199, 329, VII 111
Brederode, Francis van, defeated at Brouwershaven (1490), I 449
—— Henry, Lord of, III 194, 201 sqq.
—— Lancelot, III 236
—— Walraven, Lord of, III 640
Brederoo, Gerbrand Adrianszoon, works of, IV 718; 721
Bredow, General von, at Vionville, XI 591
Bredy, Major-General, shot at Vienna, XI 186
Breedevoort, siege of (1597), III 629
Bregaglia, preachers in, IV 46; Catholic commune of, 47; subdued by Feria, 55; 61
Bregenz, conference of sovereigns at, XI 229
Breisach, Bernard of Weimar's siege and capture of, IV 148, 376 sq.; protected by Götz, 375; Guébriant at, 381, 382; Treaty of, 383; 388; French claim to, 246, 379–80, 382, 405; ceded to France,

406, 416; 602; seized by Harcourt, 618;
v 45; 48; ceded to France, 63; 408;
Charles of Lorraine at, vi 238
Breisgau, The, French troops in, vi 241;
ceded to Modena, viii 592, ix 94
Breismann, John, Reformer, ii 161
Breitenfeld, battle of (1631), iv 205 sqq.,
209 sq., 214, 222; Horn and, 227; second
battle of (1642), 386
Breitinger, Johann Jakob, vi 625; x 384
Bremen, joins Schmalkaldic League, ii
215; resists Charles V, 262; and
Hanseatic League, iv 8; port of, demanded by Gustavus Adolphus, 191;
Danish claims on see of, 387; taken by
Königsmark, 390; given to Prince Frederick of Denmark, 365; archbishopric
of, claimed by Sweden at Osnabrück,
403; ceded to Sweden, 404, 408; trade
of, 419 sq.; duchy of, in the Hildesheim
alliance, 425; quarrel of, with Oldenburg,
427; England and, 429; Sweden signs
Rheinbund for, 432; Charles X and, 578;
580; reconquered by Bilde, 584; Cartesian philosophy at, 791; purchased by
George I, v 550; Sweden and, 562 sq.,
603; 569; 579; seized by Danes (1712),
582, 607, 610 sq.; 613; bishopric of, 615;
652; vi 21; annexed to Hanover, 23 sq.;
28; Charles XII and, 34; 36; 39; and
Sweden, 104; Prussian troops occupy,
ix 48; withdraw from, 50; embarkation
of British force at, 263; transferred to
Prussia, 264; government of, 409; Vandamme in, 515; Jews of, 588; free city
of, x 341; and the Customs' Union, 373;
xi 54; revolutionary movement at, 151;
and the German customs, xii 156
Bremen, Archbishops of :—
—— Christopher of Brunswick, ii 231
—— George of Brunswick, iii 157
—— Henry of Saxe-Lauenburg (1566-85),
iii 157
—— John Frederick of Holstein-Gottorp,
iv 89; 98
Bremgarten, vi 616
Brenkenhof, Franz Balthasar Schönberg
von, vi 733
Brenner Pass, Bavarian detachment at,
v 407
Brennier, French Commandant of Almeida,
ix 466
Brent, Sir Nathaniel, Vicar-General of
Laud, iv 279
—— William, United States Minister in
Buenos Ayres, xii 680 sq.
Brentano, Clemens, German Romanticist,
x 401 sq.; 404 sqq.; xii 818; 822
—— Ludwig, Baden revolutionary, xi
221
Brentford, sacked by Rupert, iv 308 sq.
Brenz, John (Johann Brentzen), Reformer,
ii 160, 207, 234; driven into exile, 265,
714; his principles of freedom, iii
755

Brereton, Sir William, victory of, at
Nantwich, iv 312; Fairfax and, 321;
Parliamentary General in the West,
329; surrender of Chester to, 335
Bresca, Genoese family of, iii 443
Bresci, assassinates King Humbert, xii 223
Brescia, lost by Venice (1509), i 133; recovered and lost again (1512), 136 sq.;
v 402; Prince Eugene at, 414; Wurmser
captures (1796), viii 574, evacuates, 575;
revolt at (1797), 584 sq.; xi 85; the
defence of, 95; Garibaldian prisoners at,
533
Breslau, influence of Wittenberg on, ii 161;
Frederick's manifesto issued from, iv 67;
religious liberty of, 413; Prussia and, vi
229 sq.; 235; 264; 273; Prussian defeat
at, 274 sq.; surrender of, 276; 294; 721;
Treaty of, 231, 317, 319; siege of (1806),
ix 281; University established at, 327;
328; Frederick William at, 512, 513;
French troops at, 520; Allies' troops
near, 523; University of, x 355; tumult
at, 364; disturbance at (1848), xi 157;
193; 219; supports Bismarck, 451
—— Martin Gerstmann, Bishop of (1574-
85), iii 93
Bresse, given up by France (1558), ii 94;
ceded to France, iii 419; French in
vasion of, 677; customs of, v 13
—— Philippe de. *See* Savoy, Duke of
Bresson, Count Charles, French ambassador at Madrid, xi 17; 554
Brest, relief of (1594), iii 319; Spaniards
driven from, 321, 521; development of,
v 14; 62; 187; English attack on (1694),
261 sq., 460; expedition sails from, vi
110; 112; 159; Roquefeuil's fleet at, 239;
349; naval disorders in, viii 193, 447 sq.;
451; French fleet at, 458, 466, 470 sqq.,
480; Napoleon's projected invasion of
England and, ix 210 sqq.; French ships
at, 219; Ganteaume blockaded at, 223;
blockaded by Cornwallis, 226; Ganteaume
sails from, 228; 237; British blockade
dispersed, 238; blockade renewed, 240;
French troops at, 252
—— (in Russia), Schwarzenberg retreats
to, ix 499
Brestel, Rudolf, Austrian Minister of
Finance, xii 185
Breteuil, Baron de Louis-Auguste le Tonne-
lier, French ambassador at St Petersburg,
vi 327; Minister of the Household, viii
103, 114; Chief Minister, 163; dismissed,
165
Brethren of the Common Life, i 434 sq.,
461, 627 sq.
Bretons, revolt of the, ix 564
Brett, police-sergeant, murdered, xii 65
Brewer, David Josiah, and the Venezuelan
Boundary Commission, xii 721
—— John Sherren, historian, xii 841
Brézé, Claire-Clémence de Maillé. *See*
Condé

Brézé, Henri-Évrard, Marquis de Dreux et de, Grand Master of the Ceremonies to Louis XVI, VIII 155, 157
—— Jean-Armand de Maillé, Duke of, Admiral of France, IV 599; commands French expedition to Italy, 600; death of, *ib.* sq., 609
—— Urbain de Maillé, Marquis of, Marshal of France, IV 149; and Heidelberg, 248; sent by Louis XIII to Barcelona, 649; at Maestricht, 697
Briand, Aristide, French Minister of Education, XII 113; 122 sq.; 127 sq.
Bricherasio, capture of (1594), III 417
Briçonnet (Brissonet), Guillaume, Cardinal of St Malo, I 109, 112, 177, 184, 409
—— Guillaume de (son of above). *See* Meaux, Bishop of
—— Pierre, financial minister of Louis XI, I 409
Bridge, William, Independent, IV 359
Bridgeman, Sir Orlando, Lord Keeper of the Privy Seal, V 201; 207; 334
Bridges, Colonel John, surprises Dublin Castle, IV 547
Bridgewater, taken by Fairfax, IV 331 sq.
Bridport, Alexander Hood, Viscount, admiral, VIII 471 sq.; and the French invasion (1796), 473, 475 sq.; and the Spithead mutiny, 476 sqq.
Brieg, principality of, V 652; 659; duchy of, VI 229; 230 sq.
Brienne, battle of (1814), IX 545
Brière de l'Ille, Louis-A.-E.-G., French general, in Senegal, XII 129
Briey, Austrian commander, IX 60
Briggs, Henry, mathematician, V 709
Bright, John, X 680; XI 309; 328 sq.; 339; and Ireland, 343 sq.; XII 23; resigns, 40; 43; 437; and social reform, 745
Brignole, Marquis de, Genoese plenipotentiary at Vienna, IX 599
Brihuega, Allies defeated at (1710), V 428
Brill, captured by the *Gueux de Mer* (1572), III 229–31, 233, 284; marriage of William of Orange at, 241; held by Elizabeth, 619, 670–1
Brinkley, Richard, English Hebraist, I 592
Brinon, President of Rouen, French agent in London, II 423 sq.
Brion, Philippe de, Minister of Francis I, II 97
Brisbane, convicts at, XI 790; 794 sq.; 798; industries of, XII 623
Brisegna. *See* Manrique, Isabella
Brisighello, Imperialist colonel, in the Valtelline, IV 61
Brissac, François de, French general in Italy (1551), II 86
—— Charles I de Cossé, Comte de, Marshal of France (Marshal Brissac, d. 1563), III 6
—— Charles II de Cossé, Duke of, Marshal of France (son of Marshal Brissac), III 662

Brisson, Barnabé, civil lawyer, I 577; III 50, 58
—— Henri, French politician, XII 109; 121
—— Pierre de, captive in Africa, XII 806; 808
Brissonius. *See* Brisson, Barnabé
Brissot de Warville, Jean-Pierre, VIII 213 sq.; foreign policy of, 220, 223; 240; arrested, 242; 249; at the King's trial, 258; trial and execution of, 357; 747 sq.
Brissotins, The, VIII 213 sq., 220 sq.; Ministry of, summoned, 223 sq.; 227 sq., 234, 237 sq.; arrest of, 242, 244, 248. *See also* Girondins
Bristol, exploring voyages from, I 20; Colombo at, 21; maritime importance of, 33; at the opening of the First Civil War, IV 302; Rupert at, 324; Prince of Wales at, 328; stormed by Parliamentarians, 332 sqq.; Irish troops at, 527; Whitefield at, VI 83; Reform disturbances at (1831), X 613; XII 654; University of, 763
—— Augustus John Hervey, 3rd Earl of, VI 451
—— Frederick Augustus Hervey, 4th Earl of, Bishop of Derry, VI 501 sq.; IX 693
—— George Digby, 2nd Earl of (1st cr.); created Baron Digby, IV 291; Root-and-Branch petition and, 292; flight of, to Holland, 300; Rupert and, 319; Charles I and, 332 sqq.; 338; leads English Catholics, V 100 sq.; 105; 210
—— George William Hervey, 2nd Earl of (2nd cr.), at Madrid, VI 368, 419, 426; 431; 438; Lord Privy Seal, 439; 442
—— John Digby, 1st Earl of, III 560; Buckingham and, IV 264; Charles I and, 265; at Vienna, 77; 78; at Madrid, 82; instructions to, from James I, 625; Buckingham's Spanish mission and, 641
Bristow, Benjamin H., American Secretary of the Treasury, VII 644
Britanny, relations of, with France, I 392, 396; and the Peace of Le Verger (1488), 394; allied with England, 466; Duchy of, Philip's plan concerning, III 510, 512, 524; Spanish base in, 521 sqq.; the League in, 661; English troops withdrawn from, 666; 672; Spanish expedition to, 673; Henry IV's expedition to (1598), 674 sq.; Vendôme Governor of, IV 119; taxation of, 153; claims of the Vendôme family to, 596; results of the Fronde in, 621; Estates of, V 4, VIII 39 sq., 128 sq.; disturbances in, V 9 sq., VI 130; 356; 452; and the Provincial Assemblies, VIII 112; disaffection in (1794), 379, 391, (1829), X 97
—— Anne, Duchess of. *See* Anne, Queen of France
—— Francis II, Duke of, leagued against France, I 392–4; death of, 394, 449

Britanny, Jean IV, Duke of, ɪ 392
—— Louis, Duke of, death of, v 434
British Central Africa, province of, xɪɪ 3 ;
661
—— Columbia, xɪ 771 ; united to Canada,
776 ; xɪɪ 604 sq. ; progress in, 608 ;
internal affairs of, 616 ; 650 ; 814
—— East Africa, xɪɪ 47 ; 660 sqq. ; 813
—— East Africa Company, xɪɪ 661
—— Museum, foundation of, vɪ 74
—— North Borneo Company, xɪɪ 669
—— South Africa Company, xɪɪ 49 ;
founded, 639 ; 664
Brixen, Austria receives the bishopric of,
ɪx 94
Brochero, Spanish admiral, ɪɪɪ 532
Brock, Sir Isaac, major-general, vɪɪ 337 sq.
—— Peter, Russian Minister of Finance,
xɪ 266 ; 614
Brockes, Barthold Heinrich, x 385
Broderith, Hungarian Chancellor, ɪ 96
Brodrick, Alan. *See* Midleton, Viscount
—— William St J. F. *See* Midleton,
Viscount
Broeck, Pieter van den, visit of, to Japan,
ɪv 712
Brömsebro, Peace of, signed by Christian
IV (1645), ɪv 390, 572, 574 ; Mazarin
and, 601
Brofferio, Angelo, x 126 ; xɪ 545
Broghill, Roger Boyle, Lord. *See* Orrery
Broglie, Achille-Léonce-Victor-Charles, Duc
de, x 52 ; 53 ; 54 ; and the electoral law,
57, 60 sq. ; and the liberty of the press,
58 ; and the *Société des Amis de la Presse*,
61 ; declines office, *ib.* ; 64 ; 65 ; 67 ;
goes into Opposition, 68 ; 81 ; opposes
compensation for the *émigrés*, 86 ; opposes the "law of sacrilege," 87 ; and
the Revolution of 1830, 478 ; 480 ;
Minister of Foreign Affairs, 489 ; foreign
policy of, 494 sq. ; fall of, 495 sq. ; and
Algiers, 502 ; 503 ; 508 ; and Louis-
Napoleon, xɪ 134
—— Albertine-Ida-Gustavine de Staël,
Duchesse de, x 52 ; 53
—— Charles-François, Count of, French
ambassador in Saxony, vɪ 338
—— François-Marie, Duke of, Marshal of
France, vɪ 233 sqq.
—— Jacques-Victor-Albert, Duc de, xɪɪ
106 sqq. ; defeated, 110 ; 111 ; 114 ; 116 ;
historical works of, 834
—— Victor-François, Duke of, Marshal of
France, vɪ 269 ; vɪɪɪ 51, 159, 163 ; Secretary
for War, 163 ; emigrates, 165
—— Victor Maurice, Count of, and the
Camisards, v 26
—— Maurice de. *See* Ghent, Bishop of
Broke, Sir Philip Bowes Vere, captain of
the *Shannon*, vɪɪ 342
Broken Hill, silver discovered at, xɪɪ 619 ;
628 sq.
Bromberg, Treaty of (Nov. 6, 1657), ɪv 429 ;
Tchitchagoff at, ɪx 512

Bromley, Sir Thomas, Chief Justice, ɪɪ
475
Bronitsi, Russians defeated at, ɪv 181
Bronkhorsts, faction in Gelders, ɪ 423
Brontë, Charlotte, xɪ 359 sq.
—— Emily Jane, xɪ 354
Bronzell, skirmish at, xɪ 230
Brook Farm, socialist experiment at, vɪɪ
739
—— Robert Greville, 2nd Baron, grants
of land in New England to, vɪɪ 18, 21
Brooke, Sir James, Rájah of Sarawak, xɪɪ
535 ; 669
—— John R., American general, vɪɪ 680
Brooks, James, Bishop of Gloucester, ɪɪ
531, 541
—— Preston Smith, assaults Sumner,
vɪɪ 430
Broschi, Carlo. *See* Farinelli
Brosolo, Alliance concluded at (1610), ɪɪɪ
690
Brotherhood, the Evangelical (of the
Peasants' Rising), demands of, ɪɪ 180 ;
Franconian nobles join the, 188
Brottier, André-Charles, conspiracy of, vɪɪɪ
503 sqq., 510, 512
Brouage, siege of, ɪɪɪ 32
Brouckère, Henri Marie Joseph Ghislain
de, Belgian statesman, xɪ 672
Brouet, Pascal, ɪɪɪ 586
Brougham, Henry Peter, Baron Brougham
and Vaux, vɪɪ 371 ; and the Whig party,
ɪx 687 ; and elementary education, 692 ;
influence of, x 574 ; and the income tax,
575 ; 580 ; opposes the King's divorce bill,
583 ; 585 ; and Canning, 591 ; 598 ; 601 ;
and parliamentary reform, 603 ; 604 ;
and the Reform Bills, 610 sq., 614 sq. ;
and the Irish Catholic Association, 642 ;
supports the anti-slavery movement, 658,
677 ; and the Poor Law, 660, 662 ; 663
sq. ; Scottish political tour of, 665 ; 666 ;
Melbourne and, 668 ; 673 ; and Thomas
Drummond, 677 ; 679
Broughton, John Cam Hobhouse, 1st Baron,
x 580 ; 582 ; and Bentham, 598 ; and the
Reform Bills, 610 sqq., 614
Broukère, Charles de, Belgian deputy, x
480 ; 531
Brousse, Émile, French socialist, xɪɪ 124
sqq.
Broussel, Pierre, French magistrate, arrest
of, ɪv 607 ; charge of murder against,
612 ; made Provost of Merchants, 617
Brouwer, Hendrik, Governor-General of the
Dutch Indies, ɪv 711
Brown, Benjamin Gratz, Governor of
Missouri, vɪɪ 640
—— Charles Brockden, *Wieland*, vɪɪ 741
—— George, Canadian politician, xɪ 769
sq. ; 774
—— John, raid of, at Harper's Ferry,
vɪɪ 439
—— Joseph Emerson, Governor of
Georgia, vɪɪ 522, 605, 609

Browne, Count Georg von, Russian general, VI 285

—— George, Archbishop of Dublin, III 587

—— Horace, Colonel, at Bhamo, XII 500 sq.

—— John, Massachusetts settler, VII 16

—— Count Maximilian Ulysses von, Austrian Field-Marshal, VI 254 sqq.; death of, 259; 285; 362

—— Richard, Major-General, the nickname of "The Rump" and, IV 549

—— Robert, III 340, 343, 756

—— Samuel, Massachusetts settler, VII 16

—— Sir Samuel, in Afghánistán, XII 470

—— Sir Thomas, V 332

—— Sir Thomas Gore, Governor of New Zealand, XI 799

—— William George, in Africa, XII 805; 811; 813

Browning, Elizabeth Barrett, XI 352 sqq.

—— Robert, XI 350; 352 sq.; and George Meredith, 361; 364 sq.; XII 13

Brownists, separatism and, III 340; character of, in politics, V 326

Brownrigg, Sir Robert, general, in Ceylon, IX 734

Bruce, Andrew, Bishop of Dunkeld, V 290

—— Clarence Dalrymple, traveller, XII 803

—— Sir Frederick W. A., British envoy to China, XI 817 sq.

—— James, traveller, XII 805 sq.

Brucioli, Antonio, II 379; printer at Venice, 383

Bruck, Jellačić at, XI 187

—— Baron Karl Ludwig von, Austrian Minister of Commerce, XI 190; 216; 223; 394 sq.; Minister of Finance, 402; 403; XII 176

Brue, André, African traveller, XII 806

Brühl, Count Heinrich von, Saxon statesman, VI 198 sqq.; 346

Brünn, besieged by Torstensson, IV 389 sq.; siege of (1742), VI 233; Russian troops at (1798), VIII 647; Napoleon at, IX 258; advance of Allies on (1805), 259; the Austrian *Reichstag* removed to, XI 187; Mendel's researches at, XII 766

Bruern, Richard, professor of Hebrew at Oxford, II 541

Brueys d'Aigalliers, François-Paul, French admiral, VIII 598, 604, 622 sqq.; killed, 628

Bruges, importance and decline of, 1425 sqq., 452; revolt in (1488), 448 sq.; Maximilian I in, 448; England and, 450, 454; Treaty at, between Charles V and Henry VIII (1521), II 43, 418; taken by Parma, III 618, 630; escape of Archduke Albert to, 636; surrenders to Marlborough (1706), V 416; the French at, 420; 421 sq.

Bruges, Henri-Alphonse, Vicomte de, proposed as Grand Chancellor of the Legion of Honour, IX 571

Brugghen, Justinius Jacob Leonard van der, Dutch statesman, XI 666

Brugmann, Johannes, Dutch preacher, I 435

Brugsch, Heinrich, Egyptologist, XII 845

Bruin, Lionardo, Florentine historian, I 541–2

Bruins. *See* Brun

Bruix, Eustache, French admiral, VIII 615, 630 sq., 657, 680; IX 53

Brulart, Nicholas. *See* Sillery

—— de Léon, French envoy, at Ratisbon, IV 115

Brumaire, the *coup d'état* of, and its significance for the French Revolution, Vol. VIII, Chap. XXII, 665–88

Brun, St, V 629

—— Antoine, Spanish plenipotentiary at Münster, IV 401, 715

—— Rudolf, of Zurich, II 312

Brune, Guillaume-Marie-Anne, Marshal of France, VIII 639 sq., 662, 674; IX 13; 14, 21, 68, 89, 96, 112; signs armistice with Sweden, 295; Rügen ceded to, 300; command of, 624; assassinated, X 46

Brunei, Sultan of, XII 669

Brunet, Colonel, in Paris, XI 100

Brunetière, Ferdinand, XII 119 sq.

Brunetti, Angelo (Ciceruacchio), Roman tribune, XI 74; 76 sq.

Brunfels, Otto, reformer, II 161

Bruni, Leonardo, *History of Florence*, III 471

Brunn, Heinrich, historian, XII 845

Brunnen League, of Swiss Cantons (1315), II 305

Brunner, Heinrich, historian, XII 850

—— Philip Joseph, IX 201

Brunnow, Baron Ernst Philipp von, Russian envoy in London, X 558; 564; XI 632

Bruno, Archbishop of Cologne, I 536

—— Giordano, the philosophy of, II 707 sq., 709 sq.; III 455, 466; death of, IV 668

Brunswick, attack on, by Schmalkaldic League (1542), II 243; siege of, III 644; IV 8; meeting of Lower Saxon Circle at, 85, 92 sq.; negotiations at, 96; and Christian IV, 97; subjugation of, 100; convents restored in duchy of, 112; Congress of (1714), V 610, VI 39; comprised in kingdom of Westphalia, IX 336, 411; Jews in, 412; army of, 622; and the Germanic Confederation, X 344; and the Customs' Union, 373, XI 53, 394; revolution in (1830), X 374; and Prussia, XI 228

—— House of, and Formula Concordiae, III 704; X 582

—— Charles, Duke of, deposed, X 374

—— Charles William Ferdinand, Duke of, invades Holland (1787), VIII 107, 287 sq.,

323; manifesto of, 234, 273, 409; commands the Allies (1792), 407 sqq., 414 sq., 419, 423; at Kaiserslautern, 424 sq.; IX 255; 264; Prussian envoy to Russia, 266; commander-in-chief, 273 sq.; at Jena and Auerstädt, 275 sqq.; death of, 278

Brunswick-Bevern, Frederick Francis, Duke of, Prussian general, VI 260; 264; 273 sq.

Brunswick-Calenberg, Elizabeth of Brandenburg, Dowager-Duchess of, reforms Brunswick-Calenberg, II 238; 251

—— Eric I, Duke of, II 220, 232, 235

—— Eric II, Duke of, II 251, 253, 261

Brunswick-Grubenhagen, Philip, Duke of, II 195; 216

Brunswick-Lüneburg, V 581; and Mecklenburg-Güstrow, 663

—— House of, and Gustavus Adolphus, IV 194; and the Treaty of Westphalia, 408; *Rheinbund* signed by, 431; and France, V 655; and Prussia, 662; VI 2 sq.; political record of, 4 sq.

—— Dukes of, V 37; 43; join Quadruple Alliance, 109; 161; 569; 571

Brunswick-Lüneburg, Dukes of :—

—— Christian (d. 1633), IV 79 sq.; 91

—— Christian Lewis, V 655; VI 2

—— Ernest, II 169, 195; the Protest of Speier signed by, 205; 221

—— Francis, II 195; signs the Protest of Speier, 205; 215 sq.

—— George, commander of Lower Saxon Circle troops, IV 86; Gustavus and, 207; 220 sq.; Swedish army and, 225; 227; and Bernard of Weimar, 247; Peace of Prague and, 255, 365; Saxony and, 366; neutrality of, 378; opposes the Emperor, 383; death of, 385; 408; VI 2

—— Otto of Harburg, II 195, 215 sq., 270

Brunswick-Lüneburg (Celle), Frederick, Duke of, VI 2

—— (Celle), George, Duke of, IV 194

—— (Celle), George William, Duke of, and the Grand Alliance, V 55, 244, 403; VI 2 sqq.; 7 sq.; death of, 10; 12

—— (Hanover), Ernest Augustus, Duke of, and Elector of Hanover. *See* Hanover

—— (Hanover), John Frederick, Duke of, V 651; 744; VI 3 sq.

—— (Celle), Duchess (Eleonora of Olbreuse), consort of George William, VI 3

—— Frederick Augustus, Prince of, V 662

—— Maximilian William, Prince of, V 662; VI 3

Brunswick-Oels, Friedrich Wilhelm, Duke of, IX 335; in Westphalia, 337; enters Brunswick (July 30, 1809), 357; death of, 629

Brunswick-Wolfenbüttel, House of, III 156

—— Princess Anna Leopoldovna of, VI 309; 311; 315

Brunswick-Wolfenbüttel, Prince Antony Ulric of, in Russia, VI 309

—— Duke Christian of, Bishop of Halberstadt, IV 79 sq.; at Höchst, 80 sq.; joins Mansfeld, 85; at Stadtlohn, 86; 88; resigns see of Halberstadt, 91; 92; brings reinforcements to Nienburg, 95; in Hesse-Cassel, 96; 97

—— Dowager-Duchess Elizabeth of, consort of Henry Julius, IV 93

—— Prince Ferdinand (*afterwards* Duke Charles William Ferdinand) of, VI 265 sq.; 268; 272 sq.; 277; and the Army of Observation, 408; 426; 429

—— Prince Francis of, VI 290

—— Princess Sophia Charlotte of, V 538

Brunswick-Wolfenbüttel, Dukes of :—

—— Antony Ulric, and the Grand Alliance, V 55, 403; 744

—— Charles I, VI 266

—— Frederick Ulric, IV 8; 79; 86; 91 sqq.; submission of, 98

—— Henry IV, Italian campaign of, II 58; suppression of Peasants' Revolt by, 187, 189; 195, 220, 231, 235 sq.; attack on, by Schmalkaldic League, 243, 251; recovers duchy, 259; defeats Albert Alcibiades, 275; III 157

—— Henry Julius, III 153; 156; 715; 725 sqq.; adherent of Rudolf II, IV 79

—— Rudolf Augustus, V 55; 403

Brus, Anton, Archbishop of Prague. *See* Prague

Bruslart, Louis Guérin de, French general, IX 2

Brussels, growth of, I 419; Maximilian I at, 449; Treaty of (1498), 454; abdication of Charles V at (1555), II 90, 537, III 182; meeting of States General at (1556), 185; Alva enters, 214; execution of Counts Egmont and Hoorn at, 219, 220; outlawry of William of Orange proclaimed at, 221; States General at (1569), 226, (1576), 245–6; Don John's entry into (1577), 247–8, 499; triumphal entry of William of Orange into, 248; Archduke Matthias' entry into, *ib.*; abdication of Charles V of Spanish crowns at (1556), 477; revolt of Italian regiments in, 519; taken by Parma, 618; entry of Albert and Isabel into (1599), 634; Dohna at, IV 24; Charles II in, 540; Greenville at, 555; siege of Hertogenbosch and, 691, 692; the Cardinal Infante sent to, 698; the Duke of York at, V 225; 420; 422; siege of, VI 246; 651 sq.; Congress of, 655; 656; riot in (1787), VIII 319; 320; rebellion in (1789), 329; federal constitution for a Republic drawn up at (1790), *ib.*; Austrian troops in, 336; Dumouriez occupies (1792), 299, 417, 420; evacuated by the French (1793), 421; Wellington in, IX 622, 626; provisional Government at (1814), X 520; King William enters (1815), 524; industrial

exhibition at, 533; the revolution in (1830), 534 sqq.; the National Congress at, 538; Leopold I in, 540; xi 92; 491; General Prim at, 568; conference at (1863), 672; peace conference at, xii 91; socialism at, 252; Geographical Congress at, 255; International Monetary Conference at, 484; 825

Bruyninck, secretary of William of Orange, iii 252

Bry, Jean de, French envoy, viii 642, 655 sq.

Bryan, William Jennings, nominated for the Presidency, vii 673

Bryant, William Cullen, vii 742

Bryce, James, *Holy Roman Empire*, xii 841

Brydges, Sir John, Governor of the Tower, ii 520

Brydon, William, army surgeon, escapes from Cabul, xi 733

Brynkelow, Henry, ii 490

Brzesc, Union of (1595), iv 189

Buat, Henri de Fleury de Coulan, Sieur de, execution of, v 152

Bubna, Major-general, Bohemian politician, at Nürnberg, iv 218; 233; Wallenstein and, 234

Bubna-Littiz, Count Ferdinand von, Austrian Field-Marshal, ix 359; x 118

Buccleuch, Walter Francis Scott, 5th Duke of, xi 10

Bucer, Martin, Reformer, friend of Sickingen, ii 155; in Strassburg, 160; 161; at Marburg, 207; 211; *Tetrapolitana* creed drawn up by, 212, 214, 335; Zwingli and, 216; at the Conference of Wittenberg, 234, 339; 239; draws up a scheme of comprehension at Ratisbon, 240; 244; Schmalkaldic League and, 252, 258; exiled, 265; and the French Reformers, 283, 285 sq.; the Waldenses and, 289; 328; 403; in England, 477, 502 sq., 508

Buchanan, Franklin, Confederate naval officer, vii 554, 556

—— George, Scottish Latinist, i 582; and the Portuguese Index, ii 414, 555; iii 69; *De jure regni apud Scotos*, 760.

—— James, vii 419; President of the United States, 432 sqq., 438, 446 sqq.; xi 563; xii 686

—— Robert, poet, xi 352 sq.; 357

—— William J., United States Minister in Buenos Ayres, xii 679

Bucharest, negotiations at, vi 634; Austrian army captures (1789), viii 326; reduced by Russia (1806), ix 388; Treaty of (1812), 389, 485, 487, x 169, 175, 185; xi 283; Russian Governor at, 643; International Commission at, 643 sqq.; revolutionary committee at, xii 383; 414; Treaty of (1886), 407

Buchez, Philippe-Joseph-Benjamin, x 485; xi 108

Buchholtz, Colonel, expedition of, to Lake Yamuish, v 544

Buchholz, Prussian envoy to Poland, viii 524, 537 sqq.

Buchner, Eduard, German man of science, xii 780

Bucholtz, Franz B. von, historian, xii 829

Buckingham, Edward Stafford, Duke of, executed, ii 417

—— George Nugent - Temple - Grenville, Marquis of (Earl Temple), Lord-Lieutenant of Ireland, vi 462 sq., 474, 501, 505; 467; ix 693

—— George Villiers, 1st Duke of (2nd cr.), iii 560 sq.; 566; Lord High Admiral, 567; and financial struggle, 568 sqq.; and the Spanish marriage, 575 sq.; foreign policy of, 576 sqq.; iv 88; at the Hague, 95 sq.; 131; at the height of power, 257; in Paris, 258; foreign policy and, 261 sq.; Parliament and, 263 sq.; impeachment of, 265; expedition of, to Ré, 132, 266 sq.; assassination of, 133; 641; Governor of English Company for South America, 755

—— George Villiers, 2nd Duke of, v 95; 126; and the French alliance, 191; 198; 200 sq.; and the Treaty of Dover, 203 sqq.; 207 sqq.; 216; sent to the Tower, 218

—— and Chandos, Richard P. T. N. B. C. Grenville, 2nd Duke of, x 614; xi 2 sq.

Buckinghamshire, John Hobart, 2nd Earl of, Lord-Lieutenant of Ireland, vi 495 sqq.

Buckinghamshire and Normanby, John Sheffield, Duke of, vi 11

Buckle, Henry Thomas, xii 850

Buckner, Simon Bolivar, Confederate general, vii 462, 495

Bucquoy, Charles-Bonaventure de Longueval, Count de, Austrian general, at Linz, iv 11; takes command of Ferdinand's troops, 23; invades Bohemia, 25; routs Mansfeld at Zablat, 27; summoned to defend Austrian duchies, 31; 64 sqq.; in Hungary, 71 sq.; death of, 75; 77

Buczácz, Treaty of (1672), v 353

Buda. *See* Budapest

Budaeus (Guillaume Budé), French Hellenist, i 576; ii 16, 287, 351; iii 737

Budapest, Diet at (1454), i 69; captured by Solyman (1541), ii 242; Turkish Pasha in, iii 118 sqq.; sale of prisoners at, 123; taken by Imperialists (1686), v 52, 366; 339; 345; Turkish army at, 346; 363; bridge at, x 744; the revolutionary movement at, xi 155 sq.; 208; Austrian occupation of, 210 sq.; 421 sq.

Budberg, Baron (Russian Minister), ix 272; 291; Russian Chancellor, 305

Budé, Guillaume. *See* Budaeus

Budenz, József, Hungarian scholar, xi 431

Budin, Austrian magazine at, vi 257

Budowee, Wenceslas von, iii 727

Budweis, held for the Emperor, iv 21; Austrians at, vi 234; 241

Buell, Don Carlos, American general, VII
463, 493, 495 sq.; at Shiloh, 497; 499
sqq.; proceeds to E. Tennessee, 506 sq.;
superseded by Rosecrans, 507; 583

Bülow, Prince Bernhard von, Chancellor of
the German Empire, XII 166; 171; 173
—— Friedrich Wilhelm, Count von Dennewitz, marches on Magdeburg, IX 514;
retires before Ney, 518; at Berlin, 520;
character of, 525; at Dennewitz, 529;
at Leipzig, 539; in the Netherlands,
544; 550; at Liége, 625; at Waterloo,
634 sqq.
—— Baron Heinrich Wilhelm von, German
critic, IX 266
—— General von, VI 13

Buen Ayre, the Dutch in, V 687

Buena Vista, battle of (1847), VII 396

Buenos Ayres, growth of, VI 183; 186; 391;
443; failure of expedition of Popham to,
IX 235, 753; government of, X 248 sq.;
trade of, 255, 275; 268; viceroyalty of,
274; the revolution in (1810), 278, 282,
285 sq.; 280; captured by Beresford (1806),
281; and San Martin, 291 sq.; 298;
government of (1812), 300 sq.; negotiations of, with Spain, 306; and Great
Britain, 307, 309; and the United States,
308; XII 679; the dictator Rosas in, 680;
blockade of, 681; 683; 694

Bünzli, Gregory, at Basel, II 307

Büren, Ernst Johann. See Biren

Bürger, Gottfried August, VI 830; poetry
of, 832, VIII 773, X 387; 396; 710; 716;
XI 412 sqq.; 423 sq.

Bürgi, Jobst, mathematician, V 709

Buffalo, attacked by the British (1814), VII
343; Anti-Slavery Convention at (1848),
399; railway from New York to, 694

Buffet, Louis-Joseph, French statesman,
XI 133; 491 sq.; President of the
Assembly, XII 107; 110; 115

Buford, Abraham, American colonel, VII
224

Bug river, Turkey and, VI 305; 307

Bugeaud de la Piconnerie, Thomas-Robert,
Duc d'Isly, Marshal of France, X 496;
503 sq.; XI 99 sq.

Bugenhagen, Jakob, Reformer and historian,
II 160, 162, 201, 231, 243, 250; and the
Reformation in Denmark, 611, 616

Bugey, ceded to France, III 419, 677

Bugge, Elseus Sophus, Norwegian philologer, XI 701; XII 281

Bukowina, The, ceded to Austria (1775), VI
634; 648

Bulak Museum, Cairo, XII 431

Bulavin, Kondraty, leader of Cossack revolt,
V 597

Bulawayo, captured by British, XII 639

Bulfontein, discovery of diamonds at, XI
787

Bulgákoff, Russian Liberal, XII 333

Bulgaria, Tsar Nicholas I and, XI 312;
struggle for freedom in, 634; the Church

in, 638 sq.; XII 3; 6; 10; massacres in,
32; 33; and Rumelia, 43, 341, 406; 162;
304 sq.; and Russia, 342; independence
of, 378, 427 sq.; 381; under Turkish rule,
383; massacres in, 384; 387; and the
Russo-Turkish War, 388 sq.; and Treaty
of San Stefano, 391 sqq.; and Treaty
of Berlin, 395 sqq.; Russian administration of, 403 sq.; under Prince Alexander,
404 sqq.; at war with Servia, 407; abdication of Prince Alexander, 408 sq.; 415;
421; and Macedonia, 424 sqq.

Bulgenbach. See Müller, Hans

Bull Run, battle of (1861), VII 465 sqq., 469,
(1862), 480

Bullarium Romanum, Cherubini's, III 445

Buller, Charles, and Radical party, X 676;
Secretary to Governor-General of Canada,
XI 765 sq.
—— Sir Redvers Henry, General, in South
Africa, XII 642 sq.

Bullinger, Henry, Reformer, II 234, 309;
continues Zwingli's work, 339 sq.; at
Basel, 355, 596 sq.; importance of, in
England, 597; *Decades, ib.*, 716

Bullock, Henry, pupil of Erasmus, I 580
—— J. D., Confederate foreign agent, VII
611

Bulwer, William Henry Lytton Earle (Sir
Henry Bulwer, *afterwards* Lord Dalling
and Bulwer), ambassador at Washington,
VII 434; at Madrid, XI 17; 554 sqq.;
dismissed from Madrid, 557

Bulwer-Lytton. See Lytton

Bulýgin, Russian Minister, XII 350 sq.

Bumm, English traveller at, XII 800

Bundela Rajputs, VI 517

Bundelkhand, disorder in, IX 731

Bundschuh, in the Black Forest districts,
etc., I 299; II 175

Bunge, Nicholas de, Russian Minister of
Finance, XII 317 sqq.; retires, 320

Bungo, disturbances in, XI 864

Bunker Hill, battle of (1775), VI 447, VII
167 sq., 170

Bunsen, Christian Karl Josias, Baron von,
X 360; 381 sq.; XI 163; 166 sq.;
Frederick William IV and, 191; 197;
and the Schleswig-Holstein question, 227;
249; 254; XII 820
—— Robert Wilhelm, chemist, XII 783

Bunyan, John, V 136; 207; 335

Bunzelwitz, Frederick the Great at, VI 297

Bunzlau, Russian army at, IX 516; battle at
(1813), 525

Buol, Grisons leader, sent to Innsbruck, IV
62

Buol-Schauenstein, Count Johann Rudolf
von, president of the Federal Diet, X 344
sqq.; 348; 367; succeeded by Münch-
Bellinghausen, 370
—— Count Karl Ferdinand von, Austrian
statesman, XI 232; 322; and Cavour, 372,
374; succeeds Schwarzenberg, 395; 402;
resignation of, 403

Buonaccorsi, Biagro, Florentine historian, I 200

Buonagrazia, Girolamo di Bartolommeo, Lutheran, II 381

Buonarotti, Michel, President of the Club of the Panthéon, VIII 504 sq.; X 485; 491

—— Michelangelo, I 143, 147, 382, 548, 559; statue of Pope Julius II of, 245, 249; the Sistine chapel and, II 6, 13 sq.; 28, 34; reforming sympathies of, 395; III 394, 439, 442, 457–9, 466

Buonavita, Pietro, Italian Reformer, II 383

Buoncompagni, Cardinal. *See* Gregory XIII, Pope

—— Giacomo, crown of Ireland accepted by, III 597

—— Prince Ludovisi, rights of, in Elba, IX 661

Burchard, Bishop of Oberberg. *See* Oberberg

Burchgrave, Daniel de, III 620

Burckhardt, Jakob, writings of, XI 261; XII 849

—— John, African traveller, XII 806

Burdett, Sir Francis, attack of, on Pitt, IX 681; a leader of Opposition, 687 sqq.; X 574; 599 sq.; and the dissolution of Parliament (1831), 611; 613; and Catholic Emancipation, 642

Buren, Maximilian d'Egmont, Count of (general of Charles V), II 45, 47, 78, 256, 422, 459; III 190

—— Philip William, Count of, kidnapped and conveyed to Spain (1568), III 218, 221

Burgau, Charles, Margrave of, husband of Sibylla of Jülich-Cleves, III 729

Burgdorf, school of Pestalozzi at, IX 427

Burgers, Thomas François, President of the Transvaal, XI 788

Burgess, Anthony, Presbyterian leader, IV 359

—— Mark, and the Portuguese Index, II 414

Burgevine, joins the "Taiping" rebels, XI 821

Burgh, *or* Borough (of Gainsborough), Thomas, 5th Lord, Lord Deputy of Ireland (1597), III 606

—— Walter Hussey, and the distress in Ireland, VI 495; 497

—— William, radical writer, VIII 755

Burghley, William Cecil, Lord, I 522 sq.; II 492, 495, 504 sq., 507, 517; becomes Elizabeth's secretary, 559; 565, 568; Maitland and, 573; negotiates Treaty of Edinburgh, 577, 580; III 265; policy of, towards Mary Queen of Scots, 277; position of, 280; and France, 283; character and system of, 330 sqq., 491; VI 45

Burghstead, John, regicide, V 149

Burgo, Nicholas del, nuncio to Henry VIII, II 435

Burgos, the Franco-Spanish marriages at, IV 629 sq.; depopulation of, V 376; advance of Dupont to, IX 430; 436; army of Estremadura at, 442; British at, 474–5; Wellington at, 477

—— Filipino leader, XII 529

Burgoyne, John, General, in Portugal, VI 369; 426; VII 211, 214 sqq.; surrender of (1777), 216, 232

Burgsdorf, Conrad von, Brandenburg statesman, V 642

Burgundian Circle, inclusion of the Netherlands in (1548), I 459, II 102

Burgundio, Johannes, of Pisa, 12th century Greek scholar, I 588

Burgundy, duchy of, annexed to France (1482), I 392; II 62; renounced by Francis I, 51; the Netherlands and, 102; and Spain, III 508; created a separate State, 630; the League in, 661 sqq.; recovery of, 666–7, 669; Biron Governor of, 679–80; taxation of, IV 153; *Intendants* retained in, 606; Condé Governor of, 608; 612; Tavannes in, 613; Condé exchanges Guienne for, 614; 615; Épernon Governor of, 618; and the Treaty of the Pyrenees, 620; Estates of, V 4, 13; VIII 39

—— Anthony, son of Philip the Bold of. *See* Brabant, Duke of

—— Charles the Bold, Duke of, siege of Neuss by, I 295, 390; death of, 295, 391, 410, 417; League of Public Weal and, 389; Louis XI and, 390, 422; schemes of, 390; the Swiss and, 390 sq.; Liége and, 422; 424, 430, 432; II 36; and Liége, V 488

—— John ("*sans peur*"), Duke of, I 422; II 36

—— Louis, Duke of. *See* Louis, Duke of Burgundy

—— Philip the Bold, Duke of, I 389, 418

—— Philip the Good, Duke of, I 77; increase of territory by, 389, 418–42; and Ghent and Ypres, 426–7; and the Church, 430; centralised government of, 431; military reforms of, 432; art and literature under, 432–3; II 36

—— Philip the Fair, Duke of. *See* Philip I, King of Castile

—— Margaret of, married to William VI of Hainault, I 418

—— Margaret of, and Austria, daughter of Maximilian I. *See* Savoy

—— Margaret of Maele, heiress of Artois and Flanders, Duchess of, I 418

—— Margaret of York, Duchess of, I 442–3; 460; 465; 467 sqq., 474

—— Mary, Duchess of, Louis XI and, I 437 sq., 440 sq.; the *Groote Privilegie* granted by, 438 sq.; Ghent and, 441, 443; marries Maximilian I, 295, 391, 442; death of, 392, 444

—— Maria Adelaide of Savoy, Duchess of, V 30 sq.

Burke, Edmund, and the Act of Settlement, v 275; 702; 705; vi 435; policy of, 442; 444; and America, 447; 455 sq.; Paymaster of the Forces, 457; 458; 460; resigns, 462; 464 sqq.; 476 sqq.; 581; and the trial of Warren Hastings, 471, 582 sq., 584, 585; and Indian affairs, 567; 576; 813; 816 sq.; 821; writings of, 836 sq.; vii 66, 105 sq., 108, and colonial policy, 147, 149 sq., 159, 162 sq., 172 sq., 724; viii 18, 134; *Reflections on the Revolution in France*, 755 sqq.; *Letters on a Regicide Peace*, 762; 774; and the Whig party, ix 673; and Warren Hastings, 715; 716; xii 817; 819
—— Richard, and the Penal Code, ix 694; 695
—— Robert O'Hara, Australian explorer, xi 798
—— Thomas Henry, murdered, xii 81
—— Tibbot, the MacWilliam, iii 606–7
Burkersdorf, Frederick the Great at, vi 299; fight at, xi 453
Burkes, The, hold Cathedral of Tuam, iii 593; of Castleconnell, 597; of Upper Mayo, 604
Burkhardt, George, of Spelt, ii 111, 132, 193
Burlamacchi, Francesco, ii 81; Gonfalonier of Lucca, iii 385
—— Frà Pacifico, biographer of Savonarola, i 168
Burlamaqui, J. J., Genevese publicist, ix 427
Burlet, J. de, Belgian statesman, xii 253
Burlingame, Anson, American Minister in China, xi 822
Burma, xi 724; first war with, 727 sq.; 734; second war with, 742; 802; Great Britain and, xii 4; 464; conquest of, 479; 501; 508; and Siam, 535; 793
—— Upper, annexation of, xii 43, 497; famine in, 486
Burnaby, Frederick Gustavus, visits Khiva, xii 801
Burnes, Sir Alexander, captain, and Dost Mohammad, xi 732; 733; Asiatic travels of, xii 800
Burnet, Gilbert, Bishop of Salisbury, v 136; and Queen Mary, 167; 213; 235; 255; 258; 271; and Latitudinarianism, 752; vi 6; 802; 816
—— William, Governor of Massachusetts, vii 65
Burney, Captain, in Siam, xii 535
Burnouf, Eugène, Orientalist, xii 845
Burns, Robert, poet, vi 824; 829 sq.; 832 sq.; viii 771; x 701 sq.
Burnside, Ambrose Everett, commands the Army of the Potomac, vii 483; defeated at Fredericksburg, *ib.*, 484; at Knoxville, 508, 510 sq., 513; 573 sq.
Burntisland, bombarded by the Dutch (1667), v 188; captured by Jacobites, vi 99; 102

Burr, Aaron, American politician, vii 324 sq., 372
—— Colonel, defeats the Peshwa of Poona, xi 726
Burrard, Sir Harry, sent to Spain, ix 440; 441
Burroughs, Jeremiah, Independent leader, iv 359
Burschenschaft, x 363 sqq.; 375
Burton, Henry, punishment of, iv 280
—— Sir Richard Francis, xii 809
—— Lieutenant-Colonel, at Quebec, vii 139
—— Governor of Delaware, vii 453
Bury, John Bagnell, historian, xii 845
Busaco, Wellington at, ix 460; battle of (1810), 463
Busbecq, Augier-Ghislain, iii 123; Imperial ambassador at Constantinople, vi 507
Busby, James, Resident at Bay of Islands, xi 793
Busch, John, Reformer, i 631, 639
Busche, Hermann von dem, of Deventer, i 435
Bushe, and the Irish rebellion, ix 701; and the Union, 703
Bushell, Captain, at Glasgow, vi 106 sq.
Busher, Leonard, and religious toleration, v 326
Bushire, British force at, xi 745
Busleyden, Francis van, Provost of Liége, i 454
Busolt, Georg, historian, xii 845
Bussa, explorers at, xii 807 sq.
Bussi, Corboli, Monsignor, xi 74
Bussy, François de, French envoy in London, vi 343; 345
Bussy-Castelnau, Charles-Joseph Patissier, Marquis de, vi 533; in the Deccan, 540 sq.; 543; 545 sqq.; 552; and the Nawáb of Bengal, 553; in Cuddalore, 577
Bute, parliamentary election in, x 606
—— John Stuart, 3rd Earl of, vi 298; 346; and Spain, 368, 370; 407; and George III, 417; 419 sq.; ministry of, 422 sqq.; 426 sqq.; resigns, 429; 430; 434; 437
Butera, Prince of. *See* Colonna, Fadrique
Butkoff, Vladimir, Russian official, xi 615
Butler, Benjamin Franklin, American general, vii 464, 516, 557; and "contraband," 581, 583, 600
—— Charles, secretary of the committee for Catholic relief, x 625; 632
—— Sir Edmund, iii 595
—— Sir Edward, iii 595
—— James, Duke of Ormond. *See* Ormond
—— Joseph, Bishop of Durham, vi 77 sqq.; 88
—— Pierce, deputy from S. Carolina at the Constitutional Convention (1787), vii 246, 286
—— Sir Piers. *See* Ossory, Earl of

Butler, Samuel, satirist, v 126; 133; 136
—— Simon, chairman of the United Irishmen, x 628
—— Thomas, Earl of Ossory. *See* Ossory
—— Colonel Walter, at Eger, iv 242
—— William Orlando, American general and politician, vii 399
Butlers, The, of Munster, feuds of, iii 580 sq.
Butrinto, captured by Ali of Janina, x 176
Butt, Isaac, and Irish Home Rule, xii 72 sqq.
Buttmann, Philipp Karl, ix 327
Buttstädt, army at, vi 267; 268
Buturlin, Alexander, Russian field-marshal, vi 297; 326 sq.
Buwinkhausen, ambassador of the Protestant Union, and the United Provinces, iv 33
Buxar, battle of, vi 561
Buxhöwden, Count Frederick William von, Russian general, ix 251; Kutusoff effects junction with, 257; advances on Tell-nitz, 260; 261; Russian army under, 283
Buxton, Sir Thomas Fowell, x 658 sq.
Buy, Pierre de Mornay, Seigneur de, iii 23
Buys, Paul, Dutch advocate, iii 233, 619-21, 624
—— Willem, Dutch diplomatist, v 422; 427 sq.; 429
Buzot, François-N.-L., Girondin, viii 174, 249, 251, 257, 260; suicide of, 357
Byelinsky, Vissarion, Russian writer, xii 296
Byelostók, xii 340; *pogróm* at, 367
Bylandt, Dutch merchant, Frederick Henry and, iv 699
—— Count van Willem Frederik, military Governor of Brabant, x 534
Bylling, Edward, granted land on the Delaware, vii 47
Byng, Sir George, Admiral. *See* Torrington, Viscount
—— John, Admiral, loses Minorca, vi 403 sq., 342a (in Vol. xiii)
Byrd, William, American lawyer, vii 60
Byrne, Miles, and Emmet's rebellion, ix 706
Byron, George Gordon Noel, 6th Baron, vi 825; 830; 832; x 100; 126; supports the Greek revolt, 182; influence of, in Germany, 405; influence of, in Russia, 432; 580; and Southey, 709; the poetry of, 710 sqq.; and Shelley, 713 sq.; 715; 722; influence of, upon continental literature, 725 sq.; xi 350; 354; influence of, on Pushkin, 648
—— Sir John, 1st Baron, replaces Lunsford, iv 297; refuses to surrender the Tower, 299; retreats to Worcester, 306; joined by Irish troops, 318; defeated at Nantwich, 321, 527
—— John, Vice-Admiral, vi 451 sq.

Bytown. *See* Ottawa
Byzantium, and the Greek Church, v 483 sq.; 515

Cabal Ministry, formed, v 198; 201; dissolved, 210, 214
Caballero de Rodas, Spanish general, xi 569
Cabanis, Pierre-Jean-Georges, ix 21; 24, 132
Cabarrus, Count Francis of, Spanish statesman, vi 382 sq.; viii 782
Cabet, Étienne, x 491; French politician, xi 24; 105; and socialism, xii 758
Cabezas de San Juan, revolt at (1820), x 216
Cabinda, slavery abolished at, xi 575
Cabot, John, Labrador and, i 20, 50; the three sons of, and their explorations, 33, 36; discoveries of, vii 2
—— Sebastian, discoveries of, vii 2; and the Muscovy Company, v 513
Cabral, Costa. *See* Thomar, Count of
—— Pedro Alvarez, Portuguese commander in India, i 29; discovers Brazil, 35; ix 304
Cabrera, Ramón, Carlist leader, x 237 sqq.; xii 258
Cabrinetti, José, Spanish general, xii 260
Cacault, François, sent to Rome, ix 183; recalled, 191
Cadalso, José de, Spanish poet, v 69
Cadan, Peace of (1534), ii 221 sq.; 232
Cadaval, Nunho C. A. Pereira de Mello, Duke of, defeated by Duke of Terceira, x 334 sq.
Cadè (*Gotteshaus*), Swiss league, iv 36
Cadillac, Antoine de la Mothe, Governor of Louisiana, vii 88, 93, 99
Cadiz, Drake burns shipping in harbour of (1587), iii 304, 504; English expedition to (1596), 322-5, 521, 522, 529; French naval victories near, iv 147; English expedition to (1625), 262, 267, 477 sq., 481, 483 sq., 642; commerce of Lisbon and, 650; English fleet at (1695), v 61, 262; 379; 411 sq.; vi 60; expedition from (1719), 105; 155; prosperity of, 166; 236; 351; American trade with, vii 327; Cortes of, 366; army collected at (1819), 367; Admiral Man at, viii 460; British blockade of (1797), 464 sq., 630; Rear-Admiral Linois ordered to, ix 53; Admiral Saumarez off, 54; blockade of (1804), 211, 215; Spanish treasure-ships captured off, 217-8; plague at, 218; Allied force at, 219; Villeneuve at, 223, 227; 225; Nelson arrives off, 229; plan of attack at, *ib.*; flight of French and Spanish ships to, 233; capture of French ships by Spanish insurgents at, 238; Dupont ordered to (1808), 311, 436; besieged by Soult (1810), 456, 457, 463; 464; siege of, raised, 473; arrest of deputies in, x 208; and the revolutionary movement, 213 sqq.; 220;

the Cortes at, 228; blockade of (1823), *ib.*, 308; proclamation of, revoked, 229; and the Indian trade, 256; the Central Junta at, 282; and Spanish America, 292, 305; rising of garrison at, xi 569; riots at, 570

Cadiz, Duke of. *See* Francisco de Asis

Cadogan, William Cadogan, 1st Earl, v 421; 422; 458 sq.; vi 16; 23; 27; recalled, 39

Cadorna, Raffaele, Italian general, xi 544

Cadoudal, Georges, Chouan leader, viii 379; ix 2, 14 sqq., 29 sqq.

Cadsand, taken by the French, vi 247; attacked by British (1809), ix 358

Caen, taken by Coligny (1563), iii 5; *Parlement* at, 663; strike suppressed at, x 491

Caesalpinus, Andreas, and the circulation of the blood, v 725 sq.; 734 sqq.; 738

Caetani (Cajetani), Enrico, Cardinal, iii 449, 453

Cäzis, occupation of, iv 51 sq.

Caffa, captured by the Turks (1475), i 83

Caffarelli, François-Marie-Auguste, French general, supersedes Dorsenne, ix 472

—— du Falga, Louis-M.-J.-M., French general, viii 606; 610; killed at Acre, 613

Caffè, Italian review, x 124

Cagliari, victory of Venice at, i 258; Charles V's fleet in harbour of, iii 111; Spanish expedition to, vi 29; panic of French troops at, viii 456

Cahera, Gallus, Bohemian Reformer, i 340

Cahier de Gerville, B. C., Minister of the Interior to Louis XVI, viii 222

Cahors, massacre of Protestants at, ii 303; seized by Navarre (1580), iii 33

Caianello, meeting of Victor Emmanuel and Garibaldi at, xi 390

Caiazzo, Francesco de San Severino, Count of, i 116, 120, 124

Caillard, Antoine-Bernard, French envoy at the Prussian Court, ix 36

Caillaud, John, Indian officer, defeats Shah Alam, vi 559

Caillié, René, African traveller, xii 807

Cairncross, Alexander, Archbishop of Glasgow, v 290

Cairns, Hugh McCalmont Cairns, 1st Earl, Lord Chancellor, xii 27; 30

Cairo, Napoleon at (1798), viii 603 sq., 605 sq., (1799), 614; surrenders (1801), 617, ix 72; 385; British troops prisoners at, x 547; xii 430; British troops at, 437 sq.; Lord Cromer at, 439; Gordon in, 441 sq.; Clifford Lloyd in, 444; 446; 448; Medical School at, 452; 454 sq.; 805 sq.

—— (Illinois), importance of, vii 459; Grant at, 463, 494; 471

Cairoli brothers, death of, xi 542

Caisse d'Escompte, founded by Turgot, viii 86, 694; 96; reorganised by Calonne, 97; Necker and, 695

Caistor, rising at, ii 446

Cajet river, Portugal and, xii 660

Cajetan, Cardinal. *See* Vio, Thomas de

—— Jacopo, theologian, xi 718

Calabria, ravaged by Barbarossa, iii 112; peasant revolt in (1806), ix 267, 382, 404, 406; English troops in, 270; insurrection in (1830), x 120, 122; political persecution in, xi 379; earthquake in, xii 228; 236

—— Francis, Duke of. *See* Francis I, King of the Two Sicilies

—— John, Duke of, i 104, 107, 387, 396

—— Nicholas, Duke of, i 396

Calafat, bombarded, xii 388

Calagnani, Celio, of Ferrara, ii 384

Calais, English Staple at (1494), i 452; secret Treaty of, between Charles V and Henry VIII (1520), ii 417; French capture of (1558), 93, 548, 560 sq., 566, iii 184, 260, 478; English exiles at, ii 545; Conference of (1521), 418; Elizabeth claims, iii 3, 6, 26, 263, 477; Armada anchors off, 313, 477-8; capture of, by Spain (1596), 523, 529, 628, 670; James II at, v 262

Calas, Jean, French Protestant merchant, viii 56

Calatafimi, battle of, xi 388; 533

Calatrava, José Maria, Spanish statesman, x 234; the ministry of, 238 sq.

Calcutta, settlement at, v 699; vi 531 sq.; 534 sq.; 546; 551; siege of, 552; Clive at, 555; 557; Courts of Appeal at, 568, ix 711; Cornwallis at, 710; xi 730; Burmese embassy at, 742; High Court of, 751; 816; xii 481; bubonic plague in, 487

Calder, Sir Robert, admiral, engagement of, off Finisterre, ix 225 sq.

Calderon, Felix del Rey Calleja, Conde de, Spanish general, x 216; Viceroy of Mexico, 304

—— Maria, mother of Don Juan (II) of Austria, iv 649

—— Rodrigo. *See* Siete Iglesias

—— de la Barca, Pedro, Spanish dramatist, iv 662, x 407

Caldiero, French defeat at, viii 579; Masséna attacks Austrian army at (1805), ix 258

Caledon, Du Pré (Alexander), 2nd Earl of, Governor of the Cape of Good Hope (1807-11), ix 753

Calenberg (Hanover), claim of Tilly's heirs upon, iv 408; ravages of war in, 418; vi 2 sq., 8

Calendar, The French Republican (1793), viii 358

Calhoun, John Caldwell, American statesman, vii 373 sq., 376, 380 sq., 388; Secretary of State, 393, 397 sq., 401, 403; and "nullification," 409 sqq.; 414; death of, 418

Calicut, Da Gama at, i 25; commercial importance of, 26, iv 743; Cabral and, i 29

California, VII 391; American conquest of, 395 sqq.; slavery in, 399; discovery of gold in, 400 sq., 416 sq., 433, 696; organisation of, 402, 416; admitted to the Union (1850), 421; Democrats in, 631; population of, 708; missions in, x 271; the United States and, XII 685

Calixtus III (Alfonso Borgia), Pope, I 69 sqq., 77, 552, 674, 688; II 29

—— Georg, Protestant theologian, religious reunion and, IV 424; V 648; 744

Callao, Potosí silver shipped to, x 255; 273; attacked by Cochrane, 292; royalists in, 293, 295; bombarded, XI 567, XII 678

Calleja, Felix del Rey. *See* Calderon

Calliergi, Zacharias, Cretan Hellenist, I 566

Callistus, Andronicus, Greek professor at Florence, I 543

Callot, Jacques, French etcher, XI 511

Calomarde, F. T., Spanish statesman, Minister of Justice, x 232

Calonius, Finnish lawyer, x 434

Calonne, Charles-Alexandre de, French Comptroller General, VIII 60, 69, 72, 698 sqq.; administration of, 97–103; dismissed, 104; prosecution and flight of, 106; *Requête au Roi*, 108; accused of high treason, 221; IX 362

Calvert, Leonard, settles in Maryland, VII 31 sqq.

—— *See* Baltimore, Barons

Calvi, captured by the British, VIII 458

—— Francesco (Minicio), of Pavia, II 380

—— Pier Fortunato, execution of, XI 377

Calvin, Gérard, father of John, II 349 sq., 352

—— John, influence of, in Germany, II 216; Nicolas Cop and, 285; *Christianae religionis institutio*, 287 sq., 356 sqq., 363, 376; 294–8; Confession of Faith, 295, 393; compared with Zwingli, 340, 713; *Consensus Tigurinus* of Bullinger and, 340; the Reformed Church and, Chap. XI *passim*; affinities of, with Erasmus and Luther, 349; education of, 350–2; *De Clementia*, 352 sq.; at Basel, 355; letter of, to Francis I, 356; at Ferrara, 358, 385; and Geneva, 358, 363–74; *Letter to Cardinal Sadoleto* and other writings, 363; *Ordonnances Ecclésiastiques*, 370 sqq.; system of education of, 372 sq.; special services to Protestantism of, 376; Italian refugees and, 393; controversy of, with Serveto, 411; Queen Elizabeth and, 596; 690; philosophical ideas of, 713, 715 sq.; *Commentary on the Mass*, III 74; 422, 743 sqq.; publishes *Institution Chrétienne* in French, IV 778; VI 254; 274; 798; 803

Calvinism, in the Netherlands, II 103; *see* Chap. XI, Calvin and the Reformed Church; and French Protestantism, 287 sqq., 293 sqq., 373 sq.; at Ferrara and elsewhere, 385 sqq.; in Scotland, 558

sqq.; and Knox, 573 sqq.; in Sweden, 629; as a system of thought, 715 sqq.; in Poland, III 74 sqq.; excluded from the benefits of the Religious Peace of Augsburg (1555), 141 sqq.; in Transylvania and Hungary proper, 147; in the Austrian lands generally, and in the Empire etc., under Ferdinand I and Maximilian II, *see* Chap. V *passim*; at Ghent, 250 sq.; in Europe generally, 260; in England, growth of, under Elizabeth, 340; under James I, 552 sq.; Dutch, different schools and parties arising in and from, 646 sqq.; Remonstrants and Contra-Remonstrants, 647 sqq.; under Rudolf II, 703 sqq.; political theory of, 747, 753 sqq.; and Lutheranism, in the Empire generally, IV 3 sqq.; 82, 110; recognised by the Treaty of Westphalia, 410; in Sweden, under Charles IX, 175 sq.; in general, and the Thirty Years' War and Peace of Westphalia, *see* Vol. IV *passim*; in later Switzerland, XI 234

Calvo, Carlos, and the Monroe Doctrine, XII 688

Cam, Diego, discovers the Congo, I 17

Camaldolese Congregation, reform of the, II 647

Camara, Spanish admiral, VII 679

Camarão, South American leader, V 674

Camarilla, of the absolutist reaction in Spain, x 208 sqq.

Cambacérès, Jean-Jacques-Régis de, French statesman, VIII 378, 380 sq., 386; Director, 489; Minister of Justice, 672, 677, 681; 738 sq.; IX 1; 5 sqq., 19, 32, 103; Arch-Chancellor of the Empire, 110; receives Parma, 111; appointed Napoleon's deputy, 138; 145 sqq.; and the Codes, 172–3; 616

Cambi, Giovanni, Medicean partisan, I 175

Cambodia, France and, XII 132, 524; 797

Cambon, Joseph, and French finance, VIII 73, 249, 257, 702, 704; on the *Comité de Salut Public*, 269, 366, 382; arrested, 385

—— Jules, French ambassador at Washington, VII 682

—— Paul, French ambassador in London, XII 456

Cambray, League of (1508), I 131, 246, 266, 277, III 116; Maximilian I and, I 319, 344, 456; attacked by France, II 89; Charles V and, 102; Conference of (1517), 39; Peace of (1529), 25, 59, 203; 432; siege of (1595), III 628, 669; handed over to Anjou, 706; siege of (1649), IV 612; French defeated at, 619; Congress of (1724–5), VI 39, 57, 126, 138; archbishopric of, 131; France and, V 36, 39; taken by the French (1677), 44; 45; 422; 430; Louis XVIII at, IX 643, x 44, 48

—— François de Salignac de la Mothe Fénelon, Archbishop of, writings of, V 28 sq.; 78 sq.; 88; 90; VIII 8

Cambray, Joseph de Bergaigne, previously Bishop of Hertogenbosch, archbishop of, at Münster, IV 401

Cambridge, Erasmus at, I 546; and the New Learning, 580; state of University of, II 468; destruction of libraries in, 503; Queen Mary proclaimed at, 517; Royalist tendencies at, IV 304; Cromwell at, 312; the army encamped near, 343; Crashaw at, 771; Cowley at, 773; Cartesian philosophy at, 791; Milton at, V 116; 237 sq.; VI 802; Newton at, V 721; Jacobinism at, VIII 764; Byron at, X 711; Tennyson at, XI 350; study of history at, 363; abolition of religious tests in, XII 27; 36; 762; historical study at, 820, 834

—— Platonists, V 327; 332; 749 sqq.

—— George (Electoral Prince), Duke of. *See* George II, King of England

—— George William Frederick Charles, 2nd Duke of, XII 52; 441

Camden, Gates defeated at, VII 225 sq.

—— Charles Pratt, 1st Earl, IV 431; 435; 437 sqq.; 441; dismissed, 442; 450; President of Council, 457; 462 sq.; 467; VII 147; VIII 294

—— Sir John Jeffreys Pratt, 2nd Earl and 1st Marquis of, and Catholic Emancipation, IX 678; Viceroy of Ireland, 700

—— William, antiquary, XII 816

Camelinat, French socialist, XII 125

Camera della Segnatura, Raffaelle's paintings in, II 6 sq.

Cameral Tribunal. *See Reichskammergericht*

Camerarius (Joachim Kammermeister), I 574

—— Ludwig, Palatine councillor, at Prague, IV 15; and the Palatine family, 70

—— Rudolf Jacob, botanist, V 736

Camerino, reduced by papal forces, II 75; captured by Cesare Borgia (1582), I 194, 240; duchy of, incorporated in the Italian kingdom, IX 400

Cameron, Archibald, Jacobite, VI 119

—— Charles Duncan, British Consul at Massowah, XI 753

—— Sir Duncan Alexander, general, XI 800

—— Richard, covenanter, V 286 sq.; 290

—— Simon, VII 445; Secretary of War, 450, 584 sq.; Minister to Russia, 472

—— Verney, travels of, in Africa, XII 810 sq.

—— of Lochiel, VI 105; 109; 111 sq.

Cameroons, XII 3; 41; 130; German occupation of the, 160; 658 sqq.

Camin, see of, and the Great Elector, IV 407

Caminha, English force disembarked at, X 336

Camisards, rising of the, V 26

Camoens, Luis de, *The Lusiad*, V 695

Camorra, working of the, in S. Italy and Sicily, XII 239

Camp Dick Robinson, brigade at, VII 462 sq.

—— Jackson, captured by Captain Lyon (1861), VII 458

Campagna, Spanish occupation of the (1556), II 91; brigandage in the, III 430

Campana, Francesco, III 388

Campanella, Tommaso, the *Civitas Solis*, II 707

Campbell, Sir Archibald, of Inverneil (d. 1791), colonel, VII 218 sq.

—— Sir Archibald, general (d. 1843), Governor of British Burma, XI 728

—— Colin. *See* Clyde, Lord

—— Colin, of Glendaruel, VI 105

—— Daniel, of Shawfield, VI 107

—— Sir George, Lieut.-Governor of Bengal, XII 464

—— Sir James, of Auchinbreck, VI 109

—— John A., Confederate assistant Secretary of War, VII 605

—— Thomas, poet, X 700

—— William, American colonel, VII 225

—— Admiral, IX 224

—— *See also* Argyll

Campbell-Bannerman, Sir Henry, Secretary for War, XII 52; Prime Minister, 54 sq.

Campe, peace between France and England at (1546), II 461

—— Joachim Heinrich, German writer, VIII 772 sqq.

Campeachy, contraband trade at, VI 373

—— Bay, the English in, V 687; logwood cutting in, VI 149

Campeggio, Lorenzo, Cardinal, I 489; II 16; at the Diet of Nürnberg, 171 sq., 174; 210; at Ratisbon, 326; mission to England of, 430 sqq.

—— Thomas. *See* Feltre, Bishop of

Campell, Ulric, IV 36

Camperdown, battle of, VIII 482 sq.

Camphausen, Ludolf, Prussian statesman, XI 53; 159 sq.; 191; 200

—— Otto von, Prussian Minister of Finance, XII 150

Campillo, Don Joseph del. *See* Del Campillo

Campion, Edmund, Jesuit, III 287, 350

—— Thomas, poet, III 369

Campo Florido, Spanish ambassador in Paris, VI 158; 166

—— Formio, Treaty of (1797), VIII 498, 591 sqq., 633, IX 39 sq., 56, 63, 751; Bonaparte at, 82

—— Santo, Spanish defeat at, VI 237; 241

Campomanes, Pedro Rodriguez, Count of, President of the Council of Castile, VI 382; VIII 782

Campos, Martinez, Spanish general, VII 675

Campredon, N. de, French ambassador in Russia, V 551; to Stockholm, VI 36

Camus, Armand Gaston, and French pensions (1790), VIII 72, 700; Jansenist, 196; 249
—— Lieutenant, French naval officer, XI 850
Canada, France and, V 13, 442; 684 sq.; 688; colonisation of, VI 183; 248; 342; 342a sqq. (in Vol. XIII); ceded to England, 347; 349 sq.; 351; 410 sqq.; the Peace of Paris and, 428; 461; aggressive policy of, VII 42; projected invasion of, 69; the French in, Chap. III; the conquest of, Chap. IV; General Hull invades (1812), 337; and the sealing question, 666; migration from the States into, 712; colonial empire in, IX 735; 740 sqq.; (1763–1840), Vol. X, Chap. XXI *passim*; the Catholic Church in, 625; the export wheat trade of, 760; the Federation of, Vol. XI, Chap. XXVII (2); 17; the Clergy Reserves of, 310; 336; 343; British rule in, 755 sqq.; XII 2; 21; 47; preference tariff in, 57; 603; 649 sq.; and naval defence, 649, 651; 654; and arbitration, 721 sqq.; exploration in, 814
—— Company, The, VI 533
—— Viscount. *See* Stirling, Earl of
—— François Xavier de Laval-Montmorency, Bishop of, VII 84
Canadian Pacific Railway, XII 606; 609; 615
Canale, Nicolò da, Venetian commander, I 79
Canalejas, José, Spanish journalist, VII 676
Canales, Marquez de, Spanish diplomatist, V 390
Cananor, Rajah of, the Portuguese and, I 29
Canary Islands, the Guanches of, I 10; Spain colonises, 40; Spanish fleet sent to, III 531; exports from, V 677; Spanish generals banished to, XI 569
Canby, Edward Richard Sprigg, VII 543
Canclaux, Comte Jean-Baptiste-Camille, French general, VIII 382
Candale, Sire de, I 394
Candia, siege of, by Turks (1648–69), V 36, 342 sq., 348 sq.; VI 675; British occupation of, XII 423
Candide, French journal, XI 486
Candolle, Alphonse-Louis-Pierre de, XI 260
—— Auguste de, XI 260
Candy. *See* Kandy
Canea, taken by the Turks, V 342; insurrection in, XII 419; occupied by the Powers, 420, 423
Canevaro, Italian admiral, XII 423 sq.
Canga Argüelles, José, X 218
Canisius, Egidius, Cardinal, I 560
—— (Peter Kanes), Jesuit, II 250; influence of, at the Council of Trent, 682; and the Index, 688; III 148 sq.; 155; 160 sqq.
Cannes, landing of Napoleon at, IX 615
Canning, Charles John Canning, 1st Earl, Governor-General of India, XI 329 sq.; 724; 744 sq.; 749 sqq.

Canning, George, statesman, VII 369; Foreign Minister, IX 236; in Foreign Office, 289; Napoleon's designs revealed to, 297; policy of, 298; 300, 305, 309, 321, 340; gets subsidy for the war of 1809, 358; duel with Castlereagh, 359; urges England to intervene in regard to Napoleon, 439; ode of, 681; and the Tory party, 686; 688; X 12; 33, 34; policy of, 36 sqq., 584 sq.; and the Greek revolt and Eastern Question, 184 sqq.; 197 sq.; 200; and the Spanish question, 226; and Spanish America, 308 sq.; and the United States, 309; and Portuguese affairs, 319, 321; and the European System, 371; 573; and the Ministry of 1816, 575; 580; Foreign Secretary (1822), 583; 587; 589 sq.; Prime Minister (1827), 591; and the Corn Law, 591 sq.; death of, 195, 592; and Tory principles, 600 sq.; 602; 604; 618; and Catholic emancipation, 634, 642, 645; and the abolition of slavery, 658; and the *Anti-Jacobin*, 700; policy of, on the India Board, XI 724; 755; 762; XII 682; 688
—— Stratford. *See* Stratford de Redcliffe
Cano, Melchior, Spanish theologian, II 408 sqq., 647, 659
Canosa, captured by the French (1502), I 125
—— Prince of, X 110
Canossa, Ludovico di, of Verona, II 16
Canova, Antonio, sculptor, VI 117; X 151
Cánovas del Castillo, Antonio, Spanish premier, VII 675; XI 560; XII 258; 262 sq.; 265; murdered, 266, 268; 842
Canrobert, François-Certain, Marshal of France, in the Crimea, XI 318; 322; 582; 590 sqq.; at Gravelotte, 593 sq.; 595
Canso, Gut of, toll demanded in, VII 363, 658
Cantacuzenus, Emperor of the East. *See* John V
—— Manuel (Ghin), leader of Albanians, I 75
Cantemir, Demetrius, Hospodar of Moldavia, V 604
Canter, William, of Utrecht, Dutch humanist, I 579
Canterbury, typical medieval library of Christ Church in, I 589; Convocation of (1559), resists the Reformation, II 566; (1563), accepts the Thirty-Nine Articles, 587 sq.
—— Charles Manners-Sutton, 1st Viscount, Speaker of the House of Commons, becomes Secretary of State, X 615
—— Archbishops of. *See sub nom.*
—— (New Zealand), XI 796; 799
—— Association, XI 796
Cantillon, Philip, *The Nature of Commerce*, VIII 21 sq.; X 770
—— Napoleon's legacy to, for attempted assassination of Wellington, IX 759

Canton, xi 325; 724; 734; the English in, 803 sqq.; opium trade at, 806 sq.; British attack on, 809; American trade with, 810; capture of, 812; 814 sq.; occupation of, 816; xii 526; Earl Macartney at, 796; 797

Cantons, the Swiss Catholic, League of 1524, ii 325

Cantù, Cesare, x 106; 125; *History of Italy*, xii 842

Canuel, Simon, Baron, French general, x 54

Canus, Melchior, theologian, xi 718

Canynges, William, English merchant, i 505

Cap François, French fleet at, vi 452

Capaul, Josef von, shot, iv 54

Cape Anne, trading station at, vii 15

—— Branco, discovered by the Portuguese, i 13

—— Breton Island, France and, v 443; settlement of, vi 133; 249; regained by France, 331, 538; 428; vii 75, 91; fortified, 95; history of, 112 sq.; government of, ix 746; and the Peace of Paris (1763), x 685; 687

—— Coast Castle, xii 807

—— Cod, Pilgrim Fathers at, vii 13

—— Colony, founded by the Dutch, iv 713; development of, vi 188 sq.; captured by the British (1806), ix 235, 240, 752 sqq.; retained by Great Britain, 654, 735; British occupation of, 749 sq.; the wool trade with, x 759; (1815–70), Vol. xi, Chap. xxvii (3) *passim*; 761; xii 161; affairs in, 635 sqq.; and the Transvaal, 640 sqq.; 644 sq.; and the Union of South Africa, 646; 648; 808

—— Finisterre, second Spanish Armada scattered by tempest off (1596), iii 529, 606; battle of (1805), ix 225 sq.

—— Hatteras, the *Monitor* founders off (1862), vii 563

—— Horne, settlement at, vii 15

Capel, Arthur, 1st Baron Capel of Hadham, at Colchester, iv 349, 351

—— Arthur, Earl of Essex. *See* Essex

—— Sir Henry, Baron Capel of Tewkesbury, v 321

Capella, Martianus (c. 420), *Septem Artes Liberales*, i 533

Capellari, Mauro. *See* Gregory XVI

Cape of Good Hope, Diaz discovers, i 17, 19 sq.; Da Gama and, 25, 285; Dutch occupation of, v 693 sqq.; vi 454; question of British retention of (1797), viii 498; restored to the Dutch (1802), ix 75, 752; 283; recaptured (1806), 752; retained (1814), 755, x 520; xi 667; 760. *See also* Cape Colony

—— Passaro, naval battle off, vi 33, 104, 125, 157; 419

—— St Catherine, the Portuguese reach, i 16

—— St Vincent, origin of name of, i 12; battle of, viii 461 sqq., 498; Miguelist fleet destroyed off (1833), x 333 sq.

Cape Town, and Cape Colony, vi 189; captured (1795), viii 484 sq.; surrendered (1806), xi 778; Union convention at, xii 646; 647

—— Verde Islands, discovery of, i 15; salt trade with, iii 631

—— York, overland journey to, xi 795

Capisucchi, Giovanni Antonio, Auditor of the Rota at Rome, ii 434

Capito, Wolfgang Fabricius, Zwinglian, ii 160, 211; French reformers and, 283 sq.; 310, 328; at Basel, 355

Capo d'Istria, Pietro Paolo Vergerio, Bishop of, ii 233, 394–5, 588

—— Count John. *See* Capodistrias

Capodimonte, palace at, vi 596

Capodistrias, John, Count, at the Congress of Vienna, ix 586; 600–1, 609; and the French frontier, 664; at the Conference of Aix-la-Chapelle, x 14, 16; 21; 23; 25; at the Conference of Troppau, 27; at the Conference of Laibach, 29; 34; and the Ionian Islands, 177; refuses leadership of the Greek revolt, 178; and Ypsilanti, 179; decline of the influence of, 184; 188; elected Greek President, 200; and the Greek settlement, 203; and the Spanish secret mission, 212 sq.; and Metternich, 370; 420; assassination of, 204; xi 277

Cappella, Galeazzo, ii 16

Cappello, Bianca, iii 396

Cappioni, Piero, and Charles VIII, i 113, 154 sq., 172

Capponi, Gino A. G. G., Marchese, x 108; 128; xi 65; 67; 90; 546; 548; xii 842

Caprara, Count Aeneas Sylvius, captures Neuhäusel, v 366; 369

—— Count Albert, mission of, to the Porte, v 358 sq.

—— Jean-Baptiste de, Cardinal, Papal Legate in France, ix 186–9; catechism sanctioned by, 191; debts of, paid by Napoleon, 194; 195; advice on the German Concordat, 203

Caprera, Garibaldi at, xi 390, 533, 542, xii 216

Capres, "Malcontent" of southern Netherlands, iii 251

Capri, retaken by Murat (1808), ix 382; British fleet lands a garrison at, 404; Corsican and Maltese garrison expelled from, 406

Caprivi, Georg Leo, Count von, Chancellor of the German Empire, xii 166

"Caps," Swedish party of the, Vol. vi, Chap. xxii, The Hats and Caps...

Capua, held by the Austrians, vi 153; reduced (1799), viii 658; fight at, xi 390

—— Nicholas von Schomberg, Cardinal Archbishop of, ii 23, 423, 642 sq.

—— Pietrantonio di. *See* Otranto, Archbishop of

Capuchins, introduced into Switzerland, II 341; origin of, 647; IV 4

Carabobo, battle of (1821), x 294

Caracas, Dutch trade with, v 688; the *cabildo* of, x 246 sq.; attached to Mexico, 248; and the succession to the Spanish throne, 283; 285; revolution of, 288 sq.; Bolívar in (1821), 294, (1827), 296; 297 sq.

Caraccioli, Galeazzo, Italian Reformer, II 390

—— Marino, papal nuncio at Worms (1521), II 139

Caracciolo, Antonio, chronicler, II 389 sq., 396

—— Prince Francesco, Neapolitan admiral, VIII 632, 658, 779

Caracena, Count, Spanish commander, attacks Villa Viçosa, IV 662 sq.; v 34

Carafa, Ettore, Count of Ruvo, VIII 779

Caraffa, Antonio, Cardinal, III 448

—— Antonio, Austrian field-marshal, v 367

—— Carlo, Bishop of Aversa. *See* Aversa

—— Carlo, Cardinal (nephew of Paul IV), II 91 sq.

—— Giovanni Pietro. *See* Paul IV, Pope

Caramania, conquest of, by Turks, I 81 sqq.

Carberry Hill, Prince Charles at, VI 113

Carbery, Richard Vaughan, 2nd Earl of, v 748

Carbisdale, Montrose defeated at, IV 509

Carbon, Jean, *Chouan*, IX 17; 18

Carbonari, meeting of, at Bologna, x 21; 111 sqq.; in Piedmont, 114; 123; condemned by the Papacy, 135; 138; Pius VII and, 150; persecution of, by Cardinal Rivarola, 152; and American revolutionaries, 213; in Spain, 221; excommunicated, 452; Pius IX and, XI 72, 74, 77

Carcassonne, revolt of, III 668

Carces, Comte de, III 416

Cardadeu, Reding defeated at (1808), IX 448

Cardan, Jerome, physician, v 716

Cardenas, Iñigo de, Spanish ambassador, Mary de' Medici and, IV 625

Cardew, Sir Frederick, Colonel, XII 811

Cardigan, James Thomas Brudenell, 7th Earl of, at Balaklava, XI 319

Cardona, Ramón de, Spanish viceroy of Naples, I 137 sqq., 198, 249

—— Duke of, Viceroy of Catalonia, IV 648

Cardoso, Governor of Villa-de-Conde, x 328 sq.

Carducci, Giosue, Italian writer, x 115; XI 549

Cardwell, Edward Cardwell, Viscount, Secretary for War, XII 23; and army reform, 25 sq.; 29

Carelia, ceded to Sweden, v 503; claimed by Russia, 614; Gustavus III and, VI 778; Sweden demands the restoration of, VIII 325

Carentan, surrender of (1574), III 24

Carew, Sir George, III 532, 608

—— John, arrest of, IV 447

—— Sir Nicholas, execution of, II 449

—— Sir Peter, heads rebellion against Mary, II 526 sq.

—— Thomas, poet, v 745

Carey, Arthur Douglas, in Tibet, XII 802

—— Henry Charles, American political economist, VII 699

—— Sir Robert. *See* Monmouth, Earl of

Cargill, Donald, covenanter, v 286 sq.

Caribbean Islands, grant of (1627), VII 74

—— Sea, Spanish possessions in, v 680; 688; 691; VI 59; 62; European Powers in, 185; XII 652; 655; the United States and, 684 sqq.

Caribs, The, aborigines of West Indies, I 38, 41

Carignano, Eugenio, Prince of (1859), XI 386; 536

—— *See* Savoy-Carignan

Carillo d'Acuña, Dom Alfonso, Archbishop of Toledo. *See* Toledo

Carillon. *See* Ticonderoga

Carinthia, transferred to Archduke Ferdinand, II 150; Protestantism in, III 702; Estates of, 728; Austria and, IV 204; abandoned by Austria to Italy (1809), IX 355; French province of, 418; recovered by Austria (1815), 660; and German unity, XI 173

Carisbrooke Castle, Charles I at, IV 346 sq., 350, 359

Cariteo, Neapolitan poet, III 458

Carleill, Christopher, III 301

Carlens, Jean-Pascal-Raymond, commands the Army of the Rhine, VIII 426

Carleton, Sir Dudley, 1st Baron Carleton and Viscount Dorchester. *See* Dorchester

—— Sir Guy. *See* Dorchester

Carlier, Pierre, French Prefect of Police, XI 134

Carlingford, Chichester Samuel Parkinson-Fortescue, 1st Baron, XI 343

—— Theobald Taaffe, 1st Earl of (Viscount Taaffe), defeated at Mallow, IV 345; at Knockninoss, 531; v 109

Carlisle, siege of, IV 331; Irish garrison for, 520; Prince Charles at, VI 114 sq.; 117

—— Charles Howard, 1st Earl of (3rd cr., 1661), and motion on royal marriages, v 213

—— Frederick Howard, 5th Earl of, VI 450; Viceroy of Ireland, 456, 499; 464; 467

—— George Howard, 6th Earl of (Lord Morpeth), English ambassador (1806), IX 282

—— George William Frederick Howard, 7th Earl of, x 677

—— James Hay, 1st Earl of (2nd cr.), starts on a mission of peace, IV 24; meets Ferdinand at Salzburg, 27; VII 74

Carlists, party of the, rise of, in Spain, x 231; the Carlist War (1834–40), 235 sqq.; from 1871, xii 257 sqq.

Carlo Alberto, King of Sardinia. *See* Charles Albert

Carlos, King of Portugal, xii 271 sq.

—— Don, son of Philip II, iii 168–9, 175, 268–9, 480, 484, 488–90, 685

—— Don, son of Philip III, iv 14; 69

—— Don, son of Philip V. *See* Charles III, King of Spain

—— Don (Carlos Maria Isidro de Borbóro), x 230; and the rise of the Carlist party, 231; and the succession to the throne, 232 sq.; and the Powers, 235; 237 sq.; negotiations of, with Cristina, 239; retires to France, 240; abdication of (1845), 243, xi 553; Thiers and, x 496

—— "VI," pretender to the throne of Spain. *See* Montemolin, Count of

—— Don, Spanish pretender, xii 258; 260; 262 sq.

Carlota, Doña (Louisa Carlota, of Sicily, Duchess of Cadiz), and the marriage of Queen Isabel, xi 553

—— of Naples, consort of the Infante Don Francisco de Paula, and the Spanish succession, x 231 sqq.

—— Joaquina of Spain (Princess of Brazil), Queen consort of John VI of Portugal, vi 381; x 283; 285; 310; character of, 313; 316 sq.; 322; death of, 324

Carlowitz, Treaty of (1699), v 33, 61, 364, 371, 388; xi 179; rising at, 180

—— Christopher, foments dissension in Saxony, ii 252

—— General Georg Karl von, at Moscow, v 587

Carlsbad, Peter the Great at, v 607; meeting of Ministers at (1819), x 366; Metternich and Nesselrode at (1830), 481; Decrees (1819), 22, 23, 356, 367, 370

Carlson, Frederik Ferdinand, Swedish statesman, xi 690

Carlsruhe, Ney crosses the Rhine near, ix 253; Diet at, xi 145; 147; 221

Carlstadt (Andrew Bodenstein of), German Reformer, ii 117, 138, 165 sqq., 177, 190; in Zurich, 323; visits Denmark, 606; iii 739

Carlyle, Thomas, and Scott, x 719; xi 342; the writings of, 347 sq.; 349 sqq.; 355; 357; 359; 361; *Frederick the Great,* 362; Froude's Life of, 364; historical works of, xii 838 sq.

Carmagnola, Savoyard plots in (1580), iii 408, (1588), 414

—— (Francesco Bussone), Italian general, i 279 sq.

Carmarthen, Marquis of. *See* Leeds, 5th Duke of

Carmel, Gaspard, French Reformer, ii 295

Carmelites, The Bare-footed, v 73

Carmen Sylva. *See* Elizabeth, Queen of Roumania

Carmer, Count Johann H. C., Prussian High Chancellor, vi 728

Carmine, Italian statesman, xii 227

Carnarvon, Henry Herbert, 1st Earl of (3rd cr.), ix 78

—— Henry H. M. Herbert, 4th Earl of, xi 340 sq.; 771; Colonial Secretary, xii 30; 33; and Parnell, 42, 83; 43; 84; resigns, 390; and Cape Colony, 636; 646

Carnatic, The, Clive and Warren Hastings, Vol. vi, Chap. xv (2) *passim*; 465; affairs in, ix 721–2; Nawábs of, *see* Arcot, Nawábs of

Carne, Edward, English ambassador in Rome, ii 436 sq., 564

Carné, Comte Louis Marcein de, x 500

Carnesecchi, Pietro, Italian Reformer, ii 390, 396 sq.; iii 390, 459–60, 466

Carniola, transferred to Archduke Ferdinand, ii 150; Protestantism in, iii 702; Estates of, 728; Austria and, vi 204; French province of, ix 418; recovered by Austria (1815), 660; and German unity, xi 173

Carnot, Lazare-Nicolas-Marguerite, viii 233, 249; on *Comité de Salut Public,* 344, 348, 368, 380, 385, 389; and the army, 426, 431, 434 sq.; Director, 490 sqq., 495, 498 sq.; and *Coup d'état* of 18 Fructidor, 508 sqq., 591; pamphlet of (1798), 641; ix 19; 24, 31, 96, 133; and the Restoration, 565; 572, 616, 643

—— Lazare-Hippolyte, xi 26; 39; Minister of Public Instruction, 104; retires, 114; 116; and national education, 120; 124; 131; and *Coup d'état* of December, 136; 304; 477; 489

—— Marie-François-Sadi, President of French Republic, xii 98; 112; and the Papacy, 119; assassinated, 126

—— Nicolas-Léonard-Sadi, and the theory of heat, xii 784

Carnwarth, Robert Dalyell, 6th Earl of, vi 101; 103

Caro, Annibale, iii 471

—— Ventura, Spanish general, viii 439

Caroli, Peter, Calvin and, ii 368

Carolina. *See also* Carolinas, The

—— North, Amidas and Barlow land in, vii 3; settlement in (1585–6), *ib.*; 53; trade of, 56; 162; condition of, 164; the war in (1776), 173; constitution of, 241 sq.; and custom dues, 243; and the Constitutional Convention, 245 sq., 278, 281, 283; refuses to ratify the Constitution, 303; encouragement of manufactures in, 354; and the Tariff, 377; slavery in, 386, 581; white population in (1860), 415; and secession, 453, 603; Sherman's march through, 528, 534; emancipation in, 595; opposition to Confederate policy in, 608 sq.; becomes Democratic, 642

—— South, negroes in, vii 55; trade of, 56; the war in (1776), 173; invasion of (1778), 219; constitution of, 237, 241; and Constitutional Convention, 246, 258,

263, 265, 268, 272, 277, 281 sq., 292; and the Tariff, 377 sq., 380; "nullification" in, 381, 409, 412, 414; white population of (1860), 415; secedes from Union (1860), 441, 445; 447; joins Confederacy, 453, 603; Sherman's march through, 528 sq., 534; slavery in, 588; emancipation in, 595; corruption in, 641; Republicans in, 642

Carolinas, The, v 101; foundation of, 685; vi 51, 187; trade of, 447; vii 34–8; population of, 55; religious conditions in, 58, 114; disaffection in, 169; loyalist fugitives from, 219; war in (1780–1), 223–9; and Constitutional Convention, 252, 279; cessions in, 308; in the Civil War, 471; blockade-running in, 620

Caroline affair, The, vii 390 sq.

Caroline, Augusta (of Bavaria), Empress of Austria, x 146

—— Matilda, Queen of Denmark, consort of Christian VII, vi 743; and Struensee, 745; 746; 748 sqq.; death of, 752 sq.; viii 279

—— Queen of Great Britain, consort of George II, vi 19; 42; 47; 77

—— Queen of Great Britain, consort of George IV, marriage of, ix 675; 687, 690; x 583

—— (Archduchess), Queen of Naples and Sicily, consort of Ferdinand I, viii 79, 555 sq., 644, 649; 659; 778 sq.; ix 247; 381; makes one more bid for power, 384; flight of, 404; death of, 604; treatment of, ix 648; x 110

—— Princess of Palermo. *See* Aumale, Duchesse de

—— Islands, purchased by Germany, xii 171; Spain and, 264; 666 sq.

Carolinum at Zurich, Zwingli Rector of the, ii 321

Caron, Augustin-Joseph, French colonel, x 76

—— François, Dutch trade with Japan and, iv 712; v 703

—— Noël de, Seigneur de Schoneval, iii 258

Carpaccio, Vittore, Venetian artist, i 284

Carpentaria, exploration of, xi 798

Carpenter, George Carpenter, Lord, Lieutenant-general, vi 101

Carpentier, Pieter, Dutch Governor-General of the Indies, iv 711, 739

Carpentras, siege of, by Avignon, viii 217

—— Cardinal-Bishop of. *See* Sadoleto, Jacopo

"Carpet-baggers," vii 640 sqq., 644 sq., 652

Carpi, French defeated at (1701), v 402

—— Prince of. *See* Pio di Carpi

—— Girolamo da, v 724

Carpio, Duke of. *See* Haro, Don Luis de

Carr, Robert. *See* Somerset, Earl of

—— Robert, English officer, vii 41

Carra, Jean-Louis, French politician, viii 232 sq.

Carraca, arsenal of, seized by revolutionaries (1820), x 216

Carranza, Bartolomé de, Archbishop of Toledo. *See* Toledo

Carrara, marble quarries near, iii 392

—— (Carraresi), the family of, recover Padua, i 265

—— Francesco da, Lord of Padua, war between Venice and (1378), i 258, 265; Petrarch and, iii 463

—— Jacopo da, of Padua, i 262

—— Marsilio da, of Padua, i 262 sq.

Carrel, Nicolas-Armand, journalist, and Napoleon, ix 758; x 491 sq.; 499; xi 26; 526

Carrer, Luigi, Italian poet, xi 545

Carretto, Francesco Saverio, Marquis del, Neapolitan Minister, xi 69

—— Guglielmo, Marquis del, suppresses revolt at Cilento, x 119

Carrickfergus, and the rebellion in Ulster, iv 522; Munro at, 524; surprised by "Old Scots," 532; taken by Schomberg (1689), v 312; 313; French landing at, vi 489

Carrickmacross, Lawless at (1828), x 647

Carrick-on-Suir, William III at, v 315

Carrick's Ford, Federal success at (1861), vii 457

Carrier, Jean-Baptiste, member of the National Convention, viii 249, 356; impeached and executed, 377

Carriglea, battle of (1588), iii 589, 602–3

Carrion River, Soult on the, ix 445

Cars, Duc des, French legitimist, x 486

Carstares, William, and the establishment of Presbyterianism in Scotland, v 293

Cartagena, Alva sails from (1567), iii 213; Drake before, 321; trade of, v 684; sack of (1697), 691; blockade of, ix 211; Allied force at, 219; Villeneuve at, 220; Duke of Aosta lands at, xi 572; cantonalism at, xii 261 sq.

—— de las Indias (Colombia), defence of (1741), vi 165, x 273; emigration to, 251; the Inquisition in, 253 sq.; and trade, 255; and the slave-trade, 260; buccaneers at, 272; revolution in, 285; 288; Bolivar raises troops in, 289; besieged, 290; Bolivar retires to, 296

Cartaojal, Spanish general, commands army in La Mancha, ix 448; 449; covers eastern passes, 450

Cartaxo, Saldanha at, x 336

Carteaux, Jean-François, French general, viii 348, 352

Carteret, Sir George, v 113; Lord Proprietor in New Jersey, vii 41

—— Sir George (grandson of above), Lord Proprietor in New Jersey, vii 47

—— Philip, Governor of New Jersey, vii 41, 46 sq.

—— Lord. *See* Granville, Earl

Cartesianism, *see* Vol. IV, Chap. XXVII, Descartes and Cartesianism; v 72 sq.

Cartets, Vicomte de, and Labadie, v 756

Carthage, Charles V lands at, II 69

Carthusians, execution of, under Henry VIII, II 442

Cartier, George Étienne, Canadian statesman, XI 769; 770; 775

—— Jacques, French explorer, I 44; VII 71

—— John, in India, VI 558; 566

Cartwright, Thomas, Bishop of Chester, v 234

—— Thomas, Puritan controversialist, II 594; III 340, 743, 752 sqq.; v 326

—— Edmund, inventor, IX 372

—— Major John, political reformer, VIII 755, 760; IX 688; x 576 sq.; 597

—— Thomas, Secretary of the British Legation at the Hague, x 536 sq.

—— Commander at Fort Orange (Albany), VII 39

Carvajal, Juan de, papal legate in Hungary, I 69

—— Spanish general, x 222

—— y Lancaster, Don José de, Spanish statesman, VI 361 sqq.; death of, 364

Carvalho, José da Silva, Portuguese statesman, x 326; 330

—— e Mello, Sebastian Joseph. *See* Pombal, Marquis of

Carver, William, Governor of New Plymouth, VII 14

Cary, Lucius, Viscount Falkland. *See* Falkland

—— Thomas, Governor of Carolina, VII 37

Casa Blanca, XII 12; massacre at, 133

—— Giovanni della, Archbishop of Benevento. *See* Benevento

Casal, J. Chrysostom de Villaret, Bishop of, IX 129

Casale, rising of, III 407; Imperialist forces before, IV 115; siege of, 134 sqq.; French garrison in, 148; negotiations of Mazarin before, 592; Harcourt and, 599; assigned to Mantua, 618; attack on, by Spain, 643, 673; death of Spinola at, 644; seized by the French (1681), v 48, 357; Agricultural Congress at, XI 78; 371

Casali, Battista, at the Roman Academy, II 16

Casati, Spanish ambassador, opposes Henry IV, IV 41; offers treaty to the Grisons, 45 sq.; 48; Swiss Catholics and, 51

—— Gabrio, Count de, Italian statesman, XI 90

—— Teresa, x 118

Casaubon, Isaac, Calvinist theologian, II 718; III 60

Casaux, the Seigneur de, and Marseilles (1596), III 397

Cascaes Bay, Drake in, III 318

Caselli, Charles-François, Servite, sent to France, IX 181; urges Pius VII to yield to Napoleon, 198

Caserta, palace at, VI 596

—— Gian Francesco di, Italian reformer, II 391

Cashel, Synod of, III 580; Inchiquin at, IV 531; Reconciliation meeting at (1828), x 648

Casimir III, King of Poland, West Prussia acquired by, II 635; v 632

—— IV, King of Poland, I 345

—— John. *See* John II, King of Poland

Casimir-Périer, Jean-Paul-Pierre, President of the French Republic, XII 105; 107; and the establishment of the Republic, 110; 112; 119; 126

Casket Letters, III 278-9

Caspian Sea, Russia and, v 520 sq., 544 sq.; Russian advances on, XI 273, 633, XII 491; 793

Cass, Lewis, American statesman, VII 398 sq., 400, 419; resigns Secretaryship of State (1860), 447

Cassala, XII 240; 447; relinquished by Italy, 448

Cassander, George, III 164, 172

Cassano, Prince Eugene repulsed at, v 414

Cassard, Jacques, in the West Indies, v 679

Cassegrain, N., v 721

Cassel (Montcassel), William of Orange defeated at (1677), v 44; 45

—— (Hesse), Charles XII at, v 610; 743; surrender of, VI 426; Mortier ordered to march on, IX 278; capital of the kingdom of Westphalia, 411; XI 223; Prussian troops in, 229 sqq.

—— Sir Ernest, and Egyptian hospitals, XII 453

Cassian, John, writer on monachism, I 534

Cassillis, Gilbert Kennedy, 3rd Earl of, II 456, 458

Cassini, Count, Russian Minister at Peking, XII 512

Cassiodorus, Magnus Aurelius, the *De Artibus et Disciplinis Liberalium Artium* of, I 534

Castagnetto, Count, Secretary to King Charles Albert, XI 78

Castalbajac, French Royalist politician, x 74

Castaldo, Giambattista, Austrian envoy of Charles V, contrives the murder of Martinuzzi, II 268, III 122

Castaneda, Spanish envoy at Vienna, IV 238

Castaños, Francis Xavier de, *afterwards* Duke of Baylen, Spanish general, commands the Spanish army of Andalusia, IX 437; Dupont's convention with, 438; 442; army of, remains intact, 443; in La Mancha, 448; aids Beresford, 466; x 211

Castel Delfino, ceded to Dauphiné, III 419

Castelar y Ripoll, Emilio, Spanish statesman, XI 567; 570; XII 261 sq.; 264 sq.

Castelar, Baltasar Patiño, Marquis of, Spanish diplomatist, vi 142; 149; 166
—— Spanish general, vi 362
Castelfidardo, Papal army defeated at, xi 389, 469
Castellesi, Cardinal (Adriano di Corneto), i 241, 489; ii 5, 15
Castellio, Sebastian, ii 364, 372, 375; heretical views of, 716
Castel-Melhor, Louis Souza Vasconcellos, Count of, Portuguese statesman, v 34
Castelnau, Jacques de la Mothe, Baron de, ii 297
—— Michel de, *Mémoires*, iii 65; envoy to Scotland, 269-70
Castelnaudary, Gaston's army defeated at, iv 140
Castel-Rodrigo, Francisco de Moura Cortereal, Marquis de, Governor of the Spanish Netherlands (1664–8), v 152 sq.
Castelvetro, Giammaria, Modenese Reformer, ii 387
—— Ludovico, of Modena, ii 386 sq.; iii 457, 465
Casti, Gianbattista, Italian poet, viii 778
Castiglione, battle of (1796), viii 574 sqq.
—— Baldassare, *Il Cortegiano*, i 560; ii 8, 20; iii 457, 462-4, 466
Castiglioni, Francesco Xaverio. See Pius VIII, Pope
Castile, united with Aragon, i 111, 347; institutions of, 348-9; Holy Brotherhood in, 352 sq.; war of succession in, 352; the Council of, 355; Navarre incorporated with, 367; revolt of *Comuneros* in, 357, 372 sq.; Cortes of, meet (1586), iii 508; vote subsidy for Irish expedition, 532; kingdom of, royal autocracy in, 478; traditional policy of, 479; government of, 485; condition of, 488, 513; Moors in, 494; taxation of, 496-7; burdened by imperial policy of its kings, 504, 512; desolation of, 523, 528, 537; taxed for new Holy League, 541; Philip III and the Council of, iv 634; Philip IV and the Council of, 640; flight of Philip IV and Olivares to, 643; Portugal to be a province of, 651; 655; industries in, 656; Cortes of, *ib.*; Council of, and the succession, v 392; 428; Council of, vi 137; 142; economic reform in, 383
—— (New), ix 429; territory held by French troops in, 435; operations resumed in, 455; Hill ordered to abandon (1812), 475; 479
—— (Old), Blake's army descends into, ix 438; Baird directed to join Moore in, 443; Mortier's corps in, 453; occupied by Imperial Guard, 458; disorder in, xi 562; 567
—— Admiral (Adelantado) of. See Melgar, Count of, *and* Padilla, Martin de
—— Constable of (1520). See Frias, 2nd Duke of

Castilla, Ramón, Peruvian statesman, xii 673
Castillejos, battle of, xi 564
Castillia, Gaetano, x 119
Castillo, Hernando del. See Del Castillo
Castle, informer, x 578 sq.
—— Island, fortified, vii 17
Castlehaven, Spanish ships in, iii 327, 532-3
—— James Touchet, 3rd Earl of, Vavasour defeated by, iv 526; Ireton and, 535
Castlemaine, Barbara, Countess of, v 111
—— Roger Palmer, Earl of, v 235
Castlereagh, Robert Stewart, Viscount, *afterwards* 2nd Marquis of Londonderry, viii 771; fights a duel with Canning, ix 359; dealings of, with Sicily, 384; advises intervention against Napoleon, 439; proposes Wellesley as commander of expedition to Spain, 440; Wellesley's appointment due to, 449; at Conference of Châtillon, 546; signs Treaty of Chaumont, 577; at Congress of Vienna, 579 sq.; 648, 653, 667; and the French frontier, 664; and Catholic Emancipation, 678; 681; and the Walcheren expedition, 688 sq.; succeeds Wellesley in office, 690; and the Union with Ireland, 702; 705; criticism of Treaty of Bassein, 725; 729, 733; and the French colonies, 735; x 7; 9; and the Holy Alliance, 10; and Treaty of Paris (1815), 11; and the "European System," 12; 13; at Conference of Aix-la-Chapelle, 14 sqq.; 21; protests against Carlsbad Decrees, 22; 23; 25; and Conference of Troppau, 27-9; discusses Eastern Question with Metternich, 32, 184; 36; and Consalvi, 141; 176 sq.; 186; and the Greek revolt, 187; and Vienna Congress (1819), 368; 371; and the Polish question, 445 sq.; and the union of Holland and Belgium, 519 sq.; leader in the Commons, 574 sq.; and repressive measures, 578 sq.; 580; 584; election of, for county Down, 607; and the movement for Catholic relief, 629, 634; death of, 33, 583; xii 682
Castries, Charles-E.-G. de La Croix, Marquis de, French marshal, Minister of Marine, viii 94, 96, 107
Castriotes, George. See Scanderbeg
Castro, the Barberini and, iv 685; restored to Parma, 687
—— Vireyna, silver mines at, v 682
—— Alfonso de, the *De Haeresibus*, ii 402
—— Alphonso de, Viceroy of the Indies, iii 638
—— Don Pedro de, vi 105
—— Count of, Spanish ambassador in Venice, iv 671
Catalans, Philip V and the, v 445 sq.; 452

Catalonia, constitution of, I 351; Cortes of, III 485, 496; exposed to Barbarossa's attacks, 110; revolt of (1640), IV 147 sqq., 648 sqq.; insurgents of, represented at Münster, 402; France and, 593, 598 sqq.; 612, 615; Peace of the Pyrenees and, 620, 660; Cortes of, 628, 643; Castilian troops in, 647; government of, 653; 656; 658; expense of war against, 659; pacification of, 661; the French in, V 61, 416; restored to Spain, 63; 375; 428; 451; and Philip V, 404, 436; the Allies in, 419, 426; evacuated by the Allies (1712), 434; 440; VI 34; evacuated by French, 35; 136; 383; French invade (1794), VIII 440; *émigrés* in, 782; operations in (1808), IX 239; 396; Duhesme in, 430, 435, 439; Saint-Cyr sent to, 447 sqq., 454; Augereau's failure in (1809), 457; 458; Macdonald supersedes Augereau in, 464; isolation of, 465; struggle in (1813-4), 479; Mina in, X 228; the Society of the Exterminating Angel, 229; absolutist revolt in (1828), 230; Don Carlos in, 239; Carlist rising in, XI 556; XII 258; military disorder in, 260; 263; 268

Catania, naval battle of (1676), V 44; Order of St John of Jerusalem at, IX 604; capture of, XI 92

Catarino, Ambrogio, refutes the *Sommario*, II 386

Catawba river, Cornwallis crosses, VII 227 sq.

Cateau-Cambrésis, Treaty of (1559), II 26, 88, 93 sq., 99, 566; III 6, 184, 187, 260, 263, 280, 406, 465, 477 sqq., 674, 677

Catechism, of Martin Luther, II 201, 613; of Canisius, 682

Catharine (of Aragon), Queen of England, consort of Henry VIII, marriage of, I 466, 473 sq., 476; 482, 488; II 26, 70, 416 sq., 428 sqq., 437, 440, 444

—— (of Braganza), Queen of England, consort of Charles II, marriage of, IV 621, V 105; 106; 212 sq.; Titus Oates and, 225; 698

—— (Howard), Queen of England, 5th consort of Henry VIII, II 451; executed, 453

—— (Parr), Queen of England, 6th consort of Henry VIII, II 457; marries Sir Thomas Seymour, 488

—— (de' Medici), Queen of France, consort of Henry II, marriage of, II 26, 67, 98; 219; the Reformation in France and, 296-304; 578, 581; policy and action of, III 1-45; 53; and Poland, 85; 177; and the Guises, 266, 271; and St Bartholomew massacre, 285; and Savoy, 403, 408, 413; and Philip II, 484, 486, 489 sqq.; and Don Antonio, 501 sq.

—— (d'Albret), Queen of Navarre. *See* Navarre

—— (of Austria), Queen of Poland, 3rd consort of Sigismund I, III 82

Catharine (of Austria), Queen of Portugal, marries John III, II 172

—— I, Tsarina of Russia, V 547 sq.; accession of, 549; 550 sq.; illness and death of, 551 sq.; VI 143; 302; 312

—— II, Tsarina of Russia, V 479; 505; Vol. VI, Chap. XIX; 316; and Stanislaus Poniatowski, 200; 299; 322; 340; 346; the "Greek project" of, 353, 355; 354; and Poland, 357 sq., 730 sqq.; Spain and, 378; 460; 629; and Prussia, 630 sq.; 633; and Austria, 647 sq.; 651; and Frederick the Great, 352, 702, 707 sq., 729; 742; and Denmark, 743 sq., 754; 746; 750; 753; 765 sq.; and Sweden, 769 sqq.; 778; and Finland, 782; 783; VII 232; VIII 278, 280, 292 sq.; policy of, 307 sqq.; in the Crimea, 315; after Reichenbach, 336 sq.; and Poland, Chap. XVII *passim*; death of (1796), 552, 583; and the French Revolution, 784 sq.; IX 34 sqq.; and the First Armed Neutrality, 43 sqq.; 280; attacks of, on Turkey, 385; X 172; 413; 423; 425; and the serfs, 426; 471; XI 262; 264

—— (Jagello), Queen of Sweden, consort of John III, influence of, II 630, 632; marriage of, IV 162; 166; death of, 167

—— (Stenbock), Queen of Sweden, consort of Gustavus I, death of, IV 183

—— (of Brandenburg), Princess of Transylvania, consort of Bethlen Gabor, IV 29; Russian marriage proposed for, 90; marries Bethlen Gabor, 91, 100

—— daughter of Henry II of France, III 400

—— Ivanovna, Duchess of Mecklenburg-Schwerin, V 611; VI 309

—— of Navarre, sister of Henry IV, III 413

—— Grand Duchess of Russia, Duchess of Oldenburg, *afterwards* Queen of Würtemberg, at Vienna, IX 581; X 361

—— Infanta, daughter of Philip II, consort of Charles Emmanuel, Duke of Savoy, III 413, 513; death of, 417

Cathcart, Charles Murray, 2nd Earl Cathcart, in British N. America, XI 767

—— Sir William Schaw, 10th Baron, 1st Viscount and Earl, bombards Copenhagen, IX 236; 263; at Rügen, 289; 295-6; at the Congress of Vienna, 585

Cathelineau, Jacques, Vendean leader, VIII 266, 341

Catholic Emancipation, and Pitt's resignation, IX 678 sq., 693 sqq., but *see* Chap. XXII *passim*; becomes law, X 593, *see* Chap. XIX, 620-54. *See also* Toleration

Catholique, Le, Ghent journal, X 532

Catinat de St Gratien, Nicolas de, Marshal of France, V 60 sqq.; 401 sq.; 404 sqq.

Cats, Jacob, Pauw replaced by, IV 697; poems of, 719; 721; Grand Pensionary of Holland, V 139

Cattaneo, Carlo, Italian writer, xɪ 547

Cattaro, prisoners work at, ɪx 84; ceded to France (1806), 269, 270–1, 293, 306; restored to Austria (1815), 660; Montenegrin occupation of, xɪɪ 402

Cattegat, Russo-Danish squadron in, vɪ 779

Caturce, Jean de, French Reformer, ɪɪ 291

Caub, Blücher at, ɪx 544

Caucasus, The, Russian influence in, v 545; vɪ 673 sq., 676; Orthodox mission in, x 422; Russian advances in, xɪ 273 sq.; 633; naphtha industry of, xɪɪ 321; strike in, 331; 332; 342 sq.; disturbances in, 350 sq.; 353 sq.; 373; 793

Caudebec, taken by Parma (1592), ɪɪɪ 51

Caulaincourt, Armand-Augustin-Louis de, Duke of Vicenza, ɪx 30; receives Vicenza, 111; 145; French ambassador, 307; Napoleon's directions to, 308; 310; meeting with Romanzoff, 312; 313; Napoleon's letters to, 314; 315 sqq.; summoned to St Petersburg, 485; sent to Alexander, 520; 543; suggests negotiations, 545; at Châtillon, 546; 549, 552; envoy to Alexander, 558; Minister for Foreign Affairs, 616

Caulet, Étienne-François de, Bishop of Pamiers. *See* Pamiers

Caumartin, François Lefèvre de, Bishop of Amiens. *See* Amiens

Caussidière, Marc, x 492; xɪ 99; 110

Cauvin, Jean. *See* Calvin

Cavagnari, Sir Pierre Louis Napoleon, xɪɪ 34 sq.; 469; 471

Cavaignac, Élénore-Louis-Godefroy, x 485; 491

—— Jacques-Marie-Eugène-Godefroy, French Minister of War, xɪɪ 121

—— Louis-Eugène, French general, x 485; xɪ 104; Minister of War, 112; 113; suppresses insurrection in Paris, 114; 117; and the Presidential election, 118; 121 sq.; imprisonment of, 136; 304

Cavalier, Jean, *Camisard* leader, v 26

Cavalieri, Bonaventura, mathematician, v 711

Cavallini, Pietro, ɪɪɪ 438

Cavallotti, Felice, Italian politician, xɪɪ 219

Cavan, invasion of, ɪɪɪ 605; plantation of, 614

Cave, Stephen, and Egyptian finance, xɪɪ 431, 434

Cavendish, Charles, killed at Gainsborough, ɪv 314

—— Lord Frederick Charles, Secretary for Ireland, xɪɪ 40; 81

—— Henry, man of science, xɪɪ 768

—— Lord John, Chancellor of the Exchequer, vɪ 457; 462 sqq.

—— Sir Thomas, navigator, x 272

—— Lord. *See* Devonshire, Duke of

Cavite, Spanish fleet destroyed at, vɪɪ 679, xɪɪ 530

Cavour, surrender of, ɪɪɪ 417

—— Camillo, Count di, ɪɪ 35; and Italy (1849–61), Vol. xɪ, Chap. xɪv; 79; 83; interview with Napoleon III, 307, 376, 381; 322; and Austria, 403; results of work of, 529; 530; 539; 705; death of, 392; xɪɪ 215

Cawdor, Frederick A. V. Campbell, 3rd Earl, xɪɪ 60

—— John Campbell, 1st Baron, vɪɪɪ 475

Cawnpore, xɪ 738; mutiny at, 746; massacre at, 747; 748

Cawsand Bay, English fleet leaves for Cadiz, ɪɪɪ 324

Caxton, William, the *Golden Legend*, ɪ 641

Caya river, defeat of the Allies on (1709), v 426; Soult and Marmont in front of, ɪx 468

Cayenne, French colony of, ɪv 756, v 448, 678, vɪɪ 79, 96; trade of, 327; transportations to, vɪɪɪ 506, 512 sq., xɪ 139, 304; Villeneuve ordered to, ɪx 219; reduced (1809), 240

Cayla. *See* Du Cayla

Cayuga, The. *See* Iroquois

Cazalès, J.-A.-M. de, French politician, vɪɪɪ 159, 172, 741

Cazalla, Dr Agustin, Spanish Reformer, ɪɪ 404, 407 sq.

—— Francisco de, Spanish Reformer, ɪɪ 408

—— Pedro, Spanish martyr, ɪɪ 408

Çea Bermudez, Spanish Minister, x 233

Čechs, compared with Magyars, ɪ 330 sq.; xɪ 46; 176 sqq.; 190; 216; literature of, 653 sqq.; Vol. xɪɪ, Chap. vɪɪ *passim*

Cecil, Sir Edward, commands expedition to Calais, ɪv 262

—— Sir Robert. *See* Salisbury, Earl of

—— Sir William. *See* Burghley, Lord

Cécora, Polish disaster near, ɪv 189

Cedar Creek, battle of (1864), vɪɪ 532 sq.

Celebes, The, and Dutch colonisation, ɪv 711; government of, xɪɪ 669

Céleron. *See* Bienville, Céleron de

Celestina, La, by Rojas, ɪ 379

Cellamare, Antonio Gindice, Duke of Giovenazzo, Prince of, Spanish ambassador at Paris, vɪ 33; 121; 125; 130

Celle, Queen Caroline Matilda at, vɪ 751, 753

Celles, Antoine-Charles Fiacre, Comte de Visscher de, cruelty of, as prefect of the Zuider See, ɪx 417

—— Antoine-P.-F.-G., Comte de Visscher, x 480; 527

Cellini, Benvenuto, ɪɪ 24; ɪɪɪ 394, 466, 474

Celman, M. Suarez, President of the Argentine Confederation, xɪɪ 683

Celtes, Conrad, German humanist, ɪ 323, 325, 637

Cemetery Ridge, and Gettysburg, VII 488 sq.

Cenci, Beatrice, executed, IV 668

Cennini, Bernardo, Florentine printer, I 561

Centallo, annexed to Saluzzo, III 419

Centerville, Federal retreat to (1861), VII 466

Centri, secret society, in Mantua, X 111

Centuries of Meditations, Traherne's, IV 771

Centurione, Paolo, Genoese traveller, V 512

Cephalonia, seized by Turks (1479), I 81; Fleet of Triple Alliance at (1571), III 135

Ceracchi, Joseph, IX 17

Ceram, English attempt to establish factories in, IV 735

Cerdagne, recovery of, by Spain (1493), I 111, 229, 363; Spain and, VI 141

Ceresole, French victory at (1544), II 77, 245

Ceri, Renzo da, condottiere, I 134; defends Marseilles, II 49; raids the Abruzzi, 55

Cerignola, French capture of (1502), I 125; French defeat at (1503), 195

Cerkova, Charles XII at, V 600

Ceroni, Joseph, Italian poet and captain, IX 87

Cerretani, Bartolommeo, Florentine chronicler, I 147

Cerro Gordo (Mexico), captured by Scott (1847), VII 396

Certain, George, and Lambert (William and Lewis of Nassau), III 231

Cervantes, Miguel, III 136; *Don Quixote*, 365, 546–7

Cerveira, Portuguese chronicler, I 16

Cervera y Topete, Pascual, Count de Jerez and Marquis de Santa Ava, Spanish admiral (1898), VII 679 sq.; XII 265

Cervi, island of, XI 280 sq.

Cervoni, Jean-Baptiste, French general, VIII 564 sq., 569

Cesari, Italian brigand, X 138

Cesarini, Alessandro, II 16

—— Cardinal Giuliano, at the Council of Basel, I 623

Cesarotti, Melchiore, Italian writer, VI 830

Cesena, Pius VII at, X 134; riots at (1830–1), 154, 155

Cesi, Prince Federigo, and the *Accademia dei Lincei*, V 740

—— Paolo Emilio, II 16

—— Pietro Donati, Cardinal, Bishop of Narni, III 450

Cetewayo, King of the Zulus, XII 636

Cette, harbour works at, XII 102

Cettinje, investment of, XI 636

Ceuta, taken by Portuguese (1415), I 10; fighting at, VI 151; Arab raids near, XI 564

Ceva, the Allies at, VIII 565; occupied by the French (1796), 567

Cevallos, Pedro, Spanish ambassador at Vienna, X 213

Cevennes, Protestant rising in the, V 26

Ceylon, Dutch trade with, III 638; Christian IV and, IV 567; and Dutch colonisation, 711; Portuguese in, 743 sq. ; and French colonisation, V 13; the Dutch in, 107, 696; 146; 695; Dutch colony of, taken by the English, VIII 484; retained by Great Britain, IX 75, 77, 654, 752; account of, 733 sq.; Arabi Pasha exiled to, XII 438

Cezimbra Bay, Spanish carrack captured in, III 327

Chaban, Prefect of Brussels, IX 399; work of, at Brussels, 416

Chabert, French labour politician, XII 94

Chablais, participates in Swiss neutrality, IX 660

Chabot, François, Revolutionary, VIII 213, 249, 339; trial and execution of, 363 sq.

—— L.-F.-J., French general, VIII 582

—— de l'Allier, Georges-Antoine, IX 19

Chabran, Joseph, Comte, French general, IX 60

Chabrol de Volire, Gilbert-Joseph-Gaspard, Comte de, IX 145

Chacabuco, Royalist defeat at (1817), X 292

Chaco, district of the, X 269 sq.

Chad, kingdom of, the French Congo and, XII 130

—— Lake, XII 659 sq.; exploration on, 129 sq., 806 sqq., 810 sqq.

Chadda river, and the Niger, XII 807

Chadwick, Sir Edwin, and Poor Law reform, X 660 sqq.; 681; XI 1; XII 750

Chagatái clan, VI 508

Chaikovsky, Nicholas, Russian revolutionary, XII 304

Chaireddin. *See* Barbarossa

Chait Singh, Rájah of Benares, Warren Hastings and, VI 471; 578 sqq. ; 582 sq.; IX 716

Chakdarra, attacked by the Swatis, XII 488

Chalais, Henri de Talleyrand, Comte de, execution of, IV 131

Chalcondylas, Demetrius, career of, in Italy, I 543; II 16

Chaldiran, victory of Turks at (1514), I 90

Chalgrove, skirmish at (1643), IV 313

Challemel-Lacour, Paul-Armand, French politician, XI 487

Challier, Marie-Joseph, Lyons Jacobin, VIII 340, 346

Challoner, Sir Thomas, agent of Edward VI and Mary at the French Court, II 518; III 265

Chalmers, Thomas, economic theories of, X 775; and the Disruption of the Scottish Church, XI 6

—— William, bequeaths industrial college to Göteborg, XI 684

Châlons, House of, V 669

Châlons-sur-Marne, headquarters of the League, III 39; *Parlement* of, 659, 663 sqq.; army at, 690; insurrection at (1792), VIII 251; Blücher at, IX 548; army corps at, XI 582; 585; German advance on, 594; 595

Cham, Wallenstein abandons investment of, IV 237

Chaman, railway to, XII 489

Chambarlac, General, IX 14

Chamberlain, Hugh, and a national bank, V 266; 271

—— Joseph, President of the Board of Trade, XII 36; 40; the "unauthorised programme" of, 42 sq.; and Home Rule, 44, 46; mission of, to the United States, 47; 48; Colonial Secretary, 52; and the Jameson Raid, 53; advocates Tariff Reform, 54; Colonial policy of, 57; and Parnell, 81, 84; and South African affairs, 641; 652

—— Sir Neville Bowles, Field-Marshal, XII 469

Chamberlayne, William, poet, V 136

"Chambers of Reunion," Louis XIV's, V 47 sq., 357

Chambers, Richard, refuses to pay taxes, IV 273; punishment of, 281

Chambersburg, Lee at, VII 488; burned by the Confederates, 532

Chambéry, taken by the French (1630), IV 138; added to France (1814), IX 564, 576; bishopric of, X 149

Chamblee, fort at, VII 170

Chambon de Montaux, Nicolas, Mayor of Paris, VIII 252

Chambord, Treaty of (1552), II 87, 271

—— Henri-Charles-Ferdinand-M.-D. d'Artois, Comte de, XI 133; XII 92; 103 sq.; and the Comte de Paris, 107 sqq.

Chambre Ardente, La, II 293

—— *Introuvable,* X 46

Chambres de l'Édit, III 676

Chamillart, Michel de, French financier, V 28 sq.; 417; 424

Chamisso, Adalbert von, German poet, X 404

Champ de Mars, "massacre" of the (July 17, 1791), VIII 200

Champagne, devastation of, II 87; Guise in, III 32; the League in, 661, 663; *Intendant* retained in, IV 606; Conti Governor of, 608, 614; Spaniards under Turenne in, 613; Condé in, 618 sq.; customs of, V 13; Prussian retreat from, VIII 534, 551

Champagny, Comte François-J.-M.-T. de, X 500

—— F. Perrenot de, III 237, 242; Governor at Antwerp, 245–6

—— Jean-Baptiste Nompère de, VII 332 sq.; granted duchy of Cadore, IX 111; becomes Foreign Minister, 136; 141, 195, 245, 247; Minister of Foreign Affairs, 300; 309, 321, 335, 359; Napoleon writes to, 370

Champaubert, Russian repulse at (1814), IX 547

Champeaux, French ambassador in Spain, VI 156

Champigny, truce ratified at (1575), III 28

Champion, Alexander, general, invades Rohilkhand, VI 569 sq,

Championnet, Jean-Étienne, French general, VIII 429; in Rome (1799), 652; in Naples, 653, 779; 663

Champion's Hill, Federal victory at (1863), VII 504

Champlain, Lake, exploration of, VII 72; 80; French troops at, 124 sq., 137; and the United States boundary, 307, 315; Americans checked on (1813), 341

—— Samuel de, founder of Quebec, V 684; VII 71 sq.; surrenders Quebec, 74; 75 sq.

Champnol, Emmanuel Cretet, Comte de, Governor of the Bank of France, IX 117; Minister of the Interior, 136–8; plenipotentiary for the French Concordat, 184

Champollion, Jean-François, Egyptologist, XI 525; XII 845

Chancellor, Richard, in Russia, V 512 sq.; XII 793

Chancellorsville, battle of (1863), VII 485 sq.

Chánd Bibi, Queen Regent of Ahmadnagar, VI 512 sq.

Chanda Sahib, Nawáb of the Carnatic, VI 533; 539 sqq.

Chandernagore, factory at, V 703; VI 347; 454; French rule in, 534; 544; 552; captured by the English, 553, 577; 554

Chandler, Edward Barron, Canadian politician, XI 775

—— Zachariah, American politician, VII 469, 653

Chandos, Marquis of. *See* Buckingham and Chandos, Duke of

Chang Chihtung, Chinese Viceroy, XII 505; 507; 516

Changama, Haidar Ali defeated at, VI 567

Changarnier, Nicolas-Aimé-Théodule, French general, XI 110; 119; 125; deprived of his command, 132; 134; 136; XII 106 sq.; 109

Channel, control of the, III 510–11; Armada in the (1588), 507, (1597), 529, (1598), 529–30

—— Islands, reduction of, IV 466; a centre of English commerce, IX 381

Channing, William Ellery, American Unitarian, VII 738

Chantilly, Duke of Bourbon sent to, VI 144

Chantonnay, captured by the Republicans, VIII 353

—— Thomas Perrenot de, Spanish ambassador in France, II 302, 576; III 200

Chantries Bill, The (1547), II 482

Chantry Lands, confiscation of, in England, II 502 sq.

Chanut, Pierre, French ambassador, and Christina of Sweden, IV 575 sq.; 787
Chanzy, Antoine - Eugène - Alfred, French general, XI 605 sq.; retreats to Le Mans, 607; 608 sq.; defeated at Le Mans, 610; XII 105
Chapelain, Jean, member of French Academy, IV 156
Chapelle St Lambert, Prussians at, IX 634, 637
Chaplin, Henry, and bimetallism, XII 50
Chaplitz, commands a detachment at Brili, IX 502 sq.
Chapman, Frederick Henry, in Sweden, VI 775
—— George, III 369, 380
Chaptal, Jean-Antoine, Comte de Chanteloup, IX 9; 25, 124, 133, 376; experiments of, 377; x 744
Chapu, capture of, XI 809
Chapultepec, fort of, stormed by Scott (1847), VII 396
Chapuys, Eustace, Imperial ambassador in England, II 442
Charasia, Afghans defeated at, XII 471
Charbonnerie française, secret society, x 68, 75
Charbonnières, taken by Henry IV, III 417; recaptured by Charles Emmanuel (1598), *ib.*
Charcas (Upper Peru), province of, x 249
Charenton, Synod of (1631), v 743
Charette de la Contrie, François-Athanase, Vendean leader, VIII 266 sq., 341; desertion of, 353 sqq.; accepts the terms of peace, 381 sq., 391; executed (1795), 395
"Charitable Conference," at Thorn (1645), v 743
Charlemont (Armagh), captured (1690), v 314
—— (Liége), fortified by Charles V, II 89, 102
—— James Caulfield, 4th Viscount and 1st Earl of, VI 500 sqq.; VIII 771; and the Whig Club, IX 693; 695, 701
Charleroi, v 43; restored to Spain, 45; 160; taken by the French (1667), 199; 450; 457 sq.; siege of (1746), VI 246 sq.; Jourdan besieges, VIII 435; Prussians at, IX 623; Napoleon captures (1815), 625, 626
Charles the Great, Emperor, I 9; the schools of, 534 sq., 537; v 617
—— IV, Emperor, and Brandenburg, v 621; 633
—— V, Emperor (Charles I, King of Spain), I 46, 96, 318; Spanish revenue of, 358; 368–77 *passim*; received as King in Spain, 369 sq.; the Cortes and, 370 sq.; revolts against, 372 sq.; 423, 453 sqq.; 457 sq., 477, 486, 490, 519, 658, 685, 691; character of, 378 sq.; *see passim,* Vol. II, Chaps. II and III (Habsburg and Valois), and Chaps. v–VIII (Reformation and Religious Wars in

Germany), 14, 23–5, 29, 36; possessions of, 37; character of, 38; election of, 40 sq.; meets Henry VIII (1520), 42, 416; (1522), 45, 419; 424, 426; quarrels with Henry VIII, 429; comment of, on More's execution, 443; encourages colonial trade, 100 sq.; at the Diet of Worms (1521), 139–41; dynastic aims of, 143–5, 246–8, 267; effect of reign of, on Germany, 145; the Schmalkaldic War and, 256–61; efforts of, to obtain a general Council, 249, 642; Paul III and, 661; and the Council of Trent, 663–70; advice to Mary Tudor of, 518, 522; 534, 536; close of career and abdication of, 89 sq., 537; activity of, against the Turks, III 104 sqq.; sends letter to Sultan, 109; and Paul III, 110; expedition of, against Tunis, 111 sqq.; war of, with Francis I, 113; negotiates with Barbarossa, 114, 135; with Venice, 115 sq.; Germany and, 145; Archduke Maximilian and, 166; 168; abdication of, 182 sq.; and the Netherlands, 184 sqq.; 189 sq.; and Italy, 383 sqq., 392, 395; and Savoy, 402; 410; on Castiglione, 464; policy of, 475 sq.; possessions of, 508; 540; and Ireland, 581; and Jülich-Cleves, 716; temper of, 741; v 34; 627; VI 138; 158; 507; 612; x 269
Charles VI, Emperor (Archduke), and the Spanish Succession, v 384, 388, 390 sqq., 401; and Spain, 412; 417; inherits Habsburg dominions, 419 sq.; 426 sq.; in Catalonia, 419 sq.; 429; leaves Spain, 432; and peace negotiations before Utrecht, *ib.*; elected Emperor, 434; and Peace of Utrecht, 434, 438 sqq., 450 sq.; and Peace of Rastatt, 435 sq., 452 sqq.; and the Catalans, 445 sq.; and Peace of Baden, 454 sq.; and the Tsarevich, 539; and Peter the Great, 542; 543; 704; 744; VI 21; 23; and Great Britain, 25, 37 sqq., 61 sq.; and Sardinia, 29; 30 sqq.; 35; and Vienna Treaties, 57, 60; 58 sq.; 91; and the Old Pretender, 97; 109; 123; and Sicily, 124, 126; 125; and Dubois, 131; and the Spanish claims in Italy, 138 sqq.; and the Jacobites, 142; and Spain, 145 sq., 148 sq.; 151 sqq.; 155; and Chauvelin, 163; 169; and Ostend Company, 182; and Poland, 193; and Pragmatic Sanction, 201 sqq., 228; 205 sqq.; 210; Frederick William I and, 212; 227; 249; and Russia, 308; and the Papacy, 586 sqq.; Venice and, 606; sells Finale, 608; 614 sq.; 640; 646; 741; 760; death of, 158, 204, 236; and the Austrian Netherlands, VIII 317
—— VII, Emperor (Elector of Bavaria), v 451; VI 199; marriage of, 201; and Pragmatic Sanction, 202; and the Austrian Succession, 228 sqq.; regains Bavaria, 236; 238; 240; death of, 241 sq.

Charles I, King of England (Prince of
Wales), scheme of Spanish marriage for,
III 560 sq., 575 sqq., IV 86 sq., 639 sqq.;
French marriage of, 129; and the Roman
Catholics in England, 131; and the con-
stitutional struggle (1625–40), see Chap.
VIII; during the years 1640–2, see Chap.
IX; and First Civil War (1642–7), see
Chap. X; and the Presbyterians and
Independents (1645–9), and trial and
death of, see Chap. XI; 359; suspicious
of the French Government, 378; and
projected conference at Brussels, 396; not
represented at Münster or Osnabrück,
403; 434; revives naval activity, 459 sq.;
poverty of, 461; naval disorders of reign
of, 462; reign of, and growth of
English commerce, 466; 485; and Scotland, see Chap. XVII; and Ireland, see
Chap. XVIII; 639 sq.; Spanish journey
of, 641 sq., 673; and Frederick V, 643,
646; 659; 664; Aerssens sent to, 701;
the Dutch and, 702; protests against the
"Massacre at Amboina," 739; and the
East India Company, 746; experiments
of, in colonial government, 748; 754;
and Ireland, V 103; and Portugal, 105;
216; and Scotland, 279 sq., 283 sq., 291;
and the Puritans, 325; 326; 746; VI
795 sq.
—— II, King of England (Prince of Wales),
at Bristol, IV 328; at Exeter, 333 sq.;
and Cromwell, 347; and the fleet, 350,
463; Lauderdale and, 351; invited to
Ireland by Ormonde, 435; at Worcester,
436; 446; 450; Richard Cromwell and,
450 sq.; 463; in Scotland, 466; proclaimed King in Scotland, 509 sqq.; 540;
Treaty of Pyrenees and, 542; Monck
and, 545; parliamentary writs and, 553;
goodwill to, 554; negotiations with, 555
sq.; the Convention and, 558; return of,
559; Irish Confederates and, 532; Irish
peace of 1649 and, 534; expelled from
France, 619; 620 sq.; William II of
Orange and, 724; and Algiers, 483; 591;
policy of (1667–85), Vol. V, Chap. IX;
and the government of Scotland, Chap.
X (2); in Holland, 148; lands at Dover,
280; and Portugal, 34, 105, 107, 148; and
Louis XIV, 37, 40, 42, 44 sqq., 105 sq.,
109, 154; and United Provinces, 37,
43 sqq., 107, 178 sq.; restoration and
policy of, 92 sq.; 94; 96; 98; and religious toleration, 99 sqq., 329, 333 sq.;
and Clarendon, 101 sq., 114; and Spain,
104 sq.; marriage of, 105; and Prince
of Orange, 107, 158, 163; and the Dutch
war, 108 sq.; financial difficulties of,
110 sqq.; and the peace negotiations,
112 sq.; and the army, 113, 265; and
the Parliament, 114 sq.; 124; Dryden
and, 134 sqq.; and Bishop of Münster,
150, 182; and Triple Alliance, 154, 191;
and Treaty of Dover, 154, 156; 177;

and the fleet, 178, 187 sq.; declares war
against Dutch (1665), 180, (1672), 191;
187; 190; 197; and Ireland, 301 sqq.,
310; religion of, 331; 359; and Dunkirk, 442; 650; and Brazil, 675; and
colonial affairs, 690; and East India
Company, 697; and Hobbes, 751; death
of, 230, 288; VI 6; 791; 808; and
Virginia, VII 9; and New Netherlands,
38 sq.; and Acadia, 75
Charles V, King of France, I 384, 389, 392;
communes suppressed by, 398, 411, 505,
657
—— VI, King of France, I 259, 384, 409,
414
—— VII, King of France, I 107, 384 sq.;
the Popes and, 386–7; 396, 400, 403;
taxation under, 404 sqq.; 411, 413, 430,
636; II 36
—— VIII, King of France, I 86, 107;
Italian expedition of, 108–18, 229 sq.,
303, 564, 575; Florence and, 155, 228;
170; Pisa and, 191; 362, 384, 392;
marries Anne of Britanny, 395, 450,
467; 401, 411, 413, 445, 467, 672; V 483
—— IX, King of France, accession of, II
299, 302, 581; Geneva and, 373; III 7;
marriage of, 15, 177; and England, 16
sq.; and St Bartholomew, 19; and Mary
Queen of Scots, 276, 282 sq.; and the
Netherlands, 230 sqq.; and Cosimo I,
390; death of, 24, 406; 484; 591
—— X, King of France (Charles-Philippe,
Comte d'Artois), VI 656; VIII 81, 117;
emigrates (1789), 165; accused of high
treason, 221; expedition of, to the
Vendée, 395; 398, 495, 555; IX 3; 28,
30; enters Paris, 560; made Lieutenant-
Governor, 561; views of, 566; 568 sq.; X
13; 41; 44; 49; and army reforms, 55;
tries to force a Royalist policy, 56;
58; decline of the influence of, 60; 62;
65; 67; and Richelieu, 63, 70; 65; 67;
71; accession of (1824), 85; and compensation for the émigrés, 71, 85 sq.;
and the Church, 87; consecration of, 87
sq.; 90; appoints Martignac to succeed
Villèle, 92; and Martignac, 93 sq.; and
the Polignac ministry, 96–8; character
and policy of, 97; 98; and the address
of the Liberal deputies, 99; publishes
ordinances of July 25, 1830, ib.; 162;
and the Greek Question, 189, 193; Metternich and, 371; and Revolution of 1830,
476; 477 sq.; 481 sq.; 486; XI 22; 682
—— II, King of Naples, I 108
—— III (the Little), Prince of Durazzo,
King of Naples and Hungary, I 108
—— King of Roumania, XI 645 sq.; XII
341; 387 sq.; 397; 410; 414
—— King of the Two Sicilies. See
Charles III, King of Spain
—— II, King of Spain, character and
rule of, V 34 sq.; marriages of, ib.; 45;
49; 62; and William of Orange, 244;

338; 349; accession of, 373; administration under, 374 sqq.; 377; infirmity
of, 379 sq.; 381; 383; and the succession, 384 sq., 391 sq.; death of, 393;
will of, 392 sqq., 401; 395; 459; 523;
591; and League of Augsburg, 655;
659; 664; vi 586

Charles III, King of Spain (and of the Two
Sicilies) (Don Carlos), vi 62; 126; Italian
claims of, 138 sqq.; 147 sq.; succeeds
to duchy of Parma, 149 sqq.; 152;
conquers Naples, 153; 155; marriage of,
156; 167; 202; the Two Sicilies ceded to,
203; 237 sq.; 241; 342; and the Family
Compact, 344; 346; 351; 363; reign
of, in Spain, 366 sqq.; 443; 588; and
Benedict XIV, 590; and the Jesuits,
592 sqq.; rule of, in Naples, 596 sqq.;
death of, 382; viii 778, 782; x 142;
206; and reforms in Spanish America,
274 sq.

—— IV, King of Spain (Prince of the
Asturias), vi 366; 374; 381; 384; viii
189, 782; ix 72; 302, 428; arrests his
son. Ferdinand, 429; and the revolution
of Aranjuez, 430 sqq.; forced abdication
of, 433; x 232; 283; and Mexico, 303

—— VIII (Karl Knudson), King of Sweden
and Norway, ii 600

—— IX, King of Sweden, ii 630, 632 sq.;
Sweden delivered by, iv 158; 160 sq.,
164; organises a revolt, 165; rule of,
166 sq.; 169 sq.; concludes Peace of
Teusin, 171; attacks Finland, 172; becomes King, 173; invades Livonia, 174;
government of, 175 sq.; death of, 177;
178; 179; martial reign of, 180; 183;
565; patriarchal government of, 568;
576; v 578

—— X Gustavus, King of Sweden, at
Prague, iv 394; 426; accession of, 427,
576; at Warsaw, 428; first Danish war
of, 429; second Danish war of, 432;
England and, 429, 541; reign of, 576–91;
620; and Baltic struggle, v 146 sq.; and
Denmark, 344, 562; and Poland, 344,
349, 505; 558; and the succession, 563;
and Hetman Chmielnicki, 599; 643;
death of, iv 433, 589, v 147, 344; vi
664

—— XI, King of Sweden, v 49; 527;
563; government of, 567; 568; and war
of Scania, 569 sq.; and peace treaties
of 1679, 571; character of, 572; and his
advisers, 573 sq.; and "Reduction" of
1680, 574 sqq.; domestic policy of, 576
sqq.; and Gottorp, 580; and Charles XII,
584 sq.; and Patkul, 586; and League
of Augsburg, 655; death of, 576, 579, 584

—— XII, King of Sweden, v 417; 527;
572; birth of, 576; 579; and Denmark,
580 sqq.; invades Norway, 583; character
and training of, 584 sq.; coronation of,
585; 586; and Duke of Gottorp, 580;
587; and the great Northern War, 587

sqq.; at Narva, 588 sq.; and Augustus II,
589, 592; invades Poland, 592; and
Stanislaus Leszczynski, 593; Treaty of,
with Augustus II, 595; and the Russian
peace overtures, 596; enters Grodno,
597; at Holowczyn, 598; and Mazepa,
599 sq.; in the Ukraine, 600; defeated
at Poltawa, 601; in Turkey, 602 sqq.;
at Bender, 606; rejects neutrality compact, 607; 680; and "Stettin Sequestration," 609; at Stralsund, 610 sq.;
and the third anti-Swedish league, 611;
in Scania, 612; and peace negotiations
with Russia, 613 sq.; 659; and Frederick I
of Prussia, 666 sq.; death of, 583, 614,
vi 34, 104; ib. 23 sqq.; 33 sqq.; and the
Old Pretender, 97; and the Jacobites,
104; 125; 192; and Stanislaus Leszczynski, 193, 196; 206; 695; 735; 741

Charles XIII, King of Sweden (Duke of
Sudermania), vi 779; viii 789; ix 37–8;
323, 329; xi 677; xii 281

—— XIV, King of Sweden (Jean-Baptiste-
Jules Bernadotte), Marshal of France,
viii 581 sq., 642; French Minister of
War, 671, 673 sq., 676 sq.; and Brumaire, 678, 681; ix 21–2; commander of
1st French army corps, 252; marches to
Würzburg, 253; marches to Munich, 254;
on Ingolstadt, 255; on Salzburg, 256;
pursues Kutusoff, 257; at Iglau, 258; ordered from Iglau, 260; at Austerlitz, 261;
receives Ponte Corvo, 111; 268, 274; defeats Tauenzien, 275; at Jena, 276; at
Naumburg, 277; at Zehdenick, 279; pursues Blücher, 280; at Thorn, 284; at
Mohrungen, 285; 287; at Hamburg, 296;
in Holstein, 298; 303; in Zeeland, 300;
313; choice of, as Prince Royal of Sweden,
321 sqq.; in Jutland, 322; commands
the French army, 358; becomes Prince
Royal of Sweden (August, 1810), 379;
relations of, with Alexander, 487; joins
Allies, 521; and Reichenbach plan,
522; character of, 525; attacks Oudinot,
526; at Dennewitz, 530; crosses the
Elbe, 532; 533; at Leipzig, 538; and
the invasion of France, 542; 543; besieges Hamburg, 544; and French throne,
555; and Congress of Vienna, 582;
loses Ponte Corvo, 652; ambitions of,
661; and European concert, x 19, 36;
xi 677; character and influence of,
678 sq.; constitutional position of, 680;
Norwegian policy of, 681; foreign policy
of, 682 sqq.; and the Tsar Nicholas, 684;
domestic policy of, 684 sqq.; death of,
686; 688; xii 274; 282

—— XV, King of Sweden, character and
reign of, xi 688 sqq.; death of, 690; xii
273 sq.; and Norway, 282 sq.

—— Archduke (of Austria), 3rd son of
Leopold II, vi 656; viii 336, 497, 579;
in Italy, 581 sq.; 634; at Stockach,
655 sq., 661, 663; ix 56; 68, 247, 250;

commander of the army of Italy, 250 sqq.; escapes to Bohemia, 255; in Italy, 257; retreat of, before Masséna, 258; 259; advice of, to Emperor Francis, 262; interview with Napoleon, *ib.*; army gathered in Bohemia under, 283; policy of, 288; 342, 343; Minister of War in 1805, 346; operations of, 347–55; 359, 580; x 357; 473; and the Belgian throne, 539; xi 152

Charles, Archduke (of Styria), and marriage with Mary Queen of Scots, ii 586 sq.; iii 165 sqq., 268, 698 sqq.

—— Prince of Wales. *See* Charles I and Charles II, Kings of England

—— Albert, King of Sardinia, x 114 sqq.; reforms by, 123; 129; 142; d'Azeglio and, xi 66; 70 sq.; 75 sq.; 78; grants Constitution, 80; and the war with Austria, 82 sqq.; and Italian Federation, 90; 121; 207; abdication of, 366; 367; 379; 545; 547; and Pius IX, 706; death of, 93

—— Albert, Elector of Bavaria. *See* Charles VII, Emperor

—— Edward, Prince (the Young Pretender), vi 74; 91; 106; at Paris, 110; in Scotland, 111 sqq.; in England, 114; character of, 116; retreats to France, 117; 160; 249; 817; death of, 118; x 625

—— Emmanuel III, King of Sardinia (Prince of Piedmont), v 432; vi 30; and the war with Austria, 152 sqq.; and Preliminaries of Vienna, 155; 159 sqq.; and Maria Theresa, 236 sq.; 239; 241; 243 sqq.; and Peace of Aix-la-Chapelle, 249; 362; 366; and the Papacy, 589; 608 sq.

—— Emmanuel IV, King of Sardinia, viii 644, 654, 660 sq.; ix 41; 71, 73, 79

—— Emmanuel, Duke of Savoy. *See* Savoy

—— Felix, King of Sardinia, x 116–7; 123

—— Gustavus, Count Palatine. *See* Charles X Gustavus, King of Sweden

Charles-Louis, Infante, son of the Prince of Parma, claims of, to Tuscany, ix 602

Charles, Philip of Sweden, Duke of Södermanland, iv 176 sq.; death of, 183

—— the Bold, Duke of Burgundy. *See* Burgundy

—— Madame de, ii 97

Charleston (South Carolina), founded, vii 35; threatened by Prevost, 219; siege of (1780), 222 sq.; Leslie at, 227; evacuated (1781), 231, 307; population of, 359; and the Tariff, 376, 382; and slavery, 387; Democratic National Convention at (1860), 445; forts of, 446 sqq.; Sherman captures (1865), 529, 552; 551; Federal attack on (1863), 553 sq.; naval operations at, 565; banks of, 610; blockade-running at, 620

Charlestown, settlement of, vii 16; fortified, 17

Charlet, Nicolas-Toussaint, x 489; xi 24

Charlevoix, Pierre François Xavier de, vii 90, 93, 103

Charlotte, Empress of Mexico, xi 484

—— Tsaritsa of Russia, v 538

—— Princess, daughter of George IV, engagement of, ix 690, x 541

—— Sophia, Queen of Great Britain, consort of George III, vi 434; 474 sq.; ix 690

Charlottenburg, convention signed at (1806), ix 282

Charlottetown, Confederation conference at, xi 770

Charnacé, Baron Hercule-Girard de, agent of Richelieu, iv 117; missions of, 135,142; mediator between Poland and Sweden, 187, 192; in Sweden, 194; Treaty of Bärwalde and, 198; sent to Munich,210; succeeded by d'Avaux, 402

Charnock, Job, founder of Calcutta, v 699

—— Richard, Prior of St Mary's, Oxford, i 643

Charolais, and Treaty of the Pyrenees, iv 620

Charpentier, Jean de, geologist, xi 260

Charras, Jean-Baptiste-Adolphe, French officer, xi 113; 136

Charron, Pierre, iii 70

Charterhouse, James II and the, v 335

Charters, fort at, xii 639

Chartism, rise of, x 681 sqq.; the Charter itself, 683 sq.; decline of, xi 19

Chartley, Mary in custody at, iii 291

Chartres, siege of (1591), iii 50; assembly at, 659; coronation of Henry IV at (1594), 662; German force at, xi 607

—— Charles-François de Monstiers de Mérinville, Bishop of, vi 162

—— Jean-Baptiste J. de Lubersac, Bishop of, viii 156; 179

—— Philip, Duc de. *See* Orleans, Louis Philippe Joseph, Duc de

—— Duke of (son of the Regent Orleans). *See* Orleans, Louis, Duke of

—— Sieur de Ferrières-Maligny, Vidame de, Huguenot intriguer, iii 3, 15, 19

Chase, Salmon Portland, vii 428 sq., 445; Secretary of Treasury, 450, 568 sqq., 599, 607; Chief Justice, 546, 633 sq., 653

Chashniki, Wittgenstein's advance to, ix 501

Chassé, Baron David Hendrik, Dutch general, x 537; 543

Chasseloup-Laubat, Justin-N.-S.-P., Marquis de, xii 131

Chassin, Charles-Louis, French journalist, xi 488

Chaste, Aymard de, admiral for Don Antonio, iii 501

Chastel, Jean, iii 664

Chastelain, Georges, historian, I 415, 433
Chastelard, Pierre de Boscobel de, III 268
Chasteler, J. G. J. A., Marquis du. *See* Du Chasteler
Châteaubriand, François-Auguste, Vicomte de, VI 40; 826; 830 sqq.; x 4; *Le génie du christianisme*, IX 130 sq., 188, x 5, 53, 100; *Réflexions politiques*, 43; 44; 47; 49; *La Monarchie selon la Charte*, 51; 55; and the *Débats*, 59; 60; states the demands of the Ultras, 62; 63; ambassador in Berlin, 68; influence of, 72; policy of, in Berlin, 73; ambassador in London, 74; advocates a war policy, 79; and Congress of Verona, *ib.*; Minister of Foreign Affairs, *ib.*; dismissed, 80; 82; opposes Villèle's financial scheme, 83, 86; 89; and Villèle, 90 sq.; and literature of Restoration, 100 sqq.; *Les Martyrs*, 100, XI 523; x 103; ambassador in Rome, 153 sq.; confession of faith of, 159; and Spanish affairs, 225 sq.; 230; and Spanish America, 309; 490; 494; 508; 514; XI 508; 519; 528; XII 829
Châteaubriant, Treaty of (1487), I 393
Château-Gontier, battle at, VIII 355
Châteauneuf, Catholic army at, III 11
—— Charles d'Aubespine, Marquis of, imprisonment of, IV 142; excluded from general amnesty, 593; and the Duchess of Chevreuse, 596; exiled, 607; and the House of Condé, 609; recalled, 612; 613; dismissal of, 614 sq.; death of, 618
—— Paul de l'Hôpital, Marquis de, French ambassador at St Petersburg, VI 322
—— Pierre-Antoine de Castagnères, Marquis de, French Minister at the Hague, V 610
Châteauroux, Madame de, VI 330
Château-Thierry, granted to John Casimir, III 30; Allies at, IX 547
Château-Vieux, mutiny of regiment of, VIII 192, 226
Châtelet, Florent-Louis-Marie, Duc de, VIII 162, 179
Châtelhérault, Assembly of (1605), III 681-2
—— James Hamilton, 2nd Earl of Arran, Duke of, II 454; made Regent of Scotland, 456 sq.; treaty of with Henry VIII, 458, 460; regency, 555-9; 573 sq., 575; III 261-3, 270
Chater Sing, Sikh officer, XI 741
Chatham, V 169; Dutch attack on (1667), 150 sq., 154, 188
—— John Pitt, 2nd Earl of, VIII 294, 297; lieutenant-general, commander of Walcheren expedition, IX 239, 358; and Catholic emancipation, 678; 681, 682
—— William Pitt, 1st Earl of, Vol. VI, Chap. XIII (1); 40; 42; 56; 62; 71; early years of, 73; advent to power of,

74 sqq.; 81; 87; 263; 272; Frederick the Great and, 298, 324, 328; policy of, in the Seven Years' War, 342a sqq. (in Vol. XIII); and the negotiations with France, 343, 345, 425 sq.; fall of, 346; 352; 365; 367 sq.; 423 sqq.; and Peace of Paris, 429; 430; and Wilkes, 431; and colonial policy, 433; 434 sq.; created Earl, 436; administration of, 436 sqq.; resigns, 439; 442; and America, 447; 448; 450; and Reform, 465; and Indian affairs, 567; Clive and, 570; 597; in power (1757), VII 131 sq., 137, 146 sq.; and Stamp Act, 150; 152; retirement of, 154; 155; 162; x 599; 605; 703
Châtillon, the family of, III 6, 8
—— Gaspard III de Coligny, Marshal de, at Maestricht, IV 697
—— Isabelle de Montmorency, Duchess of, influence of, on Condé, IV 609, 616; exiled, 617
—— Odet de Coligny, Cardinal de, Bishop of Beauvais, Archbishop of Toulouse, II 300; III 11
—— *See also* Coligny *and* D'Andelot
—— Chouan leader in Anjou, IX 2; 14
Châtillon-sur-Seine, Conference at (1814), IX 481, 546 sqq., 552, 577, x 9
Châtillon-sur-Sèvre, Westermann defeated at, VIII 353
Chattanooga, Buell ordered to, VII 500 sq., 506; Confederates at, 508; evacuated, 509; Rosecrans blockaded in, 510 sq.; battle of, 512 sq., 616; and the campaign of the West, 520; 551
Chatterton, Thomas, poet, VI 831; 832; x 698; 710
Chaumette, Pierre-Gaspard, Vice-President of the *Conseil Général* of the Commune, VIII 251; *Procureur*, 252, 338, 349, 356, 359
Chaumont, Treaty of (1814), VII 366, IX 550, 576 sqq., 589, 605, 646, 666-7, x 7, 9, 11, 16, 481, 519
—— Marquis de. *See* Amboise
Chauncey, Isaac, American naval officer, VII 341
Chauvelin, François-Bernard, Marquis de, French ambassador, VIII 296 sqq., 301 sqq.; ordered to leave England, 305; x 91
—— Germain-Louis de, French Foreign Minister, VI 147; 149; 156; 160; career of, 162 sq.; disgrace of, 163
Chaux de Fonds, Republican movement in, XI 253
Chaves, Soult crosses the Portuguese border near, IX 449
—— Friar Diègo de, confessor of Philip II, III 518
—— Manuel de Silveyra Pinto de Fonseca, Marquis de, x 321
Chavigny, Léon Le Bouthillier, Comte de, rival of Mazarin, IV 593; driven from the Council by *les Importants*, 596; imprisoned, 607; attached to Condé, 609;

reappears at Court, 612; Chief Minister, 614; removed, 615; death of, 617 sq.

Chavigny, French diplomatist, VI 615

Chazal, Jean-Pierre, member of the Convention, VIII 515, 677, 684, 686

Chebreïss, repulse of the Mamelukes at (1798), VIII 601

Chechen river, Russian troops on, XII 581

Chefkin, Constantine, XI 614

Cheke, Sir John, Greek professor at Cambridge, I 580, 581; committed to the Tower, II 518

Chékhoff, Anton P., Russian poet, XII 317

Chelm, diocese of, X 449; added to West Prussia (1815), 463

Chelmsford, Frederic Augustus Thesiger, 2nd Lord, XII 35

Chelnokóff, and Russian economic reform, XII 327

Chemin, Nicholas du, Calvin and, II 352

Chemistry, history of. *See* Science

Chemnitz, Banér defeats Archduke Leopold William near, IV 379; Austrians in, VI 297

—— Friedrich, poet, XI 412

—— Martin, theologian, II 714; III 704

—— Philip Bogislav von, Swedish historiographer, sent to Nürnberg, IV 216; and *De ratione status in Imperio*, 384

Chemulpo, Russia and, XII 507; 522; 579; Russian ships captured at, 580; 581

Chênedollé, Charles Julien Pioult de, IX 132

Chêng-Kwang Hall, at Peking, XII 504

Cheng-tu-fu, travellers at, XII 797

Chénier, André-Marie de, poet, VI 834; XI 520; 549

—— Marie-Joseph de, poet, *Fénelon*, VI 823; VIII 28, 366, 387; Theophilanthropist, 501; 515

Chenonceau, meeting of Don John and the Queen-Mother at, III 31

Cherasco, Peace of (1631), IV 60, 115, 117, 138, 226; and Treaty of Westphalia, 405; armistice of (1796), VIII 567

Cherbourg, British attacks on (1758), VI 342*b* (in Vol. XIII); port improvements at, IX 120; French flotilla at, 209; XI 31; naval works at, 332; 582; 587

Cherchen, Russian explorer at, XII 799; 803

Chereia, Oudinot at, IX 501

Cheriton (near Alresford), Royalists defeated at, IV 323

Cherkasky, Alexander, Prince, at Astrakhan, V 544

—— Alexis, Prince, V 557; councillor, VI 303

—— Vladimir, Prince, XI 615; 629; XII 298; 336

Cherkesses, The, and Russia, XI 274

Chernaieff, Michael, Russian general, XI 630 sq.; Commander of Servian army, XII 386

Chernaya Dolina, Tartars repulsed at, VI 305

Chernaya Napa, Swedish reverse at (1708), V 598

—— river, battle on, XI 322; 373

Chernigoff, annexed by Ivan the Great, V 479 sq.; 504; trade depression in, XII 319; 322; 327; disorder in, 353

—— Prince of, V 481

Cherniskevsky, Nicholas, Russian socialist, XI 630; XII 296 sq.; 302

Chernuisheff, Count Zachary, general in Seven Years' War, VI 294, 299, 326, 328; and Poland, 668 sq., 671; 697; 731

Chernysheff, Russian Minister of War (1830), X 465

Cherson, Catharine II at, VIII 315

Chertkoff, Governor-General of Kieff, XII 307

Cherubini, M. L. C. Z. S., IX 135

Chesapeake and *Leopard*, naval fight, VII 329 sqq., 333 sqq.

—— and *Shannon*, naval fight, VII 342

Chesapeake Bay, French fleet defeats the English at (1781), VI 453, VII 230; in the Civil War, 452, 470

Cheshire, petitions to Parliament from, IV 291; Royalist rising in, 540

Chesnelong, Pierre-Charles, French politician, XII 109; 116

Chesney, Francis Rawdon, General, X 558

Chester, James II and Tyrconnel at, V 307; William III sails from, 313; Fenians in, XI 344

Chesterfield, Philip Dormer Stanhope, 4th Earl of, V 70; VI 70; 77; 79; 84; VIII 21

Chétardie, Marquis de La. *See* La Chétardie

Chevalier, Étienne, French Minister, I 409

—— Michel, political economist, XI 298; 470; 637

Chevaliers de la Liberté, X 68

Chevert, French officer, at Prague, VI 236

Chevreul, Michel Eugène, IX 133

Chevreuse, Marie de Rohan, Duchess of, marriage of, to Luynes, IV 125; exiled, 131; and Châteauneuf, 142; excluded from general amnesty, 593; returns to Paris, 596; 597; De Retz and, 609; offended by Condé, 612

Cheynell, Francis, and Chillingworth, V 746

Chiabrera, Gabriello, Italian poet, V 69

Chiana, Val di, drainage of, VI 603

Chiaramonti, Gregorio Bernabò. *See* Pius VII, Pope

Chiari, Imperial army at, V 402

Chiasso, French army feints a crossing at, IX 61

Chiavenna, early history of, IV 35 sq.; 44 sqq.; march of Feria on, 55 sq.; 58; Treaty of Monzon and, 59; Rohan and, 61; sovereignty of the Grisons in, 63; ceded to Austria, IX 660

Chiavone, Italian brigand, XI 531

Chicago, growth of, vii 444; National Republican Convention at (1860), 445; labour disturbance at, 669 sq., 707

Chichegoff, General, Governor of Blagovestchensk, xii 521

Chicheley, Sir John, Rear-Admiral, v 196

Chichérin, Russian politician, xii 311 sq.

Chichester, William Chillingworth at, v 746

—— Arthur, Baron Chichester of Belfast, Lord Deputy of Ireland, 1603–15, iii 588, 612–6; nobility of the Pale and, iv 515 sq.

Chickahominy river, McClellan's operations on, vii 475 sqq.

Chickamauga, battle of (1863), vii 509 sqq.

Chickasaw Bayou, unsuccessful assault on (1862), vii 502

Chico, Francisco, chief of the Madrid police, xi 560

Chieregati, Francesco, papal nuncio in Germany, ii 32, 170

Chieri, retained by France (1559), ii 94, iii 400

Chièvres. *See* Croy

Chifanoja (Il Schifanoya), Venetian ambassador to England, iii 264

Chifu, negotiations at, xii 501; 512; 514

Chigi, Agostino, and Leo X, ii 10, 14; 17

—— Fabio, Cardinal. *See* Alexander VII, Pope

Chikuzen, *daimiō* of, xi 846

—— governor of, dismissed, xi 865

Child, Sir Francis, banker, v 266

—— Sir John, Governor of Bombay, v 698 sq.

—— Sir Josia, chairman of East India Company, v 699 sqq.

Childers, Hugh C. E., Chancellor of Exchequer, xii 41

Chili, the Spaniards in, v 683; Republic of, vii 368; trade of, with California, 402; and the United States, 649, 666; British expedition to, ix 753; administration of, x 248 sq.; negroes in, 260; the Indians in, 268; French settlers in, 276; revolutionary developments in, 278, 282; independent government formed in (1811–2), 287; recovered by Peru (1816), 290; invasion of, by San Martín (1817), 291 sq.; Lord Cochrane's services to, 292; royalists suppressed in (1830), 295; history of, after 1830, 300 sq.; independence of, recognised by United States, 308; Mastai-Ferretti (Pius IX) in, xi 72; xii 672; affairs in (1833–1902), 677 sqq.; 684; 689 sq.; foreign capital in, 694; arbitration by, 722

—— (China), disturbances in, xii 517

Chilianwala, battle at, xi 741

Chillingworth, William, supports Laud, iv 280; 320; v 326; 332; 745 sqq.

Chiloe, x 277; surrenders to Chilians (1826), 295

Chimkent, Russian capture of, xi 630

Chin Kiang, attack on foreigners at, xii 517

China, Dutch trade with, iii 638; tea brought to Europe from, iv 712; route to, v 512; Russia and, 544; U.S. treaty with (1868), vii 635, (1880), 649; South American trade with, x 255; British trade with, 760; intercourse of, with Western Powers, Vol. xi, Chap. xxviii (1); 259; Treaty of, with Russia (1858), 273; England and France and, 308; Napoleon III and, 476; and Japan, 823 sq.; affairs in (1858–1909), xii 500 sqq.; 4; 9 sqq.; war of, with Japan, 52; and France, 131 sq.; 345; 485; and Tibet, 490, 492; Indian troops in, 493; 498; and Annam, 524 sqq.; 543; Japan and, 552, 557 sq.; and the Macao coolie trade, 555; 556; and Korea, 567, 569 sq.; and Formosa, 572; treaty of, with Russia (1902), 576; 625; 644; 761; exploration in, 792; 793; Russian trade with, 795; the unveiling of, 796 sqq.; 801 sqq.

—— Company (French), vi 173; 533

—— Sea, Russian fleet in, xii 599

Chincha Islands, Spanish occupation of, xii 678

Chinchon, Count of, Councillor of Philip II, iii 514

Ching, Prince, xii 520

Chingis Khan. *See* Genghis Khan

Chinhai, capture of, xi 809

Chinhat, Sir Henry Lawrence at, xi 748

Chining Chow, missionaries murdered near, xii 513

Chinkiang, attack on, xi 809

Chinnampo, Japanese troops at, xii 581, 585

Chinon, Catholic force at, iii 11

Chinsura, capitulation of (1759), v 697, vi 556, 558

Chioggia, War of, between Genoa and Venice, i 258 sq.; 264

—— Bishop of (Jacopo Nacchianti), ii 666

Chios, attacked by the Venetians, v 365

Chippenham election petition, vi 72

Chippewa, American victory at (1814), vii 343

Chisholm of Strathglass, vi 105

Chitral, annexed by Great Britain, xii 52, 487; 458; 489; 802

Chittagong, xi 727 sq.

Chitu, leader of Sindhia levy, xi 725 sq.

Chiulien-ch'êng, Chinese retreat from, xii 511

Chivasso, retained by France (1559), ii 94, iii 400

Chiverny, Philippe Hurault, Comte de, Chancellor of France, iii 42, 44

Chlapovski, Stanislas, Polish general, x 472

Chlopicki, Joseph, Polish general, and the Polish revolution, x 465 sqq.

Chlum, Prussian army at, vi 242; 279

Chmel, Josef, Austrian historian, xii 829

Chmielnicki, Theophilus *or* Bogdan, Cossack leader, iv 580; Hetman of Little Russia, v 504 sq.; 599

Choate, Rufus, American lawyer, VII 744
Chobrakit. *See* Chebreïss
Choczim. *See* Khoczim
Chodkiewicz, Jan, Palatine of Samogitia, III 89
—— John Charles (son of Jan), Polish general, IV 174 sq.; in Livonia, 176; heroic defence of Khoczim by, 189
Choiseul, César, Duc de, Sieur du Plessis-Praslin, Marshal of France, in Italy, IV 601
—— Étienne-François, Duc de, French Minister of Foreign Affairs, VI 323 sq.; 330; 341 sqq.; and the Family Compact, 344 sq.; 346 sq.; and the Jesuits, 348, 592; foreign policy of, 349 sqq.; 353; Polish policy of, 354; fall of, 355 sqq.; 358 sq.; and Spain, 367 sq.; 373; and the negotiations with England, 418, 425 sqq.; and Corsica, 439; 594 sq.; VII 97; VIII 51, 82, 400
—— Count de, at Vienna, VI 343
Choiseul-Praslin, Duc de, French Minister of Foreign Affairs, VI 348
Choiseul-Romanes, Madame de, VI 341
Choisy, de, State Councillor, at Breisach, IV 382
—— French officer, VI 355
Cholat, François-Joseph-Eugène, French politician, XI 136
Cholet, Republican siege of, VIII 354
Cholmley, Sir Hugh, betrays Scarborough Castle, IV 313
—— Sir Roger, Lord Chief Justice, II 518
Chōshiu, clan and *daimiōs* of, Vol. XI, Chap. XXVIII (2) *passim*; XII 551 sq., 562
Chotek, Count Rudolph Christian, Chancellor of Bohemia and Austria, VI 639
Chotusitz, battle of, VI 234 sq.
Chouans, The, IX 2; in the West, 13; suppression of, 16 sq.
Chouet, Robert, Cartesian philosophy and, IV 791
Chow Han, Chinese writer, XII 516
Chrapovitzki, Alexander Wassiljewitch, private secretary to Catharine II, VI 699
Chrestien, Florent, III 69
Chrétien, Michael, and Gallicanism, V 76
Christ Church (Oxford), founded by Wolsey, II 434
Christensen, Jens Christian, Danish statesman, XII 293
Christian Brothers, French religious association (1680), V 79
—— Union, of Swiss Catholic States (1527), II 329 sq.
Christian I (of Oldenburg), King of Denmark, Norway and Sweden, II 600; Duke of Schleswig and Count of Holstein, 601; accession of, IV 563; XI 226
—— II, King of Denmark, Norway and Sweden, II 144; Lutheranism adopted by, 169; 203; 217; defeated by Lübeck, 228 sq.; Reformation in Denmark and, 601-8; *Stockholms Blodbad* and, 604;

flight of, 608; attempted restoration of, 614; IV 158
Christian III (Duke of Schleswig and Holstein), King of Denmark and Norway, II 77, 220, 229 sqq., 250, 444; becomes Lutheran, 611; and the struggle for the Crown, 614; accession of, 615; the Reformation in Denmark under, 615 sq.; reign of, in Norway, 619; peasant servitude and, IV 562; partition of Schleswig-Holstein and, 563; 564
—— IV, King of Denmark, and James I, III 569, 572; 644; 655; visions of, IV 6; 8; and German Protestantism, 26, 33, 70; and the war of 1623-9, 85-109 *passim*, 191; Richelieu's grant to, 129; seeks peace, 135; war of, with Sweden, 176 sq., 179; and Gustavus Adolphus, 179 sq., 182 sq., 186, 194, 211, 560; and the Peace of Lübeck, 192; offers mediation at Danzig, 193; John George of Saxony and, 225; 233; 365; mediates at Hamburg, 387, 396; and at Osnabrück, 398, 402; signs Peace of Brömsebro, 390; minority of, 564; character of, 565; relations of, with Sweden, 566; failure of, as reformer, 567; 568; 570; heroism of, 571; decline of, 572 sq.; death of, 573; 585; 676; compelled to lower Sound dues, 703; 706; VI 735
—— V, King of Denmark, accession and character of, V 561; war of, with Sweden, 44, 568, 570; and the Treaty of Fontainebleau, 571; 578 sq.
—— VI, King of Denmark, VI 738 sq.; 741 sq.
—— VII, King of Denmark, VI 742 sqq.; 746 sqq.; 755; VIII 279; IX 48
—— VIII, King of Denmark, XI 226; and the crown of Norway, 680 sq.; accession and reign of, 693 sq.; death of, 64
—— IX, Prince of Glücksburg, afterwards King of Denmark, named successor by the London Conference, XI 226 sq.; 338; and Schleswig-Holstein, 438 sq., 696; 641; XII 292 sq.
—— Prince of Denmark, death of (1647), IV 573
—— Cistercian monk, first bishop of Prussia, V 629
Christianae Religionis Institutio, by John Calvin, II 287 sq., 356 sqq., 363, 376
Christiania, occupied by the Swedes, V 583; Charles XIV in, XI 681; 688; University of, 700
Christianismi Restitutio, of Servetus, II 411
Christianopel, Peace of (1645), IV 572
Christiansborg, Slave Coast station, V 691
Christianstadt, Scanian fortress, VI 770
Christie, Charles, traveller in Asia, XII 800
—— Thomas, writer, VIII 758
Christina, Queen of Sweden, birth of, IV 186; accession of, 223; Oxenstierna and, 224; instructions of Gustavus and, 220;

Treaty of Wismar and, 370; 381; Frederick William and, 384; Imperial overtures for Peace transmitted to, 391; favours Salvius, 402; "satisfaction" of militia of, 404; minority of, 568 sq.; Swedish finances under, 570; 572; character of, 574 sq.; and the Swedish succession, 575; coronation of, 576; abdication of, *ib.*, v 146; iv 590; a pupil of Descartes, 779, 786 sq.; v 564; 744; and the Great Elector, 639, 641; ix 44

Christina of Schleswig-Holstein, Queen-consort of Charles IX of Sweden, carries on the government on death of Charles, iv 177; death of, 183

—— of Denmark. *See* Milan, Duchess of

—— of France, daughter of Henry IV, iii 685; marriage of, with Prince of Piedmont, iv 129; Duchess of Savoy, 148

—— Princess Palatine (sister of Elector Frederick IV), iii 710

Christliches Bürgerrecht (league between Zurich and Constance), ii 328–9

Christopherson, John, Bishop of Chichester, editor of Philo, i 613, 616

Chrudim, Prussians at, vi 234

Chrysoloras, Manuel, Greek scholar, i 541 sq., 546

Chrzanovski, Adalbert, Polish officer, x 468; 470; commands the Piedmontese army, xi 93

Chuartschen, bridge of, destroyed, vi 282

Chuguchak, Russian factories at, xii 796

Chuguieff, military insurrection in (1819), x 438

Ch'un, Chinese prince, xii 501; 521

Ch'ung Chi, Manchu official, xii 501

Chung K'ing, opened to trade, xii 508, 512

Chunghow, Chinese ambassador to Russia, xii 503

Chuquet, Arthur, historian, xii 834

Chur, flight of Giammastino Visconti to, iv 35; the *Gotteshaus* at, 36 sqq.; Diet at, 42; Catholics march on, 43, 44; Protestants attack, *ib.*; *Strafgericht* in, 46; 47 sq.; 52; Baldiron's march on, 55, 56; Rohan at, 61, 63

—— Carl Rudolf von Buol-Schauenstein, Bishop of, deported, ix 202

—— Hartmann II, Bishop of, iv 35 sq.

—— Freiherr Ortlieb von Brandis, Bishop of, iv 36

—— Paul Ziegler, Bishop of, claims the Valtelline, iv 36

Church Militant, The (by G. Herbert), iv 768

Church rates, English, legislation concerning, xi 345

—— Sir Richard, x 176; joins the Greek insurgents, 182; 202

—— Richard William, Dean of St Paul's, *History of the Oxford Movement*, xii 841

Churchill, John, Duke of Marlborough. *See* Marlborough

Churchill, Lord Randolph Henry Spencer, Chancellor of the Exchequer, xii 45; 46

Churrem. *See* Roxolana

Churubusco (Mexico), Scott's victory at (1847), vii 396

Churwalden, Catholic district of, iv 43 sq.

Chusan, British occupation of, xi 808 sq.; 818

Chuvas, rising of, vi 681

Chytraeus, David, Lutheran divine, iii 174, 704

Cialdini, Enrico, Italian general, xi 469; 534; 536; 542

Ciampini, Giovanni Giustino, founder of the *Accademia fisico-matematica*, v 740 sq.

Cibber, Colley, dramatist, v 129

Cibò, Caterina, Italian reformer, ii 392 sq

—— Francheschetto, i 110; 227; 233

—— Giovanni Battista. *See* Innocent VIII, Pope

—— Giulio, plots against Genoa, ii 84

Ciceruacchio. *See* Brunetti, Angelo

Cienfuegos (Cuba), port of, blockaded, vii 678

Cilento, revolt at (1828), x 119

Cimarosa, Domenico, x 131

Cincinnati, settlers at, vii 357; trade of, 360; Abolitionists in, 387; threatened by Confederates (1862), 507; Convention at (1872), 640, (1876), 645

Cinq-Mars, Henry Coiffier de Ruzé, Marquis of, conspiracy and execution of, iv 151 sq.; 155

Cinthio. *See* Giraldi, Giovanbattista

Cintra, Convention of (1808), ix 137, 318, 441; revolt at, xi 573

Circassians, Russians and, vi 674

Circles of the Empire (*Reichskreise*), i 294, 320 sq., 459

Cirillo, Neapolitan lawyer, vi 599

Cirilo, Fray, ex-General of the Franciscans, x 222

Cisalpine Club, formation of, x 626

—— Republic, viii 589 sqq., 633, 639, 645; fall of, 657; frontier of, ix 69; organisation of, 83 sqq.; x 131 sq.

Cisneros, Garcia di, Abbot of Monserrat, i 651; the *Exercitatorio de la Vida Espiritual*, ii 657

—— Leonor de, Spanish martyr, ii 408

—— Marqués de, Spanish admiral, x 285 sq.

—— Ximenes de. *See* Ximenes, Cardinal

Cispadane Republic, viii 583, 588

Cistercians, 15th century reform of the, in Spain, ii 399; in Brandenburg, v 619

Cisterna, Prince Emanuele della. *See* Della Cisterna

City Point, held by Butler (1864), vii 516; Grant at, 520; Lincoln at, 537, 544

Ciudad Real, Sebastiani defeats Cartaojal at (1809), ix 450

—— Rodrigo, captured (1706), v 416; del Parque's army falls back on, ix 455;

besieged by Ney (1810), 458 sq.; Masséna retreats to, 462, 463, 465; Wellington at, 468; revictualled by French, 469; Wellington again attacks, 470; capture of (1812), 471

"Civil script," introduced into Russia by Peter the Great, v 531

Civiltà Cattolica, Jesuit journal, xi 714; 718; 721

Cività Castellana, Neapolitan defeat at (1798), viii 652

—— Vecchia, occupied by the Imperialists (1527), ii 56; water supply of, iii 438; Stukeley sails from (1578), 597; Jesuits land at, vi 372; 593; seized by Joseph Bonaparte, ix 194 sq.; xi 71; 122; French troops recalled from, 496; xii 213; French frigate at, 239

Civitella, siege of (1527), ii 91

Clamecy, seized by the Democrats, xi 137

Clam-Martinič, Count, Bohemian politician, xii 177; 188

Clancarty, Richard le Poer Trench, 2nd Earl of, at the Congress of Vienna, ix 580; 585 sqq.

Clan-na-Gael, in America, xii 75 sq.

Clanricarde, Ulick de Burgh (Bourke), 1st Earl of, the MacWilliam, iii 584

—— Ulick Bourke (de Burgh), 5th Earl, 1st Marquis of, succeeds Ormonde as Deputy (1650–2), iv 535

Clapperton, Hugh, African explorer, xii 807

Clare election, x 645 sq.

—— John Fitzgibbon, Earl of (Lord Chancellor of Ireland), and Catholic Emancipation, ix 678; Attorney-General, 693; 697 sqq., 701, 706

Clarenbach, Adolf, Lutheran martyr, ii 202

Clarence, George, Duke of, i 464 sq.; ii 447

—— William, Duke of. *See* William IV, King of England

"Clarendon Code," v 97–103

Clarendon, Edward Hyde, 1st Earl of, Root-and-Branch petition and, iv 292; 293; on the attempt on the Five Members, 298; on parties, 305; on the Ironsides, 312; on Newcastle, 322; on the Self-denying Ordinance, 326; with Prince of Wales at Bristol, 328; on the troops, 334; 554; King submits Monck's proposals to, 555 sq.; on parliament, 558; on Monck, 559; party of, 620; v 93 sq.; and the religious settlement, 96; 97; 100; charged with high treason, 101; and Parliament, 102; opposes acts against Irish trade, 104; foreign policy of, *ib.*; and the marriage of Charles II, 105; 106; and the Dutch war, 108; 113; the fall of, 114; exile of, 115; 136; 198; policy of, 199; 201 sq.; 231; Scottish Privy Councillor, 280; 305; 333; 745

—— Edward Hyde (Viscount Cornbury), 3rd Earl of, v 255; vi 17; Governor of New York and New Jersey, vii 48

Clarendon, George William Frederick Villiers, 4th Earl of (2nd cr.), vii 636; British ambassador at Madrid, x 237; Viceroy of Ireland, xi 13; Foreign Minister, 309; 313; 322; 632; and China, 822; xii 21; 23; 28

—— Henry Hyde, 2nd Earl of, Lord Lieutenant of Ireland, v 234, 306; 247; and the Revolution settlement, 249 sq.; 255 sq.

Clarete, Ibrahim. *See* González Bravo

Clark, William, explorer, vii 326, 364

—— William Tierney, engineer, x 744

Clarke, Sir Alured, in Cape Colony, ix 749

—— Sir Andrew, Governor of the Straits Settlements, xii 532 sq.

—— George Rogers, American general, vii 221 sq.

—— Sir George Sydenham, xii 59

—— Henri-J.-G., Comte d'Hunebourg, Marshal of France, Duc de Feltre, viii 582; receives the duchy of Feltre, ix 111; 136, 271; Minister of War, 303; 307; x 47; 54

—— Richard, Major, defeats Karim Khan, xi 726

—— Samuel, vi 77 sq.

—— Father, confessor of Philip V of Spain, vi 145

Clarkson, Thomas, and the slave trade, vi 188, 472

Clary, Count, Austrian statesman, xii 202

Classics, Renaissance discoveries and printing of, i 550, 561 sq., 566, 576. *See also* Renaissance

Clauberg, Johann, Cartesian philosophy and, iv 789, 791

Claude, daughter of Louis XII of France, afterwards Queen-consort of Francis I, i 395, 454

Claudia, Archduchess, widow of Archduke Leopold (1637), iv 375

—— Felicitas, Empress, 3rd wife of Leopold I, v 211

Clausel, Comte Bertrand, Marshal of France, pursued by Wellington, ix 473; 478; retires to the Ebro, 474; pursues Mina, 476; opposed at the Dordogne, 617; command of, 624; x 496; and the colonisation of Algeria, 502 sqq.

Clausius, Rudolph Julius Emmanuel, and the theory of heat, xii 784 sq.

Clavering, Sir John, general, vi 571 sq.

Clavière, Étienne, assistant to Mirabeau, viii 150; Minister of Finance, 223 sq., 263, 339; suicide of, 357; 702

Clay, Henry, American statesman, vii 350, 367, 373 sq., 378; Tariff bill introduced by, 382; 383 sq.; and Texas, 393; compromise resolutions of, 403 sqq.; death of (1852), 418; 419

Clayborne, Maryland trader, vii 32 sq.

Clayton, John Middleton, American politician, vii 434

Clayton-Bulwer Treaty (1850), VII 434, 649, 656

Clemanges, Nicholas de, I 618

Clemenceau, Georges - Benjamin - Eugène, French statesman, XII 112 sq.; and the Dreyfus affair, 120; 122; opposes socialism, 124; 126; 128

Clement V (Bertrand de Goth), Pope, I 620

—— VII (Giulio de' Medici), Pope, I 250, 353; II 4–20; pontificate of, 21–8, 48–58; 143; Luther and, 171 sq.; Charles V and, 197, 203, 210, 219, 439; dislike of, to the General Council, 216 sq.; Francis I and, 220, 440; Zurich and, 322; João III and, 412, 414; 423 sq.; the divorce of Henry VIII and, 430–41; the Archbishopric of Lund and, 610; church reform and, 642; the question of prohibited books and, 687; III 105; friendship with France, 110, 186; and Florence, 388, 470; 460; 466; 479; XII 705

—— VII (Robert of Geneva), anti-Pope, I 108

—— VIII (Ippolito Aldobrandini), Pope, the Index and, II 687 sq.; III 397; 416; 418; 445; 450; James I and, 554 sq.; 608; Henry IV and, 660, 667, 671, 677; 702; 710; 719; and Sweden, IV 170; elected, 666; policy of, 667 sq.; death of, *ib.*; 686

—— IX (Giulio Rospigliosi), Pope, and Charles II, of England, V 202; and Jansenism, 84, 89 sq.; 202; 420; and the Peace of Baden, 454 sq.; and the Prussian monarchy, 665 sq.; 743

—— XI (Giovanni Francesco Albani), Pope, VI 97; 124; 131; 586 sq.; and the Bull *Unigenitus*, 588; 589; death of, 125

—— XII (Lorenzo Corsini), Pope, VI 150; 587 sqq.

—— XIII (Carlo Rezzonico), Pope, VI 421; 592 sq.; death of, 594; *Febronius* condemned by, X 158

—— XIV (Giovanni Vincenzo Antonio Ganganelli), Pope, VI 348; 594 sq.

—— Bulgarian Metropolitan, XII 409

—— Saxon agent in Berlin, VI 206 sq.

Clément, Jacques, III 47, 453, 766

Clercq. *See* Du Clercq

Clerfayt, François-S.-C.-J. de Croix, Comte de, Austrian general, VIII 408, 417, 420, 435; succeeds Coburg, 436 sq., 442 sq.

Clerke, Sir Philip Jennings, VI 450; 455 sq.

Clerkenwell, Fenian outrage in, XI 344, XII 65, 75

Clermont, county of, ceded to France, V 33; rising at, X 492

Clermont, The famous voyage of (New York to Albany, 1809), VII 692

Clermont, Jean-Baptiste Massillon, Bishop of, V 80

—— Louis de Bourbon-Condé, Count de, VI 246; 248

Clermont-en-Auvergne, royal commission at, V 16

Clermont-Tonnerre, Jules - Charles - Henri, Duc de, Commandant of Dauphiné, VIII 112

—— Comte Stanislas de, and the election of the States General, VIII 131; 158, 173, 178, 183, 187; *Report of* 1789, 689, 733

Cleveland, Stephen Grover, President of the United States, VII 653 sqq.; and the currency, 656 sq., 659 sq., 665, 668; 669; and the Venezuelan dispute, 670 sqq.; and Cuba, 675; XII 56; 687 sq.

Cleves, war of Charles V with (1543), II 77, 244; the French in, V 406, 650; 627 sq.; 640 sq.; acknowledges sovereignty of Brandenburg, 645; religious tolerance in, 649; 655; 668; evacuated by the French, VI 300; ceded to Murat, IX 262, 267, 409; democratic land reform in, 410; 624

—— Treaty of (1666), IV 408, V 645

—— Adolf II, Duke of, I 424

—— Adolf of. *See* Ravenstein

—— Anne of, Queen of Henry VIII. *See* Anne of Cleves

—— John I, Duke of, I 441

—— John (III) de La Marck, Duke of. *See* Jülich-Cleves-Berg

—— Philip of. *See* Ravenstein

—— Sibylla of. *See* Saxony

—— William (V) de La Marck, Duke of. *See* Jülich-Cleves-Berg

Clifford, Sir Conyers, Governor of Connaught, III 323, 606–7

—— Lady Margaret, married to Andrew Dudley, II 511

—— Sir Robert, I 468

—— of Chudleigh, Thomas, 1st Baron, V 198; 201 sq.; signs the Treaty of Dover, 204; 205; Lord Treasurer, 207; 209; and the Test Act, 210; resigns, 333

Clifton, Jacobite force at, VI 115

Clinton, Edward Fiennes de Clinton, 9th Baron, II 545, 567

—— George, American statesman and general, VII 373

—— Sir Henry, General, VII 173, 211, 215; succeeds Howe (1778), 217; 220, 222, 224 sqq., 230

—— Henry Fynes, historian, XII 836

—— Sir William Henry, IX 297; general in Portugal, X 321

Clive, Robert Clive, Lord, in India, V 697; Vol. VI, Chap. XV (3) *passim*; 438; death of, 566

Clones, Owen O'Neill defeated at, IV 526

Clonmacnoise, meeting of Catholic clergy at, IV 534

Clonmel, captured by William III (1690), V 315; Reconciliation meeting at (1828), X 648

Clontarf, meeting at, prohibited, XI 8

Clootz ("Anacharsis"), Baron Jean Baptiste du Val de Grâce, leads a deputation to the National Assembly, VIII 171; IX 363

Clot Bey, and vaccination in Egypt, XII 451

Clouet, Jean-François, professor of chemistry at Mezières, VIII 433

Clough, Arthur Hugh, XI 352; 354

Clozel, African explorer, XII 130

Clubs, French Revolutionary. See Jacobins, *Feuillants*, etc.

Clugny, William de, I 441 sq.

—— de Nuis, Jean-E.-B., French Comptroller-general, VIII 74, 88

Clusius, Carolus. See L'Écluse

Cluverius, Philip, IV 717

Clyde, Colin Campbell, Lord, at Balaklava, XI 319; 741; 746; at Lucknow, 748 sq.

Cnossus, discoveries at, XII 846

Coahuila, State of, VII 392, 394

Coalitions (against the French Revolution), the first, Vol. VIII, Chap. XIV *passim*, 398–446; the second, Chap. XXI, 633–64; the third, Vol. IX, Chaps. IX, X

Cobb, Howell, U.S.A. Secretary of the Treasury, VII 447; 605

Cobbett, William, *Political Register*, IX 688; X 576 sq.; 580 sq.; in America, 582; and Bentham, 598; 599; in Parliament, 656; 675; and the growth of London, 742

Cobden, Richard, X 680; 764; and Free Trade, 771; and Adam Smith, 777; XI 2 sq.; and the political parties, 20; 309; and the Anglo-French commercial treaty, 333 sq., 470; 325 sq.; 764; and China, 815; XII 745

Cobenzl, Count John Philip, Imperial Vice-Chancellor, VI 652 sq.; VIII 329, 419, 536; and Partition of Poland, 548 sq., 551; 591; at Rastatt, 641; succeeds Thugut, 642, 644 sq.; IX 184

—— Louis, Comte de, Austrian diplomatist, at St Petersburg, IX 41; 65; at Paris, 66; 69, 79; Foreign Minister, 248; replaced by Stadion, 262; 315

Coberger, Antony, of Nürnberg, printer, I 634, 641

Cobham, Sir Henry, III 34

—— Richard Temple, Viscount, VI 35; 70

Coblenz, Council of (1479), I 689; captured by the French (1794), VIII 437; the Prince of Prussia at, XI 396

Coburg, Luther at, II 211–4; Lannes near, IX 275

—— See Saxe-Coburg

Cocceius (Koch), Johann, theologian, V 754 sq.; 757

Cochabamba, province of, X 265; 268

Cochelet, Adrien-Louis, French consul-general at Alexandria, X 567

Cochin, fortified by Portuguese, I 30; commercial glory of, IV 743; lost to Portuguese, 744

Cochius, Christian, Prussian Court preacher, V 671

Cochlaeus, Joannes, German theologian, I 684–5; II 168, 212, 251

Cochon de Lapparent, Comte Charles, Minister of Police, VIII 490, 504 sq., 508, 510; transported, 512

Cochrane, Sir Alexander Forrester Inglis, Lord, blockades Ferrol, IX 217; sails for West Indies, 224; Rear-Admiral, 234; attacks Brest, 238; harries Duhesme in Catalonia, 239

—— John, explores Siberia, XII 794

—— Thomas, Earl of Dundonald. See Dundonald

Cockburn, Admiral Sir George, conducts Napoleon to St Helena, IX 757

Cockerill, John, engineer, X 744; 753; 757

Cocks, Richard, the Dutch and, IV 734; at Firando, 740

Coconato, Count Annibale, adventurer, III 23–4

Coddington, William, founder of Aquednok, VII 20, 24

Codes of law, English, Peel's reforms in criminal law, X 585; penal, in England and Ireland, 620 sqq.; French, *Code Louis*, V 16; projects of the civil, at the end of the Revolutionary period, VIII 740 sqq.; penal, beginnings of, at the same time, 742 sqq.; criminal, *ib.*; of Napoleon:—the Civil, IX 150 sqq.; the Criminal, 171 sqq.; the Penal, 175 sqq.; the Commercial, 176 sqq.; *Code Noir*, French Canadian, VII 101; in Italy, the Napoleonic abolished, X 137; Consalvi's attempt to get a new Civil Code, 138; Russian, Catharine II's, VI 686 sqq.; attempts at codification from 1804–15, X 417 sq.; *Svod Zakonoff*, XI 264; in Spanish America, *Cédulas*, X 250; 254 sqq.; Turkish, "Pearl" and *Multeka-ul-Ubhar*, I 98

Codrington, Christopher, Governor of the Leeward Islands, V 690

—— Sir Edward, British admiral, and the battle of Navarino, X 195–6; 197; 201

—— Sir William John, General, XI 322

Codure, John, Jesuit, II 652 sqq.; III 585–6

Cœur, Jacques, French merchant, I 409, 414, 503, 504 sq.

Coeuvres, Annibal d'Estrées, Marquis de, Marshal of France, occupies the Valtelline, IV 58 sq., 41, 129, 674 sq.

Coeverden, Dutch success at (1672), V 160

Cognac, Huguenot leaders at (1569), III 12; League of (1526), II 24, 52; effect of, on Charles V's German policy, 197; 427, 512

Coigni, François de Franquetot, Comte de, Marshal of France, VI 153 sq.; 240

Coimbra, University of, VI 388; XII 271; Moore's march into Spain by way of, IX 443; occupation of, by Masséna, 461; X 315; 322; Dom Miguel at, 335; 336

Coinage and currency, English, debased under Henry VIII, II 470; English Mint and Re-coinage Act (1696), V 268 sq.;

General Index. 299

currency difficulties between England and the American colonies, VII 68 sq.; English (1793–7), IX 675 sq.; settlement of (1819), X 587; the bimetallic question, XII 50; French (c. 1792), VIII 702 sq.; under Napoleon I, IX 121 sq.; Indian, decline of silver and its results in India, XII 483 sq.; Prussian, under Frederick the Great, VI 710 sq.; Russian, reformed (1700), V 528; after the revolutionary wars, X 414 sq.; after 1856, XII 323; Spanish, in the late 15th and early 16th centuries, I 357; in New Spain, X 258; Swedish, debased, II 622; in the United States during the Civil War, VII 569 sq., 607, 612 sq., 615 sqq.; after the war, 631, 643; 657, 668 sqq.

Coke, Sir Edward, Chief Justice, and agrarian legislation, II 469; III 563 sqq.; Parliament and, IV 263, 269; Petition of Right and, 270; V 252; Hobbes and, VI 792

—— Sir John, III 567 sqq.

Colalto, Count Rainbold von, Imperialist general, IV 60; besieges Mantua, 136

Colberg, Gneisenau's defence of, IX 332

Colbert, Charles. See Croissy, Marquis de

—— Jean-Baptiste, Marquis de Seignelay (contrôleur général), Minister under Mazarin, IV 621 sq.; under Louis XIV, V 1, 4 sq.; and Fouquet, 6; character and aims of, 6 sqq.; and taxation reforms, 8 sq.; industrial and commercial projects of, 10 sqq.; and war with Holland, 10; and French colonies, 13, 684; and internal customs of France, 13; and improvement of canals and roads, 14; and French navy, 14; creates five new Academies, 15; and administration of justice, 16; rivalry of, with Louvois, 16 sq.; 22; 25; and the municipalities, 27; 39; and the dispute with the Papacy, 85; 200; and African trade, 692; and India, 702; and the Académie des Sciences, 741; death of, 17, 28; VI 224; 532; 639; and the (French) Company of the West, VII 70, 78 sqq.; policy of, in Canada, 84 sq., 109; in West Indies, 85 sq.; VIII 8, 37, 69; IX 176; 362

—— Jean-Baptiste (the younger). See Seignelay, Marquis de

—— Comte de, French ambassador at St Petersburg, IX 103

Colbjörnsen, Christian, Danish Procurator-general, VI 756

Colborne, Sir John, 1st Baron Seaton, General, at Waterloo, IX 640

Colchester, siege of (1648), IV 349 sqq.; the plague in, V 110

—— Charles Abbot, 1st Lord, Chief Secretary for Ireland (1801), Speaker of the House of Commons (1802), IX 706; X 634

Cold Harbour, Sheridan seizes, VII 519

Coldstream, Monck at, IV 547

—— Guards, V 113

Cole, Dr Henry, expelled from New College, II 501; at Colloquy of Westminster, 568

Colebrooke, Henry Thomas, XII 845

Coleman, Edward, and the Popish Plot, V 220 sqq.

Colenso, British reverse at, XII 642

—— John William, Bishop of Natal, XI 788; XII 774

Coleraine, plantation of, III 614; offered to City of London, 615; fugitives in, V 307 sq.; 309

Coleridge, Samuel Taylor, V 122; VI 829; 832; 836 sq.; VIII 641, 766 sqq.; X 600; 704 sqq.; 710; 713 sq.; 716; 720; 722; 725; XI 347; 365

Colesberg Kopje, diamonds discovered at, XI 787

Colet, John, Dean of St Paul's, I 491, 580, 644

Colettis, Joannis, Greek statesman, X 506

Colfax, Schuyler, American statesman, VII 653

Coligny, Gaspard de, Admiral of France, I 48, 50, 55; II 92, 295; at the Assembly of Notables, 298, 302 sq.; at St Quentin, 547; III 2, 4, 5, 6–14, 16–20, 224, 232, 285

—— Louise de, 4th consort of William of Orange. See Orange

—— Jean de Coligny-Savigny, Comte de, French general, V 347

—— Odet de. See Châtillon

Colladon, Jean Daniel, physicist, XI 260

College, Stephen, conviction of, V 228

Collegiants, a community of Remonstrant dissenters, V 754

Collegium Germanicum, set up in Rome, II 655; (1552), III 149, 161, 178; and the German Jesuit colleges, IV 4

—— Romanum, founded under Julius III, II 655; III 424

Collegno, Giacinto di, X 114 sq.

Collenbach, Reichsfreiherr Heinrich Gabriel von, Austrian diplomatist, VI 346

Colletta, Pietro, Italian historian, X 111; 113; 125; XII 842

Colley, Sir George Pomeroy, in South Africa, XII 39; 637

Collier, Sir George, vice-admiral, VI 449

—— Jeremy, V 128; 130

—— Robert Porrett. See Monkswell, Lord

Collings, Jesse, XII 43

Collingwood, Cuthbert, 1st Baron, VIII 454, 463; Vice-Admiral, ordered to sail for West Indies, IX 224; meeting of Nelson with, 225; blockades Cadiz, 227; commands half the fleet at Cadiz, 229; in command at Trafalgar, 230; 233; compared with Nelson, 233; 237; 239

Collins, David, Lieutenant-Governor of New South Wales, IX 740

—— Richard Henn Collins, Lord, XII 721

Collins, Samuel, physician to the Tsar Alexis, v 513
—— William, poet, vi 824; 828; 830; 832; 834 sq.; x 698 sq.
Colli-Ricci, Baron Louis-L.-G. Venance de, Sardinian general, viii 438, 444, 558, 565, 567
Colloredo, Radolf, Graf von Waldsee, Imperial Field-Marshal, iv 240; at Prague, 394
Colloredo-Mansfeld, Jerome, Count von, guards Bohemia, ix 533
Colloredo-Waldsee, Count Francis C. von, Austrian diplomatist, xi 252
Collot, French banker, viii 677
—— d'Herbois, Jean-Marie, viii 226, 246 sq., 264; on the *Comité de Salut Public*, 344, 349 sqq., 358, 360, 362; and the fall of Robespierre, 364 sq., 369, 374 sq.; trial of, 380, 384; deported, 385
Colmar, ceded to the French, iv 143; Bernardine army at, 383; victory of Turenne at (1675), v 44
Colocci, Angelo, Roman patron of literature, ii 15
Cologne, early political insignificance of, i 299; Diet of (1505), 316 sqq., (1512), 320; Catholicism in, iii 156, 160; 171, 180; Electorate of, invaded by Prince Maurice, 673; peace congress at, 704–5; centre of Dutch immigration, 705; troubles in Electorate of, 707; Canons of, at Strassburg, 709; Matthias' policy of repression in, iv 11; death of Mary de' Medici at, 139; congress at, 396; and Avaux, 398; Chigi Nuncio at, 402; commercial and industrial insignificance of, 420; conferences at (1636), 688; treaty of, with Louis XIV (1671), v 42; peace conference at (1673), 43; election of archbishop of, 54 sq., 63; war of, with the United Provinces, 157 sq.; peace signed (1674), 161; 435; captured by the French (1794), viii 437; Electorate of, ix 93; Lutheran consistories at, 204; cessions to Prussia in, 657; Cardinal Pacca at, x 134, 355; revolutionary movement at, xi 157
—— Baron Clemens August von Droste-Vischering, Archbishop of (1835), x 381; xi 50
—— Electors of:—
—— Clement Augustus of Bavaria, vi 202
—— Ernest of Bavaria, election of, iii 708; obtains Münster, 709; 711 sq.; 719; 731 sq.
—— Ferdinand of Bavaria, iv 83; 91; 210; appeal of, to France, 226; the peace negotiations of 1634–5 and, 252; truce of Ulm and, 391; Maximilian of Bavaria and, 398; Hildesheim ceded to, 408
—— Frederick III of Saarwerden (1372), i 669
—— Gebhard I von Mansfeld, iii 156

Cologne, Electors of (*contd.*):—
—— Gebhard II Truchsess von Waldburg, iii 707, 709
—— Hermann of Hesse (d. 1508), 3rd son of Landgrave Louis II (d. 1458), i 316
—— Hermann von Wied, ii 40, 239, 243, 251 sq., 259, 682; iii 707
—— Joseph Clement, v 53 sqq.; 404; 455
—— Maximilian Henry, Bishop of Hildesheim and Liége, iv 426; supports Ferdinand Maria of Bavaria, 430; v 54
—— Maximilian, Archduke of Austria, viii 313
—— Salentin of Isenburg resigns, iii 707
Coloma (California), gold at, vii 400
Colombe, Michel (French sculptor), i 414
Colombey, battle of, xi 589
Colombia, Republic of (New Granada, Venezuela and Ecuador), vii 368; proclaimed by Bolívar (1819), x 294; 295 sq.; divided into three Republics, 297; attitude of the Indians in, 299; independence of, 308 sq.
—— Republic of (New Granada), U.S. Treaty with, rejected (1869), vii 637; purchases Swedish war-ships, xi 683; xii 672 sq.; 684; and the United States, 685 sq.; 690; 692 sqq.; 696; and the Panamá Canal, 698 sqq.
Colombo, held by the Portuguese, iv 744
—— Bartolomeo, i 21 sq.
—— Cristoforo, discovery of New World by, i 7, 21–4; 11, 34 sqq., 55
Colombus, Realdus, v 725
Colomera, Martin, Spanish general, viii 440
Colón, railway in, xii 685
Colonia del Sacramento, settlement of, vi 391; smuggling post, x 258; captured by Indian militia (1706), 270
Colonial Association (German), xii 159; 658
Colonisation and Colonies, Belgian, King Leopold II and, xii 255 sq.; of late years, *ib.*, Chap. xx *passim*
—— Danish, in the West Indies, vi 186
—— Dutch, in the earlier half of the 17th century, iv 703 sqq.; *see* Chap. xxv, The transference of colonial power to the United Provinces and England, 728–59; Vol. v, Chap. xxii *passim*; in the 18th century, vi 186 sqq.; in East India, in the 19th century, xi 667 sq.; in S. Africa, 778–89; of late years, *see* Vol. xii, Chap. xx *passim*
—— English, early schemes of colonisation in the New World, *see* Vol. i, Chap. ii; *see* Vol. iv, Chap. xxv, The transference of colonial power to the United Provinces and England, 728–59: toleration in, v 101; Council for Foreign Plantations formed (1660), 107; Chap. xxii *passim*; Walpole's policy in regard to, vi 50 sqq.; after Walpole's fall, 53 sqq.; Chap. vi, Financial experiments and colonial development, 168–90; and their relations with the French in India and America, Vol.

Colonisation and Colonies (*contd.*)
  VI, Chap. XI *passim*, 329–60; in America, and French rivalry, 410 sqq.; schemes of colonial federation, 412 sq.; in America, 18th century fiscal policy and its results, Chap. XIII (2) *passim*, 423–56; in America, *see* Vol. VII, The United States, Chaps. I–VII; *see* Vol. IX, Chap. XXIII (ii) (1783–1815); removal of trade restrictions concerning, X 586 sq.; Chap. XXI, Canada, *passim*, 685–95; Adam Smith and, 765; policy of 1841–52 concerning, XI 16 sq.; and Mr Joseph Chamberlain's policy, XII 57; in the Malay Peninsula, 531 sqq.; *see* Vol. XI, Chap. XXVII, Great Britain and her Colonies, 754–801; of late years, *see* Vol. XII, Chap. XX *passim*, 602–71; boundary of British Guiana, 687 sq.

—— European in general, preparation for the wide extension of, in Africa, the East and America, Vol. I, Chap. I, The Age of Discovery, 1–36; characteristics and fate of first schemes of colonisation; *see* Chap. II, The New World, 37–66; reaction of, on the Old World, *ib.* 47 sqq.; Vol. VI, Chap. VI, Financial experiments and colonial development, 168–90; of late years, *see* Vol. XII, Chap. XX, 602–71

—— French, early schemes of colonisation in New World, *see* Vol. I, Chap. II; under Colbert, V 12 sqq.; Chap. XXII *passim*; Vol. VI, Chap. VI, Financial experiments and colonial development, 168–90; and their relations with the English in India and America, Chap. XI *passim*, 329–60; Choiseul's relation to, 351 sq.; in America, and English rivalry, 410 sqq.; Vol. VII, Chap. III, The French in America (1608–1744), 70–113; Chap. IV, Conquest of Canada (1744–61), 114–43; effects of the Revolution in, VIII 193 sq.; taken by English (1803–15), IX 240; projects of the Consulate, 419 sqq., *see also* L'Ouverture, Toussaint; in N. Africa (from 1834), X 503 sqq.; since 1870, especially in Africa and Indo-China, XII 128 sqq.; in Annam, 523 sqq.; colonial policy in Siam, 536; of late years, *see* Chap. XX *passim*, 602–71

—— German, early colonial activity of Brandenburg, V 646–7; beginnings of modern German colonial policy, XII 159 sqq.; *see* Chap. XX *passim*

—— Italian, in Africa, the *Colonia Eritrea*, XII 240 sq.

—— Japanese, in Formosa, etc., XII 572 sqq.

—— Portuguese, in the Age of Discovery, *see* Vol. I, Chap. I; in New World, *see* Chap. II; *see* Vol. IV, Chap. XXV *passim*, The transference of colonial power to the United Provinces and England, 728–59; Vol. V, Chap. XXII *passim*; in the 18th century, VI 187, 189; *see also* Brazil; in the 19th century, XI 575; from 1875, XII 270; of late years, *see* Chap. XX *passim*

Colonisation and Colonies (*contd.*)
  —— Scottish, in New Jersey, VII 47 sq.; in the Carolines, 55; in Georgia, 62; in Acadia, 75, 112 sq.; Darien Scheme, V 296 sq.

—— Spanish, in the New World, *see* Vol. I, Chap. II; under Philip IV and Olivares, IV 655 sq.; *see* Chap. XXV *passim*, Transference of colonial power to United Provinces and England, 728–59; Vol. V, Chap. XXII *passim*; declining energy of, VI 186; 189; under Charles III, 373; Falkland Islands dispute, *ib.*; condition of, and Congress of Aix-la-Chapelle (1818), VII 366 sq.; Vol. X, Chap. VIII, Spanish Dominions in America, *passim*, 244–79; Chap. IX, The establishment of independence in Spanish America, *passim*, 280–309; loss of remainder of, XII 264 sqq.; in Philippine Islands, 528 sqq.; of late years, *see* Chap. XX *passim*, 602–71; end of Spanish dominion in Continental America, 689 sqq.

—— Swedish, in America, VII 40, 55, 57, 702

—— Venetian, *see* Vol. I, Chap. VIII *passim*
Colonna, family of the, attack on Rome by, II 53 sqq.

—— Fabrizio, I 124; captured at Ravenna, 137, 250

—— Fadrique, Prince of Butera, at Tarragona, IV 649

—— Marco Antonio, Cardinal Archbishop of Taranto, III 135; 431; 444

—— Pompeio, Cardinal, Bishop of Rieti, I 249; II 21, 57, 67

—— Prospero, and Lombardy campaign, II 44, 47 sq.

—— Vittoria. *See* Pescara, Marchioness of
Colorado, part of, ceded to United States, VII 397; and the currency question, 673; population of, 711; women's franchise in, XII 763
Colorno, Austrian check at, VI 154
Colpoys, John, Admiral, VIII 473, 475, 478
Colquhoun, Archibald Ross, in China, XII 796 sq.
Colson, John, mathematician, V 718
Coltbridge, Gardiner's Horse at, VI 112
Columba, St, at Iona, I 535
Columbanus, St (d. 615), I 535
Columbia, district of, VII 316; slavery in, 388, 402 sqq., 585 sqq.; Volunteer Militia of, 448

—— (S. Carolina), Sherman at (1865), VII 528 sq.; Sheridan at, 537

—— River, exploration of, VII 326, 364; 371, 395; operations on (1861–2), 494
Columbus (Kentucky), occupied by Confederates, VII 462 sq., 492 sqq.; evacuated, 495, 497, 559

—— Christopher. *See* Colombo
Colville, Sir Charles, General, at Hal, IX 632

Colvin, Sir Auckland, Financial Adviser to the Egyptian Government, xii 438

Colyer, Count, Dutch diplomatist, vi 32

Comacchio, occupied by Austrians, vi 586 sq., x 137, 155

Combe, Abraham, and socialism, xii 758

Combermere, Sir Stapleton Cotton, Viscount, Commander-in-chief in India, xi 729

Combes, Justin-Louis-Émile, French statesman, xii 113; 121 sq.

Combination, repeal of laws concerning, x 585; modification of the repeal, *ib.*

Combray, Marquise de, ix 136

Comenius, John Amos, educational influences of, iv 424

Coméré, Mahy de, Baron de, treatise on finance of, viii 69

Comité de Défense Générale, formed, viii 263; 268 sq.

—— *de Salut Public*, first (April 6, 1793), viii 269, 274 sq., 338 sqq., 426; second (July 10, 1793—July 27, 1794), 343 sqq., Chap. xii *passim*; reconstructed (July, 1794), 375; sphere of, reduced, 376; members of, increased to sixteen, 385; power of, increased, 387 sq., 393; and military affairs, 426; 465, 472; and the conquest of Italy, 556, 561 sqq.

—— *de Sureté Générale*, viii 349 sq., 356, 360, 362, 364, 367, 376 sq.; sphere of, reduced, 376

Commendone, Giovanni Francesco, Cardinal, Bishop of Zante, Queen Mary and, ii 519; mission to Poland of, 637; 681; papal nuncio, iii 82 sqq.; 172, 176

Commines, Jeanne de, Dame de Hallewin, i 439

—— Philip de, i 109; ambassador to Venice, 115, 282; cited, 200, 228; 393, 403; as historian and prose-writer, 415; 422, 426, 430, 438, 440; xii 830

Commission de Douze, viii 272 sqq.

Committee on the Conduct of the War (U.S.A. 1861), vii 469

Common Life, Brethren of the. *See* Brethren of the Common Life

—— Penny (*Gemeiner Pfennig*), i 304 sqq., 317

Commonwealth, the English (1649). *See under* England, Vol. iv

Commune of Paris, viii 225 sq., 228, 230, 235, 238, 240; dissolved (Aug. 30, 1792), 241; reinstated (Sept. 1), 242, 245; struggle of the Gironde and, 250 sqq., 272 sq.; and the *maximum*, 271; 338 sq.; power of, 358, 360

Communes, French, duties and powers of, before the Revolution, viii 41 sq.

—— Russian, in the 15th and 16th centuries, v 492 sq.

Comnenus, David, last Emperor of Trebizond, i 78, 82

—— John IV, Emperor of Trebizond, i 78

—— Manuel I, Emperor of the East, i 271

Como, Cardinal of, Tolomeo Gallio, Bishop of Martarano, Secretary of State under Philip II, iii 288

Compagnacci (Florentine faction), i 169, 174 sq., 181

Company of Equinoctial France, vii 79

—— of Foreign Merchants, the Dutch, formed in 1594, iv 729

—— of the Indies. *See* East India Company (French)

—— for the Islands of America, the French, iv 758; vii 70, 74, 78

—— of New France, vii 70, 73 sq.

—— of Royal Adventurers trading to Africa, v 691

—— of St Domingo, vii 91

—— of Scotland trading to Africa and the Indies, vi 91

—— of the West, Colbert's (1664), vii 70, 79, 90. *See also* East India Company (French)

—— of the West (Law's). *See* Mississippi Company

Compiègne, Edict of (1557), ii 294; the Queen-Mother at, iv 139; treaty at (1635), 144, 251, 365, 370; treaty at (1624), 675; negotiations at (1756), vi 338

Complutensian Polyglot, i 380, 578, 603, 640, 651; ii 400

Compostella, fifteenth century pilgrimages to, ii 105 sq.

Comprehension Bill (1689), failure of, v 337

"Compromise," The (1566), iii 201–3

"Compromise of 1850," The, vii 403 sqq.

Compte Rendu, Necker's (1781), viii 74, 77, 94; Lambert's (1788), 75 sq., 109 sq.

Compton, Henry, Bishop of London, v 233 sq.; 242; 255; suspended, 335; vii 59

Comte, Auguste, xi 365; 526; 707; xii 93; 850

—— François-Charles-Louis, editor of *Le Censeur*, ix 569–70

Comuneros (Spanish), revolt of the, i 357, 372 sqq.

Concha, José Gutiérrez de La. *See* La Havana, Marqués de

—— Manuel de La. *See* Del Duero, Marqués

Conciliatore, Italian review, x 124

Concini, Bartolomeo, Minister of Cosimo I, iii 388

—— Concino, *afterwards* Marquis of Ancre, and the Princes, iv 121; receives Normandy, 122; Richelieu and, 123 sq.; murder of, *ib.*; 128

—— Leonora, iv 121

Concione (Venetian Assembly), i 270

Concord (Mass.), stores at, captured (1775), vii 165

Concordats, political theory underlying, iii 758; era of, from 1816, x 139 sqq.: of the Emperor Frederick III and Pius II (1448), i 299, 687 sqq.: French, of Francis I and Leo X (1516), 388 sq.; ii 32, 38, 95, 281; abolished (1561), 300;

III 659; V 77; Napoleon I's, Vol. IX, Chap. VII, 180–207; remains in force (1818), x 56; and Jules Ferry, XII 116: Italian, of 1803, IX 189 sq.: Neapolitan, negotiations for, begun (1738), VI 588; 590: with the Kingdom of the Netherlands (1827), x 527: with Russia, Alexander I's in regard to Warsaw, etc., 424: Sardinian (1727), VI 589 sq.: Spanish, of 1851, XI 558, 709

Concordia (Lutheran), drawn up by Jacob Andreae, III 173

Condé, taken by the French (1676), V 44; 45; and the Barrier Treaties, 457 sq.; captured by the Allies (1793), VIII 347, 430; claimed by Austria, *ib.*; recaptured by France (1794), 436

—— Charlotte (de Montmorency), Princess of, wife of Henry II, III 643, 692

—— Claire-Clémence (de Brézé), Princess of, wife of Louis II, conduct of, during the Fronde, IV 610; 613; follows Condé to Flanders, 618

—— Henry I de Bourbon, Prince of, III 12, 19, 25 sqq., 155, 174, 224, 451

—— Henry II de Bourbon, Prince of, III 668 sq.; joins League of Princes, IV 119; marches to Poitou, 121; arrested, 122 sqq.; release of, 126; in central France, 127; sent against Rohan, 133; adheres to Richelieu, 134; at Roussillon, 148, 645; member of Council of Regency, 593; and New France, VII 72

—— Henri-Jules de Bourbon, Prince of (Duc d'Enghien), V 349

—— Louis I de Bourbon, Prince of, becomes a Huguenot, II 295, 297; arrest and condemnation of, 298 sq., 302; and the tumult of Amboise, 576; III 1 sqq.; killed at Jarnac, 12

—— Louis II de Bourbon (Duc d'Enghien), Prince of, trained in wars of Louis XIII, IV 149; besieges Dôle, 370 sq.; victory of, at Rocroi, 388, 594, 659; and Mercy, 389, 597; victory of, at Allerheim, 390, 597; 542; takes Thionville, 595; Orleans and, 596; in sole command, 598; at Dunkirk, 599, 703; rival of Vendôme, 601; at Court, 606 sq.; character of, 608; Retz and, 609; 610; First Fronde and, 611; imprisonment of, 612 sq.; supremacy of, 614; Second Fronde and, 615 sqq.; Spain and, 619, 660; Treaty of Pyrenees and, 620; at Seneff, V 44, 161; 45; in Franche Comté, 200, 373; 256; 340; and the Polish Crown, 349 sq.; 411; 650; VI 191

—— Louis-Joseph de Bourbon, Prince of, emigrates (1789), VIII 165; 511; IX 40

Condillac, Étienne Bonnot de, French philosopher, VI 825; XI 520

Condivi, Ascanio, II 34

Condorcet, M.-J.-A.-N.-Caritat, Marquis de, VIII 214, 249; at the King's trial, 259 sq.; suicide of, 357; *Avis aux Espagnols*, 783; 790; XII 817

Condore, English victory at, VI 548

Conegliano, Austrian army at, XI 86

—— Cima da, Venetian artist, I 284

Confalonieri, Count Federigo, x 117–9; 124; XI 75 sq.

Confederate States of America, formed (1861), VII 449; leaders in, 603 sqq.; finance in, Chap. XIX

Confederates, Irish Catholic organisation, IV 525 sqq.

Confession of Augsburg. *See* Augsburg, Confession of

—— of Faith, Calvin's, II 295

Conflans, Treaty of (1465), I 389

—— Hubert de Brienne-Conflans, Comte de (Marshal Conflans), in the Northern Circars, VI 548

Confraternities, religious, in Germany, II 108, 122

Confutationsbuch (1559), III 163

Congo, French, XII 130; 343

—— Conference, XII 161

—— Free State, XII 3; 5; 130; Leopold II and, 255 sq.; 658; 661; administration of, 662 sq.; 810

—— Reform Association, XII 663

—— river, discovery of, I 17; VI 187; the French on, XII 3, 130; 658 sqq.; explorers on, 806, 810 sq.

Congregation of Jesus Christ, II 558, 573 sqq.

Congregations of Cardinals, instituted by Sixtus V, III 446 sq.

Congress, of the (later) United States, First Continental (1774), VII 160 sqq., 181 sq., 187 sq., 201; Second (1775), 166 sq.; Third (1776), 173 sq., 207, 209, 235; composition of the, 237

Congresses (Confederate), VII 605 sqq.

Congressi degli Scienziati, XI 68

Congreve, William, dramatist, V 128; 130; 132 sq.; *Incognita* by, 136

Coni, defence of, VI 241; occupied by the French, VIII 567

Coningsby, Thomas, Baron (*afterwards* Earl) Coningsby, Irish Lord Justice, V 320

Conjeveram, Munro at, VI 576

Conjuration du 9 Mars, VIII 267 sq.

Conkling, Roscoe, American politician, VII 649 sq., 653

Connan, François, Calvin and, II 351

Connaught, religious affairs in, III 593; condition of (1592), 604; and the "Graces," IV 517; and the rebellion of 1641–2, 523 sqq.; Parliamentary party in, 530; O'Neill withdraws to, 531; final settlement of, 536 sq.; remains tranquil in 1798, 792

—— Prince Arthur, Duke of, visits China, XII 508

Connecte, Thomas, Carmelite and wandering preacher, I 676 sq.

Connecticut, English colony of, IV 747; trade of, VI 447; settlement of, VII 18 sq.,

22; regicides in, 26; charter of, *ib.*, 31; and Governor Andros, 29; defence of, 42; 53; population of, 54; religious conditions in, 57; education in, 58; effect of the Stamp Act in, 149; disaffection in, 163; British raid into (1779), 220; constitution of, 237; and custom dues, 243; and the Constitutional Convention, 246 sq., 250, 258, 260, 271, 281, 283; cessions in, 308; 336; trade of, 355; Abolition in, 361, 377, 388; negro suffrage in, 629; Democrats in, 631

Connello, "undertakers" in, III 599

Connewitz, engagement at (1813), IX 535

Cono, Johann, edits St Jerome, I 607

Conolly, Arthur, in Central Asia, XII 800 sq.

Conqueret, College of, III 54

Conquistadores, the Spanish, III 546

Conrart, Valentin, literary meetings at house of, in Paris, IV 156

Conring, Hermann, German historian and jurist, scientific work of, IV 424; XII 816

Consalvi, Ercole, Cardinal, comes to Paris (1801), IX 184; 191; claims homage for Naples, 194; resignation, *ib.*; refuses to be present at Napoleon's marriage, 197; 603; at Congress of Vienna, 586, X 2, 134 sq.; career of, 131; Secretary of Papal Conclave (1800), 132; position, influence and character of, 132; first administration of, 133; at Paris and Reims, *ib.*; opposes Napoleon, *ib.*; reinstated as Secretary of State, 134; opposes reactionary measures, *ib.*; and Metternich, 185 sq.; and the secret societies, 135; and administrative scheme of (1816), 136; and the brigands, 138; opposition to, 139; foreign policy of, 139 sqq.; and the revolutionary movements, 150; and the policy of non-intervention, *ib.*; death of, 151; and Leo XII, 152; 153; 155; O'Connell and, 635

Conscience, Hendrik, Flemish novelist, XI 673; 676

Conscription. *See* Armies

Conseil d'État, v 3

—— *des Anciens*, formed, VIII 393 sq., 489 sq.; chief members of, 507; and the *Coup d'état* of 18 Fructidor, 509, 512; 670 sqq.; and Brumaire, 676 sqq., 680 sqq. *See also* Corps *Législatif*

—— *des Cinq-Cents*, formed, VIII 393, 395, 489, 492; prominent members of, 506; and the *Coup d'état* of 18 Fructidor, 509, 512; 670 sqq.; and Brumaire, 677 sq., 680 sqq. *See also* Corps *Législatif*

—— *des Dépêches*, v 3

—— *des Finances*, v 3

—— *Privé*, v 3

Consensus Tigurinus, of Bullinger and Calvin (1549), II 340

Considérant, Victor-Prosper, x 499; XI 113

Consiglio dei Pregadi (Venetian Senate), I 271 sq.

Consilium de Emendanda Ecclesia (1537), II 33, 379, 643

—— *super Reformatione Sanctae Romanae Ecclesiae* (1537), II 644

Consistory, The, of Calvin, II 374 sq.

Consolato del Mare, IX 43

Constance, Council of (1414–8), I 295, 620, 623, 655, 677; II 107, 128, 281; Diet of (1507), I 317; refuses to publish the Edict of Worms, II 160; the Peasants' Revolt and, 179; the *Tetrapolitana* and, 212; the fathers of, III 758, 764; Horn at, IV 231, 232; IX 57; bishopric of, ceded to Baden, 94, x 361; and the revolutionary movement, XI 145; 221

—— Hugo von Hohenlandenberg, Bishop of, II 316, 324, 328, 329

Constans, Jean-Antoine-Ernest, French statesman, XII 112; 119; 125

Constant de Rebecque, Henri-Benjamin, VIII 507; 677; IX 15; 24, 427; and *Le Censeur*, 569–70; x 40; political views of, 41; *Acte-Additionnel* drafted by, 42; 45; supports the Government, 51, 60; 54; and the *Minerve*, 55; 59; 61; and the new electoral schemes, 64; 67; opposes new Press Law, 77, 89; opposes compensation for the *émigrés*, 86; *Adolphe*, 102; 103; and the Revolution of 1830, 477; XI 519

Constantine, taken by the French (1837), x 504; province of, XII 129

"Constantine, Donation of," proved spurious by Valla, I 546, 602; III 750

Constantine VIII and Constantine IX (Monomakhos), Emperors of Rome, and the Tsars, v 483 sq.

—— XII, Palaiologos, Emperor of Rome, v 482

—— Paulovich, Grand Duke of Russia, VI 674; 681; 696; 708; IX 291; policy of, 492; at Vienna, 581; Polish manifesto of, 596; x 425; divorce of, 436; and the succession to the throne, 437 sqq.; 441; and Poland, 447 sq., 451, 453 sq., 456 sqq., 466 sq.; opposes intervention in France, 465; XI 214; and the emancipation of the serfs, 615, 617; Viceroy of Poland, 629, 658 sq.

Constantino. *See* La Fuente

Constantinople, earthquake at (1509), I 89; fall of (1204), 255; captured by the Turks (1453), 281, 285; Franco-Turkish Alliance signed at, III 104; Ferdinand's embassies to, 106, 108, 118–20, 123–4; return of Solyman II to (1532), 107, (1536), 113, (1541), 119; negotiations at, 115; arrival of Venetian ambassador Badoer in, 116; adorned and improved by Solyman II, 129; rebellion in, 130; 133–4; naval preparations in, 136–7; Dutch trade with, 631; Dutch mission to (1612), 645; Bohemian and Hungarian embassy to, IV 64; Sir Thomas Roe at, 192; anarchy in, v 367; 368; 515; Treaty of (1724),

545, (1739), vi 308, (1784), viii 311; Greek Empire at, vi 506; Russian designs on, viii 278; dealings of Sweden with, ix 38; British fleet off, 235; Russian desire for, 306, 312, 313, 320, 385, 485; Queen of Naples goes to, 384; France and, 386; British fleet fails before, 388; Patriarch of, x 170, 182; Janissaries at, 171, 192; 173; Ali of Janina at, 177; 178; Russian ambassador leaves, 183; ambassadors of the Powers in, 185, 193, 195, 197; withdrawn, 198; Russian designs on, 197, 202, 546 sq., 551, 554, 562, 564; revolutions in (1808), 547; Canning in, 549; Russian fleet off (1833), 553; plots in, 556, 559; at mercy of Ibrahim, 562, 569; 565; French influence at, 567; 571; xi 276; Greek Church at, 313; xii 33 sq.; German influence in, 341; 382; revolution at, 385; conference of the Powers at, 387, 403; 389 sq.; 410; Armenian massacre in, 417; 422; revolution in (1908), 427 sq.; 435 sq.; Lord Dufferin at, 438; Young Turk party in, 455

Constantsa, port of, xii 397

Constituent Assembly. *See* National Assembly

Constitution of the Year III, viii 392 sqq., 487

—— —— *VIII. See* Consulate

—— —— *X*, ix 22 sqq.

—— —— *XII*, ix 108 sqq.

—— of *Malmaison*, drawn up by Bonaparte for Switzerland (1801), ix 98 sqq.

Constitutional Act, of Canada (1791), ix 744 sq.; x 688

Constitutional Church, of the French Revolution, civil constitution of, viii 196 sqq.; 500 sq. *See also* Chap. vii, The Concordats, *passim*

—— Society, revolutionary society (1788), vi 477

Constitutionnel, Le, French journal, x 493; xi 292

Constitutions, French, of 1791, Vol. viii, Chap. vii, 176–210

Consulate, French, of 1799, Vol. ix, Chap. i, 1–33

Consulta, Spanish, in the Netherlands, iii 198

Contarini, Alessandro, Venetian admiral (1535), iii 113

—— Alvisi, papal representative at Münster, iv 402; signs treaty between France, Venice and Sweden, 679

—— Francesco, Venetian ambassador, ii 381

—— Gasparo, Cardinal, ii 23, 33, 75; at Diet of Ratisbon (1451), 240, 398, 650; 386; Oratory of Divine Love and, 379, 641, 642; church reform and, 643 sq., 667; 648; death of, 660; iii 75, 457, 750

—— Tommaso, Venetian ambassador, iii 645

Conté, Nicolas-Jacques, French chemist, viii 606

Contemporary, Russian journal, xii 295 sqq.

Conti, Armand de Bourbon, Prince of, and Duchess of Longueville, iv 609; joins rebels, 611; imprisoned at Vincennes, 612; proposed marriage of, 613; Governor of Champagne, 614; Condé and, 615; 618

—— François-Louis de Bourbon, Prince of, v 370; 449; vi 191; 243; 246 sq.; 340

—— Louis-François-Joseph de Bourbon, Prince of, emigrates (1789), viii 165

—— General Torquato, commander of Imperial forces in Pomerania, iv 196

Continental System, ix 122 sqq.; Chap. xiii, 361–89; effects of, on British trade, 240 sqq.; and Switzerland, 425 sq.

Contra-Remonstrants (Gomarists), iii 647–55

Contreras (Mexico), Scott's victory at (1847), vii 396

—— Juan Senen de, Spanish general, defends Tarragona against Suchet, ix 465

Contrition and attrition, distinction between doctrines of, ii 126

Conventicle Act, the First (1664), v 103, 333; the Second (1670), 202, 205, 333

Convention Parliament, of 1660, v 94, 96 sq.; and church matters, 329; of 1689, 249 sqq., 259

"Convention of the Straits," of 1841, x 572

Conversino da Ravenna, Giovanni di (Latinist), i 543, 556, 558

Conway, Edward Conway, 2nd Baron, Royalist plot of, iv 314

—— Henry Seymour, Field-Marshal, vi 432; Secretary of State, 435 sqq.; 456; 463

Cony, London merchant, trial of, iv 441

Conyers, Sir John, Byron replaced by, iv 299

Conz, Bridge of, battle at, vi 4

Cook Islands, British protectorate over, xii 667

—— James, navigator, vi 182; xii 805; 814

Cooke, Edward, Under-Secretary for Ireland, ix 703

—— George, joint Paymaster of the Forces, vi 437

—— Sir George, lieutenant-general, at Quatre Bras, ix 629

Cook's Straits, xi 793

Coolgardie, gold discovered at, xii 619

Cooper, Anthony Ashley. *See* Shaftesbury, 1st Earl of

—— Fenimore, vii 742

—— Peter, Greenback candidate for Presidency, vii 646

—— Thomas, in China, xii 796

Co-operative Wholesale Society, xii 740

Cooper's Creek, exploration of, xi 795; 798; squatters in, xii 619

Coorg, annexation of, xi 730; 750
Coornheert, Dirk Volkerts, Dutch scholar, iv 718
Coote, Sir Charles, victory of, at Sligo, iv 529; 532; in Ulster, 534; Athlone surrenders to, 535; 538; in communication with Monck, 547
—— Sir Eyre, general, vi 469; 548 sq.; 554; and Mír Jafar, 558; death of, 577
—— Sir Eyre (nephew of above), viii 618; ix 358
Cop, Guillaume, royal physician, ii 351
—— Jean, Canon, ii 351
—— Michel, Protestant pastor, ii 351
—— Nicolas, Rector of University of Paris, ii 285, 351; rectorial address of (1533), 354
Cope, Sir John, lieutenant-general, vi 112 sqq.
—— officer in Indian army, vi 541
Copenhagen, University of, ii 605, 617, vi 739; *Herredag* of (1530), ii 612 sq.; recess of (1536), 620; Palatine agents in, iv 85, 89; abortive expedition of Charles X against (1658), 432, 541, 560, v 147; at Charles' mercy, iv 585; 587; relieved by Opdam, 588; negotiations at, 590; Dano-Swedish treaty signed at, 591; treaties at (1645), 602, (1660), 621, (1727), v 551; Estates at, 558; *coup d'état* at, 559 sq.; 561; 581; the plague at, 582; 583; 610 sq.; Peter the Great at, 612; vi 36; Bestuzheff at, 313; under Frederick IV, 737; under Christian VI, 738; Bernstorff at, 740; 743 sq.; 746 sqq.; 754; Conventions signed at (1780), ix 44; battle of (1801), 49 sqq., 49–50; effect of the news of, 70; bombardment of (1807), 236, 298 sq., 305; Congress proposed at, 287; important position of, 296; slow recovery of, after Napoleonic wars, xi 691; port of, xii 291; 293
Copernicus, Nicholas, i 638; ii 707; iv 777; v 708; 713; vi 792; x 137
Coppenole (of Bruges), rebel, i 446, 448 sq.
Coppermine river, exploration on, xii 814
Coppet, retirement of Madame de Staël to, ix 131; brilliant society at, 427
Coppi, Antonio, Italian historian, xii 842
Coram, Thomas, philanthropist, vii 61
Corbeil, taken by Parma (1590), iii 49
Corbet, John, Puritan author, v 331
—— Miles, regicide, v 149
Corbie, garrison at, iii 672–3
Corbière, Comte Jacques-Joseph-Guillaume-Pierre de, x 47; supports reactionary measures, 49; 54; and Richelieu, 57; 61; and the new electoral scheme, 64, 67; Minister of Education, 68; 70; appointed president of the Council of the University, 73; 74; 90
Corbon, Claude-Anthime, French politician, xi 111
Corcelles, Claude-F.-P. Tircuy de, mission of, to Rome, xi 117

Corday-d'Armans, Marie Anne Charlotte de, assassinates Marat, viii 346
Cordeliers, Club des, viii 161, 200, 267, 272
Cordier, Mathurin, French Protestant, ii 286, 351, 372
Cordilleras, mineral wealth of the, xii 692
Córdoba. *See also* Cordova
—— (Argentina), x 281; reactionary movement in, 286; 300; Treaty of (1821), 304
Cordova, scholars of, iii 545; sack of (1808), ix 437; troops at, xii 261
—— (Córdoba), Fernando Fernandez de, Spanish general, x 237, 239; xi 551; 569
—— Gonzalo Hernandez de, Prince of Venossa, Prince of Maratra y Córduba, "The Great Captain," i 115 sqq.; campaign of, in Naples, 124 sq.; 132; 196; 233; 361–5; iv 78; 80 sq.; 85; besieges Casale, 134; Ferdinand II and, 678; at Maestricht, 695
—— José de, Spanish admiral, viii 461, 463
—— or Córdoba, Luis de, Spanish admiral, vi 376; 379
Córduba. *See* Cordova
Corea, China and, xi 802; 824; 844
Corfu, devastated by Turks (1537), iii 114, 117; fleet of Triple Alliance at, 135–6; the French in, viii 590, 633; Russo-Turkish blockade of, 607, 646; revictualled, ix 237; 239; importance of, to Napoleon, 311; a centre of English commerce, 381; discussion of the fate of, 604–5; placed under British protectorate, 654
Corinne, Madame de Staël's (1807), ix 131
Corinth, siege of, by Venice (1463), i 79; occupied by the Venetians (1687), v 365
—— (Mississippi), Confederates at (1862), vii 496 sq.; Halleck's advance on, 498 sq.; battle of (1862), 501
Cork, Spanish design to seize, iii 532; trade in, 579; landing of Wolfe at (1561), 592; siege of (1569), 595; O'Donnell executed at, 596; "undertakers" in, 599; James II at, v 308; taken by Marlborough (1690), 316; the provision trade of, vi 490; Parliamentary reform in, ix 697; 705; Parnell returned for, xii 77; 88; Queen's College, 29, 71 sq.
—— Richard Boyle, 1st Earl of, Irish finance and, iv 517; Wentworth and, 518
Cormatin-Désoteux, Baron Pierre-M.-Felicité de, *Chouan* leader, viii 379
Cormenin, Louis-Marie de la Haye, Vicomte de, xi 115
Cormoy, armistice of, xi 541
Cornbury, Edward Hyde, Viscount. *See* Clarendon, Edward Hyde, 3rd Earl of
Corneille, Pierre, v 66 sqq.; 125; xi 528
Cornelio, Tommaso, Cartesian philosophy and, iv 791
Cornelius, Peter von, German painter, x 151

Cornet, Comte Matthieu-Augustin, President of the Commission of the Inspectors, VIII 677 sq.

Corneto, Adriano di, Cardinal. *See* Castellesi

Cornic-Dumoulins, Pierre-François, French admiral, VIII 466

Cornish, Sir Samuel, Vice-Admiral, VI 369; 427

Corn-laws, English, of 1815, x 590 sqq.; Irish, of John Foster (1784), VI 503 sq. *See also* Trade

Cornuda, Austrian success at, XI 86; 87

Cornudet des Chomettes, Comte Joseph, VIII 683, 686

Cornwall, rising in (1549), II 485; Spanish expeditions to, III 321, 673; condition of parties in (1642), IV 305, 314; Essex in, 323; Parliament's hold over, 332; Fairfax and Hopton in, 334; Duke of Ormond in, VI 102; parliamentary representation of, x 608; Liberalism in, XII 31

Cornwallis, Charles Cornwallis, 2nd Earl, and 1st Marquis, VI 453; in India, 475, 564, 568, 577, IX 710-5; VII 212 sq., 223 sqq.; at Yorktown, 230 sq.; VIII 92; IX 76; Viceroy of Ireland, 702; 704; death of, 730; x 629; XII 498

—— Edward, Governor of Nova Scotia, VII 121 sq.

—— Sir William, Admiral, VIII 454, 471; in charge of the English squadron off Brest (1803), IX 210 sqq.; blockades Brest, 213 sqq.

Coro, Miranda lands near, x 281; royalist city, 288

Corocoro, siver mines at, v 682

Coromandel, the Dutch and, IV 711; the Great Elector and, v 646; the Dutch in, 695, 697; coast, the, VI 534 sq.; 538; 547; 549; dynastic wars on, 551; 577

Coron, seized by Andrea Doria, III 108; negotiations for surrender of, 109

Coronel, Pablo, Spanish scholar, II 400 sq.

Corot, Jean-Camille-Baptiste, painter, XI 528

Corporation Act, of 1661, v 97; terms of the, 329

Corps Législatif, formation of, VIII 393 sqq., Chap. XVI *passim*

Corpus Christi (Texas), Taylor at (1845), VII 394

Corpus Christi Day, observation of, ceases in England, II 503

Corpus Inscriptionum Graecarum, XII 821; 844

—— *Inscriptionum Latinarum*, XII 843

—— *Juris Canonici*, new edition of, II 686; III 742

—— *Misniacum* (1559), III 150

Correro, *or* Cornaro, Giovanni, Venetian ambassador, in France, III 275

Correspondant, Le, French journal, x 500

"Corresponding" Princes, III 715 sqq.

Corrichie, battle at, III 268

Corrientes, insurgents in, XII 681

Corro. *See* Del Corro

Corryarrack, Pass of, VI 112

Corsica, given up by French (1558), II 54; offered to Cosimo de' Medici, III 386; granted to the Genoese, 478; France and, VI 439, 610, 623; Jesuits in, 593; 608 sq.; blockaded by the British (1793), VIII 458; evacuated (1796), 461; failure to grow cotton in, IX 125; bishops and priests transported to, 197

Cort, Henry, and iron manufacture, x 733

Corte, Bernardino de, betrays Milan, I 121

Cortenberg, Letter of (1312), I 419

Cortereal, Gaspard, Portuguese explorer, I 36

Cortés, Hernan, invades Mexico, I 41 sqq.; II 101

Cortese, Gregorio, Abbot of San Georgio Maggiore, Venice, II 33, 379; the Oratory of Divine Love and, 641; church reform and, 643; monastic reforms of, 647

Corti, Count, Italian Foreign Minister, XII 394; at Constantinople, 402

Cortina, Manuel, Spanish statesman, XI 551

Cortois de Pressigny, Gabriel, Bishop of St Malo; later Archbishop of Besançon, x 140

Cortona, Silvio Passerino, Cardinal of, II 56

Corunna, Spanish Armada at, III 310, 506; sack of, 318; Irish refugees at, 504; Irish Catholics at, 529; departure of new Armada from (1596), 529; VI 105; blockaded, 125; French ships take refuge at, IX 211; Villeneuve reaches, 226; Baird lands at, 443; 444; British retreat to, 445 sqq.; battle of (1809), 446; revolt at (1820), x 216; and the West Indian trade, 275

Corvetto, Count Luigi Emmanuele, French Minister of Finance, x 47; 50

Corvey, Abbey of, IX 90; acquired by Prussia, 657

Corvinus, Matthias. *See* Matthias Corvinus, King of Hungary

Coryate, Thomas, traveller, VI 515

Corzana, Count, Imperial plenipotentiary at Utrecht, v 439

Cosa, Admiral de, XI 87

Coscia, Cardinal, VI 587; 589

Cosimo I. *See* Tuscany, Grand Dukes of

Cosin, John, Bishop of Durham, *Book of Devotions*, IV 273

Cosmao Kerjulien, Baron Julien-Marie de, Spanish commodore, IX 233

Cosmati, The, III 438

Cossacks, rising of, VI 681; 695; Russia and, XI 273

Cossé, Artus de, Comte de Secondigny, Marshal of France (Marshal Cossé, brother of Marshal Brissac), III 10 sqq.; 22, 24

Costa, Andrea, Italian socialist, XII 231 sq.

Costa, Isaac da, Dutch poet, xi 676
—— de Beauregard, Count Henry of, viii 780
Costa Rica, xii 672; and the Clayton-Bulwer Treaty, 686
Coster, Samuel, Dutch dramatist, iv 720
Cotes, George, Bishop of Chester, ii 531
—— Roger, mathematician, v 720
Cotta, Johann Friedrich, Baron de Cottendorf (German publisher), ix 588; x 361
—— Frau Ursula, Luther and, ii 110
Cottbus. See Kottbus
Cotterau (Cottereau), Jean, *Chouan* leader, viii 379
Cotton, Sir Willoughby, General, xi 728
Coucy, Edict of (1535), ii 286 sq.
Coulanges, Fustel de. See Fustel de Coulanges
Coulmiers, German defeat at, xi 603; 606
Council, the Great (at Venice), closing of (1296), i 160, 271 sqq.
—— of Blood (1567), iii 216 sqq.
—— of the Forty-eight at Florence, iii 387-8
—— of Notables, viii 66; summoned, 100 sq., assembles (1787), 102 sqq., dissolved, 105; reassembled (1788), 116, dissolved, *ib.*
—— of Regency. See *Reichsregiment*
—— of Ten (at Venice), i 274 sq.; iii 137-8
—— of the Two Hundred at Florence, iii 388
—— of the North, instituted by Henry VIII, ii 448, 471
Counter-Reformation, preparation for the, see Vol. i, Chap. xviii, Catholic Europe, *passim*; growth of the movement, 677 sqq.; see Vol. ii, Chap. i *passim*, but more especially Chap. vi, Social Revolution and Catholic Reaction in Germany, 174-205; Chaps. vii *and* viii, Conflict of Creeds, etc., and War in Germany, 206-79; xii, The Catholic South, 377-415; xv, Philip and Mary, 512-49; xviii, The Church and Reform, 639-89; xix, Tendencies of European Thought in the Age of the Reformation, *passim*, 690-718; in Switzerland, ii 338; in Poland, see Vol. iii, Chap. iii, The Catholic Reaction...in Poland, 73-103; in the Empire, etc., in Hungary, Bohemia and Austria, under Ferdinand I, see *ib.* Chap. v *passim*, 140-81; under Maximilian II, *ib.*; in the Netherlands, and its connexion with the revolt, 184 sqq.; in Europe generally, 260 sq.; and Mary Stewart, Chap. viii *passim*, 260-93; in Florence, under Cosimo de' Medici, 389 sq.; Chap. xiii, Rome under Sixtus V, *passim*, 422-55; harsh side of, 466; in Ireland, importance of the movement, 587; 592 sqq.; in the Empire under Rudolf II, Chap. xxi *passim*, 696-735; and the outbreak of Thirty

Years' War, see Vol. iv, Chap. i *passim*; in re-conquered Bohemia, 73 sq.; 676 sq. See also Reformation, Jesuits, etc.
Country, Russian journal, xii 309; 337
Count's War (*Grevefeide*) (1534), ii 230, 614 sq.
Coup d'état of 18 Fructidor, viii 509 sq., 515; of 22 Floréal, 517; of 18 Brumaire, 678-88
Courbet, Amédée-A.-P., French admiral, captures Foo-chow, xii 131; 132
—— Gustave, painter, xi 528
Courcelles, French force at, xi 586
Courier de Méré, Paul-Louis, ix 270; x 103; xi 526
Courier de Turin, newspaper provided by the French Government, ix 397
Courland (Kurland), and Russia, ii 144; a semi-independent duchy, iii 73; Swedish veto upon Danish trade with, iv 177, 179; and Gustavus Adolphus, 183, 185; Charles X and, 589; v 494; 555; Charles XII in, 592; 594; Swedish occupation of (1701), 666; Prussia and, 667; vi 302; 317 sq.; 629; Russian influence in, 665 sq.; abolition of serfdom in, x 427; the Patriotic Society in, 454; Russian administration of, xii 335; 363
—— Anne, Duchess of. See Anne, Tsarina
—— Benigna (von Treiden), Duchess of, vi 302
—— Ernst Johann Biren, Duke of. See Biren
—— Frederick William, Duke of, v 550
—— Jakob III, Duke of, vi 301
Courrier, French journal, x 59; 81; 88; 102
—— des Pays-Bas, x 532
—— français, xi 486
Courrières, Count de, commissioner in England for Spanish marriage, ii 525
Court, de, French admiral, vi 160; 236
Courteen, Sir William, Assada Association and, iv 731; settlement of Barbados and, 756
Courtenay, Edward. See Devonshire, Earl of
Courthope, Nathaniel, at Pulo Run, iv 736; 745
Courtney, Hugh, arrest of, iv 447
Courtray, battle of (1302), i 426; taken by the French (1646), iv 598; Spain and, v 45, 63; taken by France (1667), 199; 416; taken by Marshal Saxe, vi 240; French victory at, viii 435
Courvoisier, Jean-Joseph-Antoine, x 67
Cousin, Victor, excluded from the Sorbonne, x 73, 78; restored to his post, 93; 103; 514; xi 23; 36; 120; as a philosopher, 526
Cousin-Montauban, Charles-G.-M.-A.-A. See Palikao, Comte de
Cousseau, Ant. Charles, Bishop of Angoulême. See Angoulême
Coutances, A.-F. de Talaru de Chalmazel, Bishop of, viii 156

Couthon, Georges, one of the *Enragés*, VIII 213; on *Comité de Salut Public*, 343, 345 sq., 351, 364, 368; arrest and execution of, 370 sq.

Contras, Huguenots' first victory at, III 43

Couza, Alexander John, Prince of Moldo-Wallachia, XI 644 sq.

Covenant, Solemn League and, adopted by Parliamentary party (1643), IV 317 sqq.; and Westminster Assembly, 358; 488; National (Scottish), IV 488 sqq.; character and early history of, 497 sqq.

Coventry, Mary Queen of Scots, imprisoned at, III 282; Cumberland's army at, VI 114

—— Henry, envoy to Sweden, V 109; and the Treaty of Breda, 112

—— Thomas Coventry, 1st Baron, ship-money and, IV 282

—— Sir William, Secretary to the navy under the Duke of York, V 113, 183; 210; 216

Coverdale, Miles, Bishop of Exeter, translation of the Bible by, II 465; 501, 539; assists in Parker's consecration, 572

Coveripak, Clive at, VI 541

Covode, John, American politician, VII 469

Cowell, John, professor of law, VI 786

Cowley, Abraham, succours Crashaw, IV 772; not a Fantastic Poet, 773 sq.; V 129; 132; and the Philosophical College, 740; 745; VI 791

—— Hannah, dramatist, X 699

—— Sir Henry Wellesley, 1st Earl, sent to Lucknow, IX 724 sq.; X 37; ambassador at Madrid, 211 sq.; ambassador at Paris, XI 333

—— Captain, and the Falkland Islands, VI 373

Cowpens, Tarleton defeated at (1781), VII 227

Cowper, Francis Thomas de Grey Cowper, 7th Earl, Lord-Lieutenant of Ireland, XII 40; 79; 81

—— William, poet, VI 79; 826; 828; VIII 765; X 699; 724

—— William Cowper, 1st Earl, V 446; 465; 469

Cox, Dr Richard, Bishop of Ely, II 557, 565, 567, 575

—— English colonel, defends Almeida, IX 459

Crabbe, George, X 700 sq.

Cracow, Compact of (1525), III 73; Protestantism in, 74, 78, 84; Canons of, 75; 76; University of, 77, 87, 102; coronation of Henry of Valois at (1574), 88–9; flight of Henry from, 90; Maximilian II declared King at (1575), 96; Báthory's supporters march to, 97; Stephen Báthory's state entry into (1576), 98; Archduke Maximilian defeated at, 450, IV 168; Palatine of, 189; taken by Charles X (1655), 581; V 480; the Swedes in, 505; 592; Augustus II crowned at, VI 191;

669; Russians expelled from (1794), VIII 542; surrenders to Prussia, 546, 548; ceded to Austria (1795), 549, 552; Schwarzenberg marches on (1813), IX 511; declared a free city, 598; Republic of, 599, 647, 655, 670; Province of, formed, X 449; Patriotic Society at, 453; Republic of, 455, 460 sq.; annexed to Poland, 461; annexed by Austria, XI 39, 46 sq., 250; journal published in, XII 339

Cracow, Franciscus Krasinski, Bishop of, and Polish Diet (1575), III 96

—— Palatine of. See Firlej, Grand Marshal of Poland

Cradock, Francis, and scheme for a national bank, V 266

—— Sir John Francis, 1st Baron Howdon, commands British troops in Portugal, IX 448; superseded by Wellesley, 449; Governor of Cape Colony, 753

Craft-gilds, in Flemish communes, I 428; 13th century importance of, 511–3

Craftsman, The, political journal, VI 71

Craggs, James, VI 41; 181

—— James, the younger, VI 30; 34; 38; 41; 181; X 625

Craig, Sir James Henry, General, in Canada, IX 745 sq.; expedition of, to Cape Colony, 749

—— John, Scottish Reformer, II 591; III 275

Craigmillar, Conference at (1566), III 273

Crail, Jacobites at, VI 99

Cramer, Charles Frédéric, Danish writer, VIII 788

—— Johann Andreas, German divine, VI 741

Crampel, Paul, African explorer, XII 130

Cranach, Lucas, German painter, II 159

Cranborne, Lord. See Salisbury, 3rd Marquis of

Cranfield, Sir Lionel. See Middlesex, Earl of

Cranmer, Thomas, Archbishop of Canterbury, I 641; II 26, 49; visits Germany, 219; 241; 433, 439 sq.; Anne Boleyn's trial and, 445; 464, 481, 484; 517, 521; imprisonment of, 538; disputation of, at Oxford, 539; trial of, *ib.*; death of, 542

Craonne, Blücher repulses the French at (1814), IX 551

Crashaw, Richard, education of, IV 771; characteristics of, 772 sq.

Craufurd, Robert, Major-General, charge of, at Busaco, IX 461; expedition of, to Chili, 753

Craven, Charles, Governor of Carolina, VII 38

—— Tunis Augustus, American naval commander, VII 555

Crawford, John Lindsay, 20th Earl of, VI 116

—— William Harris, American statesman, VII 350, 373 sq.

Crawford, William Lindsay, 18th Earl of, v 292

Crawfurd, John, envoy to the Court of Siam, XII 535

Creagh, Richard, Archbishop of Armagh, III 593

Creek Indians, The, VII 345

Creevey Papers, The, IX 687

Crefeld, taxation in, VI 221; silk manufacture at, X 732

Creighton, Mandell, Bishop of London, XII 841; 847

Crema, the French occupy, VIII 585

Crémer, Camille, French officer, XI 604; 606; 608

Crémieux, Adolphe, XI 102 sq.; Minister of Justice, 104

—— Gaston, French politician, XI 503

Cremona, siege of (1526), II 53; raid on, by Prince Eugene (1702), V 403; Elisabeth Farnese and, VI 152; 154; Napoleon captures (1796), VIII 569, (1800), IX 62; congress at, XII 235

—— Bishop of, XII 229

Crépy, Peace of (1544), II 78 sq., 245, 289, 459, 662, III 465, 477

Créquy de Blanchefort et de Canaples, Charles, Marquis de, Marshal of France, defeated (1598), III 417; at Susa, IV 135; 370

Crescentius, Peter, III 471

Crescenzio, Marcello, Cardinal, II 671 sq.

Crespin, Jean, *Livre des Martyrs,* II 293

Creswell, Father Joseph, III 533

Crete, acquired by Venice, I 255; Venetian colonisation of, 256; Turks in, V 40; 342, 344, 348; pashalik of, X 548; XI 313; 324; the Powers and, 634; disturbances in, 636; Constitution for, 637; XII 10; 382; insurrection in, 391; 392; Treaty of Berlin and, 398 sq.; 406; 415; affairs in (1878-1908), 418 sqq.; 422 sqq.; Greece and, 427 sq.; 728

Cretet, Emmanuel. *See* Champnol

Creusot, industries at, X 732, 744, 756; the Commune at, XI 503

Creutz, Count Philip, Swedish Chancellor, VI 777

Creuzé-Latouche, Jacques-Antoine, member of the National Assembly, VIII 386, 501

Creuzer, G. Friedrich, writings of, XII 821 sq.

Crèvecœur, Philip de (des Querdes), rebels against Maximilian I, I 394, 438, 446; 451

Crew, Nathaniel, 3rd Baron Crew of Stene, Bishop of Durham, V 234

—— Sir Randal, dismissal of, IV 266

Crichton, Father, III 288, 290

Crieff, burnt by Jacobites, VI 102

Crillon, Louis de Berton des Balbes de Quiers, Duke of, and Duke of Mahon, at Minorca, VI 379

Crimea, Tartars from, reinforce Imperial troops, III 107; Russia and, V 343, 368,

479, 493; VI 305; 307; 634; 648; 651; Catharine II and, 668, 672; 673; annexed by Russia (1783), 675 sq., VIII 311, 314; VI 695; ceded to Russia, 709; 778; VIII 308; Stolýpin in, XII 377

Crimea, Khan of, V 504; 506; 521; 599

Crimean War, Great Britain and the, Vol. XI, Chap. XI; 263; 266; 272; and Moldo-Wallachia, 284; 300; causes and results of, 305 sq.; 325; 346; influence of, on English literature, 351; Piedmont and, 373; Austria and, 401 sq.; 635; Greece and, 639; 764; Canada and, 769; 830; XII 294, 301, 728, 796

Crispi, Francesco, Italian statesman, XI 533; XII 215; Ministry of, 217 sq.; fall of, 218; and African affairs, 239 sqq.

Cristina (Maria Cristina of Naples), Queen Regent of Spain, X 231 sq.; policy of, as Queen Regent, 233 sq.; and Code of Cadiz, 237; negotiations of, with Don Carlos, 239; abdication of, 241; 242; XI 38; 550 sq.; and the marriage of her daughters, 553 sqq.; withdraws to Paris, 556; 557; corrupt practices of, 559 sq.; leaves Spain, 561

Critica Sociale, Italian socialist journal, XII 231

Crittenden, John Jordan, American politician, VII 581

Crivelli, Julius Cæsar, Bavarian diplomatic agent, IV 680

Crnoiević, Stephen, the maker of Montenegro, I 74

Croatia, fighting in, during the war of 1809, IX 355; French provinces of, 418; Marmont's action in, 419; revolutionary movement in, XI 156; 170; Hungary and, 173, 202; 177 sqq.; Diet of, 180; 206; 209; reaction in, 217; 399; XII 180; and the Compromise of 1868, 182, 190, of 1879, 198; 209 sq.

Crocco, Italian brigand, XI 531

Croft, Herbert, Bishop of Hereford, V 331; 334

—— Sir James, heads rebellion against Mary, II 526

Croissy, Charles Colbert, Marquis de, French ambassador in England, V 203 sq.; 209; 211

Croix, La, French journal, XII 120

Croizier, aide-de-camp to Napoleon, VIII 606

Croke, Richard, Cambridge Hellenist, I 580, 645

—— Thomas W., Roman Catholic Archbishop of Cashel, XII 85; 87

Croker, John Wilson, X 615; 655

Cromarty, George Mackenzie, 3rd Earl of, VI 117

Crome, Edward, Protestant Reformer, II 539

Cromer, Evelyn Baring, 1st Earl, XII 240; and Egyptian finance, 434; 438; Consul-General in Egypt, 439 sqq., 445 sq.; 454; retires, 456

Cromer, George, Archbishop of Armagh, III 587

Crommelin, Samuel Louis, and the Irish linen industry, VI 482

Crompton, Samuel, inventor of the spinning-mule, VII 374, IX 372, X 735

Cromwell, Henry, succeeds Fleetwood in Ireland, IV 538; resignation of, 540

—— Oliver, Protector, abolition of Episcopacy and, IV 292; Remonstrance and, 296; member for Cambridge, 304; with Essex, 311; Ironsides of, 312; at Grantham, 313; 314; victory of, at Winceby, 315; 318; and toleration, 320; Lieutenant-General, 321; at Marston Moor, 322; at Newbury, 324; Self-denying Ordinance and, 325 sqq.; at Taunton, 328; raid of, round Oxford, 329; at Naseby, 330; in Dorset, 332; in Hampshire, 333; at Bovey Tracey, 334; and Parliament, 337; 341; and the army, 342; mediates between army and Parliament, 343; and Charles I, 344 sq.; suppresses mutiny in army, 346; and Charles II, 347; at Windsor, 348; takes Pembroke, 349; at Preston, 350; King's trial and, 353; and Pride's Purge, 354; dissolves Rump, 362; Charles X of Sweden and, 429; and the Commonwealth (1649–53), 434–8; Protector, 438–48; ecclesiastical policy of, 453 sq.; revenue and, 456 sq.; militia and, 458; Irish expedition of, 463; 469; expedition of Penn and Venables and, 481; service of Shaftesbury under, 485; ascendancy of, 506; 507; in Edinburgh, 508; army of, in Scotland, 510; in Ireland, 532 sqq.; settlement of Ireland and, 536, 538; death of, 448, 540; policy of, 543; 544; Monck and, 545; 551; and Spain, 659 sq.; and Condé, 616; and Mazarin, 619; and East India Company, 746; and Portugal, V 105, 107; and Mazarin, 106; and Dutch Republic, 138, 140 sqq.; and Nieuwpoort, 146; 178; 266; and Ireland, 315; and the religious sects, 327 sq.; 333; and Spain, 372, 375, 378; 386; Elector Frederick William and, 648; 680; 697; Protestant Scheme of, VI 614; 795 sq.; 803; 805; 813; and Acadia, VII 75

—— Richard, proclaimed Protector, IV 448; Parliament and, 449 sq.; army and, 451; dissolves Parliament, 452; end of Protectorate of, 453 sq.; 539 sq.; Monck and, 545; 549; intrigue for restoration of, 553

—— Thomas, Earl of Essex, II 432; becomes King's secretary, 440 sq.; Vicar-General, 442; visitation of monasteries ordered by, 444; fall of, 451; character of, 451 sq.; the translation of the Bible and, 465 sq.; III 113; 737

Crónica Científica y Literaria, X 210; 212

Cronje, Piet Arnoldus, Boer general, XII 642

Cronsbruch, Caspar Florenz, Baron von, at Utrecht, V 439

Crook, George, American officer, in the Kanawha Valley (1864), VII 516

Cropredy Bridge, Waller defeated at, IV 323

Croquants, The, III 664

Crosa, Marquis, Sardinian envoy, X 109

Crosby, Brass, Lord Mayor of London, VI 444

Cross, Richard Assheton Cross, 1st Viscount, Home Secretary, XII 30; 481

Crowley, Robert, on agrarian reform, II 490

Crown Point, captured by the colonists (1775), VII 166

Crowne, John, dramatist, V 126 sq.; 132; 136

Croy, Prince Charles Eugène de, V 369; 589

—— Charles Philip de. *See* Havré

—— William of, Seigneur de Chièvres, I 369 sq., 452 sqq.; II 38, 43

—— William of, Cardinal, Archbishop of Toledo, I 370, 379

—— *See also* Aerschot

Crozat, Antoine, French merchant, and Louisiana, VI 172; French financier, VII 88, 92

Cruciger, Caspar, Lutheran Reformer, II 207, 250

Crusenstolpe, Swedish journalist, XI 684 sq.

Cruzada, The, Spanish tax, II 63

Crynssen, Abraham, captures Tobago, V 152

Csányi, Laszlo, Hungarian statesman, XI 212; 214

Csokonai, Michael Vitéz, Hungarian poet, XI 423

Cuba, Spanish colonies in, I 40 sq.; a Spanish possession, V 687; economic conditions of, VI 186; French in, VII 108; trade of, 327; United States and, 432, 438, 673; insurrections in (1868), 637, (1895), 674 sqq.; Spain relinquishes, 681 sqq.; Republic of, 686; and Spanish revenue, X 259; negroes in, 260; the United States and, 309; industries in, 761; XI 335; 557; proposed American purchase of, 563; XII 56; rebellion in, 264 sq.; lost by Spain, 266; 267; 530; 653 sq.; United States and, 655 sq., 685, 696 sq.

Cubières, Amedée-Louis Despans de, French general, XI 39

Cuddalore, VI 454; besieged, 577

Cuddapah, Nawáb of, VI 541

Cudworth, Ralph, Cambridge Platonist, Cartesian philosophy and, IV 791; V 750 sq.; 753

Cues, Nicholas of. *See* Cusanus

Cüstrin, Frederick V at, IV 68, 70; 196; Gustavus and, 197 sqq., 201, 203; Gallas at, 374; the Great Elector at, V 639; VI 212; arsenal of, 279; bombardment of, 280; 282; 298; Frederick William III at, IX 277; capitulates (1806), 206; evacuated, 318; fortress of, 514

Cüstrin. *See* Brandenburg-Cüstrin

Cujacius (Jacques Cujas), French Hellenist, I 577; III 58 sq.

Cujavia, Calvinism in, III 75
—— Stanislas Karnkowski, Bishop of, III 83; 90; crowns Stephen Báthory, 99

Culemburg, Count of, III 217, 222

Cullen, Government force at, VI 116
—— Paul, Cardinal, Archbishop of Dublin, XII 69

Culloden, battle of, V 326, VI 116, 246

Culmbach, V 622
—— *See* Brandenburg-Culmbach

Culmland, The, and Poland, V 629; and the German Order, 630; 634

Culmore Castle, surprised by O'Dogherty, III 613

Culpeper, Lord Thomas, Governor of Virginia, VII 9 sq., 199

Cultura Sociale, Italian journal, XII 230

Culverwell, Nathanael, Cambridge Platonist, V 752

Cum ad nihil, Bull establishing Inquisition in Portugal (1531), II 413 sq.

Cumaná, Dutch trade with, V 688; warships at, X 290

Cumberland, Prince Charles in, VI 114
—— George Clifford, 3rd Earl of, and naval war with Spain, III 319; and the English East India Company, IV 730
—— Henry Frederick, Duke of, marriage of, VI 445
—— William Augustus, Duke of, VI 114 sqq.; at Fontenoy, 242 sq.; 246 sqq.; 263; 340 sq.; 405; 408
—— Ernest Augustus, Duke of. *See* Ernest Augustus, King of Hanover
—— Richard (d. 1718), Bishop of Peterborough, V 753
—— Richard, and the Gibraltar negotiations (1799), VI 377 sq.

Cumberland Gap, Confederate troops in (1861), VII 462 sq., (1862), 507
—— River, trade on, VII 360; Fort Donelson on, 494

Cunha, Luis da, Portuguese Secretary for Foreign Affairs, VI 385
—— Tristão da, Portuguese explorer, I 32

Cuñiga. *See* Zuñiga

Cunin-Gridaine, Laurent, X 511

Cunningham, Allan, in Australia, XI 790 sq.
—— Sir James, and the English East India Company, IV 730

Curaçoa, ancient Dutch colony, IV 709 sq., 751; contraband trade at, V 684; 687; the Dutch in, VI 186; port of, closed (1804), VII 327; English capture of (1807), IX 240, 368, 750; and the trade of Venezuela, X 257

Curci, Carlo Maria, Jesuit, XI 715

Curé, Gustave, French Republican, XI 304

Curée, J. F., suggests that Napoleon should be declared Emperor, IX 31

Cureton, Charles Robert, Brigadier-general, in India, XI 741

Curie, Marie, and the discovery of radium, XII 789
—— Pierre, work of, in radium, XII 789

Curione, Celio Secondo, Reformer, II 382, 385, 391, 716

Curran, John Philpot, Irish Judge, retirement of, IX 700; 702
—— Sarah, IX 707

Currie, Sir Frederick, Indian official, XI 741
—— Dr John, of Liverpool, VIII 765

Curry, John, historian, X 627
—— J. L. M., Confederate Senator, VII 605

Curtatone, XI 86; battle of, 94

Curtis, Patrick, Archbishop of Armagh, X 650
—— Sir Roger, Admiral, VIII 479
—— Samuel Ryan, American general, VII 496

Curtius, Ernst, German historian, XII 844 sq.

Curwen, Dr Richard, preaches before Henry VIII against Peto, II 438

Curzolari, islands of, III 135

Curzon, Sir Robert, I 474 sq.
—— of Kedleston, George Nathaniel Curzon, Lord, Viceroy of India, XII 486; administration of, 488 sqq.; resigns, 496

Cusani, Augustine, Cardinal, III 449

Cusano, Benedetto, Italian Reformer, II 390

Cusanus, Cardinal (Nicholas Krebs of Cues), I 435, 599, 608, 623; the *Dialogue of Peace,* 624; 628 sq., 630 sqq., 689

Cushendun, Shane O'Neill at, III 592

Cushing, Caleb, mission of, to China, XI 810 sq.
—— William Barker, blows up the *Albemarle,* VII 564

Custine, Comte Adam-Philippe de, commands Army of the North, VIII 339, 343, 423, 429; recalled to Paris and executed (1793), 346, 430; commands Army of the Vosges (1792), 413 sqq., 417, 422 sq., 775
—— Renaud-Philippe de, French general, executed (1794), VIII 357

Custom of Paris, in Canada, VII 82

Custozza, battle of, XI 89, 122, 540

Cuvier, Georges-C.-L.-D., IX 133; XII 771

Cuxhaven, Prussia takes possession of (1800), IX 46

Cuyabá, province of, VI 390

Cuzco, centre of Inca rule in Peru, I 44 sq.; the Indians of, X 260, 263; Tupac Amaru marches on, 266 sq.; revolutionary conspiracy in (1814), 299; 301

Cyclades, The, acquired by Venice, I 255; X 202

Cyprian (Latin Father), early printed editions of, I 616-7

Cyprus, Turkish designs on, III 130-3; troops landed at, 134; taken by Turks, 134, 137, 399, 494-5; XII 33; 239; British occupation of, XI 324, XII 399, 415; 428; 499

Cyprus Convention, XII 398 sq.

Czapka, Ignaz, Ritter von Winstetten, Burgomaster of Vienna, XI 154

Czarniecki, Stephen, Polish general, defeated by Charles X, IV 582 sq.; invades Jutland, 588

Czarnkowski, Canon of Cracow (1549), III 78

Czarnovo, Russians retreat from (1806), IX 284

Czartoryski, family of, VI 193; 196; predominance of, in Poland, 198 sqq.; 354; 666 sq.

—— Prince Adam George, Polish politician and general, VIII 785 sq.; IX 35; 246; advice of, to Alexander, 259; report of Austerlitz of, 261; resignation of, 272; 337; influence of, 483; 485; at Congress of Vienna, 581; advice of, 592; X 418; curator of University of Vilna, 430, 459; and Polish Constitution, 446; 448; 457; and Polish revolution, 466 sq., 472

—— Prince Augustus, Prince Palatine, VI 198

—— Florian, Primate of Poland, VI 198

—— Prince Michael, Prince Chancellor, VI 198

Czaslau, Austrian troops in, VI 234

Czechs. *See* Čechs

Czenstochowa, Polish monastery of, Swedes fail before, IV 582

Czernovitz, meeting of Emperors at (1823), X 187 sq.

Czuczor, Georg, Hungarian writer, XI 431

Dabo, Amirs defeated at, XI 737

Dacca, Court of Appeal at, IX 711

Dacia, kingdom of, VI 674; 676

Dacke, Nels, revolts against Gustavus Vasa, II 627

Dacre, Leonard (claiming to be Lord Dacre of Gillesland), III 281 sq.

—— Thomas, Lord, Warden of the Marches, II 420

—— Thomas Fiennes, Lord, I 485

—— William, Lord, trial and acquittal of, II 441

Dada Kashji, Gwalior Minister, XI 737 sq.

Dadar, General England at, XI 735

Dadizeele, Jan van, *Bailli* of Ghent, I 443

Daendels, Hermann Willem, Dutch general, VIII 662; 787; IX 90; Governor of Java, 754

Daghestan, Russia and, V 545; annexed to Russia, X 413

Dagobert-Fontenille, Luc-Siméon-Auguste, French general in Spain, VIII 439 sq.

Dagonet, French commander in Spain, VIII 440

Daguerre, Louis-Jacques-Mandé, and photography, X 755; XII 783

Dahlberg, Erik, leads Swedes from Fünen, IV 585; V 569; 587

Dahlgren, John Adolf, American admiral, VII 527 sq.

Dahlmann, Friedrich Christoph, X 370; drafts Hanover Constitution, 374; 376; expelled from Hanover, 379 sq.; XI 49; 143; German Constitution of, 162 sq.; 164 sq.; opposes Malmoe Truce, 168; 195; withdraws from Frankfort Assembly, 200; 221

Dahomey, French conquest of, XII 129; 130; 659; explorers in, 807

Daily Telegraph, XII 810

Dain, Olivier le, I 440

Daine, Nicolas, Belgian general, X 541 sq.

Dakkar, French Governor-General at, XII 660

Dakota, North, population of, VII 711; South, and the currency question, 673

Dakotas, population of the, VII 708

Dalai Lama, of Tibet, XII 490 sq.

Dalayrac, Nicolas, IX 135

Dalberg, Emmerich Joseph, Duc de, and the French regency, IX 558; at the Congress of Vienna, 580; 584, 601

—— John von, Bishop of Worms, I 572, 634, 637

—— Karl Theodor Anton Maria von, Elector of Mainz, etc., Primate of the Confederation of the Rhine, IX 94; and the rearrangement of the German States, 202–3; 268; principality created for, 414; represented at Congress of Vienna, 587; and the Final Act, 659; X 6; 145

Dale, Sir Thomas, expedition of, to the Banda Islands, IV 735 sq.; High Marshal of Virginia, VII 6

—— Valentine, envoy to French court, III 27

Dalecarlia, seized by Sweden, II 600; 621, 624

Dales, The, Swedish mining districts, VI 779

Dalhousie, James Andrew Broun Ramsay, 1st Marquis of, VI 563; and the "railway mania," XI 4; 329; in India, 730, 740 sqq.; administrative reforms by, 744; 747; 750 sq.; XII 462

Dalkeith, castle of, taken by the Covenanters, IV 502

Dallemagne, Claude, Baron, French general, VIII 568, 638

D'Allemand, Cardinal, of Avignon, I 623

Dalling and Bulwer, Lord. *See* Bulwer

Dalmatia, Venetian power in, I 254; lost by Venice (1381), 264; recovered, 278; Turco-Venetian war in, III 117; inroads of the Uskoks in, IV 11; Venetian conquests in, V 366, 371; Turks in, VI 30; 648; 675; ceded to Austria (1797), VIII 583, 592; demanded from France, IX 272; France and (1806–9), 396–7, 418; protectorship of Franciscan Order in, 419; recovered by Austria (1815), 660; XI 47; 179 sq.; Emperor of Austria in, XII 382

—— Duke of. *See* Soult

Dalny, XII 586; 595; ceded to Japan, 601

Dalreoch, burnt by Jacobites, VI 102

Dalrymple, Sir Hew Whitefoord, sent to Spain, IX 440; agrees to convention with Junot, 441; allows French to plunder Lisbon, *ib.*; departure of, 442
— *See also* Stair
Dalton (Georgia), Confederate army at, VII 514, 521
Dalton, John, Indian officer, VI 541
— John, man of science, XII 730; 769 sq.
Dalwigk, Reinhard Karl Friedrich, Baron von, Hessian statesman, XI 397
Dalziel, Sir Thomas, at Rullion Green, V 284; 288
Damaraland, German missionaries in, XII 658; 664
Damascene. *See* John Damascene
Damascus, pashalik of, promised to Ibrahim, X 548, 553; Ibrahim enters, 549; revolt in (1834), 559; 560
Dambray, Charles-Henri, Vicomte, French Chancellor, IX 563; 565 sq.; 569; X 94
Damesme, Édouard-Adolphe-Marie, French general, XI 113
Damiens, Robert-François, attempts to murder Louis XV, VI 339, 347, VIII 50
Damietta, and Suez Canal, XII 431
Damilly, offers to betray Geneva (1586), III 414
Damjanics, János, Hungarian general, XI 207; 214
Dampier, William, seaman, VI 182
Dampierre. *See* Du Val de Dampierre
— A.-H.-M. Picot, Marquis de, VIII 428 sq.
Damville, Marshal. *See* Montmorency
Damvillers, given up by France (1559), II 93
Dan, Greene's march to the, VII 228
Danby, Earl of. *See* Leeds, Duke of
Danckelmann, Eberhard von, Prussian Minister, V 647; 658; 662 sq.
— Nicolas von, Brandenburg Minister at Vienna, V 663
D'Andelot et Coligny, François, in the Wars of Religion, II 93, 294 sq.; III 2–5, 9
Dandolo, Enrico, Doge of Venice (1192–1206), I 255
Daneau, Lambert (d. 1595), Calvinist theologian, III 749
Danewerke, The, Danes driven out of, XI 440
Dangan Hill, Preston defeated at, IV 345, 531
Dangerfield, Thomas, perjurer, V 231
Danican, Auguste, French general, VIII 396
Daniel, François, Calvin and, II 352 sq.
— Samuel, III 376
Danilevsky, Nicholas, Russian writer, XI 634
Danilo, Prince of Montenegro, XI 277; 636
Danilograd, Montenegrin victory at, XII 387
Danneskjold - Samsöe, Count Frederick, Danish Minister of Marine, VI 739
Danrémont, Comte Charles-Marie-Denis de, French general, X 504
Dan-sai, ceded to Great Britain, XII 536

Dante Alighieri, *De Monarchia* of, II 2; 35, 128; III 456–8, 463, 467; *De Vulgari Eloquentia*, 471, 473, 764
Danton, Georges-Jacques, VIII 161, 192, 200; *Procureur Substitut*, 225, 228; character of, 232; 234; Minister of Justice, 238, 241 sq.; and September massacres, 243 sq.; and National Convention, 246 sq.; at the King's trial, 260; policy of, 263 sq., 267; on the *Comité de Salut Public*, 269, 338; waning influence of, 342 sqq., 347; and Robespierre, 359 sq., 362; trial and execution of, 362 sqq.
Danube river, Turkish rule on, III 119; VI 231 sq.; Charles of Lorraine at, 235; 237; 306; opened to Russian ships, 648; military operations near (1800), IX 58, 64; Grand Army reaches (1805), 254; approached by Archduke Charles (May 10, 1809), 350; crossed by French troops (May 21, 1809), 351, (July 4–5), 352; Russian conquests on, 389; XI 314; crossed by Turkish troops, 315, 321; 323; navigation of, 643; XII 388; fortresses of, 392; Treaty of Berlin and, 898
Danubian Principalities (*see also* Moldavia, Wallachia), VI 307; 634; Catharine's designs on, 668 sq.; 672; 731 sq.; Russian evacuation of, IX 306; and the Treaty of Adrianople, X 202 sq.
Danubyu, attack on, XI 728
Danvila y Collado, Manuel, historian, XII 842
Danville, VII 539; flight of Jefferson Davis to, 541
Danzig, revolt of (1526), III 74; surrender of, to Stephen Báthory (1557), 100; and the Spanish trade, IV 105; Sigismund III at, 168, 172; Gustavus Adolphus at, 183, 186, 193; commercial prosperity of, 420; Charles X and, 428; the Dutch and, 583, 588; besieged by the Swedes (1656), V 146; Russia and, 611; Brandenburg and, 620; 629; German Order and, 631; 634; and Poland, 636; 638; Treaty of (1716), 611; VI 196; siege of (1733), 196 sq.; 630; 669; 671; Prussia and, 708 sq., 730; 732 sqq.; VIII 293, 330, 333, 523 sqq.; ceded to Prussia (1793), 535, 551; export duty levied at, IX 24; besieged (1807), 112, 284–5, 289–90; a free city, 292, 337, 338; French troops in (1808), 315; French army at (1813), 511; recovered by Prussia, 647, 656; Prussian naval station, XI 445
Daoiz, Spanish officer, killed in riot at Madrid, IX 434
Dára Shekoh, son of Emperor Shah Jehán, VI 518 sq.
Darboy, Georges, Archbishop of Paris. *See* Paris
Darby, George, vice-admiral, VI 452
— W. Evans, *International Tribunals*, XII 718

Darcy, Thomas, Lord, II 446

Dard, Henri-Jean-Baptiste, and favours to *émigrés*, IX 570

Dardanelles, passage of, VI 674; British fleet in (1807), IX 235, 368, 388; Russian claim on, 312, 313, 320; Peace of (1809), 388; Greek ships in, seized by the Porte, X 185; blockaded by Russia (1828), 201; Russia and, 203, 444; 554; closure of (1833), 555, 564; 572; XI 314 sq.; Sultan's rights in, 634; British fleet in, XII 387

Dare, Jurien van der (Georgius Aportanus), Reformer, II 160

Darfur, annexed by Egypt, XII 439; 449; 660; explorers in, 805, 811, 813

Dargai, heights of, stormed, XII 488; 489

Darien Scheme, character and results of, V 295 sqq.

—— Company (Company of Scotland trading to Africa and the Indies). *See under* Companies

Darimon, Alfred, French politician, XI 304

Darling Downs, occupation of, XI 790; 795

—— river, exploration of, XI 792, 795

Darlington, Sophia Charlotte von Kielmannsegge, Countess of, VI 19

Darmstadt, district of, and the Decree of November 19, VIII 300

Darnel, Sir Thomas, case of, IV 267

Darnley, Henry Stewart, Lord, II 458; a claimant for English throne, 582; III 269–74, 278

Darthé, Augustin-A.-J., French politician, VIII 505

Dartmouth, George Legge, 1st Lord, (2nd cr.), V 262

—— William Legge, 2nd Earl of, VI 435; Lord Privy Seal, 447

Daru, Comte Napoléon, French statesman, XI 491 sq.; 721

—— Comte Pierre-Antoine-Noël-Bruno, becomes Intendant, IX 118; Secretary of State, 141; 145, 307; historical work of, XII 829

Darwin, Charles, XI 365; *The Origin of Species*, XII 772 sq.; 774

—— Erasmus, VIII 765; X 699 sq.

Dashkoff, Princess Catharine, VI 661 sq.; 679; 697 sq.

Dashwood, Sir Francis. *See* Le Despencer, Lord

Dataria, attempts to reform, II 673

Dathenus, Peter, Protestant preacher, III 251, 252

Dati, Agostino, of Siena, I 648

—— Giuliano, the Oratory of Divine Love and, II 379

Da Torre, Count, and Pernambuco, IV 708

Daubeney, Giles, 1st Lord, I 469 sq.

Daulat Rao Sindhia, Mahárája of Gwalior, XI 726

Daun, Count Leopold Joseph Maria, Austrian Field-marshal, VI 260 sqq.; 273 sqq.; at Olmütz, 277 sq.; 280 sqq.; 287; at Torgau, 296 sq.; 299; 325 sq.; 626; 705

—— Wirich Philipp Lorenz, Count, captures Naples, V 419; 425

Daunou, Pierre-C.-F., French politician, VIII 386; IX 4; XII 829

Dauphiné, army sent to pacify (1574), III 23; held by Huguenots (1575), 27; heretics in, 400, 403 sqq.; Protestant interest in, 661; invaded by the Duke of Savoy (1692), V 60; Belleisle retreats to, VI 245; and Provincial Assemblies, VIII 111 sq.; spirit of resistance in (1788), 112 sqq., 116; and States General, 129

Dauvergne, Henri, discovers the source of the Oxus, XII 802

Davanzati-Bosticho, Bernardo, his *Tacitus*, III 471

Davel, and Vaud, VI 625

D'Avenant, Sir William, dramatist, V 125 sq.; 136; 745

Davenport, Puritan minister at New Haven, VII 20

Daventry, Ingoldsby at, IV 557

Daverhoult, Jean-A., member of *Club des Feuillants*, VIII 213

David, Jacques-L., French painter, VIII 247, 356, 364, 501; picture by, IX 60; 134, 135; X 103

—— Pierre-Jean, sculptor, X 103

Davidovich, Baron Paul, Austrian general, VIII 578 sqq.

Davids, precursors of the submarine, VII 564

Davis, Jefferson, VII 403; Secretary of War, 426; 447; Confederate President, 451, 462, 522 sq., 603 sq.; and peace negotiations, 535 sq., 542; 538; captured, 543; death of, *ib.*, 578; 581; XI 337; XII 16

—— or Davys, John, navigator, and Dutch commercial jealousy, IV 734; XII 814

—— Sir John, III 613, 615; Speaker in Irish Parliament, IV 515 sq.

—— Sir John Francis, Governor of Hongkong, XI 814

—— Thomas Osborne, and Young Ireland party, XI 7; 13

Davison, William, III 292

Davitt, Michael, Irish politician, XII 76; 81

Davos, principal seat of the *Zehngerichten*, IV 36 sq.; 41; Protestants of, 47 sq.; *Strafgericht* at, 47–8, dissolved, 50; disarmed by Baldiron, 55; de Coeuvres at, 58

Davout, Louis-Nicolas, Prince of Eckmühl, Marshal of France, IX 112; 252; crosses the Rhine, 253; 257; at Pressburg, 258; 260; commands 3rd corps, 275; at Auerstädt, 276–7; marches through Berlin, 278; Küstrin surrenders to, 280; advances to Posen, 281; 283–4; at Eylau,

286; 335; policy of, 338; 339; commander of French troops in central Germany, 346; 347-9; defeats Austrians near Markgrafen-Neusiedel, 353; letter of Napoleon to (September 2, 1810), 373; reports of, from Hamburg, 374; commander of the French army in N. Germany, 378; and the Russian campaign, 488 sqq.; 508; appointed governor on the Lower Elbe, 515; 520, 525, 530; plots communicated to, 572-3; in the War Office, 616; 645

Davy, Sir Humphry, x 741; xii 730; 769; 778

Davydoff, Denis W., Russian general, harasses French retreat, ix 497

Dawson, George, x 649

Dax, Bishop of. *See* Acqs

Day, Francis, builder of Fort St George, v 698

—— George, Bishop of Chichester, ii 501, 521

—— Thomas, writer, viii 755, 765

—— William R., American Secretary of State, vii 682

De Aar, the Boers and, xii 642

Deák, Francis, Hungarian politician, xi 172; 181 sq.; 203; and Constitutional party, 216; 400; 405 sq.; writings of, 426; xii 178 sqq.; and Hungarian demands, 182 sq.; 204; death of, 190

De Amicis, Edmondo, Italian writer, xii 231

Deane, Sir Anthony, Commissioner of English navy, v 170 sq.; 177

—— Richard, admiral, naval administration and, iv 460; 480

—— Silas, American statesman, vii 210

Dearborn, Henry, American general, vii 341

Deasy, Henry Hugh Peter, traveller, xii 804

Debbeh, Rüppell at, xii 806

Debitz, Eric, Swedish commander, iv 244 sq.

Debreczen, Kossuth at, xi 203; 204 sq.; the Hungarian Diet at, 207; 214; 425

Debry, Jean-A., member of the Legislative Assembly, viii 515

Decaen, Comte, French general, ix 67; sails for the Indies, 209; Suchet joins, 479; command of, in 1815, 624

—— Claude-Théodore, French general (1870), xi 589 sq.

Decapolis, revolt in (1834), x 559

Decatur, Stephen, American naval officer, vii 339

Decazes, Élie, Duc, x 13, 20; prefect of the Paris police, 45; Minister of Police, 47; 49; 50; electoral *coup d'état* of, 51; 52; 54; and army reforms, 55; 56; ministry of, 57-63; and the murder of the Duc de Berry, 63; estimate of, as a statesman, *ib.*; 64; 71; 73

—— Louis-C.-E.-A., Duc de Glücksberg, French ambassador at Madrid, xi 556; xii 97; 109; 114

Deccan, The, Aurangzeb and, v 699; Vol. vi, Chap. xv (2) *passim*; balance of power in, ix 722; Wellesley in, 726

Decembrio, Pier Candido, Italian writer, i 542

Decius, Milanese jurist (1512), ii 30

Decker, Pierre Jacques François de, Belgian statesman, xi 672

Declaratio Ferdinandea, iii 714

Declaration of Independence, American, Vol. vii, Chap. vi (1761-76), 175-208

—— of Indulgence, of March, 1672, v 206 sqq.; of April, 1687, 235; character and effects of, 237 sqq.; 335; reissued (May, 1688), 336

—— of Right. *See* Bill of Rights

Declaration of Sports revived, iv 279

De Clementia, Calvin's Commentary on, ii 352 sq.

Decrès, Denis, Duke, French Minister of Marine, ix 213; Napoleon's directions to, 218; advice of, to Napoleon, 228; 237, 311, 616

Decretale, character of, iii 745

Dedel, Dutch envoy in London, x 544

Dederotti, John, of Minden, founder of Bursfelde Congregation, i 631

De donatione Constantini Magni, of Lorenzo Valla, ii 694

Dee, Dr John, iii 697

Defermon des Chapelières, Jacques, *Intendant-général*, ix 118

Deffaudis, Baron, mission of, to Buenos Ayres, xii 681

Defoe, Daniel, v 396; 467; 468 sq.; vi 815 sqq.; 833

De Freyne, Arthur French, Lord, xii 89

Degáyeff, Russian terrorist, xii 311

Deggendorf, attack on, vi 238

Dego, Allies at, viii 561 sq.; surrenders, 566

De Grey, Thomas Philip de Grey, Earl, Viceroy of Ireland, xi 8

De haeretico comburendo, statute, revived, ii 540

Dejean, Jean-François-Aimé, Comte, ix 9

Dekker, E. Douwes ("Multatuli"), Dutch writer, xi 676

—— Thomas, iii 376

Delaborde, Comte Henri-François, French general, besieges Toulouse, ix 617

Delacroix, Ferdinand-Victor-Eugène, x 103; xi 528; xii 831

—— de Constant, Charles, French Foreign Minister, viii 507 sq.

Delagoa Bay, Boers at, xi 781; 782; 789; xii 635; dispute concerning, 270, 635; 640

Del Aguila, Don Juan, iii 532; leads invasion of Ireland, 608-9

Delalot, Charles, x 74; 80; 91

Delamere, Henry Booth, 2nd Lord (*afterwards* Earl of Warrington), supports the Prince of Orange, v 246

Delaroche, Hippolyte (Paul), painter, xi 528

Delauney, commands the Army of the Moselle, VIII 427

Delavigne, Jean-François-Casimir, poet, XI 528

Delaware, settlement of, VII 40 sqq., 50 sq.; 162; constitution of, 237, 242; and Annapolis Convention, 244; and Constitutional Convention, 246 sq., 252, 255, 258, 263 sq., 269, 271, 281 sq., 285 sq.; accepts Constitution, 302; representation of, 306; trade of, 355; population of, 359; upholds Tariff, 381; slavery in, 385, 585; and secession, 453

—— river, settlement from Brainford near, VII 26; Swedish colony on the south bank of, 40 sq.; Howe's operations on, 213 sq.; British base at (1813), 341; steamboats on, 351

—— Thomas West, 3rd *or* 12th Baron, Governor of Virginia, VII 5 sq.

Delbecq, Baron P. J. du Chamge, French commander, VIII 439

Delbrel, Pierre, French Commissioner with the army in Spain, VIII 440; and Brumaire, 682

Delbrück, Martin Friedrich Rudolf von, Prussian statesman, XI 394; XII 150; 152; 157

Del Campillo, Don Joseph, Spanish statesman, VI 157; 159; 166; 362; 382

Delcassé, Théophile, French statesman, XII 132

Del Castillo, Hernando, Spanish writer, I 379

Del Corro, Antonio, Spanish Reformer, II 406

Del Duero, Manuel de la Concha, Marqués, Spanish general, X 242; XI 556

Delescluze, Louis-Charles, French revolutionary, XI 106; 114; 488; 502

Delessart, Antoine de Valdec, French Minister of the Interior, VIII 216; Foreign Minister, 222; arrested, 223

Delessert, Benjamin, industrial experiments of, IX 377

—— François-Marie, French politician, XI 127

Delft, William of Orange at, III 242; Act of Federation signed at (1576), 243; William settles in, 257–9; States of Holland meet at, 617; trading Company at, 632; Archbishop Gebhard at, 708; Frederick Henry and, IV 689, 715; William II of Orange and, 725

Delhi, the interregnum at, V 697; 701; VI 508; captured by Bábar, 509; 511 sq.; 519 sqq.; seized by Bahádur Shah, 523; 524 sq.; 553; 568; capture of, by Mohammadans (1788), IX 719; and the Maráthas, 725; Bourquin defeated near, 726; siege of, 727; Shah Alam at, 730; XI 731; 746; capture of, 747; Durbar at, XII 466, 474, 495

Deligrad, Milan IV proclaimed at, XII 386

Delille, Jacques, French poet, VI 827

Delisle, Léopold-Victor, French medievalist, XII 834

Della Casa, Giovanni. *See* Benevento, Archbishop of

—— Cisterna, Prince Emanuele, X 114

—— Pergola, Bartolommeo, II 386

—— Porta, Bartolommeo (Frà Bartolommeo), Florentine artist, I 168

—— —— Egidio, follower of Zwingli, II 381

—— —— Giacomo, III 442

—— —— Giovanni Battista, V 716; 740

—— Rovere, Francesco. *See* Sixtus IV, Pope

—— —— Girolamo. *See* Turin, Archbishop of

—— —— Cardinal Giuliano. *See* Julius II, Pope

—— —— Giulio, Italian Protestant, II 382 sq.

—— Lavinia, II 384, 387

—— Torre, Giulio, Spanish agent, opposes Henry IV, IV 41

—— Valle, Andrea, II 16

Delmas, J.-F.-B., member of the *Comité de Salut Public*, VIII 269

Delmenhorst, Denmark and, VI 736; 741 sq.; 744; exchange of, 753

Del Nero, Bernardo, I 154, 173 sqq.

Delolme, Jean Louis, Swiss publicist, IX 427

Del Parque, Spanish general, ordered to advance into Leon, IX 453; remnants of the force of, 458

Delphi, excavations at, XII 845

Delphine, Madame de Staël's, IX 131

Del Principe, Island of, seized (1598), III 632

Del Pulgar, Hernando, Spanish chronicler, I 381

Del Riego, Rafael, Spanish revolutionary officer, X 215 sqq.; the hymn of, 218; 220 sq.; and the French refugees, 223 sq.; President of the Cortes (1822), 224; defeated, 228; hanged 230

Del Rio, member of the "Council of Blood," III 216, 218 sq.

Del Vasto, Alfonso Avalos, Marquis, III 105; sent on an embassy to Venice, 115; dismissed by the Signory, 116

Delvig, Baron, Russian poet, X 431

Delyánnes, Theodore, Greek statesman, at Berlin, XII 395, 398; premier, 408; 420; assassinated, 422

Delyánoff, Russian Minister, XII 315

Demarçay, French Republican politician, X 478

Dembe Wielkie, Polish success at (1831), X 470

Dembinski, Henry, Polish general, X 472; Hungarian Commander-in-chief, XI 205; 207; 210; at Szöreg, 211; 213; at Widdin, 215

Dembovski, Leon, and the Polish revolution, X 467

Demer river, French forces at, VI 246

Demerara, taken by the British (1796), VIII
484, IX 750; restored to Holland (1802),
75; lost (1803), 240; retained by Britain
(1814), 654, 755, x 520, XI 667; strike of
slaves in, 658
—— river, Dutch on, VI 186
Demerville, Dominique, Jacobin, arrested,
IX 17
Demetrius (Dmitri Samotzvanetz), the First
False Demetrius, claimant of the Russian
throne, and Sigismund, IV 175, v 497
sqq.; 524; 548
—— the Second False, IV 176; coronation
of, 189
Demmin, IV 196; taken by Gustavus
Adolphus, 199
Democracia, La, Spanish journal, XI 567
Démocratie, La, French journal, XI 488
Demoivre, Abraham, mathematician, v 716
Demonte, annexed to Saluzzo, III 419
Den, Russian journal, XI 625
Denain, battle of (1712), v 433 sq.
Denbigh, William Feilding, 1st Earl of, at
La Rochelle, IV 133
Dendermonde, Conference at (1566), III 210;
taken by Parma, 618; captured by Marl-
borough (1706), v 416; and the Barrier
Treaties, 457, 459
Denfert-Rochereau, Pierre-M.-P.-A., Colonel,
defends Belfort, XI 606, 609
Denham, Dixon, African explorer, XII 807;
810 sqq.
Denia, capture of (1708), v 426
—— Sandoval, Marquis of. *See* Lerma,
Duke of
Denifle, Heinrich Suso, German medievalist,
XII 848
Denman, Thomas, Lord, x 673; XI 9
Denmark
II xvii The Scandinavian North (1), 599–
617
IV iii The Protestant Collapse, (2) The
Lower-Saxon and Danish War
(1623–9), 85–109
v The Vasa in Sweden and Poland
(1560–1630), *passim,* 158–89
xiii The later years of the Thirty
Years' War (1635–48), *passim,*
387 sq.
xiv The Peace of Westphalia, *passim,*
395–433
xx The Scandinavian North (1559–
1660), 560–91
v xviii The Scandinavian Kingdoms,
passim, 558–83
xix Charles XII and the Great Northern War, *passim,* 584–615
VI xxi Denmark under the Bernstorffs
and Struensee, 735–57
IX ii The Armed Neutrality (1780–1801),
passim, 34–54
viii The Command of the Sea (1803–
15), *passim,* 208–43
xi The Napoleonic Empire at its
height (1807–9), *passim,* 294–340

Denmark (*contd.*)
XI xxiv Scandinavia (1815–70), (ii) Den-
mark, (iii) Dano - Norwegian
Literature (1815–65), 691–702
XII xi Scandinavia (1864–1908), 290–93
Denmark, Prince Royal of. *See* Fred-
erick VI
Dennewitz, battle of (1813), IX 529–30
Dennison, William, Governor of Ohio, VII
456
Denny, Sir Anthony, II 475
Denon, Dominique-Vivant, French anti-
quary, VIII 599; 605 sq.; 616; IX 134
Denys, Nicholas, Colonial governor and
historian, VII 110 sqq.
Deogáon, Treaty of (1803), IX 726
Depretis, Agostino, Italian statesman, XII
214 sq.; 217; 240
Deptford, Peter the Great at, v 523
De Quincey, Thomas, XI 361 sq.; 365
Derbent, Peter the Great at, v 544; 545;
evacuated by Russia, VI 304; Sir Anthony
Jenkinson at, XII 793
Derby, Lambert's army at, IV 544; Duke
of Devonshire at, v 246; Prince Charles
at, VI 114; riots at (1817), x 578
—— Charlotte de la Tremouille, Countess of (wife of 7th Earl), holds Lathom
House for the King, IV 321
—— Edward Geoffrey Smith Stanley,
14th Earl of (Lord Stanley), VII 636;
Irish Secretary, x 657 sq.; XII 71; and
the abolition of slavery, x 659; resigns,
662; 663; 666 sq.; 678; War and Colonial
Secretary (1841), XI 2; 9; and repeal of
the Corn Laws, 10 sq.; and Protection,
20; refuses office, 21; Ministry of (1852),
ib.; and France, 308; 309; 320; Ministry
of (1858–9), 328 sqq.; resigns, 331; opposes Gladstone's financial scheme, 334;
third Ministry of, 340 sqq.; retirement
of, 342; and Portugal, 574; and the
colonies, 762; and Canada, 771; XII 69
—— Edward Henry Stanley, 15th Earl
of (Lord Stanley), XI 330; 345; Foreign
Secretary, XII 30; 32 sq.; and Egypt, 40,
434; 41; 43; 141; 384; and the Eastern
Question, 387; resigns, 394
—— Edward G. V. Stanley, 17th Earl of
(Lord Stanley), Postmaster-General, XII
55
—— James Stanley (Lord Strange),
7th Earl of, repulsed at Manchester, IV
305
Dernei, Anton, printer, v 531
Déroulède, Paul, French politician, XII
121
Derreira, Poncet at, XII 805
Derrinlaur Castle, captured (1574), III
596
Derry, claimed by Tyrone, III 611; captured by O'Dogherty, 613; revolt of
(1688), v 307; 308; siege of (1689),
309, 311 sq., 315; George Dawson at, x
649

Derry, Bishop of. *See* Bristol, F. A. Hervey, 4th Earl of

Derschavin, Gabriel Romanovich, Russian poet, vi 698

Dervies, von, constructs railways in Russia, xi 619

Derwentwater, James Radcliffe, 3rd Earl of, vi 101; 103

Des Adrets, Baron, and massacre at Orange, iii 3

Desaix (*or* Dessaix) de Veygoux, L.-C.-A., commander in Egypt, viii 600 sqq., 607, 614; ix 62-3

Desalliers, French Minister in Transylvania, v 596

Desargues, Gérard, mathematician, Pascal and, iv 794; v 710

Desborough, Major-General John, iv 444; 448 sq.; Richard Cromwell and, 451 sq.

Descartes, René, ii 690 sq., 710; Christina of Sweden and, iv 574 sq.; in Holland, 722; *see* Chap. xxvii, 776–87; influence of, on French literature, v 64 sqq.; and Leibniz, 69; and Catholicism, 72 sq.; 82; and mathematical science, 710 sqq.; 714 sq.; 719; 723; 733 sq.; 739; 741; and Queen Christina, 744; 750; 752; 755; viii 5

Deschamps, Antony, x 101

—— Émile, French poet, x 101; xi 507

Deschanel, Paul, French politician, xii 126

Deseret. *See* Utah

Desèze, Raymond, barrister at Bordeaux, advocate for Louis XVI, viii 257

Desfieux, François, member of the Committee of Insurrection, viii 265, 342

Desforgues, François-L.-M. Chenain, Minister of Foreign Affairs, viii 339

Desgenettes, Baron N.-R.-Dufriche, viii 606

Desgodins, Abbé, in China, xii 797

Des Hayes, Louis, Baron de Courmenin, iv 90

Desima, Dutch factory in Japan removed to, iv 712, xii 556

Désirade, reduced (1808), ix 240

Desjardins, Paul, xii 119

Desmarets, Nicolas, French financier, and taxation, v 28; viii 69

Desmeuniers, Jean-Nicolas, and the Constitutional Committee, viii 183

Desmond, "undertakers" in, iii 599

—— the clan of, iii 529

—— Eleanor Butler, Countess of, 2nd wife of Earl Gerald, iii 595

—— Gerald Fitzjames Fitzgerald, 15th Earl of (1558–83), iii 594 sq.

—— James Fitzjohn Fitzgerald, 11th Earl of (1520–29), iii 581

—— James Fitzjohn Fitzgerald, 14th Earl of (1540–58), iii 583

—— James Fitzmaurice Fitzgerald, 13th Earl of (1534–40), murdered, iii 594

—— Sir John Fitzgerald, Captain of, iii 594 sq.

—— Sir Thomas of (Thomas Roe), iii 595

Desmoulins, Benoît-Camille, French journalist, viii 8, 161, 163, 168, 247; *Les Révolutions de France et de Brabant*, 329; and *Le Vieux Cordelier*, 360 sq.; trial and execution of, 363 sq.

Desmousseaux de Givré, Bernard-Jean-Echard, xi 41

Desna river, Lithuanian boundary, v 481

Despeña Perros, Vedel sent to secure the, ix 437

Despinoy, Comte Hyacinthe-F.-J., French general, viii 574

Desportes, Philippe, iii 61, 71, 376

Després-Crassier, E.-Philibert, general in Spain, viii 439

Des Querdes. *See* Crèvecœur

Dessau, Bridge of, Wallenstein at, iv 95; York at, ix 515; siege of (1813), 532

—— *See* Anhalt-Dessau

Dessewffy, Count Emil, Hungarian politician, xii 176

Dessoles, Jean-Joseph-Paul-Augustin, Marquis, *Commandant* of the National Guard, ix 557; 558; President of the Council, x 57; 61; resigns, 62

Destaing, J.-Zacharie, General, at Aboukir, viii 614 sq.

Destenave, African explorer, xii 129

Des Touches, French admiral, vi 453

Destournelle, Louis Deschamps, French Minister, viii 339

Destrem, Hugues, politician, and Brumaire, viii 683

Destutt de Tracy, Comte Antoine-C.-V., French Minister of Marine, xi 118

Des Ursins. *See* Orsini

Detring, official of the Chinese Customs Service, xii 526

Detroit, settlement at, vii 356

—— river, Hull crosses (1812), vii 337

Dettingen, George II at, vi 109; 238; 250

Deutsche Zeitung, xi 62

Deventer, educational work at, i 435 sq.; surrender of, iii 622; siege of (1591), 626

—— *See* Prouninck

Devereux, Captain, murderer of Wallenstein, iv 242

Deveria, Eugène, x 103

Devernaki, Ottoman force defeated at (1823), x 181

Devicota, Indian port, vi 538

Devolution, War of, v 33; origin and course of, 36 sqq.; 199 sq.; Brandenburg and, 649 sq.

Devonshire, Hopton in, iv 308, 313; petitions for a free Parliament, 549

—— Edward Courtenay, Earl of, ii 518; 520; 523–8; 544

—— Elizabeth (Foster), Duchess of (2nd wife of 5th Duke), x 138; 151

—— Spencer Compton Cavendish, 8th Duke of (Lord Hartington), xi 331; xii 23; leader of Opposition, 32; Secretary for India, 36 · 43; and Home Rule Bill,

44; 45; 52; resigns, 54; 80; 83; Secretary of State for India, 472, 475

Devonshire, William Cavendish, 1st Duke (4th Earl) of, v 216; 240; 242; 246

—— William Cavendish, 2nd Duke of, vi 13

—— William Cavendish, 4th Duke of (Marquis of Hartington), vi 75; 404 sq.; 424 sq.; resigns, 428; 431; 489

Dévots, The French, 17th century religious party, v 73

Dewey, George, American admiral, vii 679

Deza, Bishop, massacres the Moors, iii 494

Dezpuch, Ausias, nominated Bishop of Saragossa, i 658

Dharmsala, death of Lord Elgin at, xi 752

Dholpur, Dadi Kashji at, xi 738

Dhondev Pant. *See* Nana Sahib

Dhulip Sing, xi 738

Dial, The, Transcendentalism in, vii 739

Dialogue de Manant et Maheustre, iii 764

Diamantina river, squatters on, xii 619

Diamond Hill, Botha defeated at, xii 643

—— Rock (Martinique), ix 221; 224

Diario de Madrid, x 210; 229

Dias, Bartolomeo, Portuguese explorer, i 17, 19; reaches Cape of Good Hope, 20, 22, 285

—— Henrique, leader in Brazilian revolt, v 674

Diaz, Alfonso, murder of Juan Diaz by, ii 403

—— Diniz, explorer of African coast, i 14

—— Juan, Spanish Reformer, murdered, ii 254, 403

—— Pastor, and Spanish marriage question, xi 554

—— Porfirio, President of Mexican Republic, x 305; xi 477; xii 6; 676 sq.

Dickens, Charles, x 724; xi 358 sqq.

—— Guy, British *attaché* at Berlin, vi 212

Dickinson, Daniel S., member of Congress from New York, vii 398

—— John, American statesman, vii 179, 182, 203 sq., 234; at Constitutional Convention, Chap. vii *passim*

Dickson, Major, commander in Spanish foreign legion, x 227

—— African explorer, xii 807

Diderot, Denis, v 70 sq.; vi 165; and Catharine II, 678, 693; 823; 826; 833; 837; viii 5, 26 sq., 32; xi 528

Diebitsch-Zabalkanski, Ivan K. F. A., Comte de Diebitsch and de Narden (Russian general), ix 511; x 200; advances upon Constantinople, 202; 439; mission of, to Berlin, 465; 468; and the Polish revolution, 469 sqq.

Dieden, Colonel, takes Wesel, iv 693

Diedenhofen. *See* Thionville

Diedrichs, German admiral, xii 513

Diehl, Karl, German historian, xii 845

Diemen, Anthoni van, Dutch Governor-General of the Indies, iv 711; 740

Diepo Negoro, Javanese leader, xi 667

Dieppe, occupied by Ormesby, iii 3; Henry IV at (1589), 48; Pennington at, iv 260 sq.; Duc de Beaufort's fleet at, v 187; harbour of, xii 102

Dieskau, Baron Ludwig August, vii 125

Diet of the Empire, constitution of, i 290 sq.; procedure of, 291; cities represented in, 302; proposed annual meetings of, 305, 308 sq.; meetings of, at Frankfort (1454), 666, (1485), 302, (1489), *ib.*; at Nürnberg (1491), *ib.*, (1501), 311, (1522), 660; at Worms (1495), 303 sqq., (1497), 306 sq.; at Lindau (1496), 306; at Freiburg im Breisgau (1498), 307; at Augsburg (1500), 308, (1510), 319; at Cologne (1505), 316, (1512), 320 sqq.; at Constance (1507), 317; at Trier (1512), 320. (*For later meetings of the Diet see names of places*)

Diether, Archbishop, of Mainz. *See* Mainz

Dietrich, Archbishop, of Mainz. *See* Mainz

Dietrichstein, Sigismund von, councillor of Maximilian I, i 326; commander of Bohemian troops against peasants (1525), ii 182, 190

Dietz, the House of Nassau and, x 524, xi 674

Diez, Friedrich C., philologer, xii 822

—— Henry Frederick von, Prussian envoy at Constantinople, viii 316, 330 sq.

Dig, battle of (1804), ix 728

Digby, George, Baron. *See* Bristol, George, 2nd Earl of

—— Sir John, Lieutenant of Tower, i 473

—— John. *See* Bristol, John, 1st Earl of

—— Sir Kenelm, negotiates with Pope Innocent X, iv 338; 529

Digeon, Émile, French politician, xi 503

Digges, Sir Dudley, imprisonment and release of, iv 265

Digne, provisional Government at, xi 138

Dijon, *Parlement* of, iii 664, v 4, viii 47; school of sculpture at, i 414; revolt of (1595), iii 667; Napoleon's reserve army at, ix 66; the Germans at, xi 604, 606; 609

Dilke, Sir Charles Wentworth, xii 36; 40; 43

Dill, Sir Samuel, historian, xii 849

Dillenburg, birthplace of William of Orange, iii 189; exile of William of Orange at, 213, 228, 231–3; part of, added to grand duchy of Berg, ix 410; House of Nassau and, x 524, xi 674

Dillingen, Jesuits at, iii 161; Franco-Bavarian force at, v 408; 410

Dillingen Book, iv 110

Dillon, Comte Arthur de, French general, viii 412

—— John, Irish politician, xii 78; 80 sq.; and the Plan of Campaign, 85

Dillon, John Blake, and Young Ireland party, xi 7; 13
—— Harold Arthur Lee Dillon, 17th Viscount, xii 89
Dilolo, Lake, Livingstone at, xii 808
Dimitri. *See* Dmitri
Dinant, sack of, by Charles the Bold, i 422; captured by French, ii 89
Dindings, Great Britain and the, xii 532
Dingan, Zulu chief, xi 782
Dingelstedt, Franz, German poet, xi 50; 413
Ding-hu, Prjevalsky at, xii 798
Dingley, Nelson, American politician, vii 674
Dingolfing, storming of, vi 238
Dino, Dorothea de Courland, Duchesse de (Comtesse Edmond de Périgord), *afterwards* Duchesse de Talleyrand et de Sagan, x 510
Dinwiddie, Robert, Lieutenant-governor of Virginia, vii 10, 66, 120, 125
Diodati, Charles, friend of Milton, v 118
—— General, departs from Pilsen, iv 241
Dippel, Johann Conrad, pietist, v 761
Directory, The French (Nov. 1795—Nov. 1799), formed, viii 393, 397; and the army, 445 sq.; 472; Chap. xvi; and the conquest of Italy, 564, 570, 584 sq., 589, 636; and the Egyptian Expedition, 596 sq., 618; and Brumaire, Chap. xxii; finance of, 701 sq., 707; legislation of, 723 sq.; policy of, in Switzerland, ix 95 sqq.; Chap. xvi, 487-520; fall of, Chap. xxii, 665-88
Discours de la Méthode, iv 779; 781; 784; 788
Disentis, Catholic commune of, iv 36, 47, 51
Disestablishment, of Irish Church, demanded by Gladstone, xi 344 sq.
Dispositio Achillea, i 297; v 624; 656
Disputationes Camaldunenses. See Landino
Disputations, Luther's, with John Eck, ii 135. *See also* Zurich, Baden, Bern, Disputations at
Disraeli, Benjamin. *See* Beaconsfield
Dissenters, in Russia, and Peter the Great, v 529; in England, *see* Nonconformists
Dissertatio de ratione status in imperio Romano-Germanico, and its effects, iv 384
Distelmeyer, Lampert, iii 153
Ditmarschen, revolt of peasants of, ii 601; expedition of Frederick II against, iv 563 sq.
Divi, ceded to French, vi 539
Divine right of Kings, *see* Vol. iii, Chap. xxii, Political thought in the 16th century, 736-69; *also* as held by Bossuet, v 76 sq.
Dix, John Adams, American statesman and general, vii 583, 600
Dixmude, taken by the Allies (1695), v 62
Dixon, Admiral, ix 45
Djezzar, Ahmed, Pasha of Acre, viii 607 sqq.
Djokjokarta, Javanese rising in, xi 667
Djunis, Servian defeat at, xii 386
Dlotovsky, Erast, policy of, xi 629

Dmitri, son of Ivan IV, Tsar, v 495; 499
—— the False. *See* Demetrius
Dmowski, Roman, Polish patriot, xii 338 sq.; 372
Dnieper river, v 505; Cossack fortress on, 601; Turkey and, vi 305; 307; 674; 695
Dniester river, Turkey and, vi 304; 307; 676
Doáb, the Maráthas and the, ix 724; French dominion in the, 725; 727
Dobell, Sydney Thompson, poet, xi 352
Doberschütz, heights of, vi 290
Doblhoff-Dier, Baron Anton von, Austrian statesman, xi 176; 182; 186
Dobre, fight at (1831), x 469
Dobrolyúboff, Nikolai A., Russian writer, xii 297
Dobrowský, Josef, Čech writer, xi 653 sqq.
Dobrudja, The, xii 388; 392; Roumania and, 397
Dobrzyn, Palatinate of, iii 87
—— Elector of Polish Palatinate of, iii 87
Dobsen, Claude-Emmanuel, viii 272 sq.
Doctor Faustus, Marlowe's, iii 374
Doctrinaires, of the Restoration, Vol. x, Chaps. ii and xv *passim*
Docwra, Sir Henry, iii 608-9
Dóczi, Peter, Hungarian diplomatist, i 343
Doda, Prenk Bib, Mirdite prince, xii 402
Dodds, French native officer in Dahomey, xii 129
Dodge, Henry, nominated for President of the United States, vii 399
Dodington, George Bubb. *See* Melcombe, Lord
Dodoens, Rembert, botanist, v 734
Döbling, Count Széchenyi at, xi 401
Döllinger, Johann Joseph Ignatius, church historian, xi 708; 717; 719; excommunication of, 723; xii 148; 825; 848
Dömitz, Banér's fight at, iv 366; capture of fortress of (1809), ix 357
Dönhoff, Countess Sophia von, xi 193
Dörnberg, Baron W. C. von, ix 356; at Lüneburg, 515; negligence of, 626
Dörpfeld, Wilhelm, archaeologist, xii 845
Dogali, Italian defeat at, xii 240
Dogger Bank incident, xii 594; 719; 724
Dohna, Count Achatius von, at Heilbronn, iv 28
—— Christoph von, Prussian general, vi 277; 279 sq.; 287; 291 sq.
—— Count Christopher von, iv 17; and James I, 24; 29; envoy at the Hague, v 152 sq.
—— Fabian von, German general (1587), iii 43
—— Hannibal von, and George William of Brandenburg, iv 92
Dokhturoff, Russian lieut.-colonel of Hussars, defends Smolensk, ix 493; at Malo-Yaroslavetz, 499
Dol, occupied by the Vendeans, viii 355

Dolben, Sir William, vi 473

Dolder, Landammann, member of Swiss Directory, ix 97

Dôle, besieged by Condé, iv 370 sq.; Garibaldi at, xi 604

Dolet, Étienne, i 577; ii 288; death of, 291

Dolfin, Piero, Venetian merchant in Chios, i 286

Dolgoruki or Dolgorukoff, family, persecution of, vi 302
—— Alexis, Prince, v 555
—— Catharine, Princess, v 555
—— George, founder of Moscow, v 477
—— George, Prince, sent to Berlin, ix 255; interview with Napoleon, 259; 262
—— Vasili, Prince, xi 614
—— Vasily, Prince, Russian ambassador in Sweden, v 551
—— Vasily Lukich, Prince, Russian statesman, v 553 sq.
—— Vasily Vladimirovich, Prince, Russian general, v 554
—— Princes, xii 333

Dolhain, Adrian de Berghes, Lord of, iii 228 sq.

Dolman, Colonel, envoy in Holland, v 140

Dolmos, Fernam, lord of Terceira and "Antilha," i 20

Domaine d'Occident, vii 87, 91, 107

Domat, Jean, ix 162

Dombrovski, General John Henry, ix 40; x 453

Domenichi, Domenico di. *See* Torcello, Bishop of

Domenico, Frà, da Pescia, follower of Savonarola, i 147, 181 sqq.
—— Frà, da Ponzo, Franciscan rival of Savonarola, i 151, 162

Domfront, Montgomery captured at, iii 23

Domhardt, Johann Friedrich von, Prussian official, vi 733

Dominica, the French and, v 687; England and, vi 185 sq.; 426; 428; 436; taken by French (1778), 451; 464; French attack on (1805), ix 221; trade of, xii 654

Dominican Observantists, Savonarola's new Congregation, i 148 sqq.

Dominicans, Order of the, i 145, 149, 626; and the religious revival in Germany, ii 106, 161; expelled from San Marco, iii 390; at Nancy, xi 30. *See also* Religious Orders

Dominici, Giovanni, and the Renaissance, ii 3

Domitz, fortress of, vi 266

Dommartin, Elzéard-Auguste, French general, viii 444; 606

Domokós, xii 391; battle of, 422

Dompierre d'Hornoy, Charles-Marius-Albert, French admiral, xii 108

Domstädtl, Pass of, battle of, vi 278 sq.; 236

Don, river, vi 304; Turkey and, 305; Cossack district of the, xi 620

Donato, Leonardo, Doge of Venice, i 276
—— Niccolò. *See* Aquileia, Archbishop of

Donaueschingen, Kray at, ix 57; 58

Donauwörth, troubles in (1606), iii 723 sqq.; Gustavus Adolphus before, iv 214; 219; Horn and Bernard of Weimar near, 227, 229, 231; taken by Ferdinand of Hungary (1634), 244; and Thirty Years' War, 409; battle of (1704), v 409; troops at, vi 237; Grand Army crosses Danube near, ix 254; French troops ordered to concentrate at, 347; Napoleon enters (1809), 348

Doncaster, Viscount. *See* Carlisle, James Hay, Earl of

Doncourt, Germans at, xi 592

Dondukoff-Korsakoff, Prince, Russian Commissioner in Bulgaria, xii 403

Doneau, Hugues. *See* Donellus

Donegal, Spanish schemes in, iii 529, 531; plantation of, 614
—— Marquis of, and the Steelboys, vi 491

Donellus (Hugues Doneau), French legist, i 577; iii 58 sq.

Donets district, factories in, xii 320

Donetz, river, Peter the Great and, vi 305

Dongan, Thomas, Governor of New York, vii 42 sqq., 48; 88

Dongola, occupied by the Sirdar, xii 447; 805

Donker-Curtius, Dirk, Dutch statesman, xi 663; 665 sq.

Donnadieu, Gabriel, Vicomte, general, ix 21; x 50; 54; 74; 80

Donne, John, first of the Fantastic Poets, iv 760 sqq.; Herbert and, 767 sq.; and Italian poetry, 772 sq.

Donnersberg, part of, ceded to Bavaria, ix 658

Donoughmore, 2nd Earl of. *See* Hely-Hutchinson

Doornkop, Dr Jameson surrenders at, xii 641

Doppelgrund, The, Russian army at, vi 285

"Dopper" Church, in South Africa, xi 786

Doppet, François-Amédée, French commander in Spain, viii 439

Dopping, Anthony, Bishop of Meath, v 320

Dorat, Jean (Auratus), French Hellenist, i 577; iii 54 sq.

Dorchester (Massachusetts), fortified, vii 17; emigrants from, settle in Connecticut, 18
—— Sir Dudley Carleton, Viscount (Lord Carleton), iii 649; English ambassador to Paris, iv 263
—— Sir Guy Carleton, 1st Baron, Governor of Quebec, vii 171, 214, 216, 308; ix 742; x 687

Doré, Paul-Gustave, French painter, xii 831

Doreslaer, Isaac, v 138

Dorgut, Ottoman sea-captain, iii 125

Doria, Andrea (Genoese admiral), at Marseilles, II 49; and Francis I, 57 sqq., 430; aids Charles V, 59, 69; 74; at Nice, 77; at Genoa, 59, 81 sq.; III 105; seizes Coron, 107–8; with Charles V on expedition to Tunis, 111; perfidy of, 114 sqq., 135, 213, 397
—— Filippino (nephew of above), II 58
—— Gian Andrea, admiral (the younger), III 486, 541, 668
—— Giannettino, adopted son of Andrea, II 82
—— Pietro, Genoese admiral, I 258 sq.
Dormans, fight of (1575), III 28
Dormer, Jane, marries Count of Feria, II 549
Dorner, Isaac August, German theologian, XII 847
Dornès, Auguste, French politician, XI 113
Dorokhoff, Russian officer, guerrilla warfare under, IX 497
Doroszenko, Cossack Hetman, v 353; 355; 599
Dorothea of Denmark. *See* Palatinate
Dorp, Arend van, III 231 sq.
Dorpat, siege of (1625), IV 185, (1704), v 591; University of, x 431, XI 267, XII 336
Dorsenne le Paige, Jean-Marie-François, Comte, aids Marmont, IX 468
Dorset, "Bloody Assizes" in, v 232; parliamentary representation of, x 608
—— Lionel Cranfield Sackville, 1st Duke of, Lord-lieutenant of Ireland, VI 489
—— Thomas Grey, 2nd Marquis of, I 367, 480, 482
—— Thomas Sackville, 1st Earl of (3rd cr.), poems of, III 366 sq., 371
Dorsten, Treaty of (1639), IV 371
Dort, synod at (1586), III 621, (1618), 653, IV 690, v 742, 744; 753; occupied by the French (1795), VIII 436
Dorth, Colonel Jan van, lord of Horst, at Bahia, IV 704; death of, 705
Dortmund, compact at (1609), III 730; acquired by Prussia, IX 657
Dositheus. *See* Rostoff, Bishop of
Dossonville, Jean-Baptiste, police-superintendent in Paris, VIII 512
Dost Ali, Nawáb of the Carnatic, VI 532 sq.; 535
—— Mohammad, Amir of Kabul, XI 731 sqq.; 741 sq.; and Lord Dalhousie, 744; 745; XII 458 sq.; 475
Dostoievski, Feodor, Russian writer, XI 650 sq.; XII 296
Dotrenge, Theodore, x 526, 529
Douai, and Treaty of Arras, III 251; seminary at, 287, 350, 593; Archduke Albert's army at, 673; taken by French (1667), v 199, (1712), 434; 325 sq.; besieged by Marlborough (1710), 428 sq.; 746; *Parlement* of, VIII 47; Irish scholars at, x 622, 630; lace machine introduced at, 744

Douay, Abel, French general, XI 583 sq.; 586; 598
Doudart de Lagrée, explores the Mekong, XII 131
Douglas, castle of, taken by the Covenanters, IV 502
—— *See* Angus, Earl of
—— *See* Hamilton, Duke of
—— *See* Queensberry, Duke of
—— Gawain, Bishop of Dunkeld, II 691
—— Sir George, takes refuge in England, II 454, 457
—— Sir Kenneth, lieutenant-general, VIII 612
—— Lady Margaret, niece of Henry VIII, II 445; marries Lennox, 458
—— Stephen Arnold, American politician, VII 419, 426 sqq., 430, 435; and the Illinois election, 436 sq.; 439 sqq., 444 sq., 600
—— Lieut.-general, besieges Athlone, v 315
Doumer, Paul, Governor-General of Indo-China, XII 528
Doumerc, French commissary-general, VIII 416
Dourlens, submission of, III 663; siege of, 669
Douro, river, Wellesley's passage of, IX 451; and the siege of Oporto, x 328 sqq.; blockaded (1847), 339
Dover, Charles V at, II 45; Charles II lands at, v 280; Secret Treaty of (June 1, 1670), v 40 sqq., 191, 204, 207, 210, 212; Second Treaty of (" *traité simulé* ") (Dec. 31, 1670), 154, 156, 204 sq., 212
—— Straits of, VII 327; defence of the, IX 210; submarine telegraph under, XI 346
—— (New Hampshire), founded, VII 21
—— Lord. *See* Yorke, Sir Joseph
Doveton, Sir John, general, defeats the Raja of Nagpur, XI 726
Dovizi, Bernardo di. *See* Bibbiena
Dowdeswell, William, Chancellor of the Exchequer, VI 435; 437
Down, county, Schomberg lands in, v 312; the Steelboys in, VI 491
Downing, Sir George, ambassador at the Hague, v 107; 148 sq.
Downs, battle of the (1639), IV 700 sq., 707, 708
Downshire, Wills Hill, Marquis of (Viscount Hillsborough), VI 378; 424; 430; President of the Board of Trade, 437; and America (Colonial Secretary), 429 sq., 447, VII 152 sqq.; and Ireland, VI 498
Downton, Nicholas, IV 732; at Surat, 741; 745
Dózsa, George, Hungarian rebel, I 337; historical novel about, XI 427
Dozy, Reinhart P. A., historian, XII 846
Draga, Queen of Servia, XII 412 sq.
Dragashan, defeat of Ypsilanti at (1821), x 179
Drágfy, suppresses rebels in Hungary, I 337

Drago, L. M., Argentine Foreign Minister, xii 701

Dragonnades, iii 769; invented (1681), v 24; 87

Dragut, Arraiz, Turkish pirate, ii 86, 268

Drake, Admiral Sir Francis, iii 296–9; knighted, 301; expedition to West Indies, 301 sq., 304 sqq., 414, 435, 492 sq., 502 sqq., 541; vi 65; expeditions of, vii 2; x 255; 272

—— Francis, British agent at Munich (1803), ix 28; 30, 321

—— Roger, Governor of Calcutta, vi 552

Drakenberg Mountains, Natal frontier, xi 782; 783

Drakenborg, Lutheran victory over forces of Charles V at, ii 261

Drama (Macedonia), policing of, xii 426

Dramali. *See* Ali

Draper, Sir William, lieutenant-general, vi 369; 427

Dred Scott *v.* Sandford case, vii 434 sqq., 444

Dreikaiserbund (of 1872), xii 8 sq.

Dreikönigsbündniss (of 1849), xi 220 sqq.

Drente, invaded, v 150, 157

Drenteln, General, Russian police official, xii 306

Dresden, Patkul at, v 586, 594; 602; 620; vi 231; capitulates, 244; 256; 273; 287; 288; occupied by Austrians (1759), 294; 296; Treaty of (1745), 244; 318; occupied by Bavarian troops (1806), ix 279; Napoleon at (1807), 294, (1812), 487, (1813), 518, 524, 526, 530; occupied by the Duke of Brunswick-Oels (1809), 357; French troops in, 514; evacuated (1813), 515; Allies at, 518; Schwarzenberg marches on, 523; battle of (Aug. 26–7), *ib.,* 525 sqq., 528; 541; proposed conference at, xi 144, 153, 160; Metternich at, 154; 217; disturbances in, 219; Conferences of, 232 sq.

Dreux, battle of (1562), ii 584; Huguenots attempt to seize, iii 4; besieged by Henry IV (1590), 48

Dreyfus, Alfred, French officer, xii 55; 112; 120 sq.; 126

Drogheda, Poynings' Parliament at (1494), i 472; stormed by Cromwell, iv 435; the Irish rebellion at, 523; siege of, 524, 531 sq.; surrender and sack of, 533 sq.; William III at, v 261; 309; 314

Dromore, rout of Protestant force at (1689), v 307 sq.

Droste-Hülshoff, Baroness Annette Elisabeth von, xi 414

Droste-Vischering, Baron, Archbishop of Cologne. *See* Cologne

Drottningholm, Treaty of (1791), ix 37

Drouet, Jean-Baptiste, Comte d'Erlon. *See* Erlon

Drouot, François-Joseph (Lamarche), commands the Army of the North (1793), viii 429

Drouyn de Lhuys, Édouard, French Minister of Foreign Affairs, xi 118; 121 sqq.; recalls Lesseps, 125; in London, 281; 322; 474; and Convention of Gastein, 479; 480; and Rome, 534; and Syrian negotiations, 636

Droysen, Johann Gustav, German historian, xi 160; 164; 195; xii 827 sq.; 845

Drucour, Governor of Louisbourg, vii 133

Drucz, river, Charles XII crosses, v 598

Druey, Charles, Swiss statesman, xi 254

Drumann, Wilhelm, German historian, xii 843

Drumclog, Claverhouse defeated at (1679), v 285

Drumcree, Peace of (1563), iii 590

Drummond, John, English merchant in Amsterdam, v 432

—— James, 2nd titular Duke of Perth, vi 103

—— James, 3rd titular Duke of Perth, vi 109; 111 sq.

—— Lord John, 4th titular Duke of Perth, vi 109; 115; 117

—— Thomas, Under-Secretary for Ireland, x 677

—— William, of Hawthornden, denounces the trial of Balmerino, iv 493

Drumont, Édouard, *La France Juive,* xii 120

Drury, Elizabeth, and Donne's *Anniversaries,* iv 765

—— Sir William, supporter of Queen Mary, ii 514; iii 596, 601

Druses, tribe of Lebanon district, ix 385; and Maronites, xi 276

Dryander, Francis. *See* Enzinas, Francisco de

—— James. *See* Enzinas, Jáime de

Dryden, John, and Beaumont and Fletcher, iv 760; and Fantastic Poetry, 775; v 122; 125; heroic plays of, 126 sq.; comedies of, 129 sq.; 131; poems of, 132; prose writings of, 132 sq.; satires of, 133 sqq.; and Shadwell, 134; religious poems of, 135; conversion of, 135, 234; 228; x 696; 714; 724 sq.

Duane, William John, American lawyer, vii 383

Duarte, Francisca, iv 720

Du Barail, François-Charles, French general and statesman, xii 108

Du Barry, Marie-Jeanne Gomard de Vaubernier, Countess, vi 330; 356; 359; 373; 595

Du Bartas, Salluste, iii 61

Du Bellay, Guillaume, ii 284 sqq.; iii 64

—— Jean, Cardinal, ii 281, 284, 287

—— Joachim, iii 54 sqq., 71

—— Martin, iii 64

Dubienka, battle of, viii 532

Du Biez, Oudard, French marshal, besieges Boulogne, II 460
Dubitza, stormed by Loudon, VIII 325
Dublin, siege of (1534), II 442; trade with Bristol, III 579; Parliament at, 582; Tyrone submits in, 611; Tyrone and O'Cahan cited to, 612; County, English in, III 580; Cromwell at, IV 435; Parliament meets in (July 14, 1634), 518; Strafford at, 520; rebels fail to capture, 522; defence of, 523; Harcourt at, 524; return of Ormonde to, 526; Glamorgan arrested at, 529; peace proclaimed at, 530; besieged by the Confederates, 531, 532 sq.; final settlement and, 536; castle of, surprised, 547; V 261; Convention of Estates at (1660), 301; James II at, 308, 315; 312; 314; William III at, 315; disturbances in, VI 485, 489, 491; distress in, 495, 503; 497; Volunteer Convention at, 501 sq.; 504; disaffection in (1792), IX 695; University of, 696; 705; Parliamentary reform in, 697; 705; Fitzwilliam in, 698 sq.; mails for, stopped, 701; and the Union, 704; Emmet arrested in, 707; discontent in (1808), 708; Catholic traders in, x 626; Association for Catholic relief, 627 sq., 632, 639; O'Connell leaves (1798), 630; XI 7; University of, 9; XII 38; Trinity College, 29, 71 sq.; Catholic University at, 71 sq.; Parnell in, 75; 80; Phoenix Park murders in, 81; National Conference at, 82; 83; 762
Dublin Evening Post, The, x 635
Dublin Society, The, VI 484
Du Bocage, Manuel Maria Barbosa, Portuguese poet, VIII 784
Dubois, Guillaume, Cardinal, v 90; and the negotiations with Great Britain, VI 26 sq.; 29 sq.; in London, 31; 38; 123 sq.; 126; 129 sq.; ministry of, 131; 134; 144; 587; death of, 127, 131; VIII 9
—— Paul-François, French publicist, x 95
—— Captain of the Paris Watch (1788), VIII 115; Prefect of Police, IX 8; 11, 16, 21; discovers a plot (June, 1808), 137; 141
Dubois-Crancé, E.-L.-Alexis, VIII 174, 340; at Lyons, 346, 351; 366; Minister of War, 432, 678
Du Bouchage, Gabriel Gratet, Vicomte, x 47; 54
Du Bourg, Anne, executed, II 296
—— Antoine, Chancellor under Francis I, II 286, 296
Dubuisson, French physician, IX 143
Duc, Fronton Le (Ducaeus), Jesuit, I 618 sq.; edits *St Chrysostom,* III 61
Du Camp, Maxime, x 516
Du Cange, Charles du Fresne, Seigneur, III 61
Ducas, Demetrios, Cretan scholar at Alcalá, II 400
Ducasse, Jean-Baptiste, French seaman, v 59; 691

Du Cayla, Zoé Talon, Comtesse, x 69
Du Chaillu, Paul, African explorer, XII 812
Du Chasteler, J. G. J. A., Marquis, sent to recover Tyrol, IX 355
Duchâtel, Charles-Marie-Tanneguy, Comte, French Minister of Finance, x 497; 508; 511; Minister of the Interior, XI 96
—— Dutch painter, XII 249
Du Chayla, Abbé, murder of, v 26
Duchè, Jacob, American clergyman, VII 161
Duchesne, André, III 63
—— Louis, historian, XII 847 sq.
—— French general, in Tonkin, XII 131, 526; in Madagascar, 130
Ducis, Jean-François, IX 132
Duckwitz, Arnold, German politician, XI 166; 227
Duckworth, Sir John Thomas, admiral, IX 234; commands expedition to Constantinople, 235; forces passage of the Dardanelles, 388
Du Clerc, French seaman, v 679
Duclerc, Charles-Théodore-Eugène, French politician, XI 113
Du Clercq, Jacques, historian, I 430, 433
Ducos, Roger, VIII 669 sq.; and Napoleon, 675 sq., 679, 683; provisional Consul, 686; IX 1; 5, 8
—— Théodore, French politician, XI 127
Ducpétiaux, Édouard, Belgian politician, x 532; 536 sq.
Ducrest, barber, pension of, VIII 73
Ducret, the younger, chemist, IX 133
Du Croc, French ambassador to Mary Queen of Scots, III 272 sqq.
Ducrot, Auguste-Alexandre, French general, XI 598; 605 sqq.
Du Daugnon, French naval commander, holds Brouage, IV 600 sq., 618; 613; Governor of La Rochelle, 615; defeated off Ré, 617
Duddingston, Prince Charles at, VI 113
Du Deffand, Marquise, VI 767
Duderstadt, Wallenstein meets Tilly at, IV 97
Dudevant, Amantine-L.-A. *See* Sand, George
Dudley, Edmund, Minister of Henry VII, I 477 sq.
—— Lord Guilford, marriage of, to Lady Jane Grey, II 510; arrested, 518; executed, 528
—— Sir Henry, II 505; plots against Mary, 544
—— John. *See* Northumberland, Duke of
—— John William Ward, British Foreign Secretary, x 197, 200
—— Joseph, Governor of Massachusetts, VII 64 sq.
—— Lord Robert. *See* Leicester, Earl of
Dünewald, Count Johann Heinrich von, Austrian general, v 367
Düppel, XI 167; capture of, 224; 440 sq.

Dürer, Albrecht, 1 323, 325; *Triumph of Maximilian*, 326; 683; 11 159; and Erasmus, 167

Duero, Manuel de la Concha, Marqués del. *See* Del Duero

Düsseldorf, Reformed congregation at, 111 705; meeting of Estates at, 716; "Possessing" Princes in, 730; school of the Reformed Church at, v 757; reform at, 1x 410; 411; revolutionary movement at, xi 219

Du Fargis, French envoy to Spain, and the Treaty of Monzon, 1v 59, 675

Dufaure, Jules-Armand-Stanislas, French statesman, x 511; xi 98; 115; Minister of the Interior, 117, 128; 119; 126; xii 101; 105; supports Thiers, 106; 107; 111 sq.; 115; resigns, 116

Dufferin and Ava, Frederick T. Hamilton-Temple-Blackwood, Marquis of, xi 636; xii 23; and Egyptian affairs, 438 sq., 450; Viceroy of India, 477 sqq.

Duffy, Charles Gavan, and the Young Ireland party, xi 7

Dufour, William Henry, Swiss general, xi 239; 250 sq.; 255

Dufraisse, Marc, x 485; banished, xi 139

Dugommier, J.-F.-Coquille, French general, viii 352, 440

Dugonics, Andrew, Hungarian writer, xi 422

Dugua, Charles-F.-J., French general, viii 601 sq., 614

Duguay-Trouin, René, French admiral, v 59; 679; vi 391

Du Haillan, Bernard, French historian, iii 63

Du Hallier, Comte. *See* L'Hospital

Duhayet, Aubert, French ambassador to the Porte, ix 386

Duhesme, Comte Philippe - Guillaume, French general, at Naples, viii 653; in Catalonia, ix 239; 430, 435, 439; relieved by Gouvion Saint-Cyr, 448

Duhot, General, in Paris, xi 100

Duich, Loch, Jacobites at, vi 106

Duisburg, University of, iv 789, 791, v 656

Duiveland, island of, taken by Spaniards (1575), iii 242

Du Jon, François (Franciscus Junius), Calvinist, at Antwerp, iii 201; death of, 647; iv 717

Duka, Count Peter von, Austrian field-marshal, viii 575

Dulaney, Daniel, Maryland jurist, vii 59; legal arguments of, Chap. vi *passim*

Dulce, Domingo, Spanish general, xi 560; 569; xii 265

Dulcigno, ceded to Montenegro, xii 37; 390; 392; restored to Turkey, 396; 402

Du Luc, French ambassador to Switzerland, vi 613; 615

Duma, in the early days of the Muscovite State, v 484 sq., 491 sq.; council acts as a, 502; Russian modern scheme

initiated, xii 351 sqq.; Act establishing Duma, 356 sqq.; meeting of the first, 364 sqq.; the second, 372 sqq.; the third, 375 sq.; visit of leaders of, to England, 380

Dumanoir le Pelley, Comte Pierre-Étienne-René-Marie, French rear-admiral, ix 54; 234

Dumas, Alexandre, iii 548; x 101; 515; 725 sq.; xi 426 sq.; dramas of, 515; 519

—— Alexandre, *fils*, xi 516 sqq.; 548

—— Alexandre Davy de la Pailleterie, French general, holds the S. Bernard and Mont Cenis, viii 438

—— Benoît, Governor of Pondicherry, vi 533

—— Comte Matthieu, viii 213, 488, 507

—— René-François, French politician, executed, viii 371

Du Maurier, French ambassador to Maurice of Orange, iii 653

Dumay, Jean-Baptiste, Mayor of Creusot, xi 503

Dumbarton Castle, iii 282; taken by the Covenanters, iv 502; vi 92; Bushell at, 107

Dumerbion, Pierre Jadar, French general, viii 438

Dumfries, Treaty of Union burnt at, v 299

Dumfriesshire, recusants in, v 283

Dumolard, Joseph-Vincent, French deputy, viii 488, 508

Dumonceau, Jean-Baptiste, General, ix 90

Dumont, Charles-Albert-Auguste-Eugène, xii 118

—— Jean, the *Letter to an Englishman*, v 514

—— P.-Étienne-L., French publicist, viii 150, 748

Du Moulin, Peter, French divine, and James I, v 743

Dumoulin, Charles, French legist, iii 59

Dumouriez, Charles - François, French general, vi 355; Foreign Minister under Louis XVI, viii 223 sq.; Minister of War, 227, 406; resigns, 228; in Paris, 259; at Neerwinden, 268, 420 sq.; negotiates with Austria, 268, 421 sq., 503; in Belgium, 299, 415 sqq.; at Valmy, 410 sq.; in Holland, 418 sq.; in Brussels, 420; ix 30

Dun, ceded to France, v 33

Dunajewski, Julian von, Austrian Minister of Finance, xii 195

Dunamünde, Swedish victory at (1701), v 592; fortress of, vi 315

Dunbar, Mary Stewart carried to, iii 274; battle of (1650), iv 435, 510; Cope at, vi 113

—— Gawain, Bishop of Aberdeen, ii 453

—— William, poet, ii 691

—— Scottish merchant of Danzig, and Charles X, iv 580

Dunblane, Duke of Argyll at, vi 100
—— Bishop of, Catholic envoy from Mary Queen of Scots, iii 272, 275
Dunboy, ceded to King of Spain, iii 532
Dunboyne, James Butler, 2nd Lord (brother-in-law of Gerald, Earl of Desmond), iii 596
Duncan, Adam, Viscount Camperdown, viii 453 sq., 479, 481; at Camperdown, 482 sq.; ix 40
—— major-general, defeated at Fyllebro, v 569
Duncannon, captured by William III, v 315
—— Lord. *See* Bessborough
Duncker, Maximilian Wolfgang, xi 164; *History of Antiquity*, xii 846
Dundalk, Norris at, iii 606; Mountjoy at, 608; Chichester at, 613; surrendered to Inchiquin, iv 532; Schomberg at, v 312 sqq.
Dundas, Francis, General, in Cape Colony, ix 750
—— Henry. *See* Melville
Dundee, Jacobite rising at, vi 98
—— John Graham of Claverhouse, Viscount, v 285; 288; 291 sqq.; death of, 312
—— William Graham, 5th titular Viscount of, vi 98
Dundonald, Thomas Cochrane, 10th Earl of, and the Radical movement, ix 688; in South America, x 291 sqq., 295, 316
Dunes, battle of the (1658). *See* Dunkirk
Dungannon, vi 499; volunteers at, 501
—— Hugh, Baron of. *See* Tyrone
—— Matthew O'Neill (Fedoragh), Baron of. *See* Tyrone
Dungeness, Anglo-Dutch naval action off, iv 474 sq., 478; French fleet at, vi 239
Dungern, Baron Emil August von, Nassau statesman, xi 147
Dunin, Archbishop of Posen. *See* Posen
Dunkeld, Jacobite rising at, vi 98
—— Andrew Bruce, Bishop of, iii 267
Dunkirk, sack of, by French (1558), ii 93; Spanish port, iii 507; fleet of transports ordered at, 623; pirates at, 634; Cromwell and, iv 439; Anglo-French expedition against (1657), 440, 485; 540 sq.; taken by the French (Oct. 11, 1646), 598; 611; France forced to abandon, 618; invested, 619; battle of (1658), 660; Dutch expeditions against (1631), 694, (1637), 698; Spaniards retreat to, 700; surrender of, to French and Dutch, 703; 706; v 14; 104; transferred to France (1662), 106; 113; 423; 433; 440; and Anglo-French Treaty, 442; vi 23; Old Pretender at, 92 sq.; 102; 110; 159; 239; and Treaty of Aix-la-Chapelle, 249; 331; 340; fortifications of, 345 sq., 429, 436; 464; besieged by English (1793), viii 431; relieved, *ib.*; French troops at, ix 208-9; harbour of, xii 102

Dunmore, John, 4th Earl of, Governor of Virginia, vii 164, 169
Dunning, burnt by the Jacobites, vi 102
—— John. *See* Ashburton, Lord
Dunnottar Castle, prisoners in, v 289
Dunois, François, Count of, i 393
Dunoyer, Barthélemy - Charles - Pierre - Joseph, editor of *Le Censeur*, ix 569
Dunraven, Windham Thomas Wyndham-Quin, 4th Earl of, xii 89
Dunrobin, Earl of Sutherland at, vi 99
Dunstable, Cranmer tries divorce question at, ii 440
Dupanloup. *See* Orleans, Bishop of
Dupaty, C.-M. Jean-Baptiste Mercier, ix 169
Du Perron, Cardinal J. D., French diplomatist (1607), iii 684
Dupetit-Thouars, Abel Aubert, French admiral, xi 35
Duphot, Léonard, French general, viii 637; assassination of, x 132
Dupin, A.-M.-J.-J., x 91; 487; 489; and Algiers, 503; and Molé, 507; 508
—— Charles, x 493; xi 102; 116; 130
—— Claude, French farmer-general, viii 71
Du Plan, supporter of Savoy in Geneva, iii 414
Dupleix, Joseph, Governor-general of French India, vi 533 sqq.; defends Pondicherry, 538; 539; 541; fall of, 542; policy of, 543 sq.; character of, 545; 546
Duplessis-Mornay. *See* Mornay
Du Plessis-Praslin. *See* Choiseul
Dupont, Samuel Francis, American admiral, vii 554
—— de l'Eure, Jacques-Charles, x 484; 499; xi 102; 109; 124
—— de l'Etang, Comte Pierre, French general, ix 254; ordered to Cadiz, 311; at Baylen, 315; his armies at Bayonne, 430; corps of, 435-6; attacks Cordova, 437; failure and imprisonment of, 438; 439, 441; Minister of War, 557; 565; 568; succeeded by Soult, 571
—— de Nemours, Pierre-S., viii 21, 23, 86, 179; and the Court, 216; 488; 501, 515, 715
Duport, Adrien, member of the National Assembly, viii 131, 174, 182, 187, 200
Duport-du-Tertre, M.-L.-François, Minister of Justice under Louis XVI, viii 216, 222; executed, 357
Duportail, Lebègue, Minister of War under Louis XVI, viii 216; resigns, 220
Duprat, Cardinal Antoine, Chancellor of France, ii 95, 147, 284 sq.; death of, 286
—— Pascal, French politician, xi 110; 112; xii 103
Dupuis, explorer, xii 524; 797
Dupuy, Charles-Alexandre, French statesman, xii 121; 126

Dupuy, Dominique, French general, VIII 603; killed, 606

Duquesne, Abraham, French seaman, V 44; 162; 183

—— de Menneville, Marquis, Governor of New France, VII 98, 119

Durand, Sir Mortimer, mission of, to the Amir, XII 482 sq.; 487

—— Nicolas (Villegagnon), I 48 sq.

Durand-Maillane, Pierre-Toussaint, French politician, VIII 386

Durando, Giacomo, Italian Foreign Minister, XI 65, 534

—— Giovanni, Italian general, XI 84; 86

Durandus (Guillaume Durand), French Canonist, at Council of Vienne, I 620

Durango, Carlist capital, XII 260

Duranton, Antoine, Minister of Justice to Louis XVI, VIII 223

Duras, Léopold, editor of *Le National*, XI 127

—— Duc de, VI 334

Durban, capital of Natal, XI 782; Convention at, XII 646

D'Urban, Sir Benjamin, Governor of Cape Colony, XI 780 sq.

Duren, siege and capture of, by Charles V (1543), II 77, 244

Durham, Catholic Earls in, III 281

—— John George Lambton, 1st Earl of, and parliamentary reform, X 603, 608 sq., 614, 617 sq.; 655; resigns, 658; 665; XI 16; and Canada, X 690, 692 sq., XI 755 sqq.; 762; 765 sqq.; and the West Indies, XII 656

Durjan Sal, rebel Jat, XI 729

Durnovó, I., Russian Minister of the Interior, XII 313; 326

—— P., Russian Minister of the Interior, XII 360; 362 sq.; 365

Duroc, G.-C.-Michel, Duc de Friuli, VIII 564, 592, 616; IX 23; 50, 103; Napoleon's Grand Marshal of the Palace, 111; receives the Duchy of Friuli, *ib.*; at Berlin, 251; 255; interview with Lucchesini, 278; 301; Napoleon's instructions to, 302

Duroveray, Jean, Genevan democrat, assists Mirabeau, VIII 150

Duruy, Victor, French Minister of Public Education, XI 476; 479; 484; attacked by the Catholics, 485, 494; XII 93; 118; 131

Du Ryer, Pierre, French dramatic poet, V 68

Dušan, Stephen, of Servia, death of (1356), I 67

Dusaulx, Jean, French writer and politician, VIII 247

Duschek, Francis, Hungarian Minister of Finance, XI 212 sq.

Dusentschur, Anabaptist, at Münster, II 226 sq.

Dussen, Bruno van der, Dutch diplomatist, V 422; 427 sq.; 439

Dussindale, Ket defeated at, II 493

Dutch Republic. *See* Netherlands, United Provinces of the

—— Reformed Church, in S. Africa, XI 785

Duteil, Republican politician, XI 137

Du Tertre, Jean-Baptiste, VII 97

Du Tillot, Parmesan Minister, VI 593 sq.

Dutoitspan, discovery of diamonds at, XI 787

Du Tremblay, François. *See* Joseph, Père

Du Vair, Guillaume, Bishop of Lisieux. *See* Lisieux, Bishop of

Du Val de Dampierre, Henri, Comte, commands under Bucquoy, IV 23; 31

Duvelaer, Director of the French East India Company, VI 542

Duvergier de Hauranne, Abbé de Saint Cyran. *See* Saint-Cyran

—— Prosper, X 95; 507 sq.; XI 116; XII 103

Duverne de Presle, T.-Laurent-M. (Théodore Dunan), VIII 505 sq., 511

Duverney, Paris, VI 134; 144

Duveyrier, Honoré-Nicolas-Marie, French politician, IX 15

Duvivier, Franciade-Fleurus, French general, XI 104; 113

Duwall, Swedish general, IV 219; Arnim's Silesian scheme and, 236; death of, 247

Dvernicki, Joseph, Polish general, X 469; 471

Dybowski, African explorer, XII 130

Dybvad, George, Danish theologian, loses his chair, IV 567

Dyevichesky monastery, V 523

Dykvelt, Everhard van Weede, Heer van, Dutch envoy in England, V 235; 240 sq.

Dynter, Edmond of, Flemish historian, I 433

Dyson, Jeremiah, Clerk of the House of Commons, VI 424; 427; 438 sq.; 442

Dzieduszycki, Count Izydor, Polish writer, XI 657

Dzierzgowski, Primate of Poland. *See* Gnesen

Dzikowa, partisans of Stanislaus at, VI 197

Earle, Thomas, American lawyer, VII 388

—— William, General, and the Gordon relief expedition, XII 442 sq.

Early, Jubal Anderson, Confederate general, VII 531 sq.; defeated by Sheridan (1865), 537

East Africa Company (Dutch), V 647; (German), XII 661

East Anglia, spinning and weaving in, X 735 sq.

Eastern Association, The, IV 311; 314; 321

—— Bengal and Assam, province of, XII 495

—— Question, The (Near), in the 18th century, the European powers and, Vol. VIII, Chap. XI, 306–37; of early 19th century, *see* Vol. X, Chap. VI *passim*,

169–204, Chap. xvii, 545–72; of the middle 19th century, *see* Vol. xi, Chap. ix *passim*, especially 275–85, Chap. xi, Crimean war, *passim*, 309–24, *also* Chap. xxii *passim*, especially 635–47; of late 19th and early 20th centuries, Vol. xii, Chap. xiv, The Ottoman Empire and the Balkan Peninsula, 381–428; for Egypt, Chap. xv, 429–56; *see also* the Far East

East Friesland, Mansfield in, iv 85 sq.; Brandenburg and, v 647; and Hanover, ix 592, 654, 657
—— Edzard of, i 453

East India Company (Brandenburg), v 646
—— (Danish), chartered in 1614, iv 746
—— (Dutch), iii 633; 638 sq.; iv 694; 703; profits of, 710; centres of, 711; and Japan, 712; and Oriental trade, 713; Peace of Münster and, 716; 729; 731 sq.; financial position of, 735, 744 sq.; agreement of June 1619 and, 737; 738; 740; 742; Joan Maurice of Nassau and, 753; v 138; 149; 693; 702; vi 188; ix 749; end of, 754
—— (English), iii 562; rival of the Dutch, iv 713; foundation of, 729 sq.; first expedition of, 731; comparison between Dutch East India Company and, 732; financial position of, 735; agreement of June 1619 and, 737; 738; demands reparation for Amboina "massacre," 739; 740 sq.; lays foundations of British India, 742; 745; dependent on the Crown, 746; v 108; 138; 149; 178 sq.; 274; 692; operations and policy of, 697 sqq.; establishment of new Company (1698), 700; union of the two Companies, 701; 704 sq.; Vol. vi, Chap. xv (2) and (3) *passim*; 45; 49; 180; 438; 445 sq.; 465; 467; 469; vii 157 sq.; *see* Vol. ix, Chap. xxiii, The British Empire (1783–1815); x 728; 760; xi 310; 329; 724 sqq.; Crown takes the place of, 749 sqq.; and China trade, 804 sqq., 822
—— (French), attempts to organise, iii 694; v 12 sq.; vi 173 sqq.; Chap. xv (2) *passim*; vii 92 sq.; Calonne forms a new (1785–6), viii 99

East Indies, Spanish navigation to, iv 744; v 107; Dutch and English in, 108, 148 sq., 151, 154, 179; vi 57; England and, 248; Jesuits expelled from Portuguese possessions in, 387; 429; 756; British trade with, vii 4; foreign trade of, xi 15. *See also under* Indies
—— (Dutch), abolition of slavery in, xi 666; 667 sq., xii 668
—— (French), ix 209; British fleet in, 219; insurance of merchantmen for, 242

Easton, Adam, Cardinal and Bishop of Norwich, Bible Translations of, i 593, 597

Eastport, captured by the British (1814), vii 344
East Retford, and the franchise, x 601
Eaton, Theophilus, forms colony of New Haven, vii 20
Eberach, Henry, scholar at Erfurt, ii 111
—— Peter, scholar at Erfurt, ii 111
Eberlin, John, of Günzburg, ii 159 sqq.; Utopian scheme of, 183 sq.
Ebersberg, forest of, and Hohenlinden, ix 67
Eblé, Comte Jean-Baptiste, French general, ix 501
Eboli, Ruy Gomez de Silva, Prince of, iii 190; influence of, with Philip II, 476 sq.; 490; death of, 241, 514
—— Ana de Gomez de Silva Mendoza y la Cerda, Princess of, and murder of Escobedo, iii 515
Ebro river, French army of Spain on, ix 430, 441; Spanish armies on, 443
Ebusood El Amadi, iii 128
Ecclesiastical Commission, becomes permanent in England, x 673 sq.
—— Court, of James II, v 234
Echagüe, Rafael, Spanish general, xi 569
Echigo, fight at, xi 859
Echizen clan and *daimiōs*, Vol. xi, Chap. xxviii (2) *passim*
Eck, Dr Johann Maier (called Eck), controversialist, i 678; ii 29; *Obelisks* of, against Luther, 130; disputes with Luther, 134 sq.; 138; 162; *Loci Communes* of, 172; 212; 240; 326
—— John (of Trier), ii 140
—— Leonard von, Chancellor of Bavaria, ii 191
Eckeren, the Allies defeated at (1703), v 407
Eckernförde, Danish men-of-war at, xi 224
Eckhart, "Master," of Cologne, German mystic, i 434
Eckhel, Joseph Hilarius von, German numismatist, xii 816
Eckmühl, battle of (1809), ix 349
École des Chartes, xii 834
Ecuador, Spanish conquest of, i 45; Republic of, formed (1830), x 296; xii 672 sq.; 678; 696; and Panamá, 700. *See also under* Colombia
Edam, and Act of Seclusion, v 143
Eden, Sir Ashley, envoy to Bhutan, xi 752
—— Sir Frederick Morton, *The State of the Poor*, x 782
—— Sir Morton, British Ambassador at Vienna, viii 559 sq., 645, 660
—— Richard, American works of, i 52 sqq.
—— William. *See* Auckland, Lord
Edgcumbe, Richard Edgcumbe, 2nd Lord, vi 437
Edgecombe, Sir Richard, i 471
Edgehill, battle of (1642), iv 307, 311
Edgeworth, Richard Lovell, author, viii 755, 765

Edgeworth de Firmont, Abbé Henry Essex, confessor to Louis XVI, VIII 261

Edhem Pasha, Turkish commander, XII 421

Edict of Beaulieu, III 30
—— of Emancipation (1807), IX 330; 331
—— of January (1562), II 304; III 1, 2, 26
—— of July, The French (1561), II 301
—— of Nantes, III 675 sqq., 681, 754; revocation of, V 18, 21 sqq.; England and, 50; 51 sqq.; 57; 87; 166; James II and, 233; 654; VI 614. *See also* Toleration
—— of Restitution, French (1561), II 303
—— of Restitution, Imperial, IV 109–17; 233; suspended in Peace of Prague, 253; 395; Bishop of Osnabrück and, 401; 411; 414; 676 sq.; Maximilian of Bavaria and, 679; Urban VIII and, 688
—— of Toleration, withdrawn (1588) through Guise influence, III 511
—— of Villers-Cotterets (1539), II 96

Edinburgh, burnt by the English, II 459, 556; Scottish Reformation Parliament at, 579; Treaty of (1560), 577, 581, III 266, 282; Lords of the Congregation in, 264; Town Council of, 268; Mary Stewart at, 274–6; castle of, 282 sqq.; supports Scottish clergy, 551; and English Liturgy, IV 496 sq.; and "King's Covenant," 499; castle of, taken by Covenanters, 502; "Plotters" imprisoned in, 505; Charles I in, *ib.*; Cromwell in, 508, 510; Dutch naval demonstration against, V 188; 226; prisoners at, 286; the Pope's effigy burnt at, 287; executions at, 287, 289 sq.; 291; 299; castle of, VI 92; 94; 98 sq.; Porteous mob in, 108; 111; Prince Charles in, 112 sq.; 114 sq.; and John Law, 169, 175; Brougham at, X 665; Allan Ramsay's theatre at, 701

Edinburgh Review, influence of, IX 687; Lord Brougham and, X 575; 601; and Wordsworth and Coleridge, 707; and Byron, 711; 716; XI 362

Edinburgh, Alfred, Duke of. *See* Saxe-Coburg-Gotha, Duke of

Edmunds, George Franklin. American statesman, VII 653

Edrisi (Shérif al-Edrisi as-Sikilli al-Rodjari), Arab geographer, I 9

Education (*see* Schools and Universities, *but also for slighter mention*), Calvin's system of, II 372 sq.; Zwingli's system of, 318; effect of English suppression of monasteries on, 468; Edward VI's reign and, 503; in Austria, Joseph II and, IV 628; of secular clergy, 637; in Belgium, clerical seminary at Louvain under Joseph II, 649 sqq.; in Canada, work of the French and English missionaries in, VII 101 sqq.; in Denmark, under Christian VI, VI 739; in New England, VII 58 sqq.; in Ottoman Empire, under Solyman the Magnificent, III

127 sq.; in Poland, "Education Commission" of "Delegation Diet," VI 671; in Russia, under Catharine II, 692 sq.; in United States, unique character of, VII 750 sq.

Education Acts, English, of 1839, X 679; of 1870, XI 24 sq., 57; of 1902, 57 sqq.

Edward III, King of England, and Venice, I 257
—— IV, King of England, I 390, 430, 463 sq.; III 738
—— VI, King of England, I 52; birth of, II 448; reign of, Chap. XIV *passim*; Prayerbook of, V 325; and Russian trade, 513
—— VII, King of Great Britain (Prince of Wales), illness of (1872), XI 336, XII 46; marriage of, XI 338; XII 14; accession of, 53; 55; visits Ireland (1885), 82; and France, 97 sq.; and Germany, 172; 291; receives Duma leaders, 380; proclaimed Emperor of India, 495; 679; 722

Edwardes, Sir Herbert Benjamin, Major-General, in India, XI 740 sq.; 744

Edwards, Jonathan, VII 60; theological works of, 729 sqq., 732 sq.

Effiat de Chilli et de Longumkau, Antoine Coiffier de Ruzé, Marquis de, superintendent of finances, IV 130; 151

Égalité, La, French journal, XII 123

Eger, Wallenstein murdered at, IV 242 sq.; taken by Wrangel, 392; 394
—— river, attack on, IV 234; 236; 255

Eggenberg, Prince Ulric von, Imperial councillor, IV 68; 72; Wallenstein and, 94, 100, 105, in Moravia, 212, 238, 240; death of, 252; conversion of, 400

Egidio. *See* Gil, Juan

Eglinton, Alexander Montgomerie *or* Seton, 6th Earl of, march of, upon Edinburgh, IV 508

Egmont (North Holland), Descartes at, IV 788
—— Charles of. *See* Gelders
—— John Perceval, 2nd Earl of, VI 424; 430; 435; 437
—— Lamoral, Count of, victorious at Gravelines, II 93, 561; embassy to England of, 525, 530; III 48–9, 184, 188 sqq., 203 sqq., 209 sqq.; execution of, and its effects, 220, 228, 511
—— Sabina of Bavaria, Countess of, III 189

Egremont, Charles Wyndham, 2nd Earl of, VI 420; 424; 426; 430

Eguia, Francisco Ramón de, Spanish Minister of War, X 209

Eguilles, Alexandre-J.-B. de Boyer, Marquis de, VI 113

Egypt, at war with Turks, I 89; Ottoman conquest of (1517), 91, III 117; Spanish, etc. factories in, I 496; Leibniz and, V 696; VI 51; French advance into, 350; the Osmanli Sultans and, 507; Napoleon's Egyptian expedition, Vol. VIII, Chap. XIX,

594–619; the struggle for the Mediterranean (1798–9), Chap. xx, 620–32 *passim*; French designs upon (1801), ix 70; English occupation of, 72; restored to Turkey (1802), 74, 78; French and English withdraw from, 75; Sebastiani's report on 103; French feint upon (1804), 215, 217; British defeat in (1807), 235; designs of France and Russia on, 308, 310 sq., abandoned, 315; advance of Turkish authority in, 387; French loss of, 419; under Mehemet Ali, Vol. x, Chap. xvii *passim*; 172; 176; France and, 512 sq.; (1841–1907), Vol. xii, Chap. xv; British occupation of, 3, 40, 240; 5; 7; 34; Gladstone and, 49; 55; 88; 95; 132; Great Britain and, 161, 658; 428; 499; Concert of Europe and, 728; archaeological work in, 774, 845; 806; 811; 813

Ehlers, Martin, Professor of philosophy at Kiel, viii 788

Ehrenberg, Philip Adolf von, Bishop of Würzburg. *See* Würzburg

Ehrenbreitstein, besieged and taken by the French (1799), viii 641, 644, 654; ix 659

Ehrensvärd, August, Swedish naval engineer, vi 775

Ehrhard, Albert, German scholar, xii 848

Eichendorff, Joseph von, Baron, German poet, x 404 sq.

Eichhorn, J. A. F. E., Prussian statesman, and the Customs' Union, x 373; xi 51 sq.

—— Karl Friedrich, German legal historian, writings of, xii 818 sqq.; 846

Eichsfeld, The, Catholic reaction in, iii 178, 180; Prussian acquisitions in, ix 78

Eickstedt, Hans Henrik, Danish general, vi 751

Eider river, Prussian troops cross, xi 162; 338; and the Danish frontier, 693 sq.

Ein Aga, travellers at, xii 805, 813

Einarsen, Gisser. *See* Skalholt (Iceland), Bishop of

Ein feste Burg ist unser Gott, Luther's hymn, ii 201

Einsiedel, Count, Saxon Minister, x 374

Einsiedeln, pilgrimages to, ii 105; town of, and Schwyz, vi 625; political meeting at, xi 242

Eisenach, Luther's life at, ii 109 sq.; Banér at, iv 372; vi 263 sq.; Prussian force at, 265; 269

Eisleben, Luther born at, ii 109; Tilly at, iv 204

Ekaterinodár, mutiny at, xii 362

Ekaterinoslaff, Russian military colony, x 416; rising in, xii 363; 374

Elandslaagte, Boers repulsed at, xii 642

El Arish, fight at, viii 609; Treaty of (1800), 617

El Aruan, French explorer in, xii 808

Elba, occupied by Cosimo de' Medici, ii 84, 88; Cosimo's schemes in, iii 385, 391; iron worked at, 392; Spanish fortress in, vi 124; annexed by France, ix 75, 101; banishment of Napoleon to, 558–9; Napoleon leaves, 573; granted to Tuscany, 654, 661

Elbe river, the Northern Mark and, v 617; 618; 627; 646; vi 234; Frederick II crosses, 241; 242; 244; 257 sq.; 263; French troops on, 265 sq.; crossed by the Austrians, 296; 298; mouth of, to be closed to English trade, ix 374; right bank of, finally abandoned by Napoleon, 531; Allies cross (1813), 532; and Heligoland, xii 167

Elbée, M.-L. Gigot de, Vendean leader, viii 266, 353 sq.

Elberfeld, revolutionary meeting at, xi 219; 394

Elbeuf, Charles of Lorraine, Marquis of, iii 663

—— René of Lorraine, Marquis of, ii 576

Elbing, "proposition" of Gustavus Adolphus from, iv 190; capitulation of, to Charles X, 428; Treaty of, 583; v 146; acquired by Poland (1466), 634; 638; 641; 667

El Bodon, fight at (1811), ix 468

Elcho, David Wemyss, Lord, Jacobite, vi 114

Eldon, John Scott, 1st Earl of, vi 466; viii 761; ix 683; and Tory party, 686; and *Edinburgh Review*, 688; and criminal law, 692; Lord Chancellor, x 574; 580; and Canning, 591; 601; 618; and Catholic Emancipation Bill, 653

Électeur, Le, French journal, xi 488

Electoral College, i 291, 302, 309; the meeting of six Electors (*Kurfürstentag*), 291, 311; Electoral Union (*Kurfürstenverein*), 292, 311

Electors Palatine. *See* Palatinate

El Empecinado (Juan Martin Diez), Spanish guerrilla chief, x 211

Elena (of Montenegro), Queen of Italy, consort of Victor Emmanuel II, xii 414

Eleonora (of Austria), daughter of Maximilian I, Queen dowager of Portugal, Queen of France, ii 46; marriage of, to Francis I, 51, 59, 427; 73; iii 182

—— Magdalena, of Neuburg, Empress, 3rd wife of Emperor Leopold I, v 35

—— Maria, of Austria, Queen of Poland, consort of Michael Wisniowiecki, v 41; 350; married to Charles Leopold, titular Duke of Lorraine, 354 *n.*

Elfsborg, fall of, iv 163; Sweden compelled to redeem, 166; deserts Sigismund, 172; lost to Sweden, 179; in Danish hands, 180, 182

Elfsnabben, Swedish naval base, iv 571

Elgin Commission (War Office), xii 59

Elgin, James Bruce, 8th Earl of, Viceroy of India, XI 752; Governor-general of Canada, 760 sqq., 766 sqq.; in China, 812, 816 sqq.
—— Victor Alexander Bruce, 9th Earl of, Viceroy of India, XII 484 sqq.
—— Countess of, XI 767
El Goleah, railway to, XII 129
Eliaesen, Paul (Povel Helgesen), Danish reformer and scholar, II 606, 609, 613
Elias, Ney, explorer, XII 798 sq.
Elibank plot, VI 119
Elie, Jacobites at, VI 99
Elio, Don Francisco Xavier, Governor of Montevideo, X 285 sq.
Eliot, Edward Granville, Lord (*afterwards* 3rd Earl of St Germans), X 235
—— George (Mary Ann Cross), X 724; XI 360
—— Sir John, in Parliament, IV 263; imprisonment and release of, 265 sq.; 269; Petition of Right and, 270; Third Parliament and, 273; death of, in prison, 281; 318
—— John, missionary, VII 100
Eliott, George Augustus. *See* Heathfield, Lord
Elizabeth (of Bavaria), Empress of Austria, consort of Francis Joseph, XI 374; 401; XII 175; 181; Andrássy and, 190
—— Queen of England, II 93, 441, 520, 524 sq., 529 sq.; (as Princess) at Hampton Court, 535; proposed marriage of, to Archduke Ferdinand, 537; accused of plotting, 544; accession and title of, 559 sq.; Paul IV and, 564; 565 sq.; church settlement and first years, 568–98; and French Religious Wars, Vol. III, Chap. I *passim*; negotiations for a French marriage, *ib.*; relations of, with Henry IV, 666, 670 sqq.; with Netherlands, 184, Chaps. VII and XIX *passim*; with the German Princes, 710–1; with Mary, Queen of Scots, and Scotland, Chap. VIII; with her disaffected Catholic subjects, *ib.*; with Spain, Chaps. IX, XV and XVI *passim*; last years of, Chap. X; age of, in English Literature, Chap. XI; Ireland under, Chap. XVIII; Sixtus V's view of, 435; Bodin's view of, 748; principles of toleration of, 755; and Erik XIV of Sweden, IV 161, 163; and literature, 760 sq.; and religious toleration, V 325, 330; Bull against, 326; VI 701
—— (of York), Queen of England, consort of Edward IV, I 464, 466, 474
—— (Archduchess), daughter of Maximilian II, Queen of France, consort of Charles IX, marriage of, III 15, 177; and Philip II, 699
—— (of Bavaria), Queen of Prussia, consort of Frederick William IV, XI 159
—— Queen of Roumania ("Carmen Sylva"), consort of Charles I, XI 646; XII 414

Elizabeth (of Baden), Tsarina of Russia, consort of Alexander I, at Vienna, IX 581; X 436
—— Tsarina of Russia, V 543; 547; 552 sq.; VI 143, 200; 240; 252 sq.; 291; 310 sq.; character of, 312; reign of, 313 sqq.; and Frederick the Great, 327; 340; 346; 399; and Prussia, 401; 657 sq.; 660; 741 sq.; Sweden and, 761; death of, 298, 328, 661; X 426
—— (of Bourbon), Queen of Spain, consort of Philip IV, betrothed to Prince of Savoy, III 689; marriage of, to Philip IV, IV 625, 630
—— (Farnese), Queen of Spain, consort of Philip V, the Regency of, Vol. VI, Chap. V *passim*; 25; 35; 57; 60; 65; and Alberoni, 125; 126; character of, 122, 134 sqq., 167; 137; and the Italian claims, 138 sq.; 140; and Ripperdá, 142 sq.; 144; and Pragmatic Sanction, 202; schemes of, in Italy, 236; and d'Argenson, 245; 249; 361; and Charles III, 366 sq.; 596 sq.; death of, 372
—— (of Valois), Queen of Spain, 3rd consort of Philip II, II 93 sq., 566; marriage of, III 184, 264, 478, 483 sq.; death of, 490
—— (Stewart), Electress Palatine, "Queen of Bohemia," IV 29; crowned at Prague, 30; 67; exile of, 70; 78; devotion of Christian of Halberstadt to, 79; estranged from her son, Charles Lewis, 409; V 639 sq.; VI 1
—— Christina (of Brunswick-Wolfenbüttel), Empress, consort of Charles VI, V 432; 744; VI 143; 147
Elizabeth-Philippine-Marie-Hélène, Princess (Madame Elizabeth, sister of Louis XVI), executed, VIII 357; burial of, at St Denis, IX 572
Elizabeth (of Görlitz). *See* Luxemburg
Ellandonan, Jacobites at, VI 105
Ellenborough, Edward Law, 1st Baron, Lord Chief Justice, included in Cabinet, IX 685; and criminal law, 692; X 579
—— Edward Law, 1st Earl of, XI 10; President of the Board of Control, 328; and annexation of Oudh, 329 sq.; Governor-general of India, 730, 734 sqq.; recall of, 738
Ellerker, Sir Ralph, the Pilgrimage of Grace and, II 446
Ellesmere land, exploration of, XII 815
—— Sir Thomas Egerton, 1st Lord, *afterwards* Viscount Brackley, Lord Chancellor, III 560
Ellet, Charles, American engineer, VII 499
Ellice Islands, annexation of, XII 667
Elliot, Sir Charles, Admiral, XI 806 sqq.
—— Sir George, Admiral, XI 808
—— Sir Gilbert, of Minto, VI 424 sq.; Treasurer of the Navy, 442

Elliot, Sir Gilbert (son of above). *See* Minto, 1st Earl of
—— Hugh, British Minister at Copenhagen, vi 780; viii 279 sq.; and Mirabeau, 291 sq.
Ellis, George, and the *Quarterly Review*, ix 687
—— Sir Henry, historian, xii 835
—— William, Indian official, vi 560 sq.
Ellsworth, Ephraim Elmer, assassinated (1861), vii 464
—— Oliver, American statesman, at Constitutional Convention (1787), vii 246, 251, 259 sqq., 279, 288, 294, 298
Ellwangen, Vicar-general appointed at, by King Frederick I of Würtemberg, ix 202
Elmina, conquered by the Dutch, iv 751, 759
El Obeid, explorers at, xii 806, 811
Elphinston, John, Russian rear-admiral, vi 355; 673
Elphinstone, George Keith. *See* Keith, Viscount
—— Mountstuart, mission of, to Afghánistán, ix 732; Governor of Bombay, xi 725; 731
—— William George Keith, Major-general, at Kabul, xi 733; 735
Elsass, the "New League" of towns of, against Charles the Bold, i 295, 307; the south of, acquired by Charles the Bold, 390; Austria secures footing in, iii 709; French wars in, 712; troops in (1610), 731–2; iv 142; French acquisition of, 148 sq.; 246; France and, 247 sq.; 251; 368; landgravate of, assured to Bernard of Saxe-Weimar, 369 sq.; 376; 379; Erlach Governor in Upper, 382; French troops in, 390; 392; settlement of, in Peace of Westphalia, 405 sqq., 407, 416; 602; claims of Spanish Habsburgs upon, 603; Harcourt Governor of, 618; and Treaty of the Pyrenees, 620; taken by French, v 44; 47 sq.; Louis XIV and, 165, 338; 413; 416; 420; 423; 425; French troops in, 431; Peace of Ryswyk and, 453; vi 123; 141; Austria and, 238 sqq.; 623; Prussians occupy (1793), viii 352, 426; and French Revolution, 398 sq.; Custine in, 423; ix 57; Jews of, 204 sq.; proposed cession of, to Germany, 590, 653, 664; the cotton industry in, x 753; 758; xi 49; 219; workmen in, 301; 498; French army in, 581 sq.; the war in, 583 sqq.; ceded by France, 612, xii 91, 96, 135 sqq.; 145; 147; 166
Elsfleth, Duke of Brunswick-Oels embarks at, ix 357
Elsinore, Gambier appears off (1807), ix 236; British expedition at, 295
Elsintz, General, ix 58; 61–2
Elstowe, Henry, Warden of the Grey Friars, ii 438
El Teb, battle of, xii 441

Elten, claimed by Murat, ix 272
El Trab, French explorer in, xii 808
Eltz, Jakob von, Archbishop of Trier. *See* Trier
Elvas, Haro defeated at, iv 661; garrisoned by Junot, ix 440
Ely O'Carroll, plantation of, iv 513
Elz, Wallenstein's Chancellor, imprisonment of, iv 242
El Zanjón, Convention of, xii 264
Emancipation (*see also* Slavery and the Slave-trade), for the Jews, and the French Revolution, viii 790; of serfs, in Russia, and the first edition of the *Nakás*, vi 689, xi 614 sqq.; xii 294; 300 sq.; of slaves of French possessions, and the French Revolution, viii 790; of women, and the French Revolution, 790; of women in general, movement for, in the 19th and 20th centuries, xii 762 sq.
Embabeh, entrenchments at, captured (1798), viii 602; flotilla at, burned, 603
Emden, synod at (1571), iii 705
Emeric-David, Toussaint-Bernard-, ix 133
Emerson, Ralph Waldo, vii 739 sq.
Emery, Jacques-André, member of the French Ecclesiastical Commission (1809), ix 196; 198
—— Michel, Sieur de. *See* Particelli
Émigrés, French, first flight of (1789), viii 165, the second, 185; measures of the Legislative Assembly against (1791), 218 sqq.; sketch of the movement, 501 sqq.; Bonaparte and, ix 15; proposed indemnification for, x 83
Emilia, The, Murat in, ix 621; revolutionary movement in (1830), x 120; xi 386 sqq.
Emilio, Paolo, Veronese historian, iii 63–4
Emin Pasha, xii 812
Emly, William Monsell, Lord, xii 29
Emma, Queen of the Netherlands, consort of William III, xii 245; 247
Emmanuel the Great (Manoel), King of Portugal, i 31 sqq.; iii 499 sq.
—— Infant of Portugal, vi 195
—— Philibert, Duke of Savoy. *See* Savoy
Emmery, Jean-Louis-Claude, ix 151
Emmet, Robert, and the United Irishmen, ix 706 sq.; x 630 sq.; 715
—— Thomas Addis, and the United Irishmen, ix 700 sq.
Emo, Angelo, Venetian admiral, vi 606
Empaytaz, evangelist, and the Tsar, x 8
Empire, the Holy Roman
  i   ix Germany and the Empire, 288–328
     x   Hungary and the Sclavonic Kingdoms, *passim*, 329–46
     xiii The Netherlands, *passim*, 417–62
  ii ii Habsburg and Valois (i), 36–65
     iii Habsburg and Valois (ii), 66–103
  iii v   The Empire under Ferdinand I and Maximilian II, 140–81

Empire, the Holy Roman (*contd.*)
III xxi The Empire under Rudolf II, 696–735
IV i The Outbreak of the Thirty Years' War, 1–34
   iii The Protestant Collapse (1620–30), 64–117
   vi Gustavus Adolphus, 190–222
   vii Wallenstein and Bernard of Weimar (1632–5), 223–55
   xiii The later years of the Thirty Years' War (1635–48), 364–94
   xiv The Peace of Westphalia, 395–433
V xii Austria, Poland and Turkey, *passim*, 338–71
   xx The origins of the Kingdom of Prussia, *passim*, 616–38
   xxi The Great Elector and the first Prussian King, *passim*, 639–72
      [For the Spanish Succession, the War of the Spanish Succession, the Peace of Utrecht and supplementary pacifications, *see also* Chaps. xiii and xiv *passim*, 372–459]
VI xviii Joseph II, 626–56
IX ix The Third Coalition, I (1805–6), *passim*, 244–64
   x The Third Coalition, II (1806–7), *passim*, 265–93
      [*See also* Austria, Germany and the various Imperial lands, and the Emperors]
Empson, Sir Richard, Minister of Henry VII, I 477
Ems, Resolutions of (1786), x 145, 158; the King of Prussia and Benedetti at, XI 463, 578
Emser, Jerome, opponent of Luther, II 168; translation of the Bible by, 172; controversy of, with Zwingli, 321
Encina, Juan del, Spanish writer, I 380
Enckenvoert, William, Cardinal, II 21
Enckhuysen, defeat of Spanish fleet at (1573), III 237; ship-building at, 631; and the Act of Seclusion, v 143
Enclosure Commissions, in England, II 491
Encounter Bay, XI 792
Encyclopédie, The French, VIII 1, 5, 26, 56
Endegeest, castle of, Descartes at, IV 785
Enderlin, *podestà* of Tirano, death of, IV 49
Endicott, Roger, Governor of Massachusetts, VII 15 sqq., 25
Enfantin, Prosper, French politician, XI 298
Engadine, The, IV 36; 39; Protestants of the Upper, 44, 47; and Planta, 48; 52; 54; Archduke Leopold's claim on the Lower, 55; Baldiron's seizure of the Lower, *ib.*; 56; 58; 61; Austria and religious freedom in the Lower, 63
Engel, Theodor, president of Russian Government in Warsaw, x 474

Engelbrektsson, Olaf. *See* Trondhjem, Archbishop of
Engels, Friedrich, socialist, x 757; XII 123; 152; 759
Engen, engagement at (1800), IX 58
Enghien, Anne Benedicta (of Bavaria), Duchess of, v 349
—— François de Bourbon, Count of, II 77 sq., 97
—— Henri-Jules, Duc de. *See* Condé, Henri-Jules de Bourbon, Prince de
—— Louis, Duc de. *See* Condé, Louis II de Bourbon, Prince de
—— Louis-Antoine-Henri de Bourbon, Duc de, IX 30–1; murder of, 191; effect of execution of, in Russia, 221; 245, 321; execution of, defended, 761
England
I xiv The Early Tudors, 463–92
      [*See also* i, ii, xv, Economic Change, *especially* 521 sqq., xvi *especially* 580–3 and xvii *passim*]
II xiii Henry VIII, 416–73
   xiv The Reformation under Edward VI, 474–511
   xv Philip and Mary, 512–49
   xvi The Anglican Settlements and the Scottish Reformation, 550–98
III viii Mary Stewart, *passim*, 260–93
   ix The Elizabethan Naval War with Spain, 294–327
      [For Elizabeth's relations with the Dutch Republic, *see* 617–23]
   x The last years of Elizabeth, 328–63
   xi The Elizabethan Age of English Literature, 364–82
IV viii Britain under James I, 549–78
   viii The Constitutional Struggle in England (1625–40), 256–85
   ix The first two years of the Long Parliament (1640–2), 286–301
   x The first Civil War (1642–7), 302–35
   xi Presbyterians and Independents (1645–9), 336–55
   xii The Westminster Assembly, 356–63
   xv The Commonwealth and the Protectorate (1649–59), 434–58
   xvi The Navy of the Commonwealth and the First Dutch War, 459–85
   xvii and xviii *passim*, Scotland and Ireland, 486–538
   xix Anarchy and the Restoration (1659–60), 539–59
   xxv The transference of Colonial Power to the United Provinces and England, 728–59
   xxvi The Fantastic School of English Poetry, 760–75

England (*contd.*)

v   v   The Stewart Restoration, 92–115
    vi   The Literature of the English Restoration, including Milton, 116–36
    vii   The administration of John de Witt and William of Orange (1651–88), *passim*, 137–67
    viii   The Anglo-Dutch Wars (including Naval Administration under Charles II and James II), 168–97
    ix   The policy of Charles II and James II (1667–87), 198–235
    x   The Revolution and the Revolution Settlement in Great Britain [and Ireland], 236–323
    xi   Religious toleration in England, 324–37
    xiii and xiv *passim*, The Treaties of Partition, War of the Spanish Succession, and Peace of Utrecht, 372–459
    xv   Party government under Queen Anne, 460–76
    xxii   The Colonies and India, 673–705
    xxiv   Latitudinarianism and Pietism, *passim*, 742–63

vi   i   Great Britain under George I, 1–39
      (i) The Hanoverian Succession
      (ii) The foreign policy of George I (1714–21)
    ii   The age of Walpole and the Pelhams, 40–89
    iii   Jacobitism and the Union, 90–119
    vi   Financial experiments and colonial development, *passim*, 168–90
    xiii   Great Britain (1756–93), 393–478
      (1) William Pitt the Elder
      (2) The King's friends
      (3) The years of peace, and the rise of the younger Pitt (1782–93)
    xiv   [and Ireland], 479–505
    xv   [and India], 506–85
    xxiii   English Political Philosophy in the 17th and 18th centuries, 785–821
    [*See also* vii, viii, xi, xxiv *passim*]

vii   i   The first century of English colonisation (1607–1700), 1–52
    ii   The English colonies (1700–63), 53–69
    iv   The Conquest of Canada (1744–61), 114–43
    v   The quarrel with Great Britain (1761–76), 144–74
    vi   and vii, The Declaration and War of Independence (1761–83), 175–234
    ix   The struggle for commercial independence and the War of 1812 (1783–1815), 305–48

England (*contd.*)

viii   x   The foreign policy of Pitt to the outbreak of war with France, 276–305
    xi   The European Powers and the Eastern Question, *passim*, 306–37
    xiv   The General war, *passim*, 398–446
    xv   The Naval war, *passim*, 447–86
    xix   The Egyptian expedition, 594–619
    xx   The struggle for the Mediterranean, 620–32
    xxi   The Second Coalition, *passim*, 633–64
    xxv   Europe and the French Revolution, *passim*, 754–90

ix   iii   The pacification of Europe (1799–1802), *passim*, 55–80
    viii   The Command of the Sea (1803–15), *passim*, 208–43
    ix   The Third Coalition, I (1805–6), *passim*, 244–64
    x   The Third Coalition, II (1806–7), *passim*, 265–93
    xii   The war of 1809, *passim*, 341–60
    xiii   The Continental System (1809–14), 361–89
    xv   The Peninsular War (1808–14), 428–82
    xvii   The War of Liberation (1813–4), *passim*, 506–54
    xix   The Congress of Vienna, I (1814–5), *passim*, 576–602
    xx   The Hundred Days (1815), *passim*, 616–45
    xxi   The Congress of Vienna, II (1815), *passim*, 646–71
    xxii   Great Britain and Ireland (1792–1815), 672–708
    xxiii   The British Empire (1783–1815), 709–55

x   i   The Congresses (1815–22), *passim*, 1–39
    vi   Greece and the Balkan Peninsula, *passim*, 169–204
    x   Brazil and Portugal, *passim*, 310–39
    xvii   Mehemet Ali, *passim*, 545–72
    xviii   Great Britain (1815–32), 573–619
    xix   Catholic Emancipation, 620–54
    xx   Great Britain and Ireland (1832–41), 655–84
    xxi   Canada, 685–95
    xxii   The Revolution in English Poetry and Fiction, 696–726
    xxiii   Economic change, 727–62
    xxiv   The British Economists, 763–84

xi   i   Great Britain and Free Trade (1841–52), 1–21
    ix   (2) The Levant, *passim*, 275–85
    xi   Great Britain and the Crimean War (1852–6), 309–24

England (*contd.*)
xi   xii Great Britain, last years of Whiggism, Parliamentary reform (1856-68), 325-46
     xiii English Literature (1840-70), 347-65
     xxii Russia...after the Crimean War, (1) and (2), *passim*, 613-47
     xxvi India and Afghánistán (1815-69), 724-53
     xxvii Great Britain and her Colonies
          (i)   The new colonial policy (1840-70), 754-66
          (ii) The federation of Canada, 766-78
          (iii) The English and Dutch in S. Africa, 778-89
          (iv) The development of Australasia (1815-70), 789-801
     xxviii The Far East (1815-71), *passim*, 802-65
xii ii   Foreign relations of the United States during the Civil War, *passim*, 16-22
     iii Great Britain, 23-64
     xiv The Ottoman Empire and the Balkan Peninsula, *passim*, 381-428
     xv   Egypt and the Egyptian Sudan (1841-1907), *passim*, 429-56
     xvi The British Empire in India, 457-99
     xvii The Far East, *passim*, 500-36
     xx   The European Colonies, *passim*, 602-71
     xxi The Republics of Latin America, *passim*, 672-702.
          [*See also* xxii *passim*]
     xxiii Social movements, *passim*, 730-65
England, Sir Richard, general, xi 734 sq.
Enke, Wilhelmina, mistress of Frederick William II, vi 725
Ennis, Parnell at, xii 78
Enniscorthy, Parnell at, xii 77
Enniskillen, Tyrone joins Bagenel at, iii 604; taken by Maguire, 605; revolt at (1688), v 307, 308 sq., 311 sq.
Enns, occupation of the line of the, by Moreau, ix 68
Enomoto, Japanese admiral, xi 860
"**Enragés**," French faction, viii 213, 249
Ensalah, Alexander Laing at, xii 808
Enschede, siege of (1597), iii 629
Ensenada, Zeno Somodevilla, Marquis of, Spanish statesman, vi 159; 166; 361 sqq.; Charles III and, 367; 382
Entente cordiale, between France and England, after Revolution of 1830, x 29 sqq.; of recent years, xii 55, 98 sq., 172
Entragues, Catherine Henriette de Balzac de, iii 678-9; Marquise de Verneuil, 680-1; 692
Entre Minho e Douro, province of, ix 302
Enzheim, victory of Turenne at (1674), v 44

Enzinas, Francisco de (Dryander), ii 350, 401-3; translates New Testament into Spanish, 402
—— Jáime de (Dryander), Spanish Lutheran, ii 350, 387, 402 sq.
Eoban of Hesse (Helius Eobanus Hessus) (Koch?), German scholar, ii 111
Éon, Chevalier de, French spy, vi 428
Eötvös, Joseph, Baron, Hungarian politician, xi 172; 177; 181; 400; the writings of, 426 sq.; Minister of Education, xii 189 sq.; death of, 190
Eperies, submits to Austria, v 366; 367; taken by the Russians, xi 210
Épernay, Biron killed at, iii 52
Épernon, Bernard de Nogaret de La Valette, Duke of, *Parlement* of Bordeaux and, iv 611; 614; in Burgundy, 618
—— Jean Louis de Nogaret de La Valette, Duke of, iii 36 sqq., 661-3, 668 sqq., 690; and Mary de' Medici, iv 125 sq.; 127
Ephimieff, Savva, Russian anti-Polish leader, v 502
Epirus, Greek invasion of, xi 640; and the Greek frontier, xii 37, 403; Turkey and, 381; insurrection in, 391; 392; 398; the war in, 421 sq.; 428
Episcopius, Simon, iii 653; v 744
Epistolae Clarorum (or *illustrium*) *Virorum* (1514), ii 696
—— *Obscurorum Virorum*, of Crotus Rubeanus, ii 32, 696 sq.
Epworth, Wesley at, vi 86
Erasmistas, party of, in Spain, ii 401; in Portugal, 412
Erasmus, Bishop of Strassburg. *See* Strassburg
—— Desiderius (Gerrit Gerritszoon), at Deventer, i 435, 437; 460; the Reformation and, 460-2, 545, 563; the Renaissance and, 569-71, 576, 579; studies Greek, 580 sq.; and the Fathers, 606-8; edition of Josephus by, 613, 615; in England, 491, 580, 625, 637, 642 sq.; 682; Greek Testament of, 603, 645; in Rome, 564; *Julius Exclusus* and, ii 9; 10, 24, 32, 152, 162, 167 sq.; *Praise of Folly*, 280; 307 sqq.; Zwingli and, 314, 316; share of, in Reformation, 342; residence and death at Basel, 355, 414; influence of, in Spain, 400 sq.; *Annotationes*, 694; *Novum Instrumentum*, 697; letters, critical work, and religious attitude of, 697-700
Erasso, Francisco de, Lord of Mohernando, Secretary to Philip II, iii 196
Erastianism, and its Anglican interest, ii 595 sq.; in 16th century political thought, iii 742 sqq., 757
Erastus, Thomas of Bâle (Lieber), ii 195, 595 sq.; iii 154, 743, 757
Erdélyi, John, Hungarian writer, xi 427
Erdmannsdörffer, Bernhard, German historian, xii 829
Erebus, Mount, discovered, xii 815

Eregli, Prince Mustafa murdered at, III 121
Eretrea. *See* Erythrea
Erfurt, Luther at University of, II 110 sqq.; humanists of, 111; meeting of ambassadors of Protestant Princes at (1569), III 176; Aldringer at, IV 205; alliance between Gustavus Adolphus and the Weimar Dukes at, 207; Banér at, 385; sufferings of, during the War, 420; Prussian troops at, VI 265; 268 sq.; bishopric of, 704; Prussian acquisitions in, IX 78; Prussian capitulation at (1806), 277; Congress of (Oct. 1808), 137, 294, 310, 317–9, 321, 325, 335, 341, 343, 370, 388, 442; district of, 408; French troops at, 515; Napoleon at (1813), 517; Parliament, XI 222 sq., 228
Erichsen, Mylius, in Greenland, XII 815
Ericsson, John, designer of the *Monitor*, VII 550
Erie, Canal, VII 360, 691, 694
—— Lake, French claim on, VII 119; operations round, in the war of 1812, 337 sq., 340
Erigena, John Scotus, I 535
Erik VII, King of Denmark, Norway and Sweden (Erik XIII), II 600
—— XIV (Vasa), King of Sweden, II 627, 629; policy of, IV 158 sq.; character and reign of, 161 sqq.; coinage under, 166; policy of, in Livonia, 590
Eriksson, Gustaf. *See* Gustavus Vasa, King of Sweden
Erikszen, Barent, navigator, III 632–3
Eriska, Prince Charles lands at, VI 112
Erivan, province of, ceded to Russia (1828), X 444, XI 274
Erizzo, Sebastiano, of Venice (Ericius), III 468
Erlach, Hans Ludwig von, Swiss general, Bernard of Saxe-Weimar and, IV 374 sqq.; Governor of Breisach, 379; commands Bernardines, 381; 382; 392; at Lens, 599
Erlangen, students of, X 370; *Burschenschaft* at, 375
Erlau, siege of, by Turks, III 123; captured by Austrians (1687), V 367
Erle, Thomas, English general, V 421
Erlon, Jean-Baptiste Drouet, Comte de, Marshal of France, VIII 504 sq.; in the Peninsula, IX 456; plot of, 572; and the Belgian campaign, 625; at Ligny, 628; at Waterloo, 633 sqq.; X 503
Ermak Timotheevich, rebel Cossack, XII 794
Ermeland. *See* Warmia
—— (Warmia), Bishop of. *See* Hosius
Erneley, Sir Michael, transports Irish troops to England, IV 527
Ernest, Archduke of Austria, son of Maximilian II, candidate for crown of Poland, III 86 sq., 92 sq., 170; and the Netherlands, 519, 627; Governor of Upper and Lower Austria (1576), 698, 701; administration of Styria by, 702

Ernest, Augustus, King of Hanover (Duke of Cumberland), and Orange Lodges, X 671 sq.; accession of, 674; 681; absolutist action by, 379 sq.; XI 60; 148; 166; and Frankfort Assembly, 200; secedes from German Union, 222
—— Casimir. *See* Nassau-Dietz
Ernoul, Edmond, French politician, XII 108
Ernroth, General, in Bulgaria, XII 405
Errazuriz, Fed., President of Chile, XII 679
Errestfer, battle of (1702), V 590
Errington, Sir George, XII 41
Errol, Francis Hay, 9th Earl of, III 551
Erskine, David, British Minister to the United States, VII 331 sq.
—— Ebenezer, Scottish seceder, VI 108
—— Henry, Scottish advocate, VIII 770
—— John Erskine, 6th Baron, and Earl of Mar, defends Edinburgh, II 575, 577
—— Thomas, Baron Erskine, VIII 760 sqq.; Lord Chancellor, and the Libel Bill, IX 672; retirement of, 676
—— William, historian, VI 507
—— of Dun, III 263
Erving, George, United States Minister, X 213
Erythrea (Eretrea), Italian colony, XII 219; 241; 664
Erzerum, taken by Persians from Turks, III 121; war stores at, V 545; Treaty of, XI 276; XII 392; Morier at, 800
Erzgebirge, mines of the, V 738
Esbjerg, port of, XII 291
Escale, French commander at Acre, VIII 612
Eschassériaux, Baron Joseph, member of the *Comité de Salut Public*, VIII 375
Escher, Alfred, and the St Gothard tunnel, XI 260
—— von der Linth, Arnold, geologist, IX 426; XI 260
Escobar y Mendoza, Antonio, Jesuit, V 81
Escobedo, Juan de, III 497–9, 514; murder of (1578), 500, 515
Escoiquiz, Juan, Spanish statesman, tried and acquitted, IX 429; X 208; 211
Escosura, Patricio de la, Spanish Minister of the Interior, XI 562
Escurial, Treaty of the (1733), VI 63, 152; of 1790, VIII 189
Esher, Reginald Baliol Brett, 2nd Viscount, XII 59
Eslava, Viceroy of Cartagena, VI 165
Esnambuc, Pierre Vandrosque Diel de, colonial settler, VII 74
Espana, Spanish American rebel, X 276
Española, colonised by Spain, I 40
Espartero, Baldomero, Spanish general and statesman, X 235; 238; ministry of, 239 sqq.; and the Queen Regent, 241; retires to England, 242; XI 33; 550; 553; returns to office (1854), 560 sq.; resigns, 562
Espen, Zeger Bernard van, X 157

Espes, Don Guerau de, III 280 sq.
Espinosa, Victor defeats Blake at (1808), IX 443
—— Diego de, Cardinal, Bishop of Siguenza, III 490
Espoz y Mina, Francisco Xavier, Spanish commander, x 210; 227 sq.; 231 sq.
Espréménil, J.-J.-Duval de, French politician, VIII 110, 159, 172
Esprit des Lois, Le, IV 790
Espronceda, José de, x 241
Esquivel, Juan de, Jamaica colonised by, I 41
Essai pour les Coniques (by Pascal), IV 794
Essé, de. *See* Montalembert
Essek, Solyman II at, III 107; Turks at, V 359, 363; taken by the Austrians (1687), 367; 369
Essen, claimed by Murat, IX 272
Essequibo, Dutch colony of, IV 709; English reduction of (1796), IX 750, 755; ceded to Great Britain, x 520, XI 667
—— river, the Dutch on, VI 186; the Venezuelan dispute and, XII 687
Essex, The, and "broken voyages," VII 327
Essex, Lord. *See* Northampton, Sir William Parr, Marquis of
—— Arthur Capel, 1st Earl of (6th cr.), V 222; 224; 229 sq.; Lord Lieutenant of Ireland, 305
—— Frances, Countess of. *See* Somerset
—— Robert Devereux, 2nd Earl of, III 50, 325 sq., 333 sq., 376; English troops sent to besiege Rouen under, 512, 516, 521, 523, 573; in Ireland (1599), 607–8
—— Robert Devereux, 3rd Earl of, IV 290; commands Parliamentary forces, 301 sq.; 304 sqq.; occupies Worcester, 307; at Turnham Green, 308; 311 sq.; 313 sq.; at Newbury, 315; Oxford Parliament and, 319; 320; in Cornwall, 323; 324 sq.; deprived of command, 326; 328
—— Walter Devereux, 1st Earl of (5th cr.), III 601
—— Thomas Cromwell, Earl of. *See* Cromwell
Essling, exploits of French infantry at, IX 345; Napoleon at, 350; Austrians fail to take, 351; taken by the French (May 22, 1809), *ib.*
—— Prince of. *See* Masséna
Estaing, Charles-Hector Théodat, Comte de, French admiral, VI 351; 451 sq.; VII 218 sq.
Estates General, of France. *See* States General
Este, family of, in Ferrara, I 260 sq.
—— House of, IX 603
—— *See also* Ferrara *and* Modena, Dukes of
—— Cesar de, loses Ferrara, III 397
—— Charles Philibert, Marquis of (S. Martino), grandee of Spain, III 420
—— Folco de, heir of Azzo of Ferrara, I 261

Este, Francesco de, claims to Ferrara of, I 261
—— Fresco de, son of Azzo of Ferrara, I 261
—— Ippolito de (son of Hercules I), Archbishop of Gran, I 658
—— Ippolito de, Cardinal of Ferrara (son of Alfonso I), II 85, 88; at Colloquy of Poissy, 302 sq., 584; III 462
—— Isabella de (daughter of Hercules I), Marchioness of Mantua, III 458
—— Lionello de, I 558
—— Cardinal Ludovico de (son of Hercules II), III 431; 435; 451; and Tasso, 472
Esterházy, Count Maurice, Austrian statesman, XII 181
—— Count Paul, Prince of Galantha, Palatine of Hungary, V 357
—— of Galantha, Prince Paul Anton, x 25; XI 172; 180
—— Prince Nicholas, Austrian ambassador at St Petersburg, VI 253; 322; 325; 327
—— Major Count Walzin, XII 120
Esthonia, Russia and, II 144; and Sweden, IV 162, 171, 173; ceded to Poland, 174; Swedish power restored in, 176; Peace of Stolbova and, 181; the Poles and, 189; V 614; ceded to Russia, 615; Russia and, VI 206; 317; serfdom abolished in (1816), x 427; Russian administration of, XII 335
Estienne, Henri, printer, I 576, 604, 613; II 718; III 57
—— Robert, printer, I 576, 615; II 718; III 57
Estourmel, de, surrenders frontier towns of Picardy, III 662
Estouteville, Cardinal Guillaume de, I. 388
Estrades, Comte Godefroi de, and Mazarin, IV 727; French ambassador at the Hague, V 106 sq.; 149; 152
Estrées, Gabrielle de, III 418, 675, 678, 692
—— Jean de, Vice-admiral, Marshal of France, V 165; 194 sqq.; 688
—— Louis-Charles-César, Duc de, Marshal of France, VI 257; 339; 405; 426
Estremadura, the Allies in (1705), V 416, 426; Spanish battalions in, IX 435; Victor evacuates (1809), 451; Soult enters, 462; destroys Spanish army of, *ib.*; Beresford marches into, 466; Wellington in (1811), 467 sq.; Wellington marches on (1812), 471; freed from the French, 475; Carlist forces in, XII 260
Estrup, Jakob, Danish statesman, XII 293
Étampes, Turenne's victory at (1652), IV 616; German force at, XI 602
—— Anne de Pisseleu, Duchess of, II 97 sq.
Étaples, Treaty of (1492), I 111, 467 sq.; harbour of refuge at, IX 212; French ships at, 214, 215

" Eternal Edict" (Dutch), of 1667, v 152; questionable value of, 155 sq.; set aside, 157

Etherege, Sir George, dramatist, v 129 sq.

Étienne, Charles-Guillaume, x 91; editor of the *Constitutionnel*, 493

Étiolles, Lenormant de, vi 330

Etropol, monastery of, xii 408

Etruria, kingdom of, ix 69; absorbed in the French Empire, 316; Berlin Decree communicated to, 365; annexed by Napoleon, 368; 396 sqq.; offered by Napoleon to Ferdinand, 432

—— King of. *See* Parma, Louis, Duke of

—— Queen of. *See* Parma, Marie Louise, Infanta, Duchess of

Ettenheim, Johann von Werth's defeat at, iv 374; Duc d'Enghien at, ix 30

Eu, Queen Victoria at, xi 33, 37, 553

—— Gaston, Comte de, xii 675

—— Isabel, Comtesse de, xii 675

Euboea, island of, and the Powers (1829), x 202

Eucharist, doctrine of the, discussed by Luther and Zwingli, ii 209; at Colloquy of Ratisbon, 645; at Council of Trent, 671, 677 sqq.; decree concerning (issued by Diet of Speier), 330; Zwingli's writings on, 332 sq.

Euclid, v 707

Eudes de Mézerai, Jean, Abbé, v 79

Eudists, French order of the, v 79

Eudoxia, Tsaritsa, v 520; becomes "Sister Elena," 525; 537; trial of, 540; 553

Eugene, Beauharnais, Prince. *See* Beauharnais

Eugène François, Prince of Savoy-Carignan, v 61; 340 sq.; 348; joins Imperial army, 360; 366; at Zenta, 370; 401; in Italy, 402 sqq., 405, 407; 408; joins Marlborough, 409; at Blenheim, 410 sq.; in Italy (1705-6), 414 sqq.; at Vienna, 414; invades Provence, 418 sq.; attacks Toulon, 419; 420; at Oudenarde, 421; 423 sq.; at Malplaquet, 425 sq.; 429; 431; mission of, to London, 432 sq., 439; success of Villars against, 433 sq.; on the Rhine, 434 sq., 451; and Peace of Rastatt, 435, 452; 436; 450; 458; and Polish throne, 596; vi 14; 29 sq.; 91; and Ripperdá, 139 sqq.; 145; 198; 203; 206; 267; xii 400

Eugénie, Empress of the French, xi 293; 307; 384; 468; 474; supports the Government, 490; 495; acts as Regent, 496; and the peace negotiations, 498; and the Franco-German War, 583, 595; flight of, to England, 600; xii 433

Eugenius IV, Pope (Gabriele Condolmiero), i 237, 385 sq., 552, 646, 658; iii 738

Eulenburg, Count, mission of, to Japan, xi 841; 844

Euler, Leonhard, physicist, xi 260

Eupatoria, Russian capture of, vi 673

Eupen, Pierre Jean Simon van, Belgian leader, viii 329, 335

Euphrates river, mail-route to India by, x 558; Ottoman army crosses (1839), 561

Euphues, Lyly's, iii 370

Europe *in general*

I | xv | Economic Change, 493–531
  | xvi | The Classical Renaissance, 532–84
  | xvii | The Christian Renaissance, 585–619
  | xviii | Catholic Europe, 620–52
  | xix | The Eve of the Reformation, 653–92
ii | xix | European thought in the age of the Reformation, 690–718
iii | xxii | Political thought in the 16th century, 736–69
iv | xxvii | Descartes and Cartesianism, 776–99
v | xxiii | European science in the 17th and earlier years of the 18th centuries, 706–41
  | xxiv | Latitudinarianism and Pietism, 742–63
vi | xxiv | The Romantic movement in European Literature, 822–37
viii | xi | The European Powers and the Eastern Question, 306–37
  | xxv | Europe and the French Revolution, 754–90
ix | iii | The pacification of Europe (1799–1802), 55–80
  | xix | The Congress of Vienna, I (1814–5), 576–615
  | xxi | The Congress of Vienna, II (1815), 646–71
x | i | The Congresses (1815–22), 1–39
xii | i | Modern Europe, 1–15
  | xx | European colonies, 602–71
  | xxii | The modern law of nations and the prevention of war, 703–29
  | xxiii | Social movements, 730–65
  | xxiv | The scientific age, 766–91
  | xxv | Modern explorations, 792–815
  | xxvi | The growth of historical science, 816–50

Eustatia, in possession of the Dutch, v 687

Eustis, George, secretary to Confederate States Envoy, xii 18

Eutaw Springs, battle of (1781), vii 230

Euxine. *See* Black Sea.

Evald, Johannes, Danish poet, xi 697

Evangelical Brotherhood, foundation of, ii 180, 183

"Evangelical Catholics," German sect, v 743

Evans, Arthur, discoveries of, at Cnossus, xii 846

—— Sir George de Lacy, general, x 237

Evans, Australian explorer, xi 790 sq.

Evdokimoff, Nicholas, Russian general, xi 633

Eve Demaillot, Antoine-François, ix 137

Evelyn, John, v 124; and Royal Society, 740; vi 799

Evènement, Le, French newspaper, xi 127

Evening Post, The, vi 441

Everard, Sir John, Irish Catholic leader, iv 515 sq.

Everett, Edward, American statesman, vii 391, 491, 744

Evers, Sir Ralph, invades Scotland, ii 460

Evertsen, Cornelis, Dutch vice-admiral, v 183; death of, 186

—— Cornelis (the younger), Dutch naval officer, reconquers New Netherland, v 161

Every Man in his Humour, Ben Jonson's, iii 380

Evil May Day (April 30, 1517), riot in London, i 488

Evora, Spanish defeat at (June, 1663), iv 661, v 34

Evora-Monte, Dom Miguel at, x 336

Evreimoff, Russian geodesist, v 535

Evreux, Charles-Louis Salmon du Chatélier, Bishop of, x 85

Ewald, Georg Heinrich August, x 379; *History of Israel,* xii 846

Ewell, Richard Stoddard, Confederate general, vii 540

Examiner, The Whig, v 469; *The Tory,* started by St John, *ib.*; under Leigh Hunt, xi 362

Excelmans, Remy-Joseph-Isidore, Comte, Marshal of France, affair of, ix 571; negligence of, 630

Excise Scheme, Walpole's, vi 47 sq.

Exclusion Bill, introduced May, 1679, v 224; later history of, 226 sqq.

Excommunication, Bull of, issued against Henry VIII, ii 67, 440, 449; against Martin Luther, 138 sq.; against Elizabeth, iii 349

Executionsordnung (1555), iii 144, 171

Exeter, capitulates to Parliamentarians, iv 335; the Prince of Orange at, v 246

—— Henry Courtenay, Marquis of, arrested and executed, ii 449; 523

Exilles, heretics in, iii 404; surrender of (1593), 417; vi 159; battle of, 245, 362

Exmouth, Sir Edward Pellew, 1st Viscount, Admiral, viii 454; blockades Brest, 473; and mutiny, 631

Exploration, *see* Vol. i, Chap. i, The Age of Discovery, 7–36; Chap. ii, The New World, 37–66; late modern, *see* Vol. xii, Chap. xxv, 792–815

Exposcit pastoralis officii, the Bull (1550), ii 655

Extreme Unction, Sacrament of, discussed at Council of Trent, ii 672

Eyck, Hubert and John van, i 433

Eyguenots, of Geneva. ii 362

Eylau, battle of (1807), ix 195, 286, 287, 290; Scharnhorst at, 332

Eylert, R. F., Prussian bishop, x 382

Eynard, John Gabriel, and Greek independence, xi 239

Eyre, Edward John, Australian explorer, xi 795; Governor of Jamaica, xii 656

Fabbri, Count Edoardo, papal Minister, xi 89

Faber, Johann, the *Tractatus de Ruine Ecclesie planctu,* i 676; opponent of Luther, ii 168, 212, 233; Vicar-general of Constance, 316; and Zurich Disputation, 317; at Conference of Ratisbon (1526), 326

—— Stapulensis. *See* Lefèvre d'Étaples

Fabre, Auguste, editor of the *Tribune,* x 485

—— Victorin, editor of the *Tribune,* x 485

—— d'Églantine, P.-F.-Nazaire, French politician, viii 234, 247, 361, 363

Fabrice, Friedrich Ernst von, vi 20; mission of, to Sweden, 28, 34

—— Johann Ludwig von, Hanoverian councillor, vi 20

—— Weipart Ludwig von, Hanoverian judge and councillor, vi 20; 28

Fabricius, John Albert, the *Codex Apocryphus,* i 614

—— secretary of the Bohemian regents, iv 20

—— ab Aquapendente, Hieronymus, anatomist, v 724; 726; 728; 737

Fabro, Antonio (of Amiterno), ii 17

Fabvier, Baron Charles-Nicolas, French general, joins the Greek insurgents, x 182

Factory Acts, the first English, of 1802, ix 691 sq., x 659 sq.; origins of, xii 746; movement spreads to Continent, 747; in New Zealand (1894), 629; in Victoria (1896), 630

Fadinger, Stephen, Austrian peasant leader, iv 76

Faenza, surrenders to Cesare Borgia (1500), i 238; seized by Venetians (1503), 244; Sanfedists and *Carbonari* in, x 152

Faerie Queene, Spenser's, iii 373

Fagan, agent of Fouché, ix 140; 371

Fagel, Caspar, Pensionary of Holland, v 156; elected Grand Pensionary, 159; 164; 239; 245

—— Hendrik, Dutch Minister in London, x 520

Fagg, Sir John, M.P. for Steyning, v 217

Fagius, Paul, ii 265; Protestant refugee in England, 477

Faidherbe, Louis-Léon-César, French general, xi 607 sq.; 610; Governor of Senegal, xii 129

Failly, Pierre-Louis-Charles-Achille de, French general, xi 485; at Rome, 543; in the Franco-German War, 583 sqq., 596 sq.

Faipoult. *See* Faypoult

Fair Oaks, Federal repulse at (1862), VII 476 sq.

Fairfax, Ferdinando, 2nd Baron Fairfax of Cameron, Parliamentary commander in Yorkshire, IV 308, 313; at Winceby, 315; at Marston Moor, 322

—— Sir Thomas, 3rd Baron Fairfax of Cameron, recaptures Leeds, IV 308; storms Wakefield, 313; in Cheshire, 321; at Marston Moor, 322; Commander-in-chief of Parliamentary forces, 326; and New Model army, 329; at Naseby, 330; in the west, 331; takes Sherborne Castle, 332; takes Tiverton Castle, 333 sq.; surrender of Raglan Castle to, 335; 339; 341 sq.; Royalist risings and, 348 sq.; at Colchester, 351; at St Albans, 353; and Pride's Purge, 354; trial of Charles I and, 355; takes no part in the new government, 437; army and, 446; at Nantwich, 527; occupies York, 548

Fairman, Colonel, and Orange Lodges, X 671 sq.

Fajardo, Admiral, at Tunis, III 541

Faku, Pondo chief, XI 783

Falari, Duchess of, VI 131

Falconnet, Ambroise, and favours to *émigrés*, IX 570

Falk, Adalbert, Prussian *Kultusminister*, XII 148

—— Bengt, beheaded, IV 174

Falkenberg, Dietrich von, commander of Swedish troops in Mecklenburg, IV 196; at Magdeburg, 201 sqq.

Falkenstein, Johann Paul von, Saxon statesman, XI 149

—— Vogel von, Prussian general, XI 452; 455

Falkirk, march of Scotch army from, IV 436; VI 112; Jacobite victory at, 115

Falkland, Lucius Cary, 2nd Viscount, supports Laud, IV 280; Root-and-Branch petition and, 292; "Remonstrance" and, 296; and Puritanism, 306; Charles I and, 309; death of, at Newbury, 315, 318; Irish policy of, 516 sq.; V 745 sq.; 753

—— Lucius Bentinck, 10th Viscount, Lieutenant-Governor of Nova Scotia, XI 759

—— Isles, VI 373; claimed by Spain, 437; 443

Falköping, battle of, II 600

Fallières, Armand, President of the French Republic, XII 113

Falloppio, Gabriele, anatomist, II 386, 395; V 724

Falloux, Frédéric-Alfred-Pierre, Vicomte de, XI 114; French Minister of Education, 118; 119; education scheme of, 120, 126; 130; and Pius IX, 121; 123; 128; and the opposition to Napoleon III, 469; XII 92; 114

Falmouth (Cornwall), Spanish vessels at, III 493; the third Armada sails for, 529

—— (Maine), destroyed (1776), VII 169

Faludi, Francis, Hungarian writer, XI 421; 431

Famagosta, siege of, III 134; attacked by a Tuscan squadron, 399

Family Compact, The (1551), III 166; the First so-called, namely, the Treaty of the Escurial of 1733, VI 63 sqq., 152 sq.; the Second, namely, of Fontainebleau, of 1743, 159 sq.; of 1761, 344 sqq.; 368; of 1765, VIII 189, 290 sq.

—— of Love, III 755

Fanning, Edmund, Secretary of N. Carolina, VII 145

Fannio *or* Fannino, Italian martyr, II 387

Fanshawe, Sir Richard, and Portugal, V 105; in Spain, 109

Fantastic Poets, *see* Vol. IV, Chap. XXVI

Fanti, Manfredo, Italian general, XI 389

Far East, The (1815–71), *see* Vol. XI, Chap. XXVIII; Vol. XII, Chaps. XVII, XVIII *and* XIX. *See also* China, Japan, Eastern Question, etc.

Faraday, Michael, and social conditions, XII 730; 766; 786 sqq.

Fardella, Michel Angelo, Cartesian philosophy and, IV 791

Farel, Guillaume, preacher of Meaux, II 282 sq., 291 sq., 356; and Calvin, in Geneva, 358, 362 sq., 368, 375

Fargues, Henri, French politician, VIII 677, 682, 684

Farinelli (Carlo Broschi), Neapolitan singer, VI 167; 362; 364; 367

Farini, Luigi Carlo, Minister under Pius IX, X 157; XI 65; Minister of Education, 369; 371; 386; and the *Consorteria* Ministry, 535; 536; *History of the Papal States*, XII 842

Farmer, Anthony, and Magdalen College, V 238

Farnese, Alessandro, Cardinal. *See* Paul III, Pope

—— Alessandro (grandson of Paul III), Cardinal of Sant' Angelo, Archbishop of Avignon, etc., Papal legate, II 255, 662; III 450

—— Orazio, grandson of Paul III, II 82 sqq.; 269

—— *See* Parma, Dukes of

Faro, Bishop's library at, III 326; occupied by Palmella, X 333

Faroe Islands, Norway and, XI 683

Farquhar, George, dramatist, V 128; 131

Farragut, David Glasgow, American admiral, VII 498; attacks Vicksburg, 499 sq.; attacks Port Hudson, 503, 506; gains the battle of Mobile Bay, 522, 554 sqq.; at New Orleans, 552 sq., 559

Farrukhábád, General Lake's victory at (1804), IX 728

Fashoda (Kodok), French expedition at, XII 133, 448, 662, 813; 454

Fasting, Claus, Norwegian writer, xi 700
Fateh Khan, Barakzai Minister, xi 731
Fatehgarh, rebels defeated at, xi 748
Fatehpur-Sikri, Sindhia's victory at (1788), ix 719
Fauche-Borel, Swiss political agent, viii 511
Faucher, Léon, French Minister of Interior, xi 118 sq.; 123; and campaign against Republicans, 131; 133 sq.
Fauchet, Claude, author, iii 62
—— Claude, Constitutional bishop of the Calvados, viii 214, 255
Faucigny, participates in Swiss neutrality, ix 660
Faure, François-Félix, President of French Republic, xii 98; 112; 121
Fauriel, Claude, ix 24; xii 829
Favera, Guarino di. *See* Novara, Bishop of
Faversham, James II at, v 248
Favier, Bishop, Roman Catholic missionary at Peking, xii 518; 520
Favre, Gabriel-Claude-Jules, French statesman, xi 123 sq.; and the *Coup d'état* of December, 136; 305; 307; in opposition, 475, 477; 485; 489; 493; 496; negotiates with Bismarck, 497, 600; 498; signs an armistice, 499; 500; negotiates for the capitulation of Paris, 611; 612; xii 95; 103
Fawcett, Henry, Postmaster-General, xii 41
Faypoult de Maisoncelle, Chevalier G.-Charles, Minister of Finance, viii 490; envoy at Genoa, 587; at Naples, 653 sq.
Fazy, James, Genevese radical, xi 248
Febronius. *See* Hontheim
Fechen, Peter, ii 630
Feckenham, John de, ii 486; becomes Abbot of Westminster, 543; present at Elizabeth's coronation, 563, 565
Fedeli, Venetian envoy to Cosimo I, iii 389; 392 sq.
"Federal Pact," The Swiss (1815), xi 237 sqq.
Federalist, The, Alexander Hamilton writes in, vii 303
Federation, Act of, at Delft (1576), iii 243
Federigo III, King of Naples, i 118, 124, 234, 245
Fehrbellin, Banér at, iv 367; battle of (1675), v 44 sq., 568; 651
Feijoo, Antonio, Bishop of Maritana, Regent of Brazil, x 325
Feith, Rhijnvis, Dutch writer, xi 676
Fejérváry, Baron Gaza von, Austrian statesman, xii 205 sqq.; 209
Feldkirch, (Swiss) Diet at (1529), ii 330
Felix V (Amadeus VIII of Savoy), anti-Pope, i 623, 688
Felixstowe, Dutch landing at, v 189
Fellenberg, Philippe-Emmanuel de, institute at Hofwyl of, ix 427
Fellows, Sir Charles, archaeologist, xii 846
Felton, John, murders Buckingham, iv 272
Feltre, Bernardino da. *See* Bernardino, St, of Feltre

Feltre, Charles-M. A. de Goyon, Duc de, French general, xi 531
—— Marshal Clarke, Duc de. *See* Clarke
—— Thomas Campeggio, Bishop of, ii 665
—— Vittorino da. *See* Vittorino
Femern, naval battle off (1677), v 570
Fendall, Josias, Governor of Maryland, vii 33
Fénelon, François de Salignac de la Mothe, Archbishop of Cambray. *See* Cambray
Fenestrelles, capture of (1708), v 425; France and, vi 159
Fênghwangch'êng, xii 511; Russian force at, 585; 587 sq.
Fêngt'ai, Boxer disturbances at, xii 518
Fenianism, rise of, xi 343 sq.
Fenner, Thomas, iii 304 sq., 309
Fenshui pass, Japanese troops in, xii 587 sq.
Fenton, Edward, iii 300, 309
Fenwick, Sir John, execution of, v 262
—— John, settler on the Delaware, vii 47
Ferandina, Pedro de Toledo, Duke of (Marquis of Francavila), iii 470; 686; Viceroy of Milan, iv 626; 631; attacks Venice, 632 sq.
Féraud, Jean, French deputy, assassinated, viii 388 sq.
Fercullen, granted to O'Toole, iii 583
Ferdinand I, Emperor (King of Hungary and Bohemia), John Zapolya and, i 97; 343; ii 46, 66 sq., 143; Austrian territories made over to (1521), 149 sq.; 157; 169 sqq.; Peasants' Rising and, 178, 182, 190, 197; elected King of Bohemia and Hungary, 61, 198 sq.; elected King of the Romans, 66, 214, 537; 201; the Turks and, 206 sq.; 210 sq., 216; attempts to make peace with Turkey, 218, 221, 233 sqq.; treaty of, with Zapolya, 236; 267, 272; at Diet of Augsburg (1555), 275 sqq., 336, 537; 399; Council of Trent and, 674 sqq., 681 sq.; struggle as King of Hungary and Bohemia with Solyman II, Vol. iii, Chap. iv *passim*; as Emperor, *ib. and* 146–7; the Empire under, 140–65; and Archduke Maximilian, 167 sq.; and Charles V, 476 sq.; 699; and Jülich-Cleves, 716; and Bohemian religion, 727; death of, 169; v 339; 366; 625 sq.; vi 158; 507
—— II, Emperor, claims Bohemian throne, iii 568 sq.; and James I, 572 sq.; 575; 687, 699, 702, 714 sqq., 723 sqq.; Jesuit influence over, as Archduke in Styria, iv 5; and Venice, 11; and the Protestants, 13; King of Hungary, 14; and Bohemian succession, 15 sqq.; position of, in 1618, 23, 26; elected Emperor, 28; deposed in Bohemia, *ib.*; and Bohemian conflict, 31 sqq., 40; 45; 65 sq.; and German Princes, 67 sqq.; usefulness of Wallenstein to, 72 sq.; tribunal of "reformation" instituted by, 74 sqq.; and Bethlen Gabor, 75; seeks to

gain time, 77 sqq.; Palatinate in hands
of, 82; meeting of Princes convened
by, 83; 84 sqq.; 91 sq.; makes Wallenstein Commander-in-chief, 93 sq.; 98 sqq.;
Mecklenburg Dukes submit to, 101; 103;
104 sqq.; 108 sqq.; proclaims Edict of
Restitution, 111 sqq.; dismisses Wallenstein, 116 sq., 680; relations of, with
Estates of the Empire, 146; at Ratisbon,
197; Tilly in command of forces of, 198;
Convention of Leipzig and, 200; progress
of the War and, 201–12; Wallenstein
and, 213 sqq.; negotiations at Nürnberg
and, 218; 220; 238; 241; 246; 249;
Richelieu and, 250 sq., 679 sq.; Saxony
and, 252; Peace of Prague and, 253 sqq.,
365; 367; 369; 370; Amalia of Hesse-
Cassel concludes truce with, 371; death
and character of, 372 sq.; and the congress at Cologne, 396; Trautmansdorff
and, 400; Württemberg and, 409; 412;
arbitrary measures of, 414; 676 sqq.;
Mantuan succession and, 115, 678 sqq.;
tension between Urban VIII and, 681 sq.;
683 sq.; v 338; 351; xi 45
Ferdinand III, Emperor, crowned King of
Hungary, iv 91; marriage of, v 376;
elected King of the Romans, iv 115, 117,
372, 679; birth of heir to, 238; Wallenstein and, 116, 212, 239 sq.; takes
Ratisbon, 244; at Nördlingen, 245, 682;
371; accession of, 373; 375; attempts to
draw over Bernard of Saxe-Weimar, 376;
Oxenstierna and, 377; 378; refuses to
ratify Treaty of Mainz, 379; 380 sq.;
383; loyalty of *Kurfürstentag* to, 384;
Diet of Ratisbon and, 384 sq.; Denmark
and, 387; 389 sqq.; peace settlement
and, 397 sqq., 602 sq.; French claim to
Elsass and, 406 sq.; Maximilian and,
409; religious questions and, 412; territorial rights and, 413; relations of Great
Elector with, v 640 sqq.; and Poland,
344; last Diet of, iv 426; death of, 427,
429 sqq.; v 338; 340
—— I, Emperor of Austria, x 378; xi 44;
152; and the Vienna insurrection, 153
sq.; 171 sq.; and Hungary, 173; flight
of, 175; at Innsbruck, 176; returns to
Schönbrunn, 179, 182; at Olmütz, 186
sq.; abdication of, 88, 190; 193; 204;
208; 405
—— II, King of Aragon. *See* Ferdinand V,
King of Spain
—— Prince of Bulgaria, xii 342; 410 sq.;
proclaimed Tsar, 427; 578
—— I, King of Naples. *See* Ferrante
—— II, King of Naples. *See* Ferrante
—— IV, King of Naples and Sicily. *See*
Ferdinand I, King of the Two Sicilies
—— V (the Catholic), King of Spain (II
of Aragon, V of Castile), i 81, 115, 119;
at war with Louis XII, 126 sqq.; 193;
Holy League proposed by, 198; 251; 308;
316; Spain under, 346–68; 379; joins

Breton League against France (1489), 394;
Henry VII and, 466, 476; Henry VIII
and, 478–9, 483; death of, 368, 486;
656; ii 36 sq.; iii 478; 510; 738; v 483;
vi 151; 167
Ferdinand VI, King of Spain, vi 137; 139;
145; 147; marriage of, 166; 249; 342;
reign of, 361 sqq.; death of, 366; 368;
597; x 273
—— VII, King of Spain, vii 362, 365
sqq.; ix 321; arrest of, 429; and
revolution of Aranjuez, 431; Napoleon
refuses to recognise the claim of, 432;
enforced abdication of, 433; release of,
482; relations of, with Napoleon, 622;
revolt against (1821), x 74; seeks aid
of Louis XVIII, 79; and Napoleon, 205;
returns to Spain (1814), *ib.*; reactionary
policy of, 12, 141, 205 sqq.; character
of, 207; political system established by,
208 sq.; and purchase of Russian war-
ships, 209; second marriage of, 210;
plots against, *ib.*; Louis XVIII refuses
aid of, 211; and Congress of Vienna,
ib.; and British Government, 212;
and Mora's secret mission, 213; restores
the Constitution of 1812, 217 sq.; anti-
constitutional action by, 221 sq.; seeks
aid of the Allied Powers, 222 sqq.;
French loan to, 225; and the Cortes, 227
sq.; enters French camp, 228; persecution of Liberals by, 229 sq.; fourth
marriage of, 231; and King Louis-
Philippe, 231 sq.; and succession to the
throne, 232 sq.; death of (1833), 233;
282; and Spanish America, 283, 285 sq.,
290 sq., 306; seeks aid of the Allied
Powers against American revolution,
308; 316; xi 551
—— I (IV), King of the Two Sicilies, and
the Family Compact, vi 344 sq.; 366;
368; 594; 597; at Laibach (1821), vii
368; marriage of, viii 79, 555; 573, 649
sqq.; flight of, 652; returns to Naples,
658; 778 sq.; ix 68; 73, 88, 381; restoration of Naples to, 382; proposal of, to
Sicilian Parliament, 383; capitulates
to England, 384; compelled to make
way for Joseph Bonaparte, 403; throne
of Sicily guaranteed to, 604; Austrian
alliance with, 648; recognised by the
Powers, 661; restoration of (1815), x
109 sq.; negotiations with Emperor of
Austria, 110; and revolt of 1820, 112;
accepts Spanish Constitution of 1812,
24, 112; at Congress of Laibach, 29,
69, 113; returns to Naples, 114; and
Ferdinand of Spain, 224
—— II, King of the Two Sicilies, x
129; xi 18; 68; and Scientific Congresses, 69; 70; and demands for reform, 79 sq.; and Naples Constitution,
87 sq.; suppresses Sicilian Revolution,
91 sq.; and Pius IX, 121; reactionary
policy of, 379 sq.; death of, 380

Ferdinand, King of the Romans (son of Ferdinand III), death of, IV 426
—— Archduke, of Austria (son of Ferdinand I), II 537
—— Archduke, of Styria. *See* Ferdinand II, Emperor
—— Archduke, of Tyrol, III 94, 165; death of (1595), 699; quits the Landsberg League, 709; IV 1
—— Charles, Archduke, of Tyrol, and Treaty of Westphalia, IV 407, 603; and marriage of James II, V 211
—— Charles Joseph d'Este, Austrian Archduke, Prince of Modena, commands army of Germany, IX 250; 253, 254; in Bohemia, 257; watched by Bernadotte, 258; 275; commands an Austrian army, 346; ordered to occupy Warsaw, 347; in western Galicia, 354
—— Maria, Elector of Bavaria. *See* Bavaria
—— of Saxe-Coburg-Gotha, King Consort of Maria II of Portugal, X 338 sq.; XI 570 sq.; acts as Regent, 573; 575
—— Cardinal Infante of Spain, Archbishop of Toledo, IV 230; 239; at Nördlingen, 244; 246; represents Philip IV in Flanders, 644 sq.; sent to Brussels, 698; 699; successes of, 700; death of, 659, 702
—— Grand Duke of Tuscany. *See* Tuscany
Ferguson, Adam, philosopher, VIII 769
—— Patrick, colonel, VII 225 sq., 233
—— Robert, the "Plotter," V 229
Fergusson, Robert, poet, X 701 sq.
Feria, Gomez Suarez de Figueroa y Córduba, 5th Count and 1st Duke of, Spanish ambassador to England, II 549, 561 sqq., 566, 573; III 263 sq.; 283; 477 sqq.
—— Gomez Suarez de Figueroa y Córduba, 3rd Duke of, Spanish Governor of Milan, IV 41; in Milan, 48; and the Valtelline, 49 sqq.; at Innsbruck, 231; at Vienna, 234 sq.; 238; in Elsass, 246; 672
—— Lorenzo Suarez de Figueroa y Córduba, 2nd Duke of, ambassador to France and Rome, III 52; 517
Ferik Suleiman, Pasha of Plevlye, XII 401
Ferishta, Persian historian, VI 512
Fermanagh, plantation of, III 614; Commissioners of allotments in, 615
Fermat, Pierre de, mathematician, Descartes and, IV 779; 794; V 711 sq.; 715; 723
Fermo, Neapolitan defeat at (1798), VIII 652
Fermont des Chapellières, Comte Joseph-Jacques de, President of the National Convention, VIII 300
Fermor, Count William, Russian general, VI 277; 279 sqq.; 322 sqq.
Fernamond, Imperial commander, in the Valtelline, IV 61 sq

Fernandes, Alfonso, translates Erasmus' *Enchiridion* into Spanish, II 401
Fernandina (Florida), captured, VII 552
Fernando, Dom, of Portugal, death of, XI 574
Feron, Robert, II 442
Ferrand, Antoine-François-Claude, French Director-General of Posts, IX 565; 566, 570; and the *émigrés*, X 42
Ferrante (Ferdinand I), King of Naples (d. 1494), I 80 sq., 104 sq., 110, 124, 227, 387, 665
—— II, *or* Ferrantino (Ferdinand II), King of Naples (1495–6), I 114 sqq., 231 sq., 234, 245
—— Duke of Calabria, son of Federigo III of Naples, I 124
Ferrar, Nicholas, IV 280
—— Robert, Bishop of St David's, II 538 sq.
Ferrara, Venetian factories at, I 260; war of succession in, 261; Calvin in, II 358, 385; the Reformation in, 384 sqq.; colony from, in the Maremma, III 393; condition of, 401; and Savoy, 415; "the Blind Man of," 461; royal marriages at (1598), 527; duchy of, added to States of the Church, IV 667, 686; Legation of, held by French (1796), VIII 573; 583, 588; Austrian garrison at, X 137, 155; XI 71; Austrian occupation of, 77 sq.; the national movement in, 384
—— Alfonso I, d'Este, Duke of, I 137, 248 sqq.; II 43, 54 sqq.; 60 sq.; receives Reggio and Modena, 67, 384
—— Alfonso II, Duke of, III 94, 387; marries Lucrezia de' Medici, 395; death of (1597), 397, 432
—— Azzo d'Este, Marquis of, I 261
—— Borso, Duke of, III 461
—— Hercules I, Duke of, I 287; III 461
—— Hercules II, Duke of, II 81, 384 sqq.
—— Niccolo III (1481), Marquis of, I 558
—— Renée of France, Duchess of, I 457, 483; II 358; and the Reformation, 384, 387; suggested marriage of, to Henry VIII, 428, 578; III 471
—— Cardinal of. *See* Este, Ippolito de
Ferrari, Giuseppe, historian, I 341; XII 812
—— founder of the Barnabites, II 648
—— General, XI 86
—— Paolo, Italian dramatist, XI 548
Ferraris, Count Joseph, Austrian Fieldmarshal, VI 652
—— Luigi, Italian statesman, XII 217
Ferrars, John, and the London Company, VII 6
Ferré, Charles-Théophile, French communist, XI 502
Ferreni, Zaccaria, of Vicenza, II 30
Ferrero, Guglielmo, Italian sociologist, XII 231
Ferretti, Giovanni Mastai-, Cardinal. *See* Pius IX, Pope
Ferri, Enrico, Italian socialist, XII 231 sq.

Ferrières, peace negotiations at, xi 497 sq.
—— Charles-Élie, Marquis de, member of the States General, viii 146
Ferrol, Fitzmaurice sails from (1579), iii 597; fleet equipped at, 606; departure of expedition from (1597), 673; arsenal of, vi 125; 365; blockade of, ix 213, 217; Allied force at (1804), 219; Villeneuve retires to, 226; capture of French ships off, 234
Ferry, Jules, French statesman, xi 498; 502; xii 109; Ministry of, 112; 114; policy of, 116 sqq.; 121; and Tonkin, 131 sq., 527; colonial policy of, 159; 161
Fersen, Count Axel Fredrik af, Swedish statesman, vi 763 sqq.; 768; 776; 781
—— Count Axel (son of above), Swedish ambassador in Paris, vi 783; viii 789; ix 323
—— Russian commander, viii 546 sq.
Fesch, Joseph, Cardinal, ix 107; Napoleon's Grand Almoner, 111; French ambassador at Rome, 191; 193; recalled from Rome, 194; 195; member of Ecclesiastical Commission, 196; 202
Fessenden, William Pitt, American Secretary of the Treasury, vii 570
Fethard, Reconciliation meeting at (1828), x 648
Fetherstone, Richard, trial of, with More, ii 443; execution of, 444
Feth Islam, garrison of, xi 647
Feuerbacher, Matern, leader of Peasants' Rising, ii 182 sq., 188
Feuillants, revolutionary club, viii 173, 212 sq., 215 sq.; ruin of, 221; policy of, 222
Feuille du Village, La, French newspaper, xi 127
Feuillet, Octave, novelist, xi 522
Feuquières, Isaac de Pas, Marquis de, French ambassador in Sweden, v 566; 568 sqq.; 573 sq.
—— Manassès de Pas, Marquis de, French diplomatist, concludes treaty with Sweden, iv 142; at Heilbronn, 225 sq.; Kinsky and, 234; and Wallenstein, 236, 240; at the Frankfort Convention, 246 sq.; 248; Bernard of Weimar and, 249; diplomacy of, 367
Feversham, Louis de Duras, Earl of, v 232; 247 sq.
Feyt, Florentius, Jesuit, ii 631
Fez, Pisan alliance with, iii 398; xii 132; explorer in, 808
Fezensac, Duc de, ix 252
Fezzan, Hornemann in, xii 806
Fichte, Johann Gottlieb, viii 775; life and work of, ix 325–8; x 370; philosophy of, 401, 404, 410; xii 758; 818
Ficino, Marsilio, i 147, 151; and Savonarola, 188; translation of Plato by, 543; and the Platonic Academy, 559; Platonism of, ii 4, 7 sq., 16, 701
Ficker, Julius, historian, xii 823; 850

Fickler, C. B. A., Baden radical, xi 164
Ficquelmont, Count Karl Ludwig, Austrian Minister of Foreign Affairs, xi 155; 171; 174
Fidei ratio ad Carolum Imperatorem, of Zwingli, ii 335
Field of Cloth of Gold, ii 42, 417
Fielden, John, x 659; 681 sq.
Fielding, Henry, v 131; vi 833; x 718; 723; xi 361
Fields, James Thomas, editor of the *Atlantic Monthly,* vii 746
Fiennes, Nathaniel, iv 393
—— W. *See* Saye and Sele, Viscount
Fiereck, General, xi 603 sq.
Fieschi, Giuseppe, x 492
Fiesco, Gianluigi, leader of rising in Genoa, ii 81 sq.
Fiesole, Braccio Martelli, Bishop of, ii 666, 668 sq.
Fiévée, Joseph, ix 137; x 55
Fife, Jacobite successes in, vi 99
Figaro. *See* Larra
Figner, Vera, Russian revolutionary, xii 311
—— Russian officer, conducts guerrilla warfare against French, ix 497
Figueras, captured by the French (1794), viii 440, (1808), ix 430; retaken by the Catalans (1811), 465; besieged by Macdonald, 469
—— Estanislao, Spanish Republican leader, xii 260 sq.
Figueroa, Don Manuel Ventura, President of the Council of Castile, vi 374
Fiji Islands, xii 631; annexed by Great Britain, 666; 667
Filangieri, Carlo, Neapolitan general, xi 91 sq.; 380
—— Gaetano, the *Scienza della Legislazione,* viii 729, 747, 777; x 106
Filelfo, Francesco, humanist, Latin letter writing and, i 544; study of Greek at Constantinople by, 551; lectures at Florence by, 554 sq.
Filicaya, Vincenzo da, Italian poet, v 69
Filipowski, The, iii 75
Fillmore, Millard, vii 399; President of United States, 404, 432; xi 824; xii 682
Filmer, Sir Robert, iii 750, 763; *Patriarcha,* v 228, 254; vi 802 sqq.
Finale, designs of Savoy upon, iii 407; promised to Philip III of Spain, iv 14; marquisate of, v 384, 389; Genoa and, vi 249; 608
Finch, Daniel. *See* Nottingham, Earl of
—— Heneage, Earl of Nottingham. *See* Nottingham, Earl of
—— Sir John, in Parliament, iv 273; flight and impeachment of, 287
Finchley Common, army at, vi 114
Finck, General von, made Commander-in-chief by Frederick II, vi 293; 294
Findlater, James Ogilvy, 4th Earl of, vi 96

Fingal, Arthur J. Plunket, 7th Earl of, and the Irish Catholics, IX 694; 707; X 629 sqq.; 634

Fingo tribes, in Queen Adelaide Province, XI 781

Finkenstein, Napoleon at, IX 289
—— Count von, Prussian Minister of Foreign Affairs, VI 265; 293; 328; 706; 709

Finland, occupied by Sweden, II 600; bequeathed to John III, IV 160; 162; 170; Charles IV in, 172; conquest of, *ib.*; government of, 175, 181; Peace of Stolbova and, *ib.*; Peter the Great in, V 538; 603; 609; 614 sq.; VI 35; 37; 309; Swedish invasion of, 310; 314; Catharine II and, 694; 760 sq.; 770; 775 sq.; 778 sq.; Sweden and, 782; VIII 325 sq.; after the Peace of Tilsit, IX 294; Russian invasion of, 313, 322; grand duchy of, passes to Russia, 314, 323, 487, 591, X 413; and Congress of Vienna, IX 668; X 420; Russian administration of, 433 sqq.; 440; 446; XI 628; 678; 680; XII 11; Scandinavia and, 274 sq.; 277; 287; high schools in, 292; Russian policy in, 334 sq.; 355; concessions obtained by, 360; 377; 762 sq.

Finlay, George, historian, XI 280; works of, excluded from Russia, XII 300; 845

Finmark, partition of, XI 684

Finsen, Niels Ryberg, Danish physician, XII 292

Fiorella, Pascal-Antoine, French commander, VIII 575

Firenzuola, Angelo, III 394, 468

Firlej, Jan, Grand-Marshal of Poland, III 84, 87–9, 96

Firmian, Charles-Joseph, Comte de, Governor-General of Lombardy, VIII 778
—— Leopold. *See* Salzburg, Archbishop of

Firozpur, XI 732; 736; 738 sq.

Firozshahr, battle of, XI 739

First Book of Discipline (1560), II 593

First-fruits, English Act concerning (1532), II 437, 439

Fischer, Christian A., German traveller, VIII 783
—— Emil, German chemist, XII 770
—— Hannibal, Oldenburg official, XI 151; and the German fleet, 227

Fischhof, Adolf, Austrian politician, XI 153; 176

Fish, Hamilton, VII 429; American Secretary of State, 635 sq.; XII 21 sq.

Fisher, John, Jesuit, V 746
—— John, Bishop of Rochester, I 491; 580; 626; II 428, 431, 433; supports Queen Catharine, 436; the Nun of Kent and, 441; arrest, trial, and execution of, 443
—— of Kilverstone, John Arbuthnot Fisher, Lord, admiral, XII 59

Fisher's Hill, Sheridan's victory at (1864), VII 532

Fismes, Hocquincourt defeated near (1650), IV 613

Fitzalan, Henry, 12th Earl of Arundel. *See* Arundel

Fitzgerald, Earls of Desmond. *See* Desmond
—— Edward, poet, XI 354
—— Lord Edward, Irish insurrectionary leader, VIII 473, 771; IX 701
—— James Fitzmaurice (cousin of Earl Gerald), III 594 sqq.
—— Sir John, Captain of Desmond. *See* Desmond
—— Sir John Fitzedmund, III 596
—— Lord Thomas, killed at Stoke (1487), I 466
—— Lord Thomas. *See* Kildare
—— Sir Thomas, Spanish ambassador in London, VI 66
—— Vesey, and the Clare election, X 645 sq.
—— Colonel, at Blackheath, V 209

Fitzgibbon. *See* Clare, Earl of

Fitzherbert, Maria Anne, and George IV, VI 472

Fitzmaurice, Lord. *See* Lansdowne, 1st Marquis of

Fitzroy, Sir Charles Augustus, Governor of New South Wales, XI 795
—— Robert, Admiral, Governor of New Zealand, XI 793 sq.

Fitzsimmons, Walter, Archbishop of Dublin, I 472

Fitzwilliam, Charles William Wentworth Fitzwilliam, Earl, X 582; 629
—— W. *See* Southampton, Earl of
—— Sir William, Lord Justice in Ireland, III 594, 596; Lord Deputy, 604; resigns, 605
—— William Wentworth Fitzwilliam, 2nd Earl, VI 478; VIII 759; IX 76; Lord President, 674; Viceroy of Ireland, 697 sqq.

Fiume, port of, taken from Austria, IX 418

"Five Articles of Perth," IV 487 sq.; 491 sq.; abolished, 501

Five Forks, battle of (1865), VII 538

Five Mile Act (1665), V 103, 333

Five Nations, The. *See* Iroquois

"Five Scholars of Lausanne," execution of, II 293

Flacius Illyricus,Matthaeus (Mattia Vlacich), *Clavis Sacrae Scripturae*, I 609; II 383; III 150, 162; XII 816

Flacourt, Étienne de, in Madagascar, V 702

Flahaut de la Billarderie, Auguste-Charles-Joseph, Count de, XI 140

Flaminio, Marcantonio, Italian scholar, I 567; II 17, 379, 389 sq., 398; III 466

Flammock, Thomas, leader of Cornish rebels, I 469

Flamsteed, John, astronomer, V 721

Flanders, trade of, with Venice, I 257; and Burgundy, 418; revolts of communes of, 425–9; economic decline of, 429; the Council of, 431; Treaty of (1490), 449; (and Artois), ceded to Charles V (1529), II 60, 102; English commercial truce with (1528), 430; III 16, 419–20, 435; Spanish rule in, 465, 476; condition of, 495; Don John sent to, 498; return of Alva to, 500; invitation to Archduke Matthias to assume the sovereignty of, 501; and Peace of Vervins, 523; Archduke Albert of Austria and the Infanta assume joint sovereignty of, 524; after Treaty between Spain and England, 537; Province of, 618; Spanish influence in, 630; Philip's plans in, 510, 512; IV 639 sq.; Spain and, 644 sqq.; Condé in, 659; 664; Duke of Orleans in, 597; 598; 618; French advance on, 683; French in, V 62, 112, 199, 420 sqq.; French acquisitions in, 153, 373; Marlborough in, 416; 425; and Third Barrier Treaty, 459, VI 640; Marshal Saxe in, 240, 243; 246 sq.; 331; 644; boundaries of, 645 sq.; Estates of, VIII 39; agriculture in, 61, X 730, 750; campaign in (1793), VIII 428; cotton manufacture in, X 753; XI 670; anti-French feeling in, 673; education in, XII 251
—— Philip, Count of, XI 645
Flaubert, Gustave, novelist, XI 365; 509; 522; 528
Flavigny, French repulse at, XI 590
Fléchier, Esprit, Bishop of Nîmes. *See* Nîmes
Flecknoe, Richard, poet, V 134
Fleetwood, Charles, Lieut.-general, army and, IV 448; and Wallingford House party, 449 sq.; Richard Cromwell and, 451 sq.; in Ireland, 535 sqq.; Protectorate and, 539; army and, 542, 544 sq.; submits to Parliament, 548
Fleix, Peace of, III 34, 37, 665
Fleming, Charles, Jacobite envoy, VI 92
—— Herman, IV 577; will of Charles X and, 590
—— Klas Ericson, Governor of Finland, attitude of, towards the Swedish Government, IV 170, 172; 173
—— Klas Hermansson, Swedish statesman, V 573 sq.; 576
—— Klas Larson, and Oxenstierna, IV 569; death of, 571
—— Paul, German poet, V 68
"Flemish movement," XI 673, 675
Flemmyng, Robert, Dean of Lincoln, books collected by, I 597
Flers, Charles de, French general, VIII 420
Flersheim, Colonel von, sent to Paris, IV 381
Flesselles, Jacques de, *Prévôt des marchands* in Paris, VIII 164
Fletcher, Archibald, Reformer, VIII 770

Fletcher, Benjamin, Governor of New York, VII 50 sq.
—— Giles, envoy to Russia, V 514
—— John, III 381; dramatic influence of, IV 760
Fleuranges. *See* La Marck, Robert III de
Fleurus, victory of Mansfeld and Christian at (1622), IV 81; battle of (1690), V 59, 261, 661, (1794), VIII 367, 435 sq.
Fleury, André Hercule, Cardinal, French statesman, V 90; 543; VI 69; and the Jacobites, 109; 131; 134; 143 sqq.; and Spanish affairs, 148 sqq., 158 sq.; and Poland, 152; 154 sqq.; character and administration of, 161 sqq.; and Louis XV, 164; and Elisabeth Farnese, 165; and Pragmatic Sanction, 203; 204; and Austrian Succession, 228 sq.; 231; 235; 236; and Russian affairs, 308; 331; 533; death of, 109, 159, 239, 329; VIII 15, 33; X 9; 157
—— Émile-Félix, French general, XI 134
—— Joly de, French Comptroller-General, VIII 95
Flinders, Matthew, naval captain and explorer, capture of, by French, IX 739; exploration by, 740
Flinders Island, blacks deported to, XI 791
Flocon, Ferdinand, editor of *La Réforme*, XI 25; 99; 101; 109; joins the Socialist party, 114; 116
Flodden, battle of (1513), I 482
Flood, Henry, Irish politician, VI 492; 494; 497; and Irish parliamentary reform, 501 sq.
Floquet, Charles-Thomas, French statesman, XII 112
Florence, Vol. I, Chap. V (i) Savonarola, 144–89; VI (ii) Machiavelli, 190–218; the Medici expelled from (1494), 113; restored (1512), 138; war between the Visconti and, 279 sq.; cloth industry at, 496, 512; libraries founded at, 542; Platonic Academy at, 543, 559, II 702; Council of (1438), I 546; disputes between Papacy and, 661, 666; the Renaissance in, II 3; Platonism in, 4; League of Cognac joined by, 55; expulsion of the Medici from (1527), 56; establishment of a Republic in, *ib.*; fall of (1530), 25, 60, III 53, 465; restoration of the Medici in, II 60; new constitution of, III 388–9, 391, 401; art in, 394; Cosimo's rule in, 395; rule of Francis in, 396; the *Umidi* of, 470; IV 143; and Ferdinand II, 211; John Milton in, V 118; Council of, 482 sq.; Academies of, 739 sq.; Don Carlos enters, VI 150; 602; Treaty of (1801), IX 68, 364; Napoleon controls policy of the Court of, 398; French Prefect sent to, 399; historic dualism with Siena, 400; Ferdinand IV at, X 114; scientific and literary society founded at, 128; 132; XI 41; Scientific Congress at, 68; 78 sq.; Mazzini in, 91; the Austrians

in, 95; reaction in, 377 sq.; 386; becomes Italian capital, 539; financial situation in, XII 214; riots in, 220; 225 sq.; Cardinal Manning at, 230; 824

Florence, Antonino (Sant), Archbishop of, reforming influence of, I 188, 647, 649, II 3

—— Archbishop of. *See* Altoviti, Cardinal

Flores, Viceroy of Mexico, VIII 290

Florida, discovery of, I 54; expedition of de Soto to, 54; English and French in, 55 sq.; French settlement in, III 492; VI 347; ceded to Great Britain, 370; Spanish conquest of, 377; 380 sq.; 428 sq.; 453; 464; Oglethorpe's invasion of, VII 62; loyalist fugitives in, 218; Spanish, French and American claims in, 324 sqq., 362, 365; secedes from Union, 446, 603; joins Confederacy, 453; slavery in, 587; emancipation in, 595; Republicans in, 642; the United States and, XII 684; 691

Florida, Confederate cruiser and commerce-destroyer of the *Alabama* controversy, VII 565, XII 20

Florida Blanca, Don José Moñino, Count of, Spanish statesman, VI 374 sq.; and Gibraltar, 377 sqq.; 381; reforms by, 382 sq.; VIII 292, 782

Floridas, ceded by Spain (1819), x 213, 275; 686

Floriszoon, Pieter, Dutch vice-admiral, v 147

Flotte, Paul-Louis-René de, French politician, XI 131; 136

—— Comte de, Rear-Admiral, hanged at Toulon, VIII 448

Flottwell, Eduard Heinrich von, Governor of Posen, x 464

Flourens, Gustave, French politician, XI 498; 502

Floyd, Edward, III 572

—— John Buchanan, resigns Secretaryship of War, VII 447; at Fort Donelson, 495

Flushing, Philip leaves (1559), III 187; captured by the *Gueux de Mer*, 230–1, 233; demanded by Elizabeth, 619, 670 sq.; Austrian vessel stopped at, VI 643; besieged (1809), IX 139, 358; fortifications of, destroyed by the British, 359

Flying Fish, British warship, rescues the Japanese legation in Korea, XII 567

Flysteden, Peter, Lutheran martyr, II 202

Fock, Russian general, XII 586

Focktchany, conferences at, VI 634

Foere, Abbé de, x 529

Foersom, Peter Thun, Danish writer, XI 699

Fogarasi, János, Hungarian scholar, XI 431

Foggia, and the Apulian aqueduct, XII 238

Fogliani, Neapolitan Minister, VI 597

Foix, François Phébus, Count of, King of Navarre. *See* Navarre

—— Gaston de, Duke of Nemours, killed at Ravenna (1512), I 136 sq., 198, 250, 366

—— Germaine de. *See* Germaine, Queen of Spain

—— Paul de, envoy to England, III 15 sq., 18

Folembray, Decrees of (1596), III 668

Folengo, Giambattista, Italian Reformer, II 390

—— Teofilo, III 460

Foley, Sir Thomas, Admiral, VIII 626

Foligno, convention of (1801), IX 68; Pius VII at, x 134

Folkestone, action off (May 19, 1652), IV 471

Follen, Karl, revolutionary scheme of, x 364

Fombio, fight at, VIII 568

Fominskoie, French army at, IX 498

Fonblanque, Albany, x 656; 658; 665; 674

Fondi, Julia Gonzaga surprised by Turks at, III 110

Fonseca, Alonso. *See* Toledo, Archbishop of

—— Antonio de, Royalist Captain against rebel *Comuneros*, I 373

—— Diogo da, Damião de Goes and, II 415

—— Manoel Deodoro da, President of Brazil, XII 675

—— Rodrigo da, at Oporto, x 332

Fontaine, Pierre-François-Léonard, IX 134

—— Française, skirmish at (1595), III 667

Fontainebleau, Assembly of Notables at (1560), II 298; Catharine de' Medici at, III 1; royal *château* at, 53; Charles Emmanuel meets Henry IV at, 418; Biron meets Henry IV at, 680; Napoleon's return to (1809), IX 139; Pius VII imprisoned at, 200; Napoleon's policy in Treaty of, 428; 430; Napoleon at (1814), 554, 556; Napoleon leaves, 559; returns to (1815), 574; Pius VII at, x 133

—— Treaties of (1679), v 45, 571, (1745), VI 113, 159, 239, 645 sq., (Nov. 8, 1785), VIII 281, 312, (Nov. 10, 1785), 283, 321, (1807), IX 302 sq., 309, 399, 602, x 310, (1814), XI 558; Edict of (1540), II 288; Preliminaries of (1762), VI 299, 346, 428; Concordat of (1813), IX 200, 203, 207; Decrees of (Oct. 18 and 25, 1801), 372

Fontana, Domenico, architect of Sixtus V, III 426, 439 sq., 442 sqq.

Fontane, Theodor, German writer, XI 413 sq.

Fontanes, Louis, Marquis de, VIII 515; IX 15; Grand Master of the Imperial University, 128; 132, 136, 139; and the Restoration, 565; XI 528

Fontenay, captured by the Vendeans, VIII 341; higher grade school at, XII 118

Fontenay, J.-M. C. de. *See* Bourges, Bishop of

Fontenay-Mareuil, Marquis de, sent to Rome by Mazarin, IV 601

Fontenelle, Bernard le Bovier de, VIII 15

Fontenoy, seized by La Noue, III 23; by Montpensier, 25; battle of, VI 111, 242, 247, 250, 331

Fontrailles, Louis d'Astarac, Vicomte de, follower of Beaufort, IV 596; exile of, 617

Fonzio, Bartolommeo, Venetian reformer and martyr, II 381 sq.

Foochow, opening of the port of, XI 810; captured by the French, XII 131, 527

Foot, Samuel Augustus, American politician, VII 381

Foote, Andrew Hull, American admiral, VII 494 sq.

—— Sir Edward James, vice-admiral, VIII 657 sq.

—— Henry S., American Senator, VII 604

—— Solomon, American statesman, VII 429

Forbes of Pitsligo, Alexander Forbes, Lord, Jacobite, VI 114; 117

—— Duncan, of Culloden, VI 107

—— Joseph, American brigadier-general, VII 132, 135 sq.

Forbin, Count Claude de, VI 92 sq.

Forbin-Janson, Abbé C.-A.-M.-J., Comte de, x 72

—— Charles-T.-P.-A.-F., Marquis de, XI 122

Forbonnais, Sieur de. *See* Véron, François

Forcade de La Roquette, Jean-L.-V.-A. de, French Minister of the Interior, XI 490

Forckenbeck, Max von, Chief Burgomaster of Berlin, XII 146

Ford, John, dramatist, III 381; v 126

—— Patrick, editor of *The Irish World*, XII 78; 82

Forde, Francis, captures Masulipatam, VI 548; 556

Forest Cantons, Perpetual League of the (1291 and 1315), II 305

Foresta, de, Sardinian statesman, XI 369 sq.

Forey, Élie-Frédéric, French general, XI 136

Forgacz, Palatine of Hungary, IV 31

Forlì, surrenders to Cesare Borgia, I 238; revolution in (1831), x 155; 156

Forment, Damien, Spanish sculptor, I 382

Formosa, conquered by the Dutch, IV 711, 740; trade of, 712; Chinese rising in, v 696; XII 5; ceded to Japan, 52, 512, 572; French blockade of, 131, 527; 502; Japan and, 556 sqq.; progress in, 573

Formula Concordiae, of 1580, III 704, **708**, 712–3

Fornésy, Henri-François, French commander, VIII 565

Fornovo, battle of (1495), I 116 sq.

Forrest, Sir John, explorer in Australia, XI 798; XII 618

—— Nathan Bedford, Confederate cavalry commander, VII 524

Forster, George, in Central Asia, XII 800

—— Johann Georg Adam, German traveller, VIII 775

—— John, biographer and critic, XII 838

—— Thomas, Jacobite general, VI 101; 103

—— William Edward, Vice-President of the Council, XII 23 sq.; Chief Secretary for Ireland, 36; 38; resigns, 40, 81; and Parnell, 41; 77 sqq.; 82; 86

Forsyth, Sir Thomas Douglas, mission of, to St Petersburg, XII 461; 802

Fort Augustus, VI 106 sq.; 112; 116 sq.

—— Bowyer, captured by the British (1815), VII 346

—— Brown (Rio Grande), built (1846), VII 394; attacked, 395

—— Cataraqui. *See* Kingston (Ontario)

—— Donelson, Confederate stronghold on the Cumberland, VII 494; captured by Grant, 495, 558, 608, 616

—— Duquesne, skirmish near (1754), VI 332; attack on (1755), VII 123; 126; captured (1758), 135 sq.

—— Edward, English at, VII 125, 127

—— Erie, captured by the British (1814), VII 343

—— Fisher, capture of (1865), VII 528, 534, 537, 552, 556 sqq.

—— Frontenac. *See* Kingston (Ontario)

—— Fuentes, built by Fuentes, IV 42 sq.; promised demolition of, 45, 51

—— George (Inverness), VI 107; 116

—— George (Niagara), abandoned by the British (1813), VII 341

—— Haake, captured by General Fraser (1809), IX 358

—— Henry, Confederate stronghold on the Tennessee, VII 494; captured by Grant, 495, 558, 608, 616

—— James, on the Gambia, v 692, VI 464

—— Joux, ceded to the Swiss Confederation, IX 664

—— Kuropatkin, captured, XII 594

—— McAllister, Sherman captures (1864), VII 527

—— Meigs, besieged (1813), VII 340

—— Mimms, massacre at (1813), VII 345

—— Morgan, capture of (1864), VII 554 sqq.

—— Moultrie, Anderson evacuates (1860), VII 446 sq.

—— Nassau (Mouree), erected by the Dutch, IV 759

—— Orange. *See* Albany

—— Pillow, Confederates evacuate, VII 499, 559; massacre at (1864), 597

—— Pulaski, captured (1862), VII 552

—— Randolph, Confederates evacuate, VII 499

—— St David, siege of, VI 248, 537 sq., 547

Fort St George, foundation of, IV 742;
v 697; surrender of, VI 537; 552
—— St Louis (Texas), built, VII 362
—— Sandusky, besieged (1813), VII 340
—— Sommerschanz, captured, VI 197
—— Stanwix, St Leger's unsuccessful expedition against (1777), VII 215
—— Stedman, captured and recaptured (1864), VII 534
—— Stevens, Early at (1864), VII 531
—— Sumter, Anderson defends (1860–1), VII 446 sq.; surrender of, 450, 452, 454, 464 sq.; 545
—— William (India), VI 537; college at, IX 728; presidency of, XII 495
—— William (Inverness), siege of, VI 116
—— William Henry, English at, VII 125, 127; fall of (1757), 129 sqq.
Fortescue, Chichester S. P., Lord Carlingford. *See* Carlingford
Forth, Firth of, Dutch fleet in, V 188; VI 92 sq.
—— Patrick Ruthven, Earl of, Royalist commander-in-chief, IV 308
Fortiguerra, Scipione (Carteromachus), I 563
Fortis, Alessandro, Italian statesman, XII 214; 227
Fortoul, Hippolyte-Nicolas-Honoré, French statesman, XI 135; 297
Fortress Monroe, General B. F. Butler at (1861), VII 464; and Richmond campaign, 472 sq.; Jefferson Davis imprisoned in, 543; fugitive slaves at, 581 sq.
Forty-Two Articles, of Edward VI, II 508
Forwards, revolutionary journal, XII 302
Foscarari, Egidio, Bishop of Modena, II 398
Foscari, Francesco, Doge of Venice, I 276, 278 sq.; dogeship of, 281 sq.
—— Jacopo, son of the Doge, I 282
Foscarini, Antonio, Venetian ambassador in England, IV 40
Foscolo, Ugo, Italian poet, VI 824; 830; x 110; 126; influence of Byron upon, 725; XI 546; 549
Fosse, Baron van der, Governor of Brabant, x 534
Fossombroni, Count Vittorio, x 108
Foster, Augustus, British Minister to the United States, VII 333
—— John. *See* Oriel, Lord
Fotheringay, Mary, Queen of Scots, tried and executed at, III 291–2
Foucault, Léon, physicist, XII 783
—— Nicolas-Joseph, and the Protestants of Béarn, v 24
Fouché, Joseph, Duc d'Otrante, VIII 249, 351; and the *Montagnards*, 366 sq., 369; Minister of Police, 672; and Napoleon, 675, 678; IX 1; 9–11, 14–16, 21, 28–30, 107, 111, 137–40; character of, 141; 180–1, 283, 320; intrigues of, 370, 445; and the restoration, 565; conspiracy of,

572–3; 574; Minister of Police, 616; treacherous advice of, 642; policy of, 645; retirement of, x 13; 45 sq.; 48
Foucquet, Jean, French painter, I 414
Fougères, occupied by the Vendeans, VIII 355
Fould, Achille, XI 117; French Minister of Finance, 129; 131; 133; 297; 472 sq.
Foulon, Joseph-François, Minister of the Household to Louis XVI, VIII 163; murdered, 168
Fouqué, Baron Friedrich Heinrich de la Motte, German romanticist, x 404
—— Baron Heinrich August de la Motte, Prussian general, VI 279; 294
Fouquet, Basile, Abbé, and Mazarin, IV 608, 621
—— Nicolas, Vicomte de Vaux, and Mazarin, IV 608, 621; fall of, v 6
Fouquier-Tinville, Antoine-Quentin, Public Prosecutor, VIII 356 sq., 375
"Four Days' Battle," Anglo-Dutch fight (1666), v 183 sqq.
Four Elements, English play on the New World, I 51
Fourcroy, Comte Antoine-François de, man of science, VIII 433; Minister of Education, IX 127
Foureau, Fernand, African explorer, XII 812 sq.
Fourier, François-Marie-Charles, IX 133; XII 296; 758
—— Baron J.-B.-Joseph, VIII 606
Fourilles, French cavalry inspector, v 18
Fourmies, strike at, XII 125
Fournier, Claude, revolutionary, VIII 228, 232, 243
—— Captain, convention with China concluded by, XII 526
—— Sarlovese, François, IX 21
Fournière, Eugène-Joseph, French socialist, XII 123
Fourqueux, de, Comptroller-General under Louis XVI, VIII 104
"Fourteen of Meaux," execution of, II 290
Fourtou, Marie-F.-O. Bardy de, French politician, XII 106; 111; 114
Fowler, Edward, Bishop of Gloucester, v 752
—— Sir Henry. *See* Wolverhampton, Viscount
Fox, Charles James, VI 380; and the Wilkes case, 441; 445 sq.; 451; leads Reform movement, 455; 456; Secretary of State, 457; and Ireland, 458; 459; negotiates for peace, 460 sq.; resigns, 462; 463 sqq.; India Bill of, 466 sq., 581; dismissed, 467; 468 sq.; and Pitt's second India Bill, 470; 471 sqq.; 475; and Burke, 476; 477 sq.; and Ireland, 500, 504; 501; and Warren Hastings, 581, 584; VIII 284, 303, 759; IX 24; 245; succeeds Pitt, 264; 265–6; policy with France, 269; 270; and abolition of the slave trade, 613; and Whig party, 673 sqq.;

becomes Foreign Secretary, 685; death of (1806), 271; 686; and India, 711; and Warren Hastings, 716; x 360; and Irish Catholics, 631; xi 756 sq.; 766

Fox, George, Quaker, v 328; vi 799

—— Gustavus Vasa, American naval officer, vii 549

—— Henry. *See* Holland, Lord

Foxe, Edward, at Rome, ii 430

—— John, i 641; ii 533; *Book of Martyrs*, 538

—— Richard, Bishop of Winchester, i 469, 471, 620, 645

Foy, Maximilien-Sébastien, French general, pursues Mina, ix 476; pursued by Wellington, 478; x 60; 64; 67; 68; opposes compensation for the *émigrés*, 86; death of, 88; 103

Foyle, Loch, Spanish aid to the Irish Catholics sent to, iii 531, 608

Fracastan, G., Italian scholar, ii 16

Fraenckel, Léon, French politician, xi 503

Fragonard, Jean-Honoré, ix 135

Framlingham, rally of Mary Tudor's supporters at, ii 514

Francavila, Marquis of. *See* Ferandina, Duke of

Francavilla, Spanish victory at, vi 125

France

i iv Italy and her invaders, *passim*, 104–43

xii France, 384–415
[*See also* xv, Economic Change, *passim, but especially* 503 sqq., 525 sqq.; xvi, *especially* 575 sqq.; xvii, xviii *and* xix *passim*]

ii ii Habsburg and Valois (i), 36–65

iii Habsburg and Valois (ii), 66–103

ix The Reformation in France, 280–304

iii i The Wars of Religion in France, 1–52

ii French Humanism and Montaigne, 53–72

xx Henry IV of France, 657–95

iv ii The Valtelline (1603–39), *passim*, 35–63

iv Richelieu, 118–57

vii (2) Nördlingen and Prague (1634–5), *passim*, 243–55

xiii The later years of the Thirty Years' War (1635–48), *passim*, 364–94

xiv The Peace of Westphalia, *passim*, 395–433

xxi Mazarin, 592–622

xxiii Papal Policy (1590–1648), *passim*, 666–88

xxv The transference of colonial power to the United Provinces and England, *passim*, 746–59

xxvii Descartes and Cartesianism, *passim*, 776–99

France (*contd.*)

v i The government of Louis XIV (1661–1715), 1–31

ii The foreign policy of Louis XIV (1661–97), 32–63

iii French 17th century literature and its European influence, 64–71

iv The Gallican Church, 72–91

vii Administration of John de Witt and William of Orange (1651–88), *passim*, 137–67

xii Austria, Poland and Turkey, *passim*, 338–71

xiii The Treaties of Partition and the Spanish Succession, *passim*, 372–400

xiv The War of the Spanish Succession and the Peace of Utrecht, *passim*, 401–59

xxii The Colonies and India, *passim*, 673–705

vi iv The Bourbon governments in France and Spain, I (1714–26), 120–44

v The Bourbon governments in France and Spain, II (1727–46), 145–67

vi Financial experiments and colonial development, *passim*, 168–90

viii The War of the Austrian Succession, *passim*, 201–50

ix The Seven Years' War, *passim*, 251–300

xi The reversal of alliances and the Family Compact, 329–60

xv India, *passim*, 506–85

xvii Switzerland from the treaty of Aarau to the French Revolution, *passim*, 611–25

xxiv The Romantic movement in European literature, *passim*, 822–37

vii iii The French in America (1608–1744), 70–113

iv The conquest of Canada (1744–61), *passim*, 114–43

ix The struggle for commercial independence (1783–1812), *passim*, 305–34

viii i Philosophy and the Revolution, 1–35

ii The government of France, 36–65

iii Finance, 66–78

iv Louis XVI, 79–118

v The elections to the States General, 119–44

vi The National Assembly, and the spread of anarchy, 145–75

vii The constitution of 1791, 176–210

viii The Legislative Assembly, 211–44

ix The National Convention to the fall of the Gironde, 245–75

France (*contd.*)
VIII x The foreign policy of Pitt to the outbreak of war with France, *passim*, 276–305
xi The European Powers and the Eastern Question, *passim*, 306–37
xii The Terror, 338–71
xiii The Thermidorian reaction and the End of the Convention, 372–97
xiv The General war, 398–446
xv The Naval war, 447–86
xvi The Directory, 487–520
xviii Bonaparte and the Conquest of Italy, 553–93
xix The Egyptian expedition, 594–619
xx The struggle for the Mediterranean, *passim*, 620–32
xxi The Second Coalition, *passim*, 633–64
xxii Brumaire, 665–88
xxiii Revolutionary Finance, 689–709
xxiv French law in the age of the Revolution, 710–53
xxv Europe and the French Revolution, 754–90
IX i The Consulate (1799–1804), 1–33
iii The pacification of Europe (1799–1802), *passim*, 55–80
iv France and her tributaries (1801–3), 81–106
v France under the Empire (1804–14), 107–47
vi The Codes, 148–79
vii The Concordats, 180–207
viii The Command of the Sea (1803–15), 208–43
ix The Third Coalition, I (1805–6), *passim*, 244–64
x The Third Coalition, II (1806–7), *passim*, 265–93
xi The Napoleonic Empire at its height (1807–9), 294–340
xii The War of 1809, *passim*, 341–60
xiii The Continental System (1809–14), 361–89
xiv The French Dependencies, and Switzerland (1800–14), 390–427
xv The Peninsular War (1808–14), *passim*, 428–82
xvi Russia and the invasion of 1812, *passim*, 483–505
xvii The War of Liberation (1813–4), *passim*, 506–54
xviii The first Restoration (1814–5), 555–75
xix The Congress of Vienna, I (1814–5), *passim*, 576–615
xx The Hundred Days (1815), 616–45
xxi The Congress of Vienna, II (1815), *passim*, 646–71
xxiv St Helena, *passim*, 756–71

France (*contd.*)
x i The Congresses (1815–22), *passim*, 1–39
ii The Doctrinaires, 40–70
iii Reaction and Revolution in France, 71–103
v The Papacy and the Catholic Church, *passim*, 131–61
xv The Orleans Monarchy, 475–516
xvii Mehemet Ali, *passim*, 545–72
xxiii Economic Change, *passim*, 727–62
XI ii The fall of Constitutionalism in France (1840–8), 22–42
iv Italy in revolution (1846–9), *passim*, 65–95
v The French Republic (1848–52), 96–141
viii The achievement of Swiss Federal Unity, *passim*, 234–61
x Napoleon III and the period of personal government (1852–9), 286–308
xi Great Britain and the Crimean War (1852–6), *passim*, 309–24
xiv Cavour and the Kingdom of Italy (1849–61), *passim*, 366–92
xvii The Liberal Empire (1859–70), 467–506
xviii The reaction against Romanticism in French literature (1840–71), 507–28
xxi The Franco-German War (1870–1), 576–612
XII v The Third French Republic, 91–133
vi The German Empire, *passim*, 134–72
xv Egypt and the Egyptian Sudan, *passim*, 429–56
xvii The Far East, *passim*, 500–36
xx The European Colonies, *passim*, 602–71
[*See also* xxi 680 sqq.]
xxiii Social movements, *passim*, 730–65

France, Anatole, French novelist, XII 13
Francesco da Puglia, Frà, opponent of Savonarola, I 181
Franche Comté, ceded to Austria (1493), I 229, 392, 395; captured by Maximilian I, 454; invasion of, by Henry IV, III 666–7; French army in, IV 147 sq.; Condé and, 370 sq.; Bernard of Weimar in, 373 sq., 379 sq.; 593; places in, restored to Spain by Treaty of the Pyrenees, 620; Estates of, v 4; 36; 38; relinquished by France, 39, 153; 41; 43; ceded to France, 45, 165; 46; 164; 200; 220; 373; 423; 449; Prussia and, 669; VI 141
Franchet, French Chief of Police, x 93
Francia, José G. Rodriguez da, dictator of Paraguay, XII 674

Francis I, Emperor (Duke of Lorraine, *afterwards* Grand Duke of Tuscany), VI 140; 152; and Tuscany, 155 sq.; elected Emperor, 160; 203; 229; and War of Austrian Succession, 231; 242 sq.; and Treaty of Aix-la-Chapelle, 249; 257; and the Papacy, 590 sq.; 600; death of, 626

—— II, Emperor (*afterwards* Francis I, Emperor of Austria), VIII 531, 536, 579, 582, 634, 642; policy of, 644, 650 sq., 663; declines Napoleon's proposals, IX 56; 63 sqq., 92 sq., 100; policy of, 247; 248; Napoleon's threat to, 251; 256; armistice proposed by, 257; negotiations of, with Napoleon, 258; interview of, with Napoleon, 261; 262; becomes Francis I, Emperor of Austria, 269; 310, 315, 317; advised to go to Erfurt, 320; 342; prepares for war against France, 344; letter of, to King of Prussia, 352; truce of, with France, 353; Napoleon demands abdication of, 359; relations of, with Napoleon, 487; 537, 550, 555; at Congress of Vienna, 580; 596, 622; leaves Vienna, 651; feeling of, towards Napoleon, 654; and Holy Alliance, 665; signs Holy Alliance, X 9; at Aix-la-Chapelle, 14; in Italy, 20; 21; at Conference of Troppau, 27; 106; negotiations of, with King of Naples (1815), 110; at Rome, 137, 145; relations of Papacy with, 144 sq.; 146; and the execution of Gregorios, 183; at Czernovitz, 187; at Aix-la-Chapelle, 353; domestic policy of, 355 sqq.; and Magyar Diet, 371; and Galicia, 461; at Münchengrätz, 557; death of, 378; XI 44

—— I, King of France, I 43; Turkey and, 92 sqq.; 128, 140; victory of, at Marignano, 140 sqq.; 322; Leo X and, 388 sq.; 395, 458, 484, 490; II 14, 23, 26, 32, 37 sq., 49, 67, 96 sqq.; struggle between Charles V and, Chaps. II, III *passim*, 36–103; defeat and imprisonment of, 423; treaty of, with Charles V, 426; church policy of, the Concordat and, 281, the Reformation in France and, 281–92, persecution under, 347; meets Henry VIII (1520), 416 sq., (1532), 439; change of attitude to Clement VII, 216 sq.; meets Clement VII at Marseilles (1533), 68, 220, 285, 440; invades Savoy, 232; 239; death of, 82, 260; effect of, on French policy, 486; character of, 38; Calvin's letter to, 356; III 53, 64, 104 sq.; and Barbarossa, 110; and war with Charles V, 113; urged by Charles V to mediate with Sultan (1538), 115; joint Embassy of, with Charles V to Venice, 115 sq.; 399, 581, 684, 695, 758; V 625

—— II, King of France, II 93; reign of, 296–9; 499, 548, 557, 581; Council of Trent and, 674 sq.; III 261 sqq., 478, 483 sq.

Francis I, King of The Two Sicilies, appointed Regent (1821), VII 368; IX 383; assumes government (Jan. 16, 1812), 384; X 112; and revolt at Cilento, 119

—— II, King of The Two Sicilies, marriage and accession of, XI 380 sq.; 387; flight of, from Naples, 388; 389 sq.; 469

—— Infante of Spain, arrest of, IX 433; X 231

—— Charles, Archduke of Austria, XI 44; 152; and the Austrian Constitution, 174; and the succession, 190

—— Joseph, Emperor of Austria and King of Hungary, XI 88; 190; Hungarian Diet and, 202; and Hungarian campaign, 210, 213; pardons Görgei, 214; abolishes Constitution, 217; and King of Prussia, 224; and Danish succession question, 226; and Hesse-Cassel crisis, 229, 231; visits Italy, 374, 377; at Villafranca, 384; 393; 398; visits Hungary, 401; Russia and, 402; resolves on war in Italy, 403; and constitutional changes, 403 sq.; and Hungary, 404 sq.; and Prussia, 407; and German unity, 408; and Frankfort assembly of Princes, 435; and Italy, 449; and Napoleon III, 450 sq., 453; 455; visits Paris, 484; XII 14; Gladstone and, 37; 116; at Berlin, 139; character and reign of, 175; 176; and constitutional reform, 177 sq.; and Schmerling, 181; and Hungary, 182 sq.; crowned King of Hungary, 184; and the Čechs, 186; 188 sq.; Andrássy and, 190; 192; Taaffe and, 194; 196; 199; 202; and reform, 206; 209 sq.; and Bosnia-Herzegovina, 212; and Humbert I, 240; and Galicia, 337; 382; and Russo-Turkish War, 389; 401; and Prince Ferdinand of Bulgaria, 427; 433

—— Alban, Benedictine, V 237 sq.

—— St, of Assisi, II 2

—— de Sales (Saint), V 78

—— Xavier (Saint), II 652; and Japan, IV 712

—— Sir Philip, and Warren Hastings, VI 581, 584; in India, 571 sq.; 574 sqq.; writer, VIII 758, 760; IX 716

Franciscans, in England, contributions of the Order to learning, I 585–92; great preachers of, 647, 675; produce leaders of Protestant Reform, II 161; reformed in Spain, 400; in Italy, 647. *See also* Capuchins, Grey Friars, Observants, *and* Religious Orders

Francisco de Asis, King Consort of Isabel II of Spain, XI 37 sq.; marriage of, 554 sq.; 556; and Narváez, 557; 561; 569

Franck, Sebastian, sectary, II 223

Francke, August Hermann, and the Halle Pietists, V 760; VI 226; XI 710

Franckenberg, *or* Frankenberg, Johann H. de, Cardinal, Archbishop of Malines, VI 652; 656; VIII 318, 787

Franco, João, Portuguese statesman, XII 271 sq.
—— Niccolo, III 468
Franco-German War, Vol. XI, Chap. XXI
François, Marie Luise von, German novelist, XI 412
Franconia, the Hohenzollerns and, I 297 sq.; conquered by Gustavus Adolphus, IV 207; Horn in, 208; Wallenstein and, 216, 218; Bernard of Weimar in, 219; 392; ravaged in Thirty Years' War, 418; in War of Austrian Succession, VI 238; 273; and Congress of Vienna, IX 588
Frangipani, Francis, and Hungarian conspiracy, V 351 sq.
Franke, Karl Philipp, and Malmoe Truce, XI 168
Frankenhausen, defeat of Peasants' Rising at, II 188 sq.
Frankenthal, siege of (1621), IV 78; 82; in Spanish hands, 83, 603
Frankfort (on-the-Main), Diet of (1454), I 666, (1485), 302, (1489), 302, (1501), 311; Peace of (1489), 394 sq., 449; meeting of Schmalkaldic League at, II 217; negotiations with Lutherans at, 238; Diet of Schmalkaldic League at (1545), 253; submits to Charles V, 258; Turkish interpreter at, III 123; *Deputationstag* at (1590), 712; "Corresponding" Princes at, 717; meeting of Electors at, IV 27 sq.; Christian of Halberstadt at, 79; 81; "Composition" meeting at, 114, 117, 207; and Gustavus, 208; 217; Heilbronn Alliance at, 243; Bernard of Weimar at, 244; Convention, 245 sqq.; Peace of Prague accepted by, 255; occupied by Imperialists, 367; meeting of *Deputationstag* at (1643), 385; commercial recovery of, 420; Imperial election at, V 431; Diet of (1741), VI 233; Union of, 240; captured by Houchard (1792), VIII 414; surrendered, *ib.*; Diet of (1806), IX 268; and the Continental System, 373 sq., 377; grand duchy of, 413–5; Allies at, 542; Dalberg resigns grand duchy of, 587; Catholics and Jews of, at Congress of Vienna, 588; Jews of, 650; free city of, 658; Four Allied Powers at (1819), 666; Treaty of (1819), X 19, 22, 145; Commission (1819) of, 148; and Diet of Germanic Confederation (*Bundestag*), 341, 343 sqq., 362, 366 sq., (1824), 370; revolutionary plot at, 377 sq.; and European finance, 743; National Assembly at, XI 162, 164, 181, 188 sq., 191, 194 sqq., 227; *Vorparlament* at, 144, 163; Diet at (1848), 147, 162, 228; 150; Archduke John at, 166; riots in (1848), 168 sq.; Confederation meeting at, 223; 224; 233; and German navy, 227 n.; Bismarck at, 402 sq., 434; assembly of Princes at, 435; 446; 455; Constitution, 198, 200 sq., 218; Peace of (1871), 612, XII 95; 135; 159

Frankfort-on-the-Oder, retreat of Schaumburg's army to, IV 196; Tilly at, 199; capture of, 201; Cartesian philosophy in, 791; University of, V 624, IX 327, X 355; Russian and Austrian allies at, VI 292, 324; fair of, X 759
Frankfort (Kentucky), inauguration of Confederate governor at (1862), VII 507
Franklin (Tennessee), battle of (1864), VII 524
—— (Canada), district of, XI 776
—— Benjamin, and colonial federation, VI 412 sq.; 449; and peace negotiations, 460 sqq.; VII 69; 123, 145; and the Stamp Act, 149 sqq., 156 sq., 199, 204 sq.; 173; negotiates with France, 210; at Constitutional Convention, 246, 253, 257, 261 sq., 292; 730; character of, 732 sq.; XII 744; 757
—— Sir John, XII 809 sq.; 814 sq.
—— William Buel, American general, VII 469
Franquesa, Pedro, Spanish Minister, III 545
Franz Josef Land, discovered, XII 795
Franzburg, capitulation of, IV 106
Franzenskanal, XI 182
Franzoni, L. *See* Turin, Archbishop of
—— Dr, reports on Basilicata, XII 237
Frascati, Consalvi at, X 131
Fraser, Alexander George, General, captures Fort Haake, IX 358
—— Simon, of Beaufort. *See* Lovat, Lord
—— Simon, lieutenant-colonel, VII 214
Fraternities, lay, in Germany, II 108
Fraticelli, of Monte Amiata, I 151; suppressed by Pius II, 623
Frauenberg (Bavaria), siege of castle of (1525), II 188; relief of, 190
—— (Bohemia), surrender of, VI 234
Fraunhofer, Joseph, and spectrum analysis, XII 782 sq.
Fraustadt, Swedish victory at (1706), V 594
Frayssinous, Denis-Luc, Comte, Bishop *in partibus* and Grand Master of the University of France, X 78; Minister of ecclesiastical affairs, 87; 93 sq.
Frazer River, discovery of, VII 365
—— General, at Dig, IX 728
Frederica, settlement of, VII 62
Frederick II, Emperor, Venice and, I 260; V 620; 665
—— III, Emperor, I 76, 104; dynastic policy of, 294 sq.; ecclesiastical settlement of, 294 sq.; acquires Tyrol, 296; Berthold of Mainz and, 302; Matthias Corvinus and, 335, 344; 390, 442; invasion of Netherlands by, 448 sq.; 687, 689; V 623; 634
—— I (of Schleswig-Holstein), King of Denmark and Norway, attitude of, towards Lutheranism, II 169; 224, 228 sqq., 245; and the Reformation in Denmark, 608–14, and in Norway, 618 sq.; V 635

Frederick II, King of Denmark, III 151; 157; and Erik XIV of Sweden, IV 162 sq.; 166; 560; Denmark under, 561 sq.; Sweden and, 563; death of, 564

—— III, King of Denmark, Bishop of Verden, IV 89; 91; coadjutor of Osnabrück, 96; and Peace of Prague, 255; Archbishop of Bremen, 365; loses Verden, 404; commercial treaty between England and, 439; beginnings of reign of, 573 sq.; 584 sq.; 587 sq.; 590; v 558; and the *coup d'état* of 1660, 559 sq.; policy of, 560; 561; and Sweden, 146 sq., 562; 579; VI 735

—— IV, King of Denmark, accession of, v 580; and anti-Swedish leagues, 580, 587, 602; and the Great Northern War, 580 sqq.; and Treaty of Frederiksborg, 583; 607; 611 sq.; and Frederick I of Prussia, 666; VI 23; and Sweden, 28, 37; death of, 735 sq.; 737; 739; 741

—— V, King of Denmark, VI 739 sqq.; death of, 742; and Sweden, 762

—— VI, King of Denmark (Prince Royal), VI 188; 735; birth of, 743; 751; 753 sqq.; and Norway, VIII 279 sq., 788; Napoleon's letter to, IX 296; 297; English alliance refused by, 299; 300; at the Congress of Vienna, 582; and Schleswig-Holstein, x 363; 370; reign of, XI 691 sq.

—— VII, King of Denmark, XI 161; and Schleswig-Holstein, 225; accession and reign of, 694 sqq.; death of, 438, 477, 696

—— VIII, King of Denmark, XII 289; accession of, 293

—— III, of Naples. *See* Federigo

—— I, King of Prussia (Frederick III, Elector of Brandenburg), v 55; supports William of Orange, 244; 438; claims Upper Gelders as Duke of Cleves, 448; 449 sq.; 581; and anti-Swedish leagues, 593 sq.; 602; and Schwiebus Circle, 655, 658 sq.; illness of, 656; and the Great Elector's will, *ib.*; Elector of Brandenburg, 658; aspirations of, 660; and expedition of William of Orange, *ib.*; aids Emperor against France and Turks, 661; and Peace of Ryswyk, *ib.*; negotiates as to a royal crown, 663 sqq.; coronation of, 665; and Grand Alliance, 666; and Northern War, 666 sq.; alliance of, with Sweden, 667; and Poland, *ib.*; foreign policy of, 668 sq.; and Orange inheritance, *ib.*; and the Empire, 669; economic and intellectual progress under, 669 sq.; religious views of, 671; results of his reign, 672; and Academy of Sciences, 741; and Christian Wolf, 760; death of, 668; VI 6; 8

—— II (the Great), King of Prussia, v 643; 671; reign of, Vol. VI, Chap. xx; and War of the Austrian Succession, Chap. VIII (3) *passim*; and Seven

Years' War, Chap. IX *passim*; 119; invades Silesia, 158; 160; 165; 207; 210; and Frederick William I, 211 sq.; 216; policy of, 227; and War of the Austrian Succession, 310; 314; and Bestuzheff, 316; and Russia, 317 sqq., 322 sqq.; 342a sq. (in Vol. XIII); 344; and the "Reversal of Alliances," 366 sqq.; and Treaty of Hubertusburg, 346; 352; and Poland, 353, 355, 357, 665 sqq.; 358; 398 sqq.; and Treaty of Versailles, 401 sq.; and Pitt, 393, 404, 409 sq., 416, 418, 421, 437; 405 sq.; and English alliance, 407 sqq., 422; deserted by England, 427; and Benedict XIV, 589; and Swiss, 633; and Kaunitz, 629; and Russia, 630; and Bavaria, 631 sq.; meeting of, with Joseph II, 633; 646; and the *Fürstenbund*, 647; 655; and Catharine II, 658 sq., 664, 677 sq.; Peter III and, 661; 673; and Turkey, 675; 696; 699; 763; and Bernstorff, 740, 744; 767; death of, 647, VIII 282, 286, 314; and Joseph II, 309; and Poland, 523; and the neutral flag, IX 42; Napoleon at tomb of, 281; 329; x 342; *De la littérature allemande* of, 389; foundry of, 732; XII 136; 828 sq.

Frederick III, King of Prussia and German Emperor, (as Crown Prince) XI 159, 406; and Schleswig-Holstein, 440; in Austro-Prussian War, 452 sq.; supports Bismarck, 455 sq.; and the German Empire, 465 sq.; in Franco-German War, 580, 583 sq.; imperial accession and death of, XII 163 sq.; 433

—— I, King of Sweden (Landgrave of Hesse-Cassel), v 408; 555; VI 37; and Congress of Brunswick, 39; 742; 761; death of, 762

—— I, King of Würtemberg, at Congress of Vienna, IX 582; marriage of, 265; 268; x 360 sq.

—— "Hereditary Prince" of Denmark, son of Frederick V and Queen Juliana Maria, VI 749 sqq.; 755; VIII 279

—— Prince of the Netherlands, x 535 sqq.; XII 244

—— Augustus I, King of Saxony, and the *Fürstenbund*, VI 708; IX 278-9; 325; receives duchy of Warsaw, 293; 337-8; and Congress of Vienna, 582; 593 sqq.; joins in Treaty of peace (May, 1815), 647

—— Augustus II, King of Saxony, XI 59; 149; 200; and Frankfort Constitution, 218 sq.; 222

—— Augustus, Elector of Saxony. *See* Augustus, King of Poland

—— Augustus, Prince, co-Regent of Saxony, x 374; 643

—— Charles, Prince (of Prussia), in Austro-Prussian War, XI 452; in Franco-German War, 580, 585, 589 sqq., 593 sq., 599, 604, 606 sq., 609 sq.

Frederick Christian, Elector of Saxony. *See* Saxony

—— Louis, Prince of Wales, vi 66; 68 sq.; 72; 76; 210; death of, 740

—— William I, King of Prussia, v 448; and Frederick IV, of Denmark, 582 sq.; and Peter the Great, 542, 612; 611; 647; and Danckelmann, 662; 668; 671; reign of, Vol. vi, Chap. viii (2); 8; and Elector George Lewis, 17; 21; 23 sq.; and Sweden, 35 sq.; 37; and Congress of Brunswick, 39; and Hanover Alliance, 59; 143; 196 sq.; and Pragmatic Sanction, 202; 230; economic policy of, 714 sq., 717 sqq., 722

—— II, King of Prussia, reign of, Vol. vi, Chap. xx; 293; 648; 656; viii 107; accession of, 286, 288, 314; and Convention of Reichenbach, 293; 294; and the Netherlands, 322 sq.; 330, 333; character of, 400, 408; and Luxemburg, 431; and Poland, 529, 543 sq., 550 sq.

—— III, King of Prussia, viii 520, 634 sq.; ix 41; 46, 56, 73, 92; anti-French policy of, 249; offer of Hanover to, 251; French affront to, 255; 263, 264; relations of, with France, 266; with Russia, *ib.*; invited to assume title of Emperor, 272; sends ultimatum to Napoleon, 273; retreats on Weimar, 277; peace proposed to, 278; retreat of, 280; relations of, with Russia, 282; at Memel, 285; 291; peace offered to, 287; deserted by Alexander, 292; 293; and Alexander I, 308; Napoleon's demands upon, 317; 322; and Stein, 329; influence of, 331; military reform of, 332; 333; return of, to Berlin, 334; ordered to expel Stein, 335; 344; attitude of, to the war of 1809, 352; 364; accepts Trianon Tariff, 373; relations of, with Napoleon, 487; 508 sqq.; and Allies' Council of War, 527; at Leipzig, 535; 539, 542; relations of, with Austria, 550; enters Paris, 555; 556; at Vienna, 580 sq.; and the Federal Act, 650; leaves Vienna, 651; and Holy Alliance, 665; position of, after 1815, x 8; signs Holy Alliance, 9; at Aix-la-Chapelle, 14; 20; 27; 342; 348; influence of Russia and Austria upon, 349; 350; Metternich and, 352; and Francis I of Austria, 355; and Wartburg festival, 364; 365; conference of, with Metternich at Teplitz, 366; 372; and Protestant Churches, 382; and Posen, 463; and France (1830), 465, 481; death of, 382

—— —— IV, King of Prussia, (as Crown Prince) at Conference of Troppau, x 27; 381; at Münchengrätz, 557; accession of, xi 47; ideas and aims of, 48; first measures of, 49; religious policy of, 50 sqq.; constitutional schemes of, 55 sqq.; 142; and Queen Victoria, 143; and the German national movement, 63 sq., 144; proposes conference at Dresden, 144, 153; and Anhalt affairs, 150; 154; and the revolutionary movement in Berlin, 156 sqq.; and German unity, 160; 162; and "Dahlmann's Constitution," 163; 165; and Schleswig-Holstein War, 167; and Auerswald Ministry, 191; and Prussian "National Assembly, 192; and Brandenburg-Manteuffel Ministry, 193; attitude of, towards Austria, 195 sq.; chosen German Emperor, 197 sq.; declines Imperial Crown, 199; and Frankfort Constitution, 200; and Austria, 208, 224; and German Confederation, 218 sqq.; and Danish succession, 226; and Hesse-Cassel crisis, 228 sqq.; and Switzerland, 249; and Neuchâtel, 253, 255 sq.; policy of, 393, 395; and *Kreuzzeitung* party, 396 sq.; succeeded by his brother, 406; and the Papacy, 708

Frederick William, Elector of Brandenburg (the Great Elector). *See* Brandenburg, Electors of

—— William, Duke of Brunswick-Oels. *See* Brunswick-Oels, Duke of

—— Augustus, Duke of York and Albany, viii 429, 431, 662; ix 440; meets Queen Caroline, 675; and Catholic Emancipation, 679; and the opponents of Addington, 681; onslaught on, 687; relations of, with George III, 688

—— William Canal, the, v 645

Fredericksburg, Burnside defeated at (1862), vii 483 sq.

Frédéricq, Paul, Belgian historian, xii 842

Frederiksborg, royal festivities at, iv 586; Treaty of (1720), v 583, vi 37

—— (Slave Coast), Danish station, v 691

Frederikshald, attacked by Charles X, iv 589; by Charles XII, v 583; death of Charles XII at, vi 34

Frederikshamn, fortress of, vi 314; Treaty of (1809), ix 323, 487; school of Cadets at, x 434

Frederiksodde, iv 584; stormed by Wrangel, 585

Frederikssten, death of Charles XII at, v 614

Freducci, Ludovico, Lord of Fermo, ii 14

Free Bailiwicks, in Switzerland, ii 331

—— Churches, theory of, ii 200. *See also* Lutheranism, etc., *and for England*, Nonconformists, etc.

Freeman, Edward Augustus, historian, xi 363; xii 390; 397; works of, 839 sq.; 845

Freeman's Journal, Irish newspaper, xi 8

Freemasons, growth of, after 1814, x 215 sqq.; establishment of the *comuneros* in opposition to, 221; in France, under Third Republic, xii 115

Freeport (Illinois), Lincoln and Douglas at, vii 444

Frégeville, Charles-L.-J., Marquis de, VIII 677; 684

Fregoso, Cesare, French envoy, murdered, II 76; III 105, 118

—— Federigo, Cardinal, II 33; 379; tracts by Luther attributed to, 380; church reform and, 643

—— Gian-Galeazzo, Genoese in Tuscan service, III 16

Frei, Felix, Provost of Chapter at Zurich, II 310

—— Jacob, and the Reformation at Zurich, II 331

Freiberg (in Saxony), besieged by Banér, IV 387; VI 297; battle at, 299

Freiburg im Breisgau, Diet transferred to (1498), I 307; University of, 325; taken by peasants (1525), II 182; French troops in, IV 383; battles near (1644), 388, 597; V 45 sq.; ceded by France, 63; retaken (1713), 435; restored (1714), 436, 454; VI 241; 637

Freiburg (Swiss Canton), Catholicism in, III 405; and Neuchâtel, V 449; the patriciate of, VI 624; 625; Swiss Diet meets at (1803), IX 423; restores its old Constitution (1814), 600; bishopric of, X 149; XI 234; Government of, 235; reaction in, 238; the Jesuits in, 239; 240; and the Aargau monasteries, 247; 251; 257; industries of, 259

Freiligrath, Ferdinand, German poet, XI 50; 143; 413 sq.

Freinsheim, Johann, Swedish theologian, IV 787

Freire, Agostinho José, in the Azores, X 327

Fréjus, Prince Eugene at, V 419; landing of Napoleon at (1799), VIII 663, 674, IX 41

Fremantle, Australian port, XI 791

Frémont, John Charles, "the Path-finder," VII 395, 432; major-general of U.S. Army, 459 sqq.; 475; 477, 491, 493; and slavery, 583 sqq., 599

French Canal Company (Panamá), XII 698 sqq.

"French Fury, The," at Antwerp (1583), III 256–7

French Revolution. *See* France, Vol. VIII

Frenchtown, Winchester defeated at (1813), VII 339

Frend, William, Unitarian, VIII 764, 766

Frere, Sir Henry Bartle Edward, XII 35 sq.; 465; in South Africa, 636; 638

—— John Hookham, and *The Quarterly Review*, IX 687; X 700

Frère-Orban, Walter, Belgian Minister, XI 672; XII 251

Fréron, Louis Stanislas, VIII 247, 349, 352, 368 sq.; *L'Orateur du Peuple*, 374; 378

Freslon, Alexandre, French statesman, XI 115

Fresnel, Augustin-Jean, and the theory of light, XII 782

Fresnes, de, French diplomatist, III 684

Fresze, Hermann, Lutheran preacher in Norway, II 618

Frew, Prince Charles at, VI 112

Freycinet, Charles-Louis de Saulces de, French statesman, XI 602; 606; 608; XII 40; 101; premier, 117; 119; 437

Freyre de Andrade, Gomes, Portuguese general, in Brazil, V 678

—— Manoel, Spanish general, at San Marcial, IX 480; at Toulouse, 482

Freytag, Gustav, German writer, XI 414 sqq.; *Pictures from the Past*, XII 849

—— Comte F.-X.-J., French general, VIII 431

Friant, Comte Louis, French general, at Austerlitz, IX 260–1; captures Semenovskoie at the battle of Borodino, 495

Friar Bungay and Friar Bacon, Greene's, III 375

Frias, Inigo Fernandez de Velasco, 2nd Duke of, 3rd Count of Haro, hereditary Constable of Castile (1520), I 374 sq.

—— Juan F. de Velasco, 5th Duke of, ambassador to England (1604), III 536; 667

Fribourg. *See* Freiburg

Frič, Josef, *Memoirs* of, XI 656

Frid, Valentine (Paceus), I 614

Fridag, Baron, Imperial ambassador to Brandenburg, V 663

Fridericia, captured by the Prussians, XI 167; 224, 695

Friedberg, "Corresponding" Estates at, III 718

Friedjung, Heinrich, historian, XII 829

Friedländer, Ludwig, historian, XII 849

Friedland (Bohemia), Count Schlick seized at castle of, IV 71; acquired by Wallenstein, 73; Wallenstein Duke of, 134

—— (Mecklenburg-Strelitz), Swedish troops in, VI 280

—— Duke of. *See* Wallenstein

Friedland-on-the-Alle, battle of (1807), IX 290, 297

Friedlingen, Lewis of Baden at, V 406

Friedrich, Johann, *History of the Vatican Council*, XII 848

Friedrichsfelde, King Frederick Augustus I of Saxony at, IX 582

Friedrichsruhe, Bismarck's retirement at, XII 167

Friedrichstadt, capture of, XI 225

Friedwald, Treaty of (1552), II 271

"Friends of Light," Prussian Church party, XI 51 sq.

"Friends of the People," English Society (1792), VI 477; VIII 760

Fries, Jacob Friedrich, German philosopher, X 365

Friesland, Dukes of Burgundy and, I 421; subjection of, 453; annexed to the Netherlands (1523), II 102; Henry Casimir and, IV 695, 701; and the Eternal Edict, V 155 sq.; 165; socialism in, XII 248

Friesland, John William, Hereditary Stadholder of. *See* Orange, John William Friso, Prince of
—— William Frederick, Hereditary Stadholder of. *See* Nassau-Dietz
—— West, known as the North Quarter, III 621–2; discontent in, 634
—— East. *See* East Friesland
Friis, Jörgen. *See* Viborg, Bishops of
Fririon, General, IX 30
Frisch, Austrian diplomatist, VI 346
Frisia, East. *See* East Friesland
Friuli, Venice acquires (1420), I 278
Froben, John, printer at Basel, II 308, 355
Frobisher, Sir Martin, III 301; 309; 313; 319
Frochot, Comte Nicolas-Thérèse-Benoît, Prefect of the Seine, IX 126; 144
Fröbel, Julius, at Vienna, XI 188 sq.
Fröding, Gustav, Swedish writer, XII 280
Frohschammer, Jakob, philosopher, XI 712
Frohsdorf, Comte de Paris at, XII 108; 109
Froissart, Jean, I 433; XII 830
Fromentin, Eugène, painter and writer, XI 525; 528
Fronde, The, causes of, IV 603–4; Declaration of Saint-Germain and, 607; 608 sqq.; Mazarin and the old, 612 sqq.; 617 sq.; results of, 621 sq.; V 1; 21; 76; 83; VI 130
Fronsac, Armand de Maillé-Brézé, Duke of, IV 592
Fronteira, Marquis de, Portuguese general, V 426
Frontenac, Louis de Buade, Comte de, VII 81, 85; work of, in Canada, 89; death of, 90; 97
Froschauer, printer of Zurich, II 308, 312 sq., 316, 333
Frosinone, success of the French at, II 54
Frossard, Charles-Auguste, French general, XI 583; 585; at Spicheren, 586 sq.; 590 sqq.; at Gravelotte, 593 sq.
Frost, John, Chartist leader, X 683 sq.
Frotté, Comte Louis de, IX 2; 14
Froude, James Anthony, XI 363 sq.; in South Africa, XI 636; 839 sq.
—— Richard Hurrell, XI 349
Froulay, *Bailli* de, French diplomatist, VI 343
Fruin, Robert, Dutch historian, XII 249; 842
Frundsberg, Georg von, German *condottiere*, II 50, 54, 55, 190, 197
Fry, Elizabeth, visit of, to Newgate, IX 693; visits Denmark, XI 694
Fuad Pasha, Mehemed, Turkish Foreign Minister, XI 313; 636 sq.; XII 381
Fuchs, Leonhard, botanist, V 734
—— Paul von, Brandenburg statesman, V 655; 663; VI 8
Führich, Joseph, German painter, X 151
Fülek, acquired by Solyman II, III 124

Fünen (Fyen), IV 561; 571; Charles X and, 584; conquered by the Swedes, 585; 589; Swedes expelled from, V 147; serfdom in, VI 736; Spanish troops in, IX 236
Fuenterrabia, captured by the French (1521), II 44, 418; recovered by Spain (1524), 44, 46, 423; French defeat at (1638), IV 147, 149; 542, 645; marriage of Louis XIV at, 620; Franco-Spanish marriages at, 630; captured by the French (1719), VI 34, (1794), VIII 440
Fuentes (de Castilla), Pedro Henriquez de Toledo y de Acevedo, Count of, Spanish general in Lombardy (1599), III 418 sqq.; in Netherlands (1593), 519, 522; Governor of Milan (1600–10), 398, IV 41 sqq.; Venice and, 670
—— d'Oñoro, Wellington's army on the heights of, IX 466, 468
Fürst, Baron Karl Joseph Maximilian von, Prussian High Chancellor of Justice, VI 715; 728
Fürstenberg, Heinrich von, Count, Minister of Maximilian I, I 323
—— Wilhelm von, Cardinal, and the archbishopric of Cologne, V 54 sqq.
—— Wilhelm von, Count, VI 78
Fürstenbund, of 1785, signed by fifteen German governments, VI 647; 708; formation of, VIII 281 sqq., 313, 324, 529
Fürth (on the Cham), Wallenstein at, IV 237
—— (Franconia), Gustavus Adolphus and Wallenstein at, IV 216 sqq.; Austrian allies at, VI 263
Füssen, Treaty of, VI 242
Fugger, Anton, II 258
—— Count Francis, IV 393
—— Jacob, II 153
—— the brothers, of Augsburg, financiers, I 358, 506, 518, 667; II 40, 63, 127, 153, 265
Fukubari, Chōshiu councillor, XI 851; execution of, 852; 855
Fulchi, marshes of, V 604
Fulda, Jesuit seminary at, III 178; Catholic reaction at, 180; bishopric of, granted to the Prince of Orange (1802), IX 78, 90; French occupation of, 408, 414; part of, acquired by Prussia (1815), 657; Prussian troops in, XI 229 sq.
Fulgencio, Fray, Spanish monk, XI 557
Fuller, Nicholas, III 563 sq.
—— William, IV 320
—— Chief Justice (U.S.), and the Venezuelan Arbitration Commission, XII 721
Fulta, fugitives at, VI 552
Fulton, Robert, American engineer, VII 351
Fulvio, Andrea, the *Antiquitates Urbis Romae*, I 549
Funck, Johann, confessor of Duke Albert of Prussia, III 153
Furnes, the Barrier Treaties and, V 457, 459; ceded to France, VI 339
Furrah, Sir Henry Pottinger at, XII 800

Furrer, Jonas, Swiss President, xi 254

Fusan, Russia and, xii 507; 556; 581

Fuseli, Jean-Henri, art critic, viii 765

Fushimi, Chōshiu warriors at, xi 851

Fusinato, Arnaldo, Italian writer, xi 545

Fustel de Coulanges, Numa Denis, French historian, xi 525

Fyen. *See* Fünen

Fyllebro, Swedish success at (1676), v 569

Fyzabad, British troops at, vi 579

Gabbard, The, Anglo-Dutch naval action off, iv 436, 475, 478, 480 sq.

Gabel, Christopher, Danish statesman, v 561

Gabelle, French royal impost, from time of Philip of Valois, i 405 sq.; iv 153; conditions for non-payment of, 621; viii 70, 91, 692 sq., 696

Gabet, Joseph, in Tibet, xii 797 sq.

Gaboldino, Antonio, Modenese Reformer, ii 386 sq.

Gabriel, Don, Infant of Spain, vi 381 sq.

Gachard, Louis Prosper, Belgian historian, xii 842

Gacko, Montenegro and, xii 392

Gadd, Hemming. *See* Linkoeping, Bishops of

Gadebusch, Swedish victory at (1712), v 582, 608

Gadsden, James, American Minister to Mexico, vii 426

Gähler, Peter Elias, Danish general, vi 745

Gaertner, Privy-Councillor von, at the Congress of Vienna, ix 588

Gärtnerbrüder, Protestant sect of Strassburg, ii 223

Gaeta, captured by Charles VIII (1495), i 114; recaptured (1496), 118; recovered under Louis XII (1502), 125; finally lost by France (1503), 127; vi 153; surrenders to Ney, viii 652; siege of (1806), ix 267, 404; surrenders, 270; Pius IX and Leopold II at, xi 91 sqq., 121; conference at, 121, 379; fall of, 390

Gagarin, Prince, Governor of Siberia, v 535

—— Paul, Prince, xi 614

Gage, Thomas, Governor of Massachusetts, vii 159 sq., 163, 165 sq., 168

Gagern, Friedrich Balduin, Baron von, x 376

—— Hans Christoph Ernst, Baron von, viii 774; and Congress of Vienna, ix 580 sqq.; 610, 646 sq., 652

—— Heinrich von, xi 60; 62; Hesse-Darmstadt Minister, 144 sq.; 160; 162; President of *Nationalversammlung*, 164; 169; 195; succeeds Schmerling, 196; 198; 221

—— Maximilian von, xi 144; 160; 162; 165

Gages, Jean Bonaventure Dumont, Count, Spanish general, vi 160; 165; 362; 596; 608

Gainsborough, Manchester at, iv 315; flight of Nonconformists from, vii 12

Gaismayr, Michael, leader in Peasants' War, ii 190 sq.

Galabat, stormed by King John, xii 444

Galaghan, Colonel, Russian officer, v 601

Galata, surrendered to Turks (1453), i 68

Galatea, Antonio, i 624

Galateo, Girolamo, Venetian Reformer, ii 381; the *Confession*, 382

Galatz, massacres at, x 178

Galdós, Benito Pérez, Spanish writer, xii 268

Galen, B. von. *See* Münster, Bishop of

—— Claudius (ancient physician), v 723 sqq.; 737

Galeotti, Leopoldo, Italian writer, xi 65

Galgengrund, Russians at the, vi 284 sq.

Galiani, Fernando, Abbé, Italian political economist, viii 25

Galiano, Alcalá, x 210; and the Spanish revolution, 214 sqq.; and *La Fontana de Oro*, 218; negotiates with King Ferdinand, 222; 228; 231

Galicia (Austria), Joseph II visits, vi 626; 648; 669; 703; Frederick the Great and, 707; proposed cession of, to Poland (1790), viii 293, 330 sq.; 312; ceded to Austria (1775), 523; boundaries of, enlarged (1795), 549; Russian troops in, 646 sq.; extent of, ix 283; Austrian army concentrated in, 354; Russian designs on, 591; Austria retains eastern, 655; the Germanic Confederation and, x 343; under Austrian rule, 461 sq.; revolt in, xi 46 sq.; 152; the revolutionary movement in, 156; national aspirations in, 171 sq.; rising in, 174; 175; 178; and Hungary, 202; 204; 216; bishopric in, 266; 398; 402; massacre in, 658; xii 186; Minister for, 189; 195; Count Badeni's administration in, 200; 201; autonomy of, 337; 338 sq.

—— (Spain), Spanish army of, ix 435, 438; delivered from the French (1809), 453; Del Parque's army falls back on, 455; revolt in (1820), x 216; Morillo capitulates in (1823), 228; Portuguese retreat into (1828), 322; rising in, xi 554

Galigai, Leonora. *See* Concini

Galilei, Galileo, ii 707; iii 394; iv 677; scientific discoveries of, 777; condemnation of, 779; 781; 793; v 118; 708; 712; the astronomical work of, 713 sq.; 715; 718; 723; at Padua, 726; vi 792; monument erected to, at Pisa, x 129; xii 768

Galitzin (or Galitsin) family, persecution of, vi 302

—— Prince Alexander, Russian general under Catharine II, vi 682; 697

—— Prince Alexander Nicolaievich (d. 1844), Russian Minister of Education (1816), x 424; dismissed, 425; 431; 437; and the succession to the throne, 440

Galitzin, Prince Alexis, Russian ambassador to England, VI 323; 328
—— Dmitri Michailovich (d. 1738), Prince, V 553 sq.; 556
—— Prince Dmitri Alexeivich, Russian ambassador (d. 1803), VI 697
—— Dmitri Vladimirovich, Prince (d. 1844), Governor-General of Moscow, XI 270 sq.
—— Michael, Prince, Russian general, V 554
—— Prince Sergius, commands a Russian army against Austria, IX 354
—— Vasili Vasilevich, Prince, V 518; 521
—— Prince, Russian secret agent at Madrid (1817), man of letters, X 212 sq.
Gallars, Nicholas de, at the Colloquy of Poissy, II 302, 592
Gallas, Count Johann Wenzel von, Imperial envoy in London, V 432 sq.
—— Count Matthias, Austrian general, Mantua taken by, IV 115; with Wallenstein, 219, 223; succeeds Holk, 231; 234; at Leitmeritz, 237; 239 sqq.; at Nördlingen, 244 sq.; 248; 250; 367 sq.; 371 sqq.; driven into Silesia and Bohemia, 378; in Saxony, 387; resigns command, 388; 389; death of, 392; 571
Gallatin, Albert, American statesman, VII 690
Galle, Johann Gottfried, German astronomer, XII 768
—— Peter, Swedish divine, II 624 sq.
Galletti, Giuseppe, Italian politician, XI 81
Gallicanism, and Pragmatic Sanction of Bourges (1438), I 385 sqq.; and Concordat of 1516, 388 sq.; 662 sq.; old and new, II 95; and Concordat of Francis I, III 659; V 74 sqq., 85 sq.; *see* Vol. VI, Chap. XVI *passim*, 586 sqq.; Hontheim and, X 157 sq.; reaction against, 159 sqq.; and Jules Ferry, XII 116. *See also* Concordats, Pragmatic Sanction
Gallieni, Joseph-Simon, in Senegal, XII 129
Gallipoli, Turkish arsenal destroyed at, I 80; scarcity of food at, XII 238
Gallo, Marzio Mastrilli, Marchese di, Austrian envoy, VIII 582; Minister at Naples, 650
—— Niccolò, Italian Reformer, II 393
Galloway, Joseph, American loyalist, VII 162; legal arguments of, Chap. VI *passim*
Galmoy, Pierce Butler, 3rd Viscount, V 309
Galt, Sir Alexander Tilloch, Canadian Finance Minister, XI 763; 770; 775
Galton, Sir Francis, and heredity, XII 778
Galuzzi, Riguccio, Tuscan historian, VI 150
Galvez, Don Bernardo, Governor of Louisiana, VI 377; 453
Galway, plantations and, IV 520; capitulates to Coote, 535; V 316 sqq.; Articles of, 321, 323; Queen's College, XII 71
—— Henri de Massue de Ruvigny, Earl of (Marquis de Ruvigny), V 23 sq.; 321; 323; in Spain, 416, 419, 426

Gama, Vasco da, I 12; discovery of Cape route by, 24–6; 29, 30, 34, 285; IX 304
Gambetta, Léon, French statesman, XI 485; defends Delescluze, 488; 489; 491; opposes declaration of war, 495; and Franco-German War, 497 sqq., 600, 602 sqq.; XII 14; 40; 101; 103; and National Assembly, 105; Thiers and, 106; 109; 111; and clericalism, 113; 114 sq.; 121; 239; and Egyptian affairs, 436; death of, 112
Gambia, Great Britain and, XII 658
—— river, discovery of, I 15; settlements on, V 691 sq.; VI 464; trade of, XII 660; exploration on, 805 sq.
Gambier, James, 1st Baron, English admiral, character of, IX 217; attacks Denmark, 236; attacks Brest, 238
Gamble, H. R., Governor of Missouri, VII 458
Gambron (Bender Abbas), Dutch trading post at, IV 712
Gaminde, General, commander in Catalonia, XII 260
Gamonal, combat of (1808), IX 443
Gandamak, Treaty of, XII 470 sq.
Gandia, Giovanni Borgia, Duke of, I 179, 233 sq., 620
Gando, Sultan of, XII 659
Gangadhar Shastri, XI 725
Ganges river, the Dutch on, VI 556; drowning of children in, XI 730
—— canal, completion of, XI 744
Ganneron, Auguste-Hippolyte, French financier, X 495
Gansfort. *See* Wessel, John
Ganteaume, Count Honoré-J.-A., vice-admiral, VIII 615 sq.; IX 53; in command of Toulon squadron, 212–3; advice of, to Napoleon, 214; in command of Brest squadron, 216; ordered to West Indies, 222; blockaded in Brest, 223; ordered to leave Brest, 228; sent to Corfu, 237; replaced by Allemand, 239
Gapón, George, Russian priest, XII 331; 349 sq.
Garat, Dominique, French politician, VIII 746
—— Dominique Joseph (brother of above), French Minister of Justice, VIII 250; Minister of Interior, 263, 273 sq., 348, 679; IX 132
Garay, Don Martin de, Spanish statesman, X 142; appointed Secretary of Treasury, 209; 212; 219
Garcia, Carrasco Francisco, Governor of Santiago, X 287
—— Juan, Spanish Reformer, II 408
—— Fray de, Regius Professor of Divinity, Oxford, II 541
Garci-Arias, Prior of San Isidro, Spanish Reformer, II 406
Garda, Lake, Marshal Catinat at, V 402; Chasteler advances to, IX 355
Gardanne, Antoine, French general, VIII 686; IX 14

Gardes françaises, VIII 162 sqq., 166, 403
—— *nationales*, organised by Lafayette, VIII 166 sqq.; 183 sqq., 191; in 1791, 207; Lafayette resigns command of, 220; 223; reorganised, 232 sq., 236, 243; numbers of in France, 403; condition of (1799), 665; under First Empire, IX 115
—— *suisses*, VIII 162, 235 sq.; massacre of, 237, 437
Gardiner, Christopher, adventurer, VII 16
—— James, colonel of dragoons, VI 112; 114
—— Luke, and Protection in Ireland, VI 502 sq.
—— Samuel Rawson, historian, XII 840
—— Stephen, Bishop of Winchester, and pronunciation of Greek, I 581; II 430, 475; resists visitation of 1547, 481; attacks Cranmer's *Homilies*, *ib.*; 485; imprisonment of, 486; Northumberland and, 497; 501, 517; made Chancellor by Mary, 520; policy and work of, 521–35; death of, 542; III 750
—— William, the Portuguese Index and the works of, II 414
Gardner, Alan, 1st Baron, admiral, VIII 477; in command of blockade of Brest, IX 224
—— naval captain, in Ceylon, IX 733
Garfield, James Abram, President of the United States, VII 649, 652 sq.
Gargantua, Rabelais', II 287
Garibaldi, Giuseppe, in Rome, XI 94; 125; expedition of, to Sicily and Naples, 332; in London, 351; and the unity of Italy, 375; 382; in Sicily, 388; 389; and Cavour, 390, 392; meets King Victor Emmanuel, 390; 391; 462; 469; invades States of the Church, 485; Ricasoli and, 531; 532; relations of, with Rattazzi, 533; wounded at Aspromonte, 534; 535; and King Victor Emmanuel, 537 sq.; 539; and War with Austria, 540 sq.; marches against Rome, 542; at Mentana, 543; 545; in France (1870), 604, 606, 608 sq.; 705; XII 216; 681
—— Menotti, XII 240
Garielevna, Countess Anna, VI 315
Garigliano river, French defeat on (1503), I 127, 196; fight at (1860), XI 390
Gárin, Russian senator, XII 376
Garland, Augustine, IV 443
Garlike, British Minister at Copenhagen, IX 296; despatch of, to Canning, 297
Garnett, Father Henry, Provincial of Jesuits in England, and Gunpowder Plot, III 555
—— Robert Selden, Confederate general, VII 457
Garnier, François, French explorer, XII 131; 524 sq.; 796
Garnier-Pagès, Étienne-J.-L., x 485; 491; 509

Garnier-Pagès, Louis-Antoine, XI 26; and the Revolution (1848), 100 sqq.; 108; 118; 477
Garrard, Thomas, executed, II 451
Garrick, David, and Whitefield, VI 84
Garrison, William Lloyd, publisher of *The Liberator*, VII 387, 423
Garth, Sir Samuel, poet, V 70
Garz, taken by Swedes, IV 196
Garzoni, Giovanni, Italian jurisconsult, I 151
Gascoigne, George, III 367 sq., 371
Gascony, Landes of, rising in, V 9
Gaselee, Sir Alfred, general, relieves Peking legations, XII 520
Gaskell, Elizabeth Cleghorn, novelist, XI 359 sq.
Gasparin, Comte Adrien-Étienne-Pierre de, French Minister of Interior, x 497
—— Thomas-Augustin de, member of *Comité de Salut Public*, VIII 343
Gasparino da Barzizza, Italian Latinist, I 544, 556, 562
Gasquet, Abbot Francis Aidan, XII 848
Gassendi, Pierre, II 691; IV 779; philosophy of, 792 sqq.; 798 sq.
Gassion, Comte Jean de, Marshal of France, at Rocroi, IV 594; killed at Lens, 598
Gastein, Convention of, XI 445 sq., 448, 450, 479; Bismarck meets Andrássy at, XII 144
Gaston, Vendean leader, VIII 266
Gatacre, Sir William Forbes, General, at Stormberg, XII 642
Gatchina, Tsar at, IX 34, 35, 483
Gates, Horatio, American general, VII 211, 215, 225
—— Sir John, executed, II 520
—— Sir Thomas, Governor of Virginia, VII 5 sq.
Gattamelata, Stefano Giovanni, *condottiere*, I 280
Gatterer, Johann Christoph, German historian, XII 817
Gattilusio, Nicolò, Lord of Lesbos (d. 1462), I 76
Gattinara, Mercurino Arborio de, Minister of Charles V, I 371; II 52, 148, 210, 401
Gaudin, Martin-Michel-Charles, Duc de Gaëte, Minister of Finance, VIII 682, 706, 708; IX 1–2; 10, 25–6; obtains duchy of Gaëta, 111; Napoleon writes to (Oct. 13, 1807), 368; introduces French fiscal system into Piedmont, 397; liquidation of public debt by, 398; Minister of Finance, 616
Gaultier, Abbé, in London, V 430
Gaunt, John of, III 358
Gautier, Théophile, x 101; XI 509 sqq.
Gautsch, Baron Paul, Austrian statesman, XII 202 sq.; 206; 208
Gavre, defeat of Ghent by Philip the Good at (1453), I 426 sq.

Gavril Pasha. *See* Krstyovich, Gavril

Gáwilgarh, capture of (1803), IX 726

Gawler, George, Governor of South Australia, XI 792

Gay, John, poet, V 70; X 715

Gayer, Sir John, Governor of Bombay, V 700

Gay-Lussac, Joseph-Louis, scientist, XII 769

Gaza, occupied by Ibrahim Pasha, X 549
—— Theodorus, Greek professor at Forrara, I 542, 546

Gazette de France, La, in Richelieu's time, IV 155; after Oct. 1811, IX 130; at war with the Cabinet, X 94; XI 292

Gebora, battle of the (1811), IX 462

Gedimin, Lithuanian chief, V 480

Gee, Joshua, political economist, VI 50

Geer, Baron Louis de, Swedish statesman, XI 689 sq.; XII 277
—— Louis de, munition of, IV 569; 571; Swedish trade and, 725 sq.

Geertruidenburg, siege of (1593), III 627

Gefle, *Riksdag* at, VI 784

Geibel, Emanuel, German poet, XI 413 sq.; 420; 701

Geijer, Eric Gustav, Swedish historian, XI 686 sq.; XII 842

Geiler. *See* Kaisersberg

Geishiu, *daimiō* of, XI 846, 856 sq., 861

Geislingen, Pass of, V 409

Geissberger, Franz, Abbot of St Gall, II 331

Geistliche Fama, journal of Pietists, V 761

Geitzkofler, Zacharias, Imperial Controller-General, IV 5

Gelderland. *See* Gelders

Gelders, acquired by Charles the Bold (1473), I 390; factions in, 423; English expedition against (1511), 479; duchy of, falls to Duke of Cleves (1538), II 75, 236; reduced and annexed by Charles V (1543), 77, 102, 242, 244; anti-Spanish plans for, III 16; position of, 618; invaded by Maurice, 673; invaded by French (1672), V 43, 157; 148; and the Eternal Edict, 155; Prussian garrison in, 435; Peace of Utrecht and, 447 sqq.; 458 sq.; 658; VI 27; 300; Austria and, 631; Brunswick invades, VIII 287; rebellion in, 322
—— Adolf, Duke of, I 424, 441
—— Arnold, Duke of, I 424
—— Charles of Egmont, Duke of, I 131, 307, 424, 441, 450 sq., 453, 456 sq., 475; invades the Netherlands, II 43; 51, 60, 72; death of (1538), 75, 102, 236
—— Rainald IV, Duke of (d. 1423), I 424
—— William IX, Duke of (1402), I 423 sq.
—— William de la Marck, Duke of. *See* Jülich-Cleves-Berg, William V

Gelenius, Sigismund, editor of Philo, I 613, 616 sq.

Gellert, Christian Fürchtegott, V 68

Gellivare, ore fields of, XII 279

Gelnhausen, meeting of Electors and other Princes at, I 311, 313; Arnim and Oxenstierna at, IV 235

Gelt, battle of the (1569), III 282

Gemaurhof, Swedish victory at (1705), V 594

Gemblours, battle of (1578), III 249–50

Gembloux, French troops at, IX 630

Genazzano, Frà Mariano da. *See* Mariano

Gendebien, Alexandre-J.-C. de, X 480; 532; 535 sqq.
—— Jean-François, X 523

Genebrard, Albert. *See* Aix, Archbishop of

General Assembly, the Scottish, meeting of 1690, V 293 sq.

Genest, Edmond Charles, Minister from Republic of France to United States, VII 317, 320

Génestet, Petrus Augustus de, Dutch poet, XI 676

Geneva, attack on, by Duke Charles III of Savoy (1530), II 70, 330; political constitution of, under Bishop, 358 sq.; relations between Bishop of, and Savoy, 361 sq.; the Reformation in, 362 sq.; connexion of Calvin with, 358, 363, 368; government of, under Calvin, 366 sqq.; 370–5; Calvin's College and Academy at, 372 sq.; heresy in, III 400 sqq.; Savoy's attempts on, 408, 413, 420 sq., 437, 482, 683; included in Treaty of Vervins, 674; Evangelical Church in, 743; and Savoy, IV 673; Chouet Professor at, 791; Milton at, V 118; the bank of, 266 sqq.; 270; Labadie at, 756; VI 617; party conflicts in, 625; annexation of, by France, proposed (1792), VIII 437; accomplished (1798), 597, 640; revolt in (1782), 781; IX 59; excluded from Swiss Federation (1803), 104; Huguenot seminary at, 204; Swiss manufacture of clocks and watches in, 425; remains intellectual centre of French Switzerland, 427; cessions to canton of, 660; XI 234; 236; 243; radical rising in, 248; and cession of Savoy, 256; proposed episcopal see of, 258; 259; republican congress at, 485 sqq., 568; 630; *Alabama* arbitration at, XII 217, 717, 720 sq.; Russian revolutionaries at, 303
—— Joannes Franciscus of Savoy (the Bastard of Savoy), Bishop of, II 361
—— Pierre de la Baume, Bishop of, II 361

Genga, Annibale della. *See* Leo XII

Genghis Khan, conquests of, in Central Asia, I 8, VI 508

Genlis, Jean de Hangest, Seigneur de, III 17 sq., 232

Gennadios, George Scholarios, Patriarch of Constantinople, I 103

Genoa, the Ottomans and, I 68; factions in, 129; captured by the French (1507), 130; rivalry of, with Venice, 257; at war with

Venice, 258-9; Peace of (1392), 265; arms made at, 496; stormed by Imperialists (1522), II 45; new Republic established in (1528), 59; Fiesco Conspiracy at, 81 sq.; claimed by Francis I, III 110; trade of, 392; Savoy and, 400, 407, 411, 413; Spain and, 476; Revolt of, 497; Dutch trade with, 631; Habsburg influence over, 689; and the Emperor, IV 31; French victory off (1638), 147; Spain and, 687; Spanish protectorate over, V 50; John Law in, VI 169; 243; taken by Austrians, 245; and Corsica, 350, 609; siege of, 362; and the Jesuits, 593; 606; affairs in, 607 sq.; Napoleon's secret mission to, VIII 561; French control of, 587 sq., 663; government of Republic of, 778; fighting near (1800), IX 58 sqq.; Republic of, 83; French annexation of (1805), 141, 247, 249; incorporation of, in Sardinia (1814), 599; retained by Sardinia, 660, 668, 670; Piedmontese fugitives at, X 117; *fête* at, XI 75; 78; 243; Garibaldi's expedition from, 332; revolt at, 366, 375; 373; democratic congress at, 532; labour troubles at, XII 223; 225; 227

Genoa, Gulf of, Admiral Mathews in, VI 239

—— Ferdinand, Duke of, XI 91

—— Thomas, Duke of, XI 571

Genoude, Antoine-Eugène de, editor of *Gazette de France*, X 486

Genovesi, Antonio, Neapolitan lawyer, VI 588; 590; 599; VIII 777

Gensan, Russia and, XII 507

Gensonné, Armand, Girondist leader, VIII 214, 249, 251; at the King's trial, 258; trial of, 357

Gentil, Émil, African explorer, XII 130; 812 sq.

Gentile, Valentino, Italian Reformer, II 393

Gentili, Alberico, *De jure belli*, XII 707 sqq.

Gentz, Friedrich von, VIII 773 sq.; at Congress of Vienna, IX 580 sqq.; and the French frontier, 664; influence of, 671; on results of Congress of Vienna, X 2; and de Maistre's *Du Pape*, 7; 13; 150; 357; 365

Geoffroy Saint-Hilaire, Étienne, IX 133

Geography, the science of, Vol. I, Chap. I, The Age of Discovery, *passim*, 7-36; Chap. II, The New World, *passim*, 37-66. *See also* Exploration

George, Lake, French and English at, VII 125, 127; Montcalm at, 129 sq.

—— I, King of Great Britain (Elector of Hanover and Duke of Brunswick-Lüneburg), V 359; 403; commander of Imperial army, 418; 420; 425; 438; 450; and Whig leaders, 474; accession of, as George I, 476; and Sweden, 550; and the "Hanoverian Alliance," 550; and Russia, 543, 551, 555; and Great Northern War, 580; and Frederick IV of

Sweden, 582 sq.; and Peter the Great, 609, 613; forms third anti-Swedish league, 610 sq.; and the Hanoverian Succession, Vol. VI, Chap. I; character of, 41 sq.; Walpole and, 42; 43; 57; and the Earl of Mar, 97; and Spain, 123; and Gibraltar, 126, 147; and Dubois, 131; 141; 143; and Poland, 193; and Prussia, 209; 213; 445

George II, King of Great Britain (George Augustus, Electoral Prince of Hanover), V 469; created Duke of Cambridge, 474; 555; VI 2 sqq.; 10; 12 sqq.; 19; 39 sq.; character of, 41 sq.; Walpole and, 42, 395; the Civil List of, 45; 55; 61; and Pitt, 73 sq.; 106; at Dettingen, 109; 143; 147; and Don Carlos, 151; 179; and Prussia, 209; and War of the Austrian Succession, 232; 235; 237; and election of Francis I, 242; 243; and France, 249; 251 sq.; 260; and Convention of Klosterzeven, 266; 272; and Hanover, 334, 405; 340; and Prussian Alliance, 399; and Pitt's accession to office, 403; and Irish affairs, 488 sq.; death of, 416

—— III, King of Great Britain, V 462; VI 117; and Pitt, 346, 419 sq.; accession of, 416; views of, 417; character of, 423; 425; and Bute, 427; 428; sends for Pitt, 430; and Wilkes, 430 sq., 441 sq.; and Regency Act, 434; 435 sq.; 443; 445; and American Colonies, 449, 462 sq.; and Rockingham Ministry, 457 sqq.; 463; and India Bill, 467, 581; dismisses Fox and North, 467; supports Pitt, 469; and Prince of Wales, 472; illness and recovery of, 473 sqq.; and the army and navy, 476; and Ireland, 497, 500; insanity of, 505; and Frederick the Great, 702; and the *Fürstenbund*, 708 sq.; 743; and Queen Matilda, 750 sq.; 819; VII 307, 330; as Elector of Brunswick-Lüneburg, joins *Fürstenbund*, VIII 283; 285, 291, 296 sqq., 305; IX 43; 56, 102; Napoleon's overtures to, 221; 244, 245, 262; health of, 264; 266, 297, 309, 321, 367, 673; and Catholic Emancipation, 678 sq.; insanity of, 689; X 382; English Catholics and, 625; death of, 582

—— IV, King of Great Britain (Prince of Wales), Prince Regent, VI 117; and India Bill (1783), 467; 471; marriage of, 472; and Regency Bill, 473 sq.; 475; Irish Parliament and, 505; relations of, with Count Münster, IX 587; supports royal proclamation, 673; marriage of, 675; 687; and Regency, 690; Napoleon's letters to, 756; 760; and the Holy Alliance, X 10; 32; and Hanover, 374; attack upon (1817), 577; the divorce bill of, 583; visits Ireland, 637; and Catholic emancipation, 645, 650, 652; death of, 593; and Sweden, XI 683

George I, King of Greece, xi 634; election of, 641; 642; xii 420 sqq.
—— Prince of Denmark, v 230; 247; 460; death of, 428, vi 12
—— Prince of Georgia, son of Heraclius, annexation of territories of, ix 48
—— Prince, of Greece, xii 420; High Commissioner in Crete, 423
—— Prince Regent. *See* George IV
—— Petrovich (Kara George). *See* Kara
—— of Trebizond. *See* Trapezuntius
George, David Lloyd, Chancellor of the Exchequer, xii 62
—— Henry, and socialism, xii 759
Georgia (Europe), Russia and, v 545, vi 648, 672, 676; Russia and Turkey in, viii 316; Sultan acknowledges suzerainty of Russia over, ix 385; annexed by Russia, x 413; General Alikhánoff in, xii 363
—— (America), vi 51; foundation of, 54 sq.; 66; the Wesleys in, 82; 83; 149; settlement of, vii 61 sqq.; 105; 149; representation of, in Congress, 160, 164, 166; invaded (1778), 218 sq.; Constitution of, 237; and Constitutional Convention, 246, 252, 258, 263, 268, 277, 281, 283; representation of, 306; cessions in, 308; and the Tariff, 377, 380; slavery in, 386 sq., 587; secedes from Union (1860), 446; joins Confederacy, 452, 603; in Civil War, 471, 513, 522 sq.; and Sherman's march, 533 sq.; emancipation in, 595; opposition to Confederate policy in, 608 sq.; blockade-running in, 620; reconstruction in, 633; becomes Democratic (1871), 642
Georgia, "commerce-destroyer," vii 565 sq.
Georgian bay, proposed canal to, xii 608
Georgians, The (Caucasus), xii 342
Gerald, Joseph, political reformer, viii 770
Geraldino, Don. *See* Fitzgerald, Sir Thomas
Gérando, Joseph-Marie, Baron de, ix 24; 132; member of Extraordinary Junta for Tuscany, 399
Gerard, Balthasar, *alias* François Guyon, iii 258 sq.
Gérard, Comte Étienne-Maurice, Marshal of France, and Belgian campaign, ix 625; 627; x 478; 494; 542
Gerbert. *See* Sylvester II, Pope
Gerbet, Olympe-Philippe, Bishop of Perpignan. *See* Perpignan
Gerhardt, Paul, hymns of, iv 425; v 648; 758
Géricault, J.-L.-T.-A., French painter, ix 135; x 103
Geringer, Baron Karl Gabriel von, Governor of Hungary, xi 216
Gerlach, Leopold von, Prussian general, xi 51; 191; 396 sq.
—— Ludwig von, Prussian politician, xi 51; 160; 192 sq.; 220; and *Kreuzzeitung* party, 396; 397; xii 826
Germ, The, Pre-Raphaelite organ, xi 357

Germain, George Sackville. *See* Sackville, Viscount
Germaine de Foix, 2nd consort of Ferdinand V (II), King of Spain, i 127; dowry of, 363; 366, 377
German Order (of Knights), i 293, 343, 345; conversion of territory of, into duchy of Prussia, ii 169; 599, 635; collapse of, and restoration to Poland of lands of, iii 73; transfer of rights of, in Livonia, by Kettler, v 493 sq.; 621, 624 sq.; work of, in Prussia, 630 sqq.; decline of, 632 sqq.; 665; Grand Master of, and Imperial Recess of 1803, ix 94
Germania, of Valencia (brotherhood of trade-guilds), rebellion of, i 376 sq.
Germanic Confederation, The, ix 659 sq.; 667; (1852–62), Vol. xi, Chap. xv (1); 459
Germanos, Archbishop of Patras. *See* Patras
Germantown, Washington attacks, vii 213, 217
Germany
i   ix   Germany and the Empire, 288–328
     xv   Economic Change, *passim,* 493–531
     xvi The Classical Renaissance, *especially* 571–4
          [*See also* xvii, xviii *and* xix, *passim*]
ii   ii   and iii, Habsburg and Valois, *passim,* 36–103
     iv   Luther, *passim,* 104–41
     v   National Opposition to Rome in Germany, 142–73
     vi   Social Revolution and Catholic Reaction in Germany, 174–205
     vii Conflict of Creeds and Parties in Germany, 206–45
     viii Religious War in Germany, 246–79
     xix Tendencies of European Thought in the Age of the Reformation, *passim,* 690–718
iii v   The Empire under Ferdinand I and Maximilian II, *passim,* 140–81
     xxi The Empire under Rudolf II, *passim,* 696–735
iv   i   The Outbreak of the Thirty Years' War, *passim,* 1–34
     iii The Protestant Collapse (1620–30), *passim,* 64–117
     vi   Gustavus Adolphus, *passim,* 190–222
     vii Wallenstein and Bernard of Weimar (1632–5), *passim,* 223–55
     xiii The later years of the Thirty Years' War (1635–48), 364–94
     xiv The Peace of Westphalia, 395–433
     xx   The Scandinavian North (1559–1660), *passim,* 560–91

Germany (*contd.*)
v xiv (i) The War of the Spanish
       Succession, (ii) The Peace of
       Utrecht and the Supplementary
       Pacifications, *passim*, 401–59
    xx The Origin of the Kingdom of
       Prussia, 616–38
   xxi The Great Elector and the first
       Prussian King, 639–72
  xxiv Latitudinarianism and Pietism,
       passim, 742–63
vi viii The War of the Austrian Suc-
       cession, *passim*, 201–50
    ix The Seven Years' War, *passim*,
       251–300
  xviii Joseph II, *passim*, 626–56
  xxiv The Romantic movement in
       European literature, 822–37
viii xxv [The *Aufklärung* in Germany],
       772 sqq.
ix ix The Third Coalition, I (1805–6),
       passim, 244–64
    x The Third Coalition, II (1806–7),
       passim, 265–93
   xix The Congress of Vienna, I (1814–
       5), *passim*, 576–602
   xxi The Congress of Vienna, II (1815),
       passim, 647–71
       [*See also* Chaps. iv, xi, xiv, *and*
       Prussia]
x   xi The Germanic Federation (1815–
       40), 340–82
   xii Literature in Germany, 383–412
  xxiii Economic Change, *passim*, 727–62
xi iii Liberalism and Nationality in
       Germany and Austria (1840–8),
       43–64
    vi The Revolution and the Reaction
       in Germany and Austria, I
       (1848–9), 142–201
   vii The Revolution and the Reaction in
       Germany and Austria, II 202–33
   xv Austria, Prussia, and the Ger-
       manic Confederation
       (1) Reaction and Reorganisa-
           tion (1852–62), 393–410
       (2) German Literature (1840–
           70), 411–20
  xvi Bismarck and German Unity,
       432–66
  xxi The Franco-German War (1870–1),
       576–612
xii vi The German Empire (1871–1910),
       134–73
   xx The European Colonies, *passim*,
       602–71
  xxiii Social movements, *passim*, 730–65
       [*See also* the Empire *and* the
       various German States, *especi-
       ally* Prussia]
Germersheim, Mansfeld at, iv 80; 84;
   Charles of Lorraine at, vi 240
Geroldseck, Diebold von, controversy between Zwingli and, ii 321; death of,
   at Kappel, 337

Gerona, taken by French (1694), v 61,
   (1711), 428; fortress of, Duhesme attacks
   (1808), ix 439; besieged by Saint-Cyr
   (1809), 448, 454–5; fall of, *ib.*, 457
Gerry, Elbridge, Massachusetts deputy at
   Constitutional Convention (1787), vii
   246, 274 sq., 280, 285, 289, 293 sq., 321
Gerson, Jean, ii 281
Gerst, Republican rising in, xi 137
Gerstenberg, Heinrich Wilhelm von, x 386
Gertruydenberg, peace negotiations at, v
   427, 430, 452; captured by French
   (1793), viii 419, (1795), 436
Gervinus, Georg Gottfried, expelled from
   Hanover, x 379 sq.; xi 62; 164; xii
   826
Gesenius, F. H. Wilhelm, German Hebraist,
   x 382; xii 846
Gesner, Conrad, bibliographer and natural-
   ist, i 611, 615; 618; and botanical
   studies, v 734, 736, 738
—— Jean, Swiss scholar and botanist, vi
   625
Gessi, Egyptian officer, xii 439; 441
Gessner, Solomon, Swiss poet and man of
   letters, viii 781
Gettysburg, battle of (1863), vii 488 sqq.,
   616
Geulincx of Antwerp, at Louvain, iv 789
Gewitsch, Field-marshal Daun at, vi 277
   sq.
Gex, Savoy recovers, iii 405, 419; ex-
   changed for Saluzzo, 677
Geyer, Florian, leader of Franconian
   peasants, ii 182, 188; death of, 190
Gezzar, kills Sultan's messengers at Acre,
   ix 385; death of, 387
Ghadames, explorers in, xii 808
Ghazipur, opium factory at, xii 485
Ghazni, xi 731; captured, 732; 733; 735
Ghent, struggle between Philip the Good
   and, i 427; gilds at, 428; rivalry between
   Bruges, Ypres and, 428–9; Peace of
   (1492), 450; Charles V and, 458; rebellion
   of 1539 in, ii 74 sq., 98, 236; suppressed,
   238; Charles V at (1540), iii 114; Pacification of, 181, 246–7, 250–1; Chapter of
   Golden Fleece assembled at (1559), 187;
   Egmont and Hoorn imprisoned at, 215,
   218; States of Flanders at, 244; Congress at, 245 sq.; Spaniards expelled
   from, 248, 250 sqq.; taken by Parma,
   618; 630; restored to Spain (1679), v 45;
   captured by French (1678), 164, 219,
   420; captured by Marlborough (1706),
   416; 421 sq.; 457 sq.; vi 243; seized by
   Belgians, 652; Peace of (1814), vii
   347, 349, ix 622; and the fisheries dispute, vii 362 sqq.; Austrian defeat at
   (1789), viii 329; Louis XVIII at, x 44;
   industries at, 524, 533; 526; plots at,
   539; 746; and the Liberal cause, xi 674;
   socialism at, xii 252; 755
—— Maurice de Broglie, Bishop of, x
   525 sq.

Gheria, pirate stronghold, vi 531
Ghiberti, Lorenzo di Cino, Florentine sculptor, i 548
Ghilzais, The, Afghan tribe, xi 733
Ghislieri, Michele. *See* Pius V, Pope
—— Marquis, Austrian ambassador, x 132
Ghulám Kádir, official at Delhi, ix 719
Ghyka, Prince Alexander, Hospodar of Wallachia, xi 282
—— Prince Gregory, Hospodar of Moldavia, xi 284; 643
Giacinto, Corsican leader, vi 609
Giacometti, Paolo, Italian playwright, xi 548
Giacomini, Antonio, Florentine captain, i 191, 197
Gialong, King of Annam, xii 523
Giammaria, Count of Verrucchio, ii 18
Gianni, Tuscan minister, vi 602
Giannone, Pietro, Neapolitan historian, vi 588 sq.; 594
Gibbon, Edward, historian, vi 837; viii 18; xi 363; xii 817; 845
Gibbs, Josiah Willard, physicist, xii 785
Giberti, Giammatteo. *See* Verona, Bishops of
Gibraltar, Bay of, fleet under Santa Cruz in, iii 500; Spanish fleet attacked at (1607), 539, 639; scheme for occupation of, iv 484; capture of (1704), v 413; siege of (1705), *ib.*, 416; 444; Alberoni and, vi 31; 35; 38 sq.; 57 sq.; siege of (1727), 59, 145, 342*a* (in Vol. xiii), 376, 379 sq.; 452; Treaty of Seville and, 60; 63; 65; British fleet at, 68; George I and, 126; Spain and, 138 sqq.; 147 sqq.; 157; Admiral Haddock at, 236; 239; 350; 365; 376; secret negotiations concerning, 377 sq.; 381; 464; Spanish blockade of (1781), vii 231; 331; threatened (1779-83), viii 92; Danish ships searched at, ix 45; Ganteaume passes Straits of, 53; Saumarez withdraws to, 54; strategic importance of, 210; Villeneuve near, 220; Nelson near, 225; ships despatched to, 229; Nelson and, 230; a centre of English commerce, 381; plot at, x 230; General Prim lands at, xi 569
Gibson, Thomas Milner, and Conspiracy Bill, xi 328
Gide, Charles, French socialist, xii 124
Gié, Pierre de Rohan, Marshal de, French general at Fornovo, i 117
Gielgud, Anton, Polish general, x 472
Gien, Court at, saved by Turenne, iv 616
Gierke, Otto, German historian, xii 850
Giers, Nicholas de, Russian Foreign Minister, xii 313
Giesebrecht, Wilhelm von, German historian, xii 827
Gieseler, Johann Carl Ludwig, German historian, xii 846
Gifford, Gilbert, priest, iii 291
—— William, editor of *Quarterly Review*, ix 687; x 699

Gil, Juan (Egidio), Spanish reformer, ii 404 sq.
Gilbert, Sir Humphrey, iii 300; colonisation projects of, vii 2, 52
—— Ralegh, expedition of, to New England, vii 12
—— Sir Walter Raleigh, lieutenant-general in India, xi 740 sqq.
—— William, physician to Queen Elizabeth, v 716
Gilbert Island, annexation of, xii 667
Gilds. *See* Craft-gilds
Giles, Ernest, Australian explorer, xii 618
Gilgit, British agency at, xii 487; 802
Gillot, Jacques, iii 70
Gilmore, James Roberts, American author, vii 578
Gilyan, Russia and, v 544 sq.
Gindely, Anton, on Ranke, xii 827
Ginetti, Cardinal, at Cologne, iv 396
Gingi, fortress of, vi 539
Ginguené, Pierre-Louis, ix 132
Ginkel, Godert de, 1st Earl of Athlone. *See* Athlone
Gioberti, Vincenzo, ii 35; x 128; writings of, 166 sq.; 168; *Primato*, xi 65 sq.; *Prolegomeni al Primato*, 67 sq.; 70 sq.; 73; 76; 90; Ministry of, 93, 546 sq.; and Pius IX, 705; 712
Giocondo, Frà, ii 12
Giöri, Valtelline general, at Misox, iv 48 sqq.
Gioia, Melchiorre, Italian writer, x 128
Giolitti, Giovanni, Italian statesman, xii 218 sq.; 223; Ministry of, 225 sqq.
Giordani, Pietro, Italian writer, x 128
Giordano, Italian brigand, xi 531
Giorgio, Domenico, Italian Lutheran, ii 387
Giorgione (Giorgio Barbarelli), i 284
Giorgis, de, Italian general, in Macedonia, xii 426
Giovenale, Latino, the Oratory of Divine Love and, ii 379
Giovio, Paolo (Paulus Jovius), i 545, 560, 568; ii 15, 21; iii 114, 394; v 512
Gipps, Sir George, Governor of New South Wales, xi 795
Giraldi, Giovanbattista (Cinthio), iii 467 sq., 472
Girard, Albert, mathematician, v 710
—— Grégoire, Swiss Franciscan friar, xi 239
—— Baron Jean-Baptiste, French general, ix 525-6
—— Philippe-Henri de, inventor of flax-spinning machine, ix 125, x 755
Girardin, Émile de, x 492; xi 127; 526; xii 110
Giraud, Charles, French statesman, xi 135
—— P.-F.-F.-J., French writer, viii 380
Girodet-Trioson, Anne-Louis Girodet de Roussy, painter, ix 135; xi 528
Giron, Pietro, leader of *Comuneros*, i 374

Gironde. *See* Girondins
Girondins, VIII 213, 248 sqq.; failure of, 253 sq., 256 sq.; and the King's trial, 254 sqq., 259, 262; responsibility of, for the King's death, 261; Danton and, 264, 267, 269; 270 sq.; fall of, 275, 338 sq.; 346; proscription of, 350; trial and end of, 357
Girton College, XII 762
Gislikon, battle at, XI 251
Gistera, Carl, Austrian Minister of Interior, XII 185 sq.
Gitschin, acquired by Wallenstein, IV 73; Wallenstein and Bubna at, 234; XI 452; Prussians in, 453
Giudice, Cardinal, VI 123
Giusti, Giuseppe, poet, X 126; XI 68; 546
Giustiniani, A., ambassador at Rome (1502), I 240
—— Lorenzo, 1st Patriarch of Venice, I 267
—— Paolo, reformer of the Camaldolese, II 647
—— Taddeo, I 259
—— Papal Nuncio, X 142
Giza, Pyramids of, XII 433
Gizzi, Pasquale, Cardinal-Legate at Forlì, X 156; Papal Secretary of State, XI 76 sq.; 703
Gjatsk, Napoleon at, IX 494
Gjoe, Mogens, High Steward of Denmark, II 611, 614
Gladstone, Herbert John Gladstone, Viscount, Governor-General of South Africa, XII 648
—— William Ewart, X 110; 655; 667; Under-Secretary to Board of Trade, XI 2; 4; and Maynooth College grant, 9; 10; 21; first Budget of, 310 sq.; resigns, 320; opposes Divorce Bill, 326 sq.; 328; 330; Chancellor of Exchequer (1859), 331; 333; financial policy of, 334 sq.; 337; introduces Reform Bill of 1866, 339; rivalry of, with Disraeli, 342 sq.; and Irish Disestablishment, 344 sq.; 345; and Neapolitan trials, 379; 577; 764 sq.; and Anglo-French Treaty of Commerce, 470; XII 14; policy of, 23 sq.; Ministry of (1868–74), 23 sqq.; and Disraeli, 30; 31; anti-Turkish agitation by, 32; 34 sq.; Ministry of (1880–5), 36 sqq.; 42; Home Rule Bill of (1886), 43 sq.; resigns, 45; Ministry of (1892–4), 49 sqq.; retires, 51; 61; disestablishes Irish Church, 65 sq.; and Irish land question, 67, 70; and Irish education, 70 sqq.; 77; Irish Land Act of, 79 sq.; 81 sq.; resigns (1885), 83; and Irish Home Rule, 84, 87; and Germany, 161; and Montenegro, 402; and Greece, 403, 408; and Armenian question, 416, 418; and the "Bulgarian Atrocities," 384; and Egyptian affairs, 437, 439; and the Sudan, 440; and Gordon relief expedition, 442; 444; 458; 472; and Free Trade, 743; 760

Glamorgan, Edward Somerset (Lord Herbert), 6th Earl and 2nd Marquis of Worcester, titular Earl of, IV 328; Irish treaty and, 338; and Ormonde, 528; arrest of, 529; 530
Glandèves, naval commander at Toulon, VIII 448
Glanfynne, lands of, III 613
Glanvill, Joseph, divine, V 752
Glapion, Jean, II 148
Glareanus. *See* Loriti
Glarus, Zwingli at, II 307 sqq.; manufacture of cotton goods at, IX 425; industrial legislation in, XI 260
Glasgow, Darnley at, III 273; V 285; covenanting students at, 287; Union riots in, 299; VI 99; Malt Tax riot in, 107; 115; and Irish trade, 496; riot at (1820), X 582; financial crisis in, XI 327; University, XII 71
—— Archbishop of. *See* Cairncross
—— Assembly, IV 284; 500 sqq.
Glatz, VI 229; ceded to Prussia, 235, 244; 242; and Peace of Aix-la-Chapelle, 249; 279; capitulates, 294; 297 sq.; regained by Prussia, 300; 326; 339 sq.; 632
Glauber, Johann Rudolf, chemist, V 731
Glayon, Seigneur de, Dutch Councillor of State, III 194
Gleichman, Johan George, Dutch Finance Minister, XII 244
Gleim, Johann Wilhelm Ludwig, German poet, VIII 773
Glencairn, Alexander Cunningham, 5th Earl of, II 558, 573; III 271
—— William Cunningham, 4th Earl of, II 456 sqq.
Glencoe, massacre of (1692), V 294
Glenconkein, forest of, III 609
Glenelg, Charles Grant, Lord, influence of, IX 717; and East India Company, 728 sqq.; President of Board of Trade, X 645
Glenfinnan, Prince Charles in, VI 112
Glenmalure, battle of (1580), III 598, 602
Glenshiel, Pass of, Jacobites in, VI 106
Glisson, Francis, anatomist, V 729; 733
Globe, Le, French journal, X 95; 98; 103
Globig, H. A. F. von, Saxon plenipotentiary at Congress of Vienna, IX 587
Glogau, given to Wallenstein, IV 213; taken by Swedes, 386; V 593; principality of, 654; VI 229 sq.; Kyau's retreat to, 274; 275; taken by Jerome (1806), IX 281; evacuation of, demanded (1808), 318; Reynier at, 512; fortress of, 514
Gloucester, Parliamentary garrison at, IV 314; siege of, 315, 317, V 746
—— Humphrey, Duke of, I 598
—— William, Duke of (son of Queen Anne), V 275; VI 6; 8
—— William Henry, Duke of, marriage of, VI 445
Glücksburg, Christian, Prince of, XI 226 sq.
—— Duc de. *See* Decazes, Louis-C.-É.-A.
Glutz, Robert, Swiss historian, XI 261

Gmunden, Treaty of (1514), between Maximilian I and Tsar Wasiliei Ivanovič, I 343

Gneisenau, Augustus Neidhardt, Count, Prussian Marshal, defender of Kolberg, IX 291; 328, 332; favours alliance of Austria with Prussia, 344; in Silesia, 514; character of, 524; 542, 543; illness of, 551; advice of, 592; 631; hesitation of, before Waterloo, 637; x 349; 365

Gneist, H. Rudolph von, historian, XII 850

Gnesen, Canonry of, III 75; shrine at, v 629

Gnesen, Archbishops of (Primates of Poland):—
—— Jacob Uchanski (1562–81), III 81; 84; Interrex of Poland, 90, 96
—— Michael Stefan Radziejowski, Cardinal, v 592
—— Nicholas Dziergowski (1546–59), III 78
—— Stanislas Karnkowski (1581–1604) (Bishop of Cujavia), III 83, 90

Goa, capture of, by Alburquerque, I 31 sq.; Dutch adventurers at, III 632; Stevens at, IV 729; Anglo-Dutch expedition to, 738; Portuguese and, 744, IX 717; British occupy, 731

Gobelins factory, v 11

Gobi, desert of, XII 792; 802; 805

Goch, John of. *See* Pupper

Godard, F., French advocate, VIII 733
—— Thomas, Indian general, VI 576

Godefroi, Denys and Jacques, III 58

Godeheu, Director of French East India Company, VI 542 sqq.

Goderich, Viscount. *See* Ripon, Earl of

Godfrey, Sir Edmund Berry, murder of, v 221 sq., 224, 334

Godolphin, Sidney Godolphin, 1st Earl of, v 247; and James II, 262; 271; 274; 298; 427; and Marlborough, 428 sq., 460 sq.; 440; character of, 461; and party government, 463 sqq.; and Harley, 465; 466; dismissal of, 469; 595; 701; VI 11
—— Sir William, English ambassador in Spain, v 220

Godoy, Manuel de, Duke of Alcudia, Prince of the Peace and of Bassano, Spanish statesman, VIII 442, 782; IX 301–2; proclamation of (1806), 428; alarm of, 430; fall of, 431 sqq.; his rule, 434; and Spanish arsenals, 435; x 207; in Rome, 213

God's World, Russian journal, XII 313

Godunoff, Boris, Tsar. *See* Boris
—— Theodore, Tsarevich, v 499

Godwin, Sir Henry Thomas, commander in the Burmese War, XI 742
—— William, writer, VIII 761; 765; x 700; 712; 774; *Political Justice*, VI 836, VIII 767 sqq., x 778 sq.

Göben, August von, German general, XI 586 sq.; 610

Göding, retreat of Russians and Austrians to (1805), IX 261

Göhlsdorf, fighting at (1813), IX 530

Göhrde, French defeated on the (1813), IX 530

Göldli, George, leader of the forces of Zurich, II 337
—— Heinrich, Zwingli and, II 307

Göllersdorf, Wallenstein at, IV 212

Goens, Ryklof van, Dutch naval commander, v 695

Görgei, Arthur von, XI 185; career of, 203; and Kossuth, 203 sq., 212; Hungarian Commander-in-chief, 205; 206; Minister of War, 207; defeated at Pered, 210; at Arad, 211; surrenders to the Russians, 212 sq.; interned at Klagenfurt, 214

Görlitz, VI 264; 268; 274; Austrian army in, 282; 289 sqq.; Macdonald at, IX 525; Blücher at, 531

Görres, Joseph von, *Rothes Blatt*, VIII 775; IX 91; editor of *Rheinischer Merkur*, 577, x 352; IX 595; x 160; *Athanasius*, 165; 341; and Federal Diet, 347; 350; 353; 362; 365; recalled by Ludwig I, 371; ecclesiasticism of, 380; 401 sq.; XI 49; XII 848

Görtz, George Henrik, Baron, Swedish statesman, v 582; 609; 613 sq.; VI 26 sqq.; execution of, 34; 104
—— Johann Eustach, Graf von Schlitz, Prussian ambassador to the Hague, VIII 286; at Rastatt, 641

Görz, the Counts of, Venice and, I 263 sq.

Goes, Damião de, Portuguese Reformer, II 414 sq.

Goëss, Count, Imperial envoy at the Hague, v 432

Goesvort. *See* Wessel, John

Göta canal, XI 684 sq.

Göteborg, Charles IX and, IV 176 sq.; 208; 561; attacked by Christian IV, 571; Charles X at, 586, 589; VI 755; 779 sq.; port of, VIII 280; threatened by the Danes, 325; General Moore at, IX 322; industrial college at, XI 684; 685; fortifications of, XII 277; University of, 280

Goethe, Johann Wolfgang von, v 755; 763; VI 824; 826 sqq.; 832 sqq.; VIII 773 sq.; Napoleon's interview with, IX 319; 335; x 383; and Herder, 386; *Götz von Berlichingen, ib.*, 386 sqq.; *Die Leiden des jungen Werthers*, 387 sq.; 389; at Court of Saxe-Weimar, 389; in Italy, 389 sq.; Schiller and, 390 sqq.; 400; 403 sq.; and Romantic movement, 407 sqq.; death of, 410; 411; XI 347; 365; 411 sqq.; 415; 418; 420; 424; 430

Götter, Baron, Prussian envoy to Vienna, VI 229

Göttingen, Wallenstein near, IV 94; 96 sq.; evacuation of, VI 426; Bernadotte marches from, IX 253; University of, 329, 411, x 379; students' disturbance at, 364;

Hainbund at, 387; historical study at, XII 817, 823, 827

Götz, Christian, Austrian general, XI 206
—— Count von, Imperialist general, devastates Hesse-Cassel, IV 371; 375 sq.; superseded, 377; 389

Goez, Benedict, in the Pamirs, XII 800; 802

Goëzman, Louis-Valentin, and Beaumarchais, VI 358

Goffe, William, regicide, VII 25

Gogh, Vincent van, Dutch painter, XII 249

Gogol, Nicholas, Russian writer, XI 262; 649 sq.

Gohad, Rájah of, IX 726 sq.

Gohier, Louis Jérôme, Director, VIII 669 sq., 675, 678 sqq.

Goislard de Monsabert, French politician, VIII 110

Goito, French force at (1701), V 402; battle of (1848), XI 86

Gokla, Indian general, XI 726

Golab Sing, ruler of Kashmir, XI 740

Golconda, War of, with Aurungzeb, V 697 sq., VI 522; Shah Jehán and, 518; 519; 520; 521

Gold Coast, discovery of, by Gomes, I 16; Dutch voyages to, III 631 sq.; English forts on, IV 759; settlement on, V 691; trade with, VI 187; Great Britain and, XII 658; 660

Goldbach, French position along the (1805), IX 260
—— secretary to Bestuzheff, VI 317

Goldberg (Silesia), Poles in, III 78
—— (Mecklenburg), Saxons repulsed at, IV 366

Golden Book, of Venice, I 273
—— Bull (1222), V 367, (1356), I 291 sq.
—— Fleece, Knights of, quarrel with Maximilian I, I 446; III 698; VI 140
—— Horn, Russian warship in, V 527

Goldenberg, assassinates Prince Kropotkin, XII 306

Goldoni, Carlo, Italian dramatist, VI 606

Goldsborough, Schofield advances on, VII 528; Sherman at, 530

Goldsmith, Oliver, VI 828; 833; X 697; 701; 724

Goletta, captured by Spaniards, II 69

Golfe Jouan, French fleet in, VIII 458

Goliad (Texas), massacre at (1836), VII 392

Golokhvástoff, and Russian reform, XII 313

Golombo, Czarniecki defeated at, IV 582

Golos, St Petersburg journal, XI 625

Golovin, Alexander, Russian Minister of Education, XI 624; XII 295; 299; 315
—— Count Theodore, Russian statesman and field-marshal, V 523; 527; 588

Golovkin, Gabriel Ivanovich, Count, Russian Grand Chancellor, V 555; VI 303
—— Count Grigorii, IX 36; 38
—— Count Jourij, X 427

Golovkin, Count, Russian ambassador in Sweden (1728), V 555

Golovnin, Zemstvo president in Moscow, XII 327; 329; at the Moscow congress, 355 sq.

Goltz, Augustus Frederick Ferdinand, Major von der, IX 292; concludes alliance between Austria and Prussia (1809), 344; X 346
—— Count Bernard Wilhelm von der, Prussian envoy, VIII 441
—— Colmar, Baron von der, German general (1870), XI 589
—— Robert Heinrich Ludwig von der, Count, XI 396; Prussian ambassador in Paris, 483

Goluchowski, Count Agenor, Austrian statesman, XI 404; XII 178; 206; 211

Golymin, battle at (1806), IX 284

Gomarus, Franciscus (F. Gomar), III 646 sq.

Gomes, Fernam, explores Gold Coast, I 16, 19

Gomez, Ruy. *See* Eboli, Prince of
—— Carlist general, X 238

Gomez Labrador, Don Pedro, at the Congress of Vienna, IX 584; 589, 602, X 211; and the slave trade, IX 614; 652

Gomperz, Theodor, German historian, XII 845

Gonçalvez, Antam, Portuguese explorer, I 12 sq.

Gondar, James Bruce at, XII 805

Gondi. *See* Retz

Gondokoro, XII 439; explorers at, 809

Gondomar, Diego Sarmiento d'Acuna, Count of, ambassador to England, III 559-61; returns (1620), 567 sq., IV 34; James I ruled by, III 567 sq., 574 sq., IV 626, 640 sq.; and Ralegh, 754 sq.

Gondrin, Archbishop of Sens. *See* Sens

Gonesius, Peter, Polish Reformer, II 637

Gontaut Biron, Anne-Armand-Élie, Vicomte de, XII 107

Gonzaga, Marquises and Dukes of Mantua. *See* Mantua
—— Dukes of Nevers. *See* Nevers
—— Ercole di, Cardinal of Mantua, at the Council of Trent, II 394, 676 sqq.; death of, 682
—— Elizabeth di, Duchess of Urbino. *See* Urbino
—— Fernando (Ferrante) di, Count of Guastalla, Governor of Sicily, II 70, III 114; of Milan, II 81, III 400; and Piacenza, II 83 sqq.; 88, 268
—— Julia (wife of V. Colonna), Duchess of Traietto, II 33, 390 sq.; III 109; 466
—— Mary di. *See* Mary di Gonzaga, Queen of Poland
—— Vincent di, Duke of Guastalla (1702), V 403

Gonzales, Juan, Spanish Reformer, II 406

González Bravo, Luis ("Ibrahim Clarete"), journalist, x 241; Spanish Minister, xi 550 sq.; 558; 566; 568; Ministry of, 569

Gonzalo de Cordova. *See* Cordova

Gooch, Daniel W., American politician, vii 469

Goodman, Christopher, ii 585, 591, 596

Goodrich, Sir John, British ambassador in Sweden, vi 770

—— Thomas, Bishop of Ely, ii 517

Goodwin, John, works of, burnt at Oxford, vi 807

—— Thomas, Westminster Assembly and, iv 319; Independent leader, 359

Googe, Barnaby, iii 367

Gookin, Daniel, and St Brandan's Isle, iv 756

Gora, taken by Poniatovski (1809), ix 354

Gorani, Count Joseph, Italian publicist, viii 778

Gorboduc, by Sackville and Norton, iii 367

Gorchakóff, Alexander, Prince, Russian Chancellor, at Vienna, xi 321; 434; and Prussia, 456, 577; 628; Asiatic policy of, 630 sqq.; and Crete, 634; and Poland, 660; 843; and France, xii 97, 141; 138; 343; 387; at Congress of Berlin, 394; and Russian advance in Asia, 464; death of, 313

—— Prince, removed from Viatka (1908), xii 376

Gordon Castle, Jacobite rising at, vi 98

—— riots, v 337; x 622; 625

—— Alexander, of Auchintoul, Jacobite general, vi 103

—— Alexander Gordon, 2nd Duke of (Marquis of Huntly), vi 98; 102

—— Charles George ("Chinese Gordon"), xi 821; xii 40; in Egypt, 439 sqq.; in Khartum, 442 sq.; 444; 812

—— George Gordon, 1st Duke of, v 290 sq.

—— Lord George, iii 268, 270; vi 455

—— Lady Jane, iii 274

—— John, Colonel, at Eger, iv 242

—— John B., Confederate general, vii 540 sq.

—— Lady Katharine, marriage of Perkin Warbeck to, i 469

—— Lord Lewis, Jacobite, vi 115

—— Patrick, in Russia, v 523

—— Sir Robert, x 21; 32

—— Thomas, Jacobite agent in Russia, v 543

—— Thomas, colonel, joins the Greek insurgents, x 182

—— Admiral, at Danzig, vi 197

Gordonsville, Confederate army at (1862), vii 472

Goree, taken by Dutch (1617), iv 759; v 60; 179; ceded to France (1678), 692; retained (1762), vi 347, 428; abandoned to British (1779), 452; ceded to France (1783), 464

Goremýkin, Russian Minister of Interior, xii 326; 328; Prime Minister, 365 sq.; 368

Gorgast, Prussian army at, vi 280

Gorges, Sir Ferdinando, and the settlement of Maine, vii 21 sq.; death of, 24

—— Ferdinando (grandson of above), vii 27

Gorham, George Cornelius, Vicar of Brampford Speke, xi 18

—— Nathaniel, Massachusetts deputy at the Constitutional Convention (1787), vii 246, 257, 266, 268, 282, 295, 297

Goria, annexed by Russia, x 413

Goring, George, the elder. *See* Norwich, Earl of

—— Colonel George, Baron Goring, plot of, iv 289 sq.; 304; surrenders Portsmouth, 305; and Puritanism, 306; 319; 321; at Marston Moor, 322; 324; in the West, 330 sqq.; in France, 334

Gorka, Andreas, Castellan of Posen, ii 636; iii 75

Gorky, Maxim, xii 13; 330

Gorst, Sir John Eldon, Under-Secretary for India, xii 45

—— Sir Eldon, and Egyptian affairs, xii 450; 456

Gortchakoff, Pierre, Prince, at Shevardino, ix 494; at Bautzen, 519

Goschen, George Joachim Goschen, 1st Viscount, xii 23; 29; 36; mission of, to Constantinople, 37; 43; Chancellor of Exchequer, 45 sqq.; First Lord of Admiralty, 52; 403; and Egyptian Finances, 434

Goslar, Brunswick-Lüneburg Dukes at, iv 408; acquired by Hanover, ix 658

Gospels, The Apocryphal, early printed editions of, i 613

Gossembrot, Sigismund, of Augsburg, i 324

Gosson, Stephen, iii 372

Gotha, army at, vi 265; 266; 270; "Union" meeting at, xi 221; socialist congress at, xii 153

Gothenburg. *See* Göteborg

Gothofredus (Denys Godefroy), French scholar, i 577

Gothus, Laurentius Petri. *See* Upsala, Archbishops of

Gotland, iv 561; ceded to Sweden (1645), 572; West, v 569

Gotō, Japanese Minister of Public Works, xi 861; 865

Gotthelf, Jeremias. *See* Bitzius, Albert

Gottorp, ducal line of, iv 563; 572; and Denmark, vi 736, 741. *See also* Holstein-Gottorp

Gottsched, Johann Christoph, German critic, v 68; x 384; 396; 406

Gouda, convention at (1610), iii 647; the Princess of Orange arrested near, viii 287

—— de, papal envoy, iii 267

Goudanus (Nicholas Floris), iii 149

Goudchaux, Michel, French politician, xi 26; 99; Minister of Finance, 104; 304

Gough, Sir Hugh Gough, 1st Viscount, in India, xi 738 sqq., 745

Goujon, Jean-M.-C.-Alexandre, French politician, viii 388

Goulard, Marc-Thomas-Eugène de, French Minister of Interior, xii 106

Goulburn, Henry, x 585 sqq.; 615; Chief Secretary for Ireland, 637; 642; Chancellor of Exchequer, xi 2; 762; 790

Gourara, French occupation of, xii 129

Gourgaud, Gaspard, Baron, French general, at St Helena, ix 757; 759; xi 102

Gourmont, Gilles de, French printer, i 576

Gournay, Vincent de, French economist, viii 22, 24

Gouvion, Jean-Baptiste, French politician, viii 213

—— Saint-Cyr, Laurent, French marshal, viii 638, 659; withdraws from Otranto, ix 193; 254; surrender of Rohan to, 258; takes Rosas, 448; besieges fortress of Gerona, 454; replaced by Augereau, 457; and the Russian campaign, 488; 499; at Berlin, 512; 514; guards Dresden, 523; 526, 529; holds Erzgebirge, 530–2; x 20; 54; scheme of, for army reform, 55; 57; 61; resigns, 62

Govea, André de, at Bordeaux, iii 69

Governolo, occupied by King Charles Albert, xi 88

Govind Ráo (of Gujarat), ix 726

—— Chandra, Rájah of Kachar, xi 730

Gower, Earl. *See* Stafford, Marquis of

—— George Granville Leveson-Gower, Lord (*afterwards* 1st Duke of Sutherland), viii 292, 296; recalled from Paris (1792), 297 sq.

Gowrie, William (Lord Ruthven), Earl of, iii 550

Goyon, Charles-M.-A. de. *See* Feltre, Duc de

Gozzadini, Giovanni, ii 17

Graaf, Regnier de, anatomist, v 731

Graaff-Reinet, Boers of, surrender, ix 749; district of, xi 778

Grabovski, Stanislaus, Polish statesman, x 452

Gradenigo, Pietro, Doge of Venice, i 261, 268, 273

—— Venetian captain, iii 113

Grado, patriarchate of, created, i 267

Gradovsky, Russian politician, xii 311

Graeff, Cornelis de, v 145

Grätz, Imperial Court withdraws to, iv 389; seminary at, vi 637; revolutionary movement at, xi 155; 187

Graf, Arturo, Italian writer, xii 231

—— Carl Heinrich, German orientalist, and Old Testament study, xii 846

Grafenfehde (*Grevefeide*) (Count's War), ii 230, 614

Grafton, Augustus Henry Fitzroy, 3rd Duke of, vi 415; 424; 431; 435 sqq.; and East India Company, 438; 439; 442;

444; resigns, 447; 448 sq.; Lord Privy Seal, 457; 459; 463; 467; vii 152, 154, 173

Grafton, Charles Fitzroy, 2nd Duke of, Lord-lieutenant of Ireland, vi 485

—— Henry Fitzroy, 1st Duke of, v 247

Graham, Sir Gerald, in Egypt, xii 441

—— Sir James Robert George, and parliamentary reform, x 603; 614; 662 sq.; 667; 678; Home Secretary, xi 2; and Corn Laws, 3 sq., 9 sq.; and Factory Acts, 4 sq.; 7; and Dublin University, 9; 21; resigns, 320; 765

—— John, of Claverhouse, Viscount Dundee. *See* Dundee

—— General Thomas. *See* Lynedoch

Grahovo, Turkish defeat at, xi 636, xii 414

Grain Coast, trade with, vi 187

Gramido, Convention of (1847), x 339

Grammont, Gabriel de. *See* Tarbes, Bishop of

—— West Indian buccaneer, v 691

Gramont, A.-A.-Alfred, Duc de, Foreign Minister, xi 493, 578; 495

Grampound, disfranchisement of, x 601; 605

Gran, captured by Ferdinand, ii 207; Solyman demands keys of, iii 108; surrender demanded by Solyman from Ferdinand, 118; taken by Turks, 119; captured from the Turks (1683), v 363

—— Peter Pázmány, Archbishop of, iv 75

Granada, conquered by Ferdinand and Isabella (1492), i 224, 358 sq., 361 sq.; Treaty of (1500), 124; Moors in, iii 493–4; Philip V at, vi 166; corps of Sebastiani at, ix 457; kingdom of, 469; tablets and parchments of, xi 713

—— Ferdinand de Mendoza y Talavera, Archbishop of, i 360; 651

—— Luis de, ii 409

—— Pedro Guerrero, Archbishop of, at the Council of Trent, ii 676 sq., 680

—— New. *See* New Granada

Granby, John Manners, Marquis of, vi 426; 434; Commander-in-chief, 437; 439; 442

Grand Alliance, of 1689, v 35, 57 sqq.; England and, 249; campaigns of, from the English point of view, 260 sqq.; of 1701, formation of, 398 sqq., 403, vi 9

—— Gulf, captured (1863), vii 503; 559 sq.

—— Remonstrance, of 1641, iv 295 sqq.

—— Trunk Pacific Railway, xii 608 sq.; 613

—— Vezirate, growth of power of, i 101

Grandmaison, Michel (Moreau de), French revolutionary, viii 682

"Granges," American political societies (1872), vii 646, 706

Granja, La, Queen Isabel at, xi 556

Granson, victory of Swiss at (1476), i 391

Grant, Charles. *See* Glenelg
—— James, General, at St Lucia, vi 451; at Fort Duquesne, vii 136
—— James, explores the Nile, xii 809
—— General Sir James Hope, in India, xi 749
—— Ulysses Simpson, captures Paducah, vii 463; early services of, 494; captures Forts Henry and Donelson, 495; 499 sqq.; and Vicksburg campaign, 501 sqq.; proceeds to Chattanooga, 510 sqq.; at Washington (1864), 514 sq.; and campaign in East (1864), 514 sqq.; 527 sq.; and Richmond campaign, 531, 533 sqq.; in Petersburg, 539; Lee surrenders to, 541; in Washington, 545; President of United States, 631 sqq.; and San Domingo, 637, 639; character of, 639; proposed election of (1876), 644, 652 sq.; xii 21; 95; 689
Grantham, Cromwell at, iv 313
—— Thomas Robinson, Lord, vi 75; 149; Secretary of State, 462
Grantley, Fletcher Norton, Lord, Speaker of the House of Commons, vi 443; 455
Granvelle, Antoine Perrenot, Sieur de, Cardinal, Bishop of Arras, ii 93; iii 34; 114; 134; influence of, in Netherlands, 183 sq., 188, 190–8; 218; 221; 227; counsels murder of Orange, 253; 265; 477; 481; 489; death of (1586), 514
—— Nicholas Perrenot, Sieur de, Minister of Charles V, ii 240 sq., 243, 250, 253, 258, 260, 268
Granville (of Potheridge), John, Lord (2nd son of John Granville, Earl of Bath, cr. 1702, d. 1707), vii 37
—— John Carteret, Earl (Lord Carteret), at Stockholm, vi 36 sq.; 39; 44; 71; enters the Cabinet, 73; 74 sq.; succeeds Walpole, 235; 238; 394; 396; 405; 417; and Pitt, 420; 424; Lord-lieutenant of Ireland, 485; death of, 428
—— Granville Leveson-Gower, 1st Earl, diplomatist, at Memel, ix 298; negotiations with Russia, 305–6; and Corn Law of 1815, x 771
—— Granville George Leveson-Gower, 2nd Earl, vii 671; xi 331; 577; and Afghan frontier, 632; 633; 801; Colonial Secretary, xii 23; Foreign Minister, 28, 36; 31 sq.; 40; 161; and Egyptian affairs, 436, 438, 440 sq., 444
Graspan, Boers defeated at, xii 642
Grasse, Comte de. *See* Grasse-Tilly
Grassellini, Monsignor, Governor of Rome, xi 76
Grasse-Tilly, François-Joseph-Paul, Marquis de, French admiral, vi 453 sq.; 462; vii 231
Grassi, Francesco, ii 83
Grassis, Paris de, i 252
Gratius, Ortuinus (Ortwin de Graes), and *Letters of Obscure Men*, i 637; ii 696

Gratry, Joseph-Alphonse, Oratorian, xi 721; 723
Grattan, Henry, vi 458 sq.; 474; 494; 496; and Irish trade, 497; and Irish Independence, 498 sqq.; 502; 504 sq.; viii 771; and Whig Club, ix 693 sqq.; retirement of, 700; and Union, 705; 708; x 574; and movement for Catholic emancipation, 631, 633 sq., 635 sq.; 657
Graubünden. *See* Grisons
Graudenz, Frederick William III at, ix 280, 281; fortress of, demanded by Napoleon (1806), 282; investment of (1807), 284; blockade raised, 285; surrender demanded, 291
Gravamina Germanicae Nationis, by Jakob Wimpheling, ii 29
Grave, falls into Parma's hands, iii 620; siege of (1602), 636; French possession, v 43
—— Pierre-Marie, Marquis de, Minister of War to Louis XVI, viii 223, 406
Gravel, Balthasar, Abbot of Fulda, iii 178
—— Robert de, Seigneur de, v 38
Gravelines, interview between Henry VIII and Charles V at (1520), ii 42, 417; battle of (1558), 93, 561, iii 184; engagement with Armada off (July 29, 1588), 313, 315, 507; Anglo-French Treaty and, iv 440; taken by French (1644), 597; abandoned (1652), 618 sq.; ceded to France, 620; the Old Pretender lands at, vi 103
Gravelotte, xi 590; battle of, 593 sqq., 600 sq.
Graves, Thomas Graves, Lord, Admiral, vi 453; vii 230
—— Sir Thomas, admiral (nephew of above), ix 53
Gravina, Charles, Duc de, Spanish admiral, joins Villeneuve, ix 223
—— Papal Nuncio, x 142, 208
Gravosa, Osuna attacks Venetians off, iv 632
Gray, John, economic theories of, x 781
—— Thomas, poet, vi 825; 828; 830; x 698 sq.; xi 351; 357
—— William, Bishop of Ely, collector of books, i 597
—— Boston ship-captain, vii 326, 364
—— Justice (U.S.), xii 714
Gray's Mill, Prince Charles at, vi 112
Graz. *See* Grätz
Graziosi, Canon, xi 73
Grazzini, Anton Francesco (Il Lasca), iii 467 sq., 470
"Great Awakening, The," American religious revival (1740), vii 737
Great Britain. *See* England for affairs in common
Great Contract, The, iii 557
—— Fish River, discovered by Diaz, i 17; passed by Gama, 25; vi 189
—— St Bernard, Napoleon crosses the (1800), ix 59, 60

Grebel, Conrad, Anabaptist, opponent of Zwingli, II 322
—— Jacob, executed, II 322
Greece, conquest of, by Ottomans, I 74; 79; Venetian successes in, v 365 sq.; influence of French Revolution in, VIII 789; and Congress of Vienna, IX 661; Vol. x, Chap. VI *passim*; and Congress of Verona, 33 sq., 39; attitude of France towards, 91, 506; Palmerston and, XI 18; under King Otho, 277 sqq.; Tsar and, 312; 313; military revolt in, 533; Alexander II and, 634; and Crete, *ib.*, XII 419 sq., 427 sq.; rupture of, with Turkey, XI 636; misgovernment in, 639 sq.; succession in, 641; new Constitution of, 642; brigandage in, 643; Roumania and, 646; XII 10 sq.; 37; Great Britain and, 43; 304; 381; and Russo-Turkish War, 390 sq.; 393; and Treaty of Berlin, 394, 398 sq.; frontier settlement of, 402 sq.; 406; coast of, blockaded, 408; and Bulgaria, 411; and Cyprus, 415; at war with Turkey, 420 sqq.; and Macedonia, 424, 426; and the European Concert, 728; 762; researches in the history of, 821, 842, 845
Greek, controversy as to the pronunciation of, I 581; Classics, search for MSS of, 549 sq.; Aldine editions of, 562; early French printed editions of, 576; Roman printed editions of, 566; scholarship, revival of, 540–2. *See also* Renaissance
Greeley, Horace, editor of *New York Tribune*, VII 425, 577, 590; Presidential campaign of, 640, 643 sq.; death of, 653
Green, John Richard, historian, XII 840
—— Thomas Henry, teaching of, XII 765
—— Cay island, XII 20
—— Ribbon Club, v 218; 228 sq.
"Greenback" Party, VII 646, 648, 652 sq.
Greene, Nathaniel, American general, VII 223 sqq., 227 sqq.
—— Robert, dramatist and novelist, III 371, 375
Greenland, fishery disputes in, III 644; Christian IV and, IV 567; whale fisheries of, VI 49, 181; Norway and, XI 683; exploration of, XII 815
—— Company, America and, IV 749
Greensborough, Jefferson Davis at, VII 542 sq.
Greenshields, James, and Book of Common Prayer, VI 94
Greenwich, Treaty of (1543), III 261
Greenwood, John, III 333, 345
Greg, S., Russian Minister of Finance, XII 309
Gregg, William, clerk to Robert Harley, v 465
Grégoire, Ernest, Belgian revolutionary leader, x 537
—— Henri, Comte, Constitutional Bishop of Blois, member of the Convention, VIII 249, 382, 501, 733, 790; IX 182; 186;

x 60 sq.; motion to annul election of, 62; 71; 486; XI 72
Gregorios, Patriarch of Constantinople, execution of, x 183
Gregorovius, Ferdinand, historian, quoted, II 19, 25, 28; *City of Rome*, XII 849
Gregory I, Pope, III 752
—— VII (Hildebrand), Pope, III 422; 439; 752
—— IX (Ugolino, of Anagni), Pope, I 260, 666, 668; II 2
—— XI (Peter Roger de Beaufort), Pope, opposition to taxation of, I 669
—— XII (Angelo Correr), Pope, I 268
—— XIII (Hugo Buoncompagni), Pope, I 325; Carranza and, II 410; John III of Sweden and, 631 sq.; III 18; 20; and Catholic League, 38; 136; and Counterreformation, 178; attacks Elizabeth, 286 sqq.; 349; 414; and Cardinal di Montalto, 426 sqq.; new Calendar of, 424, 707; 497; and Ireland, 596 sq.; Concordat of, with Duke William V of Bavaria, 709; v 494
—— XIV (Nicolas Sfondrato), Pope, and the Catholic League, III 50, 659; 442; 710
—— XV (Alessandro Ludovisi), Pope, rescues Klesl, IV 22; fears Spanish supremacy in Italy, 53; 672 sqq.; death of, 57, 674
—— XVI (Mauro Capellari), Pope, the pontificate of, x 154 sq.; and Lamennais, 163 sq.; and the Jesuits, 167; and Prussian marriages controversy, 381; 488; and Guizot, XI 37; 67 sq.; 71; condemns Articles of Baden, 246; 703; and Antonelli, 705; 716; death of, 70, *also* x 168
—— Saint, printing of the works of, III 445
—— of Tours (d. 595), I 534
—— Sir Augustus Charles, in Australasia, XI 798
—— James, mathematician, v 721
Greifswald, IV 196; siege of (1631), 199, 203; a Swedish possession, 404; lost by the Swedes, v 652; Treaty of, VI 26
Greig, Sir Samuel, Russian admiral, VI 673; VIII 325
Greiz, Liberal movement at, XI 149
Gremonville, Nicolas Bretel, Sieur de, French envoy at Vienna, v 38; 349; 351 sq.
Grenada, the French in, v 687; VI 185 sq.; 346; British occupation of, 426; ceded to Great Britain (1763), 428; reduced by d'Estaing, 452; retained by Great Britain (1782), 464; insurrection in (1796), VIII 484; negroes in, XII 653; 654; 656
Grenadines, ceded to Great Britain, VI 428
Grenelle, powder factory at, VIII 433; disaffection at (1796), 504 sq.
Grenfell, George, African explorer, XII 811
—— John Pascoe, captain in the Brazilian navy, x 316

Grenier, Comte Paul, French general, IX 67; marches towards Berlin, 511

Grenoble, capture of, III 416 sq.; *Parlements* of, 415, V 4, VIII 47; provincial assembly at, 91; disturbances in (1788), 112 sq., (1816), X 50; IX 196

Grenville, George, statesman, VI 424 sqq.; and Prussia, 427; 428; succeeds Bute, 430; 431; 434; and John Wilkes, 441; 442; death of, 443; VII 147 sqq., 152

—— James, joint Vice-treasurer of Ireland, VI 437

—— Sir John. *See* Bath, Earl of

—— Sir Richard, and the *Revenge*, III 319; expedition of, to Virginia (1585-6), VII 3

—— Sir Richard, 1st Baronet (grandson of above), in Munster, IV 524

—— Thomas, mission of, to Paris, VI 461

—— William Wyndham, Baron Grenville, VIII 288, 294; Foreign Secretary, 295 sqq., 301, 303 sqq., 496, 559 sq., 648 sq., 651; ministry of, IX 288; 291, 299; and Catholic Emancipation, 678; 680; and peace, 681; and Pitt, 682; 683; forms Ministry, 685; resignation of, 686; influence of, 687; 690; and Ireland, 697 sqq.; and Canada, 744; X 574; 580; and the Irish Catholics, 631; 666

—— (Greenville *or* Greynvile), Irish "Undertaker" (1586), III 600

Greppo, Jean-Louis, French politician, XI 124; 136; 139

Gresham College, V 740

—— Thomas, III 211

Gretser, Jacob, *Defensiones*, IV 4

Greuze, Jean-Baptiste, IX 135; XI 528

Greville, Charles Cavendish Fulke, X 587

Grévy, François-Paul-Jules, XI 116; 132; President of the National Assembly, 500; 600; President of the French Republic, XII 92; 107; succeeds Mac-Mahon, 112; 116

Grew, Nehemiah, botanist, V 735 sq.

Grey, Lady Catharine, II 574; III 534

—— Sir Charles, General, VIII 484

—— Charles Grey, 2nd Earl, VI 472; 476; VIII 759 sq.; succeeds Fox in Foreign Office, IX 271; and reform, 672; 676; leader of Whig party, 687; 690; and the Polish revolution, X 474; and Algiers, 502; 574; attacks Canning, 591; Ministry of (1830-4), 594, 655 sq.; and parliamentary reform, 599, 603, 607 sq., 610, 612; resigns, 614; recalled to office, 615; 618; resigns, 663; and dismissal of Melbourne, 666; 668; and O'Connell, 669; 673 sq.; and Queen Victoria, 678; XI 755

—— Sir George, Governor of Cape Colony, XI 784; 786; in South Australia, 792, 795; in New Zealand, 794 sqq., 799 sq.

—— Henry George Grey, 3rd Earl (Viscount Howick), X 679; XI 10; Secretary for Colonies and for War, 14, 16; colonial

policy of, 759 sqq., 763 sqq.; and New Zealand, 796 sq.

Grey, Lady Jane, marriage of, to Guilford Dudley, II 510; proclaimed Queen, 514; arrested, 518, 520; executed, 528; III 359

—— Sir John, General, in Gwalior, XI 738

—— Lord Leonard (6th son of Thomas, 1st Marquis of Dorset), executed, II 452; 471

—— Sir Thomas, executed, II 528

—— Thomas, *styled* Lord Grey of Groby (son of Earl of Stamford), IV 314

—— Thomas Philip de. *See* De Grey

—— William de. *See* Walsingham, Lord

—— de Wilton, Arthur, 14th Baron, Lord Deputy of Ireland, III 265, 298, 598, 602

—— de Wilton, Sir William, 13th Baron, II 505 sq., 517, 577

Grey Friars Observants, suppression of, by Henry VIII, II 441

—— Leagues. *See* Grisons

Greyerz, and Freiburg, VI 625

Gribaldi, Matteo, Italian Reformer, II 393

Gribeauval, Jean-Baptiste Vaquette de, French general, VI 349

Gribovo, Greeks defeated at, XII 422

Griboyedoff, Alexander, Russian poet, X 431; XI 614

Gridley, Jeremiah, American lawyer, VII 178 sq.

Grieg, Edvard, Norwegian musician, XII 281

Griffenfeld, Count Peter Schumacher von, Danish statesman, V 560 sqq.; 571; 578

Griffin, Thomas, Admiral, VI 538

Griffith, Maurice, Bishop of Rochester, II 531

—— Rice ap, disaffection of, II 471

Grigorovich, Alexander, XI 614

Grijalva, Hernando di, coast of Mexico explored by, I 41

Grillenzone, Giovanni, founder of Modenese Academy, II 386

Grillparzer, Franz, Austrian dramatist, X 407; XI 414 sqq.

Grimaldi, Luciano, Prince of Monaco, holds Monaco against Genoa, I 129

—— Napoleone (Genoese admiral, 1380), I 259

—— Philip II's agent in Genoa, III 497

—— Cardinal-Legate at Forlì, X 156

Grimaldo, Marquis de, Spanish Minister of Foreign Affairs, VI 136 sq.; 139; 142; 145; at Paris, 368, 370; 371; retires, 374; 375

Grimani, Marco, Cardinal Legate to Scotland, II 458

—— Cardinal Domenico, II 15

Grimm, Baron Friedrich Melchior, and Catharine II, VI 678, 698 sq., VIII 784 sq.

—— Jacob, X 379; expelled from Hanover, 380; 402; 404; XI 49; 164; XII 822 sq.; 849

Grimm, William, x 379; 402; 404; xi 49;
xii 822
Grimmelshausen, Christoph von, iv 425
Grimnitz, Treaty of (1529), iv 104
Grindal, Edmund, Archbishop of Canter-
bury, iii 340 sq.
Grinevetsky, assassinates Alexander II, xii
310
Gringmuth, Russian politician, xii 314;
373
Gringore, Pierre, *Le Jeu du Prince des Sots
et Mère Sotte*, ii 281
Gripenstedt, Johan August, Swedish Minister
of Finance, xi 688; 690
Grippenberg, General, in the Russo-Japanese
War, xii 596 sq.
Griqualand East, Treaty State of, xi 783
—— West, annexation of, xii 635
Grisel, Georges, betrays Babeuf conspiracy,
viii 504 sq.
Grisons, The, ii 306; the Reformation in,
328; iii 466, 684; Vol. iv, Chap. ii *passim*;
129; 373; canton of, vi 614; and France
(1798), viii 640 sq.; French army in (1800),
ix 64, 68; xi 234; 236
Gritti, Alvise, iii 109
—— Andrea, Venetian general, i 87
—— Lorenzo, iii 115
Grobbendonck, Anthony Schets, Lord of,
siege of Hertogenbosch and, iv 692 sq.
—— Gaspar Schets, Lord of, iii 195
Grochov, battle of (1831), x 469 sq.
Grocyn, William, at Oxford, i 491; 579;
and L. Valla, 602; orthodoxy of, 643
Grodno, Diet of, dissipated, v 555; 594;
Charles XII enters, 597; Diet of (1793),
viii 537 sqq.; province of, x 420; 440;
Russian administration of, 459 sq.;
placed under martial law, 469
Gröben, Count Karl von der, Prussian
general, xi 221; 230 sq.
Groenewegen, Dutch colonial leader, iv
755
Groenloo, attempt to capture, iii 628; siege
of (1597), 629
Groll, siege of (1606), iii 638; Dutch cap-
ture of (1627), iv 691
Grolmann, Karl Wilhelm Georg von, ix
332; xi 50
Gronberg, Imperialist commander, iv 393
Groningen, siege of (1590), iii 626; dis-
content in, 634; Henry Casimir and, iv
695, 701; Cartesian philosophy and, 789;
besieged (1672), v 43; and the Eternal
Edict, 155 sq.; 160; 165; University of,
ix 417
Groot, Hugo de. *See* Grotius
—— Pieter de, Pensionary of Rotterdam,
v 156; mission of, to Paris, 156 sqq.
Groote, Gerard, founder of fraternity at
Deventer, i 434 sq., 627 sq.
Groote Privilegie, granted by Mary of
Burgundy (1477), i 438
Gropper, Johann, Catholic divine, ii 240,
243, 667

Gros, Antoine-Jean, ix 135
—— Baron Jean-Baptiste-Louis, xi 812;
816; 818; xii 681
Gross, Russian resident at Berlin, vi 319
Gross-Beeren, battle of (1813), ix 526, 528,
530
Grossenbrode, Danish capitulation at, iv
102
Gross-Enzersdorf, French troops advance
from (1809), ix 352
Grosseteste, Robert, Bishop of Lincoln, in-
terest of, in Greek studies, i 537, 585–7,
657
Grosseto, fair at, iii 393
Grossfriedrichsburg (Guinea Coast), v 647;
691
Gross-Görschen, battle of (1813), ix 517
Gross-Hennersdorf, Austrians repulsed at,
vi 244
Gross-Jägerndorf, battle of, vi 264, 322
Gross-Kamin, Prussian troops at, vi 281 sq.;
285 sq.
Grossi, Tommaso, x 126; xi 545; 548
Grosswardein, Treaty of (1538), ii 236, 242;
v 61; surrenders to the Turks (1660),
345; 348; Görgei at, xi 214
—— George Martinuzzi, Bishop of, ii 242;
murder of, 268 sq., iii 122–3
—— Pasha of, and Tökölyi, v 366
Grosvenor, Lord Robert, xi 339
Grote, George, historian, x 598; 655 sq.;
supports the Poor Law Bill, 662; 675 sq.;
xi 250; xii 830; 836; 844
—— Baron Thomas von, Hanoverian
envoy in London, vi 14
Grotefend, Georg Friedrich, xii 845
Groth, Klaus, German poet, xi 414; 420
Grotius, Hugo (Huig van Groot), *De Jure
Belli et Pacis*, i 579; *Mare Liberum*
(1609), iii 644; moves resolution in
States of Holland, 648; 650–2, 655,
740, 763, 767; iv 144; mission of,
to Paris, 250, 369; 389; and Queen
Christina, 575; works of, 717 sq.; v
745; 754; viii 29; and Gentili, xii
707 sq.; method of, 709 sqq.
Grottammare, birthplace of Sixtus V, iii
425
Grouchy, Emmanuel, Marquis de, Marshal
of France, viii 474, 654; advance of,
on Valence, ix 617; commands cavalry
reserve, 625; 627, 630; despatches of,
633 sqq.; responsibility of, 641 sq.; at
Paris, 643
Grudzinska, Joanna (Princess Lovicz), x
436; 448
Grün, Anastasius. *See* Auersperg, Count
Anton Alexander von
Grüneberg Manuscript, The. *See* Königinhof
Grünne, Count von der, Austrian adjutant-
general, xi 398; 403
Grüsch, Protestant-Venetian party at, iv
52; de Coeuvres at, 58
Gruet, Joachim am, ii 322, 375

Gruieff, Bulgarian officer, xii 408

Grumbach, Wilhelm von, ii 190, 274; iii 151 sq.; *Grumbachsche Händel*, 151, 172 sq.

Grumbkow, General von, Prussian statesman, vi 210 sqq.

Grundtvig, Nikolai Frederik Severin, Danish writer, xi 692; 698

Grynaeus, Simon, *Orthodoxographa*, i 617; ii 355

Gryphius, Andreas, German poet, v 68

Guadagni, Abbé, iii 24

Guadagnoli, Antonio, Italian writer, xi 545

Guadalajara (Spain), Philip II meets Elizabeth of France at, iii 483; Ripperdá at, vi 139; Absolutist force marches on (1823), x 227

—— (Mexico), Court established at, x 248

Guadalupe Hidalgo, Treaty of (1848), vii 397, 426

Guadarrama, canal of, vi 383; pass of, Estremaduran army sent to, ix 444; French troops cross, 445

Guadeloupe, French settlement of, iv 758, vii 78 sq., 85; failure of English attack on, v 60; an English possession (1759-63), vii 96; ceded to France, vi 428; captured by English (1794), viii 484, ix 749; recaptured, *ib.*; restored to France (1801), 75; blockaded (1804), vii 327; reduced (1810), ix 240, 752; restored to France (1815), 653; xii 652; France and, 656

Guadet, Marguerite Élie, Girondist leader, viii 214, 231, 249, 256, 271; executed, 357

Guadiana river, Victor halts in valley of, ix 450

Guaira, Jesuit government in, x 269 sq.

Gualterio, Cardinal, Jacobite agent at Rome, vi 97

Gualterotti, Francesco, supporter of Savonarola, i 154

Guancavelica, quicksilver mines at, v 682

Guanches, The, of the Canary Islands, i 10

Guanica (Porto Rico), Miles lands at, vii 680

Guaraní Indians, in Paraguay, xii 674

Guararapes hills, Dutch defeat in (1647), v 675

Guarini, Giovanni Battista, *Pastor Fido*, iii 467

Guarino (da Verona), humanist, i 543, 546, 550, 558, 562

Guastalla, French victory at, vi 154; 366; administered by Moreau de St Méry, ix 398; duchy of, assigned to Empress Marie-Louise, 602, 660; reversion of, secured to Infanta Marie-Louise (1817), x 212

—— Duke of. *See* Gonzaga, Fernando de

—— Vincent di Gonzaga, Duke of. *See* Gonzaga

Guasto, Count del. *See* Vasto

Guatemala, administration of, x 248; independence of, 305; State of, xii 672

Guayaquil, Hollanders defeated at, iv 642; x 273; and Bolívar, 295 sq.

Guben, Frederick the Great at, vi 288

Guchen, caravan route to, xii 793; 799; 802

Guchkóff, Russian politician, xii 360; 375 sq.

Gudmundarsen, David, ii 621

Guébriant, Jean-Baptiste Budes, Count de, Marshal of France, joins Bernard of Weimar, iv 375; 379; 381 sqq.; 385 sq.; difficulties and death of, 388 sq.; 595

Gueffier, French envoy, in Grisons, iv 45 sqq.; Catholics urged on by, 51; 54

Guelders. *See* Gelders

Guelfs and Ghibellines, revived in Savoy, iii 401, 412; 438

Guénégaud, Henri, Marquis de Plancy, French Secretary of State, v 5

Güns, defended against Solyman, ii 218, iii 107

Günther, Johann Christian, x 385

Guérande, Treaty of (1365), i 393 *n.*

Guercino, "King of the Campagna," iii 431

Guericke, Otto von, and the air-pump, v 715

Guérin, Gabriel-Christophe, ix 135

—— Pierre-Narcisse, Baron, xi 528

Guerra, Italian brigand, xi 531

Guerrazzi, Francesco Domenico, *L'Assedio di Firenze*, x 127; xi 78; and government of Tuscany, 90 sq.; 94; trial of, 337 sq.

Guerrero, Pedro. *See* Granada, Archbishop of

Guesde, Jules, French socialist, xii 119; 123 sqq.

Guest, Lady Charlotte, and *Mabinogion*, xi 352

Güstrow, recovered by Mecklenburg Dukes, iv 204

—— Duke of. *See* Mecklenburg-Güstrow

Guetaria, French naval victory near, iv 147

Gueugnon, feudal Courts in, viii 49

Gueux de Mer, iii 203-4, 206; 229-30, 237, 239-40, 284, 286, 493, 509

Guevara, Doña Anna de, and Olivares, iv 654

—— Antonio de, iii 548

—— Louis Velez de, iv 663

Guiana, Ralegh's expedition to, iii 562; iv 754; Dutch trade in, iii 633; Dutch colonies in, iv 709, 756; Harcourt's colony in, 755; the French in, vii 74, 79, 97, 108, ix 576, 653; Great Britain and, x 520, xi 667

—— British, xii 653 sq.; and Venezuela, 655, 687, 721; government of, 656 sq.

—— French, and Brazil, xi 655

Guibert, Jacques-Antoine-Hippolyte, Comte de, ix 280

Guicciardi, The, Valtelline nobles, IV 48

Guicciardini, Francesco, Florentine historian, I 147, 150, 170, 176, 184, 186, 200, 363, 368; II 1, 9, 21, 23 sq.; III 387 sqq., 457

—— Count Francesco, Italian statesman, XII 228

—— Piero, I 169, 176

Guichen, Count de, French naval officer, VI 453

Guidal, Maximilien-Joseph, French general, IX 14; 144

Guidi, Carlo Alessandro, Italian poet, V 69

Guidiccioni, Giovanni, Cardinal, and the Jesuits, II 653

Guidocerius, Agacius, Roman Hebraist, II 17

Guienne, revolt in, I 396; and the States General, 399; and the *Parlement* of Bordeaux, 401; administration in, 403, 407 sq.; English invasion of (1512), 479 sq.; revolts against the *Gabelle* (1548), II 96, 492; IV 613; and Condé, 614; restored to Epernon, 618

—— College of, III 69

Guieu, Jean-Joseph, French general, VIII 582

Guildford, battle of (1781), VII 228 sq.

Guilford, Francis North, 1st Lord, V 232

—— Frederick North, 2nd Earl of (Lord North), VI 377 sq.; 380; 427; 431; joint Paymaster of the Forces, 437; Chancellor of the Exchequer, 438; 439; 442; and the East India Company, 445, 570 sq.; and America, 447; 450; and Ireland, 455; resigns, 456; 457 sq.; 460 sq.; 463; Home Secretary, 464; 465 sq.; dismissed, 467; 468; and Irish affairs, 495, 498 sq.; 501; 581; VII 154; American policy of, 157 sqq., 161 sqq., 217

—— 4th and 5th Earls. *See* North

Guillemot (*Chouan*), shot (1805), IX 136

Guinard, Auguste-Joseph, X 491

Guinea (Bilad Ghana), I 9, 15, 17; slave trade in, 10, 14 sq.; colonising of, 11, 16; V 179; Brandenburg trade with, 647; 677; settlements in, 691 sqq.; Upper Senegal united to, XII 130

—— Gulf of, XII 807; 811

—— Coast, and the slave trade, VI 187; Great Britain and, XII 658

—— Company (French), V 445; (English), 691; VI 173, 533; X 260

Guinegaste, defeat of Louis XI at (1479), I 391, 413, 443; victory of Henry VIII (battle of the Spurs) (1513), 140, 457, 481

Guines, captured by French, II 93, 546; Treaty of (1520), 416; meeting of Henry VIII and Francis I at, 417; fall of, III 670

—— Adrien-Louis de Bonnières, Duc de, VIII 87

Guipuzcoa, and Spanish Succession, V 384, 389; fishermen of, VI 344; guerrilla warfare in (1794), VIII 440

Guirigay, El, Spanish journal, XI 550 sq.

Guise, siege of, II 92

—— House of, of Lorraine, Diane de Poitiers and, II 98; the Reformation in France and, 296–9; III 2, 16, 25, 33; characteristics of, 262; power of, 265–6, 289, 451, 483 sqq., 501 sqq., 550, 657 sqq.

—— Charles of Lorraine, 4th Duke of (Prince of Joinville), and Catholic League, III 45–50; 397; 517; 659 sqq.; 681; at La Rochelle, IV 133; rebellion of, 150

—— Charles de, Cardinal of Lorraine (*from* 1550), Archbishop of Rheims, II 83, 91, 93, 98, 294, 296 sq., 302, 574; at Council of Trent, 680 sqq.; death of (1574), III 25; 263; 268; 406; 489; 591

—— Claude of Lorraine, Count of (*afterwards* 1st Duke of Guise), II 47; 98

—— Francis, 2nd Duke of, II 87, 91 sqq., 98, 297; Triumvirate made by, 300; invasion of Italy by, 545 sq., 574; III 1 sqq.; takes Calais, 184; murder of (1563), II 683, III 5

—— Henry of Lorraine, 3rd Duke of, leader of Catholic League, III 8–44; murder of (1588), 45, 415, 452, 511; 170; and English plots, 288, 502

—— Henry II of Lorraine, 5th Duke of, Naples and, IV 482, 601, 657

—— Louis the elder, of Lorraine, Cardinal of, Archbishop of Sens (d. 1578), III 1

—— Louis the younger, of Lorraine, Cardinal of, murder of (1588), III 45, 452

Guitry, Huguenot commander, III 23 sq., 27, 52

Guizot, François-Pierre-Guillaume, X 43; and Louis XVIII, 44; 48; 50; and electoral changes, 51 sq.; and *Doctrinaires*, 52 sqq.; 55; 64; and new electoral scheme, 66; 67; dismissed from Council of State, 68; excluded from Sorbonne, 78; restored to his post, 93; writings of, 102, 513; 103; 167; and Revolution of 1830, 476 sqq.; 480; supports Casimir Périer, 487; Minister of Public Education, 489 sq.; 493; 495 sq.; recalled to office, 497 sq.; and Algeria, 503 sq.; and Molé, 507; and the coalition against Molé, 508 sq.; 511; 516; ambassador in London, 565 sq.; and Turko-Egyptian Question, 566 sqq.; Foreign Minister, 570; 572; Vol. XI, Chap. II *passim*; 16 sq.; and the Jesuits, 67; and the Opposition, 96; dismissal of, 97 sq.; 118; Education Act of, 130; 131; and Switzerland, 249, 252; 297; 305; and Spanish marriages, 554 sq.; 707; and China, 812; XII 683; writings of, XI 524, XII 831 sq., 849

Gujarat, landing of Turks at, III 117; the Dutch in, V 695; annexed by Emperor Akbar, VI 512; Peshwa's rights in, leased, IX 726; XI 742; Afghans at, 744

Guldberg, Ove Höegh, Danish statesman, vi 735; 749 sqq.; 754; fall of, 755; 756; viii 279; dismissed, 280

Guler de Weineck, Jean, iv 49; Grisons under, 50 sq.

Gullberg, Christian repulsed from, iv 179

Gum Coast, trade with, vi 187

Gumble, Thomas, *Life of Monck*, iv 559

Gunfleet, English fleet at the, v 181, 186; 183

Gunning, Peter, Bishop of Ely, v 97

Gunpowder Plot, iii 555

Gunter, Edmund, mathematician, v 709

Guntersville, Hood at, vii 524

Gunthorpe (Gundorp), John, Dean of Wells, books collected by, i 597

Gurkhas, treaty with, ix 718; war with, 732

Gurko, General, Governor-general of St Petersburg, xii 307; 336; 369; 388 sq.; 404

Gurney family, of Earlham, viii 765

Gurzno, victory of Wrangel near, iv 186

Gusinje, xii 392; acquired by Montenegro, 396; 401 sq.

Gustafsburg, Bernard of Weimar in, iv 367

Gustafsson, Gustaf, of Vasaborg, iv 178

Gustavus I (Vasa), King of Sweden, ii 228 sq., 245, 615; early life of, 603 sq., 621; accession of, 622; the clergy and, 624–7; iv 158–61; 166 sq.; 170; 173; 179; v 578; vi 771; 779

—— II Adolphus, King of Sweden, the Protestant Union and, iv 12; and Christian of Anhalt, 17; 26; 65; 68; 71; inherited wars of, 89 sq.; Danish negotiations of, 92; 99; 100; 103; and Hanse Towns, 105; and Stralsund, 107 sq.; in Pomerania, 114; concludes Truce of Altmark, 115; 117; and Richelieu, 140 sq.; 159; 171; 174; 176; becomes King, 177; character of, 178 sq.; Russian War of, 180 sq.; Polish War of, 182 sq.; home government of, 184; Prussian War of, 185 sq.; economic policy of, 187 sq.; 189; from 1630–2, see Chap. vi; 232 sq.; Bohemian policy of, 234; 243; 246; Grotius and, 250; Charles I and, 275; 277; 364; victorious advance of, 365; officers trained under, 366, 370, 375, 386; arbiter of war in Empire, 395; 401 sqq.; 410; 415; 418; 427; rivalry between Christian IV and, 560, 566; 570; 574; 575 sqq.; and Urban VIII, 676, 681 sq.; results of death of, 223 sqq., 568 sq.; 682, 696 sq.; Louis de Geer and, 725; schemes of, in West Indies, 759; v 338; 562 sq.; 577 sq.; 637; and Elector Frederick William, 639; vi 622; 761; 768

—— III, King of Sweden, Vol. vi, Chap. xxii; 354; visits France, 358; 676; marriage of, 741; 753 sqq.; *coup d'état* of (1772), viii 309, 315, 325, (1789), 326; 336; 399; murder of (1792), 400; 528;

and French Revolution, 788 sq.; and Catharine II, vi 678, ix 37; 43–5, 321; x 434

Gustavus IV Adolphus, King of Sweden, viii 789; relations of, with Tsar Paul, ix 38, 46, 48, 50; 250; 263; makes war on Prussia, 266; 289; renews war against France, 295; sues for armistice, 300; deposition of, 321; xi 677; 681

—— V, King of Sweden, xii 288; 290

Gutenberg, Johann, Latin Bible printed by, i 634, 639; 689

Guthrie, James, Scottish "protester," v 282

Gutierrez, Antonio Garcia, Spanish writer, x 241

Gutschmid, Alfred von, German archaeologist, xii 846

Guttstadt, Ney retreats from, ix 290

Gutzkow, Karl Ferdinand, German writer, x 410 sq.; xi 411; 414 sqq.

Guy, John, settler in Newfoundland, vii 52, 74

Guyenne. See Guienne

Guyomard, Pierre, French politician, viii 682

Guyon, Jeanne-Marie Bouvier de la Motte, v 88; 761

—— Richard Debaufre, general in the Hungarian army, xi 215

Guyton-Morveau, Louis-Bernard, French chemist, viii 269; ix 133

Guzman, A. M., member of the Committee of Insurrection, viii 265

—— Doña Anna *or* Louise Francisca de, *afterwards* Queen of Portugal, iv 651 sq.

—— Fernando Nuñez de. See Pintianus

—— Gaspar de. See Olivares

Guzman de Alfarache, by Mateo Aleman, iii 482

Gvadányi, Count Joseph, xi 422

Gwalior, captured (1780), vi 576; State of, ix 720; surrender of fortress of, by Sindhia, 726–7; xi 726; Ellenborough's policy in, 737; 738; 749

Gwyn, Nell, v 205; 266

Gyldenløve, Ulrik Christian, Danish admiral, v 580; 581

—— Ulrik Frederik, v 561; 569 sq.

Gyldenstjerne, Knud. See Odense, Bishops of

Gyllenborg, Carl, Count, Swedish Minister in London, v 612; vi 27; 104; 759

Gyllenhielm, Karl Karlsson, captured by Poles, iv 174; 185; Oxenstierna and, 569

Gyllenstierna, Christina, defends Stockholm against Christian II, ii 603

—— Johan Göransson, Swedish statesman, v 567; 569 sqq.; death of, 571; and Charles XI, 572 sq.

Gyöngyösi, Stephen, Hungarian poet, xi 422

Gyraldus, Lilius, *Historia Poetarum*, i 567

Gyulai, Count Franz, Austrian general,
xi 403
—— Count Ignaz, ix 259
—— Paul, Hungarian writer, xi 430

Haakon VI. *See* Hakon
—— VII, King of Norway (Prince Charles
of Denmark), xii 289 sq.
Haan, Jan de, Dutch vice-admiral, v 162
—— Johann de, supporter of Oldenbarneveldt, iii 651
Haarlem, siege of, iii 235; surrender of
(1573), 236; restored, 248; cloth and
linen trade at, 631; Remonstrants in,
651; William II of Orange and, iv 725;
and the Act of Seclusion, v 143
—— lake, drainage of, xi 664 sq., 668
Haas, de, Dutch painter, xii 249
Habibulla, Amir of Afghánistán, xii 490
Habington, William, poetry of, iv 760;
768
Habsburg, House of, iii 85; 386; 397;
450; 678; 684 sqq., 717 sq.; claim of, on
Naples, 465; and Bohemian succession,
iv 15 sq.; 129; 135 sq.; 141; French
policy and, 144 sq., 157, 369 sq., 372;
maritime designs of, 190 sqq.; Spanish
branch of, and Gustavus Adolphus, 208;
364; Pope Urban VIII and policy of,
365; 400; and Elsass, 405 sqq.; Hanse
Towns and, 414; 415; Protestantism
and, 416; 417; 425; 426; Polish question and, 429, 433; Mazarin and, 430
sq.; 623 sq.; 631; 640; 643; 665;
Paul V and, 672; Richelieu and, 674;
hostility of Urban VIII towards, 676 sq.,
679, 682 sq.; Frederick Henry and, 690;
Spanish branch of, 623–65; v 338 sqq.;
ix 248; 253, 309, 315 sqq., 341; Napoleon
and, 505; 591, 660
Hacke, Baden Minister, x 344
Hadamar, and Luxemburg, xi 674
Hadden Rig, success of the Scots at,
ii 455
Haddick, General, ix 61; 62
Haddington, seized by the English (1548),
ii 488; recovered (1549), 495; Scottish
Parliament at, iii 262; Cope at, vi 113
Haddock, Nicholas, Admiral, vi 66 sq.; 157;
236
Hadersleben, Prussians at, xi 167
Hadik, Count Andreas von Futák, Austrian
Field-marshal, vi 268; 292 sq.
Hadj, pilgrims from the, xii 452
Hadjach, Ukrainian fortress, v 600
Haebelin, leader of the Peasants' Rising,
ii 179
Häffelin, Baron Kasimir von, Bavarian
Minister in Rome, x 146
Händel, George Frederick, vi 19; 43
Hänlein, von, Prussian diplomatist, x 348
Häring, Wilhelm (Wilibald Alexis), novelist,
xi 417; 420
Häusser, Ludwig, German historian, xii 827
Haffs, The, v 629; 652

Hafiz Rehmat Khan, Rohilla chief, vi
569 sq.
—— Pasha, invades Syria, x 561
Hagelanden, Boreel van, Dutch politician,
xi 663
Hagelburg redoubt, vi 197
Hagelsberg, Girard at, ix 526
Hagen, Steven van der, iii 638
Hagenau, Compact of (1505), i 127; Con-
ference at (1540), ii 645; the Compromise
of (1604), iii 709; Mansfeld at, iv 78, 80;
406; Allied sovereigns at, x 45
Hagenbach, Peter von, i 390
Hagerup, G. F., Norwegian statesman, xii
286 sq.
Hague, The, Peace Conferences at (1607),
iii 540, 558, 640 sq.; Oldenbarneveldt an
advocate at, 624; Cloister Church at,
seized for Contra-Remonstrants, 650;
Buckingham at, iv 262; Concert, the
First, 432; Second, *ib.*, 541; missions of
Korfits Ulfeld to, 573 sq.; 587 sq.;
Frederick Henry at, 693; Henrietta
Maria at, 702; 714; Prince William II
at, 726 sq.; peace negotiations in (1613,
1615), 736; Sir William Boswell at, 749;
Coalition of (1672), v 43; murder of
the brothers de Witt at, *ib.*, 159;
"Association" formed at (1683), 49;
English embassy to, 138; Prince of
Orange at, 156; Treaty of Partition
signed at (1698), 384; Grand Alliance
signed at (1701), 397 sq., 403, 437; peace
negotiations at (1709), 422 sq., 427, 432;
Treaty of Guarantee (1681), 577; George I
at, vi 18; 26; 324; conference at (1760),
343; occupied by the French, viii 436;
Treaty of (1794), 543 sqq., 550; Prince
of Orange enters (1813), ix 550; risings
at, x 517; administration at, 525;
Supreme Court of Appeal at, 533; treaty
signed at (1842), 544; Peace Conference
at (1899), xii 133, 247, 715, 719 sq.,
722 sqq.; Peace Conference at (1907), 1,
4, 56, 133, 701, 716, 719 sq., 723 sqq.,
729; Permanent Court of Arbitration at,
12, 289, 617, 695, 723, 725 sqq.
Haguenau, Coigni's troops in, vi 240
Haicheng, Japanese army at, xii 589
Haidar Ali, ruler of Mysore, vi 549; 567;
576; death of, 469, 577; ix 723 sq.
Haidarábád, kingdom of, founded, vi 524,
532; the French at, 540; 541; Bussy at,
543; 546; 567; xi 734; 736; Outram's
defence of, 737; 743
—— Nizám of (1766), vi 567
—— Nizám of (1818), xi 727
—— Nizám Ali of, relations of, with
Tipu, ix 710; 714; with Cornwallis, 715;
power of, 717; war with the Maráthas,
720; power of, 721 sqq.; 731
Haileybury College, closed as Indian Civil
Service College, xi 751
Hainault, Philip the Good accepted by,
i 419 sq.; Margaret of Valois in, iii 84;

and the Treaty of Pyrenees, IV 620; Louis XIV and, V 36; 50; 200; Estates of, VI 652; Walloons in, X 521; agitation in (1828), 530; agriculture in, 731, 750; coal-mining in, 755 sq.

Hainault, William VI, Count of (*and* of Holland, Zeeland and Friesland), I 418 sq.

Hainköi, pass of, XII 388

Hainspach, Prince Henry of Prussia at, VI 705

Haiphong, captured by the French, XII 525

Haiti. *See* San Domingo

Hai-Yang, naval engagement off, XII 511

Hajji Dimitr, Bulgarian leader, XI 638

—— Loja, at Sarajevo, XII 400

Hakím, Mirza, son of the Emperor Humáyun, VI 512

Hakluyt, Richard, *Voyages* of, Spanish influence upon, III 548

Hakodaté, Japanese port, XI 829 sq.; opened to foreign trade, 833; 841; 843

Hakon VI, King of Norway, married to Margaret of Denmark, II 600

Hal, taken by the French (1691), V 59; General Colville at, IX 632

Halberstadt, see of, IV 91, 111 sqq., 407; Wallenstein in, 94; 111 sqq.; 407; bishopric of, V 642; taxation in, VI 221; Prussian forces near, 265; 266; 267; 269; 339

—— Christian, Bishop of. *See* Brunswick-Wolfenbüttel, Duke Christian of

Hald. *See* Frederikshald

Haldane, Richard Burdon, Secretary for War, and army reform, XII 60

Haldimand, Sir Frederick, lieutenant-general, Governor of Canada, IX 741; 747; X 687

Hale, John, Vicar of Isleworth, executed, II 442

—— John Parker, American statesman, VII 399

—— Sir Matthew, Lord Chief Justice, V 96; 201

Haleby, Ibrahim, Code of Law made by, I 98

Halepa, Pact of, XII 418 sq.

Hales, Sir Edward, Governor of Dover, V 233

—— John, *Discourse of the Common Weal,* I 525; II 490 sqq.

—— John, Canon of Windsor (*the Ever-memorable*), Laud supported by, IV 280; V 332; 744; 747

Halifax, founding of, VII 115, 121; Loudon at, 128 sq.; Boscawen at, 133; Howe retreats to (1776), 172

—— Charles Montagu, Earl of (2nd cr.), and the national finances, V 265 sqq.; and the currency, 269; and the Bank of England, 270; 274; impeachment of, 275; 461 sq.; 466 sq.; Earl of Oxford and, 470, 474; 700; VI 12; 45; 56

—— Charles Wood, Viscount, XI 14 sq.

Halifax, George Montagu Dunk, 2nd Earl of (3rd cr.), VI 424; 425; First Lord of the Admiralty, 427; 428; 430; and John Wilkes, 432; and the Regency Act, 434; 442; Lord-lieutenant of Ireland, 489, 492; death of, 444

—— George Savile, 1st Marquis of, V 136; 208; 210; 213; opposes the Non-resisting Test, 216; 222; 224; and Shaftesbury, 225; opposes the Exclusion Bill, 226; 227 sq.; and the municipal charters, 229; 230; and James II, 231, 262; dismissal of, 232, 260; *Letter to a Dissenter* of, 235, 239, 335; *Anatomy of an Equivalent* of, 336; 337; and Dykvelt, 240; and invitation to William of Orange, 242; at Council of Peers, 247; 249; and Revolution settlement, 249 sq.; 252; 255 sqq.; Lord Privy Seal, 258; 277

Halil Pasha, X 551

Halim Pasha, proposed as Khedive, XII 444

Halkett, Sir Colin, General, at Waterloo, IX 639

Hall, Carl Christian, Danish statesman, XI 696

—— Charles, *Effects of Civilisation*, X 780

—— Charles, American Arctic explorer, XII 815

—— Edward, III 374

—— Floris Adrian van, Dutch Minister of Finance, XI 662; 665 sq.; 668

—— Robert, Baptist, VIII 764

Hallam, Arthur Henry, XI 350

—— Henry, historian, XII 834; 836 sq.

Halland, ceded to Sweden (1645), IV 572; Treaty of Roeskilde and, 586; V 569

Halle (on the Saale), Catholic Confederation at (1533), II 220, 232; Cartesian philosophy at, IV 791; League of (1533), V 626; University of, 670, VI 226, IX 327, 411, X 355; V 760; military drill at, VI 216; Austrian troops in, 295; Blücher at, IX 532; meeting of Old Liberals in, XI 451

Halleck, Henry Wager, American general, VII 480 sq., 483 sq.; on the Mississippi (1861), 492 sq., 495 sq.; transferred to Washington, 500 sq., 506, 532; 583

Haller, Albrecht von, Swiss scholar, VI 625; 827; XI 260

—— Berthold, Zwinglian reformer, II 315, 327

—— Emmanuel de, French commissioner, VIII 637

—— Karl Ludwig von, Swiss writer, VIII 782; political doctrines of, X 160; conversion of, to Rome, 380; *Restoration of Political Science*, 370; XII 826

Hallett, Holt S., explores the river Menam, XII 797

Halley, Edmund, astronomer, V 719; 721 sq.

Hallier, Comte du. *See* L'Hospital

Hallom, John, in Pilgrimage of Grace, II 447

Hallue river, battle of, XI 607, 610

Halma, Nicolas, librarian to the Empress Josephine, XII 829

Halmstad, Diet at (1678), v 572

Hals, Frans, Dutch painter, IV 723

Ham, given up to France (1559), II 94; castle of, III 669 sq., XI 286

Hamah, Turkish defeat at (1832), x 550

Hamann, Johann Georg, x 386

Hambach, revolutionary demonstration at (1832), x 375, 377

Hamburg, English Merchant Adventurers at, IV 8; and Christian of Denmark, 89; 91; neutral, 99; and Spanish trade, 105; designs of Christian IV on, 194; negotiations at, 373, 376 sq., 378, 380, 383, 396 sqq., 402; blockade of (1643), 387; trade of, 419 sq., v 646; IX 41; Danish forces in, 48 sqq.; seizure of British envoy at (1804), 249; ceded to Prussia, 264; Mortier captures (1806), 282; Bernadotte at, 296, 324; 364; trade of, 374, 377 sq.; municipal patriotism of, 409; abandoned by Eugene Beauharnais (1813), 514; by Wallmoden, 520; isolated, 530; besieged by Bernadotte (1813), 544; a free city, x 341; and the Customs' Union, 373; Bank of, 746; cotton shipped to, 759; revolutionary movement in, XI 151; 227; shipping trade of, XII 156

Hamelin, Philibert, French reformer, II 292

—— West Indian buccaneer, v 691

Hameln, siege of, IX 263

Hames, Nicholas de, III 201 sq.

Hami, caravan route to, XII 793; 799; 802

Hamilton (Lanarkshire), recusants at, v 285

—— (Ontario), industries of, XII 612

—— the House of, III 275, 277

—— Alexander, American statesman and commander-in-chief, legal arguments of, Vol. VII, Chap. VI *passim*; 231, 244; and the Constitutional Convention, Chap. VIII *passim*; 316, 355, 692, 699, 730; x 280

—— Andrew, colonial governor, VII 48

—— Anthony, and Charles II, v 124

—— Emma Lyon, Lady, wife of Sir William Hamilton, VIII 648 sqq., 659; IX 229

—— Lord George, Earl of Orkney. *See* Orkney

—— Henry, Lieutenant-Governor of the North-West, VII 222

—— James, 3rd Marquis and 1st Duke of, at Stettin, IV 203; 209; 347; Scottish army and, 349; at Preston, 350, 507 sq.; Royal Commissioner, 498 sq.; presides over General Assembly at Glasgow, 500; 502; 503; "Plotters" and, 505

—— James Douglas, 4th Duke of, v 297; VI 92 sq.

Hamilton, John, Archbishop of St Andrews, II 558, 595

—— Patrick, Scottish Protestant martyr, II 555 sq.

—— Richard, in Ireland, v 307 sqq.

—— Sir William, metaphysician, VI 811

—— Sir William, British Minister at Naples, VIII 621, 631 sq., 650 sqq., 658 sq.

—— William Douglas, 3rd Duke of, v 291 sq.

—— Count, general, in Pomerania, VI 280; 287

Hamilton's Horse, VI 112; 114

Hamm, taxation in, VI 221

Hammer-Purgstall, Baron Joseph von, *History of the Ottomans*, XII 829

Hammond, Colonel Robert, Charles I and, IV 346

Hampden, Henry B. W. Brand, 1st Viscount, Speaker of the House of Commons, XII 38; 79

—— John, IV 266 sq.; ship-money and, 283; 287; 289; 291; Root-and-Branch petition and, 292; impeachment of, 297; 504

—— John, the younger (grandson of the above), v 229; 259

—— John Hampden Trevor, 3rd Viscount, British ambassador at Turin, VIII 559

—— Renn Dickson, Bishop of Hereford, XI 18

Hampshire, "Bloody Assizes" in, v 232

Hampton (New Hampshire), founded, VII 21

—— Court, Elizabeth at, II 535; Treaty (1543) with Charles V, confirmed at, 457; Treaty of (1562), between Elizabeth and Condé, 584; reception of Tyrone by James I at, III 611

—— Court Conference (1604), III 553, v 743, VII 12

—— Roads, the *Monitor* and the *Merrimac* in, VII 472, 496, 561; 530; peace negotiations at (1865), 536, 601

Hamsa, General of the Sultan Mohammed II, I 70

Hamza Pasha, Turkish envoy, I 82

Han river, Japanese gunboat in, XII 558

Hanau, besieged by Imperialists, IV 370 sq.; Pragmatic army at, VI 238; French occupation of, IX 408; incorporated in Grand Duchy of Frankfort, 414; Liberal movement at, XI 146 sq.; 229

Hancock, John, Boston merchant, VII 153

—— Thomas, II 480

—— Winfield Scott, American general, VII 652

Handasyde, lieutenant-general, in Scotland, VI 114 sq.

Haner, German reformer, suggests Marburg Conference, II 333

Hangchow, opened to trade, XII 512

Hangest, Charles and Jean de. *See* Noyon, Bishops of

Hanikoff, P., Russian admiral, VIII 481

Hanka, Václav, Čech writer, xi 654 sq.

Hankow, captured by rebels, xi 820; railway at, xii 505, 797; missionaries murdered at, 508

Hannart, Franz, Chancellor of Charles V, ii 156 sq., 171

Hannecken, General, defeated at Waghäusel, xi 221

Hannen, James Hannen, Lord, and the Behring Sea arbitration, xii 721

Hanoi, xii 131; French explorers at, 524 sq.; 796

Hanotaux, Gabriel, French statesman, xii 124; 343; 834

Hanover, Protestant Union in, iv 12; Louis XIV and, v 42, 54; 432; and Sweden, 607, 614 sq.; and the third anti-Swedish league, 610 sq.; 612; 666; Vol. vi, Chap. i *passim*; 73; and Mecklenburg, 206; 207; 213; and War of the Austrian Succession, 231 sq.; 235; and Convention of Westminster, 251, 254; 252; 260; and Seven Years' War, 263; 323; French in, 266; 318; France and, 334; Austria and, 339 sq.; 355; 405; Pitt and, 407 sq.; George III and, 416; 703; Alliance of, 59, 141, 147, 395; Convention of, 243; and the *Fürstenbund*, viii 282 sq.; Prussian troops occupy, ix 48; withdraw from, 50; French occupation of, 244, 249; Prussian desire for, 250; 251, 256, 262, 264; French army in, 252; Allies in, 263; annexed by Prussia, 265; 266, 270; offered to England, 271; Mortier invades, 282; seized by Bonaparte, 364; part of the French Empire, 408-9; British expedition to, 439; and Congress of Vienna, 587; 592, 597, 609 sqq.; and Federal Act, 650; 654, 657 sq.; and the Papacy, x 148; and Prussia, 341; connexion of, with England, 343, 354, 379; and the Germanic Confederation, 344, xi 220 sqq.; political system of, x 363; and Customs' Union, 373, 379, xi 53, 394; constitutional reforms in, x 374; separated from Great Britain, *ib.*, 674; revolutionary movements in, xi 60, 148; 167; and Frankfort Constitution, 218; 227; and Schleswig-Holstein, 337; 454; and Austro-Prussian War, 452; 455; anti-Prussian feeling in, xii 137; 147

—— Ernest Augustus of Brunswick-Lüneburg, Elector of, reversion of see of Osnabrück granted to, iv 408; becomes Elector of Hanover, v 55; 244; 662; vi 2 sqq.; 6; 19

—— George Lewis of Brunswick-Lüneburg, Elector of. *See* George I, King of Great Britain

—— Sophia, Electress of, v 251; and Act of Settlement, 275; 298; 474; 662; and Leibniz, 670; vi 1 sqq.; character of, 5; and English Succession, 6 sqq.; 12; death of, 17; 18 sqq.

Hanoverian Alliance (1725), v 550 sq.; 555

Hanovertown, Grant at (1864), vii 519

Hanriot, François, commander of *Gardes nationales*, viii 273 sq., cashiered, 342; 361 sq.; arrested and executed, 370 sq.

Hanseatic League, decline of, in late 15th century, i 292-3; quarrel of, with the Netherlands, 456; settlement of, in Bergen, 496; in London, *ib.*; loss of Novgorod trade to, 502; Protestant tendencies among cities of, ii 160; Reformation and social and political ferment in, 227 sqq.; the supremacy of the Baltic and, 228 sq., 614; naval rivalry of, with Denmark, 599; league of Dutch Republic with, iii 644; decay of, in the early 17th century, iv 8; 105; concessions to, by Treaty of Münster, 414, by Treaty of Osnabrück, *ib.*; v 623; and the German Order, 632 sqq.; 646; coercion of, ix 364; Hanseatic departments and the French Empire, 408 sq.; and *Zollverein*, x 379, xi 53; x 747; and tariff uniformity, xii 156

Hansemann, David Justus Ludwig, Prussian statesman, xi 53; 58; at Heppenheim meeting, 62 sq.; 159 sq.; 191

Hansen, Mauritz Christopher, Norwegian poet, xi 700

Hanyang, captured by rebels (1853), xi 820

Haouran, revolt in the, x 559, 561

Harbarovsk, founded, xi 273

Harbin, railway at, xii 344; 578 sq.; 587

Harbord, Sir William, and the Irish rebellion, v 311

Harborne, William, in Turkey, iv 729

Harcourt, François-Eugène-Gabriel, Duc de, mission of, to Gaeta, xi 121 sq.; 126

—— Henri I, Duc de, Marshal of France, ambassador in Spain, v 382 sq.; 384 sq.

—— Henri de Lorraine, Comte de, in Italy, iv 148; 149; in Catalonia, 599; 611; in southern France, 616; seizes Breisach, 618

—— Sir Simon, in Dublin, iv 524

—— Simon Harcourt, 1st Viscount, Lord Chancellor, vi 16; 18

—— Simon Harcourt, 1st Earl, Lord-lieutenant of Ireland, vi 494 sq.

—— Sir William G. G. V. V., Home Secretary, xii 36; 43; 46; Chancellor of the Exchequer, 49, 51

Hardee, William J., defends Savannah against Sherman, vii 527, 529

Hardenberg, Charles Augustus, Prince of, Prussian Minister, vi 728; viii 441, 544; ix 249 sq.; policy of, 255; 263 sqq., 282, 287 sqq., 296, 328, 329, 331; succeeds Stein at Berlin, 335; policy of, 510; 512; signs Treaty of Chaumont, 577; at Congress of Vienna, 580 sqq.; 648 sqq.; proposals of, 663; at Conference of

Aix-la-Chapelle, x 14; at Conference of Troppau, 27; 50; in Rome (1821), 148; and the freedom of the Press, 347; 349; political views of, 350 sq.; 352 sq.; and Wartburg festival, 364; and murder of Kotzebue, 365; and Grand Duke Karl August of Saxe-Weimar, 366; death of, *ib.*; xi 57; 59

Hardenberg, Friedrich Ludwig von (Novalis), x 160; 398 sqq.; death of, 401; 402 sq.; 405; 407; xi 49

Hardinge, Sir Henry Hardinge, Viscount, at Albuera, ix 467; x 611; in India, xi 738 sqq.

—— Sir John, Queen's Advocate, xi 337

Hardouin, Jean, French scholar, xii 817

Hardwicke, Philip Yorke, 1st Earl of, vi 75; 404; 407; 424 sqq.; and Prussia, 427; 428; 435

—— Philip Yorke, 3rd Earl of, Viceroy of Ireland, ix 706

Hardy, Sir Charles, the younger, Admiral, vi 376; 452; vii 128

—— J., French general, viii 476

—— Thomas, shoemaker, viii 760 sq.

—— Thomas, novelist, xii 13

—— Sir Thomas Duffus, medievalist, xii 835

Hare, Francis, Bishop of Chichester, v 429; 431

Hargraves, Edward Hammond, gold miner, xi 795

Hargreaves, James, inventor of the spinning-jenny, vii 374; x 735

Hari Rud river, and the Afghan frontier, xii 477 sq.

Harington, Sir John, iii 328, 611

Harkány, defeat of Turks at (1687), v 367

Harlan, Justice (U.S.), xii 721

Harlay, Achille de, iii 59

Harlay-Chanvallon, François de, Archbishop of Paris, v 20, 24

Harley, Robert, Earl of Oxford. *See* Oxford

—— Thomas, missions of, to Hanover, vi 13 sqq.

Harman, Sir John, English admiral, v 192 sq.

Harmignies, William of Orange routed at (1572), iii 232-3

Harnack, C. G. Adolf, German theologian, xii 847

Harneca, Dutch banking house of, vi 769

Haro, Don Gonzalo Lopez de, Spanish navigator, viii 290

—— Inigo de Velasco, Count of. *See* Frias, 2nd Duke of

—— Don Luis de (de la Paz), Duke of Carpio, iv 660; at Elvas, 661

Harper's Ferry, John Brown seizes (1859), vii 439; burned (1861), 454; Confederate camp at, 464 sq.; 475, 481, 530 sq.

Harpsfield, Nicholas, ii 501

Harrach, Baron Charles von, iv 73

Harrach, Ernest Albert von. *See* Prague, Archbishop of

—— Count Joseph, President of Imperial War Council, vi 204

—— Count, Imperial ambassador at Madrid (1700), v 381; 391 sq.

Harrar, annexed by Egypt, xii 439

Harrington, James, *Commonwealth of Oceana*, iv 544, vi 796 sq.; founds Rota Club, iv 546; 556; and Revolution settlement, v 252 sq.; 264; vi 801; 813; 820

—— William Stanhope, 1st Earl of, at Madrid, vi 32, 58; 61; 124; 126; 141 sq.; 145; 149

Harriot, Thomas, mathematician, v 709 sq.; 714

Harris, George Harris, 1st Baron, general, campaign of, against Tipu, ix 723

—— George F. R. Harris, 3rd Baron, Governor of Trinidad, xii 653

—— Sir James. *See* Malmesbury, 1st Earl of

—— Townsend, American Consul-general in Japan, xi 831 sqq.; 836; 842; 853

Harrisburg (Penn.), National Convention at (1827), vii 377

Harrison, Benjamin, President of United States, vii 660 sq., 665 sqq.

—— Thomas, regicide, iv 437; arrest of, 447; vi 799

—— William Henry, American general, vii 338, 340, 388; President of United States, 389 sq.

Harrison's Landing, Federal retreat to (1862), vii 479, 500; Lincoln at, 480

Harrow School, the New Learning at, i 582

Harrowby, Dudley Ryder, 1st Earl of, sent to Berlin, ix 263; leaves Berlin, 264

Harsch, Austrian Quartermaster-general, vi 289 sq.

Hart, Sir Robert, in China, xii 523, 527

Harte, Francis Bret, vii 747

Hartenau, Count. *See* Alexander, Prince of Bulgaria

Hartford, meeting at (1814), vii 348

"Hartford Wits," The, vii 741

Hartington, William Cavendish, Marquis of. *See* Devonshire, 4th Duke of

—— Lord. *See* Devonshire, 8th Duke of

Hartley, David, and taxation of the Colonies, vii 162

Hartwell, Louis XVIII at, ix 561; de Blacas at, 565

Harvard College, vii 727, 744 sq.

Harvey, Beauchamp Bagenal, commands "Army of the People," ix 701

—— Gabriel, iii 368 sq.

—— Sir John, Lieutenant-Governor of Nova Scotia, xi 759

—— William, physiologist, v 725 sqq.; 733; vi 792

Harville, L.-A. Juvenal des Ursins, Comte de, French commander, viii 416, 421

Harwich, dockyard at, v 169

Harwood, Sir Edward, Colonel, IV 696
Hasan, Uzun, Turcoman prince, I 78, 82 sq., 88
Hasanzai tribe, XI 743
Hase, Karl August, German theologian, XII 847
Hasegawa, Japanese general, XII 600
Haslach, Dupont retreats from, IX 254
Hasner, Baron Leopold, Austrian Minister of Education, XII 185; 187
Hasper, Peter, IX 355
Hassan, Muley, ruler of Tunis, II 69
—— Governor of Bosnia, slaughtered at Sissek, III 700
—— Abyssinian prince, XII 440
Hasselt, the Allies at, VI 246
Hassenfratz, Jean-Henri, French chemist, VIII 606
Hassenhausen, Davout at, IX 276
Hassenpflug, Hans Daniel, Hesse-Cassel Minister, XI 228 sq.; 232 sq.
Hastenbeck, battle of, VI 263, 341
Hastings, Francis Rawdon, 1st Marquis of, in America, VII 229 sq.; in India, XI 724 sqq.; resignation of, 727; 730; 743; 750; 753
—— Frank Abney, Captain, destroys a Turkish squadron, X 196
—— Henry. *See* Huntingdon
—— Warren, Governor-General of India, VI 445; 465 sq.; 471; 559 sq.; 564; Indian career of, 566 sqq.; impeachment of, IX 715 sqq.; and Free Trade, 733; XI 731; XII 5; and Tibet, 490; 798
Hastwell, Sir Edmund, English ambassador in Venice, II 383
Hatch, Edwin, ecclesiastical historian, XII 847
"Hats and Caps," The, in Sweden, Vol. VI, Chap. XXII
Hatsuse, Japanese battleship, sunk by mines, XII 587
Hattem, Pontiaan van, and Spinoza, V 754
Hatteras Inlet, captured by Federals (1861), VII 552
Hatton, Sir Christopher, III 332 sq.; 600
Hattorf, Philip von, Hanoverian Minister, VI 20
Hatzfeldt, Prince Franz Ludwig von, Governor of Berlin, IX 281; X 370
—— Melchior, Imperialist general, at Wittstock, IV 372; 389; sent to Poland, 429
Hauer, Baron, Governor of Galicia, X 462
Hauff, Wilhelm, German writer, X 406; XI 417
Haugwitz, Count C. A. H. Kurt von, Prussian Minister, VIII 534, 536, 543 sq., 635; IX 74; 249; policy of, 255; 259, 262 sqq.; arrives at Paris, 265-6; agitation against, 272; advice of, 282; 329
—— Count Friedrich Wilhelm, Chancellor of Bohemia and Austria, VI 639
Hauksbee, Francis, man of science, V 722

Haupt, Moritz, German philologist, XII 823
Hausrath, Adolf, German historian, XII 847
Hausruck, The, ceded to Austria (1815), IX 658
Haussen, battle at (1809), IX 349
Haussmann, Baron Georges-Eugène, Prefect of the Seine, XI 303
—— Nicolas, French politician, VIII 415, 422
Hautefort, Marie de, and Richelieu, IV 150
Hauteval, French political agent, VII 321
Hautpoul, Alphonse-Henri Beaufort, Marquis de, French general, XI 129
Havana, Spanish ships built in, III 520; VI 64; 142; 346; capture of, 369, 426; restored to Spain, 370; 428 sq.; 453; the U.S.S. *Maine* at, VII 676, XII 696; Willaumez at, IX 234; naval fortress of, X 248, 256; buccaneers at, 272; the trade of, 275; General Prim in, XI 566; XII 18
Havelberg, fight near (1627), IV 100; taken by Gustavus, 203; by Banér, 366; see of, 407, V 618; Peter the Great at, 612; Treaty of, VI 206
Havelland, drainage of, VI 225
Havelock, Sir Henry, major-general, at Cawnpore, XI 747 sq.
Haverman, Hendrik J., Dutch painter, XII 249
Haveron, Jean, Rector of University of Paris, I 636
Havet, Louis, and the Dreyfus affair, XII 120
Haviland, William, general, VII 143
Havlíček, Karel, Čech journalist, XI 656
Havre, Le, English expedition to (1562), II 584, III 3, 6; Condé and, IV 612; 613; development of, V 14; French troops at, IX 208; trade in, 242; XI 15; threatened by the Germans, 607; harbour works at, XII 102
Havré, Charles Philip de Croy, Marquis of (brother of Aerschot), III 245 sq.
Hawaii, U.S. treaty with (1884), VII 649; XII 666; and United States, 667 sq.
Hawaiian Islands, the United States and, VII 667 sq., 673
Hawick, Jacobite force at, VI 101
Hawke, Edward Hawke, Lord, VI 248; 250; and the naval operations of the Seven Years' War, 342a sqq. (in Vol. XIII); and the battle of Quiberon Bay, 342c (*ib.*); First Lord of Admiralty, 437; 444
Hawkes, Thomas, Protestant martyr under Mary, II 338
Hawke's Bay, Province of, XI 799
Hawkesbury, Lord. *See* Liverpool, Robert Banks Jenkinson, 2nd Earl of
Hawkins, Sir John, relief of Huguenot settlers in Florida by, I 55; III 295-7; 300; 313 sqq., 492 sq.; VII 2; X 253
—— Sir Richard (son of Sir John), III 801; VI 516; X 254; 278

Hawkins, William, Mayor of Plymouth (brother of Sir John), III 297; 493
—— William, in India, IV 741
Hawkshaw, Sir John, and Suez Canal, XI 638
Hawkwood, Sir John, English *condottiere*, I 265
Hawley, Henry, lieutenant-general, in Scotland, VI 115
Haworth, fortified, III 282
Hawthorne, Nathaniel, VII 745 sq.
Haxthausen-Abbenburg, Baron August F. L. M. von, XI 266; 274
Hay, John, Marquis of Tweeddale. *See* Tweeddale
—— John, Lincoln's private secretary, VII 577
Hayd, Khevenhüller's force at, VI 235
Haydon, Benjamin Robert, painter, X 721; the autobiography of, XI 362
Hayes. *See* Des Hayes
—— Rutherford Birchard, President of the United States, VII 645 sq.; XII 686
Haymerle, Baron Heinrich Carl von, Austrian statesman, XII 192; 394
Haynau, Baron Julius Jacob von, Austrian general, XI 95; 188; in Hungary, 209 sqq.; recalled, 215 sq.
Hayne, Robert Young, American politician, VII 376, 381, 412, 414, 418
Hayti, attempted occupation of, IX 749; abandoned (1798), 750; Bolívar in, X 293; Republic of, XII 7
Hayward, George, geographer, XII 802
Hazara, Sikh possessions in, annexed, XI 740
Hazrat, Russian advance on, XI 630
Head, Sir Edmund Walker, Governor-General of Canada, XI 768
—— Sir Francis Bond, Governor of Upper Canada, X 692; XI 755
"Heads of the Proposals," IV 343 sqq.; 353
Hearne, Samuel, at the Coppermine river, XII 814
—— Thomas, antiquary, XII 816
Heath, Nicholas, Bishop of Worcester and Archbishop of York, II 467; the first Prayer Book attacked by, 484; 501, 521; made Chancellor, 543; 564 sq., 568, 571
—— Sir Robert, case of Darnel and, IV 268; VII 34
Heathfield, George Augustus Eliott, Lord, VI 379 sq.; 452; VII 232
Hebbel, Friedrich, German poet, X 405; 407; XI 414 sqq.; 420
Hébert, Jacques-René, VIII 234; *Procureur Substitut*, 252, 262; arrested, 272 sq.; 338, 348, 356; executed, 362; *Le Père Duchesne*, 373
—— Michel-Pierre, French Minister of Justice, XI 42
Hebrew learning, in England, in the Middle Ages, I 590

Hecker, Friedrich Franz Karl, Baden radical, XI 61 sq.; 145; 163
Heckerens, faction in Gelderland, I 423
Heckscher, Johann Gustav Moritz, German politician, XI 166; 168 sq.
Hedenström, discovers New Siberia Islands, XII 795
Hedges, Sir Charles, Secretary of State, V 465
Hedin, Sven, XII 280; travels of, 798, 804
Hedio, Caspar, of Strassburg, Zwinglian, II 207, 328, 333
Hedjaz, pilgrims in the, XII 453
Hédouville, Comte Gabriel-Marie-Théodore de, commander of the 'Army of England,' attempts to pacify France, IX 3; 13 sq.
—— Nicolas-Jean-Charles, Comte de, French diplomatist at Frankfort, IX 414
Hedwig Eleonora of Holstein-Gottorp, Queen of Sweden, consort of Charles X, IV 578; 590; V 562; 564
Heeckeren, Baron Georges d'Anthès de, XI 472
Heemskerk, Jacob van, navigator, III 632, 639
—— Dr J., Dutch statesman, XI 667; XII 243 sqq.
Heemstra, Baron van, Dutch statesman, XI 666
Heer, Oswald, German botanist, XI 260
Heeren, Arnold H. L., German historian, XII 817; 823
Hefele, Karl Joseph von (Bishop of Rottenburg), XI 719; 722; *History of the Councils*, XII 848
Hegel, Georg Wilhelm Friedrich, II 714; VI 827; 836; VIII 773; X 361; 374; influence of, on German literature, 410; XI 365; XII 135; 155; 847
—— Karl, German historian, XII 850
Hegius, Alexander, head of Deventer School, I 435 sq., 461, 634; opponent of Luther, II 168
Hegner, Ulrich, Swiss novelist, IX 427
Hegyes, engagement at, XI 211
Heiberg, Johan Ludvig, Danish dramatist, XI 699
—— Peter Andreas, VIII 788
Heidanus, Cartesian philosophy and, IV 789
Heideck, George von, II 270
Heidegger, John Conradin, Burgomaster of Zurich, VI 615 sq.
Heidelberg, II 238; League of (1553), 274; surrender of (1622), III 575, IV 80 sqq.; Calvinist refugees in, III 703; University and Library of, 713; Erastian Controversy in, 758; theologians of, IV 5; Dohna at, 24; 77; the Catholic League at, 113; taken by Werth, 248 sq., 367; Cartesian philosophy in, 786; sacked (1689), V 56; University of, 628; ceded to Baden, IX 94; secret clubs at, X 375; school of romantic writers, 401 sqq.; political meetings at, XI 144, 162

Heidelberg Catechism, The (1564), III 154, 163, 646 sq., 653

Heilbronn, supports the Protest of Speier, II 205; meeting of princes at (1594), III 714 sq., 722; Protestant Union at, IV 11 sq., 28, 69; Mansfeld at, 67; Alliance of (1633), 142, 225 sqq., 234, 236, 243, 245, broken up, 246, 247 sqq., 365, 399, 401; Oxenstierna at, 682

Heiligerlee, battle of (1568), III 223

Heilmann, Josué, XI 901

Heilsberg, Charles XII at, v 593; Bennigsen at, IX 290

Heimburg, Gregor, opposition to Rome and submission of, I 624, 633, 680, 689

Hein, Pieter Pieterzoon, of Delfshaven, vice-admiral at Bahia, IV 704 sq.; captures Spanish treasure fleet, 706; death of, ib. sq.; 750

Heine, Heinrich, x 375; 405; 410 sqq.; influence of Byron upon, 726; XI 411; ballads of, 413

Heinse, Johann J. W., novels of, v 388; 399; 403

Heinsius, Anton, Grand Pensionary of Holland, v 257 sq.; 269; and Spanish Succession, 384 sqq., 432; and accession of Philip V of Spain, 395 sq.; and Grand Alliance (1701), 398; 403; and French overtures for peace, 417, 422 sq., 427; and Sweden, 591; VI 31; death of, 32

—— Daniel, Dutch scholar, I 579; IV 717; v 68

Heintzelman, Samuel Peter, American general, VII 476

Heke, Maori chief, XI 793; 795

Held, Gustav Friedrich, Saxon Minister, XI 149

—— Matthias, Vice-Chancellor of Charles V, II 235 sq., 238

Helding, Michael. See Mainz, suffragan-bishop of

Helen Glinskaia, consort of Vasili III, Tsar of Muscovy, v 487

Helena (Arkansas), Confederate repulse at (1863), VII 505

—— Grand Duchess of Russia, XI 617

—— of Servia, driven out by Mahmud Pasha (1457), I 70

Helfenstein, Count Ludwig von, killed in Peasants' Rising, II 187

Helfert, Baron Joseph Alexander von, German historian, XII 829

Helgesen, Povel. See Eliaesen, Paul

Heligoland, captured by England (1807), IX 368; and the Continental System, 374, 381; ceded to Great Britain, 654; ceded to Germany, XII 47, 167

Heliopolis, Turkish defeat at, VIII 617

Hellenic movement, of early 19th century, Vol. x, Chap. VI passim, 169–204. (For the earlier literary movement see Renaissance)

"Helluland," discovered by Northmen, I 50

Helmfelt, Simon Grundel, Baron of, Swedish general, v 569 sq.

Helmholtz, Hermann von, XII 785

Helmont, Jean-Baptiste van, chemist, v 730; 733 sq.

Helmstedt, Calixtus at, IV 424; University of, v 744

Helsingborg, recovered by Sweden, v 570; Danes defeated at (1710), 581, 603

Helsingfors, VI 761; Gustavus III at, 778

Helst, Bartholomaeus van der, art of, IV 723

Helvetia, project of kingdom of, IX 425

Helvetic Confederation, recognised at Osnabrück and Münster, IV 410

—— Confession, the First (1536), II 339; embraced by Lutomirski, III 74

—— Republic, VIII 639, 645; creation of, IX 95; coups d'état, 97–9; dissolution of, 104; liquidation of debt of, 426; effects of establishment of, XI 235 sq. See also Switzerland

—— Society, VI 625

Helvétius, Claude-Adrien, French philosopher, VI 826; VIII 9, 24, 26, 29, 32; farmer-general, 71; influence of, upon Bentham, x 595

Helvoetsluys, Rupert sails from, IV 463; Tromp sails from, 473; Herbert sails from, v 245

Hely-Hutchinson, John (afterwards 2nd Earl of Donoughmore), general, commands in Egypt, VIII 617 sq.; diplomacy of, IX 288; 693

Hembyze, revolutionary leader at Ghent, III 248, 250, 252

Hemerken, Thomas. See Kempis, à

Hemmingsen, Nils, IV 562

Hénault, Charles-Jean-François, historian, XII 817; 829

Henderson, Alexander, Covenant drawn up by, IV 317; at Glasgow, 501

Hendrik of Zutphen, Prior of Dort, I 460

Hendrikszoon, Admiral Boudewyn, at San Salvador, IV 705

Heneage, Sir Thomas, III 619

Henley, Joseph Warner, President of Board of Trade, XI 331

—— Robert. See Northington, Earl of

Henneberg, Berthold of, Elector of Mainz. See Mainz

—— Count William of, accepts the peasants' Articles, II 188

Hénon, Jacques-Louis, French Republican, XI 304

"Henrican Articles," The, III 86 sqq.

Henrico, settlement of, VII 6

Henrietta Maria, Queen of England, consort of Charles I, treaty of marriage of, III 577; marriage of, IV 129; 131; 258; 263; 266; reconciled with the King, 272; Prynne's Histriomastix and, 279; 303; 304; 306 sq.; at York, 311 sq.; 319; 323; 328; 331; 334; and France, 336,

338; 340; 488; Hyde and, 620; 642; in
Holland, 702; 773; v 93; jointure of,
95; 106; and France, 112
Henrique, of Portugal (Prince Henry the
Navigator), i 10; colonising plans of,
11–5, 17; death and will of, 15 sq.
Henriquez, Don Martin, Viceroy of Mexico,
iii 296
Henry IV, King of Castile, i 352, 354, 379
—— IV, King of England, i 10
—— VI, King of England, i 427, 464, 641
—— VII, King of England, the Cabots
and, i 33; siege of Boulogne by, 111;
Italian League joined by, 118; Britanny
and, 393–5; 450–5; Chap. xiv *passim*;
ii 555; iii 580, 749
—— VIII, King of England, i 51; Holy
League joined by, 136, 366; at war with
France, 140; 456; Chap. xiv, (ii) *passim*,
580, 644; ii 26; meetings of, with
Francis I and Charles V (1520), 42, 49;
52 sq., 56 sq., 67, 71, 75; invades France
(1544), 77 sq.; 220; allied with Lübeck,
229; the Lutheran Princes and, 238 sq.;
death of, 82, 260; reign of, Chap. xiii
passim; will of, iii 266; and Ireland,
580–7, iv 513 sq.
—— II, King of France, i 396; marriage
of, ii, 26, 67, 219; royal credit under,
65; 76; 78; accession of, 82 sqq., 86;
invades Lorraine, 87; and the German
Princes, 87, 271; 199, 269; invades Germany, 271; the French Protestants and,
292 sqq.; 486 sq., 492 sq.; Scotland and,
499; 505; Mary Tudor and, 526; 545
sq.; Elizabeth and, 560; death of, 296,
574; Council of Trent and, 670 sq.;
included in peace of 1547, between Emperor and Porte, iii 120; 166, 184, 263
sq., 286, 399, 477 sq., 482
—— III, King of France (Duke of Anjou),
projected marriage of, with Queen Elizabeth, ii 525; Duke of Anjou, iii 11 sqq.;
King of Poland, 85–95; King of France,
24 sq.; 26; and Catholic League, 31
sqq., 43 sqq.; 62; 170; 177; 238; 242;
and Emmanuel Philibert, 406 sq.; 414
sq., 430; 451 sqq.; 501; 510; murder of
(1589), 47, 511; 597, 695, 710 sq.; and
Poland, v 494
—— IV (of Navarre), King of France, i
525; iii 3, 11; heir after the Valois to
the French throne, 15; becomes King of
Navarre, 18; share of, in the religious
troubles in France before the death of
Henry III, 19–45 *passim*; Casimir's treaty
with, 711; won over by Emmanuel Philibert, 406; recognised by Henry III as his
successor, 45; contest of, with the League,
47–52, 68, 70, 385, 397 sq.; and Charles
Emmanuel, 415 sqq., 437; and Sixtus V,
451 sqq., 511 sqq., 540, 558; War of,
with Spain in alliance with the United
Provinces, 627 sqq.; and the Twelve Years'
Truce, 641–2; account of reign, policy

and character of, Chap. xx, 657–95; relations with the Protestant Princes of
Germany, 711 sq., 722 sqq.; the hero of
legitimism, 751 sq.; assassination of, vi
2; and the Grisons, 41 sqq.; anti-
Habsburg policy of, 40, 50, 56; 57;
effects of death of, 118 sqq.; 125; 129;
131; 137; accomplishment of designs of,
144; 152; 155; 624 sq.; 667; papal
succession and, 668; Paul V, Venice and,
670; v 72; 702; 744; vi 612
Henry I (the Fowler), of Saxony, German
King v, 617; 639
—— Cardinal, King of Portugal, iii 499
sq.
—— Prince, of Germany, at Peking, xii
504 sq.
—— Prince Consort of Holland, xii 248
—— d'Albret, King of Navarre. *See*
Albret
—— Prince (of the Netherlands), in
Luxemburg, xi 674 sq.; xii 244; 433
—— Prince of Prussia, in the Seven
Years' War, vi 262, 267 sq., 277, 279,
287 sqq., 297 sq.; victory of, at Frei-
burg, 299; 324; 326; 357; 632; and
Catharine II, 678; 696; in Saxony, 703;
705 sq.; 730; at St Petersburg, 668 sqq.,
731; 732 sqq.
—— Prince of Wales (son of James I),
iii 558; iv 625
—— Casimir, Stadholder of Friesland.
See Nassau-Dietz
—— Frederick, Duke of Cumberland. *See*
Cumberland
—— Patrick, Virginian patriot, vii 145,
149; character of, 151; 161, 164; threatens
violence, 169; 303
—— Colonel, and the Dreyfus affair, xii
121
—— of Costessey, *Commentary on the
Psalms*, i 587, 591 sq.
Hentzi, Heinrich, Austrian general, xi 208
Henzi, Samuel, Swiss revolutionary, vi 625
Hepburn, James, 4th Earl of Bothwell.
See Bothwell
Heppenheim, Nationalist assembly at, xi
62, 144
Herat, proposed Franco-Russian expedition
by way of, ix 48; xi 731; siege of, 732;
733; captured by Persia, 745; Sher Ali
at, xii 459; 465 sq.; Ayub Khan at,
475; 479; caravan route to, 793; 800 sq.
Hérault, Republican rising in, xi 137
—— de Séchelles, Marie-Jean, member of
the National Convention, viii 249, 342
sq.; trial and execution of, 363; 375
Herbersdorf, Baron Adam von, iv 76
Herberstein, Siegmund, Baron von, Imperial
ambassador at Moscow, v 487; 512
Herbert, Arthur, Earl of Torrington. *See*
Torrington
—— Sir Edward, iv 297
—— George, iv 280, 760; characteristics
of, 766 sqq.

Herbert, Henry, Lord (son of Earl of Pembroke), marriage of, to Lady Catharine Grey, II 510

—— Thomas, Earl of Pembroke. *See* Pembroke

—— William, Earl of Pembroke. *See* Pembroke, 1st Earl of

—— Sir William, III 600 sq.

—— Lord (1645). *See* Glamorgan, Earl of

—— of Cherbury, Edward Herbert, Lord, VI 791

—— of Lea, Lord (Sidney Herbert), Secretary of the Admiralty (1841–5), x 667; Secretary at War (1845–6, 1852–4), Secretary of State for War (1859–61), XI 2; 10; 21; 320; and the panic of 1859, 333

Herborn, University of, IV 789, 791

Herbst, Eduard, Austrian Minister of Justice, XII 185; 201

Herbsthausen, battle of (1645), IV 390, 597

Herculaneum, discovery of, VI 596; 600

Herculano de Carvalho, Alexandre, *History of Portugal*, XII 843

Herder, Johann Gottfried, VI 827; 830; 832; VIII 773 sq.; x 383; importance of, in German literature, 385 sq.; 387; 391; 396; 400 sq.; 404; XI 414; XII 817 sq.; 849 sq.

Hérédia, José Maria de, French poet, XI 515

Hereford, surrenders its charter, v 229

Hereros, The, rebellion of, XII 664

Heresbach, Conrad, II 236

Herford, abbey of, Elizabeth Princess Palatine and, IV 786; Labadie at, v 756

Hergenhahn, August, Nassau politician, XI 147; 198

Hergenröther, Joseph von, Cardinal, *Anti-Janus*, XI 719; XII 848

Héricourt, success of Swiss at (1474), I 390

Herigonus, Petrus, mathematician, v 710

Herjedalen, acquired by Sweden, IV 572

Herman, Jakob. *See* Arminius

Hermandad, in Castile and Aragon, I 352 sq.

Hermann, Gottfried, philologer, XII 821 sq.

—— M.-J.-A., President of the Revolutionary Tribunal, VIII 356 sq.

—— Russian general, VIII 662

—— of Hesse. *See* Cologne

—— of Ryswyk, Dutch heretic, I 460

Hermannstadt, XI 173; occupied by Russians, 206

Hermes, Georg, x 380 sq.

Hermogenes, Patriarch of Moscow, v 501 sq.; 506

Hermonymus, George, Greek scholar, I 597

Hernád river, Görgei at, XI 211

Hernandez, Julian, Spanish Reformer, II 406 sq.

Herrasti, Governor of Ciudad Rodrigo, IX 458

Herrenhausen, Treaty of (1725), v 550, VI 59

Herrezuelo, Spanish Reformer, II 407

Herries, John Charles, x 610

—— Lord (Sir John Maxwell), 4th Baron, III 278

Herrnhut, Moravian community in, v 762; John Wesley at, VI 82

Herschell, Farrer Herschell, Lord, XII 46; 86; 484; 721

Hersfeld, Tilly at, IV 86; Leopold William secures, 112; ceded to Hesse-Cassel, 408; Prussian troops at, XI 230

Hertford, Edward Seymour, Earl of. *See* Somerset, Duke of

—— Francis Charles Seymour-Conway, 3rd Marquis of, IX 270 sq.

—— William Seymour, 1st Marquis of (*later* 2nd Duke of Somerset), Charles I and, IV 305; in South Wales, 308; 313

Hertogenbosch, captured by Frederick Henry, IV 115, 691 sqq.; 698 sq.; captured by Pichegru, VIII 436

Hertz, Heinrich, and wireless telegraphy, XII 787

—— Henrik, Danish poet, XI 699; 701

Hertzberg, Count Ewald Friedrich von, Prussian Foreign Minister, VI 346; 648; 707; 709; 734; VIII 293, 322 sqq.; policy of, 329 sq.; 333; and Poland, 525, 529

Hervet, Gentien, French scholar, I 619

Hervey, Frederick Augustus. *See* Bristol, 4th Earl of

Hervilly, Comte Louis-Charles de, VIII 391

Herwarth von Bittenfeld, Karl Eberhard, Prussian general, XI 452

Herwegh, Georg, German poet, XI 50; 413

Herz, Henriette, VIII 773

Herzegovina, I 71; acquired by Turks, 73; XI 533; insurrection in, 636; XII 3; 9; rising in, 32; 172; annexed by Austria, 175 sq., 192, 211 sq., 378, 400, 427 sq.; 198; insurrection in, 382 sq.; 385 sqq.; Austria and, 389, 394; 390; Treaty of San Stefano and, 392; Treaty of Berlin and, 396 sq., 399 sq.

Herzen, Alexander, Russian journalist, and *Memoirs of Catharine II*, VI 658; and *Kolokol*, XI 625 sq.; XII 294; 296; 298; 302

Herzog, Hans, Swiss general, XI 257

Hesdin, surrenders to France, II 72; captured by Charles V, 89; retained by Spain (1559), 94; siege of, 420

Heselrige, Sir Arthur, impeachment of, IV 297; 449; Richard Cromwell and, 451 sq.; army and, 545, 547; Parliament and, 548, 550; 557; v 94

Hesse, Brandenburg and landgravate of, v 627; and the German Empire, XI 465

—— Agnes of. *See* Saxony

—— Landgraves of, refuse *Formula Concordiae*, III 704, 715

Hesse, Philip, Landgrave of, II 156, 169, 187; Peasants' Rising and, 189, 191; Protestant League formed by, 195 sq.; breach with Zwingli averted by, 204; Protest signed by, 205 sqq., 211, 213; at Schmalkalden, 215, 220 sq.; invasion of Würtemberg by, 224; 234, 236, 239; scandal of second marriage of, 194, 240 sq., 241 sqq.; won over by Charles V, 244, 252–9; surrenders to Charles V, 261; imprisoned, 268, 275; 329; Zwingli and, 333 sqq., 338; leader of Protestant Princes, III 157, 163; 193; and William of Orange, 210, 222

—— William, Landgrave of, II 270 sq.

Hesse-Cassel, IV 66, 85 sq.; represented at Brunswick, 96; V 414; 435; VI 240; 242; Convention of Westminster and, 254; 447; included in kingdom of Westphalia, IX 336; rising in (1809), 356–7; 411; military life in, 412; subsidy treaty with, 672; X 343; and Germanic Confederation, 344, XI 221 sqq.; X 346; reaction in, 363; and Customs' Union, 372 sq., 378; constitutional changes in, 374; the revolutionary movement in, XI 146 sq.; crisis in, 228 sqq.; 233; reaction in, 397; 450; 454 sq.

—— Amalia Elizabeth, of Hanau, Landgravine of, IV 370; concludes truce with the Emperor, 371, 379; consents to neutrality, 383; 390; 392; and Peace of Westphalia, 408; death of, *ib.*

—— Prince Charles of, VI 743; 755; 779 sq.

—— Prince Frederick of, XI 226

Hesse-Cassel, Electors of:—

—— Frederick William I, XI 60; 146 sq.; 228 sq.; 231; 233

—— William I, receives Mainz territory, IX 94; 273; deposition of, 278; at Congress of Vienna, 582; 610; X 13; 19; and the Diet, 346; 374; XI 209

—— William II, XI 60; 146

Hesse-Cassel, Landgraves of:—

—— Charles, V 55; 244; 403; VI 28; 59

—— Frederick I. *See* Frederick, King of Sweden

—— Frederick II, VI 425

—— Maurice, III 713; and Henry IV, 722; and Protestant Union, 725; and Gustavus Adolphus, IV 12; 25; at Heilbronn, 28; 66; 67; 69; and Christian of Halberstadt, 79; 82; 96

—— William IV, III 173 sq.; 241; 711; death of (1592), 713

—— William V, Gustavus Adolphus and, IV 195; at the Leipzig convention, 200; 204; 208; friendly towards Sweden, 225; 247; 249 sq.; Peace of Prague and, 255; 365; 368; and France, 370; loses his landgravate, 371; and dies (1637), 401

—— William VI, joins *Rheinbund*, IV 431 sq.; V 743

—— William VIII, VI 266

Hesse-Darmstadt, and Protestant Union, III 725; and Turkish grant, IV 10; joins France, IX 253; accedes to Defensive Triple Alliance, 597; X 343; and Germanic Confederation, 344, XI 221 sqq.; X 362; and Customs' Union, 372 sq.; and Hanover, 380; XI 60; revolutionary movement in, 144 sq.; 163; reaction in, 397; 450; 454; and Austro-Prussian War, 457

—— Prince George of, at Congress of Vienna, IX 582

Hesse-Darmstadt, Landgraves of:—

—— Ernest Lewis, V 403

—— George II, IV 114; and Saxony, 211, 252; administrator of Hesse-Cassel, 371; and Treaty of Ulm, 391

—— Lewis V, III 731; IV 33; and Union, 69; 80; 84

Hesse-Darmstadt, Lewis I, Grand Duke of, cessions to, IX 658

—— Lewis II, Grand Duke of, XI 60; 145

—— Lewis III, Grand Duke of, XI 145

Hesse-Homburg, and Germanic Confederation, X 343

—— Landgrave Frederick VI of, and Federal Act, IX 651

—— Prince Lewis of, IX 538

Hesse-Philipsthal, Louis, Landgrave of, defends Gaëta, IX 404

Hessels, member of "Council of Blood," III 216 sq., 251

Hessus, Helius Eobanus. *See* Eoban of Hesse

Hetairia Philike, Greek secret society, X 176; 178 sq.

Hetherington, Henry, X 682 sq.

Hetzendorf, Castle of, Queen of Naples dies at (1814), IX 384; Windischgrätz at, XI 188

Hetzer, Ludwig, German theologian, II 223

Heu, Gaspard de, II 297

Heuglin, Theodor von, African explorer, XII 811

—— Lutheran martyr, II 202

Heusenstamm, Sebastian von. *See* Mainz, Electors of

Heusken, American interpreter, XI 831; murder of, at Yedo, 841 sq.

Hewett, Dr John, execution of, IV 447

—— Sir William, Admiral, XII 441; 444

Hexham, General Wade at, VI 114

Heyden, Count, Russian admiral, X 199

—— Count, and Russian reform, XII 328; 355; 360; and the first Duma, 365; Stolypin and, 369

Heydt, August von der, Prussian statesman, XI 193; 230

Heylin, Peter, ecclesiastical writer, VI 798 sq.

Heynlin, John, Rector of University of Paris, I 637

Heyse, Paul, novelist and poet, XI 414 sq.; 417; 419 sq.

Heytesbury, William A'Court, 1st Baron, at Madrid, x 226; at Lisbon, 317, 321; at St Petersburg, 474; xi 731

Heywood, Thomas, *A Woman killed with kindness*, iii 380

Héze, Willem van Hoorn, Baron de, iii 245, 251

Hicks, Thomas H., Governor of Maryland, vii 453

—— William, general (Hicks Pasha), xii 440; 443

Hicks-Beach, Sir Michael Edward, *later* Viscount St Aldwyn, Chief Secretary for Ireland, xii 45; 46; Chancellor of Exchequer, 52; 74 sq.

Hidalgo, Baltasar, Spanish general, xii 259

—— Manuel, x 303 sq.

Hideyoshi, and Japanese invasion of Korea, xii 556, 564

Hierapetra, Italian occupation of, xii 423

Hierta, Swedish journalist, xi 685

Higgins, D., physician to Philip V of Spain, vi 145

High Commission, Court of, under Whitgift, iii 342 sqq.; and Laud, iv 278 sqq.; abolished, 291; v 234; revived in Scotland (1664), 283. *See also* Ecclesiastical Commission

"Highland Host," in Ayrshire, v 285

Highlands, iv 491; royalist rising in, 511

Higo, *daimiō* of, xi 832; 852

Hikoné clan, xi 851; 864

Hildesheim, see of, ceded to Elector of Cologne, iv 408; 412; Alliance (1652), 425, 431; designs of Frederick II of Prussia upon, vi 254; bishopric of, ceded to Prussia, ix 78; acquired by Hanover, 658

—— Adam Adami, Bishop Suffragan of, historian of Münster Congress, iv 401

Hildreth, Richard, American historian, xii 841

Hill, Benjamin H., Confederate senator, vii 605

—— General Sir Rowland, Viscount, ordered to watch Soult, ix 468; in Estremadura, 471; and the bridge of Almaraz, 472; at Madrid, 473–4; ordered to Salamanca, 475; guards passes of Roncesvalles and Maya, 479; victory of, at Saint Pierre, 481

—— Sir Rowland, and the Post-office, x 679

Hiller, Johann, Baron von, at Eckmühl, ix 350

Hillsborough, Viscount. *See* Downshire, Marquis of

Hilmi Pasha, Turkish Inspector-General, xii 426

Hilprecht, Hermann von, discoveries of, at Nippur, xii 846

Himalaya mountains, xii 793; exploration in, 798

Himbercourt, Sire de, Count of Meghem, i 440 sq.

Himeji, Japanese noble, xi 832

Hinckeldey, Karl Ludwig Friedrich von, Berlin president of police, xi 395

Hincks, Edward, Assyriologist, xii 845

Hindmarsh, Sir John, Admiral, Governor of South Australia, xi 792

Hindu Kush mountains, xii 793

Hindustán, growth of trade in, iv 712; power of Sindhia in, ix 719; British in, 726; 727

Hinojosa, Juan de Mendoza, Marquis de La, iv 626

Hinschius, Paul, and study of Canon Law, xii 847

Hinterpommern. *See* Pomerania, Prussian

Hiōgo, port of, xi 833; 841; 853 sq.; 855; opening of, 856; 859; xii 546

Hipler, Wendel, leader in Peasants' Rising, ii 184, 187 sq.

Hippel, Theodor Gottlieb von, German writer, viii 790

Hippolithus a Lapide, *pseud. See* Chemnitz

Hiroshima, xi 852; trial of Chōshiu at, 854; Japanese army at, xii 510

Hirschberg, linen industry at, vi 721

Hirschfeld, Karl Friedrich von, Prussian general, ix 526

—— Karl U. F. W. M. von (son of above), Prussian general, xi 221

Hirzel, Bernhard, Swiss pastor, xi 246

Hislop, Sir Thomas, General, xi 726

Hispaniola, French in, v 687, 688, 690

Histoire littéraire de la France, xii 829

Historische Zeitschrift, xii 827

Historisch-politische Zeitschrift, Ranke's, x 376

History, the study and writing of, Introductory Note, i 1–6; modern, sphere and scope of, *ib.*; Machiavelli and, Chap. vi *passim, especially* 199–218; Maximilian I and, 326; in Spain, in the late 15th and early 16th centuries, 381; Lorenzo Valla and historical criticism, 546, 602; ecclesiastical, the Magdeburg Centuriators, Baronius, etc., 608 sqq.; indirect effects of the St Bartholomew massacre on, iii 62 sqq.; Cosimo de' Medici and, 394; influence of the Renaissance on, 473 sq.; Gibbon and, vi 837: American writers, Irving, vii 741; Hickling, Prescott, Motley, etc., 744 sq.: French, of the Restoration, x 102 sq.; from 1830–40, 513 sq.; in the 19th century, xi 523 sqq.: in Hungary, 431; Italian, in the middle 19th century, 548; in Switzerland, in the 19th century, 261; *see* Vol. xii, Chap. xxvi, Growth of Historical Science, 816–50

Hitotsubashi, Japanese noble, Vol. xi, Chap. xxviii (2) *passim*

Hizen, *daimiō* (Japanese feudal lord) of, xi 825; 832; clan of, 863, xii 562

Hlawsa, John, Hungarian Reformer, i 340

Hoadly, Benjamin (Bishop of Bangor and of Winchester), iii 746
—— John, Archbishop of Armagh, vi 488
Hoang-ho river, exploration on, xii 798 sq.; 803
Hobart, settlement founded at (1803), ix 740
—— Robert, Baron (*afterwards* 4th Earl of Buckinghamshire), Governor of Madras, ix 721
—— Pasha, xi 636
Hobbes, Thomas, ii 691; iii 742; the *Leviathan*, 747 sqq., 762 sqq.; v 254; 331; 561; 751; 753; and Spinoza, 754; Vol. vi, Chap. xxiii *passim*; viii 711
Hobhouse, Arthur Hobhouse, Lord, and Sher Ali, xii 467
—— John Cam. *See* Broughton, Lord
Hobkirk Hill, battle of (1781), vii 229 sq.
Hobson, William, Captain, Governor of New Zealand, xi 793
Hoby, Sir Philip, ii 495
Hochberg, Countess von. *See* Baden
Hoche, Lazare, viii 351, 380, 391; and the Quiberon expedition, 392; commands the Army of the Moselle, 427 sq., 432; and the invasions of England (1796–7), 472 sqq., 497 sq., 508, 772; death of (1797), 482, 497, 508; at Neuwied, 498 sq.
Hochelaga, settlement of, vii 71
Hochfeld, fight at (1638), iv 378
Hochkirch, vi 271; battle of, 289 sqq.
Hochstädt, Styrum defeated at (1703), v 408; 410; French victory gained at (1800), ix 64
Hocquart, Gilles, *Intendant* of New France, vii 103
Hocquincourt, Charles de Monchy de, Marshal of France, defeated by Turenne, iv 613; by Condé at Bléneau, 616; 619
Hodges, Sir G. Lloyd, Colonel, commander of Portuguese force, x 326 sq.; 329
Hodgkin, John, suffragan of Bedford, assists in Parker's consecration, ii 572
—— Thomas, historian, xii 841
Hodgskin, Thomas, economic theories of, x 781; xii 758
Hodgson, Bryan Houghton, xii 845
Hodson, William Stephen Raikes, at Delhi, xi 747
Hoë von Hohenegg, Matthias, Court-preacher at the Saxon Court, iv 5 sq.; at the Leipzig convention, 200; 204
Höchst, battle of (1622), iv 81; Gustavus at, 208
Höchstetters, German trading company of Augsburg, i 523
Hög, Justus, at Münster, iv 402
Hoeks, supporters of Jacqueline of Hainault, i 420, 423, 445, 449
Hölderlin, Johann Christian Friedrich, viii 773; poetry of, x 396; 400; 403
Hoen, Cornelius von, ii 332 sq.

Höpken, Count Anders Johan von, Swedish Chancellor, vi 762
—— Baron Daniel Niklas von, Swedish statesman, vi 759
Hörschelmann, Governor-General of Moscow, xii 376
Hoeschel, David, editor of Philo, i 613
Hofer, Andreas, commands Tyrolese army (1809), ix 355; death of, 356; x 355
Hoffmann, Conrad, ii 314, 320
—— Ernst Theodor Wilhelm (Amadeus), x 405
—— Gotthelf, author of the *Kutschkelied*, xi 413
—— John Godfrey, and Congress of Vienna, ix 585
—— Weimar official, sent to Bernard of Weimar, iv 376
—— Imperial Minister, resident in England (1687), v 241; 243; 247 sq.
—— von Fallersleben, August Heinrich, German poet and politician, xi 412
Hoffraeus, Paul, iii 161
Hofmann, Alois, editor of the *Wiener Zeitung*, viii 776 sq.
—— Melchior, Protestant revolutionary, ii 224 sq., 229, 611
Hofmeister, Zwinglian, preaches at Schaffhausen, ii 327
Hofwyl, institute of Fellenberg at, ix 427
Hogendorp, Dirk van, reforms suggested by, ix 754
Hogland, Isle of, battle off, vi 778
Hohenelbe, Austrian army at, vi 706
Hohenems. *See* Altemps
Hohenfriedberg, Austrians repulsed at, vi 242
Hohenkrähen, capture of, by Swabian League (1512), i 321
Hohenlinden, battle of (1800), ix 67–8, 181; Napoleon's account of, 761
Hohenlo, Count, Dutch general (1586), iii 622, 625
Hohenlohe, Adolf, Prince von, Prussian statesman, xi 410
—— Prince Conrad, Austrian statesman, xii 203; 208
—— Georg Frederick von, with Thurn, iv 31; 65; ban pronounced upon, 68; 71
—— Gustav, Cardinal, xii 148
Hohenlohe-Ingelfingen, Frederick Louis, Prince of, ix 274; commands Prussian army, 275; at Jena, 276–7; at Ruppin, 279
Hohenlohe-Kirchberg, Friedrich Wilhelm, Prince von, Austrian commander, viii 408, 412, 419 sq., 423
Hohenlohe-Schillingsfürst, Prince Chlodwig, Bavarian Foreign Minister, xi 719; Chancellor of the German Empire, xii 166 sq.; 171
Hohenstaufen dynasty, in Naples, iii 464 sq. *See also* Frederick II, Emperor
Hohentwiel, taken by Bernard, iv 375

Hohenwart, Count E. de, Austrian states-man, XII 187 sqq.; 192

Hohenzollern principalities, annexed by Prussia, XI 227

—— House of, v 622; and Prussia, 616, 643; IX 330; 334

—— Anton, Prince von, Prussian states-man, XI 406

—— Eitelfritz, Count of, I 323

—— Frederick of, Burgrave of Nürnberg. *See* Brandenburg

Hohenzollern-Hechingen, x 343; and the customs treaty, 373; revolutionary move-ment in, XI 150

Hohenzollern-Sigmaringen, x 343; and the customs treaty, 373

—— Charles, Prince of. *See* Charles, Prince of Roumania

—— Leopold, Prince of, XI 462 sq.; 495; 571; 578; 648

Hokianga, French mission at, XI 793

Hokutai, captured by the Russians, XII 596

Holbach, Paul Henri Thyry, Baron de, VI 826; VIII 26

Holberg, Ludwig, Baron von, Danish writer, VI 739; XI 697 sq.; 700

Holburne, Francis, Admiral, 342b (in Vol. XIII), VII 128

Holck, Count Conrad, and Christian VII, VI 744; 746

Holcot, Robert, scholastic theologian, II 251

Holcroft, Thomas, trial of (1794), VIII 761

Holden, William W., VII 605; head of the peace party (1863), 609

Holdernesse, Robert D'Arcy, 4th Earl of, VI 406; 409; 417; 425; and Indian affairs, 542

Holdich, Sir Thomas, XII 722

Holgate, Robert, Bishop of Llandaff, *later* Archbishop of York, II 448, 452, 471, 521

Holinshed, Raphael, III 374

Holk, Count Henry, Imperial Field-Marshal, at Stralsund, IV 107; near Dresden, 219; 223; 231; 234; raids Voigtland, 235; 237

Holkar, Jaswant Ráo, IX 725; war with, 727 sqq.

—— Malhar Ráo, Maharaja of Indore (1811-33), XI 726

—— Tukaji, and Indian politics, IX 717-9; 720

Hollabrunn, Austrian army at, v 361; fight at (1805), IX 257

Holland (Province and State, *but see also* Netherlands), Philip the Good and, I 419; prosperity of, 420 sq.; power of gilds in, 428; III 16; countship of, accepted by Orange (1584), 617; im-portance of, 618, 620, 625; commercial prosperity of, 630-1; 641; relations of, with England, 644; and the exiled "King

of Bohemia," IV 70; represented at Mün-ster, 401; admiralty of, 469, 473; 691 sq.; Frederick Henry and, 694; 697; 700; Henrietta Maria in, 702; 705; King of Portugal and, 714; and Treaty of Mün-ster, 715 sq.; 718; (State of), philosophy and art in, 722 sq.; opposed to William II, 724 sqq.; hegemony of, 727; Descartes in, 779, 785, 787 sq.; (State of), shipping and trade of, v 11 sq.; relations of, with the States General, 137; States of, and peace negotiations with England, 140; and Act of Seclusion, 142 sqq.; financial reforms in, 145; 146; and restoration of Charles II, 148; and the young Prince of Orange, 148, 151; the "Eternal Edict" passed by, 152; 157; William elected Stadholder of, 157; French Protestant refugees in, 166; (and Netherlands in general), and Spanish Succession, 275, 377 sq.; and Scottish exports, 288; 296; 378; and Peace of Utrecht, 439; (Nether-lands), rise of Latitudinarianism and Pietism in, 742, 744, 753 sqq., 757; trade of, with England, VI 50; and Hanover Alliance, 59; 60; 124; and the West Indies, 186; 187; (Netherlands), and the Powers of Europe, 202; 217; 246; 248; 308; 318; and Brazil, 389; 407; and American trade, 448; and India, 546; 555 sq.; King Theodore of Corsica in, 609; 640; 703; Prussian intervention in, 709; 724; 773; Goldsmith and, 828; Anglo-Russian expedition in, IX 41; Allied forces in, 56; relations of, with France, 88-91, 252, 391; annexation of, 141; naval losses of, 243; Napoleon and, 364, 369 sqq., 416 sq.; the French abandon, 550; and Congress of Vienna, 605; Belgium incorporated with, 655, 668; 670; Vol. x, Chap. XVI *passim*; agriculture in, 730; roads and canals in, 745; common lands in, 749; emigration from, 762

Holland, modern Kingdom of, officially Kingdom of the Netherlands, Vol. XI, Chap. XVI (1), Holland (1839-70), 661-8; Chap. XXVII (3), The English and Dutch in S. Africa (1815-70), 778-89; Vol. XII, Chap. IX, The Low Countries (1870-1905), 243-50; and Siam, 534; historical re-search in, 816. *See also* **Netherlands** *and the* Batavian Republic

—— Henry Fox, Lord, VI 75; 403 sqq.; 423; 424; 428; created Lord Holland, 429; 435

—— Henry Richard Vassall Fox, 3rd Baron, VI 472; letters of Fox to, IX 676; x 512; 581 sq.; 600; and the Re-form Bill, 610; 679

—— Sir Henry Rich, 1st Earl of, in Paris, IV 263; and Hull, 294; 349

Holles, Denzil, 1st Baron Holles of Ifield, IV 281; impeachment of, 297; 343; am-bassador at Paris, v 109; 112

Hollis, Thomas, VIII 755

Hollond, John, naval writer, iv 462
—— John, Governor of Madras, ix 710; 715
Holm, Adolf, German historian, xii 845
Holman, James, traveller, xii 794
Holmby House, Charles I at, iv 340, 342
Holmers, Jan Frederik, Dutch writer, xi 676
Holmes, Charles, Rear-Admiral, vii 139
—— Oliver Wendell, vii 746
—— Sir Robert, English admiral, v 108; African expedition of, 149, 179; 206
—— Theophilus H., Confederate general, vii 505
Holowczyn, battle of (1708), v 598
Holstein, duchy of, at war with Denmark, ii 599; Christian IV and, iv 86, 97, 109; invaded by Wallenstein, 101 sq.; Swedes in, 387, 571 sq., 584; Danish army in, v 587; 609; vi 736; 744; Bernadotte in, ix 296-7, 303, 324; and Federal Act, 650; and Germanic Confederation, 659, x 344, xi 223; 224; German troops in, 439; ceded by Denmark, 442; Austria and, 449; Prussian troops in, 450. *See also* Schleswig-Holstein
—— House of, refuses *Formula Concordiae*, iii 704
—— Adolphus, Duke of, iii 151
—— Frederick I, Duke of. *See* Frederick I, King of Denmark and Norway
—— Frederick II, Duke of, administers the see of Hildesheim, iii 157
Holstein-Gottorp, v 403; Charles XII and, 588; 611; Denmark and, 560 sq.; 579 sqq.
—— House of, and Sweden, v 562; vi 741 sqq., 761 sq.
Holstein-Gottorp, Dukes of:—
—— Adolphus, at Magdeburg, iv 202; death of, 205
—— Adolphus Frederick. *See* Adolphus Frederick, King of Sweden
—— Charles Frederick, v 550 sqq.; 614; vi 28; 37; 39; 741
—— Christian Albert, v 568
—— Frederick III, iv 98; and the Emperor, 99; and Torstensson, 387, 571; 578; King Frederick III and, 584; Treaty of Roeskilde and, 586 sq.; v 513; 558
—— Frederick IV, v 579 sqq.; marriage of, 581, 587; death of, 581, 592
Holstein-Gottorp, Anne (Petrovna), Duchess of, v 547; 550; 552 sq.; vi 311, 658
—— Prince Carl August of, vi 657 sqq.
—— Hedwig Sophia, Duchess of, v 580; 587
—— Princess Johanna Elizabeth of. *See* Anhalt-Zerbst, Princess Elizabeth of
—— John Frederick of. *See* Bremen, Archbishop of
Holstein-Sonderburg-Plön, John Adolphus, Duke of, v 569; 579

Holt, Joseph, American Postmaster-General and Secretary of War, vii 447 sq.
—— William, iii 287
—— Irish leader in Wexford, ix 701
Holum, Jon Aresen, Bishop of, leader of Icelandic revolt, ii 621
Holwell, John Zephaniah, Governor of Bengal, vi 552; 559
Holy Alliance, The, of 1815, ix 664 sqq.; x 9 sq.; 16 sqq.; 22; 39; principle of, repudiated by France (1830), 120; Cardinal Consalvi and, 136; 188; 195; and Spain, 211, 226; President Monroe and, 309; 371; 479 sq.; 725
—— Brotherhood. *See* Hermandad
"Holy Discipline," controversy concerning, iii 757
Holy League, The (1511), i 198, 319, 366, 479, 486; of Cognac (1526), ii 24
Holyoake, George Jacob, and cooperation, xii 740
Holyrood, Mary Stewart at, iii 273-4; Chapel Royal of, v 290 sq.; Catholic press at, *ib.*; James VIII proclaimed at, vi 113
Holzapfel. *See* Melander
Holzhausen, fighting at (1813), ix 539
Homburg, and Germanic Confederation, xi 223
Home, Duncan, at Delhi, xi 746
Home Government Association, in Ireland, xii 73
—— Rule. *See* Ireland
—— Rule League, in Ireland, xii 73
Homestead (Penn.), strike at, vii 707
Homonnay, Drugeth de, enters Upper Hungary with Polish Cossacks, iv 31
Hompesch, Baron Ferdinand de, ix 40
Homs, Turkish defeat at (1832), x 550
Honau, battle at, xi 251
Hondschoote, battle of, viii 431
Honduras, vi 64; disputes in, 66; foundation of, 183; 365; 367; British rights in, 370; 377; 380; 429; logwood cutting in, 464, 471; xii 672; Great Britain and, 686
—— British, government of, xii 656 sq.
Hone, William, trial of, x 579 sq.
Hongkong, xi 805 sq.; 808; ceded to Great Britain, 809; 816; 819
—— and Shanghai Banking Corporation, xii 513
Honoratus, St, and the Insulani, i 534
Honorius III (Cencio Savelli), Pope, v 629
Hontheim, Johann Nikolaus von (Justinus Febronius), vi 636; x 6; 145; 148; doctrines of, 157 sq.; death of, 158; 159
Hood, John Bell, Confederate general, vii 521 sqq.; at Spring Hill, 524; at Nashville, 525
—— Sir Samuel Hood, 1st Viscount, Admiral, vi 453 sq.; occupies Toulon, viii 348, 457 sq.; 454
—— Thomas, poems of, xi 353
Hooft, Pieter Corneliszoon, Muiden Circle and, iv 719 sqq.; writings of, 721

Hooft, Dutch politician, v 164

Hoogendorp, Gisbert Charles van, x 517 sq.; 522

Hoogerbeets, sent by Holland to support Utrecht, III 651 sq., 655

Hooghley, factory at, v 698; sack of, VI 532; taken by the English, 552; 556

Hooglide, Austrian defeat at, VIII 435

Hoogstraten, Antony van Lalaing, Count of, III 194; 204; 210 sqq.; 217 sqq.; died (1568), 224

—— Jacob van, Dominican, I 460

Hoogvorst, Emanuel van den Linden, Baron de, x 535 sqq.

—— Joseph van den Linden, Baron de, x 535 sq.

Hook of Holland, waterway through, XI 666

Hooke, Nathaniel, French agent in Scotland, VI 91 sq.

—— Nathaniel, historian, XII 817

—— Robert, physicist, v 722; 728; 735; 739

Hooker, Joseph, commands the Army of the Potomac, VII 484 sqq.; at Chattanooga, 510 sqq.

—— Sir Joseph Dalton, XII 773

—— Richard, III 329, 347 sq.; 742; 757; 762; 768; VI 795; 801; XII 707 sqq.

Hooper, John, Bishop of Gloucester, II 497 sq.; promoted to see of Gloucester, 502; 539; trial and death of, 563

Hoorn, shipbuilding at, III 631

—— Philippe de Montmorency, Count of, proposes league against Granvelle, III 192; 194; 195; 197; 200 sqq., 215 sqq.; arrest of, 215; trial of, 219; execution of, 220, 222 sqq.

—— Dowager Countess of, III 218, 227-8

Hop, Jacob, Dutch envoy at Vienna, v 389 sq.

—— van der, Dutch commander, VIII 287

Hope, Sir James, Admiral, XI 843

—— Sir James Archibald, General, IX 358

Hopes, Amsterdam financial house of the, x 743

Hopf, Karl, German historian, XII 845

Hopkins, Stephen, legal arguments of, as to British and American relations, Vol. VII, Chap. VI *passim*

Hopkinson, Francis, American politician, VII 724

Hopton, Ralph, 1st Baron, IV 304; in Cornwall, 308; 311 sqq.; 315; 318; defeated at Cheriton, 322; at Exeter, 334; v 746

Horatian Ode of Marvell, IV 775

Hori, Japanese Commissioner for Foreign Affairs, XI 844

Horki, Charles XII at, v 599

Hormuz, commercial importance of, I 28; Portuguese factory at, 32

Horn, Cape, route discovered, IV 713

—— Arvid, Count, Swedish statesman, v 542; 555; 593; Chancellor, VI 759 sq.

—— Bengt, Swedish general, v 570

—— Evert, killed at Pskoff, IV 181

Horn, Gustaf Karlsson, Count of Björneborg, Swedish general, besieges Dorpat, IV 185; takes Kolberg, 196; 199; in Franconia, 208; captures Bamberg, 213; 223; career of, 227 sqq.; in southern Swabia, 238; at Augsburg, 244; at Nördlingen, 245; 387 sq.; 571

—— Klas Kristersson, death of, IV 163

Horne, John. *See* Tooke, John Horne

—— Robert, Bishop of Winchester, II 568, 586, 593 sq.

Hornemann, Friedrich, African traveller, XII 806 sq.

Horner, Francis, and *Edinburgh Review*, IX 687; and the currency, 689

Horrocks, Jeremiah, astronomer, v 714

Horsens, proposed conference at, IV 567

Horsley, Samuel, Bishop of St Asaph, VIII 763 sq.

Horsman, Edward, politician, XI 339

Horton, Anne (*née* Luttrell), marries the Duke of Cumberland, VI 445

—— Thomas, at St Fagan's, IV 349

Horváth, Michael, Bishop of Csanad, XI 209; 214; 431; Hungarian Minister of Justice, XII 189

—— de Pálóc, Adam, Hungarian poet, XI 422

Hosemann, Andreas. *See* Osiander

Hosier, Francis, Admiral, VI 60; 142; 147

Hosius (Osio) Stanislaus, Cardinal, Bishop of Kulm and Ermeland (Warmia), II 631, 636 sq.; at Council of Trent, 676, 682; III 79, 81-4

Hosiwu, engagement at, XII 520

Hostalrich, captured by Augereau (1810), IX 457

Hoste, Sir William, 1st Baronet, naval captain, IX 239

Hôtel de Rambouillet, IV 777

Hôtel des Invalides, established, v 19; rioters at (1789), VIII 164

Hotham, Sir Charles, British envoy at Berlin, VI 210 sqq.

—— Sir Henry, vice-admiral, VIII 459 sq.; IX 226

—— Sir John, secures Hull, IV 299; 301; arrest of, 313

—— William Hotham, Lord, admiral, VI 451

Hotman, Charles, III 42, 58 sq.

—— François, *Letter sent to the Tiger of France*, II 297, III 70; *Franco-Gallia*, 62, 760

Hotta, Japanese Councillor of State, XI 831 sqq.; 836; dismissal of, 837

Hottentots, in Cape Colony, XI 780; rebellion of, XII 664

Hottinger, Nicholas, II 319

Hottinguer, French political agent, VII 321

Hotze, David van, Austrian general, VIII 661

Houchard, Jean-Nicolas, commands the Army of the North, VIII 346; executed (1793), 357; captures Frankfort (1792),

414; 424; succeeds Kilmaine (1793), 430 sq.

Houdon, Jean-Antoine, ix 134

Hough, John, President of Magdalen College, Oxford, v 238

Houghton, Daniel, African traveller, xii 806

—— John, Prior of the Charter House, ii 442

Hougoumont, and the field of Waterloo, ix 632 sqq.

Houssaye, Henry, French historian, xii 834

Houten, Samuel van, Dutch statesman, xii 246 sq.

Houtman, Cornelis, iii 632; Eastern expedition of, iv 729

Hoverbeck, Freiherr von, German politician, xii 146

Howard, family of, iii 559–60, 566. *See also* Arundel, Carlisle, Norfolk, Northampton, Nottingham, Suffolk and Surrey, Earls *or* Dukes of

—— Catharine, Queen of England. *See* Catharine (Howard), Queen of England

—— Charles, Earl of Carlisle. *See* Carlisle

—— Lord Edward, i 479; killed in attack on French fleet (1513), 480 sq.

—— Philip Thomas, Cardinal, v 235

—— Lord Thomas, *afterwards* Earl of Surrey. *See* Norfolk, 2nd Duke of

—— Lord Thomas (son of 2nd Duke of Norfolk), attainder and death of, ii 445

—— Lord Thomas, 1st Earl of Suffolk, 1st Baron Howard de Walden. *See* Suffolk

—— William, Viscount Stafford. *See* Stafford

—— of Effingham, Charles, 2nd Lord, 1st Earl of Nottingham. *See* Nottingham, Earl of

—— of Effingham, Francis, Baron, Governor of Virginia, vii 9 sq.

—— of Effingham, William, 1st Baron, Lord Admiral, ii 513; Governor of Calais, 517; defends London against Wyatt, 528

—— of Escrick, William, 3rd Baron, v 213; 229 sq.

—— John, philanthropist, influence of, ix 693

—— Oliver Otis, American general, vii 526

—— Rhode Island loyalist, legal arguments of, as to British and American relations, Vol. vii, Chap. vi *passim*

Howden, John Hobart Caradoc, Lord, mission of, to Buenos Ayres, xii 681

Howe, George Augustus, 3rd Viscount, vii 134 sq.

—— John, puritan divine, and Declaration of Indulgence, v 238; 332; 335

—— John Grubham, M.P., v 259

—— Joseph, Nova Scotia statesman, xi 762

Howe, Richard Howe, 1st Earl, English admiral, relieves Gibraltar, vi 379 sq., 452; and American War, 448, 451; First Lord of Admiralty, 468; vii 212; viii 454, 465 sqq.; and mutiny at Spithead, 476 sqq.; naval victory of (June 1, 1794), ix 226; 737

—— Robert, American general, vii 218

—— William, 5th Viscount, vii 166, 168, 172; character of, 211, and American campaign (1776–8), 212 sqq., 217

Howick, Viscount (1806). *See* Grey, Charles, 2nd Earl

—— Henry George Grey, Viscount (1839). *See* Grey, 3rd Earl

Howley, William, Archbishop of Canterbury, x 679

Hoya, Count Johann von, commander of forces of Lübeck, ii 230

Hoyos-Sprinzenstein, Count Johann Ernst von, Governor of Vienna, xi 175

Hrabowsky, Baron Johann, Hungarian general, xi 180; 184

Hradschin, The (at Prague), iii 701

Hsien Fêng, Chinese Emperor, xii 501; 503

Hsiuyen, Chinese retreat from, xii 511; 587

Hua, Eustache-Antoine, French deputy, viii 213

Huber, Alfons, German historian, xii 829

—— Aloysius, French revolutionary, x 501; xi 104; 109

Hubertusburg, Peace of, vi 300, 346, 428, 430, 663, 702, 710, 713, 715, 720, 725, 729

Hubmaier, Balthasar, reformer, ii 178

Huc, Evariste, in Tibet, xii 797 sq.; 803 sq.; 808

Hudde, Johan, opposes the Prince of Orange, v 165

Huddersfield, riots at, x 578, xi 2

Huddlestone, John, and Charles II, v 230

Hudelist, Josef von, at Congress of Vienna, ix 583

Hudson, River, fighting on (1776), vii 212; 220; steamboats on, 351; 360

—— Michael, royalist divine, vi 798

Hudson's Bay, settlements on, v 442; French occupation of, vii 89; railway schemes and, xii 608

—— Bay Company, v 63; vi 179; ix 747; xii 608 sqq.

—— Bay Territory, ceded to Canada, xi 776; 777

Hué, French occupation of, xii 526

Hübner, Count Joseph Alexander von, xi 190; Austrian ambassador at Paris, 381

Hühnerwasser, Austrian repulse at, xi 453

Hüningen, French army at, v 406; 425; besieged by Wrede (1813), ix 544; fortifications of, rased, 664

Huescar, Duke of, mission of, to Paris, vi 161; 364

Huet, Peter Daniel (*afterwards* Bishop of Avranches), I 616

Hughes, Sir Edward, Admiral, VI 454; 469; 577

—— Thomas, and cooperation, XII 740

Hugo, Gustav, German historian, XII 818

—— Victor, VI 828; 831 sq.; 834; X 88; 101 sq.; 130; 499; 514 sq.; and Sir Walter Scott, 726; XI 24; 127; and Montalembert, 131; 134; and *Coup d'état* of December, 136; 365; influence of, on Hungarian literature, 427; the writings of, 507 sqq., 515, 519, 522, 528, XII 831

Hugonet, Chancellor (of Mary of Burgundy), I 440 sq.

Hugue, Clovis, French socialist, XII 124

Huguenin, Sulpice, revolutionary, VIII 234

Huguenots, *see* Vol. II, Chap. IX, The Reformation in France, 280–304; 346 sqq.; *see* Vol. III, Chap. I, Wars of Religion in France, 1–52; Chap. II, French Humanism, *passim*, 53–72; Chap. XX, Henry IV of France, *passim*, 657–95; for the theoretical side of the movement *see* Chap. XXII *especially* 760 sqq.; embassy of, to Germany, 164 sq., 177; appealed to by William of Orange, 224; 265; and Savoy, 404 sq.; 491 sqq., 501 sqq.; later relations with German Protestants, 710 sqq.; Ranke's view of political position of, IV 691; Revocation of Edict of Nantes and persecution of, V 21 sqq., 233; 74; 116; Bossuet and, 86 sq.; in the Netherlands, 166; and England, 233; in Denmark, 579; in Brandenburg, 646; 685; VI 163; 188; in America, VII 55, 88, 114; VIII 52, 56, 108 sq., 141, 194, 734; Napoleon I and, IX 203 sq.

Hugues, Bezanson, Genevese statesman, II 362

—— Victor, recaptures Guadeloupe, IX 749

Huguet, Antoine, Constitutional Bishop, VIII 505

Hui-li-chau, Colborne Baber at, XII 797

Hulin, Pierre-Augustin, Comte, General, IX 31; 144

Hull, the Commons and, IV 294; importance of, 299, 300; Charles I and, 301, 305; Parliamentary stronghold, 313 sqq.; 774; merchants of, IX 375

—— William, American general, VII 337 sq.

Hulst, siege of (1591), III 626, (1596), 628; victory of Guébriant at (1642), IV 386; captured by Dutch (1645), 598

Humanism, rise of, I 532 sq.; origin of name, 538; 540, 564, 572; in Erfurt, II 111; breach between Reformers and, 168; French, *see* Vol. III, Chap. II, 53–72. *See also* Renaissance, the Classical

Humann, Jean-Georges, French Minister of Finance, X 489

Humáyún, Moghul (*or* Mongolian) Emperor of Delhi, III 117; VI 507; 510 sq.; 514

Humbert I, King of Italy, accession of, XII 216; 219; assassinated, 223; 240

—— J.-J.-Amable, general, French invasion of Ireland under, VIII 476, 772; lands at Killala, IX 702

"Humble Advice, The," IV 359 sq.

"Humble Petition and Advice, The," IV 444 sqq.

Humboldt, Baron Alexander von, X 260, 268, 271, 278, 374; XII 797

—— Baron Friedrich Wilhelm von, VIII 711, 773; Minister of Public Instruction, IX 326; 327; at Congress of Vienna, 580; 585, 609; and Germanic Constitution, 648–9; and French frontier, 664 sq.; and Diet, X 348 sq.; resignation of, 366; 393; XII 822

Hume, Alexander Hamilton, Australian explorer, XI 790 sq.

—— David, VI 589; 817; *Essays on Political Questions*, 819 sqq.; VIII 769; X 770; XII 817; 836

—— Joseph, X 656; 662; and Orange Lodges, 672; 675; 680; XI 3; and Trade Unionism, XII 748

Hu-mên-chai, Treaty of, XI 810

Humières, Jean de, Governor of Péronne, III 30

Hummelauer, Baron, mission of, to England, XI 88; 92

Hummelberg, Zwinglian reformer at Ravensburg, II 160

Hummelshof, battle of (1702), V 590

Humphrey, Laurence, Puritan, II 592

Humphreys, Andrew Atkinson, American general, VII 538

Hunan, anti-foreign feeling in, XII 516

Hunfalvy, Paul, Hungarian scholar, XI 431

Hung Sin-tsuen, and the "Taiping" rebellion, XI 820

Hungary, the Ottoman invasion of (1454), I 69; (1526), 96; Solyman and, 93, 95 sq.; internal decay of, 329; acquired by the Habsburgs, *ib.*; compared with Bohemia, 330 sq.; provinces annexed to, 331 sq.; political structure of, 332; mistaken foreign policy of, 343 sqq.; 658; Turkish wars in (1551), II 86, (1529), 206 sq., (1532), 218 sq.; defeat of, at Mohács (1526), 61; causes of defeat, 197 sq.; Turkish conquest of (1541–2), 242; treaty of Ferdinand I with (1538), 236; Bohemia and, 197–9; struggle between Austria and Turkey for, Vol. III, Chap. IV *passim*; Báthory's design to unite with Poland, 103; under Ferdinand I, 146–7; advance of Protestantism in, 175; under Rudolf II, 719 sqq.; Estates of, IV 1; Protestants in, 2; and Peace of Zsitva-Torok, 8; Ferdinand II, King of, 14; 23 sqq.; invaded by Bethlen Gabor, 31; Bucquoy in, 71; sectaries take refuge in, 75; 77;

Wallenstein in, 98 sq.; revolt of, against Emperor Leopold I, v 35; and the Turks, 36, 40, 49; Habsburg rule in, 52, 339 sq.; frontier of, 342; 343; Turkish invasion of, 346 sq.; Austria and, 348; conspiracy in, 350 sqq.; 355 sq.; conciliatory measures in, 357 sq.; Austrian successes in, 366 sq.; 368; Turkish successes in, 369; and Peace of Carlowitz, 371; 401; insurrection in (1703), 407; 432; 435; and Russia, 482; Turks in, 626, 661; religious intolerance in, 743 sq.; Hanoverian troops in, vi 4; 30 sq.; and Pragmatic Sanction, 201; 204; and Austria, 250; Frederick the Great and, 277; Turkish victories in, 307; 507; Joseph II and, 626 sq., 653 sq.; insurrection in, 628, 655, 710; viii 293; hostility to Joseph II in, 327, 329; influence of French Revolution in, 777; Austro-Russian army retreats to (1805), ix 261; Archduke John withdraws to (1809), 355; revolt (1849) in, x 39; Germanic Confederation and, 343; and Austria, 356, 371; 382; literature of (1686–1900), Vol. xi, Chap. xv (3); Palmerston and, 17; 47; Revolution in (1848), 93, 95, 152, 155 sq.; 170; Ministry of, 172; 174; 178; relations of, with Austria, 179 sqq.; Diet of, 180 sqq.; Slav invasion of, 183 sq.; Austria declares war against, 185; and the accession of Francis Joseph, 190 sq.; 200; progress of the Revolution in, 202 sqq.; Republic proclaimed in, 207; and Italy, *ib.*; and Russian intervention, 209; suppression of Revolution in, 209 sqq.; reaction in, 216; customs union with Austria, 223, 394; 285; Schwarzenberg and, 393; Austrian rule in, 398 sqq.; 402 sq.; effect of "October Charter" in, 404; under leadership of Deák, 405 sq.; 456; and Italy, 531, 537 sqq.; xii 1; 6; 11; Chap. vii, Austria-Hungary, 174–212; 842

Hungary, Palatines of. *See under their names, and compare* List 136

Hun-ho valley, xii 593; 596 sqq.

"Hunkers," at U.S.A. Democratic Convention (1848), vii 399

Hunsdon, Henry Carey, 1st Lord, iii 6; 282; 291

Hunt, Henry, and the Radical movement, ix 688; x 576 sq.; 580 sq.; in prison, 582; and Bentham, 598; 599; 615

—— James Henry Leigh, and the Regent, ix 690; x 720; writings of, xi 361 sq.

Hunter, David, American general, vii 491, 530, 533, 587 sq.

—— John, Vice-Admiral, Governor of New South Wales, ix 738

—— Robert, colonial governor, vii 49

Huntingdon, Henry Hastings, Earl of, ii 510; and the succession, 560, 582

Huntington, Ellsworth, American traveller, xii 803

Huntly, George Gordon, 4th Earl of, iii 262, 268

—— George Gordon, 5th Earl of, iii 272 sq., 274 sqq.; 551

—— George Gordon, 1st Marquis of, and Highland disorder, iv 491; 501 sq.

—— Marquis of. *See* Gordon, 2nd Duke of

Huntsman, Benjamin, and steel manufacture, x 733

Hunyady, John, saves Belgrade from the Turks (1456), i 69 sq., 72; 335

Hurlbut, Stephen Augustus, American general, vii 510

Hurons, The, Indian tribe, vii 75 sq., 101

Hurst Castle, Charles I in, iv 354

Hurter, Friedrich von, German historian, xii 829

Hus, John, ii 175; and Zwingli, 313; v 633

Huse, Caleb, Confederate foreign agent, vii 611

Huskisson, William, and the currency, ix 689; x 200; 573; 584 sq.; and colonial policy, 585 sqq.; financial and tariff reforms by, 588 sqq.; 593; 602; 618; xi 3; 762

Huss, Magnus, xi 688

Hussein Pasha, Turkish commander-in-chief, x 549 sq.

Hussey, Thomas, Roman Catholic Bishop of Waterford and Lismore, vi 377 sq.

—— inventor of a reaping machine, vii 695

Hussula, Swedish meeting at, vi 778

Hut, Hans, German revolutionary, ii 224

Hutchinson (Anne Marbury Wheelwright), Mrs, in Boston (Mass.), vii 17 sqq., 25

—— Lucy, *Life of Colonel Hutchinson*, v 116

—— Thomas, Governor of Massachusetts, vii 148 sq., 154 sqq., 159

Hutten, Ulrich von, and *Epistolae Obscurorum Virorum*, i 573; attacks the Papacy, 667; *Julius Exclusus* attributed to, ii 9; 32, 152, 155 sq., 314, 694, 696; new edition of the works of, forbidden, x 370

Hutton, James, *Theory of the Earth*, xii 771

Huxelles, Nicolas du Blé, Marquis de, Marshal of France, v 427; 439; vi 31; 129; 146

Huxley, Thomas Henry, xii 772 sqq.

Huy, allied French and Dutch in, iii 628; taken by the Allies (1695), v 62, by Marlborough (1703), 407, by Villeroi (1705), 414; capture of (1746), vi 247

Huyghens, Christian, inventions of, iv 722; v 713; *Horologium Oscillatorium*, 718; 722 sq.; xii 781

—— Constantine, career of, iv 720 sq.; Descartes and, 787; 794; and William of Orange, v 167

Huysmann, Roelof. *See* Agricola, Rudolf
Huyssens, tutor of the Tsarevich Alexis,
    v 537; 595
Hwayuenk'ow, Japanese force at, xii 511
Hyde, Anne. *See* York, Anne, Duchess of
—— Edward, Earl of Clarendon. *See*
    Clarendon
—— Edward, Governor of N. Carolina,
    vii 37
—— Henry, Earl of Clarendon. *See*
    Clarendon
—— Laurence, Earl of Rochester. *See*
    Rochester
—— Lawrence, member of Parliament
    (1601), iii 357
—— Nicholas, Chief Justice, iv 266
—— de Neuville, Jean-Guillaume, Baron,
    ix 13 sqq.; x 91; 92
Hyde Park, Reform meeting in, xi 340 sq.
Hydra, Island of, x 196
Hypsilanti. *See* Ypsilanti

Iaroslav, Grand Duke of Russia, the Code
    of, v 515
Iaroslavl, annexed by Ivan the Great, v
    479; 502; 604
Ibarra, Don Diego de, Secretary in Belgic
    Provinces, iii 519
Ibell, Charles von, attempted assassination
    of, x 366
Iberville, Pierre le Moyne (*or* Lemoine),
    Sieur de, French Canadian, vii 88 sqq.
—— de, French diplomat, v 472
Ibrahim, Ottoman Sultan, and Rákóczy, iv
    389; v 342 sq.; xi 275
—— Lord of Caramania, i 81 sq.
—— Lodi, Afghan Sultan, vi 508 sq.
—— Mameluke Bey, viii 600 sqq., 607 sq.
—— Pasha of Buda, v 362 sq.
—— Pasha, Grand Vezir of Solyman the
    Magnificent, i 96, 101; in command of
    Persian expedition (1533), iii 104 sq.,
    109; 112 sq., 120; fall of (1536), 113
—— Pasha (of Egypt, 1825), expedition
    of, to Greece, x 181, 189 sqq.; and the
    battle of Navarino, 196; evacuates the
    Morea, 201; in Syria, 547, 549 sqq., 559,
    569, 571; defeats the Turks at Nezib,
    562; 565; xii 429; 447
Ibsen, Henrik, Norwegian dramatist, xi
    699; 701 sq.; xii 13; 281
Iceland, Bristol trade with, i 33; Breton
    sailors and, 414; the Reformation in,
    ii 621; xi 683; Constitution for, 694;
    early law courts of, xii 712
Ich'ang, opened to foreign trade, xii 502;
    508
Idaho, and the currency question, vii 673;
    women's franchise in, xii 763
Iddesleigh, Stafford Henry Northcote, 1st
    Earl of, Chancellor of the Exchequer,
    xii 30; 35; Foreign Secretary, 45; death
    of, 46
Idées Napoléoniennes, Les, ix 758
Idéologues, The, and Napoleon I, x 40 sq.

Idiaquez, Don Juan de, iii 514, 526
Idstedt, battle at, xi 225, 695
If, Château, iii 397; surrendered by Tus-
    cany, 674
Iffland, August Wilhelm, German dramatist
    and actor, x 388; 394
Iganie, Polish success at (1831), x 470
Igelström, Count Joseph, Russian general,
    viii 541 sq., 545
Igis, Protestants at, iv 52; 61
Iglau, Bernadotte at, ix 258; Haugwitz
    at, 259; Bernadotte recalled from, 260;
    Archduke Charles withdraws to, 353
Igli, railway to, xii 129
Ignateff, Yakoff, confessor of the Tsarevich
    Alexis, v 538; 541
Ignatieff, Count Nicholas Paulovich, Russian
    ambassador at Constantinople, xi 634;
    xii 381, 386; Minister of the Interior,
    304; 312 sq.; 317
Ignatius, Saint. *See* Loyola
Iguala, "plan" of, x 304
Iho Ch'ilan, Society of Boxers, xii 517
Ii Kamon no Kami, *daimiō*, xi 825; 829;
    833 sq.; 836 sqq.; murder of, 841; 844
Il fermo proposito, Encyclical of Pius X,
    xii 230
Ilanz, iv 52; Jenatsch at, 54
Ilbersheim, Convention of (1704), v 411
Ilbert, Sir Courtenay Peregrine, xii 477
Île de Bourbon. *See* Bourbon, Île de
Île de France, towns recaptured in, iii 47;
    government of, 668; customs of, v 13;
    agricultural population in, viii 61
Île de France (Mauritius). *See* Mauritius
Île de Saint Jean. *See* Prince Edward
    Island
Île Royale. *See* Cape Breton Island
Ilerda, Francesco Romolino, Bishop of,
    i 184
Ilgen, Heinrich Rüdiger von, Brandenburg
    Secretary of State, v 602; 664; 667
Ilha de Villagalhão, French Protestant
    colony at, i 48
Ili, Russian expedition to, xi 273
Illeshazi, Stephen, iii 701, 721
Illinois, enters the Union (1818), vii 359,
    386, 421; and the slavery question, 424,
    601; election campaign in (1858), 436;
    population of, 444, 695; in the Civil
    War, 471; coal in, 704
Illuminati, The, viii 772, 776
Illyria, Napoleon's dealings with, ix 417-9;
    condition of, 418; kingdom of, 660
Illyricus, Matthaeus Flacius. *See* Flacius
—— Thomas, French Reformer, ii 291
Ilow, Christian, Freiherr von, and Wallen-
    stein, iv 239 sqq.; murdered at Eger,
    242
Ilten, Jobst Hermann von, Hanoverian
    statesman, vi 20
Imam Baksh, and the Holkar host, xi 736
—— Ghar, fortress of, xi 736
Imas, Governor of Badajoz, surrenders, ix
    462

Imbert-Colomès, Jacques, VIII 509, 511
Imeretinsky, Prince, and Poland, XII 337
Imeritia, suzerainty of Russia over, IX 385;
annexed to Russia, X 413
Imitation of Christ, The, I 628, 641
Immaculate Conception, dogma of, XI 712 sq.
Immensa, Bull remodelling the Inquisition,
II 650
Immermann, Karl Lebrecht, X 412; XI 411
Immortale Dei, Encyclical of Leo XIII, XII
118
Imola, attacked by Cesare Borgia (1499), I
238; surrendered to Julius II (1503), 196;
riots at, X 154; Mastai (Pius IX) at, XI
72
Imperial Cameral Tribunal. *See Reichs-
kammergericht*
—— Institute, founded to commemorate
Queen Victoria's Jubilee (1887), XII 47
—— Recess of 1803, IX 95
Impey, Sir Elijah, Chief Justice of Bengal,
VI 466; trial of, 471; 568; 571; and
Nuncomar, 573, 583
In Coena Domini, Bull, VI 637
Inama-Sternegg, Karl Theodor von, his-
torian, XII 850
Inca, The, natives of Peru, I 44 sq.
Inchbald, Elizabeth, novelist, VI 836
Inchinnan, the Earl of Argyll at, V 289
Inchiquin, Murrough O'Brien, 6th Baron,
1st Earl of, IV 527; Presidency of Munster
and, 528; 531; declares for the King,
532; 533 sq.
"Incident, The," Scottish conspiracy (1641),
IV 505
Indemnity Bill, The English, of 1660, V
94
Independencia, Peruvian man-of-war, dis-
patched to Japan, XII 555
Independents, English party and sect, rise
of, in 1643, IV 319 sq.; Chap. XI, Presbyterians and Independents (1645-9),
336-55; 453-4; politically discredited at
the Restoration, V 99 sq., 103; and the
growth of toleration, 327 sqq.; and New
England, VII 12, 57; difficulties of 1763,
144. *See also* Nonconformists
Index expurgatorius, of the Sorbonne, II
288; to be distinguished from the *Index
librorum prohibitorum,* 687
—— *librorum prohibitorum,* Portuguese,
II 414; papal, history of, 379; 686 sqq.;
Paul IV's, 674; revised by the Council of
Trent and re-issued as the Tridentine,
676, 687 sq.; Canisius' attitude towards,
688; Cassander and, III 164; effect on
literature of, 465; Congregation of the,
and de Thou, 64; and France, V 74
India, Saracens in, I 9; Diaz and the sea
route to, 17; Vasco da Gama reaches,
24 sqq.; trade with, in Middle Ages, 27;
Cabral's expedition to, 29; Portuguese
settlement in, 30 sq.; Dutch, IV 711;
British, 740 sqq.; Portuguese, 744; (1650-
1744), Vol. v. Chap. XXII (2); France

and, 13; rivalry of England and France
in, 57; Portuguese possessions in, 372;
384; Russia and, 544; the Moghul Empire, Vol. VI, Chap. XV (1); English and
French in (1720-63), Chap. XV (2); Clive
and Warren Hastings in, Chap. XV (3);
51; 299; French and English rivalry
in, 332; 347; 350; Franco-British War
in, 454; 465; Fox's Bill, 466 sq.; Pitt's
first Bill, 468; 469; Pitt's second Bill,
470; 475; 643; French possessions in,
VIII 80; French expedition to (1796), 473;
Napoleon's designs on, 608 sq., 618, IX
47, 70, 80, XI 637; Tsar Paul proposes
to invade, IX 47; proposed Franco-
Russian expedition to, 308; 311, 315,
386; products of, 363; British Empire in
(1783-1815), 709-35; Russia and, X 169
sq., 202 sq., 545; British trade with, 760;
Adam Smith's views on, 765; (1815-69),
Vol. XI, Chap. XXVI; United States trade
with, 15; 259; Sepoy Mutiny in, 326;
schemes for the government of, 329; 633;
790; British Empire in (1869-1910), Vol.
XII, Chap. XVI; 5; 7; 32; Russia and,
56, 343; emigration to Australia from,
625; 657; factory legislation in, 747;
761 sq.; 792; caravan route to, 793;
800; 803
Indian Civil Service, XII 26
—— National Congress, XII 494 sqq.
—— Territory, VII 462
Indiana, enters Union (1816), VII 359, 421;
and the slavery question, 424; population of, 695; wheat in, 696 sq.; coal
in, 704
Indianapolis, Conference at (1896), VII
673
Indians (North American), treatment of,
by French, English, and Spanish colonists,
VII 97 sqq.
Indies, The, Spanish treasure and, III 319
sqq.; trade with, 537, 540, 641-2; Dutch
enterprise in, 631, 715, 725; Spanish
policy in, IV 697, 702 sq., 713; 462;
free trade in, 716; Dutch in, 751;
English in, 756 sq.; French and Dutch
in, 758; West Africa and, 759. *See also*
East Indies *and* West Indies
—— (Spanish), under Charles V, II 101
—— Company. *See* Perpetual Company
Indigirka river, XII 794
Indore, Murray seizes, IX 727
—— Maharaja of. *See* Holkar
Indulgences, sale of, in Germany, II 121;
origin of, 123-6; abuse of, 127; Luther
and, 120 sqq.; Zwingli and, 313
Indus, river, navigation of, XI 736; and
the Indian frontier, XII 489
Infallibility, papal claim to, and doctrine
of, opposed to medieval high papalist
theory, III 744; *see* Vol. XI, Chap. XXV,
Rome and the Vatican Council, 703-23
Infantado, da Silva, Duke of, tried and
acquitted, IX 429

Infessura, Stephano, Italian historian, I
221
Inflation Act, The (1874), VII 643
Ingemann, Bernhard Severin, Danish no-
velist, XI 698
Inghirami, Tommaso Fedra, II 8, 15, 16
Ingle, Richard, leads a raid into Maryland,
VII 33
Inglis, Sir John Eardley Wilmot, major-
general, at Lucknow, XI 748
Ingogo, battle of, XII 637
Ingoldsby, Col. Richard, at Daventry, IV
557; sent to New York, VII 45
Ingolstadt, University of, founded, I 622;
advance of Charles V on, II 256; Diet of
(1563), III 159; Jesuits in, 160; Archduke
Ferdinand at, 699; new Catholic League
at (1614), IV 13, (1632), 210; death of
Tilly at, 214; 366; besieged (1704), V
410; VI 233; 237; fall of (1743), 238;
Moreau besieges (1800), IX 64; surrender
of, 65; Grand Army crosses Danube near,
254
Ingres, Jean-Auguste-Dominique, French
painter, IX 135; X 103
Ingria, conquest of, by Sweden, IV 180;
Peace of Stolbova and, 181; V 503;
Russian invasion of (1699), 588, 590 sq.;
597; 614; guaranteed to Russia by Prussia
(1718), VI 206; ceded to Russia by Sweden
(1721), V 615
Inishannon, Irish retreat to, III 609
Inishowen, disputed overlordship of, III
589, 591
Inkerman, battle of, XI 319, 364
Inn river, IX 65; Moreau occupies the line
of (1800), 68; Austrian troops cross
(1805), 252
Innerrhoden, the Suter affair at, VI 625
Innocent III (Lothario Conti), Pope, I 656;
III 422, 757
—— IV (Sinibaldo Fieschi), Pope, III 745;
749
—— VI (Étienne Auber), Pope, taxation
of German clergy by, I 669
—— VIII (Giovanni Battista Cibò), Pope,
I 86, 104, 221 sqq., 448, 657 sq., 666;
III 128
—— X (Giambattista Pamfili), Pope, re-
presented by Chigi at Münster, IV 402;
protests against Peace of Westphalia in
Bull *Zelo Domus Dei*, 415, 688; 529;
600; 687; V 84
—— XI (Benedetto Odescalchi), Pope,
supports the Emperor, V 51; and Louis
XIV, 52, 55; and Cologne election, 54;
and James II of England, 58, 235,
335; 76; and the dispute with France,
85; and William of Orange, 244; and
Hungary, 356; assists Austria, 359; 364;
and Spanish Succession, 392; XI 713
—— XII (Antonio Pignatelli), Pope, and
James II of England, V 58; 88; VI 586
—— XIII (Michele Angelo Conti), Pope,
VI 131; 587

Innsbruck, Austrian Diet at (1518), I 314,
322; flight of Charles V from, II 88;
Spanish troops at, IV 32; Alexander beheaded at, 55; Valtelline negotiations at,
62 sq.; Feria at, 231; V 407; Charles VI
at, 432; VI 37; seminary at, 637; battles
before (1809), IX 355; re-conquered by
Austria, 356; Emperor Ferdinand at, XI
175 sq.; 180
Innviertel, The, VI 707
Inouyé, Marquis Kaoru, Japanese statesman,
XI 860; 865; visits England, XII 546;
549; 569; administration of, in Korea,
570 sq.
—— Lieutenant, at Peking, XII 519
Inquisition, the papal, in France, futile
attempts to establish (1555-7), II 294;
in Italy, in Venice in 13th century,
I 269; re-organised and extended over
Italy (1555), II 33, 381 sqq., 649 sqq.;
Cosimo de' Medici and, III 390; Emmanuel
Philibert and, 404; Congregation of the,
446; general effects on literature of, 465;
470 sqq.; and Giordano Bruno, IV 668;
loses censorship of the Press in Tuscany, VI 601; in Mexico, Lima (from
1570), and Cartagena (from 1763), X 253
sq.; in Netherlands, under Charles V,
II 103; under Charles and Philip II,
III 164, 184 sqq., 193, 199, 201 sqq., 630;
in Spain, under Ferdinand and Isabel,
I 356, 359 sq.; 371; 578; 661; later, in
its Spanish form and in Spain, II 99,
399 sqq.; Bartolomé de Carranza and,
409 sq.; 650; under Philip II, III 448,
478 sqq., 487 sq., 491, 495; in Aragon
less pliant than in Castile, 514; results
of working of, 517 sqq.; Moriscos and,
543; 545; 743; 769; under Charles II,
V 375; under Charles III reduced in
power, VI 373
Insalah, French occupation of, XII 129
Inshiu, *daimiō* of, XI 832; 834; 846; and
Chōshiu, 850; 852; 864
Institute of Egypt, established by Bonaparte
in 1798, VIII 605 sq.
Institutio Christianae Religionis, of Calvin,
II 356-7; published in French (1540), IV
778
Institution of a Christian Man. See Bishops'
Book
"Instrument of Government," IV 438
Intendants, French, V 4 sqq.; VIII 37 sqq.
Inter innumeras, Encyclical of Leo XIII,
XII 119
Interim, The Augsburg (1548), II 84; and
its results, 264 sqq.; recognised by Paul
III, 260; the Leipzig, 266
Introduction to Christian Doctrine, by
Zwingli, II 320
Inveraray, Jacobites at, VI 99 sq.
Inverness, Jacobite rising at, VI 98; 100
sqq., 105; Cope at, 112; 115 sq.
Invernizzi, Monsignor, President of the
Romagna Commission, X 152

"Invincibles," Irish secret society, XII 81
Ionian Islands, seized by France (1797),
VIII 590 sqq., IX 751; conquest of, by
Russia (1799), 41; independence of, recog-
nised (1801), 75; reduced (1809) by the
British, 239; ceded to France (1807),
293, 306; British Protectorate in, 665;
x 173, 176 sq.; Greece and, XI 280 sq.,
634; 640 sqq.; XII 415
Iowa, and the slavery question, VII 402;
enters Union (1846), 421; population of,
695
Ipek, Patriarchate of, XII 424; 426
Ipswich, Wolsey's college at, II 434
Iraghticahan, disputed possession of, III
611
Irakli, Prince of Georgia, VI 676
Irányi, Joseph, Hungarian politician, XI
156
Irbit Fair, x 428
Ireland, Lambert Simnel in, I 465'sq.; Perkin Warbeck in, 468 sqq.; pacification
of, 471 sq.; monachism in, 534 sq.;
policy of Henry VIII in, II 471 sq.;
rebellion in (1543), 442; history of, to
Settlement of Ulster, Vol. III, Chap.
XVIII; papal volunteers in, 298; rebellion
in, 286-7, 530-1; Philip II's designs
upon, 517 sq., 529 sq.; and Strafford,
IV 285, 288; rebellion in, 295, 297;
Charles I and, 318, 328, 334 sqq., 345,
347; 350; 501; Cromwell in, 435, 463;
represented in Parliament, 437, 440;
Instrument of Government and, 438;
446; revenue of, 457; 466; Charles II
proclaimed in, 509; from Plantation of
Ulster to Cromwellian settlement, *see*
Chap. XVIII; Henry Cromwell and, 540;
(1659-60), 545, 547, 552; 677; (1660-
1700), Vol. v, Chap. x (3); French intervention in, 58; and the Restoration, 103
sq.; restrictions on the trade of, 104;
260; William III in, 261; 265; in the 18th
century, Vol. VI, Chap. XIV; 52; reinforcements drawn from, 99, 100; 455 sq.;
disturbed condition of, 457; Parliament
in, 458 sq.; 470; Regency Bill in, 474;
476; settlers from, in America, VII 221;
disaffection in, VIII 92; 276, 453; French
expeditions to (1796-8), 473, 475 sq., 650;
influence of French Revolution in, 771
sq.; French designs upon (1801), IX 70;
(1803), 214; (1804), 216, 218; and Regency, 693; disaffection in, 695; rebellion
in, 701; project of Union with, 702 sqq.;
condition of, 708; and movement for
Catholic emancipation, Vol. x, Chap. XIX
passim; (1832-41), Chap. xx *passim*;
141; parliamentary representation in,
606 sq., affairs in (1841-8), XI 7 sqq.;
310; Fenianism in, 343; Disestablishment in, 344 sq.; Roman Catholic Church
in, 711; and Home Rule Movement, Vol.
XII, Chap. IV, 65-90; 1; 11; Gladstone
and, 24; 27; University Bill for, 29;

and Liberal party, 31; Parliament and,
38 sq.; Phoenix Park murders, 40; 41
sq.; Home Rule Bill (1886), 43 sq.; 46;
48; Home Rule Bill (1893), 49 sq.;
Unionist policy in, 61; population of,
63; and co-operation, 741; 751
Ireton, Henry, and Parliamentary army, IV
343; 345; 351; draws up the "Remon-
strance of the Army," 353; 355; Lord
Deputy of Ireland, 435, 534; death of,
535
Irgai, battle of, XI 631
Irish Agricultural Organisation Society,
XII 88
—— Land League, formation of, XII 36;
38; dissolved, 41; 76 sqq.
—— National League, XII 41; 82; 84
—— Reform Association, XII 89
—— Republican Brotherhood, XII 75
—— Sea, submarine telegraph under, XI
346
—— Unionist Alliance, XII 89
Irish World, newspaper, XII 78
Irkutsk, post-road through, XII 792; 794
Iron Duke, British warship, at Yokohama,
and *Maria Luz* traffic in Chinese labour,
XII 554
Iroquois Indians, The, I 38, 44; Dutch
trade with, IV 709; VI 412; VII 39,
42 sq., 69; and the colonists, 75 sqq.,
80; rising of, 89, 115; punitive expe-
dition against, 220
Irrawaddy river, XI 727; British expedition
on, XII 479; 798; 805
Irtysh river, v 495
Irun, Franco-Spanish marriages at, IV 630;
captured by French, 645
Irurzon, Spanish defeat at, VIII 440
Irving, Washington, VII 740 sqq.
Isabel, Isabella:—
—— Queen of Castile (the Catholic), I
126, 316, Chap. XI *passim*; encouragement of learning by, 379 sq.; 394, 476,
656; II 399; III 478; x 279
—— (of Castile), Queen of Denmark
(sister of Charles V), II 169, 602
—— (of Castile), Queen of Portugal, I 362,
453
—— II, Queen of Spain, x 232 sq.; 237;
242 sq.; French aid to, 495 sq.; XI 17;
33; 37 sq.; 462; proclaimed of age, 550;
negotiations for marriage of, 552 sqq.;
marriage of, 554 sq.; and Serrano, 555
sqq.; relations of, with her husband,
556; gives birth to a son, 557; gives
birth to a daughter, 559; 560; opposes
sale of Church lands, 561; and O'Donnell,
562, 567; character of, 563; and Mexican
affairs, 565 sq.; and Italy, 566; 567;
Pius IX and, 568; private life of, *ib.*;
569; dethronement of, 570; 575; the
Papacy and, 709; XII 258; 264
—— (of Braganza), Queen of Spain,
consort of Ferdinand VII, x 210; 212;
231

Isabel, Isabella (*contd.*):—
—— (of Bourbon), Queen of Spain, consort of Philip IV, and Olivares, IV 649 sqq.; Regent, 653; 654; death of, 658
—— (of Portugal), Queen of Spain, II 53, 74, 424
—— Clara Eugenia, Infanta of Spain, III 303; 413; 415; 489; 504 sqq., 520 sqq., 533 sqq.; 627 sqq.; marriage of, 630; 673; 697; at Brussels, IV 78, 81; 83; 99; 230; 644; Frederick Henry and, 694, 696; death of, 697. *See also* Archdukes, the
—— Maria, Infanta of Portugal, x 320 sq.
Isabella (Spanish colony in Española), abandoned, I 40
Isabey, French painter, IX 135
Isandhlwana, battle of, XII 35; 636
Iselberg, battles on the (1809), IX 355–6
Iselin, Isaac, Swiss writer, VIII 781
Isenburg, and the "Central administration of reconquered territories," IX 587
Isernia, fight at, XI 390
Ishak Khan, rebellion of, XII 482
Isidore, Bishop of Seville. *See* Seville
Island No. 10 (Mississippi), fortification of, VII 497; surrendered by the Confederates (1862), 498, 559
Islay, Earl of. *See* Argyll, 3rd Duke of
Isle de Riez, Soubise defeated at, IV 128
—— of France. *See* Mauritius
—— of Pines, Avellaneda meets English fleet near, III 322
Isly river, French victory on, XI 35
Isly, Duc de. *See* Bugeaud de la Piconnerie
Ismail, Russians capture (1770), VI 673, (1790), VIII 336, (1810), IX 485; fort of, demolished, X 175
—— 1st Shah of Persia (the Sofi), I 88 sq.; at war with Selim I, 90
Ismáíl Beg, at Fatehpur Sikri, IX 719
Ismaïl Pasha, Khedive of Egypt, XI 637 sq.; XII 431 sqq.; deposed, 435; Gordon and, 439 sq.; 446; 450; 453; and education, 454
Ismailia, British fleet at, XII 437
—— (Gondokoro). *See* Gondokoro
Ismailovo, Russian royal residence, VI 302
Isnard, Maximin, Girondist, VIII 214; 249; 273; 384
—— Achille Nicolas, economist, experiments of, and beet sugar, IX 377
Isny, joins the League of Protestant cities (1529), II 205
Isola della Scala, victory of the French at (1512), I 136
Isolani, Croat cavalry general, IV 371
Ispahan, Russian Minister at, V 544; Morier at, XII 800
Israels, Josef, Dutch painter, XII 249
Issik-Kul, Lake of, XI 273; 631; Prjevalsky at, XII 799
Issoire, capture of, III 32
Istria, taken by Osuña, IV 631; Venetian, VI 648; gains of Austria in (1797), VIII 583, 592

Istúriz, Francisco Javier de, Spanish statesman, XI 554 sq.
Itagaki, Japanese Councillor of State, XI 865; Minister, XII 549 sq.
Itakura, Japanese Minister, XI 850
Italy
I   iv   Italy and her invaders, 104–43
     xv   Economic change, *passim*, 493–531
     xvi   The Classical Renaissance, *passim*, 532–84
     xvii The Christian Renaissance, *passim*, 585–619
     xviii Catholic Europe, *passim*, 620–52
     xix   The eve of the Reformation, *passim*, 653–92
           [*See also* Florence, Rome, Venice]
II   i   Medicean Rome, *especially* 27–35
     ii and iii Habsburg and Valois (I) *and* (II), *passim*, 36–103
     xii   The Catholic South, *passim*, 377–99
     xviii The Church and Reform, *passim*, 639–89
     xix   Tendencies of European Thought in the Age of the Reformation, *passim*, 690–718
III xiv   The end of the Italian Renaissance, 456–74
           [*See also* Tuscany, Savoy *and* Rome]
IV   ii   The Valtelline (1603–39), *passim*, 35–63
     iv   Richelieu, *passim*, 118–57
     xxii Spain and Spanish Italy under Philip III and Philip IV, 623–65
     xxiii Papal policy (1590–1648), 666–88
V   xiii The Treaties of Partition and the Spanish Succession, *passim*, 372–400
     xiv   The War of the Spanish Succession, *passim*, 401–59
VI   iv and v The Bourbon governments in France and Spain (1714–46) (I) *and* (II), *passim*, 120–67
     xvi   Italy and the Papacy, 586–610
VIII xviii Bonaparte and the conquest of Italy, 553–93
     xxi   The Second Coalition, *passim*, 633–64
           [*See also* Naples]
IX   iii   The pacification of Europe (1799–1802), *passim*, 55–80
     iv   France and her tributaries (1801–3), *passim*, 81–106
     ix   The Third Coalition, I (1805–6), 244–64
     xiv   The French Dependencies, and Switzerland (1800–14), *passim*, 390–427

Italy (*contd.*)

ix   xix   The Congress of Vienna, I (1814–5), *passim*, 576–602
The Congress of Vienna, II (1815), *passim*, 646–71
[*See also* the various States of Italy under their names]

x   iv   Italy (1815–46), 104–30

     v   The Papacy and the Catholic Church, *passim*, 131–61

xi   iv   Italy in Revolution (1846–9), 65–95

     xiv   Cavour and the Kingdom of Italy (1849–61), 366–92

     xix   The completion of Italian Unity
(1) The successors of Cavour (1861–70), 529–44
(2) The Literature of the *Risorgimento* and after (1846–70), 544–9

xii   viii   United Italy, 213–42
[*See also* Venice, Rome, etc.]

Itamaraca, Dutch victory of (1640), iv 708
Itō, Marquis Hirobumi, Japanese statesman, xi 848; 860; 865; xii 509; career of, 546 sq.; death of, 547; 548 sq.; Minister-President, 550 sq.; 570; 572
—— Japanese admiral, xii 512
Ittig, Thomas, editor of Josephus, i 613
Iturbide, Augustin, Mexican general, x 304
Itzstein, Johann Adam von, Baden politician, xi 61
Iuka, battle of (1862), vii 501
Ivan III (Vasilovich) (the Great), Tsar of Russia (1462–1505), conquest of Novgorod by, i 502; v 477 sqq.; and Lithuania, 481; relations of, with the West, *ib.*; marriage of, *ib.*; and title of Tsar, 483; 484 sq.; policy of, 486; 493; 507; 515
—— IV (the Terrible), Tsar, iii 85; treats for peace with Stephen Báthory (1581), 101; iv 164; 166; annexes Kazan and Astrakhan, v 479, 493; 483 sq.; accession and reign of, 487 sqq.; and the *Oprichnina*, 490 sqq.; and foreign affairs, 493; and Livonia, 493 sq.; and Siberia, 494 sq.; 498; 503; 506; 512; relations with England, 513, 516; xii 793 sq.; death of (1584), iii 103, 171, v 495
—— V, Tsar, v 518 sq.; 523; death of, 524; 547; 556
—— VI, Tsar, accession of, vi 309; 311; 315
—— eldest son of Ivan IV, v 495
—— the Black, of Montenegro, i 74
Ivory Coast, Portuguese explorers and, i 16; trade with, vi 187; annexed by France, xii 129; 660
Ivry, battle of (1590), iii 48, 454, 511, 658 sqq.
Iwakura, Tomomi, Japanese statesman, xi 858; 864 sq.; envoy to Europe, xii 542; 545 sq.; Minister of Left, 549; death of, 550; 557 sq.

Iyemitsu, Japanese *Shōgun*, xi 825
Iyenari, Japanese *Shōgun*, xi 825
Iyesada, Tycoon of Japan, xi 832
Iyeyasu, Japanese *Shōgun*, xi 825; 827; xii 538
Izdbienski, Benedict, Bishop of Caminiecz, later of Posen, iii 75
Izmailoff, Lev, Russian envoy to Pekin, v 544
Izquierdo de Ribera y Lezaun, Eugene, Spanish agent, ix 301 sq.

Jablonsky, Daniel Ernst (Bishop of Brandenburg), v 671
Jablyak, xii 392; acquired by Montenegro, 396
Jacatra, the Dutch at, iv 736, 742
Jackman, Charles, explorer, xii 795
Jackson (Mississippi), Federals occupy (1863), vii 504 sq.
—— Andrew, American general, vii 345; 350, 373 sq.; President of United States, 378 sqq., 382 sq., 387, 389; significance of election of, 407 sq., 412, 420 sq.
—— Claiborne Fox, American statesman, Governor of Missouri, vii 493
—— Francis J., British Minister to United States, vii 332; sent to Kiel, ix 299
—— Thomas Jonathan ("Stonewall"), vii 475, 477; and the Seven Days' Battles, 478; and Chancellorsville, 485 sq.
—— British Minister at Rome, ix 194
—— French agent in England and Ireland, imprisonment of, ix 697
Jacob of Baden. *See* Trier, Electors of
—— of Jüterbok, at Erfurt, ii 111
—— of Liebenstein. *See* Mainz, Electors of
Jacobi, Friedrich Heinrich, German philosopher, viii 773; x 388
Jacobi-Kloest, Baron von, viii 641; Prussian Minister in London, ix 282; at Congress of Vienna, 585
Jacobin Club, viii 185 sq., 211 sq., 239, 245, 251, 267, 359; closed (1794), 376 sq.; and the army, 404; records of, xii 834
Jacobites, Oxford and St John (Bolingbroke) and, v 472 sqq.; and Peter the Great, 543; intrigues of 1713–4, vi 14 sqq.; party of, eclipsed after the rising of 1715, 21; influence of (1715–21), 43 sq.; in a minority, 69; 71 sq.; the "45," 74; Chap. iii, Jacobitism and the Union, 90–119, 142, 159 sq.
Jacobsbrüder, ii 105 sq.
Jacoby, Johann, German politician, xi 53; 157
Jacquard, Joseph-Marie, inventor of loom, ix 125
Jacqueline (Jacobaea) of Bavaria, heiress of Hainault, Holland, etc., i 419 sq., 423
Jacqueminot, Jean-François, Vicomte, French general, xi 97

Jacqueminot, Jean-Ignace, IX 150
Jäger, Johannes, of Drontheim. *See* Rube-
anus, Crotus
Jägerndorf, principality of, **v** 625; 653;
659; duchy of, VI 229; 230
—— George, Prince of. *See* Branden-
burg-Ansbach, Margrave George of
—— George Frederick, Prince of. *See*
Brandenburg
—— John George, Prince of. *See* Bran-
denburg-Ansbach
Jaffa, captured by Bonaparte, VIII 609;
Egyptian fleet at, X 549
Jaffé, Philipp, German historian, XII 823
Jagello, Polish House of, succeeds to Hun-
gary and Bohemia, I 331, 336, 344; II
198; III 73; line of, 76; Court of, 88;
unite Lithuania and Poland, v 480; VI
198
—— Catharine. *See* Catharine, Queen of
Sweden
—— Prince of Lithuania, **v** 480
Jahde, The, closed to English trade, IX 374
Jahn, Friedrich Ludwig, German publi-
cist, X 365; 370; XII 818
Jaipur, State of, XI 726
—— Partáb Singh, Rájah of, and Sindhia,
IX 719
Jaitpur, annexation of, XI 743
Jajce. *See* Yaytse
Jakobsson, Peter. *See* Sunnenvæder, Peter
Jalalabad, XI 733; relief of, 734; 735;
British force at, XII 470
Jalandar, XI 740; mutiny at, 746
Jalapa, American army in (1847), VII 396;
the fair of, X 254
Jalès, federation of (1790), VIII 197 sq.
Jamaica, colonised by Esquivel, I 41;
Penn and Venables in, IV 482; seized
by the English (1655), 660, **v** 680; 34;
Charles II and, 101, 104; 110; contra-
band trade in, 684; 687 sq.; progress of,
689 sq.; 691; smuggling in, VI 64, 351;
Maroons of, 185; England and, 186;
879; opened to foreign shipping, 436;
453 sq.; development of, VII 78, 108;
French designs on, IX 218, 222; government in, 750; lost by Spain (1655), **x**
255, 272; the negroes in, 260; and the
contraband trade in Spanish America,
273; 276; Bolívar in, 290; and the
abolition of slavery, 658 sq., 677 sq.;
and the sugar trade, 761; XI 757; negroes
of, 761; XII 653 sq.; government of,
657
Jamais, Émile, French politician, XII 124
James, river, Grant crosses, VII 520, 533;
530
—— I, King of England, and VI of Scotland, early life of, in Scotland, Vol. III,
Chap. VIII *passim*; Elizabeth refuses to
recognise as her successor, 358 sqq., 503,
521, 534 sqq., 542, 544; Britain under,
Chap. XVII; Ireland under, 609 sqq., 637,
644; resemblance of, to Rudolf II, 697,

731; theories of sovereignty of, 750 sqq.;
Spanish marriage negotiations of, IV 2,
83 sqq., 87 sqq., 625 sq., 640 sq., 673;
and Bohemian succession, 17 sq., 23 sq.,
29 sq.; 67; 77 sqq.; and Denmark,
191; 256; France and, 258; 259 sq.;
274; *Declaration of Sports*, 279; and
the militia, 304; growth of English commerce in the reign of, 466; and Scotland,
486 sq.; 488; last years of, 491 sq.;
Scottish ecclesiastical affairs and, 494
sqq.; 508; and Ireland, 514 sqq.; 629;
sides with Venice against Paul V, 670;
733; 745; and the colonies, 748; Ralegh
and, 754; methods of government of, in
Scotland, v 279 sqq.; and religious toleration, 325; 743; *True Law of Free Monarchy*, VI 803; and Virginia, VII 6 sq.;
72
James II, King of England, and VII of
Scotland, (as Duke of York), IV 306; sent
prisoner to London, 335; escape of, 348;
519; goes to Boulogne, 540; and the
French Protestants, v 24 sq.; 40; 49;
supports Louis XIV, 50 sqq.; flight of,
to France, 56; Louis XIV and, 57 sq.,
244 sq.; and the Papacy, 58; and battle
of La Hogue, 59; marriage of, 93; and
Royal African Company, 108, 113; 149;
Dryden and, 135; and West Indies, 149;
163; 166; and naval administration,
Chap. VIII (1); at battle of Lowestoft,
181; at battle of Southwold Bay, 190,
192 sq.; accession, character and policy
of, Chap. IX; Declaration of Indulgence
of, 235, 237 sqq.; and the Universities,
237 sq.; and Parliament, 240; and Prince
of Orange, 240 sq.; and the Seven
Bishops, 242; brings Irish troops into
England, 243; concessions by, 245; and
landing of William of Orange, 246;
flight of, 247 sqq.; 250 sq.; impolicy of,
255; in Ireland, 261; at St Germain,
262 sq.; and Crown of Poland, 263,
354; 264 sq.; 271 sq.; 277; Scottish
High Commissioner, 286 sq.; accession
of, 288, 334; rule of, in Scotland, 289
sq.; the Scottish Convention of Estates
and, 291; and Highland chiefs, 294;
and Ireland, 306 sq.; and Tyrconnel,
307; in Ireland, 307 sqq.; at the siege
of Derry, 308 sq.; at Dublin, 310 sq.;
313; at the Boyne, 314; flight of, from
Ireland, 315; at Versailles, 316; 326;
conversion of, 333; and religious toleration, 335 sq.; Marlborough and, 460 sq.;
Godolphin and, 461; and colonial affairs,
690; 757; death of, 275; VI 6; 9; 43;
abdication of, 794 sq., 808; 815; and
New England, VII 28 sq., 69; New York
granted to, 38, 41 sqq., 45; claims of, on
New Jersey, 46 sq., 49; and Penn, 50
—— IV, King of Scotland, Warbeck aided
by, I 469; 471, 479, 481; killed at Flodden, 482; 484; II 553

James V, King of Scotland, I 485; makes peace with England (1534), II 441; marries Madeleine of Valois, 448, 455; 453; disputes with Scotch nobles, 454; marries Mary of Guise, 455; and England, 456, 555; 553; death of, 456

—— Francis Edward Stewart, Prince of Wales (the Old Pretender), birth of, V 241 sq., 290; 246 sqq.; 250; 275; recognised by Louis XIV, 399; 423; 441; and Peter the Great, 472; 543; VI 6; 15; 21 sq.; 26; illness of, 27; 30; Alberoni and, 31; 57; at Saint-Germain, 91; sails from Dunkirk, 92 sq.; 96; relations of, with the Powers, 97; and Earl of Mar's rising, 98; in Scotland, 102 sq.; in Italy, 104; marriage of, 105; 106; 109 sqq.; 113; 117; Regent Orleans and, 123; and Dubois, 131; 142; 289; death of, 118

—— Duke of York. *See* James II, King of England

—— Edwin John, barrister, XI 328

—— Frank, African traveller, XII 813

—— William, *Some Varieties of Religious Experience*, XII 775

—— of Hereford, Lord (Sir Henry James), XII 43; 52

Jameson, Leander Starr, and the Transvaal Raid, XII 53, 641

Jamestown (Virginia), English colony at, IV 747; settlement of, VII 6; Nathaniel Bacon in, 9

—— (St Helena), landing of Napoleon at, IX 757

Jamet, Léon, at the Court of Ferrara, II 384

Jamna river, XI 726

Jamrud, railway to, XII 489

Jan of Leyden. *See* John of Leyden

Janda Khaur, regent in Lahore, XI 738

Jane (Seymour), Queen of England, 3rd consort of Henry VIII, II 445; death of, 448

Janina, reaction in, X 173; Kurshid Pasha at, 178, 181; and the Greek frontier, XII 403; 421

Janissaries, revolt of (1481), I 85; support Selim I, 89 sq.; organisation of, 99 sqq.; changes in constitution of, V 342; 347 sq.; at Vienna, 362; IX 386-9; revolt of the (1826), X 192

Jankau, Swedish victory at (1645), IV 389

Jankoji, Rájah of Gwalior, XI 737

Janovitch (Besme), murderer of Coligny, III 19

Jansen, Cornelius, and Jansenism, V 82 sqq.

Jansenism, Richelieu adverse to, IV 157; Pascal and, 794 sqq.; V 82 sqq., 88 sqq.; VI 163; the *Parlement* and, 347; in popular movements, French especially, 587 sqq.; 590 sq.; and fall of the Jesuits, 595; results of controversy in regard to, VIII 8 sq.; 56, 194, 196; and modern Ultramontanism, X 157

Janssen, Johannes, *History of the German People*, XII 848

Janssens, Jan Willem, Dutch general, surrender of Cape Town by, IX 752; surrender of Java by, 754

Janus, Döllinger's, XII 848

Japan, Dutch East India Company in, IV 712; English factory at Firando in, 740; treaty of the United States with, VII 434; (1842-71), Vol. XI, Chap. XXVIII (2); 259; 802; the Regeneration of, Vol. XII, Chap. XVIII; and the War with Russia, Chap. XIX; progress of, 4 sq.; alliance of, with Great Britain, 9 sq., 55 sq.; 14; and war settlement with China, 52; 342; at war with Russia, 345 sq., 348, 354, 521 sq.; 379; and China, 502; and Korea, 509 sq.; at war with China, 510 sqq.; China and, 515, 522; and the Philippine Islands, 529 sq.; 609; Canada and, 650; and Hague Court of Arbitration, 727

Jaquess, James F., United States volunteer colonel, VII 578

Jarmetz, ceded to France, V 33

Jarnac, battle of, III 11-2, 224

Jaroměř, Austrian army at, VI 705; Field-Marshal Benedek at, XI 453

Jaromirez. *See* Jaroměř

Jaroslav, burning of, IV 189

Jarzé, Chevalier de, Condé and, IV 612

Jassy, burnt by Solyman II, III 117; Peter the Great at, V 604; VI 308; Treaty of (1792), 676, VIII 289, 295, 337, 530, IX 385; Prince Ypsilanti at, X 178; entered by the Turks, 179; riot at, XI 283; 643

Jaubert, Hippolyte-François, Comte, X 503; 508

Jaucourt, Arnail-François, Marquis de, VIII 213

Jaureguy, Juan, III 255, 258

Jaurès, Jean, French politician, XII 119 sq.; 122 sqq.; and Dreyfus affair, 126; 127 sq.

Java, Dutch ventures to, III 632; spices of, IV 734; agreement of June 1619 and, 737; English in, 740; Dutch in, 742; captured (1811), IX 240; occupation of, 732; restored to Holland, 735; Stamford Raffles in, 754; rebellion in (1825), X 528; trade with, 761; Dutch rule in, XI 667 sq.; XII 534; trade of, 668

Javogues, Charles, revolutionary, VIII 505

Jay, John, American statesman, VI 461; VII 316, 319 sq., 328

Jeanne d'Albret, Queen of Navarre. *See* Navarre

Jeannin, Pierre, President, III 52; envoy to Holland, 640-2, 685, 691, V 702; Minister under Mary de' Medici, IV 118 sq.; superseded, 122, 625

Jebb, John, democrat, VIII 755

Jechna Doab, XI 741

Jedburgh, burnt by English (1523), II 422; Jacobites at, VI 101

Jedda, disturbance at, XI 635

Jedrzejow, **Diet of** (1576), III 97–8
Jefferson, Thomas, VII 166, 316, 320; President of United States, 324 sqq., 331, 369, 372 sq.; 407; 730; V 277; X 281; XII 744; 757
—— City, governor chased from (1861), VII 458
Jefferyes, James, Captain, mission of, to St Petersburg, VI 34
Jeffrey, Francis Jeffrey, Lord, editor of *Edinburgh Review*, IX 687; XI 347
Jeffreys, George, Lord Chief Justice, V 230 sqq.; 234; VI 805
Jefremoff, Major-general, at Zorndorf, VI 281
Jehángir, Moghul Emperor, IV 741; admits Dutch traders at Surat, 743; VI 515 sqq.; death of, 517
Jellachich (Jellačić) von Buzim, Baron François von, Austrian general, IX 255; surrender of, to Augereau, 258; 347
—— —— Joseph, Count, *Banus* of Croatia, XI 177; 179; and Croatian Diet, 180 sq.; 182; invades Hungary, 183 sq.; 185; marches on Vienna, 187; at Schwechat, 189; invades Hungary, 202 sq.; 206; 209; 211; 217
Jem (son of Mohammad II), conflict with Bayazid, I 85, 224; imprisoned in Europe, 86, 114; death of, 87, 115
Jemappes, battle of, VIII 299, 417, 534
Jemmingen, battle of (1568), III 223
Jemteland, acquired by Sweden, IV 572
Jena, Prussian army near, IX 274; Hohenlohe at, 275; battle of (1806), 276 sq., 326, 329, 331–2, 428, 592; University of, 325, X 364, 375, XI 150
Jenatsch, George, Grisons Preachers headed by, IV 46, 52, 54; escape of, 55; 61 sqq.
Jenckes, Thomas Allen, of Rhode Island, American politician, VII 635
Jenkins, Sir Richard, Resident of Nágpur, XI 726
—— Robert, English mariner, VI 48; 64; 66; 149; 157
Jenkinson, Sir Anthony, in Russia, XII 793
—— Charles. *See* Liverpool, 1st Earl of
Jenner, Edward, discoverer of vaccination, XII 779
—— Bernese Federalist, IX 97
Jensen, Adolf, German song-writer, XI 413
—— Peder, Danish scholar, II 609
—— Nicolas, printer at Venice, I 284, 561
Jephson, Major-general William, IV 443
Jermyn, Henry, Earl of St Albans. *See* St Albans
Jerningham, Sir Robert, II 429 sq.
Jerome (Hieronymus), execution of, II 451
Jersey, French attacks on, VI 452
—— Edward Villiers, 1st Earl of, V 430
—— Frances (Twysden), Lady, wife of 4th Earl, influence of, IX 675

Jerusalem, occupied by Ibrahim Pasha (1832), X 549; Protestant bishopric at, XI 6; the Holy Places of, 305, 311, 313, 324, 635
—— Paisios, Patriarch of, V 508
Jesuits (Society of Jesus), in the New World, I 62; constitution, organisation, and spread of, II 33, 651 sqq.; at Council of Trent, 667 sqq.; learning of, 688; introduced into Switzerland, 341; in Sweden, under Johan III, 631 sq.; in Poland, 637; and the Catholic reaction, III 83 sq.; Stephen Báthory uses in education, 102 sq.; in France, work of, in the cause of Christian and Renaissance learning, 61; and Henry IV, 664, 681; 140; and Ferdinand I, 145 sqq.; colleges of, at Mainz and Heiligenstadt, 155; in Bavaria, 160 sq.; and Maximilian II, 167, 178; Klesl's work in Austria, 701 sq.; 723; and the propaganda in England under Elizabeth, 286 sqq., 350 sqq.; in Florence, 389; in Savoy, under Emmanuel Philibert, 404 sq.; and the *Collegium Romanum*, 424; 435; and Sixtus V, 447 sqq., 455; in Ireland, failure of first mission, 585 sq.; second mission and its importance, 592 sqq.; political theories of, *see* Chap. XXII, *passim, especially* 765 sqq.; excluded from Venice, 774; and Catholic reaction in Empire, IV 4 sqq.; banished for short time from Bohemia (1618), 21; in re-conquered Bohemia, 73 sq.; 82; and Scioppius, 113; and Sigismund III of Poland and Sweden, 170; banished from Venice, 676 sq.; Pascal and, 795 sq.; Gui Patin and, V 73; 76; methods of, 80 sqq.; and Jansenism, 81 sqq.; and Popish Plot, 220 sqq.; 331; and James II of England, 335 sq.; and Emperor Leopold I, 341; and the Russian Pretender, 497 sqq.; 504; in America, 676 sqq., 683 sq.; 743; at Oxford, 746; and Jean de Labadie, 755 sq.; in France, on Louis XIV's death, VI 121, 127; Frederick William I and, 208; expelled from France (1764), 348, 592; rebellion of, in Paraguay, 364; expelled from Spain and Spanish America (1767), 372; use of confiscated property of, in Spain, 383; general attack upon by Carvalho in America and Portugal, 386 sq.; in Brazil, 390, 392; the Papacy and, 591 sq.; expelled from Naples, 593; expelled from Parma, 594; suppressed by Clement XIV, 595; confiscated wealth of, in Poland, 671; Catharine II and, 693; Frederick the Great and, 721; 806; in Canada, VII 72, 77, 81, 83 sq., 98 sqq.; in the West Indies, 96 sq.; exploration of Marquette, 362; VIII 8, 53, 789; reconstituted by Pius VII, X 6, 134; in France (c. 1824), 83 sq., 89 sq.; 94, 153, 162; in Modena,

107; excluded from Bavaria, 147; and education in Papal States, 152; and Conclave of 1829, 154; attack Gioberti, 166; Gregory XVI and, 167, 381; in Spain (*c.* 1815), 141 sq., 207; (*c.* 1820), 219; again expelled (1835), 236; expelled from Lisbon (1833), 335; in Spanish America, 247, 253, 271, 298; Paraguay missions of, 269 sq.; English Catholic Emancipation Act and, 654; in France (*c.* 1840), XI 23, and Guizot, 34 sqq., 67 sq.; Gioberti and, 65 sqq.; in Switzerland, 67, 239, 247 sqq.; in Rome, 76, 79, 81; 126; at Grätz, 155; and the dogma of the Immaculate Conception, 713; the *Civiltà Cattolica* of, 714; decree of expulsion of, from France (1880), XII 117; excluded from the German Empire (1872), 148; in Portugal, 271; in China, 514; in Siam, 534 sq.; in Japan, 542; in Canada, 614; in Tibet, 797

Jeunesse, La, French journal, XI 486

Jew of Malta, The (Marlowe's), III 374–5

Jewel, John, Bishop of Salisbury, II 161, 588; *Apologia,* III 348

Jewett, William Cornell, adventurer, VII 577

Jews, in Spain, I 359 sq.; in England, V 328; readmitted to Brandenburg, 648; in Russia, attitude of Peter the Great towards, 529; Indemnity Acts and, VI 44; Frederick William I and, 208; in Naples, 599; in Austria, 636; in Prussia, 711; in France, before the Revolution, VIII 52; and the Revolution, 732 sqq., 790; Napoleon I and, IX 204 sqq.; persecution of, in the States of the Church, X 152; in Rome, XI 74; Hungarian Diet and, 210; in Switzerland, 256; in Moldavia, 283; in Roumania under Constitution of 1866, 646; in Sweden, 680; in Tuscany, 706; in Austria, XII 193; in Russia, 339 sq., 351, 359; in later Roumania, 397 sqq.; researches in the history of, 846

Jezierski, John, Count, Polish deputy, X 467; 469

Jhansi, annexation of, XI 743; 746; 749

Jibuti, exploration from, XII 813

Jičin. *See* Gitschin

Jingo, mythological Empress of Japan, XII 564

Joan of Brabant, I 418, 423

Joanna, Queen of Castile. *See* Juana
—— I, Queen of Naples (d. 1382), I 108
—— II, Queen of Naples (d. 1434), I 108
—— Queen of Naples, widow of Ferdinand I, I 476
—— Queen of Naples, widow of Ferdinand II, I 476

João (John) I, King of Portugal, I 10
—— II, King of Portugal, I 16 sq., 20, 24
—— III, King of Portugal, II 172, 412 sq.
—— Dom, Prince of Portugal, death of, XI 574

Jochmus, A., German politician, XI 200

Jodelle, Estienne, III 55

Jodhpur, State of, XI 726
—— Bijai Singh, Mahárája of, IX 719

Jönsson, Thure, revolts against Gustavus Vasa, II 626 sq.

Joffrin, French socialist, XII 124

Johannesburg, beginnings of, XII 639; railway to, 640

Johannot, Joseph-Jean, French deputy, VIII 380, 385

John XXII (Jacques d'Euse of Cahors), Pope, I 656; V 621
—— King of Abyssinia, XII 240; 440; 444
—— II, King of Aragon, I 347
—— II, King of Castile, I 347, 351, 379
—— King of Denmark, I 456
—— V, Cantacuzenus, Emperor of the East, I 540
—— II, King of France, I 389
—— Zápolya, King of Hungary, I 96 sqq., 317, 336 sq.; leads national party in Hungary, II 198; defeated by Ferdinand I, 199; 206 sq., 220, 236, 242; Turkish vassal, III 106–7; keeps the Hungarian Crown by the Peace of 1533, 109; death of (1540), 118; and Transylvania, V 339
—— d'Albret, King of Navarre. *See* Navarre
—— Albert, King of Poland (1492–1501), and Wladislav II of Bohemia, I 336; 345
—— (II) Casimir, King of Poland, arrested, IV 378; sues for aid at Vienna, 427; and Prussian sovereignty, 429; Charles X and, 579 sqq.; renounces claim to Swedish Crown, 590; V 344; 349 sq.; 504; VI 664
—— III (Sobieski), King of Poland, V 41; 49; 341; 350 sq.; defeats Turks, 353 sq.; elected king, 345; 355; makes peace with Turkey, 355; and Louis XIV, 356; and the Emperor, 356, 362 sq.; aids Austria against Turks, 359, 361; 364 sq.; death of, 365, 370; 651; VI 105; 191 sq.
—— IV (Duke of Braganza), King of Portugal, Rupert and, IV 463 sq.; proclaimed King, 651 sq., 713; Holland and, 714; and Brazil, 753; V 105; 372; 674; VI 389
—— V, King of Portugal, death of, VI 384
—— VI, King of Portugal, marriage of, VI 381; becomes Regent, 388; rule of, as Prince Regent, IX 72, 301 sqq.; in Brazil, 304, x 310 sq.; succeeds to throne (1816), 311; 312; returns to Lisbon, 313; 317; and independence of Brazil, 317, 319; death of, 320
—— King of Saxony, XI 59; 455
—— III, King of Sweden, II 627, 629–32; candidate for Crown of Poland, III 91, 94;

policy of, IV 158; Finland bequeathed to, 160; marries Catherine Jagello, 162; 164; revolts, 165; becomes King, *ib.*; 166 sqq.; death of, 169, 173

John, Archduke of Austria, IX 65-7; 258; commands the army of Inner Austria, 346-7; 353-5; desires renewal of war, 359; 580; x 357; XI 152; elected *Reichsverweser*, 165; 166 sqq.; 171; Regent of Austria, 176; 178; 189; Frankfort Assembly and, 194; 199 sq.; resigns office, 230; 222

—— Don, of Austria, natural son of Charles V, II 409; III 18; 31; at Lepanto, 134 sqq., 494 sq.; at Tunis, 497; sent to Netherlands, 244 sqq., 286, 302; 490, 498; death of (1578), 499, 500 sq.; 515; 597

—— Don, of Austria (natural son of Philip IV, d. 1679), IV 619; child of Señora Calderon, 649; sent to Naples, 657 sq.; 659 sq.; in Catalonia, 661; Court faction of, 665; v 34 sq.; 45

—— of Baden. *See* Trier

—— of Bavaria. *See* Liége

—— Sigismund, Elector of Brandenburg. *See* Brandenburg

—— Don, of Brazil, Prince Regent of Portugal, demands the retrocession of Olivença, IX 605

—— of Capistrano, Italian preacher, I 69, 77, 629, 647

—— Infante of Castile, I 453

—— son of Frederick I of Denmark, II 229

—— Damascene, works of, I 586 sq.

—— Philip, Rhinegrave, III 3, 5; death of, 13; IV 375

—— Sigismund Zápolya, crowned as infant, II 242; heir of Hungary, III 118, 170 sq.; Transylvania adjudged to (1562), 123; annexes Szatmar, 125; does homage to Solyman II, 126

—— of Goch. *See* Pupper

—— of Leyden (Jan Beuckelssen), II 225 sq.; III 740, 755

—— of Lorraine, Cardinal, Archbishop of Rheims. *See* Lorraine

—— of Parma, the Blessed, I 663

—— of Ragusa, Cardinal, I 599

—— of Salisbury, medieval scholar and writer, I 536

—— of Speyer, printer at Venice, I 284, 561

Johnson, Andrew, VII 469, 543; President of the United States, 546, 598; policy of, 625 sqq.; rupture of, with Congress, 628 sqq.

—— Joseph, publisher, VIII 765

—— Reverdy, United States Minister to Great Britain, VII 636; XII 21

—— Samuel, VI 84; 610; x 697; 701

—— Samuel (Whig divine), his works burnt at Oxford, VI 807

—— Sir William, VII 95, 98, 124 sqq.

Johnson, William Samuel, deputy for Connecticut at Constitutional Convention, VII 246, 257, 271

—— W. H., Indian Survey official, XII 801

Johnston, Albert Sidney, Confederate general, VII 462; killed at Shiloh, 497

—— Archibald, of Warriston, *afterwards* Lord Warriston, at the General Assembly at Glasgow, IV 500

—— Sir Harry Hamilton, XII 811

—— Joseph Eccleston, VII 452; and Bull Run, 465 sqq.; 468; retreats to Gordonsville, 472; 474 sqq.; at Fair Oaks, 476; 504 sq.; succeeds Bragg, 514, 516; retreats to Atlanta, 521; censured, 522; in North Carolina, 529 sq.; surrender of, 542

—— Major, in New South Wales, IX 739

Johnstone, George, Commodore, VI 377 sq.; 454; 565

—— Sir Nathaniel, Governor of Charleston (Carolina), VII 37

—— Robert, son of Sir Nathaniel, Governor of South Carolina, VII 38

Joinville, Guise at, III 1, 31; treaty at (1585), 37

—— François-F.-P.-L.-M. d'Orléans, Prince de, XI 505

Jókai, Maurice, Hungarian novelist, XI 430 sq.

Joliet, Louis, French-Canadian explorer, VII 362

Jomard, Edme-François, Orientalist, VIII 605

Jomini, Baron Henry, Russian general, at the Congress of Vienna, IX 587

Jonas, Justus, Lutheran theologian, II 201, 207

Joner, Wolfgang, Abbot of Kappel, II 320, 337

Jones, Griffith, Welsh divine, VI 81

—— Sir Harford, ambassador to Persia, XII 800

—— Col. John, in Ireland, IV 547

—— John Paul (John Paul), naval adventurer, VI 449; VII 220

—— Michael, defends Dublin, IV 531 sq.; defeats Ormonde at Rathmines, 533; 534

—— Richard, political economist, x 783

—— Roger, Lieutenant, burns Harper's Ferry Armoury (1861), VII 454

—— Col. Theophilus, IV 547

—— Sir William, M.P., v 228

—— Sir William, writer, VIII 755

—— Sir William, Orientalist, XII 845

Jonesborough, Confederates defeated at (1864), VII 522

Jongestal, Allard Pieter, Dutch envoy to England, v 141

Jonker-Franzen War (1488-91), I 449

Jonköping, Assembly at (1599), IV 172; threatened by Danes, 179; Treaty of (1809), IX 323

Jonquière, Clement de Taffanel, Marquis de La, in New France, VII 119

Jonson, Ben, III 329, 380; IV 760; 762; V 745

Jordan, Camille, member of the *Conseil des Cinq-Cents*, VIII 506 sq.; IX 24; X 42; 47; and the *Doctrinaires*, 52-3; and press censorship, 54; 55; 56; issues election proclamation, 57; 60; 63; and new electoral proposals, 66; 67; dismissed from Council of State, 68; 73; 103

—— Sir Joseph, English vice-admiral, V 192 sq.

—— J. L. von, at the Congress of Vienna, IX 585

—— Sylvester, Professor at Marburg, X 374; 377

José, Dom, son of Pedro III of Portugal, VI 388

Joseph I, Emperor, V 47; crowned King of Hungary, 367; 401; and Charles XII, 417, 597; 419; and peace negotiations, 422 sqq., 427, 457; and Clement XI, 454; recognises Stanislaus Leszczynski, 596; and Augustus II, *ib.*; Treaty of, with Sweden, 607; death of, 429, 431; VI 97; 201; 586

—— II, Emperor, V 455; 516; Vol. VI, Chap. XVIII; 346; 354 sq.; 470; and Clement XIV, 594; 600; and Tuscany, 601; 603; and Switzerland, 616; 664; and Poland, 668 sq.; and Catharine II, 675, 678, 708; 676; 703; in Bohemia, 704; and War of the Bavarian Succession, 705 sq.; and Austrian Netherlands, 710; 731; VIII 277, 280 sqq.; invades Holland, 287; and Frederick the Great, 309; policy of, 310 sqq.; in Crimea, 315; declares war on Turkey (1788), 316 sq., 324 sqq., 524; and Austrian Netherlands, 317 sqq., 327 sqq.; and Turkey, IX 385; revolt against policy of, 415; X 135; 144 sq.; and "Punctations of Ems," 158; and the Church, 357; 406; and Galicia, 461; 520; XI 399; 401; 422; 431; 653; antipapal policy of, 708; death of, VI 654; VIII 292, 332

—— I, King of Portugal, VI 166; 368; reign of, 384 sqq.; death of, 375, 388

—— King of Spain. *See* Bonaparte, Joseph

—— Archduke, Palatine of Hungary, IX 41; XI 673

—— Clement. *See* Cologne, Joseph Clement, Elector of

—— *le Père* (François Leclerc du Tremblay), at Ratisbon, IV 115, 138, 141, 680; Richelieu and, 123; 135; death of, 149; notice of, 150; Grotius and, 250; 376

—— Michael, leader of Cornish rebels, I 469

Joséphine, Empress (de Beauharnais, *née* Tascher de la Pagerie), consort of Napoleon I, VIII 563; 678; IX 23-4; 32, 107, 113, 139-40

Josephstadt. *See* Jaroměř

Josephus, early printed editions of, I 612 sq.

Jósika, Baron Nicolas, Hungarian writer, XI 426; 430

—— Baron Samuel, XI 152; 216

Joubert, Barthélemy-Catharine, French general, VIII 444, 566, 580, 582 sq., 654; succeeds Macdonald, 657; killed, 659, 672

—— French Lutheran, burnt at Paris, II 284

—— and Egyptian finances, XII 434

Jouffroy, Théodore-Simon, X 95; 103; 514

Joule, James Prescott, and theory of heat, XII 784

Jourdan, Comte Jean-Baptiste, Marshal of France, VIII 351; commands Army of the North, 431; and Army of the Sambre and Meuse, 435 sqq., 442, 497 sq.; *Fructidorien*, 515; at Stockach, 656; in the *Cinq-Cents*, 673, 676 sq.; IX 71; 112; at Talavera, 452; director of King Joseph's armies, 476; at Burgos, 477; strengthens garrison of Pampeluna, 478

—— Mathieu Jouve, Avignon bandit, VIII 218

Journal des Débats, IX 130, 570, X 59, 91, 97, 490, 507, XI 34, 292

—— *de l'Empire*, IX 130

—— *de Paris*, IX 130

—— *du Peuple*, XI 24

Jovanovich, Baron, XII 400

Jove-Llanos, Gaspar Melchor de, Spanish dramatic poet, V 69; VI 823; VIII 782

Jovius, Paulus. *See* Giovio, Paolo

Joyce, Cornet George, IV 342

Joyeuse, Anne, Duke of, III 36 sq., 40; death of, 43

—— François de, Cardinal, III 433; 452; IV 671

—— Henry, Duke of, Marshal of France, III 668, 684

—— William, Vicomte de, Marshal of France, III 3, 20 sqq.

Joyeuse Entrée, VI 651 sq.

Juan, Jorge, X 273

—— Don, of Austria. *See* John

Juana, Princess of Castile (*La Beltraneja*), I 352, 363

—— *la Loca*, Queen of Castile, I 362-4, 368, 373, 379, 453, 455, 475-7, 484, 490

—— Doña, sister of Philip II, III 479-80, 484, 490

Juárez, Benito Pablo, Mexican statesman, X 305; XI 476 sq.; 479; and Maximilian, 484; 565; President of Mexico, XII 676; and Porfirio Díaz, 677

Jub river, Germany and, XII 661

Jubé, Auguste, Baron de La Pérelle, Adjutant-general of the Directorial Guard, VIII 677

Jud, Leo, II 316, 318

Judenburg, truce at (1797), VIII 582, 585

Jühlke, African explorer, XII 160

Juel, Jens, Danish admiral, v 571; 579
—— Niels, Danish admiral, v 561; 570
—— Owe, negotiates with Charles X, iv 587
Jülich, siege of (1610), iv 118; and the Treaty of Cleves, 409; War of, 426; 433; taken by Archduke Leopold, 624; acquired by Duke of Neuburg, v 33; 350; the Allies at, 409; 627 sq.; 643; and War of the Austrian Succession, vi 231; 339
Jülich and Berg, Maria, heiress of, marries John III of Cleves, ii 236, iii 716
—— —— William IV, Duke of, ii 236
Jülich-Cleves, duchy of, ii 75, 236, 239, 243 sqq.; the disputed succession in, iii 558, 686 sqq., 715 sqq.; siege of Jülich by Maurice, 643; taken by Archduke Leopold, 688; Archduke Albert cuts off access to, 689; Henry IV's designs upon, 687 sqq.; exposed to Dutch immigration, 705; "Possessing" Princes in, 730-2; succession in, iv 2, 5; 10; 12 sq.; 100; 104; and Peace of Westphalia, 408; France, Brandenburg and, 428; 578; 624
Jülich-Cleves-Berg, partition of, vi 231
—— Anna of (daughter of William V), claim to the duchies, iii 716
—— Antonia (Duchess of Lorraine), 2nd consort of Duke John William of, iii 722; regent, 729
—— Jacobaea of Baden-Baden, 1st consort of John William, Duke of, iii 715 sq.
—— John III (de La Marck), Duke of, ii 75; unites the duchies, 236; iii 716
—— John William, Duke of, death of (1609), iii 642, 686, 729; Bishop of Münster, 705; 709; insanity of, 715 sq.; 722
—— Magdalena of (daughter of William), iii 716
—— Maria (of Austria), Duchess of, married to William V, ii 244
—— Maria Eleonora (daughter of William V), claimant to the duchies, iii 716, v 636
—— Sibylla (daughter of William V), as possible claimant, iii 716; second marriage of, 729
—— William V (de La Marck), Duke of (*also* of Gelders), ii 75; submits to Charles V, 77, 244 sq., i 424; becomes Lutheran, ii 236 sq., 243; excluded from Schmalkaldic League, 239, 241; 252; 450 sq.; iii 156; 172; 705; insanity of, 715; succession to, 716; v 636
Jüterbok, Treaty of (1611), iii 733; Gallas defeated at, iv 388
Julian the Apostate, iii 752
Julian, George W., of Indiana, vii 469
Juliana Maria, Queen of Denmark, consort of Frederick V, vi 746; 749 sqq.; 754; viii 279
Juliers, William IX, Duke of, and of Gelders. *See* Gelders

Julius II (Giuliano della Rovere), Pope, i 110, 177; an enemy of the Borgia, 184; 221; Perugia and Bologna attacked by, 128, 245; Venice and, 129-34, 196, 244 sqq., 268; and League of Cambray, 131, 246 sq.; War between France and, 135 sq., 197 sq., 248 sqq.; Maximilian I and, 139, 319; Cesare Borgia and, 195 sqq., 242 sq.; and Holy League, 198, 248 sq., 366, 479; death of, 139, 252; character of, 243 sq.; Gallican Church and, 388; 491, 548; Church reform and, 620 sq.; 655, 657; a pluralist, 659; 657, 665, 667; 670; sale of offices by, 672; 690; art under, ii 5-10; 30, 281, 426; iii 737
—— III (Giovanni Maria del Monte), Pope, ii 85 sqq., 90; sends Council back to Trent, 266; 399; sends Pole to England, 518 sq.; death of, 534; and the Jesuits, 655; 663, 668, 670, 672
Julius Exclusus, attack on Julius II in, ii 9
Jullian, Camille, French historian, xii 834
Jung Bahadur, xi 749
—— Joachim, naturalist, v 734
Jungbunzlau, school of Bohemian Brethren, iii 703; Austrian magazine at, vi 257
Junge Pfalz. See Sulzbach
Jungfernhof, Saxons defeated at (1700), v 587
Jungius, Jacob, man of science, iv 425
Jungman, Josef, Čech writer, xi 653 sq.
Junisbeg, Turkish ambassador at Venice, iii 113
Junius, Franciscus. *See* Du Jon, François
Junius, Letters of, vi 441
Junker, Wilhelm, African explorer, xii 811 sq.
Junot, Andoche, Duc d'Abrantès, French general, viii 564, 585 sq., 611; ordered to Lisbon, ix 303-4; French in Portugal commanded by, 343; Italian peasant revolt crushed by (1806), 398; attacks Lisbon, 428, x 310; in possession of Portugal, ix 429 sq.; 435-6; and campaign of 1808, 439; proposals to British, 440-1; 456; at Busaco, 461; and Russian campaign, 488 sqq.; occupies Lisbon, x 310
"Junto," becomes exclusively Whig (1697), v 274
Jura, Swiss manufactures in, ix 425; disturbances in, xi 240; 242; 246; 259
Jureff, Nikita Romanovich, v 496
Jurieu, Pierre, v 76; 87
Jurischitz, Hieronymus, iii 108 sq.
—— Nicholas, heroic defence of Güns by, iii 107
Jussieu, lecturer in the French School of Medicine, excluded, x 78
Jussuf, Grand Vezir (1711), v 606
—— Grand Vezir (1788), viii 325 sq.
Justamond, John O., writer, vii 96
Justicia, in Aragon, i 351

Justification by Faith, doctrine of, at Trent, II 645, 667 sq.

Justinian, *Institutes*, XII 704

Jutland, rising in (1534), II 614 sq.; IV 102 sq.; restored to Denmark, 109; Swedish reduction of, 387; 561; 567; 571; 584 sq.; invaded by Frederick William, 588; 589; V 607; 609; agricultural condition of, VI 737; XI 167; lost by Danes, 441; provincial Diet of, 692

Juusten, Paulus. *See* Viborg, Ordinary (and Bishop) of

Juxon, William, Archbishop of Canterbury, Bishop of London, IV 279; Lord Treasurer, 283

Kaarden, Paul van, III 638

Kabardia (Kabardine district), VI 304; acquired by Russia, 674

Kabeljaauws, party in opposition to Jacqueline of Hainault, I 419 sq., 423, 445

Kabul, the Emperor Bábar at, VI 509; 510; occupied by Humáyun, 511; 512; 517; Shah Jehán's army at, 518; 524; 527; XI 731; evacuation of, 733; 735 sq.; Russian envoy at, XII 34, 469, 801; 37; 459; 466; Cavagnari murdered at, 471; 475; Sir Mortimer Durand at, 483; caravan route to, 793; 800

Kabylia, rising in, XII 129

Kachar, invaded, XI 727; 730

Kachovski, Peter, Russian officer, X 443

Kärst, Julius, German historian, XII 845

Käser, Leonard, Lutheran martyr, II 202

Käuffi, Kilian, Abbot of St Gall, II 331

Kaffa, Crimean port, VI 305

Kaffirs, War with (1834-5), XI 780; restored to their land, 781; War with (1850-3), 784; Transkei, England makes war on, XII 636

Kaffraria, British, XI 786

Kafiristan, valleys of, XII 805

Kaga, *daimiô* of, XI 832

Kagg, Field-Marshal Lars, IV 589

Kagoshima, British squadron at, XI 846; 849; naval expedition to, 853; 864; the Satsuma clan and, XII 562; 563

Kaim, Austrian general, IX 62

K'aip'ing, XII 505; Japanese army at, 588 sq.

Kaiser Wilhelm Canal, XII 171

Kaisersberg, Johannes Geiler von, I 323; preaches on *Ship of Fools*, 683; II 29, 106

Kaiserslautern, French in, IV 144; taken by the Imperialists, 367; Brunswick at, VIII 424; battle of (1793), 427 sq.

Kaiserswerth, siege of (1702), V 406

Kaja, and the battle of Gross-Görschen (1813), IX 517

Kakhánoff, Commission of, XII 313; 318

Kakoun, fight at, VIII 609

Kalahari desert, XI 783; crossed by Livingstone, XII 808

Kalakaua, King of Hawaii, VII 667

Kalamâs river, the Greek frontier and, XII 398, 403

Kalamata, captured by Venetians, V 365

Kalands, The (German associations), II 108

Kalat, Khan of, and Quetta, XII 467

Kaláyeff, murders Grand Duke Sergius, XII 350

Kalb, French agent in America, VI 352

Kalckreuth, Count Friedrich Adolph of, Prussian envoy, VIII 412; 415; Prussian Marshal, Governor of Danzig, IX 289; 292, 307

Kalckstein, Ludwig Karl von, Prussian general, IV 230

Kalgan, XII 792; caravan route to, 793; 796; Younghusband at, 802; 804

Kalgoorlie, gold discovered at, XII 619; 634

Kalinjar, Sher Shah killed at, VI 511

Kalisch, Swedes defeated at (1706), V 595; Convention of (1813), IX 513; 579, 592, 596; Kutusoff at, 514-5; part of department of, ceded to Prussia, 655-6; X 449; 455

Kállay, Baron Benjamin von, Austrian Minister of Finance, XII 199 sq.; 400

Kalm, Peter, Swedish traveller, VII 102 sq.

Kalmar, Union of (1397), I 293, 502, II 228, 600, IV 170, 561; Court of Erik at, 161; Statute of (1587), 168 sq.; taken by Swedes, 172 sq.; war of (1611), 177, 179, 560, 565 sq.

Kálnoky, Count Gustave, Austrian statesman, XII 199; 211

Kalpi, rebels defeated at, XI 749

Kaltenborn, Rudolph Wilhelm von, *Letters of an old Prussian Officer*, VI 713

Kaluga, retreat to (1812), IX 497-9

Kama river, Russian boundary, V 481

Kameke, General von, XI 586 sq.; 589

Kameniec, taken by Turks (1672), V 353; 354 sq.; 365; restored to Poland (1699), 371

Kamenskoi, Michel Fédorovitch, Count, Russian Field-Marshal, orders Russian retreat, IX 284; succeeded by Bennigsen, 285

—— Count Nikolai, and War with Turkey, IX 485

Kames, Henry Home, Lord, VIII 769

Kamienie, plain of, III 86

Kamimura, Japanese admiral, XII 588

Kammergericht, of Frederick III, I 304, 313; of Maximilian I, 313, 315. *See also Reichskammergericht*

Kammermeister, Joachim. *See* Camerarius

Kampschulte, F. Wilhelm, German historian, XII 847

Kamptz, K. C. A. H. von, Prussian statesman, X 377

Kámrán, son of Emperor Bábar, VI 510 sq.

Kamran Shah, ruler of Herat, XI 731

Kamschatka, survey of, V 535; Russian fortress in, XI 272

Kanagawa, xi 833; 836; opened to trade, 840; 842
Kanakas, in Queensland, xii 625; 633
Kanaris, Constantine, Greek admiral, x 186; xii 391
Kanawha valley, Crook in, vii 516; Hunter retires to, 531
Kandahar, reduction of, by Bábar, vi 509; 511; taken from the Persians, 512; 518; lost to the Moghuls, 519; 524; 527; xi 731; Shah Shuja crowned at, 732; 733 sqq.; relief of, xii 37; 459; 470 sq.; Roberts's march to, 475; caravan route to, 793; 800
Kandy, King of, Dutch treat with, iv 711; British troops in (1803), ix 734
Kanem, the French Congo and, xii 130
K'ang Yuwei, Chinese Reformer, xii 517
Kangaroo Island, xi 792
K'anghsi, Emperor of China, xii 514
Kánhoji, Gáekwár, holds Baroda, ix 726
Kankrin, Count Jegor, Russian Minister of Finance, x 422; 428; xi 265 sq.
Kano, explorers at, xii 807 sq.
Kansas, creation of Territory of, vii 427; the struggle in (1854–6), 430, 434 sq., 458; refused admission to Union, 435; in Civil War, 462; negro suffrage in, 629; population of, 708, 711
Kansas-Nebraska Act (1854), vii 427 sqq., 444
Kan-su, exploration in, xii 797
Kansuh Ghuri, Mamluk Sultan of Syria, defeated by Selim I, i 91
Kant, Immanuel, writings of, vi 727 sq.; 825 sqq.; 834 sq.; 837; viii 772 sq.; ix 325; 328; *Project of a Perpetual Peace*, 669; Schiller and, x 391; 393; 400; xii 155
Kápolna, Hungarians repulsed at, xi 205
Kappel, forces of Zurich at, ii 331; First Peace of (1529), 332; battle of, 196, 216, 217, 337; death of Zwingli at, 209, 216; Second Peace of (1531), 338
Kappeyne, Joannes, Dutch statesman, xii 243 sq.
Kara Sea, exploration of, xii 795
—— George Petrovich, Servian leader, ix 387; x 172; xi 284 sq.
—— Ibrahim, Grand Vezir, v 366 sq.
—— Mustafa, Grand Vezir, succeeds Ahmad Kiuprili, v 355; 358; marches against Austria, 359; 360; besieges Vienna, 360 sqq.; retreat of, 363; death of, 364
—— Osman, Mediterranean pirate, iii 541
Karabusa, retained by Venice, v 349
Karachi, xi 346; 732; capture of, 736
Karageorgevich, Alexander. *See* Alexander
—— Peter. *See* Peter
Karagué, explorers in, xii 809
Karakorum, ruins of, xii 792
—— pass, xii 801
Karakozoff, D., attempts to assassinate Tsar Alexander II, xi 626, 630, xii 295; 298; 303

Karamsin, Nicolai Mikhailovitch, Russian historian, viii 784; treatise of, ix 487; x 438; xi 262; xii 842
Karashahr, travellers at, xii 799, 802 sq.
Karatheodori, Alexander, at Congress of Berlin, xii 394; Provincial Governor of Crete, 419
Karauli, State of, xi 726
Karaveloff, Regent of Bulgaria, xii 409
Kardis, Peace of (1661), v 344, 505, 562 sq., 587
Karikal, France and, vi 347, 464, 533
Karim Khan, Pindari chief, xi 725 sq.
Karl, Duke of Sudermanland. *See* Charles IX of Sweden
Karlshamn, recovered by Sweden, v 570
Karlskrona, Swedish naval station, v 578; 610; vi 28; new docks at, 775 sq.
Karlstad, built by Charles IX, iv 176; conference at, xii 289
Karlsten, fortress of, v 583
Kármán, Joseph, Hungarian writer, xi 423
Karnkowski, Bishop of Cujavia. *See* Cujavia
Karpóvich, Russian student, xii 315
Kars, Turkish army crosses Euphrates near, iii 121; ceded to Russia, xii 342, 398; 389; 392
Karski, John, Polish officer, x 453
Karwonski, family of, iii 75
Kaschan, submits to Emperor Leopold I, v 366
Kashgar, Russia and, xi 632; xii 343; caravan route to, 793; 796; 800 sqq.
Kashgaria, China and, xii 502
Kashirsk iron-works, v 533
Kashmir, under Moghul dynasty, vi 511, 512; in 1747, 524, xi 731; and the Sikhs, 732, 740; xii 485; 793; exploration in, 800, 802
Kasimbazar, factory of, seized, vi 551; 553
Kasimir IV, King of Poland. *See* Casimir
Kaskaskia, captured by Clarke (1778), vii 221 sq.; 356
Kassange, Livingstone at, xii 808
Kassassin, Egyptian defeat at, xii 437
Katak, capture of (1805), ix 726
Katharina Alexeievna, Grand Duchess of Russia. *See* Catharine II, Tsarina
Katkoff, Michael, Russian journalist, xi 625 sq.; 629; editor of the *Moscow Gazette*, xii 296; 298; 300; 311; opposes Ignatieff, 313; 314
Katona, Joseph, Hungarian dramatist, xi 424; 430 sq.
Katséna, explorers at, xii 810
Katt, de, reader to Frederick the Great, vi 281; 290
Katte, Hans Hermann von, Prussian officer, vi 212
Katunga, explorers in, xii 807
Katwijk, naval action off (1653), iv 476
Katzbach, French reverse at (1813), ix 524, 528

Kaufmann, Constantine von, Governor of Russian Turkestan, XI 631 sq.; XII 461; 470

Kaulbars, Alexander, Russian general, Bulgarian Minister of War, XII 405; in the Russo-Japanese War, 597 sqq.; on the Pamirs, 802

—— Nicholas, Russian major-general, in Bulgaria, XII 409 sq.

Kaunitz, Wenzel Anton, Prince von, Austrian Chancellor, VI 249; 252 sqq.; and Franco-Austrian alliance, 320, 331, 335 sqq., 400 sq.; 341 sqq.; and Prussia, 398 sq., 647 sq., 656, 702; rejects British overtures, 427; 615 sq.; and Joseph II, 627; 628; and Russia, 629 sq.; 631; 633; and Turkish alliance, 634; 635; 639; and United Provinces, 640; and Antwerp, 642; 651; 654 sq.; 670; and Frederick the Great, 708; 783; VIII 221, 277 sq., 310, 313 sq., 319, 399; retires (1792), 533; originates idea of the Concert of Europe, X 3

Kavanaghs, The, III 583

Kawamura, Japanese general, XII 585; 597 sq.

Kawerau, G., German historian, XII 847

Kay, Prussian defeat at, VI 292, 324

—— John, and the weaver's loom, X 735

—— Robert, and the weaver's loom, X 735

Kayserling, Count, Russian Minister at Warsaw, VI 200; 667

Kazalinsk Fort, XI 273

Kazan, annexed to Russia, V 479; 502; 531; illegal taxation in, X 426; University of, 431; student disturbances at, XII 315

Kazembe, embassy to, XII 808; 809

Kazeneck, Count, Austrian Minister, VIII 282

Kazinczy, Francis, Hungarian poet, VIII 777; XI 423 sqq.; 431

Kazvin, Morier at, XII 800

Keane, John Keane, Lord, British major-general at New Orleans, VII 345; Commander-in-chief at Bombay, XI 732

Kearny, Philip, American general, VII 395

Kearsarge, The, fights the "commerce-destroyer" *Alabama*, VII 566

Keate, Robert William, Governor of Natal, XI 787

Keats, John, VI 830, 834 sq.; the poetry of, X 720 sqq.; XI 350

Keble, John, X 657; and Oxford Movement, XI 348; 354; 711

Kedah, Great Britain and, XII 536

Keeling, William, in India, IV 741

Keely. *See* Quaelly

Keenan, Augustus H., Confederate Senator, VII 605

Keene, Sir Benjamin, English ambassador at Madrid, VI 65 sqq.; 146 sq.; 149; 155; 157; and Patiño, 166; 167; 363 sq.; death of, 365

Kehl, captured by French (1703), V 407; 408; 410; ceded by France, 436; 450; 454

Keigwin, Richard, revolt of, at Bombay, V 698

Keiller, James, manufacturer, XI 684

Keiskama river, XI 780

Keith, George Keith Elphinstone, Viscount, Admiral, expedition of, to Cape Colony, VIII 484 sq., IX 749; VIII 617, 632; IX 51; 53, 58; defends Straits of Dover, 210

—— James Francis Edward (Marshal Keith), VI 105; at Prague, 259; 280; 306 sq.; death of, 289

—— Sir Robert Murray, Colonel, English Minister at Copenhagen, VI 737; 750; VIII 277

Keksholm, ceded to Russia by Sweden (1595), IV 171, (1721), V 615; IV 176; Peace of Stolbova and, 181

Kelantan, Great Britain and, XII 536

Kelat-i-Ghilzai, evacuation of, XI 735

Keller, Augustine, and suppression of Aargau monasteries, XI 246

—— Count D.-L.-Christophe von, VIII 429

—— Count Émile, French politician, XI 469; 472

—— Ferdinand, archaeologist, XI 261

—— Gottfried, X 405; XI 261; 417 sqq.

—— Count, Russian general, XII 587 sqq.

Kellermann, François-Christophe, Duc de Valmy, Marshal of France, VIII 346, 351; commands the Army of the Centre, 409 sqq., 413, 415; and War with Sardinia, 437, 443 sq., 570

—— François-Étienne, Duc de Valmy (son of above), French general, at Waterloo, IX 636 sqq.

Kellett, Sir Henry, Vice-Admiral, XII 795

Kelley, Benjamin Franklin, Federal general, VII 457

Kellgren, Johan Henrik, Swedish poet, VIII 789

Kellie, Alexander Erskine, 5th Earl of, VI 117

Kelly, George, Jacobite, VI 111

—— impostor at Court of Rudolf II, III 697

Kelso, attacked by the English (1522), II 420, (1542), 456, (1544), 460; Jacobites at, VI 99, 101

Kelung, French occupation of, XII 131

Kelvin, William Thomson, Lord, XII 784 sq.; 787

Kemble, John Mitchell, historian, XII 835

Kemény, Sigismund, Baron, XI 426 sq.; 430

Keményi, John, Prince of Transylvania. *See* Transylvania

Kempen, Stephen, Reformer, II 161

Kempenaar, de, Dutch Liberal, XI 663

Kempis, Thomas à, the *Imitation of Christ*, I 625, 628; V 755

Kempten, abbots of, II 176; risings of peasants at (1525), 179; the 14 Protestant cities joined by, 205

Kempthorne, Sir John, Vice-Admiral, v 192 sq.

Kendal, Jacobite force at, VI 101
—— Ehrengard Melusina von der Schulenburg, Duchess of, VI 19; 484

Kenesaw Mountain, fighting at (1864), VII 521

Kenia, Mount, XII 809

Kenmare, Thomas Browne, Viscount, and the Irish Catholics, IX 694; x 627; 640

Kenmure, William Gordon, 6th Viscount, VI 101; 103

Kennebec river, Popham and Gilbert land at, VII 12; boundary of Acadia, 20, 75, 89

Kennedy, Edmund B., Australian explorer, XI 795

Kennemer, The (inhabitants of North Holland), I 420

Kenner, Duncan F., Confederate senator, VII 605

Kennicott, Robert, in Yukon district, XI 633

Kenninghall, Mary Tudor at, II 514

Kent, rising in, under Wyatt, II 527; Kentish Petition sent from, IV 300; Royalist rising in, 348 sq.
—— Island (Maryland), dispute concerning, VII 32 sq.
—— Edward Augustus, Duke of, x 674
—— Victoria Mary Louisa, Duchess of, x 674 sq.

Kentish Knock, victory of Blake off the, IV 436, 473, 478, 480

Kentucky, settlers in, VII 221, 356 sq.; trade and manufacture in, 353 sq.; becomes a State (1791), 357; population of, *ib.*, 359, 689; enters Union (1792), 359, 413, 421; upholds Tariff, 381; resolutions of (1798), 410 sq.; and secession, 453, 461, 470; invaded by Confederates (1861), 462 sq., 492; Bragg invades (1862), 507; slavery in, 581, 584 sqq.

Kenyérmezö, defeat of Turks at (1479), I 335

Kenyon, Lloyd Kenyon, 1st Baron, Chief Justice, and question of Libel, IX 672; and Catholic Emancipation, 678

Keogh, John, and the Irish Catholics, IX 694–5, x 627 sqq.

Keon, Myles, and Back-lane Parliament, x 628

Kepler, Johann, astronomer, II 690; III 697, 707; v 708; 711; 713 sqq.; 719

Keppel, Arnold Joost van, Earl of Albemarle. *See* Albemarle
—— Augustus Keppel, 1st Viscount, Admiral, VI 437; 450 sq.; 462; resigns, 463; First Lord of Admiralty, 464

Ker, John, of Kersland, VI 92

Kerch, Russia and, VI 634, 673 sq.

Kerdrel, Vincent-Paul-Marie-Casimir Audren de, French politician, XII 106

Kergorlay, Comte Louis-Florian-Paul de, x 488

Keria, Russian explorer at, XII 799; 803

Kerjean, de, French officer in India, VI 541

Kern, J. Conrad, Swiss statesman, XI 256

Kerner, Georg, VIII 773

Kéroualle, Louise de, Duchess of Portsmouth. *See* Portsmouth

Kerry, O'Moores and O'Conors in, III 588; "undertakers" in, 599

Kerrykurrihy, granted to Earl of Desmond, III 594; invaded by Fitzmaurice, 595

Kersaint, Gui-Pierre de Coetnempren, Comte de, French admiral, VIII 247, 251, 449; IX 363

Kersausie, Joachim-R.-T. Gaillard de, x 491 sq.; 499

Kervyn de Lettenhove, Baron J. M. B. C., XII 848

Keshen, Chinese Commissioner, XI 809

Kesselsdorf, Prussian victory at, VI 244

Ket, Robert, rebellion of, II 492

Ketteler, Freiherr Wilhelm Emmanuel von, Bishop of Mainz. *See* Mainz
—— Baron von, German Minister at Peking, XII 520 sq.

Kettenbach, Henry of, Reformer, II 161

Kettler, Gotthard, High Master of the Teutonic Order, III 73; v 493 sq.

Key West, in the Civil War, VII 552

Keyes, Erasmus Darwin, American general, VII 476

Keyser, Rudolf, Norwegian historian, XI 701

Kezanlik, Bulgarian raid on, XI 638

Khaibar, Afridis in, XII 488; 489 sq.
—— Pass, XII 469 sqq.; 475

Khair Eddin (Chaireddin). *See* Barbarossa II

Khalifa, The, XII 443; 447 sq.

Khaltúrin, Russian revolutionary, XII 307 sq.

Khan Jehán Lodi, Afghan commander, VI 517

Kharaj, The (Turkish capitation tax), I 102

Kharkoff, Russian military colony, x 416; XII 329; peasant disturbances in, 333; 376

Kharram, Prince. *See* Shah Jehán

Khartum, Gordon at, XII 40, 442 sq.; 41 sq.; 441; fall of, 443; 444; the Khalifa at, 447; 448; 811

Khátmándu, Ochterlony at, IX 732

Khelat, English traveller at, XII 800

Kherson, arsenal of, VI 648; Russian military colony, x 416

Khevenhüller, Count Ludwig Andreas, Austrian Field-Marshal, VI 233 sqq.; 236

Khilkóff, Prince, and Russo-Japanese War, XII 346; 358

Khiva, Russia and, v 544; XI 273; Khan of, and the Tsar, 630; Russian conquest of, 631 sq.; absorbed by Russia, XII 460; 464; 491; 793; political mission to, 800; 801

Khoczim, defended by Chodkievicz, iv 189; the Turks defeated at (1673), v 354, 364; fortress of, vi 307 sqq.; fortress of, captured by Austrians (1788), viii 325, 334

Khokand, principality of, vi 509; Khan of, xi 273; Russian conquest of, 632; absorbed by Russia, xii 460

Kholm, diocese of, xii 339

Khomyakóff, President of third Duma, xii 375

Khorasan, Russia and, xii 492

Khoten, Russian explorer at, xii 799; 800 sqq.

Khozhend, taken by the Russians, xi 631

Khrustalyéff, Russian politician, xii 361 sq.

Khuen-Héderváry, Count, Hungarian statesman, xii 199; 204

Khulm, Moorcroft at, xii 800

Khusrev Pasha, x 549; 562; 567

Khusru, son of Emperor Jehángir, vi 515

Kiachta, Russian army at, xi 816 sq.; postroad to, xii 792; 795

Kianghung, State of, xii 508

Kiangsu, province of, xi 821; xii 507; disturbances in, 517

Kiaochow, German occupation of, xii 4, 513; 132; 170

Kibálchich, Russian revolutionary, xii 304; 308; 310; hanged, 311

Kibet, explorer at, xii 811

Kido, Japanese Councillor of State, xi 865; xii 549 sq.

Kieff, occupied by Russia, v 353; 358; 477 sq.; and Lithuania, 480; 484; ceded to Russia (1667), 505; 511; 516; 519; 531; Russian retreat to (1706), 594; 595 sq.; Russian administration of, x 459; University of, xi 267; 625; revolutionary propaganda in, xii 304; 305 sq.; Osinsky hanged at, 307; 358 sq.; mutiny at, 362

Kiel, University of, vi 753; Jackson sent to, ix 299; Peace of (1814), 582, 656, x 19, xi 682 sq., xii 281; Provisional Government at, xi 161; 225; 445

Kielce, school of mining in, x 449

Kieler Blätter, xi 692

Kielmannsegge, Baroness Sophia Charlotte von. *See* Darlington, Countess of

—— Baron von, Master of the Horse, vi 20

Kienmayer, Baron Michel de, Austrian Field-Marshal, ix 254

Kierkegaard, Sören Aaby, Danish writer, xi 699

Kieser, D. G. von, German professor of medicine, x 364 sq.

Kikemba, Cameron at, xii 810

Kildare, English in, iii 580

—— Gerald FitzGerald, 8th Earl of, i 466, 468, 471-2

—— Gerald Fitzgerald, 9th Earl of, Lord Deputy of Ireland, ii 442, 471; iii 581

—— Gerald Fitzgerald, 11th Earl of, iii 590

—— Thomas Fitzgerald, 10th Earl of, ii 442, 471; iii 581

Kildare, 20th Earl of. *See* Leinster, 1st Duke of

Kilia, captured by Stephen the Great, i 83; seized by the Turks (1484), 84; demolition of forts at, x 169, 175

Kilimanjaro, Mount, xii 809

Kilkenny, Confederation of, iii 610; Ormonde's Treaty at (1649), iv 435, 532; General Assembly of Confederated Catholics at (1642), 525; Rinuccini at, 529 sq.; 531; 534; Articles of, 535

Killala, French force lands at, ix 702

Killiecrankie, battle of (1689), v 293; Pass of, vi 116

Killybegs, arrival of Spanish vessel at, iii 608

Kilmacrenan, O'Dogherty killed at, iii 613

Kilmaine, Charles-Joseph, French general, at Arlon (1793), viii 429; succeeds Custine, 430

Kilmainham gaol, Parnell in, xii 80

Kilmarnock, William Boyd, 4th Earl of, vi 114; 117

Kilpatrick, Hugh Judson, American general, vii 527

—— John, Major, vi 541; at Plassey, 554 sq.

Kilrush, Irish rebels defeated at, iv 524

Kilsyth, Royalist victory of (1645), iv 332

Kilwarden, Arthur Wolfe, 1st Viscount, and Emmet's rebellion, ix 707

Kimberley (S. Africa), foundation of, xi 787; xii 635; Cecil Rhodes at, 638; 639; siege of, 642

—— (Australia), gold discovered at, xii 619; 814

—— John Wodehouse, 1st Earl of (Lord Wodehouse), xi 343

Kimbolton, death of Catharine of Aragon at, ii 444

—— Lord. *See* Manchester, 2nd Earl of

Kim-ok Kiun, Korean rebel, xii 510

Kinbergen, Dutch admiral, viii 295

Kinbuck, Jacobite force at, vi 100

Kinburn, vi 305; acquired by Russia, 674; besieged by the Turks (1787), viii 316

Kinchow, occupied by the Japanese, xii 511; 586

Kinder, Claude William, and Chinese railways, xii 505

Kineyri, fight at, xi 740

King, Philip Gidley, Governor of New South Wales, ix 738

—— Richard, ride of, to Grahamstown, xi 782

—— Rufus, Massachusetts deputy at the Constitutional Convention (1787), Vol. vii, Chap. viii *passim*, 364

—— William, Archbishop of Dublin, vi 481 sq.; 486 sq.

—— William, Chief of the Ngati-Awa, xi 799

King William Island, explorers at, xii 814 sq.

Kinglake, Alexander William, xi 364; xii 439

King's Book, The, or *A Necessary Doctrine for any Christian Man*, ii 448

—— Mountain, Ferguson defeated at (1780), vii 225 sq.

Kingsley, Charles, writings of, xi 359; at Cambridge, 363; xii 774

Kingston (Ontario), built, vii 85; lost, 89; 125; captured by Bradstreet (1758), 135 sq.; University of, xi 778; industries of, xii 612

—— Sir Anthony, plot against Mary by, ii 544

—— Sir William, Lieutenant of the Tower, ii 435

Kingswood, Whitefield at, vi 83

Kinizsi, Paul, Hungarian general, i 335, 337

Kinker, Johannes, Dutch writer, xi 676

Kinsale, Spanish ships in (1601), iii 532, 608; wines unshipped at, 594; Rupert at, iv 463, 532; James II lands at, v 308

Kinsky, Count Francis Ferdinand, Chancellor of Bohemia, vi 204

—— Rudolf, Prince, xi 655

—— Count William, Wallenstein and, iv 233 sq., 236, 240; murder of, 242

Kiong-Lyng, Russia and, xii 507

Kiôto, Vol. xi, Chap. xxviii (2) *passim*; Japanese Court at, xii 537; 563

Kirbekan, engagement at, xii 443

Kircher, Athanasius, German scientist and physicist, v 739

Kirchhoff, Gustav Robert, German chemist, xii 783

Kirchner, von, Imperial envoy at Utrecht Congress, v 439

Kirghiz, The, and Russia, xi 273; and the Cossacks, xii 343

Kirkcaldy, Sir William, of Grange, warns Cecil, iii 265; joins the party of Mary, 282 sqq.

Kirke, Sir David, in Newfoundland, vii 52, 74

—— Lewis and Thomas (brothers of the above), attack Quebec, vii 74

—— Percy, Lieutenant-general, v 232; 243; relieves Derry, 312

Kirkholm, Polish victory at (1605), iv 175, 188

Kirki, battle at, xi 726

Kirk o' field, iii 273-4

Kirkpatrick, Major James Achilles, in India, ix 722

—— William, General, mission of, to Nepál, ix 718

Kirman, English traveller at, xii 800

Kiruna, ore fields of, xii 279

Kirwan, Dean, ix 693

Kisfaludy, Alexander, Hungarian poet, xi 423

—— Charles, Hungarian poet, xi 424 sq.; 431

Kishinéff, *pogróms* at, xii 340

Kishiu, Prince of, xi 825, 832; 836; heir to the Tycoon, 837; 852; 855

Kiss, General, execution of, xi 214

Kisséleff, Paul, Count, Russian Administrator of Moldo-Wallachia, xi 282

Kitchener of Khartum, Horatio Herbert Kitchener, Viscount, xii 130; occupies Dongola, 447; 448; in India, 496; in South Africa, 642

Kitchin, Anthony, Bishop of Llandaff, ii 571

Kiu-kiang, captured by the "Taipings," xi 820

Kiuprili, The family of, v 33, 36

—— Ahmad, Grand Vezir, v 40; succeeds his father, 346; invades Hungary, 346 sq.; in Candia, 348; 352; invades the Ukraine, 353 sq.; death of, 355; 366

—— Mohammad, Grand Vezir, v 40; 343; and Transylvania, 344 sq.; death of, 346

—— Mustafá, Grand Vezir, v 61; 368 sq.

—— Neuman-, Grand Vezir, v 604

Kiutayeh, Egyptian advance to, x 552; Convention of (1833), 553, 558; Kossuth at, xi 215

Kizil-Arvat, railway to, xii 801

Kjöge, bay of, v 570

Klagenfurt, Görgei interned at, xi 214

Klapka, George, Hungarian general, xi 204 sq.; 207; capitulates at Komorn, 213

Klausenburg (Kolozsvár), Montecuculi at, v 345; 346; xi 173; captured by Bem, 205

Kléber, Jean-Baptiste, French general, viii 353, 355 sq.; at Fleurus, 436, 446; and the Egyptian expedition, 599 sq., 603, 608 sq., 611 sqq.; in command, 616 sq.; assassinated (1800), 617

Klein, American newspaper correspondent in Samoa, vii 662

Klein-Schnellendorf, Convention of, vi 232 sq.; 235

Kleist, Heinrich von, German dramatic poet, vi 827; ix 335; x 402 sq.; 407; xi 415 sq.

—— von Nollendorf, Emilius Friedrich, Count, at Nollendorf, ix 528; at Leipzig, 535-6; army of, 623

—— von, of Zeblin, vi 217

Kleist-Retzow, Hans von, Prussian politician, xi 160; 192

Klenau, Austrian general, at Leipzig, ix 535

Klesl, Melchior, Cardinal, Bishop of Neustadt and Vienna, iii 701; 720; 726 sq.; policy of, iv 1, 9 sqq.; arrest and death of, 22; 25

Klewitz, W. A. von, Prussian financier, x 351

Klimowicze, Russian military colony, x 416

Klinger, Friedrich Maximilian von, German poet, x 386; 388

Klingsporre, Swedish agent at St Petersburg, ix 38

Klissow, battle of (1702), v 581, 592

Klitzing, General von, iv 383

Klondyke, gold discovered in, xii 608; 617

Klopp, Onno, *Fall of the House of Stewart*, xii 848

Klopstock, Friedrich Gottlieb, German poet, vi 741; 754; viii 773 sq.; x 384 sqq.

Klostergrab, Protestants in, iv 15, 19

Kloster-Grüssau, Silesian army at, vi 280

Klosterzeven, Convention of, vi 263 sq., 266, 272; battle of, 341

Klutsjino, battle of (1610), iv 176

Knäred, Peace of (1613), iv 179 sq., 183

Knajajevats, burned, xii 386

Knesebeck, K. F. von dem, Prussian Field-Marshal, ix 359; interview of, with Alexander, 513; at Vienna, 585; x 47

Knezevich, attempts assassination of Milan of Servia, xii 412

Kniazhevich, Alexander, Russian Minister of Finance, xi 619

Kničanin, Stephan Petrovich, Servian general, xi 211

Knickerbocker Magazine, The, vii 742

Knies, Karl Gustav Adolf, German economist, xii 850

Knigge, Baron Adolf F. F. Ludwig von, viii 772

Knight, Charles, publisher, x 673

—— William, secretary to Henry VIII, Bishop of Bath and Wells, ii 429

—— cashier of the South Sea Company, vi 181

Knights, The, in the Empire. *See* Reichsritterschaft

—— The German. *See* German Order

"Knights of Labour," and the American railway strike, vii 707

Knights' War (1522–3), ii 155 sq.

Kniperkrona, Swedish Minister at Moscow, v 587

Kniphausen, Swedish Marshal, iv 199; in the Weser lands, 225, 237

Knipperdollinck, Anabaptist, Burgomaster of Münster, ii 226 sq., 624

Knobelsdorff, Baron von, Prussian ambassador at Paris, ix 272

Knockninoss, victory of Inchiquin at (1647), iv 531

Knodsenburg, siege of (1591), iii 626

Knollys, Sir Francis, iii 277–8; 591

—— Francis, the younger, iii 301

Knoop, L., and the Russian cotton industry, xi 272; xii 321

Knoque, the Barrier Treaties and, v 457 sqq.

Knorring, Russian general, ix 47

Knorringen, Heinrich von, Bishop of Augsburg. *See* Augsburg

Knowles, James Sheridan, dramatist, xi 352

"Know-Nothing" party, vii 425, 431 sq., 437, 439

Knox, Alexander, *Thoughts on the Will of the People*, viii 772

—— John, influence of Geneva on, ii 374; 495; bishopric of Rochester offered to, 502; at Frankfort and Geneva, 556–8; returns to Scotland, 558 sq. ; *First Blast of the Trumpet*, 560; in Scotland, 573–7; 591–6; *First Book of Discipline*, 593; 691; iii 262 sqq., 270 sqq., 549; political theories of, 755–6; and ritual, iv 494 sq.; 497

—— Indian officer, defeats Shah Álam, vi 559

Knoxville, Burnside at, vii 508, 510; besieged (1863), 511

Knudson, Karl. *See* Charles VIII, King of Sweden and Norway

Knuyt, John van, at Münster, iv 401, 715

Knyphausen, Baron Dodo Heinrich von, vi 328; Prussian ambassador in Paris, 338

—— Baron Friedrich Ernst von, Prussian envoy at Stockholm, vi 36

Knyvet, Sir Thomas, naval commander, i 480

Kobdo, caravan route to, xii 793; 798

Kōbé, occupation of, xi 859; opened to foreign trade, xii 546; 805

Kobekó, Commission of, xii 358

Koch, Baron, private secretary to Empress Maria Theresa, vi 254

—— John Lewis von, ix 201

Kochanovski, Michael, Polish senator, x 467

Kochubei, Count Victor, Russian Minister, influence of, on Alexander I, ix 483; x 427; xi 264

Kodok. *See* Fashoda

Köhler, Dutch general, xii 243

Kölcsey, Francis, Hungarian poet, xi 424

Kölner Wirren, and the German Catholics, x 165

Koen, Jan Pieterszoon, Dutch Governor-General of the Indies, iv 711

Königgrätz, vi 242; 257; Frederick the Great at, 279; 705; battle of (Sadowa), xi 340, 453, 457, 480 sq., 483, 494, 540, 576, xii 182 sq.

Königinhof, Čech poems and Grüneberg MS. found at, xi 654

Königsberg, spread of Lutheranism in, ii 160; University of, iii 74, 78; Funck executed at, 153; Treaty of (1656), iv 428, 582; foundation of, v 630 sq.; 634 sq.; Great Elector at, 640; 644; 647; 658; Frederick I crowned at, 665; Stanislaus Leszczynski at, vi 197; 264; ix 280; threatened by French, 284, 285, 290–1; Convention signed at (1807), 292; Pestalozzian school started at, 326; University of, 327; *Tugendbund* formed at (1808), 328; Frederick William at (July 18, 1809), 352; political agitation at, xi 53; 54; 157

Königsegg, Count Lothar Joseph Georg von, Austrian Field-Marshal, at Madrid, VI 142; 145 sq.; 148 sq.; in Italy, 154

Königshofen, defeat of Peasants' Rising at, II 190; taken by Gustavus, IV 207

Königsmarck, Johann Christoph, Count von, Swedish Field-Marshal, IV 386 sq.; 390; joined by Bernardines, 392; attacks Prague, 393

—— Countess Marie Aurora von, V 668; VI 240

—— Count Otto Wilhelm von, V 365; 569 sq.

Königstein, Frederick Augustus II, King of Saxony, at, XI 219

Könneritz, Julius Traugott Jakob von, Saxon statesman, XI 149

Köpenick, Treaty of (1638), V 638, 641

Körber, Ernst von, Austrian statesman, XII 202 sq.

Körner, Karl Theodor, German poet, IX 335; death of, 510; X 403 sq.; XII 818

Kössenick, Brandenburg-Polish treaty at (1638), IV 378

Köthen, York at, IX 515. *See also* Anhalt-Köthen

Kötschenbroda, truce of (1645), IV 390

Koevorden, siege of (1592), III 626

Koh-i-nur diamond, taken by Ranjit Sing, XI 732

Koh-Kut, ceded to Great Britain, XII 536

Kohlschütter, Karl Christian, Saxon privy councillor, influence of, IX 595

Kok, Adam (II), Griqua leader, XI 783

—— Jörgen, reforming Burgomaster of Malmö, II 610

Kokang, ceded to Great Britain, XII 508

Koko-nor, travellers at, XII 797 sqq.; 803 sq.

Kokoschkin, Russian brigadier, VI 286

Kokóshkin, F., Russian politician, XII 327; 333; 356

Kokóvtseff, Russian Minister, XII 350; 353

Kokura, clan of, XI 849 sq.

Kolaba, XI 743

Kolbe, Johann Casimir. *See* Wartenberg, Count von

Kolberg, taken by Gustaf Horn, IV 196; port of, V 641; VI 287; captured by the Russians (1761), 297; 326; 328; besieged by the French (1807), IX 288, 396; surrender demanded, 291

—— Heath, battle of (1644), IV 387, 571

Kolding, *Rigsraad* summoned to, IV 101; Christian IV at, 102

Kolettes, John, Greek statesman, XI 279

Kolhapur, State of, XI 727

Kolima river, XII 794; exploration on, 795

Kolin, battle of, VI 261 sq., 263, 265, 341

Kollár, Jan, Slovak poet, XI 655; XII 842

Kołłataj, Hugo, Polish writer, VI 671

Koller, Colonel, Danish politician, VI 751

Kollontai, Henry, Polish patriot, VIII 786

Kolokol (The Bell), Russian journal, XI 625 sq.; XII 296; 298

Kolokotronis, Theodorus, Greek patriot, VIII 789

Kolowrat-Krakowsky, Johann Karl, Count, Austrian Field-Marshal, IX 260–1

Kolowrat-Liebsteinsky, Franz, Count, X 378; XI 44; 152 sqq.; resigns, 155, 171

Kolozsvár. *See* Klausenburg

Kolychéff, Russian envoy at Berlin, IX 36; at Paris, 47

Komburlej, Governor of Volhynia, X 421

Kommissároff, Russian gendarme, XII 363 sq.; 367

Komorn (Komárom), Emperor Francis ratifies armistice at (1809), IX 353; 355; in Hungarian occupation, XI 184; 204 sq.; relief of, 206; 210; Klapka at, 213; 214

Komura, Baron Juichiro, negotiates peace with Russia, XII 600 sq.

Konarski, Stanislaus, Polish educational reformer, VI 199

—— Bishop of Posen. *See* Posen

Kondratenko, General, in Port Arthur, XII 586, 590, 595

Kong, exploration in, XII 129; 812

Kongeaa, river, Danish frontier, XI 695 sq.

Kongsvinger, fort of, XII 289

Konia, captured by Turks (1473), I 82; fight at (1559), between sons of Solyman II, III 124

Konieh, railway at, XII 342

Konoyé, Japanese noble, XI 837; 839; 844

Konstantinović, Michael, Bosnian historian, I 72 sq.

Kootenay, mining district of, XII 608

Kopet Dagh, Russia and, XII 343

Kopidlansky, Vladyk of Kopidlno (Bohemia), I 338

Kopienski, Ilia, Polish printer, V 529

Kopp, Eutychius, Swiss historian, XI 261; XII 843

Koprili. *See* Kiuprili

Kora, Shuja-ud-daulá and, VI 563; 568; 569

Koraim, Sheikh, at Alexandria, VIII 600

Korais, Adamantios, X 174

Korat, railway to, XII 536

Kordofan, Egyptian rule in, XII 439; 440; the Khalifa in, 448; 806

Korea, XII 4 sq.; Russia and, 345, 507, 521 sq.; relations of, with China and Japan, 508 sqq.; Japan and, 552, 556 sqq., 561; affairs in (1876–95), 564 sqq.; Russian aggression in, 576 sq.; and the Russo-Japanese War, 579 sqq.; 600 sq.

—— Straits of, XII 588

—— King of, XII 567 sqq.; 571

—— Queen of, XII 566; murdered, 570; 571

Koregaon, Peshwa's army repulsed at, XI 726

Korff, Modest, Baron, XI 614

Köriyama, chief of, XI 842

Kormönd, Archduke Charles at, IX 258

Korolyénko, Vladimir G., Russian writer, xii 333
Koron, taken by Venetians (1685), v 365
Kororarika, xi 793; burned, 794
Korsakoff, Alexander, Russian general, viii 660 sqq., 674
Korti, Gordon relief expedition at, xii 442; 805
Kosa (Kaffirs), and white settlers, vi 189; destruction of, xi 786
Koscielski, Polish political leader, xii 167
Kosciusko, Thaddeus, viii 532, 541 sqq., 545 sqq., 786; ix 24; 36; meeting with Napoleon, 283; distrusts Napoleon, 338; Polish general, x 471
Kosegarten, Ludwig Gotthard, German poet, x 394
Koser, Reinhold, German historian, xii 829
Kosheléff, Alexander, Russian writer, xi 625; Slavophil scheme of, xii 309
Kosheloff, Ivan, Russian explorer, xii 795
Kosloff, Crimean port, vi 305 sq.
Kosova. *See* Kossovo
Kosseir, Baird at, ix 734
Kossovo, victory of the Turks at (1389), i 71, 82, 100; xii 383; 425 sq.
Kossuth, Francis, Hungarian statesman, xii 207; 209
—— Louis, xi 18; 152; and the revolutionary movement (1848), 153, 155 sq.; and Hungarian Ministry, 172; and the Slavs, 173; 180; financial measures of, 181 sq.; 183; and Lamberg, 184; 187; and the siege of Vienna, 188; and Görgei, 203 sq., 212; 205; appointed "Governor-President," 207; 209 sqq.; abdication and flight of, 212; 213 sq.; in exile, 215; England and, 351, 393; 400; 405; writings of, 426, 431; xii 178; 207
Kostka, Jan, Palatine of Sandomeria, iii 87, 90–1, 96
Kostromá, xii 306; trade depression in, 319; 329
Kota, Zálina Singh, Regent of, ix 727
Kotoshikhin, Grigory Karpov, Russian traveller, v 513
Kottbus, General Laudon at, vi 282; assigned to Saxony (1807), ix 292; circle of, ceded to Prussia (1815), 656
Kotzebue, August Friedrich Ferdinand von, viii 773; assassination of, x 21, 352; 364 sq.; 394; 438; influence of, on English literature, 710; xi 699
Koumoundoûros, Greek statesman, xii 391
Kovno, Napoleon crosses the Niemen at, ix 490; Murat at, 504; xii 336; strike in, 350; 373
Kowloon peninsula, England and, xi 813, xii 514
Kozloff, P. K., Russian explorer, xii 799
Kozminek, Synod of, iii 79
Kozodavleff, Joseph, Prince, Russian Minister of Interior, x 428
Krabbe, Gregers, at Münster, iv 402

Krämer, Heinrich, *Malleus Maleficarum*, i 642
Kraevsky, Andrew, Russian journalist, xi 625
Kraievski, Alexander, Polish patriot, x 433
Kramarz, Dr, in Poland, xii 378
Krapf, Johann Ludwig, missionary at Mombasa, xii 809
Krasicki, Ignatius, Polish writer, vi 671
Krasnaia-Pakhra, Russian army at, ix 497
Krasnogura, Victor at, ix 501
Krasnoi, French concentration at, ix 500 sq.
Krasnoiarsk, strike at, xii 331; founded by Cossacks, 792; 795
Krasnovodsk, railway at, xii 801
Krassow, Ernst Detlof von, Swedish general, v 597; 601; 603; 607
Kratt, ceded to Great Britain, xii 536
Kraus, Franz Xavier, German historian, xii 848
Krauss, Baron Philip von, Austrian Minister of Finance, xi 187; 190; 217
Kravchinsky, Serge Michaelovich (Stepniak), xii 306
Kray de Krajof, Paul, Baron von, Austrian commander, viii 659; ix 56 sqq.; 64–5
Krefeld, silk-weaving in, xi 259
Krell, Nicolas, German Chancellor, iii 711, 713
Kremlin, at Moscow, v 482; 493; 519; 557
Kremsier, the *Reichstag* at, xi 190 sq., 196
Kreusler, Wolrad, German song-writer, xi 413
Kreuznach, taken by Gustavus, iv 213; by Longueville, 383
Kreuzzeitung, Prussian journal, xi 192; 396
Kreyenberg, von, Hanoverian resident in London, vi 16
Kristersson, Klas. *See* Horn
Kristianopel, recovered by Sweden, v 570
Kristianshavn, privileges of, v 559
Kristianstad, taken by the Danes, v 569 sq.
Kristich, Servian Minister, xii 407
Kristoffy, J., Hungarian statesman, xii 205
Kriza, John, Hungarian writer, xi 427; 429
Krizhanich, Iuri, Servian scholar, v 516
Kroja, captured by Turks (1478), i 80
Krok, Cech journal, xi 654
Krolévetz, peasant rising in, xii 361
Kronach, Murat at, ix 275
Kronborg, taken by Swedes, iv 587 sq.; Queen Matilda at, vi 750
Krones, Franz X., German historian, xii 829
Kronstad (Kronslot), built, v 590 sq.; expedition from, vi 673; occupied by Russia, xi 206; French fleet at, xii 9, 98; mutiny at, 360; 369
Kropotkin, Prince, Governor of Kharkoff, xii 306
Krossen, Peter the Great at, v 607
Kroumirs, The, brigandage by, xii 129

Krstyovich, Gavril, Secretary-General of Eastern Rumelia, XII 405 sq.

Krüdener, Burkhard Alexis Constantine, Baron von, IX 41

—— Julia de Wietinghoff, Baroness von, IX 665; X 8; 424

Krüger, Admiral, and the Odessa mutiny, XII 355

Krug, Wilhelm Traugott, German philosopher, one of the founders of Tugendbund (1808), IX 328

Kruger, Stephen John Paul, President of the Transvaal, XI 785 sq.; XII 55; 248; 640 sq.; death of, 643

Krukoviecki, John, Polish general, X 472 sq.

Krumbacher, Karl, German historian, XII 845

Krumpen, Otte, general of Christian II, II 603

Krusovać, Turks routed at (1454), I 69

Krzyzak, Felix, III 79

Krzyzanovski, Severin, lieut.-general of the Polish Guards, X 454; 457

"Ku Klux Klan," American Secret Society of night-riders (from 1866), VII 641 sq.

Kuban, Russia and, V 343, VI 648; V 527; VI 305; 709

—— Tartars, territories of, VI 304

Kudlich, Hans, Austrian politician, XI 179

Kübeck, Baron Karl von, Austrian Minister, XI 155; 182; 217

Kuenburg, Michael von, Archbishop of Salzburg. See Salzburg

Kuenen, Abraham, Dutch theologian, XII 249; 846

Küper, Sir Augustus Leopold, Admiral, XI 846

Küster, von, Prussian diplomatist, at Congress of Vienna, IX 585

Küstrin. See Cüstrin

Kufara, Gerhard Rohlfs at, XII 813

Kujo, Chief Minister of the Mikado, XI 837 sqq., 844

Kukawa, explorers in, XII 807, 810

Kulali, hospitals at, XI 321

Kulangsu Island, XI 809

Kuli Khan. See Nádir Shah

Kuliscioff, Anna, and socialism, XII 231

Kulja, Russian occupation of, XI 632; China and, XII 502 sq.; 796; travellers at, 799, 803

Kulm, fighting at, IX 527; battle of (1813), 528, 541

Kulturkampf, in the first years of the German Empire, XII 147 sqq.

Kumamoto, daimiō of, XI 847; 861

Kumassi, mission to, XII 807

Kunduz, Moorcroft at, XII 800

Kunersdorf, battle of, VI 292 sq., 296 sq., 324 sqq.

Kung, Prince, Chinese plenipotentiary, XI 819; XII 506; 514; and French Treaty with Annam, 525; 526

Kungura, copper mines of, V 553

Kunishi, Japanese noble, XI 851 sq.; 855

Kurakin, Boris Ivanovich, Prince, Russian ambassador, V 543; 555; 611 sq.

—— Russian diplomatist (1808), IX 317

Kuram valley, British force in, XII 470 sq.; 489 sq.

Kurbatoff, Alexis, V 526

Kurbski, Prince, V 489 sq.

Kurdistan, Russia and, X 545

Kurdla, battle of (1795), IX 720

Kurile Islands, Japan and, XII 574

Kurla, travellers at, XII 799, 802

Kurland. See Courland

Kurnool, Nawáb of, VI 541

Kuroki, Baron, Japanese general, XII 581; defeats Zasulich, 583 sq.; 585; 587 sqq.; at battle of Liaoyang, 591 sq.; 593; 597; at battle of Mukden, 598

Kuropatkin, Alexei Nicolaevich, General, Governor of Trans-Caspia, XII 344; 348; in Russo-Japanese War, 581 sqq., 585 sqq., 589 sqq., 596 sqq.; resigns, 598; 601; on the Pamirs, 802

Kursk, peasant disorders in, XI 268, XII 353

Kurtz, Count, Imperial plenipotentiary, at Hamburg, IV 383, 396

Kuruman, missionaries at, XII 808

Kurumé, daimiō of, XI 846

Kutaitsoff (Kutaisoff), Turkish valet of Paul I, VIII 645, 648; IX 40

Kutch, State of, XI 727

Kutchuk-Kainardji, Treaty of, VI 358, 634, 674, 676, 681, VIII 308, 310 sq., IX 386, X 169, 173, XI 282

Kuttenberg, Diet of (1485), I 340; Prussian troops in, VI 234

Kutusoff, Michael Larivonovitch Golenitchef, Prince of Smolensk, Russian Field-Marshal, IX 250; at Braunau, 255 sq.; retreat of, 257; defeats Mortier, ib.; 259; at Slobodzeia, 485; and invasion of 1812, 489 sqq.; Commander-in-Chief of Russian army, 507; marches on Plock, 511; at Kalisch, 514–5; death of, 516

Kutzdorf, bridge of, destroyed, VI 282; 285

Kutzo-Vlachs, The, in Macedonia, XII 415; 424 sqq.

Kuwana clan, XI 851; 858

—— Japanese noble, XI 832; 854; 859

Kuyper, Abraham, Dutch statesman, XII 243; 246; 248

Kuzé, Japanese statesman, XI 844

Kwang Chow Wan, France and, XII 514

—— Hsü, Chinese Emperor, XII 502; 504 sq.; and reform, 517; 518; 520; death of, 523

Kwangsi, outrages in, XII 517; 526

Kwantung peninsula, XII 526; Russian troops in, 583; 585 sq.

Kwei-hsiang, Chinese general, XII 504

Kwei-hwa-cheng, post-road through, XII 792; 798

Kwo Sungtao, Chinese envoy in London, XII 501; 503

Kyaikhalo, attack on, XI 728

Kyau, Baron Friedrich Wilhelm von, Prussian general, vi 274

Kyd, Thomas, iii 375

Kykduin, sea-fight at (1673), v 161

Kymmene river, vi 314; Finnish boundary, 761; 778

Kyrdjali, ceded to Turkey, xii 408

Kyritz, victory of Torstensson at, iv 367

Labadie, Jean de, v 755 sqq.

Labat, Jean Baptiste, missionary, vii 97, 102

Lábatlan, Gregory, Hungarian Minister, i 343

La Baume, Pierre de. *See* Geneva, Bishops of

Labbey de Pompières, Guillaume-Xavier, French deputy, x 476 sq.

Labédoyère, Charles - Angélique - François Huchet, Comte de, execution of, x 48

La Belle Alliance, and Waterloo, ix 632 sqq.

La Besnardière, Jean-Baptiste de Goney, Comte de, at the Congress of Vienna, ix 580; 584

Labiau, Treaty of (1656), iv 428, 583

Labiche, Eugène, French dramatist, xi 518

La Bisbal, José Henrique O'Donell, Conde de, *afterwards* Count of Lucena, in Catalonia, ix 457; and Spanish revolutionaries, x 215 sq.; 227; xi 560 sq.; Ministry and resignation of, 562; forms new Ministry, 563; in Moroccan campaign, 564; created Duke of Tetuan, *ib.*; and Mexican affairs, 565; resigns (1863), 566; and Prim, 566 sq.; recalled (1865), 567; death of, 568

Laborde, Alexandre de, x 91; 476

Laborie, Fernand-Gustave-Gaston, French advocate, xii 120

Labouchère, Pierre-César, Dutch financier, ix 370

Laboulaye, Édouard-René Lefebvre de, French politician, xii 109 sq.

La Bourdonnais. *See* Mahé de la Bourdonnais

La Bourdonnaye, Comte François-Régis de, x 47; 49; and de Serre, 59; 60; 80; 91; 97; Minister of the Interior, 98

—— Comte A.-François-Auguste de, French commander, viii 416

Labrador, de la Roche and, vii 71; and the fisheries dispute, 363, 365, 657; under the Newfoundland Government, x 685

—— P. Gomez. *See* Gomez

Labriola, Antonio, and socialism, xii 231

—— Arturo, Italian socialist, xii 231

La Brossé, French ambassador in Scotland, ii 458

La Bruyère, Jean de, ii 711; v 67; 71; 79; viii 8, 15

Labuan, ceded to Great Britain, xii 669

La Cadie, French colony of, vii 71

La Calandria, by Bibbiena, ii 11, 14

La Cava, Giovanni Tommaso de Sanfelice, Bishop of, ii 390, 666 sq.

Lacépède, Bernard-Germain-Étienne de la Ville, Comte de, ix 133

La Chaise, François de, confessor of Louis XIV, v 24; 89; 221

La Chalotais, Louis-René de Caradeuc de, Attorney-general of the *Parlement* of Rennes, vi 356

La Chapelle, Michel Marteau de (La Chapelle-Marteau), iii 42, 44–5

La Charité, taken by German troops, iii 12; Huguenot stronghold, 20; granted to Alençon, 30; siege of (1577), 32

La Chastre, Claude de, Baron de Maison-Fort, iii 662, 665

Lachat, Eugène, Bishop of Basel. *See* Basel

La Chétardie, Joachim-Jacques, Marquis de, French ambassador at St Petersburg, vi 308 sqq.; 315 sq.; 761

Lachlan river, exploration of, xi 792

Lachmann, Karl, German scholar, x 404; xii 823

—— German Reformer, ii 160

Lacizi, Paolo, Italian Reformer, ii 391

La Cloche, James, mission of, to Rome, v 202

La Colle Mill, British success at (1814), vii 343

La Concha, José Gutiérrez de. *See* La Havana, Marqués de *and* Del Duero, Marqués

Lacordaire, Jean-Baptiste-Henri, x 163; 164; and Liberal Catholics, 165; 500; xi 23; 27; 120; and opposition to Napoleon III, 469

La Corona, Masséna repulsed at (1796), viii 574; Austrian retreat to, 575; French driven from, 580

Lacoste, Élie, Commissioner to Army of the Moselle, viii 427 sq.

—— Baron Jean de, French Minister of Marine, viii 223

La Cour, Edmond de, French ambassador at Constantinople, xi 313

Lacretelle, J.-C.-Dominique de, viii 515

Lacroix, J. F. de (d'Eure-et-Loir), French deputy, viii 249, 267, 269, 348; trial of, 363

—— Silvestre-François, ix 133

Lacuée, Gérard-Jean, Comte de Gessac, ix 145

La Cuesta, D. Gregorio Garcia de, Spanish general, reduces his army to order, ix 448; Victor sent against, 449; 450; Wellesley and, 451 sqq.; invalided, 455

Lacy, Luiz, Spanish general, leader of insurrection in Spain, x 210; 215

—— Maurice, Austrian Field-Marshal, vi 626; 632; 705

—— Maurice, Russian general, withdraws troops from Naples, ix 263

—— Count Peter, Russian general, vi 196; 303; 305; in the Crimea, 306; 310; 322

Ladakh, xii 800; travellers at, 801 sqq.

Ladenberg, Adalbert von, Prussian statesman, xi 230

Ladenburg, burnt by the French (1689), v 57; 409

"Ladies' Peace," The (1529), ii 25

Ladislaus I (Wladislav), King of Hungary and Bohemia (Archduke of Austria), i 69 sq.; ii 198

—— II, King of Hungary and Bohemia, i 296, 317 sq., Chap. x *passim*

—— III, King of Poland and Hungary, x 458

—— IV, King of Poland, iv 174; becomes Tsar, 176, v 501, 504; retires, iv 189; Prussian provinces and, 570, v 638, 641; military successes of, iv 579 sq.; v 743

Ladjard, Pierre-Auguste de, French Minister of War, viii 406

Ladmirault, Louis-René-Paul de, French general, xi 589 sqq.; at Gravelotte, 593 sq.

Lado, leased to King Leopold II, xii 661

Ladoga, canals of, v 548, vi 302

Ladrones, The, and the United States, vii 681 sq.

Lady Margaret Hall, Oxford, xii 762

Ladysmith, siege of, xii 642 sq.

Laetus, Julius Pomponius, the Roman Academy of, i 560; ii 32

Lafargue, Paul, French socialist, xii 123; 125

La Farina, Giuseppe, and the unity of Italy, xi 375

Lafayette, Louise de, and Richelieu, iv 150

—— M.-J.-P.-Roch-Yves Gilbert Motier, Marquis de, vii 211, 230; viii 61, 101, 104; Commandant of National Guard, 165 sq., 168 sq., 184 sq., 187, 191; commands Army of the Centre, 220, 222, 405 sqq.; at the bar of Assembly, 230 sq., 238; taken prisoner by Austrians, 239, 409; ix 137; and *Le Censeur*, 569; and General Excelmans, 571; and Chambers at Paris, 642; x 40 sqq.; at Hagenau, 45; 54; 56; 61; and new electoral scheme, 65; 66; 68; associated with military conspiracies, 76; 91; popularity of, at Lyons, 97; promises assistance to General Pepe, 119; and Polish revolutionaries, 454, 465, 473; and Revolution of 1830, 478 sq.; 480; 483 sq.; at La Grange, 750

La Fère, siege of (1580), iii 33, (1596), 628, 670; Spanish garrison in, 663

Laferté-Gaucher, battle at (1814), ix 553

La Ferté-sous-Jouarre, Condé at, iii 1

Laffitte, Jacques, x 58; 65; 67; and Revolution of 1830, 477; 480; resigns, 484; and fall of Molé, 510; xii 832

La Fin (agent of Biron), iii 680

La Flèche, Descartes at, iv 778, 780; military school established at, vi 349

Lafoes, João de Braganza, Duke of, viii 378

Lafon, Jean-Baptiste-Hyacinthe, Abbé, ix 143

—— de Ladébat, André Daniel, President of the *Anciens*, viii 215, 509, 512

La Fontaine, Jean de, v 66 sqq.; 70

La Fontana de Oro, Madrid patriotic society, x 218; 220 sq.

La Force, Henri Nompar de Caumont (in 1652), Duc de, and Condé, iv 615

—— Jacques Nompar de Caumont, Duc de, Marshal of France, Rhinegrave Otto Lewis and, iv 248; 251; 367

—— (Huguenot leader under Henry of Navarre), iii 664, 690

Laforest, French ambassador at the Porte (1536), iii 104

—— French envoy to Prussia, ix 264; 266

La Forge, Étienne de, French Protestant martyr, ii 354

La Fuente, Constantino Ponce de, Spanish Reformer, ii 404 sqq.

Lafuente, Modesto, Spanish historian, xii 842

La Gallissonière, Roland Michel Barrin, Marquis de, vii 93 sqq., 107, 112, 117, 119

Lagarde, Baron Joseph-Jean, Secretary of Directory, viii 679

—— Paul de, German orientalist, xii 846

La Garde, Paulin de, French ambassador to Solyman II, iii 118

—— French ambassador at Madrid, x 225

La Gardie, Jacob de, captured by Poles, iv 174; in Moscow, 176; in Ingria, 180; victory at, of, at Bronitsi, 181; 184 sq.; 569

—— Count Magnus Gabriel de, and Queen Christina, iv 575; in Baltic Provinces, 582; chancellor, 590; policy of, v 565 sq.; and Charles XI, 567; 568; 572

Lagena, Charles XII at, v 588

Lagerlöf, Selma, Swedish writer, xii 280

Laghouat, French boundary at, xii 129

Lagny-sur-Marne, Huguenot army at, iii 9; seized by Parma (1590), 49

La Goletta, Charles V at, iii 111; 114; taken by the Turks, 497; corsairs destroyed at, 541

La Gorce, Pierre de, French historian, xi 324; xii 834

Lagos, centre of Portuguese Slave Trade, i 13; Napier at, x 333; Great Britain and, xii 658; 660; explorer at, 811

Lagrange, Charles, French politician, xi 110; 136

—— Comte Joseph, guards Brandenburg, ix 511; at Berlin, 512

—— Comte Joseph-Louis, ix 133; xii 767

—— d'Arquien. *See* Arquien

Lagrené, Théodore-M.-M.-J. de, mission of, to China, xi 811

La Guaira, conspiracy in (1797), x 276; British frigate at, 283

La Guéronnière, Louis-Étienne-Arthur, Vicomte de, xi 382; 387; 467 sq.

La Harpe, Amédée Emmanuel, viii 564, 566 sq.; killed, 568

—— Frédéric César de, Swiss politician, viii 639, 646, 781 sq., 785; ix 95, 97; tutor to Alexander I, 483; influence of, 581; at Congress of Vienna, 587; 600; x 8; 9; 21; xi 239

—— Jean-François de, French poet, vi 823; viii 33, 515, 725

La Havana, José Gutiérrez de la Concha, Marqués de, xi 569

La Haye, de, French admiral, v 696; 703

—— Sainte, and Waterloo, ix 632 sqq.

—— Sainte-Hilaire, ix 136

La Hève, settlement at, vii 111

La Hitte, Lieutenant-Governor of Saluzzo, iii 414

La Hogue, battle of (1692), v 59, 261, 263

La Hontan, Baron Armand Louis de Delon-darée, *Nouveaux Voyages dans l'Amérique*, vii 104

Lahore, vi 509; 517; 523; Afghan troops at, 524; xi 731; affairs in, 738; peace with, 740; 741

La Horie, French chief of staff, ix 144

Laibach, Conference of (1821), vii 368, x 12, 29–31, 69, and Naples revolt, 113, 116; the Papacy and, 150; and Great Britain, 186; and south German States, 369; French *lycée* at, ix 418

Laignelot, Joseph-François, French deputy, viii 247

Laillier, Jean, heretical writer (1485), i 681

Lainé, Joseph-Henri-Joachim, Vicomte, ix 146; x 44; 47; succeeds Vaublanc as Minister of Interior, 50; 51; 54; and Royer-Collard, 55; 57; 59; and expulsion of Grégoire, 62; 63; and new electoral scheme, 64; 67; 68

Laing, Alexander, African explorer, xii 807 sq.

—— Samuel, Finance Minister in India, xi 752

Laing's Nek, British repulse at, xii 39, 637

Laïot, Prince of Wallachia, i 83

La Jaunaie, Peace of (1795), viii 381

Lajolais, General, ix 29; 32

Lake, Gerard, 1st Viscount Lake of Delhi and Leswarree, General, and Irish re-bellion, ix 700; in Hindustán, vi 525, ix 726 sqq.; xi 720

—— Sir Thomas, iii 567

—— of the Woods, and United States boundary, vii 364 sq.

La Kéthulle, de, African traveller, xii 812

Lakhta, Peter the Great at, v 548

Lalaing, Count, envoy of Philip II in Eng-land, ii 525

—— Antony van. *See* Hoogstraten, Count of

Lalaing, George, Count of Renneberg. *See* Renneberg

Lalande, Joseph-Jérome le Français de, French astronomer, ix 133

Lallemand, Baron Charles-François-Antoine, French general, plot of, ix 572

—— Henri-Dominique, Baron, French general, ix 572

Lally, Thomas Arthur, Comte de, in India, vi 546 sqq.; execution of, 549

Lally-Tollendal, Trophime-Gérard, Marquis de, member of the National Assembly, viii 131, 173, 178 sqq.; resigns, 183; pamphlet of, ix 562

Laloi, Pierre-Antoine, member of the *Comité de Salut Public*, viii 375

La Loo, Antony de, private secretary to Count of Hoorn, iii 216

Lalor, Peter, Speaker of the Victorian As-sembly, xi 798

La Loutre, Joseph Louis, Abbé, vii 122

Lal Sing, Sikh chief, xi 734; 738 sq.

Lálsot, defeat of Sindhia at (1787), ix 719

La Luzerne, Comte César-Henri de, Minis-ter of Marine, viii 107; dismissed, 163

La Mabilais, Peace of (1795), viii 382, 391

La Mancha, Castaño's army in, ix 448 sq.; Sebastiani in, 451; Madrid threatened by army of, 452; Venegas takes refuge in, 454; occupied by French detach-ments, 455; freed from French, 475; Carlist forces in, xii 260

La Marche, Olivier de, Flemish historian, i 430, 443, 446

Lamarche. *See* Drouot, François-Joseph

La Marck, Évrard de (brother of Robert II). *See* Liége, Bishop of

—— John de. *See* Cleves, John III, Duke of

—— Robert II de, Lord of Bouillon and Sedan (d. 1535), ii 43, 60, 89

—— Robert III de, Lord of Fleuranges (son of above (d. 1537)), defends Peronne, ii 71

—— Robert IV, Count of (d. 1556), taken at Hesdin, ii 89

—— William de. *See* Cleves, William V Duke of

—— William de, Lord of Lumey, iii 229; 233; 236

—— William de (Aremberg), i 440, 444

—— Count de, vi 28; 34; French am-bassador in Spain, 156; 157

Lamarck, Jean-Baptiste-P.-A. de Monet, Chevalier de, ix 133; xi 365; xii 771 sq.; 776

La Marmora, Alfonso Ferrero, general, xi 366 sq.; sails for Crimea, 373; 385; 536; Ministry of, 539 sq.; and War with Austria, 540 sq.

Lamarque, Maximilien, Comte, French gene-ral, x 480; 488

Lamartine, Alphonse de, vi 832; x 88; 100 sq.; influence of Byron upon, 725; 499;

and fall of Molé, 510; writings of, 514 sq.; xi 32; 39 sq.; and Revolution of 1848, 102 sqq.; foreign policy of, 106, 109; and Constituent Assembly, 108 sqq.; 113; and Republican Constitution, 116; 124; 305; 508; *Histoire des Girondins*, 524; xii 833

La Maurienne, invasion of, iii 417

Lamb, William, Confederate colonel, vii 556

Lamballe, M.-T.-L. de Savoie-Carignan, Princesse de, viii 80

Lamberg, Franz Philipp, Count von, Austrian Field-Marshal, murder of, xi 184

Lambert, Charles Guillaume, French Comptroller-General, viii 75, 107

—— François, Reformer, ii 200

—— John, major-general, iv 321; in Yorkshire, 350; and Constitution, 437; brings forward the "Instrument of Government," 438; 443 sq.; dismissed, 447; return of, 539; 540 sq.; 542; 544; *coup d'état* of, 545 sq.; meets Monck, 547 sq.; 551; sent to Tower, 554; escape and rising of, 557; imprisoned, v 94

—— Commodore, at Rangoon, xi 742

Lambessa, Miot transported to, xi 139

Lambeth, Whitgift's conference at (1595), iii 346; v 227

Lambinus (Denys Lambin, 1520-72), French Latinist, i 577; iii 54, 59

Lamboy, William de, Imperial general, in France, iv 150 sq.; defeated on Rhine, 377; at Hulst, 386; in Hesse, 393; in Flanders, 598

Lambros, Spyridion, historian, xii 845

Lambruschini, Luigi, Cardinal, Papal Secretary of State, x 156; 157; xi 703

Lambton, John George. *See* Durham, Earl of

La Meilleraye, Charles de la Porte, Duc de, Marshal of France, commander under Richelieu, iv 149; Governor of Britanny, 592; in Italy, 601; Controller-General, 606; 613

Lamennais, Hugues-Félicité Robert de, Abbé, x 43-4; 54; *Essay on Indifference in Matters of Religion*, 72; 94; 103; 149; doctrines of, 162-3; founds *L'Avenir*, 163; and the Papacy, 163-4; writings of, 499; 500; 514; xi 27; 115; 707; 717

Lamentabili, syllabus of Pius X, xii 230

Lameth, Alexandre, French politician, viii 174, 182, 186 sq., 200

L'Ami des Hommes, viii 21

La Mina, Marquis de, Spanish general, in Paris, vi 155 sqq.; recalled, 158; 165 sq.; in Italy, 362

Lamoignon, Chrétien François de, French Keeper of the Seals, viii 103, 105, 108; dismissed, 115

—— Guillaume de, French judge, viii 743

La Molle, favourite of Alençon, iii 23-4

Lamoricière, Christophe-Léon-Louis Juchault de, French general, xi 113; 135 sq.; 389

Lamormain, Guillaume Germeau de, Jesuit confessor of Ferdinand II, iv 74; 111; 113; 212; 238; peace negotiations (1634-5) and, 252

La Mothe, de, French general, v 422

—— de Canillac, Vicomte de, v 16

La Mothe-Fénelon, Bertrand de Salignac, Marquis de, French ambassador in England, iii 15

La Motte, Emmanuel-Auguste de Cahideuc de Dubois de, French admiral, vii 128

—— Fouqué. *See* Fouqué

La Motte-Houdancourt, Philip, Count of, Marshal of France, in Catalonia, iv 599; 653, 658

La Motte Pérouse, French brigadier, vi 197

—— Rouge, Joseph-Édouard de, French general, xi 602 sq.

Lamourette, Adrien, constitutional bishop of Lyons, viii 230

Lampadius, Jacob, at Congress of Westphalia, iv 401

Lampe, Friedrich Adolf, German theologian, v 757

Lampedusa, cession of, demanded by Great Britain, ix 103

Lamprecht, Carl, *German History*, xii 850

Lanark, cotton-spinning at, x 735

Lanarkshire, insurgents in (1666), v 284

Lancashire, Catholicism in, iii 284; Royalist rising in, iv 540; Jacobites in, vi 101, 114; 504; parliamentary representation of, x 608; xii 21; distress in, 730; 744

Lancaster, vi 101; Prince Charles at, 115

—— Sound, explorers in, xii 814 sq.

—— James, iv 729; first expedition of English East India Company and, 731

—— Joseph, and elementary education, ix 692

Lan-chau-fu, travellers at, xii 802, 804

Lancius (Jesuit), at Munich, iii 161

Landabum, Spanish officer, x 224

Landais, French admiral, viii 466

Landau, threatened by Bernardines, iv 383; taken by French, 389, 597; v 63; besieged by the Allies (1702), 406, by Tallard (1703), 408, by the Allies (1704), 411, by Villars (1713), 435; ceded to France, 436, 454; 452; Custine retreats to, viii 415, 422 sq.; relief of, 428; acquisition of, by Bavaria, ix 658-9; fortress of, transferred to Germany, 664

Lande, French envoy to Grisons, iv 61

Landen. *See* Neerwinden

Lander, John, African traveller, xii 808; 811

—— Richard, African traveller, xii 807 sq.; 811

Landes, The, drainage of, xi 299

Landfriede, The, I 294, 304

Land Goshen, established by Boers, XII 638

Landguard Fort, Dutch attack on (1667), V 189

Landino, Cristoforo, Italian humanist, *Disputationes Camaldunenses*, I 559; II 701

Landois, Pierre, executed, I 393

Landor, Arnold, at Lake Manasarowar, XII 798

—— Walter Savage, VI 834; VIII 764, 767; X 709 sq.; 713; 720; XI 350

Landrecies, besieged by Charles V, II 77, 457; invested by Prince Eugene (1712), V 433; captured by the Allies (1794), VIII 435; recaptured, 436

Landriani, Gherardo, discoverer of Cicero's rhetorical treatises, I 550

Landriano, defeat of the French at (1529), II 59

—— Antonio, treasurer of Ludovico *il Moro*, I 121

Landrieux, adjutant-general, VIII 572, 585

Landsberg (on the Warthe), VI 281; Russians at, 286; 287; 291; capitulates to Gustavus, IV 200

—— League, The (1558), III 159, 176, 709

Landshut, Bavarian Diet at (1553), III 159; taken by Gustavus Adolphus, IV 214; fight at, VI 294, 326; Bavarians driven out of, IX 348; Austrians retire upon, 349

—— Succession War, The (1504), I 315

Landsknechte, improvement of, by Maximilian I, I 325

Landskrona, V 147; captured by Denmark, 569 sq.

Landstad, Magnus Brostrup, Norwegian writer, XI 701

Landstuhl, Sickingen besieged in, II 156

Landucci, Luca, Florentine annalist, I 153, 169, 176, 188

Lane, Ralph, settlement of, in Virginia, VII 3

Lanfrey, Pierre, French historian, XII 834

Lang, Matthaeus. *See* Salzburg, Archbishop of

—— Philip, favourite of Rudolf II, III 697

—— Admiral, commander of the Chinese fleet, XII 507

Langara, Don Juan de, Spanish admiral, defeated by Rodney, VI 376; VIII 457 sq.

Langdale, Marmaduke, 1st Baron, IV 349 sq.

Langdon, John, deputy from New Hampshire at the Constitutional Convention (1787), VII 246, 279

Lange, François, French jurist, IX 165

—— John, Erfurt scholar, II 111 sq.

Langen, Joseph, German historian, XII 848

—— Rudolf von, German humanist, I 664

Langenau, General von, at the Congress of Vienna, IX 587

Langensalza, fight at, XI 452

Langeron, Comte Andrault de, Russian general, character of, IX 524; attacks Marmont, 539

Langharne, Rowland, in South Wales, IV 348

Langholm, Jacobites at, VI 101

Langlois, Captain, purchases Banks' Peninsula, XI 793

—— Jean, heretic (1491), I 681

Langport, Goring and Fairfax at, IV 331

Langres, Allies at, IX 544

Langside, battle of (1568), III 277

Langson, XII 131; French occupation of, 526 sq.

Languedoc, governed by Damville, III 23; the Estates of, 25; held by Montmorency (Damville), 40; the League in, 661, 668; IV 126; Rohan in, 127, 132 sq.; rebellion in, 135, 139, 153; *Intendant* retained in, 606; Estates of, V 4, VIII 39 sq.; canal of, V 14; Spanish troops in, VI 159

Languet, Hubert, at Court of Ferrara, II 384; 578; and William of Orange, III 221

Lan-ho, valley of, Japanese army in, XII 589

Lanjuinais, Comte Jean-Denis, VIII 187, 251, 255, 257 sqq., 273, 275; returns to the Convention (1795), 384, 386, 397; 488; and General Excelmans, IX 571; President of Chamber, 620

—— Victor-Ambroise, Vicomte, XI 126 sq.

Lannes, Jean, Duc de Montebello, Marshal of France, VIII 568 sq., 606, 608 sq., 612 sqq.; and Brumaire, 677, 679; IX 60; 62, 252; joins Ney at Stuttgart, 253; invests Ulm, 254; at Austerlitz, 260–1; at Coburg, 275; at Jena, 276; at Potsdam, 278; at Zehdenick, 279; at Thorn, 281; 283–4; at Friedland, 290; receives Sievre, 339; defends Essling, 351; killed, 352; defeats Castaños and Palafox at Tudela, 443; and Saragossa, 444; 447

Lannoy, Charles de, Prince of Sulmona, Viceroy of Naples (1522), II 48, 55 sq.

—— Philip de, Prince of Sulmona (son of above), Spanish commander in Netherlands, III 211–2

La Noue, François de, III 9; 13–4; 16; 20 sqq.; 27; 31; 47 sqq., 65; 471

Lansac, the younger, captures English merchantmen, III 32

Lansdowne, Lord Henry Petty-Fitzmaurice, 3rd Marquis of, Chancellor of Exchequer, IX 685; X 574; 668; XI 309; 320

—— William Petty, 1st Marquis of (Lord Fitzmaurice, 2nd Earl of Shelburne), VI 380 sq.; 425; President of Board of Trade, 430; 431; dismissed, 432; 435 sqq.; and East India Company, 438; resigns, 439; 445; 450; and Ireland, 455; 457 sqq.; Ministry of, 461 sq.; resigns, 463; 464; 466; created Marquis, 467; 468; 476; 501; and Warren Hastings, 581; VIII 755, 760; and Whig party, IX 674; 676; 710

Lansdowne, Henry C. K. Petty-Fitzmaurice, 5th Marquis of, xii 39; Secretary for War, 52; Foreign Secretary, 53; and Egyptian affairs, 456; Viceroy of India, 481 sqq.; 594

Lansing, John, New York deputy at Constitutional Convention (1787), vii 246, 264, 270 sq., 304

Lanskoi, Count Sergei, xi 614 sq.

Lanza, Giovanni, Italian statesman, xi 543

Lanzarote, Portuguese discoverer of Guinea, i 13 sq.

Laon, siege of (1594), iii 663; battle of (1814), ix 551

La Palice, harbour works at, xii 102

—— Jacques de Chabannes, Sire de, i 125, 133, 137 sq.

La Palisse, seized by Democrats, xi 137

La Palud, Convention of (1815), ix 617

La Paz, Juan Orendayn, Marquis de, vi 137 sq.; 141 sq.; 145

La Peña, Spanish general, sent to Tarifa, ix 464

Laplace, Pierre-Simon, Marquis de, xii 767; 770 sq.

Lapland, Sir Hugh Willoughby in, v 512

Laplanders, pasturage privileges of, xii 289

La Plata, trade of, vii 327; disaffection in, ix 752; college for Indian nobles in, x 263; administration of, 274; governor of, deposed, 284

La Prévalaye, *Chouan* leader, ix 2; 14

Laptieff, Dmitri, Russian explorer, xii 795

—— Khariton, Russian explorer, xii 795

Lapukine. *See* Lopukhina

La Quadra, Alvaro de. *See* Aquila, Bishop of

—— *See* Villarias, Marquis of

La Ramée, Pierre de, ii 710; iii 57, 59; iv 776

La Ravardière, Daniel de la Tousche, Sieur de, vii 74

La Renaudie, Godefroy de Barry, Seigneur de, ii 297

Larevellière-Lépeaux, Louis-Marie de, viii 249, 300, 386; Director, 489 sq., 492 sq., 496, 501, 669

La Reynie, Nicolas-Gabriel de, Lieutenant of Police, v 16

Larissa, Turkish occupation of, xii 421; 422

La Rive, Arthur Auguste de, physicist, xi 261

La Rivière, Abbé de, iv 608; dismissal of, 612

Larkin, Michael, Fenian, xii 65

Larmor, Sir Joseph, man of science, xii 789

Laroche, Lenoir, Minister of Police, viii 508

La Rochefoucauld, Dominique de, Comte de Saint-Elpis, Cardinal, viii 158

La Rochefoucauld, François VI, Duke of, Prince of Marsillac, iv 609; joins the rebels, 611; 613; 615

—— d'Enville, Louis-Alexandre, Duc de La Roche-Guyon et de, viii 131, 179, 226

La Rochefoucauld - Liancourt, François-Alexandre-Frédéric, Duc de, viii 179

La Rochejaquelein, Henri-Auguste-Georges du Verger, Marquis de, xi 469; 472

—— Comte Henri du Verger de, Vendean leader, viii 266, 340, 354 sq.; ix 136; death of, 624

La Rochelle, revolt of (1542), ii 96; fall of (1628), iv 57, 133-5, 137; 59; significance of the fall of, 108, 115; Huguenot assembly at (1612–3), 119, (1620), 127; 128; 130; 132; English expeditions to (1627), 266 sq., (1628), 272, 643; 691; military disaffection at, x 76

La-Roche-sur-Yon (Napoléon-Vendée), town created by Napoleon, ix 120

La Romana, Marquis de, Spanish general, in Fünen, ix 236; 322; troops of, at Santander, 442; rallies Blake's army, 443; succeeds Blake, 445; falls back on Astorga, 446; reorganises his army, 448; retires northward, 449; fights with Ney, 451; 455; Wellington borrows troops from, 460

Laromiguière, Pierre, ix 132

La Rothière, battle of (1814), ix 545

La Rovière, de, French printer, i 613

Larra (*Figaro*), Mariano José de, x 241

Larrey, Baron Dominique Jean, French surgeon, viii 606, 613 sq.

La Rue, Isidore-Étienne, Chevalier de, member of *Conseil des Cinq-Cents*, viii 506, 512

La Salle, Robert Cavelier, Sieur de, descent of Mississippi, vii 87 sq., 118, 362; xii 810

Lasalle, Comte Antoine-Charles-Louis de, French general, takes Stettin, ix 279

Lasca, il. *See* Grazzini

Lascaris, Constantine, the Greek grammar of, i 546

—— John, Greek scholar, i 543, 563, 566, 575; ii 16 sq.

Las Casas, Bartolomé de, ii 101; v 682

Las Cases, Emmanuel-A.-D.-M.-J., Marquis de, at St Helena, ix 757 sqq.; x 1

Lasco, John à. *See* Laski

La Serna, José de, Viceroy of Peru, x 293; 295

Lasker, Eduard, German Liberal leader, xii 146

Laski, Adalbert, Palatine of Siradia, iii 83, 85, 98

—— Jan (John à Lasco), Polish Reformer, in England, ii 477, 502, 593, 617; in Poland, 636 sq., iii 74

Las Palmas, English attack on, iii 321

Lassalle, Ferdinand, German socialist, xii 153; 758

Lassen, Christian, German historian, xii 845

Lasser von Zollheim, Baron Joseph von, Austrian Minister of the Interior, xii 188; 192

Lassy, rout of insurgents at (1567), iii 212

Last Judgment, The, of Michelangelo, ii 34

Laswári (Leswarree), battle of, ix 726

Laszki, Hieronymus, envoy to the Sultan, iii 118

Latalski, Bishop of Posen. *See* Posen

Lateran, The, *omnium ecclesiarum mater,* iii 440; Apostolic palace of, guaranteed to Pope, xii 229

—— Council, The (732), i 267; the Fifth (1512–7), 136 sq., 139, 249, 251, 489, 621, 651 sq., 678, 680, 690, ii 8 sq., 30 sqq., 639, 641

Lathom House, siege of, iv 321

Latimer, Hugh, Bishop of Worcester, ii 161, 445; sermons of, 490; arrest of, 521; 538; trial and death of, 541

Latin Fathers, The, early reprints of, i 616

—— scholarship, in Middle Ages, i 536; progress of, 543–5. *See also* Renaissance, the Classical

Latins, intellectually contrasted with Teutons, ii 692 sq.

Latitudinarianism, English, and growth of Toleration, v 327; among bishops, 467–8; *see* Chap. xxiv, 742–63

La Tortue, pirates' headquarters at, v 691

Latouche-Tréville, Louis de, commands squadron at Toulon, ix 215

La Tour, Charles Saint-Étienne de, in Acadia, vii 23, 110 sq.

La Tour, General de, Piedmontese commander, x 117

La Tour d'Auvergne. *See* Bouillon

—— d'Auvergne Lauragais, Charles, Prince de, xi 126

La Tour du Pin, Comte de, at Congress of Vienna, ix 584

—— du Pin Gouvernet, Jean-Frédéric de (Comte de Paulin), Minister of War (1789), viii 186 sq.

Latour, Count Maximilian Baillet von, Austrian general, viii 497

—— Count Theodor Franz Baillet von, Austrian Minister of War, xi 174; 176; 182; 185; murder of, 186; 188

Latour-Maubourg, Marie-Victor de Fay, Marquis de, French general, and Russian campaign, ix 488; Minister of War, x 62

La Trémouille, Claude, Duc de, iii 665, 670, 674, 679 sqq.

—— Charlotte de. *See* Derby, Countess of

—— Louis de, French general in Italy, i 116, 122, 126, 139 sq., 394

Lattanzi, Milanese editor, hints at annexation of Etruria, ix 396

Lauban, Field-Marshal Daun at, vi 292

Laube, Heinrich, German writer, xi 411; 414 sqq.

Laud, William, Archbishop of Canterbury, principles of, iii 737, 742, 758, 765; and Montague, iv 261, 268; Bishop of London, 272; Wentworth and, 277; and Puritanism, 278; Archbishop of Canterbury, 279; 280; 282 sq.; impeachment of, 287; 293; 295; trial and death of, 327; 493; 495 sq.; 504; v 117; 326; 330; 746; and Massachusetts, vii 17

Lauderdale, James Maitland, 8th Earl of, viii 760, 770; ix 271; and Whig party, 674

—— John Maitland, 2nd Earl and 1st Duke of, iv 342; 351; v 198; 201; 204 sq.; created Duke, 207; 209 sq.; 213; Secretary for Scottish affairs, 280; and Earl of Middleton, 282; and Earl of Rothes, 282, 284; 283; and Scottish recusants, 284 sq.; 286

Laudon, Baron Gideon Ernst von, Austrian Field-Marshal, vi 271; 278; 282; 288; at Kunersdorf, 292 sqq.; in Silesia, 297; 324; 326; 328; 626; 632; 648; in Bohemia, 704; 705 sq.; viii 325, 331; Turks defeated by, ix 385

Laudonnière, René, French coloniser in Florida, i 55; vii 71

"Laud's Liturgy," imposed on Scottish Church (1637), iv 495 sqq.

Lauenburg, Estates of Circle summoned to, iv 91; Mansfelders at, 95; Wallenstein in duchy of, 101; 102; held by Sweden, ix 266; part of duchy of, ceded to Denmark, 656, 661; to Prussia, 657; joins Germanic Confederation, 659; lost by Denmark, xi 338, 442; 445; 691; 694; 696

—— Duke Francis Albert of, and Gustavus, iv 221; 236; 241 sq.

Lauer, Austrian general, ix 65

Lauffeldt, vi 248; battle of, 250, 331

Lauffen, fight at, ii 221

Laugier, Cesare de Bellecour, Comte de, Italian general, xi 84; 94

—— French officer, at Acre, viii 611

—— naval captain, killed at Venice (1797), viii 586

Laun, armistice at (1634), iv 252

Launay, de la Haye de, Chief of Prussian Customs (1766), vi 712 sqq.; 720; 723

—— B.-R. Jourdan de, Governor of the Bastille, viii 164

—— Gabriele de, General, Sardinian Minister, xi 366 sq.

Laurel Hill, Garnett retreats from (1861), vii 457

Laurentian Library, The, iii 394

Laurentius (the Norwegian), Jesuit, ii 631

Laureo, Vincenzo, Bishop of Mondovi, Cardinal and papal nuncio in Poland, iii 88 sqq.; banished from Poland but returns on death of Maximilian, 99; becomes Cardinal (1578), 100; sent as nuncio to Scotland, 272; returns to Italy, 275

Laurie, Gawen, settler in New Jersey, vii 47

Laurier, Sir Wilfrid, Canadian statesman, xii 607

Lauriston, Jacques Alexandre Bernard Law, Marquis de, French Marshal, aide-de-camp to Bonaparte, ix 75; embarks at Toulon, 218; negotiations of, 498; taken prisoner, 540; x 68

Lausanne, Treaty of (1564), iii 405; French army leaves, ix 59; advance of Federalists on, 100; International Congress at, xi 486

Lautour-Boismaheu, Jean-Aimé, aide-de-camp to Masséna, viii 569

Lautrec, Odet de Foix, Vicomte de, ii 24, 44 sq., 57 sqq., 97, 429 sq.

Lauzun, Antonin Nompar de Caumont, Duc de, in Ireland (1690), v 314 sqq.

Laval, University of, xi 778

Laval-Montmorency. *See* Canada, Bishop of

Lavalette, Père, Jesuit, vi 348

—— Antoine-M.-C., Comte de, Napoleon's aide-de-camp, viii 588, 683; disaffection of, ix 572; x 49

La Valette, Bertrand de, iii 415 sq.

—— Charles-J.-M.-F., Marquis de, xi 474

—— Louis de Nogaret d'Épernon, Cardinal de, commander under Richelieu, iv 149; at Langres, 251; with Bernard of Saxe-Weimar, 367 sq., 370 sq.; in Catalonia, 645

La Vallière, Françoise-Louise, Duchesse de, v 19; 73; vi 330

Lavardac, rising at, xi 137

Lavater, Johann Kaspar, Swiss physiognomist, vi 625; viii 781 sq.

—— Rudolf, Zurich leader at Kappel, ii 337

La Vauguyon, Duc de, vi 356

Laveran, Alphonse, and malaria, xii 779

L'Averdy, Clément-Charles-François de, French Controller-General, vi 356

La Verendrye, Gautier de, vii 94

Lavergne, Bernard-Martial-Barthélemy, French politician, xi 132

—— Léonce de, French politician, xii 110

Lavicomterie de Saint-Samson, Louis de, French deputy, viii 247

La Vieuville, Charles, Marquis de, French Minister, dismissed, iv 128 sq.; Finance Minister, 615; death of, 618

Lavigerie, Charles-Martial Allemand, Cardinal, xii 117

La Ville, Abbé de, vi 335

La Villeheurnois, Berthelot de, viii 505 sq., 512

Lavoisier, Antoine-Laurent, French chemist and farmer-general, viii 71, 695; x 755; xii 768

La Vrillière, Louis Phelypeaux, Sieur de, Secretary of State (1661), v 5

—— Louis Phelypeaux, Duc de, Minister 1770 (Count of Saint-Florentin), vi 358

Lavroff, Peter, Russian political writer, xi 630; xii 302 sq.; 307

Law, *see* Codes; *but also* for French law generally in the age of the Revolution, Vol. viii, Chap. xxiv, 710–53; *and* for international law, Vol. xii, Chap. xxii, 703–29

—— Jacques-François, surrenders at Trichinopoly, vi 541 sq.; 546

—— Jean, French commander at Kasimbazar, vi 553

—— John, financier, v 705; vi 38 sq.; 128 sqq.; effect of system of, 133; character of, 169, 177; system of, 169 sqq.; leaves France, 176; 182; and Company of the Indies, 532 sq.; vii 92; viii 9, 39, 86

—— William, mystic, author of *A Serious Call*, v 751; 759; vi 77 sq.; 81; 88

Lawes, Henry, musician, v 116

Lawford, Commodore, ix 45

Lawless, John, x 641; at Ballybay, 647 sq.

Lawrence, Charles, General, vii 132

—— Sir Henry Montgomery, British Resident at Lahore, xi 740; 742; in Oudh, 748

—— James, Captain of the *Chesapeake*, vii 342

—— John Laird Mair Lawrence, Lord, Governor-General of India, xi 740; 742; 744; 752 sq.; xii 457; and Afghan question, 458 sqq.; 465; 469; 489

—— Stringer, major-general, in India, vi 541; 548

Law's Company. *See* Company of the Indies

Lawson, Vice-Admiral Sir John, victory of, off the Gabbard, iv 436; 541; 547; v 190

—— William, Australian explorer, xi 790 sq.

Layard, Sir Austen Henry, xii 37; 845

Laynez, Diego (Jacobus), General of the Jesuits, at Colloquy of Poissy, ii 302, 652–7; at Council of Trent, 667 sq., 671, 679 sq.; iii 161, 389, 592; disputation of, on episcopal rights at the Council of Trent, 751, 765

Layton, Brian, raids Scotch border, ii 460

Lazarillo de Tormes, iii 482, 547

Lazowski, Polish refugee, insurrectionary Brissotin, viii 228, 232, 265

Lazzarone, Valtelline Chancellor, iv 49

Lea, Henry Charles, American historian, xii 847

Leach, Dryden, Wilkes' printer, vi 439

Leade, Jane, pietistic writer, v 762

League, Catholic, the French, *see* Vol. iii, Chap. i *passim*, the Wars of Religion, 1–52; and Sixtus V, 451 sqq.; dissensions in, 512; and Philip II of Spain, 517, 522; and French monarchy, 658 sqq.; retains centres in Poitou, etc. (1598), 674; put down in Anjou and

Lorraine (1598), 675; original members,
728 sq.; 732; later political theories of,
764 sq.
League, Catholic, the German, proposed, ii
195; growth of, iii 729; and the outbreak
of the Thirty Years' War, *see* Vol. iv,
Chap. i *passim*; kept alive (1621), 77;
84, 113 sq.; and Urban VIII, 681
[For the action of the forces of the
League *see* the various campaigns of
the Thirty Years' War]
—— of Freedom, in Italy (1525), ii 23
—— of God's House, The Swiss, ii 306
—— of the Five Catholic Cantons (1524),
ii 325
—— of the Ten Jurisdictions, The Swiss,
ii 306
Leake, Sir John, English admiral, v 413;
416; captures Minorca, 426, 444
—— William Martin, and Greek archaeo-
logy, xii 821
Learmonth, George, xi 649
Leavitt, Humphrey H., American judge,
vii 573
Lebanon, administration of, xi 276; 636
Le Bas, P.-F.-J., French politician, viii
249, 364, 370
Lebeau, Jean Louis Joseph, Belgian Minister for Foreign Affairs, x 532; and election of Leopold I, 540; 541 sq.; xi 669
Leblanc, Nicolas, French chemist, ix 125;
x 755
Lebœuf, Edmond, Marshal of France, xi
495 sq.; 541; and army reform, 581;
590 sq.
Lebon, Joseph, revolutionary, at Arras,
viii 372
—— Philippe, inventor of gas-lighting
system, ix 125
Lebrija *or* Lebrixa. See Nebrissensis
Lebrun, Charles François, Duke of Piacenza,
ix 5 sqq.; Napoleon's Arch-Treasurer,110;
receives Piacenza, 111; Napoleon's letter
to (Aug. 20, 1810), 373; appointed Lieutenant-General in Holland, 416-7
—— Écouchard, ix 132
—— Pierre-H.-H.-M.-Tondu, Minister for
Foreign Affairs, viii 238, 263, 297 sqq.,
302 sq.; suspended, 339; executed, 357
Lebus, see of, v 618
Lebzeltern, Count Lewis, Austrian diplo-
matist, ix 198; x 25; and Consalvi, 136;
183
Le Cap, and Toussaint L'Ouverture, ix 421
Le Carlier, M.-J.-F.-Philibert, French
commissioner in Switzerland, viii 640
Le Catelet, given up to France (1558),
ii 94
Lecce, the *Adelfi* in, x 111; political per-
secution in, xi 379; xii 236; and the
Apulian aqueduct, 238
Le Censeur, ix 569; 573
Le Chapelier, Isaac-René-Guy, Rennes
deputy to States General, viii 152, 154,
178, 201, 691

L'Échelle, Jean, French general, viii
354 sq.
Le Chevalier, French royalist, ix 136
Lecky, William Edward Hartpole, xii 300;
writings of, 840, 849
Le Clerc, Jean (Bussi), iii 42
Leclerc, Jean, burnt at Metz, ii 283
—— Pierre, French Reformer, ii 290
—— Victor Emmanuel, French general,
viii 604, 677; commands expedition to
San Domingo, ix 421
Le Clercq, Chrétien, Récollet missionary,
vii 100, 104
Leclercq, Arnoul, *hooftman* of Ghent, i
449 sq.
L'Écluse, Charles de, naturalist, v 734
Lecointre, Laurent, French politician, viii
379 sq., 384; arrested, 385
Lecomte, Claude-Martin, French general,
xi 501
Leconte de Lisle, Charles-Marie, French
poet, xi 512; 514 sq.
Lecourbe, Comte Claude-Joseph, French
general, viii 661; in Jura, ix 624
Lecouteulx de Canteleu, Jean-Barthélemy,
viii 677
Le Coz, Claude, revolutionary bishop,
protests against reduction of the French
sees, ix 186
Lede, Marquis de, vi 33; 35
Ledeganck, Karel, Flemish poet, xi 676
Ledenburg, secretary of States of Utrecht,
iii 652
Lederer, Baron, General, at Pest, xi 180
Ledesma, Spanish envoy, iii 420
Le Despencer, Francis Dashwood, Lord,
vi 424 sq.; Chancellor of the Exchequer,
427; resigns, 429; x 599
Ledru-Rollin, Alexandre-Auguste, xi 25;
40; 97; 102; Minister of Interior, 103;
106; and the elections, 107; and Constituent Assembly, 108 sqq.; 114; 123;
and Social Democratic party, 124 sq.;
126; 132
Ledyard, John, in Yakutsk, xii 794; 806
Lee, Arthur, American statesman, vii 59,
210
—— Charles, American general, vii 211,
217 sq.
—— Edward, Archbishop of York, i 682;
ambassador in Spain, ii 426; 452
—— Henry, American general, vii 228
—— Nathaniel, dramatist, v 127; 131
—— Robert Edward, vii 452; Confederate
general-in-chief, 455 sqq., 464, 475;
succeeds Johnston, 476; 478; wins the
second battle of Bull Run, 480; invades
Maryland, 481; at Fredericksburg, 483;
at Chancellorsville, 485; invades Pennsylvania, 486 sq.; at Gettysburg, 488 sqq.;
and the campaign in the East (1864),
514, 516 sqq.; and Richmond campaign
(1864-5), 531 sqq.; evacuates Richmond,
538 sq.; retreat of, 539 sq.; surrender of,
541; services of, to the South, 621

Lee, Roland, Bishop of Coventry and Lichfield, II 471
—— Samuel P., American admiral, VII 576
Leeds, petitions from, IX 369 ; parliamentary representation of, X 601 sq., 613; pauperism in, XI 2; Gladstone at, XII 80; University of, 763
—— Francis Osborne, 5th Duke of (Marquis of Carmarthen), VI 468; Foreign Secretary, VIII 277, 282 sqq., 286, 294; resigns (1791), 295; 323; IX 673
—— Thomas Osborne, 1st Duke of (1st Earl of Danby, Marquis of Carmarthen), Lord Treasurer, V 210; financial policy of, 214 sq.; and Non-resisting Test, 216 sq.; 218 sq.; 221 sq.; fall of (1678–9), 222 sq.; 227; 230; and James II, 231; and Dykvelt, 240 sq.; signs invitation to William of Orange, 242; 246; and Revolution settlement, 249 sq.; 255; President of Council, 259; 260; and the Bank of England, 268; resignation of, 274; 334
Leeuwenhoek, Antony van, Dutch naturalist, IV 722; V 727; 729; 735; 737
Leeward Islands, settlement of the, IV 756; V 442; 687 sq.; government of, 690; VI 186; XII 653 sq.; federal constitution of, 656; 657
Lefebvre, François-Joseph, Duc de Danzic, Marshal of France, VIII 672, 677 sqq., 686; IX 14; granted duchy, 112; besieges Danzig, 289; 349; defeats Blake, 443
Lefebvre-Desnouettes, Comte Charles, French general, IX 438; captured at Benavente, 445
Lefèvre, Nicolas, chemist, V 730
—— Pierre, III 160
—— Pierre, first disciple of Loyola, II 652 sq.
—— d'Étaples (Faber Stapulensis), Jacques, printer, I 614, 619, 640, 681 sq.; preacher at Meaux, II 282; French translation of the Gospels by, 283 sq.; death of, 287
—— de Saint-Remy, Jacques, historian, I 433
Leflô, Adolphe-Charles-Emmanuel, French general, XI 136; ambassador at St Petersburg, IV 97
Lefort, François, Swiss general, and Peter the Great, V 520; 522 sqq.; 530
Le Franc, Jeanne, mother of Calvin, II 350
Lefranc, Édouard-Edmé-Victor-Étienne, French Minister of Interior, XII 106
Lefrançais, Gustave, French politician, XI 502
Legations, The, in 1814–5, recovered by the Pope, IX 603; X 132; and the Congress of Vienna, 135; Consalvi's administrative scheme and, 136; 155; 156; XI 71, 74; 468; Garibaldi invades, 485
Legendre, Louis, French politician, VIII 228, 247, 340, 362, 366

Legge (Bilson-Legge), Henry, Chancellor of the Exchequer, VI 425
—— William, dismissal of, IV 333
Leghorn, failure of Maximilian I at (1496), I 172; trade of, III 385, 392; seized by Vitelli, 387; 397; free trade and religion in, 399; Napoleon at (1796), VIII 573; commerce of, IX 302; reform agitation at, XI 78; revolt at, 90; the Austrians at, 95; 378
Legion of Honour, created (May 19, 1802), IX 20; 110, 112
Legislative Assembly, The (Oct. 1791–Sept. 1792), constitution and powers of, VIII 202 sqq., 209 sq.; Chap. VIII *passim*; finance of, 701; legislation of, 735 sqq.
Legists, School of, in France, II 95
Legnago, Austrian retreat to, VIII 579; French occupation of, IX 68; fortress of, XI 82
Legrand, Antoine, *Apologia pro R. Descartes*, IV 791
—— Jérôme, French deputy, VIII 153
—— French general, IX 260–1
Le Gray, Gustave, and photography, XII 783
Le Guen de Kérangal, G.-G.-F.-M., French deputy, VIII 715
Lehmann, Max, German historian, XII 829
—— Orla, Danish politician, XI 167; 693
Lehnin, foundation of, V 620
Lehrbach, Count Ludwig Konrad von, Austrian envoy at Congress of Rastatt, VIII 641
Lehwaldt, Hans von, Prussian commander-in-chief, VI 264; 266; 273; 276 sq.
Lehzen, Louise, Baroness, X 674
Leibniz, Gottfried Wilhelm von, II 691, 707; Cartesian philosophy and, IV 791; and Pascal, 794; V 69; Bossuet and, 87; and Peter the Great, 532; 648; influence of, at Prussian Court, 670 sqq.; *Consilium Aegyptiacum*, 696; and mathematical science, 712, 718; and Newton, 717 sq.; 723; 739; and scientific societies, 741; 744; 758; 760; VI 2 sq.; 6; 8; and the English Succession, 14, 16 sq.; 19; 77; XII 816 sq.
Leicester, Robert Dudley, Earl of, II 518; Queen Elizabeth and, 582; III 17; in the Netherlands, 37, 290, 502, 619–23; 269, 280; 296; and the Puritans, 491, 500, 710; death of, 332
—— Robert Sidney, 2nd Earl of (4th cr.), sent to Paris, IV 276
Leichhardt, Friedrich W. L., Australian explorer, XI 795
Leigh, Charles, and South American colonisation, IV 755
Leighton, Sir Ellis, secretary to the Lord Lieutenant of Ireland, V 305
—— Alexander, IV 278
—— Robert, Archbishop of Glasgow, V 281
Leiningen, Charles, 3rd Prince of (d. 1856), XI 166

Leiningen-Westerburg, Count Charles of, executed, xi 214

Leinster, rebellion in, iv 523 sqq., **535**
—— James Fitzgerald, 1st Duke of (Earl of Kildare), vi 488; 498
—— William Robert Fitzgerald, 2nd Duke of, and Whig Club, ix 693

Leipheim, Peasants' Rising at (1525), ii 181 sq.

Leipzig, Poles in, iii 78; Convention of Protestant Princes at, iv 195, 197, 200, 204, 205; 206; 207; Wallenstein at, 219, 221; 373; besieged by Torstensson, 386; the Swedes hold, 390; the War and, 420; Cartesian philosophy at, 791; University of, v 760; Prussian magazines at, vi 267 sq., 273; 721; battle of (1813), ix 201, 425, 534–41; Blücher at, 515; Napoleon occupies, 517; Allies march on, 532; Napoleon at, 533; Count Radetzsky at, 583; 598; and German literature, x 384; fair of, 759; xi 59; disturbances in, 148 sq.; 219; *Reichsgericht* moved to, xii 150; Ranke at, 824; Mommsen at, 844
—— Disputation, The, between Luther and Eck, ii 135 sq.

Leipzig Interim. See *Interim*

Leiria, captured by Saldanha (1834), x 336

Leisewitz, Johann Anton, x 386

Leisler, Jacob, usurpation of, in New York, vii 44 sq., 69

Leissèques, Corentin-Urbain-Jacques-Bertrand de, French rear-admiral, ix 234

Leith, captured and burnt (1544), ii 459; fortified, 575; siege of (1560), 577; battle of (1560), iii 483; Cromwell in possession of, iv 510; Jacobites at, vi 99; 112; 116
—— Sir James, lieutenant-general, at Badajoz, ix 471

Leitmeritz, negotiations at (1634), iv 243, 252; Austrian magazine at, vi 257

Leitrim, plantation of, iv 513

Leitzkau, Assembly of Clergy at (1512), ii 129

Leix, rebellion in, iii 585, 587; plantation of, 588, 599, v 323

Le Jay, Claude, Jesuit Father, ii 652 sqq.; iii 160

Lejonhufvud, Axel, imprisonment of, iv 169

Leland, John, antiquarian, ii 469

Le Large, Amable, French admiral, viii 466

Lelevel, Joachim, Polish historian, and the Polish revolution, x 466 sq.; xi 657; xii 842

Le Maire, Isaac, Amsterdam merchant, v 702
—— James (son of Isaac), voyages of, iv 713

Le Maistre de Saci, Isaac-Louis, iv 795

Le Mans, feudal courts in, viii 49; Vendean defeat at, 355; strike suppressed at, x 491; xi 604; 607 sqq.; battle of, 610
—— Claude d'Angennes, Bishop of, iii 46

Le Marois, Comte, French general, ix 195; ordered to Ancona, 400

Lemberg, taken by Turks (1672), v 353; Polish victory at (1675), 355, 364; Russians advance towards (1809), ix 354; under Austrian rule, x 461 sq.; popular council at, xi 174
—— Sokolowski, Archbishop of, iii 103

Lemercier, Jean-Louis-Anatole, Comte, xi 469
—— Comte Louis-Nicolas, President of the *Anciens*, viii 677

Le Mètre, French engineer, v 601

Lemierre, Antoine-Marin, French dramatist, vi 831

Lemnos, taken by Venetians, v 342

Lemos, Pedro Fernandez de Castro (Marquis de Sarria), Count of (son-in-law of Lerma), iv 629
—— Pedro A. F. de Castro, 10th Count of (Marquis of Sarria, Duke of Taurisano), Spanish Viceroy in Peru, v 681; 683

Lena river, xii 794; exploration on, 795

Lenau, Nikolaus, German poet, x 407; xi 411

L'Enclos, Ninon de, viii 4

Lénin, Russian socialist leader, xii 330 sqq.

Lennep, Jacobus van, Dutch writer, xi 676

Lennox, Esmé Stewart, Seigneur d'Aubigny, Duke of, iii 287 sq.; 550
—— James Stewart, 4th Duke of (1st Duke of Richmond), iv 496
—— John Stewart, 3rd *or* 11th Earl of, ii 454
—— Lady Margaret Douglas, Countess of, ii 565; iii 269
—— Matthew Stewart, 4th *or* 12th Earl of, ii 457 sq., 555 sq.; iii 274 sq.; accuses Mary, 278; Regent of Scotland (1570), 282; 285; murder of, 549

Leno, Giuliano, architect, ii 12

Lenoir-Dufresne, French cotton manufacturer, ix 125

Lenoncourt, Philip de, Cardinal, Archbishop of Rheims (d. 1591), iii 40

Lens, truce of (1477), i 442; taken by French, iv 598; battle of (1643), 599, 602, 606

Lenthall, William, Speaker, iv 344 sq.; 548

Lenz, Jakob Michael Reinhold, x 386 sq.; 396; 400

Leo X (Giovanni de' Medici), Pope, i 32, 92, 113, 139, 153, 250, 323; Concordat with Francis I, 388; 489, 545, 548, 550; the Renaissance and, 565 sq.; Church reform and, 621, 678; 661; policy of, 665; sale of offices by, 670, 672; 690; ii 4, 8, 10–19, 27; art under, 12 sqq., 22, 30 sqq., 40 sqq.; Indulgences of, 121; Luther's Theses and, 131; Luther and, 132; death of, 418, 426, 610; prohibited books and, 687; iii 128; 468; 470; x 143
—— XI (Alessandro de' Medici), Pope, iv 669

Leo XII (Annibale della Genga), Pope, opposes Consalvi, x 139; in Paris, 139 sq.; 142; and Church affairs in Hanover and States of Upper Rhine, 148; and Switzerland, 149; election of (1823), 151 sq.; and Consalvi, 152; reactionary policy of, 152 sq.; death of, 154; and Lamennais, 163; Concordat of, with the King of the Netherlands, 527; xi 72; 716

—— XIII (Vincent Joachim Pecci), Pope, and Ireland, xii 48, 82; and France, 118 sq.; Bismarck and, 152; election of, 216; and Italian monarchy, 229; and Belgium, 251; 264; 725; death of, 225

—— Heinrich, German historian, xii 826

—— the Philosopher, *The Art of War*, v 529

Leoben, preliminaries of peace signed at (1797), viii 498, 553, 582 sq., 591

Leogane (San Domingo), and French Revolution, viii 193

Leon, Blake's army rallied in, ix 443; Marshal Soult and, 444; 453; Del Parque ordered to, 455; guarded by the French, 458; Marmont in, 469; Sanchez in, *ib.*; delivered from the French, 473; Graham descends into, 476

—— Diego, Spanish general, x 242

—— Fray Luis Ponce de, Spanish Reformer, ii 409

—— Juan Ponce de, Spanish Reformer, ii 406

—— Ponce de, discoverer of Florida, i 54

Léon y Pizarro, José, Spanish statesman, x 212

Leonard, David, Boston loyalist lawyer, vii 196

Leoninus, Dr, Dutch politician, iii 237

Leontieff, Abyssinian governor, xii 343

Leopardi, Giacomo, Count, x 127, 725; xi 546; 549

Leopold I, Emperor, elected, iv 430 sq., 587; 590; 619; and Louis XIV, Vol. v, Chap. ii *passim*, 364; relatives of, 34 sq., 41, 52, 350, 377, 381, 384; and Turks, 40, 49, 51 sq., 60 sq., 368, 370; and coalition against France, 43; and Treaty of Nymegen, 45, 356, 571; the German Princes and, 46; and Truce of Ratisbon, 49 sq.; and Augsburg Alliance (1686), 52; and Elector Maximilian Emmanuel of Bavaria, 52 sq.; and Cologne election, 54; and Revolution in England, 55, 57 sq.; captures Belgrade, 56; joins Grand Alliance (1689), 58; and the neutralisation of Italy, 62; and Peace of Ryswyk, 63; English mission to, 109; and United Provinces, 157, 161, 164, 166; and English expedition of William of Orange, 244; alliance of, with Brandenburg, 353; and France, 357, 650 sq.; and Hungary, 356 sq., 367, 369; and Elector Frederick Augustus I of Saxony, 369 sq.; and Turkish attack on Transylvania, 345; illness of, 346; 347; marriage of, 349,

377; election of, 338, 644; jurisdiction of, 339; assists Dutch (1673), 340; accession and character of, 340 sq.; 343; and Poland, 344, 349 sq., 354, 356; secret treaty of, with France, 349, 353; goes to Passau, 360; 361; and John III of Poland, 362 sq.; signs Holy League against the Turks, 364; and Queen Maria Anna of Spain, 381; and Spanish Succession, 377, 387, 389 sqq., 664; and accession of Philip V of Spain, 395 sq., 401; and Grand Alliance, 397 sq., 403; and Duke of Savoy, 408, 448; Spanish claims of, 412; and Elector Frederick William, 652 sq.; and Elector Frederick III, 661 sq.; and crown of Prussia, 663 sqq.; and Vienna *Academia*, 741; death of, 414; and Elector George Lewis of Hanover, vi 3; 4; 6 sq.; and Switzerland, 616; and the succession, 201; ix 328

Leopold II, Emperor (Grand Duke of Tuscany), reign of, in Tuscany, vi 600 sqq.; 645; reign of, 656 sq.; 710; 783 sq.; viii 778; accession of, 293, 332 sqq.; and war with France, 218, 221; and Poland, 528 sqq.; death of, 223, 398, 531; makes terms with Turkey, ix 385; x 142

—— III, Duke of Austria, etc. *See* Austria

—— I, King of the Belgians, at Congress of Vienna, ix 583; and Greek State, x 203 sq.; 338; 490; 506; elected King (1831), 540; character of, 541; and Dutch invasion, 542; 570; and Queen Victoria, 674; xi 669 sqq.; death of, 672; xii 160; 225; 718

—— II, King of the Belgians, xi 645; accession of, 673; xii 3; 250; 252; and army organisation, 254; and Congo Free State, 255 sq., 658 sq., 661 sq., 810; death of, 256

—— I, Grand Duke of Tuscany. *See* Leopold II, Emperor

—— Archduke (of Tyrol), Bishop of Passau and Strassburg, Rudolf's vicegerent in Jülich, iii 558, 688, 690, 730 sqq.; iv 24; and bishoprics of Strassburg and Passau, iii 699, 702, 709; 720; 728; in Bohemia, 733 sqq.; lessened importance of, iv 26; Ferdinand's vicegerent in Vienna, 27; 31; 55; 57; 80; 84; and Edict of Restitution, 112 sq.; in Grisons, 673 sqq.

—— of Coburg, Prince. *See* Leopold I, King of the Belgians

—— of Hohenzollern-Sigmaringen, Prince. *See* Hohenzollern-Sigmaringen

—— Ignatius, Archduke. *See* Leopold I, Emperor

—— Prince of Palermo, xi 553

—— William, Archduke, and Halberstadt, iv 91, 111 sqq.; 375; defeated near Chemnitz, 379; 385; at Breitenfeld, 386; defends Upper Austria, 389; 391 sq.

Leopoldine Caroline, Archduchess of Austria, x 313

Leopoldstadt, fortress of, v 350; 359

Lepanto, taken by Turks (1499), I 87 sq.; battle of (1571), III 134–5, 137, 170, 294, 315, 391, 410, 486, 495, 540, v 342

Le Peletier, Claude, French financier, v 28

Lepelletier de Saint-Fargeau, F.-L.-Félix, Comte, VIII 395 sq., 504

—— —— Louis Michel, Jacobin martyr, VIII 131

Le Pesant, Pierre. *See* Boisguillebert

Le Play, Pierre-Guillaume-Frédéric, economist, XII 94

Lepsinsky, Russian trade at, XII 796

Lepsius, Carl Richard, German Egyptologist, XII 845

Leri, Cavour at, XI 385

Lerida, French defeated before, IV 599; Spanish defeated before, 653; captured by Spain, 658; captured by Suchet (1810), IX 457

Lérins, islands of, occupied by Spain, IV 147

Le Rivière (Jean le Maçon), Huguenot pastor, II 293

Lerma, Francisco Gomez de Sandoval y Rojas, Marquis of Denia, 1st Duke of, III 397; 418–9; favour of, with Philip III, 526–8, 530–1; mistaken policy of, 534–8; 540–5; IV 623 sqq.; power of, 626; Philip III and, 627 sqq.; disgraced, 629, 633; 635 sqq.; 640; 650; coinage and, 656; 670

—— Pedro de, Spanish scholar, II 401 sq.

Lermontoff, Michael, Russian writer, XI 648 sq.

Leroux, Pierre, socialist, X 485; 499; XI 24; 108; 110

Lersundi, Francisco, Spanish general, XI 559

Lesage, Alain-René, French novelist, VI 833; X 717 sq.

Lesage-Senault, J. H., French politician, VIII 386

Lesbos, annexed by Turks (1462), I 76

Les Cayes, holds out for Rigaud, IX 420

Lescot, Fleuriot, Mayor of Paris, VIII 364, 371

Lescun, Thomas de, Count of Comminges, Maréchal de Foix (brother of C. de Lautrec), I 393; II 45, 97

Lescure, Louis-Marie, Marquis de, VIII 354

Lescuyer, anarchist leader at Avignon, VIII 218

Lesdain, Comte de, French explorer, XII 803

Lesdiguières, François, *afterwards* Duc de Lesdiguières, Constable of France, Huguenot leader, III 41; in Savoy, 414–9, 661, 672–3, 690

—— François de Bonne de Créquy de Blanchefort, Duc de (grandson of above, son of Charles, Marshal Créquy), Marshal of France, aids Savoy, IV 123, 626;

supports the Court, 127; 128; death of, 131; 633; v 44

Lesghians, The, and Russia, XI 274

Lesley, John, Bishop of Ross, III 278; 283

Leslie, Sir Alexander, 1st Earl of Leven, at Stralsund, IV 107, 192; in Bohemia, 209; at Hanau, 371; Dunse Law and, 284; commands Scottish army, 320; at York, 321; invests Hereford, 331 sq.; 334; 349; at Dunbar, 435; 504; 510; 527

—— Alexander, general, VII 227

—— Charles, non-juror and controversialist, III 746; VI 807; 816

—— David, at Marston Moor, IV 322; victory of, at Philiphaugh, 332 sq., 506

—— John, Duke of Rothes. *See* Rothes

—— Walter (*afterwards* Count and Field-Marshal), at Eger, IV 242

L'Espée, Prefect de, killed at St Étienne, XI 503

Lesseps, Vicomte Ferdinand de, VII 649; mission of, to Rome, XI 94, 123, 125 sq.; and Suez Canal, 637 sq., XII 430 sq.; 433; 437; 439

Lessines, Marlborough at, v 420

Lessing, Gotthold Ephraim, v 69; 71; 131; VI 713; 823; 827; 832 sq.; VIII 772 sq., 790; x 383; position of, in German literature, 384 sq.; 386; 389; 395 sq.; XI 411; 415 sq.; *Education of the Human Race*, XII 817

Lessius, Leonard, Jesuit, v 82

Lestock, Richard, admiral, VI 239

L'Estocq, Anton Wilhelm von, Prussian general, IX 284–5; at Eylau, 286; 290–1; 315

Lestocq, Armand, French physician, VI 311; 315

L'Estoile, Pierre de (Stella), Calvin and, II 352; III 58

L'Estrange, Sir Roger, v 233; 290; 331

Lestwitz, General von, Governor of Breslau, VI 274

Leszczynska, Maria. *See* Maria Leszczynska

Leszczynski, Raphael, III 75, 79

—— Stanislaus. *See* Stanislaus I, King of Poland

Letcher, John, Governor of Virginia, VII 454

Le Tellier, François-Michel. *See* Louvois, Marquis de

—— Michel, confessor of Louis XIV, v 90

—— Michel, French Minister of War, IV 593; 599; and Mazarin, 608; 612; 614 sq.; v 5 sq.; 17; Chancellor of France, 24

Letellier, Barthélemy's valet, VIII 512

—— de St Just, L., Lieutenant-Governor of Quebec, XII 614

Lethington. *See* Maitland

Letort, French general, IX 568

Letourneur, Pierre, French translator, VI 830

—— C.-L.-F.-Honoré, Director, VIII 249; 442; 489, 491, 495

Letter to Sir Hercules Langrishe, IX 695
Letterkenny, O'Neill defeated at, III 591
Letters from the Cape of Good Hope, IX 761
Letters of Indulgence, in Scotland, First, 1669, Second, 1672, Third, 1679, V 284 sqq.; James II's, 290
Letters of Majesty, of 1609, to Bohemia and Silesia, III 727–8, 734; IV 2 sq.; 14 sqq.; 74 sq.
Leu, Joseph, assassinated, XI 247
Leubelfing, page of Gustavus, IV 221
Leuchtenberg, Augustus (Beauharnais), Duke of, X 338; 539
—— Nicolas Maximilianovich, Duke of, XI 641
Leuthen, battle of, VI 275; 277; 280; 282 sq.; 291; 341; 706
Leuzen, Prussian force at, V 666
Levant, Dutch trade with, III 631; French Consuls in trading stations of, 694; French Company of, V 12; ports of, VI 350; Vol. XI, Chap. IX (2); after the Crimean War, Chap. XXII (2); Austrian Lloyd service in, 394
Levasseur, Émile, French economist, XII 850
Levellers, Section of Independents (1647), IV 345 sqq.
—— in Ireland. *See* Whiteboys
Leven, David Melville, 3rd Earl of, VI 92
—— Earl of. *See also* Leslie, Alexander
Leventina, Val, and Uri, VI 625
Lever, Thomas, sermons of, II 490
Le Verger, Peace of (1488), I 394
Leverrier, Urbain-Jean-Joseph, XII 768
Leveson, Sir Richard, III 327
Leveson-Gower. *See* Granville
Levin, Rahel A. F. (Madame Varnhagen von Ense), VIII 773
Lévis, François Gaston, Duc de, Marshal of France, VII 126, 129; 135, 141 sqq.
Levski, Vasil, Bulgarian patriot, XII 384
Lew, Zdenko, of Rozmital, Bohemian politician, I 338
Lewal, Jules-Louis, French Minister of War, XII 96
Lewenhaupt, Adam, Swedish general, V 594; 597 sqq.; 603
—— Carl Emil, Swedish general, VI 760 sq.
Lewis, Jacobites in, VI 105
—— IV (the Bavarian), Emperor, V 620 sq.
—— I, the Great, King of Hungary, XI 421; 429
—— II, King of Hungary and Bohemia, III 105; V 625
—— Margrave of Baden-Baden. *See* Baden-Baden
—— Count of Nassau. *See* Nassau
—— Elector Palatine. *See* Palatinate
—— Sir George Cornewall, X 676; XI 765; and Niebuhr, XII 821
—— Matthew Gregory, X 698; 710; 716; 718
—— Meriwether, explorer, VII 326, 364

Lexington, battle of (1775), VI 447, VII 165; captured (1861), 460
Leyden, siege of (1574), III 239–40, 498; Separatist Congregation formed at, 346; cloth and linen trade at, 631; Remonstrants in, 651–2; University of, IV 717, 789, V 753 sq., IX 417; and Act of Seclusion, V 143; 639; 734
—— Jan of. *See* John of Leyden
Leyrit, de, Governor of Pondicherry, VI 547
Leyva, Alonso de, III 307, 314
—— Antonio de, Spanish general, II 44, 48; defence of Pavia by, 50 sq.; 53, 58 sq., 70; death of, 72
Lhassa, British expedition to, XII 4, 490; travellers at, 797 sq.; 799; 803 sq.; Treaty of, 492
L'Hôpital (*or* L'Hospital), Michel de, Chancellor of France, II 297, 301, 303, 347; III 2, 6; and the *Politiques*, 7–8, 11, 21, 67; political theories of, 753; IX 176
L'Hospital (*or* L'Hôpital), François de, Comte du Hallier, Marshal of France, at Rocroi, IV 594
—— Guillaume-François-Antoine de, Marquis de Saint-Mesme *and* de L'Hospital, mathematician, V 718
—— *See also* Vitry
L'Hoste, Secretary of Villeroy, III 682
Lhuillier, Louis Marie, French politician, VIII 234, 252
Liancourt, Duc de. *See* La Rochefoucauld-Liancourt
Liane, French flotilla in the, IX 228
Liao-Tung peninsula, XII 4; Japan and, 52; 511 sq.; 576 sq.; ceded to Japan, 601
Liaoyang, XII 346; Kuropatkin at, 581 sqq.; 587; battle of, 591; 601
Liapunoff, Prokopi, Russian anti-Polish leader, V 501
Libau, port of, VI 666
Libel of Reformation, of Emperor Ferdinand I, II 675, 678, 680
Liber Pontificalis, XI 718
Liberation, Russian journal, XII 333
Liberator, Boston newspaper, VII 387
Liberia, colony of, planted, VII 386; negro republic of, XII 660
Libertas, Bull of Leo XIII, XII 118
"Libertines" (liberal Calvinists in northern Netherlands), and William the Silent, III 646
—— followers of Montaigne, VIII 4
Liberty of a Christian Man, Luther's, II 136
Libraries, services of Benedictines as guardians of books, I 534 (*see also* the monastic schools in general); and search for MSS, 549; Filelfo's Greek library, 551; collection of Niccolo de' Niccoli, 551 sq.; public, Cosimo de' Medici first great founder of, 552; the great libraries of Florence, *ib.*; beginnings of Vatican

Library, 552 sq.; private, of 15th century, 553; of Christ Church, Canterbury, at close of 13th or opening of 14th century, 589 sq.; of Ramsey Abbey, 590; and the age of collection, 594 sqq.; Vatican, in the 15th century, 595 sq.; other Italian of this early period including that of San Marco, 596; French, at St Denis, at Corbie, at Avignon (the papal), and beginnings of the Bibliothèque Nationale of Paris, 597; English collectors and collections, including those of certain colleges of Oxford and Cambridge, 597 sq.; of Basel, 599; German, including that of Cues, 599 sq.; in 16th century, 611 sq., 619; lending, 639; catalogue of Vatican MSS. begun under Benedict XIV, VI 589; American, VII 744 sq.; Russian, in villages, XII 327

Libre Parole, La, French journal, XII 120

Libri-Bagnano, G., editor of the *National* (Belgian journal), x 532 sqq.

Libussa, Princess, XI 654

Libyan desert, travellers in, XII 813

Licet ab initio, Bull (1542), II 381, 649

—— *debitum pastoralis officii* (1549), II 655

Lichfield, troops at, VI 114

Lichnowsky, Felix, Prince, murder of, XI 169

Lichtenbergers, faction in Utrecht, I 423

Lichtenstein, G. von, Minister of Maximilian I, I 324

Lie, Jonas, Norwegian novelist, XII 281

Lieber, Franz, German writer, XII 820

Liebermann, Felix, XII 850

Liebig, Justus, Baron von, x 741

Liebknecht, Wilhelm, socialist politician, XII 153

Liebler, Thomas. *See* Lüber

Liechtenstein, and Germanic Confederation, XI 223

—— Prince Charles of, Governor of Bohemia, IV 71 sqq.

—— Prince Wenceslas (Wenzel) von, Austrian ambassador at Paris, VI 228

—— Prince, Austrian general, IX 260; sent to Vienna (Sept. 25, 1809), 359

—— Prince, XII 195 sq.

Liefkenshoeck, fort of, VI 641 sqq.

Liége, sack of (1468) by Charles the Bold, I 389 sq., 422; Charles V and, II 102; Prince-Bishopric of, Ernest of Bavaria elected to (1581), III 708; taken by Marlborough (1702), V 406; 488; siege of (1746), VI 247; Prince-Bishopric of, 647; occupied by the French (1792), VIII 417; Prussians at, IX 623; Bülow at, 625; trade of, x 524; William I at, 531; Belgian retreat to (1831), 542; the iron industry of, 755 sq.; Walloons in province of, 521; unrest in (1828), 530; International Congress at, XI 486; socialism at, XII 252

Liége, Bishops of:—

—— Ernest of Bavaria, III 708

—— Évrard de La Marck, II 102

—— George (bastard son of Emperor Maximilian I), II 102

—— John of Bavaria (son of Albert of Holland and Hainault), I 421-2

—— Louis of Bourbon, I 422, 440, 444

Liegnitz, Saxon victory at, IV 244, 247; principality of, V 652; 659; Prussia claims duchy of, VI 229; 275; battle of (1760), 294 sq., 297, 326

Liers, attacked by the French, VI 247

Liestal, attack upon, XI 245

Lieven, Christoph Andreievich, Prince, x 22; and Greek Question, 186 sq., 190, 193 sq., 197, 199, 202; in London, 474

Life, Russian journal, XII 330

Lifford, stormed by O'Neill, III 591

—— James Hewitt, Viscount, Lord Chancellor of Ireland, VI 505

Ligham, Dr, Dean of Arches, II 431

Lightfoot, Joseph Barber, Bishop of Durham, XII 847

Ligne, Charles Joseph, Prince de, VI 697; 699; IX 580

—— Eugene Lamoral, Prince d'Aubise et d'Epinay, Prince de, x 536

Ligny, fight at, IV 81; Blücher defeats French at (1814), IX 544; Blücher at, 625; battle of (1815), 627 sqq.

Ligonier, John Ligonier, 1st Earl of, VI 75; 114; 248; 424

Ligorio, Pirro, III 442

Liguria, French influence in, IX 69; nobility of, 397; French Concordat and, 401

Ligurian Republic, VIII 588, 592, 633; reconstituted by Bonaparte, IX 83

Ligurio, Alfonso, follower of Servetus, II 411

Li Hungchang, Chinese statesman, XII 501; railway policy of, 505 sq.; and Russia, 507; 509; and Treaty of Shimonoseki, 512; at St Petersburg, 513; 520; negotiates with France, 526; and negotiations with Japan, 570; death of, 521

Lilburn, John, IV 280

—— Colonel Robert, IV 449

Liliencron, Baron Detlev von, German song-writer, XI 413

Liliestråle, Joachim Vilhelm, Swedish Vicar-general, VI 774

Liliuokalani, Queen of Hawaii, VII 667 sq.

Liljencrantz, Johan, Swedish President of Finance, VI 773 sq.; 776 sq.

Lille, Treaty of (1513), I 483; taken by French (1667), V 38, 199; captured by Allies (1708), 421 sq.; 447; 457 sq.; action at, VI 240; siege of (1792), VIII 415; 435; peace negotiations at (1797), IX 39; Drouet at, 572; cotton industry at, x 753; 758; XI 31; Republican banquets at, 40; 602

Lillieroth, Baron, Swedish representative at the Hague, v 591

Lillo, George, dramatist, vi 823

Lilly, William, English Hellenist, i 580, 582

Lima, under Spanish rule, v 681; 682; 684; *consulado* of, x 247; University of, *ib.*; administration of, 248, 250, 275; clerical disorder in, 253; the Inquisition in, 253 sq.; Indians in, 263; Indian conspiracy in (1750), 266; 284; San Martín in, 293; Bolívar in, 295 sq.; Chilian troops in, xii 679

Limanowski, Polish socialist, xii 337

Limburg, duchy of, annexed to Brabant (1288), i 419; restored to Spain, v 45; 447; vi 631; frontiers of, 645; 647; and Decree of November 19, viii 300; Belgium and, x 505, 542 sqq.; and Germanic Confederation, xi 223; 667; 669; 674

Limerick, "undertakers" in, iii 599; Ireton besieges, iv 534 sq.; Cromwellian Settlement and, 536; besieged by Ginkel (1691), v 58, 261, 817 sqq.; by William III (1690), 315 sq.; Treaty of (1691), 319 sqq.

Limoëlan, *Chouan* conspirator, ix 17–8

Limoges, the Commune at, xi 503

Limousin, peasants' rising in, iii 664; Turgot *Intendant* of, viii 83, 127

Limpopo river, xi 782; the Transvaal and, xii 639

Lin, Chinese Commissioner, xi 807; 810

Linacre, Thomas, English Hellenist, i 491, 563, 579, 582, 643

Linares, Duke of, vi 361

Lincoln, Abraham, vii 436 sq.; President of United States, 440 sqq.; early history of, 443 sqq.; description of, 449 sq.; administration of, during Civil War, Chaps. xiv and xv *passim*; meets Grant, 515; and peace negotiations, 535 sqq.; at Richmond, 544 sq.; death of, 545 sqq.; work of, 547 sq.; 576; and slavery, 580, 583–602; views of, on secession, 625; xi 336; xii 16

—— Mrs Abraham (Mary Todd), vii 545

—— Benjamin, American general, vii 219, 313

—— Edward Fiennes de Clinton, 1st Earl of (7th cr.), iii 18

—— John de la Pole, Earl of, i 465 sq.; killed at Stoke, 467

—— Robert Todd, American politician, vii 545

Lindau, Diet of (1496), i 306; ii 205; and the *Tetrapolitana*, 212; Treaty of (1622), iv 56 sqq., 129

Linden, Würtemberg diplomatist, at Congress of Vienna, ix 609

Lindenau, Bertrand at, ix 535; French retreat through, 540

Lindesay, Thomas, Archbishop of Armagh, vi 486

Lindet, Robert, viii 249, 256, 269, 340; on *Comité de Salut Public*, 343 sq.; 368; 385; and *Société des Égaux*, 504

Lindholm, Treaty of (1393), ii 600

Lindley, John, Professor of Botany, xi 10

Lindman, S. A. A., Swedish statesman, xii 278

Lindner, F. L. L., *Manuskript aus Süddeutschland*, x 369

Lindsay, Sir David, Scottish poet, ii 555, 691

—— William, Earl of Crawford. *See* Crawford

Lindsey, Robert Bertie, 1st Earl of, at La Rochelle, iv 133; Royalist general, 307

Linevich, Lieutenant-general, in the Russo-Japanese War, xii 583, 596 sqq.

Ling, Peter Henrik, Swedish poet, xi 686

Lingard, John, historian, xii 836

Lingen, siege of (1597), iii 629; captured by Spinola (1605), 637; countship of, v 668; ix 410

Lingg, Hermann Ludwig Otto, poet, xi 414

Liniers, J. A. M., Viceroy of Buenos Ayres, x 281; 285 sq.

Linköping, Treaty of (1598), iv 172; Swedish Estates at, 173 sq.; see of, vi 774

Linköping, Bishops of:—

—— John Brask, ii 603, 622 sq., 624 sqq.

—— Hemming Gadd, ii 603, 607

—— Martin Olafsson, ii 631

Linlithgow, elections in, vi 93; 115

Linois, Comte Charles-Alexandre-Léon-Durand de, French rear-admiral, ix 53–4

Linschoten, Jan Huyghen, his *Itinerarium*, iii 632

Linth, victory of Soult on the, viii 661

Lintin, opium smuggling at, xi 806

Linyanti, Livingstone in, xii 808

Linz, homage of Austrian Estates to Rudolf at, iii 701; meeting of Archdukes at, 719; embassy from Union at, 726; assembly of Austrian Estates at (1614), iv 11; Maximilian at, 64; 76; v 347; Holy League signed at (1684), 364; Bavarian troops at, vi 232 sq.; 277; Napoleon at, ix 257; revolutionary movement at, xi 155

Lionne, Hugues de, Marquis of Berny, and Mazarin, iv 608, 614; dismissed, 615; French ambassador, 686; 688; Secretary of State, v 1; 5; 39; 102; 153

Liotard, Victor, in Africa, xii 130

Li Pinghêng, Governor of Shantung, xii 513

Lippa, on the Marosch, taken by Mohammad Sokolli, iii 122; Turkish garrison departs from, 123

Lippe-Bückeburg, Count William of, vi 369; 387; 426

Lippe-Detmold, the revolutionary movement in, xi 150

Lippomani, Aloisio (Aloysius Lippomannus), the *Lives of the Saints*, ɪ 610; nuncio to Poland, ɪɪ 637, ɪɪɪ 80

Lippomano, Nicholas. *See* Bergamo, Bishop of

Lipsius, Justus (Joest Lips), Dutch scholar, ɪ 579; ɪv 717

Lipski, iron-works at, v 533

Lipstorpius, Daniel, ɪv 791

Liptay, Baron Anton, Austrian Field-Marshal, vɪɪɪ 558, 568, 575

Liria, Duke of, vɪ 142; Spanish ambassador in Russia, 145; 150 sq.

Lisbon, English repulse at (1589), ɪɪɪ 318, 511; Irish refugees at, 504; jealousy among Spanish officers at, 505; departure of Armada from, under command of Medina Sidonia (1588), 506 sqq.; organisation of new Armada at, 529; desolation at, 530; Rupert at, ɪv 463 sq.; 467; revolution in, 651, 713; trade and, 728; vɪ 155; 369; earthquake at, 385; 388; a centre of English commerce, ɪx 302; Junot marches to, 303–4, 428 sq.; 363; French at (1807–8), 367, 435 sq., 439; Wellesley sets out for, 440; 441; Moore orders a retreat on, 443–4; British at, 448; Wellesley at, 449 sq.; guns from, 459; Masséna advances on (1810), 461; retreats from, 462; Cardinal Pacca in, x 134; revolutionary agents in, 213; occupied by the French (1807), 310; revolt at, 312; King John returns to (1821), 313 sqq.; leaves (1823), 317; Sir Charles Stuart at, 319; Saldanha threatens, 320; Dom Miguel at (1828), 322; revolt at, 324; 325; defence of, against Dom Pedro, 328; 330; Napier's advance on (1833), 331 sqq.; Dom Pedro in, 334 sqq.; revolution (1836) in, 338; xɪ 281; 572; cholera in, 574; xɪɪ 270; King Carlos murdered at, 272

—— Roderic da Cunha, Archbishop of, and Portuguese independence, ɪv 651

Lisgar, Sir John Young, Lord, Governor-General of Canada, xɪ 775

Lisieux, Guillaume Du Vair, Bishop of, *La Philosophie Morale des Stoïques*, ɪɪɪ 70, v 72

Lisle, Sir George, death of, ɪv 351

—— John Dudley, Viscount. *See* Northumberland, Duke of

L'Isle Adam, Villiers de, Grand Master of the Knights of Rhodes, ɪ 94

Lismanini, Francisco, religious Reformer in Poland, ɪɪ 635, 637

Lisola, Baron Franz Paul von, Austrian diplomatist, ɪv 427; 429; v 112; 349; 648

Lissa, French defeated off (1811), ɪx 239; naval battle at (1866), xɪ 541

List, Friedrich, political economist, x 354; and *Zollverein*, 372; xɪ 54

Lista, Alberto, x 229

Lister, Joseph Lister, Lord, xɪɪ 780

Liston, Sir Robert, British ambassador at Constantinople, x 175; 177

Lit, van der, Russian ambassador in London, v 608

Literature (General), effect of the discovery of the New World upon, ɪ 62 sqq.; and the Renaissance, *see* Chaps. xvɪ, The Classical Renaissance, *passim*, and xvɪɪ, The Christian Renaissance, *passim*; Machiavelli in, *see* Chap. vɪ, *especially* 199–218; political thought in, *see* Vol. ɪɪɪ, Chap. xxɪɪ, Political Thought in the 16th century, 736–69; science in, in the 17th and 18th centuries, Vol. v, Chap. xxɪɪɪ, 706–41 *passim*; the Romantic movement in European, Vol. vɪ, Chap. xxɪv, 822–37; ecclesiastical, of the earlier 19th century, x 157 sqq.; and the Hellenic movement of the early 19th century, 174 sq.; and Byron, 182; xɪ 13

—— English, under Elizabeth, theological, ɪɪɪ 347 sq.; Chap. xɪ, The Elizabethan Age of English Literature, 364–82; *see* Vol. ɪv, Chap. xxvɪ, The Fantastic School of English Poetry; Vol. v, Chap. vɪ, The literature of the English Restoration, including Milton; political philosophy in, in the 17th and 18th centuries, Vol. vɪ, Chap. xxɪɪɪ, 785–821; the great Reviews, ɪx 687 sq.; Vol. x, Chap. xxɪɪ, The Revolution in English poetry and fiction, 696–726; (1840–70), Vol. xɪ, Chap. xɪɪɪ, 347–65; of late years, xɪɪ 64

—— French, in the 15th century, ɪ 414 sq.; *see* Vol. ɪɪɪ, Chap. ɪɪ, French Humanism and Montaigne, 53–72; Vol. v, Chap. ɪɪɪ, French 17th century literature and its European influence, 64–71; of philosophy, and the French Revolution, Vol. vɪɪɪ, Chap. ɪ, 1–35; and the French Revolution, Chap. xxv, 754–90; under the First Empire, ɪx 129 sqq.; censorship, *ib.*; literary men in political opposition, 130 sqq.; of the Restoration, glory of, x 100 sqq.; from 1830–40, 513 sqq.; Vol. xɪ, Chap. xvɪɪɪ, The reaction against Romanticism in (1840–71), 507–28

—— German, Maximilian I and, ɪ 326; of the German Reformation, ɪɪ 136; failure of press censorship over the, 158 sqq.; in the age of the Reformation, Chap. xɪx *passim*; and the Thirty Years' War, ɪv 425; at the opening of the 19th century, ɪx 335; ecclesiastical views of the Romantic, x 160 sqq.; in the 18th and early 19th centuries generally, *see* Chap. xɪɪ, 383–412; (1840–70), Vol. xɪ, Chap. xv (2), 411–20

—— Hungarian (1686–1900), Vol. xɪ, Chap. xv (3), 421–31

—— Italian, and the greatness of Venice, ɪ 284 sq.; under Leo X, ɪɪ 16 sq.; 27 sq.; in Tuscany, under Cosimo de' Medici, ɪɪɪ

394; the end of the Italian Renaissance, Chap. xiv, 456–74; Romanticism in, x 124 sqq., 166 sqq.; of the *Risorgimento* and after (1846–70), xi 544–9

Literature, in the Netherlands under the Burgundian Dukes, i 432 sqq.; transcription of mss and the humanistic scholarship of the Brethren of the Common Life, 435 sqq.; (1800–70), xi 675 sq.

—— Norwegian (and Danish) (1815–65), xi 697–702; in the later 19th century, xii 281

—— in the New England colonies, vii 59 sq.

—— Polish, and Young Russia, x 432; (and Bohemian), xi 653–60; journalistic, xii 339

—— Russian, Catharine II of Russia and, vi 698 sq.; and Young Russia in the early 19th century, x 431 sq.; (1800–1900), xi 648–52; journalistic, of the later 19th century, xii 296 sqq.; recent tendencies in, 302 sq.; journalistic, 347

—— Spanish, in the late 15th and early 16th centuries, i 379 sqq.; in the second half of the 16th and early 17th centuries, iii 545 sqq.; during the last forty years, xii 268 sq.

—— Swedish, in the late 19th century, xii 280

—— Swiss, in the early 19th century, ix 427; in the 19th century, xi 261

—— in the U.S.A., early efforts and growth in, vii 740 sqq.

—— See also History, etc.

Lithuania, Grand Duchy of, iii 73, 83–5, 87; Russia and, iv 580; Peace of Oliva and, 591; v 480; and Ivan the Great, 481; 485; 498; Russia and, 504; Charles XII in, 592; 596; German Order and, 632 sq.; vi 192; 221; 664; 671; Russian army in, viii 531; Russian occupation of (1794), 546; proposed grand-duchy of, ix 486; forced conversions in, x 425; the secret societies and, 432, 453; and Poland, 446, 450 sq.; 464, 467; Russian rule in, 456 sq., 459 sq.; expedition to (1831), 472; xi 622; repressive measures in, 629; language movement in, xii 336; 337

—— Alexander, Great Prince of, v 481

—— Jagello, Prince of. *See* Jagello

Litta, Count Giulio, ix 39

—— Laurent de, Cardinal, papal nuncio in St Petersburg (1797), ix 39; x 139; and Irish Catholics, 635

—— Pompeo, Count, historian, xii 842

Little Gospel, The (German devotional treatise), ii 107

Littledale, St George, travels of, xii 802

Littler, Sir John Hunter, lieutenant-general, xi 739

Littleton, Sir Edward, in Bengal, v 700

—— Edward John, and Irish tithe, x 662; 663

Littleton, Sir Thomas, the elder, v 216

Littré, Maximilien-Paul-Emile, French writer, xii 93

Liu Ming-chuan, Chinese Viceroy, xii 505

Liverani, Eusebio, Monsignor, xi 531

Liverdun, Treaty of (1632), iv 226

Liverpool, and Irish trade, vi 496; and the franchise, x 605; the cotton trade of, 759; financial crisis in, xi 327; 336; and Manchester railway, 4; xii 20; Home Rule meeting at, 75; University of, 763

—— Charles Jenkinson, 1st Earl of, vi 424; Treasurer of the Ordnance Office, 427; 429; 437 sq.; Secretary at War, 450; President of the Board of Trade, viii 285

—— Robert Banks Jenkinson (Lord Hawkesbury), 2nd Earl of, viii 297; Foreign Minister, ix 71; 100–1, 681; and Catholic Emancipation, 678; at the Foreign Office, 681; at War Office, 689; Prime Minister, 690; and Canada, 746; and Napoleon, 759; x 194; 574; 584; 589; illness of, 591; and Ireland, 637; xi 790

—— Plains (Australia), xi 790

Livigno, and Valtelline War, iv 39, 50, 54, 61

Livingston, Robert R., United States Minister to France, vii 325

Livingstone, David, in Africa, xii 658, 808 sqq., 812

Livonia, influence of Charles V's policy on, ii 144; ceded to Poland (1582), iii 73; 101; and Sweden, iv 162 sqq.; invaded by Charles IX, 174 sq.; Mansfeld in, 176; 181 sqq.; and Truce of Altmark, 187; 188 sq.; Gustavus and, 191 sqq.; 366; 378; 383; 578; 580 sq.; 583 sq.; confirmed to Sweden, 590; 591; Charles X and Polish claim to, 589; Russian conquest of (1557–60), v 493 sq.; surrendered to Poland, 494; and Russia, 505, 512, 527; Swedish rule in, 577; Patkul and, 586; invaded by the Saxons (1699–1700), 587; Russian invasion of (1701–2), 590 sq.; 602; 610; 614; ceded to Russia (1721), 615; 630; 652; vi 35; the Treaty of Havelberg and, 206; 207; 253; 301; 317; and 1st Partition of Poland, 669; 694; Sweden and, 778; abolition of serfdom in, x 427; repressive measures in, xi 629; Russian administration of, xii 335; 363

—— Knights of, and Lithuania, v 480 sq.

Livorno, prosperity of, vi 600; 606; closed to English vessels by Napoleon, ix 398

Livry, Abbé de, French diplomatist, vi 140

Lizard, Knights of the, v 633

Lizet, Pierre, President of the *Chambre Ardente*, ii 288

Llandaff, Henry Matthews, Viscount, Home Secretary, xii 45

Llorente, Alejandro, Spanish Minister of Finance, xi 559

Llorente, Juan Antonio, Spanish historian, VIII 783; XII 842

Lloyd, Clifford, mission of, to Egypt, XII 444

Loanda, Portuguese settlement, VI 187; Livingstone at, XII 808

Loano, battle of, VIII 444, 558 sq., 562

Loaysa, Garcia de, Cardinal, II 26, 217
—— Archbishop of Toledo. *See* Toledo

Lobanoff, Prince, IX 291; sent to Tilsit, 292
—— Prince, Russian Foreign Minister, XII 418; and Li Hungchang, 513

Lobanoff-Rostovski, Prince Dmitrij, Russian Minister of Justice, X 440

Loban, the French at (May, 1809), IX 350, 352
—— Comte Georges Mouton de, Marshal of France, and the Belgian campaign (1815), IX 625; 627, 633, 641; X 488

Lobeck, Christian August, German scholar, XII 822

L'Obel, Matthias de, botanist, V 734

Lobengula, King of the Matabele, XII 49; 639

Lobkowitz, August Longin, Prince von, Governor of Galicia, X 462
—— Prince George Christian, Austrian Commander-in-chief, VI 234 sqq.; 241; 308; in Italy, 596 sq.
—— Wenceslas, Prince von, Austrian statesman, V 341; 349; 352 sq.
—— Zdenko von, Bohemian High Chancellor, III 727; IV 16; 18; 19
—— Prince von, Austrian general (1800), IX 62
—— Prince von, Austrian adjutant-general (1848), XI 182

Lob-nor, caravan route to, XII 793; 799; 802

Lobo de Silveira, Chevalier, at the Congress of Vienna, IX 584

Lobositz, Prussian troops in, VI 255; 257; 262

Local Government Board, established, XII 27

Loch, Henry Brougham, Lord, in China, XI 819

Loches, meeting between the Queen-Mother and Anjou at, III 28

Lochleven, Mary Queen of Scots imprisoned at, III 276; her escape from, 277

Lochmaben, the Old Pretender proclaimed at, VI 98

Loch-na-Nuagh, VI 112; Prince Charles at, 117

Loci Communes, of Melanchthon, II 165, 233; translated into Italian, 380; John Eck's counter-publication, 172

Locke, John, philosopher, II 691; III 749; 760; 764; 767; V 125; and Revolution settlement, 252 sqq.; 264; and currency, 269; 271; theory of government of, 273; 275 sqq.; 332; 334; 467 sq.; VI 787; 795; 802 sqq.; 807; 809 sqq.; style of, 811 sq.;

813 sqq.; 817 sq.; 825; scheme of constitution for Carolina (1667) attributed to, VII 35; VIII 5, 7, 10, 757

Lockhart, George, of Carnwarth, VI 106
—— John Gibson, XI 362
—— Sir William, envoy in France, IV 439; 540; Treaty of the Pyrenees and, 542
—— Sir William S. A., general, XII 488

Lockhorsts, faction in Utrecht, I 423

Locle, Le, Republican movement in, XI 253

Locré de Roissy, Jean-Guthrum, Baron, IX 8; 151

Lodenstein, Jodocus van, and Pietism, V 755

Lodge, Sir Oliver, and wireless telegraphy, XII 787
—— Thomas, III 371

Lodi, Peace of (1454), between Venice and the Sforza, I 281; taken by French (1523), II 48; Elisabeth Farnese and, VI 152; 508; 510; battle of (1796), VIII 569 sq.

Lodovisio, Lodovico, Cardinal. *See* Ludovisi, Luigi

Lodz, growth of, XII 337

Löffler, Jacob, Swedish diplomatist, in Paris, IV 247 sqq.; Heilbronn Alliance and, 251; and Gustavus, 401

Löscher, Valentin Ernst, and Pietism, V 760

Loevestein, escape of de Groot from (1621), III 655; Jacob de Witt imprisoned at, V 138

Löwendahl, General, VI 243; 247 sq.

Löwenhielm, Count Gustaf Karl F., at Congress of Vienna, IX 586; 661

Löwenörn, Paul Vendelbo, Danish statesman, VI 738

Löwenwolde, Count Carl Gustaf, Russian envoy to Warsaw, VI 194; 302
—— Count Frederick Casimir, Russian resident at Warsaw, VI 194 sq.
—— Reinhold, Russian officer, VI 302

Lofft, Capel, writer, VIII 758

Lofö, peace negotiations at (1718), V 613

Loftus, Adam, 1st Viscount Loftus of Ely, Irish finance and, IV 517; 520

Logan, James, in Pennsylvania, VII 51-2
—— John Alexander, American general, VII 524

Logique de Port-Royal, IV 790

Logroño, siege of (1521), I 378

Lohelius. *See* Prague, Archbishop of

Lohmann, Prussian official, XII 155

Loigny, French repulse at, XI 605

Lois Castle, Charles XII at, V 591

Loisel, Antoine, III 59

Loisy, Alfred, and patristic study, XII 848

Loja, revolt at, XII 267

Lollio, Alberto, founder of Ferrarese Academy, II 384

Lombard, Johann Wilhelm, Prussian statesman, Cabinet Secretary, IX 249; unpopularity of, 272; 282

Lombard, French socialist, XII 123

Lombardo-Venetia (*see also* Lombardy), martial law in, XI 152; 170; political trials in, 372; under the rule of Radetzky, 376 sq.; 382

Lombardy, Alva raises troops in, III 8; and the Duke of Savoy, IV 624, 642; occupied by the French, V 401 sq.; VI 124; Alberoni in, 125; 154; 159 sqq.; 197; war in, 236; Charles Emmanuel and, 245, 249; 601 sq.; Don Philip invades, 608; Switzerland and, 611; overrun by the French (1796), VIII 553, 779; 556, 588 sq.; Austrian province, 778; Napoleon plans to attack, IX 59; occupied by French troops, 62–3; Count Melzi and, 85; Bonaparte's plans for, 87; Napoleon assumes the crown of (1805), 247; 397; Austrian designs on, 591; Austrian rule in, X 104 sqq., 109; conspiracies in, 117 sq.; Church government in, 144 sq.; XI 70; hostility to Austria in, 75 sq.; 78; 81; war in, 82, 84 sqq.; union of, with Piedmont, 90; and Austria, 92; 332; 384; 388; relinquished by Austria, 407; Garibaldi in, 533

Lombe, Sir Thomas, silk manufacturer, X 733

Lombroso, Cesare, XII 231

Lome, Dupuy de, Spanish Minister to United States, VII 676

Loménie, Louis Léonard de, biographer of Mirabeau, VIII 150

—— de Brienne, Étienne-Charles de, Archbishop of Sens and Toulouse, VIII 74; and *Compte Rendu* of 1788, 75, 689; Chief of Council of Finance, 104 sqq.; 108, 110 sqq., 114; retires (1788), 115; 160; 198

—— —— Henri-Louis, Comte de, Secretary of State under Louis XIV, V 5

—— —— L. M. A., Comte de (brother of Archbishop), Minister of War, VIII 107

Lomza, Russians retreat to, IX 284

Lonato, battle of, VIII 575

Lonck, Hendrik Corneliszoon, IV 707

London, trade of, with Venice, I 257; literary club formed in (1579), III 368; gates of, shut on report of Spanish landing, 531; Constable of Castile in, 536; estimated growth of trade to (1619), 567; offer of Coleraine lands to City of, 615; ordered to supply ships, IV 266; 272, 278; "Root-and-Branch" petition and, 291; Irish rebellion and, 295; 296 sq.; at opening of first Civil War, 302 sq.; 304; 308 sq.; taxation and, 282, 310; 311; Royalist plot in, 314; 315 sqq.; 323 sq.; 333; 335; Presbyterians and, 337 sqq.; 342; and Parliamentary army, 343 sq.; 347 sq.; 354; Petition of, 356; 443; 505; Commissioners of Solemn League and Covenant in, 506; 545 sq.; 548; 550

sqq.; 557 sqq.; 736; the plague in, V 110; the Great Fire of, 110, 303; loan by, to Charles II, 111; 222; deprived of its charter, 229; captured by the Tories, *ib.*; 232; its charter restored, 245; 247; Prince Eugene in, 432; increase of shipping in, 439; "the Invisible College" in, 740; entry of George I into, VI 18; John Law in, 169; 253; 333; "No Popery" riots in, 455; flight of Nonconformists from, VII 12; merchants of, and the Pilgrim Fathers, 13; press-gang in, 328; preliminaries of peace signed (1801) in, IX 75; peace reports from, 102; meeting of French bishops in, 186; alarm in (1805), 223; 225; Count Starhemberg leaves, 309; 320; stores of bullion in, 372; Turkish embassy established at, 386; deputies from the Asturias arrive in, 440; merchants of, 676; trial of Warren Hastings in, 715; Cardinal Consalvi in, X 134, 140 sq.; Spanish revolutionary agents in, 213; Francisco Miranda in, 280; Spanish American loans raised in, 307; Queen Maria II of Portugal in, 322, 326; Pedro I of Brazil in, 326; University of, charter of incorporation, 668; centre of European finance, 728, 742 sq.; and development of agriculture, 730; retail trade in, 759; and wool trade, 760; peace negotiations at, XI 224; 300; Orsini in, 308; Orsini Plot in, 327; reform meetings in, 340; Garibaldi in, 351, 538; King Victor Emmanuel in, 373; Cavour in, 374; Mazzini in, 376; Exhibition (1862) at, 486; Workmen's International Association at, *ib.*; 596; 625; XII 12; coal dues abolished, 48; legislation for, 61; Karl Marx in, 152; Armenian meetings in, 416; 480; conferences of colonial premiers in, 651; municipal expenditure of, 734; 758; 762; 781

London, Treaty of (1518), I 490, (1520), II 417, (1674), V 197, (1827), X 195, 199, (1852), XI 696, (1904), XII 132; Conference of (1814), X 519 sq., 523 sq., (1827), 194, (1828), 200 sqq., (1830–1), 483 sq., 538 sqq., (1838), 506, (1852), XI 255; Convention of (1814), 778, (1833), X 543, (1840), 568 sq., (1884), XII 637, 640; Protocol of (1852), XI 226, 436 sq., 439 sqq., 477, (1877), XII 387; Mexican Convention in (1861), XI 565; Schleswig-Holstein Conference in (1864), 441 sq.; Canadian Conference in (1866), 771; Luxemburg Conference in (1867), 483, 667, 674; Black Sea Conference in (1871), 634, 639, XII 28, 382; Declaration of (1909), 729

—— Company, The, IV 747, VII 4 sqq.; extinguished (1623), 7; 72

—— Corresponding Society, VI 477

—— County Council, established, XII 48

—— Missionary Society, XI 779; 783; XII 808

London Museum, and the *Letters of Junius,* VI 441
—— *Magazine,* XI 362
—— *Review,* XI 362
Londonderry, 2nd Marquis of. *See* Castlereagh, Viscount
—— Charles Stewart Vane-Tempest-Stewart, 6th Marquis of, XII 87
—— Charles William Stewart (Vane), 3rd Marquis of, at Conference of Troppau, X 27 sq.; at Conference of Laibach, 29 sq.; at Conference of Verona, 34; 45; 611; 667 sq.
Long Parliament, The, of Charles I, etc., Vol. IV, Chaps. VIII–XII, XIX; of Charles II, Vol. V, Chap. V *passim*; Chap. IX *passim*
Longfellow, Henry Wadsworth, VII 745 sq.
Longford, plantation of, IV 513
—— Castle, captured by O'Donnell (1595), III 605
Long Island, Duke of York and, V 108
Longjumeau, Peace of, III 10
Longland, John, Bishop of Lincoln, II 433
Longpré, Biron at, III 672; Spanish attack on, repulsed, 673; Biron's tactics at, 679
Longstreet, James, Confederate general, VII 511, 513, 540
Longuet, Charles, French political writer, XI 486
Longueville, ducal House of, V 449
—— Anne-Geneviève de Bourbon, Duchesse de, IV 596; 609 sq.; First Fronde and, 611 sq.; 615; 618; V 89
—— Henry I d'Orléans, Duke of, III 47–8
—— Henry II d'Orléans, Duke of, IV 119; 121; obtains Picardy, 122; 124; 126; at Breisach, 377; assumes command of Bernardines, 383; at Münster, 402; 602; First Fronde and, 611 sq.; death of, 618
—— Louis d'Orléans, Duke of, captured at battle of the Spurs (1513), I 481
Longwood, Napoleon at, IX 757 sqq.
Longwy, fall of, VIII 241, 409
Lónyay, Meinhard, Hungarian Minister of Finance, XII 189 sq.
Loo, Provisional Treaty of (1788), VIII 289, 324
Lookout Mountain, and Chattanooga, VII 511 sq.
Loos, Admiral, at Pernambuco, IV 708
Loots, Cornelis, Dutch writer, XI 676
Lopatin, Russian revolutionary, XII 311
Lope (Felix) de Vega (-Carpio), Spanish dramatist, IV 662
Lopez, Francisco, Dictator of Paraguay, XII 674
—— Dr Roderigo, III 335
Lopukhin, Russian police official, XII 376
Lopukhina, Eudoxia, Tsaritsa. *See* Eudoxia
—— Natalia, exiled to Siberia, VI 315
—— Mlle, mistress of Paul I, VIII 645, IX 41
Lord, Percival Barton, at Kunduz, XII 800

"Lords of the Articles," the Scottish, IV 487 sqq.
Loredano, Antonio, Venetian admiral, defends Skutari (1474), I 80; death of, 87
—— Venetian admiral, at battle of Gallipoli (1416), I 278
Lorentz, Hendrik Antoon, Dutch physicist, XII 789
Loreto (Loretto), Sanctuary of, III 438; Bishopric created at, *ib.*; the Madonna of, sent to France, VIII 581; Pius IX and, XI 706
Loria, Achille, Italian economist, XII 231
Lorient, VI 247; arsenal at, 349; French fleet at, IX 212; 238; Allemand sent to, 239
Loriol, Duc d'Angoulême defeats imperialists at (1815), IX 617
Loris-Melikoff, Count Michael, General, Russian statesman, XII 308 sqq.; resigns, 312; 313 sq.; and peasant reform, 317 sq.; 389
Loriti, Heinrich (Glareanus), II 308, 314
"Lorme, M. de" (Abbé Gaultier), V 430
Lorne, Archibald Campbell, Lord. *See* Argyll
Lornsen, Uwe Jens, Schleswig official, XI 692
Lorraine, IV 132; Montague seized in, 133; French invasion of, 139 sqq.; French conquests in, 146 sqq., 151, 226, 230, 246; 251; 367 sq., 370; 388; 598; Condé in, 619; Treaty of the Pyrenees and, 620; a desert, 621; V 33, 47; ceded by France, 62 sq.; suzerainty of, 164; and Spanish Succession, 391; VI 62; the Old Pretender in, 96, 104; 155 sq.; 158; 162; 167; annexed to France, 203; 238 sqq.; and France, IX 653; loss of, 758; XI 49; 498; French army in, 581 sqq.; the war in, 585, 587; ceded by France, 612; XII 91; Peace of Frankfort and, 95; German annexation of, 135, 137, 145, 147
—— Bishoprics (Toul, Metz and Verdun), occupied by France (1552), II 87
Lorraine, Dukes of:—
—— Anthony, puts down the peasants of Alsace, II 190 sq., 195
—— Charles II, III 511, 663, 665
—— Charles III (IV), IV 137; 139; forfeits his duchy, 142 sq.; Richelieu and, 147, 226; defeated at Pfaffenhofen, 230; at Nördlingen, 245; 248; 250; attempt of, to recover his duchy, 367 sq.; 371; defeated at Sennheim, 377; Leopold William and, 392; and Charles II, 535; and Peace of Westphalia, 405, 603; 616 sq.; arrest of, 427, 619; havoc wrought by, 621; V 43; 350; 354
—— Charles IV (V) (Charles Leopold), V 45; 341; 348; and the Polish Crown, 350, 354; marriage of, 354; campaign of, against Turks, 360; at siege of Vienna, 361; 363 sq.; successes of, against Turks, 366; and the Elector of Bavaria, 367 sq.; goes to the Rhine, 368; 661

Lorraine, Dukes of (*contd.*):—
—— Francis. *See* Francis I, Emperor
—— Leopold Joseph Charles, v 389; 454
—— Nicolas Francis, Cardinal, escapes to Florence, iv 143
—— René II (of Vaudémont), i 391, 393; ii 87
Lorraine, Prince Charles of, vi 234; 237; in Bavaria, 238; 240; at Dresden, 244; in Netherlands, 246 sq.; 257 sq.; at battle of Prague, 259; 262; 264; in Silesia, 273 sqq.; 277; 646
—— Cardinal Charles of, Bishop of Metz (d. 1599, brother of Henry, Duke of Lorraine), iii 709
—— Cardinal of. *See* Guise, Charles of (Archbishop of Rheims)
—— Christina of Denmark, Duchess of, ii 87
—— Christine of, married to Ferdinand de' Medici, Grand Duke of Tuscany, iii 42; 396; 413
—— John of, Cardinal of Lorraine (d. 1550) (son of René II), holder of pluralities, i 659; ii 98; 281
—— Margaret of. *See* Orleans
—— Mary of. *See* Mary of Guise, Queen of Scotland
—— Nicole, Duchess of, 1st wife of Duke Charles III, iv 143
—— Renée of, iii 193
Losada, Cristóbal de, Spanish Reformer, ii 406
Los Castillejos, Marquis of. *See* Prim, Juan
Los Gelves, captured and lost by Spain, iii 486
Loshnitza, Tchitchagoff advances to, ix 502
Lostwithiel, capitulation of, iv 323, 331
Los Velez, Fernandes Joaquin Fajardo de Zuñiga y Requesens, 6th Marquis of, commands Spanish army against Catalans, iv 648; defeat of, 649
—— Pedro Fajardo, 3rd Marquis of, and the Moriscos, iii 494
Lothar II, Emperor, v 618
Lothringen. *See* Lorraine
Lotzer, one of the leaders of German Peasants' Rising, ii 180
Loubet, Émile, President of the French Republic, xii 112; and the Papacy, 119; 121 sq.; at Rome, 242
Loudon, James, Governor-General of the Dutch East Indies, xi 668
Loudoun, John Campbell, 1st Earl of, Chancellor of Scotland, marches on Edinburgh, iv 508
—— John Campbell, 4th Earl of, vi 115 sqq.; 426; and Louisburg, 342*b* (in Vol. xiii), vii 126 sqq., 132
Loudun, Conference of (1616), iv 122
Loughborough, Alexander Wedderburn, 1st Baron, and 1st Earl of Rosslyn, vi 425; 441; 444; 450; and India Bill, 467; 478; vii 157 sq.; and Whig party, ix 673 sq.

Louis, King of Bavaria. *See* Ludwig
—— VI (the Fat), King of France, i 384
—— IX, King of France (St Louis), i 384; xii 705
—— XI, King of France, Italy and, i 107 sq., 301; compared with Matthias Corvinus, 335; 362; Chap. xii *passim* (384–416); Mary of Burgundy and, 417, 437–42; Edward IV and, 463; 636; Pope Paul II and, 663; ii 36; iii 695, 738; v 623
—— XII, King of France (Duke of Orleans), claims Milan, i 108; 115; accession of, 118; occupies Milan, 119–23, 192; attacks Naples, 123–4, 193; Ferdinand of Spain expels, 125–7, 195; Genoa attacked by, 129–30; joins League of Cambray, 131; Venice attacked by, 132–3; Swiss and, 134, 136, 248; Pope Julius II and, 135–6, 198; 190, 192, 194–5, 197, 236, 306, 315, 336, 344, 363, 384; the Church and, 388, 393 sqq.; reforms of justice under, 403; finance of, 410 sq.; army of, 413; marries Mary Tudor, 140, 483; death of, 458, 484; ii 9, 281, 308; iii 695
—— XIII, King of France, iii 547, 577 sq.; iv 53; 58; 87; and Mansfeld, 88; accession of, 118 sq.; attains majority, 120; and Luynes, 124 sqq.; subdues Béarn, 127; 129 sq.; and the Huguenots, 128, 132 sqq.; character of, 136; and Richelieu, *ib.* sqq.; and Gaston, 140 sq.; 144 sq.; 148 sqq.; 153; and Sweden, 247 sq.; Charles I and, 258, 262 sq., 266, 272, 284; Bernard of Weimar and, 368 sqq., 380 sq., 382; Preliminary Treaty and, 398; and Peace of Westphalia, 404 sqq.; 608; marriage of, 625; Barcelona and, 649, 653; and Urban VIII, 677; and Duke of Nevers, 678; 697; death of, 388, 593, 659, 702; v 376; vi 612
—— XIV, King of France, iii 695; and Elsass, iv 406; joins *Rheinbund*, 432; accession of, 593; 604; and the Fronde, 608 sqq., 613; majority of, 615; re-enters Paris (Oct. 21, 1652), 617; authority of Mazarin and, 618; marriage plans for, 620, 660; and Mazarin's death, 622; 659; 688; Age of, Vol. v; domestic policy of, *ib.*, Chap. i *passim*; foreign policy of (1661–97), Chap. ii; and Pope Alexander VII, 76; the religion of, 77; Court preachers of, 79 sq.; and the Jansenists, 84, 89 sq.; and religious uniformity, 85; and Portugal, 105 sq.; and Charles II of England, 106, 109, 201, 209, 223; detaches Charles II from the Triple Alliance, 154; subsidises Charles II, 212, 214, 217 sqq., 227, 230; aids Dutch against England, 109, 182; joins England against Dutch, 112; and United Provinces, 152 sq., 156 sqq., 161, 180; makes proposals for peace, 162; 165; invades Spanish Netherlands (1667), 199; Triple Alliance and, 200; and Peace of Aachen, 200, 373; and Treaty of Dover, 203 sq.;

205; 208; and James II, 211, 217, 231, 235, 243 sqq., 260, 262 sq., 275, 308, 399; and English expedition of the Prince of Orange, 244; and Ireland, 307 sq., 314, 316; Romanising policy of, 331; 339; and Austria, 344, 347; and Emperor Leopold I, 349, 353; and Hungary, 352 sq.; and Poland, 350, 354 sq.; and Queen Mary of Poland, 356; 359; and Turkey, 360; 368; and Treaty of Ryswyk, 370; and Spain, 200, 374; marriage of, 376 sq.; and Spanish Succession, 380 sqq., 401; and accession of Philip V of Spain, 394 sqq.; Grand Alliance (1701) and, 398, 404; recognises "James III," 399; and William III, *ib.*; 403; alliance of, with German Princes, 404; 411; and Convention of Milan, 415; makes overtures for peace (1706-10), 417, 422 sq., 427; recognises Protestant Succession in England, 422; appeals to France against the Allies, 424; and peace negotiations (1711), 430; and Peace of Rastatt, 435 sq., 452; and Peace of Utrecht, 434, 439; and Treaty with Great Britain (April 11th, 1713), 441 sqq.; 444; and Princess Orsini, 447; and Spanish Netherlands, 447; and Sicily, 448; and Neuchâtel, 449; and principality of Orange, *ib.*; and negotiations with the Emperor (1713), 450 sq.; and Peace of Baden, 455; and Griffenfeld, 561; and Sweden, 566, 568, 570 sq., 577; and Charles XI, 573; 596; and Elector Frederick William, 648 sq.; 650 sq.; 659; Leibniz and, 696; and Brazil, 675; and settlements in America, 684; and Indian Company, 702 sq.; establishes *Académie des Sciences*, 741; 743; Sophia of Hanover and, vi 1 sq.; and the Old Pretender, 9, 17; and Great Britain, 22; 25; and the Jacobites, 91 sq., 97, 111, 120 sq.; and Madame des Ursins, 122; 127 sq.; 132; 138; standing army of, 216; 229; 239; 329; and the *Parlement*, 347; 391; 586; Clement XI and, 588; and Switzerland, 613 sqq.; 624; 640; 711; 718; death of, 97, 120; and Canada, vii 81, 87 sq.; viii 5 sq.; last years of, 8, 14; power of, 36; 43 sq.; xii 534

Louis XV, King of France, v 31; 91; 441; 543; vi 25; betrothal of, 39; 63; and the Jacobites, 109 sq., 112 sq.; accession of, 120 sq.; 126 sq.; 131 sq.; 134; and the Infanta, 140; marriage of, 143 sq.; dismisses Bourbon, 144; 146; illness of, 148; 152; 158; and the Old Pretender, 159; Francis I and, 160; 161; and Chauvelin, 162 sq.; character of, 164; 165; 194; and Stanislaus Leszczynski, 196; and Austrian Succession, 229; 239; and Maria Theresa, 243, 325, 400 sq.; and d'Argenson, 247; and Frederick the Great, 250, 266, 299, 702; and Seven Years' War, 260; 262; army of, 269; 303; 323; desires peace, 327; and death of Fleury, 329;

330; and Peace of Aix-la-Chapelle, 331; 334; and Treaty of Versailles, 336; 338 sq.; 340 sqq.; and the *Parlements*, 347, 359; and Choiseul, 349, 352; 351; and Austria, 353; 356 sqq.; 360; Charles III of Spain and, 368; 411; 546; 588; and the clericals, 591; and the Jesuits, 592; and Switzerland, 613; 711; and Sweden, 768; death of, 359, 616; and French colonies, vii 117, 119; viii 19, 22, 44, 59

Louis XVI, King of France, vi 144; marriage of, 356; and Switzerland, 616; Joseph II and, 631; and Scheldt dispute, 644 sq.; 704; 782; 784; and United States, vii 317; viii 48; condition of the peasants under, 62 sq.; and finance, 66, 75; Chap. iv *passim*; and elections of 1789, 123, 127 sq., 132; and meeting of the States General, 146 sq., 152; holds a "royal session," 155 sqq.; and National Assembly, 165, 179, 183; leaves Versailles for Paris, 185; and the Church, 197 sqq., 219; arrested at Varennes, 200; and Constitution of 1791, 201, 208, 211, 215; and the *émigrés*, 218 sq.; growing unpopularity of, 219; and mob in Tuileries (June 20), 229 sq.; leaves Tuileries, 236 sq.; in Temple, 240; trial of, 254 sqq.; execution of, 261 sq., vi 477; ix 572; x 732; xii 523

—— XVII, son of Louis XVI of France, imprisonment of, viii 378; restoration of, proposed, 387, 389; ill-treatment and probable death of, 389 sq.

—— XVIII, King of France ("Monsieur"), vi 783 sq.; and Congress of Troppau, vii 368; character of, viii 81, 103; flight of, to Brussels, 200; accused of high treason, 221; impolitic attitude of, 390 sq., 394 sq.; and Brottier's conspiracy, 505; 555; at Mittau, 635; and Bonaparte, ix 18; 28; established at Mittau by Paul, 40; 138, 143, 181, 186; proposed restoration of, 560; at Hartwell, 561; return of, 562; Ministry of, 565; and the Church, 569; suspicions against, 572; 573; and Napoleon, 573-4; flight of, 575; 594; and Order of St John of Jerusalem, 604; army of, 618; policy of, 619; returns to France, 643 sqq.; and Congress of Vienna, 617, 646, 653, 662-3; and proposed general Alliance, x 17; 41; 42; at Ghent, 44; at second Restoration, 44-5; 46; 50; and the *Doctrinaires*, 55; and army reforms, *ib.*; 56; 57; and Decazes Ministry, 57; and elections of 1819, 60; 62; dismisses Decazes, 63; ill-health of, 69; 70; 71; and reaction, 73; 74; 75; and intervention in Spain, 79; dismisses Chateaubriand, 80; 81; and compensation for the *émigrés*, 82; death of (Sept. 15, 1824), 85; 87; 96; 97; 140; negotiations of, with Papacy, 143 sq.; 207; and Spanish

aid (1815), 211; and Spanish affairs, 222
sq., 225 sqq.; 230; xi 174; 681; and
Sweden, 683

Louis I (the Great), King of Hungary, i
264, 342
—— II, King of Hungary and Bohemia,
i 93, 95; drowned after Mohács, 96 sq.;
331, 337 sqq., 343; ii 66, 198
—— King of Portugal. *See* Luiz
—— King of Spain. *See* Luis
—— Archduke of Austria (1836). *See*
Ludwig
—— Duke of Burgundy, grandson of
Louis XIV (Dauphin, 1711–2), v 28;
30 sq.; 88; 421; 434; vi 127
—— Dauphin of France (son of Louis XIV),
v 30; 391; 434
—— Dauphin, son of Louis XV, vi 144;
148; marriage of, 156, 199; 160; and
the Jesuits, 348; death of, 356
—— Ferdinand, Prince of Prussia, ix 267;
272; killed at Saalfeld, 275

Louis-Napoleon, Emperor of France. *See*
Napoleon III

Louis-Philippe, King of the French (Duke
of Chartres, Duke of Orleans), viii 417;
ix 384; plot in favour of, 573; x 119 sq.;
and rebellion in Papal States, 155; 167;
and Ferdinand VII of Spain, 231 sq.; and
Spanish affairs, 235, 237; 382; attitude
of the Powers towards, 465, 481 sq.; and
Portugal, 324 sq.; and ex-Emperor Dom
Pedro of Brazil, 326; offer of Crown
to, 477 sqq.; character of, 479; checks
Republican extremists, 480; relations of,
with England, 482; and Belgium, 483,
506, 539 sq.; foreign policy of, 484;
and Casimir Périer, 487; and republican
revolt in Paris, 488; and Guizot, 489;
attempted assassination of, 492; and
Third Party, 493; 494; and de Broglie,
and Thiers, 495 sq.; recalls Guizot to
office, 497; and Count Molé, 497 sq.,
507 sq.; and maintenance of peace, 505;
opposition to foreign policy of, 508 sqq.;
and Soult Ministry, 511; and Egyptian
Question, 512 sq.; and Thiers Ministry,
513; and the crisis with Great Britain
(1840), 570; and Spanish marriages, xi
17, 553 sqq.; 22; 28 sq.; and Tahiti, 35;
and Thiers and Guizot, 37; Thiers and,
40 sq.; 73; 81; 96; dismisses Guizot, 97
sq.; and Thiers, 98 sq.; and Revolution
of 1848, 100 sqq.; abdicates, 101; and
Switzerland, 249; 288; 556; 671; 793;
xii 410
—— Louis-Dominique, Baron, finance of,
ix 566–7; x 20; 44; appointed Minister
of Finance, 57; 61; resigns, 62; and the
Revolution of 1830, 478

Louisa, Louise:—
—— (of Great Britain), Queen of Denmark, consort of Frederick V, vi 739
—— (of Hesse-Cassel), Queen of Denmark,
consort of Christian IX, xi 695 sq.

Louisa, Louise (*contd.*):—
—— (of Sweden), Queen of Denmark,
consort of Frederick VIII, xii 290
—— (of Hesse-Darmstadt), Queen of
Prussia, consort of Frederick William II,
vi 726
—— (of Mecklenburg-Strelitz), Queen of
Prussia, consort of Frederick William III,
viii 634; influence of, ix 267; 278; re-
treat of, 280; meets Napoleon, 292;
Alexander I and, 308; return of, to
Berlin, 334; influence of, 336; 581; death
of, 336; x 350; xi 151
—— of Savoy. *See* Angoulême, Duchess
of
—— Dorothea, Prussian Princess, vi 7
—— Elisabeth, Queen of Spain, consort
of Luis, vi 39; 126; 137; 140
—— Elisabeth, Duchess of Parma. *See*
Parma
—— Juliana, Electress Palatine. *See*
Palatine
—— Marie, Queen of the Belgians, con-
sort of Leopold I, xi 671
—— Ulrica, Queen of Sweden, consort of
Adolphus Frederick, vi 668; 671 sq.

Louisburg, fort of, built, vii 95, 113;
capture of (1745), 114 sqq.; restored to
France, 121; Loudoun and, 128 sq.; the
English attacks of 1757–8 upon, vi 342a
sq. (in Vol. xiii); capitulates (1758), *ib.*,
415, vii 132 sqq.

Louisiana, and French colonisation, v 13;
John Law and, vi 172 sq.; 183; 352;
troubles in, 373; 410 sqq.; 429; Mississippi Company and, 532; foundation of,
vii 70, 114; Crozat in, 88, 92; development of, 92 sq.; ceded to Spain (1763),
vi 347, 370, 422, vii 93; to France (1800),
ib., 324 sq., to United States (1803), 93,
143, 326; enters Union (1812), 359, 413;
slavery in, 361 sq., 386, 590; upholds
Tariff, 381; secedes from Union (1860),
446; joins Confederacy, 453, 603; and
Vicksburg, 502; emancipation in, 595,
598; contraband trade in, 620; new
government set up in, 625; Republicans
in (1876), 642; sale of, to United States,
ix 26, 244, 741; French colonial expedition
to, 80; purchased from Spain, 419; United
States and, xii 684

Louisville, trade of, vii 360; Confederate
headquarters at, 463; Federals occupy
(1862), 507

Loulé, Terceira at, x 333
—— Marquis of, Portuguese statesman,
x 327; 330; xi 571; 574 sq.

Lourdes, miracles of, xi 714, xii 114

Lourés, Duke of Cadaval at, x 334

Loustallot Elysée, *Révolutions de Paris*,
viii 168

Louth, English in, iii 580; invasion of,
605; election, x 644

Louvain, foundation of University of, i
419, 436, 622; Confession of, enforced by

Charles V, II 80; College at, III 593; opposes William of Orange, 232; University of, IV 789; Jansenism at, v 82, x 157; siege of, VI 246; 248; seminary of, 637, 649 sq.; VIII 318, 320, 327; University of, transferred to Brussels, 318; Dumouriez at (1793), 420; doctors of, and Erastianism, IX 415; *Collegium Philosophicum* at, x 526; French advance on (1831), 542

Louvel, Louis-Pierre, assassinates the Duc de Berry, x 23; 63; 67

L'Ouverture, Toussaint, negro ruler of San Domingo, VI 185; VIII 484; IX 420 sq., 750; death of, 422

Louvet de Couvray, Jean-Baptiste, VIII 249; accuses Robespierre, 253; 384, 386

Louville, Charles-August d'Allonville, Marquis de, French envoy in Spain, VI 123

Louvois, François-Michel le Tellier, Marquis de, v 1; 5; 7; rivalry of, with Colbert, 16 sq.; character of, 17, 19; army administration of, 18 sq.; 20; and persecution of the Protestants, 24; death of, 28; 39; 43 sq.; and devastation of Palatinate, 56 sq.; 59; 405

Louvre, Meeting of Estates of France at (1593), III 517

Lovat, Simon Fraser, 12th Lord Lovat, VI 100 sq.; 109; 117

Lovedale, Free Church educational mission, Sir George Grey and, XI 786

Lovejoy's Station, Confederates at, VII 522 sq., 526

Lovel, Francis, Viscount, flight of, to Flanders, I 465

—— Sir Thomas, II 417

Lovelace, Francis, Governor of New York, VII 41 sq.

Lovicz, Princess. *See* Grudzinska, Joanna

Low Countries, The. *See* Netherlands, Holland, Belgium, etc.

Lowe, Sir Hudson, forced to surrender Capri, IX 382; at St Helena, 760

—— Robert. *See* Sherbrooke, Viscount

Lowell, James Russell, VII 745 sq.

Lower, Richard, physician, v 727 sq.; 733 sq.

Lower Saxon Circle, and War of 1623-9, IV 85-109; 567

Lowestoft, battle of (1665). *See* Southwold Bay

Lowestoft, The, reaches Quebec (1759), VII 142

Lowicz, Conference at, III 84; principality of, granted to Davout, IX 339; school at, x 449; Paskevich at, 472

Lowther, James, Irish Secretary, XII 76

Loyalty Islands, slave trade in, XII 666

Loyola, St Ignatius (Inigo Lopez de Recalde), I 651; the *Spiritual Exercises*, 625; II 401; supports Roman Inquisition, 650; early life of, 651 sq.; Caraffa and, 652 sq.; rule of Order of Jesuits by, 654-9; the *Spiritual Exercises* of, 657 sq.; III 425, 585; IV 777

L'Oyseleur, Pierre, Seigneur de Villiers, III 253

Lualaba, river, discovered by Livingstone, XII 809; 810; 812

Lubecki, Prince Ksavery (František), Polish Minister of Finance, x 454 sq.; and Tsar Nicholas I's proposed French campaign, 465; and Polish revolution, 466 sq., 469; XI 658

Lubienski, Archbishop, Primate of Poland, VI 354

Lubina, fight at (1812), IX 493

Lublin, Union of, III 83-4, v 480, VI 671; occupied by Poniatovski (1809), IX 354; Polish province, x 449, 461; disorder in, XII 354

Lubomirski, Stanislas Heraclius, Polish commander-in-chief, v 350

Lucan, George Charles Bingham, 3rd Earl of, XI 330

—— Richard Bingham, 2nd Earl, surprised by Holkar, IX 727

Lucas, Sir Charles, and Royalist rising in Essex, IV 349; death of, 351

—— Charles, Irish patriot, VI 492; 494

—— Frederick, editor of *The Tablet*, XII 69

—— William, in Africa, XII 806

Lucca, entry of Charles VIII into, I 113; the Reformation in, II 391 sq.; Vermigli in, *ib.*; republic of, III 385; Reformers at, 389; trade of, 392; Habsburg influence over, 689; VIII 778; granted to Élise Bonaparte, IX 247; creation of duchies in, 268; Élise Bonaparte and, 398-9; assigned to Tuscany, 602-3; assigned to Infanta Marie Louise, 661; XI 69 sq.; national movement in, 75; and union with Piedmont, 84; 88

—— Don Carlos, Prince of, x 301

Lucchesini, Jérôme, Marquis de, Prussian Minister, VIII 293, 412, 425, 441; ambassador in Paris, IX 73; 249, 251, 271-2; interviews Duroc, 278; joined by Zastrow, 281

Lucena, Count of. *See* O'Donell, José Enrique

Lucerne. *See* Luzern

Lucero, Diego Rodriguez, Grand Inquisitor, rebellion of Cordova against, I 360

Luch Ali, Calabrian renegade, III 497

Luchaire, Achille, French medievalist, XII 834; 850

Luckau, Bülow at IX 520

Luckner, Count Nikolaus, French marshal, VIII 222; executed (1794), 357; commands Army of the Rhine (1791), 405, 407; recalled, 409

Lucknow, VI 553; 572; Henry Wellesley sent to (1801), IX 724; mutiny at, XI 746; relief of, 748; 749

Luçon, Vendean defeat at, VIII 353

Luddite riots, x 576

Luden, Heinrich, x 364 sq.; *History of the German people*, XII 824

Luder, Peter, German humanist, at Erfurt, II 111
Ludewig, Johan Peter von, anti-papal Manifesto of, v 666
Ludiana, attack on, XI 739
Ludlow, Edmund, Cromwell and, IV 347, 443, 448; leader of Republicans, 449 sq.; in Ireland, 535; 538; 545; Committee of Safety and, 546; 547 sq.; 550; 556 sq.; 557; at Amsterdam, v 110
Ludovica (of Modena), Empress of Austria, 3rd consort of Francis I, IX 580
Ludovico *il Moro. See* Milan, Dukes of
Ludovisi, Luigi (nephew of Gregory XV), Cardinal Archbishop of Bologna, and the Valtelline, IV 57, 674; and Catholic Reaction, 672 sq.
Ludwig I, King of Bavaria, as Crown Prince opposes Montgelas' constitutional scheme, x 146, 359; 204; opposes Metternich, 368; accession of, 371; enlightened measures of, 371 sq.; and Ultramontanes, XI 61 sq.; abdication of, 146; and Greece, 278
—— II, King of Bavaria, XI 397; 465 sq.
—— Archduke of Austria, x 378; XI 44; 152 sqq.; retirement of, 171
Ludwig, Otto, German dramatist, XI 415 sqq.; novels of, 419; 420
Lübeck, size and importance of, I 299; struggle of, for commercial supremacy in Baltic, 456; Schmalkaldic League joined by, II 216; municipal revolution in, 228, 231; rivalry between Dutch and, 228; war between Scandinavian North and, 229 sq.; declaration of war against Christian II by, 607, 622; commercial decay of, IV 8, 420; Denmark and, 89, 91, 98 sq., 163, 561; and Spanish trade, 105; 107; Peace of (1629), 109, 192; and Sweden, 158; meeting of Hanse Towns at, 108, 195; congress held at (1651-2), 578; v 579; and German Order of Knights, 630; taken by Danish troops (1801), IX 48; 94; captured by French (1806), 280; Scharnhorst at, 332; 367; annexed to France (1810), 374; government of, 409; Jews of, 588; free city of, x 341; the revolutionary movement in, XI 151
Lüber *or* Lieber, Thomas (Erastus). *See* Erastus
Lüderitz, Bremen trader in Africa, XII 160
Lüders, Alexandre Nicolaievich von, Russian general, XI 206; 211; 659
Lüdinghausen, Baron Friedrich von. *See* Wolff, Father
Lüneburg, Estates of Lower Saxon Circle at, IV 86; 91 sq.; 98; convents restored in, 112; defeat of Morand at (1813), IX 515
—— Dukes of. *See* Brunswick-Lüneburg
Lütkeman, Archdeacon. at Stockholm, VI 772
Lützen, battle of (1632), IV 221, 223, 231 sq

Lützow, "Free Corps" of, IX 510
—— Count Rudolf von, Austrian Minister in Rome, XI 71; 77
—— Count von, Imperial Councillor, at Hamburg, IV 397 sq.
Lugard, Sir Frederick, XII 811
Lugnetz, Catholic commune of, IV 36, 47, 51
Lugo, Soult and Ney concentrate at, IX 451
Lugos, XI 211; fight at, 213
Luis, King of Spain (Don Luis), VI 126; 135; accession of, 137; death of, *ib.*; 138; 139; 146
Luitpold, Prince (of Bavaria), XI 146
Luiz I, King of Portugal, XI 534; 570 sq.; accession of, 574; XII 270 sq.
Lujan, Don Francisco de, III 296
Lukasinski, Valezy, Polish officer, x 453 sq.; 458; 470
Luk'ou, British officers assaulted at, XII 518
Luleå, railway from, XII 279
Lumbres, Gillain de Fiennes, Seigneur de, III 229
Lumley, John, 1st Baron (2nd cr.), III 281
—— Richard, Earl of Scarborough. *See* Scarborough
Luna, Alvaro da, Spanish statesman, I 354
—— Juan de, rising in Siena against, II 83
—— Don Sancho de, III 420 sq.
—— Count di, Spanish ambassador to Council of Trent, II 683; III 168
Lund, dispute concerning Archbishopric of, II 610 sq.; 616; battle of (1676), v 44, 570; Peace of (1679), 579; Görtz at, VI 28; University of, XII 273
Lund, Archbishops of:—
—— Aage Sparre, II 610
—— Diederik Slaghoek, and Stockholm *Blodbad*, II 603; 604; death of, 607; 610
—— Gunnar Berger, II 603, 605, 610
—— Jörgen Skodborg, II 610
Lunden. *See* Lund
Lundi Kotal, British troops in, XII 489
Lundy, Robert, Governor of Derry, v 308 sq.
Lundy's Lane, battle of (1814), VII 343
Lunéville, cavalry school at, VIII 446; Treaty of (1801), IX 18, 66, 69-71; and Austria, 74, 79; and Germany, 81, 92; and Switzerland, 98, 100; 245; and Bavaria, 253; rising at, x 492
Lungchow, opened to foreign trade, XII 506
Lunge, Vincent, Norwegian commander, II 618 sqq.
Lunsford, Sir Thomas, Lieutenant of the Tower, IV 297
Lupetino Baldo, Italian Reformer, II 383
Lupfen, Countess von, Peasants' Rising and, II 177
Lupset, Thomas, on agrarian reform, II 490
Lusatia, joined with Hungary (1477), I 331; and Ferdinand, IV 22 sqq.; 28; 32; Saxony and, 34, 75; Saxons in, 204, 209; Wallenstein in, 237; and Peace of Prague, 252 sq.; and Brandenburg, v 620; VI

256 sq.; 262; Duke of Bevern in, 264; Austrian forces in, 265; 266 sqq.; 282; 291 sq.; Maria Theresa and, 244; 327; Frederick the Great and, 704; 705 sq.; Catharine II and, 707

Luserna, Count of, III 403

Lusignan, captured by Montpensier, III 25; opposition to Napoleon III at, XI 473

Luther, Hans, father of Martin, II 109 sq., 116

—— Martin, and Indulgences, I 322; 340; influence of, in Hungary, 340; Wessel and, 437; 638; *Deutsche Theologie*, 641; 652; translation of New Testament by, 684; II 8, 19, 21; Chap. IV *passim*; expresses popular feeling, 147 sq.; 152 sqq.; activity of, 162 sq., 174; attitude of, towards Peasants' Revolt, 192 sqq., 233; comparison between Machiavelli and, 194; 206; at Conference of Marburg, 207 sq., 213, 215, 217, 223; Bullinger and, 234; Philip of Hesse and, 241; 243; 250; death of, 252; statue of, at Worms, 208, 309 sqq., 339, 613; as a Reformer, 343 sq.; compared with Zwingli, 208 sq., 313 sqq., 345 sq.; with Erasmus, 700; philosophical ideas of, 713 sqq.; writings of, 136, 201; *Babylonish Captivity*, 148, 158; *Karsthans*, 159; *Neukarsthans*, *ib.*; translation of Bible by, 164; the hymns of, 201, 690; *Catechism*, 201; III 106, 422; revolutionary theories of, 736, 738 sqq., 750; Church theory of, 753, 757, 759, 764 sq.; IV 5; V 635; VI 254; 274

Lutheranism, from the time of Luther himself, Vol. II, Chaps. IV, V, VI, VII and VIII *passim*; in the Netherlands, under Charles V, 103; in France, 285 sq.; Zwingli and, 319; criticism of, 343 sq.; in Italy, 380 sqq.; in England, and Elizabeth, 588 sq.; in Denmark, 611 sqq.; in Norway, 618 sqq.; in Sweden, 624 sqq., 633; in Poland, 635 sqq.; as a system of thought, 713 sqq.; and Sigismund I, in Poland, III 74 sqq.; and the Religious Peace of Augsburg (1555), 140 sqq.; in Transylvania and Hungary proper, 147; position of, in Austrian Church, Empire, etc. under Ferdinand I and Maximilian II, *see* Chap. V *passim*; under Rudolf II, 703 sqq.; political side of, Chap. XXII, Political Thought in the 16th century, 736–69 *passim*; in Empire, IV 3 sqq.; 82 sqq.; in Sweden, and Upsala Resolution, 170 sqq.; and Peace of Westphalia, 411 sqq. [*See also* the Lutheran Princes in the Thirty Years' War *and* Toleration]

Lutomirski, Stanislas, Canon of Konin, III 74, 81

Lutsk, Tormassoff at, IX 490

Lutter, battle of (1626), IV 97 sqq., 110

Lutternberg, battle of, VI 426

Luttrell, Colonel, and John Wilkes, VI 440

Lutzingen, and battle of Blenheim, V 410

Lux, Adam, deputy to the Convention, VIII 775

Luxemburg, acquired by Philip the Good of Burgundy, I 421; invaded by French (1542), II 76 sqq., (1552), 87; the Allies in, III 628, 666; leave granted for French army to pass through, 690; IV 369; and Treaty of the Pyrenees, 620; Louis XIV and, V 36, 47, 62, 165; town of, besieged (1681), 48 sq., 230, 364; restored to Spain, 63; 389; 447; 450; seminary at, VI 637; 641; 647; Austrian retreat to, 652; defences of, VIII 281; Austrian troops in (1790), 329, 335; besieged (1794), 437, 442; ceded to France (1801), 369; devotion to Austria in, 415; the duchy and Federal Act, 650, 659; assigned to King of Netherlands (1815), 655; and Netherlands, X 343, 354; and Germanic Confederation, 344; 369; Belgium and, 483, 505 sq., 540 sqq.; assigned to King of Holland, 524, 539; and *Zollverein*, XI 53; neutralisation of, 462; France and, 483; 580; 667; Belgium and, 669; 674 sq.; Germany and, XII 95

—— Alliance, The (1682), V 35

—— Charles, Duke of. *See* Charles V, Emperor

—— Charles Emmanuel Sigismond, Duc de, VIII 158

—— Elizabeth of Görlitz, Duchess of, I 421

—— François-Henri de Montmorency, Duke of, Marshal of France, V 45; at Fleurus, 59, 261; 60; death of, 62; 160; Dutch campaign of (1672), 164 sq.; 256; 262; 340; 405

—— François Louis, Duke of, envoy to Rome (1589), III 443, 453

—— John of, and Margravate of Brandenburg, V 621

—— Wenceslas of, I 421

Luynes, Charles, Marquis d'Albert, Duke of, Constable of France, IV 124 sq.; and Richelieu, 126; 145; death of, 127, 640

—— Charles-Philippe d'Albert, Duke of (d. 1758), VI 165

—— Marie de Rohan, Duchess of. *See* Chevreuse

Luzac, Dutch Liberal, XI 663

Luzan y Guerra, Ignacio de, Spanish writer, V 69

Luzern, Diet at (1521), II 315, (1524), 324; Treaty of (1560), III 405; IV 51; Diet at (1621), 54; and Bündners, 56; and Neuchâtel, V 449; canton of, VI 613; 625; restores its old Constitution, IX 600; and Congress of Vienna, 601; negotiations for a bishopric of, X 149; XI 234; government of, 235; 237; reaction in, 238; 240; joins *Siebnerkonkordat*, 242; 244 sq.; and Articles of Baden, 246; and Aargau monasteries, 247; anti-Jesuit risings in, *ib.*; 251

Luzh, Russian geodesist, V 535

Luzhenovsky, Russian official, XII 363

Luzon (Philippines), and United States, VII 684; American troops in, XII 530; 531

Luzzara, battle of (1702), V 406

Luzzatti, Luigi, Italian statesman, XII 217; 225; 227 sq.; debt conversion scheme of, 234

Lybecker, Georg, Swedish general, V 597; 609

Lycia, researches in, XII 846

Lydenburg, district of, XI 785

Lyell, Sir Charles, geologist, XII 730; 771 sqq.

Lyesna, battle of (1708), V 598 sq.

Lyly, John, III 344, 370-1, 373; Spanish influence upon, 548

Lyme Regis, Monmouth lands at, V 232

Lynar, Count zu, Saxon statesman, VI 730

Lynch, Comte Jean-Baptiste, Mayor of Bordeaux, IX 617

Lynchburg, Federal advance on, VII 530 sq.; 537; Lee's retreat to, 539 sq.

Lynden van Sandenburg, Count Constantius Theodorus van, Dutch statesman, XII 244 sq.

Lyndhurst, John Singleton Copley, 1st Baron, Lord, Chancellor, X 615; 655; 667; and municipal reform, 671; XI 2

Lynedoch, General Thomas Graham, 1st Baron, British commissioner at Austrian headquarters, VIII 572; at Cadiz, IX 463; sent to Tarifa, 464; in command of a corps, 476; with Wellington, 477

Lynn Canal, and Klondyke, XII 617

Lyon, George, African traveller, VII 807

—— Nathaniel, Federal captain, VII 458 sq.; killed at Wilson's Creek, 460

Lyons, silk trade at, encouraged by Louis XI, I 414; financial centre at, II 64 sq.; spread of Lutheranism in, 291; in hands of the Huguenots, III 3; visited by Charles IX and his mother, 7; Peace of (1601), 397, 419 sq., 683; Henry III and Navarre at (1574), 25; trade at, 392; Henry IV proclaimed at, 417; the League at, 661 sq., 665 sq.; entry of Henry IV into, 668 sq.; population of, VIII 60; disaffection in (1793), 268, 270, 339 sq.; open war in, 345 sq., 431; fall of, 351; massacre at (1795), 387; inhabitants of, declared *émigrés*, 502; Commission meets at (1802), IX 85; Napoleon at (1815), 574; *fédérés* of, 619; disturbances at (1816), X 50, (1817), 54; popularity of La Fayette at, 97; revolts at (1831), 487, (1834), 491 sq.; silk industry of, 754, XI 259; 31; Louis-Napoleon at, 134; 243; 290; Gambetta at, 498; Commune at, 503; 601; 608 sq.; XII 96; President Carnot assassinated at, 112, 126; 124; Socialist Congress at, 127; 236

—— Pierre d'Espinac, Archbishop of, III 45 sq., 52, 452

Lyra, Nicholas de, Hebrew scholar, I 591; II 111, 694

Lyttelton, Sir Edward, IV 283

—— George Lyttelton, Lord, VI 71; 434

Lytton, Edward George Earle Lytton Bulwer-Lytton, 1st Baron, X 655; 724; Colonial Secretary, XI 330; dramas of, 352; novels of, 358

—— Edward Robert Bulwer, 1st Earl of, and Afghan War, XII 34; 36; Viceroy of India, 460; and Afghánistán, 466 sqq.; administration of, 472 sqq.; 476; 478; and Indian Civil Service, 480; 482; and Punjab, 490

Lyveden, Lord. *See* Smith, Robert Vernon

Ma, Chinese general, XII 511

Maager, Transylvanian politician, XII 177

Maanen, Cornelis Felix van, Dutch Minister of Justice, X 531; 533 sq.; dismissal of, 535

Maasdam, Van der Duyn van, Dutch politician, X 517

Maassen, Friedrich, German canonist, XII 848

—— Karl Georg, and Prussian financial reform, X 354 sq.; and tariff reform, 372 sq.; Minister of Finance, 378

Mabillon, Jean, French Benedictine, V 79; XII 816

Mabinogion, Lady Charlotte Guest's translation of, XI 352

Mably, Abbé Gabriel Bonnot de, VIII 1, 26, 33 sq.

Macadam, John Loudon, X 738

Macao, Portuguese and, IV 733, 744; expedition to (1809), IX 781; slavery abolished at, XI 575; 804; death of Napier at, 805; 806; 810; 819; Portuguese occupation of, XII 506 sq.; 554 sq.

Macarthur, Captain John, and Australian wool, IX 738; XI 791

Macartney, George Macartney, 1st Earl, Governor of Madras, VI 577; IX 710; embassy of, to China, 718; Governor of Cape Colony, 749; mission to China, XII 796

Macassar, Dutch and, IV 711; V 146

Macaulay (Catharine Sawbridge), Mrs, VIII 755, 758

—— Thomas Babington, Lord Macaulay, VI 802; 818; IX 264; X 601 sq.; and parliamentary reform, 609, 614, 618; 655; enters Melbourne Ministry, 678; XI 361 sqq.; 751; XII 837

—— Zachary, and the slave trade, VI 472, X 584; 658

MacCarthies, The, of Munster, III 581

McCarthy, J., explores the Menam, XII 797

MacCarthy Mor, III 607

McCausland, John, Confederate officer, VII 532

McClellan, George Brinton, General-in-Chief of the U.S. army, VII 456 sq., 463;

takes command, 467 sqq.; in Virginia (1862), 472 sqq.; and the Seven Days' Battles, 477 sqq.; in Washington, 481, 493; at Antietam, 481 sq.; relieved of his command, 483; 579; candidate for Presidency, 593, 600 sq.

Macclesfield, Charles Gerard, 2nd Earl of, vi 8

McClure, George, American general, vii 341

McCormick, Cyrus Hall, inventor of the reaper, vii 415, 695

—— Richard, and United Irishmen, x 629

McCulloch, Benjamin, Confederate general, vii 460

—— Hugh, American Secretary of the Treasury, vii 631

—— John Ramsay, economist, x 598; on Irish absenteeism, 776; 784; xii 745; 759

Macdonald, Æneas, Jacobite, vi 111

—— Alexander, of Glencoe, v 294

—— Sir Claude Maxwell, and Wei-Hai-Wei, xii 514; 520

—— Sir Donald, of Sleat, vi 100

—— Étienne-J.-J.-Alexandre, Duc de Tarente, viii 435, 446, 654; and War of 1799, 656 sq.; and Brumaire, 679 sq.; ix 60; 68; receives Taranto, 111; 353; supersedes Augereau, 457; cooperates with Suchet, 464; departs for Figueras, 465; in Catalonia, 469-70; and Russian campaign, 485; 505; relations of, with York, 510; at Danzig, 511; 520; abandons line of Katzbach, 524; crosses the Bober, 525; at Leipzig, 535 sqq.; guards French frontier, 543; 547; envoy to Alexander, 558; on Council of War, 565; adheres to Bourbons, 621; x 66

—— Sir John, Jacobite, vi 111

—— Sir John Alexander, Premier of Canada, xi 769 sqq.; 775; xii 605 sqq.; 614 sq.

—— of Clanranald, vi 105; 111 sq.

—— of Glencoe, vi 111 sq.

—— of Keppoch, vi 101 sq.; 111 sq.

Macdonell of Glengarry, vi 111 sq.

Macdonnel, Scottish general, in Portugal, x 335

Macdonnell, Antony Patrick Macdonnell, Lord, xii 90

McDonnell, Aeneas, x 641

MacDonnell, Alaster, with Montrose, iv 527

—— James, iii 591

—— Sorley Boy (brother to James), iii 591 sq.

MacDonnells of the Isles, The, iii 591

McDougall, William, Canadian politician, xi 769; 775

McDowell, Irvin, at Bull Run, vii 465 sq.; 469; 473; ordered to join McClellan, 475, 477

Macedonia, insurrection in, x 180; xii 10; Austrian trade in, 211; Turkish misrule in, 342; 381; 391; 393; Treaty of

Berlin and, 396; 398 sq.; Bulgarian propaganda in, 410; 411; Kutzo-Vlach movement in, 415; 421; affairs in (1878-1908), 424 sqq.; 428; the Powers and, 728

Macerata, duchy of, incorporated in Italian kingdom, ix 400

Macfarland, E. J., secretary to Confederate States envoy, xii 18

MacGahan, Januarius, visits Khiva, xii 801

McGee, Thomas D'Arcy, Canadian politician, xi 770; 775

MacGibbon, Maurice, titular Archbishop of Cashel, iii 595

McGill University, xi 778

Macgregor (*or* Drummond), William, of Balhaldie, Jacobite, vi 109 sq.

Machabaeus (John Macalpine), Scottish divine, ii 555

Machault d'Arnouville, Jean-Baptiste de, French statesman, vi 332; 334 sq.; 348; viii 25

Machiavelli, Niccolò, i 87, 170, Chap. vi *passim*; Cesare Borgia and, 237, 240, 242; eulogies of German cities by, 298 sq.; views of, on trade, 516; 624, 649; ii 5; *Il Principe*, 34 sq., 118, iii 464-6; Bacon and, 377; 390 sq.; 456; 742; 762; 766-7; vi 790; 793; 798; 820

—— Secretary of Margaret, Duchess of Parma, iii 217

Maciejowice, battle of (1794), viii 546

Mack von Leiberich, Baron Charles, German general, viii 421, 429; Chief of Staff to Coburg, 435; at Naples, 650 sqq.; ix 248; conference of, with Tsar Alexander I's envoy, 250; advice of, to the Emperor, 253; capitulates at Ulm, 254-5

Mackay, Baron Aeneas, Dutch statesman, xii 245

—— Hugh, General, v 246; at Killiecrankie, 293

McKenna, Theobald, Irish Catholic writer, viii 772

Mackenzie, district of, xi 776

—— river, exploration on, xii 814

—— Sir Alexander, explorer, vii 365; ix 748; xii 814

—— Alexander, Canadian politician, xii 605

—— Sir George, *Jus Regium*, vi 800

—— James Stewart, vi 424; 430

—— John, missionary, in South Africa, xii 638

—— Sir Morell, and Emperor Frederick III, xii 163

—— William Lyon, organises rebellion in Canada, x 692 sq.

—— British diplomatic agent at Tilsit, ix 297-8

Mackinaw, on Lake Huron, captured by the British (1812), vii 337, 343

McKinley, William, vii 664; President of United States, 673; and Cuba, 675 sqq.; and Philippines, 684 sq.; 722

McKinley Tariff, The, VII 664, 669
Mackinnon, Laird of, VI 105
Mackintosh, Sir James, *Vindiciae Gallicae,*
VI 477, VIII 758; 762, 774; x 580; 584
sq.; 601; XII 837
—— William, of Borlum, VI 98 sq.; 101;
103
Maclaurin, Colin, mathematician, v 718
MacLean, Sir Donald, New Zealand states-
man, XI 799
Maclean, Sir Hector, of Duart, VI 111
McLeod, Alexander, and burning of the
Caroline, VII 390
Maclure, Sir Robert, makes the North-West
passage, XII 814
MacMahon, Ever, Bishop of Clogher, IV
534
Macmahon, Marie-E.-P.-M., Comte de, Duc
de Magenta, Marshal of France, XI 496;
582 sq.; at Wörth, 584 sq.; 586 sq.; forms
army of Châlons, 595; marches to Meuse,
596 sq.; at Sedan, 597 sq.; 599 sqq.;
XII 97; succeeds Thiers, 107; 109; 111;
resigns, 112; 115 sq.; and Carlists, 261;
and Delagoa Bay dispute, 270, 635
MacMahons, of Monaghan, The, III 588
Macnaghten, Edward Macnaghten, Lord,
XII 722
—— Sir William Hay, XI 731; 733
—— Lady, XI 733
MacNeven, William James, and United
Irishmen, IX 700 sqq.; x 629
Mâcon, retaken by Royalists, III 3; ban-
quet to Lamartine at, XI 40
Maçon, Jean le, Huguenot pastor. *See* Le
Rivière
Macpherson, David, *Annals of Commerce,*
x 783
—— James, *Ossian,* VI 830 sqq., XI 352;
x 698; 710
—— John, in India, IX 709 sqq.
McPherson, James Birdseye, American
general, VII 503, 520
Macquarie river, exploration of, XI 792
Macquarie, Laghlan, major-general, Go-
vernor of New South Wales, IX 739; XI
789
Macquart, François, French general, VIII
443
McQueen, James, geographer, XII 807
McRae, C. J., Confederate foreign agent,
VII 611
Macrae, James, Governor of Madras, VI 532
MacWilliam, Earl of Clanricarde. *See*
Clanricarde, Earl of
Madách, Imre, Hungarian dramatist, XI
430
Madagascar, Dutch adventurers at, III 632;
French in, v 13, 702 sq.; European
pirates at, VI 531; 535; French colonial
expedition to, IX 80; XI 778; France and,
XII 3, 47; 456; Russian fleet at, 598; an-
nexed by France, 130 sq.
Madalinski, Antoine, Polish general, VIII
542

Maddalena, French repulse at (1793), VIII
456
—— Bay, Nelson's base on, IX 216, 219
Madden, Sir Frederic, historian, XII 835
Madeira, Portuguese general, x 315
Madeira Islands colonised by Spain, I 40,
49; Breton trade with, 414; handed over
to Britain, IX 236
Madeleine of France and Navarre, sister
of Louis XI, I 366
—— (of France), Queen of Scotland, consort of James V, II 455
Madier de Montjau, Noel-François-Alfred,
French politician, XI 124; 136
Madison, James, President of United States,
at Constitutional Convention, Vol. VII,
Chap. VIII *passim*; and Federal Republicans, 316; President, 331 sqq., 360; 369;
407; and Virginia Resolution (1798), 410;
x 281; XII 696
Madox, Thomas, English historian, XII 816
Madoz, Pascual, Spanish politician, XI 551
Madras, v 698 sq.; 704; VI 248; evacuated
by French, 249; 427; 445; 529; growth
of, 532; 534 sq.; captured by French,
536; restored to England, 538; 539;
French attack on, 547 sq.; 552 sq.;
Haidar Ali at, 567; misrule in, 576;
577; 582; Lord Macartney at, IX 710;
Lord Mornington and, 722; reform in,
728, 732; Pindaris in, XI 725; High
Court of, 751; military system of, 752
sq.; frontier of, XII 485; 496 sq.
Madrid, Philip's return to (1586), III 514;
Perez in, 515; disorders in, 518; English
enterprise discussed in, 533; transfer of
capital from, to Valladolid, 537; Prince
Charles' visit to, 575–6, IV 641 sq., 673;
222; condition of, 630; protest of Venice
at, 632, 633; death of Philip III at,
634; 636; 638; poverty in, 644; 650;
651 sqq.; 658; 661 sq.; social condition
of, 663; art in, 664; death of Philip IV
at, 665; Clement VIII and Court of,
666, 668; 670; 678; Cabinet of, and
Urban VIII, 681; v 376; occupied by
the Allies, 416, 428; the Old Pretender
at, VI 105; 141; 145; decay of, 166;
entry of Charles III into, 366; 371; the
King and Queen leave (1808), IX 430;
Ferdinand goes to, 431; 432; insurrection at, 433; Murat at, 434; stores
of, 435; French forces in, 436; the
French evacuate, 438–9; 441; Napoleon
captures, 443 sqq.; Victor and, 451;
Venegas and, 452; 453; Areizaga and,
455; Wellington enters (1812), 473; re-
occupied by French, 475; evacuated
(1813), 477–8; revolt in (1822), x 79,
224 sq.; recaptured by French, 80, 227;
arrest of Liberal deputies in, 205; improvements in, 210; Liberal hopes in,
216; new municipality of, 217; patriotic
societies of, 218; Riego in, 220; sedition
in, 222; Queen Maria Cristina enters,

231; disaffection of troops in (1837), 238-9; revolution in (1840), 241; 242; Central Junta at, 282; revolutionary risings in, xi 556 sqq.; martial law in, 559; revolution in (1854), 560, 570; fighting in, 562; mutinies in, 566 sq.; University of, 567

Madrid, Treaties of (1526), ii 51, 426, (1617), iv 11, 38, (1621), 53 sq., (1630), 275, (1670), x 272, (1721), vi 39, (1801), ix 75, 602

Madrid Gazette, Charles IV's manifesto in the, ix 429

Madruzzo, Christoforo, Cardinal-Bishop of Trent, ii 661 sqq.

—— Ludovico, Bishop of Trent. *See* Trent

Madura, Dupleix and, vi 540; administration of, xii 668 sq.

Madvig, Johan Nikolai, Danish scholar, xi 699

Maes, Jacques, Pensionary at Antwerp, iii 183

Maestricht, siege of (1579), iii 252, 705; Ban of (1581), 253, 258; besieged by Frederick Henry, iv 695 sq.; Thomas of Savoy at, 697; 699; a French possession, v 43; 56; 158; taken by the French (1673), 161; 164; 455; ceded by France (1678), 45, 46; vi 247 sq.; Joseph II and, 643 sqq.; besieged (1793), viii 265, 419; claims of Joseph II to, 277, 281, 312; Belgium and, x 483, 539 sqq.

Maeterlinck, Maurice, Belgian dramatic poet, xii 13

Mafeking, siege of, xii 642 sq.

Maffei, Annibale, Count, at Utrecht Conference, v 439

—— Francesco Scipione, Marquis, Italian poet, v 69

Mafia, The, suspicion of members of, vii 666; working of, in S. Italy and Sicily, xii 239

Magalhães, Fernão de, i 12; circumnavigates the world, 36

Magallon, Charles, French agent in Egypt, viii 595

Magdala, storming of, xi 753, xii 664

Magdalen Islands, and the fisheries dispute, vii 363, 365, 657

Magdeburg, the "Magdeburg Centuriators" and their Church history, i 609; Synod of (1451), 631; pictures at, seen by Luther, ii 109 sq.; Schmalkaldic League joined by, 215; question of protectorate of, 252; siege of, by Maurice of Saxony, 262, 269; fall of, 270; see of, held by Cardinal Archbishop Albert, iii 152; Protestant Administrator of, and Diet, iv 10; Christian William of Brandenburg and, 195 sq.; 197; Tilly at, 199; Gustavus and, 200; siege and fall of, 201 sqq., 214, 217; rebuilding of, 207; Saxony and, 218; and Peace of Prague, 252 sq.; Conference at (1635), 255; Banér in, 366; archbishopric of, and Brandenburg, 407;

commercial recovery of, 420; archbishopric of, v 623, 626 sq., 642, 644; taxation in, vi 221; in Seven Years' War, 256, 260, 263, 265 sqq.; 327; 339; colonisation in, 716; 718; Conference (1688), 4; Prussian retreat to (1806), ix 277; capitulation of, to Ney (1806), 280-2; 292, 337; rising in, 356; 357; chief fortress of kingdom of Westphalia, 411; new corps formed at, 514; French troops at, 515

Magdeburg, Albert of Brandenburg, Archbishop of, v 625 sq.

—— Frederick of Beichlingen, Archbishop of, i 631

—— Günther II of Schwarzburg, Archbishop of, v 623

—— Joachim Frederick of Brandenburg, Administrator of, iii 153, 706, 710, 714

—— Ludolf, Archbishop of (12th century), v 620

Magee, John, proprietor of *Dublin Evening Post*, x 635

—— College, Londonderry, xii 71 sq.

Magellan Straits, Chili and, xii 679

—— Ferdinand, xii 528 sq.

Magenta, battle of, xi 383, 403, 468

—— Duc de. *See* Macmahon

Magersfontein, British reverse at, xii 642

Maggior Consiglio, of Venice, i 272

Maghreb, France and, xii 131 sq.

Magic, in Empire, iv 6; after Thirty Years' War, 423

Magnan, French ambassador at St Petersburg, vi 303

—— Bernard-Pierre, Marshal of France, xi 134

Magne, Pierre, French statesman, xi 133; 297; xii 108

Magni, Joannes (Johan Magnusson). *See* Upsala, Archbishops of

Magno, Marcantonio, Italian Reformer, ii 390

Magnus, son of Gustavus Vasa of Sweden, iv 161; madness of, 164, 166

Magnus Intercursus, The (1496), i 452, 455, 473; iii 643

Magnusson, Johan. *See* Magni, Joannes

—— Peter. *See* Vesterås, Bishop of

Magon de Clos-Doré, Charles-René, French admiral, ordered to sail for West Indies, ix 223

Magrath, Andrew G., Confederate judge, vii 605

Magruder, John Bankhead, Confederate general, vii 474

Maguire, Connor or Cornelius, 2nd Baron of Enniskillen, Irish rebellion and, iv 522

—— John Francis, Irish politician, xi 344

—— of Fermanagh, the clan of, iii 588, 590

—— of Fermanagh, Cuconnaught, iii 612

—— of Fermanagh, Hugh, Lord of Fermanagh, iii 603 sqq.; killed (1600), 608

Magus Muir, Archbishop Sharp murdered on, v 285

Magyars, contrasted with the Čechs, i 330 sq., 332

Mahaffy, John Pentland, historian, xii 845

Mahan, Alfred Thayer, naval historian, xii 842

Maharajpur, British force at, xi 738

Maháráshtra, region of, vi 521

Mahdi, the (1881). *See* Mohammad Ahmad

Mahé, France and, vi 347, 454, 464, 533

—— de la Bourdonnais, Bertrand-François, French naval officer, vi 535 sqq.; 542; 546

Mahmud I, Sultan of Turkey, vi 304

—— II, Sultan of Turkey, ix 389; and Mehemet Ali, Vol. x, Chap. xvii *passim*; 512; and Treaty of Bucharest, 169; disputes of, with Russia, 175; orders execution of Gregorios, 182 sq.; seeks aid of Mehemet Ali, 189; and revolt of the Janissaries, 192; declares a holy war and repudiates Treaty of Akkerman, 198; 512; death of, 562; xi 275; 278

—— Neddim, Grand Vizier, xii 385

—— Pasha (Beglerbeg of Rumelia), i 70 sqq., 79

—— Shah, ruler at Kabul, xi 731

Mahon, Barbarossa carries off booty from, iii 112

—— Viscount. *See* Stanhope, 3rd Earl

Mahr, Treaty of (1796), ix 720

Mai, Angelo, Cardinal, historian, xii 842

Maid (Holy) of Kent. *See* Barton, Elizabeth

Maida, English victory at (1806), ix 270, 404

Maid's Tragedy, The, by Beaumont and Fletcher, iii 381

Maidstone, Fairfax disperses Royalists at, iv 349

Maier (*or* Mayer), John, of Eck. *See* Eck, Johann

Maignet, Étienne, French politician, viii 372

Mailáth, George, Hungarian Chancellor, xii 182

—— Count N. Janos, Hungarian historian, xii 842

Mailhe, Jean-Baptiste, French politician, viii 255

Maillard, Oliver, Franciscan preacher, ii 280

—— Stanislas, leads mob to Versailles (Oct. 1789), viii 184, 264

Maillebois, Jean-Baptiste-François Desmarets, Marquis de, Marshal of France, vi 154; 161; 165; 232; retires into Bavaria, 235; 236; in Piedmont, 243; 245; 362; 608; Napoleon's indebtedness to, viii 576 sqq.

Mailly, Louise-Julie de Nesle, Comtesse de, and Louis XV, vi 164; 330

Main, river, British troops on, vi 237 sq.; 273; 277

Maine (France), the League in, iii 663; customs of, v 13; feudal courts in, viii 49

—— (U.S.A.), expedition of Popham and Gilbert to (1607), vii 12; settlement of, 21 sq.; annexed by Massachusetts, 24 sq., 27; and the Indians, 28; boundary of, 320, 390 sq.; conquest of eastern (1814), 344; enters Union, 362; abolition in, 388; State of, xi 777

Maine, U.S.S., blown up at Havana, vii 676 sq., xii 696

Maine, Anne-Louise-Bénédicte de Bourbon, Duchess of, vi 33; 125; 128 sq.; and Cellamare, 130; 132

—— Charles II, Count of, i 108

—— Sir Henry James Sumner, vi 814; 821; xii 460; 711; *Ancient Law*, 850

—— Louis-Auguste de Bourbon, Duke of, v 31; vi 120 sq.; 128

—— de Biron, François-P.-G., xi 526

—— *See also* Mayenne

Maintenon, Françoise d'Aubigné, Marquise de, v 19 sqq.; and Revocation of Edict of Nantes, 23 sq.; 31; 77; 87; and Père La Chaise, 89; 423; 447; vi 92; 121; 132

Mainville, French officer in India, vi 541

Mainz, and the Religious Peace, iii 142–3; Protestants expelled from, 178; headquarters of Gustavus Adolphus, iv 208 sq.; Bavaria and, 210; 211; negotiations at, 216; siege of (1635), 367 sq.; Treaty of (1638), 379; and Condé, 389; a French possession, 597; taken by Germans (1689), v 57, 661; 409; 435; Pragmatic army at, vi 238; archbishopric of, 704; and Decree of November 19, viii 300, 305; surrenders to the Allies (1793), 347, 423, 430; captured by Custine (1792), 414; besieged (1794), 437, 442; captured by French (1797), 641; French Commissioner at, ix 92; territory of, 94; reduced to position of a suffragan see, 202; Lutheran consistory at, 204; magazine formed at, 252; Mortier at (1806), 274; Stein at, 329; and the Continental System, 377; French army at (1813), 540; Bavarian designs on, 592; importance of, 596; federal fortress of, 659; revolutionary movement at, xi 145; 228; claimed by France, 457, 483; Napoleon III and, xii 136

—— Commission, The, x 367; 369 sq.; 378

Mainz, Electors of:—

—— Albrecht of Brandenburg, Cardinal, i 674, 678, 685; ii 40 sq.; indulgences farmed by, 121; Luther's Theses sent to Rome by, 131; 133; Luther and, 158, 162 sq., 169; 195, 220, 235, 238, 243; death of, 251; iii 152; v 625 sq.

—— Anselm Casimir von Umstadt, iv 210 sq.; 218; consents to Treaty of Ulm, 391; Maximilian of Bavaria and, 398

Mainz, Electors of (*contd.*):—
—— Berthold von Henneberg, the unity of the Empire and, I 292; attempts at governmental reform by, 300 sqq.; death of, 316; censorship of press and, 685; II 142, 149
—— Daniel Brendel von Homburg, III 176
—— Diether von Isemburg, I 675, 688 sq.
—— Dietrich von Erbach, I 631, 633, 688
—— Emerich Joseph von Breitbach-Bürresheim, x 158
—— Frederick Charles Joseph, Freiherr von Erthal, VI 708; IX 56
—— Jakob von Liebenstein, I 316
—— Johann von Cronenburg, IV 73; 81; 83 sq.; 88
—— Johann Philipp von Schönborn, IV 430; the *Rheinbund* and, 431; v 43
—— Karl Theodor A. M. von Dalberg (last Elector). *See* Dalberg
—— Lothar Franz von Schönborn, v 403; VI 202
—— Philipp Karl von Eltz, VI 231
—— Sebastian von Heusenstamm, II 251, 671
—— Wolfgang von Dalberg, III 706, 731, 734
Mainz, Michael Helding, suffragan Bishop of, II 264
—— Wilhelm Emmanuel, Baron von Ketteler, Bishop of, XI 721
Maipú, battle of (1818), x 292
Máiquez, Isidoro, x 210
Maison, Nicolas Joseph, Marquis, Marshal of France, x 201
Maistre, Casimir, African explorer, XII 812
—— Joseph-Marie, Comte de, VI 837; *Considérations sur la France*, VIII 780 sq.; 789 sq.; IX 133; x 4; *Du Pape*, 6; doctrines of, 43 sq., 161; 45; and Roman claims in France, 72; 141; and King Victor Emmanuel I of Sardinia, 142; 160; 162 sqq.; views of, on the situation in Italy, 165 sq.; 167; and the Papacy, XI 707
Maitland, Rear-Admiral Sir Frederick Lewis, surrender of Napoleon to, IX 243; at Rochefort, 644; and Napoleon, 756
—— Frederic William, XII 841; 850
—— John, Duke of Lauderdale. *See* Lauderdale
—— Sir Peregrine, General, at Waterloo, IX 639–40
—— Sir Thomas, in Portugal, XI 572
—— Colonel, at Savannah, VII 219
—— of Lethington, Sir William, II 550, 558, 573, 575 sq., 595; III 263; and Mary Stewart, 267–8, 273–5, 278–9, 282, 286
Maiwand, British reverse at, XII 37; 475
Majorca, v 446; reactionary excesses in, x 207
Majuba Hill, battle of, XII 39; 637
Makarieff Fair, x 428
Makaroff, Admiral, at Port Arthur, XII 581; 588

Makhran, fight at, XI 632
Makilolo tribe, Livingstone and, XII 808; 809
Maklakoff, Russian delegate at Prague Congress, XII 378
Makrinitsa, fall of, XII 391
Maksutoff, Prince, Governor of Alaska, XI 632
Malabar, the Dutch on the coast of, III 638, IV 711; Portuguese and Dutch in, v 695 sq.
Malacca, outpost of Eastern trade, I 27 sq.; Albuquerque in, 31; siege of (1606), III 638; conquered by Dutch (1640), IV 711; captured by British (1795), VIII 484, IX 750, XII 532; 533
—— Straits of, Great Britain and, XI 667
Malachovski, Casimir, Polish general, x 472
Malaga, Rupert at, IV 464; corps of Sebastiani at, IX 457; socialistic riots at, XI 570
Malagrida, Gabriel, Jesuit, VI 387
Malakand, attacked by Swatis, XII 488; 489 sq.
Malakhoff, capture of the, XI 322 sq.
—— Aimable-J.-J. Pélissier, Duc de, Marshal of France, XI 322; 328
Malalos, captured by American troops, XII 531
Malartie, General, and Tipu, IX 722
Malaspina, papal legate, IV 171
Malassise, Sieur de, III 14, 33
Malatesta, Lamberto, III 430, 432
—— Frà Sacramoro, and Savonarola, I 188
—— Sigismondo, Lord of Rimini, I 624
Malaxa, bombarded, XII 420
Malay Archipelago, Dutch trade with, III 632, 638; v 696; Dutch in, x 761, XI 667
—— Peninsula, XII 4; affairs in, 531 sqq.
—— States (Federated), XII 532 sq.
Malays, in Cape Colony, XI 778
Malby, Sir Nicholas, President of Connaught, III 604
Malcolm, Sir John, in India, IX 722; 726; mission of, to Persia, 732, XII 800; XI 726
—— Sir Pulteney, British admiral, x 554
"Malcontents," Dutch Catholic party, III 251–2
Maldachini, Donna Olimpia (sister-in-law of Innocent X), IV 687
Malden, British post at, VII 337
Malebranche, Nicolas de, II 691; develops "occasionalism," IV 789; 790; v 65; 78 sq.; 86
Malesherbes, Chrétien-G. de Lamoignon de, VIII 24; Minister of King Louis XVI's Household, 82, 84, 87; resigns, 87 sq.; 106; 257
Malet, Claude-François de, French general, conspiracy of, IX 137, 143–4, 504
—— Sir Charles Warre, resident at Poona, IX 710

Maleville, François-Jean-Léon de, French Minister of Interior, xi 118; 127; 133
—— Jacques, Marquis de, *Analyse...du Code Civil*, viii 742; ix 150; 160
Malghera, fort of, captured, xi 95
Malherbe, François de, iii 71–2; literary ideals of, iv 777; v 64 sqq.; 69; xi 508
Malietoa, King of Samoa, vii 662 sq.
Maligny, Jean de, ii 298
Málik Ambar, Abyssinian Minister, vi 515
Malindi (port on East Coast of Africa), Da Gama at, i 25
Malines, Court of Appeal set up at, ii 102; surrendered to William of Orange, iii 232–3; plundered by Alva's soldiers, 234; vi 248; seminary at, 651; 652; seminary of, closed, viii 327; Pichegru captures, 436; Mainz ecclesiastically subordinate to, ix 202; Catholic Congress at, xi 714
—— Francois-Antoine, Comte de Méan, Archbishop of, x 526
—— Cardinal-Archbishop of. *See* Franckenburg
Malipiero, Domenico, Venetian historian, i 284, 287
Mallarmé, F.-R.-Auguste, French politician, viii 368
Mallet du Pan, Jacques, *Mercure Britannique*, viii 1; 34; 216, 373, 781 sq.
Mallinckrodt, Heinrich von, German politician, xii 147
Mallory, Stephen Russell, vii 447; Confederate Secretary of the Navy, 605
Mallow, Lord Taaffe defeated at, iv 345
Malmaison, Bonaparte at, ix 24, (1815), 643, 756; Constitution of (1801), 98–9
Malmesbury, James Harris, 1st Earl of, ambassador at St Petersburg, vi 460; 470; 472; viii 278; at the Hague, 282, 286 sqq., 543 sq.; 322 sq.; at Lille, 494, 498; 759; ix 43; and Whig party, 673 sqq.
—— James Howard Harris, 3rd Earl of, Foreign Secretary, xi 21; 328; 331
Malmoe, Peace of (1512), i 457; blockaded by Horn, iv 387; 560; siege of (1676), v 570; Truce of (1848), xi 166; 168; 224
Malo, commandant of French dragoons, viii 505
Maloggia, Pass of, iv 35, 39; Grisons Preachers cross the, 46; 49
Malon, Benoît, French politician, xi 502; 505; xii 123 sq.
Malone, Anthony, Chancellor of the Exchequer in Ireland, vi 489
Malony, John Baptist, x 621
Malou, J., Belgian statesman, xii 250 sq.
Malouet, Pierre Victor, Baron, Commissioner in West Indies, vii 97; viii 124, 132; at States General, 149, 152; assaulted in National Assembly, 170, 173, 201; and the Court, 216
Malo-Yaroslavetz, battle at (1812), ix 499
Malpighi, Marcello, v 727; 729; 734; botanical studies of, 735 sq.; 737

Malplaquet, battle of (1709), v 425 sq., 436, 668, vi 206
Mals, conference at (1496), i 118
Malseigne, Chevalier Guyot de, and the mutiny at Nancy, viii 192
Malta, given to the Knights of St John, ii 60, 68; defended against Turks (1565), iii 125, 489, 540; Knights of, and Paul V, iv 669; Knights of, and Turks, v 342; Great Britain and, 444; Knights driven from (1788), ix 604; French designs on, viii 591, 595 sqq.; captured (1798), 598, 621, 623, 645, ix 40, 751; recaptured (1800), viii 629, ix 41 sq.; Russia and, viii 645, 648, ix 39, 69, 181; restored to Knights of Malta (1801), 74 sqq., 751; British retention of, 103, 209; strategic importance of, 210, 244–5; 263; a centre of English commerce, 381; cession of, to Great Britain (1814), 654, 755; vicissitudes of, 751; British fleet at, xi 313; 753; Indian troops in, xii 33, 394, 468; Mediterranean fever in, 780
Malte-Brun, Conrad, geographer, viii 788
Malters, fight at, xi 247
Malthus, Thomas Robert, viii 768; x 598; and Corn Laws, 773; writings and influence of, 774 sqq.; and Godwin's *Political Justice*, 778; xii 817
—— the elder (father of above), viii 768
Maltitz, Johannes von. *See* Meissen, Bishop of
Malus, commissariat Staff-officer to Dumouriez, viii 416, 419
Malus Intercursus, The (1506), i 454 sq.
Malvasia, surrendered by Venice, iii 116
Malvenda, Fray Pedro de, ii 251; discussion with Diaz of, 403
Malvern Hill, Federal victory at (1862), vii 479
Malý, Jakub, Čech political writer, xi 656
Malygin, Lieutenant, Russian explorer, xii 795
Mameli, Goffredo, x 126; xi 545
Mamelukes, rise of, in Egypt, ix 385; fall of, 387; viii 600
"Mamelukes," *or* Savoyard party at Geneva, ii 362
Mamiani, Terenzio della Rovere, Count, Italian statesman, xi 89; 93
Man, Isle of, reduction of, iv 466; Wesley in, vi 83
—— Robert, Admiral, viii 460 sq.
—— Dr, iii 491
Manabé, member of the Council, at Kiōto, xi 837 sqq.
Manahiki Islands, British protectorate over, xii 667
Manasarowar lake, explorers at, xii 798
Manassas (Virginia), Confederate camp at, vii 464; Federal advance to, 465; 472 sq.; 474 sq.
Manasséin, N., Russian Minister of Justice, xii 316; 336

Manchester, outbreak of Civil War at, IV 301; Strange repulsed at, 305; Jacobites at, VI 101; 114; 496; Radical meetings at, X 578; "massacre" at, 581; parliamentary representation of, 601 sq., 613; Corn Laws Repeal Association in, 680; use of machinery in, 734 sq.; insanitary state of, XI 1; disturbances at, 2; Fenians in, 344; murder of Police-Sergeant Brett at, XII 65, 74 sq.; 73; University of, 763

—— Edward Montagu, 2nd Earl of, commander of Eastern Association, IV 314; 315; on Committee of Both Kingdoms, 320; at York, 321; at Marston Moor, 322; 324 sqq.; Parliamentary army and, 344; 557; V 93; 100

—— Henry Montagu, 1st Earl of (Viscount Mandeville) (1620), III 571

Manchuria, XII 4; 56; Russian occupation of, 345; 513; 521 sq.; Russian aggression in, 576 sq.; Russo-Japanese War in, 578 sqq., 594; post-road through, 792

Mancini, Hortense, Duchesse de Mazarin, IV 542; V 106

—— Laure. *See* Mercoeur

—— Marie, IV 620; and Louis XIV, V 19

Mandalay, British agent withdrawn from, XII 479; 793

Mandat, Jean-Antoine-Galyot, *Commandant Général* of the *Gardes Nationales*, VIII 235 sq.

Mandavi, XI 743

Manderscheid, John zu, Bishop of Strassburg. *See* Strassburg

Mandeville, British *Chargé d'affaires* at Constantinople, X 552

Manet, Édouard, painter, XI 528

Manetti, Gianozzo, translator of Bible, I 679

Manfredi, Astorre, Lord of Faenza, murdered, I 238

Manfredini, Federigo, Prime Minister of Tuscany, VIII 778

Mangalore, Treaty of, VI 577, IX 710; French land at, 721

Mangan, James Clarence, poet, XI 352

Mangasciâ, Ras, XII 240

Mangin, Étienne, French Reformer, II 290

Manhattan Island, trading ports on, IV 709

Manhes, Charles-Antoine, Comte, French general, severity of, in Calabria, IX 406

Manifestácion, prison of the, III 513, 516

Manila, VI 369; restored to Spain, 370; 373; 427; 430; Dewey captures, VII 679, 681, 683 sqq., XII 530; trade of, X 255; 259; 275

Manin, Daniel, X 111; XI 76; and the revolution in Venice, 82; 84; 86; restored to office, 90; at Venice, 95; 374; and Italian unity, 375; 488

—— Lodovico, last Doge of Venice, VIII 586, 593

Manique, Portuguese *Intendant* of Police, VIII 784

Manitoba, La Verendrye in, VII 94; Province of, XI 776 sq.; XII 605; 610; provincial rights of, 614 sq.

Manners, Thomas Manners-Sutton, 1st Baron, Chancellor of Ireland, IX 707

Manners-Sutton, Charles. *See* Canterbury, 1st Viscount

Mannheim, surrender of (1622), III 575; a French possession, IV 144; captured by Bernard (1632), 208; sacked (1689), V 56; 409; 435; Frederick William I at, VI 212; occupied by the French (1794), VIII 437, 442; surrendered (1795), 443; ceded to Baden, IX 94; Davout at, 253; Kotzebue assassinated at, X 365; effect of the French Revolution (1848) in, XI 145; 147

Manning, Henry Edward, Cardinal, and the Syllabus, XI 716; XII 230

—— Thomas, visits Lhassa, XII 798

Mano Negra, Spanish secret society, XII 267

Manoel. *See* Manuel

Manrique, Alfonso, Inquisitor-General, II 401

—— Iñigo, Bishop of Sigüenza. *See* Sigüenza

—— Isabella, of Brisegna, II 390

—— Jorge de, Spanish poet, I 381

Månsdotter, Karin, married by Erik XIV of Sweden, IV 163 sq.

Mansell, Sir Robert, III 564, 567

Mansfeld, Luther at, II 109

—— Countess Agnes von, III 707

—— Count Albrecht von, II 196, 215, 259, 261

—— Count Ernest von, English assistance to, III 573 sq., 577 sq.; serves Bohemian Directors, IV 24; defeated at Zablat, 27; with Christian of Anhalt, 64 sq.; and Emperor Ferdinand II, 67; 77 sq.; raids Darmstadt, 80; hesitations of, 81; in Low Countries, 85; in East Frisia, 86; 87 sq.; English levies of, 92; 258; summoned to Paris, 93; 95; at Dessau Bridge, 97; subsidised by Richelieu, 129; and Bohemian throne, 233; pursued into Hungary by Wallenstein, 98; death of, *ib.* sq.; 101; 128; 243

—— Count Gebhard von, II 196, 215

—— Count Gebhard von, Archbishop of Cologne. *See* Cologne

—— Count Peter Ernest von, III 194 sq., 218, 245, 519, 627; IV 24

—— Count Philip von, Imperial general, IV 250

—— Count Wolf von, IV 377

—— Count Wolrad von, III 12 sq.

Mansfield, David Murray, 2nd Earl of (Viscount Stormont), ambassador at Paris, IV 378; 449 sq.; President of Council, 464

—— Sir James, Lord Chief Justice (Solicitor-General), XII 713

—— William Murray, 1st Earl of (Lord Mansfield), VI 188; 403; 405; 424; 426; and Wilkes, 432; 434 sq.; 441 sq.; and America, 447; 472

Mansfield, Sir William Rose. *See* Sandhurst

Manso, Giovanni Battista, and Milton, v 118

Manson, Sir Patrick, and malaria, xii 779

Mantegna, Andrea, Italian painter, i 284

Mantes, garrisoned by Montmorency's Company, iii 23; Edict of (1591), 675; Articles of (1593), 675

Manteucci, Pellegrino, African explorer, xii 811

Manteuffel, Baron Edwin Hans Karl von, Prussian field-marshal, xi 191; 409 sq.; mission of, to St Petersburg, 456; in Franco-German War, 606 sq.; 609 sq.

—— Baron Otto von, Prussian statesman, xi 193; 198; and Hesse-Cassel crisis, 229 sqq.; at Dresden Conference, 232 sq.; 395 sq.; 403; William I and, 406

Manton, Thomas, Nonconformist divine, v 201

Mantua, Congress of (1459), i 78, 655, 666, 669; Council of (1535), ii 394; iii 401; 476; House of, favourably disposed towards Henry IV, 683; House of Savoy linked with, 686; succession in, iv 115, 117, 134 sq.; besieged by Colalto (1629), 136, 138; 145; 148; Charles Emmanuel in, 626; French force at, v 402; 403; French evacuate (1706), 415; duchy of, 451; claimed by the King of Sardinia, vi 152; 153 sq.; Leopold II at, 656; besieged by the French (1796), viii 553, 556, 572 sq.; siege of, abandoned, 574 sq.; fall of, 580; surrenders to the Allies (1799), 659; ceded to France (1801), ix 69; Andreas Hofer shot at, 356; Austrian revenue from, 393; *Centri* in, x 111; Duke Francis IV at, 120; xi 82; investment of, 84; 85 sq.; 88; conspiracy in, 376 sq.; 384; elections at, xii 226

—— Benedetto of, ii 389

Mantua, Dukes of [di Gonzaga]:—

—— Charles IV (Duke of Nevers), Mantuan claim of, iv 115; 119; in Champagne, 122; 124; becomes Duke of Mantua, 134 sq., 138; death of, 148; hostile to Austria, 643; 678; alliance between Richelieu, Venice and, 679; acknowledged in Mantua, 680; v 349; 401

—— Federigo II, Marquis, *afterwards* Duke of, ii 48, 57, 60; invested with Montferrat, 68, 72

—— Ferdinand, Montferrat restored to, iv 626

—— Francis IV, and Montferrat, iv 626

—— Vincent II, iv 134, 643; 678

—— William, iii 387

Mantua, Giovanni Francesco Gonzaga, 1st Marquis of (General of Holy See), i 280; patron of Vittorino da Feltre, 557

—— Margaret of Savoy, consort of Francis IV, Duchess of, Regent of Portugal, iv 650; Braganza and, 651 sq.; 654

Manucci, Teobaldo Pio. *See* Manuzio, Aldo

Manuel (the Great), King of Portugal. *See* Emmanuel

—— King of Portugal, xii 272

—— Jacques-Antoine, x 54; 56; attacks Government, 60; 61; 66; 68; funeral of, 90; 486; xii 832

—— Don Juan, incites Philip the Fair (of Burgundy and Castile) against Ferdinand, i 363; Maximilian supported by, 364, 367

—— Nicholas, ii 327, 332

—— Pierre - Louis, *Procureur Général Syndic*, viii 225; suspended, 230; reinstated, *ib.*; 242, 246 sq.; at the King's trial, 260; executed (1793), 357

Manuskript aus Süddeutschland, Lindner's, political importance of, x 369

Manuzio, Aldo (Teobaldo Manucci), Venetian printer, i 561 sqq.; aided by the *Neacademia* of, *ib.*

—— Paolo (son of the above), i 563

Manwaring, Roger, Bishop of St David's, iv 268; impeached and pardoned, 271 sq.; vi 803

Manwein, Margary murdered at, xii 501

Manz, Felix, Anabaptist opponent of Zwingli, ii 322 sq.

Manzioli, Angelo, *Zodiacus Vitae*, ii 384

Manzoni, Alessandro, Italian writer, vi 831; x 100; 125; writings of, 166; xi 546 sqq.

Maori, The, and the Settlement of New Zealand, xi 792 sq.; 799 sq.; xii 624

Mar, John Erskine, 17th Earl of (*or* 1st of new cr.), Regent of Scotland, death of (1572), iii 285, 549

—— John Erskine, 22nd (*or* 6th) Earl of, Scottish Secretary of State, v 299; vi 43; 96 sq.; rising of, 98 sqq.; attainted, 103; 106

Mara, William de, early Hebrew scholar, i 590

Maracaibo, captured by Grammont (1679), v 691

Maradas, Don Balthasar, Spanish commander, iv 65; 72; in Prague, 209; 219

Marajo, French settlement on, vi 389

Maranham. *See* Maranhão

Maranhão, conquered by Dutch, iv 753, 755; revolt in (1684), v 678; settlement in, 679; reduced for Pedro I (1823), x 316

—— and Pará Company, vi 385 sq.

Maranhão-Pará, State of, vi 389 sq.

Maranoa river, exploration of, xi 795

Marãnos, the Crypto-Jews of Spain, i 624

Marans, taken by Mayenne, iii 32; fortified by Navarre, 41; besieged and taken by Catholic party (1587), 42

Marassé, Jean René Blandine de, viii 422

Marat, Jean-Paul, publisher of *L'Ami du Peuple*, viii 168 sq., 192, 213, 234, 373; in the National Convention, 239, 243, 247, 251, 262; trial of, 271; assassinated, 346

Maráthas, The, English treaty with (1674),
v 698; rise of, vi 518; 521 sq., 529,
531 sq., 541; defeated at Panipat (1761),
524, 568; defeated by Lake (1803), 525;
546; Warren Hastings and, 567, 569,
582 sq., xi 725; and Emperor Shah
Alam, vi 568; 577 sq.; war of Tipu
against, ix 710; 715, 717; military
power of, 718 sqq.; and Sindhia, 718 sq.;
at war with the Nizám, 720 sq.; Wellesley and, 725 sqq.

Marathon, brigandage at, xi 643
Marbeck, John, musician, ii 466
Marbella Point, naval engagement off (1705),
v 413
Marbois. *See* Barbé-Marbois
Marbot, Antoine, French general, viii 672
Marburg, University of, ii 201, ix 411; Con-
ference of (1529), ii 207 sqq., 333; the
Articles of, 209; Archduke John at, ix
258; Savigny's lectures at, xii 822
—— succession, secured to Hesse-Cassel,
iv 408
Marceau, François-Séverin des Graviers,
French general, viii 355, 497
Marcel, Étienne, Estates General and, i
399
Marcellus II (Marcello Cervini), Pope, ii
90, 534; the Jesuits and, 655, 663 sqq.,
672 sq.
March, Ausias (Spanish poet), i 379
"March Days" of agitation in Berlin, xi
157 sq.
Marchand, Jean-Baptiste, in Africa, xii 55;
129 sq.; 343; 448; 812 sq.
—— Comte Jean-Gabriel, French general,
meets Del Parque near Salamanca, ix
455
Marchangy, Louis-Antoine-F. le, King's
procurator in France, x 76
Marches, The (Italian), brigandage in, iii
430; favours bestowed by Sixtus V on,
438; rebellion in, x 155; national move-
ment in, xi 384; 387; 390; invasion of,
469; 530; annexed to Italy, 709
Marchfeld, battle fought on the (1809), ix
350
Marchiennes, depot of the Allies, v 433 sq.
Marciano, defeat of Piero Strozzi at, ii 88
Marck. *See* La Marck
Marcks, Erich, German historian, xii 829
Marco y Catalan, Governor of Rome, x 152
Marconi,Guglielmo, and wireless telegraphy,
xii 787
Marcora, Giuseppe, Italian politician, xii
227
Marcos de Obregon, by V. Espinel, iii 547
Marcoussis, rebel Princes removed to, iv
613
Marcy, William Learned, American Secre-
tary of State, vii 426
Mardefeld, Gustav von, Prussian Minister
at St Petersburg, vi 316; 658
Marderfeld, Arvid Axel, Swedish general,
v 595

Mardyk, Anglo-French treaty and, iv 440,
485; 598; 618; handed over to England,
619; harbour at, v 442; war-port at, vi
23; 26
Maréchal, Sylvain, French journalist, viii
504
Maremma, The, draining of, iii 393, 395,
399, 437–8; attempt to colonise, vi 601;
603
Marengo, battle of (1800), ix 15–6, 33, 42,
62 sqq., 150, 346
Marescalchi, Ferdinand, ix 84
Maresio, Giulio, Italian martyr, ii 397
Maret, Hugues Bernard, Duc de Bassano,
French ambassador, viii 299, 302 sq.,
305, 498
Marfori, Carlos, Marquis of Loja, xi 568 sq.
Margaret, Queen of Denmark, i 502;
marriage of, with Hakon of Norway, ii
600; becomes Queen of Sweden (1393),
ib.
—— Empress, consort of Leopold I, v
349; 377
—— (of Valois), Queen of France, 1st
consort of Henry IV, marriage of, iii 15,
18; 22 sq.; 33 sq.; 484; 489; divorce of,
678
—— Duchess of Alençon, and Queen of
Navarre, ii 284 sq., 287, 353; *Mirror
of a Sinful Soul*, 354, 384, 426
—— (Tudor), Queen of Scotland, consort of
James IV, i 484 sq., 488; ii 419 sq., 422;
divorce and re-marriage of, with Henry
Stewart, 453 sq.; death of, 455, 555; 560
—— (of Austria), Queen of Spain, consort
of Philip III, iii 527; iv 626
—— Archduchess, daughter of Maximilian II, dies in a Carmelite nunnery, iii
699
—— of Austria and Burgundy, Duchess
of Savoy, i 111, 131; birth of, 443;
marriage of, 445; 450 sq., 453; Governor-
General in Netherlands, 455–9, 477;
Henry VIII visits, 479; 481, 483; ii 40,
42, 59, 66, 102, 143, 424
—— (of Valois), Duchess of Berry, *afterwards* consort of Emmanuel Philibert of
Savoy, and humanism, iii 58; marriage
of, 400; 403; 406 sq.
—— Duchess of Parma. *See* Parma
Margarita, Clemente Solaro della, xi 70 sq.;
75
Margarites, Apostolos, xii 424
Margarot, Maurice, radical, viii 770
Margary, Augustus Raymond, murdered by
Chinese, xii 500 sq.; 796
Margate, Spanish designs on, iii 308; sick-
ness in English fleet at, 316; Arthur
O'Connor seized at, ix 701
Margeret, Jacques, French officer in Russia,
v 513
Margotti, editor of *Unità Cattolica*, xi 714;
xii 226
Marguerite, Jean-Auguste, French general,
xi 598

Marheineke, P. K., Lutheran theologian, x 382

Maria, Marie:—

—— (de' Medici), Queen of France, 2nd consort of Henry IV, III 544; 558; 678; appointed Regent, 690, 732; IV 34; 56; Regent, 118 sq.; 121; and Richelieu, 123 sqq.; escapes to the Netherlands, 139; death of, *ib.*; 141; 625 sq.; 640; in England, 592; 645; v 72

—— (Leszczynska), Queen of France, consort of Louis XV, marriage of, VI 143 sq.; 146; 148; 156; 164; 194; 196; 199

—— Queen of Hungary (sister of Charles V), Regent of the Netherlands, I 458; II 66, 74, 102, 235; censured by the Pope, 239; 267, 273, 448; resignation of, 537; III 182; 185; 187; 190

—— (d'Arquien), Queen of Poland, consort of John Sobieski, v 350; 354; 356; 365

—— (di Gonzaga), Queen of Poland, consort of John Casimir, v 349

—— I, Queen of Portugal, VI 375; 381; 388; insanity of, IX 301; sails for Brazil, x 310; death of, 311

—— II, Queen of Portugal, x 235; 320 sq.; in London, 322 sq.; returns to Brazil, 323; in England and France, 326; 328; in Lisbon, 336; marriage and reign of, 338 sq.; XI 572 sq.

—— (of Bavaria), Queen of the Two Sicilies, consort of Francis II, XI 380

—— Amalia (Archduchess), Empress, consort of Charles VII, VI 201

—— Amalia (of Saxony), Queen of Spain, consort of Charles III, VI 156; 367; 596 sq.; death of, x 231

—— Amélie (of Naples), Queen of the French, consort of Louis-Philippe, XI 101

—— Amélie, Queen of Portugal, consort of Carlos, XII 271 sq.

—— Anna (of Spain), Empress, consort of Ferdinand III, v 340; 376

—— Anna (of Spain), Queen of Portugal, consort of Joseph, VI 375; 388

—— Anna (of Austria), Queen of Spain, 2nd consort of Philip IV, marriage of, IV 664; faction of, 665; v 34 sq.; 45; 373

—— Anna (of Neuburg), Queen of Spain, 2nd consort of Charles II, v 34 sq.; illness of, 379; and the Spanish Succession, 381; 385; 391 sq.

—— Antoinette (of Austria), Queen of France, consort of Louis XVI, marriage of, VI 356; 616; 644; 783 sq.; character and influence of, VIII 79 sqq.; opposes Turgot, 87; opposes Necker, 90; opposes Calonne, 103; and meeting of States General, 146; in Paris, 185; enmity of Madame Roland against, 214; and insurrection of June 20, 229; quits Tuileries, 236 sq.; trial and execution of, 356 sq.; burial of, at St Denis, IX 572; x 732

Maria, Marie (*contd.*):—

—— Antonia, Queen of Portugal, consort of John V, Regent, VI 384

—— Caroline, Queen of Naples. *See* Caroline

—— Casimiria, Queen of Poland, VI 191

—— Cristina (Archduchess), Queen Regent of Spain, XII 257; 264

—— Eleonora (of Brandenburg), Queen of Sweden, consort of Gustavus Adolphus, IV 29, 68; marriage of, 89, 184; 185; 191; 203; at Mainz, 209; 220; excluded from government, 224; 568; v 639

—— Feodorovna (Sophia Dorothea of Würtemberg), Tsarina of Russia, consort of Tsar Paul, VI 696; IX 36; Empress Dowager, 305; and Napoleon, 486; foundress of institutions, XI 263, 625

—— Frederica Amelia (of Oldenburg), Queen of Greece, consort of Otto, XI 639 sqq.

—— Henriette (of Orleans), Queen of Belgium, consort of Leopold II, XI 673

—— Josepha (of Bavaria), Empress, consort of Joseph II, VI 630 sq.

—— Josepha (Archduchess), Queen of Poland, consort of Augustus III, VI 201

—— Louisa Augusta, Princess of Prussia. *See* Augusta of Weimar, German Empress

—— Louise (Archduchess), Empress of the French (Duchess of Parma), IX 140; 144–5, 147, 360; Napoleon's marriage with, 369; proposed regency of, 556; Parma, Piacenza, and Guastalla granted to, 559; 573, 581, 602; receives Parma, etc., 660; rule of, in Parma, x 107; 118; 120; XI 69

—— Louise Beatrix (of Este), Empress of Austria, 3rd consort of Francis II, IX 310; supports Stadion, 341, 359

—— Luisa (of Parma), Queen of Spain, consort of Charles IV, v 34 sq.; VIII 442, 783; IX 431; arrives at Bayonne, 432

—— Luisa (of Savoy), Queen of Spain, 1st consort of Philip V, v 447; VI 122

—— Miloslavskaia, Tsaritsa, consort of Alexis, v 506

—— Nagaia, Tsaritsa, consort of Ivan the Terrible, v 495 sq.

—— Pia (of Italy), Queen of Portugal, consort of Luis, XI 534; 574

—— Sophia (of Neuburg), Queen of Portugal, consort of Pedro II, v 35

—— Teresa (Infanta), Queen of France, consort of Louis XIV, IV 620; 658; marriage of, 660 sq.; v 19; death of, 20; 30; 33; and the Spanish Netherlands, 36, 152; 376 sq.

—— Theresa, Queen of Hungary, Empress, v 354; 543; and the War of the Austrian Succession, Vol. VI, Chap. VIII (3) *passim*; and the Seven Years' War, Chap. IX *passim*; 57; 139 sqq.; 155; 159 sq.; and acceptance by the Powers of Pragmatic Sanction, 203; accession of, 204; 310;

Maria, Marie (*contd.*):—
315; and Frederick the Great, 316, 338, 398; 317; 323; and Marshal Soltikoff, 324; 325; and the Empress Elizabeth, 325, 327; 331; and Count Kaunitz, 335; 336; 339; 341; 343; France and, 345; 346; and Poland, 355, 630, 669, 732; 366; and the Franco-Austrian alliance, 400 sq.; 427; and Clement XIII, 594; and the Jesuits, 595; 596; and Naples, 597; 600; 626 sqq.; 632; and Bavaria, 633; and reform, 637 sqq.; and Netherlands, 649; and Catharine II, 677, 699; 707; 724; death of, 634; viii 79 sq., 277, 309, 311; and Poland, 523; xi 421 sq.
—— of Austria, daughter of Ferdinand I. *See* Cleves
—— Archduchess, consort of Archduke Charles of Styria, iii 699
—— Infanta, daughter of Philip III, and Prince Henry, iii 559, iv 625; Charles I and, iii 575; iv 641, 643
—— of Portugal, marriage of, with Alexander, Duke of Parma, iii 200
—— Grand Duchess of Russia, daughter of Paul, at Vienna, ix 581
—— Amalia, Archduchess, consort of Ferdinand, Duke of Parma, viii 79
—— Anna (of Bavaria), Dauphine, v 41
—— Anna Victoria, Infanta of Spain, betrothed to Louis XV, vi 39, 126; repudiated, 140, 143
—— Beatrix of Este (Modena), Archduchess, Duchess of Massa-Carrara, ix 603
—— Christina, Archduchess, consort of Albert of Saxe-Teschen. *See* Saxe-Teschen
—— Cristina of Naples. *See* Cristina, Queen of Spain
—— Eleonora of Jülich-Cleves, consort of Duke Albert Frederick of Prussia. *See* Prussia
—— Francisca of Braganza, consort of Don Carlos, x 230; and the Spanish Succession, 231 sq.
—— Isabel, Princess of Asturias, *afterwards* Queen of Spain. *See* Isabel II
—— Josèphe, Dauphiness, vi 199; 338
—— Louise (of Parma), Princess of Bulgaria, xii 410
—— Louise, Grand Duchess of Tuscany. *See* Tuscany
—— Luisa Fernanda, Infanta. *See* Montpensier, Duchesse de
—— Magdalena, Archduchess, consort of Wolfgang William of Neuburg. *See* Neuburg
—— Theresa, Order of, ix 604
—— Theresa, Infanta, Dauphiness (1744), vi 156; 160
—— Thérèse Charlotte, Madame Royale, daughter of Louis XVI, viii 390, 503 sq. *See also* Mary

Maria à Jesu de Agreda, Philip IV and, iv 658
—— da Fonte, revolution of (1846), x 339
Maria Luz, Peruvian ship engaged in the Chinese labour traffic at Yokohama, xii 554 sq.; 559
Marialva y Menezes, Antonio Luis, Count de Castanhede, Portuguese general, v 34
Marian persecution, ii 533, 538 sqq.
Mariana, Queen of Portugal. *See* Maria Anna
—— Juan, Jesuit writer, i 360; ii 659; iii 763, 766; viii 3 sq.
Mariana Victoria (of Portugal), married to Don Gabriel, vi 381 sq.
Mariane, French *Chargé d'affaires* in Switzerland, vi 616
Mariano, Frà (servant to Leo X), ii 13, 17
—— da Genazzano, Frà, rival of Savonarola, i 147, 150 sq., 174
Maribö, suppression of the convent at (1521), ii 617
Marie, Alexandre-Thomas, xi 26; 39; 102; Minister of Public Works, 104; 108; 118
Marie Galante, reduced (1808) by the British, ix 240
Marienbourg (Belgium), built by Charles V, ii 102; captured by France (1523), 89; restored to Spain (1559), 93; ceded to France, v 33; ceded to Netherlands, x 22, 524
Marienburg (West Prussia), taken by Gustavus Adolphus, iv 207; Treaty of (1656), 428, 583; v 632; siege of (1410), 633; 634 sq.
Marietta, settlers at, vii 357
Mariette, F. Auguste F., French Egyptologist, xii 845
Marignano, battle of (1515), i 141, 486, vi 611 sq., 621
—— Gian Giacomo, Medichino, Marquis of, ii 88; iii 390
Marigny, truce at, iii 28
Marillac, Charles de. *See* Vienne, Archbishops of
—— Louis de, Marshal of France, execution of, iv 138; 155
—— Michel de, exile of, iv 138
—— *Intendant* of Poitou, 1681, and the *dragonnades*, v 24
Marinelli, confessor of Pius IX, xii 216
Marino, Giovanni Battista, Crashaw influenced by, iv 772 sq.
Marion, Francis, American general, vii 226
Mariotte, Edme, physicist, v 715
Maris, the brothers, painters, xii 249
Marischal, George Keith, 5th Earl, iii 550
—— George Keith, 10th Earl, vi 98; 103 sqq.
Marivaux, Pierre Carlet de Chamblain de, vi 833; xi 528
Mark, and Treaty of Cleves, iv 409; countship of, added to grand duchy of Berg, ix 410

Marklissa, Field-Marshal Daun at, VI 291; 292

Markoff, Russian diplomatist, IX 245

Marlar, Anthony, printer, II 466

Marlborough, Province of, XI 799

—— George Spencer, 4th Duke of, VI 424; Lord Privy Seal, 430

—— George Spencer-Churchill, 6th Duke of, X 593

—— John Churchill, Duke of, envoy to Louis XIV, V 231; at Sedgmoor, 232; and Prince of Orange, 243, 247; 246; 255; and James II, 262; 266; in Ireland, 316; and religious toleration, 334; and Grand Alliance (1701), 398; character and military genius of, 405, 436 sq., 460 sqq.; in Netherlands (1702), 406 sqq.; march of, to Danube, 409; at Blenheim, 410 sq.; 412 sq.; returns to Netherlands, 414; designs of, on Toulon, 412, 414, 419, 426; at Ramillies, 415 sq.; and peace negotiations, 417, 420, 422 sq., 427; visits Charles XII, 417, 596 sq.; in the Netherlands, 418; at Oudenarde, 420 sq.; 424; at Malplaquet, 425; declining influence of, in England, 428; 429; successes of, against Villars, 431; dismissal of, 431, 471; 432; 440; 457 sq., and party government, 462 sqq.; created duke, 463; 465 sq.; Earl of Oxford and, 470 sq.; Peter the Great and, 595; 609; missions of, to Berlin, 666 sq.; VI 7 sq.; 11; 14; 16 sq.; 91; 206; 267

—— Sarah, Duchess of, V 428; 460; 462; 565 sq.

Marliano, Bartolommeo, *Urbis Romae Topographia*, I 549

Marlowe, Christopher, III 373 sq.

Marmont, Auguste-F.-L. Viesse de, Duc de Raguse, Marshal, VIII 564; 602, 616; and Brumaire, 679; IX 60-3; 252; joins Bernadotte, 253; invests Ulm, 254; ordered to Salzburg, 256-7; guards Styria, 258; 289, 355; Dalmatia transferred to, 396; 419; Masséna superseded in Portugal by, 466; joins Soult, 467; at Badajoz, 468; at Leon, 469; 471; falls back on the Douro, 472; wounded, 473; at Möckern, 536-7; at Schönefeld, 539; guards French frontier, 543; at Sezanne, 549; defeat of, 552; defends Paris, 553; surrender of, 557-8; advice of, to Napoleon, 574; X 54; 100; and revolution of 1830, 475 sq.

Marmora, Sea of, British fleet in, XII 390

Marmotan, French politician, XI 502

Marnix, John de, Lord of Thoulouse, III 211

—— Philip de. *See* Sainte-Aldegonde

Marongio Nurra, Emmanuel, Bishop of Cagliari, XI 368

Maronites, The, and the Druses, XI 276

Marot, Clément, II 286; in Ferrara, 384; 690

Maroto, Rafael, Carlist general, X 240

Marquesas Isles, France and, XI 35; 793; government of, XII 668

Marquette, Jacques, French Jesuit and explorer, VII 362

Marramaque, Antonio Pereira, writings of, II 414

Marrast, Armand, editor of *Tribune*, X 485; 491 sq.; XI 26; 39; 102 sq.; 108; 110; and Republican Constitution, 115; President of Assembly, 118; 124

Marsaglia, battle of (1693), V 61

Marsala, Garibaldi at, XI 388, 533

Marschalk, Nicholas, first German printer of Greek, II 111

Marschall von Burgholzhausen, Count Ernst Dietrich von, Austrian general, in Lusatia, VI 264 sq.; 268; 278

Marsden, Samuel, in Australia, XI 791, 793

Marseillaise, French journal, XI 492

Marseilles, siege of, by Bourbon (1524), II 49, 423; Conference of, between Clement VII and Francis I (1533), 68, 220, 285, 440, III 110; troubles at (1591), 397, 410, 416; Spanish designs on (1596), 668, (1601), 683; the plague at, VI 128; 348; arsenal at, 349; VII 60; *fédérés* from, 232 sq., 252, disaffection in (1793), 268, 270, 340, 348 sq., 431; the Terror at, 372; the "White Terror" at, 387; trade of, 486; inhabitants of, declared *émigrés*, 502; military plot at, X 76; Mazzini at, 121; Duchess of Berry lands at, 488; rising at, 492; XI 31; 114; 137; land-bank at, 298; 302; Commune at, 503; working men's Congress at, XII 123; 430

Marsh, Francis, Archbishop of Dublin, and Committee on Irish affairs, V 316

—— James, discovers gold in California, VII 400

—— John, American jurist, VII 304

—— Stephen, Presbyterian leader, IV 359

Marsiglio of Padua, and the Papacy, I 655

Marsin, Comte Ferdinand de, Marshal of France, V 409 sqq.; 414; 416

—— Jean-Gaspard-Ferdinand, Comte de, arrest of, IV 612; in Catalonia, 615; 618

Mars-la-Tour, XI 589; battle at, 590 sqq.; 594 sq.;

Marston, John, English dramatist, III 380

Marston Moor, battle of (1644), IV 312, 321 sqq., 327, 506

Marstrand, captured by Tordenskiold (1719), V 583

Martaban, capture of, XI 728, 742

Martel, Louis-Joseph, Vice-President of the French Assembly, XII 110

—— de, French rear-admiral (1673), V 195 sq.

Martell, Liberal Spanish priest, X 219

Martelli, Camilla, and Cosimo de' Medici, III 396

Martens, Frederick de, jurist, XII 373; 721

Martens, Georg Friedrich von, at the Congress of Vienna, ix 583; 587, 609
Martha, Tsarevna, imprisonment of, v 525
Martignac, Jean-Baptiste-Silvère-Gaye, Vicomte de, x 85; succeeds Villèle, 92; career and character of, *ib.*; Ministry of, 93-6; 97; 153
Martin V (Otto Colonna), Pope, i 237, 646; ii 29; iii 439
—— Alexandre (*dit* Albert). *See* Albert
—— C. R. D., jurist, x 364
—— (of Strassburg), Édouard, xi 99; 101; 110
—— François, founder of Pondicherry, v 703
—— Henri, the *History of France*, x 514
—— Joseph, French deputy, viii 155
—— Josiah, Governor of N. Carolina, vii 173
—— Luther, Maryland deputy to the Convention, vii 246, 250, 255, 270, 277, 281, 295, 297
—— Pierre, Comte, French admiral, viii 458 sq., 466
"Martin Marprelate" Controversy, iii 344 sq.
Martineau family, of Norwich, viii 764
—— Harriet, and women's employment, xii 762
Martinengo, Abbot, papal nuncio for England, ii 583, 586
—— Count Massimiliano Celso, Italian Reformer, ii 391
—— Sciarra, Savoyard general, iii 24, 28; 416
Martinet, French infantry inspector, v 18
Martinez de la Rosa, Francisco, Spanish statesman, x 219; 221; 224; Ministry of, 234 sq.; 236 sq.
—— de Campos, Arsenio, Spanish general, xii 262; 264 sq.
—— Marina, Francisco, x 206; 219
Martini, Ferdinand Heinrich Wilhelm, naturalist, vi 626; 635
Martiniana, Cardinal, ix 181
Martinique, settled by French, iv 758, vii 78 sq., 85; failure of English attack on, v 60; a French possession, 687 sq., vii 96 sq., 107; vi 346; 348; 351; conquest of (1762), 421, 426; ceded to France (1763), 428; 453 sq.; and French Revolution, viii 193; taken by British (1794), 484, ix 749; restored to France (1801), 75; 221 sqq.; 234; 238; blockade of (1804), vii 327; reduced by British (1809), ix 240, 752; restored to France (1815), 653; xii 652 sq.; France and, 656
Martinitz, Jaroslav von, iii 727; and *Letter of Majesty*, iv 16; Regent in Bohemia, 18 sq.; the "defenestration" of, 20 sq.
Martinovics, Ignatius Joseph, Slav democrat, viii 777
Martins, Domingues José, revolutionary leader in Brazil, x 312

Martinsburg, Patterson at, vii 465
Martinuzzi, George. *See* Grosswardein, Bishop of
Martyr, Peter. *See* Vermigli
—— Peter, of Anghera. *See* Anghera
Martyrology, Crespin's, ii 293
Marvell, Andrew, iv 767 sq.; literary work of, 774 sq.; v 132; 216; 218
Marx, Karl, in England, x 757; and early English socialists, 778, 780, 782; xi 53; *Das Capital*, xii 123; 124; 152; 252; influence of, in Russia, 329; propaganda of, 758 sq.
Mary of Burgundy, Empress, consort of Maximilian I. *See* Burgundy, Mary, Duchess of
—— of Burgundy, Empress, consort of Maximilian II (daughter of Charles V), iii 145; 166 sq.
—— I, Queen of England, i 53, 488, 489; ii 42 sq., 53, 89; marriage of, 92 sq.; 274, 428, 445, 470; Protector Somerset and, 485; 492, 499, 503; reign of, Chap. xv *passim*; death of, 559; iii 167, 182, 184, 189, 260, 264, 476-7
—— II, Queen of England, v 44; 46; 128; 211; proposed marriage of, 213; marriage of, 163, 219; and William III, 167; coronation of, *ib.*; 239; 243; 249 sq.; proclaimed Queen, 251; character and influence of, 258; death of, *ib.*; 261; and Scottish Crown, 292; 315; vi 6 sq.
—— (of Modena), Queen of England, consort of James II, marriage of, v 211; 232; 234; gives birth to a son, 241 sq.; flight of, to France, 247 sq.; 255
—— Queen of Hungary. *See* Maria
—— (Tudor), sister of Henry VIII, Queen of France, i 456, 477, 481, 483 sq.; marriage of, with Charles Brandon, Duke of Suffolk, ii 560
—— (Stewart), Queen of Scotland, ii 93; birth of, 456, 555; proposed marriage of, with Edward VI, 493, 556; 510; and the English throne, 535; marriage of, with Francis II, 548, 558; widowed, 580; returns to Scotland, 581, 595; Vol. iii, Chap. viii, 243, 328, 350, 436, 478, 483-4, 489, 492, 498; recognises Philip as her heir (1586), 502-3; 591, 760
—— Princess Royal of England (daughter of Charles I). *See* Orange
—— (of Guise *or* Lorraine), Queen of Scotland, consort of James V, marriage of, ii 455; 457, 486, 548, 555 sq.; rule of, 557; 567, 572 sq.; death of, 577; policy of, iii 261 sqq.; 266, 268
Mary Rose, The, loss of, ii 460; and Henry VIII's naval policy, 472
Maryland, English colony of, iv 747; Labadists in, v 756; vi 52; trade of, 447; settlement of, vii 31-4; 53; political conditions in, 54 sq.; economic conditions in, 55 sq.; religious conditions in,

58; disaffection in, 163; and confederation, 235; Constitution of, 240; and Constitutional Convention, 246 sq., 255, 271, 281, 283, 286, 298, 300; and trade regulations, 310; boundary of, 311; slavery in, 403; and secession, 453 sq., 470, 581; Lee invades (1862), 481; and emancipation, 585 sq., 598

Masampo, xii 521; Japanese naval base at, 599

Masaniello. *See* Aniello

Mascaron, Jules, French preacher, v 79

Mascov, Johann Jacob, German historian, xii 817

Masena, Barth at, xii 810

Masham, Abigail (Hill), Lady, v 465 sq.

Mashin, Colonel, Servian conspirator, xii 412

Mashonaland, xii 47; Matabele raids on, 639; 664

Masih Pasha, siege of Rhodes by, i 84

Masino, Count of, iii 412

Mason and Dixie line, The, vii 361

—— George, Virginian delegate at Constitutional Convention (1787), Vol. vii, Chap. viii *passim*

—— James Murray, American envoy to Europe, vii 470; xi 335; xii 18

—— Sir John, and Somerset's reforms, ii 496

—— Captain John (d. 1635), and settlement of New Hampshire, vii 21, 31, 46

—— John (d. 1672), leader of expedition against Pequods, vii 19

Masovia (province of Poland), iii 76; Election Diet of 1573 in, 85–7

—— Conrad, Duke of, v 630

Maspero, Gaston, Egyptologist, xii 845

Mass, abolition of, in Switzerland, ii 321; in England, 571; in Scotland, 579; change of language in, in England, 482; and First Prayer-Book of Edward VI, 484 sq.; discussion of, at Council of Trent, 679

Massa, duchy of, assigned to Este, ix 603

—— Isaac, Dutch writer on Russia, v 513

—— Prince, Neapolitan insurrection and (1657), iv 657 sq.

Massachusetts, settlement of, vii 13 sqq.; charter of, obtained (1629), iv 747, vii 15; control of, over Maine, 22, 24 sq., 27; regicides in, 26; charter of, annulled, 28; and Governor Andros, 29; new charter granted to, 30; population of, 54; religious conditions in, 57; education in, 58; relations of, with Crown, 64 sqq.; disaffection in, 152 sqq., 161 sqq.; writs of assistance in, 177 sqq.; Constitution of, 239 sqq.; and Constitutional Convention, 245 sqq., 251, 255, 263 sq., 278, 292, 298 sq.; and Constitution, 303; cessions in, 308; paper money in, 312 sq.; elections in, for Annapolis Convention, 314; 336; abolition in, 361; 388; manufactures in, 375 sq.; and the Tariff, 377; factory legislation in, xii 747

Massachusetts Bay, Assembly of, vi 439; 446 sq.

—— Company, iv 748, vii 15

Massari, Giuseppe, Neapolitan patriot, xi 536

Massaro, Vincenzio, Como priest, ii 381

Mass-book, Swedish (*Ordo Missae Sueticae*), ii 628

Masséna, André, Duc de Rivoli, Prince d'Essling, Marshal of France, viii 438; and conquest of Italy, 443, 558, 566, 569, 574 sq., 578, 582; in Rome, 638; in Switzerland, 661 sq.; ix 21; 47, 57–9, 61–2, 68, 70, 96; created Prince of Essling, 112; Saint-Cyr joins, 193; 254; convention proposed by, 257; marches on Naples, 262; on Narew, 289; defends Aspern against Austrians (May, 1809), 351; also (July, 1809), 353; helps Joseph Bonaparte, 404; commands in Spain, 457; army of, 458; besieges Almeida, 459; at Torres Vedras, 460; occupies Coimbra, 461; retreats to Ciudad Rodrigo, 462–3; operations of, 465; at Fuentes d'Oñoro, 466

Massenbach, Christian von, Prussian colonel, ix 279

Massey, Sir Edward, Presbyterian general, iv 341

Massillon, Jean-Baptiste. *See* Clermont

Massin, forest of, vi 281 sq.

Massinger, Philip, English dramatist, iii 381

Massmann, H. F. M., at the Wartburg festival, x 364

Masson, Frédéric, French historian, xii 834

Massoneria, secret society in Italy, x 111

Massow, Ludwig Joachim Valentin von, Marshal of the Prussian Court, xi 191

Massowah, Italian occupation of, xii 240, 444; assigned to Egypt, 439; 805

Mastai, Paolino, Monsignor, and Pius IX, xi 72

Mastai-Ferretti, Giovanni Maria, Cardinal Count. *See* Pius IX, Pope

Master, Sir Streynsham, in India, v 698

Masuda, leader of Chōshiu warriors, xi 851 sq.; 855

Masulipatam, English factory at, iv 742, v 703; ceded to the French, vi 539; 546; taken by the English, 548

Mataafa, King of Samoa, vii 662

Matabele, The, Boers massacred by, xi 781; 782

—— War, xii 639

Matabeleland, xii 47; 49; Cecil Rhodes and, 638 sq.

Matamoras (Mexico), captured by Taylor (1846), vii 394 sqq.

Matanzas, Bay of, Spanish treasure fleet in the, iv 706; 707

Matari, Napier at, xi 737

Matelief, Cornelis, Dutch admiral, iii 638

Mathé, Félix, French politician, xi 139

Mathematics, history of. *See* Science

Mather, Cotton, vii 726; *Magnalia Christi Americana*, 727 sq.; 729

—— Increase, Independent minister, vii 29, 729

Mathew, Father Theobald, x 677; influence of, in Ireland, xi 8; 12

Mathews, Thomas, Admiral, vi 160; 237; 239

Mathias, Thomas James, poet, x 700

Mathon de La Cour, Charles Joseph, *Collection des comptes-rendus*, viii 74

Mathy, Karl, Baden statesman, xi 61 sqq.; 145; 164; 166; at Gotha meeting, 221; 446

Matignon, Charles-Auguste de Goyon, Count of (Comte de Gacé), Marshal of France, vi 92

—— Royalist commander in French Religious Wars, iii 23, 40-1

Matilda, Countess of Tuscany, i 251, 260

Matra, James Maria, and New South Wales, ix 736

Matricula (Imperial army tax), i 317 sq.

Matsudaira, Japanese Councillor of State, xi 832; 834

Matta, Chilian Minister of Foreign Affairs, vii 666

Mattei, Alessandro, Cardinal, x 132; 139

Matthew of Vendôme, on Pope's power, i 654

Matthews, Henry. *See* Llandaff, Viscount

Matthias, Archduke, *afterwards* Emperor, iii 181; sovereignty of Netherlands offered to, 248-9, 501, 687, 704; early career of, 698, 700-2, 715; heads Archdukes against Rudolf II, 718 sqq., 731 sqq.; crowned King of Bohemia, 734; elected Emperor, iv 1; rule of, 2 sq.; 9; and Diet of Ratisbon (1613), 10 sq.; and Klesl's policy, 13 sq.; Bohemian Protestants and, 15; at Dresden, 17; in Hungary, 18; 22; death of, 25

—— Corvinus, King of Hungary, i 70 sqq.; fails against Turks, 73; 81; conquests of, in Bohemia and Austria, 293, 335 sq.; the Papacy and, 658; death of (1490), 296, 336, 395; character of, 335; ii 198; xi 421

Matthys, Jan, Anabaptist, ii 225 sq.

Matto Grosso, province of, vi 390

Matun, British success at, xi 728

Maturin, Charles, writer, x 718

Matvieeff, Andrei, Russian envoy in London, v 595; 608

—— Artemon, Russian statesman, v 516 sqq.; murder of, 519

Matyúshenko, Russian mutineer, xii 355

Matyushkin, General, captures Baku, v 545

Maubeuge, ceded to France, v 45; and Barrier Treaties, 458; siege of (1793), viii 431 sq.

Mauburnus (Johannes Momboir) of Brotherhood of Common Life, ii 657

Maud, Queen of Norway, xii 290

Maudslay, Henry, and the screw-cutting lathe, x 734

Mauguin, François, French deputy, x 91; 476; 478; 480; and Algiers, 503; 508

Maumee Rapids, Indians defeated on the (1794), vii 357

Maundsaur, Treaty of, xi 726

Maupas, Charlemagne-Émile de, Prefect of Haute-Garonne, xi 134 sqq.; 141; Minister of Police, 291 sq.

Maupeou, René-Nicolas-Charles-Augustin de, Chancellor of France, vi 356 sqq.; viii 82

Maurepas, Jean-Frédéric Phélypeaux, Count de, French statesman, vi 113; 535; viii 82, 87, 89, 94 sq.; death of, 96

Maurer, George Ludwig von, German historian, xii 850

Maurevel, Charles de Louvier, Seigneur de, murderer of Mouy, iii 19

Maurice, Landgrave of Hesse-Cassel. *See* Hesse-Cassel

—— Prince of Nassau-Orange. *See* Orange

—— Prince Palatine. *See* Palatine

—— of Savoy, Cardinal. *See* Savoy

—— Frederick Denison, xii 740

Maurienne, occupied by Lesdiguières, iii 673

Mauritius, vi 133; the French in, 534 sq.; and French Revolution, viii 194; French colonial expedition to, ix 80; reduced (1810) by British, 240, 732, 754; retained (1814), 564, 576, 735, 755; Tipu's envoys to, 721

Mauritsstad, Dutch capital in Brazil, iv 708

Maurus, Rabanus, Abbot of Fulda, influences monastic studies, i 535

Maury, Jean-Siffrein, Cardinal, *afterwards* Archbishop of Paris (Abbé Maury), viii 173, 748; ix 181; member of Ecclesiastical Commission, 196; and vacant French sees, 198-9

Mautern, Kutusoff at, ix 257

Mauthausen, Elector Charles Albert of Bavaria at, vi 232

Mauve, Anton, Dutch painter, xii 249

Mauvillon, Major Jacob, German author, viii 150

Mavrocordato, Alessandro, Prince, x 181; 506; xi 279

Maxen, Prussian defeat at, vi 294 sq.

Maxim the Greek, v 508

Maximilian I, King of the Romans and Emperor-Elect, i 92; Chap. iv *passim*; failure of, in Italy (1496), 172; Chap. ix *passim*; Hungary and, 336, 339; Eastern policy of, 343 sq.; 363 sq.; marries Mary of Burgundy, 391 sq.; allied with Britanny, 393 sqq., 442-62; hostile to Henry VII, 467, 470; Treaty of, with Henry VII, 475, 477; Henry VIII and, 481 sqq., 487, 490; the Papacy and, 672, 690; and Council of Pisa, ii 29; death of, 37, 40, 139; 39; 132 sq., 176, 198; iii 716; iv 36; v 487; 624; 635

Maximilian II, Emperor (Archduke of Austria), II 267, 269, 537, 681; III 15, 20, 91 sq.; Polish candidature of, 95–101; treaty with Solyman II, 125, 130–1, 147, 149, 153, 161, 164; character of, 165 sqq.; religious views of, 167 sqq.; the reign of, 169 sqq.; death of, 181, 218, 224, 238, 252, 395–6, 698, 703, 706, 716

—— I (Maximilian Joseph), King of Bavaria (1805), VIII 648, 776; joins France, IX 253; recognised as King, 262; 265, 268; at Congress of Vienna, 582; X 359

—— II, King of Bavaria, accession of, XI 146; 200; and Hesse-Cassel, 229; 397; XII 827

—— Emperor of Mexico (Ferdinand Maximilian Joseph, Archduke), Governor of Lombardo-Venetia, VII 535; XI 374; 377; proclaimed Emperor, 477; 479; death of, 483 sq.; 565; XII 676 sq.

—— Archduke, Governor of Tyrol and Anterior Austria, III 450, 687; early career of, 698 sqq.; renunciation by, of claim to Polish throne (1592), 714; 719; 723; 725; 729, 731; IV 1; 10; at the *Reichstag* of Linz, 11; 13; 22 sq.; death of (1618), 26; and Polish succession (1587), 168

—— Ernest, Archduke, of Styria, III 719

—— Henry. *See* Cologne

—— Joseph, Elector of Bavaria. *See* Bavaria

Maxwell, James Clerk, XII 785 sqq.

—— Robert, Lord, invades England (1542), II 456

Maybach, Prussian Minister of Public Works, XII 157

Mayence. *See* Mainz

Mayenfeld, Protestants at, IV 52; 55; Austrian garrison in, 56; 58

Mayenne, occupied by the Vendeans, VIII 355

—— Charles de Lorraine, Duke of, General of Catholic League, III 32, 36 sq., 40 sq., 46, 48, 50, 52; and assassination of Elizabeth, 288; 414 sq.; self-seeking of, 511 sq.; 659; struggle of, with Henry IV, 661 sqq.; accepts Henry IV, 668; serves him, 673, 675, 679

—— Henri de Lorraine, Duke of, IV 119; 124; in Guienne, 126 sq., 625

—— *See also* Maine

Mayflower, pilgrims of the, IV 747

Mayhew, Jonathan, Boston minister, VII 144

Maynard, François, French poet, V 69

—— Sir John, and the Revolution settlement, V 249 sq.

Mayne, Cuthbert, III 287

Mayneville, factotum of the Guises in Paris, III 47

Maynooth, College of, established, IX 700; XI 9; XII 67; 71

Maynwaring, Bishop of St David's. *See* Manwaring

Mayo, County, boycotting in, XII 38; 89

—— Richard Southwell Bourke, 6th Earl of, Governor-General of India, XII 458; and Sher Ali, 460 sq.; rule of, 462; assassinated, 463; 464; 468; 478; 482

Mayow, John, chemist, V 728; 732

Mayr, Martin, II 29

Mazandevan, ceded to Russia, V 545

Mazarin, Jules, Cardinal, IV 138; succeeds Richelieu, 152, 388, 399; and Civil War in England, 328; 334; and Charles I, 336; 338; and Bavaria, 391 sq.; 402; and Treaty of Westphalia, 405 sq.; 426; policy of, 429 sqq.; and *Rheinbund*, 431; Vaudois persecution and, 439; 540; 542; *see* Chap. XXI; 656; 658; political difficulties of, 659; 660; and Anne of Austria, 702; and William II of Orange, 727; 754; and Louis XIV, V 1; 5; and Fouquet, 6; 14; and marriage of Louis XIV, 19; policy of, 32; 106; and Clarendon, 199; and Leopold I, 338; 756; VIII 36; IX 93

—— Michel (brother of the Cardinal), in Catalonia, IV 600

Mazarini, Giulio. *See* Mazarin, Jules

Mazar-i-Sharif, death of Sher Ali at, XII 470

Mazarquivir, Spanish possession, VI 380

Mazaruni river, gold discovered in, XII 654

Mazas, prison of, XI 136

Mazeievich, Arseni, Archbishop of Rostov, VI 679

Mazepa, Ivan, Cossack Hetman, V 596 sqq.; and Charles XII, 599; and Peter the Great, 599 sqq.; 601 sqq.

Mazochi, Jacopo, *Epigrammata*, I 549

Mazza, Antonio, secretary to Venetian Embassy in England, II 513

Mazzini, Giuseppe, X 106; at Genoa, 117; and "Young Italy," 121–2; and literary movement in Italy, 126, 127, 128; 166; 378; 483; XI 65; *Giovine Italia*, 67, 69; appeals to Pius IX, 78; in Florence, 91; in Rome, 93 sq.; 121 sq.; and French intervention, 125; 245; 351; 366; in Milan, 372; 374; and Genoa rebellion, 375; in London, 376; 377; 380; and Sicilian Revolution, 388 sq.; 391; Ricasoli and, 531; 532; and King Victor Emmanuel, 537 sq.; 539; 542; 547; 705; XII 214

Mazzolini, Sylvester (Prierias), and Luther's Theses, II 131, 138

Mazzoni, Giuseppe, Tuscan triumvir, XI 91

Meade, George Gordon, commands Army of the Potomac, VII 487 sqq.; 510; and campaign in east (1864), 514, 516 sq.; at Petersburg, 537

Meadows, Sir William, General, in India, VI 469; 475

Meagher, Thomas Francis, Irish Nationalist, XI 13

Méan, François-Antoine, Comte de. *See* Malines, Archbishop of

Meath, English in, III 580

Meaux, the preachers of, and the Sorbonne, II 283; execution of the Fourteen of, 290; Condé at, III 1; Parma at, 49; concessions granted to, 666; the Enterprise of, 9

—— Guillaume de Briçonnet, Bishop of, I 674; II 282 sq.

—— Jacques-Bénigne Bossuet, Bishop of, and Montaigne, v 64 sq.; and Descartes, 65; 66; and Cartesianism, 73; 74; 76; as a preacher, 80; 81; 84; and dispute with the Papacy, 85 sq.; writings of, 86; and the Huguenots, 86; 87; and Fénelon, 88; 90; 743; VIII 6; *Exposition de la Foi Catholique*, x 160; XII 848

Mecca, I 91; pilgrim route to, v 699; capture of (1804), IX 387; taken by Mehemet Ali (1811), x 547; cholera brought by pilgrims from, XII 439, 452; 806

Mechlin. *See* Malines

Mechnikoff, Elias, Russian pathologist, XII 780

Mecklenburg, Gustavus in, IV 196, 199, 204; Peace of Prague and, 253; and compact at Stuhmsdorf, 366; 374; 378; claimed by Sweden at Osnabrück, 403 sq.; 418; v 435; Stenbock in, 608; 610 sq.; 667; Russian force in, VI 26; 28; 34; Peter the Great and, 206; 220; 267; 276; Swedish troops in, 280; 742; constitutional system of, x 363; and *Zollverein*, 379; reaction in, XI 397

—— Dukes of, on Protestant side, III 157, 704, IV 98 sqq.; 104; 116; 194; 197; restoration of, 203 sq.; and the Kurmark, v 618. *See also* Mecklenburg-Schwerin *and* Mecklenburg-Güstrow

—— Albert, Duke of, II 230, 615

—— George, Duke of, II 269 sq., 273

—— Henry, Duke of, II 196, 203

—— Johann Albrecht I, Duke of, II 270

Mecklenburg-Güstrow, Gustavus Adolphus, Duke of, v 663

—— Duke John Albert of, submits to Emperor Ferdinand II, IV 101

Mecklenburg-Schwerin, becomes Lutheran, II 238; x 343; and Germanic Confederation, 344; and tariff reform, 373; XI 59; revolutionary movement in, 150 sq.

—— Duke Adolphus Frederick of, submits to Emperor Ferdinand II, IV 101; obtains Schwerin and Ratzeburg by Treaty of Westphalia, 407–8

—— Catharine, Duchess of, v 550

—— Elizabeth Catharine Christina, Princess of. *See* Brunswick-Wolfenbüttel, Princess Anna Leopoldovna of

—— Charles Leopold, Duke of, v 550; 611 sq.; VI 26

—— Frederick, Duke of, VI 266

—— Frederick Francis I, Grand Duke of, x 373

Mecklenburg-Schwerin, Frederick Francis II, Grand Duke of, XI 150; in Franco-German War, 603 sqq., 607, 610

—— Princess of, proposed as bride of Gustavus IV Adolphus of Sweden, IX 38

Mecklenburg-Strelitz, Swedish troops in, VI 280; x 343; and Germanic Confederation, 344; XI 59; revolutionary movement in, 150 sq.

—— Charles, Prince of, x 350; 376

—— George, Grand Duke of, XI 151

Médard, St, miracles of, v 91

Medellin, battle of (1809), IX 450–1

Medemblik, William II of Orange and, IV 725

Medicean conspiracy, The (1497), I 175 sq.

Medici, House of, Vol. II, Chap. I *passim*; Florence restored to, II 60

—— Alessandro de', Duke of Florence, II 25, 60; III 187; murdered (1537), II 72, III 387

—— Catharine de'. *See* Catharine de' Medici, Queen of France

—— Cosimo de' ("*Pater Patriae*"), convent of San Marco established by, I 145; 150, 164 sq.; libraries founded by, 552; II 3 sq.; Platonic Academy of Florence and, 702

—— Cosimo I de', Grand Duke of Tuscany. *See* Tuscany

—— Garzia de', death of (1562), III 395

—— Giovanni de'. *See* Leo X, Pope

—— Giovanni de', son of Grand Duke Cosimo I, Cardinal, early death of, III 390, 395

—— Giovanni de' (delle Bande Nere), II 44, 48, 50, 54, 61; III 387; IV 36

—— Giovanni Angelo de'. *See* Pius IV

—— Giuliano de' (brother of Lorenzo the Magnificent), murder of, I 186, 661; II 22

—— Giuliano de' (son of Lorenzo the Magnificent), I 140, 199, 217; II 15

—— Giulio de'. *See* Clement VII, Pope

—— Ippolito de', Cardinal, II 26

—— Isabella de', wife of Paolo Giordano Orsini, murder of, III 396, 427

—— Lorenzo de' (the Magnificent), death of, closes an epoch, I 104, 110; 141; Savonarola and, 147 sqq.; 158, 176, 217; Innocent VIII and, 223 sqq.; Platonic Academy and, 559, 702; 661; II 3, 8, 22; III 387 sq.; 390; 394; poetry of, 458 sq.; 470

—— Lorenzo de' (grandson of Lorenzo the Magnificent), II 13

—— Lorenzino de', III 387

—— Lucrezia de', daughter of Cosimo I, III 395

—— Ludovico de', Duke of Sarto, Neapolitan statesman, x 143

—— Piero de' (son of Lorenzo), I 110, 113, 127, 148 sqq., 166, 174, 185, 193, 228, 230

Medici, Pietro de' (son of Cosimo I), iii 397 sq.

Medicine, science of, in Russia, under Peter the Great, v 531; and Surgery, advance of, xii 778 sqq. *See also* Science

Medina, capture of (1804), ix 387; taken by Mehemet Ali (1811), x 547

Medina-Celi, Juan Francisco Tomas de la Cerda, 8th Duke of, Spanish statesman, v 35

—— Luis de la Cerda, 6th Duke of, in the Netherlands, iii 234; defeated off Tripoli, 486

Medina del Campo, Peace of (1489), i 467

—— Sidonia, Alfonso Perez de Guzman, 7th Duke of, commands Armada, iii 308–15, 505 sqq., 521; iv 652 sq.

Meditationes de prima philosophia, iv 779; 782

Mediterranean Sea, power of the Saracens in, i 9; Muslim pirates in, ii 68 sq.; war in (1536), 72; Sultan's power in, iii 540; French supremacy in, v 44, 53, 61; British fleet in (1694), 61 sq., 426; Dutch fleet in, 161; England and, 262, 419, 694; the Turks in, 349; France and, 404; the Allies in, 411 sqq.; British fleet in, vi 32; 239; 337; 350; suppression of piracy in, 381; 452; British trade with, vii 1; campaign in (1792–6), viii 456; the British abandon (1796), 461, 583, 598, 643; the struggle for (1798–9), Chap. xx; British surrender of posts on (1802), ix 77; xii 239; Italy and, 241; 430; 703

Medjerda, valley of, the French in, xii 129

Medun, Turks defeated at, xii 387

Medway, the Dutch in the (1667), v 113, 150 sq., 172, 188 sq.

Meerman, John, embassy of, to England, v 152

Meerset, Colonel van der, defeats the Austrians at Turnhout, vi 652

Meerut, mutiny at, xi 746 sq.

Meeus, Ferdinand, x 536

Meghem, Charles de Brimeu, Count of, iii 194 sq.; 203; 206; 211; 213; 223

Mehedia (headquarters of Mediterranean pirates), captured by Spain (1550), ii 86

Méhée de la Touche, arrives in London (1803), ix 28

Mehemet, Pasha of Aleppo, x 550

—— Ali, Pasha of Egypt, Vol. x, Chap. xvii *passim*; 172; 176; aids Sultan against Greeks, 180 sq.; 189; evacuates the Morea, 201; 494; 512 sq.; xi 636; xii 429; and railway construction, 430; 432; 439; 451; and education, 453; revolt of, 728

—— Ali, Ottoman commander, xii 388; 394; murdered, 401

—— Ruchdi, Grand Vizier, xii 385

Mehidpur, engagement at, xi 726

Mehlen, Bernhard von, ii 623

Mehul, Étienne-Henri, ix 134–5

Meier, family of (in Luzern), vi 625

Meier, Jacob, of Basel, ii 334

—— Sebastian, Zwinglian Reformer, ii 327

Meikle, Andrew, and the threshing-machine, x 741

Meilhan, Senac de, viii 9

Meinders, Franz von, Brandenburg Privy Councillor, v 663

Meissen, Allies at, ix 518

—— Johannes von Maltitz, Bishop of, ii 238, 243

Méjean, Comte Étienne, sent to help the Viceroy of Italy, ix 395

Mekong river, exploration of, xii 131, 524, 796 sq.; 485; 536

Mekran, caravan route to, xii 793

Melanchthon, Philip, *Discourse*, i 574; at Wittenberg, ii 132; 162; 189; *Loci Communes*, 165, 233, 380; and Peasants' Rising, 193; 194, 212; attempts conciliation, 213; at Diet of Ratisbon, 240–4; 250, 265 sq.; French Reformers and, 285 sq.; 402, 698, 713; death of (1560), iii 140; influence of, on Elector Augustus of Saxony, 150; and Flacius, 162; 167; 179; and exorcism, 711; and monasticism, 741 sq.

Melander, Count Peter von Holzapfel, Hessian general, in Westphalia, iv 247; peace policy of, 380; 383; succeeds Gallas, 392 sq.

Melanesia, partition of, xii 667

Melas, Michael F. Benedict, Austrian general, viii 558, 659, 663; in Italy, ix 57 sq.; and Marengo, 62 sq.

Melâs, Paul, Greek leader in Macedonia, xii 426

Melbourne, founding of, xi 792; 795; industries of, xii 623; 624 sq.; University of, 627

—— William Lamb, 2nd Viscount, vii 391; x 570; and parliamentary reform, 603; 614; career and character of, 664 sq.; Ministry of, 664 sqq.; dismissal of, 666; second Ministry of, 668 sqq.; and Brougham, 668; 674; and Queen Victoria, 675; resumes office (1839), 678; resigns, 680; and the Queen's marriage, 681; and Trades Unions' demonstration, 682; xi 15; 20; 731; xii 734; 736

Melchthal, Arnold von, xi 261

Melcombe, George Bubb Dodington, Lord, vi 424 sq.; 427

Meldrum, Sir John, iv 314; at Newark, 321

Melegnano, battle at, xi 383

Melendez, Valdes, Spanish poet, viii 783

Melfort, John Drummond, Earl of, v 289; 308

Melgar, Fadrique Henriquez, 2nd Count of, hereditary Admiral of Castile (1520), i 374

—— Luis Henriquez de Cabrera, Count of (*later* Duke of Medina del Rio Seco), Admiral of Castile, v 35

Melgar, Juan Tomas Enriquez de Cabrera, Count of (Duke of Medina del Rio Seco), Admiral of Castile, v 35

Melikoff. *See* Loris-Melikoff

Melilla, Moorish attack on, vi 374; Arab raids near, xi 564

Méline, Félix-Jules, French statesman, xii 99; 119; and the Dreyfus case, 120, 126

—— Jules, French politician, xi 502

Mellifont, submission of Tyrone at, iii 609

Mellini, Celso, ii 16

Mello, Francisco de, Portuguese ambassador to England, v 105

Melo, Francisco de, Spanish general, at Rocroi, iv 594

Melouna pass, fighting in, xii 421

Melun, Edict of (1533), ii 285

—— Vicomte de, xi 120

Melville Island, xi 790; explorers at, xii 814

Melville, Andrew, ii 691; iii 550-1; 743; 757

—— Henry Dundas, 1st Viscount, vi 465 sq.; Treasurer of the Navy, 468; 581; Home Secretary, viii 297 sq.; First Lord of the Admiralty, ix 217; vote of censure on, 222; resignation of, 223; and Loughborough, 673; and Catholic emancipation, 678 sq.; Addington and, 682; resignation of, 684; and India, 710; 716-7, 724, 729; and Francisco Miranda, x 280

Melzi d'Eril, Francis, Duke of Lodi, viii 779; ix 84 sqq.; 190, 192; correspondence of, 393; Napoleon and, 394

Memel, Swedish possession, iv 186; Truce of Altmark and, 187; Treaty of Königsberg and, 428; v 630; dues of, 638, 641; vi 264; blockaded, 409; Frederick William and Alexander I at (1802), ix 256; 285; peace negotiations at (1807), 287; 297; 327; Edict of Emancipation signed at (1807), 330; and Milan Decree, 368

Memling, Hans, Flemish painter, i 433

Memmingen, meeting of leaders of peasants at (1525), ii 179 sq.; 205; *Tetrapolitana* and, 212; Zwinglian Congress at (1531), 216

Memminger, Christopher Gustavus, Confederate Secretary of Treasury, vii 604, 606 sq., 613 sq.

Memphis, Spanish claim to, vii 315; Polk's headquarters at, 458; captured by Federals (1862), 498 sq.; Hurlbut at, 510; 551

Menabrea, Federigo Luigi, Italian statesman, xi 542 sq.

Menam river, blockaded, xii 49; 534; French blockade of, 536; explored, 796 sqq.

Ménard, Philippe-Romain, French general, viii 639

Mendel, Gregor, Abbot of Brünn, experiments of, xii 766; 776 sq.

Mendeléeff, Dmitri Iwanowitsch, chemist, xii 770; 790

Mendeléyeff, Russian writer, xii 321

Mendizabal, Juan Alvarez, Spanish statesman, x 215; 234; Ministry of, 236 sq.; 326; 332; xi 555 sq.

Mendoza, Bernardino de (2nd son of Alonso Suarez de Mendoza, Count of Coruña), Spanish ambassador, in France, iii 42, 46, 49, 52; in England, 288-91; dismissed by Elizabeth, 290-1, 299, 301

—— Diego Hurtado de, royalist commander against Spanish rebels, i 377

—— Diego Hurtado de (son of 1st Marquis of Mondéjar), poet and diplomatist, manuscripts of, i 613; in Italy, ii 82 sqq., 88

—— Francisco Hurtado de (son of 3rd Marquis of Mondéjar), Admiral of Aragon, iii 634; taken prisoner (1600), 636

—— Francisco Xavier de, Portuguese statesman, vi 385

—— Inigo Hurtado de (Bishop of Burgos), Imperial ambassador to England (1528), ii 429

—— Pedro (Pero) Gonzalez Hurtado de, Cardinal Archbishop of Toledo (d. 1495), i 355; 651; (Bishop of Sigüenza), 658; iii 399

—— P. G. de, Bishop of Salamanca. *See* Salamanca

—— y Talavera. *See* Granada, Archbishop of

Menelik II, Emperor of Abyssinia, xii 240 sq.; 343

Menéndez y Pelayo, Marcelino, Spanish historian, xii 269; 842

Mengaud, A., Swiss patriot, viii 639

Mêng-tzu, opened to foreign trade, xii 506

Menin, Dutch garrison in, v 63; surrenders to Marlborough (1706), 416; the Barrier Treaties and, 457 sqq.; Marshal Saxe in, vi 240; French victory at (1794), viii 435

Meno, Prégent, Perkin Warbeck and, i 468

Menot, Michel (Franciscan preacher), ii 280

Menotti, Ciro, x 119-20; 126; 483

Menou, Baron Jacques-François de, French general, viii 389, 396 sq., 599, 603, 616 sqq.; ix 397; and Tuscany, 399; capitulates in Egypt, 438

Mensdorff-Pouilly, Count Alexander, General, Austrian Foreign Minister, xi 444; 448

Menshikoff, Alexander Danilovich, Russian statesman and general, v 525; 547; 549; and the succession to Catharine I, 551 sq.; administration of, 554; banishment and death of, 553; 594 sq.; 597 sqq.; vi 302

—— Alexander Sergeievich, Prince, xi 306; mission of, to Constantinople, 313 sq., 316; in the Crimea, 317, 319

—— Maria, v 552; 554

Mentana, Garibaldi defeated at, xi 485 sq.; 543

Menting, Ludwig, financier, i 507

Menzala, Lake of, XII 431
Menzel, Saxon official, VI 254
Menzies of Shian, VI 113
Menzini, Benedetto, Italian poet, V 69
Meppen, Charles Lewis at, IV 378
Mequinenza, captured by Suchet (1810), IX 457
Meran in Tyrol, peasants' parliament at, II 184
Mercantilism, Walpole and, VI 48 sqq.; and English Revolution of 1688, V 264; and Continental System, IX 361 sqq.; Adam Smith's criticism of, X 764 sqq. *See also* Trade
Mercantini, Luigi, Italian poet, XI 545
Mercator, Gerard, V 716
Mercedes, Queen of Alfonso XII of Spain, XII 264
Mercer, John, Maryland deputy at Constitutional Convention (1787), VII 246, 278
Merchant Adventurers, The English, I 429, 508
Mercier de Lostende, French ambassador at Madrid, XI 571
—— de la Rivière, F.-F.-J.-H., "Economist," VIII 23 sq.
Mercœur, Philippe-Emmanuel of Lorraine, Duke of, a leader of the *League*, III 661, 663, 666, 668; holds Nantes, 675
—— Laure Mancini, Duchess of, marriage of, IV 609, 612
—— Louis, Duke of. *See* Vendôme, Louis, Duke of
Mercy, Field-Marshal Franz von, commands Bavaro-Imperialist army, IV 388 sqq.; 597
—— Count Claude Florimond, Austrian field-marshal, campaign of 1709, V 425, VI 615, 623; killed, 154
Mercy-Argenteau, Count Florimond Claude von, Austrian diplomatist, and Marie-Antoinette, VI 644; VIII 189
—— Count Florimond Claude von (brother of above), Austrian general, VIII 558, 565 sq., 572
Méré, Jean Poltrot de, III 5
Mereczko, Peter the Great at, V 596
Meredith, George, XI 361; XII 13
Merezhkovsky, Dmitry S., Russian writer, XII 333
Meridian (Mississippi), Sheridan's expedition against, VII 520
Mérilhou, Joseph de, X 480
Mérimée, Prosper, X 101–2; XI 520 sq.
Mérindol, Conference of Protestant churches at (1560), II 297
Mérinville, C.-F. de M. de. *See* Chartres, Bishop of
Merlin (of Douai), Comte Philippe Antoine, VIII 249, 350, 378, 380 sq.; Minister of Justice, 490, 496, 503, 507 sq.; Director, 510, 669; criminal code of, 746
—— (of Thionville), Antoine-Christophe, VIII 249, 366, 415, 422

Merlot, Abbé, President of the Commune, VIII 733
Mermillod, Gaspard, *curé* of Geneva, XI 258
Mérode, Comte Felix de, X 535 sqq.
Merode, Saverio de, Monsignor, XI 389; 705
Merrimac, The, VII 455; and the *Monitor* (1862), 472, 496, 560 sqq.; abandoned, 474; design of, 560
Merritt, Wesley, American general, VII 679; Governor of Philippines, XII 530
Merry, Robert, English dramatist, X 699
—— British *chargé d'affaires* at Copenhagen (1800), IX 45
Mersch, Jean André van der, Belgian general, VIII 328
Merseburg, Frederick the Great at, VI 270; 271
Mers-el-Kebir, conquered by Spain (1505), I 365
Mersenne, Father Marin, IV 779
Mertz, Friedrich Wilhelm von, Austrian field-marshal, XI 184
Méru, Charles de Montmorency, Seigneur de, III 22, 25; 29; 32
Morv, XII 343; Russian occupation of, 477; 793
Merveldt, Maximilian, Count von, Austrian general, VIII 582, 584
Merven, Henry van der, defends Heidelberg, IV 82
Mery-sur-Seine, fighting at (1814), IX 549
Mesdag, Hendrik Willem, Dutch painter, XII 249
Meseritz, General Fermor at, VI 279
Meshcherski, Prince Peter, Procurator-General of the Synod, X 424
Meshed, caravan route to, XII 793
Mesnager, Nicolas, French diplomatist, V 420; 430; 432; 439
Mesonero Romanos, Ramón de, X 217; 219
Mesopotamia, annexed to Ottoman empire (1516), I 91; conquered by Selim I, III 117; Russian and British agents in, X 556; Turkey and, XII 4; 774
Mespelbrunn, Julius Echter von. *See* Würzburg
Messejana, Duke of Terceira in, X 333
Messenger of Europe, Russian journal, XII 298
Messenhauser, Wenzel, commander of the Viennese National Guard, XI 188 sq.
Messenia, insurrections in, XI 279
Messenius, Arnold, IV 576
Messina, straits of, Barbarossa in, III 109; fleet of Triple Alliance sails from, 135; returns to, 136; return of Doria's fleet to, 541; naval battle off (1675), V 162; VI 32 sq.; Spanish occupation of, 153; political feeling at, IX 381; rising at, XI 79 sq.; 85; capture of, 92
Meszáros, Lazar, General, Hungarian Minister of War, XI 204; 210; 213; at Widdin, 215

Metacam (Philip), Pokanchet chief, vii 27 sq.
Metaphysical Society, founded, xii 774
Metastasio, Pietro Bonaventura, xi 423
Metaxas, Greek party of, x 506
Metcalfe, Sir Charles Theophilus Metcalfe, 1st Lord, and Ranjit Singh, ix 732; in India, xi 729, 731; Governor of Canada, 759, 767
Metella, Cecilia, tomb of, iii 443-4
Metemma, Gordon relief expedition at, xii 442; 443; 805
Methodists, and Conventicle Act, v 336 sq.; the Wesleys and, Vol. vi, Chap. ii (2) *passim*
Methuen, John, ambassador extraordinary to Portugal, v 412
—— Sir Paul, English ambassador to Spain, v 378; 412
—— Paul Sanford Methuen, Lord, general, in South Africa, xii 642
—— Treaty (1703), v 412; vi 386 sq.; viii 284 sq.
Methven, Henry Stewart, Lord, marriage of, with Margaret Tudor, ii 454
Methwold, William, iv 733; 745
Metternich, Melanie, Princess, x 380; xi 154
Metternich-Winneburg, Clement W. N. L., Prince of, viii 429, 641; ix 242; 309-10, 316; policy of, 320; 341-3; and war with France, 344; peace influence of, 359; after Stadion's retirement, 360; policy of, 507; 521-2, 528, 542-3, 546, 555; proposes a congress at Vienna, 564; and Fouché, 573; signs Treaty of Chaumont, 577; at Congress of Vienna, 580 sqq.; 646 sqq.; and Napoleon's envoy, 618; and French frontier, 664; and Holy Alliance, 665; Oriental policy of, 668; 671; x 7; 9; and Holy Alliance, 10; 13; at Conference of Aix-la-Chapelle, 14 sqq.; 20; distrusts Russia, 21; repressive policy of, 22 sq.; and the revolts in Spain and Naples, 23-7; at Conference of Troppau, 27 sq.; influence of, over the Tsar, 34; and policy of Great Britain, 37; and intervention in Naples, 72, 113; Italian policy of, 105, 106, 120, 130, 483; and Count Confalonieri, 118; and Cardinal Consalvi, 135 sq.; 151; and the Sanfedists, 135; policy of, towards Papacy, 144 sq., 150; in Rome, 145; and ecclesiastical affairs in Germany, and Bavaria, 145-6; and Congress of Verona, 151; and French intervention in Papal States, 156; and Italian independence, 165; and Greek revolt, 176, 179, 182 sq., 187 sq., 193 sqq.; conference of, with Castlereagh, 184; and the independence of Greece, 188, 201, 203; and Spanish affairs, 35, 225, 230, 237; and German unity, 340; and the Diet, 345 sq., 347; and Prussian politics, 351 sq., 355; and Austrian conservatism, 356 sqq.; foreign policy of, 358; and France, *ib.*; and King Frederick I of

Würtemberg, 360; and Baden, 148 sq., 362; 363 sq.; dominant position of, 365; and murder of Kotzebue, *ib.*; at Teplitz Conference, 366; and Carlsbad meeting, *ib.*; and Conference at Vienna (1819), 367 sq.; height of prosperity of, 370; and Hambach demonstration, 375; and the principle of intervention, 376; and Hanoverian absolutism, 380; 382; and Dom Miguel, 321; and Polish revolution, 473; and French revolution of 1830, 481; Louis-Philippe and, 494; 505; and the French occupation of Ancona, 506; and Convention of Münchengrätz, 557; and the Eastern Question, 31 sqq., 563 sq., 572; and Palmerston, xi 17; 39; 41; 44; and Prussia, 48; 56; and Italy, 71; and Pius IX, 75, 77 sq.; fall of, 81; 143; 152; 153; resignation and flight of, 154; 233; and Bern, 236; and Switzerland, 244 sq., 249 sq.; 658; and Gregory XVI, 703; 708; xiii 829
Metz, occupied by the French (1552), ii 87, 144; siege of, by Charles V, 87, 273 sq.; bishopric of, ceded to France, iv 404; 602; *Parlement* of, v 4, viii 47, 745; and States General, 125; French army at (1792), 407, 409; xi 464; Bazaine in, 496; 580; Napoleon III at, 582; French army in (1870), 588 sqq.; German advance on, 599; capitulation of, 498, 603; 604; ceded by France, 612, xii 136
Metzenheim, Hans (Bogbinder), adviser of Christian II, ii 604
Metzler, George, leader of Peasants' Rising, ii 182, 187
Metzovo, and Greek frontier, xii 403
Meucci, Filippo, Italian song-writer, xi 545
Meudon, royalists at, iii 657
Meulan, besieged by Mayenne, iii 48
Meurs, siege of (1597), iii 629; recaptured by Maurice (1601), 636
Meurthe, arrests in, xi 138
Meuse river, campaign on, v 406 sq.; Charles of Lorraine at, vi 247; 248; and Holland, x 519; navigation of, 543 sq.; xi 589 sqq.; German army corps at, 594; Macmahon's march to, 595 sqq.
Mevissen, Gustav, German Liberal leader, xi 53
Mexico, races inhabiting, i 38 sq.; mineral wealth of, 40, 518; discovery of, 41 sqq.; 52 sq.; religion of, 61; Catholic Church in, 60 sq.; v 375; Spanish rule in, 681 sqq.; 688; Indian slavery in, 692; vi 183; and Napoleon III, 352; boundary of, vii 362; Republic of, 368; at war with United States (1846), 391, 394 sqq., 406; makes peace (1848), 397; California and, 402; land purchased from, 405, 426; the French in (1865), 535, 635; city of, American march on (1847), vii 396 sq.; occupied, *ib.*; administration in, x 246 sq., 248, 252; University of, 247; the Inquisition in, 253 sq.; languages in,

261; city of, Indian quarters in, 263, 268; the *consulado* of, and the mint, 274 sq.; revolutions in (1808-22), 302 sqq.; and Guatemala, 305; and Spain, 306; Spanish troops in, 307; independence of, recognised by United States and Great Britain (1822), 308 sq.; xi 447; Napoleon III and, 476 sq., 479, 481, 484; 554; European intervention in, 565 sq.; 683; xii 6; French intervention in, 21 sq.; and Japan, 544 sq.; 672; affairs in, 676 sq.; United States and, 685; 689 sq.; development of, 690; 692 sq.; foreign capital in, 694; 696; Panamerican Congress at, 700; 702; and Hague Court of Arbitration, 727. *See also* New Spain

Mexico, Gulf of, vi 350 sq.; xii 691

Meyer, Conrad Ferdinand, xi 261; 412
—— Eduard, German historian, xii 845 sq.
—— Gerold, ii 337
—— Hans, of Knonau, ii 313
—— Dr Martin, Chancellor of Mainz, i 688
—— Marx, Admiral, of Lübeck, ii 229, 614 sq.

Meyerskappel, battle at, xi 251

Mezaros de Szoboszló, Johann, Austrian field-marshal, viii 578 sq.

Mézentseff, General, Russian police official, xii 306

Mezières, French army corps at, xi 598; 600; 609

Miani, British victory at, xi 737
—— Girolamo, ii 648

Miaoulis, Andreas Vokos, Greek admiral, x 181; 189

Miari, Bailiff of the Order of St John, ix 604

Micara, Cardinal, xi 703

Michael Romanoff, Tsar of Muscovy, and Peace of Stolbova, iv 181; not represented at Münster or Osnabrück, 403; election of, v 502; 503; 506; 516 sq.
—— Wisniowiecki, King of Poland, election of, v 41; 350 sq.; 353; death of, 354; vi 198
—— Grand Duke of Russia (General, 1831), x 471; xii 433
—— Grand Duke of Russia (son of Nicholas I), Viceroy of Caucasus (1863), xi 633
—— III Obrenovich, Prince of Servia, xi 285; 634; 647 sq.; xii 412

Michalov, added to West Prussia, x 463

Michanowich, Charles XII at, v 598

Michaud, Joseph, historian, viii 515; x 89; xii 829

Michel de Bourges, French Republican lawyer, x 492; 499; xi 132; 134; 136

Michelangelo. *See* Buonarotti

Michelborne, Sir Edward, iv 730

Michelet, Jules, French historian, x 102; 516; xi 34; 36; 39; 509; 523 sq.; xii 830 sq.; 833; 838

Micheli, Vitalis, Doge of Venice (d. 1173), i 255

Michell, Abraham Ludwig, Prussian ambassador in London, vi 402
—— Sir Francis, iii 570-1

Michelsen, Chr., Norwegian statesman, xii 288

Michiel, Antonio, Venetian merchant, i 285
—— Giovanni, Venetian ambassador in England, ii 513, 529, 534, 536, 542, 547 sq.

Michieli, Joannes, Cardinal, nephew of Pius II, i 657

Michigan, abolition in, vii 388; enters the Union (1837), 421; population of, 695, 708
—— Lake, and the United States boundary, vii 307, 315

Michillimackinac, Jesuit mission-station at, vii 84

Michni Pass, under British control, xii 471

Mickievicz, Adam, Polish poet, x 432; 448; 459

Micronesia, partition of, xii 667

Micronius, Martin, Protestant refugee in England, ii 502

Middelburg, Sea Beggars and, iii 230, 239; William I of Orange at, 257; William III of Orange at, v 155; 756; capitulates to the British (1809), ix 358

Middlesex, Reform meetings in, vi 455
—— Earl of (Sir Lionel Cranfield), iii 567-8, 573, 577

Middleton, Admiral Sir Charles. *See* Barham, Lord
—— David, iv 741
—— John Middleton, 1st Earl of, v 281 sqq.
—— Thomas, iii 380

Midhat Pasha, xii 383; 385; fall of, 387; 416

Midland Association, The, iv 311; 314

Midleton, Alan Brodrick, 1st Viscount, vi 487
—— Alan Brodrick, 2nd Viscount, vi 487
—— William St John Fremantle Brodrick, 9th Viscount, Secretary for War, xii 53; 59

Midlothian, Gladstone in, xii 35 sqq.

Mieroslawski, Ludwig, Polish general, xi 46; in Sicily, 92; in Baden, 221; xii 294

Mietzel river, Russian army at, vi 281 sq.; 285

Mignet, François-Auguste-Marie, x 95; 96; writings of, 514, xi 524, xii 832 sq.

Miguel, Dom, usurping King of Portugal, x 235; 313; absolutist movement and, 316 sq.; withdraws to Vienna, 317; and the Portuguese regency, 320 sqq.; returns to Lisbon as Regent, 322; proclaimed King of Portugal, *ib.*; character of, 323; the Powers and, 324; popularity of, 324 sq., 327; 326; and siege of Oporto, 330, 335; and fall of Lisbon, 335; surrender and exile of, 336 sq.
—— Infante of Portugal, i 453

Mikhailoff, Alexander, Russian revolutionary, xii 306

Mikhailovsky, Russian philosophical writer, xii 302

Mikhelson, Russian commander, in Turkey, ix 485

Mikkelsen, Hans, favourite of Christian II, ii 604, 610

Milan, duchy of, i 105 sqq.; claim of Orleans to, 108, 232, 236, 287; embassy from, in Paris, *ib.*, 110; partition of, 120; occupied by French (1499), 121, 123, 237, 249, 308; and Treaty of Blois (1504), 127, 131; French driven from (1512), 138, 250; Swiss in, 139, 141; French in possession of (1516), 142; and Venice, 279 sqq.; seized by Charles V (1521), ii 44; siege of citadel of, 53; importance of, to Charles V, 62; revenues of, 64; given up by France (1559), 94; ambassadors murdered at, iii 105; disputed claims to, 116; 386, 465; granted to Spain (1546), 476, 687; Condé at, 689; objective of Duke of Savoy, 690; and Valtelline, Vol. iv, Chap. ii *passim*; 118; and Savoy, 123 sq.; Spinola in, 136; 145; French expedition against (1647), 601; in Spanish hands, 666; 672 sq.; 682 sq.; 687; and Spanish Succession, v 383 sq., 388 sqq., 398; 402; 407; 417; and Peace of Utrecht, 450; Convention of (1707), 415; vi 139; 151 sqq.; 159; assigned to Sardinia, 160; 161; 167; 201; evacuated by the Spaniards, 245; Don Philip at, 608; 617; duchy of, viii 554; Rights of Man in, 556 sq.; French in (1796), 570 sq., 574, 588 sq.; the Allies enter (1799), 656; Napoleon at (1800), ix 61, (1805), 87, 247, (1807), 367; Archbishopric of, offered to Caprara, 189; Austrian revenue from, 393; Eugene Beauharnais and, 395; Cathedral of, 396; Austrian government in, x 105; the *Gazette* of, 106; the *Anti-Eugeniani* in, 111; Berchet escapes from, 126; xi 75 sq.; rising in, 79; revolution in, 81; and Piedmont, 83, 85 sq.; 88 sq.; disturbances at, 152; Austrians in, 182; 243; 373; 374; under rule of Radetzky, 376 sq.; 383; xii 218 sq.; riots in, 220; 223; strike at, 225 sq.; progress of socialism at, 231; bank of, 235; 236

—— II Obrenovich, Prince of Servia, xi 285

—— IV, King of Servia, xi 634, 648; xii 385 sq.; 390; 407; abdication of, 411; death of, 412; 413

Milan, Dukes of:—
—— Filippo-Maria (Visconti), i 278 sqq.
—— Francesco I (Sforza), i 105 sq., 109
—— Francesco II (Sforza), i 486; ii 43, 45, 52 sq., 57, 60, 69, 232
—— Galeazzo-Maria (Sforza), i 106
—— Gian-Galeazzo (Sforza), i 106, 111; 113

Milan, Dukes of (*contd.*):—
—— Gian-Galeazzo (Visconti), i 108, 265 sq., 278; iii 385; and the Valtelline, iv 35
—— Ludovico *il Moro* (Sforza), i 106 sqq., 109, 115, 122, 156, 171 sqq., 177, 191, 228, 232; expelled from Milan, 236 sq., 238, 245; imprisoned in France, 308; and the Valtelline, iv 36
—— Massimiliano (Sforza), i 138, 142, 251, 486; ii 308; and the Valtelline, iv 36

Milan, Bona of Savoy, Duchess of, i 106
—— Christina of Denmark (niece of Charles V), Duchess of, ii 69 sq., 87
—— Isabella of Naples, Duchess of, i 106
—— St Carlo Borromeo, Cardinal Archbishop of, ii 341, 659, 674, 678, 681; iii 414, 445
—— Federigo Borromeo, Cardinal Archbishop of, iv 48
—— Giovanni Angelo Arcimboldo, Archbishop of, and Christian II, ii 606
—— Decree (1807), The, vii 331, 333; ix 368, 378

Milanese, The, vi 236; Don Philip's claims in, 239; 243; 245

Milano, Agesilao, attacks the King of Naples, xi 380

Milaslovski, Ivan, and the conspiracy against Peter the Great, v 522

Milazzo, battle at, xi 388

Miles, Nelson Appleton, American general, vii 681
—— William Augustus, diplomatist, viii 291, 303

Mileto, Garibaldi lands near, xi 534

Milhaud, French cavalry officer, at Waterloo, ix 636; 640

Militia, Ordinances of 1642, iv 300 sqq.; regulations of 1660, v 97; royal control of, 252; after the Revolution of 1688, *ib.*

Miliutin, Nicholas, Russian statesman, xi 613 sq.; 621; 629

Mill, James, and elementary education, ix 692; and Ricardo, x 772, 778; and Bentham's political theories, 597 sq.; 599; Macaulay and, 601; 612; *History of British India*, xii 836
—— John Stuart, iii 764; vi 814; x 600; 676; and Ricardo, 772, 774; and Malthus, 776; 778; and India, xi 329; and Ireland, 343 sq.; autobiography of, 362; xii 66; works of, excluded from Russia, 300; 731; and socialism, 759; *Subjection of Women*, 762

Millar, John, Professor of Law at Glasgow, viii 769

Millau, meeting of Protestants at, iii 25

Millborne, Jacob, executed, vii 45

Milledgeville, Sherman at, vii 527

Miller, Johann Martin, German author, x 387
—— John, Massachusetts clergyman, vii 144

Miller, Ralph Willett, captain of the *Theseus*, VIII 610

—— William, officer of marines, x 292 sq.; 295

Millerand, Alexandre, French statesman, XII 113; 121; and socialist movement, 124 sqq.; Minister of Commerce, 127 sq.

Millesimo, Austrians driven from (1796), VIII 566

Millet, Jean-François, French painter, XI 528

Millevoye, Charles-Hubert, French lyric poet, IX 132

Milliken's Bend (Mississippi), Sherman's camp at, VII 502 sqq.

"Millions," Spanish excise-tax, III 505

Millot, French general, in Annam, XII 526; 797

Mills, Roger Quarles, American politician, VII 660

—— Colonel, and Cromwell's title, IV 444

Mill Springs, Zollicoffer at, VII 462; Federal victory at (1862), 495

Milne, Walter, Scottish Protestant martyr, II 558; III 264

Milner, Alfred Milner, Viscount, XII 641

—— Dr John, Vicar Apostolic of the West of England, X 633

Milnes, Lieutenant-Governor of Canada, IX 741; 744

Miloradovich, Michael, General, Governor-General of St Petersburg, x 440 sq.

—— Russian general, and Russian retreat, IX 496 sqq.; 511; at Zeitz, 518

Milosh Obrenovich, Prince of Servia, IX 387; XI 284 sq.; 647

Miloslav, Prussian reverse at, XI 164

Miltitz, Karl von, opponent of Luther, II 134 sq., 168

Milton, John, III 752–3, 766; change of temper of towards Church and State, IV 280; 293; 363; religious toleration and, 543; 545; opposes Restoration, 556; 763 sq.; 766; Marvell and, 774; Spanish translations of, v 69; 81; 116; early poems of, 117; travels of, 118; prose works of, 119 sq.; later poems of, 120 sqq.; Dryden and, 125; 132; 253; 263; 271; political writings of, VI 795 sq., 803, 807, 813; 831; German controversy on, x 384; XI 351

Milyukóff, P. N., Russian politician, XII 315; 333; 348; and Union of Unions, 352 sq.; 355; and Zemstvo Liberals, 357; 360; and first Duma, 365; and Shipóff, 368; 372; and third Duma, 375; 377 sq.; at Mansion House, 380

Milyútin, Dmitry, Russian general, XII 295; 312

—— Nicholas, and Poland, XII 336

Min river, French fleet in, XII 131

Mina, San Jorge da, first Portuguese port on Guinea Coast, I 16

—— Francisco Espoz y, Spanish guerrilla chief, in Navarre, IX 469; pursued by

Clausel and Foy, 476; leads force into Mexico, x 303 sq.

Minadois, Germano, Italian Reformer, II 390

Minas Geraes, created a captaincy, v 678; gold in, VI 390; centre of Brazilian separatism, x 314 sq.

Minciaky, Russian envoy, x 188; 192

Mincio river, crossed by Prince Eugene, v 402; the Allies cross, VI 154; French boundary on, IX 63; Austrian retreat from, 68; French occupation of district of, 69; XI 85; war on, 86; 89

Mindelheim, Saxony and, VI 632

Mindello, Dom Pedro disembarks at, x 328, 333

Minden, see of, restored to Catholic occupancy, III 709; Tilly master of (1625), IV 93; bishopric of, 111 sq., 407 sq., v 642; French defeat at, VI 342

Minerve, The, conducted by Benjamin Constant, x 55

Minghetti, Marco, Italian statesman, x 168; XI 71; 81; 89; and *Consorteria* Ministry, 535; Ministry of, 536 sqq.; dismissed, 539; XII 214, 216

Mingrelia, suzerainty of Russia over, IX 385

Minho, insurrection at (1826), x 321; province of, occupied by Napier, 336

Minin, Fedor, Russian explorer, XII 795

—— Kuzma, Russian anti-Polish leader, v 502

Minkin, Nastasia, x 427

Minneapolis, Convention at (1892), VII 665

Minnesota, enters Union (1858), VII 438; negro suffrage in, 629; population of, 702, 708, 711

Mino da Fiesole, II 13

Minorca, surprised by Barbarossa, III 112; French occupy, v 411; captured by the Allies (1708), 426; ceded to Great Britain, 444; Sir George Byng at, VI 32; 57; 66; 68; 139 sqq.; 239; seized by Marshal Richelieu (1756), 337; 338; 342a (in Vol. XIII); restored to Spain (1763), 347; 365; 376; captured by French (1782), 379, VIII 92; VI 380 sq.; 403; 428; blockaded, 452; ceded to Spain (1783), 464; offered to Russia, VIII 278, 314; re-captured by British (1798), 630; restored to Spain (1801), IX 75; strategic importance of, 210

Miñoz, Sigismundo, Reformer, II 390

Minsk, district of, VI 669; captured by Russians (1812), IX 501; province of, x 428; Russian rule in, 459 sq.; martial law in, 469; labour organisation in, XII 331; 339

Minszka, Maria, consort of the Pretender Dmitri (the False Demetrius), v 497, 499, 548

Mint, The English. *See* Coinage

Minto, Gilbert Elliot, 1st Earl of, British ambassador at Vienna, VIII 660 sq.; 759;

and Whig party, IX 673; 685; in India, 731 sqq.; Governor-General, 754; policy towards Baluchistan, XI 731

Minto, Gilbert Elliot, 2nd Earl of, envoy to Italy, XI 17, 78

—— Gilbert J. M. K. Elliot, 4th Earl of, Viceroy of India, administration of, XII 496 sq.

Miollis, Sextius-Alexandre-François, French general, IX 58; 68; occupies Castle of Sant' Angelo, 195–6; and Pope Pius VII, 401

Miot, Jules-François, French Republican, XI 136; 139

Miquel, Johannes, Prussian Minister of Finance, XII 146; 157; 166

Miquelon, island of, VI 346; ceded to France, 428, 464; British capture of (1793), IX 749; XI 776

Mirabeau, André-B.-L. de Riquetti, Vicomte de, VIII 172

—— Honoré-Gabriel de Riquetti, Count, VI 721; 723; VIII 58, 61; and States General, 133, 149–54, 157 sq., 170; position of, in National Assembly, 174 sq., 178, 182, 186 sqq.; and Family Compact, 189, 290 sqq.; death of, 199; 694; on testation, 730; 755

—— Victor Riquetti, Marquis de, VIII 21 sqq., 27, 50, 71, 735

Mirabilia Romae, medieval guide-book, II 106, 128

Mirabocco, fort of, III 404

Miraflores, Marquis of, Spanish statesman, XI 554; 566

Miramón, Miguel, Mexican statesman, XI 565

Miran, son of Mír Jafar, VI 555; 559

Miranda, captured by Spaniards, VI 369

—— Francisco, Spanish-American general, serves in French revolutionary army, VIII 419, 421, 510; career of, X 280 sq.; and Caracas revolution, 288 sq.

—— Sancho Carranza de, attack on Erasmus by, II 400

Mirandola, siege of, by Julius II (1511), I 135, 248 sq.; under French protection, II 72, 78; Henry II of France and, 85 sq.; duchy of, V 451; granted to Duke Francis IV, IX 603

—— Pico della. *See* Pico della Mirandola

Mirari vos, encyclical of Gregory XVI, X 164

Mirepoix, Gaston-C.-F. de Lévis, Duc de, French ambassador in London, VI 333; 542

Mir Jafar, Nawáb of Bengal, VI 553 sqq.; Clive and, 557 sq.; deposed, 559; restoration of, 561; death of, *ib.*

—— Kasim, Nawáb of Bengal, VI 559 sq.; deposed, 561

Mirko, Prince, of Montenegro, XII 413

Miroménil, Armand-T. Hue de, Keeper of the Seals, VIII 82, 87; on Council of Finance, 96, 101; dismissed, 103

Miron, Henry III's physician, III 39

—— Swiss politician, IV 54

Mirror of a Sinful Soul, of Margaret of Navarre, II 354

Mirsky, Prince. *See* Svyatopolk-Mirsky

—— Russian revolutionary, XII 306

Mirtschea the Great, Prince of Wallachia, and the Turks, I 82

Mishchénko, Russian general, XII 376; 587; 589; 596

Mishmee hills, Thomas Cooper at, XII 796

Misiones, frontier dispute in, XII 676

Missiessy, Édouard-Thomas Burgues, Comte de, Admiral in command of Rochefort squadron, IX 219; sails for Antilles, 221; reaches Martinique, 221; recall of, 222; replaced by Allemand, 225; 240

Missionary Ridge, VII 511; fighting at (1863), 512 sq.

Mississippi, State of, Spanish claims in, VII 315; emigration to, 356; enters Union, 359, 413; and Tariff, 381; secedes from Union, 446; joins Confederacy, 453; in Civil War, 462, 522; emancipation in, 595, 626; new Constitution in, 632 sq.; becomes Democratic (1875), 642

—— river, VII 183; contraband trade on, 373; Spanish successes on, 377; Treaty of Paris and, 429; 462; exploration of, VII 85, 87, 89, 93, 108 sq., 119, 691; navigation of, 232, 303; trade of, 323 sqq.; British force at, 345; steamships on, 351, 360, 692; survey of, 364; in Civil War, 452, 458, 462, 470 sq.; operations on (1861), 491 sqq., (1862), 501, (1863), 502 sqq.; Confederates evacuate, 506, 522, 616; naval operations on, 558 sqq.; economic importance of, 691 sqq., 704, 711

—— Bubble, The, VIII 9

—— Company and scheme, VI 128; 131; 172 sqq.; 532

Missolonghi, defence of (1825–6), X 181, 190; Byron at, 712

Missouri, State of, enters Union (1821), VII 359, 413, 421; slavery in, 361 sq., 402; settlers from, in Kansas (1854–6), 430; and secession, 453; in Civil War, 458 sq., 462, 470; and emancipation, 584 sqq., 598; reaction in (1870), 639, 642; population of, 695; Department of, created, 491; Compromise (1820), 362, 386, 406, 418; repeal of, 427 sq., 435, 441, 444

—— river, exploration of, VII 326; trade on, 360

—— valley, immigration to, XII 610 sq.

Mitchel, John, Irish Nationalist, XI 13

Mitchell, Sir Andrew, ambassador to Prussia, VI 284; 321; 338; 401; 409

—— Sir Thomas Livingstone, Australian explorer, XI 792; 795

Mitchelstown, affray at, XII 85

Mitford, John Freeman, and Catholic Relief agitation, X 626

Mitford, William, *History of Greece*, XII 835 sq.

Mito, Prince of, XI 825; 838 sqq.; 847; 849; 852

Mitre, Bartolomé, Constitutional President of the Argentine Confederation, XII 683

Mitrowitz, Russian consul shot at, XII 425

Mittau, V 556; Articles of, 557; captured by Russians (1705), 594; Louis XVIII at, VIII 635, IX 40, 562

Mittel-Pöllnitz, Prussian retreat to (1806), IX 275

Mittermaier, Karl Joseph Anton, President of *Vorparlament*, XI 163 sq.

Mitylene, occupied by the Powers, XII 426

Mitzlaff, Colonel Joachim von, IV 98 sq.; in Moravia, 101; 228

Mizen Head, French fleet at, VIII 474

Mizon, African explorer, XII 130

Mlodetsky, Russian revolutionary, XII 309

Mniszech, Marina. *See* Minszka, Maria

Mobile, Spanish capture of, VI 377; French settlement at, VII 362; attack on, planned (1862), 500, (1864), 514, 552; submarines built at, 564 sq.; banks of, 618; the *Oreto* at, XII 20

—— Bay, battle of (1864), VII 522, 554 sqq.

Mobillier, Grelle de, visits Russian prisons, X 422

Mocenigo, Pietro, Doge of Venice, I 80, 279

Mocha, Dutch trade and, IV 712 sq.

Mockel, Swedish agent, at Benfeld, IV 381

Mocquard, Jean-François-Constant, French politician, XI 135; 387

Modder river, Lord Methuen crosses, XII 642

Modena, captured by Julius II (1510), I 135, 248; seized and kept by Ferrara (1531), II 56, 67, 219; the Reformation in, 386 sq.; favourably disposed to Henry IV, III 683; House of Savoy linked with, 686; Habsburg influence over, 689; and Ferdinand II, IV 211; rebellion of, 686 sq.; VI 153; 243; acquired by Maria Theresa, 246; 586; revolt in (1797), VIII 588; military school at, IX 86; prefect sent to, 394; duchy of, granted to Duke Francis IV, 603; Austrian influence in, X 105; under Francis IV, 107; King Victor Emmanuel I of Sardinia at, 116; conspiracy at (1830), 119–20, 126; 123; 155; XI 69 sq.; national movement in, 75; and union with Piedmont, 83, 386; 84; 88; 381; 468

—— Giovanni de Morone, Bishop of, II 33, 52; at Conference of Worms (1540), 240; at Modena, 366, 641; 398; imprisoned, 399; 645, 660; at Council of Trent, 661, 682; III 457

Modena, Dukes of:—

—— Alfonso IV (of Este), IV 620

—— Ercole (Hercules) III (of Este), VIII 554, 571, 583, 592

—— Ferdinand (of Habsburg), receives the Breisgau and Ortenau (1803), IX 94

Modena, Dukes of (*contd.*):—

—— Francis II (of Este), V 403

—— Francis III (of Este), VI 171; 237; 243; 249

—— Francis IV (of Habsburg), claims of, at Congress of Vienna, IX 603; restoration of, 621; X 107; and Menotti's revolutionary scheme, 119 sq.; and smuggling, 154

Modena, Charlotte - Aglae (of Orleans), Duchess of, wife of Francis III, VI 133

Modène, François-Charles de Raimond, Count of, French ambassador to Sweden, VI 765 sq.

Modernism, in Italy, papal attitude towards, XII 230

Modlin, surrender of fortress of (1831), X 473

Modon, Ibrahim Pasha lands at, X 190

Modrzewski, Polish Reformer, II 636

Modyford, Sir Thomas, Barbados and, IV 757

Moe, Jörgen, Norwegian writer, XI 701

Möckern, battle of (1813), IX 536-7

Möhler, Johann Adam, *Symbolik*, XII 847

Möllendorf, Richard J. Heinrich von, Prussian field-marshal, VIII 437, 441; in Poland, 535; 544; IX 277

Möller, Heinrich, of Zutphen, Reformer, II 160

Mörike, Eduard, German poet, X 406; XI 414; 420

Moero, Lake, Livingstone at, XII 809

Mörs, countship of, V 668; evacuated by French, VI 300

Möser, Justus, political economist and historian, VI 205; VIII 773; X 404

Mösskirch, engagement at (1800), IX 58

Moffa di Lisio, Guglielmo, X 114

Moffat, Robert, in Africa, XII 808

Moga, Johann, Hungarian general, XI 184; 189; 203

Mogador, bombarded by the French, XI 35

Moghul empire, Vol. VI, Chap. XV (1)

Mogileff. *See* Mohileff

Mohabat Khan, Moghul general, VI 517

Mohács, Hungarians defeated by Turks at (1526), I 96, 338, 345, II 61, 197, III 73, 105; battle of (1687), V 52, 367

Mohammad I, Ottoman Sultan, I 68, 278, 281

—— II, Ottoman Sultan, Constantinople taken by (1453), I 67; Servia attacked and conquered by, 68, 70; Venetian Treaty with, 69; Hungary and, *ib.*; Scanderbeg and, 70 sq.; Bosnia and Herzegovina taken by, 72 sq.; conquest of Greece by, 74 sq.; seizure of Trebizond by, 78; at war with Venice, 79; attacks Italy (1480), 81; wars of, in Roumania and Moldavia, 82 sq.; siege of Rhodes by, 84; death of, *ib.*; III 126; V 361; X 171

—— III, Ottoman Sultan, III 700

—— IV, Ottoman Sultan, V 36; 343; makes war on Poland, 353; and France, 355; and Austria, 359; 364; 367; 369

Mohammad V, Ottoman Sultan, xii 428
—— Sultan of Malacca, defeated by Albuquerque, i 31
—— Abu Jafar, Imam at Cairo (1516-7),
i 91
—— Aga of Dorkovo, xii 384
—— Ahmad (Mahdi, 1881), xii 40, 400
sqq., 447
—— Ali, Nawáb of the Carnatic (of
Arcot), 1750-95, vi 540; 544; affair of
the debts of, 576, ix 709, 721; death of,
724
Mohawk valley, defeat of St Leger in (1777),
vii 215; 356; migration up, 357
Mohawks, The. *See* Iroquois
Mohileff, Charles XII at, v 598; meeting
of Joseph II and Catharine at, viii 311;
captured by Davout, ix 492; archbishopric
of, x 424; province of, 459; xii 339;
strike in, 350
—— Stanislaus Siestrzeńcewicz, Archbishop of, x 141
Mohl, Robert von, xi 164; Prussian Minister
of Justice, 166
Mohmand tribe, xi 743; raids of, 488
Mohr, Maximilian, Rudolf von Planta and,
iv 46
—— schoolmaster at Wittenberg, ii 166
Mohrungen, engagement at (1807), ix 285
Moir, James, of Stonywood, Jacobite, vi
115
Moira, Francis Rawdon-Hastings, 2nd Earl
of, and Whig party, ix 690; in India,
732 sqq.
Mojaisk, Napoleon at (1812), ix 496; Cossacks threaten, 497; Napoleon's retreat
to, 499
Mola, fight at, xi 390
Moldau river, Austrians cross, vi 257; 258
Moldavia, and Turkish Wars, i 83 sq.;
Solyman's changes in, iii 117; and the
Turks, iv 188 sq., v 344; vi 307 sq.; 672;
674; Joseph II and, viii 324; Russian
designs on, ix 308, 485; ceded to Russia
(1808), 320; hospodars of, 386; invaded
by Ypsilanti (1821), x 30; and Treaty
of Bucharest, 169; revolt in (1821), 178
sq.; 188; occupied by Russia (1829),
444; Hungarian invasion of, xi 211; 281
sqq.; Napoleon III and, 306; Russian
occupation of (1853), 314, 316 sq., 401;
321; independence of, 323; union of,
with Wallachia, 633, 643 sq.; xii 392;
395; the Jewish question in, 397. *See
also* Danubian Principalities
—— Hospodar of (1711). *See* Cantemir
—— and Wallachia, Prince of. *See* Couza
Molé, Matthieu, appointment of, iv 615;
621
—— Comte Louis-Mathieu de, ix 145; x
54; and opposition to despotic measures,
81, 87; 478; Minister of Foreign Affairs,
497 sq.; conciliates Republicans and
Catholics, 500 sq.; 502; and Algeria, 504;
505; and occupation of Ancona, 506;

character of Ministry of, 507; coalition
against, 508 sq.; defeat of, 510; 511;
xi 33; 98; 130; 133
Molembo, slavery abolished at, xi 575
Molesworth, Sir William, x 655 sq.; and
Orange Lodges, 672; 675 sq.; xi 16; 764
sqq., 976
Molière, Jean-Baptiste Poquelin de, iii
548; v 65; 67 sq.; 128 sq.; xi 516
Molina, Luis, ecclesiastical theories of,
iii 757-8, 765
—— Count of, Spanish ambassador in
England, v 214
Molinés, Cardinal, arrested, vi 124
Molinet, Jean, French chronicler, i 417,
433, 447
Molinier, Auguste, French medievalist, xii
834
Molinists, The, viii 9, 12
Molino del Rey (Mexico), Scott's victory at
(1847), vii 396
Molinos, Michael de, and Quietism, v 88
Molins de Rey, Spanish defeat at (1808), ix
448
Molise, peasant movement in, xi 536
Molitor, Comte Gabriel-Jean-Joseph, French
marshal, ix 351; x 80; xi 119
Molla Khusrev, code of laws, "the Pearl,"
drawn up by, i 98
Mollelos, Viscount de, Portuguese general,
x 333 sqq.
Mollenbeck, Anabaptist, ii 226
Molleville, Bertrand de. *See* Bertrand de
Molleville
Mollien, Comte Nicolas-François, ix 117;
120, 363, 372, 380; x 83
Mollio, Giovanni, Italian Reformer, ii 390
Mollwitz, battle of, vi 230 sqq.
Moltke, Count Adam Gottlob von, Danish
statesman, vi 735; 740 sq.; dismissed, 743
—— Count Christian Frederick von,
Danish grand marshal, vi 749
—— Count Helmuth K. B. von, xi 406;
mission of, to Florence, 448; and Austro-
Prussian War, 452 sq.; 456; and army
reform, 579; plan of campaign of, 580;
conduct of Franco-German War by, 582
sqq.; xii 139
—— Count Karl, Danish statesman, xi
168; 694 sq.
Moluccas, The, spice trade of, ii 101, x 761;
Dutch trade with, iii 632, 638; Dutch
dominion in, iv 710, 733 sqq.; agreement of June 1619 and, 737 sq.; war in,
740; Dutch in, v 695 sq.; revolt in
(1672), 696
Molyneux, William, v 320; and Dublin
Philosophical Society, 740; *Case of Ireland*, vi 480, 494; 484 sq.; 491
Molza, Francesco Maria, ii 15; iii 459,
466
Mombasa, Da Gama at, i 25; railway at,
xii 662; 809; 812
Mombello, provisional treaty signed at
(1797), viii 588

Momein, caravan route to, xii 793; 796

Mommsen, Theodor, xii 828; 843 sq.; 850

Mompesson, Sir Giles, iii 570-2

Mon, Alejandro, Spanish Minister of Finance, xi 551 sq.; 559; 566

Monacacy river, battle at (1864), vii 531

Monaco, siege of (1507), i 129

Monaghan, Catholic demonstrations in, x 647 sq.

Monasteries, suppression of the, in England, ii 444, 448 sqq.; results of suppression, 467 sqq.; partial revival of, in Mary's reign, 543; suppression of, in the canton of Zurich, 321; reform of, in Spain, 400; spoliation of, in Norway, 618; Swedish, attacked by Gustavus Vasa, 625 sq. *See also* Religious Orders

Monastir, scheme of reform for, xii 425; 426

Monboddo, James Burnett, Lord, viii 769

Moncada, Hugo de, with Armada, iii 313

—— Ugo de, regent of Charles V, ii 53; death of, 58; 197

Moncalieri, proclamation of, xi 367

Moncey, Bon-Adrien Jeannot de, Duc de Conegliano, French marshal, viii 440, 442; ix 61; receives duchy of Conegliano, 111; occupies Biscay and Navarre, 430; suppresses riot in Madrid, 433, *and see* x 80; ix 435–6

Monciel, A.-M.-René Terrier de, French Minister of the Interior, viii 228, 231

Monck, Charles Stanley Monck, 4th Viscount, 1st Baron in United Kingdom, Governor-General of Canada, xi 768 sq.; 775

—— George, Duke of Albemarle. *See* Albemarle

Monckton, Robert, Lieutenant-general, vi 426

Monclar, J.-P.-F. de Ripert, Marquis de, viii 727

Moncontour, battle of, iii 13, 224

Moncorvo, captured by Spaniards, vi 369

Monde (Le), ou Traité de la Lumière, iv 779

Mondego Bay, British force lands in (1808), ix 439–40

Mondelheim, Marlborough at, v 409

Mondevergue, Marquis de, in Madagascar, v 703

Mondovi, University at, iii 412

—— Bishop of. *See* Laureo, Vincenzo

Mondragon, Christopher, Spanish commander in Netherlands, iii 234, 239, 242, 244, 519–20, 628

Monembasia (in the Morea), besieged and taken by Turks, ii 72, 74; surrenders to Venice (1690), v 365

Monganagh, lands of, iii 613

Monge, Gaspard, Comte de Péluse, viii 238; Minister of the Navy, 502; 595, 605 sq., 616, 674

Mongolia, Russian privileges in, xi 819; xii 792; Russian trade in, 796; 803 sq.

Moniteur, French official organ, ix 15; 31, 101, 103, 107, 130, 188, 192, 266; for May 12, 1811, 418; 570, 574, 580, 589

—— *Ottoman*, x 549

—— *Westphalien*, ix 412

Monitor and *Merrimac* in Hampton Roads (1862), vii 472, 496; 550, 560 sqq., 616

Monjuich, surrendered to French, iv 649; captured by the Allies (1705), v 416; prisoners tortured at, xii 268

Monkswell, Robert Porrett, Lord, xi 337; xii 29

Monkton, Robert, Lieutenant-general, vii 137, 139 sq.

Monmouth, James Scott, Duke of, v 101; 134; 207; 212; banished to Holland, 225; 226; and Green Ribbon Club, 229; exiled, 229; 230; invades England, 232; execution of, *ib.*; at Bothwell Bridge, 285 sq.; and Argyll's invasion of Scotland, 289; 306; 334; 654

—— Sir Robert Carey, 1st Earl of, iii 361

Monnard, Charles, historian, xi 261

Monnier, Jean-Charles, Comte, French general, at Marengo, ix 62

—— Madame, abduction of, by Mirabeau, viii 149

Monod, Gabriel, French historian, xii 120; 831; 834

Monopolies, under Elizabeth, iii 356 sq.; under James I, 569 sqq.; the Monopoly Act, 577

Monroe, James, vii 316, 320, 325; President of United States, 350, 367 sqq., 373; x 39; 309; xii 687

—— Doctrine, vii 369 sq., 671 sq.; xii 684 sq.; 687; development of, 688 sq.; 691; 693 sqq.; application of, 696; 700

Mons, taken by Count Lewis of Nassau (1572), iii 17, 230; besieged by Alva, 17–18; captured by Alva, 21; besieged by Don Frederick of Toledo, 231–2; surrendered, 233–4; taken by Duke of Anjou (1578), 249; besieged by French (1678), v 45, 164 sq.; captured by Louis XIV (1691), 59; recovered by Spain, 63; 422; captured by the Allies (1709), 425 sq.; Barrier Treaties and, 458; besieged by French (1746), vi 246; 339; occupied by French (1792), viii 417; defence of (1815), ix 623

Monsell, William. *See* Emly, Lord

Monson, George, member of Indian Council, vi 571 sq.

—— Colonel William, advance of, into Máliva, ix 727

Monstrelet, Enguerrand de, French chronicler, i 433; xii 830

Montagu, Charles, Earl of Halifax. *See* Halifax

—— Edward, Earl of Sandwich. *See* Sandwich

—— Sir Edward, Lord Chief Justice, ii 475, 518

Montagu, Sir Henry. *See* Manchester, Earl of
—— Lady Mary Wortley, vi 175
—— Ralph, English ambassador in Paris, v 223
Montague, Sir George, Admiral, viii 467, 470
—— Henry Pole, Lord, arrest and execution of, ii 449
—— Richard, case of, iv 259 sqq.; 268; Bishop of Chichester, 272
—— Walter, English agent to Savoy and Lorraine, seized by Richelieu, iv 132 sq.
Montaigne, Michel Eyquem de, influence of New World on, i 58; Americans and Europeans compared by, 59; 63, 577; ii 690, 711 sq.; iii 65, 69, 72; his criticism of Tasso, 473; 759; iv 777 sq.; influence of, on French literature, v 64 sqq.; viii 4, 32
Montalban, Juan Perez de, plays of, iv 662
Montalcino, defeat of Siennese at, ii 88; given to Tuscany (1559), 94; occupied by Cosimo de' Medici, iii 386
Montalembert, André de, Seigneur d'Essé, iii 262
—— Charles Forbes, Comte de, x 163; 164; and Liberal Catholics, 165; 500 sq.; xi 27; 34; Guizot and, 40; 114; 120; and the Pope, 121; 126; 128; Victor Hugo and, 131; and Napoleon III, 296, 469; 297; 371; 714; and Vatican Council, 721; xii 847
Montalivet, Jean-Pierre Bachasson, Comte de, French Minister of Interior (1809), ix 139
—— Marthe-Camille Bachasson, Comte de, French Minister of Interior (1830), x 480; 487; 489; 496; xii 110
Montalto, town of, sacked (1518), iii 425; bishopric created at, 438
—— Cardinal Alessandro di, iii 38
Montalvo, Garcia Ordoñez de, Spanish author, i 381
Montana, and currency question, vii 673; population of, 711
Montanaro, xi 86; battle of, 94
Montanelli, Giuseppe, Italian politician, xi 65; 69; 90 sq.; 377
Montargis, d'Andelot brings German reinforcements to, iii 4; force under Martinengo cut up at, 28; rising at, xi 137
Montarlot, Cugnet de, x 221; 223 sq.
Montauban, resists entry of Joyeuse, iii 20; Calvinists in, 676; besieged (1621), iv 127 sq.; revolt of, 130, 134 sq.; Provincial Assembly at, viii 91; conflict between Catholics and Protestants at (1790), 197
—— Charles-G.-M.-A.-A. Cousin-. *See* Palikao, Comte de
—— de, in Madagascar, v 703
Montbazon, Marie de Bretagne, Duchess of, iv 596; exile of, 617

Montbéliard (Mümpelgard), ceded to French (1634), iv 143; added to France (1814), ix 564, 576
Montberon, Gabriel de, iii 5
Montbrun, Charles Dupuy, Lord of, ii 297; captured and executed, iii 27
Montcalm, Gozon de Saint-Véran, Louis Joseph, Marquis de, vii 126 sqq., 134 sq., 137 sqq.
Montcassel, battle at (1677), v 162 sq.
Mont Cenis Pass, captured by Dumas, viii 438; French enter Piedmont by, ix 61; road over, 119; Tunnel, xi 371
Montchoisy, French general, ix 99
Monte, Giambattista del, nephew of Pope Julius III, ii 85 sq.
—— Giovanni Maria del, Cardinal. *See* Julius III, Pope
Montebello, fight at (1800), ix 62; battle of (1859), xi 383
Monte Carlo, Gapón at, xii 350
—— Caseros, Rosas defeated at, xii 682
Montecuculi, Count Raymond of, Imperialist commander, iv 393; 432; v 44; 341; defeats Rákóczy, 344; campaign of, against Turks, 345 sqq.; 353; death of, 360; 366; 369
Monte dei Nove, in Siena, ii 83
Monte di Pietà, the first established in Rome (1494), i 647
Montefeltro, Federigo of. *See* Urbino
—— Guidobaldo di, Duke of Urbino. *See* Urbino
Monteigne, George, Archbishop of York, iv 272
Monteil, African explorer, xii 129
Monte Legino, French success at, viii 565
Monteleone, Marquis of, mission of, to Versailles and London, vi 138
Montélimar, Duc d'Angoulême at (1815), ix 617
Montemar, General, in Italy, vi 153 sq.; 159; 165; 596
Montemolin, Carlos Luis, Count of (Carlos VI), x 243; xi 553; 564
Montemurlo, fight at, iii 387
Montenegro, resists Turks, i 74; Napoleon's designs on, ix 269; Turkey and, xi 277; 533; disturbances in, 636; xii 37; Italy and, 242; and Russia, 342; 381 sq.; at war with Turkey, 383, 385 sqq.; and Treaty of San Stefano, 392 sq.; and Treaty of Berlin, 396 sq., 399; and Albanians, 401 sq.; affairs in (1880–1910), 413 sq.; 427 sq.
—— Marquis di, Imperialist commander, iv 87
Montenotte, Austrian repulse at, viii 566, 576
Montereau, defeat of Allies at (1814), ix 549
Monterey (California), Convention at (1849), vii 402
—— (Mexico), captured by Taylor (1847), vii 396
Monterotondo, Garibaldi at, xi 542 sq.

Monte San Giovanni, siege of (1495), I 114
Montes Claros, battle of (1665), v 34, 105
Montespan, Françoise-Athénaïs, Marquise de, v 19 sq.; 23; 31
Montesquieu, Charles de Secondat, Baron de la Brède et de, IV 790; v 2; 275; VI 165; 167; and Law, 177; 589; 687; 811; VIII 1, 14, *Lettres Persanes,* 17; *L'Esprit des Lois,* 18; 19 sqq., 36, 137; 743 sq.; and Irish Union, IX 702; x 40; XI 524; XII 817; 819
Montesquiou, captain of Anjou's guard, III 12
Montesquiou-Fezensac, Anne-Pierre, Marquis de, commands Army of the South, VIII 437
—— François-Xavier-Marc-Antoine, Abbé de, member of French Provisional Government, IX 556; Minister of Interior, 565; advice of, 574; x 42 sq.; and the negotiations with the Papacy, 140
Monteverde, Juan Domingo, Spanish naval officer, x 288 sq.
Montevideo, founding of, VI 391; British failure at (1806), IX 753, x 281; held by Royalists, 285 sq.; lost (1814), *ib.,* 290; 300; Portuguese garrison expelled from, 316; siege of, XII 680 sqq.
Montez, Lola, XI 61; 145 sq.
Montezuma, v 380
Montfaucon, Bernard de, VI 589
Montferrat, given to Mantua (1559), II 54, 94, III 402; Savoy's designs on, 407–8, 411, 413; war in, IV 134 sqq.; seized by Savoy (1613), 626; French in, 642; Charles Emmanuel claims, 678; Nevers obtains, 680
—— Boniface, Marquis of, rights of, over Crete and Salonika, bought by Venice, I 255
—— Giovanni Giorgio Palaologus, Marquis of, death of, II 68
Montfort, Count of, III 401
Montgelas, Count Maximilian - Joseph Garnerin von, Bavarian Minister, VIII 776; reform of Church under, IX 201–2; 253; policy of, 582; 658; x 146; 343; policy of, 359
Mont Genèvre, Lesdiguières crosses, III 416
Montgomerie, Thomas George, Colonel, and Tibetan exploration, XII 798
Montgomery (Alabama), Convention at (1861), VII 447, 449, 471
—— Comte Gabriel de, kills Henry II of France, II 296; Huguenot commander, III 3; 9; 13 sq.; 19 sqq.; 23 sq.
—— George, Bishop of Derry, Raphoe and Clogher, III 611
—— Richard, American general, VII 170 sq.
Montgon, Charles-Alexandre de, Spanish envoy to France, VI 146
Montholon, Charles Tristan, Marquis de, at St Helena, IX 757
—— French envoy, and Treaty of Madrid, IV 54

Monthoux, envoy of Savoy, negotiates with Protestant Union, IV 17
Monti, Antonio Felice, Marquis de, French ambassador in Poland, VI 193 sq.; 196 sq.
—— Vincenzo, Italian poet, VI 830; *Bassvilliana,* VIII 778 sq.; XI 549
Montigny, Floris de Montmorency, Baron of, III 194 sq.; 205; 207; 217; 227; 251
Montijo, Count, Spanish diplomatist, VI 166
Montils-lèz-Tours, Charles VII's ordinance of, I 403, 449
Montlosier, François-Dominique de Reynaud, Comte de, VIII 8; x 90
Montluc (*or* Monluc), Blaise de, Marshal of France, defends Siena, II 88; III 14; 64 sq.
—— Jean de, Sieur de Balagny. *See* Balagny
—— Jean de. *See* Valence, Bishop of
Montmartre, Blücher at (1814), IX 553
Montmédy, given up by France (1559), II 93
Montmélian, fortified by Savoy, III 410; French capture of (1600), 418, 677
Montmollin, George de, Chancellor of Neuchâtel, 7 449
Montmorency, Anne de, Marshal and Constable of France, II 49, 71; invasion of Savoy by, 73; 92 sq.; influence and career of, 97 sqq.; 296; Triumvirate joined by, 300; 505; 517; captured at St Quentin, 547; III 4–6, 8; death of (1567), 9
—— Diana of Angoulème, Duchess of (wife of Duke Francis), III 46
—— Floris de, Baron of Montigny. *See* Montigny
—— Francis, Duke of, Marshal of France, III 15 sq., 22; sent to Bastille, 24; released, 28, 30, 46
—— Henry, Count of Damville, Marshal of France, Duke of, III 5 sqq.; Governor of Paris, 20 sqq.; 30; Duke of Montmorency, 41; Governor of Languedoc, 406 sq., 413 sqq.; *politique,* 661; 666
—— Henri II, Duc de, IV 126; seizes Ré and Oleron, 131; Gaston and, 139 sq.; death of, 140; 154 sq.; 609
—— Matthieu-J.-F. de Montmorency-Laval, Duc de, x 34 sq.; French Minister of Foreign Affairs, 74; and intervention in Spain, 79; dismissed from office, *ib.*; at Verona, 225
—— Philip de, Count van Hoorn. *See* Hoorn.
—— *See* Méru *and* Thoré (sons of Anne, Duke of)
Montmorin-Saint-Hérem, Comte Armand-Marc de, Foreign Secretary, VIII 104, 124, 132; dismissed, 163; returns to the Foreign Office, 188, 216; resigns, 216, 222; 288
Montmors, Claude de, friend of Calvin, II 351

Montobbio, Castle of, surrendered by the Fieschi to Genoa, II 82

Montojo, Spanish admiral, VII 679

Montpellier, besieged by Joyeuse, III 3; Calvinists in, 676; Peace of, signed (1622), IV 56, 58, 130; siege of (1622), 128; 134

Montpensier, Anne-Marie-Louise d'Orléans, *la Grande Mademoiselle*, IV 608; at Orleans, 616; battle of Saint-Antoine and, 617; V 650

—— Antoine-Marie-Philippe-Louis d'Orléans, Duc de, marriage of, XI 17, 33, 37 sq., 553 sqq.; 101; ordered to leave Spain, 569; 570

—— Charles, Count of. *See* Bourbon

—— Francis of Bourbon, Duke of, III 51 sq.

—— Henry of Bourbon, Duke of, III 674, 679

—— Louis I de Bourbon, Comte de, I 114, 116 sq.

—— Louis II de Bourbon, Duke of, III 11 sq.; 23; 25; 241

—— Marie de Bourbon, Duchesse de, IV 130

—— Marie-Louise-Fernande de Bourbon, Duchesse de, marriage of, XI 17, 33, 37 sq., 553 sq.; 557; and the Mexican throne, 565; ordered to leave Spain, 569

Montreal, trading-post at, VII 76 sq., 94; Amherst's expedition against (1759), 137, 139, 141 sqq.; Montgomery's expedition against (1775), 170; disaffection at, 337; Wilkinson's expedition against (1813), 341; British in, IX 747; X 687; 689; industries of, XII 612

Montrésor, Claude de Bourdeille, Comte de, one of *les Importants*, IV 596

Montreuil, besieged by the English (1544), II 78, 459

—— Jean de, agent of Mazarin in England, IV 338 sq.

Montrevel, Nicolas-Auguste de la Baume, Marquis de, Marshal of France, V 26

Montrond, surrendered to the Crown, IV 613; Condé at, 615; capitulation of (1652), 617

—— envoy of Napoleon, IX 618

Montrose, Jacobite rising at, VI 98; 102 sq.

—— James Graham, 1st Marquis and 5th Earl of, plot of, IV 316; victories of, 328, 330, at Kilsyth, 332; defeat of, at Philiphaugh, 337, 506; Charles I and, 333, 338, 339; at Glasgow, 500; 502 sq.; "Plotters" and, 505; taken prisoner, 509; 527

Monts, Pierre du Guast, Sieur de, Lieutenant of the King in New France, VII 71

Mont St Jean, Wellington at (1815), IX 631 sqq.

Montserrat, V 110; the English in, 687; captured by the French, VI 454; 464; cultivation of limes in, XII 654

Monza, King Humbert assassinated at, XII 223

Monzon, Cortes at (1563), III 488; Philip II at, 513 sq.; Treaty of (1626), IV 38, 57, 59 sqq., 88, 130, 675 sq.; Philip IV at, 643; in French hands, 653

Mookerheide, fight at (1514), III 239

Moon, Mountains of the, XII 812

Moor, The (Wolsey's palace in Hertfordshire), Treaties of (1525), II 425, 427

Móor, Hungarian defeat at, XI 203

Moor, Corneille de, printer of the *Spectateur Belge*, X 529

Moorcroft, William, horse-dealer and traveller, XII 798; 800 sq.

Moore, James, attacks St Augustine (Florida), VII 36 sq.

—— Sir John, General, at Göteborg, IX 322; sent to Spain, 440; commander in Portugal, 442; at Salamanca, 443 sqq.; campaign of Corunna, 445 sq.

—— Thomas, Governor of St Lucia, IX 750

—— Thomas, poet, lampoons of, on the Regent, IX 690; 706; X 669; 715

Moors of Spain. *See* Moriscos

Mora, José Joaquin de, X 210; secret mission of, to Italy, 212 sqq.

Morád, Prince, son of Shah Jehán, VI 519

Morales, Don Juan Ventura, Spanish *Intendant* at New Orleans, VII 325

Morand, Charles-Antoine-Louis-Alexis, Comte, French general, defeated at Lüneburg, IX 515

Morard de Galles, J. Bonaventure, French admiral, VIII 450, 465 sq.; and the English invasion, 473 sq.

Morat, siege of, by Charles the Bold (1476), I 391; battle of (1802), IX 100

Morata, Olympia, at Court of Ferrara, II 384, 387

Moratin, Nicolas Fernandez de, Spanish dramatic poet, V 69

Morato, Fulvio Peregrino, II 384

Moravia in the 15th century, I 329; ceded to Matthias Corvinus, 331; Diet of, 335; Estates of, III 721; ceded to Archduke Matthias, 726, 733; moderate policy of, IV 22; revolts, 26, 28, 64; Anhalt in, 65; Wallenstein in, 72; 74; reaction in, 75; 87; 101; effects of War in, 417, 421; VI 204; Prussian invasion of, 233 sqq.; 255; 277; Prussian army in, 279; 280; 286; 310; 339; Joseph II visits, 626; insurrection in, 628; 638; 706 sq.; Suvóroff in, IX 41; Napoleon in, 258; XI 171; and Hungary, 202; Austrian troops in, 448, 452; electoral parties in, XII 188; 195; 200 sq.

—— Jodocus, Margrave of, V 621 sq.

—— Procopius, Margrave of, V 621

Moravian community, at Herrnhut, V 762 sq. *See also* Pietism

Moray, Alexander Stewart, 5th Earl of, Scottish Secretary of State, V 290

Moray, James Stewart, 2nd Earl of, II 554, 558, 573, 581, 595; relations with Mary, III 263, 266–8; flies to England, 270 sqq., 275; Regent of Scotland, 276 sqq.; assassinated (1570), 282; 549

Morbegno, capital of *Squadre*, IV 35 sqq.; 41; Serbelloni at, 62

Mordaunt, Charles, Earl of Peterborough. *See* Peterborough

—— Sir John, supporter of Queen Mary, II 514

—— John, *afterwards* Baron and Viscount, Royalist conspirator, IV 447; 540

—— Sir John, English commander (d. 1780), VI 342*b* (in Vol. XIII)

Mordvinoff, Count Nicolas, Russian admiral, X 427; 441

More, Alexander, VI 798

—— Hannah, VIII 763

—— Henry, Cambridge Platonist, IV 791; V 750 sq.; 754

—— Sir Thomas, influence of New World on, I 56; *Utopia*, 56–8, 491, 626, 641, V 325; II 421, 432; becomes Chancellor, 436; resigns office, 438; Nun of Kent and, 441; arrest and imprisonment of, 441 sq.; trial and execution of, 443; character of, *ib.*

Morea, The, conquest of, by Turks (1462), I 75 sq., 285; Venetian conquests in, V 365, 371; VI 4; Turks in, 30; Venice and, 605 sq.; 675

Moreau, Jean Victor, French general, VIII 435; captures the Dutch fleet, 436; 497, 509, 511; in Italy (1799), 656 sq., 677 sq.; and Brumaire, 678, 680; IX 21–2; 29, 32, 57–8, 61, 64, 66–8, 137

—— de St Méry, Médéric-Louis-Élie, Administrator of Parma, etc. (1802), IX 398

Moreira, confessor of Joseph I of Portugal, VI 386

Morel, François, French Reformer, II 295, 302, 573

—— Frederic, editor of Philo, I 613, 617

—— Gilles, editor of Latin Fathers, I 618

Morellet, André, Abbé, reports on French India Company, VI 549 sq.; VIII 727, 755

Morelli, Michele, and Neapolitan insurrection, X 112

Morelly, *Code de la Nature*, VIII 16, 32 sq.; 26

Morelos, José Manuel, Mexican leader, X 303 sq.

Moreman, English divine, imprisoned, II 501

Moreno, Garcia, President of Ecuador, XII 673

—— Don Juan, Spanish vice-admiral, IX 54

Moreto, Augustin, plays of, IV 662

Moreton, William, Bishop of Kildare, V 320

Morette, ambassador of Savoy, III 274

Morgan, Sir Charles, Colonel, IV 99; defeats Spanish fleet off Tertolen, 695; 696

Morgan, Daniel, American general, VII 215, 227

—— Edwin Dennison, U.S. Senator from New York, VII 599

—— Henry, Bishop of St David's, II 531

—— Sir Henry, buccaneer, V 691; X 272

—— Jacques de, discoveries of, at Susa, XII 846

—— Thomas, adherent of Mary, Queen of Scots, III 291

—— William, New York bricklayer, VII 379

Morgarten, battle of (1315), II 305; French repulse at (1798), VIII 640

Morges de Roux, P.-F. de Sales-Déagut, Comte de, VIII 116

Morgue, Austrian general, IX 62

Morier, James, travels of, in Persia, XII 800

Morigia, founder of the Barnabites, II 648

Morillo, Pablo, Spanish commander, X 227 sq.; in South America, 290 sqq.; returns to Europe, 294; 306

Moriones, Domingo, Spanish general, XII 260

Moriscos, in Spain, persecution of, II 99; III 105; revolt of, 131; deputation to Constantinople (1569), 132, 493–4, 496; Valentian, 542; expelled from Aragon, Andalusia, Castile, etc., 543–4, 682; expelled from Spain, V 376

Morison, Robert, botanist, V 734

Morisson, Charles-F.-G., French advocate, VIII 255

Moritz, Karl Philipp, *Anton Reiser*, X 388; 399

Morlaix, burnt by the English (1522), II 420

Morley, George, Bishop of Winchester, V 334 sq.

—— Colonel Herbert, IV 545, 547

—— of Blackburn, John Morley, Viscount, Secretary for Ireland, XII 43 sq.; 46; 49; 87; Secretary for India, 496 sq.

Mormons, The, VII 402 sq., 738

Mornay, Philippe de, Seigneur du Plessis-Marly, III 22; leader of stricter Huguenots at Béarnese Court, 38, 46, 52, 62, 670, 681; probable author of *Vindiciæ contra Tyrannos*, 760 sqq.

Mornington, R. C. Wellesley, Earl of. *See* Wellesley, Marquis of

Morny, Charles-Louis-Joseph, Duc de, XI 131; 134 sq.; Minister of Interior, 136; 137 sq.; President of Chamber, 294; 297; 299; 327; supports Napoleon III, 471; 472; 482

Moro, Domenico, X 122

Morocco, factories in, I 496; Florentine trade with, 507; Portuguese invasion of, III 499; Treaty of Holland with (1609), 645; Ripperdá in, VI 143; XI 16; French policy in, 35; Spanish War in, 564; 565 sq.; XII 3; 9; 55; 129; later French policy in, 132 sq.; Germany and, 171 sq.; 266;

misgovernment in, 456; 659; the Powers and, 660; 664; shipwrecked captives in, 806; 808; 811

Morone, Cardinal Giovanni de. *See* Modena, Bishop of

—— Girolamo, II 23; conspiracy of, 52

Morosini, Francesco, Venetian general, v 348; 365

—— Jean-François, Cardinal, III 44, 46, 449, 452

—— Michele, Doge of Venice, I 269

Morozoff, Boris, and Tsar Alexis, v 517

—— Russian merchant, XII 346

Morpeth, Lord. *See* Carlisle, Earl of

Morrill, Justin Smith, Republican politician, VII 606

Morris, Gouverneur, Pennsylvanian deputy at Constitutional Convention, Vol. VII, Chap. VIII *passim*; American Minister at Paris, 319, 328; VIII 34

—— Thomas A., Federal general, VII 457

—— William, poet, XI 357

Morrison, Robert, missionary, XI 812

Morse, Nicolas, Governor of Madras, VI 536

—— Samuel Finley Breese, VII 415

Mortara, Agricultural Congress at, XI 75

Mortemart, Casimir-Louis-V. de Rochechouart, Duc de, x 484

Mortensen, Klaus, Danish Reformer, II 610

Mortenssön, Jens, II 618

Mortier, Édouard-A.-C.-Joseph, Duc de Trevise, Marshal of France, VIII 661; receives Treviso, IX 111; defeated by Kutusoff, 257; at Vienna, 258; at Mainz, 274; ordered to march on Cassel, 278; takes Hamburg, 282; besieges Kolberg, 288; at Friedland, 290; corps of, 441; 453, 463; left in Moscow, 498; guards Lindenau, 537; at Bar-sur-Aube, 545; defends Paris, 553; in office under Louis-Philippe, x 494

Morton, James Douglas, 4th Earl of, Regent of Scotland, III 271, 279, 285-6; executed (1581), 287, 549-50

—— John, Cardinal, I 477

—— Oliver Perry, Governor of Indiana, VII 624

—— Thomas, Bishop of Durham, v 328

—— Thomas, squatter at Horne Bay, VII 15 sq.

—— William Thomas Green, first employs ether, XII 779

Morveau, Guyton de. *See* Guyton-Morveau

Morville, Charles-Jean-Baptiste Fleurian, Count of, French Minister for Foreign Affairs, VI 146

Morvilliers, J. de, Bishop of Orleans. *See* Orleans

Morwen, Dr John, President of Corpus Christi College, Oxford, imprisoned, II 501

Moryson, Fynes, III 696

Moscherosch, Johann Michael, IV 425

Moscow, origin and growth of, v 477 sqq.; 480 sq.; 483; Patriarchate of, 484, 506; 487; and *Oprichnina*, 490; 492; burnt (1571), 493; 499; besieged (1606), 500 sq.; Poles driven out of, 502; Polish attack on (1618), 504; 508; foreigners in, 511, 513, 517; rising in, 515; 516; education in, 529; improvements in, 530 sq.; 534; Catharine I crowned at, 548; Peter II crowned at, 554; 556; 587; the Academy of Sciences at, 741; Tsarina Elizabeth at, VI 311 sq.; 681; Legislative Commission at, 687; 688; 695; 699; coronation of Tsar at (1796), IX 36; Rostopchin at, 40; campaign of, 380, 396; march of Grand Army on (1812), 489 sqq.; French entry into, 496, 506; evacuation of, 498; military administration of, x 420; secret societies in, 433; Constantine I declared Tsar at, 440; mutiny in, 441; Nicholas declared at, 442; XI 266; serfs at, 267; 270; 615; 618; local government in, 621; 625; Pan-slavist Congress at, 634, XII 304; 298; 301; revolutionary spirit in, 303, 305 sq., 308; strike in, 319; 320; 325; improvements in, 327; 331; the *Besyeda* club at, 333; 346; 348; 350; 353; congresses in, 354 sq., 358; Zemstvo Congress at, 362; rising at, 362 sq.; 365; 375 sq.; Richard Chancellor in, 793

—— Nikon, Patriarch of, v 503; 506 sq.; ecclesiastical reforms by, 508 sq.; 517 sq.

—— Philaret (I) (Theodore Romanoff), Patriarch of, v 497; 500; power of, 502 sq., 506; 516

—— Philaret (II) Patriarch of (1821), x 423; 437

Moscow, Slavophil journal, XII 298

—— *Gazette,* XI 625 sq.; XII 359

Moselle river, XI 580; the French retire behind, 588; 589; 592

Moser, Johann Jacob, statesman, historian, and pietist, v 762

Mosheim, Johann Lorenz von, German historian, v 760; XII 817

Moshesh, Basuto chief, XI 783; 787

Mosquito Coast, and the Clayton-Bulwer Treaty, XII 686

"Mosquito fleet," The, VII 679

Mosquito Indians, Great Britain and, XII 685

Mossel Bay, Da Gama at, I 25

Mossorin, Hungarian reverse at, XI 211

Mosto, Ca da, Venetian captain, discovers Cape Verde Is., I 15

Mostovski, Count Thaddaeus, Russian Minister of Home Affairs, x 449

Motecuhzoma, ruler of Mexico, I 41 sq.

Motien Pass, Japanese troops in, XII 587 sq.

Motley, John Lothrop, American historian, VII 745; XII 842

Motz, F. C. A. von, Prussian Minister of Finance, x 372 sqq.; **378**

Moucheron, Balthasar de, and North-West passage, III 631–3

Moulai-Hafid, defeats Abd-el-Aziz, XII 133

Moulaya valley, French occupation of, XII 133

Moulins, Jean-F.-Auguste, Director, VIII 669 sq., 675, 679 sq.

Moulins-sur-Allier, Assembly at (1566), III 8; French opposing armies at, 29; Montmorency at, 30

Mounet, General, IX 358

Mounier, Baron Claude-Édouard-Philippe, X 52; created a peer, 58; chief of the Police, 63

—— Jean-Joseph, French politician, VIII 1, 113, 116; and reform, 122, 129; and States General, 149, 152, 155; and Right Centre, 173; 178, 180, 182 sq.; retires to Geneva, 185

—— French general, at Naples, VIII 653

Mountcashell, Justin MacCarthy, Viscount, V 312

Mountjoy, Charles Blount, 8th Baron, *afterwards* Earl of Devonshire, III 323; 533; Lord Deputy of Ireland, 608–9

—— William Stewart, 1st Viscount, V 309

Mount Lyell, copper discovered at, II 619

—— Morgan, gold discovered at, XII 619

Mountmorres, William Browne de Montmorency, 5th Viscount, XII 38

Moura, Don Cristobal de, III 499, 514, 526, 529

Mousa, Kaimakam, Pasha, Janissaries helped by, IX 388

Mousehole, in Cornwall, burned by Spaniards, III 321

Mousinho da Silveira, Portuguese statesman, in the Azores, X 327; reforms by, 337 sq.

Moustier, Léonel, Marquis de, French ambassador at Berlin, XI 403; Foreign Minister, 483

Mouvans, Antoine de, Huguenot leader, II 297; III 11

Mouy, Huguenot leader, murdered in Niort, III 14; 16, 19

—— Madame de, III 16

Mowat, Sir Oliver, Canadian politician, XI 769

Moy Hall, Prince Charles at, VI 116

Mozaffar Jang, ruler of the Deccan, VI 539 sq.

Mozambique, Da Gama at, I 25; Anglo-Dutch expedition to, IV 738; XI 574; European settlement at, 575; 778; XII 3; 640; Portuguese in, 657, 660; 663

Mstislavl, district of, VI 669

Mstislavski, Prince Ivan, V 491; 496 sqq.

Muata Yánvo, embassy to, XII 808; 809

"Mud March," Burnside's (1863), VII 484

Mudki, Sikh force at, XI 739

Mücheln, Soubise at, VI 270 sq.

Müffling, Frederick Ferdinand Karl, Baron von, illness of, IX 551

Mühlbacher, Engelbert, German historian, XII 829

Mühlberg, victory of Charles V at, II 81, 261, III 120; effect of, on French policy, II 492

Mühlhausen (Elsass), annexed to France (1798), VIII 597, 640

—— (Thuringia), Münzer and Pfeiffer in, II 186; surrendered (1525), 189; Catholic Princes at, IV 32, 110

Mülheim, Protestant settlement at, IV 11

Mülinen, Grisons commander, IV 50 sq.

Müllenhoff, Carl V., German philologist, XII 823

Müller, Adam, X 357; 363; and Prussian tariff reform, 373; conversion of, to Rome, 380; XII 826

—— Hans, of Bulgenbach, leader in the Peasants' Rising, II 178 sq., 182, 190

—— Johann. *See* Regiomontanus

—— Johannes von, Swiss historian, VI 625; VIII 781; IX 335; 425; completes *History of Swiss Confederation*, 427; XI 261; XII 817; 843

—— Otfried, German scholar, XII 821; 824; 844

Müllern, Chancellor of Sweden, VI 34

Münch-Bellinghausen, Count Joachim von, President of Federal Diet, X 370

Münchengrätz, Daun at, VI 291; Convention of (1833), X 376, 546, 557, 563, 565; Austrian repulse at, XI 453

Münchhausen, Baron Gerlach Adolph von, Hanoverian statesman, VI 4

Münnich, Burkhard Christoph von, Russian commander-in-chief, VI 196 sq.; 302 sqq.; 309; arrested and banished, 311 sqq.; 322

Münsingen, political meeting at, XI 240

Münster, Anabaptist movement at (1535), II 103, 222, 224 sqq., III 740; siege and capture of (1535), II 227; bishopric of, III 705; Ernest of Bavaria elected Prince Bishop of, 709; Christian of Halberstadt at, IV 79, 86; Peace conference and Treaty of (1648), 146, 398 sqq., 433, 598, 659, 715 sq., 723 sq., 744, 787, V 52, 166, 675; war of, with United Provinces, 157 sq.; 161; Treaty of, and the Scheldt, VI 641 sqq., VIII 281; Prussian acquisitions in (1802), IX 78; bishopric of, 93; Prussian portions of, 410

—— Bishops of:—

—— Christoph Bernard von Galen, IV 426; *Rheinbund* signed by, 431; V 37; and Charles II of England, 109, 111; invades United Provinces, 109, 150 sq., 182; 187; 569; and Sweden, 571; and Great Elector, 649, 651

—— Ernest of Bavaria, III 709

—— Franz von Waldeck, II 220, 224 sq.

Münster, Ernst F. H., Count von, Hanoverian statesman, at the Congress of Vienna, IX 587; 609 sqq., 647 sqq.; X 374

—— Sebastian, the *Biblia Hebraica* of, II 355; V 493

Münzer, Thomas, Anabaptist, II 166 sq., 177; Peasants' Rising and, 182, 186–9; 323; III 739

Mürzsteg, programme of, XII 211, 426

Mufti, in Ottoman State under Mohammad II, I 101; under Solyman the Magnificent, III 127 sq.

Muggleton, Lodowick, V 330

"Mugwumps," in Presidential election of 1884, VII 653

Muir, Thomas, advocate, VIII 770

—— Sir William, and Sher Ali, XII 466

Mukden, railway at, XII 344; 354; Russian troops in, 587; 591; Russians retire on, 592; 597; battle of, 598; 600

Mukhtar, explorers at, XII 808

Muktija Effendi, XII 400

Mulder, Gerrit-Jan, and Dutch bishoprics, XI 665

Muldraugh's Hill, Sherman occupies (1861), VII 463

Muley Hassan, Tunis taken from, III 110; reinstated in Tunis, 111

Mulgrave, Lord. *See* Normanby

Muller, Baron Jacques-Léonard, commands the Western Army of the Pyrenees, VIII 440

Mullingar, Ginkel at, V 317

Mulraj, Governor of Multan, XI 740

Multan, rebellion at, XI 740 sq.

"Multatuli." *See* Dekker

Multeka-ul-ubhar (Turkish code of laws), I 98

Mun, Adrien-Albert-Marie, Comte de, XII 94; 115; 119

—— Thomas, IV 733; in the East, 745

Munch, Andreas, Norwegian poet, XI 701

—— Peter Andreas, Norwegian historian, XI 701

Mundinus, physician, V 724

Munglem, State of, XII 508

Munich, Bavarian Diet at (1556), III 159; Jesuits at, 161; Catholic Union formed at (1609), 728; meeting of Catholic League at, 732; IV 210; Gustavus Adolphus at, 215; capitulates, VI 233; 238; 647; Moreau advances on, VIII 497; Court of, IX 202; Bernadotte marches on (1805), 254; wedding of Eugene Beauharnais at, 265; Treaty of (1816), 658; Lamennais at, X 164; Görres recalled to University of, 371; improvements in, by Ludwig I, 372; XI 61; revolutionary movement in, 145 sq.; 712 sq.; Old Catholic Congress at, XII 148; 847

Munk, Christina, marriage with Christian IV, IV 573 sq.

Munkács, V 366; surrenders to Austria (1687), 367; surrenders to the Russians (1849), XI 213

Muñoz y Sánchez, Agustín Fernando. *See* Riánzares, Duke of

—— Torrero, Diego, X 219

Munro, Sir George, at Kirkby Lonsdale, IV 350

Munro, Sir Hector, General, VI 454; 561 sq.; 576

—— Robert, in Holstein, IV 102; 107; at Carrickfergus, 524; 527; defeated by Owen O'Neill, 530; 531

—— Colonel, at Fort William Henry, VII 129 sq.

Munster, religious condition of, III 593; Plantation of, 599–601; and rebellion of 1641–2, IV 523 sqq.; 526; Inchiquin and Presidency of, 528; 531; 533 sq.; VI 490; agrarian crime in, 504; and Irish rebellion, IX 702

Murad I, Ottoman Sultan (1375), I 67, 99, 258; XII 383

—— II, Ottoman Sultan (1421–51), I 68, 70, 74

—— III, Ottoman Sultan, III 139, 170

—— IV, Ottoman Sultan, IV 211

—— V, Ottoman Sultan, XII 383; 385

—— Mameluke Bey, VIII 600 sqq., 607, 614

Murád, Prince, son of Emperor Akbar, VI 513

Murano, school of painting of, I 284

Murat, Caroline Maria (*née* Bonaparte), IX 267; 406

—— Joachim, King of Naples, Marshal of France, VIII 396, 564, 603, 611, 615 sq.; and Brumaire, 677, 679, 686; IX 31; 62–8, 87, 110; receives Cleves and Berg, 111; Napoleon's letters to, 196; commander of French cavalry, 252; crosses the Rhine, 253; joins Ney at Stuttgart, *ib.*; pursues Austrian army, 255; 257; joins Napoleon, 258; at Austerlitz, 260–1; receives the grand duchy of Berg, 267; at Diet of Rhenish Confederation, 268; claims Essen, Werden, and Elten, 272; at Jena, 274 sqq.; at Weimar, 276; at Zehdenick, 279–80; enters Warsaw, 284; advances on Königsberg, 290; succeeds Joseph Bonaparte in Naples, 381; and Queen Maria Caroline of Naples, 382; in Russia, 384; imprisons Pope, 401–2; prefers throne of Naples to that of Portugal, 406–7; and the grand duchy of Berg, 409 sq.; at Burgos, 430; at Madrid, 431 sqq.; returns to France, 436; at Paris, 446; and Russian campaign, 488 sqq.; at Posen, 511–2; 533; at Leipzig, 534 sqq.; and General Excelmans, 571; in Italy, 598; 603–4; defeat of, 621; escapes to Toulon, 622; declaration of war against, 648; X 111; and idea of an Italian kingdom, 165

—— Napoleon-Lucien-Charles, Prince, XI 119

Muratori, Ludovico Antonio, historian, VI 589; 599; XI 706; XII 816

Murav1éff, Michael, and the emancipation of the serfs, XI 614 sq.; in Lithuania, 629

—— Nicolai, Governor-General of Eastern Siberia, XI 272 sq.; XII 344

—— Nikita, Russian officer, X 432

Muraviéff, Count, mission of, to the Porte (1832), x 551 sq.
—— Count, Russian Foreign Minister (1898), xii 341
—— Lieutenant, Russian explorer, xii 795
Muraviéff-Apostol, Hippolytus, x 442
—— Matthew, x 442
—— Sergius, Russian lieutenant-colonel, x 442 sq.; 454
Murchison river, gold discovered on, xii 619
Murcia, lost by the Allies, v 419; retreat of Spanish troops to (1809), ix 456 sq.; struggle in (1811–2), 470; anarchy in, xii 261
Murciélago, El (The Bat), Spanish journal, xi 559 sq.
Muret, Marc-Antoine (Muretus), iii 55, 69
Murfreesborough, battle of (1862), vii 507 sq.
Murillo, Bartolomeo Esteban, art of, iv 664
—— Juan Bravo. *See* Bravo Murillo
Murinais-d'Auberjon, A.-V.-Augustin, Comte de, French general, viii 512
Murner, Thomas, Franciscan preacher, i 675; ii 159 sq., 162, 168, 174 sq., 331; the *Heretics' Calendar*, 334
Múromtseff, Russian politician, xii 327; 356 sq.; President of Duma, 366 sq.
Murphy, Father John, and Irish rebellion, ix 701
Murray river, exploration of, xi 792, 795
—— Lord George, Jacobite general, vi 112 sqq.
—— James, General, Governor of Minorca, vi 379; 452; at capture of Quebec, vii 137, 141 sqq.; Governor of Canada, ix 741
—— John, and *Quarterly Review*, ix 687
—— Sir John, General, beats off Suchet, ix 479; sails for Catalonia, *ib.*; and the war with Holkar, 727
—— Sir John, of Broughton, vi 109; 111; 114
—— Robert, and a national bank, v 266
—— William. *See* Mansfield, 1st Earl of
—— Admiral, expedition of, to Chili, ix 753
—— de Melgum, Count Joseph Jacob, Austrian commander, Governor of the Austrian Netherlands, viii 319 sq.
Murri, Romolo, and *Cultura Sociale*, xii 230
Murshidábád, treasury of, vi 555, 558, 568, 582; Court of Appeal at, ix 711
Murviedro, xii 257; Don Alfonso proclaimed at, 262
Murzuk, explorers at, xii 806 sqq., 811
Musaffar-ed-dín. *See* Muzaffar-ed-dín
Muscat, held by Portugal, iv 744
Muscovy, jealous of annexations of Poland, iii 82; Stephen Báthory in, 101; Báthory's designs upon, 103. *See also* Russia
—— Company of England, v 513
—— Tsars or Grand Dukes of. *See* Michael and Alexis Romanoff

Musculus, Wolfgang, editor of Eusebius, i 616
Music. *See* Art
Musin-Pushkin, Count Ivan, v 530
Muskeyn, Fleming in the French service, viii 481
Musquiz, Don Miguel, Spanish Minister of Finance, vi 371
Musset, Louis-Charles-Alfred de, x 101; 516; xi 508; 512; poetry of, 513; comedies of, 515
Mussi, Muzio, xii 220
Musso, the war of (1531), ii 336
Mustafa II, Ottoman Sultan, v 369 sq.
—— III, Ottoman Sultan, vi 355
—— IV, Ottoman Sultan, ix 388
—— (son of Mohammad II), defeats Uzun Hasan, i 82
—— Prince, murder of, iii 121, 124
—— Lala, iii 131, 134
—— Pasha of Skutari, x 548
—— Kamel, Egyptian agitator, xii 454 sq.
Mustagh, glacier pass of, xii 802
Musurus, Marcus, printer in Venice, i 562, 565 sq.; ii 16
Muthill, burnt by Jacobites, vi 102
Mutianus, Conrad, scholar of Erfurt, i 435, 624
Mutiny, Indian. *See* India, *also* Sepoy
—— Act, English, effects of passing of, v 259
—— Bill, Irish, of 1781, vi 499; Grattan's *Observations* on, *ib.*
Mutkuroff, Lieut.-colonel, Regent of Bulgaria, xii 409
Mutsu Hito, Mikado of Japan, accession of, xi 855; 856 sqq.; xii 539; 545; 548 sq.; grants a Constitution, 551; 556 sq.; and Saigō, 561; 563
Mutti (Muth), Conrad (Mutianus Rufus), scholar at Erfurt, ii 111
Muzaffar-ed-dín, Amir of Bokhara, xi 630 sq.
—— Shah of Persia, xii 344
Muzzarelli, Carlo, Monsignor, xi 91
Mycenae, excavations in, xii 845
Myconius, the "Reformer of Weimar" (Oswald Geisshüssler), ii 104 sq., 130, 161; at the Conference of Marburg, 207; 310, 318; in Basel, 355
Myedè, Burmese army at, xi 728
Myers, British officer at Albuera, ix 467
Myle, van der, Dutch ambassador to Venice (1609), iii 645
Myngs, Sir Christopher, English vice-admiral, v 190
Myroure for Magistrates, A (Thomas Sack-ville's), iii 366
Mysore, vi 540; 541; Haidar Ali in, 549; 567; 577; campaigns in, ix 715; 723; British administration in, xi 730; government of, xii 476
Mytho, ceded to France, xii 524

Naarden, destruction of (1572), iii 234–5; captured (1673), v 161

Nabókoff, V., Russian Minister of Justice, xii 309; 312; 333

Nacchianti, Jacopo. *See* Chioggia, Bishop of

Nachod, Prussian army at, vi 279, 632, 705; xi 452; fight at, 453

Nachtigal, Gustav, traveller in Africa, xii 160; 811

Nádasdi, Th., Hungarian Reformer, i 340

Nadasdy, Franz Leopold, Count, Austrian field-marshal, vi 273; 275 sq.

—— Francis, and the Hungarian conspiracy, v 351 sq.

Nadaud, Martin, French deputy, xi 136

Nadin, surrendered by Venice to Turks, iii 116

Nádir Shah (Kuli Khan), and Russia, vi 304; 307; 524; 527

Näfels, battle of, vi 617

Nägeli, Karl Wilhelm, botanist, xi 260

Nagano Shuzen, retainer of Ii Kamon no Kami, xi 837

Nagasaki, foreign traders at, xi 823; Dutch factory at, 828, xii 556; xi 830 sq.; port of, opened, 833; 839 sq.; 843; British firm at, 846; 848; 859; Roman Catholic mission at, 861 sq.; xii 567

Nagera, Duke of, rebels against Ferdinand of Spain, i 365

—— Duke of (son of above), viceroy of Navarre, i 378

Nágpur, position of (1785), ix 719; xi 725 sq.; annexation of, 743

Nagy Sarlo, Austrian defeat at, xi 206

Nagyvárad. *See* Grosswardein

Naharro, Torres de, Spanish writer, i 380

Nahuatlacá, The, of Mexico, i 38 sq., 43

Nairn, the Duke of Cumberland at, vi 116

Nairne, John Nairne, Lord, Jacobite, vi 103; 113

Naissance, La, de la Paix, iv 787

Nakagawa, Prince, the Mikado's chief adviser, xi 849

Nakai, defends British Minister at Kiōto, xi 861

Nakas, The, of Catharine II (1767), vi 686 sqq.

Nakhichevan, ceded to Russia (1828), x 444, xi 274

Naláczy, Joseph, Hungarian writer, xi 422

Naldi, Dionigi di, Venetian general, i 132

Namaqualand, German missionaries in, xii 658; 664

Nambu clan, xi 859

Namling, visited by Englishmen, xii 798

Namur, county of, purchased by Philip the Good, i 419; defence of, by Charles V, ii 89; seized by Don John of Austria (1577), iii 247, 499, 501, 515; Thomas of Savoy defeated near, iv 697; captured by French (1692), v 60, 261; taken by William III (1695), 62, 661; 63; 422; 450; Barrier Treaties and, 457 sqq.; siege of (1746), vi 247; 647; 656; socialism at, xii 252

Namur, Albert Ludovic de Lichtervelde, Bishop of, vi 650

Nána Farnavís, and Marátha War, ix 710; relations of, with Sindhia, 718 sqq.; death of, 725

Nana Sahib (Dhondev Pant), xi 727; 731; at Cawnpore, 747 sq.; 749

Nancré, Marquis de, French envoy to Madrid, vi 30

Nancy, defeat of Charles the Bold at, i 391; Charles IX at, iii 7; Louis XIII at, iv 140; a French possession (1633), 143; 246; 620; ex-King Stanislaus at, vi 199; *Parlement* of, viii 47; mutiny at (1790), 192, 194, 404; Comte d'Artois at (1814), ix 560; xi 30; political demonstrations at, 137; 586; 589; German force at, 592

—— Anne-L.-H. de la Fare, Bishop of, viii 146, 151, 689

Nanking, British force at, xi 809; 813; the "Taipings" at, 820 sq.; Treaty of, 807, 811; travellers at, xii 796 sq.

Nanningfu, foreign trade at, xii 506

Nansen, Fridtjof, xii 281; 795; 815

—— Hans, Burgomaster of Copenhagen, v 559

Nanshan, xii 585; battle of, 586

Nantes, the Conspiracy of (1560), ii 292; viii 60; assaulted by the Vendeans, 341, 353; Carrier at, 356, 377; the Duchess of Berry at (1832), x 488, 490; harbour of, xii 102

—— Edict of. *See* Edict

Nantwich, Royalist defeat at (1643), iv 312; (1644), 321, 527

Napier, Sir Charles, x 331; in command of Dom Pedro's fleet, 332 sq.; at Lisbon, 334; 335; in Minho, 336; 337; in the Levant, 569, 571; in Baltic, xi 317

—— Sir Charles James, Commander in Sind, xi 735 sqq.; 745

—— Sir Joseph, Attorney-General for Ireland, xii 69

—— Robert Cornelis, Lord Napier of Magdala, xi 749; 753

—— Sir William Francis Patrick, as a historian, xi 364

—— William John, Lord Napier, mission of, to China, xi 805; 810

—— of Merchiston, Francis Napier, Lord, in India, xii 463

—— of Merchiston, John, v 708 sqq.

Naples (state and city), in 15th century, i 104 sq.; French claim to, 108 sq., 287; Charles VIII at (1495), 115, 231 sq.; French expelled from (1496), 117; designs of Louis XII on, 123; French occupation of (1501), 124, 127, 239; Spanish occupation of (1503), 142, 362; academy of, founded by Pontanus, 560; siege of city of (1528), ii 58 sq.; subsidy voted to Charles V at, 71; rebellion of (1548), 83; the Reformation in, 387–91; ravaged

by Barbarossa, III 109; brigandage in, 430; 454; rival dynasties in, 464–5; Philip II proclaimed King of (1554), 476; raided by Turks, 486; revolt at (1565), 489; Don John in, 497 sq.; Philip orders ships from, 504; Dutch trade with, 631; expedition of Guise to, IV 482; Osuña and, 631, 633; revolt of (1647), 600 sq., 639, 656 sqq.; 666; 669; Urban VIII and, 682 sq.; 685; 687; Cartesian philosophy in, 791; Louis XIV and, V 53; Milton in, 118; 402; insurrection in (1702), 403; captured by Imperialists (1707), 419; 450; Tsarevich Alexis at, 539; the *Academia Secretorum Naturae* of, 740; (the Two Sicilies), and Spanish Succession question, 383 sq., 389; 398; 417, 422; Sir George Byng at, VI 32; Don Carlos in, 62, 153, 167; 151 sq.; 155; and Pragmatic Sanction, 203; 233; 237; 241; 366; anti-clericalism in, 588; and Concordat (1741), 590; 594; Genoa and, 607; (the Two Sicilies), 139; ceded to Don Carlos, 203; the Papacy and, 586 sqq.; 597; under Charles III, 596 sqq.; 600; War between France and (1798), VIII 607, 649 sqq.; revolt in (1798–9), 631; French occupation of (1799), 653 sq.; liberal ideas in, 777 sq.; Tsar Paul and, IX 42; 68; evacuated by French, 75; 88; neutrality of, 193; guarded by Nelson, 220; Masséna and, 262; Napoleon and Court of, 262–3; French troops enter (1806), 267; creation of duchies in, 268; compelled to exclude British commerce, 364; Berlin Decree and, 365; 384; French Monarchy in, 397; Pope claims suzerainty over, 401; 403; British fleet and, 404; Archbishop of, *ib.*; taxed by Joseph, 405; result of French rule in, 406 sq.; Murat receives crown of, 410, 604; action of (1815), 621; Austrian troops in, 648; with Sicily (*i.e.* the Two Sicilies), and final decision of Congress of Vienna, 661, 667 sq.; revolution (1820) in, VII 368, X 24, 112 sqq., 120; attitude of the Powers towards (the Two Sicilies), 25 sqq.; French intervention in, 69; 72; and restoration of 1815 (in the Two Sicilies), 109 sq.; the *Carbonari* in, 111 sq.; the Spanish Constitution of 1812 imposed upon, 120; and the Papacy, 132, 143, 150 sq.; Spanish Constitution proclaimed at, 223; Metternich's supremacy in, 370; XI 41; 69 sq.; 75; movement for reform in, 79 sq.; and the war with Austria, 84 sq.; Constitutional *régime* in, 87 sq.; 89 sq.; 240; Garibaldi in, 332; 375; reaction in, 379 sq.; King Victor Emmanuel in, 389 sq., 533 sq.; difficulties of government in, 530; 531; brigandage in, 535 sq.; Pius IX and, 706; annexed to Italy, 709; strike at, XII 225; 226; socialism in, 232; 237 sq.; Ismail at, 435

Napoleon I, Emperor of the French, VI 215 sq.; 295; and the Corsicans, 350; 352; and Prussia, 725; 728; 830; Mexican schemes of, 352; VII 322; and Louisiana question, 324 sqq.; Decrees of, 330 sqq.; American sympathy for, 335; 336; 348, 366; at Toulon (1793), VIII 352; 396 sq.; in Army of Italy, 438; 456 sq.; and invasion of England, 483, 494 sqq.; 497 sqq.; and *Coup d'état* (1797), 508 sq., 512; and conquest of Italy, Chap. XVIII, 703; and Egyptian expedition, Chaps. XIX and XX; in Switzerland, 639; lands at Fréjus, 663, 674 sq.; and Brumaire, Chap. XXII *passim*; and French finance, 707 sq.; and Consulate, Vol. IX, Chap. I *passim*; 37, 39, 40; attempts to separate Tsar Paul I from England, 41 sq.; 42, 47, 48 sq., 50; forms flotilla in Channel, 51; war policy of, 55 sq.; plans of campaign (1800), 57 sqq.; schemes against England, 70 sqq.; and Peace of Amiens, 74 sqq.; and Tributary States, 81–106; and Switzerland, 97–106; friction between Britain and, 101–4; marriage of, 107; power of, 108–9; creation of nobility by, 110–3; army system of, 114–6; and finance, 116–20; economic policy of, 121–6; and education, 127–9; and regulation of theatres and newspapers, 129–30; and Chateaubriand, 131; and the *Idéologues*, 132; makes changes in the *personnel* of government, 136; Spanish policy of, 137; Spanish visit of, 138; relations of, with Fouché, 139; assassination of, attempted, *ib.*; divorces Josephine, 139–40; second marriage of, 141; Ministerial changes by, 140–1; internal policy of, 141–2; growing unpopularity of, 142; and the invasion of Russia, 143; reported death of, 144; returns to Paris, *ib.*; new Ministry of, 145; addresses Legislative Body, 146–7; home policy of, Chap. V; and the French Codes, Chap. VI; and Concordats, Chap. VII; coronation of, 191–2; quarrels with Pius VII, 193–200; and the German Church, 201–3; relations of, with non-Roman and non-Christian subjects, 203–6; relations of, with the Churches, 206–7; and prohibition of British trade, 240–3; makes overtures to George III, 244–5; assumes kingship of Italy, 247; relations of, with Austria, 248; schemes of, for invading England, 251–2; Austrian campaign (1805), 253 sqq.; enters Vienna, 257; joins Murat, 258; critical position of, *ib.*; negotiations of, with Russia, 259; policy towards Prussia, 265–6; Italy, 267; Holland, *ib.*; Germany, 268; Turkey, 269; England, *ib.*; 270; designs of, on the Mediterranean, 270; on Prussia, 272; Prussian campaign, 274 sqq.; annexation of territory by, 278 sqq.; policy of, towards Poland, 281–3; peace negotiations

with Prussia, 281–2; attitude of, towards Great Britain, 283; at Warsaw, 284; difficulties in 1807, 288; at Friedland, 290; peace negotiations with Russia, 292; and Prussia, 292–3; policy of, towards Denmark, 296 sqq.; Portugal, 300 sqq.; Prussia, 307–8; 317 sqq.; Eastern schemes of, 308 sqq.; at the Congress of Erfurt, 318; and War of 1809, Chap. XII *passim*; and Continental System, Chap. XIII *passim*; called to the throne of Italy, 394; advice of, to Eugene Beauharnais, 395; builds up "a French Italy," 397; controls Court of Florence, 398; issues *Senatus Consultum* (February 17, 1810), 402; dealings of, with Naples, 404–7; with Germany, 407–15; with Belgium, 415–6; with Holland, 416–7; with Illyrian provinces, 417–9; with San Domingo, 419–22; with Switzerland, 422–6; political schemes of, 428; and Spanish Royal Family, 429–33; makes Joseph King of Spain, 434; army of, in Spain, 435–43; attacks Madrid, 444; pursues Moore, 445–6; returns to France, 447; orders of, to Soult, 456–7; recalls Augereau, 457; supersedes Masséna, 466; recalls troops from Spain, 471; 475, 481; sends Soult to Spain, 478; releases Ferdinand VII, 482; and Russian invasion of 1812, Chap. XVI *passim*; influence of, in Russia, 484 sqq.; health of, 489; march of, on Moscow, 490 sqq.; enters Moscow, 496; retreat of, 498 sqq.; reaches Paris, 504; position of, after Moscow, 507 sqq.; and War of Liberation, Chap. XVII *passim*; at Gross-Görschen, 517; at Bautzen, 519; proposes armistice, 520 sqq.; plans of, 522 sq.; at Dresden, 524 sqq.; hesitation of, 529; abandons right bank of Elbe, 531; at Leipzig, 536; retreat of, 540; terms offered to, 542–3; anxiety of, about Paris, 549; at Laon, 551; at Rheims, 552; abdication of (April 6, 1814), 554; deposition of, 556 sqq.; banishment of, to Elba, 558 sq.; and the Church, 569; landing of, at Cannes, 615; during the Hundred Days, Chap. XX *passim*; at Quatre-Bras, 627 sqq.; at Waterloo, 632 sqq.; at Paris, 642; second abdication of, 643; flight of, 644; agents of, at Congress of Vienna, 646; decrees abolition of slave trade, 662; schemes of, in the East, 714; abandonment of Louisiana by, 741; at St Helena, Chap. XXIV; Apologia of, 763 sqq.; death of, 769; achievements of, *ib.*; contemporary view of, 770; legacy of, to France, 770–1; ideal of a political system for Europe of, x 1; 9; 11; and the *Idéologues*, 40; and Necker, 40; 42; 132; and Cardinal Consalvi, 133; 134; and the Guelfs, 135; and finances of the Papal States, 136; and Catholic Church in France, 139; and unity of Italy, 165;

169; 173; and Ferdinand VII of Spain, 205; in Madrid, 282; Mexico and, 303; 341; 344 sq.; and German States, 359 sq.; and Portugal, 310; and Poland, 445; and Bank of France, 746; and French industries, 750, 753; XI 24; and Helvetian Republic, 235 sqq.; 259; 287; 292; 296; 302; and Prussian army, 579; and India, 637; and Gallican Church, 707; and Suez Canal, XII 430; and historical research, 829; 834

Napoleon II, François-Charles-Joseph, Duke of Reichstadt, birth of, IX 142; 380; 645, 762; x 45; plot in favour of (1821), 76; 488

—— III, Emperor of the French, sentiments of, towards America, VII 470; 636; IX 410; Palmerston and, XI 18; 21; 24; elected to Constituent Assembly, 110 sq.; 117; elected President, 118; and Pius IX, 121, 128; 378, 468, 478; and Italian expedition, 123, 126; 127; appoints a new Ministry, 129; and Education Acts, 130 sq.; measures by, against the Republicans, 131 sq.; autocratic aims of, 133 sqq.; and the *Coup d'état* of December, 135 sqq.; promulgates the Constitution of 1852, 140; proclaimed Emperor, 141; 246; mediates between Prussia and Switzerland, 255 sq.; character and aims of, 286 sq.; foreign policy of, 287 sq., 305 sq.; administration of, 288 sqq.; and imperial family, 292 sq.; marriage of, 293; and the Church, 295 sq.; 297 sqq.; and improvements in Paris, 303; attempted assassination of, 304, 327, 375; 306; and Great Britain, 307, 328 sqq., 338; and the French claims in Jerusalem, 311 sq.; and Nicholas I, 312; and the peace negotiations (1855), 322 sq.; 370; and Cavour, 371; and Italy, 306 sq.; 373; alliance of, with Piedmont, 376, 381 sq.; and War with Austria, 383 sq.; 385; annexes Nice and Savoy, 386 sqq.; 389; and kingdom of Italy, 390; and Austria, 393, 403, 407; proposes a Congress, 436; 445; meets Bismarck at Biarritz, 446 sq.; 448; and Italo-Prussian alliance, 449; and Austro-Prussian War, 450 sq.; 453 sqq.; and Luxemburg, 462, 483, 675; personal policy of, 467; Italian policy of, 468, 474, 478, 484 sq.; clerical opposition to, 468 sq.; and Anglo-French Treaty of Commerce, 469 sq.; continued opposition to, 471 sqq.; and Poland, 475; and Mexican affairs, 476 sq., 484, 565 sq.; and Schleswig-Holstein, 477; and the North German Confederation, 480; 482; visits Emperor of Austria, 484; and army reform, 487, 494; compelled to grant constitutional reforms, 489 sqq.; and *plébiscite*, 493; and crisis with Prussia, 494 sq.; deposed, 500; Victor Hugo and, 510; and Italy, 530 sqq.,

544; and cession of Venetia, 540; Bismarck and, 540; 547; Spain and, 564; and Spanish Succession, 570; humiliates Portugal, 574; attitude of, towards Prussia, 576 sq.; and European situation in 1870, 577; declares war against Prussia, 463 sq., 578; plan of campaign of, 581 sq.; conduct of War by, 583 sqq.; appoints Bazaine to command, 588; retires to Verdun, 590; at Châlons, 594 sq.; at Sedan, 496, 597 sq.; 600; Bismarck negotiates with, 611; and Alexander II, 633; and Suez Canal, 638; and Moldo-Wallachia, 644; and Charles XV of Sweden, 690; and occupation of Rome, 706 sq.; and Pius IX, 708; and Victor Emmanuel, 709; 714; and Vatican, 717; XII 8; and United States, 21; 93 sq.; 131; and Germany, 135 sq.; 433

Napoleon, Eugène-L.-J.-J., Prince Imperial, at Saarbrücken, XI 583; XII 92; 108

—— Louis, Prince Royal of Holland. *See* Napoleon III, Emperor of the French

—— Prince. *See* Bonaparte, Napoleon-J.-C.-P.

Napoléon-Vendée. *See* La-Roche-sur-Yon

Napoléonville. *See* Pontivy

Napoli di Romania. *See* Nauplia

Naquet, Joseph-Alfred, French politician, XII 103

Narbonne, revolt of, III 668; Commune at, XI 503

—— Comte Louis de, Minister of War to Louis XVI, VIII 220 sqq., 405 sq.; dismissed, 223

Narbrough, Sir John, English admiral, V 171

Nardi, Jacopo, Italian historian, I 200

Narentine pirates, defeated by Venice, I 254

Nares, Sir George, Arctic expedition of, XII 815

Nariaki of Mito, XI 828; 832; opposes Tycoon, 834; 836 sqq.; death of, 841; 844

Národni Noviny, Čech journal, XI 656

Narodnoye Dyelo, Russian journal, XI 630

Narragansett Bay, Roger Williams founds colony at, VII 17

Narragansetts, The, Indian tribe, VII 19

Naruishkin, Alexis, founder of iron-works in Russia, V 533

Naruszewicz, Adam Stanislas, Polish writer, VI 671

Narva, taken from Russia (1581), IV 167; ceded to Sweden, 171 sq.; 180; siege of (1704), V 537, 591; 547; battle of (1700), 588 sq., 666; 631; British vessels escape from, IX 46

Narvaez, Ramón Maria, Duke of Valencia, X 237; 239; 242 sq.; Ministry of, XI 551 sqq.; 554; returns to office (1847), 556 sq.; retires, 557; 558; and Bravo Murillo, 558 sq.; 560; forms Ministry (1856), 562; dismissal of, 563; Ministry of (1864-5),

566 sq.; fifth Ministry of, 567 sq.; death of, 568

Narvaez, Pamphilo de, in Florida, I 54

Narvik, railway to, XII 279; 289

Naryn, fortress at, XI 632

Naseby, battle of (1645), IV 330 sq., 337, 506

Nash, Thomas, English dramatist and novelist, III 376-7

Nashville, Johnston at, VII 462 sq.; evacuated (1862), 495; Rosecrans at, 507; 521, 523; Schofield at, 524; battle of (1864), 525, 528

Nasi, Miquez, III 131

—— Italian Minister, XII 239

Nasir Jang, ruler of the Deccan, VI 539 sq.

Nasirabad, mutiny of, XI 746

Nasmyth, James, engineer, X 734

Nassau, sufferings of, during the Thirty Years' War, IV 418; Church government in, IX 201; and Grand Duchy of Berg, 410; contingent of, with Wellington, 622; and Prussia, X 341; 343; and Germanic Confederation, 344, XI 222; Constitution (1818) of, X 362; the revolutionary movement in, XI 144; 147; and Austria, 450; 454 sq.

—— (Bahamas), blockade of, VII 552, 620

—— House of, and principality of Orange, III 190, V 449; IX 583; 592; XI 674

—— Adolf, Count of (1481), I 443

—— Adolf, Duke of, XI 147

—— Adolf, Count of (1568), III 223

—— Engelbert, Count of, I 449, 452

—— Frederick, Duke of, IX 268; 657

—— Frederick Henry of. *See* Orange

—— Henry of (the elder), III 189 sq.

—— Henry of (the younger), brother of William the Silent, III 12, 224, 239

—— Count John of, III 707; commands Spanish fleet, IV 694 sq.

—— Count Justin of, III 309, 313, 507

—— Count Lewis of (brother of William the Silent), III 12 sq.; negotiates with Charles IX, 16 sq.; and Alençon, 22; supports William, 201 sqq., 209 sqq., 217 sqq.; and the Compromise, 207; invades Friesland, 222 sqq.; in France, 228 sqq.; 238; death of (1574), 239

—— Count Lewis Günther of, at the battle of the Dunes, III 635 sq.

—— Marie of, III 213

—— Prince Maurice of. *See* Orange

—— Prince Maurice of, Governor of Brazil. *See* Nassau-Siegen, John Maurice

—— Count Philip of, killed (1595), III 628

—— Count William of. *See* Orange, Prince of

Nassau-Dietz, Albertina Agnes, Countess of, daughter of Frederick Henry, Prince of Orange, marries William Frederick, IV 701; V 668

—— Ernest Casimir, Count of, III 635; succeeds as Stadholder of Friesland, 655; at Hertogenbosch, IV 693; death of (1629), 695

Nassau-Dietz, Count Henry Casimir of, IV 695; defeated by the Spaniards, 699; death of, 701
—— Henry Casimir II, Prince of, Hereditary Stadholder of Friesland, V 150; 164 sq.
—— John William, Prince of. *See* Orange, John William Friso, Prince of
—— Prince William Frederick of, Hereditary Stadholder of Friesland, IV 701; 726; V 143 sq.; 150
—— William Lewis of, Stadholder of Friesland, etc., adviser of Maurice, III 625 sq.; opposes Oldenbarneveldt, 634, 637, 640; Calvinist, 649; death of (1640), 655
Nassau-Dillenburg, John, Duke of, III 157, 210, 222; 232; 239; 251; 254
—— Prince William of, VI 247
Nassau-Hadomar, Count, *afterwards* Prince, John Lewis of, IV 400
Nassau-Orange, House of, V 449
Nassau-Siegen, Prince John Maurice of, Governor-General in Brazil, IV 708; 714; 751 sqq.; 759; V 150; 153; 674 sq.; VI 389
"Nat Turner's Insurrection," VII 387
Natal, ceded to Great Britain, VI 429; Boers in, XI 781 sq.; a British colony, 782 sq.; 788; self-government granted to, XII 49, 644; development of, 640; and Boer War, 642; 645; and Union of South Africa, 646; 648; and native affairs, 649
Natalia, Republic of, XI 782
—— Tsaritsa, V 516 sq.; 519
—— Grand Duchess of Russia (sister of Peter II), V 553; 555
Natalie, Queen of Servia, XII 411 sq.
Natchez, The (Indian tribe), VII 92
Nathanson, Russian politician, XII 322
Nation, The, Irish newspaper, XI 7 sq.
National, Le, French journal, under Carrel, X 491; 499; changed point of view of, XI 26 sq.; 34; 36; 42; 96; 99; 102; 127
—— Belgian ministerial journal, X 532 sqq.
National Assembly (June 1789–Sept. 1791), VIII 153, Chap. VI *passim*; and the Constitution of 1791, Chap. VII *passim*; closed, 201; and army, 403 sqq.; and navy, 448 sq.; finance of, 691–701; legislation of, Chap. XXIV *passim*
—— Colonisation Society, XI 792
—— Convention (Sept. 1792–Oct. 1795), Vol. VIII, Chaps. IX, XII and XIII *passim*; closed, 397, 489; and army, 424, 426; detestation of, 487 sqq.; finance of, 701 sqq., 730; legislation of, 738 sq., 741 sq., 746, 752
—— Debt (English), bill for government loan (1693), V 266
—— League, in Ireland, XII 48
—— Liberal Federation, XII 49
Nationalities, modern growth of, *see* Vol. XI

Nat-padi, capture of, XI 728
Nau, Secretary to Mary, Queen of Scots, III 292
Naulin, Marc-Claude, arrest of, VIII 367
Naumburg, Lutheran Convention at (1555), II 276; meeting of Protestant Princes at (1561), III 163, 168; Austrians in, VI 297; Prussian troops at, IX 273–4; French at, 275
—— Nicholas Amsdorf, Bishop of, II 117, 201, 242 sq.
—— Julius Pflug, Bishop of, II 240, 242, 264 sq., 667; III 146; 152
Nauplia, besieged and taken by Turks, II 72, 74, III 116 sq.; taken by Venetians (1686), V 365; fall of (1822), X 185; and piracy, 186; Admiral Codrington at, 195; King Otto lands at (1833), 204; French occupation of, XI 277; 278; 640
Nauwport, taken by Boers, XII 642
Navagero, Andrea, Venetian Latinist, I 567; II 16
—— Cardinal Bernardo, II 682
Navarino, battle of (1827), X 91, 195–7; effect of, 198, 201, 371, 417
Navarra, Pedro, Count of Navarro, I 125, 137, 140; African expedition and death of, 365 sq.
Navarre, seized by Ferdinand of Aragon, I 366 sq.; invaded by Henri d'Albret, 378; France and, in 1558, II 94; VI 136; Spain and, 141; occupied by Marshal Moncey, IX 430; Napoleon's army in, 443, 458; Mina in, 469; occupied by the Carlists, X 235, XII 260
—— Antony of Bourbon, King-consort of. *See* Bourbon
—— Catharine d'Albret, Queen of, I 366
—— François Phébus (Count of Foix), King of, I 366
—— Henri d'Albret, King of, I 378; invades Navarre, II 43, 51
—— Jean d'Albret, King of, I 366
—— Jeanne d'Albret, Queen of (wife of Antony of Bourbon), early betrothed to William of Cleves, II 75, 239; widowed, III 6; and Moncontour, 11, 13; death of, 17 sq.
—— Margaret of Valois, Queen of. *See* Margaret of Valois, Queen of Henry IV
Navarro, Admiral, VI 160; 236
Navies, Dutch, *see* Vol. IV, Chap. XVI *passim,* the first (Anglo-) Dutch War, 466–85; English; under Henry VIII, II 472; under the Tudors, *see* Vol. III, Chap. IX, The Elizabethan Naval War with Spain, 294–327; administration of, under James I, 564; *see* Vol. IV, Chap. XVI, The Navy of the Commonwealth and the first Dutch War, 459–85; Vol. V, Chap. VIII, The Anglo-Dutch Wars, (1) Naval administration under Charles II and James II, 168–78; and Admiralty, VI 443 sq.; 448; British squadrons (1811–5), VII 338;

during Wars of the French Revolution, Vol. VIII, Chap. XV *passim*, Chap. XX *passim*; in 1803, IX 210 sq.; Chap. VIII *passim*; Bill of 1889, XII 48; increased strength of, 60 sq.; French, under Colbert, V 14 sq.; Choiseul's reforms in, VI 348 sq.; disorders in, in 1790, VIII 192 sq.; 207; under Louis XVI, 447 sqq.; during Revolutionary Wars, Chap. XV *passim, also* Chap. XX *passim*; in 1803, IX 209 sqq.; Chap. VIII *passim*; German, late growth of, XII 170 sq.; Italian, of recent years, 234; Japanese (1904), 578; (1905), 599; Russian, created by Peter the Great, V 520 sqq.; during and after the Wars of Revolution, X 417; in the Far East (1904), XII 578 sq.; Savoyard, under Emmanuel Philibert, III 410; Spanish, *see* Chap. IX, The Elizabethan Naval War with Spain, 294–327; of the Spanish Indies, X 256; Swedish, under Charles XI, V 578; of the U.S.A., and the Civil War, Vol. VII, Chap. XVII, 549–67

Navigation Laws (1651), IV 436, 470; re-enacted 1660, V 94; 103; and Dutch carrying trade, 139; effects of Act of 1662, VI 52; Constitutional Convention of U.S.A. and, VII 279, 282 sq.; and Colonies (1764), VI 432 sq.; English relaxation of, X 586; old code of, repealed, XI 15 sq.

Navy Board. *See* Navies, English

Naxos, held in fief by Nasi, III 131

Nazareth, French success near (1799), VIII 611; revolt in, X 559

Neacademia, The, of Aldo Manuzio, I 561, 563

Neale, Edward Vansittart, and co-operation, XII 740

Neander, J. August W., *History of the Church*, XII 846 sq.

—— Joachim, German pietist, V 757

—— Michael, I 614

Neave, James, murder of, IV 172

Nebel river, and battle of Blenheim, V 410

Nebenius, K. F., X 354; drafts Baden Constitution, 362

Nebraska, creation of Territory of, VII 427; population of, 708, 711

Nebrija, Alfonso de, II 400

—— Antonio. *See* Nebrissensis

—— Francisca, Spanish scholar, I 379

Nebrissensis, Antonio Nebrija (Lebrija *or* Lebrixa), Spanish Hellenist, I 379, 381, 578

Necessary Doctrine for any Christian Man (King's Book), II 448

Necháyeff, Russian revolutionary, XII 303

Necker, Jacques, VI 550; Gustavus III and, 782; VIII 25; and French finance, 45, 56, 71 sqq., 689 sqq.; *Compte Rendu* of, 74 sq., 77, 94, 97, 690; Director of Treasury, 89 sqq.; *Administration of the finances of France*, 98 sq.; exiled, 99, 104; Minister of Finance (1788), 115 sqq.;

122; inaction of, 123 sq., 127 sq., 132; at States General, 147 sq., 156 sq.; dismissed, 163 sqq.; in National Assembly, 182 sq.; resigns, 194; and Napoleon I, X 40

Nedlitz, Eugene Beauharnais at, IX 515

Needs of the German Nation, II 185

Neerwinden (Landen), William III defeated at (1693), V 61; battle of (1793), VIII 268 sq., 420 sq.

Negapatam, Dutch settlement, VI 454; French and English at, 535; 547

Negreiros, Vidal de, leader in the Brazilian revolt, V 674

Negri, Francesco, of Bassano, follower of Zwingli, II 381

—— Girolamo, II 20

—— Sembilan, the, sultanate of, XII 532 sq.

Négrier, French general, in Tonkin, XII 131

Negro river, settlements on, VI 390

Negropont, fort of, captured by Turks (1470), I 79 sq., 286; attacked by Venetians (1688), V 365

Neile, Richard, Archbishop of York, IV 279

Neipperg, Count Albert Adam von, IX 65; X 107

—— Count Wilhelm von, Austrian field-marshal, VI 230; 232

Neisse, witches burnt in, IV 423; fortress of, VI 229 sq.; 232 sq.; 278; siege of, 289 sqq.; conference at, 633; 668; 703; 731

Nejd, Abbas Pasha's troops driven from, XII 429

Nelidoff, Mademoiselle, mistress of Paul I, VIII 646; IX 36; 40–1

Nelson (New Zealand), XI 793; 796; 799

—— Horatio Nelson, Viscount, methods of, VIII 454 sq.; at Cape St Vincent, 461 sqq.; and Egyptian Expedition, 598 sq., 604; and Mediterranean campaign (1798–9), Chap. XX, 643, 648; at Naples, 649 sqq., 657 sqq.; IX 48 sqq.; 73; French fear of, 209; in charge of Mediterranean squadron, 210; Napoleon's plans to mislead, 214 sqq.; blockades Toulon, 216; hampered by Orde in Mediterranean, 219; despatches for, captured by Villeneuve, 220; in ignorance of French movements, 223; sails for West Indies, 224; makes move on Trinidad, 225; returns to Europe, *ib.*; starts for Cadiz, 227; joins fleet, 229; and battle of Trafalgar, 230 sqq.; death of, 233; mourning for, 234; and Turkey, 386

Nemiroff, Peace Congress at, VI 307

Nemours, treaty at (1585), III 39

—— Charles-Amadeus of Savoy, Duke of, IV 615; joins Condé, 616; killed in duel, 617

—— Charles Emmanuel of Savoy, Duke of, III 661, 666; death of, 668

—— Jacques d'Armagnac, Duke of, I 397

Nemours, James of Savoy, Duke of, III 12, 19, 406
—— Louis I d'Armagnac, Duke of, I 124
—— Louis-Charles-P.-R. d'Orléans, Duke of, and Belgian throne, x 484, 539; in Algeria, 504; XI 32; 101
—— Marie de Longueville, Duchess of, V 449
Nenagh, Reconciliation meeting at (1828), X 648
Neo-Platonists, The, II 701
Nepál, Gurkhas of, IX 718
Nepluyeff (Neplyneff), Ivan Ivanovich, Russian ambassador to the Porte, V 545; VI 304
Neptune, discovery of, XII 768
Nérac, conferences at (1578–9), III 33; agreement of, 665
Nerchinsk, silver mines of, V 533; post-road through, XII 792, 796
—— Treaty of, XII 795
Neri, Pompeo, Tuscan statesman, VI 602
Nerli, Jacopo, Florentine printer, I 149, 154
Nero, Bernardo del. *See* Del Nero
Nes, Jan Jansse van, Dutch admiral, V 190
Nesselrode, Charles Robert, Count von, signs Treaty of Chaumont, IX 577; at Congress of Vienna, 580 sqq.; at Conference of Aix-la-Chapelle, X 14; 29; 50; and Eastern Question, 194, 197 sqq.; 376; and English intervention in Polish-Russian affairs, 474; and French revolution of 1830, 481; and Dardanelles question, 555; XI 633; 828
Nestoroff, Alexis, Russian upper-fiscal, V 535; 546
Nethenus, Samuel, pietist, V 757
Netherlands, the seventeen Provinces of the, to 1579. [*See also* Netherlands, United Provinces of the; Netherlands, Spanish and Austrian; Netherlands, Kingdom of the; Holland *passim*; *and, for later periods*, the Batavian Republic *and* Holland and Belgium, Kingdoms of]
I xiii The Netherlands, 417–62
II ii *and* iii Habsburg and Valois (I) *and* (II), *passim*, 36–103
III vi The Revolt of the Netherlands, 182–220
  vii William the Silent, 221–59
Netherlands, the Spanish (*afterwards* Austrian)
III vi The Revolt of the Netherlands, *passim*, 182–220
  vii William the Silent (and the separation of the northern and southern provinces), *passim*, 221–59
IV xxi Mazarin, *passim*, 592–622
  xxii Spain and Spanish policy, *passim*, *especially* 644 sq., 658 sq.

Netherlands, the Spanish (*contd.*)
V ii The Foreign policy of Louis XIV (1661–97), *passim*, 32–63
  xiii The Treaties of Partition and the Spanish Succession, *passim*, 372–400
  xiv The War of the Spanish Succession, *passim*, 401–59
Netherlands, the Austrian (*formerly* Spanish)
VI viii (2) The War (of the Austrian Succession), *passim*, 228–50
  xviii Joseph II, *passim*, 626–56
VIII xi The European Powers and the Eastern Question, *passim*, 306–37
  [*See also* Netherlands, Kingdom of the, *and* Belgium]
Netherlands, United Provinces of the
III vi The Revolt of the Netherlands, *passim*, 182–220
  vii William the Silent, *passim*, 221–59
  xix The Dutch Republic, 617–56
IV xiv The Peace of Westphalia, *passim*, 395–433
  xvi The Navy of the Commonwealth and the First Dutch War, 466–81
  xxiv Frederick Henry, Prince of Orange, 689–727
  xxv The transference of Colonial Power to the United Provinces and England, 728–59
V ii The foreign policy of Louis XIV (1661–97), *passim*, 32–63
  v The Stewart Restoration, 107 sqq.
  vii The administrations of John de Witt and William of Orange (1651–88), 137–67
  viii (2) The Anglo-Dutch Wars (1664–74), 178–97
  ix The policy of Charles II, *passim*, 198–220
  xiv The War of the Spanish Succession and the Peace of Utrecht, *passim*, 401–59
  xxii The colonies and India, *passim*, 673–705
VI i (2) Foreign policy of George I, *passim*, 21–39
  viii (2) The War (of the Austrian Succession), *passim*, 228–50
  xviii Joseph II, *passim*, 626–56
VIII xi The European Powers and the Eastern Question, *passim*, 306–37
  xiv The general war, *passim*, 398–446
IX ii The Armed Neutrality, *passim*, 42 sqq.
  [*See also* Batavian Republic, Netherlands, Kingdom of the, *and then* Holland]

Netherlands, Kingdom of the [*i.e.* Holland and Belgium, 1815–30, 1830–9]
IX   xix   The Congress of Vienna, (I) (1814–5), 605 sq. *and* (II) 654 sq.
X   xvi   The Low Countries, *passim*, 517–44 [*i.e.* Holland only since 1839]
XI   xxiii   (1) Holland (1839–70), 661–8 xxvii   (3) The English and Dutch in S. Africa (1815–70), 778–89
XII   ix   The Low Countries [1] (1870–1905), 243–50
Netherlands, King of the. *See* William I
Neto, Bras, Portuguese agent in Rome, II 413
Nettement, Alfred, and the opposition to Napoleon III, XI 469
Nettuno, the Old Pretender at, VI 105
Neu-Brandenburg, sack of (1631), IV 199 sqq.
Neubreisach, military arrests at, X 76
Neuburg, and the Landshut War, I 315; religious disturbance in, III 724; secedes from the Protestant Union, IV 12; 214; Gustavus at, 219; obtains Jülich and Berg, 409, 428
—— Counts Palatine of the House of, III 704
—— Anna, Countess Palatine of, III 716
—— Charles Philip, Duke of, VI 97
—— John William, Duke of. *See* Palatinate, John William, Elector Palatine
—— Maria Magdalena, Archduchess, consort of Wolfgang William, III 398, 733
—— Philip Lewis, Count Palatine and Duke of, claim of, to Jülich-Cleves, III 642 sq., 687 sq., 716, 724 sq.; 735; V 628
—— Philip William, Duke of. *See* Palatinate, Philip William, Elector Palatine
—— Wolfgang William, Count Palatine of, II 264; claim of, to Jülich-Cleves, III 716, 729 sq.; converted to Rome, 733, IV 5, 10; new Catholic League and, 13; and possession of Jülich-Cleves, 408, V 643
Neuchâtel (Neuenburg), and Prussia, V 449, 669, 671; and Franco-Swiss alliance, VI 617; ceded to France (1805), IX 262; canton of, formed, 601; ceded to Prussia (1815), 656; forced into Swiss Confederation, 668; Frederick William IV of Prussia and, XI 143, 227, 234, 242, 245; surrendered by King of Prussia, 255 sq.; rising at, 152; 234; 236; Constitution of, 238; 242; submits to Confederation, 245; 250 sqq.; revolution in, 253; 259
Neue Preussische Zeitung. See Kreuzzeitung
Neuenaar, Count Adolf von, Stadholder of Gelderland, Utrecht, and Overyssel, III 620–1, 625, 711
—— Count Hermann von, III 707

Neufchâteau, French retreat to, XI 585
—— François de, Minister of the Interior, VIII 508; 510, 517, 642, 644
Neugebauer, Martin, tutor of Tsarevich Alexis, V 537; in Swedish service, 603
Neuhäusel, captured by Turks (1663), V 346, 348; 355; 359 sq.; taken by Austrians (1685), 366
Neuhof, Baron Theodore von, King of Corsica, VI 609
Neuhuys, Dutch painter, XII 249
Neuilly, Louis-Philippe at, X 477
—— Étienne de, one of "the Sixteen" at Paris, III 42
—— Foulques de, preacher, I 676
Neumann, Baron, Austrian ambassador in London, X 566
Neumarkt (Upper Austria), victory of Austrian peasants at, III 702
—— (Silesia), Frederick the Great at, VI 275
Neu-Ruppin, Swedish troops in, VI 287
Neuss, siege of, by Charles the Bold (1474), I 295, 390; held by Calvinists, III 450; captured by Parma, 712
Neustadt (Lower Bavaria), Davout's army ordered to, IX 349
—— (Moravia), meeting of Joseph II and Frederick II at (1770), VI 633, 668, 703
—— (Pomerania), Banér and Wrangel meet at, IV 374
—— (Silesia), capture of, VI 242; 731
—— (Upper Palatinate), John Casimir at, III 703
Neuwied, battle of, VIII 498
Neva river, and St Petersburg, V 529, 590; 552; Charles XII and, 596
Nevada, ceded to United States (1848), VII 397; silver mines of, 643
Nevers, Land-bank at, XI 298
—— Charles di Gonzaga, Duke of. *See* Mantua
—— Francis I of Cleves, Duke of, III 4; killed at battle of Dreux, 5
—— Louis di Gonzaga, Duke of, III 19–20, 45, 47, 407, 669
—— Philippe-Jules-François, Duke of, VI 165
Nevesinye, revolt at, XII 382
Nevill, Surveyor-General for Ireland, VI 488
Neville, Sir Henry, II 505
Nevis, colonised by English, V 687; captured by French, VI 454; 464
New Amstel, colony established at, VII 41
—— Amsterdam. *See* New York (City)
Newark (England), relieved by Rupert, IV 321; Charles I at, 333 sq.; 338 sq.; parliamentary representation of, X 604 sq.
—— (Canada), burnt by McClure (1813), VII 341
New Biscay, administration of, X 248
—— Brunswick, development of, VII 113; government of, IX 746; X 688 sq.; timber trade of, 760; XI 757; 763; union of, with Canada, 770 sq.; 777; industries of, XII 611; 615

Newburn-on-Tyne, Leslie's victory at (1640), IV 504

Newbury, battle of (1643), IV 315, (1644), 324

New Caledonia, XII 631; France and, 666 sqq.

Newcastle (Australia), XI 790; Labour unions of, XII 628

—— (Penn.), Assembly at, VII 51

Newcastle-under-Lyme, Cumberland's army at, VI 114

—— Thomas Pelham-Holles, 1st Duke of (and of Newcastle-upon-Tyne), VI 54; Secretary of State, 59; Principal Secretary, 61; 62 sq.; and Spain, 65 sqq.; 70; 72 sq.; resigns, 74; Ministry of, 75; Pitt and, *ib.*; 333; 346; character of, 396 sq.; 398; 401; Ministry of, 402 sqq.; 405; First Lord of Treasury, 406; 407; 417; 419; retires, 422; 424 sqq.; and Prussia, 427; 428; 434; Lord Privy Seal, 435; 436; and Indian affairs, 542; death of, 442

—— Henry Pelham Fiennes Pelham Clinton, 4th Duke of, X 604

—— Henry Pelham F. P. Clinton, 5th Duke of, Colonial Secretary, XI 763; 765; 800

Newcastle-upon-Tyne, Scottish army at, IV 339 sq.; Propositions of, 339, 346; Leslie at, 504; 547 sq.; V 209; 238; VI 97; 113; General Wade at, 114 sq.; programme, XII 49

—— William Cavendish, Earl, *later* Duke, of, IV 305; repulsed at Bradford, 308; at Newark, 309; 311 sqq.; raises siege of Hull, 315; 320; in York, 321; leaves England, 322; V 95

New England, English colony of, IV 747–8; self-government in, 756 sq.; and British trade, VI 52 sqq.; VII 10 sqq.; political conditions in, 54; economic conditions in, 55 sq.; religious conditions in, 57 sq., 144, 726 sq.; literature in, 59 sq., Chap. XXIII *passim*; trade of, 67; currency in, 68; condition of (1748), 118; opposes the war of 1812, 338, 344, 348; prosperity of, 350; and slavery question, 386, 424; fisheries in, 434, 688; ideals of, 726 sqq.; French Canadians in, XII 611

—— —— Company, VII 12, 15, 18

—— —— Confederation, VII 23

Newfoundland, Breton fishers and Banks of, I 414; Verrazzano and, 43; Cabot and, 50; Gilbert and, VII 2; settlement of, 52; 71; 79; d'Iberville in, 89; England and, V 60, 422, 427, 443; fishery rights in, VI 344, 367, 370, 380, 465, 494, VII 232, 363 sqq., 657, IX 75, XI 776; assigned to England, VI 411, VII 95; French rights in, VI 464; British conquests in, VIII 484; XI 757; 771; government of, 776; XII 47; 55; Anglo-French agreement and, 456; development of, 611; fishery dispute in, 617

New France, discovery of, I 43; V 684 sq.; Vol. VII, Chap. III *passim*

New Gazette, Russian journal, XII 312

New Granada, discovery of, I 40; viceroyalty of, V 683; government of, X 248, 267, 273; revolt in (1780), 275; revolution in, 288 sq.; reconquered by Morillo, 290 sq.; 293; Bolívar in (1819); 294; 297 sq. *See also* Colombia

—— Granada Confederation, XII 685

—— Guinea, Dutch exploration of, IV 713; Germany and, XII 41, 160 sq.; Australia and, 631; partition of, 666 sq., 668 sq.; unexplored regions in, 814

—— Hampshire, settlement of, VII 20 sq., 27; and the Indians, 28; population of, 54; disaffection in, 163; writs of assistance in, 181; Constitution of, 241 sq.; and Constitutional Convention, 246; accepts Constitution, 302; and trade regulations, VI 447, VII 310 sq., 354; abolition in, 361, 387; manufactures in, 375

—— Harmony, Owen's socialist settlement, X 780

—— Haven, settlement of, VII 20, 22 sq.; influence of Restoration in, 25 sq.; and Connecticut, 26

—— Hebrides, Anglo-French agreement and, XII 456; 625; Australia and, 631; 666 sq.

—— Holland, discovery of, IV 713

—— Inverness, settlement of, VII 62

—— Jersey, settlement of, VII 41 sq., 46 sqq.; religious conditions in, 57 sq.; education in, 59; and Continental Congress (1774), 164; and custom dues, 243; and Annapolis Convention, 244; and Constitutional Convention, 245 sqq., 249, 252 sqq., 255, 258, 271, 282 sq.; trade of, VI 477, VII 355; population of, 359; abolition in, 361, 593; manufactures in, 375; urges protection, 377

Newlands, John Alexander Reina, chemist, XII 770

Newlyn, burned by the Spaniards, III 321

New Madrid (Missouri), evacuated by Confederates (1862), VII 497

Newman, John Henry, Cardinal, II 34; and Oxford Movement, XI 5 sq., 710 sq.; 347 sq.; influence of, 349; 355; sermon by, 709; 713; and Syllabus, 716; 721; XII 71

—— Thady, III 593

Newmarch, William, completes *History of Prices*, X 783

Newmarket, Charles I at, IV 342

New Mexico, VII 394; annexed by United States (1846), 395 sqq.; slavery in, 399, 401, 416; boundary of, 403 sq.

—— Netherlands. *See* New York (State)

Newnham College, Cambridge, XII 762

—— Alderman, and Prince of Wales, VI 472

New Orleans, founded, VI 133, VII 92; trade of, 324 sq., 360, 691 sq.; insurrection at, VI 373; British attack on (1814), VII

345 sqq.; in Civil War, 471; captured by Farragut (1862), 498, 552 sq.; banks of, 610, 618

New Plymouth (America), settlement of, vii 14 sq., 23; attacked by Indians, 27; and Governor Andros, 29; incorporated in Massachusetts, 30

—— —— (Australia), province of, xi 796; 799 sq.

Newport (Mon.), "Treaty of" (1648), iv 352, 555; 354; Chartist attack on, x 683

—— (Rhode Island), occupied by British, vii 218

—— Mountjoy Blount, Baron Mountjoy, Earl of, iv 297

—— Pagnell, Rupert at, iv 315

New Republic, established by Boers, xii 638

New Road, Russian journal, xii 333

Newry, death of Burgh at, iii 606; Irish rebels and, iv 522, 524, 533

New Siberia Islands, discovered, xii 795

— South Wales, founding of, ix 736 sqq.; xi 16; British administration in, 789 sq.; development of, 791 sq.; 795; gold in, 796; 797; population of, 799; development and progress of, xii 619 sqq.; 634; and Sudan War, 651; and arbitration, 751

— Spain, i 42; administration of, x 244 sq., 247, 248, 274; *Gachupines* in, 251; trading regulations in, 255 sq.; mining in, 258 sq.; native population of, 261, 268; missions of, 271; chamber of mining in, 275. *See also* Mexico

— Testament, The, printed Greek texts of, i 603 sq.; Erasmian text of, 603, 606, ii 699; translations of, Luther's, 164; Spanish (by Enzinas), 402; (by Perez, etc.), 406; Tyndale's, 464 sq.; Danish (by Mikkelsen and Pedersen), 610; Icelandic, 621; Swedish (by Andreae and Petri), 625

Newton, Sir Isaac, v 237; and the currency, 269; 712 sqq.; 716; and Leibniz, 717 sq.; theory of gravitation of, 719; *Principia*, 720, 722; 721 sqq.; vi 19; 826; xii 767; and theory of light, 781 sq.

Newtown Butler, defeat of James' army at (1689), v 312

New Word, Russian journal, xii 313; 330

New York (New Netherlands), State of, settlement in, iv 709, vii 22, 38 sqq.; Dutch West India Company and, iv 749; 757; seized by English (1664), v 149, vii 38 sq.; Treaty of Breda and, iv 740, vii 80; v 151; 161; vii 53; political conditions in, 54; economic conditions in, 55; religious conditions in, 57; education in, 59; attacked by Frontenac (1690), 90; by Montcalm (1757), 129; effect of Stamp Act in, 149; and Mutiny Act, 152; importance of, 164; writs of assistance in, 181; Constitution of, 237,

242; and custom dues, 243; and Annapolis Convention, 244; and the Constitutional Convention, 245 sqq., 250, 255, 258, 264, 271 sqq., 286; cessions in, 308; opposes taxation, 309; invaded by Prevost (1814), 343; migration into, 357; population of, 359; abolition in, 361, 388; manufactures in, 375; and the Tariff, 377; Democrats in, 631, 646

New York (New Amsterdam), City of, settlement of, vii 22; captured by English (1664), v 149, 179 sq., 189, vii 39 sq.; v 197; 685; Convention at (1690), vii 69; Congress at (1765), 149; Assembly of, vi 438; Howe at, 451, vii 212; menaced by French fleet (1781), 230; a British city, 231, 307; merchants of, 310 sq., 319; chosen as seat of government, 314, 316; 321; communication with, 351, 694; banks at, 352 sq.; imports of, 355; emigration from, 359; financial panic in (1837), 385, (1857), xi 327, (1884), vii 647; conscription riots in (1863), 573; politics in (1871), 639; literature in, 747; xii 95; municipal expenditure of, 734

New York Herald, xii 809 sq.

New Zealand, discovery of, iv 713; Constitution of, xi 16, 796; 760; British rule in, 761; development of, 792 sqq.; progress of, 799; 801; xii 1; 603; development and progress of, 618 sqq., 626 sqq.; and Australian federation, 631 sq.; 634 sq.; and naval defence, 649, 651; 666; and Pacific Islands, 667; local government in, 734; social movements in, 747, 751, 753, 755, 763

—— —— Association, xi 793

—— —— Company, xi 793; 796

Ney, Michel, Duc d'Elchingen, Prince de La Moskowa, Marshal of France, viii 652, ix 100 sq.; 112, 252; crosses the Rhine, 253; 254; sent to Tyrol, 256; in Carinthia, 258; 274, 277; Magdeburg capitulates to, 280; at Thorn, 284; guards Warsaw, 284; approaches Königsberg, 285; at Guttstadt, 290; and the Diet of Fribourg, 423; 441; pursues British, 446-7; holds Galicia, 449; concentrates at Lugo, 451; 452; evacuates Galicia, 453; attacks British, 461 sqq.; and the Russian campaign, 488 sqq.; on the lower Main, 516; 518; at Bautzen, 519; resignation of, 520; sent to Berlin, 529; at Dennewitz, 530; at Laon, 551; at Notre Dame, 561; on French Council of War, 565; joins Napoleon, 574-5; envoy to Alexander, 558; and the Hundred Days, 621; 625; at Quatre-Bras, 626 sqq.; at Waterloo, 635 sqq.; x 49

—— Napoléon - Henri - Edgar, Comte, French general, xi 128

Neyen, Father, iii 639, 641

Nezib, defeat of Turks at (1839), x 512, 562

Ngami, Lake, discovered, XII 808
Ngan-si-chau, travellers at, XII 803
Niagara, fort at, VII 89, 125; Prideaux's expedition against (1759), 137, 141
—— intrigue, The, VII 577 sq.
Nibelungenlied, study of the, XII 823
Nicaragua, U.S. Treaties with (1868), VII 637, (1884), 649, 656; 673; XII 672; and Clayton-Bulwer Treaty, 686; 699
Niccoli, Niccolo de', collector, I 551, 594
Niccolini, Agnolo, and Savonarola, I 185
—— Agnolo, Archbishop of Pisa. *See* Pisa
—— Giovanni Battista, patriotic dramas of, X 125; 128; XI 70; 545; 548
Nice, Truce of (1538), II 73, 235 sq., 288; siege of, by French and Turks (1543), 77, III 112; claims of Philip II over, 400, 402, 407; Duke of Savoy at, 410, 416; Guise repulsed from (1600), 418; V 389; restored to Savoy, 437, 448; regained by Sardinia, VI 249; occupied by French (1792), VIII 299, 305, 437, 555, 780; XI 88; Great Britain and, 332, 334; ceded to France, 386 sqq., 468; 577
Nicene Creed, reaffirmed at Council of Trent, II 665
Nicholai, Bishop, in Yezo, XII 575
Nicholaievsk, port of, XI 272
Nicholas III (Giovanni Gaetano), Pope, I 663
—— IV (Jerome of Palestrina), Pope, III 427, 440
—— V (Tommaso Parentucelli of Sarzana), Pope, I 76 sq., 78; influence on Renaissance of, 546; 552; library of, 594 sqq., 646, 679; III 439, 444, 757
—— I, Tsar, X 39; and French foreign policy, 98; and Turkish Question, 191 sqq., 198 sqq.; and Treaty of London, 195; and battle of Navarino, 197; blockades the Dardanelles, 201; and Treaty of Adrianople, 202; Metternich and, 371; and Prussia, 372; and navy, 417; 425; reactionary educational policy of, 430 sqq.; and Finland, 435 sq.; marriage of, 436; and succession to throne, 437, 439 sq.; accession of, 440; suppresses risings of December, 441 sqq.; foreign policy of, 444; and Poland, 448, 456 sqq.; at Warsaw, 458 sq.; and Lithuanian provinces, 460; 462; and Polish army, 465 sq.; and Polish revolution, 467 sqq., 473 sq.; and French revolution of 1830, 481; and Louis-Philippe, 482; 505; and integrity of Ottoman empire, 546; and Turko-Egyptian Question, 552, 563 sqq., 570; at Münchengrätz, 557; and Great Britain, 558; and Gregory XVI, XI 71; and Metternich, 154; 189; and Prussia, 200; aids Austria, 208 sqq.; 213; and Görgei, 214; and Emperor Francis Joseph, 217; and King Frederick William IV of Prussia, 224, 395; and Schleswig-Holstein, 225 sq.; 228; and Hesse-Cassel,

229 sq.; character and policy of, 262 sqq.; legal reforms by, 264 sq.; and the serfs, 268 sq.; results of reign of, 274; and Turkey, 277, 312 sq.; and Napoleon III, 307, 312; and causes of Crimean War, 314 sqq.; 321; 324; and Austria, 402; 613 sq.; 622; and Sweden, 684, 687; death of, 321; XII 294; 296; and Finland, 334; and the Jews, 339
Nicholas II, Tsar, X 39; visits France, XII 98; 225; 247; 315; accession of, 322; 326; and Finland, 335; 336; visits Warsaw, 338; 342; 347; and reform, 348 sq.; 350; and reforms of 1905, 351; deputation to, 354; dismisses Trépoff, 359; and the Duma, 366 sqq.; plot against, 373; 376; at Cowes, 380; and King Alexander of Servia, 412; and Crete, 423; 513; 594; and the Peace Conference, 723 sqq.
—— Grand Duke of Russia, XII 351; 373; 376; 390
—— Prince of Montenegro, XII 383; 385 sqq.; captures Nikshich, 389; 390; 392; 397; Albanians and, 402; 407; 414; 427
—— Sir Edward, V 93
—— of Cusa. *See* Cusanus, Cardinal
—— of Trier, finder of the codex of Plautus, I 550
Nicholls, Sir George, poor law commissioner, X 662; 676
Nicholson, Sir Francis, Lieutenant-Governor of Virginia, VII 10; sent to Carolina, 38; Deputy-Governor of New York, 43 sqq.; 59; captures Port Royal (1710), 112
—— John, Brigadier-general, at Delhi, XI 746 sq.
Nicolai, Christoph Friedrich, VIII 772 sq.
—— Swedish resident at Dresden, and Bohemian malcontents, IV 234
Nicolas, Sir Nicholas Harris, XII 835
Nicolay, Aymard. *See* Verdun, Bishop of
Nicole, Pierre, Pascal and, IV 795
Nicolls, Sir Jasper, Commander-in-chief in Bengal, XI 734
—— Richard, Governor of New York, V 108; 180; VII 39 sqq.
Nicopolis, victory of Turks at (1396), I 82, 259
Nicotera, Baron Giovanni, Italian statesman, XII 214; 217
Niebuhr, Barthold Georg, historian, VIII 773; influence of, IX 326; at Berlin University, 327-8; Prussian Minister at Rome, X 147 sq.; 349; 352; 374 sq.; 404; XII 817; work and influence of, 819 sqq.; 824; 835 sq.; 843
—— Carsten (father of the above), Eastern traveller, VIII 773, 788
—— Marcus C. N. von (son of the above), X 191; secretary to Frederick William IV, 396
Nied river, French position on, XI 588
Nieder-Schönfeld, Bavarian army capitulates at, VI 238

Niel, Adolphe, Marshal of France, xi 487; 577; 581

Nielly, Baron Joseph-Marie, French admiral, viii 470

Niemcewicz, Julian Ursin, vi 671; x 432; 467

Niemojevski, Vincent, Polish deputy, x 452; 455

Niepce, Joseph Nicéphore de, and photography, xii 783

Nieroth, Carl Gustaf, Swedish general, v 593

Niese, Benedictus, German historian, xii 845

Nieszava, Statute of (1454), i 345

Nieuport, battle of (1600), iii 535, 635–6; the First Barrier Treaty and, v 457; ceded to France, vi 339

Nieuwenhuis, Domela, Dutch socialist, xii 245

Nieuwpoort, William, Dutch envoy to England, v 141; 143; 145 sq.

Nievo, Ippolito, Italian writer, xi 548

Nièvre, revolt at, xi 137

Nifo, Agostino, Italian scholar, ii 16

Niger river, xii 3; exploration on, 120, 805 sqq., 810 sq.; 658; colonisation on, 659

Nigeria, xii 47; 129; 456; protectorates of, 660; explorers in, 807

Nightingale, Florence, xi 321

—— Major-general, proposed Governor of New South Wales, ix 739

Nigra, Cavaliere Constantino, Sardinian Minister of Finance, xi 369

Nigri, Philip, Commissioner for marriage treaty of Philip and Mary, ii 525

Nihilism, growth of, in Russia, xi 629 sq.; short formulae, and continued growth of, xii 297 sqq.

Niigata, port of, xi 833; 841; opened, 863

Nijni-Novgorod, and anti-Polish movement, v 501 sq.; banishment of Speranskii to, ix 487; Fair, x 428; conference at, xii 328; 330; 354

Nijō, Japanese noble, xi 834

Nikitenko, Alexander, xi 626

Nikolaieff, Major, Rumelian officer, xii 406

Nikolsburg, Peace of (1621), iv 75, 87, 98; peace negotiations at (1805), ix 261, (1866), xi 455 sq., 483; armistice of, 541; Convention of, 576

Nikon, Patriarch of Moscow. *See* Moscow

Nikosia, taken by Turks (1570), iii 134

Nikshich, xii 387; captured, 389; 392

Nil Sorski, Russian monk, v 507 sq.

Nile river, French power on, ix 72; battle of, 209, viii 604 sq., 649; xii 439; Lord Wolseley on, 442 sq.; Barrage of, 446; 448 sqq.; rivalry of the Powers on, 658 sqq.; 662; exploration on, 805 sq., 809, 811 sq.

—— the Western. *See* Senegal

Nilsson, Nils, Swedish finances and, iv 575

Nîmes, University of, founded by Margaret of Navarre, ii 291; reverse of Catholics near, iii 3; captured by Huguenots, 14; resists Joyeuse, 20; holds out for Huguenots, iv 134; conflict between Catholics and Protestants at (1790), viii 197; Duc d'Angoulême at, ix 617

—— Esprit Fléchier, Bishop of, v 16; 79

Ning-hia-fu, Huc at, xii 797; 798

Ningpo, capture of, xi 809; 810

Niño, Rodrigo, report of Venice (1535) by, ii 378

Niort, Huguenot army at, iii 11; siege of, raised, 13; Huguenot forces at, 14; La Noue fails to take, 27

Nios, surrendered by Venice to Turks, iii 116

Nippur, discoveries at, xii 846

Nisard, Armand, French ambassador to Vatican, xii 122

—— Jean-Marie-Napoléon-Désiré, x 514

Nish (Nissa), xii 390; assigned to Servia, 392; 396; military conspiracy at, 413

Nishinomiya, town of, xi 855

Nisida, prisons of, xi 379

Nithard, Johann Everard, Cardinal, confessor of Queen Marie-Louise of Spain, v 35

Nithsdale, William Maxwell, 5th Earl of, vi 101; 103

Nitti, Francesco Saverio, Italian economist, xii 237

Nitzsch, Carl Wilhelm, German historian, xii 850

Niuchwang, treaty port of, xii 511; 522; Russian troops at, 583

Nive, battles on (1813), ix 480 sq.

Nivernais, The, Huguenots levy contributions on, iii 30; customs of, v 13; lawyers in, viii 49

—— Duc de, mission of, to Berlin, vi 334 sq.; in London, 346, 428; 400

Nivière-Chol, Mayor of Lyons, viii 340

Nizám-ul-Mulk, Viceroy of Southern India, vi 524; 532; 539

Nizhny Novgorod. *See* Nijni-Novgorod

Nizza, captured by Lewis of Baden (1689), v 368; recaptured by the Turks (1690), 369

Noailles, Adrien Maurice, Duke of, Marshal of France, vi 128 sq.; 154; mission of, to Madrid, 161; 165; 167; 238 sq.; 411

—— Alexis, Count de, arrested, ix 197; at Congress of Vienna, 584; 602

—— Anne-Jules, Duc de, Marshal of France, v 59; 61; 428

—— Antoine de, French ambassador in England under Mary, ii 513, 518, 524 sq., 536, 541; implicated in plots, 544; recall of, *ib.*

—— F. de. *See* Acqs, Bishop of

—— Gilles de, French ambassador in England, ii 575

—— L. A. de. *See* Paris, Archbishop of

—— Louis-Marie, Vicomte de, viii 179, 692, 715

Nobrega, Jesuit, founder of São Paulo, vi 390

Nocedal, Cándido, General, Spanish Minister of Interior, xi 562 sq.; xii 258

Nodier, Charles, x 101; xi 507

Nodzu, Count, Japanese general, xii 588 sq.; at battle of Liaoyang, 591 sq.; 593

Noel, Sir Gerard Henry Uctred, Admiral, xii 423

Nöldeke, Theodor, German scholar, xii 846

Nördlingen, joins Protestants (1529), ii 205; battle of (1634), iv 50, 60, 143, 244 sqq., 247 sq., 252, 644, 682 sq.; Tilly at, 208; 220; effect of battle of, 276; 373; taken by French, 390; 392; French victory of (1645), 597; conference of Circles at (1702), v 403

Nöteborg, surrenders to Swedes, iv 180 sq.; taken by Peter the Great (1702), v 590

Nogara, French retreat to, v 402

Nogaret, Jacques Ramel de, French Minister of Finance, viii 490, 507 sq., 699, 703 sqq.

Nogent river, Prussian boundary, v 634

Nogi, Baron Ki-Teu, Japanese general, xii 587; 589; at siege of Port Arthur, 590 sq.; 594; captures Port Arthur, 595; 596 sq.; at battle of Mukden, 598

Noir, Victor, French journalist, xi 491 sq.

Noircarmes, Philip de, Governor of Hainault, iii 212, 216, 217, 226

Noisseville, French repulse at, xi 599

Nola, revolt at (1820), x 112

—— Antonio de, discovers Cape Verde Is., i 15

Nolcken, Erik Mattias von, Swedish statesman, vi 311

Nollendorf, fighting at (1813), ix 527; 528

Nombre de Dios, Drake's attack on (1572), iii 298; taken by Drake (1596), 322

No me olvides, Spanish periodical, x 241

Nonconformists, under Elizabeth, iii 340 sqq.; and Clarendon Code, v 98 sqq.; and schemes of 1668, 201 sq.; and Declaration of Indulgence of 1672, 207; and Non-resisting Test, 216; and Second Declaration of Indulgence, 238 sq.; *see* Chap. xi *passim*; and Hanoverian Succession, vi 21; and Indemnity Acts, 44; in American colonies, and outbreak of War of Independence, vii 144 sq.; sects in U.S.A., 738 sq.; and French Revolution, viii 763 sqq. *See also* the various sects and Toleration

Nonnen, Edward, agriculturist, xi 684

Non-resisting Test, introduced in the Lords (1675), v 216 sqq.

Noot, Henri van der, Belgian politician, vi 651 sqq.; 656; viii 319 sq., 328 sq., 335 sq., 415, 786

Nootka Sound, discovery of (1778), vii 365; seizure of British ships in, vi 475, vii 328, viii 188, 289 sq., 448; Convention at (1790), 292; trading settlement at, ix 748

Norby, Sören, Norwegian admiral, ii 608, 623

Nordenskjöld, Adolf Erik, Swedish traveller, xii 280; 795

Nordhausen, meeting of Schmalkaldic League at (1531), ii 217

Nordheim, capture of, by Tilly, iv 100

Nordin, Prebendary Carl Gustaf, and Gustavus III, vi 777 sqq.

—— Baron, Swedish financier, xi 684

Nore, The, mutiny at (1797), viii 476, 479 sq., ix 676

Norfolk, Thomas Howard, Earl of Surrey and 2nd (Howard) Duke of, i 471; victorious at Flodden, 482

—— Thomas Howard, Earl of Surrey and 3rd Duke of, overcomes Andrew Barton in the Downs, i 479; made Earl of Surrey, 482; ii 45, 47, 78, 417; sack of Morlaix by, 420; invasion of Picardy by, ib.; invasion of Scotland by, 422, 456; the Pilgrimage of Grace and, 446 sq.; 462; 471, 475, 520, 527

—— Thomas Howard, 4th Duke of, ii 567; iii 278, 280 sq.; executed (1572), 283, 285

—— (Virginia), burnt (1775), vii 169; Navy Yard at, seized by Confederates (1861), 454, 560; abandoned (1862), 474, 552

—— Island, penal establishment at, xi 791, 794

Noris, Enrico, Cardinal, vi 589

Norman, George, Reformer in Sweden, ii 629

—— Sir Henry Wylie, and Sher Ali, xii 467

Normanby, Constantine Henry Phipps, Marquess of (Lord Mulgrave), viii 660 sq.; x 677

Normandy, Coligny goes to, iii 5; Royalist army in, 6; cessation of active hostilities in, 24; Duke of Montpensier tries to secure for Henry IV, 51; Essex leads a small army to (1590-1), 334; the League in, 661, 663; *Parlement* of, iv 611; 612; customs of, v 13; 25; bread riots in, vi 144; 452; 783; agricultural population in, viii 61; disaffection in (1793), 268, 340, 345; visit of Bonaparte to, ix 80

—— Charles, Duke of. *See* Aquitaine

Norris (or Norreys), Sir Henry, iii 15

—— (Norreys), Sir John, expedition of, to Spain, iii 317-8, 511; in Ireland, 600, 605 sqq.

—— Sir John, Admiral, vi 24; 26; 28; in the Baltic, 34, 36; 110; 239

—— Sir William, envoy to India, v 701

Norrköping, Diet of (1604), iv 174, 177; Swedish *Riksdag* at, vi 766

Norrland, iron ore fields of, xii 289

North, Sir Dudley, the *Discourses upon Trade*, x 770

—— Edward, 1st Lord, ii 475

—— Francis. *See* Guilford, Lord

North, Frederick, Lord. *See* Guilford, 2nd Earl of

—— Frederick, Lord (*afterwards* 4th Earl of Guilford), and the Quebec Act, x 686

—— Frederick (*afterwards* 5th Earl of Guilford), 1st Governor of Ceylon (1798), ix 734

—— Roger, iv 755

North American Review, vii 744

Northampton, Henry Howard, 1st Earl of, (3rd cr.), iii 559–60

—— William Parr, 1st Marquis of, ii 475; second marriage of, 480, 493, 499; and the trial of Somerset, 506 sq.; 517

North Anna river, Lee entrenched behind, vii 519

—— Berwick, Jacobites at, vi 99

North Briton, vi 429 sqq.; 441

Northbrook, Thomas George Baring, 1st Earl of, xii 34; mission of, to Egypt, 444; Viceroy of India, 463 sqq.; resigns, 466; 472; 476

Northcote, Sir Stafford. *See* Iddesleigh, Earl of

North-East Passage, Willoughby and Chancellor search for, i 53

Northern Star, Chartist newspaper, x 683

Northern War, The Great (1699–1721), *see* Vol. v, Chap. xix *passim*; Russia and, 527 sq.; 580 sqq.; Brandenburg and, 666 sqq.; end of, vi 34 sqq.

North German Confederation, xi 220; 455; formation of, 457 sqq.; and southern States, 464 sq.; Napoleon III and, 480; xii 134 sq.

Northington, Robert Henley, 1st Earl of, Lord Chancellor, vi 425; 434 sqq.; President of the Council, 439

—— Robert Henley, 2nd Earl of, Viceroy of Ireland, vi 464; 501 sqq.

North Island, New Zealand, xi 795 sq.; 799 sq.

—— Pole, expeditions to, xii 795, 814 sq.

—— Sea, submarine telegraph under, xi 346; xii 171; Dogger Bank incident in, 723 sq.

—— Sea Convention, xii 290 sq.

Northumberland, Whitecoats raised in, iv 305

—— Algernon Percy, 10th Earl of, iv 557

—— Henry Algernon Percy, 6th Earl of, ii 434, 439, 454

—— Hugh (Smithson) Percy, 1st Duke (3rd cr.) (*and* 4th Earl) of, vi 424; 437; 492

—— John Dudley, Duke of (Earl of Warwick), ii 458, 460, 475, 488, 491 sq.; defeat of Norfolk rebels by, 493; plots against Somerset, 494 sqq.; rule of, as Protector, 499–511; foreign policy of, 499 sq.; progress of Reformation under, 502–3; leads forces against Mary, 515; arrest of, 518; executed, 520

—— Thomas Percy, 7th Earl of, iii 278, 281

North-West Company, The, ix 747

—— —— Frontier Province, Lord Lytton and, xii 474

—— —— Passage, Frobisher seeks, i 53 sq.; Dutch attempt to discover (1596), iii 632

—— —— Provinces, xi 751; formation of, xii 495

—— —— Territories, xi 771 sqq.; 776 sq.; xii 605

—— —— Territory, vii 308, 357; slavery prohibited in, 386, 406

Norton, Sir Fletcher. *See* Grantley, Lord

—— Thomas, iii 366–7, 371

Norumbega, settlement of, vii 71

Norway

ii xvii The Scandinavian North, 599–602
    (2) Norway, 617–21

iv xx The Scandinavian North (1559–1660), *passim*, 560–91

v xviii The Scandinavian Kingdoms, *passim*, 558–83
    [*See also ib.*, 613]

vi xxi Denmark under the Bernstorffs and Struensee, *passim*, 735–57

ix xix and xxi The Congress of Vienna, I and II, *passim*, 576–615, 646–71

xi xxiv Scandinavia (1815–70)
    (i) Sweden and Norway, 677–90
    (iii) Dano-Norwegian Literature (1815–65), 697–702

xii xi Scandinavia, 280–90

Norwich, captured by Ket, ii 492; and the First Civil War, iv 302; spinning industry at, x 735

—— George Goring, Earl of, and the Royalist rising in Kent, iv 349; 351; recalled from France, 597

Noskowski, Bishop of Plock. *See* Plock

Nota, Alberto, Italian playwright, xi 548

Notables, Assembly of (1596), iii 671

Nothomb, Jean Baptiste, Belgian statesman, x 532; 542; xi 669 sq.

Notre Dame, Cathedral of, consecrated to worship of Reason, viii 359; Temple of the Supreme Being, 514

Nott, Sir William, General, Commander at Kandahar, xi 733 sqq.

Nottingham, King's standard raised at, iv 302; 304 sqq.; Cromwell at, 314; Leven at, 331; surrenders its charter, v 229; Luddites at, ix 692; Castle, burnt (1831), x 613

—— Charles Howard, Earl of (5th cr.) (Lord Howard of Effingham), and the Armada, iii 309–11, 313 sqq.; 361; 538; 559; 564; 567

—— Heneage Finch, 1st Earl of (6th cr.), v 210; 233

—— and Winchelsea, Daniel Finch, 2nd and 6th Earl of, v 243; 247; Secretary of State, 258; dismissal of, 274; 277; 336 sq.; and the "tack," 464; 471; vi 435

Nouvelle Minerve, French literary journal, x 499

Nova Colonia, established, v 680; ceded to Spain, vi 386

Novaliches, Don Manuel Pavía, Marquis of, xi 569

Novalis. *See* Hardenberg, Friedrich Ludwig von

Novara, siege of (1495), i 117; (1513), 139; Preliminaries of Vienna and, vi 155; battle of (1849), x 116 sq., xi 93 sqq., 121, 207, 366 sq.

—— Guarino di Favera, Bishop of, the *Thesaurus Linguae Graecae*, ii 17

Nova Scotia, French settlement in, vii 71; restored to France (1697), v 63; assigned to England (1713), vi 411, vii 112; the fall of Louisburg and, 115 sq.; importance of, 120 sq.; French intrigues in, 121 sqq.; fishery dispute and, 363, 434, 657 sqq.; settlers in, ix 743; x 685; "Loyalists" in, 687; divided (1784), 688; industry of, 689; xi 757; 759 sq.; union of, with Canada, 770 sq.; industries of, xii 611; 616. *See also* Acadia

—— Zembla (Novaia Zemlia), Dutch adventurers in, iii 632; discovery of, xii 793; 795

Novéant, German force at, xi 589

Noveschi, Siennese faction, ii 83

Novgorod, Treaty of (1611), iv 176; v 477 sq.; annexed by Ivan the Great, 479 sq.; 484; massacre at, 488; Sweden and, 501, 502; 588; recruiting in, x 415, 416; 468

Novgorod-Sieverski, annexed to Russia, v 479

Novgorodtseff, Russian Liberal, xii 333

Novi, battle of (1799), viii 659; Desaix and, ix 62-3

Novibazar, Sandjak of, xii 386; 392; 396; Austrian occupation of, 400 sq.; 424; evacuated by Austria, 427

Novik, Russian cruiser, xii 591

Novikoff, Nicolas Ivanovich, Russian writer, vi 699; viii 784 sq.

Novion, Nicolas Potier, Sieur de, v 16

Novisima Recopilación, x 208

Novo-Archangelsk, Russian settlement at, vii 371

Novoberdo, captured by the Turks (1455), i 69

Novoë Vremya, Russian journal, xii 314; 331; 346; 376

Novogrod, Russian retreat to, ix 284

Novorossiisk, mutiny at, xii 362; 363

Novossilzoff, Count Nicolas, ix 246; 248; expelled from St Petersburg (1807), 306; influence of, 483; Russian envoy in England (1804), x 3; 15; and the proposed Russian Constitution, 437 sq.; and Polish affairs, 446, 448, 450 sqq., 455; at Vilna, 459

Nowell, Alexander, Dean of St Paul's, ii 585, 592

Nowe-Miasto, Archduke Ferdinand at, ix 354

Noy, William, Attorney-General, iv 281; and ship-money, 282

Noyers, Sublet de, rival of Mazarin, iv 593

Noyon, Treaty of, between Charles V and France (1516), i 247, 369, 487; ii 39, 143; Calvin born at, 349; besieged by Henry IV, iii 50

Noyon, Bishops of:—

—— Charles de Hangest, ii 350

—— Jean de Hangest, ii 350

Nubar Pasha, xii 434; General Gordon and, 439; 442; 450

Nueces river, boundary of Texas, vii 394

Nürnberg, i 299; Council of Regency at, 310; Diet of (1491), 302, (1501), 311, (1522), 660, ii 152 sq., (1524), 156, 171; *Reichsregiment* at (1521), 151, (1524), 156; spread of reformed doctrines in, 170; Peasants' Revolt at, 177; the original Protestants and, 204 sq.; the Augsburg Confession signed by, 211; Religious Peace at (1532), 218, 221, 232; Catholic League of (1538), 235, 237; quits Landsberg League, iii 709; religious disturbance in, 724; Protestant Union joined by, 725; meeting of Electors in (1611), 735; Protestant Union at, iv 4, 12, 33; bank of, 7; besieged by Tilly, 208; and Gustavus Adolphus, 207; 214 sq.; Gustavus and Wallenstein before, 216 sqq.; meeting of *Kurfürstentag* at, 384; Treaty of Westphalia wound up at (June, 1650), 415; commercial state of, 420; Bavaria and, v 51, ix 269; v 610

—— Conrad II, Burgrave of, v 622

—— Frederick III, Burgrave of, v 622

—— Frederick VI, Burgrave of. *See* Brandenburg, Frederick I, Elector of

Nueva, João de, Portuguese explorer, defeats the Zamorin of Calicut (1500), i 29

Nugent, Count Laval, Austrian field-marshal, ix 359; xi 84; 86

"Nullifiers," party in S. Carolina (1831) against the tariff, vii 381 sq.

Nuncomar, Sir Elijah Impey and, vi 471; and Warren Hastings, 572 sqq.; 583; ix 715, 716

Nunez, Fernan, Spanish envoy at Lisbon, vi 377

Nuñez, Fernando de Guzman. *See* Pintianus

—— R., President of Colombia, xii 673

Nupé, xii 660; Hornemann lost at, 806

Nupieds, rebellion of the, in Normandy, iv 153

Nur Jehán, wife of Emperor Akbar, vi 516 sq.

Nur Mohammad, Syad, Afghan ambassador, xii 467 sq.

Nushki-Seistan trade route, xii 492

Nuytz, Canonist, xi 712

Nyangivé, Livingstone at, xii 809; 810

Nyantics, The, Indian tribe, vii 23

Nyassa, Lake, xii 661; 663; Livingstone at, 809
Nyassaland, exploration of, xi 575
Nyborg, Dutch victory at (1659), iv 432, 589, v 147
Nye, Philip, Westminster Assembly and, iv 319; Independent leader, 359
Nyenskans. *See* Slottburg
Nyköping, Swedish Estates at, iv 177
Nymegen, Maurice's attempt to capture, iii 626; the Allies at, v 406; Peace of (1679), 23, 36, 45 sqq., 49, 52, 63, 162, 165 sq., 220, 356, 454, 570 sq., 577, 652, 688, vi 4
Nymphenburg, Treaty of, vi 231
Nyon, Treaty of (1564), iii 405
Nyssens, Albert, Belgian politician, xii 253
Nystad, Peace of (1721), v 542, 615, vi 37, 758, 782

O, François, Marquis de, *Surintendant*, iii 47
Oakboy disturbances in Ireland, vi 490
Oastler, Richard, x 659; 681 sq.
Oates, Titus, v 220 sqq.; 224; 227; sentence on, 231; 306; 334
Ob river, Cossacks on, xii 794; 795
Obdam de Wassenaer. *See* Wassenaer
Oberberg, Burchard, Bishop of, iii 156
Oberglauheim, and battle of Blenheim, v 410 sq.
Oberhalbstein, Catholic commune of, iv 47
Oberkampf, Guillaume-Philippe, French manufacturer, ix 125
Oberländer, Martin Gotthard, Saxon Minister, xi 149
Oberlin, Jacobin member of Swiss Directory, ix 97
Oberstein, Count, and the "Spanish Fury" at Antwerp, iii 245
Obok, French colony of, xii 343; 664
Obrenovich, House of, xi 647
—— Milosh. *See* Milosh
O'Brien, James (Bronterre), Chartist, x 684; xi 19
—— Murrough, 1st Earl of Thomond and Baron Inchiquin. *See* Thomond
—— Teig, iii 607
—— William, Fenian, xii 65
—— William, Irish politician, and Plan of Campaign, xii 85; 89
—— William Smith, Irish Nationalist, xi 8 sq.; and repeal of Corn Laws, 11; 13
Obschütz, French army at, iv 270 sqq.
O'Byrne, Fiagh MacHugh, iii 598
O'Cahan, the clan of, in Londonderry, iii 588
—— Sir Donnell, Lord of Iraghticahan, iii 611 sqq.
Ocaña, Duchess of Mantua interned at, iv 654; victory of King Joseph at (1809), ix 455–6; revolt at (1820), x 216
Occasional Conformity Bill, and "tack" of 1704, v 464; passed, 471
Ochakoff, fortress of, vi 305; 307; captured by Russia (1788), 676, viii 292 sqq., 325, 337, 528; razed, 295

Ochiali, Pasha, Ottoman sea-captain, iii 125, 135 sq.
Ochiltree, James Stewart, Lord, vii 112
Ochino, Bernardino, Italian Reformer, ii 390, 392 sq.; in England, 477; Elizabeth and, 563; influence in Poland of, 637, iii 80; ii 716; *Labyrinth*, 716
Ochrida, Lake, xii 392
Ochs, Peter, Swiss democrat, viii 639, 781 sq.; ix 96
Ochsenbein, Ulrich, Swiss politician, xi 247 sq.; 251; 253 sq.
Ochterlony, Sir David, in Nepál, ix 732; at Bhartpur, xi 729
O'Connell, Daniel, and the Irish Union, ix 707 sq.; and Catholic Emancipation, x 141, 629 sqq.; Leo XII on, 153; 593; and Bentham, 598; election of, for County Clare, 607, 646 sq., 654; career of, 629 sq.; defence of Magee, 635; opposes Plunket's Bill, 636; policy of, *ib.*; and visit of George IV to Ireland, 637; founds a new Association (1823), 639 sqq.; 642; and Goulburn's Act, 643; and Waterford election, 644; 649; 652 sq.; in Parliament, 656; 657 sq.; and Coercion Bill (1834), 663; Earl Grey and, 664; and second Melbourne Ministry, 669; and Lord John Russell, *ib.*; and Irish Poor Law Reform, 676; 677; and Working Man's Association, 683; Lord Mayor of Dublin, xi 7; and Young Ireland, 7 sq.; and Repeal campaign of 1843, 8; convicted of sedition, *ib.*; 9; death of, 12; 13; xii 72 sqq.; and the Papacy, 82
O'Connor, Arthur, viii 473, 772; and the United Irishmen, ix 700 sq.
—— Fergus, Chartist, x 683 sq.; xi 19
O'Conor, Brian, iii 583, 587
—— Cahir, iii 587
—— Charles, and Catholic Emancipation, x 627
Octennial Act, vi 493
Oczakoff. *See* Ochakoff
Odell, Moses F., American politician, vii 469
Odense, *Herredag* of (1527), ii 612 sq.; Diet of (1657), iv 584
Odense, Bishops of:—
—— Jens Andersen (Beldenak), ii 603 sqq., 613
—— Knud Gyldenstierne, ii 608, 613 sq., 616, 619
Odenwald, districts in, ceded to Bavaria, x 346
Oder river, boundary of Mark Brandenburg, v 618; 627; and Frederick William Canal, 646; vi 274; 279; Russians and Prussians on, 280; 292 sqq.; 326; French garrisons on, ix 325
Odescalchi, Benedetto. *See* Innocent XI
Odessa, vi 676; Catharine II and, 692; the *Hetairia Philike* founded at, x 176; Gregorios buried at, 183; 554; and wheat trade, 760; local government in, xi 621;

625; revolutionary propaganda in, xii 304; 305; 307 sq.; strike in, 331; 340; naval mutiny at, 355; 358 sq.; 367

O'Devany, Cornelius, Catholic Bishop of Down and Connor, execution of, iv 515

Odoevsky, Prince, v 534

O'Dogherty, Sir Cahir, Lord of Inishowen, iii 612 sq.

O'Donel, José Enrique. *See* La Bisbal, Conde de

O'Donnell, the clan of, in Tyrconnell, iii 589, 601 sq.

—— Calvagh, iii 589 sqq., 602

—— Con, iii 591, 602

—— Edmund, Jesuit, iii 596

—— Sir Hugh, chief in Tyrconnell, iii 602 sq.

—— Hugh MacDiaganach, iii 603

—— Hugh Roe, chief in Tyrconnell, iii 521, 529, 531 sq.; death of (1602), 533, 611; 603 sqq.; 609

—— Joan, iii 603

—— Manus, chief in Tyrconnell, iii 583, 587

—— Sir Niall Garv, iii 608, 612 sq.

—— Rory, 1st Earl of Tyrconnell. *See* Tyrconnell

O'Donojú, Juan, Viceroy of Mexico, x 304

Odowalski, Count, in Prague, iv 393

O'Driscoll, clan of, iii 532 sq.

Odyk, William Adrian, Lord of, v 156

Odyniec, Antoni Eduard, Polish poet, xi 658

Oebli, Hans, *Landammann* of Glarus, ii 331 sq.

Oechsli, Zwinglian Reformer, ii 325

Oecolampadius, John (Hausschein), Reformer, ii 155, 161; at Marburg, 207; 216, 234; and the French Reformers, 283; and Waldenses, 289; Zwingli and, 316; at Disputation of Baden (1526), 326 sq.; at Basel, 355; 698

Oedenburg, Diet at (1681), v 357, 367

Oeder, Georg Christian, vi 747

Oehlenschläger, Adam Gottlob, Danish poet, vi 831; xi 692; 698 sq.

Öland, sea-fight at (1676), v 162; 569

Örebro, Synod of (1529), ii 628; Charles IX meets his Estates at (1610), iv 177; Gustavus holds Diet at (1614), 181 sq.; Diet at (1810), ix 324

Oersted, Hans Christian, Danish scientist, xi 699; xii 786

Oesel, a Danish possession, iv 561; ceded to Sweden (1645), 572

Östergötland, Duke John of, heir to Swedish throne, iv 174; 177; death of, 183

Oetinger, Friedrich Christoph, German metaphysician, v 762

Oettingen, House of, joins the Protestant Union, iii 725

Oettingen-Wallerstein, Ludwig Kraft Ernst, Prince of, xi 61

Oeyras, Count of. *See* Pombal, Marquis of

Ofen. *See* Buda

Offaly, rebellion in, iii 585, 587, 599; plantation in, 588, v 323

—— Thomas Fitzgerald, Lord, iii 581

Offenburg, Radical gathering at, xi 62 sq.

Offuz, and battle of Ramillies, v 415

Ōgaki, clansmen of, xi 851

Ogasawara, Japanese Minister, xi 848; 850; 854

Ogden (Utah), railroad centre, vii 705

Ogé, Vincent, leader of rebellion in San Domingo, viii 193

Ogéron de la Bouère, Bertrand Denis de, vii 86, 91

Ogilvie, William, philosopher, viii 769

—— General, at Narva, v 591; 594 .

Ogilvy, James, Earl of Seafield. *See* Seafield

Ogle, Charles Chaloner, in Greece, xii 391

—— Thomas, Episcopacy and, iv 320

Oglethorpe, James, founder of Georgia, vii 61 sqq.

—— James Edward, Commander of Wade's Horse, vi 115

Oglio river, French force at, v 402

O'Gorman, Purcell, x 641

Ogowé river, xii 130; exploration on, 812

O'Hagan, Thomas, Lord, Lord Chancellor of Ireland, xi 8

Ōhara, Japanese noble, xi 845 sq.

O'Higgins, Bernardo, x 292

Ohio, encouragement of manufactures in, vii 354; enters Union (1803), 358, 421; population of, 359; and the slavery question, 361, 424; favours protection, 377, 381; militia of, 456; and Vallandigham, 574 sq.; negro suffrage in, 629; Democrats in, 646

—— river, importance of, vii 108; expedition to (1749), 119; French on, 131, 136; Clarke's campaigns on, 221 sq.; steamboats on, 351, 360, 690; settlers on, 357; Grant's operations on, 463; railway from, to Baltimore, 694

—— Company, vii 95

—— valley, colonisation in, vi 183; 462

Ohm, Georg Simon, German physicist, xii 786

Oil river, Great Britain and, xii 659; 660

Ojetti, Ugo, Italian writer, xii 231

Oken, Lorenz, x 364 sq.

Okey, John, regicide, v 149; vi 799

Okhotsk, sea of, xi 272; trade route to, xii 794

Ōki of Hizen, Japanese vice-Minister, xi 865

Oklahoma, settlers in, vii 711

Oku, Baron, Japanese general, xii 585 sqq.; at battle of Liaoyang, 591 sq.; 593; 596 sq.; at battle of Mukden, 598

Ōkubo, Japanese statesman, xi 861; 864 sq.; xii 549 sq.

Ōkuma, Japanese Councillor of State, xi 865; xii 549 sq.

Olaf, King of Denmark and (*later*) of Norway, ii 600

Olafsson, Martin. *See* Linkoeping, Bishops of

Olavide, Don Pablo Antonio José, Count of Pilos, *El Evangelio en triumfo*, VIII 783

Old Catholics, The, and Döllinger, XII 147 sqq.

Old De Beers, diamonds discovered at, XI 787

"Old League," of Swiss Highlanders, I 295

"Old Roman Catholic" Church, the remains of Jansenism in Holland, V 91

Oldenbarneveldt, Johan von, Grand Pensionary of Holland, III 540, 621 sqq., 629, 633 sq., 637, 640 sqq.; *Remonstrantie* of, 651, 652 sq.; execution of (1619), 654; character of, 654 sq., 656; and Swedish alliance, IV 690; party of, 723; policy of, 729; V 139; 702

—— Regnier de, Lord of Groenveld, III 656

—— William de, Lord of Stoutenburg, III 656

Oldenburg, Christian of. *See* Christian I, King of Denmark

—— Count Christopher of, leader of forces of Lübeck, II 230, 259, 261, 614 sq.

—— Paul Frederick Augustus, Grand Duke of, XI 151; 279

—— Peter I, Grand Duke of, deposed, IX 375

—— Henry, Secretary of Royal Society, V 754

Oldensworth, Stenbock capitulates at (1713), V 582, 609

Oldenzaal, siege of (1597), III 629; captured by Spinola (1605), 637

Oldham, John, poet, V 135

—— John, trader, murdered by Indians, VII 19

Oldmixon, John, VII 108

Olearius, Adam, V 511; 513

Olesnicki, Nicholas, III 75

Olevian, Caspar, III 154 sq.

Olga Bay, Sir James Hope at, XI 843

Olier, Jean-Jacques, Abbé, V 78 sq.

Olinda, Dutch at, IV 707, 750; rivalry of, with Reciff, V 678; captured by Dutch, VI 389

Oliphant (Margaret Oliphant Wilson), Mrs, novelist, XI 360

Oliva, Barbarossa at, III 109; Peace of (1660), IV 433, 589 sqq., 621, V 344, 349, 563, 593, 643, 649; Cistercian convent of, 629; 632

Olivares, Gaspar de Guzman, Count of Olivares, Duke of San-Lucar de Barrameda, Spanish statesman, III 540; 575; IV 82; aggressive policy of, 191; influence of, 628 sq.; character and ascendancy of, 635 sqq.; Buckingham and, 641; finance and, 642 sq., 656; 644; Catalonia and, 645, 647 sqq.; combination against, 650; Braganza and, 651 sq.; in Aragon, 653; fall of, 654 sq.; 658; 662

Olivares, Count Henry de Guzman de, Spanish ambassador, III 46; 289; 430; 434 sq.; 448; 451 sqq.

Olivença, ceded to Spain (1801), IX 72, 605; restoration of, to Portugal, 652, 661, 670

Oliver, Peter, Chief Justice of Massachusetts, VII 156

—— Richard, Alderman of London, VI 444

—— informer, X 579

Olivier, François, Chancellor of France, II 297

—— Juste, poet, XI 261

Olkusz mines, X 449

Ollanda, Francesco de, II 34

Ollivier, Émile, French statesman, XI 304; 472 sq.; 475; 480; rivalry of, with Rouher, 481 sq.; 485; Ministry of, 490 sqq.; 578; retirement of, 588; XII 109

Olmütz, Peace of (1477), I 331, 335; taken by Torstensson (1642), IV 386; VI 233; siege of (1758), 277 sq., 707; 280; 289; seminary at, 637; march of Kutusoff on, IX 257; and Austerlitz, 260–1; Archduke Ferdinand retires upon, 354; Metternich at, XI 154; 190; 217; conferences at, 225; the punctation of, 231, 393

Olney, Richard, American Secretary of State, VII 671 sq.; XII 687 sqq.

Olona, revenue raised from, IX 393

Olonets iron-works, V 533; 548

Oloron, Gérard Roussel, Bishop of, II 282, 284 sq., 287, 353

Olózaga, Salustiano de, Spanish statesman, X 242; XI 550; elected to Cortes, 555; 556; draws up Liberal Constitution, 561; arrested, 555; 566

Olympia, excavations in, XII 845

Omagh, fort established at, III 609

Oman, the sultanate of, XII 491

Omar Pasha, relieves Corinth (1463), I 79

—— Pasha, Turkish general, XI 277; 283; crosses the Danube, 315; 317; 636

Omdurman, taken by Lord Kitchener, XII 448

O'Meara, Barry, at St Helena, IX 757; 768

Omichand, and conspiracy against Siráj-uddaulá, VI 554 sq.

O'More, Gilapatrick, III 587

—— Rory, Irish rebellion and, III 588, IV 522

Omsk, post-road through, XII 792

Oñate, Carlist university at, XII 260

—— Count, Spanish ambassador, *afterwards* Viceroy of Naples, IV 22; at Vienna, 238; 239 sqq.; 240; 241

Oneglia, captured by the French (1792), VIII 457

Oneida, The. *See* Iroquois

O'Neills, The, of Tyrone, III 580, 588

O'Neill, Sir Art, III 608

—— Brian, III 589; murdered, 590

O'Neill, Con Bacach, 1st Earl of Tyrone. *See* Tyrone, Earl of
—— Sir Cormac, III 612
—— Hugh, Baron of Dungannon, 2nd Earl of Tyrone. *See* Tyrone, Earl of
—— Hugh, joins Ormonde, IV 533 sq.
—— John. *See* Tyrone, Earl of
—— Matthew (Fedoragh). *See* Dungannon
—— Owen Roe, Irish rebels and, IV 522, 525; in Ulster, 525; defeat of, at Clones, 526; Rinuccini and, 530; 531 sqq.
—— Sir Phelim, IV 534
—— Shane, Earl of Tyrone. *See* Tyrone, Earl of
—— Turlough Luineach, III 590, 601 sqq.
Onondaga, The. *See* Iroquois
Onslow, Arthur, Speaker of the Commons, VI 70; 72
Ontario, Hull invades (1812), VII 337; and Confederation, XI 770; 771; 774; XII 604; industries of, 611 sq.; railways in, 613; 614
—— Lake, war on (1813), VII 341
Ootmarsum, siege of (1597), III 629
Opatoff, Archduke Ferdinand withdraws to, IX 354
Opdam, Dutch admiral, succeeds Tromp, IV 476; relieves Copenhagen, 588
Opechancanough, Indian chief, VII 7 sq.
Opequon, battle of (1864), VII 532
Opie (Amelia Alderson), Mrs, VIII 764
Opinion nationale, La, French journal, XI 487
Opitz, Martin, German poet, V 68
Opium trade, Commission on, in regard to India, XII 485 sq.; with China, 516 sq.
Oporto, riots in, VI 386; Wine Company of, 385; Soult captures (1809), IX 449 sq.; Wellesley at, 451; revolt at (1820), X 312; Saldanha at, 320, 322; Santa Martha evacuates, 328; siege of (1832), 329 sqq.; raised, 335; 336; insurrectionary Junta at, 339; XI 572; Republican rising at, XII 270 sq.
Oppède, Jean Meynier, Seigneur de, persecutes the Waldenses, II 290
Oppeln, duchy of, IV 75, 98; principality of, V 625
Oppenheim, burnt by the French (1689), V 57
Oppert, Julius, German Assyriologist, XII 845
Opra Pitrachand, Siamese Minister, XII 534
Opressa, Charles XII at, V 600
Oprichnina, administrative expedient established by Ivan IV, V 490 sqq., 499 sq.; 502
Oquendo, Admiral Antonio de, at the battle of the Downs, IV 700; at Pernambuco, 707 sq.
—— Miguel de, III 307, 312, 314
Oram Bey, III 137, 138
Oran, conquest of, by Spain (1509), I 365, (1731), VI 151; 380; revolt in, XII 129
Orange, principality of, V 449 sq.

Orange, House of, and Peace of Münster, IV 716; 720
Orange, Princes of:—
—— Frederick Henry of Nassau, III 637; 644; 649; succeeds to Maurice, 656; occupies Herford, IV 10; at Worms, 66; takes Rheinberg, 230; 257; 311; Guébriant and, 386; policy of, 401; death of, 598; *see* Chap. XXIV *passim*; V 137; 622; 640 sq.; 668
—— John II of Châlons, (1485-7), I 393
—— John William Friso (of Nassau-Dietz), V 425; 668
—— Maurice of Nassau, III 225; 519 sq.; 533 sqq.; 619 sqq.; military achievements of, 625-9, 631, 634-8; and the Peace, 640 sqq.; and Oldenbarneveldt, 649 sqq.; death of, 656; IV 3; and Frederick V, 29, 70; 81; death of, 689; 690; 692; 694; Breda and, 698; 778; V 137
—— Philibert, II 55 sqq.
—— Philip William of Nassau, III 190, 653
—— William (the Silent), of Nassau, II 71, 78; in France with the German auxiliaries to the Huguenots, III 12, 37, 138, 164, 174, 177, 179, 182; early life, 189-204, 206 sqq.; proposes German Protestant league, 210; leaves Netherlands, 213, 217 sqq.; career of, Chap. VII, 221-59, 290, 498, 501, 618, 621, 704, 708, 710; V 137; 449; 628
—— William II of Nassau, betrothal of, IV 290; 468; marriage of, 701; 720; 724; States General and, 725 sq.; death of, 466, 727; V 137 sq.; 612
—— William III of Nassau. *See* William III, King of England
—— William IV, Stadholder, VIII 321
—— William V, VI 709; VIII 106, 276, 286 sq.; at the Hague (1787), 288, 321 sqq., 429, 787; X 77; 90, 92, 749
—— William Frederick. *See* William I, King of Netherlands
Orange, Amalia von Solms, Princess of, married to Frederick Henry, III 656; IV 689 sq.; changes sides, 697; V 107; 144; 151
—— Anne (of Egmont), 1st consort of William of, III 190
—— Anne (of Saxony), 2nd consort of William of, III 179; marriage of, 193; 222; frenzied, 225; 241
—— Charlotte (de Bourbon), 3rd consort of William of, marriage and character of, III 179, 241; death of, 255
—— Prince Frederick of, at Hal, IX 632
—— Louise (de Coligny), 4th consort of William of, marriage and character of, III 256 sqq.; and Arminians, 649; and Oldenbarneveldt, 653; death of, 655
—— Mary, Princess of (daughter of Charles I), IV 290; marries William II of Orange, 701 sq.; V 107; 144; 148; 151

Orange, Wilhelmina (of Prussia), Princess of, consort of William V, VI 709; arrest of, VIII 107, 287, 322 sq.

Orange-Châlons, Philibert, Prince of, III 190

—— René of Nassau, Prince of, II 78; III 190, V 449

Orange Free State, founded, XI 784; 786 sqq.; and Confederation, XII 636; 637; 640 sq.; annexed by Great Britain, 643. *See also* Orange River Colony

—— River Colony, Boer emigration to, XI 781 sq.; 783; XII 644; and Union of South Africa, 646; 648

—— River Sovereignty, XI 783 sq.

—— Societies, first founded, IX 700; Lodges, Parliamentary action concerning, X 671 sq.

Oranienburg, castle, V 622; 641

Oratio de Reformandis Moribus, of Pico della Mirandola, II 31

Oratory, Congregation of the, welcomes Cartesian philosophy, IV 789 sq.; nursery of clerical scholars, V 78 sq.

—— of Divine Love, II 379, 640, 647

Orbetello, ceded to Spain, III 385; Spanish troops at, VI 159, 236

Orchan, Ottoman Sultan (1326–60), I 67, 99, 101

Orco, Remirro de, III 113

Orczy, Baron Laurence, Hungarian writer, XI 422

Ord, Edward Otho Cresap, American general, VII 536 sqq.

Orde, Sir John, 1st Baronet, Admiral, in command off Cadiz, IX 219; nearly captured by French, 223; removed from command, 224

—— Thomas. *See* Bolton, Lord

Ordener, General, IX 30

Order, Russian journal, XII 309

Order of the Black Eagle, Prussian, V 665

—— of German Knights. *See* German Knights

—— of the Sword, collapse of, and cession of Livonia to Poland, III 63. *See also* Religious Orders

Ordinal, The (of 1550), II 503

Ordinaries, The, in Sweden, replace Bishops, II 629

Ordin-Nashchokin, Athanasius, Russian statesman, V 516 sqq.

Ordonnances Ecclésiastiques, Calvin's, II 370 sqq.

Oregon, settlement in, VII 326; British and American claims in, 364 sq., 391; Russian claims in, 370 sq.; American occupation of, 393, 398, 406; slavery in, 399; enters the Union (1859), 438; boundary dispute, XI 17, 777

O'Reilly, Alexander, Spanish general, VI 373 sq.; 382

—— Count Andrew, Austrian field-marshal, at Marengo, IX 62

—— III 603, 605

Orél, disorder in, XII 353

Orenburg, railway to, XI 619, XII 343

Orendayn, Juan. *See* La Paz, Marquis de

Orense, La Romana at, IX 448; Soult takes refuge in, 451

Orfa, fortress of, X 560

Orford, Edward Russell, Earl of, Admiral, V 59; 61; 241; at La Hogue, 261; 262; 274; impeached, 275; 461

—— Horace Walpole, 4th Earl of, VI 98; 423; 460 sq.; and Indian Nabobs, 570; and Benedict XIV, 589; 832; VII 146; VIII 18, 27, 63; X 698; 710; 718; 725; XI 355

—— Sir Robert Walpole, 1st Earl of (2nd cr.), and party government, V 463; Secretary at War, 465; 466; 469; 474; Ministry of (1722–42), Vol. VI, Chap. I (1); 22; 39; resigns, 72; 109; 157; and South Sea Company, 179 sqq.; and Pragmatic Sanction, 202; 235; 237; 394; Pitt and, 395 sq.; policy of, *ib.*; 417; and Irish affairs, 485 sq.; and East India Company, 530; 809; 817 sq.; VII 58; X 703

Oribe, Manuel, President of Uruguay, XII 680 sqq.

Oriel, John Foster, Lord, and Irish corn laws, VI 503 sq., XII 67; and Union with Ireland, IX 704

Orinoco river, gold mine on, III 562; X 269 sqq.; Bolivar near, 293 sq.

Oriskany, St Leger's success at (1777), VII 215

Orissa, regained by France, VI 464; British influence in, 556; 564; famine in, XI 752

Orkney, Bishop of, III 275–6

—— Elizabeth Villiers, Countess of, V 257; 274

—— Lord George Hamilton, 1st Earl of (3rd cr.), V 410; 425

Orléanais, the *capitation* in the, V 28

Orleans, the Estates at (1439), I 411, (1561), II 299 sqq.; alliance of House of, with Armagnac (1410), 36; Synod of (1510), 29; spread of Protestantism in, 291; 674; the Ordinance of (1561), 300; siege of (1562), III 2, (1563), 5; Edict of, 7 sqq.; League in, 43, 662; concessions granted to, 666; saved by Mlle de Montpensier (1652), IV 616; XI 602 sqq.; recaptured by Germans, 605 sq.; 607

Orleans, Bishops of:—

—— Arnoul, I 669

—— Felix-Antoine-Philibert Dupanloup, XI 118; 120; 296; opposes Emperor, 469; 484; 709; and Syllabus, 716; XII 103; 106; 115

—— Jean de Morvilliers, III 11

—— Ludovic-F.-J. de Senac d'Orgeval, VIII 198

Orleans, Dukes of:—

—— Charles I (of Valois) (d. 1465), I 415

—— Charles II, invades Luxemburg (1542), II 76; death of (1545), 80, 461

Orleans, Dukes of (*contd.*):—
—— Ferdinand-Philippe-Louis, x 483; marriage of, 500; 501; 503; xi 30; death of (1842), 32
—— Gaston-Jean-Baptiste, first marriage of, iv 130 sq.; character of, 137; second marriage of, 139 sq., 142 sq.; schemes of, 150 sqq.; at Court, 592; Lieutenant-general, 593; 596 sqq.; Fronde and, 608; stands by the Court, 611 sq.; 613 sqq.; joins the rebels, 616; Lieutenant-Governor, 617; death of (1660), 620; lampoons of, 777
—— Henry. *See* Henry II, King of France
—— Louis, murdered (1407), ii 36
—— Louis (Duke of Chartres) (d. 1752), vi 134
—— Louis. *See* Louis XII, King of France
—— Louis-Philippe. *See* Louis-Philippe, King of France
—— Louis Philippe Joseph (*Égalité*), viii 81, 90, 108, 158; conspiracy of, 161 sq., 184 sq., 247; proscribed (1793), 350; guillotined, 357
—— Philip I, v 55 sq.; 106; 162
—— Philip II, Regent of France, v 31; 90; 419; 441; Vol. vi, Chap. iv *passim*; 25 sqq.; 29 sq.; Alberoni and, 33; 35; and Great Britain, 38; and Jacobites, 97, 102; character of, 127; 140; and Law's System, 169, 172 sq.; Spanish policy of, 350; 394; death of, 127, 131 sq.; viii 8, 59
Orleans, Duchesses of:—
—— Charlotte Elisabeth (Princess Palatine), 2nd wife of Philip I, v 55; 63; vi 132 sq.; 164; viii 8
—— Hélène-Louise-Elisabeth of Mecklenburg-Schwerin, wife of Ferdinand-Philippe-Louis, xi 32; 101
—— Princess Henrietta of England, 1st wife of Philip I, at Exeter, iv 323; v 106; 198; 203 sq.
—— Margaret of Lorraine, marriage of, to Gaston of Orleans, iv 139, 143, 592
—— Valentina Visconti, wife of Louis I, i 108, 281
Orleans, Prince Henry of, in China, xii 796; in Central Asia, 803
Orloff, Count Alexei (1796), vi 662 sq.; 673; 679; ix 35
—— Aleksei, Prince (1857), xi 614
—— Prince Alexis Feodorovich, General, at Constantinople, x 554, 556
—— Count Gregori, vi 355; and Catharine II, 660, 662; 679; 696
Ormea, Charles-François-Vincent Ferrero, Marquis of, Sardinian diplomat, vi 589 sq.
Ormesson, Lefèvre de, French Comptroller-General, viii 96; elected Mayor of Paris, 252
Ormond, James Butler, 12th Earl, 1st Duke of, and Confederate Catholics, iv 435, 527 sqq.; 463; 521 sq.; at Kilrush, 524; at Ross, 526; defeated at Rathmines,

533; 534; Charles II and, 555; v 93; 105; 230; Lord-Lieutenant of Ireland, 302; 304; recalled, 305; reappointed Lord-Lieutenant, 305 sq.; 310; vi 486
Ormond, James Butler, 2nd Duke of, v 247; 412; in Flanders, 433; 440; 458; vi 14; 18; 97 sq.; 102; and Alberoni, 104 sq.; expedition of, to England, 125; 142
—— Mary, Duchess of, wife of 2nd Duke, v 475
—— Thomas Butler, 10th Earl of, iii 590; 594; 596 sq.; 607
Ormonde, Sir James, supporter of Warbeck, i 470
Ormuz, English capture of (1622), iv 732, 742 sq.
Ornano, Jean-Baptiste de, Comte de Montlaur, Marshal of France, iv 131
Oropesa, Don Manuel Joaquin Alvarez de Toledo, 8th Count of, Marquis of Frechilla, Spanish statesman, v 35; 58; 376
Oroquieta, Don Carlos defeated at, xii 260
Oroshi, burned, xii 402
O'Rourke, Sir Brian, chief of Leitrim, iii 604
—— Brian Oge, iii 604–5, 607
Orr, James Lawrence, Confederate Senator, vii 605
Orrery, Roger Boyle, 1st Earl of (Lord Broghill), and Richard Cromwell, iv 451; and Monck, 538; 547; v 136
Orry de Fulvy, Commissary of Perpetual Company of Indies, vi 533; 537
Orseolo, Pietro II, Doge of Venice, i 271
Orsini, family of, i 126, 227; war of Alexander VI with, 233 sq.
—— (des Ursins), Anne Marie de la Trémouille, Princess, v 447; 455; vi 122
—— Felice, Italian revolutionary, xi 291; 304; attempts to assassinate Napoleon III, 307; 308; 327; execution of, 375; 376
—— Giovanni, Cardinal, death of, i 240
—— Ludovico, iii 430
—— Niccolò, Count of Pitigliano, Captain-General of Church, i 114, 117, 133
—— Paolo, supporter of Medici, i 153
—— Paolo Giordano, iii 396, 427–9
—— Virginio, advises Piero de' Medici, i 110; purchases territory from Cibò, *ib.*, 227; captured by the French, 115; escapes, 117; at war with Alexander VI, 233
Orsova, blockaded by Loudon, viii 326; ceded to Austria, 334; Kossuth at, xi 212
Ortega, Jaime, Captain-General of the Balearic Islands, xi 564
Ortenau, ceded by Austria to Modena, ix 94
Ortenburg, Joachim, Count of, iii 160; the "Ortenburg conspiracy," *ib.*
Orthez, capture of (1569), iii 13; battle of (1814), ix 481, 550
Ortlieb (Freiherr von Brandis). *See* Chur, Bishop of
Oruba, the Dutch in, v 687; vi 186

Oruro, silver mines at, v 682

Orvieto, Pope Clement VII escapes to, II 24, 57, 429; occupied by the Italian army, XI 389

Orvilliers, Louis Guillouet, Count, French admiral, VI 376; 450 sq.

Ory, Matthieu, Inquisitor-General, II 288; Renée of Ferrara and, 386

Orzechowski, Stanislaus, III 75, 79

Osaka, Vol. XI, Chap. XXVIII (2) *passim*; XII 563

Osborne, Thomas, Duke of Leeds. *See* Leeds

Oscar I, King of Sweden, XI 682; 686; accession and reign of, 687 sq.; XII 282

—— II, King of Sweden, reign of, XII 273 sqq.; and Norway, 280, 283 sqq.; death of, 290

Osgoode, William, Chief Justice in Canada, IX 744

O'Shaughnessy, Arthur William Edgar, poet, XI 365

Osiander (Andreas Hosemann), Reformer, II 169, 207, 265; III 153; v 635

Osinsky, Russian revolutionary, XII 306 sq.

Oslo, Hans Reff, Bishop of, II 619 sq.

Osma, Pedro de, Spanish heretic, I 680

Osman Digna, XII 440; 443

—— Pasha, at Plevna, XII 388

Osnabrück, see of, restored to Catholic occupancy, III 709; coadjutorship of, IV 89; peace negotiations and conference at, 146, 398 sqq., 433; and Louis XIV, v 42; Treaty of, 596, 641

—— Bishop of. *See* Hanover, Ernest Augustus, Elector of

Osorio, Francisco, Spanish revolutionary officer, x 216

Ossegg, monastery of, IV 15

Osselin, Charles-Nicolas, French deputy, VIII 247

Ossetian mission in Caucasus, x 422

Ossian, poems of, x 698

Ossory, Piers Butler, Earl of, II 442, 471

—— Thomas Butler, Earl of (d. 1680), v 196; 213

Osten, Count Adolphus Sigfried, Danish Minister for Foreign Affairs, VI 747; 751

Ostend, siege of (1601–4), III 535, 636–7; capitulation of, 537–8; 634–5; captured (1706), v 416; 422; 457; British headquarters at, VI 243; 246; ceded to France, 339; 644; defences of, VIII 281

—— Company, v 703 sq.; VI 49; 57 sqq.; suppressed, 60; 138 sqq., 145 sq.; 149; Charles VI and, 182; Spain and, 202; 209

Osterman, Andrei Ivanovich, Russian Vice-Chancellor, v 551 sq.; and Peter II, 553; and foreign affairs, *ib.*; 554 sqq.; 613 sq.; Foreign Minister, VI 302 sqq.; 309 sq.; arrested, 311; death of, 312; 313 sq.

—— Count Ivan Andreivich, VI 682; ambassador to Sweden, 766; Russian Chancellor, VIII 548, 551

Ostermann-Tolstoi, Alexander Ivanovich Tolstoi, Count, Russian general, IX 261; 492, 527

Osterode, Council held at (1806), IX 282; French headquarters at, 287

Ostia, reduced (1497) by Gonzalo de Cordova, I 233; Cardinal della Rovere at, 110; to be given up by the Papacy (1527), II 56; Khair Eddin Barbarossa at, III 112; seized by Napoleon (1806), IX 194

Ostolaza, Canon, x 209

Ostrolenka, Bennigsen's retreat to, IX 284; battle of (1831), x 472

Ostrorög, John, Polish Reformer, II 634

Ostroviza, captured by the Turks (1454), I 69

Ostrovno, fight at (1812), IX 492

Ostrovski, Ladislas, Count, and the Polish revolution, x 467, 469

Ostrovsky, Russian Minister, XII 317; 326

O'Sulivan, John, Colonel, Jacobite, VI 111

O'Sullivan, Irish chieftain, relations of, with Spain, III 532–3

Osuña, Pedro Giron, Duke of, Governor of Naples, IV 631; and Paul V, 632; and the Venetian plot, 671; 633, 636

Osuna (Ossun), Marquis de, French Minister at Madrid, VI 343 sq.

Oswald, James, politician, VIII 769

—— Richard, and the peace negotiations (1782), VI 461; VII 232

Oswego, fort at, VII 125; captured by Montcalm (1756), VI 403, VII 126; British failure at (1814), 343

Otago, province of, XI 796; 799

Otaheite. *See* Tahiti

Othman, Sultan of Ottomans (1299–1326), I 99

Otho, King of Greece, x 204; 506; XI 18; accession and reign of, 277 sqq.; 533; 639 sq.; deposed, 641

Otis, James, VII 149, 153; and the writs of assistance, 179 sq., 185; 189 sqq., 193

O'Toole, Turlough, III 583

Otori, Japanese Minister, XII 510

Otranto, captured by Turks (1480), I 81, 104, 286, 666; Saint-Cyr withdrawn from, IX 193; Straits of, XII 242

—— Pietrantonio di Capua, Archbishop of, II 390

Otrepieff, Grishka, and the false Dmitri, v 497, 499

Otricoli, revolutionary force at, XI 72

Ott von Batorkez, Baron P. C. von, Austrian general, IX 58; 61–2

Ottawa, seat of Government, XI 769, 773; conference of colonial premiers at, XII 651

—— river, XII 604; 608; French population on, 611

Ottmachau, taken by Prussia, VI 230

Otto I (the Great), Emperor (936–73), I 536; v 617 sq.; 639

—— (of Bavaria), King of Greece. *See* Otho

Otto, Louis Guillaume, Comte de Mosloy, French diplomatist, ix 71; 101-2
Ottoboni, Pietro. See Alexander VIII, Pope
Ottokar II, King of Bohemia, v 631
Ottoman empire. See Turkey
Ottomond, tomb of, v 416
Otway, Thomas, dramatist, v 127; 130 sq.
Ouargla, French boundary at, xii 129
Oubril, Count, Russian envoy, sent to London, ix 256; sent to Paris, 270-1; disgraced, 272
Oudenarde, revolt of (1539), ii 74; restored to Spain, v 45; captured by Marlborough (1706), 416; battle of (1708), 420 sq., 668
Oudenburg, capture of, iii 635
Oudewater, taken by Spaniards (1575), iii 241
Oudh, the Begams of, vi 471, 578 sqq.; 524 sq.; 561; a "buffer" State, 563; 568 sq.; 570; Hastings' policy in, 582 sqq.; military defence of, ix 714; exactions from, 716; Shore and, 721; Mornington and, 724 sq.; annexation of, xi 329, 743; British intervention in, 730; 745; 748; 750 sq.; xii 480; combined with North-West Provinces, 495
—— Nawáb Wazir of, Cornwallis and, ix 714; Mornington and, 724
Oudinot, Charles-Nicolas, Duc de Reggio, Marshal of France, viii 661; receives duchy of Reggio, ix 111; at Austerlitz, 260; at Erfurt, 319; 351; and Russian campaign, 488; 501 sqq.; sent to Berlin, 520; 525-6; at Dennewitz, 530; defeat of, at Bar-sur-Aube, 550; x 80; in Italy, xi 94, 122 sq., 125 sq.; 706
Ouessant (Ushant), naval engagement off, vi 451 sq.
Oultremont, Henriette, Countess de, xi 661 sq.
Our Life, Russian journal, xii 347
Ourthe river, Schérer defeats Clerfayt at, viii 436
Ouseley, Sir William Gore, mission of, to Buenos Ayres, xii 681
Outram, Sir James, at Haidárábad, xi 737; 743; 745; at Lucknow, 748 sq.
Ouvrard, Gabriel Julien, French financier, ix 116; 140, 371
Ovando, Don Nicholas, Spanish Governor in West Indies, i 41
Overbeck, Friedrich, German painter, x 151
Overbury, Sir Thomas, iii 560; iv 734
Overend and Gurney, bank of, xi 340
Overmaas, France and, v 164
Overton, Major-General Robert, iv 545
Overyssel, province of, iii 618; Remonstrants in, 647; invaded by English (1665), v 37, 43, 150; 155; French invasion of (1672), 157; 161; Republicans in, viii 287
Ovidius Naso, Publius, xi 422
Oviedo, Matthew de (titular Archbishop of Dublin), iii 608
Owari clan, xi 857; 864

Owari, daimiō of, xi 825; 832; 836 sq.; expedition of, against Chōshiu, 852; 858
Owen, Hew, iii 289
—— John, works of, burnt at Oxford, vi 807
—— Robert, socialist, and Factory Act, ix 692; x 576; 681 sq.; 684; 778; the work of, at New Lanark, 779 sq.; and social reform, xii 738, 744, 750; and socialism, 758
—— Samuel, man of science, xi 684
Oxenden, Sir George, Governor of Bombay, v 698
Oxenham, John, seaman, iii 298-9; x 254
Oxenstierna, Axel, Swedish Chancellor, iv 68; heads Heilbronn Alliance, 142; 143; 178 sq.; 184 sq.; administration of West Prussia and, 186; 193 sq.; at Mainz, 209; 216; at Nürnberg, 217 sq.; Gustavus Adolphus and, 219 sq.; 222; directs Swedish Government, 223 sq.; 225; and Heilbronn and Franco-Swedish Alliances, 226 sqq.; 234; at Gelnhausen, 235 sq.; 240; 243 sqq.; Louis XIII and, 247 sq.; Worms Convention and, 249; sends Grotius to Paris, 250; Treaty of Compiègne and, 144, 251; 252; Peace of Prague and, 254; Magdeburg and, 255; 365 sq.; 369; returns to Sweden, 370; 372 sq.; and France, 377; 381; Christian IV and, 387, 568; 389; 392; 569 sq.; makes war on Denmark, 571 sq.; decline of supremacy of, 555; 574; Charles X and, 576; death of, 577; Polish policy of, 578; 682; 697; 718; Louis de Geer and, 726; colonies founded by, 759; v 562 sq.
—— Bengt, Swedish statesman, v 570; 573; 576 sq.; and Charles XII, 585; 591
—— Erik, iv 577; Treaty of Elbing and, 583
—— Count John, Swedish plenipotentiary at Osnabrück, iv 402 sq.
Oxford, the New Learning at, i 580; University of, ii 468, 503, iii 326, 447, v 238, 245, 254, 334, vi 805; martyrs at, ii 538-42; Lerma detained at, through plague, iii 536; Parliament at (1625), iv 261, (1644), 319 sq., (1681), v 227; Laud Chancellor of, iv 278; Royalist, 304; 306; Charles I at, 308; negotiations at (1643), 309 sq.; 312 sq.; 315; 321 sqq.; negotiations at (1644), 327 sq.; 329 sq.; 332 sqq.; 337 sq.; surrender of, to Parliamentary forces (1646), 335, 339; 342; 454; Confederate agents at, 528; Cartesian philosophy expelled from, 791; v 740; 746; 760; the Wesleys at, vi 82; 807; Toryism in, viii 763; Shelley at, x 712; Clough and Matthew Arnold at, xi 354; study of history at, 363, xii 820, 834, 839 sq.; abolition of religious tests in, 27; 36; 762
Oxford and Cambridge Magazine, xi 357
Oxford Movement. See Tractarian Movement

Oxford, Robert Harley, 1st Earl of (2nd cr.), v 429 sq.; 462 sq.; Secretary of State, 464; intrigues and dismissal of, 465; 466; forms Ministry, 469 sq.; created earl, 470; character of, *ib.*; and fall of Marlborough, 471; and the Old Pretender, 472; 473; 474; dismissal of (1714), 475; 595; vi 11; Lord Treasurer, 12; and Succession, 14 sqq.; dismissal of, 17; George I and, 18; 96; and South Sea Company, 177

—— Robert de Vere, 19th Earl of, iv 696

Oxley, John, Australian explorer, xi 790 sqq.

Oxus river, Emperor Bábar's troops on, vi 508; Russian advance on, xi 632

Oxyrhynchus papyri, xii 846

Oyama, Marquis, Japanese field-marshal, defeats Chinese, xii 511; 589; and battle of Liaoyang, 591 sq.; 593; 596 sq.; at battle of Mukden, 598; 601

Oysé, François Ignace de, French engineer officer, viii 422 sq.

Oysonville, Baron de, at Breisach, iv 382

Ozanam, Antoine-Frédéric, French writer, and religious revival, x 500; xii 847

Ozarowsky, Polish envoy to Paris, vi 197

Ozeroff, Ladislas, Russian poet, vi 830; 832

Ozora, Austrians surrender at, xi 185

Paardeberg, surrender of, xii 642

Paardekraal, Boer rebellion at, xii 637

Pablo de Segovia, iii 547

Pac, Count Ludvik, Polish general, x 467

Pacca, Bartolomeo, Cardinal, ix 96; imprisoned at Fenestrella, 196; 200; reactionary policy of, x 134–5; 139 sq.; and *Febronianism,* 159; xi 703

Pacciotti, Italian engineer, iii 410

Pace, Dr Richard, secretary to Wolsey, i 486

Pachacamac (*or* Pumacagua), Mateo García, defeated and hanged, x 299

Pache, Jean Nicolas, French Minister for War, viii 259 sq., 263, 412, 416, 430; Mayor of Paris, 264, 271 sq., 274, 356, 362

Pachecho, Pedro de Montalvan, Cardinal, ii 656, 668, 670, 673

—— Italian engineer, iii 230

Pacheco, Duarte, "the Portuguese Achilles," defeats the Zamorin of Calicut, i 30

—— Francisco, Spanish politician, xi 554; Ministry of, 555 sq.; expelled from Mexico, 565

Pachobey, Turkish official, x 177

Pacific Islands, xii 631; the European Powers and, 666 sqq.

Pacifico, David, Greek trader, xi 18; 280 sq.

Pack, Otto von, Landgrave Philip of Hesse and, ii 201 sq.

Packe, Sir Christopher, iv 443

Padavino, Giovanni Battista, and the Valtelline, iv 35, 38, 42 sq.; 45 sq.

Paderborn, see of, restored to Catholic tenure, iii 709; Christian of Halberstadt

in, iv 79; Friedrich von Spee at, v 758; bishopric of, ceded to Prussia, ix 78

Padilla, Cristóbal de, Spanish Reformer, ii 407

—— Juan de, leader of rebel *Comuneros,* i 372–5

—— Juan de, report of, on the Indians in Peru, v 683

—— Martin de, Admiral of Castile, iii 529–32

Padre Cobos, El, Spanish journal, xi 561

Padua, acquired by Venice (1402), i 266; siege of, by Maximilian I (1509), 133, 246; Botanical garden at, iii 394, v 734; the *Infiammati* of, iii 470; captured by Austrians, xi 87; 152

Paducah (Kentucky), Grant occupies, vii 463, 494

Paez, Antonio, Governor of Venezuela, x 293 sq.; 296; and Bolívar, 297; 298

—— Pedro, Portuguese Jesuit, xii 805

Pagan, Burmese defeated at, xi 728

Pagano, Mario, viii 777, 779

Paget, Sir Augustus Berkeley, British Minister at Copenhagen, xi 337

—— Sir Henry William. *See* Anglesey

—— Sir William Paget, 1st Baron, ii 474 sq., 493 sqq.; sequestered, 505 sq.; 516; and Spanish marriage, 525; 531, 543

—— William Paget, 7th Baron, v 371

Pagnani, Santi, Latin translation of Bible by, ii 383

Pagnerre, Laurent-Antoine, French politician, xi 26; 100; 108; 118

Pago Pago, coaling station at, xii 666

Pahang, sultanate of, xii 532 sq.

Pahlen, Count Peter, ix 49–50

—— Count, Russian Minister, xii 300; 309

Paine, Thomas, vi 477; *Rights of Man,* 836, viii 758 sqq.; *Common Sense,* vii 173, 207; viii 762 sq., 765; circulation of *Rights of Man,* ix 673; x 704

Painting. *See* Art

Pais, Ettore, Italian historian, xii 842

Paisios, Patriarch of Jerusalem. *See* Jerusalem

Paisley, pauperism in, xi 2

Pakenham, Sir Edward Michael, General, at Salamanca, vii 345 sq.; at New Orleans, ix 473

Pakhoi, opened to foreign trade, xii 502

Paklat, factory at, xii 534

Palacký, František, Bohemian historian, xi 46; 173; at Slav Congress, 177; 191; 216; writings of, 653, 655 sq.; xii 842 sq.

Paladines, Louis-J.-B. d'Aurelle de, French general, xi 603 sqq.; 608

Palafox y Melzi, Joseph, Saragossa defended by, ix 438 sq.; 442; withdraws defeated to Saragossa, 447

Palaiologos, Andrew, v 483

—— Thomas, v 482

—— Zoe (Sophia). *See* Sophia, Tsaritsa

Palais-Royal, and the Revolution, VIII 161, 163

Palamos, captured by French (1694), V 61

Palatinate, The, III 568; Spinola sent to, 569; feeling of House of Commons towards, 572–3; danger of, in 1621 and following years, 573 sqq.; Calvinism in, 710; Upper, Lutheran agitation in, 713; Upper, Christian of Anhalt governor of, 717; and Protestant hegemony, IV 2, 5; 34; and War of 1620–3, 64–84; 86–91, 95; army of Bernard of Weimar in, 247 251; Peace of Prague and, 253; 642; Charles I and, 643, 646; Upper, 66; 69; 78; 82 sq.; Maximilian to keep, 409; Lower, and Don Carlos, 69; 81 sqq.; assigned to Elector Palatine Charles Lewis, 409; desolation of, 418; 641; French in (1674), V 44, (1688), 56 sq.; 418, 453; 63; 414; persecution of Calvinists in, 664; 672; 743; Upper, allied armies in (1742), VI 235; X 361; Bavarian, 346, 375, XI 221; 218

Palatinate, The:—
Counts Palatine of Birkenfeld (*not Electors*). *See* Birkenfeld
Counts Palatine of Neuburg (*not Electors*). *See* Neuburg
Counts Palatine of Zweibrücken (*not Electors*). *See* Zweibrücken; *see also* Sulzbach

Palatinate, The:—
Electors Palatine:—
—— Charles Lewis, imprisonment of, IV 148; and Heilbronn Alliance, 226; attempts to recover Palatinate, 378, 381; obtains Lower Palatinate, 409; 418; and Imperial succession, 430; V 648; 755; VI 5
—— Charles Philip, VI 202 sq.; 231
—— Charles Theodore, VI 240; 246; 631
—— Frederick I the Victorious, I 296, 311
—— Frederick II, Danish marriage and claims of, II 229, 245, 250, 619; submits to Charles V, 258, 262; and Interim, 264
—— Frederick III, II 595; III 154–5, 163–4, 172 sqq., 189, 210, 241; death of, 703
—— Frederick IV, III 687–8, 708 sqq.; death of (1610), 734, IV 2
—— Frederick V, James I and, III 559; 568 sq.; guardian of, 734; King of Bohemia, IV 3; 6; deserted by Union, 12; opposes succession of Ferdinand, 17; 24; 28; elected King of Bohemia, 29 sq.; 32; and James I, 33 sq.; and War in Bohemia and the Palatinate (1620–3), 64–84; Gustavus Adolphus and, 90; 95; 206; demand for restoration of, 215; death of, 224; 414; Philip IV and, 640; Charles I and, 643; 779
—— John William (Duke of Neuburg), V 381; and Grand Alliance, 403; 435; 438; 448; and Peace of Utrecht, 450; 660; 664

Electors Palatine (*contd.*):—
—— Lewis V, II 40; 155; 203; 220; 238; III 154; 703; 708; 710
—— Otto Henry, II 244; 256; III 154
—— Philip, I 311; acquires the *Junge Pfalz*, 315 sq.
—— Philip William (Duke of Neuburg), IV 426; *Rheinbund* signed by, 431; V 33; 41; 43; and Polish Crown, 350, 354; 645

Palatine Princes, etc.:—
—— Anne di Gonzaga, Princess, and the Fronde, IV 610, 613 sqq.
—— Christopher, Count, III 22 sq.; defeat and death of, 239, 703
—— Dorothea, Electress, daughter of Christian II of Denmark, II 245, 251
—— Elizabeth, Princess, and Descartes, IV 779, 785 sq.; 787; V 640; 755 sq.; VI 5
—— Lewis Philip, Prince, IV 226; 247
—— Louisa Juliana, Electress, wife of Frederick IV, III 713; IV 29; Gustavus Adolphus and, 203; V 628
—— Maria Anna Louisa, Electress, wife of John William, VI 138
—— Maurice, Prince (son of Frederick V), IV 304; in Dorset, 313; 321; 335; in the Mediterranean, 465
—— Count Philip of (brother of Elector Otto Henry), II 221
—— Rupert, Count, the Landshut succession and, I 315
—— Rupert, Prince (son of Frederick V). *See* Rupert

Pale, The English, III 580, 609–11

Paleario, Aonio, Italian Reformer, II 395 sq.; III 457, 465

Palen, Constantine, and Emancipation of Serfs, XI 615

Paleocapa, Pietro, Venetian Liberal leader, XI 76

Paleologus, Constantine XII, last Emperor of the East, I 103
—— Demetrius, tyrant of the Morea, I 74
—— John VI, Emperor of the East, the Venetians and, I 258
—— Manuel II, Emperor of the East, I 541
—— Thomas, tyrant of the Morea, I 74

Palermo, the Dutch defeated at (1675), V 162; captured by Spain, VI 32; 124 sq.; 153; Jacobin plot in, VIII 556; flight of the King and Queen of Naples to (1798), 652, (1805), IX 263; political interests of, 381; British threaten (1812), 384; insurrection at, XI 77, 80; 92; Garibaldi at, 388, 533, XII 217; XI 541

Palestine, archaeological work in, XII 774

Palestrina, Giovanni Pierluigi de, the *Missa di Papa Marcello*, II 686

Palestro, battle at, XI 383

Paley, William, theologian, VI 88; *Moral and Political Philosophy*, VIII 763; *Evidences of Christianity*, XII 775

Palffy von Erdoed, Count Aloys, Governor of Venice, xi 82

Palfrey, John Gorham, historian, xii 841

Palgrave, Sir Francis, historian, xii 835

Palikao, Charles-G.-M.-A.-A. Cousin-Montauban, Count de, xi 473; 588; and the war with Germany, 595 sqq.; flight of, 600

Palissy, Bernard, ii 292; v 738

Palizzolo, Sicilian criminal, xii 239

Palladio, Andrea, his *Caesar*, iii 471

Palladius. *See* Sjælland, Bishop of

Pallavicini della Priola, Emilio, Marquis, Italian general, xi 534

Pallavicino, Giambattista, Lutheran, ii 380 sq.

—— Giorgio, x 119; and Italian unity, xi 375

—— Cardinal Pietro Sforza, and Julius II, ii 9; and Leo X, 10

Palliser, Sir Hugh, Admiral, vi 451

Palm, Johannes Henricus van der, Dutch writer, xi 676

—— Johann Philipp P., Nürnberg bookseller, murder of, ix 272; 326

Palma, *autos de fé* at, v 375; Gulf of, Nelson at, ix 220

—— Estrada, President of Cuba, xii 697

—— Jacopo, Venetian painter, i 284

—— (*alias* Bando), Spanish brigand, xii 259

Palmairas, on San Francisco river, v 677

Palmella, Pedro de Souza Holstein, Duke of, Portuguese statesman, at Congress of Vienna, ix 584; x 317; in London, 322 sqq., 326; at Terceira, 324; in the Azores, 327; missions of, to London, 330; 331 sq.; at Faro, 333; 335; Minister of Maria II, 338; xi 572

Palmer, gold discovered at, xii 619

—— Sir Henry, iii 309

—— Roger, Earl of Castlemaine. *See* Castlemaine

—— Sir Thomas, accuses Somerset, ii 505; execution of, 520

—— Thomas Fysche, Anglican clergyman in Dundee, viii 770

—— William, and the Nizám of Haidárábad, xi 727

Palmerston, Henry John Temple, 3rd Viscount, vii 391; x 156; and Greek Question, 204; 232; 234; and Portuguese affairs, 326, 330; and Polish revolution, 474; and Belgian Question, 484, 506, 543 sq.; and France, 495; 505; and Mehemet Ali, 511; and rivalry with Russia in Central Asia, 556; and Turko-Egyptian Question, 551, 555, 557, 561 sqq., 566 sqq.; 593; and parliamentary reform, 603; 614; and Catholic emancipation, 642; 666; 675; Eastern policy of, 679; xi 2; 10; Foreign Secretary, 14; foreign policy of, 16 sqq.; dismissal of, 18; 21; Thiers and, 36; 37 sq.; 77; and Austrian policy in Italy, 92;

106; and Hungary, 209; and Switzerland, 250, 252; and the Don Pacifico incident, 281; and Napoleon III, 307; 310; and the causes of Crimean War, 315 sq.; succeeds Lord Aberdeen, 320; and Crimean War, 321 sqq.; 325; and Divorce Bill, 326 sq.; defeat of, 328; 329; returns to office (1859), 331; Italian policy of, 331 sq.; and France, 333; and Gladstone's financial scheme, 334 sq.; and Schleswig-Holstein, 224 sq., 337 sq.; 379; Schwarzenberg and, 393; 470; 529; and Spanish marriages, 38 sq., 554 sq.; and Spain, 556 sq.; and Persia, 633; and Suez Canal, 638, xii 430, 433; and Black Sea, xi 639; and China, 805, 807 sq., 814 sq.; death of, 338 sq.; xii 31

Palmier, Pierre. *See* Vienne, Archbishops of

Palmieri, Matteo, Italian Renaissance scholar, i 596

Palmstruch, Livonian banker, iv 578

Palo Alto, battle of (1846), viii 395

Paludan-Müller, Frederick, Danish poet, xi 699; 701

Palz, John von, professor of theology, ii 114

Pamfili, Giovanni Battista. *See* Innocent X

Pamiers, Étienne François de Caulet, Bishop of, v 84 sq.

Pamirs, The, frontier settlement in, xii 52; 343; Russian aggression in, 482; 483; 485; 793; exploration in, 800 sqq.

Pampeluna (Pamplona), surrender of, to Spain (1512), i 366; French in (1808), ix 430; stores of, 435; Palafox and, 442; French retreat to, 478; captured by Wellington (1813), 480; Olózaga arrested at, xi 555

Pamplona. *See* Pampeluna

Panama, attack on (1671), v 691; and Peru, x 248 sq.; trade with, 255; burnt by Morgan (1670), 272; smuggling in, 273; xii 685; and Clayton-Bulwer Treaty, 686; Colombia and, 698; independence of, 699; United States and, 699 sq.

—— Canal, xii 698 sq.

—— Isthmus of, iii 322, vii 433, 438, 637

Pancarte, established and abolished, iii 694

Pancemont, A. F. X. Mayneaud de. *See* Vannes, Bishop of

Panchamal, acquisition of, by Portuguese, ix 718

Pandolfini, Angelo, and Savonarola, i 147

Panin, Count Nikita Ivanovich, Russian statesman, vi 662 sq.; Foreign Minister, 668 sq.; 678 sq.; 682; and *Nakâs* of Catharine II, 686; 697; and Poland, 730; 732; 753; 765; and Swedish *coup d'état*, 772; viii 309 sq.; ix 40; 43, 49-50

—— Count Peter, Russian general, vi 673; 697

Panipat, vi 509; Maráthas defeated at, 524, 568, xi 725

Panis, Étienne-Jean, member of Commune, VIII 225; 234, 247

Panitsa, Major, court-martial on, XII 410

Panizzi, Antonio, XI 380

Panjáb. *See* Punjab

Panmure, James Maule, 4th Earl of, VI 98; 103

Panshino, Russian army at, V 521

Panslavism, origin of, XI 653 sqq.; 656; Russia and, 274, 633 sq.; Balkans and, 284–5; 638–9

Pantaleoni, Diomede, negotiates with Cavour, XI 392

Pantano, Odoardo, Italian politician, XII 221 sq.; 228

Panvinio, Onofrio, work of, on Basilicas, I 610

Panzani, Gregorio, in England, IV 280; 287

Paoli, Pasquale de', Corsican general, VI 350; 439; 609 sq.; VIII 352, 560

Paoting Fu, XII 509; outrages near, 518

Papacy, The, and the Papal State. *See* Rome, Ecclesiastical State of, *and also* individual Popes

Paparrigopoulo, Konstantino, Greek historian, XII 842

Papillon, Thomas, and East India Company, V 700

Papineau, Louis Joseph, and French Canadian party, X 693; XI 768; 775; XII 604

Papino, Frà Girolamo, Inquisitor, II 387

Pappenheim, taken by Horn, IV 229

—— Count Godfrey Henry zu, Bavarian general, IV 76; takes Wolfenbüttel, 102; 196; at Magdeburg, 201 sqq.; 204; at Breitenfeld, 205; at Leipzig, 219; 220 sq.; death of, at Lützen, 221; 696

Pará, commercial monopoly in, V 678; 679; seat of Government at, VII 390

Parabosco, Girolamo, Italian novelist, III 468

Paracelsus, P. A. T. Bombast von Hohenheim, V 730

Parachin, Prince Milan at, XII 386

Paradol, Prévost, French writer, XI 526

Paraguay, Jesuits in, VI 364, 372, 386, 593; administration of, X 249; Indians in, 268; missions of, 269; independence of, 286; despotism in (1810), 297; XII 674; Argentina and, 680; 684; 690

Paraiba Company, VI 385

Paraná, capital of Argentine Confederation, XII 683

—— river, Indians of, V 683; Anglo-French squadron in, XII 681; 682

Paravicini, Giovanni Maria, IV 48 sq.

Paray-le-Monial, pilgrimages to, XII 114

Pardo, The, Convention of, VI 67 sq., 147; Francisco de Asís at, XI 556

Paré, Ambrose, III 19

—— Jules François, Minister of the Interior, VIII 348

Parenti, Piero, historian, I 169, 183, 187

Parentucelli, Tommaso. *See* Nicholas V, Pope

Pares, Bernard, *Russia and Reform*, XI 625

Parga, surrendered to Ali of Janina (1814), X 176; placed under British protection, *ib.*; restored to Ali Pasha (1817), 177

Parieu, Marie-L.-P.-F. Esquirou de, French Minister of Public Instruction, XI 129 sq.

Parini, Giuseppe, Italian poet, VIII 778 sqq.; XI 549

Paris, University of, resists Papacy, I 635 sq., 667; placards of, II 286; Edict of (1543), 288; Protestant Church organised at (1555), 293; first Synod at (1559), 295; entered by Guise (1562), III 1; assault upon, by Coligny and Condé, 4; Massacre of St Bartholomew at (1572), 19; disorder in, 27; return of King Charles IX to, 29; clergy of, preach a "boycott" of the Huguenots, 30; intrigues of the League in, 39; government of the "Sixteen" in, 42; Guise master of, 43–4; receives news of murder of Guise, 46; invested by army of Henry III (1589), 47; besieged by Henry IV, relieved by Duke of Parma, 49, 659 sqq.; the "Sixteen" in control of, 50; Jesuit conference in, 288; revolt of, 452; Catholics in, 510–1; deposes Henry III, 511; Perez in, 516; murder of Henry IV in, 690; sanitation of, 693; meeting of States General at (1614), IV 120; assembly of French clergy at, 143; Buckingham at, 131; alliance with the United Provinces concluded at (1635), 144; 147; Löffler at, 247; 251; 368; Bernard at, 369; 371 sq.; 375; Erlach at, 376, 379; 381; in revolt, 599; 602; 604 sqq.; 609 sq.; and the Court (1649), 611 sqq.; Condé leaves, 614 sq.; fight in, 617; return of Mazarin to (Feb. 1653), 618; 621; march of the Cardinal Infante to, 698; 718; 727; disorders in, V 16; 740 sq.; Peter the Great in, VI 28; 97; the Young Pretender in, 110; 111; 121; growth of, 133; disturbances in, 144; famine in, 162; 169; Law's System in, 175; 308; 315; Count Kaunitz at, 335; 338; Family Compact signed at, 344; military school at, 349; 358 sq.; 783; population of, VIII 60; disorder in (1787), 106, (1789), 123; elections in (1789), 130 sqq.; becomes focus of the Revolution, 160 sq.; outbreak of Revolution in (July), 163 sqq.; (October 5 and 6), 184 sq.; *fédérés* in (1790), 191; the Church in, 196; affairs in (1792), 225 sq., 233; monarchical feeling in, 238; the September massacres in, 242; National Convention in, Chap. IX *passim*; the Terror in, Chap. XII *passim*; condition of, after the Terror, 378 sq., 382; the Allies and, 429, 431 sq., 434; royalists in, IX 16; concentration of government at, 33; Baron Reuterholm in, 37; German Princes at (1802), 93; Helvetian Club formed at, 95; improvements in, 120; theatres in,

129; republican plot in, 137; unemployed in, 143; fraudulent bankruptcy in, 177; Spina in, 181; Napoleon's coronation in (1805), 191; Pope Pius VII in, 192; Papal Legate leaves, 195; chancery of Archbishop of, 197; Congregation of, 197; action of Chapter of, 198; financial crisis in, 258; Turkish ambassador at, 386; 397; archives of, 411; censor at, 417; criticism in, 419; representatives from colonial chambers in, 422; intrigues at, 445; 447; capitulation of (1814), 482; entry of Napoleon into (1812), 508; Prussian envoy sent to, 512; Napoleon leaves, 516; the Allies and, 549 sqq.; Louis XVIII and, 562; Charter of (1814), 563; art galleries of, 564; Imperial guard removed from, 567; discontent in, 569, 571–2; flight of Louis XVIII from, 575; *fédérés* of, 619; Allies advance on (1815), 643–4; artistic spoils of, 666; disturbances in (1822), x 76, (1830), 99–100; Cardinal Consalvi at, 133 sq., 140; Cardinal della Genga at, 139; revolution of 1830 in, 475 sqq.; riots (1831) in, 484; insurrections in (1832), 488, (1834), 492; and development of agriculture, 730; mechanical industry in, 744; the Bourse of, 748; retail trade in, 759; events in, during the Republic, 1848–52, Vol. xi, Chap. v *passim*; 31; 290; banks in, 298; 300; improvements in, 302 sq.; 333; 371; King Victor Emmanuel in, 373; the defence of, 497 sqq.; political demonstration in, 485; 488; Commune in, 502 sqq.; 578; 580; and War with Germany, 594 sqq.; investment of, 600 sqq.; bombardment of, 608; the last sortie from, 611; 851; xii 12; Irish Republican Brotherhood in, 75; Commune in, 91; 93; 95; fortresses of, 96; Universal Exhibition at, 101; 103; 106 sq.; Collectivist meetings at, 125; 126; King Alfonso XII in, 264; Russian Liberators in, 347; Armenian meetings in, 416; Dogger Bank arbitration at, 594; Venezuelan Boundary Commission at, 688; Behring Sea arbitration at, 721; municipal expenditure of, 734; University of, xi 67, 297, xii 762; 792; 822; 832

Paris, *Parlement* of, Constitution of, i 401 sq.; (1521), proclamation of, ii 283; the Protestants and (1542), 288; (1555), refuses to set up the Inquisition, 294; objects to persecution (1559), 296; declares Huguenots rebels, iii 2; demands modification of Edict of Amboise, 6; censures Trent Decrees, 7; 662 sqq., 672; action of, in 1614–5, iv 120 sq.; 139; on death of Louis XIII, 593; and government of Mazarin, the Fronde, etc., 604 sqq.; v 3; vi 146; in 18th century, 347 sq.; 356; viii 47, 66, 73; opposition of, to Turgot, 87; to Crown, 106 sqq., 111, 115; 745

Paris, Treaties of (1623), iv 57; (Franco-Swedish, 1634), 248 sqq.; (1657), 619; (1778), vi 449; (1787), viii 323; (1806), ix 265 sq.; (1810), 323; (1814), ix 658, x 9, 519; (1856), xi 276, 308, 323 sqq., 577, 611, 614, 633 sqq., 639, 643, 647, 745, xii 28, 298, 382, 388, 392; Preliminaries of (1727), vi 146 sq.; Peace of (1763), v 443, vi 346 sq., 349, 422 sq., 428, 430, vii 70; and French colonial possessions, vi 549, 561, vii 113, 143, x 685; First Peace of (1814), ix 576 sq., 588, 591, 604, 614, 618, 647, 653, 664 sq.; Second Peace of (1815), 653, 665, 669, vii 366, x 11, 16 sq., 48, 524; Convention of (1808), ix 318, (1815), x 177; Congress of (1856), xi 306, 374, 380, xii 143; Conference at (1858), xi 306, 633, 649; (1869), 634, 636; Declaration of (1856), xii 16; 18; 715

Paris, Archbishops of:—
—— Christophe de Beaumont, vi 347; 591
—— Denis-Auguste Affre, xi 113
—— Georges Darboy, xi 505; 719; 721
—— Jean-Baptiste-Joseph Gobel, viii 158, 359
—— Jean-S. Maury, Cardinal. *See* Maury
—— Louis-Antoine de Noailles, v 89 sq.

Paris, Louis-Philippe-Albert d'Orléans, Comte de, xi 101 sq.; xii 92; 103; and Comte de Chambord, 107 sq.; 112; 271
—— François de, deacon, viii 9
—— Matthew, evidence of, as to Greek studies, i 537
—— George van, execution of, ii 501

Pâris brothers, French financiers, vi 174

Parisio, legate appointed to open Council of Trent, ii 661

Park, Mungo, African explorer, vi 188; xii 806 sqq.; 811

Parkány, defeat of the Poles at (1683), v 363

Parke, John G., American general, vii 538

Parker, Sir Hyde, British admiral, vi 452; ix 48 sqq.
—— Matthew, Archbishop of Canterbury, consecrated, ii 571, 576, 597
—— Sir Peter, Admiral, viii 477
—— Richard, leader of the Nore mutiny, viii 454, 479 sq.
—— Samuel, Bishop of Oxford, Descartes and, iv 791; and Nonconformists, v 331; vi 656
—— Theodore, American clergyman, vii 744

Parkes, Sir Harry Smith, in China, xi 815 sq.; 819; in Japan, 853, xii 543 sq.
—— Sir Henry, and New South Wales, xii 626; 631

Parkman, Francis, American historian, vii 100, 745; xii 841

Parlamento, the Florentine, and reforming work of Savonarola, i 155 sqq.

Parlement of Paris. *See* Paris, *Parlement* of

Parlements, French provincial, v 1 sqq., 74; viii 47, 65; reinstated (1774), 82, 86 sq.; and corn tax, 85; 100, 104 sq.; contest between Crown and (1787), 106 sqq., 111, 115; unpopularity of, 116, 139; end of, 167, 177; 711

Parliament of Great Britain. *See* England

Parliamentary Reform, English, and Place-Bills, v 273; projects of (1766-83), vi 455 sq., 458 sq., 465; motion for, by Marquis of Blandford, x 593; Lord Grey and, 594; general movement for, 594 sqq.; passage of Bill (1832), 616; its results, 616 sqq.; organisation and first action of Reform League, xi 340 sqq.; Reform Bill of 1867, *ib.*, 345 sq.; extension of County franchise (1884), xii 41 sq.; Irish, in 1782-3, vi 458 sq., 501 sq., 505, *see also* Ireland, Home Rule

Parma, acquired by French (1499), i 121; annexed by Julius II (1512), 251; acquired by the Papacy (1521), ii 44; given to Pierluigi Farnese, 80; disputed between Paul III and Charles V, 83-6; War of (1642-4), iv 600; Prince Eugene in, v 403; vi 29; 60; Elisabeth Farnese and, 122; 126; claims to, 138; 139; Don Carlos succeeds to, 149 sq.; 152; War in, 153 sq.; 155 sq.; 159; taken by Spain, 160; Don Philip and, 167, 239, 249 sq., 608; Treaty of Seville and, 202; taken by Duke Francis III of Modena, 243; 245; relinquished by Maria Theresa, 246; 366; the Papacy and, 587, 594; 600; French annexation of (1808), ix 141, 247, 398; creation of duchies in, 268; Austria assumes administration of, 647; 652; assigned to Empress Marie-Louise (1814), 559, 660, x 105 sqq.; Marie-Louise flies from (1830), 120; Papal territory demanded for, 132; revolution in, 155; and Infanta Marie-Louise, 212; under Empress Marie-Louise, xi 69 sq.; 75; union of, with Piedmont, 83, 386; 84; 88; 381; 468; xii 226; socialism in, 232

Parma, Dukes of:—
—— Alexander Farnese (Prince of, *afterwards* Duke), marriage of (1565), iii 200; Commander in Netherlands (1578-92), 249 sqq., 289, 503 sq., 618, 620 sqq.; and English succession, 358; 385; 423; 450; and invasion of England, 504 sq.; attacks Aachen, 705, Neuss, 712, 450; invades France (1590), 49 sqq.; at Rouen, 517; death of (1592), 51, 517
—— Antonio Farnese, vi 138; 147; 149
—— Charles. *See* Charles III, King of Spain
—— Ferdinand (of Bourbon), vi 593 sq.; viii 79, 555, 570; death of (Oct. 1802), ix 398
—— Francesco Farnese, vi 35; 38; 122; 125; and Spanish claims, 138 sq.; 586
—— Louis, King of Etruria, ix 69; 87, 302, 398, 602

Parma, Dukes of (*contd.*):—
—— Odoardo I, and Spain, iv 373; quarrel between the Barberini and, 685; excommunicated, 686 sq.
—— Ottavio Farnese, ii 72, 75, 83 sqq., 87, 269; iii 187; relations of, with Charles V and Philip II, 476
—— Philip, vi 139; 141; 158; in Italy, 159 sqq., 167; 237; and the Family Compact, 239, 344 sq., 368; 250; at Parma, 245; 339; 363; 366; the Franco-Austrian alliance and, 401; 597; 608
—— Pierluigi Farnese (son of Paul III), ii 69, 72, 80, 82; murder of, 83, 263; iii 187; relations of, with Charles V and Philip II, 476
—— Rinuccio I, a vassal of Spain, iv 666; and Clement VIII, 668

Parma, Henrietta (of Modena), Duchess of, wife of Antonio, vi 147
—— Louisa Elisabeth (*or* Marie-Louise), Duchess of (daughter of Louis XV), wife of Infant Philip, vi 158
—— Margaret, Duchess of (daughter of Charles V), marriage of, to Alessandro de' Medici, ii 25; marriage of, to Ottavio Farnese, 72; Regent of the Netherlands, 578 sq.; 582, iii 187 sq.; account of her rule, 191-217 *passim*; quits the Netherlands, 217; 228; 234; 265; 481; 489; death of (1586), 514
—— Marie-Louise (Infanta), Duchess of (Queen of Etruria), ix 88; 398; deposed, 399; Queen Dowager, 584; 602; Lucca assigned to, 661; provision for, x 212

Parnell, Charles Stewart, xii 36; 40 sq.; and Lord Carnarvon, 42; 48; and the "Manchester martyrs," 65; 74 sqq.; in America, 77; 78; trial of, 79; and the Irish Land Act, 80; imprisoned, 80 sq.; and the Phoenix Park murders, 81 sq.; 83 sqq.; death of, 87
—— Sir Henry Brooke, xi 3
—— Sir John, dismissed from Exchequer, ix 703
—— Thomas, poet, x 697

Paros, surrendered by Venice to Turks, iii 116

Parpaglia, Vincent, appointed Nuncio to Elizabeth, ii 578; stopped by Philip, 579; 586 sq.

Parr, Catharine. *See* Catharine
—— Samuel, viii 763, 765

Parrasio, Gianpaolo, ii 16

Parris, Robert, and the purchase of Maori lands, xi 799

Parry, Sir William Edward, Polar expeditions of, xii 814

Parsdorf, convention at (1800), ix 64

Parsons, Sir Lawrence, and the Irish rebellion, ix 701; and the Union, 703
—— Robert, iii 287-90, 350, 353, 528, 533
—— Sir William, Lord Justice, iv 521; 534

Parthenay, captured by the Vendeans, VIII 340

Parthenopean Republic, The, VIII 653, 779; fall of, 657. *See also* Naples

Particelli, Michel, Sieur d'Emery, finances and, IV 605; dismissal of, 606

Partition Treaties, of Poland, the First, VI 630; Vol. x, Chap. xx (2), 729–34, 669 sq.; for the Second and Third, namely, The extinction of Poland, Vol. VIII, Chap. XVII, 521–52

—— Treaties, of the Spanish monarchy. *See* Spain, *especially* Vol. v, Chap. XIII, The Treaties of Partition and the Spanish Succession

Partouneaux, Louis, Comte, surrender of, IX 503

Party-government, in England, "Petitioners" and "Abhorrers" (1679), v 226; under Queen Anne, Chap. xv, 460–76; under Walpole, VI 70 sq.; under William III and Anne, 815 sqq. *See also* England, etc.

Paruta, Paolo, historian, III 114, 457

Pas de Calais, coal mining in, XII 100

Pascal, Blaise, II 711; VIII 4; life and work of, IV 794 sq.; *Lettres Provinciales*, 795, x 134; *Pensées*, IV 796; 798; and Montaigne, v 64 sq.; 73; 84 sq.; and mathematical science, 710, 712; 715; 744; 748; x 154; 159; 166; XI 526

Pascendi Dominici Gregis, Encyclical of Pius X, XII 230

Paschal, Charles, French envoy to the Grisons, IV 43 sqq.

Pascual, Mateo, Professor of Theology at Alcalá, II 401

Pashek, John, of Wrat, Bohemian politician, I 338

Pasini, Valentino, XI 76; and the defence of Venice, 95

Paskiévich, Ivan Feodorovich, Russian marshal, x 472 sq.; Viceroy of Poland, 474; in Hungary, XI 210 sq.; 213 sq.

Pasolini, Count Giuseppe, Italian statesman, XI 72 sq.; 81

Pasquali, Carlo. *See* Paschal, Charles

Pasquier, Estienne, III 63, 753–4

—— Étienne-Denis, Duc de, IX 141; 144; x 48; 50; Chancellor of France (1817), 51; 52; and the *Doctrinaires*, 54–5; 56; Minister of Foreign Affairs, 62; 63; and the new electoral proposals, 65; 67; 68; urges dissolution, 70; and intervention abroad, 74; 83; and the re-establishment of religious bodies, 84; opposes the "law of sacrilege," 87; and the revolution of 1830, 478

Pasquier-Brouet, Jesuit, II 652, 654, 656

Passagio, plundered by Venetians, I 80

Passaglia, Carlo, Jesuit, XI 392; 531; 715

Passano, Giovanni Joachino, Seigneur de Vaulx, in England, II 423 sqq., 427

Passarowitz, Peace of, VI 32; 125; 203; 308; 587; and Venice, 605

Passau, Conference at (1552), II 272; Treaty of (1552), 273, 672, III 141, 718, 724, IV 108, 410; Leopold I at, v 360; taken by Elector of Bavaria, VI 231; 236

—— Archduke Leopold, Bishop of, III 642, 702

Passerat, Jean, III 69

Passeyer, home of Andreas Hofer, IX 355

Passive obedience, doctrine of, III 752 sqq.

Passos, Manuel, Portuguese statesman, x 338

Passy, François, French deputy, XI 98

—— Hippolyte-Philibert, x 493; 495; and Algiers, 503; 511; French Finance Minister, XI 118

Pasteur, Louis, XII 779 sqq.

Paston Letters, The, I 492

Pastor, Ludwig, German historian, XII 847 sq.

Pastor Aeternus, the Bull (1516), II 31

Pastoret, Claude-E.-J.-P., Marquis de, VIII 213, 488

Pastrengo, Austrian attack on, XI 84

Pasvan Oglu, Pasha of Widdin, x 172

Patagonia, Magalhães and the coast of, I 36; Chili and, XII 679; 692

Patarenes, The. *See* Bogomils

Pater, Adrian Janszoon, at Pernambuco, IV 707 sq.

Paterno, Pedro, negotiates with Aguinaldo, XII 530

Paterson, Eliza, wife of Jerome Bonaparte, IX 107; 193

—— James, and the Darien scheme, v 296

—— William, founder of the Bank of England, v 267; 271

Patin, Gui, and Cartesianism, v 73; 86

Patiño, Don José de, Spanish statesman, VI 64 sq.; 126; 142; 145 sqq.; and England, 151, 155; 157; 159; Elisabeth Farnese and, 166; 382; death of, 156

Patkul, Johann Reinhold von, Swedish statesman, v 577; 580; and Charles XI and Augustus II, 586; and the league against Sweden, 586 sq.; at Moscow, 587; 590; 592 sqq.; execution of, 595

Patna, seizure of, VI 560; 561; Court of Appeal at, IX 711; opium factory at, XII 485

Patras, taken by Doria, III 108; Turkish defeat at (1687), v 365; Greek rising at (1821), x 179; French occupation of, XI 277

—— Germanos, Archbishop of, x 179

Patrick, Simon, Bishop of Ely, v 753

Patrie, La, French newspaper, XI 123; 292

Patriot King, Bolingbroke's, VI 71

"Patriots," English party of, v 71; theories of, and the *Craftsman*, 818 sq.

Patrizzi, Francesco, II 707

Patrocinio, Sor Maria de los Dolores, XI 557; 561

Patterson, Robert, VII 464; attacks Harper's Ferry, 465; 466

Patterson, William, American politician, Vol. VII, Chap. VIII *passim*

Patton, Philip, Admiral, VIII 453, 479

Pau, *Parlement* of, V 4, VIII 47

Paul, St, II 712 sq.

—— II (Pietro Barbo), Pope, I 71, 80, 560, 624; George Podiebrad and, 655; taxation of the Church under, 662; great wealth of, 666; III 469

—— III (Alessandro Farnese), Pope, I 567, 662; II 15, 21, 23, 32 sqq., 69 sqq.; intrigues of, for Pierluigi Farnese, 80, 83; 90; attempts reform, 233; 235; 239; denounces Diet of Speier, 249; summons Council of Trent, 249, 643, 661; 251, 255, 260; the *Interim* and, 265; the *Consilium de Emendanda Ecclesia* and, 379; Bull *Licet ab initio* of, 381; 385; the Portuguese Inquisition and, 414; Henry VIII and, 444, 449, 474; Church reform and, 642 sq., 644; Inquisition set up in Rome by, 650; the Jesuits and, 653; the Council of Trent and, 662–70; elected (1534), III 110; prepared to defend Rome against Barbarossa, 112; included in the Peace with Porte (1547), 120, 187; 390; and St Peter's, 442; and the Inquisition, 446; 465; 479; and Ireland, 585, 592

—— IV (Giovanni Pietro Caraffa), Pope, II 33 sq.; reign of, 89–92; the Oratory of Divine Love and, 379; proceeds against reformers, 381 sq., 387; 399; and Spain, 534, 545; Pole and, 546; Elizabeth and, 564, 636, 640; Church reform and, 643 sq., 648, 673; Loyola and, 652 sq., 655 sq.; Council of Trent and, 674; the *Index Librorum Prohibitorum*, 687; III 6 sq.; animus of, against Habsburgs, 123, 145, 168, 476, 479; 186; 191; and Elizabeth, 263–4; 390; 425; and Inquisition, 465, 488; death of, 482; IV 683; V 118

—— V (Camillo Borghese), Pope, I 270, 660; III 440; and the Moriscos, 542; 684; and Spain, 686, 688; 710; and Matthias, 721, 727; 729; and Venice, 744; and the Emperor, IV 31; 629; Osuña and, 632; 643; 669; quarrel of, with Venice, 670 sq.; and the Valtelline question, 672; death of, *ib.*; 674

—— I, Tsar, VI 340; 658 sqq.; 662; 679; accession of, 681; 696; 700; 743; signs the Treaty of Exchange, 753; VIII 547, 552, 583, 635, 643; policy of, 644 sqq., 785 sq.; IX 40 sqq.; 47 sqq.; 69; assassination of (1801), 70; and Charles Emmanuel IV King of Sardinia, 71; 181; 297; and Turkey, 385; and Asia Minor, 386; and the navy, X 417; 423

Paulding, Hiram, American admiral, VII 454

Paulet, *or* Poulet, Sir Amias, III 31–2, 292

—— adviser of Henry IV, from whom the *Paulette* took its name, III 695

Paulette, The, French tax, III 695; IV 120; and the opening of the Fronde, 605 sq.

Paulinist Order, III 75

Paulus, Nicholas, German historian, XII 847

—— Pierre, Dutch politician, VIII 787

Pauncefote, Sir Julian, *afterwards* Lord, VII 672; XII 687; 699; 723

Paunsdorf, Reynier at, IX 539

Pauvan, Jacques, preacher of Meaux, II 284

Pauw, Adrian, Lord of Heemsteede, Dutch representative at Münster, IV 401, 715; 697; Grand Pensionary of Holland, V 139

—— Reinier, III 650 sq.; 655

Pavani, Vicar-General of the Jesuits, X 154

Pavia, Council of (1423), I 677; the battle of (1525), 94, II 23, 50 sq., 423 sq.; effect of, on Peasants' Rising, 181; effect of, in Switzerland, 326; captured by Lautrec (1527), 57; Treaty of (1617), IV 124, 129; Peace between Savoy and Spain at, 626, 631; seminary at, VI 637; riot in (1796), VIII 571; military school at, IX 86; King Charles Albert at, XI 82; riots in (1898), XII 220

—— Manuel, Spanish Republican general, XII 261 sq.

Pavillon, Nicolas, Bishop of Alet. *See* Alet

Pavlovsk, Tsar at, IX 34; railway to, XI 266

Paxton, Charles, Surveyor and Searcher of the Port of Boston, VII 177

Payan, Claude François de, *Agent National*, VIII 364, 371

Payer, Julius, Austrian explorer, XII 795

Payne, Lewis, attempts to assassinate Seward, VII 546 sq.

Pays, Le, French newspaper, XI 292

Pays de Gex, persecution in, V 22, 25

Paz, Duarte de, resists the Inquisition, II 413

Pázhukin, Russian Minister, XII 314; 316; 318 sq.

Pázmány, Peter, Archbishop of Gran. *See* Gran

Pazzi, conspiracy of the, I 661

Pea Ridge, Federal victory at (1862), VII 496

"Peace of the Church," The, of Clement IX, an attempt to end Jansenist trouble, V 743

"Peace of Monsieur," The, III 30

Peacham, Edmond, III 565

Peachell, John, Vice-Chancellor of the University of Cambridge, V 237 sq.

"Pearl," Turkish code of laws, I 98

Pearl of the Passion, II 107

Peary, Robert E., Polar expeditions of, XII 815

Peasants' Revolt, The German (1524–6), origin, course, and results of, II 174 sqq.; demands of (1525), 180, 183 sq., 185 sq.; results of, 191 sq.

—— War, The, in the Netherlands (1492), I 450; in Hungary (1514), 337

Pe-chi-li, Gulf of, XII 792
Pechlin, Baron Carl Fredrik, Swedish statesman, VI 763 sq.; 768; 781
Peckham, Sir Edmund, II 544
—— Sir Henry, plots against Mary, II 544
Pecquet, Jean, anatomist, V 727
Pecquigny, defences of, III 672
Pécs, Georga Szakmáry, Bishop of, I 336
Péczeli, Joseph, Hungarian poet, XI 422
Peddie, Major, on the Nunez river, XII 807
Pedersen, Christian, translator of New Testament into Danish, II 610
Pederssön, Gebel. *See* Bergen, Bishop of
Pedro I, Emperor of Brazil (Pedro IV of Portugal), Prince Royal, x 313; Regent in Brazil, 313 sqq.; declared Emperor, 316; character and policy of, 317 sqq.; and the settlement with Portugal, 319 sq.; and Portuguese succession, 320; 321; and Great Britain, 323; 324; abdication of (1831), 325; in England and France, 326; in the Azores, 327; lands in Portugal, 328; besieged in Oporto, 329 sqq.; at Lisbon, 334 sqq.; and surrender of Dom Miguel, 336; death of, 337
—— II, Emperor of Brazil, x 325; XII 674 sq.
—— II, King of Portugal, V 35
—— III, King Consort of Portugal, VI 388
—— IV, King of Portugal. *See* Pedro I, Emperor of Brazil
—— V, King of Portugal, x 339; XI 573 sq.
Peel, General Jonathan, Secretary for War, XI 341
—— Sir Robert, 1st Baronet, and the Factory Act, IX 691; x 584
—— Sir Robert, 2nd Baronet, and Canada, IX 746; x 557; reforms by, 585; 587; and Canning, 591; 593; and Bentham, 598; 601; and Reform Bills, 610 sq., 615; and Catholic emancipation, 634, 642, 645, 650 sqq.; policy of, as Chief Secretary for Ireland, 636 sq., 655; 657; supports the Poor Law Bill, 662; Ministry of, 666 sqq.; resignation of, 668; 669; and municipal reform, 671 sq.; and Dissenters' marriages, 673; and Queen Victoria, 678, 681; 680; influence of Ricardo on, 773 sq., 777; Ministry of (1841-6), XI 1 sqq.; resignation of (1846), 11; 15 sqq.; 19; death of, 20; and political parties, *ib.*; 309 sq.; 320; and Colonial dues, 762; XII 68; 71; and Free Trade, 743; 760
—— Sir Robert, 3rd Baronet, Irish Secretary, XI 343; 529
—— Sir William, naval captain, at Lucknow, XI 748
Peele, George, the tragedy of *Edward I*, III 375
Peereboom, J. van den. *See* Van den Peereboom
Pegram, John, Confederate general, VII 457
Pegu, British annexation of, XI 742, XII 479
Pehtang, American envoy at, XI 817; 818

Peiho river, XI 808; 815 sq.
Peirpoint, Francis H., Federal Governor of Virginia, VII 455 sq.
Peitsang, engagement at, XII 520
Peitz, Danckelmann at, V 662
Peixoto, Floriano, General, Vice-President of Brazil, XII 675
Peking, Russian envoy to, V 544; mission, x 422 sq.; XI 753; European representatives at, 802; 803; Convention of (1860), 812; 813; 815; 817 sq.; 823; establishment of Legations at, 819; 822; foreign representatives at, XII 501 sq., 504; railway at, 505 sq.; science school at, 506; 508; 517; legations besieged at, 519 sq.; Japanese embassy to, 557; the Boxer movement in, 575; 792; 796; Central Asiatic routes to, 802 sqq.
Peking Gazette, XII 518
Pelagius II, Pope, I 267
Pelcl, František, Čech writer, XI 654
Pelew, Germany and, XII 667
Pelham, battle between Lincoln and Shay's "Regulators" at, VII 313
—— Henry, statesman, colonial policy of, VI 58 sq.; 71 sq.; Ministry of, 74 sq.; 396; death of, 402
—— Sir William, III 597
Pelim, Münnich banished to, VI 312
Pélissier, Aimable-Jean-Jacques. *See* Malakhoff, Duc de
Pélisson, Paul, and the Huguenots, V 22
Pelletan, Eugène, French journalist, XI 487
Pellew, Admiral. *See* Exmouth, Viscount
Pellican, Conrad, Reformer, II 161, 356
Pellico, Silvio, x 124; *Mie Prigioni*, 127; XI 79; 547
Pelloux, Luigi, General, Italian statesman, XII 221 sq.
Pelly, Sir Lewis, at Peshawar, XII 467
Pemba island, British protectorate over, XII 661
Pemberton, John Clifford, Confederate general, VII 504 sq.
Pembroke, town of, taken by Cromwell, IV 349; French force lands in (1797), VIII 475
—— Thomas Herbert, 8th Earl of, V 250
—— William Herbert, 1st Earl (2nd cr.), II 475, 495, 499, 505 sq., 517, 530
Penafiel, Miguelist force repulsed at (1832), x 329
Penance, Sacrament of, II 125; considered at Council of Trent, 672
Penang, British occupation of, XII 532
Peñaranda, Count Guzman de, IV 401, 715
Peneios river, Greek frontier and, XII 398
Penjdeh, XII 42; 343; claimed by Russia, 478
Penn, Richard, envoy of American Congress, VI 447
—— Sir William, Admiral, IV 468; appointed, 478 sq.; in West Indies, 481 sq.; Gibraltar and, 484; V 190
—— William, quaker, V 234 sq.; 237; 238; 255; 262; 336; 692; 756; VII 29, 47 sq.; character of, 49 sqq.

Penning, agent of Cardinal Pole in England, II 519

Pennington, Sir John, Admiral, IV 258; 261; imprisoned, 646; at the battle of the Downs, 700

Pennsylvania, trade of, VI 51; 447; settlement of, V 685, VII 49 sqq.; 53; political conditions in, 54; education in, 59; 125; and Continental Congress, 164; writs of assistance in, 181; General Assembly of (1765), 183; charter of, 198 sq.; Constitution of, 239, 241 sq.; and Annapolis Convention, 244; and Constitutional Convention, 246 sq., 251, 253, 255, 263 sq., 275, 298 sq.; encouragement of manufactures in, 354 sq.; population of, 359; 360; slavery in, 361; coal in, 375; and Tariff, 377, 381; Lee invades (1863), 487; Confederate raid into (1864), 532; Democrats in, 631; builds Portage railroad, 695; coal in, 704

Penny, Nicholas, Brigadier-General, in India, XI 740

Penobscot river, American fleet destroyed in (1779), VI 449; settlement on, VII 111, 220; British successes on (1814), 344

Peñon de la Gomera, captured by Spain (1508), I 365

—— de Velez, battle of (1564), III 391; Moorish attack on (1774), VI 374

Penrith, Jacobite force at, VI 101

Penruddock, John, rising of, IV 441

Penry, John, III 343, 345

Penryn, and the franchise, X 601

Pensacola, ceded to Spain, VI 126; 377; 453; Spanish settlement, VII 88; British force at (1814), 345; navy-yard at, taken by the Secessionists (1860), 446; recaptured (1862), 552

Pentagouet, French settlement at, VII 111

Pente Pegadia, battle of, XII 421

Penterriedter, Baron von, Austrian envoy at Hanover, VI 29 sq.

Pentland rising (1666), V 110, 284

Penzance, burned by Spaniards, III 321

People's Business, The, revolutionary journal, XII 303

Pepe, Gabriele, X 128

—— Guglielmo, and the Naples revolt, X 112; defeated by the Austrians, 113–4; and General La Fayette, 119; 121; 221; XI 85; 87

Pepin, Guillaume, Dominican preacher, II 280

Peplin, convent of, V 632

Pepoli, Giovanni, III 431

Pepperell, Sir William, VII 116

Pepys, Samuel, IV 549; the Restoration and, 554 sq.; 557; V 124 sq.; 168 sq.; secretary to the Admiralty Commission, 170 sq.; and naval administration, 172 sqq.; 183; 190; 195; 248; 266

Pequods, The, Indian tribe, VII 19, 27

Perak, sultanate of, XII 532 sq.

Perambakam, battle at (1780), IX 714

Perault, Cardinal Raimund, II 112

Perceval, Spencer, Solicitor-general, IX 681; leader of the Tories, 686; 688 sq.; death of, 690

Perche, customs of, V 13

Percier, Charles, French architect, IX 134

Percy, Henry, Lord, II 559

—— Hugh (*afterwards* 2nd Duke of Northumberland (3rd cr.)), VII 165

—— Thomas, Bishop of Dromore, VI 830 sq.; X 698; 710; XI 414; 429

Perczel, Moritz, Hungarian general, XI 185; 203 sqq.; resumes command, 206; 213; at Widdin, 215

Pered, Hungarians defeated at, XI 210

Pereira, commissary-general in Ireland, V 314

Péreire, Émile, French financier, XI 298

—— Isaac, French financier, XI 298

Perekop, lines of, VI 305 sq.; 308; 673

Perényi, Emericus, Hungarian noble, I 336

—— Baron Sigmund von, Hungarian politician, XI 214

Pères de la Foi, suppressed, IX 190

Peretti, Camilla, III 427

—— Francesco, III 427

—— Maria, wife of Fabio Damasceni, III 421

Perevolchna, Swedish surrender at (1709), V 602

Pereyaslavl, Lake of, Peter the Great at, V 520; Treaty of, VI 695

Perez, Antonio, III 113, 407, 498, 500, 514 sqq., 527

—— Juan, Spanish Reformer, New Testament translated by, II 406 sq., 411

Pergola, Bartolommeo della. *See* Della Pergola

Périer, Casimir, X 67; opposes Villèle's financial scheme, 83; 88; opposes proposed Press Law, 89; 120; sends French troops to Ancona, 155 sq.; and the Polish revolution, 474; and revolution of 1830, 476, 478; Ministry of, 485 sqq.; foreign policy of, 487 sq.; death of, 488; 489; 496; and Algiers, 502; 506

Perignon, Dominique Catharine, Marquis de, VIII 440

Périgord, rising in (1575), III 27; peasants' rising in (1594), 664

Périgueux, seized by the Catholics (1581), III 37

Perivolakia, conference on the island of, X 192

Perizonius, Jacobus, Dutch scholar, XII 817

Perm, post-road to, XII 794

Pernambuco, expedition of West Indian Company to, IV 706 sq.; Dutch and, 750 sq., VI 389 sq.; Spanish expedition to (1639), IV 708; 714; V 146; civil war in (1710–1), 678; Company, VI 385; insurrection in (1817), X 312; Portuguese garrison in, 315

Pernau, Erik XIV and, IV 162; 183; Charles XII at, V 588; 590; 603

Pernes, Miguelist force defeated at (1834), x 336

Pernstein, William of, Bohemian politician, i 338

Péronne, Treaty of (1477), i 440; siege of (1536), ii 71; granted to Condé, iii 30; siege of (1871), xi 610

Perote (Mexico), captured by Scott (1847), vii 396

Perotti, Nicholas, Latin Grammar of, i 546; 558

Perovski Fort, attack on, xi 630

Perovsky, Count Basil Alexeievich, Governor-General of Orenburg, xi 273

—— Sophia, Russian revolutionary, xii 307; 310 sq.

"Perpetual Edict" (1577), iii 247

Perpetual Company of the Indies (French), vi 533

—— League, of the Forest Cantons (1315), ii 305

Perpignan, besieged by Francis I, ii 76; Henry IV's designs upon, iii 683

—— Olympe-Philippe Gerbet, Bishop of, xi 469

Perraudi, Cardinal (Raymond Pérault or Péraud), i 311

Perrault, Charles, x 384

Perre, Paulus van der, Pensionary of Middelburg, v 139; 141

Perrégaux, François-Alexandre-Charles de, French general, x 504

Perrenot, Jérome, brother of Cardinal de Granvelle, iii 190

—— See Champagny, Chantonnay and Granvelle

Perrinchief, Richard, royalist divine, v 331

Perron, French officer, and the Marátha war, ix 720 sqq.

Perrone, Ettore, Italian general, xi 93

—— Giovanni, theologian, xi 713

Perrot, Sir John, iii 595-6, 602-4

Perry, Matthew Galbraith, American commodore, negotiates with Japan, vii 434; xi 824; 827 sqq.; 834; 836; 839; xii 565

—— Oliver Hazard, American commodore, vii 340

Perryville, battle at (1862), vii 507

Persia, Turks and, i 88 sq.; War of, with Egypt (1514), 90 sq.; Turkish Campaign in (1548), iii 120; Bayazid flies to, 124; in alliance with Spain, 541; Ferdinand's embassy to Shah of, 118; countermove of, against Turkey, 120–1; Dutch and English in, iv 743; Russia and, v 544 sq., vi 672, x 175; under Safevi kings, vi 507; 508; disturbances in, 512; 524; 527; French Treaty with (1807), ix 289; and Russian advance in Asia, x 203; 413; Russian War with (1827-8), 444; xi 274, 633; Russian intrigues in, x 545; 556; attacks Herat (1838), 558, xi 732; and Turkey, 276; 733; British War with, 745; xii 4; 34;

56; Russia and, 343 sq., 378 sq.; 485; relations of, with Great Britain and Russia, 491 sq.; 498; early travellers in, 793; exploration in, 800 sq.

Persia, Shah of, ix 289

Persian Gulf, xii 342; Lord Curzon visits, 491 sq.; 499

Persigny, Jean-Gilbert-Victor Fialin, Duc de, xi 134 sq.; 140; 296; ambassador in London, 328; 472 sq.; dismissed, 476

Persson, Göran, Ministry of, iv 162 sq.; 164

Perth, Knox' preaching at, iii 264; convention at (1569), 279; Pacification of (1573), 286; Five Articles of, iv 487 sqq.; march of Cromwell on, 510; taken by the Jacobites, vi 98; Earl of Mar at, 99 sqq.; 102 sq.; Prince Charles at, 112; 115 sq.

—— capital of Western Australia, xi 791

—— titular Duke of. *See* Drummond

—— James Drummond, 4th Earl of, Lord Chancellor of Scotland, v 290

Pertz, Georg Heinrich, German historian, xii 823; 827

Peru, race inhabiting, i 38, 44 sq.; supplies of silver from, 40, 513, v 682, x 250 sq., 258, 268; conquest of, i 45 sq.; Catholic Church in, 60 sq.; 62; v 375; 381; 683; 688; 692; and European trade, 684, vi 183; 190; 351; rebellion in, 381; Republic of, vii 368; under Spanish rule, x 244 sq., 247, 273; power of Viceroy of, 248 sq.; trading regulations in, 255 sq.; native population of, 261 sqq.; French trade with, 272, 274; chamber of mining in, 275; royalist strength in (1811), 287, 306; 290; invasion of, by San Martín (1820), 291 sqq.; Bolívar in, 294 sqq.; independence of (1824), 295 sq.; 297; attitude of the Indians in, 299; 301; and Japan, xii 554 sq.; coolie trade of, 555; 672 sq.; Chili and, 677 sqq.; 689; progress of, 690; 692; 696; 718

Perugia, surrender of, to Julius II (1506), i 128, 245; Cesare Borgia at, 194; Alexander VI at, 232; revolt of (1540), ii 75; University founded at, ix 402; xi 384; occupied by Italian army, 389

Peruzzi, Baldassare, ii 12

Pery, Edmund Sexton Pery, Viscount, vi 494

Pesaro, restored to the Pope, ix 189

—— Giovanni Sforza, Lord of, husband of Lucrezia Borgia, i 234

—— Admiral, iii 114

Pescadores, The, xii 131; ceded to Japan, 512, 572

Pescara, Ferdinando Francesco d'Avalos, Marquis of, ii 23 sq., 44, 48 sqq., 52 sq.

—— Vittoria Colonna, Marchioness of, ii 23, 33 sq., 390, 393, 398; iii 458

Pescatori, Laura, and Queen Elisabeth of Spain, vi 122

Peschiera, Prince Eugene at, v 402; fortress of, xi 82, 85; siege of, 86; 88; 384

Pescia, Domenico da. *See* Domenico, Frà

Peshàwar, Persian descent on, vi 524; Dost Mohammad in, xi 732; 734; Afghan conference at, xii 467; 488

Pessard, Hector, French journalist, xi 303, 477

Pest, siege of (1542), ii 242; occupied by Ferdinand's troops, iii 118; Ferdinand sends an army to, 119; seminary at, vi 637; tumult at, xi 180; murder of Lamberg at, 184; 188; Austrian troops in, 203; 206; 210. *See also* Budapest

Pestalozzi, Johann Heinrich, Swiss writer, viii 781; ix 325–6; schools of, at Burgdorf and Yverdon, 427; xi 260

Pestel, Paul, Russian colonel, x 432 sq.; execution of, 443

Pet, Arthur, explorer, xii 795

Petalidi, French force at, x 201

Petau, Denys, iii 61

Peter I, the Great, Tsar, the Turks and, v 370; 371; and Denmark, 580 sqq.; and Patkul, 586; and league against Sweden, 587; and Great Northern War, 588 sqq.; aids Augustus II of Poland, 593; seeks mediation of the Powers, 595 sq.; and Mazepa, 599 sq.; at Poltava, 601 sq.; and second anti-Swedish league, 602; captures Riga, 603; and War with Turkey, 604 sqq.; at Krossen, 607; in Holstein, 609; conquers Finland, *ib.*; and third anti-Swedish league, 610 sq.; and Mecklenburg compact, 611 sq.; abandons Scanian expedition, 612; alliance of, with Frederick William I, *ib.*; and George I, 613; alliance of, with France and United Provinces (1717), 613; and Sweden, 613 sq.; and Peace of Nystad, 615; 477; 484; 510; 515 sq.; proclaimed Tsar, 517; early years of, 518 sqq.; marriage of, 520; Azoff expeditions of, 521 sq.; conspiracy against, 522; embassy of, to the West, 523; and revolt of the *Strieltzy*, 523; 524; and Tsaritsa Eudoxia, 525; in Amsterdam, *ib.*; reforms by, 526, 528, 531 sq., 536, 545 sqq.; makes peace with Porte, 526 sq.; and War with Sweden, 528; religious toleration by, 529; promotes education, *ib.*; abolishes Patriarchate, 506, 530; and development of trade, 533 sq.; measures by, against peculation, 534 sq.; and his son Alexis, 537 sqq.; proclaimed Emperor, 542; alliances of, with Sweden, France, and England, 542 sq.; operations of, in Asia, 544 sq.; and the succession, 547; crowns Catharine Empress, 547 sq.; death of, 548; 549 sq.; and Peter II, 553; and Frederick I of Prussia, 667; 741; and the Baltic, vi 24; and Sweden, 26, 28, 37; and George I, 27; in Paris, 28; 33 sqq.; 125; 143; and Poland, 191, 193; 200; and Prussia, 206; and the

army, 217; 298; 302; conquests of, in Persia, 304; 305; 312 sq.; 321; 663; and Turkey, 672; 677; 681 sq.; Catharine II and, 691; 693 sq.; 698; 700 sq.; 741; x 371; and the nobles, 429; and Russian serfdom, 436; xi 264

Peter II, Tsar (Grand Duke), v 538; 547; 549; accession of, 552; education of, 553; 554; and the Dolgorukis, 554 sq.; death of, 555; vi 303; 311

—— III, Tsar, vi 252; and Frederick the Great, 298 sq.; 300; accession of, 328, 346; and Poland, 353; 427; marriage of, 658 sq.; 660 sq.; murder of, 662 sq.; 665; policy of, 679 sqq.; and the nobility, 685; 729; 741 sq.; ix 34; xi 267

—— I Karageorgevich, King of Servia, xi 648; xii 386; 407; 412; accession of, 413

—— Arbues, St, murdered, i 359

—— Leopold, Grand Duke of Tuscany. *See* Leopold II, Emperor

—— Martyr. *See* Anghera, Peter Martyr of

—— Martyr. *See* Vermigli, Pietro Martire

Peter Plymley's Letters, ix 690

Peterborough, Charles Mordaunt, 3rd Earl of, v 211; 416; 432

Peterhead, the Old Pretender lands at, vi 102

Peterhof, Peter II at, v 554; Tsarina Anne at, vi 309

Petermann, Andreas, iv 791

Peters, Karl, African explorer, xii 160

Petersburg (Virginia), Manufacturing Society of, vii 354; Butler advances on (1864), 516; 520; siege of, 531, 533, 537 sqq.; evacuation of (1865), 539

Petersen, Frederik Christian, Danish philologist, xi 699

—— Johann Wilhelm, pietist, v 762

—— Johanna Eleonora, pietist, v 762

Peterwardein, taken by the Turks (1526), i 96; Sultan Solyman at (1551), iii 122; Austrians capture (1687), v 367; 368 sqq.; surrenders to Russia (1849), xi 213

Petherick, John, explores the Bahr-el-Gazal, xii 811

Petiet, Claude, French statesman, viii 508; ix 84

Pétion de Villeneuve, Jérôme, viii 174, 186; 188; Mayor of Paris, 220, 225 sq.; and the insurrection of June 20, 228 sqq.; 235 sq., 242 sq.; refuses the Mayoralty (1792), 252; suicide of, 357

Petite République Française, French journal, xii 125

Petition of Right, iv 270 sq.

Petitioners, party of (1679), v 226. *See also* Party-government

Peto, William, preaches against Henry VIII, ii 438; appointed legate to England, 546

Petöfi, Alexander, Hungarian poet, xi 211; 423; 428 sqq.

Petrarca, Francesco (Petrarch), i 264, 536 sq., 538 sqq., 549; death of, 553; iii 457–8, 463; xi 423

Petrashevtsy, The, Russian socialists, xii 296

Petre, Edward, Jesuit, v 233; 235; 255

—— William, Lord Petre, v 220

—— Sir William, Secretary of State, ii 480, 495, 525

—— Dr (Cromwell's deputy as Vicar-General), ii 445

Petri, Henricus, printer, i 617

—— Laurentius (Lars Petersson). *See* Upsala, Archbishops of

—— Olaus (Olaf Petersson), Swedish Lutheran, ii 624 sq., 628, 630

Petrie, W. M. Flinders, Egyptologist, xii 845

Petrików. *See* Piotrkow

Petrobey, Chief of the Maina, x 185

Petropavlovsk fortress, Decembrists in, x 441, 443; xi 272

Petropávlovsk, Russian battleship, sinking of, outside Port Arthur (1904), xii 346; 581

Petrosa, Petrus, iv 175

Petrovich, Bojo, Montenegrin general, xii 386 sq.

Petrucci, Cardinal Alfonso, ii 14

—— Pandolfo, Lord of Siena, i 193

Petrunkévich, Russian politician, exiled, xii 306; 322; Shipóff and, 328; 333; 360

Pett, Sir Phineas, English navy commissioner, v 171

Petty, Dr (Sir) William, Irish survey of, iv 537; v 266; 303; vi 481

Petty-Fitzmaurice, Lord Henry. *See* Lansdowne, Marquis of

Peucker, General Eduard von, Prussian Minister of War, xi 166; 221

Peurbach, George, German astronomer, i 632

Peutinger, Conrad, German humanist, i 323, 325; ii 29

Peynier, Comte de, Governor of San Domingo, viii 193

Peyronnet, Charles-Ignace, Comte de, x 77; and the Press Laws, 89 sq.; 92; 99

Peyton, Edward, Commodore, vi 535; 537

Pézenas, Damville at, iii 24

Pezuela, Juan de la, x 242

Pfaffenbrief, The (1370), ii 311

Pfaffenhofen, Charles of Lorraine defeated at, iv 230

Pfefferkorn, Johann, attacks Reuchlin, i 573, ii 696

Pfeffinger, Dr, Saxon councillor, ii 122

Pfeiffer, Heinrich, revolutionist preacher in Mühlhausen, ii 186; death of, 189

Pfeil, African explorer, xii 160

Pfinsterer, Gulielmus Groen van, Dutch politician, xii 243

Pfintzing, Melchior, printer of Nürnberg, i 326

Pfizer, Paul, German publicist, x 376

Pfleiderer, Otto, German theologian, xii 847

Pflug, Julius. *See* Naumburg, Bishop of

Pfordten, Baron Ludwig Karl Heinrich von der, xi 149; 232; 397

Pforr, Franz, painter, x 151

Pfuel, Ernst Heinrich Adolf von, Prussian general, xi 158; 164; Ministry of, 192

Pfyffer, Edward, Mayor of Luzern, xi 244

—— Kasimir, Luzern statesman, xi 243

—— Ludwig, the Borromean League founded by, ii 341

—— Colonel, iii 9

Phalange, French journal, x 499

Phalaris, Epistles of, xii 816

Phalis, Guillaume de, French scholar, i 636

Phanariots, Greek settlers in Constantinople, i 103

Pharsalos, Greeks defeated at, xii 422

Phaulkon, at Court of Siam, xii 534

Phauser, Sebastian, and Maximilian II, iii 167–8

Phélippeaux, Antoine Le Picard de, French engineer, viii 610, 612

Phelippes, decipherer, iii 291

Phelips, Sir Robert, foreign policy and, iv 261 sq.; Parliament and, 263

Phelypeaux, Antoine, French Secretary of State, v 5

—— *See* La Vrillière, *also* Pontchartrain

Philadelphia, founding of, vii 50; 51; effect of the Stamp Act in, 149; Continental Congresses at, 160 sq., 166, 237; occupied by Howe (1777), 213; quitted by Clinton, 217; Constitutional Convention at (1787), 245, 246–304, 314; 268; merchants of, 311; chosen as seat of Government, 316, 325; communication with, 351; banks at, 352; encouragement of manufactures at, 353; imports of, 355; emigration from, 359; manufactures in, 375; Anti-Slavery Society in, 387; Freemasons of, and the *Carbonari*, x 213

Philaret (I), Patriarch of Moscow. *See* Moscow

—— (II), Archbishop of Moscow. *See* Moscow

Philaster, by Beaumont and Fletcher, iii 381

Philip I (the Fair), Duke of Burgundy, and King of Castile, i 119, 126, 303, 306, 316, 318; intrigues in Spain, 362 sqq.; 434, 446 sqq., 450 sq., 452–5, 458, 467, 473, 475 sqq.

—— II (Augustus), King of France, i 384

—— IV (the Fair), King of France, i 384, 404, 407, 411

—— VI (of Valois), King of France, i 405

—— II, King of Spain, i 46, 53, 419, 459; ii 75, 84, 89 sqq., 244; and Imperial succession, 267; and repression of heresy, 409; 516; arrives in England, 530; reign of, with Mary in England, Chap. xv *passim*; Elizabeth and, 535, 544, 561; Council of Trent and, 675 sq., 677 sq.; iii 6–7; receives the news of St Bartholomew, 20; formation of French Catholic League reported to, 31; Treaty with

League (1585), 37; and the French succession, 49–50; seeks to secure French throne for Infanta, 52; attempts to procure peace from Solyman, 124; commands relief of Malta, 125, 131–6, 138; and Imperial succession, 145, 165–9, 175–8; and Netherlands, Chaps. VI and VII *passim*, and 617–30; 260, 263–5, 269–71, 274, 276, 280–3, 286, 288; intrigues in England, 289–92; the naval war with England, Chap. IX; suggested as successor to Elizabeth, 358, 385, 390, 395, 397, 400, 404–5, 408, 413–8, 430; relations of, with Sixtus V, 434–6, 448–54; Spain under, Chap. XV; death of (1598), 525–30, 534, 536, 542, 544, 595, 597, 605–6; relations of, with Henry IV, 659, 666 sqq., 754–5; Spanish power at death of, IV 666; 678; Paul IV and, 683; V 372; 516; 740; VI 152; 389; effect of, on Belgium, X 522

Philip III, King of Spain, III 397–8, 418–21, 513; Spain under, Chap. XVI, 558–61, 608, 641–2, 665; and the Austrian succession, 699, 719, 721, 733; IV 2; 3; represented at Linz *Reichstag*, 11; 14; and the Emperor, 31; 53; Spain under in later life, Chap. XXII *passim*; death of, 635; Leo XI and, 669; and Paul V, 670; V 376; X 269

—— IV, King of Spain, III 538, 576, 686; IV 82; 104 sq.; aggressive policy of, 191; Ferdinand II and, 211; Spanish Netherlands and, 230, 698; sends ambassadors to Cologne, 396; represented at the Congress, 401; Spain under, Chap. XXII; American dominions of, 703; loses Portugal, V 34; 36; and Charles II of England, 104; 372 sq.; 376; and the succession, 377; death of, 34, 37, 109, 182; testament of, 379, 385; 675

—— V, King of Spain (Duke of Anjou), V 30 sq.; accession of, 275, 393 sqq.; 340; 392; Grand Alliance (1701) and, 398; Emperor Leopold I and, 401; reception of, in Spain, 404; in Italy, 406; 412; 416; 417; and the peace negotiations, 420, 422 sq.; 427; position of, in Spain, 426, 428; renounces his claims on France, 434, 441; 436; and Peace of Utrecht, 440; and Treaty with Great Britain (1713), 444 sq.; and Sicily, 445, 448; and the Catalans, 445 sq.; Princess Orsini and, 447, 455; and Spanish Netherlands, *ib.*; 450; 452; and Peace of Baden, 455; 591; Vol. VI, Chaps. IV and V *passim* (1714–46); 25; invades Sardinia, 29; and the "Plan," *ib.*; 33 sq.; and Quadruple Alliance, 35; 38; and Gibraltar, 39; and Hanover Alliance, 59; 65; and Old Pretender, 105; 110; and Pragmatic Sanction, 202; 350 sq.; 361; Clement XI and, 586; death of, 161, 249, 597; X 232; 272; and Spanish America, 279

—— son of Charles III of Spain, VI 366

Philip the Good of Burgundy. *See* Burgundy, Dukes of

—— Landgrave. *See* Hesse

—— Pokanchet chief. *See* Metacam

Philip, John, missionary, XI 781

Philip (Filipo) Neri, St, III 425

Philiphaugh, Parliamentary victory of, IV 332 sq., 506

Philipoff, Terty, Russian writer, XI 625

Philippeaux, Pierre, VIII 249, 360 sq.; trial and execution of (1794), 363 sq.

Philippeville, fortified by Charles V, II 89, 102; ceded to France, V 33; added to the Netherlands (1815), X 22, 524

Philippi (West Virginia), Confederates routed at (1861), VII 456

Philippine Islands, VI 344; lost by Spain, 346; 351; 427; United States and, VII 679, 681 sqq.; cession of (1898), 684 sqq.; 750; nominally controlled by Viceroy of New Spain, X 248; missions in, 255; affairs in (1520–1905), XII 528 sqq.; American rule in, 5; 12; lost by Spain, 266; 666 sq.; 670; acquired by the United States, 697

Philippopolis (Rumelia), Turkish defeat near, XII 389; 406 sq.; 422

—— (South Africa), mission station, XI 783

Philippovich, Baron von, Austrian general, XII 400

Philippsburg, and France, IV 142 sqq.; 147, 246; captured by Imperialists, 250; taken by Condé, 389; 405; ceded to Bishop of Speier, 407; 416; 597; 602; lost by France, V 44, 45; taken by French (1688), 55; restored (1697), 63; Allies at, 411; captured by French (1792), VIII 414; surrender of (1800), IX 65

Philips, Edward, IV 451

Phillip, Captain Arthur, Governor of New South Wales, IX 737 sqq.

Phillips, Georg, and history of canon law, XII 848

—— Wendell, American orator, VII 744

—— William, General, VII 230

Phillpotts, Henry, Bishop of Exeter, X 673; XI 18

Philo, early printed editions of, I 612 sq.

Philosophy. *See* Political Philosophy, *also* Descartes

Philothei, monk of Pskoff, V 483

Philpot, John, Protestant Reformer, II 539

Phipps, Sir William, Governor of Massachusetts, VII 64, 89 sq., 111

Phoenix Park, murders in, XII 40, 81 sq., 86

Photiádes Pasha, Governor of Crete, XII 419

Photius, Archimandrite, X 423; 424; 452

Phoûrka pass, Turks in command of, XII 422

Phra Narai, King of Siam, XII 534

Phull, General von, military policy of, IX 490 sq.

Physics, history of. *See* Science

Physiocrats, The, VIII 22 sqq.; Turgot and, 83; 135, 140

Physiology, history of. *See* Science
Piacenza, submits to French (1499), I 121; annexed by Julius II (1512), 251; added to Papal territory (1521), II 44, 56; given to Pierluigi Farnese, 80; murder of Pierluigi at, 83; 84 sq.; agricultural colony from, III 393; Spain and, 476; VI 29; Elisabeth Farnese and, 122; 152; 154 sq.; 159 sq.; Spanish defeat at, 161; Don Philip's rights in, 239; 243; 245 sq.; acquired by Don Philip, 249; 362; 366; 597; 609; taken by French (1800), IX 62; French annexation of duchy of (1808), 141, 247, 398; creation of duchies in, 268; assigned to Empress Marie-Louise (1814), 602, 660; x 212
Piaggia, Carlo, African traveller, XII 811
Piagnoni (Savonarolists), I 169 sq., 174, 181 sq., 564
Piale, Pasha, Ottoman sea-captain, III 125, 131, 133
Pianori, Giovanni, XI 304
Piauhi, conquest of, v 679
Pibrac, Guy du Faur de, III 59
Picard, Aymon, French Protestant martyr, I 681
—— Jean, French astronomer, v 722
—— Louis-Joseph-Ernest, French politician, XI 305; 475; 485; 488; 493; member of the Provisional Government, 497 sq.; 612
Picardy refuses to receive Condé, III 30; Philip proposes to take, 510; the League in, 661–3; garrisons in, strengthened, 672; Henry IV's recovery of, 674; Longueville and, IV 122; invaded by Spanish and Imperial forces, 147, 370 sq.; 606; customs of, v 13; agricultural population in, VIII 61
Piccadilly, riot in, XII 43
Piccolomini, Aeneas Sylvius. *See* Pius II, Pope
—— Alfonso, III 430
—— Ottavio d'Arragona, Prince, Duke of Amalfi, Austrian field-marshal, at Lützen, IV 221; in Pilsen, 239 sqq.; in Franconia, 245; at Saalfeld, 383; 385; 393; in Dunkirk, 598
Pichegru, Charles, VIII 351, 385; commands the Army of the Rhine, 426 sqq., 432; commands the Army of the North, 434 sqq.; commands the Army of the Rhine and Moselle, 442 sq.; treachery of, 442 sq.; member of Council of Five Hundred, 506; and *coup d'état* (1797), 509 sqq.; transported, 512; and Cadoudal's conspiracy, IX 29 sqq.
Pichler, Aloys, German historian, XII 848
Pickering, Sir William, agent of Edward VI and Mary at the French Court, II 518
Pico della Mirandola, Count Galeotto, II 72, 387
—— della Mirandola, Gianfrancesco, I 678
—— della Mirandola, Giovanni, I 147, 151, 559, 572, 596, 605, 615, 680; the

platonism of, II 4, 7, 702; and Leo X, 16; *Oratio de reformandis moribus*, 31; 308; character and achievements of, 694 sq.
Picquanet, George, *hooftman* of Bruges, I 449
Picquart, Georges, French officer, XII 120 sq.
Pictet, Marc-Auguste, founds *Bibliothèque britannique* in Geneva, IX 427; at Congress of Vienna, 601
—— de Rochemont, Charles, IX 427
Picton, Sir Thomas, General, at Busaco, IX 461; at Badajoz, 471; at Roncesvalles and Maya, 479; at Ligny, 628; at Waterloo, 635; Governor of Trinidad, 750
Pidal, Pedro José, Marquis of, Spanish statesman, XI 550; 559
Pie, Monsignor, XI 469; 484
Piedade, battle at (1833), x 334
Piedmont (Italy), and the Wars (1522–9), II 62, (1536–7), 73; held by France, 89; relinquished (1558), 94; occupied by French, III 399, 402, 404; Spaniards in, 400; cleared of French garrison, 406; Cardinal of Lorraine in, *ib.*; militia in, 411; Cardinal Borromeo in, 414; threatened by Lesdiguières, 416–7; Spanish troops in, 419; policy of rulers of, 423; Louis and Richelieu in, IV 137 sqq.; 148; Turenne's conquest of, 388; Mazarin in, 592; 600 sq.; v 61; Duke Victor Amadeus of Savoy in, 411, 414; evacuated by the French (1706), 415; 425; VI 237; Franco-Spanish attack on, 241; 243; 245; and Papacy, 589; 608; liberal rising in (1821), VII 368; and French (1794), VIII 438; 555; Jacobin plot in, 557; French occupation of (1798–9), 654, IX 69; 61; annexation of, 71, 78 sq., 82; organisation of, by Bonaparte, 83, 104; a Franco-Italian province, 397–8, 400; and French Concordat, 401; rising in (1821), x 72, 114–7, 120, 150; the Restoration in (1814), 108–9; revolt in, and Count Confalonieri, 117; *pronunciamiento* of militia of (1833), 122; conspiracy in army of, 123; opposition of, to Papal aims, 142; Metternich's supremacy in, 370; (1849–61), Vol. XI, Chap. XIV *passim*; situation in, 70; and the Papal State, 71; national movement in, 75, 78; 83 sq.; and Italian Federation, 89; union of, with Lombardy and Venetia, 90; 92; defeat of, by Austria, 93; and Swiss Sonderbund, 249; Napoleon III and, 306 sq.; sends troops to Crimea, 322; 332; appeals to France and England, 367; and union with central Italy, 386, 388; 403; 468; alliance of, with Prussia, 479; 535; 706; the Siccardi Laws in, 708; education in, XII 237
—— Princes of. *See* Savoy, *also* Sardinia, King of

Piedmont (W. Virginia), victory of Hunter at (1864), VII 531

Pieni l' animo, Encyclical of Pius X, XII 230

Pier, the Great, "admiral of the Zuiderzee," I 453

Pierce, Franklin, President of the United States, VII 419, 425 sq.

Piero di Sacco, Alessandro da, Venetian Reformer, II 381 sq.

Pierson, Nicolas Gerard, Dutch Minister of Finance, XII 246 sq.

Pietermaritzburg, capital of Natal, XI 782

Pieter's Hill, stormed by General Buller, XII 643

Pietism, in Holland and Germany, Vol. v, Chap. XXIV *passim*, 742–63

Pietra Santa, silver mines of, III 392

Pietro, Michele di, Cardinal, imprisoned, IX 200; X 133

Pievtsoff, Russian explorer, XII 799

Pigeau, Eustache-Nicolas, IX 166; 169

Pighino. *See* Siponto, Archbishop of

Pighius, Albert, II 667, 717

Pignatelli, Antonio. *See* Innocent XII

—— François, Prince of Strongoli, Governor of Naples, VIII 652

Pigneau de Behaine, Bishop, XII 523

Pigot, George Pigot, Lord, Governor of Madras, VI 548; 565; 576

Pikhnó, Russian official, XII 373

Pilat, Austrian publicist, editor of *Oesterreichischer Beobachter*, IX 583; X 357

Pilatus, Leontius, Greek teacher of Boccaccio, I 541

Pilc, Polish journalist, XII 337

Pilgrim Fathers, The, VII 13 sq.

Pilgrimage of Grace (1536), II 446 sq.

Pillau, port of Königsberg, seized by Gustavus, IV 186 sqq., 193; 194; 197; Treaty of Königsberg and, 428; tolls of, V 638, 641; 647; Russian magazine at, VI 297

Pillersdorff, Baron Franz von, Austrian statesman, XI 155; 170 sq.; resigns, 175; 179; 189

Pillnitz, Convention of (1791), VI 656, VIII 296, 399, 530

Pillow, GideonJohnson, Confederate general, VII 462, 495

Pilsen, Mansfeld in, IV 24, 65, 67; Wallenstein at, 239 sq., 241 sqq.; Treaty of (1647), 391; surrender of, VI 234; Allies at (1813), IX 520

Pimentel, Eleonora, VIII 779

Pimentelli, Spanish ambassador, and the conversion of Christina of Sweden, IV 576

Pinckney, Charles, American politician, VII 246 sq., 272, 281, 287, 289 sqq.

—— Charles Cotesworth, American statesman and soldier, VII 246, 272, 282, 320 sq.; and the Presidential election of 1800, 324, 372; VIII 493

—— Thomas, United States Minister to Great Britain, VII 328, 372

Pinczow, Calvinist Synod at (1550), III 79

Pindaris, measures against the, XI 724 sqq.; 753

Pindemonte, Giovanni, Italian poet, VI 835

—— Ippolito, Italian poet, VIII 778

Pinel, Philippe, IX 132

Pinerolo, II 73; retained by France (1558), 94, III 400, 406, 478; retroceded to Savoy (1574), 25; France seizes (1631), IV 60, 115, 138 sq., 405, 679, 685; Fouquet imprisoned at, V 6; 415

Pinet, Jacques, Army commissioner, VIII 440

Pingone, Emmanuel Philibert, Italian historian, III 412

Ping-shan, H.M.S. *Woodcock* at, XII 796

Ping Yang, captured by the Japanese, XII 511

Pinkie Cleugh, battle of (1547), II 487, 556

Pinneberg, taken by Imperialists (1627), IV 102

Pintianus (Fernando Nuñez de Guzman), Spanish Hellenist, I 379, 578

Pinto. *See* Serpa Pinto

Pinto-Ribeiro, João, Portuguese statesman, Portuguese independence and, IV 651

Pinturicchio (Bernardino Betti), Umbrian painter, I 233

Pinzon, Vicente Yañez, discoverer of Brazil, I 34 sq.

Pio di Carpi, Alberto, Prince of, I 562, 573; II 15 sq.

—— —— Lionello, Prince of, I 562

—— —— Rodolfo, Cardinal, Bishop of Faenza, I 656; III 425

Piombino, II 84, 88; Savoy's claim to, III 385; 395; alum worked at, 392; 398; promised to Philip III, IV 14; Jacopo VI of, III 385; principality of, IX 661

Piombo, Sebastian del, III 466

Piotrkow, meeting at (1552), II 636, III 78; Catholic Synod at (1555), 79; Diet of (1558), 80; (1562), 82; Augustus II at, V 595

Piper, Carl, Count, Swedish statesman, V 600

Pippin, son of Charles the Great, the Venetian Republic and, I 260

Piraeus, Anglo-French occupation of, XI 640

Pirch, English officer, at Waterloo, IX 638

Pirkheimer, Wilibald, German humanist, I 325; II 138, 160; opposes Luther, 168, 698

Pirna, negotiations at, IV 252; 379; VI 244; Saxon army at, 255, 338

Piro, Portuguese conquest of (1791), IX 718

Pirot, Servian victory at, XII 389; 396; 407

Pisa, rebellion of, against Florence, I 113, 155, 171 sq., 191; besieged by Maximilian I (1498), 119; Council of (1469), 620, (Sept. 1511), 249, 251, 479, 651, 677; Second Synod of (May, 1511), II 29; Florentine conquest of, III 385; seized by Vitelli, 387; docks built at, 391-2; School

of Botany at, 394; botanic gardens at, v 734; scientific congress at (1839), x 128–9; 131; and the Jesuits, xi 69

Pisa, Agnolo Niccolini, Archbishop of, iii 386, 388

—— Francesco Salviati, Archbishop of, iii 390

Pisacane, Carlo, Italian revolutionary, xi 375; 380

Pisani, Frederick, dragoman, x 552

—— Giorgio, Venetian politician, vi 607

—— St Goard, Marquis de, French ambassador at Rome, iii 443, 452, 461

—— Vettor, Venetian commander, i 258 sq.

Pisania, English factories at, xii 806

Pisareff, Russian writer, xii 297; 302

Piscataqua river, settlements on, vii 21

Pisek, surrender of, vi 234

Pishin, British retreat to, xi 734; district of, xii 471

Pistoia, factions in, iii 388, 391; Diocesan Synod at, vi 605

—— and Prato, Scipione Ricci, Bishop of, vi 603 sqq.; x 142

Pistoris, Maternus, Italian humanist, in Erfurt, ii 111

Pistorius, Johannes, confessor of Rudolf II, iii 710

Pithou, Pierre, iii 59 sq., 63; *Satyre Ménippée* and, 69 sq.

Pitigliano, Niccolò of, iii 386

—— *See* Orsini

Pitoño, Spanish brigand, xii 259

Pitsani, mounted police at, xii 641

Pitschen, Maximilian defeated at (1588), iv 168

Pitt, John, in Madras, v 700

—— Thomas ("Diamond Pitt"), Governor of Madras, v 699 sq.; vi 394

—— William, Earl of Chatham. *See* Chatham

—— William, the younger, rise of, Vol. vi, Chap. xiii (3); 45; 48; 66; and Ireland, 503 sq.; and Clive, 561 sq.; and Warren Hastings, 580; India Bill of, 582; and Catharine II, 677; and American trade, vii 309, 328; foreign policy of (1783–93), Vol. viii, Chap. x, 322 sq.; policy of, in the East, 331 sq., 337, 528; and peace with France, 496, 498, 559; 643; and French monarchy, 648; and the reformers, 759, 761 sq.; ix 41; retirement of, 71; appoints Lord Barham First Lord of Admiralty, 224; 243; and Third Coalition, 245–6; 256, 263, 362; repressive period of, 672 sq.; resignation of, 679 sq.; return of, 683; death of, 264; 685; and Poor Relief, 691; and Ireland, 693 sq.; and the Union, 702 sq.; and India, 710; 717, 730, 733; and Canada, 744; x 3; 141; and Spanish America, 280 sq.; 574; 579; 583; and parliamentary reform, 599; 612; and Catholic emancipation, 625, 631, 633;

657; and Canada, 685, 688 sq.; 703; and Adam Smith, 765, 771

Pittenweem, Jacobites at, vi 99

Pittone, Philip, Baron, Austrian general, viii 558

Pitt-Rivers, Augustus H. L. Fox, archaeologist, xii 850

Pittsburg, fort built at, vii 120; trade of, 360, 375, 692; convention of Free-Soil party at (1852), 419. *See also* Fort Duquesne

—— Landing, Grant moves to, vii 496 sq., 559; Halleck at, 498

Pitzuwo, Russian troops at, xii 583; 585

Pius II (Aeneas Sylvius Piccolomini), Pope, i 72, 76 sqq., 78; goes on crusade, 79, 655 sq.; 92, 145, 285, 387; issues his Bull for protection of ruins of Rome, 547; 623, 632 sq.; nepotism of, 647; at Congress of Mantua, 655; 664, 688; ii 29, 355; iii 757

—— III (Francesco Piccolomini), Pope, i 126, 195, 242

—— IV (Giovanni Angelo de' Medici), Pope, ii 550, 576, 578 sq.; Elizabeth and, 583; the Inquisition and, 650; the Jesuits and, 656; Council of Trent and, 674–86; prohibited books and, 687; iii 145, 148, 154, 168–9, 191, 266–7, 270–1, 386, 390, 403, 405, 482, 592; issues Bull for erection of Catholic colleges in Ireland, 593

—— V (Michele Ghislieri), Pope, ii 33, 397; Carranza and, 410; 656; Congregation of the Index set up by, 687; League of, against the Turks, iii 133, 494; death of (1572), 18, 136; 172; 175, 178; and Mary, Queen of Scots, 272, 275–6; and Elizabeth, 281 sqq., 349; and Cosimo I, 386, 390, 396; policy of, 424 sqq.; 429; and Sixtus V, 441, 455; and Carnesecchi, 466; 468; v 325

—— VI (Giovanni Angelo Braschi), Pope, iii 438; visits Vienna, vi 636; viii 197, 573, 581; deportation of, 636 sqq., 790; 778; x 143; and Consalvi, 131; at Florence, 132; 143; 153; and *Febronius*, 158; 159

—— VII (Gregorio Bernabò Chiaramonti), Pope, ix 88; 107; and the Concordats with France, 180–90; crowns Napoleon, 191–2; quarrel of, with Napoleon, 193–7; imprisoned at Avignon, 196; at Savona, *ib.*; resistance of, 198; imprisonment of, at Fontainebleau, 200; reconciliation of, with Napoleon, *ib.*; released (1814), 201; and German Church, 201–3; effect of imprisonment of, 206–7; character of, 207; 400; declines to join alliance against England, 401; declines to recognise Joseph Bonaparte as King of Naples, 404; 586; and Order of St John of Jerusalem, 604; restoration of, 621; and Final Act, 662–3; reconstitutes the Jesuits, x 6; and Holy Alliance, 10;

returns to Rome (1814), 131; elected Pope (1800), 132; Consalvi's influence upon, 132; 133; at Fontainebleau, *ib.*; reinstates Consalvi as Secretary of State, 134; and restoration of Papal government (1814), *ib.*; 137; 139; and negotiations with France, 140; friendly attitude of, to England, 141; and reaction in Spain, 142; and settlement with France, 143–4; and Emperor Francis, 145; and Bavaria, 146–7; and Prussia, 148; and States of Upper Rhine, 148–9; and Netherlands, 149; death of, 151; as a lover of art, *ib.*; 153; consents to ecclesiastical taxes in Spain, 209; Concordat of, with Tsar, 424, 449; and Belgian bishops, 526; and Irish Catholics, 635; xi 72; 703

Pius VIII (Francesco Xaverio Castiglioni), Pope, x 139; pontificate of, 154; 381

—— IX (Giovanni Mastai-Ferretti), Pope, definition of Papal attitude in the *Syllabus* (1864) of, x 6; 124; 156; 164; 167; election (1846) of, 168; pontificate of (1846–70), Vol. xi, Chap. xxv *passim*; and English bishoprics, 19; 38; and Guizot, 40; election of, 71; character and career of, 72 sq.; Amnesty of, 74; further reforms by, 76; and Metternich, 77; and Great Britain, 78; and Rome, 79 sqq.; and War with Austria, 84, 87 sq.; 89; flight of, 91; 93 sq.; restoration of, 95, 378; and France, 121 sq., 125 sq.; and Napoleon III, 128, 468, 474, 478; and Piedmontese ecclesiastical Courts, 367 sq.; 371; reactionary policy of, 378; at Gaeta, 379; 387; and struggle for Temporal Power, 389, 391 sq.; 469; aided by France, 484 sq.; and Œcumenical Council, 494; hostility of, to Italy, 530 sq.; publishes *Syllabus*, 539; 541; and dogma of Infallibility, 543; 545; Concordat of, with Spain, 558; and Isabel of Spain, 568; 574; and Holland, 665; xii 93; 103; and Germany, 148 sq.; and the Italian monarchy, 229; and Alfonso XII, 263; and Ecuador, 673; and Ultramontanism, 848; death of, 152, 216

—— X (Giuseppe Sarto), Pope, xii 122; 225

Pi y Margall, Francisco, Spanish Republican leader, xii 261

Pizarro, Fernando, Francisco and Gonzalo, Spanish explorers, ii 101

—— Francisco, invasion of Peru by (1532), i 45 sq., 58; death of, ii 101; x 246

Pizzighettone, Bonaparte captures, viii 569

Placards, the Parisian, of 1534, ii 285 sqq.

—— issued by Charles V and Philip II in Netherlands, against heresy, iii 184 sqq., 199 sqq.

Place, Francis, and Radical movement, ix 688; and elementary education, 692; x 598 sq.; 612; and Reform Bill agitation, 615; 656; xii 734; and Trade Unionism, 748

"Place of Battles." *See* Rasboieni

Placentia, French settlement in Newfoundland, vii 52

Placentius, John, iv 791

Plade, Peder (Palladius). *See* Sjælland, Bishop of

Pläswitz, armistice at (1813), ix 508, 520–1

Plague, the bubonic (1896), in India, xii 486 sq.

Planchenoit, Blücher at (1815), ix 637; Young Guard at, 641

Planck, Gottlieb Jacob, German Church historian, xii 846

Planitz, H. von der, Saxon Chancellor, ii 170

Planta, Pompeius von, supports Spanish party in Grisons, iv 45; 47 sq.; 52

—— Rudolf von, supports Spanish party in Grisons, iv 45; 46 sqq.; 55

Plappeville, fort of, xi 591 sq.

Plasencia, Soult's march on, ix 453

—— Philip Sega, Cardinal Bishop of, Legate in France, iii 52

Plassey, battle of, vi 554 sq.

Plate river. *See* Rio de la Plata

Platen, Countess of, vi 19

Platen-Hallermünde, Count August von, poet, x 412; xi 413

Plater, Count Louis, x 430; 453

Platina (Bartolommeo Sacchi), i 552, 624

Plato, Renaissance study of, ii 701 sq.; v 739; 749

Platoff, Count, Hetman of Cossacks, at Borodino, ix 495; pursues Grand Army, 499 sq.

Platonism, introduced into Florence, ii 4; Platonists, 4, 702

Platt, Thomas Collier, American politician, vii 649

"Platte country," vii 427

Platter, Thomas, printer of Basel, ii 355

Plattsburg (N.Y.), captured by British (1813), vii 341

Plauen, list of grievances drawn up at, iii 712

—— Henry of, High Master of German Order, v 633

Plava, Montenegro and, xii 392, 396, 401 sq.

Playfair, Lyon Playfair, Lord, xi 10

—— William, writer, viii 771

Plébiscite, see Vol. ix, Chap. i, The Consulate, *passim*

Plehve, W. K., Russian statesman, xii 309; 311; 315 sq.; Minister of Interior, 326; 328 sq.; and labour movement, 331; Secretary of State for Finland, 335; and Armenian Church, 342; assassinated, 346; 376

Pléiade, The, iii 54, 368

Pleissenberg, fortress of, v 593

Plekhánoff, Russian socialist, xii 307; 329 sq.

Plempius, Vopiscus Fortunatus, iv 789

Plener, Ignatius von, Austrian Minister of Finance, xII 176
Pleskow. *See* Pskoff
Plessen, Baron L. E. H. von, at Congress of Vienna, IX 588
—— Wolrad von, IV 40
Plessis-les-Tours, Treaty of (1580), III 254
Plethon, Gemistos, Platonist, I 542; II 701
Pletinckx, Karl, Belgian revolutionary leader, x 536 sq.
Pléville Le Pelay, Georges René, Minister of Navy, VIII 508
Plevlye, xII 396; Austrian occupation of, 400 sq.
Plevna, xII 32; siege of, 388, 391 sq.
Plichon, Charles-Ignace, French politician, xI 469; 472; Minister of Public Works, 493
Pliusa, truce of (1583), IV 167
Plock, electors of Palatinate of, III 87; ceded to Poland (1582), 101; Kutusoff marches on, IX 511; Polish province, x 449; martial law in, 469 sq.
—— Noskowski, Bishop of, III 83
Plön, Duke of. *See* Holstein-Sonderburg-Plön
Ploeshti, insurrection at, xI 646
Plombières, Napoleon III and Cavour at, xI 307, 376; 381
Plowden, Edmund, jurist, II 586
Plunket, Sir Nicholas, IV 535
—— Oliver, Catholic Archbishop of Armagh, v 228; 306
—— William Conyngham, 1st Baron, and Irish rebellion, IX 701; and the Union, 703; and Bill for Catholic relief (1821), x 636; Attorney-General, 637; 642; 677
Plunkett, Sir Horace Curzon, xII 88; 90; 741
Plymouth, seizure of Spanish ships at, III 225; English fleet at, 309–11, 316; Flemish ships' cargoes seized in harbour of (1589), 317; Spanish vessels at, 493; Anglo-Dutch naval engagement off, IV 472; the *Mayflower* pilgrims at, 747, VII 13; Franco-Spanish fleet at, VI 376, 452; French ships carried into, IX 234; Portuguese refugees at, x 322, 324
—— Company, and North America, IV 747, VII 4, 12 sq.
—— (Massachusetts), settlement of Separatists in, III 562
—— (N. Carolina), the *Albemarle* destroyed off (1864), VII 563 sq.
Po river, Austrian troops on, VI 153 sq.; 241; 245; Italian troops cross, xI 84, 86
Pobieda, Russian battleship, xII 581
Pobyedonóstseff, Constantin, tutor of Alexander III, xII 312; Procurator of Holy Synod, 313; 314 sqq.; 323; opposes reform, 326, 328; 331; and Finland, 335; 348
Pocahontas, daughter of Indian chief Powhatan, VII 7

Pocock, Sir George, Admiral, VI 369; 426; 547 sq.
Podewils, Prussian Minister, VI 421; 658
Podgoritsa, Montenegro and, xII 392, 396
Podhorzan, Frederick II at, VI 234
Podiebrad, George, King of Bohemia, I 293, 296, 331, 655, 689; II 198
Podlasia, Polish Palatinate of, III 87; province of, x 449
Podolia, incorporated in Poland (1431), III 73; Palatine of, 91; ceded to Turks (1672), V 353; 355; 365; restored to Poland (1699), 371; Austria and, VI 630; Russian administration of, x 459 sq.; martial law in, 469; disorder in, xII 354
Poe, Edgar Allan, VII 742 sq.
Pöhlmann, Robert, German economic historian, xII 845
Poel, claimed by Sweden at Osnabrück, IV 403 sq.
Pöltenburg, Baron Ernst von, Hungarian general, xI 213
Poerio, Alessandro, Italian poet, x 126; xI 545
—— Carlo, Italian Liberal, xI 379
—— Giuseppe, x 114
Poggio Bracciolini (Giovanni Francesco), Italian humanist (1380–1459), I 545; his *Urbis Romae Descriptio*, 547; 549; 565; visits England, 598
Poincaré, Raymond, French Minister of Finance, xII 113; 124
Point Isabel (Texas), operations near (1846), VII 394 sq.
—— Lévis, batteries erected on, VII 138 sq.
Pointis, Jean-Bernard-Louis Desjean, Baron de, French seaman, v 59; 307; 413
Poiret, Pierre, pietist, v 762
Poisseuille, Jean-Louis-Marie, physiologist, v 727
Poissy, Colloquy of (1561), II 301 sq., 568, 581, VIII 68
Poitiers, Synod of French Church at (1561), II 300; siege of (1569), III 13; submission of, 663; Edict of (1577), 665; attempt to seize, 672; Mazarin at, IV 616; University of, 778
—— Diane de, II 97 sq.; the Guises and, 296; 486; III 263
Poitou, spread of Protestantism in, II 292; the League in, III 661, 663; Protestants threaten trouble in, 674; Mercœur's strength in, 675; and Condé, IV 122; 123; 126; 128; rebellion of (1636–7), 153; customs of, v 13; 24; scarcity in, VI 162
Pokanchets, The, Indian tribe, VII 27
Pokrovsky monastery, v 525
Pokzóvskoe, peasant rising in, xII 361
Pola, victory of Genoese at (1379), I 258 sq.
—— Giambattista Vergerio, Bishop of, II 394

Poland

I   x   Hungary and the Sclavonic kingdoms, 329–46

II   Note on the Reformation in Poland, 634–8

III   iii The Catholic Reaction, and the Valois and Báthory elections, in Poland, 73–103

IV   v   The Vasa in Sweden and Poland (1560–1630), 158–89

     vi Gustavus Adolphus (1630–2), *passim*, 191 sqq.

     xiv The Treaty of Westphalia, *passim*, (Treaties of Königsberg, Marienburg, etc.), 427 sqq.

     xx The Scandinavian North (1559–1660), *passim*, 578 sqq.

V   xii Austria, Poland and Turkey, 338–71

     xix Charles XII and the Great Northern War, *passim*, 584–615

     xx The Origins of the Kingdom of Prussia, *passim*, 616–38

VI   vii Poland under the Saxon Kings, 191–200

     x Russia under Anne and Elizabeth, *passim*, 301–28

     xi The Reversal of Alliances and the Family Compact, 353–8

     xix Catharine II (of Russia), *passim*, 664–701

     xx (2) Poland and Prussia, 729–34 [*See also* 150 sqq., 628 sqq.]

VIII   xvii The extinction of Poland (1788–97), 521–52 [*See also* 786]

Note. *For later history of Poland after the annexations, see* IX 337 sqq.; 485 sq.; 491, 591 sqq.; 663; Congress of Vienna and, 655 sq.; 667 sq.; and Polish revolution, Vol. x, Chap. XIV *passim*; 8 sq.; Catholic Church in, 141; 164; administration of Prussian, 353; ecclesiastical reaction and, 425; 426 sq.; literary development of, 432; 438; at war (1831) with Russia, 444; attitude of France towards, 483, 488; literature of, Vol. XI, Chap. XXII (4); revolutionary movements in, 46 sq.; 71; France and, 109, 308, 475 sq.; *Vorparlament* and, 163; Hungary and, 208; 323; Bismarck and revolution in, 434; 436; 456; land tenure in, 616, 628; 622; political parties and Russian concessions in, 657 sq.; insurrection (1863) in, 537, 628 sq.; 660; XII 1, 11; Germany and, 139, 162, 167; Sweden and, 274; 294; schools in, 299; 324; Russian policy in, 336 sqq.; 351; strikes in, 353; agitation and martial law in, 360 sqq.; and second Duma, 372; 373; ideas of 1908 in, 377 sq.; 842. *See also* Warsaw, Grand Duchy of

Poland, primate of. *See* Gnesen

Polar exploration, XII 814 sq.

Pole, The, journal, XII 339

Pole, Edmund de la. *See* Suffolk, Earl of

—— Sir Geoffrey, arrest of, II 449; 523

—— Reginald, Cardinal and Archbishop of Canterbury, II 33, 85, 239, 379, 398 sq., 446–9; 501; Papal legate to England, 518; unwise advice of, to Mary, 519 sq.; 522, 525, 529; 532; treatment of Protestants by, 533, 536, 543; relations of, with Paul IV, 546; death of, 549; 641; Church reform and, 643; and Council of Trent, 660–8; III 466

—— Richard de la (titular Earl of Suffolk), I 481; death of, II 426

—— William de la, I 505

Polentani, The, Lords of Ravenna, I 281

Polenz, George von. *See* Samland, Bishop of

Polianovka, Treaty of (1634), V 504

Polignac, Armand de, IX 29; 32

—— Auguste-Jules-Armand-Marie, Prince de, Ministry of, x 97–9; foreign schemes of, 98; 475; 486; and Algiers, 502

—— Jules de, IX 29; 32

—— Melchior de, Cardinal, V 427; 439; VI 191

—— Yolande M. Gabrielle de Polastron, Duchesse de, VIII 80

Poligny, riot at, XI 137

Politian (Angelo Ambrogini Poliziano), I 18, 545; edits Justinian's *Pandects*, 546; *Miscellanea*, 550; 553–6; *Orfeo*, 584; II 16, 18, 701; III 458

Politica, Chevalier de, Russian Minister to the United States, VII 370

Political Philosophy, possibilities of change in, I 56 sq., Vol. II, Chaps. VI, 174–205, and XIX, 690–718, *passim*; in the 16th century, Vol. III, Chap. XXII, 736–69; English, in the 17th and 18th centuries, Vol. VI, Chap. XXIII, 785–821; Philosophy and the [French] Revolution, Vol. VIII, Chaps. I, 1–35; xxv, *passim*, 754 sqq.; Vol. x, 40 sqq.

Politique, Liége journal, x 532

Politiques, French, party of the, III 7 sq., 21 sq., 37, 50, 67–8; political theories of, 753–4, 756

Polk, James Knox, VII 393; President of the United States, 395, 397, 401

—— Leonidas, Confederate general, VII 457 sq., 462

Pollard, Edward Albert, editor of the *Richmond Examiner*, VII 550, 605, 607

Pollilore, engagement at, VI 577

Pollock, Sir George, Field-Marshal, XI 734 sq.

Polo, Marco, travels of, I 8; XII 793; in China, 796; 798; 802 sq.

Polock. *See* Polozk

Polotski, Russian monk. *See* Sitianovich, Simeon

Polozk, Peter the Great at, V 594; district of, assigned to Russia, VI 669; Saint-Cyr evacuates (1812), IX 499

Poltáva, battle of (1709), v 536, 581, 601
sqq., 607, 667, vi 192, 311; peasant
disturbances in, xii 333
Poly, François-C.-G.-Louis, Baron de, viii
505 sq.
Polynesia, France and, xii 666 sq.
Pomaks, The, xii 406; 408; 426
Pomare, Queen of Tahiti, xi 35
Pombal, Sebastian Joseph de Carvalho e
Mello, Marquis of (Count of Oeyras),
Portuguese statesman, vi 187; and the
Jesuits, 592; Ministry of, 384 sqq.; fall
of, 375, 388; and Brazil, 391 sq.; and
the Papacy, 594; viii 783; x 311
—— Cardinal, vi 594
Pomerania, refuses *Formula Concordiae,*
iii 704; iv 104; Imperial troops in, 106;
108; and Gustavus Adolphus, 115, 193
sq., 196 sq., 215 sq., 218, 220, 244;
Treaty of Prague and, 254 sq.; and
compact at Stuhmsdorf, 366; 374; 378;
claimed by Sweden at Osnabrück, 403 sq.;
and Brandenburg, v 620, 626; Spielhagen's writings on, xi 420. *See also*
Pomerania, Prussian, *and* Pomerania,
Western
—— Eastern. *See* Pomerania, Prussian
—— Prussian, passes to Brandenburg
(1648), iv 404, 426; taxation in, vi 221;
263; Swedes in, 266 sq., 280, 287, 295,
409; Russian troops in, 287, 289, 297,
326; evacuated by Russia (1762), 298;
economic conditions in, 715
—— Swedish. *See* Pomerania, Western
—— Western, cession of, to Sweden (1648),
iv 404, 429, v 562; Brandenburg and,
iv 430, 432 sq., v 40, 359, 569, 643, 651
sq., 666; and Peace of Saint-Germain,
571, 652; part of, assigned to Denmark
(1715), 582, 611, vi 24; Prussian designs
on (1756), 251; Prussians invade, 276;
Swedish army in, 294; peasant proprietors in, 220; Prussian designs on
(1803), ix 250; part of, evacuated by
Sweden, 300, 322; restored to Sweden
(1810), 323; Swedish army in, 507;
annexed to Prussia (1815), 592, 656, xi
680
Pomerania, Dukes of:—
—— Barnim (d. 1573), ii 170; assists
Christian II, 230; makes peace with
Charles V, 262
—— Bogislav X (d. 1523), ii 170
—— Bogislav XIV (d. 1637), iv 104;
signs capitulation of Franzburg, 106;
108; 194; death of, 366; 404; v 637;
641
—— George (d. 1531), ii 170
Pomerania-Stettin, Otto III, Duke of, v 624
Pomerania-Wolgast, Dukes of, v 631
—— Duke Philip Julius of, iv 104
Pomerelia, German Order and, v 631
Pomeroon, Dutch settlement on the, iv 755
Pomfret Castle, surrenders to rebels (1536),
ii 446

Pommereul, Baron François-René-Jean de,
French general, becomes General Censor
(1811), ix 141
Pommersfelden, victory of Albrecht Alci-
biades at, ii 275
Pomore, loyalty of the, v 500
Pompadour, Jeanne-Antoinette Poisson le
Normant d'Étioles, Marquise de, vi 164;
254; 330; 333; and French politics, 334;
335; and Austrian alliance, 336; and
Count Starhemberg, 338; 339; 341; 348;
and Choiseul, 356; 400 sq.; and the
Church, 591; 592; viii 24, 72
Pomponazzo, Pietro (Peretto), ii 4, 702 sq.;
Immortality of the Soul, 704; iii 466
Pomponne, Simon Arnauld, Marquis de,
French ambassador in Sweden, v 566
Ponce (Porto Rico), Miles at (1898), vii 681
Poncet, Charles, African explorer, xii 805
—— Jules, African explorer, xii 811
Ponda, acquisition of, by Portuguese, ix 718
Pondicherry, captured by Dutch (1693), v
696; restored to France (1697), 63; 703;
France and, vi 347; 532; French rule
in, 534; 535 sq.; siege of (1748), 538;
539 sq.; Dupleix at, 544 sq.; 547; taken
by British (1761), 427, 549, 577; evacuated
by France (1778), 454; regained by France
(1783), 464; recaptured by British (1793),
475, ix 714; retained by Great Britain,
240; French soldiers at, xii 535
Ponet, John, Bishop of Winchester, ii 501
Poniatowski, Joseph Antoine, Prince, Polish
general, ix 354; and Russian campaign,
488 sqq.; drowned at Leipzig, 540
—— Stanislaus, Count Palatine of Ma-
zovia, v 603 sq.; 606; vi 193; 196 sq.
—— Stanislaus Augustus. *See* Stanislaus
II, King of Poland
Ponikau, agent of Bernard of Weimar, signs
agreement at Paris (Oct. 1635), iv 368
Ponsonby, George, leader of Whigs, ix 687;
and Whig Club, 693; 698–9; retirement
of, 700; and Polish Question, x 446
—— John, Speaker of Irish House of
Commons, vi 489; 494
—— John Ponsonby, Viscount, British
ambassador at Constantinople, x 512;
554 sqq.; 560; 563; 570
—— Sir William, Major-General, at Water-
loo, ix 635; and Whig Club, 693; 698–9
Pont-à-Mousson, German force at, xi 588 sq.;
592
Pontanus, Jovianus (Giovanni Gioviano
Pontano), of Naples, i 560, 624; ii 16;
iii 470
Pontarlier, Bernard of Weimar at, iv 379;
380; 382
Pontchartrain, Louis Phelypeaux, Comte
de, v 28; 30
Pont de Grésin, Savoy and, iii 419, 420
Pontecorvo, vi 494; restored to Papacy,
595; Naples occupies, viii 650; principality of, declared by France to belong
to Church, ix 189; granted to Bernadotte

(1806), 194, 268; resigned by Bernadotte, 324; reverts to Holy See, 652; claimed by Naples, x 132; revolution in (1821), 150

Pontécoulant, Comte Louis-Gustave Doulcet de, French politician, viii 515; x 45

Ponte Ferreira, fight at (1832), x 329
—— Lagoscuro, Papal party defeated at (1644), iv 686
—— Longone (in Elba), the fortification of, iii 683

Pontenuovo, battle of, vi 350, 610

Pontine marshes, iii 437

Pontivy (Napoléonville), town created by Napoleon, ix 120

Pontoglio, Prince Eugene at, v 402

Pontoise, meeting of Estates at (1561), ii 301; acknowledges Henry IV, iii 662; *Parlement* transferred to (1652), iv 617; vi 130 sq.; *Parlement* banished to (1753), 347

Pontremoli, occupied by French (1495), i 116

Pont-Saint-Esprit, captured by de Luynes, iii 32

Ponts de Cé, treaty at, iii 675

Poona, Marátha insurgents in, vi 524; 575; French envoy at, 576; Malet sent to, ix 710; relations of, with the Nizám, 714; Sindhia at (1792), 719 sqq.; Brahman oligarchy at, 720; capture of (1802), 727; 731, (1817) xi 726

Poor Law, English, Elizabeth's, iii 356; Pitt's suggestions, ix 691; Justices at Speenhamland, *ib.*; Commission of 1832 and its report, x 660 sqq.; reform of 1834 carried, 662; agitation against new law, 682; Irish, reformed (1838), 676; extension of functions under, xii 753 sq. (For the charitable system of the Middle Ages, *see* ii 108)

Pope, Alexander, *Essay on Man*, iv 768; v 70; 467; vi 822; 826; x 696 sqq.; 701; 714; 723; xi 423
—— John, commands Army of Virginia, vii 477 sq., 480, 500, 506; on the Mississippi (1862), 497 sqq.

Poperinge, ceded to France, v 45

Popham, Edward, admiral, naval administration and, iv 460; in Portugal, 464
—— George, expedition of, to New England, vii 12
—— Sir Home Riggs, captures Cape Colony, ix 235; expedition of, to Cape Colony, 752; expedition of, to Buenos Ayres, *ib.*; x 280; expedition of, to the River Plate, 281
—— English officer in India, storms Gwalior, vi 576

Popish Plot, The so-called (1678), v 220 sqq.; 334

Poplawski, Polish publicist, xii 338 sq.

Populaire, French journal, x 491

Population, Malthus on, x 775; lowered death-rate in, xii 781; overflow of, from

Europe, 12; in Empire, especially Germany, after Thirty Years' War, iv 418; of England, in 1642, 302; of England, Scotland and Ireland, from 1852, xi 70, 346; during last few years, xii 63; in France, declining birth-rate in, 102; Prussian, Frederick William I's measures to increase, vi 218 sq.; Spanish, during earlier 16th century, i 357

Pordage, Samuel, poet, v 132

Porlier, Juan Diaz, Marqués de Montarosa, Spanish guerrilla chief, in Cantabrian hills, ix 469; x 210

Porro, Luigi, x 124

Porta, Carlo, Italian writer, xi 545
—— *See also* Della Porta

Portal, Gerald, mission of, to Abyssinia, xii 444
—— José, organises rising at Seville, xi 557
—— Pierre-Barthélemy, Baron, French Minister of Marine, x 57; 60

Portalis, Jean-É.-Marie, French politician, viii 507, 727, 742; ix 150 sqq.; 160, 188
—— Comte Joseph-Marie, x 56; 63; 92

Port Arthur, in the Russo-Japanese War, Vol. xii, Chap. xix *passim*; 132; railway to, 344; 345 sq.; taken by Japan, 348, 511 sq.; leased to Russia, 513; 521 sq.; ceded to Japan, 601
—— Augusta, projected railway to, xii 634
—— Dalrymple, settlement founded at, ix 740
—— Darwin, founded, xi 798
—— Egmont, Spanish attack on, vi 373; 437; 443

Porteous, Beilby, Bishop of London, viii 763
—— John, Captain of the Edinburgh City Guard, vi 48; 108

Porter, Sir Charles, Lord Chancellor of Ireland, v 317; 320 sq.
—— David Dixon, American admiral, vii 500, 502 sq., 505, 537, 544, 557
—— Endymion, iii 575
—— Fitz-John, American general, vii 480
—— George, and plot against William III, v 262
—— George Richardson, political economist, x 783 sq.

Port' Ercole, France retains, iii 385

Porterfield, G. A., Confederate colonel, defeated at Philippi (1861), vii 456

Port Essington, Australia, xi 795
—— Gibson, captured (1863), vii 503
—— Hamilton, British occupation of, xii 509
—— Hudson, Federal attack on (1863), vii 503; surrender of, 506; 559

Portici, conference at, xi 379

Port Jackson, Captain Phillip at, ix 737

Portland, naval battle off (1653), iv 436, 475, 478 sqq.

Portland, William Bentinck, 1st Earl of, v 163; 167; 275; ambassador in France, 381 sq.; 397; 422; 655
—— William Henry Cavendish Bentinck, 3rd Duke of, vi 431; Lord-Lieutenant of Ireland, 458 sq., 500 sq.; 461; resigns, 462 sqq.; and the Regency Bill, 474; supports Pitt, 476; 478; 501; viii 759; Cabinet of, ix 299, 301, 439, 688; and the Whig party, 673 sqq.; and Catholic emancipation, 678; Home Secretary, 697 sqq.
—— Bay, Sir Thomas Mitchell at, xi 792
Port Macquarie, xi 790 sq.
—— Mahon (Minorca), v 426; 444; vi 342a (in Vol. xiii), 350; capitulates, 452
—— Natal, discovered by Da Gama (1497), i 25; besieged by the Boers, xi 782
Porto, Francesco, Cretan scholar, ii 384 sq.
—— Bello, death of Drake near, iii 322; and Peruvian trade, v 684; vi 60; capture of, 72; 142; pestilence at, x 251, 255; fair of, 272, abolished, 274
Porto-Carrero, Cardinal, v 383; 392 sq.
Porto Ferraio, model naval port, iii 385, 391, 398; Ganteaume's attempt on (1801), ix 53; ceded to France, 75
—— Longone, fortified, iii 398
—— Novo, English victory at, vi 577
—— Praya, naval engagement off, vi 454
—— Rico, Drake beaten off, iii 321; a Spanish possession, v 687, xii 685, 696; penal settlement, vi 186; 378; 380; naval demonstration at (1898), vii 679; expedition to, 680 sq.; ceded to United States, 682; xii 655, 697; emancipation in, 653; 656
—— San Stefano, Emperor Leopold II retires to, xi 91
—— Seguro (Brazil), discovered by Cabral (1499), i 35
Port Phillip, discovery of, ix 740; xi 790; 796
—— Royal (Nova Scotia). *See* Annapolis
—— Royal (S. Carolina), captured (1861), vii 470, 552, 582
Port-Royal des Champs, Abbey of, iv 621; Pascal and, 794 sq.; Cartesian philosophy and, 790; 796; 798; convent of, v 83 sq.; 89
Port Royal Sound (South Carolina), French Protestant colony at, i 50
—— Said, foundation of, xii 431
—— Santiago, British occupation of, xii 529
Portsmouth, iv 266; Buckingham murdered at, 272; surrendered by Goring, 305, 308; 323; dockyard at, v 169; Whig plan to seize, 225; corporation of, x 670; Treaty of (1905), xii 357; 574; 600 sq.
—— Louise de Kéroualle, Duchess of, v 205; 215
Port Sudan, harbour of, xii 449

Portugal
 i   i   The Age of Discovery, *passim*, 7–36
 iii xv Spain under Philip II, *passim*, 499 sqq.
 iv   xxii Spain...under Philip III and IV, *passim*, 623–65
      xxv The transference of colonial power to the United Provinces and England, *passim*, 728–59
 v   xiv The War of the Spanish Succession and the Peace of Utrecht, *passim*, 401–59
      xxii The Colonies and India, *passim*, 673–705
 vi   xii (1) Spain under Ferdinand VI and Charles III, *passim*, 361–84
          (2) Portugal (1750–93), 384–8
          (3) Brazil (17th and 18th centuries), 389–92
 ix   xi The Napoleonic Empire at its height (1807–9), *passim*, 294–340
      xv The Peninsular War (1808–14), 428–82
      xix The Congress of Vienna, I, *passim*, 576–615
 x   x   Brazil and Portugal, 310–39
 xi   xx The course of revolution in Spain and Portugal (1845–71), 550–75
 xii x   The Iberian Peninsula (1871–1908), 269–72
      xx The European Colonies, *passim*, 607–71
Porzio, Simon, Italian scholar, ii 16
Posada Herrera, Juan, Spanish politician, xi 563
Poschiavo, ceded to Bishop Hartmann, iv 36; 39; Spaniards expect attack from, 50
Posen, burning of Hussite preachers at, iii 74; Protestant Synod at (1560–1), 81; Jesuits in, 83, 102; seized. by the Swedes, v 505; 594; Russians in, vi 291, 325; 326; 629; Prussia and, 708 sq.; district of, ceded to Prussia (1793), viii 535; Treaty of (1806), ix 279; Davout advances to, 281; Napoleon at, 284; Murat at, 511; Eugene (Beauharnais) evacuates (1813), 512; part of, ceded to Prussia (1815), 655, x 445; withdrawn from the Confederation, 349; created a grand duchy, 353; Freemasons in, 453; under Prussian rule, 462 sq.; 473; Polish conspiracy in, xi 46; Prussia and, 160; 163; rising in, 164; 192; 434; German settlers in, xii 162
Posen, Archbishops of:—
—— Konarski, iii 83
—— Latalski, iii 77
—— Martin von Dunin, x 381; xi 50
Posse, Count Arvid, Swedish statesman, xii 277
"Possessing" Princes, The (Jülich-Cleves), iii 642–3, 730–3

Possevino, Antonio, Jesuit, II 631; sent as Nuncio to mediate between Tsar Ivan IV and Poland, III 101; second mission to Poland and Russia, 103; negotiates Russo-Polish treaty, V 494; 498

Possiette, Captain, at Nagasaki, XI 831

Post, The, American colonial, question of, and War of Independence, VII 205; English penny-post created, X 679; Great Elector's system of, in Prussia, VI 205

Postel, Guillaume, Syriac New Testament and, I 604; the *Protevangelium* and, 613

Potagos, Papagiotis, African traveller, XII 811

Potchefstroom, Boer government at, XI 782; *Grondwet* of, 785

Potemkin, Prince Gregori Alexandrovich, Russian statesman, VI 352; 674 sq.; and Catharine II, 678; 696; and Frederick II, 708; 753; VIII 293, 309, 314; at Oczakoff, 325; death of, 337; IX 34; 43

Potenza, Giovanni Francesco di, Nuncio to Christian II, II 607

—— political persecution in, XI 379

Potgieter, Andries Hendrik, Boer leader, XI 782

Pothier, Robert-Joseph, IX 162; 165

Poti, ceded to Russia (1829), X 202, 444, XI 274

Potocki family, VI 200

—— Count Ignatius, VIII 786

—— Count Nicholas, VI 197

—— Count Severin, X 430

—— Count Stanislaus, Polish Minister of Education, X 452

—— Count Theodore, Polish statesman, VI 193 sqq.; 197

—— Polish general, defeated by Wrangel near Gurzno, IV 186

—— Count, and the Polish National League (1891), XII 338

—— Count, Austrian President of the Council (1870), XII 187; 192

Potomac river, reconnaissance on, VII 468; Confederate batteries on, 469; Federal troops on, 473; operations on (1862), 482, (1863), 490; Army of, 467 sq., 472, 480

Potosi, lawlessness in, V 681, X 250 sq.; decay of, 255, 259; the *mita* of, 264 sq.

Potsdam, Edict of (1685), V 646; 667; VI 215; the Duc de Nivernais at, 335; 718; Alexander I at (1805), IX 256, 308; Napoleon at, 281

Potter, John, Archbishop of Canterbury, VI 77

—— Louis de, Belgian politician, X 532; 537 sq.

Potteries, disturbances in the, XI 2

Pottinger, Major Eldred, at siege of Herat, XI 732

—— Sir Henry, British Governor of Hongkong, XI 807; 809 sq.; Asiatic travels of, XII 800

Pouancé, French Royalist chiefs at, IX 3

Pouilly, de, French historian, XII 817

Poulain, Nicholas, III 42–3

Poulet, Sir Amias. *See* Paulet

Poupry, French repulse at, XI 605

Pourtalès, Count Albert, Prussian politician, XI 396

—— Count, German ambassador in St Petersburg (1908), XII 378

Pourtalès-Steiger, Count Louis August, XI 255

Poussielgue, Jean-Baptiste, Secretary of the French Legation at Genoa, VIII 595

Poussin, Nicolas, French painter, XI 528

Poutrincourt, Jean de Bienville, Sieur de, in New France, VII 71, 75

Pouyer-Quertier, Augustin-Thomas, French statesman, XI 470; XII 95

Povsinski, Bartolomeus, IV 170

Povyenets, state mines at, V 529

Powell, Mary, wife of John Milton, V 123

Power, Lord, III 596

Powerscourt, Castle of, III 583

Powhatan, Indian chief, VII 7

Powick Bridge, victory of Rupert at (1642), IV 307

Powis, William Herbert, 1st Marquis of, V 220

Powle, Henry, opposes Non-resisting Test, V 216

Pownall, Thomas, Governor of Massachusetts, VII 98, 108

Poyer, John, dismissal of, IV 348

Poyet, Guillaume, Chancellor of France, II 288

Poynings, Sir Adrian, III 3

—— Sir Edward, Deputy Lieutenant in Ireland, I 472; 479; III 580

—— Acts, The, I 472; IV 515; 519; 528; V 320; 690; considered and repealed in fact, VI 458 sq.; 493; 499 sq.

Poyntz, Sydenham, Parliamentary general, IV 329, 332; at Rowton Heath, 333

Pozharski, Dmitri, Prince, V 502

Pozsony. *See* Pressburg

Pozzo di Borgo, Charles André, Count, Corsican refugee, IX 283; in Paris, 558; policy of, 586; X 15; 21; 47; 56; and the reaction in Spain, 230; and the Polish Patriotic Society, 454

Prado, Don Juan de, Governor of Havana, VI 369

Pradt, Dominique Dufour de, Abbé, ambassador to Warsaw, IX 338; Chancellor of Order of Legion of Honour, 568

Praemonstratensian Order, in Brandenburg, V 619

Praemunire, III 556, 565

Praet, Louis de Flandre, Sieur de, Imperial ambassador in England, II 424

Prätigau, The, Protestants of, IV 44, 47, 52; 55; revolt of, 56; 58

Praga, Polish Diet at, VI 195; in the hands of the Poles, IX 354; ramparts of, removed, X 449; 468

Pragmatic Sanction, of Bourges (1438), i 385 sqq., 671, ii 29; of 1516, i 671, ii 32, 281; of St Louis (so-called), i 386; of Charles V (1549), 459, ii 102

—— Sanction, Austrian, of Charles VI, Vol. vi, Chap. viii (1); 57; 139; 149 sq.; 152; 155; Augustus III of Poland and, 195; 228 sq.; 310

Prague, Ferdinand I crowned at, ii 199; ratification of Austro-Turkish treaty at (1562), iii 123; battle of, 569; botanical and zoological gardens at, 697; residence of Rudolf II at, 701; Archdukes at, 719; advance of Archduke Matthias on, 725–6; meeting of Princes with Rudolf II at (1610), 731; Rudolf II at, 733; riot in (1611), 733; entry of Matthias into (1611), 734; death of Rudolf II at, 735; Scultetus at, iv 6; 15; Christopher von Dohna at, 17; and Bohemian succession, 18 sqq.; 65; 66; 68; Anhalt's papers seized at, 71; Catholic reaction in, 73 sq.; 93; 200; 209; Wallenstein in, 101, 213, 215, 221, 223; 241 sq.; 247; John George in, 252; negotiations at, 255; 393; Emperor Ferdinand II and, 365; George William of Brandenburg and, 366, 403; Bernard of Weimar and, 376, 378; Calvinist Estates to be admitted to, 379 sq.; 384, 390, 395, 397, 400, 407, 409 sqq.; Silesia and, 417; vi 232; 234 sq.; fall of (1743), 236; 241; battle of, 257 sqq.; 283 sq.; 341; seminary at, 634; 721; Congress of, ix 288, 577, 583; revolutionary movement at, xi 153, 156; Metternich at, 154; 171; 176; Slav Congress at, 177, xii 378; insurrection at, xi 177 sq.; 187; 203; 216; Russian influence in, 653; University of, xii 195

—— Peace of (1635), iv 144, 146, 243, 252, 364, v 637; (1866), xi 457, 461, 541, 576, xii 139, 290

Prague, Archbishops of:—

—— Anton Brus, iii 147

—— Ernest Albert von Harrach, and the Catholic reaction, iv 73

—— Lohelius, iv 15; banished, 21; returns, 71

Praia, English mercenaries at, x 327

Praise of Folly, by Erasmus, ii 280

Prati, Giovanni, poet, x 126; xi 546 sq.; 549

Pratica, the Florentine, and Savonarola's reforms, i 159 sqq.

Prato, captured by Pope's forces (1512), i 199; vi 604; riot in, 605

—— S. Ricci, Bishop of. *See* Pistoia

—— Vecchio, Giovanni da, Finance Minister of the Medici, i 147

Pratt, Sir Charles. *See* Camden, 1st Earl of

Pratteln, engagement at, xi 245

Pravo, Russian journal, xii 347

Prax-Paris, Joseph-Marie-Adrien, French politician, xii 106

Prayer-Book, English, reformed uses, ii 482 sq.; Edward VI's First Book of Common Prayer, 484 sq.; Second Book of Common Prayer, 508; Elizabeth's Book, 569 sqq.; 587 sqq.; revision of 1661, v 98 sq.

Prazmowski, Andrew, iii 75

Préamenu. *See* Bigot de Préameneu

"Precedence," as system in Muscovite State of 16th and 17th centuries, v 485 sq., 489

Préciosité, in French 17th century life, v 73, 79 sq.

Precursore, Italian Liberal newspaper, x 127

Precursors, The, Irish society, xi 7

Précy, Comte Louis F. Perrein de, French general, viii 345, 351

Predestination, philosophy of, ii 717

Prégent de Bidoux, French admiral, i 480, 483

Pregnani, Abbé, in London, v 203

Preititz, captured by Ney (1813), ix 519

Prendergast, Sir Harry N. D., general, in Burma, xii 479

—— United States naval commander, xii 680 sq.

Prentiss, Benjamin Mayberry, American general, vii 505

Prenzlau, Swedish capture of, vi 280; 287; surrender of Hohenlohe at (1806), ix 279

Preobrazhenskoe, Peter the Great at, v 519 sqq., 524, 587

Presbyterianism, elements and beginnings of, ii 592 sqq.; Calvin, Knox and, *ib.*; in England, under Elizabeth, iii 340 sqq.; political theory of, 743, 753 sqq.; in England in 1643–4, iv 318 sqq.; Chap. xi, Presbyterians and Independents (1645–9), 336–55; and Westminster Assembly, *see* Chap. xii *passim*, 356–63; at accession of Charles II, v 96 sq., 101 sqq.; and Declaration of Indulgence of 1672, 207; opposed to toleration, 326 sqq.; attitude of, generally, during Restoration period, 329 sqq.; in Scotland, at Restoration, 279 sqq.; 290; William's recognition and establishment of, 292 sqq.; in Ireland, at Restoration, 304 sq.; in Ulster, disabilities of, vi 483. *See also* Nonconformists

Prescott, Robert, General, Governor of Canada, ix 744

—— William Hickling, historian, vii 745; xii 841

Presidi, The, retained by Spain, ii 88, iv 152; 155; ceded to Tuscany, 597

Présidiaux, The, in France, ii 96

Presles, College of, iii 58

Prespa, Lake, xii 392

Press and printing, for Renaissance publications in general, classical, patristic and other, *see* Vol. i, Chaps. xvi *and* xvii *passim*; great influence of, in this period, 684 sqq.; in Canadian French colonies, late establishment of, vii 102 sq.; in

Denmark, under Struensee and later, vi 752, 756; English, Act of 1662, v 98; freed from censorship, 271 sq.; results of this, under Anne, 467; question of the freedom of, vi 444; prosecutions of 1817, x 580; French, at opening of Revolution, viii 122 sq., 168 sq.; copyright law in age of Revolution, 724 sq.; under First Empire, censorship of, ix 129 sq.; clerical, 190; liberty of, x 59; 73; legislation for control of, 77; new Press Law of 1826 withdrawn, 89 sq.; censorship re-established, *ib.*; under Napoleon III, xi 291 sq.; statute of 1868 concerning, 487 sq.; the German, under Federal Act, x 347; early Italian, at Venice, that of Aldo Manuzio and its great publications, i 561 sqq.; other Italian presses, *ib.*; at Rome, 566; and Vatican in 19th century, xi 714; Japanese, influence of, xii 544, 547; in Kingdom of the Netherlands, x 529 sqq.; Polish, censorship of, from 1820, 452; Prussian, freedom of, under Frederick the Great, vi 713; Russian, and Peter the Great, v 529, 531; censorship of, in 19th century, xi 267; outbreak of journalistic activity under Alexander II, 625; censorship of, 625 sq.; law of 1865, xii 295; activity of censorship of (1865–79), 300; 312; censorship of, from 1882, 314 sqq.; interval in working of censorship (1904), 346; renewed activity of, 349; 353; Witte and, 361

Pressburg, Ferdinand I elected King of Hungary at, ii 199; Alliance of (1608), iii 721; iv 21; 31; Diet at (1620), 64; Habsburgs and, v 339; 346 sq.; 352; attacked by Tökölyi (1683), 361; 363; Diet at (1687), 367; coronation at, viii 327, 335; Austrian retreat to, ix 257; Archduke John retreats to (1809), 355; King of Saxony at, 582, 599
—— Peace of (1491), i 344, 395; (1626), iv 98; (1805), ix 261 sq., 341, 355
Presse, La, French journal, x 499; xi 127
Prester John, i 8, 14
Preston, battle of (1648), iv 350 sqq., 507; Jacobites at, vi 101; 102; 114; disturbances at, xi 2
—— Thomas, and Irish rebellion, iv 525 sqq.; 530; at Dangan Hill, 531
—— Captain, at Boston, vii 154
Prestonpans, battle of, vi 113
Pretoria, xii 640; Lord Roberts at, 643; 647
—— Convention, The, xii 637
Pretorius, Andries W. J., Boer leader, xi 782 sqq.
—— Marthinus Wessel, President of Transvaal, xi 785; 788 sq.
—— Stephan, Lutheran divine, v 758
Preussische Jahrbücher, xi 451
Preussisches Wochenblatt, xi 396

Prevesa, stormed by Tuscan squadron, iii 399; captured by the Venetians (1684), v 365; captured by Ali of Janina, x 176; xii 403; bombarded, 421
Prevost, Augustine, Governor of East Florida, vii 219
—— Sir George, Governor of Canada, vii 335, 338, 343; ix 746
—— Johann Baptist (Zambra), iv 46 sq.
—— J. M., Colonel, vii 219
Prévost d'Exiles, Antoine-François, French Abbé, vi 824
Priboy, Austrian troops at, xii 396
Price, John, iv 559
—— Richard, philosopher, viii 755 sq., 764
—— Sterling, Confederate general, vii 460 sq.
Pride, Colonel Thomas, "Pride's Purge," iv 354
Prideaux, John, Brigadier-general, vii 137, 141
Prie, Madame de, vi 134; 143 sq.
Priè, Marquis of, x 114
Priebus, Wallenstein obtains lordship of, iv 103; Hadik and Laudon at, vi 292
Priepolye, Montenegro and, xii 392; 396
Prierias. *See* Mazzolini, Sylvester
Priesten, fighting at (1813), ix 528
Priestley, Joseph, philosopher, becomes French citizen, viii 764; nominated for Convention, 247; 755, 758, 765; influence of, upon Bentham, x 595; 700; discovers oxygen, xii 768
Prieur, Pierre-Louis (*de la Marne*), deputy to National Convention, viii 249, 343, 375
Prieur-Duvernois, Claude-Antoine (*de la Côte-d'Or*), viii 249, 344, 380; and the army, 426
Prikazy, machinery of central Russian administration, v 515 sq.
Prim, Juan, Count of Reus, Marquis de los Castillejos, Spanish captain-general, x 242; xi 558; 563; in Moroccan campaign, 564; in Mexico, 565 sq.; declines office, 566; and O'Donnell, 566 sq.; plots against dynasty, 566 sqq.; escapes to Portugal, 567; retires to Geneva, 568; 569; in search of successor to Isabel, 570 sq.; assassinated, 571; xii 259
Primo de Rivera, Fernando, Spanish general, xii 265
Prina, Comte Joseph, ix 86
Prince, The, of Machiavelli, i 212 sq.
Prince Edward Island, French in, vii 112 sq.; government of, ix 746; ceded to Britain (1763), x 685; xi 757; 770 sq.; united to Canada, 776; industries of, xii 611
Prince Potemkin, Russian warship, mutiny on, xii 355
Principia Philosophiae, iv 779; 786; 793
Prinkipo, British fleet off, xii 390
Prinsterer, Gulielmus Groen van, Dutch historian, xi 664; 666

Prior, Matthew, in Paris, v 430; 467; vi 830

Pritchard, Benjamin D., American colonel, vii 543

—— George, consul at Tahiti, xi 35

Prittwitz, Karl L. W. E. von, Prussian general, xi 158 sq.

—— Rittmeister, and Frederick the Great, vi 324

Priuli, Girolamo, mission of, to France (1620), iv 50

—— Luigi, ii 379, 398

—— Lorenzo, iii 425, 428, 432

—— historian, i 285

Privas, surrender of (1629), iv 135

Privy Council, of Edward VI, composition of, ii 475; committee of, for Foreign Affairs, set up (1625), iv 257; courts of criminal jurisdiction of, 291; (*see also for criminal jurisdiction of*, Star Chamber); of 1660, v 93; action of, under Charles II, Chap. v *passim*; reorganised in committees (1668), 201; reorganisation of 1696 in regard to commerce and colonies, 264; constitution and powers of, under William III, 272; 464; for later history of, *see* England

—— Six (*Heimliche Rath*), in Zurich, ii 322

Prjevalsky, Nicolai, travels of, xii 798 sq.; 802 sq.

Probstheida, French at, ix 538

Proctor, Henry A., General, vii 339 sqq.

—— Vermont senator, vii 676

Prodol, Austrian repulse at, xi 453

Prokesch-Osten, Anton, Count von, x 552

Prokopovich, Theophan, Bishop of Pskoff. *See* Pskoff

Prolétaire, Le, French journal, xii 123

Proly, P. J. de, Member of Committee of Insurrection, viii 265, 342

Prome, British occupation of, xi 728; 742

Pronchisheff, Russian explorer, xii 795

Prondzynski, Ignaz, Polish officer, x 468; 470 sq.

Pronis, coloniser of Madagascar, v 702

Prony, G.-C.-F.-M. Riche de, Director of School of Bridges, etc., ix 120

Propertius, Sextus Aurelius, xi 422

Prossnitz, Prussian army at, iv 278

Protectorate, The, of Oliver Cromwell, Vol. iv, Chap. xv, 434–58, Chap. xvi, 459–85, 511 sq., 533 sqq.

Protest against decisions of Diet of Speier (1529), ii 204; Signatories of, 205; 330

Protot, French politician, xi 502 sq.

Proudhon, Pierre-Joseph, French socialist, xi 24; 99; 110; 114; 300; 304; 474 sq.; funeral of, 478

Prouninck, Gerard (Deventer), iii 620 sqq.

Proust, Louis-Joseph, French chemist, ix 376

Prout, William, chemist, xii 770

Provana, Andrea, Lord of Leynì, iii 401, 410, 412–3

Provençe, invaded by Charles V (1536), ii 71; Épernon appointed governor of, iii 40; Savoy's designs on, 415–6, 437, 510; the League in, 661–3; taxation of, iv 153; 600 sq.; 606; 613; Condé claims, 614; pacified, 620; Estates of, v 4, viii 129; invaded by Prince Eugene (1707), v 418 sq.; vi 159; 350; invasion of (1746), 362; Fouché banished to, ix 371

—— Comte de. *See* Louis XVIII

Provera, Giovanni, Marquis de, General, viii 557, 566, 580, 636

Providence (Bahamas), relinquished by Spain, vi 464

—— (Rhode Island), settlement of, vii 19 sq., 24; occupied by the Americans, 218

—— Lake, and canal project, vii 503

—— Plantations (Providence, Portsmouth and Newport), incorporated, vii 24; trade of, vi 447

Providien, naval engagement off, vi 454

Provincia Cisplatina, x 316

Provincial Assemblies, The, Turgot and, viii 86; Necker and, 91, 94; instituted (1787), 102, 109 sq.; 209

Prozorovski, Russian commander, in Turkey, ix 485

Prudhomme, Louis-Marie, French writer, viii 251

Prussia

v   xiv   The War of the Spanish Succession and the Peace of Utrecht, *passim*, 401–59

     xix   The Great Northern War, *passim*, 584–615

     xx   The Origins of the Kingdom of Prussia, 616–38

     xxi   The Great Elector and the first Prussian king, 639–72

vi   viii The War of the Austrian Succession, 201–50

     ix   The Seven Years' War, 251–300

     x   Russia under Anne and Elizabeth, *passim*, 301–28

     xi   The reversal of Alliances and the Family Compact, *passim*, 329–60

     xiii Great Britain (1756[-63]), *passim*, 393–428

     xix   Catharine II (of Russia), *passim*, 657–701

     xx   Frederick the Great and his successor
           (1) Home and foreign policy (1763–97), 702–28
           (2) Poland and Prussia (1763–91), 729–34

viii xi   The European Powers and the Eastern Question, *passim*, 306–37

     xiv   The General War, *passim*, 398–446

     xvii The extinction of Poland (1788–97), 521–52

     xxi   The Second Coalition, *passim*, 633–64

Prussia (*contd.*)

IX ix The Third Coalition, I (1805-6), *passim*, 244-64

   x The Third Coalition, II (1806-7), *passim*, 265-93

   xi The Napoleonic Empire at its height (1807-9), *passim*, 294-340

  xvii The War of Liberation (1813-4), 506-54

  xix The Congress of Vienna, I (1814-5), *passim*, 576-602

  xx The Hundred Days (1815), *passim*, 616-45

  xxi The Congress of Vienna, II (1815), *passim*, 646-71

X i The Congresses (1815-22), *passim*, 1-39

   xi The Germanic Federation (1815-40), *passim*, 340-82

  xiv Poland and the Polish Revolution, *passim*, 445-74

  xxiii Economic Change, *passim*, 727-62

XI iii Liberalism and Nationality in Germany and Austria (1840-8), *passim*, 43-64

  vi The Revolution and the Reaction in Germany and Austria, I (1848-9), *passim*, 142-201

  vii The Revolution and the Reaction in Germany and Austria, II, *passim*, 202-33

  xv Austria, Prussia, and the Germanic Confederation
(1) Reaction and Reorganisation (1852-62), 393-410
(2) German Literature (1840-70), 411-20

  xvi Bismarck and German Unity, 432-66

  xxi The Franco-German War (1870-1), 576-612

XII vi The German Empire, *passim*, 134-73
[*See also, especially after* 1871, *Germany*]

Prussia, East, creation of duchy of, I 293; II 169; III 74 sq.; the Reformation in, 153; IV 185; and compact of Stuhmsdorf, 366; Great Elector and, 581; Treaty of Königsberg and, 582 sq.; Treaty of Oliva and, 590; VI 217 sq.; immigration to, 219; 220 sq.; 225; troops in, 256; Russians in, 264; 266; 277; Frederick the Great and, 294, 300; 297 sq.; Russian troops in, 322; 716; 729; 732; revolutionary movement in, XI 157

—— **West** *or* Polish, surrendered to Poland (1466), I 293; III 87; and Gustavus Adolphus, IV 185; and Great Elector, 428 sq., 433; and Charles X, 580 sqq.; Treaty of Oliva and, 590; Frederick II and, IV 251; 277; 291; taxation in, 712; 716; 729 sq.; 733; VIII 522; annexed by Prussia (1775), 523

Prussia, Duke of. *See* Brandenburg, Albert, Margrave of

—— **Dukes of.** *See also* Brandenburg, Electors of

—— **Albert** of Brandenburg(-Ansbach), Grand Master of Teutonic Order, 1st Duke of, I 691; II 162; secularises possessions of Order, 169, 635; 198; and Christian III of Denmark, 230, 611; 239; 262; 270; 571; III 73 sqq.; and Osiander, 153 sq.; V 625 sq.; 635 sq.

—— **Albert Frederick, Duke of,** III 716; IV 25; V 636 sqq.

—— **John Sigismund, Duke of.** *See* Brandenburg, John Sigismund, Elector of

—— **Dorothea, Duchess of,** V 635

—— **Maria Eleonora** of Jülich-Cleves, Duchess of, III 716, 729; V 636

—— **Prince Henry of,** IX 327

—— **Prince William of** (son of Frederick William II), appeals to Napoleon, IX 307; at Erfurt, 318; proposed as Governor of Saxony, 594

—— **Prince of.** *See* William I, German Emperor

Prussian Academy of Sciences, XII 821

Pruth, river, campaign of (1711), V 604 sq.

Prutz, Robert Ernst, German writer, XI 50

Pruyn, American Consul-General in Japan, XI 842

Prynne, William, IV 273; 278; punishment of, 279 sq.; release of, 291; and Parliament, 549, 553; Restoration and, 554; the *Histriomastix,* V 128; writings of, VI 813

Przegląd Polski (Polish review), XI 660

Przemysl, ecclesiastical seminary of, X 462

—— **Peter,** Bishop of, III 77-8

Pskoff, besieged by Stephen Báthory (1581), III 101, V 494; progress of Swedes arrested at, IV 180; annexed to Russia, V 478 sqq.; State of, 484; 500; 590; Rumyantseff's army at, VI 773

—— **Theophan Prokopovich,** Bishop of, V 536

Psychical Research Society, founded, XII 775

Ptolemy, astronomer, V 707 sq.; XII 812

Public Advertiser, VI 441; 444; 493; 495

Public Weal, the French and Burgundian, League of, I 389; War of, 396 sq.

Publicius, Jacob, German humanist, II 111

Pucci, Antonio, Cardinal, II 30, 413

—— **Giannozzo** (Medicean partisan), I 175

—— **Lorenzo,** Cardinal, II 413

Puchheim, Imperial general, defeats Rákóczy, IV 389

Puchmajer, Antonin, Čech poet, XI 653

Puchner, Baron Anton von, Austrian general, XI 206

P'uchün, Chinese heir-apparent, XII 518

Puebla, captured by Scott (1847), VII 396; taken by the French, XI 476

Puerto de Santa Maria, revolutionaries at, x 215 sq.
—— Real, Spanish ships destroyed at, III 325
Pütter, Johann Stephan, German historian, XII 817
Pufendorf, Samuel, German historian and publicist, v 648; 655; 670
Pugacheff, Yemelian, insurrection of (against Catharine II), v 505; VI 674; 680 sq.; 689; 701; VIII 784; XI 263
Puget, Captain, and Brest, IX 217
Pugin, Augustus W. N., English architect, XI 355
Puglia, Francesco da. *See* Francesco da Puglia
Puig Moltó, Antonio, Spanish officer, XI 563
Puisaye, Comte Joseph - Geneviève de, *Chouan* leader, VIII 379, 391; and Quiberon expedition, 472
Puisieux, Pierre Brulart, Marquis de, IV 127 sq.
Pularoon, English and Dutch claims in, v 108; 112; 149; 151; 179; retained by Dutch, 189
Pulci, Luigi, III 458, 460–1
Pulgar, Hernando del. *See* Del Pulgar
Pulicat, English and Dutch and, IV 737, 743
Pulli, Spanish brigand, XII 259
Pulo Run, IV 736; Treaty of Breda and, 740
Pulo-condore, islands of, ceded to France, XII 524
Pulszky, Ferencz Aurel, Hungarian leader, XI 188; 204; 214
Pulteney, William. *See* Bath, Earl of
Pultusk, the Jesuits installed at, III 83; Swedish victory at (1703), v 592; Russian army at, IX 284; 290
Punitz, battle at (1704), v 593
Punjab, The, Emperor Bábar in, VI 509; 510 sqq.; invaded by Sikhs, 523; Persian invasion of, 524; and Marátha confederacy, IX 725; XI 724; 727; 731 sq.; annexation of, 742; 744; 751; and north-west frontier, XII 458; 474; 480; and north-west frontier districts, 489 sq.; agrarian reform in, 493
Punniar, engagement at, XI 738
Punta del Rey, English trade with, III 633
Punto Obligado, fort of, XII 681
Pupper, John (of Goch), German theologian, I 437, 626, 652
Purandhar, Treaty of, VI 575
Purishkévich, and the third Duma, XII 375
Puritanism, beginnings of, and Vestiarian Controversy, II 590 sqq.; John Knox and, *ib.*; English Church and, 597; under Elizabeth, III 340 sqq.; under James I, 553 sq.; and 16th century political thought, 755; and Laud, IV 278 sqq.; becomes Nonconformist, v 99; and New England, VII 11, 17. *See also* Nonconformists
Pusey, Edward Bouverie, XI 349; 711

Pushkin, Alexander, Russian poet, x 431; XI 262; 648 sq.
Puteo, Jacopo, legate at the Council of Trent, II 676
Putiatin, Count, Russian admiral, in China, XI 816; in Japan, 828, 830; 839
Putiloff factory, strike at, XII 349
Putiloff, Russian general, in the Russo-Japanese War, XII 593 sq.
Putivl, rebellion at, v 500
Putte, Francis van de, Dutch Colonial Minister, XI 666; 668
Puttkamer, Robert Victor von, German statesman, XII 163
Puy-de-Dôme, experiment of the, IV 794
Puyrredón, Juan Martin, x 301
Puységur, L. P. de Chastenet, Comte de, Secretary for War, VIII 163
Pyasina river, exploration on, XII 795
Pyat, Félix, French politician, XI 99; 114; 502
Pyatigórsk, rising in, XII 363
Pyeshkoff, removed from Kharkoff, XII 376
Pyhäjoggi, Pass of, v 588
Pym, John, III 574; Petition of Right and, IV 270; in the Short Parliament, 284 sqq.; 287 sq.; 289 sqq.; Root-and-Branch petition and, 292; Ten Propositions carried by, 293; 294 sq.; impeached, 297 sq.; 299; 305; taxation and, 311; 314; 316; death and character of, 318; 319; English West India Company and, 758
Pyramids, battle of the, VIII 602 sq.
Pyrenees, The, timber trade of, v 12; Peace of (1659), IV 157, 432 sq., 541, v 33 sq., 105, 373, 446, provisions of, IV 620, 660 sq.

Quadra, Alvaro de la, Bishop of Aquila. *See* Aquila
Quadrilateral, The, Austrian army in, XI 82, 84 sq.
Quadruple Alliance, of 1666, v 37, 109; of 1718, VI 30 sqq., 124; of 1834, x 234, 336
Quaelly (Keely), Malachias, Archbishop of Tuam, killed at Sligo, IV 529
Quakers (Society of Friends), v 101 sqq.; and Declaration of Indulgence of 1672, 207; and Second Declaration of Indulgence, 238; and principle of toleration, 327; and Labadism, 756 sq.; Indemnity Acts and, VI 44; in New England, VII 24 sqq., 57; in Pennsylvania, 49; and the Indians, 100. *See also* Nonconformists
Quam Memoranda, Bull of Pius VII, IX 401
Quanta Cura, Papal Encyclical of 1864, XI 712 sqq.
Quarantotti, Cardinal, Vice-Prefect of the Propaganda, x 141; and Ireland, 635
Quarterly Review, The, IX 687; x 716; XI 362
Quatre-Bras, battle of (1815), IX 626 sqq.
Quatremère de Quincy, Antoine-Chrysostome, IX 133

Quebec, fort erected at, v 684, vii 71; surrender of (1629), 74; 76 sq.; 81; attacked by Phipps (1690), 90; 94; government of, 117; capture of (1759), vi 342, 342a sqq. (in Vol. xiii), 415, vii 136 sqq.; province of, extended, vi 446; government of, 476; Montgomery's expedition against (1775), vii 170 sq.; affairs in, ix 742 sqq.; boundaries of province of, x 685; French and English in, 688; Confederation Convention at, xi 769 sqq.; 771; 774; 777; xii 604; 606 sq.; French population of, 611; industries of, 612; 614
—— Act, The (1774), ix 743, x 686
Quedlinburg, abbey of, v 668
Queen Adelaide, South African province of, xi 780; 786
Queensberry, James Douglas, 2nd Duke of, v 298 sq.; vi 93
—— William Douglas, 1st Duke of, v 289
Queen's Colleges, Ireland, established, xi 9
Queensland, xi 761; founding of, 795; population of, 796, 799; separated from New South Wales, 798; 801; development and progress of, xii 619 sqq.; constitution of, 632; 666
Queenstown (Niagara), van Rensselaer attacks (1812), vii 338
Queen's University, in Ireland, xii 71, 75
Quercy, peasants' rising in, iii 664
Querdes, Des. *See* Crèvecœur
Quérel, police agent, ix 29
Queretaro, death of Emperor Maximilian at, xi 483
Querini, Venetian ambassador, viii 592
Querno, Camillo, ii 18
Quesnay, François, viii 21 sqq.; teachings of, ix 362; Adam Smith and, x 763, 766, 769; 770
Quesnel, Pasquier, *Réflexions*, v 89 sq.; x 157
Quesnoy, captured by Prince Eugene (1712), v 433, recovered, 434; surrendered (1793), viii 431; recaptured (1794), 436
Questenberg, Gerhard von, Imperial ambassador, iv 210; 238 sq.
Questions of Life, Russian journal, xii 333
Quetta, British occupation of, xii 460, 467; 470; 489
Quevedo, Francisco Gomez de, factotum of Osuña, iv 632; literary skill of, 633
Quiberon, expedition to (1795), viii 391, 471 sq.
—— Bay, the battle of, vi 342c sq. (in Vol. xiii)
Quietism, in France, v 88; 761. *See also* Quakers, etc.
Quignon, Cardinal, reformed Breviary of, ii 484
Quilimane, Livingstone at, xii 808
Quincy, Josiah, American lawyer, vii 154
Quinet, Edgar, and Napoleon, ix 758; x 102; 481; 492; xi 34; 36; xii 833
Quinipiac river, settlement at, vii 20

Quintana, Juan de, ii 411
—— Manuel José, Spanish poet, viii 783
Quintanghona, French slaver seized at, xi 574
Quiroga, Antonio, Spanish revolutionary officer, x 216 sq.
—— Father, Capuchin diplomatist, Wallenstein and, iv 239
—— Spanish Index of prohibited books of, ii 687
Quito, v 679; 683; government of, x 248; insurrection in, 258; languages in, 261; revolutionary movement in (1809), 284, 286; royalists in, 290; 294 sq.; and republic of Ecuador (1830), 296
Quitzow, family of, v 622
Quod nunquam, Bull of Pius IX, xii 149
Quosdanovich, Peter Vitus von, Austrian general in Italy, viii 574 sq.
Quotidienne, The, x 80; 94

Raab, Turkish fugitives at, v 362, 363; Austrians attack (1809), ix 355, 396; captured by Austrians (1849), xi 210
—— river, battle on (1664), v 347 sq.
Raabe, Wilhelm, German novelist, xi 417; 419 sq.
Rabago, Jesuit, confessor of Ferdinand VI, vi 361; 364
Rabah, Zobeir, defeat of, xii 130
Rabaut de Saint-Étienne, J.-P., viii 21, 183; on *Commission de Douze*, 272; executed (1793), 357
Rabelais, François, the *Gargantua*, ii 287; 690, 710 sq.; iii 460
Rabenhaupt, Karel, Baron de Sucha, v 160
Rabutin, François de, French historian, iii 64
—— Austrian ambassador in Russia (1726), v 552
Raby, Lord. *See* Strafford, 3rd Earl of
Racan, Honorat de Bueil, Marquis de, French poet, v 69
Racconigi, Count Bernardino de, iii 403, 412–3
Rachol, Portuguese conquest of (1791), ix 718
Racine, Jean, v 65; 68; 125; vi 831
Racova, Turkish defeat at (1475), i 83
Raczynski, Count, at Diet of Posen, x 463
Radak, Prince, of Bosnia, i 73
Radcliffe, Ann, novelist, vi 832; x 698; 716; 718; 725
Radetzky, Johann J. W. A. F. Karl, Count von Radetz, Austrian field-marshal, at Congress of Vienna, ix 583
—— Count Joseph, Austrian field-marshal, x 357; xi 68; in Italy, 71; retreats from Milan, 81 sq.; 84; and Italian War, 85 sqq.; at Novara, 93; 170; 182; 187; 189; 208 sq.; 357; conference of, with King Victor Emmanuel, 366; 374; rule of, in Lombardo-Venetia, 376 sq.
—— Russian general, xii 389

Radevynszoon, Florentius, establishes fraternity at Deventer, I 434 sq., 627

Radishcheff, Alexander Nikolaevich, *Journey from St Petersburg to Moscow*, VI 690; 699; *Ode to Liberty*, VIII 785

Radnor, Sir John Robartes, 1st Earl of (Lord Robartes), V 93; 101; 305

Radolt, Erhardt, Venetian printer, I 284

Radom, Confederation of, VI 667; Polish troops posted near, IX 354

Radowitz, Joseph Maria von, Prussian statesman, XI 48; 50 sq.; ambassador at Carlsruhe, 60; and German national movement, 63 sq.; 144; at Vienna, 153; 160; 165; Frederick William IV and, 191; character of, 220; and *Dreikönigsbündniss, ib.*; and Germanic Confederation, 222 sqq.; and dispute with Austria, 228 sqq.; Minister of Foreign Affairs, 229; resigns, 230; mission of, to England, *ib.*; and Switzerland, 252; 396

Radstadt, siege of (1526), II 190 sq.

Radu, Prince of Wallachia, I 83

Radziejowice, Calvinistic community at, III 75

Radziejowski, Cardinal. *See* Gnesen, Archbishops of

—— Polish exile, IV 581

Radzivil (Radziwill), Anton Henry, Prince von, Governor of Posen, X 353; 463

—— Barbara, Queen of Poland, consort of Sigismund II, III 76, 78, 82

—— Prince Bogislav, in Lithuania, IV 580; in Poland, 581

—— Prince Christopher II, IV 183; commands Polish army, 185

—— Prince Michael (Black Radziwill), III 76, 82

—— Michael, Prince, Polish commander-in-chief, X 469 sq.; XI 277

Raemond, Florimond de, II 296

Räzüns, Catholic forces at, IV 51 sq.; 55

Raffaelle Sanzio, of Urbino, I 143; made Inspector-General of Antiquities at Rome, 548; II 4; the *Camera della Segnatura*, 6 sqq.; portraits of Leo X and of Clement VII by, 12 sqq., 22; 18; 28; III 439

Raffet, Denis-Auguste-Marie, X 489; XI 24

Raffles Bay, XI 790

Raffles, Sir Thomas Stamford, Governor of Java, IX 754; XI 668

Raffron du Trouillet, Nicolas, French deputy, VIII 247

Raggi, secret society, in Bologna, X 111

Ragkavês, Alexander, Greek delegate at Berlin, XII 395

Raglan, Fitzroy James Henry Somerset, Lord, envoy in Spain, X 226; in command in the Crimea, XI 317 sq.; 322

Ragnone, Lattanzio, Italian Reformer, II 390

Ragusa, seized by Napoleon (1806), IX 269; 271; French occupation of, 306; 418

—— Duke of. *See* Marmont

Raievskii, Russian officer, and invasion of 1812, IX 492 sq.

Raiffeisen, Friedrich Wilhelm, and co-operative banks, XII 742

Raimondi, Marcantonio, engraver, II 28

Rain, battle near (1632), IV 214; 219

Rainalaiarivony, Madagascar Minister, XII 131

Rainaldus, *Annales Ecclesiastici*, III 444

Rainborow, Thomas, Vice-Admiral, IV 347

—— William, at Sallee, IV 482

Rainer, Archduke of Austria, XI 405

Raja, The, III 129

Rajput clans, VI 508 sq.; 512; 523; 525

Rajputana, Dára Shekoh in, VI 519; famine in, XII 486

Rákóczy, House of, V 339

—— Princes of Transylvania. *See* Transylvania

Rakonitz, IV 65; Wallenstein and Arnim at, 213, 215

Rålamb, Erik, IV 178

Ralegh, Sir Walter, settlers of, III 302; expedition to Cadiz and, 323; 376; 521; James I and, 561 sq.; 600; 633; second expedition of, to Guiana, IV 754; execution of, 755; VI 65; and American colonisation, VII 2 sq.

Raleigh (N. Carolina), "regulators" at, VII 145; surrender of Johnston at, 452; Sherman's march to, 528, 530

Ralph Roister Doister, by Nicholas Udall, III 366, 371

Ramainvilliers, commander of the guard of the Tuileries, VIII 229 sq.

Rambaud, Alfred Nicolas, French historian, XII 845

Rambeaud, French officer, at Acre, VIII 612

Rambouillet, Louis XV at, VI 164; Decree (1810), VII 332

—— Hôtel de, IV 156

Ramel, Jean-Pierre, French general, VIII 505 sq., 509; transported, 512; assassinated, X 46

—— de Nogaret. *See* Nogaret, Jacques Ramel de

Ramezay, Claude de, Governor of Quebec, VII 141

Ramillies, battle of (1706), V 415 sq., 668, VI 91

Rammekens, demanded by Elizabeth, III 619; Dutch force assembled at, IV 698

Ramnagar, battle at, XI 741

Ramond de Carbonnières, Louis F. E., Baron, VIII 213

Ramorino, Italian rebel leader, attempts invasion of Savoy, X 122; at Novara, XI 366 sq.

Rampolla, Mariano, Marquis del Tindaro, Cardinal, XII 225

Rampon, Comte Antoine Guillaume, French general, VIII 565

Rámpura, capture of (1804), IX 727

Ramsay, Allan, poet, X 701

—— James, Bishop of Ross, VI 94

—— Sir James, at Hanau, IV 370 sq.

Ramsay, Sir William, XII 770; 790
—— William Mitchell, XII 847
Ramu, British repulse at, XI 727
Ramus. *See* La Ramée, Pierre de
Rána Sanga, of Udaipur, VI 509 sq.
Ranc, Arthur, French politician, XI 502
Rancé, Armand-Jean le Bouthillier de, Abbot of La Trappe, V 262 sq.
Rand, The, National Union organised on, XII 640
Randall, Samuel Jackson, leader of the Protectionist Democrats, VII 651
Randolph, Edmund, Virginian deputy at Constitutional Convention (1787), Vol. VII, Chap. VIII *passim*
—— Colonel Edward, III 591
—— Edward, special commissioner to New England, VII 28
—— G. W., Confederate Secretary of War, VII 605
—— Sir Thomas, English ambassador in Scotland, II 579 sq.; sent to France, III 30
Randon, Count Jacques-Louis-César-Alexandre, Marshal of France, XI 135
Rangone, Giulia, Countess, II 384
Rangoni, Papal Nuncio at Moscow, V 498
Rangoon, XI 728; captured, 742
Ranjit Singh, relations of, with British, IX 730; XI 731; 732; 736; death of, 738
Ranke, Leopold von, II 7; V 373; 384; 639; 662; VI 227; 732; X 374; founds *Historisch-politische Zeitschrift*, 376; 404; XII 135; work and influence of, 824 sqq.; 843 sq.
Rankine, William John Macquorn, and the theory of heat, XII 784
Rantzau, Count Christoph von, converts John Frederick of Hanover, V 744
—— Daniel, in Småland and Östergötland, IV 164; 179
—— Johann, general of Christian III, II 230, 615
—— Josias, Comte de, Marshal of France, IV 388; imprisoned, 611
Rantzau-Ascheberg, Count Schack Charles, VI 744 sq.; recalled, 746; 749 sqq.
Ranvier, French politician, XI 502
Raoul-Duval, Charles-Edmond, French politician, XII 108
Rapallo, victory of French at (1494), I 112; defeat of the French at (1495), 117
Rapidan, river, Confederate and Federal armies on (1863), VII 491, 515
Rapinat, Commissary in Switzerland under the Directory, VIII 518, 640, 670
Rapp, Comte Jean de, French general, IX 100; commands Army of the Rhine, 624; in Strassburg, 645
Rappahannock river, Burnside advances from, VII 483; Confederate and Federal armies on (1863-4), 514
Rasboieni, victory of Turks at (1476), I 84
Rascia, town of, XII 401
Rasenghien. *See* Vilain

Rasin, Sezyma, and Wallenstein, IV 206, 233
Rask, Rasmus Kristian, philologer, XI 699; *Icelandic Grammar*, XII 822
Raskolniki, The, Russian schismatics, V 509 sqq.; in Altai mountains, XII 794
Raslawice, victory of Kosciusko at, VIII 542
Raspail, François-Vincent, X 491; 499; XI 105; 108; 117
Rassam, Hormuzd, imprisoned by King Theodore, XI 753
Rastatt, Peace of (1714), V 435 sq., 447, 449, 452 sq., VI 614; Congress of (1797), VIII 519, 592 sq., 634, 641 sq., 644, IX 39, 95, 577; murder of French envoys at, VIII 655; XI 50; 219; surrender of, 221
Rastell, William, II 501
Rastoul, French politician, XI 502
Rasul, Sikh force at, XI 741
Rasumovski, Prince Andreas, Russian representative, refused admittance at Rastatt, IX 39; at Congress of Vienna, 586
Raszyn, Poles defeated at (1809), IX 354
Rathbone, Major H. R., VII 545
Rathenow, Swedes expelled from, V 651
Rathlou, Joachim Otto Schack, Danish statesman, VI 751
Rathmines, Ormonde defeated at (1649), IV 533
Ratibor, duchy of, IV 75; 98
Ratisbon, meeting of Catholic princes at (1524), II 172, 326; becomes Lutheran, 238; Catholic League at, IV 12; 82 sqq.; 91; *Kurfürstentag* at (1630), 110, 114-7, 138, 141, 150, 197, 679 sq.; Tilly at, 198; 213; 217; Bernard of Weimar in, 231 sq., 235, 237 sq.; 242 sq.; capitulation of, to Ferdinand of Hungary, 244; 246; Bavaria and, V 52, 407; Truce of (1684), 49 sqq., 56, 61, 653; VI 237; and France, 247; Dalberg transferred to see of, IX 94, 202; granted to Bavaria, 269; French army approaches, 347; campaign at (1809), 348-50; 359; part of Dalberg's principality, 414
—— Diet of (1532), II 218, III 107; Diet or Religious Conference of (1541), II 33, 75, 240, 645, 650, 660; (1546), 80, 253; (1556-7), III 162; (1576), 177, 180-1; (1593), 713 sq.; (1597), 715; (1603), 718; (1608), 724; summoned by Rudolf (1611), 735; (1640), IV 384 sq., 397 sq.; (1653), 415, 426; (1664), V 347; (1675), 651, 743; (1713), 451; (1801), IX 92 sqq.
—— Frederick of Nürnberg, Bishop of, I 669
—— Philip, Bishop of, III 161
Ratmiroff, and plot against Nicholas II, XII 373
Ratona, death of Mansfeld at, IV 98
Rattazzi, Urbano, Italian statesman, XI 366; 370 sq.; Keeper of the Seals, 372; 386 sq.; the laws of, adopted, 529; Ministry of,

532 sqq.; and Garibaldi, 533; resignation of, 535; confiscates church property, 542; and religious Orders, 708; xii 213; death of, 214

Ratzeburg, bishopric of, iv 112; ceded to Mecklenburg-Schwerin, 408

Ratzel, Friedrich, German anthropologist, xii 850

Rauch, Friedrich Wilhelm von, Prussian adjutant-general, xi 191; 199

Raucourt, Françoise Clairien, *alias* Saucerotte, *alias* Raucourt, actress, ix 572

Raule, Benjamin, and Brandenburg navy, v 646 sq.

—— Jacob, and Brandenburg navy, v 647

Raumer, Friedrich L. G. von, historian, xii 824

—— Karl Otto von, Prussian Minister of Education, xi 395

Rauscher, Joseph Othmar von, Austrian cardinal, xi 398; 401

Ravachol, French anarchist, xii 125

Ravaillac, François, iii 643, 690; iv 624 sq.

Ravardière, La. *See* La Ravardière

Ravenna, victory of French at (1512), i 137, 198, 250, 365, 479; occupied by Venice, 281, 287; Inquisition at, x 134; Cardinal Riverola at, 152; 155 sq.

Ravensburg, and Treaty of Cleves, iv 409; the Great Elector and, v 645

Ravenstein, Adolf (of Cleves) zum, i 439, 441, 449 sqq.

—— Philip (of Cleves) zum, i 441, 448 sqq., 454

Ravez, Simon, President of Chamber of Deputies, x 57; 68; 91; 94

Ravina, Amedeo, *Canti Italici*, x 126

Rawa, Peter the Great at, v 526

Rawal Pindi, Sikhs surrender at, xi 742; the Amir at, xii 478

Rawdon, Sir Arthur, at Dromore, v 307

—— Lord. *See* Hastings

Rawitz, Charles XII at, v 593

Rawka, Polish defeat at, viii 546

Rawling, Cecil Godfrey, in Tibet, xii 804

Rawlinson, Sir Henry Creswicke, xii 460; 801; 845

Ray, John, naturalist, v 734 sqq.

Rayleigh, John William Strutt, Lord, xii 770

Raymond, McPherson occupies (1863), vii 504

—— George, in the East, iv 729

—— Michel-Joachim-Marie, French general, and Marátha War, ix 720 sqq.

Raynal, Guillaume Thomas François, French historian, vii 93, 96; viii 26 sq.

Rayneval, Alphonse Gérard de, French diplomatist, xi 121 sq.; 126; Minister for Foreign Affairs, 129

—— Comte François-M. Gérard de, x 74

—— Joseph-Matthias Gérard de, French diplomatist, vi 380; 461

Raynouard, François-Juste-Marie, xii 829

Rayón, Ignacio Lopez, x 303

Razilly, Claude Delaunay de, Governor of Acadia, vii 110 sq.

Razin, Stenka, Cossack leader, v 505

Razumoffsky, Count Alexis, husband of Tsarina Elizabeth, vi 311

Ré, Isle of, Buckingham's expedition to, iv 132, 266 sq.; victory of Vendôme off (1652), 617

Reaal, Laurens, Governor of Dutch East Indies, iv 720; Courthope and, 736

Reaction, The, after the French Revolution, Vol. x *passim*

Read, George, American statesman, vii 246, 252, 258

Reade, Charles, writings of, xi 359

Reading, Charles I at, iv 308 sq.; taken by Essex (1643), 312; 315; 324

Reagan, John Henninger, Confederate Postmaster-General, vii 543, 605

Réal, Comte Pierre François, viii 677 sq.; ix 29; 32, 151

Rebecqui, François-Trophime, French deputy, viii 249, 250, 340, 357

Rebmann, missionary at Mombasa, xii 809

Recalde, Juan Martinez de, iii 298; 307; 312

Récamier, Mme Jeanne-Françoise-J.-A.-B., ix 24; 131; x 101; 514

—— failure of firm of, ix 171

Rechberg, Count Johann Bernard, Austrian statesman, xi 403; 436; and Schleswig-Holstein, 437, 439 sqq.; fall of, 444

Reciff, the Dutch and, iv 750 sq., vi 389; de With defeated at (1648), iv 753; lost by Dutch (1654), v 146, 675; 678

Récollets, The Franciscan, in New France, vii 72, 77

Récsey von Récse, Baron Adam, Hungarian general, xi 185

Recurt, Adrien, French Minister of Interior, xi 113; 118

Red Book of Sweden (*Röda Boken*), ii 630, 632

—— River (Mississippi) expedition, vii 520; Farragut at, 559

—— River (of the North) rebellion, xi 777; Lord Selkirk's colony on, xii 604

—— River (Tonkin), exploration on, xii 524 sq.; 797

—— Sea, xii 430; 499; Italy and, 664

Redan, The, British attack on, xi 322 sq.

Redei (Rhedey), Francis, Prince of Transylvania. *See* Transylvania

Rederijkers (Rhetoricians), in the Netherlands, i 434

Redesdale, John Freeman Mitford, 1st Baron, Lord Chancellor of Ireland, ix 706

Redi, Francesco, naturalist, v 737

Reding, Aloys, Baron de, Swiss patriot, viii 640; ix 99 sq.

—— Rudolf, *Landammann* of Schwyz, vi 621

Reding, Theodore, Marshal and Grandee of Spain (brother of Aloys), victorious at Baylen, IX 437; defeated at Cardadeu, 448; mortally wounded at Valls, *ib.*

Redmond, John Edward, Irish politician, XII 89

Reed, Sir Thomas, General, in India, XI 746

—— Thomas Brackett, Speaker of House of Representatives in Congress of 1889, VII 663

—— American Minister in China, XI 816

Reeves, John, legal historian, VIII 760

Reff, Hans, Bishop of Oslo. *See* Oslo

Reflections on the Revolution in France, Burke's, IX 716

Reform Bills, The English, of 1832, etc. *See* Parliamentary Reform

Reformatio Legum Ecclesiasticarum, II 508; failure of, 589

Reformation, The, in Hungary and Bohemia, I 340; preparation for, in the Netherlands, 434 sqq., Chap. XVII, The Christian Renaissance, *passim*, Chap. XVIII, Catholic Europe, *passim*, Chap. XIX, The Eve of the Reformation; early ideas of and demand for, II 2, 29; balance of religious and political forces of 16th century in, 104; in Germany, 25 sq., 158 sq., Chaps. IV–VIII *passim*; in France, Chap. IX *passim, also* 346–9; in Switzerland, Chap. X *passim, also* 362; Calvin and, Chap. XI *passim*; in the South of Europe, Chap. XII *passim*; in Venice, 381; in Ferrara, 384; in Modena, 386; in Naples, 387; in Lucca, 391; in Spain, 399–412; in Portugal, 412; in England, 463–8; under Edward VI, Chap. XIV; the Scottish and Anglican Settlement, Chap. XVI *passim*; in Denmark, 602–17; in Norway and Iceland, 617–21; in Sweden, 621–33; in Poland, 634–8; connexion of, with the Peasants' Revolt in Germany, 175; European Thought in the Age of, Chap. XIX *passim*; connexion and distinction between the Renaissance and, 282, 691; in Austrian lands, Empire, etc., and the Counter-Reformation under Ferdinand I and Maximilian II, Vol. III, Chap. v *passim*, 140–81; in Ireland, 586 sq.; in Poland, 74 sqq.; influence of, on political thought, *see* Chap. XXII *passim*, Political Thought in the 16th century, 736–69

Reformation without Tarrying for Any, III 756

Réforme, La, French newspaper, XI 24; 27; 34; 42; 96; 99; 101

Reformed Church, The, Calvin and, Vol. II, Chap. XI *passim. See also* Reformation

Régale, The French, V 77, 85

Regel, Alexander, visits Turfan, XII 802

Regensburg. *See* Ratisbon

Regent Inlet, explorers at, XII 814

Reggio, duchy of, awarded to Ferrara (1531), II 67, 219; granted to Duke Francis IV, IX 603

Reggio, Duke of. *See* Oudinot

—— di Calabria, Austrian force at, VI 32; rising at, XI 79; 388

—— nell' Emilia, birthplace of Ariosto (1474), III 460–1; revolt in (1797), VIII 588; XII 226; socialism in, 232, 235

Regimini militantis ecclesiae, Bull constituting Society of Jesus, II 653

Regiomontanus (Johann Müller), I 571, 632, 638

Regis, Colonel Michele, X 114; 117

Regius. *See* Roy, Henry de

—— Urbanus, Reformer, II 183

Regnault, Baron Jean-Baptiste, French painter, IX 135

Régnier, Claude Ambrose, Duc de Massa, VIII 677; IX 9; 30, 31; granted duchy of Massa, 111; President of the Legislative Body, 145; 146; Joseph Bonaparte aided by, 404

Regnier, Mathurin, III 71; XI 508

Regulating Act, Lord North's, VI 571 sqq.

Rehbinder, Baron, Russian Secretary of State for Finnish affairs, X 433

Rehnskjöld, Carl Gustaf, Swedish general, V 593 sq.; 598; at Poltawa, 601; 603

Reichard, Christian Gottlieb N., German geographer, XII 807

Reichenbach, VI 299; 656; Convention of (1790), 710, 725, VIII 289, 292 sq., 333 sqq.; Treaty of (1813), IX 506, 521–2, 579, 591

—— Prussian resident in London, VI 210 sq.

Reichenberg, domains of, IV 73

Reichensperger brothers, German politicians, XII 147

Reichsdeputationstage, III 143

Reichshofrath, institution of, I 313 sqq.; III 723, 729–30

Reichskammergericht, institution of, I 304; opposition to, 305 sqq.; 311, 313, 317, 327; II 149, 151, 153 sq.; reconstitution of (1531), 214; 217, 221; rejected by Protestants, 222; 232 sq., 243; reconstitution of, by Charles V (1547), 263

Reichsmünzordnung (1559), III 142

Reichsregiment (Council of Regency), institution of, I 309; 311, 320; II 145, 149 sqq.; revolt of cities against, 153 sq.; failure of, 156 sq., 222

Reichsritterschaft (Imperial knights), II 154 sq.

Reichstadt, granted to Empress Marie Louise, IX 602; agreement of, XII 389, 394, 396

—— Duc de. *See* Napoleon II

Reichstag. See Diet of the Empire

Reid, Thomas, philosopher, VIII 769; X 43

Reille, Comte Honoré-C.-M.-J., Marshal of France, VIII 569; IX 470; and Belgian campaign, 625; at Waterloo, 633 sqq.

Reimarus, Hermann Samuel, XII 816

Reims. *See* Rheims

Rein, Jonas, Norwegian writer, XI 700

Reina (or Reyna), Cassiodoro de, Spanish Reformer, ɪɪ 411, 592
Reinach, Joseph, and Dreyfus affair, xɪɪ 120
—— Field-Marshal von, ɪv 377
Reingoud, Jacques, ɪɪɪ 620 sq.
Reinhard, Anne, marries Zwingli, ɪɪ 313
—— Count Charles Frederic, Napoleon's words to, ɪx 424
—— Hans von, at Congress of Vienna, ɪx 568; 600
—— Martin, Lutheran theologian, in Denmark, ɪɪ 606
Reinoso, Felix José, and the *Colegio de San Mateo*, x 229
Reis, Dragut, Barbary corsair, ɪɪɪ 486
Reitwein, castle of, Frederick the Great at, vɪ 293
Religious Orders, in New World, ɪ 62; in 15th century Italy, 144 sqq.; and Universities in pre-Reformation days, 643 sq.; religious revivals and, 647 sq.; gilds and brotherhoods, 648 sq.; 652; the older, in Germany, ɪɪ 106; religious confraternities, 108; and Reforming movement, 161 sq.; drastic reform of, in Spain, 399 sq.; and Church reform, 646 sqq.; foundation of new Orders, *ib.*; in Austria, Joseph II's action towards, vɪ 636 sq.; in Belgium, Joseph II and, 649; in France, and edict of 1765, vɪɪɪ 53; character of, in 18th century, 56; suppression of (1790), 195; Napoleon I and, ɪx 190 sq.; Villèle and, x 83 sq.; and education, in 19th century, xɪɪ 92; attack on Congregations in France, 117, 121 sq.; and French Schools, 113 sqq.; and policy of Jules Ferry, 117; in Russia, numbers enrolled in (1825), x 422 sq.; in Spain, after Revolution, 141 sq.; agitation against, in 1834, 236; in early Spanish America, 252 sq. *See also* Jesuits, Theatines, Capuchins, etc., and the older Orders individually
Rély, Jean de, French translator of Bible, ɪɪ 283
Rembrandt (Rembrandt Hermanszoon van Rhijn), art of, ɪv 722
Remieulx of Ghent, ɪ 449
Remonstrantie, The (1610), ɪɪɪ 647
Remonstrants, and Contra-Remonstrants, in Dutch Reformed Church, ɪɪɪ 647 sqq.; and Latitudinarians, v 744
Rémusat, Comtesse C. E. J. de, ɪx 23
—— Comte Charles de, x 52 sqq.; 59; 95 sq.; Under-Secretary of State for Public Works, 497; 508; xɪɪ 105; 107
Remyro, Greek emissary of King Ferdinand (1540), ɪɪɪ 118
Renaissance, The, Vol. ɪ *passim, especially* Chap. xvɪ, The Classical Renaissance, 532–84: in Italy, 537–68, 571, 583 sq.; in Northern Europe, 568–71; in Germany, 571–5; in France, 575–8; in Spain and Portugal, 578; in Netherlands, 579; in

England, 579–83: Chap. xvɪɪ, The Christian Renaissance, 585–619: in Italy, 592–6; in France, 597; in England, 585–92, 597 sq.; in Switzerland, 599; in Germany, 599 sq., *see also* Bible, Libraries, etc. *and* for briefer references to the movement as a whole, Chaps. xvɪɪɪ, Catholic Europe, *passim*, and xɪx, The Eve of the Reformation, *passim*; *also* the following:—Maximilian I and, 325 sqq.; in Hungary, 339 sq.; in Spain, 379 sqq.; preparation for, of Brethren of the Common Life in Netherlands, 435 sq.; and Erasmus, 460 sqq., 568 sqq.; in England, early beginnings of, 491 sq.: Vol. ɪɪ, Chap. ɪ, Medicean Rome, *passim*; Chap. xɪx, Tendencies of European Thought in the Age of the Reformation, *passim*; at Erfurt, 111 sq.; at Wittenberg, 167 sq.; in France, 281 sqq., 346 sq.; and Zwingli, 308, 345 sq.; at Basel, 355 sq.; 377 sq.; the French, Vol. ɪɪɪ, Chap. ɪɪ, French Humanism, etc., 53–72; the English, Chap. xɪ, The Elizabethan Age of English Literature, 364–82; Rome and, 422, 438 sq.; the later Italian, Chap. xɪv, The end of the Italian Renaissance, 456–74; Spain and, 546 sqq.; for Renaissance influence on Reform movements in general, *see also* Reformation *and* Counter-Reformation
Renan, Ernest, xɪ 509; 523 sq.; 527; xɪɪ 93; 114; 119; 846 sq.
Renard, Simon, Spanish ambassador in England, ɪɪ 509, 513, 516, 523 sq., 533; ɪɪɪ 197
Renault, Pierre-Hippolyte-Publius, French general, xɪ 100
Rendsburg, Christian IV at, ɪv 101; fall of (1627), 102; fortress of, xɪ 161 sq.
René, King of Sicily, etc. *See* Anjou, René, Duke of
Renée of France. *See* Ferrara, Renée, Duchess of
Reneri, Henry, Dutch philosopher, ɪv 788
Renneberg, George Lalaing, Count of, ɪɪɪ 251–2
Rennefort, Urbain Souchu de, in Madagascar, v 703
Rennes, surrender of (1491), ɪ 450; *Parlement* of, v 4, vɪ 130, 348, 356, vɪɪɪ 47; 112; disorder in, 129; "libel plot" at, ɪx 21; Dreyfus trial at, xɪɪ 121
—— Louis Guido Guérapin de Vauréal, Bishop of, ambassador to Spain, vɪ 159 sqq.; 167
Renouvier, Charles-Bernard, the *Manuel républicain* of, prohibited, xɪ 114; xɪɪ 94
Renwick, James, Scottish covenanter, v 290
Renzi, Pietro, Italian politician, xɪ 65; 69
Repeal Association, founded by O'Connell, xɪ 7 sq.; 11
Repnin, Prince Anikita Ivanovich, Russian ambassador in Poland (1768), vɪ 354, 628, 667

Repnin, Prince Nikita Ivanovich, Russian field-marshal (1716), v 612
—— Prince Nikolai, Russian envoy, VIII 643
—— Prince Vasily, Russian general, VI 318
Repnin - Volkonski, Nicolas - Grigorievich, Prince, IX 579; Governor of Saxony, *ib.*; at Vienna, 586
République, La, French newspaper, XI 127
Requesens y Zuñiga, Don Luis de, Viceroy of the Netherlands, III 237 sq.; 240 sqq.; 286; 495 sq.; died (1576), 498
"Request," The Dutch (1566), III 203–4
Resaca de la Palma (Texas), battle at (1846), VII 395
Rescht, seized by the Russians (1722), v 545
Rescissory Act, Scottish, of 1661, v 281
Reservatum ecclesiasticum, III 141–2, 152–3, 162, 180
Reshid, Mustafa, Pasha, Turkish general, X 181; 549; defeated at Konieh, 551; 559 sq.; XI 275 sq.
Restif de la Bretonne, Nicolas-Edmé, VI 833
Restoration, The, after the French Revolution, Vol. X *passim*; the English (1660), Vol. IV, Chap. XIX
Rethymno, Russian occupation of, XII 423
Retief, Pieter, Boer leader, XI 782
Retusaari, island of, v 591
Retz, Albert de Gondi, Comte de (*afterwards* Marshal of France), III 19; 27
—— Jean-François-Paul de Gondi, Cardinal de, IV 607 sq.; Beaufort and, 609; joins the rebels, 611; 612 sqq.; and the Court, 617 sq.; *Memoirs,* VI 130
Retzius, Gustaf, Swedish man of science, XII 280
Reuchlin, Johann, German Hebraist, I 572 sq., 605 sq., 637, 684; II 32, 695 sq., 697; *De Rudimentis Hebraicis,* 696
Reumont, Alfred von, German historian, II 33
Reus, revolt at (1843), X 242
—— Count of. *See* Prim, Juan
Reusch, Franz Heinrich, German theologian, XII 848
Reuss, Princes of, v 633
—— Henry XX, Prince of, XI 149
—— Eduard W. E., German theologian, XII 846
Reuter, Fritz, German humanist, XI 417; 420
Reuterholm, Baron, Swedish diplomatist, banished, VIII 789; at Swedish Court, IX 37–8
Reutern, Count Michael, Russian Minister of Finance, XI 619; XII 319
Reutlingen, signs the Augsburg Confession, II 205, 211
Reval, becomes Swedish, IV 162; 166 sq.; John III and Sigismund at, 169; v 534; 547; British fleet at, 551; 590; captured by Russians (1710), 603; port of, VI 35 sq.; 680; strike in, XII 350; 379
Réveil, Le, French journal, XI 488

Réveillon, wall-paper manufacturer, attacked by Paris mob, VIII 161
Revel, Count, Sardinian ambassador in London, XI 77
—— General di, XI 541
Reveni, battle at, XII 421
Reventlow, Count Christian Ditlev Frederick, VI 742 sq.; 746; 756
—— Count, Danish general, v 581
Reventlow-Preetz, Count Frederick von, XI 161
Reverdil, Elias Solomon Francis, Swiss philosopher, VI 744; 746 sqq.
Rèves, Jacques de (Revius), opposes Descartes, IV 789
Révolution, La, French journal, XII 123
Revue de Paris, XI 485
—— *politique,* French journal, XI 487
—— *pour tous,* French journal, XI 486
—— *Républicaine,* founded by Dupont, X 499
Rewbell, Jean-François, VIII 381, 385, 415, 422; member of Directory, 489 sqq., 494, 496, 517; retires, 519, 667
Reybaz, Étienne Salomon, collaborator with Mirabeau, VIII 150
Reydaniya (near Cairo), victory of Turks at (1517), I 91
Reynier, Jean L. Ebenezer, Comte, French general, VIII 600 sqq., 608 sq.; defeated at Maida, IX 270; attacks Wellington's right centre at Busaco, 461; at Warsaw, 511; surprised by Russians, 512; at Gross-Beeren, 526; at Dennewitz, 530; at Leipzig, 539; 540
Reynolds, Edward, Bishop of Norwich, v 96
—— John Fulton, at Gettysburg, VII 488
—— J., *De Justa Reipublicae Christianae Potestate,* III 764
—— Dr Richard, executed, II 442
Reynst, Dutch Governor-General in Banda, English traders and, IV 735
Reyphins, Belgian deputy, x 526; 529
Rezonville, XI 589; battle at, 590 sq.
Rhaetian Leagues, The, I 308
Rhálles, Greek statesman, XII 421
Rhegas (ὁ Φεραῖος), Greek poet, VIII 789; x 174
Rhegenius, Michael, German philosopher, IV 791
Rheims, Henry III crowned at (1575), III 26; Douay College removed to, 287, 350; the League in, 662; attempt to seize, 672; Louis XV consecrated at, VI 131; Young's impressions of, VIII 60; Napoleon at (1814), IX 552; consecration of Charles X at, X 88; Cardinal Consalvi at, 133; French army at, XI 595; labour congress at, XII 124
—— Jean of Lorraine, Archbishop of, pluralist, I 659
Rheinberg, siege of, by Maurice (1597), III 629; by Mendoza, 634; recovered by Maurice (1601), 636; taken by Spinola (1606), 638, 722; access to Jülich-Cleves

cut off at, 689; occupied by Spanish troops, 712, 718; captured by Allies (1702), v 406

Rheinbot, Prefect of Moscow, xii 376

Rheinbund, The, signed (15 Aug. 1658), iv 431 sq., v 33; Louis XIV fails to prolong (1668), 38; 42, 46, 351, 644. *See also* (for Napoleon's scheme) Rhine, Confederation of the

Rheinfelden, battles of (1638), iv 375

Rheinische Zeitung, xi 53

Rheinthal, Captain, Russian traveller, xii 802

Rhenanus, Beatus, German humanist, ii 313

Rhenish Mercury, suppressed, x 352

Rhigas. *See* Rhegas

Rhine river, Dutch privateers on, iii 705; Lower, foreign invasion upon, 712; war on (1688), v 55 sqq., 60 sq., 63; campaigns on (1702), 406, (1703), 408 sq., (1707), 418 sq., (1713), 451; and Peace of Utrecht, 438; campaigns on (1727), vi 59, (1741), 232, (1743), 237 sq., (1744-5), 240 sqq., (1746), 246, (1758), 277, (1747), 318, (1784), 645; left bank of, granted to France (1795), viii 441, (1798), 642; right bank of, French claims on, 644; and rectification of frontiers, ix 56; and French Revolutionary action, 91 sqq., 278; Congress of Vienna and, 549, 588; and France, 564, xi 338, 457; Prussia and, ix 592, 596, 657; xi 49; and Prussian plan of campaign, 580; 664; xii 136

—— Confederation of the, ix 201; 268, 273, 279; Prussia and, 307; 316, 336, 339; contingent of, 344; 346; Princes of, 347; 407, 408, 409, 507; proposal for abolition of, 521; 727

Rhinegrave, Otto Lewis von Kyrburg, Wildgrave and, and battle of Nördlingen, iv 248

Rhineland, unhappy state of, i 298 sq., 301; political agitation in, xi 52 sq.

Rhins, Dutreuil de, French explorer, xii 803

Rhode Island, settlement of, vii 20, 23 sq.; and Quakers, 25; charter of, 26, 31; and Governor Andros, 29; Constitution of, 54; shipbuilding in, 56; religious conditions in, 57; education in, 58; 60; effect of Stamp Act in, 149; disaffection in, vi 447, vii 163; French fleet off (1778), vi 451, vii 218; Constitution of, 237; declines Confederation, 245 sq.; representation of, in Senate, 263, 306; judges in, 277; accepts Constitution, 302; trade regulations in, 311 sq.; slavery in, 361, 388; manufactures in, 375; and the Tariff, 377

Rhodes, besieged by the Turks (1480), i 84, (1522), 93 sq.; capture of, 94, ii 46

—— Cecil John, xi 788; xii 3; and British South Africa Company, 49; and Jameson Raid, 53; in South Africa, 638 sq., 641; death of, 643; 645; 812

Rhodes, James Ford, American historian, xii 841

Rhodesia, expansion in, xii 639; 644

Rhodope, The, Turks take refuge in, xii 389; Pomaks in, 405 sq.; 408

Rhone, royalist feeling on the (1815), ix 616-7

Riall, Sir Phineas, Major-general, vii 343

Riancey, Henri-Léon Camusat de, French politician, xi 120

Riánzares, Agustín Fernando Muñoz y Sánchez, Duke of, and Queen Cristina, x 241, xi 551; 559 sq.

Riario, Girolamo, Pazzi conspiracy and, i 661

—— Piero, Cardinal, i 658 sq.

—— Raffaelle Sansoni, Cardinal (of San Giorgio), imprisoned by Florentines, i 661; ii 8, 15, 17

Riaz Pasha, Prime Minister of Egypt, xii 438

Riazan. *See* Ryazán

Ribagorza, fief of, iii 514

Ribault, Jean, attempts to found Huguenot colony in America, i 50, 55; vii 71

Ribe, Treaty of (1460), xi 693

Ribe, Bishops of:—

—— Hans Tausen ("the Danish Luther"), ii 609 sq., 611 sq.; the Confession of Faith of, 613; 615 sq.

—— Ivar Munk, ii 611

—— Wandel, German Reformer, ii 616

Ribera, José (L'Espagnolet), iii 546; art of, iv 664

Ribeyrolles, French journalist, xi 25

Ribot, Alexandre-Félix-Joseph, French statesman, xii 119

Ricardo, David, and currency, ix 689; x 598; theories and influence of, 772 sqq.; 782; xii 758 sq.

Ricardos, Count Antonio, Spanish general, viii 439

Ricasoli, Baron Bettino, Italian statesman, xi 378; 386; succeeds Cavour, 530; policy of, towards Rome, 530 sq.; resigns, 532; President of Ministry, 540; resigns, 542

Ricci, Giuseppe, Count, x 123

—— Lorenzo, Jesuit, vi 592 sq.

—— Matteo, missionary in China, xii 515

—— Paolo (Lisio Filino, Reformer), ii 386

—— Scipione, Bishop of Prato and Pistoia. *See* Pistoia

Rich, Richard, Lord, ii 475, 506

—— Sir Robert, speech of, on foreign policy, iv 261

Rich Mountain, Federal success at (1861), vii 457

Richard II, King of England, iii 580; 749

—— III, King of England, i 393, 447, 464

—— Albert, French politician, xi 492

—— François, ix 125

—— Spanish insurrectionary, attempts to assassinate Ferdinand VII, x 210

Richardet, French deputy, xi 139

Richardot, Jean, President of Archduke Albert's Privy Council, iii 640-1

Richardson, James, African traveller, xii 810

—— John, and Irish language, vi 487

—— Samuel, novelist, vi 823 sq.; x 698; 717 sq.; 724

—— American Secretary of the Treasury, vii 643

—— murder of, near Yokohama, xi 845 sq.

Richecourt, Governor of Tuscany, vi 600

Richel, Bavarian ambassador, correspondence of, with Elector Maximilian I, iv 238

Richelieu, Armand-Jean du Plessis, Cardinal, Duke of, iii 577; iv 50; rise of, 56; and Valtelline, 58 sqq.; First Minister, 88; 90; and Christian IV, 92; and Mansfeld, 93; 99; and Edict of Restitution, 111; 115; concludes Treaty of Cherasco, 117; Ministry of, *see* Chap. iv; 192; and Italy, 194, 198; Gustavus Adolphus, the German War and, 210 sqq.; 222; 225 sq.; Wallenstein and, 234, 239 sq.; anxious to avoid war with Austria, 246; Bernard of Weimar and, 249; 250 sq.; makes terms with Spain, 264; 266; promises toleration to Huguenots, 272; States General and, 275; England and, 258, 262, 276, 284, 311; anti-Habsburg designs of, 365; 367 sqq.; 373 sq.; 381; later German War and, 383; designates Mazarin as his successor, 388; 396; 399; D'Avaux agent of, 402; 592 sq.; 595 sqq.; 600; 602; financial situation at death of, 603; *Parlement* and, 604; 622; 637; and Austria, 640, 642; Spain and, 643 sq., 645; Catalonia and, 644 sq.; 648 sq.; 656; and *Conseil du Roi*, 674; and Treaty of Monzon, 675; concludes Franco-Hispano-Papal Treaty (1627), 677; and Mantuan succession, 678 sqq.; 681 sqq.; 691; and United Provinces, 697 sq.; death of, 388, 653, 659, 702; v 3 sqq.; 14; 19; policy of, 32; 72; and the Church, 75; 331; 338; 373; and Canada, 442; colonial policy of, 702 sq.; 743; vi 229; 622; and Canada, vii 73 sq.; viii 36, 38

—— Armand-E.-S.-S. du Plessis, Duc de, succeeds Talleyrand, ix 664; opposes contraction of French frontier, 665; x 13 sq.; at Conference of Aix-la-Chapelle, 14 sq.; 18; 25; 38; succeeds Talleyrand, 47; signs Second Peace of Paris (1815), 48; opposes punitive measures, 49; 50; and electoral schemes, 51; 54 sq.; liberates France from army of occupation, 56; resignation of (1818), 57 sq.; overtures to, from French government, 61; second Ministry of, 63-70; resigns, 70; 71; concessions of, to ultra-Royalists, 73; foreign policy of, attacked, 74; resignation and death of, *ib.*; and the settlement with Papacy (1819), 143 sq.

Richelieu, Armand-Jean (de Vignerot) du Plessis, 2nd Duke of, iv 592; Condé and, 612

—— Louis-François-Armand du Plessis, 3rd Duke of, Marshal of France, vi 132; 239; in Seven Years' War, 263, 265 sq., 267, 269; 337; 356; viii 59

Richepance, Antoine, French general, ix 67

Richer, Edmond, French theologian, v 75 sq.

Richery, Joseph de, French admiral, viii 473

Richmond (Surrey), Queen Elizabeth dies at, iii 360-1

—— (Virginia), cotton-mill at, vii 354; Confederate capital (1861), 471, 609; campaign against, *ib.*, 472 sqq.; Burnside advances against (1862), 483; Hooker advances against (1863), 485; Grant advances against (1864), 514, 516 sqq., 533; evacuation of (1865), 538 sq., 541; Lincoln at, 544 sq.; railway communication with, 551

—— (Yorks), Henry (Fitzroy, son of Henry VIII), Duke of, ii 427, 445, 470

—— and Lennox, Charles Lennox, 3rd Duke of (4th cr.), vi 424; 434; leads movement for Reform, 455, x 597; vi 461 sqq.; 465; and India Bill, 467; 468; viii 294, 297

—— Charles Lennox, 4th Duke of, becomes Lord-Lieutenant of Ireland, ix 707; x 635

—— Charles Gordon-Lennox, 5th Duke of, x 611, 614; resigns, 662 sq.

—— Duchess of, wife of 4th Duke of, ball of, on eve of Waterloo, ix 625

Richter, Æmilius Ludwig, German canonist, xii 847

—— Eugen, German politician, xii 146; 157

—— Johann Paul Friedrich ("Jean Paul"), vi 824; 833; viii 773; x 388; 394; 411

Richthofen, Ferdinand von, Prussian geographer, xii 797

Ricord, Jean François, Commissioner, and Bonaparte, viii 561

Ricotti, Ercole, Italian historian, xi 548

—— Magnani, Cesare, Italian general, xii 233

Ridley, Nicholas, Bishop of London, ii 484, 501, 503; arrested, 521; 538; disputation of, at Oxford, 539; trial and death of, 541

Ridolfi, Cosmo, Marquis de, Tuscan Minister, x 128; xi 78; 90

—— Giovanni Battista, Savonarolist, i 169, 183

—— Niccolò, Medicean, i 175

—— Roberto, conspirator and Florentine banker, iii 283-4

Riebeck (Riebeek), Antoni van, founds Cape Colony, iv 713

—— Jan van, and Cape of Good Hope, v 695

Ried, Treaty of (1813), IX 587, 591, 658
Riedberg, castle of Plantas at, IV 47, 52
Riederer, Galius, IV 52
Rieger, Francis Ladislas, Čech politician, XI 178; XII 186; 195
Riego, Rafael del. *See* Del Riego
Riehl, Wilhelm Heinrich von, German writer, XI 417; 419 sq.; XII 849
Riel, Louis, Canadian insurgent leader, XI 777; XII 606
Rienzi, Cola di, I 539
Rieti, battle near (1821), X 114, 116
Rietz, Prussian Groom of the Chamber, VI 726
Rieux, Marquis de, guardian of Britanny, I 394
Riezler, Sigmund, German historian, XII 829
Riga, Jesuits established in, III 102; Charles IX and, IV 174; trade and, 177; captured by Sweden (1621), 183; 185; V 570; attacked by Saxons (1700), 587 sq.; 590; 594; 597; captured by Peter the Great (1710), 603; XII 335; strike in, 350
Rigaud, mulatto chief in San Domingo, IX 420
Rigault, Nicholas, editor of Tertullian and Cyprian, I 616 sq.; III 61
—— Raoul, French politician, XI 502
Rigby, Edward, claims Maine, VII 24
—— Dr E., traveller in France, VIII 60, 63
—— Richard, Master of Irish Rolls, VI 424; 439
Right, Russian journal, XII 346
Rigny, Comte de Henri Gauthier, French admiral, X 91; 196
Riley, General, military governor of California, VII 402
Rimini, captured by Venetians (1503), I 224; XI 65; revolt at, 69; 88
Rimnik, The, Turkish defeat on, VIII 326
Rin, William, Flemish rebel, I 446 sq.
Rincon, Antonio, murder of (1541), II 76; III 105, 118
Rinhuber, Laurence, writer on Russia, V 513
Rink, Melchior, Dutch Anabaptist, II 624
Rinuccini, Giovanni Battista, Papal Nuncio in Ireland, IV 338, 529 sq.; 532
Rio de Janeiro, French attacks on, V 679, VI 391; 184; 390; Court of Portugal at (1807), X 310 sq.; Portuguese troops in, 312, 314 sq.; revolutionary outburst in (1821), 313; Treaty signed at (1825), 319; Panamerican Congress at, XII 700 sq.
Rio de la Plata, discovered by Solis (1515), I 36, 43; Spain and, VI 375, 390; Popham's expedition to, X 281; Protectorate of, 285; revolution in region of, 287; 290 sq.; Capitalism and Provincialism in, 298; history of region of, after 1830, 300 sq.; XII 267; Dom Pedro II and, 674; 682; 684
Rio Grande (del Norte), French claim to, VII 362; Texan boundary, 394, 397, 403 sq., 406; 470

Rio Grande do Sul, city of, VI 391; revolt in, XII 675
Rions, d'Albert, Comte de, French naval commander, VIII 192, 448
Ríos Rosas, Antonio de los, Spanish politician, XI 562; 568
Riou, Captain Edward, at battle of Copenhagen, IX 52
Rioult, Louis-Édouard, French painter, XI 511
Rio Verde, victory of Moors at (1501), I 361
Ripley, Eleazar Wheelock, American general, VII 343
Ripoli, taken by the French (1691), V 59
Ripon, Frederick John Robinson, Viscount Goderich, 1st Earl of, and the Eastern Question, X 197; 198; 584; 588; raised to House of Lords, 591; succeeds Canning, 592; and parliamentary reform, 603; 645; resigns, 662 sq.; XI 3; 792
—— George Frederick Samuel Robinson, 1st Marquis of, Viceroy of India, XII 36; 475 sqq.; 494
Ripperdá, Jan Willem, mission of, to Vienna, VI 139 sq.; created Duke, 141; fall of, 142 sq.; 145 sq.; Elisabeth Farnese and, 166
Ripperda, Captain, defender of Haarlem, III 235 sq.
Riquet, Pierre-Paul, Baron de Bonrepos, V 14
Risorgimento, Italian paper, XI 83
Risquons-Tout, French revolutionaries at, XI 671
Rist, Johann Georg, Danish diplomatist, VIII 788
Ristich, Jovan, Servian statesman, XII 411
Ritchie, Charles Thomson Ritchie, Lord, Chancellor of Exchequer, XII 54
—— Joseph, African traveller, XII 807
Ritschl, Albrecht, *History of Pietism*, XII 847
Ritter, August Heinrich, and history of Greek philosophy, XII 822
—— Carl, German ethnologist, XII 850
—— Moriz, German historian, XII 828
Ritterschaft, the German knightly order. *See Reichsritterschaft*
Riukiu Islands, Japan and, XII 555 sqq.
Rivadavia, Bernardino, X 301
Rivarol, Antoine, French writer, VIII 8
Rivarola, Cardinal, Papal legate, X 134; 139; 152
Rivarolo, Corsican refugee, VI 609
Rivas, Angel de Saavedra, Duke of, X 241
Rive Gauche, La, French journal, XI 486
Rivera, José Fructuoso, President of Uruguay, XII 680
Rivers, Anthony Woodville, Earl, I 441
—— Richard Savage, Earl, VI 12 sq.
Rivet, Jean-Charles, French politician, XII 103; 105
Riviera, the Allies on the, VI 243

Rivière, Charles-François de Riffardeau, Marquis, *afterwards* Duc de, IX 29; 32
—— French commandant in Annam, XII 131; 525
—— *See* Mercier de la Rivière
Rivoli, Marshal Catinat at, V 402; battle of (1797), VIII 580
Rizzio, David, II 595; III 271 sqq.
Roanoke Island, Amidas and Barlow land at, VII 3; captured by Burnside (1862), 483, 552
Robartes, Sir John, Earl of Radnor. *See* Radnor
Robecchi, Luigi, African traveller, XII 813
Roberjot, Claude, French envoy, VIII 655 sq.
Robert, Pierre-F.-J., French deputy, VIII 234, 247
Roberts, Richard, machinist, X 734 sq.
—— Colonel, in India, IX 722
—— of Kandahar, Frederick Sleigh Roberts, Earl, at Kandahar, XII 37; 39; 59; in Afghánistán, 470 sq.; 482 sq.; in South Africa, 642 sq.
Robertson, William, historian, XII 817
Roberval, Gilles Personne de, IV 779
—— Jean François de la Roque, Sieur de, attempts to establish colony of "New France" (1542), I 44, 50, VII 71 sq.
Robespierre, Augustin, VIII 247, 370 sq.
—— Maximilien Marie Isidore, VIII 20, 32, 34; in National Assembly, 174, 186, 188; 234; character of, 239 sq., 747; and Commune, 239 sqq.; and National Convention, 246 sq., 250 sqq.; Louvet's attack on, 253; at Louis XVI's trial, 255 sq., 258; 271; policy of, 343, 345, 347, 358, 364 sq.; and Danton, 359 sqq.; supremacy of, 364 sqq.; coalition against, 367 sqq.; arrest and execution of, 370 sq.
Robethon, Jean de, Hanoverian councillor, VI 14; 20
Robilant, Count di, Italian Minister of War, XII 240
—— Count di, Italian officer, in Macedonia, XII 426
Robinson, Frederick John. *See* Ripon, Earl of
—— Henry Crabb, VIII 768
—— John, Bishop of Bristol (*and afterwards* of London), at Utrecht, V 438; in Sweden, 586
—— Mary, poet, X 699
—— Thomas, Lord Grantham. *See* Grantham
Robortellus, Francesco, Hellenist, I 567; II 391
Robsart, Amy, death of, II 582
Robustelli, of Grossotto, Valtelline leader, IV 48 sq.; 54; 58 sq.
Roca, Julio A., General, President of the Argentine Confederation, XII 679; 683
Roccasecca, defeat of French at (1503), I 126

Rocca Sparviera, annexed to Saluzzo, III 419
Rocci, Papal Nuncio, at Ratisbon, IV 679 sq.
Rochambeau, Jean-Baptiste-Donatien de Vimeur, Count of, Marshal of France, VI 453; commands Army of the North, VIII 222, 405
Rochdale, cooperation in, XII 738 sq.
Roche, Ernest, French socialist, XII 123
—— Father Philip, and the Irish rebellion, IX 701
—— Marquis de la. *See* Roberval, Jean
Rochefort, development of, V 14; expedition against, VI 342b (in Vol. XIII), VII 132; French ships at, IX 211 sqq.; Allemand sails from, 225; returns to, 234; 238; Napoleon escapes to (1815), 644, 756
—— Henri, XI 488 sq.; 491; arrested, 492; 600
Rochelle, Huguenot stronghold, III 10–11; siege of, 20–1, 32; Edict of, 21; 22 sqq.; retained by Huguenots (1598), 676
Rochester, James II at, V 248
—— John Wilmot, 2nd Earl of, V 124; 132
—— Laurence Hyde, 1st Earl of (2nd cr.), V 231; dismissal of, 234; 235; and William III, 275; 464; VI 11
—— Sir Robert, II 525
Rochford, George Boleyn, Viscount, trial and execution of, II 445
—— William Henry Zuylestein, 4th Earl of, VI 439; 443; 447
Rochussen, Charles, Dutch painter, XII 249
—— Jacob Jan, Dutch statesman, XI 666
Rockhill, Woodville, in Tibet, XII 804
Rockingham, Charles Watson-Wentworth, 2nd Marquis of, VI 424; 428; 434; First Lord of the Treasury, 435; 438; and Chatham, 442; 444 sq.; 448; 450; and Ireland, 455; 456; Ministry of, 457 sqq.; 501; and Warren Hastings, 581; death of, 460 sq., 466, 501; VII 147, 149
Rocky Mountains, United States boundary and, VII 326, 364 sq.; 395
Rocquebertin, deputy-governor of Genoa (1506), I 129
Rocroi, victory of Enghien at (1643), IV 388, 594, 599, 659 sq., 702; and Treaty of the Pyrenees, 620
Roda, Jérome de, III 244
Rodach, Protestant Conference at (1529), II 206
Rodbertus, Johann Karl, Prussian economist, XI 218
Rode, Henne, and the Eucharistic controversy, II 332
—— John, German Reformer, I 631
Rodez, Saignelay-Colbert de Castle Hill, Bishop of, VIII 156
Rodich, Baron, Austrian statesman, XII 383
Rodicheff, Russian barrister, XII 322; 333
Rodney, George Brydges Rodney, 1st Baron, Admiral, VI 342d (in Vol. XIII); 376 sq.; 379; conquers Martinique, 426; 452; in the West Indies, 453 sq., 462; VII 231

Rodriguès, Olinde, x 485
Rodrigues, Simão, Jesuit, II 415, 652
Rodrigues Graça, Joaquim, occupies Angola, XI 575
Roe, Sir Thomas, IV 192; at Hamburg, 378; 734; and English East India Company, 737; ambassador to Great Moghul, 741 sq.; V 698; VI 515
Roebuck, John Arthur, x 656; 675; 676; and Crimean War, XI 320; 764
Roederer, Comte Pierre Louis, VIII 8, 66, 236, 667; and Brumaire, 676, 680 sq.; IX 4; 12, 390; improves Neapolitan finance, 405
Roëll, Jonkheer Johan, Dutch statesman, XII 247
Roelofs, Willem, Dutch painter, XII 249
Römer, Friedrich, Würtemberg politician, XI 62; 148
—— Olaus, Danish astronomer, V 715
Rœmond, Florimond de, II 296
Rœnnov. See Roskilde, Bishops of
Röntgen, Conrad Wilhelm, discoverer of X-rays, XII 788 sq.
Roer river, Coburg defeats French at, VIII 419; the Austrians driven across, 436
Roermonde, taken by William of Orange (1572), III 232 sq.; taken by Marlborough (1702), V 406; Austria and, VI 631; proposed bishopric of, XI 665
Roeskilde, Treaty of (1568), IV 166, 429, 541, 585 sqq.; (1658), V 147, 558
Röust, Diethelm, Burgomaster of Zurich, II 327
—— Marcus, Burgomaster of Zurich, II 315, 318, 322
Rogeard, Louis-Auguste, French journalist, XI 486
Roger II, King of Sicily, I 9
—— du Nord, Comte Édouard, French politician, XI 136
Rogers, James Edwin Thorold, economist, XII 850
—— John, Protestant martyr, II 533, 538
—— John, arrest of, IV 447
—— Robert, VII 127
Roget, French nationalist, XII 121
Roggenburg, stormed by peasants, II 181
Rogier, Charles, Belgian statesman, x 532; 535 sqq.; XI 670 sq.; returns to office, 672; policy of, 673; 674
Rohan, Armand-Gaston-Maximilien de, Cardinal, VI 131
—— Henri, 1st Duke of, IV 41; Valtelline campaign of, 59 sqq.; 683; rising of, 115; leader of Princes, 122; 124; in Poitou, 126 sq.; 130; 132 sqq.; 148 sq.; at Rheinfelden, 375
—— Hercule, Duke of, III 690
—— Jean, Sire de, I 394
—— Marguerite de Béthune, Mme de, *Messieurs du Marais* at house of, IV 156

Rohan, Prince de, Grand Master of Knights of St John, IX 39–40
Rohan-Chabot, Louis M. Bretagne Dominique, Duke of, VIII 751
Rohan-Guemené, Charles-Alain-Gabriel, Duc de Montbazon, Austrian general, surrender of, IX 258
Rohault, Jacques, French Cartesian philosopher, IV 791
Rohilkhand, VI 524; campaign in (1774), 569 sq.; danger of, to Oudh, IX 724; campaign in (1858), XI 749
Rohillas, The, VI 569 sq.; 572; 582 sq.
Rohlfs, Gerhard, African explorer, XII 811; 813
Rohrbach, Jäcklein, leader in Peasants' Rising, II 182 sq., 187 sqq.
"*Roi Soleil*," The, III 769
Rojas, Fray Domingo de, Spanish Reformer, II 407 sq., 410
—— Fernando de, *Celestina*, I 380
Rokelle river, exploration on, XII 807
Roland, Philippe-Laurent, French sculptor, IX 134
—— *Camisard* leader, V 26
—— de la Platière, Jean-Marie, Minister of Interior to Louis XVI, VIII 223 sq., 227, 231, 238; arrest of, 242, 244; in National Convention, 250 sq.; at King's trial, 256; resignation of, 263; death of, 357
—— de la Platière, Madame Manon Jeanne, VIII 213 sq., 249; arrest of, 274; death of, 357
Rolandis di Castel-Alfeo, di, leader of Jacobin plot in Bologna, VIII 557
Roliça, Wellesley attacks (1808), IX 440
Roll, Zwinglian theologian, II 327
—— *Schultheiss*, of Solothurn, VI 615
Rollin, Charles, French historian, XII 817
Roma, Jean de, persecution of Waldenses by, II 289
Romagna, Cesare Borgia and, I 238, 242, II 1; Julius II and, I 128, 246; brigandage in, III 430, 432; Legation of, ceded to Venice (1797), VIII 583; revolutionary movement in (1830), x 120, 122, 123, 150; rebellion in (1831), 155; freebooters in (1843), 156; *Precetto Politico* in, 168; national movement in, XI 384; 386; 388; annexed to Italy, 709; socialism in, XII 232
Romagnosi, Gian Domenica G. G., x 124; 128
Romaine, William, popular preacher, VI 79
Roman de la Rose, I 415
Romanin, S., Italian historian, XII 842
Romano, Haddick at, IX 61
—— Francesco, Italian Austin friar, II 391
—— Giulio, Italian painter, II 13, 28
—— Paolo, Italian sculptor, II 13
Romanoff, House of. See Russia, and the Tsars under their several names

Romanoff, Alexis, Tsar. *See* Alexis
—— Michael, Tsar. *See* Michael
—— Theodore. *See* Philaret
Romanovsky, Dmitry, Russian general, xi
631
Romans (Dauphiné), Assembly at (1788),
viii 116 sq., 129
Romantic movement in European literature,
The, Vol. vi, Chap. xxiv; and the French
Revolution, viii 776; Vol. x, Chap. xxii,
The Revolution in English poetry and
fiction, *passim. See also* Literature
Romanzoff, Count Nicholas, Russian
Minister of Foreign Affairs, ix 305;
policy of, 307; 311, 312; at Erfurt, 319;
321
Rome, The ecclesiastical state of
i   vii Rome and the Temporal Power,
          219-52
      xviii Catholic Europe, *passim*, 620-
          52
      xix The Eve of the Reformation,
          passim, 653-92
          [*See also* xvi *and* xvii, The Classi-
          cal *and* Christian Renaissance]
ii   i   Medicean Rome, 1-35
          [*See also* xii *and* xviii, The
          Catholic South *and* The
          Church and Reform, *passim*]
iii   xiii Rome under Sixtus V, 422-55
iv   xxiii Papal Policy, 666-88
vi   xvi Italy and the Papacy, 586-610
ix   vii The Concordats, 180-207
       xiv The French Dependencies, 400
          sqq.
      xix and xxi The Congress of Vienna,
          passim, 576-615, 646-71
x   iv   Italy, *passim*, 104-30
       v   The Papacy and the Catholic
          Church, 131-61
xi   iv   Italy in Revolution (1846-9),
          passim, 65-95
       xiv Cavour and the Kingdom of
          Italy (1849-61), *passim*, 366-
          92
       xix The completion of Italian Unity
          (1846-70), *passim*, 529-49
       xxv Rome and the Vatican Council
          (1846-70), 703-23
xii   v   [*and*] The Third French Re-
          public, *passim*, 91-133
       viii United Italy, 229 sq.
       xxii The modern Law of Nations and
          the prevention of war, *passim*,
          705 sqq.
Rome, city of, entered by Charles VIII
(1494), i 114, 230; Vatican Library at,
552; Academy of, founded by Laetus,
560; sack of (1527), 567, ii 24, 28, 33,
55 sqq., iii 466 sq., 470; under Medici
Popes, Vol. ii, Chap. i; Charles V
in, 29; attack on, by Colonna (1526),
54; Luther summoned to, 132; Luther
in, 117 sq.; University of, 16 sq.; iii
447, 454, x 137; Charles V's troops in,

iii 105, 454; alarmed by approach of
Barbarossa, 112; League against Turks
formed in (1538), 114; seminary at, 287;
394; under Sixtus V, Chap. xiii *passim*;
James I sends agent to, 555; influence
of Charles Emmanuel at, 686; Richelieu
in, iv 123; 592; 601; De Retz and, 615,
618; threatened, 686; Milton in, v 118;
740; Jacobites in, vi 110, 113; Alberoni
at, 125; 586; Jesuits in, 595; 626; rising
in (1797-8), viii 637; ix 42; French
influence in, 69; condition of, under
Pius VII, 88; negotiations in (1801),
183; annexed by Napoleon (1809), 196-7;
return of Pius VII to (1814), 201, x 131;
French occupation of, ix 343, 390, 400,
x 132; Miollis in (1808), ix 401;
second city in French Empire, 402;
King and Queen of Spain in, 433; Murat
occupies (1815), 621; street lighting in,
abolished, x 13; interregnum (1814) in,
134; Francis I in, 137; brigands in,
138; executions in, 152; Bonaparte plot
in, 154; Metternich in, 365; 1846-70,
Vol. xi, Chap. xxv *passim*; Nicholas I
at, 71; government reform in, 79; 80;
the situation in, 84; Republic in, 91,
93 sq.; French intervention in, 94 sq.,
121 sqq., 125 sqq.; Lombard Legion
in, 367; reaction in, 378; French troops
in, 384, 462, 494, 530, 538; evacuated
by the French, 485, 541; 387; as
capital of Italy, 391, 539; 392; 469;
Napoleon III and, 478; second French
expedition to, 485 sq.; policy of Ricasoli
towards, 530 sq.; policy of Rattazzi towards, 534; Garibaldi marches against,
542; reunited to Italy, 544; xii 115;
first Italian parliament at, 213; riots at,
217; democratic demonstrations in, 219;
225 sq.; Pius IX and, 229; 230; socialist
congresses at, 231 sq.; President Loubet
at, 242; 820; 824; Archaeological Institute of, 843
Rome, "King of." *See* Napoleon II
Romeo and Juliet, iii 378
Romero, Julian de, iii 233; 520
Romilly, Sir Samuel, viii 149, 755; becomes Solicitor-General, ix 685; and
criminal law, 692; 396; x 598; 604
Romme, Gilbert, French deputy, viii 388,
784
Romney, Henry Sidney, Lord Sidney and
Earl of, v 242; Lord-Lieutenant of Ire-
land, 320; vi 493 sq.
Romny Fair, x 428
Romolino, Francesco, Bishop of Ilerda. *See*
Ilerda
Romont, lost by Savoy, iii 405-6
—— Count de, ally of Charles the Bold,
i 390, 446
Romorantin, Edict of (1560), ii 298
Roncali, Federico. *See* Alcoy, Count of
Roncesvalles, French attack (1813), ix 479
sq.

Ronciglione, the Barberini and, IV 685
Roncourt, French force at, XI 592
Rondeau, Claudius, English political agent in Russia, V 555 sq.; VI 306; 308
Rondinelli, Frà, Franciscan opponent of Savonarola, I 181
Ronge, Johannes, religious Reformer, XI 52; 146
Ronnow, Charles of Lorraine at, VI 234
Ronquillo, Don Pedro, Spanish ambassador in England, V 217
—— Rodrigo, Spanish judge, I 373
Ronsard, Pierre de, III 54–6; 61; 71; 376; 467; and Malherbe, V 65; 68
Ronsin, Charles-Philippe, Republican general, VIII 360, 362
—— Père, Jesuit, X 72; 94
Rooke, Sir George, Admiral, V 411 sqq.
Roon, Albrecht Theodor Emil, Count von, Prussian field-marshal, Minister of War, XI 406 sq.; 409 sq.; and Schleswig-Holstein, 440; 449; 456; 579; XII 149
Roos, Lord (John Manners). See Rutland
Roosebeke, battle of (1382), I 425 sq.
Roosevelt, Theodore, President of United States, XII 531
"Root-and-Branch" Petition and Bill, IV 291 sqq.
Roper, Margaret, daughter of Sir Thomas More, II 443
Ropscha, murder of Peter III at, VI 662 sq.
Roquefeuil, Count de, French naval officer, VI 110; 239
Rorke's Drift, defence of, XII 636
Rosaeus, III 648
Rosas, capitulation of, to French (1645), IV 599; Old Pretender at, VI 105; taken by Saint-Cyr (1808), IX 448
—— Juan Manuel, Argentine dictator, rule of, X 301; XII 674; 680 sq.; defeat of, 682; 683
—— Juan Martinez de, X 278
Roscher, Wilhelm, German economist, XII 850
Roscoe, William, VIII 765
Roscrea, Reconciliation meeting at (1828), X 648
Rose, George, Secretary to Treasury, IX 679; 682
—— Sir George Henry (son of above), British Minister to the United States, VII 332 sq.
—— Sir Hugh Henry. See Strathnairn, Lord
—— Sir John, and Alabama controversy, VII 636
Rosebery, Archibald Philip Primrose, 5th Earl of, Secretary for Foreign Affairs, XII 43, 49; Ministry of, 51 sq.; 87 sq.; and Chitral, 487
Rosecrans, William Starke, victory of, at Rich Mountain (1861), VII 457; succeeds Buell, 507 sqq.; at Chickamauga, 509 sq.; 578
Rosen, Baron, Russian general, X 468; 470

Rosenberg, Peter of, Bohemian politician, I 338
Rosenblüt, Hans, German poet, II 175 sq.
Rosenburg, Count, Austrian envoy to St Petersburg, VI 317
—— Prince, defeated by Davout (1809), IX 353
Rosendal, compromise of (1503), I 451
Rosenkampff, Gustav, Baron, and codification of Russian Laws, X 418
Rosenkrans, Olaf, author of Apologia nobilitatis Daniae, V 579
Rosenkrone, Baron Marcus Gerhard, Danish Foreign Minister, VI 754
Rosenroll, Christopher, IV 52
Rosenthal, Nedermeyer van, Dutch politician, XI 662
Roses, Wars of the, I 309, 463
Rosetta, Dugua occupies, VIII 601, 606; British defeat at (1807), IX 235
Rosicrucians, Society of, IV 4; and Frederick William II of Prussia, VI 725 sqq.
Rosily, French admiral, supersedes Villeneuve, IX 229
Roskilde, Bishops of:—
—— Joachim Roennov, II 614, 616
—— Lage Urne, II 609, 613
Rosmini, Antonio, II 35; writings of, X 128; and Church reform, 168; and Italian Federation, XI 89 sq.; and Pius IX, 705
Rosne, Seigneur de, French refugee and Spanish commander in Netherlands, III 628; League captain, 663, 670
Rosny. See Sully, Duke of
Rospigliosi, Giulio. See Clement IX
Ross, victory of Ormond at (1643), IV 526
—— Bishop of. See Lesley, John
—— Alexander Stewart, Duke of, I 485
—— Sir James, Polar expeditions of, XII 814 sq.
—— Sir John, Arctic expedition of, XII 814
—— Robert, British general, VII 344 sq.
—— Ronald, Major, and malaria, XII 779
—— Major, in New South Wales, IX 737
Rossbach, battle of, VI 270 sqq., 280, 286, 290, 295, 299, 408
Rossem, Martin van, invades Netherlands (1542), II 76; commands troops of Cleves, 242
Rossetti, Christina Georgina, XI 354
—— Dante Gabriel, XI 351; 353; the poetry of, 357; 365
—— Gabriele, Italian poet, X 112; 126; XI 545
Rossi, Ernesto, Italian actor, XI 548
—— Cav. Giovanni Battista de, Italian archaeologist, XII 847
—— Count Pellegrino Luigi Odoardo, X 165; French ambassador at Rome, 167; XI 68; 74; 81; the administration of, 90; murder of, 91, 117; 93; 705
—— Pietro de', Italian general, I 262

Rossignol, Jean-Antoine, VIII 228, 234; in
Vendée, 346, 353, 360; and Babeuf con-
spiracy, 504
Rossini, Gioacchino, x 103, 129
Rossitz, League at (1607), III 721
Rosslyn, Earl of. *See* Loughborough
Rostock, congress summoned to (1563), IV
163; 196; 204; capitulates to Tott (1631),
207
Rostoff, annexed by Ivan the Great, v 479
Róstoff-on-the-Don, murders in, XII 305;
332; 363
Rostopchin, Count Feodor Vasilievitch, IX
35; 40 sqq.; plot of, 487; Governor of
Moscow, 496
Rostov, Archbishop of. *See* Mazeievich
—— Dositheus, Archbishop of, v 540
Rostovtseff, Jacob, XI 614 sq.
Rota Club, founded by Harrington, IV 546
Rothembourg, Count of, French ambassador
at Madrid, VI 146 sq.; 150; 155
Rothenburg, joins Evangelical Brotherhood,
II 188; recovered from peasants (1525),
190; Meeting of the Protestant Union
at (1608), III 726; (1611), IV 2; (1619),
29; Austrians at, VI 292
Rothenthurm, French repulse at (1798),
VIII 640
Rothes, John Leslie, 7th Earl and 1st
Duke of, v 282; 284
Rothschild, House of, x 357; 369
—— Lionel Nathan de, Baron Rothschild,
XI 330; 345
—— Nathan, financier, x 742 sq.
—— Nathan Meyer Rothschild, Lord, XI
330
Rotrou, Jean, French dramatic poet, v
68
Rotteck, Karl Wenceslas Rodecker von, x
351; 361; 377; *Universal History*, XII
826
Rotterdam, Oldenbarneveldt Pensionary of,
III 624; trading companies at, 632;
Contra-Remonstrants driven from, 648;
Remonstrants driven from, 652; "anti-
synod" at, 653; interests of port of,
IV 466; favours the Stadholder, VII 287;
occupied by the French, 436; jealousy of
Antwerp against, x 533; and Eastern
trade, 761; port of, XII 249
Rottman, Bernard, Reformer of Münster,
II 224 sq.; theocratic ideas of, III 755
Rottweil, Guébriant wounded at, IV 388
Roubaix, socialism at, XII 125
Roucoux, battle of, VI 247, 331
Rouen, *bourse* started at, II 65; Lutheran-
ism in, 291; siege of (1562), III 3;
Assembly held at (1563), 6; Archbishop
attempts to address Protestant congre-
gation at, 30; besieged by Essex (1591),
50-1, 512; relieved by Farnese (1592),
517, 626, 659-60; acknowledges Henry
IV, 663, 665-6, 672; *Parlement* of,
661, 664, 672, v 4, VI 348, VIII 47 sq.;
and Canada, VII 71, 77; Republican

banquets at, XI 40; 114; 602 sq.; the
Germans in, 606 sq.; 610; XII 101;
harbour of, 102
Rouget de L'Isle, Claude-Joseph, and
French Restoration, IX 565
Rouher, Eugène, French Minister of
Justice, XI 129; 131 sqq.; 140; and
Anglo-French Treaty of Commerce, 470;
Minister of State, 477; 480; rivalry of,
with Ollivier, 481 sq.; 485; President of
Senate, 490; 492; 543; XII 106 sqq.
Rouillé, Antoine-Louis, French Minister of
Foreign Affairs, VI 333; 335; 338
Rouland, Gustave, French statesman, XI
478
Roumania, Napoleon III and, XI 306, 308;
formation of, 633; Constitution of, 646;
Germany and, XII 166; Russia and, 305;
381; insurrection in, 384; and Turkey,
388; 392; 394; and Treaty of Berlin,
395, 397 sqq.; affairs in (1881-1907),
414 sq.; and Kutzo-Vlachs, 424; 428;
762
Roumans, I 83; in Hungary, XI 173, 180,
207; rising of, 202; 217
Roumelia, Russian designs on, IX 306;
Eastern, XII 3; union of, with Bulgaria,
43, 341, 406, 408; Treaty of Berlin and,
395; 399; government of, 405 sq.
Roundway Down, battle of (1643), IV 313,
316
Rous, Francis, Provost of Eton, v 753
—— Sir John, VI 456
Rousseau, Jean-Baptiste, XI 423
—— Jean-Jacques, III 747, 765, 767; v
70 sq.; 277; VI 165; 795; writings
of, 823 sqq., 828 sqq., 834 sqq.; influence
of, in America, VII 174; VIII 1 sqq.;
Contrat Social, 7, 29 sq., 173 sq., 177,
180 sqq., 208; 15, 26, 27-32; 136;
teachings of, IX 361-2; influenced by
English writers, 427; x 8; 40; 698; 710;
725; XI 423; 508; 519; 528; XII 744;
757 sq.; 817
—— Pierre-Étienne-Théodore, painter, XI
528
Roussel, Gérard. *See* Oloron, Bishop of
Rousselin. *See* Saint-Albin
Roussillon, ceded to Spain (1493), I 111,
229; 362; 366; French occupation of
(1542), II 76; Edict of, III 7; French
in, IV 147 sq., 645, 647; lost to Spain,
650, 653, 662; Peace of the Pyrenees
and, 660, v 33; Spain and, VI 141;
Spanish troops occupy (1793), VIII 432
Roussin, Albin-Reine, Baron, French admiral, in the Tagus, x 325 sq.; ambassador at Constantinople, 512, 552 sq.
Roux, Jacques, Revolutionary, VIII 342
Rovere. *See* Della Rovere.
Rovère, J.-S.-François-Xavier, French
deputy, VIII 340, 512
Roveredo, Austrian defeat near (1796), VIII
578
Rovière, de La. *See* La Rovière

Rovigo, taken by the Austrians, xi 87
Rovuma river, Livingstone on, xii 809
Row, John, iv 491
Rowton Heath, battle of (1645), iv 333
Roxburghe, John Ker, 1st Duke of, vi 107
Roxo, Cape, Portugal and, xii 660
Roxolana, iii 121; procures murder of Ahmad Pasha, 124
Roy, Comte Antoine, French Minister of Finance, x 62; opposes compensation for the *émigrés*, 83
—— Henry de, iv 788
—— Pierre Le, iii 69–70
Royal African Company, formation of, v 108; 149; 178 sq.; 689; 692 sq.; vi 187 sq.
—— Niger Company, xii 3; 659 sq.
—— Society of London, v 124; 132; 740 sq.; 752; 754; and Maltese fever, xii 779
Royer-Collard, Pierre-Paul, ix 133; x 42 sqq.; 47; supports Richelieu and the Crown, 48 sqq.; electoral plan of, 51 sq.; and the *Doctrinaires*, 52 sq.; 54; defends army reform proposals, 55; and the proposed Concordat, 56; 57 sqq.; resignation of, 60; declines office, 61 sq.; 63 sq.; and new electoral proposals, 65 sqq.; and de Serre, 67 sq.; dismissed from Council of State, 68; 69 sq.; 73; opposes new Press Law, 77; President of Chamber, 93; and Polignac Ministry, 98; 102; opposes *Doctrinaires*, 492; 502; and fall of Molé, 510
Rózanoff, Russian writer, xii 333
Rozhdestvensky, Zinivy Petrovich, Russian admiral, xii 594 sq.; 598 sq.
Ruamps, Pierre-Charles, French politician, viii 388
Rubeanus, Crotus (Johannes Jäger of Drontheim), *Epistolae Obscurorum Virorum* and, i 573, 684, ii 696; scholar at Erfurt, 111
Rub-el-Khali, desert of, xii 805
Rubi, Marquis of, Governor of Madrid, vi 382
Rubino, Joseph, Roman historian, xii 843
Rucellai, Bernardo, *Api*, iii 468, 470
—— Tuscan Minister, vi 602
Rucherath, Johann. *See* Wesel, Johann
Rudbeck, Olaus, v 576; 728
—— Thure, Marshal of Swedish Diet, vi 764; 776
Rude, François, x 103
Rudinì, Marchese di, Italian statesman, xii 217
Rudiszcze, Charles XII at, v 600
Rudolf, Lake, discovered, xii 813
—— I (of Habsburg), Emperor, v 622
—— II, Emperor, iii 161; becomes King of Romans and of Hungary, 179–80; Sixtus V and, 449–50, 519; and Henry IV, 687–8; the Empire under, Chap. xxi; death of, iv 1; 9; privilege granted by, as to Bohemian forfeitures, 72; 79; 624
—— Crown Prince of Austria, xii 175
Rudolff, Christoff M., German mathematician, v 709

Rue, besieged by Parma, iii 51
Rüchel, Ernst Friedrich Wilhelm Philipp von, Prussian general, ix 274–5; 282
Rückert, Friedrich, German poet, and national feeling, ix 335
Rueda, Lope de (1550), Spanish playwright, i 380
Rüdiger, Count Fedor Wassiliewich, Russian general, xi 213
Rügen, iv 104; 106; Wallenstein on, 107; 192; allotted to Sweden, 404; defence of (1676), v 569; 570; 579; Swedes in, 608; 611; lost by Swedes (1678), 652; Sweden and, vi 37; 276; Lord Cathcart at (1807), ix 289, 295; ceded to France, 300; restored to Sweden (1810), 323; ceded to Prussia (1815), 656; Spielhagen's writings on, xi 420
Rueil, French Court at, iv 607; Treaty of (1649), 611
Rüppell, Wilhelm Eduard, German traveller, xii 806; 810 sq.
Rütimeyer, Ludwig, Swiss zoologist, xi 260
Ruffo, Fabricio Denis, Cardinal, Neapolitan general, viii 631 sq., 657 sq., 779; x 135
Rufus, Mutianus. *See* Mutti, Conrad
Ruga, Milanese advocate, one of Cisalpine Triumvirate, ix 84
Ruge, Arnold, German democrat, xi 50
Ruhl, Philippe-Jacques, viii 300, 388
Ruiz del Padrón, Antonio José, x 219
Rukavina, Georg, Baron von Widovgrad, Austrian general, viii 558
Rullion Green, Pentland rising suppressed at (1666), v 110, 284
Rullo, Donato, at Viterbo, ii 398
Rumbold, Sir George, ix 249
—— Richard, and Rye House plot, v 229 sq.
"Rumes" (or *Rumi*), general Eastern name for European traders, i 27
Rumpf, Wolfgang von, iii 697
Rumsey, John, Colonel, and Rye House plot, v 229
Rumyantseff, Count, Russian statesman, ix 485
—— Alexander, Russian general, v 539; vi 307
—— Peter, Russian general, vi 280; in Pomerania, 286 sq.; 328; 647; 697; 773
Runeberg, Johan Ludwig, Finnish poet, x 434
Rupert, Count Palatine. *See* Palatinate
—— Prince Palatine, iv 304; at Powick Bridge, 307; sacks Brentford, 308; 312; storms Bristol, 313; 315; 319; relieves Newark, 321; at Marston Moor, 322, 324; 329; at Naseby, 330; 331 sqq.; in Ireland, 463, 532; at Lisbon, 464 sq.; 467 sq.; at battle of Lowestoft, v 181; in naval campaign of 1666, 183 sqq.; 190; in naval campaign of 1672–3, 194 sqq.; 210
Rupert's Land, Canada and, xi 771
Rupp, Julius, German theologian, xi 51

Ruppa, Wenceslas William von, provisional rule of, in Prague, IV 21; 28; 66; 71

Ruppin, Hohenlohe at, IX 279

Ruremonde. *See* Roermonde

Rus, Russian journal, XII 309; 354

Rusca, Nicholas, Archpriest of Sondrio, killed, IV 46 sq.; avenged, 49

Rusconi, Antonio, Cardinal, x 150

Rusdorf, Johann von, and Palatine family, IV 70; 90; 209

Rush, Richard, United States Minister to Great Britain, VII 369

Rushe, Sir Francis, III 613

Ruskin, John, XI 355 sq.

Russell, Edward, Earl of Orford, Admiral. *See* Orford

—— John. *See* Bedford, Earl of

—— Earl (Lord John Russell), VII 636; x 512; 593; and parliamentary reform, 600 sqq., 609 sq.; and Reform Bills, 610, 613 sq., 617 sq.; 655; and Irish Tithe Bill, 662, 668; 663; 666; Home Secretary, 669; and O'Connell, *ib.*; and municipal reform, 670 sq.; 672; and Dissenters' marriages, 673; and Queen Victoria, 678; Colonial Secretary (1839), 679; and Free Trade, 680; 683; and Canada, 692; XI 10; Ministry of (1846-52), 11 sqq.; and Palmerston, 18; resigns, 21; and Aberdeen Ministry, 309 sq.; and Russia, 312; and causes of Crimean War, 316; resigns, 320; at Peace Conference, 321 sq.; 325; 328 sq.; Foreign Secretary, 331; Italian policy of, 331 sq.; 333; and *Alabama* incident, 337, XII 720; and parliamentary reform (1860), XI 339; defeat of, 339 sq.; 529; and Morocco, 564; and the colonies, 758 sq., 762, 764 sq.; and China, 815; and United States, XII 19, 21; 31; 69

—— Lord Odo. *See* Ampthill, Lord

—— Thomas, organises revolt in Ulster, IX 706 sq.

—— Thomas Wallace, Irish politician, XII 89

—— Sir William, Lord Deputy of Ireland, III 605

—— William, Lord Russell, v 216; 222; and Exclusion Bill, 226; 239; execution of, 230; 259

—— Lord William, and Dom Pedro, x 335

—— Colonel, imprisonment of, IV 447

Russia

IV   v   The Vasa in Sweden and Poland, *passim*, 158-89

xx   The Scandinavian North, *passim*, 578-91

v   xii   Austria, Poland, and Turkey, *passim*, 338-71

xvi   Russia (1462-1682), 477-517

xvii   Peter the Great and his pupils (1689-1730), 518-57

xix   Charles XII and the Great Northern War, 584-615

Russia (*contd.*)

VI   vii   Poland under the Saxon Kings, *passim*, 91-200

ix   The Seven Years' War, *passim*, 251-300

x   Russia under Anne and Elizabeth, 301-28

xviii   Joseph II, *passim*, 626-56

xix   Catharine II, 657-701

xx (1)   Frederick the Great and his successor, Home policy, 702-28

xx (2)   Poland and Prussia, *passim*, 729-34

xxii   The Hats and Caps and Gustavus III, *passim*, 758-84

VIII   x   The foreign policy of Pitt, *passim*, 276-98

xi   The European Powers and the Eastern Question, *passim*, 306-37

xvii   The extinction of Poland (1788-97), *passim*, 521-52

xxi   The Second Coalition (against the French Revolution), *passim*, 633-64

xxv   Europe and the French Revolution, 784 sqq.

IX   ii   The Armed Neutrality (1780-1801), *passim*, 34-54

iii   The pacification of Europe (1799-1802), *passim*, 55-80

ix   The Third Coalition, I (1805-6), *passim*, 244-64

x   The Third Coalition, II (1806-7), *passim*, 265-93

xi   The Napoleonic Empire (1807-9), *passim*, 294-340

xiii   The Continental System, *passim*, 361-89

xvi   Russia under Alexander I, and the invasion of 1812, 483-505

xvii   The War of Liberation (1813-4), *passim*, 506-54

xviii   The First Restoration (1814-5), *passim*, 555-75

xix   The Congress of Vienna, I (1814-5), *passim*, 576-602

xxi   The Congress of Vienna, II (1815), *passim*, 646-71

x   i   The Congresses (1815-22), *passim*, 1-39

vi   Greece and the Balkan Peninsula, *passim*, 169-204

xiii   Russia, 413-44

xiv   Poland and the Polish Revolution, *passim*, 445-74

xvii   Mehemet Ali, *passim*, 545-72

XI   ix   Russia and the Levant

(1) Russia under Nicholas I, 262-74

(2) The Levant, *passim*, 275-85

xi   Great Britain and the Crimean War (1852-6), *passim*, 309-24

Russia (*contd.*)
xi   xxii Russia and the Levant after
            the Crimean War
            (1) Russia and the period of
            reform, 613–34
            (2) The Balkan Lands, 635–
            47
            (3) Russian Literature (1800–
            1900), 648–60
      xxviii The Far East (1815–71), 802–65
xii   vi   The German Empire, *passim*,
            134–73
      xii Reaction and Revolution in
            Russia, 294–345
      xiii The Reform movement in
            Russia, 346–80
      xiv The Ottoman Empire and the
            Balkan Peninsula, *passim*,
            381–428
      xvi The British Empire in India,
            passim, 457–99
      xvii The Far East, *passim*, 500–36
      xix The Russo-Japanese War, 576–
            601
Russia, Little, v 504 sq.; 596; Catharine II
    and, vi 693 sqq.; land tenure in, xi 616;
    xii 339
—— Red, iii 73; vi 630; 669
—— White, v 504 sq.; vi 630; 669 sq.;
    xii 337; Poles in, 339
Russian Academy of Sciences, vi 697
—— American Company, xi 632
—— Company, in Berlin, vi 324
Russian Courier, journal, xii 312
—— *Gazette*, xii 314
—— *Messenger*, xi 625
—— *Review*, journal, xii 314
—— *Word*, suppressed, xii 295; 297
Russo, Vincenzo, viii 779
Rustchuk, Russian capture of (1810), ix
    485; Turkish troops at, xi 283; Midhat
    Pasha at, xii 383; 409
Rustem Pasha, Grand Vezir, and Peace
    of 1547, iii 120; conspires for murder of
    Prince Mustafa, 121; replaced in office
    of Grand Vezir, 124
Ruthenes, The, Count Stadion and, xi
    175
Ruthenia, forced conversions in, x 425
Rutherford, Ernest, and radio-activity, xii
    790
Rutherglen, rising of recusants at (1679),
    v 285
Ruthven, Raid of, iii 288, 550
—— Patrick, 3rd Lord, iii 271
—— William. *See* Gowrie
Rutland, Charles Manners, 4th Duke of,
    Lord-Lieutenant of Ireland, vi 468, 503;
    Lord Privy Seal, 468; death of, 474,
    505
—— John Manners, Lord Roos, 1st Duke
    of, v 212
Rutledge, John, deputy for South Carolina
    at Constitutional Convention (1787), vii
    246, 265, 267, 281, 284, 290, 296, 302

Rutledge, Walter, Jacobite, vi 111
Ruuth, Eric, Swedish President of Finance,
    vi 777 sq.
Ruvigny, Henri de Massue, 1st Marquis de,
    French ambassador in England, v 211;
    217 sq.
—— Henri de Massue, 2nd Marquis de,
    Earl of Galway. *See* Galway
Ruwenzori, Mount, discovered, xii 812
Ruysbroeck, Johannes (Rusbroek), Flemish
    mystic, i 434, 627
Ruysch, Frederik, anatomist, v 738
—— Nicolas, Secretary to the States
    General, v 145
Ruyter, Michael Adriaanzoon de, Dutch
    admiral, victory of, off Plymouth, iv
    472; 473; 476; 478; 589; seizes Swedish
    ships in South, 591; v 43; on coast of
    Guinea, 108, 149, 179; in Medway, 113,
    150 sq., 188; blockades Swedish fleet,
    147; at Southwold Bay, 158, 192 sq.; at
    Schooneveld, 161; in Mediterranean, 161
    sq.; 178; 181; at Bergen, 182; in naval
    campaign of 1666, 183 sq.; 186 sq.; 189;
    in naval campaign of 1672–3, 194 sqq.;
    death of, 44, 162
Ryazán, annexed to Russia, v 479; 500 sq.;
    Milyukóff banished to, xii 315
—— Stephen Yavorsky, Archbishop of, v
    530; 535 sqq.; 547
Rybinski, Michael, Polish general, x 473
Rydberg, Viktor, Swedish writer, xii 280
Rye House plot, v 229 sq.; 259
Ryer. *See* Du Ryer
Ryhove, iii 248, 250
Ryland, George, secret mission of, from
    Canada, ix 746
Ryléieff, Condratij, Russian poet, x 431 sq.;
    and December insurrection, 440 sqq.;
    execution of, 443
Rymer, Thomas, author, v 133
Rysakóff, attempts to assassinate Alexander
    II, xii 310
Ryswyk, Contra-Remonstrants at, iii 648
—— Peace of (1697), v 32 sq.; 45; 62 sq.;
    274; 370; 374; and Spanish Succes-
    sion, 379 sq.; 382; 397; 399; 450; 453;
    Sweden and, 584; and Hispaniola, 688;
    691; 703; vi 12; 32; 151; and Acadia,
    vii 90, 111; viii 15, 68
Rzevuski, Henryk, Polish novelist, xi 658

Saádat Ali, Wazir of Oudh, exactions from,
    ix 721
Saale river, Soubise at, vi 268, 270 sqq.;
    297
Saarbrücken, engagement at, xi 583, 585 sq.
Saardam, Peter the Great at, v 523
Saargemünd, French force at, xi 586
Saarlouis, retained by France, v 63; fortress
    of, transferred to Germany, ix 664
Saba, captured by English (1665), v 110;
    in possession of Dutch, 687
Sabaeus, Faustus, of Brescia, librarian of
    Vatican, i 617

Sabará, discovery of gold at, vi 390
Sabathier, Abbé, and *Etats Généraux*, viii 106, 108
Sabina of Bavaria. *See* Egmont
Sabinus, Petrus, lecturer in Academy of Rome, ii 17
Sablé, Abel Servien, Marquis de, French plenipotentiary at Münster, iv 402 sqq.; at the Hague, 602; and Mazarin, 608; 612; 614 sq.; death of, 621
Sabran, Madame de, vi 134
Sabugal, defeat of French at (1811), ix 463; Wellington at, 468
Sabúroff, Russian Minister of Public Instruction, xii 309; 312
Sacchi, Bartolommeo. *See* Platina
—— Ettore, Italian statesman, xii 225; 228
Sacheverell riots, v 337
—— Henry, v 429; 467 sqq.; vi 47; 78; 80; 815; 817
—— William, v 216; 222
Sachs, Hans, *Wittenbergische Nachtigall*, ii 159
Sa-chu, travellers at, xii 799, 802 sq.
"Saci, M. de." *See* Le Maistre de Saci
Sacile, Franco-Italian army defeated at (1809), ix 355
Sack, Samuel Gottfried, Prussian Bishop, x 382
Sacken, F. G. von der Osten, Prince, Russian general, in Poland, ix 514, 524; at Leipzig, 539; at La Ferté, 547
—— Baron von, Saxon ambassador to Russia, vi 704
Sackett's Harbour, British repulse at (1813), vii 341, 343
Sackville, George Sackville Germain, Viscount (Lord George Germain, *formerly* Sackville), vi 377 sq.; 435; 447; 449; vii 211, 214, 231
—— Lionel Sackville Sackville-West, 2nd Baron, British Minister to United States, vii 660 sq.
—— Thomas. *See* Dorset
Saco (Maine), settlement at, vii 22
Sacramento, capture and restoration of, vi 370; 374 sq.
—— river, gold discovered on, vii 400
Sacraments of Penance, and Indulgences, ii 125 sq.; discussed at Council of Trent, with Extreme Unction, 672; of Orders, 680, 683; of Matrimony, 683
Sacred College, The, iii 446, 449–51, 453
—— Promontory, town founded by Dom Henrique on the, i 11, 12
Sacy, Baron Antoine-Isaac Silvestre de, xii 846
Sá da Bandeira, Bernardo de Sá Nogueira, Viscount de, Portuguese statesman, x 328; Ministry of, 338 sq.
Sadiya, caravan route to, xii 793; 796
Sadler, Michael Thomas, x 659 sq.
—— Sir Ralph, English ambassador in Scotland, ii 458, 574

Sadoleto, Jacopo, Cardinal-Bishop of Carpentras, i 560, 564, 605; ii 8, 15 sqq., 20, 24, 28, 30, 33; Oratory of Divine Love and, 379, 640; 386; Catholic reform and, 397 sq.; 449, 641 sqq., 660
Sadolin, Jörgen, Danish Reformer, ii 610, 613
Sadowa, battle of. *See* Königgrätz
Sadras, vi 454; conference at, 542
Sadulapur, battle of, xi 741
Sadusain, battle at, xi 740
Saez, Spanish Minister, x 229 sq.
Šafařík, Paul Josef, Bohemian historian, xi 46; 654; xii 842
Saffi, Aurelio, Triumvir in Rome, xi 94; xii 214
Saffron Walden, Parliamentary army encamped at, iv 341
Saftingen, vi 642; Austrian vessel stopped at, 643; 645
Sagallo, fort of, xii 343
Sagan, principality of, iv 103
Sagasta, Praxedes Mateo, Spanish premier, vii 675; xii 263 sq.
Saghalin, Russia and, xii 344; Japan and, 574; 577; 591; 601 sq.
Sagredo, Venetian historian, iii 114
Sagres, Drake at, iii 305
Sagunto, battle of (1811), ix 470
Sahagun, Moore at, ix 445
Sahara, The, France and, xii 47, 129; travellers in, 807 sq.; 812 sq.
Sahuguet, French general, ix 53
Saïd Pasha, Viceroy of Egypt, xi 638; xii 430 sq.; 433 sq.; 434
Saida, revolt in (1834), x 559
Saigō Kichinosuké, Japanese politician, xi 838; 865
—— Takamori, Japanese Minister, xii 549 sq.; 561 sq.; rebellion of, 563; 564
Saigon, occupied by French, xii 4, 131, 524; 525; 796
Sailor's Creek, Confederate force captured at (1865), vii 540
St Albans, council of officers at, iv 353
—— Earl of. *See* Bacon, Francis
—— Henry Jermyn, 1st Earl of (2nd cr.), v 112
St Alban's Head, action with Armada off (July 23, 1588), iii 312
Saint-Albin, A.-C. Omer Rousselin de Corbeau, Comte de, journalist, viii 367
St Amand, storming of (1815), ix 627
Saint-André, Jean Bon, viii 249, 343 sq., 375, 449 sq.; at Brest, 465
—— Count, Austrian general, vi 281
St André d'Albon, Marshal of France, joins (Guise) Triumvirate of 1561, ii 300; 303; iii 4–5
St Andrews, Castle of, siege of, ii 462
St Angelo, Castle of, i 233, 242; ii 24, 54 sqq.; Clement VII in, 428; iii 428 sqq.; occupied by French, ix 195
St Angelo in Malta, holds out against Turks, iii 125

Saint-Arnaud, Jacques-Achille Leroy de, Marshal of France, xi 133 sqq.; in Crimea, 317 sq.
St-Arnoul, besieged by Huguenots, iii 4
St Aubin du Cormier, battle of (1488), i 394, 466
St Augustine (Florida), captured (1862), vii 552
St Bartholomew, island of, viii 280
—— Massacre of (1572), i 56; iii 7, 19–20, 59, 61–2, 86, 177, 232, 257, 285, 404, 406, 550, 596, 753, 760; v 326
St Bartholomew's Day (Aug. 24, 1662), and English Nonconformists, v 99
St Baseul, Council of (992), i 669
St Bernard Pass, captured by Dumas, viii 438; 443 sq.
St Bris, Conference of, iii 42
St Castein, Baron de, vii 509, 111
St Catherine's, action with Armada off (July 25, 1588), iii 312
St Chaumont, Marquis de, at Hamburg, iv 377
St Christopher's. *See* St Kitt's
St Clair, Anglo-Polish adventurer, and "Pomak Republic," xii 406
Saint-Cloud, royal army at, iii 47, 657, 660; Declaration of (1589), 664, 675; Bonaparte at, ix 24; Senate goes to, 32; Council of State at, 172; treaty constituting Rhenish Confederation at (1806), 268; Napoleon III at, xi 286; 611; higher grade school at, xii 118
St Croix, sold by France, vi 738
Saint-Cyr, military school at, ix 127, 410, 568
—— Laurent. *See* Gouvion
Saint-Cyran, Duvergier de Hauranne, Abbé de, and Richelieu, iv 123; v 82 sq.; x 159
St Denis, Greek learning at the Abbey of, i 588; Huguenot forces at, iii 9; League attempts to recover, 50; Henry IV hears mass at (1593), 52; coronation of Maria de' Medici at, 690; burial of Louis XVI at, ix 572
St Denys, battle of (1678), v 45, 165
St Dizier, siege of (1544), ii 78, iii 190; captured by Charles V (1544), ii 245, 459; attack on (1814), ix 545
St Domingo. *See* San Domingo
St Dominique, France and, vi 351 sq.
St Donats, miracle of, iii 284
Ste Aldegonde, Philip de Marnix, lord of, iii 201–2; advocate for William of Orange, 231, 233; 237; 241; 755
Sainte-Aulaire, Louis-Clair de Beaupoil, Comte de, x 47
Sainte-Beuve, Charles-Augustin, and Napoleon's writings, ix 762; x 101; 516; xi 365; 525 sq.; 548; xii 832; 849
Ste Catherine, fortress of, iii 415; destroyed (1600), 418, 677
Sainte-Croix, battle at (1814), ix 553
Ste Foy, assembly of 1594 at, iii 675
St Elmo (Malta), taken by Turks, iii 125

St Elmo (Naples), Tsarevich Alexis at fortress of, v 539
Sainte Marie aux Chènes, xi 593
Sainte Marthe, Charles de, French Reformer, ii 292
Sainte-Menehould, negotiations at (1614), iv 120
Saint-Étienne, rising at, x 492; the Commune at, xi 503; labour congress at, xii 124
St Eustatia. *See* St Eustatius
St Eustatius, captured by British (1665), v 110; vi 186; 448; captured by French, 454
Saint-Evremond, Charles de Marguetel de Saint-Denis, Seigneur de, v 70; 74; 126 sq.; letters of, 132 sq.; 136; viii 4
St Fagan's, Horton's victory at (1648), iv 349
Saint-Florent, Stofflet at, viii 382
St Foy, battle of (1759), vii 142
Saint-Fremont, General, defeat of, v 402
St Gall, ii 205; joins Christian Civic League, 329; riotous proceeding at, 331; cotton manufacture in, ix 425; xi 234; 236; 240; joins *Siebnerkonkordat*, 242; 243; and Articles of Baden, 246; 248; 259; and insurance against unemployment, xii 755
—— Abbots of, ii 307, 331, vi 614 sq.
St George, Knights of (of Swabia), i 292
St Germain, Comte Claude Louis de, French general, vi 742 sq.; 745; Minister for War, viii 82, 88; 400
St Germain-en-Laye, Conference at (1562), ii 303; Peace signed at (1570), iii 14; Edict of (1594), 675; Declaration of (1648), iv 607, 610 sq.; Peace of (1632), and New France, vii 74; Treaty of (1679), v 45, 571, 647, 652, 660; peace conference at (1668), 153; Old Pretender at, vi 91; military school of, ix 410, 568
St Gilles, fight at (1815), ix 624
St Gothard (Hungary), battle of (1664), v 40, 347 sq., 350
Saint Gothard (Switzerland), Pass of, ix 59, 61; road over, xi 239; tunnel, 259
St Helena, mutiny at, v 698; Napoleon at, ix 428, 756 sqq.
St Helen's, Prince Rupert at, v 184
St Helens, Alleyne Fitzherbert, Baron, vi 380; viii 278, 292; ix 50
Saint-Hilaire, Barthélemy, French Foreign Minister, xii 403; 436
—— Gilbert de, iv 27
—— L.-V.-J. Le Blond, Comte de, ix 260
Saint-Huruge, Marquis, leader of Paris mob, viii 228
St Jacob on the Birs, battle of, vi 612
St James' Chronicle, vi 440
St Jean d'Angely, besieged by Anjou, iii 14; surrender of (1621), iv 127
St Jean-de-Losne, relief of, iv 371
St Jean de Maurienne, Treaty between France, Venice and Sweden at (1630), iv 679

St Jean Pied-de-Port, siege of (1516), I 369; capture of (1521), 378

Saint John (Île de Saint Jean). *See* Prince Edward Island

St John (New Brunswick), social and commercial centre, x 689

—— river (Canada), boundary of Quebec, x 685; settlements on (1778), 687

—— Knights of, besieged at Rhodes by the Turks, I 84; treaty with Turks, 86, 224; *see also* Rhodes; established at Malta and Tripoli, II 60; 69, 451; Tsar and, IX 39 sqq., 69, 73; 94; 604; 654

—— Henry, Viscount Bolingbroke. *See* Bolingbroke

—— Oliver, Chief Justice, envoy at the Hague, v 138

—— Sir Oliver, *afterwards* Viscount Grandison, Irish policy of, IV 516

—— William Paulet, Lord. *See* Winchester, Marquis of

St John's (Quebec), fort of, captured (1775), VII 170

—— (Newfoundland), capture of, VI 426

—— river (Florida) (the River of May), French settlement at (1564), I 55

St Julien, Treaty of (1603), III 421

Saint Julien, Count, IX 63; Austrian representative in Paris, 65

Saint-Just, Antoine-L.-Léon de, VIII 249, 255, 271; on the *Comité de Salut Public*, 343, 345, 351, 361 sqq., 368 sqq.; arrest and execution of, 370 sq.; 426; IX 362

St Kitts, French settlement of, IV 758; v 110; ceded to England (1713), 442 sq.; 687 sq.; British fleet at, VI 452; 454; 464; settlements on, VII 74, 78

Saint-Lambert, Jean-François, Marquis de, poet, VI 827; IX 132

St Lawrence, Indian revolt at, XII 606

—— Gulf of, attempts to explore, I 44; fishing rights in, VI 428, VII 657 sq.

—— river, the French on, v 684 sq., VI 183, VII 71, 108 sq., 117; British expedition up, 90; defence of, 95; navigation of, XI 776, XII 612

St Leger, Sir Anthony, Lord Deputy of Ireland, II 471, 496, III 582, 584–6

—— Barry, expedition of, against Fort Stanwix, VII 215

—— Sir Warham, III 608

St Louis, Lewis and Clark start from, VII 326; trade of, 360; in Civil War, 458, 471; Halleck at (1861), 493; Republican National Convention at (1896), 672; 691

Saint-Luc, François d'Espinay, Seigneur de, holds Brouage (1585), III 41; 673

—— François d'Espinay, Marquis of, IV 616

St Lucia. *See* Santa Lucia

St Luke, Academy of, VI 589

St Luziussteig, the French hold the, IV 58, 61

St Malo, English attack on (1692), v 261; the Old Pretender at, VI 102; 342*b* (in Vol. XIII)

St Mandé, socialist meeting at, XII 127

Saint-Marsan, French ambassador at Berlin, IX 512

St Martin, French and Dutch in, v 687; reduced (1810), IX 240

—— Louis-Claude de, IX 133

St Mary's (Maryland), seized by Clayborne and Ingle, VII 33

St Maur les Fossés, Treaty of (1465), I 389; treaty between Henry III and the Leaguers at (1585), III 39

St Maur-sur-Loire, Benedictines of, XII 816

—— Congregation of (1627), v 79

St Michel, Fort, holds out against Turks, III 125

St Nazaire, harbour works at, XII 102

St Omer, Iconoclastic riot at (1566), III 208; failure of siege of, IV 147; France and, v 39, 44; 45; 162; 220; Dutch claims on, 422; Charles X at, x 90; O'Connell at, 630

Saintonge, peasants' rising in, III 664

St Ouen, Louis XVIII at (1814), IX 562

Saint-Paul, Governor of Champagne for the League, III 669

St Paul's Cross, Whitgift's sermon at, III 342

—— School, the New Learning at, I 582

St Peter's, at Rome, the rebuilding of, II 5 sq., 10, 12, 32

St Petersburg, origin of, v 529, 590; 531; 533 sqq.; 542; death of Peter the Great at, 548; Peter II and, 555; Charles XII and, 591, 596; 595; 597; 605; 609; Academy of Science at, 741; British mission to (1718–9), VI 34; 197; Stanislaus Poniatowski at, 200; 253; Russian Court moved to, 303; 312; 314; Botta-Lopukhina conspiracy at, 315 sq.; 318; the Marquis de Châteauneuf at, 322; 324; 326 sq.; 657 sq.; revolution in, 662; Prince Henry of Prussia at, 668, 731; 669; the centre of government, 682; 688; the Russian capital, 700; 732; 778; Free Economic Society of, 689; Stanislas in, IX 36; Gustavus IV's visit to, 38; British diplomacy at, 39; Count Litta at, 39; Bavarian representative at, 40; Court Gazette of, 46; Gustavus IV again at, 46 sqq.; Prussian declaration sent to, 266; change of Ministry at, 272; Savary at, 305; deputation of Finns to, 314; Frederick William III of Prussia in (1809), 344; Speranskii in, 484; Protocol of (1826), x 191 sqq., 202; Public Library of, 431; University of, *ib.*, XI 624; secret society in, x 432 sq.; 434; Nicholas I married at, 436; military insurrection at (1820), 438; December insurrection at (1825), 440 sq.; local government in, XI 263, 621; 266; industrial policy at, 270; 321; 615; reforms in, 618; 625; incendiary fires in, 627; demonstration in, XII 295; 301; 303; revolutionary propaganda

in, 304; 306 sq.; student disturbances in, 315; trade depression in, 319; 321; 325; strike in, 330; 332; Finnish deputation at, 335; 337; the Jews in, 341; Ferdinand of Bulgaria at, 342; 346; political conference in, 347; 348; Gapón's demonstrations in, 349; Union of Unions Congress at, 355; 360; martial law in, 362; 365; 368; Anglo-Russian Chamber of Commerce at, 380; 478; Li Hungchang at, 513

St Petersburg, Convention of (1755), vi 320; (1780), ix 44; Treaty of (1747), vi 318; (1772), 630; (1801), ix 73; (1805), 246; (1826), xi 684; Conference of (1824), x 189; Congress of (1794), viii 548; 551

Saint-Pierre (Basses-Pyrénées), battle of (1813), ix 481

—— (Newfoundland), vi 346; ceded to France, 428, 464; captured by British (1793), viii 484, ix 749; and fishery dispute, xi 776

—— Abbé Charles-Irénée Castel de, vi 702, viii 15; the *Projet de...la paix perpétuelle* of, x 2 sq.; 9

—— Jacques-Henri Bernardin de, vi 827; viii 501; xi 528

St Pölten, Elector Charles Albert of Bavaria at, vi 232

Saint-Pol, François de Bourbon, Count of, ii 58 sq.

—— Comte Louis de, executed by Louis XI, i 415

Saint-Priest, Emmanuel-Louis-Marie Guignard, Vicomte de, x 486

—— François-Emmanuel Guignard, Comte de, viii 163; French ambassador at Constantinople (1768-76 *and* 1778-85), 595

St Privat, xi 592; battle at, 593

St Quentin, battle of (1557), ii 91 sq., 294, 547, iii 184, 399 sq.; seditious attempt on (1597), 672; returned to France (1559), ii 94; captured by the Germans, xi 610

Saint-Quentin, French general in Italy (1500), i 123

Saint-Réjant, *Chouan* conspirator, ix 17-8

St Roch, affair of Church of, ix 572

St Ruth, General, in Ireland, v 316 sqq.

St Sacrament, colony of (in Uruguay), v 456

St Saphorin, British Minister at Vienna, vi 30; 39

St Sauveur, settlement at, vii 72; destroyed, *ib.*

Saint-Sévérin, French plenipotentiary at Aix-la-Chapelle, vi 331

Saint-Simon, Comte Claude-Henri de, French socialist, vi 836; viii 8; ix 133; xi 526; xii 93; 758

—— Louis de Rouvroi, Duke of, v 25; 86; vi 127 sq.; 132; 135 sq.; publication of *Mémoires* of, xi 523

St Stephen, Order of, iii 391-2

Saint-Sulpice, seminary of, v 78 sq.

St Thomas, taken by the Danes (1671), v 688

St Thomé, captured by the Dutch (1675), v 696

St Trond, meeting at (1566), iii 207

St Ursula's Schifflein, German religious association, ii 108, 122

St Venant, captured by the Allies (1710), v 429

St Venceslas, Treaty of (1517), i 338

St Vincent, Cape. *See* Cape St Vincent

—— island of, claimed by French, v 687; vi 185; 332; capture of (1762), 346; 426; assigned to Great Britain, 428; reduced by d'Estaing (1779), 452; 464; captured by British (1796), viii 484; xii 654; government of, 656

—— John Jervis, Earl of, viii 454, 460 sq.; in West Indies, 484; 498; 620 sq.; First Lord of Admiralty, ix 210; 217, 681, 684; and slave trade, 751

St Vincent de Paul, Society of, xi 473

Sakai, massacre at, xi 859

Sakhar, English troops at, xi 734 sq.

Sákharoff, General, killed, xii 363

Sala, Giuseppe Antonio, Cardinal, x 153; 168

Salabat Jang, Subahdar of Deccan, vi 540; 546; 549

Saladin, J.-B.-Michel, French deputy, viii 488

Salahiyeh, fight at, viii 604

Salamanca, Treaty of (1505), i 364; University of, iii 447, 593; Vendôme at, v 428; Moore's army at (1808), ix 443, 445; Soult marches from (1809), 453; Dorsenne joins Marmont near, 468; fall of, 471; siege of (1812), 472; battle of, 472-3; Wellington retires from, 475

—— José de, Spanish Minister of Finance, xi 555 sq.; 559 sq.

—— Cardinal Pedro Gonzalez Hurtado de Mendoza, Bishop of (d. 1574), ii 677

Salamis, naval revolt at, xii 422

Salamonius, iii 737

Salandra, Antonio, Italian statesman, xii 227

Salas, Montealgro di, Neapolitan statesman, vi 596 sq.

Salasco armistice, The, xi 89 sqq.; 93

Salbai, Treaty of (1782), vi 576 sq., ix 710

Salces. *See* Roussillon

Saldanha, Cardinal, and the Jesuits, vi 386, 592

—— de Gama, Count of, Portuguese plenipotentiary at Congress of Vienna, ix 584; x 222

—— Oliveira e Daun, João Carlos, Duke of, Portuguese statesman, x 320; 322; leaves England, 324; 327; at defence of Oporto, 331 sq.; and defence of Lisbon, 335; 336; Minister of Maria II, 338; insurrection by, 338 sq.; head of the Ministry, 339; Minister of War, xi 572; Prime Minister, *ib.*; and Thomar, 572 sq.; fall of, 573 sq.; returns to Portugal, 575

Saldern, Caspar von, and Schleswig-Holstein question, VI 753

Sale, Sir Robert Henry, at Jalalabad, XI 733; 734; 739

Salem (Mass.), Roger Williams at, VII 17; Congress at (1774), 163; skirmish at (1775), 165; and "broken voyages," 327

—— (New Jersey), founded, VII 47

Salemé river, André Brue on, XII 806

Salerno, revolt in (1828), X 119

—— Ferrante Sanseverino, Prince of, III 471, 472

Salicetti, Christophe, French politician, VIII 352, 564, 570, 573; IX 83

Salinguerra, Taurello, holds Ferrara against Venice, I 260

Salis, Grisons family, IV 42

—— Hercules von, at Venice, IV 50

Salisbury, royal army at, V 218

—— James Cecil, 3rd Earl of, V 218

—— Margaret Plantagenet, Countess of, II 447, 449; execution of, 452; 523

—— Sir Robert Cecil, 1st Earl of (5th cr.), Minister of Elizabeth, III 332, 354, 356; and James I, 534 sqq.; 737; 755; IV 256

—— Robert Arthur Talbot Gascoyne Cecil, 3rd Marquis of (Lord Cranborne), VII 661, 671; XI 340; and Disraeli's Reform Bill, 341 sq.; XII 11; 14; Secretary for India, 30; 33; Ministry of (1885–6), 42; 43; Ministry of (1886–92), 45 sqq.; Ministry of (1895–1902), 52 sqq.; death of, 54; 83; and Irish Home Rule, 84 sq.; 87; and Tunis, 239; and Portugal, 270; at Congress of Berlin, 394 sqq.; 400; and Bulgaria, 406; and Armenian question, 418; and Egyptian question, 445, 447; and Afghánistán, 465 sq.; and India, 473; and Chitral, 487; and China, 504, 506; and Venezuelan dispute, 687; and arbitration, 727 sq.; 734; 782

—— (South Africa), fort at, XII 639

Salis-Soglio, Ulrich von, commander of the Sonderbund forces, XI 250 sq.

Salkeld, Philip, at Delhi, XI 746

Sallee, blockaded by Rainborow (1637), IV 482

Salles, Jean-Baptiste, French deputy, VIII 357

Salmasius (Claude de Saumaise), III 752; and Christina of Sweden, IV 575; VI 798

Salmeron, Alfonso, Jesuit, II 391, 652, 654; at Trent, 667, 671; III 160; 585; 592

Salmerón, Nicolás, resigns professorial chair, XI 567; President of Republic in Spain, XII 261

Salo, fight at, VIII 585

Salomon, Rabbi, III 137–8

Salonika, acquired by Venice, I 255; contraband in, IX 389; consuls murdered at, XII 385; Austria and, 401; 425 sqq.

Salsette, island of, British occupation of, VI 575; 576

Salutati, Coluccio de', Chancellor of Florence (1375), I 544

Saluz, Philipp, IV 36

Saluzzo, seized by France (1548), II 84; retained by France (1559), 94; French claim to, III 397, 402, 478; flight of dissenters to, 404; Savoy's designs on, 407 sq., 411, 413, 437; seized by Savoy, 414 sq., 674; attacked by Lesdiguières, 417; kept by Savoy, 419, 677

—— Louis II, Marquis of, I 118

Salvadori, Milanese democrat, VIII 585

Salvandy, Narcisse-Achille, Comte de, X 59; XI 36

Salvati, Giuseppe, and Naples revolt, X 112

Salvatierra, Pedro de Ayala, Count of, I 375

Salverte, Anne-Joseph-Eusèbe Baconnière, French deputy, X 476 sq.

Salviati, Archbishop of Pisa. *See* Pisa

—— Alamanno, Savonarolist, I 169

—— Jacopo, Savonarolist, I 169

—— Lucrezia (de' Medici), I 175

Salvini, Tommaso, Italian actor, XI 548

Salvius, Johan Adler, conducts Swedish diplomatic affairs, IV 373, 396 sqq., 402

Salvotti, Anton, X 118

Salwey, Richard, IV 548

Salwin river, exploration of, XII 797 sq.

Salza, Hermann von, High Master of German Order, V 630

Salzburg, Peasants' Revolt in, II 190; Jesuits in, III 161; Ferdinand (II) meets Doncaster at, IV 27; 393; religious intolerance in, V 743; emigration from, VI 218; 647; annexed to Austria (1797), VIII 633, 642; archbishopric of, obtained by Tuscany (1803), IX 94; Bernadotte advances on, 256; annexed by Austria (1805), 262; General Jellachich's army at (1809), 347; Austria's gains in (1815), 658; Austria's appropriation of, X 346; Napoleon III at, XI 484

Salzburg, Archbishops of:—

—— Ernest of Bavaria (the elder), III 161

—— Johann Jakob Kuen von Belasy, II 681; III 161

—— Leopold, Count Firmian, V 743; VI 218

—— Michael von Kuenburg, III 161

—— Matthaeus Lang, Cardinal, I 184, 323 sq.; II 29, 147; Peasants' Rising and, 184

Salzwedel, Torstensson quartered at, IV 386

Sam, Conrad, Zwinglian Reformer, II 333

Samara, bacteriological institute in, XII 327

Samarin, George, and emancipation of serfs, XI 615, 622; *Frontiers of Russia*, XII 298

Samarkand, captured by Russians, XI 631; 632; XII 343; Russian occupation of, 459; 801

Sambaji, Marátha chief, VI 521 sq.

Sambalpur, annexation of, XI 743

Sami Bey, envoy of Mehemet Ali, X 567

Samland, George von Polenz, Bishop of, II 160, 162

Samoa, affairs in (1885–9), VII 661 sqq.;

U.S. Treaty with (1878), 649; Germany and, xii 41, 160; Australia and, 631; 666 sq.

Samogitia, German Order and, v 633

Samori, The. *See* Zamorin

Samoyede mission, x 422

Sampson, Thomas, English Puritan, ii 592

—— William Thomas, American naval officer, vii 679 sq.

Samson Bernardin, and Zwingli, ii 313

San Bonifazio, Austrian army at, xi 86

San Caetano, Ignacio de, Grand Inquisitor of Portugal, vi 388

San Carlos de la Rápita, Ortega lands at, xi 564

Sancerre, refuge for Protestants of central France, iii 20

—— Count of, French general, surrenders St Dizier, ii 78

Sanchez, Francisco, Spanish Latinist, i 578

—— Juan, Spanish martyr, ii 408

—— Julian, Spanish guerrilla chief, in Leon, ix 469

San Cristovão (Cape Verde Islands) discovered, i 15

Sancroft, William, Archbishop of Canterbury, v 234; 242; deposed, 259; 330; 336; vi 798

Sanctae Inquisitionis artes aliquot detectae, ii 406

Sanctis, Francesco de, Italian writer, xi 548 sq.

Sand River Convention, xi 784 sq., xii 39, 41

Sand, George (Amantine-L.-A. Dudevant), x 102; 411; 499; 515; xi 112; 139 sq.; the writings of, 519 sq.; 522

—— Karl, x 22 sq.; assassinates Kotzebue, 365

Sande Bakhuysen, Julius J. van de, Dutch painter, xii 249

Sandepu, fighting at, xii 597

Sanders, Dr Nicholas, iii 285–6, 597–8

Sanderson, Sir William, historian, vi 807

Sandhurst, Sir William Rose Mansfield, 1st Baron, Commander-in-chief in India, xi 752

Sandör, General, hanged, xi 214

Sandomeria, Palatine of. *See* Kostka, Jan

San Domingo, foundation of, i 40; attacked by Penn and Venables, iv 482, 660; failure of British attack on, v 60; 684; 687; Republic of, vi 189; French in, vii 86; Company of, vi 173, 533, vii 91; prosperity of, 96 sqq.; press in, 103; 104; 107; disorder in (1790), viii 193, 216 sq.; Spain receives part of (1795), 442; 484; revolutionary armies sent to (1801), ix 20; French fleet at, 209; British blockade of (1803), 211; 219; French at (1805), 221; independence of, 244; produce of, 372; Napoleon and, 419–22; ruled by Toussaint L'Ouverture, 420–1; French expedition to (1801), 422; Spanish portion of, restored (1814), 576;

proposed annexation of, by United States, vii 637; and Caracas, x 248; criminals migrate to, 257; French *boucaniers* of, 272; independence of, 276; trade with, 586; 761; a Spanish colony, xi 566; and Haiti, xii 652, 655; 695

Sandomir, Consensus of (1570), ii 637, iii 83; *Rokosz* of (1606), iv 189; Austrian and Prussian claims to, viii 548; occupied by Poniatowski (1809), ix 354; province of Poland, x 449; annexed to Poland, 461

Sandoval, Prudencio de, iii 106

Sandwich, Edward Montagu, 1st Earl of, joins Blake, iv 483; 484 sq.; Charles II and, 540; 541; 552; v 93; 105 sq.; 181; in command of English fleet, 182; 183; 192

—— John Montagu, 4th Earl of, at Aix-la-Chapelle, vi 331; 424; 430; First Lord of Admiralty, 430; 431; 443 sq.; 456

Sandys, Edwin, Archbishop of York, ii 567

—— Sir Edwin, and London Company, vii 6

—— Samuel Sandys, Lord, vi 425

Sanfelice, Giovanni Tommaso. *See* La Cava

San Fernando (Spain), revolt at (1820), x 216

—— (Venezuela), captured by Bolívar (1818), x 293

San Fernando de Omoa, vi 378

San Filippe (Cape Verde Islands) discovered, i 15

San Francisco river, v 677 sq.

Sangallo, Antonio, ii 12 sq.; iii 442

San Gennaro, Order of, vi 598

Sangha river, France and, xii 130

San Giacomo, captured by the Allies (1795), viii 444

San Gil barracks, xii 259

Sangster, Scottish officer in service of Sindhia, ix 718

Sanhedrin, the Grand, ix 205

San Ildefonso, Philip V at, vi 134, 137, 146; 166; Family Compact ratified at, 344; 361; 391; Treaty of (1795), ix 217, 420; (1796), viii 460; Secret Treaty of (1800), vii 93, 324 sq.

Sanitation, science of, in Russia, under Peter the Great, v 531; progress of, in general, xii 780 sq.

San Jacinto, battle of (1836), vii 392

San Jacinto, United States ship of war, the steamer *Trent* and, xii 18

Sanjaks, Turkish, in Hungary, iii 119

Sanjō Saneyoshi, Japanese statesman, xi 837; 839; 849 sq.; 863 sq.; 865; xii 549 sq.

San Juan (Porto Rico), blockaded (1898), vii 680

—— Island, acquired by United States, xi 777, xii 28

—— —— Fernando de, Spanish Reformer, ii 406

San Juan, Spanish general, murder of, IX 448

—— —— de Lua. *See* San Juan d' Ulloa

—— —— de Nicaragua river, XII 686

—— —— d' Ulloa (Mexico), attack on Hawkins at, III 295 sq., 492; captured by Scott (1847), VII 396

San Lazzaro, Order of, III 410

San Lourenço, Count of, X 331

San Luis, Count Luis José Sartorius of, XI 559 sq.

San Marcial, Soult repulsed at (1813), IX 480

San Marco, friars of, ejected, III 390; Cosimo's gardens near, 394

San Martín, José de, career of, X 291 sq.; in Peru, 292 sqq.; retirement of, 295; 302; 306

San Martino, battle at, XI 383

—— Count Ponza di, Viceroy of Naples, XI 536

San Marzano, Count Carlo di, X 114 sqq.

San Maurizio, Order of, III 410

Sanmên, Italy and, XII 514

San Miguel, Evaristo, Spanish officer, X 215; 226 sqq.

Sannazaro, Jacopo, II 16; III 458, 462, 470; *Arcadia*, X 718, 724

Sannikof, Jacob, explorer, XII 795

San Paulo, V 676; discovery of gold in, 678 sq.; settlement at, VI 390; a centre of Separatism, X 314; 315

San-po river, XII 798; explored by Sven Hedin, 804

Sanquhar, Cameronians at, V 286

San Remo, Emperor Frederick III at, XII 163

San Roman, Francisco de, Spanish Reformer, II 403

Sansac, L. Prénst, Sieur de, III 13

San Salvador, State of, XII 672

—— (Bahia). *See* Bahia

Sansanding, explorers at, XII 807

San Sebastian, captured by French (1719), VI 34, (1794), VIII 440; siege of (1813), IX 239, 478, 480; governor expelled from, 430; stores of, 435; Queen Isabel at, XI 569

San Severino, Francesco. *See* Caiazzo, Count of

—— Galeazzo di, I 120 sqq.

—— Stanislao, Cardinal, X 150

Sanseverino, Frederic, Cardinal, I 250

Sanson, executioner of Louis XVI, VIII 261

Sansovino, Andrea, II 12 sq., 15; III 471

Sanssouci, Frederick William IV at, XI 159

San Stefano (Tuscany), falls to Philip II, III 385

—— (Turkey), Russian headquarters at, XII 390; Treaty of, 33, 142, 391 sqq., 398, 400 sq.

—— Neapolitan Minister, VI 596

Santa Agueda, Cánovas murdered at, XII 266

Santa Anna, Antonio Lopez de, Mexican general and politician, VII 392, 396, 406, 426; X 304

Santa Catarina, heights of, stormed by Allies (1707), V 419

Santa Catharina, island of, captured by Spain, VI 375, 391

Santa Coloma, Spanish Viceroy of Roussillon, IV 647 sq.; death of, *ib.*

Santa Cruz (Teneriffe), Blake at, IV 484

—— (West Indies), Dutch in, IV 758; in French occupation, V 687; Danes in, VI 186; and emancipation, XII 652

—— Islands, annexed by Great Britain, XII 667

—— Alvaro de Bazan, Marquis of, III 294, 300, 302, 305–6, 308, 500; defeats Don Antonio's ships, 501; urges a strong naval policy on Philip, 502–3; fleet of, in the Tagus, 504; death of (1588), 505

—— Alvaro de Bazan, Marquis of, succeeds Spinola (1630), IV 644

—— de Marzenado, Alvar de Navia Osorio, Marquis de, Spanish general, VI 151

—— Marquesa de (1843), XI 550

—— de, Spanish priest, XII 260

Santa Fé, captured by Kearny (1846), VII 395; and the Spanish American frontier, X 269; 300

Santa Lucia (Verona), King Charles Albert at, XI 85

—— (West Indies), France and, V 687, VI 185; 186; 332; 347; British occupation of, 426; assigned to France, 428; 451; 464; taken by British (1794), VIII 484, IX 749; recaptured (1795), VIII 484, IX 749; retaken by British (1796), VIII 484; (1803), IX 240, 244; retained by England, 564, 576; cultivation of cocoa in, XII 654

—— Bay, annexed by Great Britain, XII 636

Santa Marta, Royalist port, at war with Cartagena, X 290

Santa Martha, Portuguese general, X 328 sqq.

Santa Maura, seized by Turks (1479), I 81; captured by Venetians (1684), V 365

Santander, Spanish squadron at, VI 125; disturbance in, IX 315; La Romana's troops at, 442; Masséna retires to, 462

Sant' Antonino. *See* Antoninus, Archbishop of Florence

Santarem, French and (1810), IX 462–3; 466; Macdonnel besieged in (1833), X 335; Dom Miguel at, 336

Santarosa, Pietro di, Sardinian Minister, XI 369

Santa Severina, Cardinal Santoro di, III 443

Santerre, Antoine-Joseph, VIII 228, 232; *Commandant* of the *Gardes Nationales*, 257, 260

Santhià, exchanged for Vercelli, III 400; evacuated by Philip, 407

Santiago, Order of, I 11, 353

—— de Chile, Council formed at, X 285; 287

Santiago de Cuba, I 41; taken by English (1662), V 105; capture of (1898), VII 680 sq., XII 697
—— de los Caballeros (Española), I 41
—— Island (Cape Verde Islands), discovered, I 15; passed by Da Gama (1497), 25
Santo Domingo. *See* San Domingo
Santorre di Santarosa, X 114; 116 sq.
Santo Stefano, prison of, XI 380
Santucci, Vincenzo, Cardinal, XI 392
Sant' Uffizio. *See* Inquisition
Sanudo, Marino, the *Diarii*, I 284; II 380
Saorgio, Sardinian camp at, VIII 437 sq.
Sapieha, Casimir, Grand Hetman of Lithuania, VI 192
—— Leo, commands Polish army, IV 185
Sapienza, island of, XI 280 sq.
Saracco, Giuseppe, President of the Italian Senate, XII 222 sq.
Saracenus, Johannes, Abbot of Vercelli, I 588
Sarafoff, Boris, President of the Macedonian Committee, XII 425
Saragossa, burning of Aragonese at, III 516; Los Velez sent to, IV 648; battle at (1710), V 428; disturbance in (1808), IX 315; 326; campaign centred at, 438; Palafox defends, 443; Lannes sent to, 444; 447; Blake's defeat before (1809), 454; Suchet retires to (1810), 457; Ferdinand VII at, X 205; revolt at (1820), 216; 293; rising at, XI 559
Sarajevo, siege of, XII 400
Sarakhs, Boundary Commission at, XII 477
Sarátoff, strike in, XII 350; 363; 366
Saratoga, battles of (1777), VII 215 sq.; surrender of Burgoyne at, 216
Saravia, Hadrian, Protestant refugee in England, II 597
Sarawak, Sir James Brooke in, XII 669
Sardinia, Spanish invasion of, VI 29; 35 sq.; 124; transferred to Victor Amadeus, 126, V 437, 445; VI 139; 154; and Pragmatic Sanction, 203; 213; and Austrian Succession, 228 sq.; 239; and Lombardy, 245; and Peace of Aix-la-Chapelle, 249; 250; and Great Britain, 477; and the Papacy, 589 sq., 594; Naples and, 597; 608; and Corsica, 609 sq.; 623; declares war on France, VIII 437, 442, 456, 559; under Victor Amadeus III, 555; army of, 557; neutrality of (1796), 567; makes peace, 569; interest taken by Tsar Paul in, IX 42; strategic importance of, 210; and Defensive Triple Alliance, 597; incorporation of Genoa in (1815), 599, 615, 660, 667; XI 209; 244; and Switzerland, 249, 252; and Treaty of Zurich, 385; and Crimean War, 373; 468; socialism in, XII 232. *See also* Piedmont
—— King of. *See* Savoy, Victor Amadeus II *and* Victor Amadeus III, *also* Victor Emmanuel I
Sardou, Victorien, dramatist, XI 518; 548

Saris, John, and expedition to Japan, IV 740
Sarmatia, the "iron-bastion" of Christendom, III 94
Sarmiento d'Acuna. *See* Gondomar, Count of
Sarnen, League of, XI 242 sqq.; dissolved, 245
Sarnico, Garibaldians imprisoned at, XI 533
Saros, county of, VI 703
Sarpi, Pietro (Frà Paolo), Pope Paul V and, I 270, IV 671; II 10 sq., 644; III 744; VI 594
Sarrans, Bernard, French politician, XI 125
Sarria, Marquis of, Spanish general, VI 368
Sarrien, Jean-Marie-Ferdinand, French Minister of Justice, XII 113
Sarsfield, Patrick, titular Earl of Lucan, V 313; 315 sq.; 318
—— Spanish general, X 215 sq.
Sartines, Antoine-R.-J.-G.-Gabriel de, Comte d'Alby, French Minister of the Navy, VIII 02, 04
Sartorius, Georg (Baron von Waltershausen), German historian, IX 595; 612; XII 824
—— Sir George Rose, in command of Dom Pedro's fleet, X 326 sqq.; and the defence of Oporto, 331 sq.
—— Luis José. *See* San Luis, Count of
Sarzana, surrendered to Charles VIII (1494), I 113, 153
Sarzec, Ernest de, discoveries of, at Tello, XII 846
Sasawa river, Prussian troops at, VI 241; 259
Sasbach, death of Turenne at, V 44
Sas de Ghent. *See* Sas-van-Gent
Sasebo, Japanese troops embarked at, XII 580
Saskatchewan, district of, XI 776; XII 610; province of, 615
—— river, La Verendrye at, VII 94; XII 606; 609
Sassari, Alexander Dominic Varesini, Bishop of, XI 368
Sasselti, Filippo, III 474
Sastrow, Bartholomew, II 262
Sasun, massacres in, XII 416
Sas-van-Gent, landing of Maurice at, III 635; taken by Dutch (1644), IV 597
Satanovski, Arsenius, translator of Russian Bible, V 516
Satara, annexation of, XI 743
—— Rájah of, Sindhia and the, IX 718
Sat-Cho combination, The, in Japan, XII 551
Sathas, Constantine N., historian, XII 845
Satlaj river. *See* Sutlej
Satschan, Lake of, and Austerlitz, IX 261
Satsuma, *daimiō* and clan of, Vol. XI, Chap. XXVIII (2) *passim*; XII 551 sq.; Saigō and, 561; rebellion of, 562 sqq.
Sattler, Philip, envoy of Gustavus Adolphus, IV 194, 216
Satyre Ménippée, La (1593), III 69-70, 661

Saugnier, captive in Africa, XII 806; 808
Sauli, Marquis, Sardinian Minister in Vienna, XI 75
Sault Ste Marie, Jesuit mission station at, VII 84; and home trade, 718
Saulx, Comtesse de (1591), III 416
Saumaise, Claude. *See* Salmasius
Saumarez, James Saumarez, Baron de, British admiral, VIII 454; IX 54; commander in the Baltic (1810), 379
Saumur, remains loyal, III 46; Huguenot Assembly at (1611), IV 119; captured by Vendeans, VIII 341; military plot at, X 76
Saunders, Sir Charles, Admiral, First Lord of Admiralty, VI 437; at Quebec (1759), VII 138
—— Thomas, Governor of Madras, VI 541
Saunier, Antoine, Calvin and, II 372
Sauret, French commander, VIII 574
Saurin, William, Attorney-General of Ireland, IX 707
Sauroren, battle of (1813), IX 480
Saussure, Horace-Bénédicte de, Swiss physicist, IX 427; XI 260
Sauvage, Jean Le, Chancellor of Charles V, I 370, 371
Sauve, Madame de, III 27
Sauveur, Joseph, French mathematician, V 722
Sauzet, Jean-Pierre-Paul, French jurist, X 493; 495; XI 101
Savage, conspirator under Babington, III 291
Savannah, captured by British (1778), VII 219; besieged, *ib.*; siege of, abandoned, *ib.*; French fleet repulsed at, VI 452; evacuated by British (1781), VII 231, 307; 346; and the campaign in west (1864), 520; Sherman captures (1864), 527 sq.; 552
Savanore, Bussy at, VI 546
—— Nawáb of, VI 541
Savary, Anne-Jean-Marie, Duc de Rovigo, French general, IX 31–2; receives Rovigo, 111; succeeds Fouché, 141; imprisoned, 144; at St Petersburg, 305; interviews Ferdinand VII, 432; takes Murat's place, 436; sends reinforcements to Dupont, 437; evacuates Madrid, 438; 441; X 503
—— Daniel, French commodore, VIII 476
—— member of Swiss Directory, IX 97
Savello, Duke of, Imperialist general, at Wittenweier, IV 376; 380
Savenay, Vendean defeat at (1793), VIII 356
Saverne. *See* Zabern
Savigny, Friedrich Karl von, professor of jurisprudence at Berlin University, VIII 776, IX 327; X 374, 404; XII 819 sq.; 822; 827; 835
Savile, Sir George, and Act of 1778, VI 454; X 625
—— Sir George, Marquis of Halifax. *See* Halifax
—— Thomas, Viscount (*afterwards* Earl of Sussex), IV 305 sq.

Savoja, Italian humanist, II 15
Savona, meeting at, between Kings of France and Naples (1507), I 130; Savoy's designs on, III 407; Maillebois' forces at, VI 245; de Vins repulsed at, VIII 444; Napoleon at, 561; Pius VII and, IX 196 sqq.; 201
Savonarola, Girolamo, Vol. I, Chap. V *passim*; character of, 145; *Apology*, 178; *Triumphus Crucis*, 179; 233; ideas and visions of, 649; methods and disciples of, 650; attitude of, towards Renaissance, II 2 sqq.; 5, 29; III 389; V 508
Savornin-Lohman, Alexander Frederick de, Dutch politician, XII 246
Savoy, importance of, to France, II 62; invaded by French (1536), 70, 232; (1537), 73; 89; given up by French (1559), 94; III 260; under Emmanuel Philibert [q.v.] and Charles Emmanuel [q.v.], 399–421; 478; Henry IV's policy toward, 683; French alliance with, 688; and Valtelline, Vol. IV, Chap. II *passim*; and Peace of Monzon, 88; 95; conquered by Richelieu, 115; 123 sq.; 130; 132 sqq.; 138 sq.; 145; invaded by French, V 59; and Spanish Succession, 389; 422; peace negotiations and, 429 sq.; and Peace of Utrecht, 439 sq.; 448; Quadruple Alliance and, VI 31, 124; 139; 149; France and, 152; 158 sq.; regained by Sardinia, 249; and Genoa, 608; and Switzerland, 623; invaded by Sardinia (1793), VIII 437; French in (1792), 555; enfranchisement in, 720; influence of French Revolution in, 780; and Treaty of Frankfort, X 22; attempted invasion of, by Ramorino, 122; France and, XI 88, 376; the *Lyonnais* in, 106; Polish invasion of, 245; ceded to France, 256, 386 sqq., 468; Napoleon III and, 332, 334; 577. *See also* Piedmont *and* Sardinia
—— Conference (1661), V 97; 330
—— House of, and Geneva, II 358–62; marriage alliances of, with Modena and Mantua, III 686
Savoy, Dukes of :—
—— Amadeus VI, I 264
—— Charles III, II 60, 70, 73
—— Charles Emmanuel I, III 7; 25; 397; birth of, 406; accession of, 412; policy of, 412–21, 437; son-in-law of Philip II, 510 sq., 513, 673 sq.; at war with France, 679; negotiates with France, 683, 686 sqq., 689 sq.; IV 17; and the Imperial succession, 18; allows Mansfeld to enter Bohemian service, 24; 27; veers towards Catholic coalition, 34; 40; failure of ambitions of, 118; 119; 129; renews claim to Montferrat, 134 sqq.; death of, 138; and Lombardy, 624; and Spain, 626; 631; 642 sqq.; 666; Paul V and, 669; 673; alliance between Spain and, 678 sq.; 683; alliance between France and, 687
—— Charles Emmanuel II, and Treaty of the Pyrenees, IV 620

Savoy, Dukes of (*contd.*):—
—— Charles Emmanuel III, King of Sardinia (Prince of Piedmont), v 432
—— Emmanuel Philibert, II 89, 92; III 131, 134, 182–4, 187, 385, 387; work of reconstruction of, 399–408; policy of, 409–11; character of, 412
—— Francis Hyacinth, death of, IV 148
—— Philibert II, the Fair, I 455
—— Philip II, de Bresse, I 118
—— Victor Amadeus I, IV 678
—— Victor Amadeus II (King of Sicily, *afterwards* King of Sardinia), v 58; 60 sqq.; and Grand Alliance, 370, 408; and Spanish Succession, 380, 388, 393; 401; and Louis XIV, 404; and War of the Spanish Succession, 411; 412; 414 sqq.; 419; 425; and Sicily, 427, 445, 448; meeting of Emperor Charles VI with, 432; 434; and Peace of Utrecht, 437; VI 30; 32 sq.; 124 sq.; 169; and Clement XI, 587; 589 sq.
—— Victor Amadeus III, King of Sardinia, VIII 555, 559, 780
Savoy, Duchess Anna Maria of, VI 8
—— Beatrice (of Portugal), Duchess of, II 70
—— Bona of. *See* Milan, Duchess of
—— Catharine (Infanta of Spain), Duchess of, III 25, 513
—— Princess Clotilde of, marriage of, to Prince Napoleon, XI 376, 381
—— Louise of. *See* Angoulême, Louise, Duchess of
—— Margaret (of Austria and Burgundy), Duchess of. *See* Margaret
—— Maurice of, son of Charles Emmanuel I, Cardinal, III 686
—— Yolande (sister of Louis XI), Duchess of, I 390 sq.
Savoy-Carignan, House of, VI 6
—— Prince Eugene of. *See* Eugene
—— Eugenio, Prince of. *See* Carignano
—— Prince Thomas of, and France, IV 593, 600; returns to Piedmont, 601; 656; 697
Savoy-Nemours. *See* Nemours
Sawbridge, John, Lord Mayor of London, VI 465; VIII 755
Saxe-Altenburg, Frederick William, Duke of, III 712, 714
—— George, Duke of (1848–53), XI 150
—— Joseph, Duke of (1834–48), XI 150
Saxe-Coburg, Princes of, X 343
—— Prince Augustus of, XII 410
Saxe-Coburg-Gotha, and Prussia, XI 228; and Schleswig-Holstein, 438
—— Alfred, Prince, Duke of Edinburgh, Duke of, and Greek throne, XI 641; XII 408; 467
—— Ernest I, Duke of, at Congress of Vienna, IX 583
—— Ernest II, Duke of (born 1818), XI 143; 224; 397

Saxe-Coburg-Gotha, Ferdinand, Prince of (born 1816). *See* Ferdinand
—— Leopold, Prince of (born 1824), XI 33; 553 sqq.
—— Leopold, Prince of (born 1790). *See* Leopold, King of the Belgians
Saxe-Coburg-Saalfeld, Ferdinand, Prince of, at Congress of Vienna, IX 583
—— Prince Frederick Josias of, VIII 268, 325 sq., 347, 415; defeats French at the Roer, 419; at Neerwinden, 420 sq.; at Valenciennes, 429 sq.; at Fleurus, 435 sq.
Saxe-Gotha, extinction of line of, X 343
—— John Frederick, Duke of, III 150; and Grumbach troubles, 151, 163
Saxe-Hildburghausen, Prince Joseph of, VI 263 sq.; 265; 267 sq.
Saxe-Lauenburg, Duke Frederick of (d. 1586), III 708
—— Duke Henry of, Archbishop of Bremen. *See* Bremen
Saxe-Teschen, Albert Casimir, Duke of, VI 649; Viceroy of Austrian Netherlands, VIII 318 sq.; 415 sqq.
—— Duchess Maria Christina of (wife of above), VI 649; 651; VIII 318 sq.
Saxe-Weimar, Duke Bernard of, and Margrave George Frederick of Baden, IV 80; 102; in Netherlands, 103; taken into French pay, 148; 197; at Leipzig Convention, 200; 204; 206; takes Mannheim, 208; holds Swabia, 216; 219; commands Gustavus' army, 221; later years of, *see* Chap. VII; 365; 367; compact between French and, 368 sq.; 370 sqq.; 373 sq.; before Breisach, 375 sqq.; 378 sq.; death of, 380; army of, 381 sqq.; 392; 418; 682; 686
—— Prince Bernard of, at Frasnes, IX 626–7; at Waterloo, 632
—— Duke Ernest the Pious of, IV 80; acts as Regent in Franconia, 229
—— Duke Frederick of, with Mansfeld, IV 80; prisoner at Stadtlohn, 86
—— Duke John of, sons of, IV 80; and Gustavus Adolphus, 195, 207
—— Duke John Ernest of, in the Netherlands, IV 80, 96; joins Mansfeld, 97 sq.; Bernard and, 376; 381
—— Duke John Frederick of, insane, IV 227
—— John William, Duke of, III 10, 173, 179
—— Karl August, Grand-Duke of, X 343; and Diet, 346 sq.; and University of Jena, 364; liberalism of, 366; and tariff reform, 373; 389; XI 150
—— Duke William of, with Mansfeld, IV 80 sq.; under Christian of Halberstadt, 86; at Leipzig Convention, 200; 207; 217; 219; and John George, 230; 247; Peace of Prague and, 255; 365; joins the Imperialists, 366; 381
Saxony, II 237, 252; (Ernestine), invaded by Maurice and Ferdinand (1546), 257;

III 142; troubles in, 712; Jesuits in, 723; Ernestine line of, 704; claim of, on Jülich-Cleves, 716; IV 4; and Protestant hegemony, 5; 10; 12 sqq.; and Peace of Prague, 253, 255, 417; sufferings of, during War, 418 sq.; native industries in, 421; and Austria, 430; alliance of, with France, V 33; Swedish army in, 417; 420; and Great Northern War, 586 sqq.; Denmark and, 609; and the third anti-Swedish league, 611; and Brandenburg, 618 sq., 623, 627; 666; 743; and Seven Years' War, Vol. VI, Chap. IX *passim*; 33; and War of the Polish Succession, 196 sq.; under Count von Brühl, 198; 206; army of, 213; and Pragmatic Sanction, 228, 310; and War of the Austrian Succession, 231, 250; 235; 243; Russia and, 315; Frederick the Great declares war against, 317; 318; 320; Prussian invasion of (1756), 321, 326, 338 sq., 403; 632; and Polish Succession, 665, VIII 522, 527, 529; later relations of Prussia and, VI 703 sqq.; and Peace of Teschen, 707; 720; 725; 734; makes peace with France (1795), VIII 442; Prussian troops in, IX 273; Kottbus assigned to, 292; French troops in, 347; invaded by Duke Ferdinand of Brunswick-Oels, 357; possibilities in (1813), 482; Metternich and, 507; protection of, by Napoleon, 516; proposed Prussian annexation of, 579; 593 sqq.; and Congress of Vienna, 587; 609, 615; duchy of, acquired by Prussia, 657; kingdom of, and Germanic Confederation, X 344; Grandducal and Ducal Houses of, *ib.*; and Prussia, 353; constitutional system of, 363; 364; constitutional reforms in, 374; and the *Zollverein*, 373, 378 sq., XI 54, 443; industrial undertakings in, X 732, 744, 751, 753 sq., 757; banking in, 746; agriculture in, 750; political conditions in, XI 59 sq.; revolutionary movement in, 148 sq.; 160; tumults in, 192; 200; and Frankfort Constitution, 218; 219; and German union, 220 sq., 408; and Schleswig-Holstein, 337; reaction in, 397; and Austro-Prussian War, 452; 454 sq.; and Austro-German Alliance, XII 145; 150

Saxony, Dukes of:—
—— Albert of Meissen (founder of the Albertine line), I 297, 449 sq., 452 sq.
—— George (son of Albert of Meissen, d. 1539), I 453; 475; II 135, 148, 156, 163, 169, 170, 186, 195, 201, 215, 220; joins League of Nürnberg, 235; death of (1539), 237; 252
—— Henry (d. 1541), II 237, 252
—— Henry the Lion, V 618; VI 2
—— Henry the Proud, V 618
Saxony, Electors of:—
—— Augustus, II 275; V 627
—— Christian II, IV 2

Saxony, Electors of (*contd.*):—
—— Ernest (founder of the Ernestine line), I 297
—— Frederick I the Valiant, I 297
—— Frederick III the Wise, I 297, 310, 316, 321; II 41, 116, 121, 132, 147, 155 sqq., 158, 166, 169, 186, 189, 194
—— Frederick Augustus I. *See* Augustus II, King of Poland
—— Frederick Augustus II. *See* Augustus III, King of Poland
—— Frederick Augustus III. *See* Frederick Augustus, King of Saxony
—— Frederick Christian, VI 199
—— John, II 169, 186; Peasants' Rising and, 189; Protest signed by, 205; at Augsburg, 211, 213; at Schmalkalden, 215
—— John Frederick, the Magnanimous, II 211, 233–45; draws up "Wittenberg Reformation," 250; 253, 257; defends electorate against Maurice, 258; successes of, 259; taken prisoner at Mühlberg, 260 sqq.; 286
—— John George I, IV 2 sq.; 9; agrees to succession of Ferdinand II, 17; 22; 28 sq.; joins Ferdinand, 33 sqq.; 68; 73; 83; 92; mediator at Brunswick, 96; 110; and Edict of Restitution, 111 sqq.; quiescence of, 195, 197 sq.; Convention of Leipzig and, 200; 201; Magdeburg and, 202; 204 sqq.; and Gustavus Adolphus of, 205 sqq.; in Bohemia, 209; 211; 213; 215; 220 sq.; Oxenstierna and, 224 sq.; Heilbronn Alliance and, 226; 230; 232; 233; 234 sqq.; at Leitmeritz, 243; makes peace with Emperor Ferdinand II, 251; at Prague, 252; Peace of Prague and, 254 sq., 395; 366; at Wittstock, 372; and French, 390; and Treaty of Westphalia, 408, 410
—— John George III, V 55; 244; 359; in Vienna, 362
—— Maurice, II 86, 241 sqq., 252–75; invades Electorate, 257; deserts Charles V, 269; death of, 275; V 627
Saxony, Agnes (of Hesse), Duchess of (consort of Maurice of Saxony), II 252
—— Prince Antony of, at the Congress of Vienna, IX 582
—— Duke Augustus of, Administrator of Magdeburg, IV 407, V 644
—— Duke Frederick of (d. 1511), V 634
—— Maria Antonia Walpurgis, Electress of, VI 199
—— Princess Mary of, VI 316
—— Maurice, Count of (Maurice de Saxe), Marshal of France, V 555; VI 110 sq.; 232; in the Low Countries, 239 sq., 242, 246 sqq.; 318; 362; 640
—— Sibylla (of Cleves), Electress of, II 237
—— Prince Xavier of, VI 354
Say, Léon, French politician, XII 107; 112; 130

Saye and Sele, William Fiennes, 1st Viscount, refuses shipmoney, IV 283 sq.; V 93; land in New England granted to, VII 18, 21

Sayers, Dr Frank, nonconformist, and French Revolution, VIII 764

Sayf ad-Din, Sultan of Egypt, I 89

Sayle, William, Governor of South Carolina, VII 36

Sayn-Wittgenstein, Count John von, representative of Frederick William of Brandenburg at Congress of Münster, IV 401

—— Louis Adolph. *See* Wittgenstein

Sazónoff, assassinates Plehve, XII 346

Scala, Antonio della, Lord of Verona, I 265

—— Can Grande della, Lord of Verona, I 262

—— Martino della, Lord of Verona, I 262

Scales, Edward Woodville, Lord, I 394, 466

Scaliger, Joseph, II 718; III 59 sq.; IV 717; XII 816; 844

Scalvini, Giovita, X 126

Scanderbeg (George Castriotes), Albanian chief, I 70 sq., 100

Scandinavia, Vol. IV, Chap. XX; (1815–70), Vol. XI, Chap. XXIV; (1872–1909), Vol. XII, Chap. XI. *See also* Norway, Sweden, *and* Denmark

Scania, IV 560 sq.; the Swedes and, 571; Treaty of Roeskilde and, 586; 590 sq.; war of (1675–9), V 562, 569 sq., 578 sq.; under Swedish rule, 577; 583; Danish invasion of (1709), 603; 610; 612; Denmark and, VI 735; Swedish troops in, XI 683

Scarborough, British vessels captured by Paul Jones off (1778), VII 220

—— Richard Lumley, 1st Earl of (Lord Lumley), V 242

—— Richard Lumley-Saunderson, 4th Earl of, VI 431

Scariffholis, O'Neill's army destroyed at (1650), IV 534

Scarlett, Sir James Yorke, general, XI 319

Scarron, Madame. *See* Maintenon, Marquise de

—— Paul, V 20

Schack-Staffeldt, Adolph Wilhelm, Danish poet, XI 697

Schadow-Godenhaus, Friedrich W., German painter, X 151

Schäffle, Albert Eberhard Frederic, XII 155; Austrian Minister of Commerce, 187

Schaep, Gerard, Dutch envoy to England, V 139

Schaepman, H., Dutch politician, XII 246

Schärtlin zu Burtenbach, Sebastian, commander under Schmalkaldic League, II 255 sq., 270

Schässburg. *See* Segesvár

Schäufelein, Hans Leonard, German engraver, I 326

Schafarik. *See* Šafařík

Schaffgotsch, Hans Ulrich, Freiherr von, general, imprisonment of, IV 242

Schaffhausen, joins Swiss Confederacy (1501), I 308; IX 57; rising at, 95; Canton of, XI 234; 240

Schanfig, Catholic district of, IV 43

Schappeler, Christoph, Zwinglian preacher at Memmingen, II 160, 177, 179

Scharding, Austrians defeated at (1703), V 407; Bavarian repulse at, VI 233; 236

Scharnhorst, Gerhard Johann David von, Prussian general, VIII 774; IX 275; 328; reforms of, 331–2; life of, 332 sqq.; favours Austrian alliance, 344; recall of, 510; in Silesia, 514 sqq.; death of, 523; XI 579

Schatzlar, Pass of, Prussian army at, VI 242

Schaub, Sir Luke, diplomatist, VI 30 sq.

Schauenburg, Count Anton von, III 155

Schaumann, Eugene, assassinates Bóbrikoff, XII 335

Schaumberg, Count Adolf of, II 259

Schaumburg, Haimbald von, Imperial commander at Garz, IV 196; 199

Schaumburg-Lippe, Georg, Prince von, X 373

Schawli, Alexander and Frederick William at, IX 291

Scheele, Karl Wilhelm, and photography, XII 783

Scheffel, Joseph Victor von, German poet, XI 414; 417; 420

Scheffer, Count Carl Fredrik, Swedish statesman, VI 762 sq.; 767

—— Friedrich H. E. L., Hesse-Cassel Minister, XI 146

Scheldt river, VI 247; 470; navigation of, 641 sqq.; 652; Joseph II and opening of, VIII 277, 279, 281, 312, 318; the French and opening of, 300 sqq., 304; British expedition to (1809), IX 358; Peace of Paris and, 614–5; opened to Belgian trade, X 522, 542, 745; blockaded (1832), 543; XI 669; abolition of tolls on, 672

Schelling, Friedrich Wilhelm von, II 714; VIII 773; X 382; 401; 404; 410; 706

Schenck von Nydeggen, Martin, III 711 sq.

Schenectady, fortified, VII 42; massacre at, 45; destroyed by the French (1690), 90

Schenk, Burchard von, II 380

Schenkendorf, Max von, X 403

Schepper, Cornelius, Ferdinand's ambassador in Constantinople, III 108–9

Scherbatoff, Prince, VI 688

—— Prince, Governor-General of Moscow, XI 270

Scherenburg, Rudolf von, Bishop of Würzburg. *See* Würzburg

Schérer, Barthélemy-L.-J., VIII 436, 444; Minister of War, 508, 518; commands the Army of Italy, *ib.*, 562 sqq.; and the war of 1799, 656, 670

Scherer, Edmond-Henri-Adolphe, XI 525

Scherpe Resolutie, The (1617), III 650

Schets, Gaspar, Seigneur de Grobbendonck. *See* Grobbendonck

Scheuchzer, Jean-Jacques, naturalist, v 738
Scheurer-Kestner, and the Dreyfus affair, xii 120
Scheurl, Christoph, German priest, ii 134
Scheveling, Eberhard, iv 791
Scheveningen, naval action off (1653), iv 476, 480 sq.; Charles II sails from, v 148
Schiedlow, Austrian forces near, vi 292
Schieringers, The, Frisian faction, i 421
Schifer (Severus), iii 166
Schill, Friedrich von, patriotic attempt of (1809), ix 335; in Westphalia, 337; 356; takes Stralsund, 357
Schiller, Johann Christoph Friedrich von, vi 827; 830 sq.; 834; viii 773 sq.; x 100; Italian translations of dramas of, 124; 383; *Die Räuber*, 386, 388 sq.; *Don Carlos*, 389 sq.; the poetic development of, 390 sq.; and Goethe, 390 sqq.; 400; 407 sq.; 411; 706; 710; xi 411; 413; 415 sq., 423 sq.
Schimmelmann, Henrik Karl, Baron, vi 751
Schimmelpenninck, Roger Jean, Count, Grand Pensionary of Holland, viii 787, ix 267; Dutch ambassador, 77; xi 663
Schinner, Matthias, Cardinal of Sion, i 135, 138, 141, 487; ii 309, 315
Schippenbeil, Convention of Bartenstein signed at (1807), ix 287
Schism Act, Bolingbroke's (1714), v 474 sq.
Schlachter's Nek, affair of, xi 779
Schlegel, August Wilhelm von, German critic, ix 427; x 398 sqq.; in Austria, 406; 407; xii 818
—— Elias, x 396
—— K. W. Friedrich von, viii 776, 790; x 357; 363; conversion of, to Rome, 380; 396; 398 sqq.; 403; 407; 410 sq.; xi 49; xii 818; 845
Schleiermacher, Frederick Ernest Daniel, viii 776; teacher of theology at Berlin University, ix 327; x 370; 382, 401, 404
Schleiz, Prussian defeat at (1806), ix 275
Schleswig, iv 101 sq.; restored to Denmark, 109; Denmark and, v 550 sq., 582 sq., vi 37, 736; 661; 743; xii 290 sq.
—— Christian, Duke of. *See* Christian III of Denmark
Schleswig-Holstein, Frederick II and, iv 562; question of, 563 sq.; Denmark and, v 53 sq., 579; 581; 610; vi 741 sq.; 753; union of, with Denmark, x 343, 354; dispute of, with the King of Denmark, 363, 370; xi 38; Prussia and, 64, 160 sqq.; anti-Danish rising in, 161 sq.; the *Vorparlament* and, 163; the National Assembly and, 167; 194; the war in, 224 sq., 440 sqq., 695; and the succession question, 226 sq.; 231 sqq.; Great Britain and, 337 sq.; 412; the Powers and, 436 sqq.; new Constitution for, 437 sq.; ceded by Denmark, 442, 696; Austro-Prussian administration of, 442

sqq.; 454; 477; 479; 537; the national movement in, 692 sqq.; Mommsen and, xii 844
Schleswig-Holstein, Paul, Duke of. *See* Paul I, Tsar
Schleswig-Holstein-Augustenburg, Prince Christian Augustus of, ix 323
Schleswig-Holstein-Noer, Frederick, Hereditary Prince of, xi 161
Schlettstadt, ceded to the French, iv 143 sq.
Schley, Winfield Scott, American commodore, vii 679 sq.
Schleyer, Johannes von, Würtemberg statesman, xi 148
Schlick, Count Heinrich, captures Danish horse, iv 102; Wallenstein and, 238; 392
—— Count, defeats General Meszáros (1849), xi 204; 205 sq.
—— General, defeated at Scharding (1703), v 407
Schlieff, Colonel Anton von, imprisoned, iv 242
Schliemann, Heinrich, researches of, xii 845
Schlippenbach, General, defeat of, v 590
Schlitz-Görtz, Baron Friedrich Wilhelm von, Hanoverian statesman, vi 20
Schlözer, August Ludwig, German historian, viii 772 sqq.; xii 817
Schlosser, Friedrich Christoph, German historian, xii 826 sq.; 849
Schlüsselburg, v 553; capture of (1702), 590; prison of, vi 660 sq.; 680; fortress, Lukasinski imprisoned in, x 454
Schlumberger, Gustave L., historian, xii 845
Schmalkalden, meeting of Protestant Princes at (1530), ii 214 sq.
—— League of, ii 26, 67; formed (1532), 215 sqq.; power of, in N. Germany, 217 sq.; Diet of (1535), 233, 235, 256; split in, 242; Henry of Brunswick and, 243; 251; internal weakness of, 252; Diet of (1545), 253 sq., 255; War of (1546), 256 sq., iii 145, 147, v 626; iii 741
Schmalz, T. A. H., Rector of Berlin University, ix 327; x 352; 364
Schmedding, John Henry, ix 201
Schmerling, Anton, Baron von, Austrian statesman, xi 155; 162; 166; 171; 188; and the execution of Blum, 189; and the Frankfort Assembly, 196; Ministry of, 404 sq.; and German unity, 408; Minister of the Interior, 444; xii 178; and Hungary, 180 sqq.; resigns, 182; 184; 188 sq.; 192; electoral system of, 196 sq.; 205
Schmettau, Privy Councillor von, v 661
Schmid, Felix, Burgomaster of Zurich, ii 322
Schmidt, Michael Ignaz, German historian, xii 817
—— Austrian general, viii 655
—— Lieutenant, and Sevastopol mutiny, xii 362
Schmitt, President of Austrian *Reichstag*, xi 173

Schmoller, Gustav, German economist, xii 155; 850

Schmottseifen, Prussian camp at, vi 292

Schnaebele, arrest of, xii 112

Schneckenburger, Max, *Die Wacht am Rhein*, x 379; xi 49; 412

Schneider, John George (Eulogius), viii 775

Schnepf, Erhard, Lutheran theologian, ii 234; driven into exile, 265

Schoelcher, Victor, French politician, xi 136

Schön, Theodor von, vi 209; ix 330–1; Chief President of East Prussia, xi 53

Schönborn, John Philip von. *See* Mainz

Schönbrunn, attempt to assassinate Napoleon at (1809), ix 139; Imperial decree issued from, 196; Napoleon takes up residence at, 257; receives Haugwitz at, 262; Peace of, *or* of Vienna (1809), 337, 339, 356, 359, 486; discussions at (1805), 364; xi 179; 182; the Emperor leaves, 186; Jellačić at, 187; 188

Schönefeld, Marmont at (1813), ix 539

Schönfeld, Prussian general, vi 656

Schönwalde, Frederick William II at, viii 293

Schofield, John McAllister, American general, vii 520, 524, 528, 530

Scholastic Philosophy, decline of, i 532; influence of, in 13th century, 536

Schomberg, Charles de, Duke of Hallinn, Marshal of France, in Catalonia, iv 600

—— Frederick Herman, Duke of, Marshal of France, in Portugal, iv 661 sq.; v 34; in England, 209; 244; 246; in Ireland, 312 sqq.; death of, 314; 655; 660

—— Comte Henri de, Marshal of France, defeats Gaston in Lorraine, iv 140

—— Nicholas von. *See* Capua, Archbishop of

Schoockius, Martin, iv 788

Schools, monastic, in general, i 533 sqq.; of Charles the Great, 535 sq.; of Brethren of the Common Life (*especially* Deventer), and of Windesem Congregations, 435 sqq.; 627 sqq.; the Renaissance and, Chap. xvi, The Classical Renaissance, *passim*, *especially* 556 sqq., 574, and for English schools, 581 sq.; German, in the pre-Reformation period, 637 sq.; Italian, of the same period, 649; later:—Belgian, religious instruction in, xi 669 sq., 671 sq.; attempt to secularise education in, xii 251 sqq.: in Canada, x 695: in China, xii 522: Danish, spread of, 292: Egyptian, and Mehemet Ali, 453 sq.: English, associations for the advancement of elementary education (1810–13), ix 692; and Education Acts of 1870–2, xii 24 sq., 733; Act of 1902, 57 sqq.; better administration of, 752 sq.: in Empire, after Thirty Years' War, iv 424 sq.: French, under First Empire, ix 126 sqq.; law of 1833 concerning, x 490; struggle concerning, from 1840, xi 26 sqq.; and the "Falloux'

Act," 129 sqq.; under Napoleon III, 297; and clerical reaction, xii 114; and policy of Third Republic, 117 sq.: in India, under Lord Ripon, 476: Irish, Act of 1831, 71: Polish, after 1815, x 449; under Russia, after 1863, xii 336 sq.; Polish language in, 353: Prussian, under Frederick William I, vi 225: Russian, founded under Peter the Great, v 529; from 1802–3, x 430; under Alexander II, xi 624 sq.; and Count Dmitry Tolstoi, xii 298 sq.; 315 sq.; and Provincial Zemstvo Board of Moscow, 327; and Zemstva generally, 330; in Baltic Provinces, 336; for Jews, 340: in Spain, just before absolutist reaction, x 229: Swiss, of Pestalozzi, ix 427; of 19th century, xi 260 sq.

Schooneveld, sea-fight at (1673), v 161, 194; 195

Schoonhoven, taken by the Spaniards (1575), iii 241

Schooten, Franciscus van, v 711

Schopenhauer, Arthur, x 410

Schoppe, Caspar, and Giordano Bruno, ii 708; attacks the Jesuits, iv 113

Schorch, Grisons leader, at Innsbruck, iv 62

Schorlemer, Freiherr von, German politician, xii 147

Schott, Andreas, editor of *Bibliotheca Patrum*, i 618

Schouten, Willem C. van, voyages of, iv 713

Schouwen, island of, taken by the Spaniards (1575), iii 242, 244

Schrader, Clemens, and Syllabus, xi 715

—— Hanoverian envoy to Sweden, vi 34

Schröder, Andreas, Baron von, Russian ambassador at Dresden, xi 232

Schroeder, General, defeated at Turnhout, vi 652

Schröderheim, Elis, Swedish vicar-general, vi 776

Schrötter, Prussian Minister, ix 334

Schubart, Christian F. D., poet, viii 772 sq.

Schüpfheim, fight near, xi 251

Schürer, Emil, German historian, xii 847

Schütte, Anton, Austrian agitator, xi 174

Schütz, Baron Georg Wilhelm Helvig von, Hanoverian envoy in London, vi 15 sq.

—— Baron Ludwig Justus von, vi 4; Hanoverian envoy in London, 9; 12

Schulenburg, Friedrich Albrecht, Count von der, at Congress of Vienna, ix 587

—— Ehrengard Melusina von der. *See* Kendal, Duchess of

—— Count Matthias Johann von, General, in Poland, v 594

Schulin, Johann Sigismund, Danish statesman, vi 740; 742

Schulte, Johann Friedrich von, German canonist, xii 848

Schulz, General, defeats Tökölyi, v 366

Schulze-Delitzsch, Franz Herman, German economist and politician, xii 146; 742

Schumacher, Peter. *See* Griffenfeld

Schurf, Jerome, II 117

Schurz, Carl, American statesman, VII 653

Schusterinsel, occupied by French, VI 623

Schutt, island of, Montecuculi in, V 346

Schuurman, Anna Maria van, IV 720; V 756

Schwabach, Protestant Congress at (1529), II 207; Articles of (1529), 209 sqq.

Schwach, Konrad Nicolai, Norwegian poet, XI 700

Schwäbisch Hall, meetings of Union at, III 689, 730, 731

Schwan, Theodore, American general, VII 680

Schwarz, Danish missionary, influence of, IX 724

Schwarzach, battle at (1553), II 275

Schwarzburg-Rudolstadt, and Germanic Confederation, X 344; 373

Schwarzburg-Sondershausen, and Germanic Confederation, X 344; tariff-treaty of, with Prussia, 372; the revolutionary movement in, XI 149

—— Günther, Prince of, XI 149

Schwarzenberg, Count Adam zu, Brandenburg Minister, IV 100, 201, 366; death of, 384; V 637; 640; 642

—— Charles, Prince, XI 217

—— Felix, Prince, Austrian Foreign Minister, XI 92; 95; 183; Ministry of, 189 sq.; and Frankfort Assembly, 196 sq.; 200; 206; and Russian intervention, 208 sq.; 216 sq.; and Prussia, 218, 220; and Germanic Confederation, 222 sq.; 224; and Prussia, 227 sqq.; and Hesse-Cassel crisis, 228 sqq.; at Dresden Conferences, 232 sq.; reactionary policy of, 393 sq.; 395; 398; and Hungary, 398 sq.; death of, 215, 394

—— Frederick, Prince, XI 249

—— Karl Philipp, Prince von, IX 344; commands Austrian troops, 488; retires to Brest, 499; at Warsaw, 511; in Silesia, 514; in Bohemia, 523; 525; at Dresden, 526–7; effect of Kulm on, 528; hesitation of, 531 sqq.; at Leipzig, 536 sqq.; 543; and invasion of France, 545 sqq.; in Paris, 556; X 116; 357

—— Otto Henry, Count of, III 252

Schwarzwald, desolation of the, IV 418

Schwechat, battle at, XI 189, 202 sq.

Schwedt, Gustavus Adolphus at, IV 199; occupied by Russians, V 280, 286

Schwegler, Friedrich Carl Albert, German historian, XII 821; 843

Schweidnitz, siege of, VI 264; 273; 275 sq.; 297; 299; 328

Schweinfurt, Gustavus Adolphus at, IV 213

Schweinfurth, Georg, African explorer, XII 811

Schwendi, Lazarus, Baron von (commissioner of Charles V), II 272; III 170

Schwerin, bishopric of, recovered by Rome, IV 112; ceded to Mecklenburg-Schwerin, 408

—— Count Henry of, II 599

—— Count Kurt Christoph, Prussian field-marshal, VI 227; 248; 256 sqq.; death of, 259

—— Count Maximilian von, Prussian statesman, XI 58; 159; Minister of the Interior, 406

—— Freiherr Otto von, Brandenburg statesman, V 642; 655

—— Count Otto von (the younger), V 649 sq.

—— Duke of. *See* Mecklenburg-Schwerin

—— Provost, Swedish financier, XI 684 sq.

Schwiebus Circle, Elector of Brandenburg and, V 654; 655; 658 sq.

Schwyz, canton of, rises against Louis XII, I 136; dissatisfaction in, 141; VI 613; in 1766, 625; revolt in (1798), VIII 640; government of, XI 238; 239; disturbances in, 242; 243; reunited, 245; and the Aargau monasteries, 247; 251

Science, in general, effect of discovery of New World upon, I 62 sq.; under Cosimo de' Medici, III 394; Spanish contributions to, in late 15th and early 16th centuries, 548; advance of, in early 17th century, IV 777 sqq.; Descartes and, 778 sqq.; Vol. V, Chap. XXIII, European Science in the 17th and earlier years of the 18th centuries; in France, under the First Empire, IX 133; in Italy, after the French Revolution, X 128 sq.; scientific Congresses from 1839–47 and political propaganda, XI 68 sq.; in Switzerland, in 19th century, 260 sq.; Hungarian Academy of (1825), 425 sq.; Vol. XII, Chap. XXIV, 766–91

Scilly Islands, reduction of, IV 466; Wesley in, VI 83

Scio, Turkish defeat off, VI 673; massacre at (1822), X 185, 186

Scioppius. *See* Schoppe, Caspar

Sclopis, Count Federigo, *History of Legislation*, XII 842

Scodra. *See* Skutari

Soolnek, taken by Turks (1552), III 123; acquired by Solyman II, 124

Scone, Charles II crowned at (1651), IV 510

Scory, John, Bishop of Chichester, II 490, 502, 521, 567, 572

Scot, Thomas, Secretary of State, IV 548; 556 sq.

Scotland [*for affairs of Great Britain in common see* England], and England, II 419–22; 453–62, 548; attempted union of 1547, 487; France and, 499, 574 sq.; the Reformation in, Chap. XVI *passim*; condition of, in 1560, 551; rebellion in (1559), 572 sq.; Calvinism in, III 260 sqq.; Catholicism in, 262 sq., 271, 492; and Mary Stewart, Chap. VIII *passim*; Guise's

scheme of invasion of, 503; Kirk of, 549 sqq.; political and ecclesiastical changes in, 550 sqq.; and England, 549, 555 sq.; *see also* James VI of Scotland and I of England; IV 283 sqq.; and Strafford, 288; Charles I in, 293 sqq.; 297; 301; 315; Parliamentary negotiations with, 316 sq.; Solemn League and Covenant and, 318; 357; 327 sq.; 333; and France, 338; 342; Royalism in, 349; Cromwell in, 350; Church of, 359; Charles II proclaimed in (1649), 435; subjugated by Monck, 436; representation of, 437, 440; "Instrument of Government" and, 438; 446; revenue of, 457; from accession of Charles I to Restoration, *see* Chap. XVII; 522; opposes army, 545; Monck and, 546 sq., 552; 554; 1660-1707, Vol. v, Chap. X (2); and the Restoration, 103; effect of Dutch War in, 110; risings in, 187, 225; James II and, 312; 465; 474; 612; Jacobitism and Union in, Vol. VI, Chap. III *passim*; 34; Wesley in, 83, 86; 169; Jacobite rising in, 243; 469; 476; intellectual activity of, VIII 769 sqq.; parliamentary representation in, x 606 sq.; municipal reform in, 670; vernacular poetry of, 701; agriculture in, 739 sq.; banking in, 744; Disruption in, XI 5 sqq., 18; XII 1; Education Act (1872) in, 25; 27; Liberalism in, 31; parliamentary representation of, 42; Secretaryship for, established, *ib.*; and disestablishment, 49; Unionist majority in, 53; 762 sq.

Scott, Edmund, IV 734
—— John, Earl of Eldon. *See* Eldon
—— Sir John, Judicial Adviser in Egypt, XII 450
—— Robert Falcon, Antarctic expedition of, XII 815
—— Sir Walter, VI 831 sqq.; and *Edinburgh Review*, IX 687; x 102; literary influence of, 402; 708; poetry of, 716 sq.; novels of, 717, 719, 724, XII 834; x 722; influence of, upon continental literature, 725 sq.; XI 355; 358; 361; 426; influence of, on French literature, 519, 523; *Quentin Durward*, XII 824; *Ivanhoe*, 830
—— Sir William. *See* Stowell, Lord
—— Winfield, American general, in Mexico, VII 396 sq., 419; 447, 455 sq., 465, 467; retirement of, 468; 477
—— Colonel, at Nágpur, XI 726
Scotti, Marquis, Parmesan envoy to Spain, VI 139
Scott-Moncrieff, Sir Colin, and the Nile Barrage, XII 446
Scribe, Augustin-Eugène, dramatist, XI 515 sq.
Scriptoris, Paul, professor at Tübingen, I 682
Scripture and tradition, discussed at the Council of Trent, II 665 sq. *See also* Bible, New Testament, etc.

Scroggs, Sir William, Lord Chief Justice, v 225
Scrooby, flight of Nonconformists from (1606), VII 12
Scrope, George J. Poulett, x 655
Scudéry, Madeleine de, x 718; 724
Scully, Dennis, and the movement for Catholic emancipation, x 629 sq.; 631 sq.
Scultetus, Abraham, IV 5; at Prague, 6; 31
Scutari. *See* Skutari
Seabury, Samuel (Bishop of Connecticut), legal arguments of, Vol. VII, Chap. VI *passim*
Seafield, James Ogilvy, 1st Earl of, Lord Chancellor of Scotland, v 299
Seaforth, William Mackenzie, 5th Earl of, VI 100; 102 sq.; 105
Sebald, Carl Fredrik, Gustavus III and, VI 769
Sebastian, King of Portugal, III 499
Sebastiani, François-Horace-Bastien, Comte, Marshal of France, IX 103; reports on Egypt, 211; brings about rupture between Russia and Turkey, 281; at Constantinople, 388; and La Mancha, 449; defeats Cartaojal, 450; and Victor, 451; and Venegas, 452 sqq.; at Granada and Malaga, 457; x 120; 476; 478; supports Louis-Philippe, 480; 489; and Algiers, 502; ambassador in London, 565
—— Jean-André-Tiburce, Vicomte, French general, XI 97; 100
Sebottendorf van der Rose, Karl Philipp, Baron, Austrian lieutenant field-marshal, VIII 558, 568 sq.
Sechelles, Condé's envoy in England, II 584
Seckendorf, Friedrich Heinrich, Count von, Austrian field-marshal, VI 210 sq.; 236; 238; in Bavaria, 241 sq.
Secretan, Louis, IX 97
Sects, growth and persecution of, in Germany, II 223 sq. *See (for England)*, Nonconformists, *also* Vaudois, etc.
Sécus, Frédéric, Baron de, x 536
Sedaine, Michel-Jean, French dramatic poet, v 70; VI 823; VIII 725
Sedan, Bouillon retires to, III 681; Elector Palatine at, IV 81; 150; compensation for, 616; French army at (1792), VIII 238, 407, 409; capitulation of, IX 758; XI 465; battle of, 496, 544, 595, 597 sq., 600 sq., 612, XII 91, 187, 191, 213
Seddon, James A., Confederate Secretary of War, VII 605
Sedgmoor, battle of (1685), v 232
Sedlnitzky, Josef, Count, chief of police in Vienna, x 357; XI 154
Seebohm, Frederic, historian, XII 835; 850
Seehaufen, The (bands of rebellious peasants), II 179
Seeley, Sir John Robert, historian, XI 363; writings of, XII 840 sq.
Séez, Jean Bertaut, Bishop of, III 71
Sega, Philip. *See* Plasencia, Bishop of
Segesvár, battle of, XI 211, 428

Segovia, Philip at, III 208; Montigny imprisoned at, 228; depopulation of, v 376; Ripperdá at, VI 143; Estremaduran army sent to, IX 444
—— Martin Perez Ayala, Bishop of, II 680
Séguier, Antoine-Jean-Matthieu, Baron, IX 166
—— Antoine-Louis, French advocate-general, III 59; VIII 106
—— Pierre, President of the Parliament of Paris, II 294; III 59
—— Pierre, Chancellor of France (1643), IV 593
Ségur, Louis-Philippe, Comte de, French ambassador at St Petersburg (1768), VI 697
—— Louis-Philippe, Comte de, Grand Master of Ceremonies (1805), IX 111
—— Philippe-Henri, Marquis de, Minister of War, VIII 95 sq., 107, 402
Segur d'Aguesseau, Joseph-Paul-Louis, XI 474
Ségur-Pardailhan, emissary of Navarre, III 36, 708, 710
Sehested, Hannibal, Norway under, IV 572; 573 sq.
Seicentisti, The, and French influence in Italy, v 69
Seignelay, Jean-Baptiste Colbert (the elder), Marquis of. *See* Colbert
—— Jean-Baptiste Colbert (the younger), Marquis of, French Minister of Marine, v 59; VII 87, 109
Seistan, Sher Ali and, XII 464; Russia and, 492; 800
Seklucyan, Jan, III 74
Selangor, sultanate of, XII 532 sq.
Selborne, Roundell Palmer, 1st Earl of, Lord Chancellor, XII 27
—— William Waldegrave Palmer, 2nd Earl of, in South Africa, XII 644
Selden, John, case of Darnel and, IV 267; 281; Root-and-Branch petition and, 292; VI 800
Self-denying Ordinance, The, IV 325 sqq.
Selim I (the Great), Ottoman Sultan (1512–20), I 84; conquests of, 90 sq., III 17; becomes Caliph, I 91; death of, 92, III 126; X 548
—— II, Ottoman Sultan, III 124, 127–8, 130 sqq., 136; death of (1574), 139, 170
—— III, Ottoman Sultan, VIII 294, 326; declares war on Russia, IX 235; 289, 293, 306; accession of, 385; organises his forces, 386–7; deposes the hospodars of Moldavia and Wallachia, 388; appeal of Tipu to, 723; X 171
—— Prince. *See* Jehángir, Moghul Emperor
Selimé, travellers at, XII 805; 813
Selkirk, Thomas Douglas, 5th Earl of, settlements in Red River valley attempted by, IX 747, XII 604; X 691
Sella, Quintino, Italian statesman, XI 537; Finance Minister, 543 sq.; XII 213; 215

Seller, Abednego, *History of Passive Obedience*, VI 807
Selling (*or* Sellyng), William Tilley of, Prior of Christchurch, Canterbury, I 491, 579, 598, 643
Selmer, Christian August, Norwegian statesman, XII 283 sq.
Selz, conferences at (1798), VIII 642, 644
Semblençay, Jacques de Beaune, Sieur de, French Minister of Finance, I 409 sq.; II 95 sq.
Semendria (Smederevo), besieged by the Turks (1454), I 69; captured (1458), 70, 72; reduced by Loudon, VIII 326; garrison at, XI 647
Semigallia, recognised as Polish fief, III 73
Semirechensk, province of, XI 631
Semler, Johann Salomo, New Testament studies of, XII 816
Semliki river, exploration on, XII 812
Semlin, taken by Solyman the Magnificent (1521), I 93; III 125
Semmes, Raphael, Confederate naval commander, VII 565 sq.
Sémonville, Charles-Louis Huguet, Marquis de, IX 89–90
—— French politician, VIII 677
Sempach, battle of, VI 617
Sempill, Francis, Jacobite, VI 109 sqq.
Senafé, Italian success at, XII 240
Senarcleus, Claud de, II 403
—— Louis de, Reformer, II 403
Sénart, Jules, XI 110; 118; 123
Sendai Bay, XI 860
Sendai, clan, XI 859
—— *daimiō* of, XI 836
Seneca, The. *See* Iroquois
Senece, Baron de, III 45
Seneff, battle of (1674), v 44, 161
Senegal, reconquered by France (1694), v 60; France and, VI 347; 428; 452; ceded to France, 464; Company of, 173, 533; gum trade of, VII 327; lost by France (1809), IX 240; XII 95; French administration in, 129; 130; 448; 812
—— river (Western Nile), discovery of, I 14; French settlements on, v 691 sq.; France and, XII 658 sq.; 805 sq.
Senegambia, the English in, VI 187
Senez, Jean Soanen, Bishop of, v 90
—— Captain, in Yunnan, XII 524
Senfft von Pilsach, Baron, XI 51
Seniavin, Russian admiral, IX 235; 304
Senior, William Nassau, X 660 sq.; economic principles of, 784; XI 1; and social reform, XII 745
Senlis, Council of (1240), I 668; Treaty of (1493), 111, 392, 451; fight at (1589), III 47
Sennar, Egyptian rule in, XII 439; 805 sq.
Senneterre, Count, French diplomatist, VI 35
Sennheim, Charles of Lorraine defeated at (1638), IV 377

Sens, Provincial Synod of (1528) suppresses heresy, II 284; slaughter of Huguenots at, III 1; Cossé at, 14; concessions of Henry IV to, 666
—— Louis-Henri de Pardaillan de Gondrin, Archbishop of, v 22
—— Archbishop of. *See* Loménie de Brienne
Seoul, Russia and, XII 507; 567; Chinese influence in, 570; 571; occupied by the Japanese, 580; 581
Sepoy rebellion, XI 745 sqq.
Septizonium, The, of Severus, destroyed by Sixtus V, III 443-4
Septuagint, Roman edition of, II 688; publication of, by Sixtus V, III 445
Serafino, Frà, of Ferrara, II 386
—— of Aquila, III 458
Seraphim, Archbishop of St Petersburg, x 423 sqq.; 452
Serbelloni, commands Spanish troops in Valtelline, IV 58, 61 sq.
—— Austrian general, VI 257; 260; 277
Serbs, XI 179; rising of, 180; 182; 206; 217; 285; and Austria, 399
Sercey, Pierre-C.-C.-Guillaume, Marquis de, French admiral, VIII 466
Sercognani, General, XI 72
Seres, policing of, XII 426
Sergent, Antoine-François, member of the Commune, VIII 225, 234, 300
Sergius, Grand Duke of Russia, XII 331; murdered, 350; 376
Seringapatam, attack on (1792), VI 475; captured (1799), IX 723
Seripando, Girolamo, Cardinal, II 676 sqq.; at the Council of Trent, 667 sq.
Sermoneta, Michelangelo Caetani, Duke of, XI 79
Serpa Pinto, Alexandre Alberto de la Rocha, Portuguese explorer, XII 663; 811
Serra, Correa da, botanist, VIII 783
—— de Pilar, and the siege of Oporto, x 328 sqq.
Serrano, Francisco, Duke of La Torre, Spanish statesman, XII 260; 262
—— Bedoya, Spanish general, XI 569
Serrano Dominguez, Francisco, Duke of La Torre, and Queen Isabel, XI 555 sq.; Captain-General of Granada, 556; banished, 568 sq.; elected Regent, 570
Serre, Comte Pierre-François-Hercule de, x 47 sq.; supports Government, 49 sq.; President of Chamber, 51; and electoral schemes, 51 sq.; and *Doctrinaires*, 52 sq.; 55; 57; Minister of Justice (1818), 57; and electoral proposals, 58, 60 sq.; 59; and Decazes Ministry, 61 sq.; health of, breaks down, 62; 63 sq.; defends new electoral proposals, 65 sqq.; and Royer-Collard, 67 sq.; 69; 70 sq.; 73; 103
Serres, Olivier de, I 525; III 70; his work on agriculture, 694
Serristori, Battista, Savonarolist, I 175
Sertini, agent of Italian *Carbonari*, x 213

Sérurier, Jean-M.-Philibert, French marshal, VIII 443 sqq., 564, 567, 656, 685
Servan de Gerbey, Joseph, Minister of War to Louis XVI, VIII 227, 406 sq.; recalled, 238, 412, 439
Servatus, Lupus, Latinist, I 535
Servetus (Miguel Serveto y Reves), II 375, 411 sq., 716; III 755; V 725 sq.
Servia, under Stephen Dušan, I 67; Mohammad I attacks, 68 sq.; conquest of, by Turks, 70; reconquered by Turks (1690), v 61; 367; Austrian invasion of, 368 sq.; Tartar invasion of, VI 673; 675; Joseph II and, VIII 324; claimed by Russia, IX 312; and Treaty of Bucharest, x 169; gains autonomous government, 172; (1858-69), XI 647 sq.; 284 sq.; Russia and, 312, 634, XII 342, 378; XI 533; 636; XIII 10; 32; 381; at war with Turkey, 383, 385 sqq.; 389; coalition Ministry in, 391; 392; and Treaty of Berlin, 396; at war with Bulgaria, 406 sq.; affairs in (1888-1906), 411 sqq.; 421; and Macedonia, 424; 427 sq.; Ranke's History of, 824
—— Alexander Karageorgevich, Prince of, XI 285; 647
—— Milan, Prince of. *See* Milan
—— Milosh Obrenovich, Prince of. *See* Milosh
Servicio, Spanish tax, II 99
Servien, Abel. *See* Sablé
Seslavin, Russian officer, guerrilla warfare of, IX 497
Seso, Carlos de, Reformer, II 407 sqq.
Sessa, fight at, XI 390
—— Luis de Corduba, Duke of, Imperial ambassador in Rome, II 21
—— Duke of, III 454
Sestri Levante, Alberoni at, VI 125
Seton Castle, Jacobites at, VI 99
Seton, John (Gardiner's chaplain), II 501
Settele, Giuseppe, Italian astronomer, x 137
Settembrini, Luigi, *Protesta del popolo delle due Sicilie*, XI 69, 79; 87; 380
Settimo, Ruggiero, resigns office, IX 384; Sicilian leader in 1848, 385; XI 80
Settle, Elkanah, English dramatist, v 134
Seume, Johann Gottfried, German humourist, x 403
Seurre, allotted to Mayenne, III 668
Sevastopol, VI 648; port of, 675 sq.; defences of, VIII 295, 313; 315; XI 316 sq.; siege of, 318 sq.; fall of, 322; 323; naval mutiny at, XII 362; 382
"Seven Days' Battles," The (1862), VII 478 sq.
Seven Pines, Federal repulse at (1862), VII 476 sq.
—— Years' War, The Northern (1563-70), IV 163 sqq.
—— Years' War, The (1756-63), Vol. VI, Chap. IX, 251-300; results of, VIII 51, 307

Severia, Swedish army in, v 598

Severoli, Cardinal, x 139

Sèves, Octave-Joseph-Anthelme (Suleiman Pasha), French colonel, x 548; 569

Sévigné, Marie de Rabutin-Chantal, Marquise de, v 7; 9

Seville, has monopoly of colonial trade, II 100; silk industry of, *ib.*; Reformation in, 404–7; defence of, III 324; trade of, 492, 496; Philip in, 494; seizure of private property by Government at, 512; depopulation of, v 376; 684; Spanish Court at, VI 166; Dupont sent to reduce (1808), IX 436 sq.; Victor and, 449; taken by French (1810), 456; Soult and, 468; Junta of, 438, 448, 451–2, 455; Freemasons of, x 215; Cortes at, 227 sq.; 239; the *consulado* of, 247; and Indian trade, 254 sqq.; and slave trade, 260; Junta of, 282, 285; capture of, by French (1810), 286; Junta of, and Mexico, 303; rising at, XI 557

—— Treaty of (1729), v 555, VI 60 sq., 64, 149, 202

—— Caspar de Zuñiga, Cardinal Archbishop of. *See* Zuñiga

—— Fernando de Valdés, Archbishop of, II 405, 408 sq.

—— Isidore, Bishop of (d. 636), I 534

—— Don Enrique, Duke of, XI 553 sqq.; cashiered by Narváez, 557

Sèvres, Austro-French negotiations at, VI 335; normal school at, XII 118

Seward, Anna, VIII 767

—— William Henry, "Higher Law" speech of, VII 403, 428 sq., 440, 445; Secretary of State, 450, 479, 536; attack on, 545 sq.; 575; 589 sq., 592; foreign policy of, 635 sqq., 653; XII 16 sq.; 19; 21; and Mexico, 676; and *Alabama* dispute, 720

Sext, The, III 745. *See also* Codes

Sextus Empiricus, II 712

Seydlitz, Friedrich Wilhelm von, Prussian general, VI 265; 270 sqq.; 283 sqq.

Seymour, Charles, Duke of Somerset. *See* Somerset

—— Sir Edward Hobart, Admiral, in China, XII 519 sq.

—— Francis, on foreign policy, IV 261; 263

—— Sir George Hamilton, British ambassador at St Petersburg, XI 312; at Lisbon, 573

—— Lord Henry, III 309, 313

—— Horatio, Governor of New York, VII 632

—— Jane. *See* Jane, Queen of England

—— Sir Michael, Admiral, XI 325

—— Sir Thomas, Lord Seymour of Sudeley, Lord High Admiral, II 242, 477; plots and execution of, 488

Sézanne, skirmish at (1814), IX 547; Blücher defeats Marmont at, 549

Sèze, Paul Victor de, French deputy, VIII 488

Sfondrato, Francesco, Cardinal, II 670

Sforza, Francesco, Galeazzo Maria, Gian Galeazzo, Ludovico Maria, Massimiliano. *See* Milan, Dukes of

—— Cardinal Ascanio, I 110, 123, 177, 196, 226

—— Bianca Maria, consort of Maximilian I, I 106, 111

—— Caterina, I 113, 238, 624; III 387

—— Giovanni. *See* Pesaro

Shabatz, garrison of, XI 647; King Peter proclaimed at, XII 412

Shackleton, Sir Ernest, Antarctic expedition of, XII 815

Shadwell, Thomas, dramatist, v 127; 130; 133 sq.

Shafiroff, Peter Pavlovitch, Baron, Russian Vice-Chancellor, v 546; negotiates with the Porte, 605 sqq.; 612 sq.

Shafter, William Rufus, American general, VII 680

Shaftesbury, Anthony Ashley Cooper, 1st Earl of, and Cromwell's title, IV 443; 485; v 93; 101; Otway's caricature of, 131; Dryden's satire on, 134; and French Alliance, 191; 198; 201; Lord Chancellor, 207; 208 sq.; and the Test Act, 210; dismissal of, *ib.*; and the Prince of Orange, 213; opposes Non-resisting Test, 216 sq.; as leader of Opposition, 218; sent to Tower, *ib.*; opposes the Duke of York, 222 sq.; President of Privy Council, 224; 225 sqq.; accused of high treason, 228; 229; Locke and, 253; 274; 306; and Treaty of Dover, 333; and succession, 334; 336; death of, 230; VI 808; land in New England granted to, VII 34

—— Anthony Ashley Cooper, 7th Earl of, x 659 sq.; 681; XI 5; 353; XII 744

Shah Álam, Moghul Emperor, VI 524; invades Bengal, 559; 561; 563; and Maráthas, 568; 569

—— Jehán, Moghul Emperor, VI 515; 517 sq.; deposed, 519; 520

Sha-ho river, Russo-Japanese War on, XII 592 sqq.

Sha-ho-pu, captured by Japanese, XII 593

Shahryar, son of Emperor Jehángir, VI 517

Shakespear, Richmond, in Afghánistán, XII 800

Shakespeare, William, III 547, 553; Lessing and, x 385; Herder and, 386; Schlegel's translation of, 399; XI 353; 415; 421; in Hungarian literature, 424 sq., 429 sq.; Danish translation of, 699

Shakhovskóy, Prince D., XII 333

Shakir Pasha, and the Armenian massacres, XII 417

Shalavroff, Russian explorer, XII 795

Shalderque, William, United States agent in Leghorn, x 213

Shales, Henry, Commissary-general in Ireland, v 313 sq.

Shamil, surrender of, xi 633

Shanghai, xi 807; capture of, 809; 810; 816; attacked by "Taipings," 821; Kim-ok Kiun murdered at, xii 510; 512; 526 sq.; Court of Appeal at, 541; 796

Shan-hai-Kwan, projected railway to, xii 505

Shannon, Henry Boyle, Earl of, vi 448 sq.; 494

Shantung, Germany and, xii 171; 512; 517

Shapuri island, British occupation of, xi 727

Shari river, discovered, xii 807; 811 sq.

Sharington, Sir William, frauds on the Mint by, ii 488

Sharp, Granville, and abolition of slavery, vi 188; 472; viii 755

—— James, Archbishop of St Andrews, v 281 sqq.; 284; murder of, 285

—— John, Dean of Norwich, v 234

Sharpe, Sir Alfred, xii 811

—— James, Restoration and, iv 553 sq.

Shashih, opened to trade, xii 512

Shaw, Lemuel, Chief Justice of Massachusetts, vii 735

—— Robert, Indian tea-planter, xii 801

—— William, Irish politician, xii 77

Shawia, French occupation of, xii 133

Shawnee, The (American Indians), vii 337

Shaxton, Nicholas, Bishop of Salisbury, ii 467

Shayévich, organises strike at Odessa, xii 331

Shays, Daniel, leader of "Regulators," vii 313

Shchepkin, at Moscow Congress, xii 356

Shcherbatóff, Prince, xii 327

Sheares, Henry, and Irish rebellion, ix 701-2

—— John, and Irish rebellion, ix 701-2

Sheb, travellers at, xii 805, 813

Sheerness, fortification of, v 112; de Ruyter at, 188; flight of James II to, 247

Sheffield, steel manufacture in, x 733; University, xii 763

—— Edmund Sheffield, Lord, ii 475

Sheikh-ul-Islam, The, position of, i 101; (1644), xi 275

Sheil, Richard Lalor, x 634; 637; and new Catholic Association, 639 sq., 641; 643; 649; and Coercion Bill, 657

Shein, Alexei, Russian general, v 522 sq.; 525

Shelburne, 2nd Earl of. *See* Lansdowne, 1st Marquis of

Shelbyville (Tennessee), Confederate retreat to (1862), vii 508

Sheldon, Gilbert, Archbishop of Canterbury, v 100; 331; 753

Shellabargar, Samuel, Republican leader, vii 628

Shelley, John, Treasurer of Household, vi 437

Shelley, Percy Bysshe, vi 825; 828 sqq.; 834 sq.; viii 768; x 580, 709 sq.; the poetry of, 712 sqq.; and Byron, 713 sqq.; 722 sqq.; xi 350 sq.; 362

Shelton, John, Colonel, defeated by Afghans, xi 733

Shemak, Russian agent at, v 544; 545

Shenandoah, The, "commerce destroyer," bought in England, vii 565 sq.; question of, xii 20

Shenandoah Valley, Stonewall Jackson in, vii 475, 477; Sigel in (1864), 516; importance of, 530 sq.; Early in, 532; Sheridan in, *ib.* sq.

Shendy, travellers at, xii 805 sq.

Shenstone, William, poet, vi 830; x 698

Shepheards Calender, Edmund Spenser's, iii 366, 369-70

Shepstone, Sir Theophilus, and Transvaal, xii 35, 636

Sher Ali, Amir of Afghánistán, xii 459 sqq.; relations of, with England and Russia, 464 sqq.; 471; 475; death of, 470

Sher Shah, Afghan chief, vi 510 sq.

Sher Sing, Sikh rebel, xi 741

Sherborne Castle, stormed by Parliamentarians, iv 332 sq.

Sherbrooke, Robert Lowe, Viscount, xi 339 sq.; 764 sq.; Chancellor of Exchequer, xii 23; 29

Sheremetieff, Boris Petrovich, Boiar, Russian field-marshal, v 524; suppresses revolt at Astrakhan, 531; 588; defeats the Swedes, 590; captures Dorpat, 591; 594; 598; campaign of, against Turks, 604 sq.

Sheridan, Philip Henry, American general, vii 518 sq.; in Shenandoah Valley, 532 sq., 537; at City Point, 537; in pursuit of Lee, 539 sqq.

—— Richard Brinsley, vi 462 sq.; Treasurer of Navy, 464; viii 298, 760; ix 102; 439; and Whig party, 676; and peace, 681; 685; and Regency, 690; and Warren Hastings, 715

—— Sir Thomas, Jacobite, vi 111

Sherif Pasha, Prime Minister of Egypt, xii 435

Sheriffmuir, battle of, vi 100; 102

Sherman, John, American Secretary of the Treasury, vii 643, 653, 668

—— Roger, deputy at Constitutional Convention, Vol. vii, Chap. viii *passim*

—— William Tecumseh, vii 463, 466; at Shiloh, 497; captures Jackson, 505; 510 sq.; at Chattanooga, 511 sqq.; and campaign in the West (1864), 514, 520 sq.; captures Atlanta, 522 sq.; marches to sea, 526 sqq., 533 sq.; at City Point, 537; and peace negotiations, 542; 583

—— Act, The, vii 668

Shiel, Loch, Prince Charles at, vi 112

Shigatse, travellers in, xii 798, 803 sq.

Shiites, The, persecution of, by Selim I, i 90

Shikarpur, occupation of, XI 736
Shiloh, battle of (1862), VII 497
Shimada Sakon, retainer of the *Kwambaku*, XI 837
Shimadzu Saburō, Japanese statesman, XI 844; mission of, to Yedo, 845; 846; 851; 864; XII 549
Shimidzu, Japanese noble, XI 825
Shimoda, Japanese port, XI 829 sqq.; opened to foreign trade, 833
Shimonoseki, naval expedition to, XI 848; 853; bombardment of, XII 546; Treaty of, 345, 512 sq., 572
—— Straits of, XI 848; 851
Shinshiu, disturbances in, XI 864
Ship of Fools, The, of Sebastian Brant, I 683; II 280
Shipka Pass, XII 388 sq.
Ship-money, levy of (1628), IV 268, 282 sqq.
Shipóff, Dmitry, and Russian reform, XII 327 sqq.; 347; 352; 354; and Count Witte, 360; 365; invited to form a Cabinet, 368; Stolýpin and, 869
Shipoff, Colonel, captures Rescht, V 545
Shippen, William, Jacobite, VI 395
Shiré river, XII 660; Livingstone on, 809
Shirley, Sir Anthony, III 541
—— James, English dramatist, III 381
—— Sir William, Governor of Massachusetts, VII 69, 115 sq., 124 sq.
—— Dr, Chancery action by, V 217
Shirwa, Lake, discovered, XII 809
Shishkoff, Alexander, Russian admiral, Secretary of Council of State, IX 488; Minister of Education, X 425
Sholingar, English victory at, VI 577
Shōnai clan, XI 859
Shore, Sir John, Lord Teignmouth, and Bengal, IX 713; Governor-General of India, 717 sqq.
Shovel, Sir Cloudesley, Admiral, V 412; 416; 419
Shrewsbury, Charles Talbot, 1st Duke of, V 240 sq.; and invitation to William of Orange, 242; 255; Secretary of State, 258; 259; and James II, 262; 274; 430; and Peace of Utrecht, 440; Lord Chamberlain, 469; influence of, in 1714, 475; Lord Treasurer, 476
—— George Talbot, 4th Earl of, puts down Pilgrimage of Grace, II 446; 513, 517
Shuiski, Princes of family of, V 487, 491, 496
—— Andrew, murder of, V 487
—— Prince Skopin, V 500 sq.
—— Vasili. *See* Vasili IV, Tsar
Shujah, Prince, son of Shah Jehán, VI 519
Shuja-ud-daulá, Nawáb Wazir of Oudh, VI 555; 561; 563; and Hastings, 569; and Rohillas, 570; 578 sq.
Shuldham, Thomas, Colonel, XI 728
Shumacher, family of, VI 625
Shumla, Turkish force at, X 202; Kossuth at, XI 215

Shungaku, Prince of, XI 844; President of Council, 845; at Kiōto, 847; 850; 851
Shurur, victory of Turks over Persians at (1502), I 88
Shuvaloff, Alexander, VI 311
—— Peter, VI 311
—— Peter, Count, Russian ambassador in London, XI 631 sq.; XII 142, 394; and Poland, 337
Siam, Dutch trade with, III 638, IV 711; China and, XI 802; XII 4; and France, 49, 132; Anglo-French agreement and, 456; 498; 508; affairs in (1511–1907), 534 sqq.; 797
Si-an-fu, Chinese Court at, XII 520
Sibbern, Norwegian Minister, XI 690
Sibbes, Richard, IV 279
Siberia, Russian acquisitions in, V 494 sq.; 531; banishments to, 552, 554, VI 312, 315, 690, XI 628; V 595; Orthodox mission of, X 422; XI 270; population of, 273; newspapers in, 625, 651; XII 4; emigration to, 318; 321; development of, 344 sq.; 873 sq.; opening up of, 794
Siberian Railway, XII 324; 326; 331; 344 sq.; 362; and Russo-Japanese War, 578, 592, 600
Sibi, district of, XII 471
Sibir, Tartar capital, V 494 sq.
Sibthorpe, Robert, IV 268; VI 803; 807
Siccardi, Giuseppe, Sardinian politician, XI 367 sqq.
—— Laws, Cavour and, XI 367 sqq.; 708
Sich, community of, VI 695
Sicily, visit of Charles V to (1535), II 70; the Emperor unable to defend against Barbarossa, III 110; independence of, 476; raided by Turks, 486; Don John at, 497; Philip orders ships from, 504; Mazarin born in, IV 592; disaffection of, 600; 626; French in, 601; 666; Louis XIV and, V 53, 417, 422; Dutch fleet at, 161; 427; ceded to Duke Victor Amadeus of Savoy (1713), 437, 445, 448; with Naples (the Two Sicilies), and the Spanish Succession question, 383 sq., 389, 398, 417, 422; VI 29; Spanish attack on, 32 sqq.; 38; Spain and, 124 sq.; transferred to Emperor Charles VI, 126; 151 sqq.; 596; with Naples (the Two Sicilies), 139; ceded to Don Carlos, 167, 203; the Papacy and, 586 sqq.; 597; under Charles III, 600; Constitution forced on (1820), VII 368; Napoleon's designs on, IX 270; 272; importance of, to Napoleon, 311; 321; departure of British forces from, 367; a centre of English commerce, 381; British in, 382 sqq.; Joseph Bonaparte and, 405; Murat's invasion of, 406; guaranteed to Ferdinand IV, 604; and Naples (*i.e.* the Two Sicilies) and Congress of Vienna, 603; 661, 667–8; Church government in, X 143; Palmerston and, XI 18; 69; 75; movement for

reform in, 79; revolution in, 80; and War with Austria, 85; 88 sq.; revolution in, suppressed, 91 sq.; Garibaldi's expedition to, 332; 380; revolution in (1860), 388, 469; votes for annexation, 390; 531; 534 sq.; annexed to Italy, 709; xii 214; insurrections in, 218; socialism in, 232; condition of, 238 sq.

Sicily, Crown Prince of. *See* Francis I, King of Naples and Sicily

Sickel, Theodor von, German historian, xii 823; 829

Sickingen, Franz von, attacks Worms, i 321 sq.; ii 41, 43; feud of, with Trier, 154 sq.; iii 739

Siculus, Marineus, and Geraldino, Italian scholars, i 379, 381

Siddi, Moghul admiral, vi 531

Sidgwick, Captain Robert, vii 111

Sidmouth, Henry Addington, Baron, ix 71; 77 sqq.; proposal of, for war contribution, 677; Prime Minister, 679 sqq.; resignation of, 683; re-enters Cabinet, 690; Home Secretary, x 578 sq.; 584

Sidney, Algernon, iii 749; Charles X and, iv 541; at Amsterdam, v 110; 229; execution of, 230; 259; writings of, vi 791, 803 sqq., 815, 818

—— Sir Henry, ii 505; Lord Deputy of Ireland, iii 591, 594, 609–10

—— Henry, Earl of Romney (Viscount Sidney). *See* Romney

—— Sir Philip, iii 18, 369, 371 sq., 376, 622; v 116

Sidon, fall of, to Crusaders, i 254

Siebenpfeiffer, P. J., German journalist, x 375

Siècle, Le, French newspaper, ix 758; xi 127; 292; 487

Siegen, town, under rule of two sovereigns, x 362; relinquished by William I (1815), 524; and Luxemburg, xi 674

Siegwan-Müller, Constantin, Mayor of Luzern, xi 247 sq.

Siem-reap, ceded to France, xii 536

Siena, Council of (1423), i 657; (1424), 677; revolt in (1545), ii 83; revolt against Spain and conquest of (1552–5), 88; ceded to Savoy, iii 385–7, 395, 397–8; Reformers in, 389; conquest of, by Spain, 465, 476–7; *Intronati* of, 470; granted to Medici, 478; claims to, vi 138; 152; and Florence, ix 400; Leopold II at, xi 91; and Clement VII, xii 705

—— St Bernardino of. *See* Bernardino

Sieniawska, Pani, marries Prince Augustus Czartoryski, vi 198

Sieniecki, Grand Marshal of Diet of Warsaw (1575), iii 97

Sierck, taken by French, iv 595

Sierra Bullones, Marquis of. *See* Zabala

—— Leone, Great Britain and, xii 658; 660; 807; 812

—— Leone Company, vi 188, ix 751

Sierra Morena, defence of, ix 437 sq.; Cartaojal takes shelter in, 450; Areizaga's army in, 455; Soult and, 456

—— Parda, Diaz at (1486), i 17

Siete Iglesias, Rodrigo Calderon, Marquis de, rules Spain, iv 626; 628 sq.; execution of, 636

Sievers, Count Johann Jakob, Russian Minister, vi 683; 692; plenipotentiary in Poland, viii 537 sqq.

Sievershausen, battle of (1553), ii 275

Sieverski, v 500; retained by Poland, 504

Siewakowski, Jan, iii 83

Sieyès, Comte Emmanuel-Joseph, Abbé, viii 2, 20, 122 sqq.; and States General, 132 sq., 149; and National Assembly, 153 sq., 158, 176, 178, 182; on Constitutional Committee, 183; and Brissotins, 213 sq.; in National Convention, 249; *Montagnard,* 366; *Indépendent,* 378; 381; and Directory, 489, 507, 515; elected Director, 519 sq., 668; and Brumaire, 675 sq., 679 sq., 683; provisional Consul, 686; ix 1 sqq.; 17, 21; x 41; 85

Sigbrit, "Mother," favourite and adviser of Christian II, ii 604

Sigel, Franz, commands in Shenandoah Valley (1864), vii 516, 533; Baden revolutionary (1849), xi 221

Sigismund of Luxemburg, Emperor, i 289 sq., 297, 424; v 621; 623; 632

—— I, King of Poland, i 343, 345; ii 198, 632; iii 74 sqq.; v 635

—— II Augustus, King of Poland, ii 270, 635; Reformation and, 636 sq.; iii 76; relations of, to Reformed Catholic reaction in Poland, 78–84; iv 162 sq.; v 354; 494; 636

—— III, King of Poland and Sweden, loses Sweden, ii 632; iii 450, 698 sq., 714; iv 23; elected King of Poland, 168; 169 sqq.; King of Sweden, 170 sqq.; and Charles IX, 173 sq.; Charles and Tsar Basil allied against, 176; 177; and Gustavus Adolphus, 179; 180 sqq.; and Turks, 183; 185 sq.; makes peace with Sweden, 187; rule of, in Poland, 188; *Rokosz* of Sandomir and, 189; 192; v 343; 498; invades Russia, 500; 501; death of, 504; 636

—— Archduke, Duke of Tyrol, i 294 sq.; Nicholas of Cusa and, 632 sq., 689

Signory, the Florentine, and reforming work of Savonarola, i 155 sqq.

—— the Venetian, iii 114–6; cautious in regard to Henry IV, 689

Sigüenza, Iñigo Manrique, Bishop of, i 658

—— Mendoza, Bishop of. *See* Mendoza, Pedro Gonzalez Hurtado de

Sikhs, The, in Punjab, vi 523; 524; wars with, xi 731; 739 sqq.

Si-kiang river, xii 796

Sikkim, Tibetan invasion of, xii 490; travellers at, 798, 803

Siku arsenal, captured, xii 519

Silesia, becomes part of Bohemian kingdom, i 329, 331; meeting of Estates of (1608), with Pressburg Allies, iii 721; and *Letters of Majesty*, iv 2; Diet of, 17; 22; 26; 33; occupied by Saxons, 34; sends troops to Bohemia, 22; and Ferdinand, 28, 64; Frederick V in (1620), 68; 75; Christian of Halberstadt in, 86; 97 sqq.; subdued by Wallenstein, 103; 200; 206; controlled by Leslie, 209; 216; 237; 240; 242; Swedish troops in, 247, 370; 253 sq.; 374; 378; 386; and Treaty of Westphalia, 403, 412 sq.; effects of the War upon, 417, 421; Brandenburg and, v 359, 624; Bohemia and, 621; 625; 644; Great Elector and, 654; and War of Austrian Succession, Vol. vi, Chap. viii (3) *passim*; effects of Frederick II's attack on, 158; 197; 204; 206; 209 sq.; acquired by Prussia, 250; 276; 280; 288; Austrians in, 289; 310; 316 sqq.; Soltikoff in, 325 sq.; 327; 338 sq.; Treaty of Hubertusburg and, 346; 352; 398; 401; Prussian army in (1790), viii 293; 308; levy on, ix 307; connexion with Prussia threatened, 308; 336; Napoleon's troops in (1808), 316; Prussian forces in, 514; Russian forces in, 516; defence of, 520; campaigns in (1813), 522 sqq.; freed, 525; 542; defeat of army of (1814), 548; industries in, x 732, 751, 754 sqq.; sheep-breeding in, 750; unrest in, xi 52; 171; 450 sq.; xii 136; Catholic party in, 147; 201

—— Austrian, insurrection in, vi 628; 629; Prussian army in (1778), 704 sq.; 707; 709; industries of, 718 sq.; 721; 724; economic conditions in, 715 sq.; 729

—— George William, Duke of, v 652

Silhouette, Étienne de, Commissary of French India Company, vi 542

Silistria, Russian capture of, ix 485; fortress of, xii 397

Silla, Mungo Park at, xii 806

Sillery, Nicolas Brulart, Marquis de, Secretary of Henry III, iii 40; Chancellor of France, iv 118; superseded, 122; 127 sq.

Silva, Frey Diogo da, Inquisitor-General in Portugal, ii 413

—— de, Spanish ambassador in Scotland, iii 272–5, 280

Silvaplana, Grisons leaders at, iv 62

Silvela, Manuel, Spanish statesman, xi 570

Silverton, gold and silver at, xii 619

Silvester I, Pope, v 484

—— monk, favourite of Ivan IV, v 489; 515

Simanca, Spanish Papalist, iii 757

Simancas, murder of Montigny at, iii 228; death of Hugh O'Donnell at, 533; archives from, at Paris, ix 120

Simbach, surrender of, vi 238

Simcoe, John Graves, Lieutenant-Governor of Upper Canada, ix 746

Siméon, Comte Joseph-Jérôme, viii 507, 509; ix 153; Minister of the Interior, x 63

Simla, treaty at (1838), xi 732; Afghan conference at, xii 464; 494

Simnel, Lambert, imposture of, i 465; defeated at Stoke-upon-Trent (1487), 466; iii 579

Simon, Antoine, French politician, viii 234, 356, 371

—— Heinrich, German politician, xi 52; 200

—— Jules, and Education Commission, xi 120; 127; 475; 485; and defence of Paris, 497; xii 111 sq.; 114 sq.

—— Père Richard, French theologian, v 79; 87; Hebraist, xii 816

—— French general, ix 21

Simoneau, Louis, Mayor of Étampes, viii 225, 227

Simonetta, Cicco, Milanese Minister, i 106

—— Luigi, legate at Council of Trent, ii 676–82

Simplon, Pass of, ix 59; road over (1807), 119, xi 239

Simpson, General Sir James, xi 322

—— Sir James Young, and the use of chloroform, xii 779

Simson, Eduard, President of Frankfort National Assembly, xi 196; 198 sq.

Si-nan-fu, Richthofen at, xii 797

Sinapius, Johann, court physician at Ferrara, ii 384

—— Kilian, in Ferrara, ii 384 sq.

Sinclaire, Baron Malcolm, murdered, vi 309

Sind, Emperor Humáyún in, vi 511; 512; xi 724; 727; annexation of, 731; 732; 734; war with, 736 sq.

Sindhia, Daulat Ráo, position of, ix 720; 725; defeat of, 726

—— Madhoji Ráo, power of, ix 714 sqq.; death of, 720

Singapore, acquired by Great Britain, xi 667; 727; Great Britain and, xii 532; 536

Sinigaglia, capture of (1502), i 195, 240; Pius IX at, xi 71 sq.

Si-ning-fu, travellers at, xii 804

Sinn Fein, xii 90

Sinope, surrenders to Turks (1457), i 285; Turkish fleet destroyed at, xi 306, 315 sqq.

Sinsheim, victory of Turenne at (1674), v 44

Sintius (Sintheim), Johannes, i 436

Sinzendorf, Count Philipp Ludwig von, Imperial ambassador at the Hague, v 439 sqq.; 432; and the Utrecht negotiations, 450; 451; 457; vi 139 sq.; 204; 229

Sipahis, Turkish cavalry, i 99; changes in the constitution of, v 342

Siponto, Sebastiano Pighino, Archbishop of, ii 671

Sipyágin, Russian Minister of Interior, XII
314; 326; 329; 376
Siráj-ud-daulá, Nawáb of Bengal, VI 551
sqq.; death of, 555; Clive and, 556 sq.
Sir Darya, Russia and, XI 273; 630 sq.
Sirhind, Emperor Humáyún at, VI 511
Sirleto, Cardinal, III 450
Sirmond, Jacques, III 61
Sismondi, Jean-Charles-Léonard Simonde
de, IX 132; 427; X 40; XI 261; XII 830
Sisophon, ceded to France, XII 536
Sissek, slaughter of Hassan and his troops
at, III 700
Sistine Chapel, decoration of, by Michel-
angelo, II 6, 14, 34
Sistova, Peace of (1791), VI 656, VIII 277,
289, 293, 295, 334, IX 385; XII 388;
Bulgarian Assembly at, 405
Sitabaldi Hills, XI 726
Sitia, French occupation of, XII 423
Sitianovich, Simeon (Polotski), Russian
monk, V 516 sq.
Si Tlemcen, revolt of, XII 129
Sittard, victory over Imperialists at (1543),
II 242
Sittich, Mark, of Ems, *Vogt* of Bregenz,
II 329
Situ. *See* Chitu
Sivaji, Marátha leader, V 698; VI 521
Siverson, Captain, at Bantam, IV 734
Siwa, subdued by Ibrahim Pasha (1820), X
548; Hornemann at, XII 806
"Six Acts," The English, of 1819, X
581 sq.
"Sixteen," The, revolutionary government
of, in Paris, III 42, 50, 659, 661–2
Sixtus IV (Francesco della Rovere), Pope,
I 80, 108; nepotism of, 221, 237; Venice
and, 268; Spain and, 359; 387; the
Vatican Library and, 552; 560; Mat-
thias Corvinus and, 658; Pazzi con-
spiracy and, 661; Indulgences issued by,
662; war of, with Naples, 666; sale of
offices by, 670; the press and, 685;
Spanish Inquisition and, II 650; prohibited books and, 686; III 439–40,
444
—— V (Felice Peretti), Pope (Cardinal di
Montalto), Inquisition and, II 650; Congregation of the Council of Trent established by, 686; succeeds Gregory XIII
(1585), III 38, 40 sq., 46 sq., 50; and
attack on Elizabeth, 289, 303, 349; and
Geneva, 414; 415 sq.; Rome and, Chap.
XIII; character and achievements of, 455;
promises money for Philip's invasion of
England, 504 sqq.; 710; 764; death of,
IV 666; treasure of, 681
—— of Siena, the *Bibliotheca Sancta*,
I 611
Sjælland, Peder Plade (Palladius), Bishop
of, II 616
Skaleni, Greeks defeated at (1821), X 179
Skalholt (Iceland), Gisser Einarsen, Bishop
of, II 621

Skalich, charlatan at Prussian Court, III
153
Skalitz, fight at, XI 453
Skara, Vincent Bellenack, Bishop of, exe-
cuted in Stockholm *Blodbad*, II 604
Skeffington, Sir William, Lord Deputy of
Ireland, II 442
Skelton, John, Poet Laureate to Henry VIII,
II 423
Skiernewicze, the three Emperors at, XII
158; 162
Skippon, Philip, IV 304; Major-general,
326; 341; 349
Skipworth Moor, muster of rebels on (1536),
II 446
Skirving, William, Secretary of Edinburgh
Convention, VIII 770
Skobeleff, Michael, Russian general, XI 632;
XII 313; 389; 581
Skodborg, Jörgen. *See* Lund, Archbishops of
Skovronskaya, Martha (Catharine I). *See*
Catharine I
Skram, Peder, Danish admiral, II 230, 615
Skrzynecki, John, Polish commander-in-
chief, X 470 sqq.
Skuratoff, Lieutenant, Russian explorer, XII
795
Skutari (Bosporus), Florence Nightingale
at, XI 321
Skutari-in-Albania (Scodra), besieged and
taken by Turks (1474), I 80 sq.;
abandoned by Venice (1479), 74, 286;
Pashalik of, IX 418; X 202; Convention
of, XI 636; Prince Nicholas at, XII 390
—— Lake of, XII 414
Skyros, surrendered by Venice to Turks,
III 116
Skytte, Benedict, V 656
—— John, tutor of Gustavus Adolphus,
IV 178; 182
Sladen, Sir Edward Bosc, on Chinese
frontier, XII 500
Slaghoek, Diederik. *See* Lund, Archbishops
of
Slatin Pasha, and Sudan, XII 447
Slave Coast, settlements on, V 691
—— Trade, movements for abolition of,
VI 188; legislation on, 472 sq.; regulated,
ib.; and Peace of Ghent (1814), VII 347;
at Congress of Vienna, IX 662; British
Abolition Act, 751; and Conference of
Aix-la-Chapelle, X 19; with Spanish
America, review of, 259 sq.
Slavery, in the U.S.A., and question of
representation, VII 266 sqq.; 281 sq.;
struggle in Republic concerning, 361 sq.;
Chap. XII *passim*; for the great struggle,
Civil War, and emancipation, Chaps.
XIII–XIX, 405–621; state of affairs after
the War, Chap. XX *passim*; in Spanish
America, X 260; British movement for
abolition of, 658 sqq. *See also* Slave
Trade *and* Emancipation
Slavinetski, Epifany, translator of the
Russian Bible, V 516

Slavonia, v 352; Austrians in, 366; xi 170; Hungary and, 173; 177 sqq.; disturbances in (1848), 182; 202; 206

Slavs, in Germany, v 617; and Liberal movement, xi 46; Hungary and, 173; Slav Congress at Prague, 177; 178 sq.; 207; 399; 404; Vol. xii, Chaps. vii and xiv *passim*

Slawata, Count William, iii 727; and the Catholic party in Bohemia, iv 16; regent, 18 sq.; "defenestration" of, 20 sq.; 72

Sleeman, Sir William Henry, Indian official, xi 743

Slidell, John, Confederate States envoy to Europe, vii 447, 470; xi 335; xii 318

Sligo, surrenders to James (1689), v 309; lost by James, 312; recovered, 313; Castle, taken by O'Donnell (1595), iii 605

—— O'Conor, iii 604–5, 607

Slingelandt, Govert van, Pensionary of Dort, v 145

Slingsby, Sir Henry, execution of, iv 447

Slivnitsa, battle of, xii 407

Slobodzeia, Turks surrender at (1811), ix 485

Slocum, Henry Warner, American general, vii 526

Slottburg, captured by Russians (1703), v 590

Sloughter, Colonel Henry, Governor of New York, vii 45

Slovaks, at Croato-Slavonic Diet, xi 179; 202; 399; Slovak writers, 654 sq.

Slovenes, xi 173 sq.; at Croato-Slavonic Diet, 179

Slovenia, a proposed kingdom of, xi 174

Sluys, siege of (1492), i 449 sq.; taken by Protestants (1604), iii 535, 538, 637; taken by Parma (1587), 623; taken by French, vi 247

Smerwick, so-called Papal volunteers land at (1580), iii 298; Fitzmaurice entrenched at, 597; surrender of (1580), 598

Smet de Naeyer, Comte de, Belgian statesman, xii 253 sqq.

Smeton, Mark, execution of, ii 445

Smidt, Senator, at Congress of Vienna, ix 588

Smirnoff, Russian general, in Port Arthur, xii 586

Smith, Adam, political economist, v 689; vi 45; 51; and Colonial System, 56; vii 83; viii 71, 276, 769; advocates Irish Union, ix 702; x 354 sq.; *The Wealth of Nations*, 763 sqq.; 782; xi 311; xii 817

—— Caleb B., Secretary of Interior, vii 450

—— Donaldson, African explorer, xii 813

—— Edmund Kirby, Confederate general, vii 507; surrender of, 543

—— Erasmus, Irish educationist, xii 71

—— Goldwin, historian, xii 839

Smith, Sir Harry George Wakelyn, xi 739; Governor of Cape Colony, 783 sq.

—— James, of Deanston, x 741

—— John, Cambridge Platonist, v 750

—— John, and Virginia, vii 4, 7

—— Sir Lionel, General, xi 726

—— Dr Richard, ii 501

—— Robert Vernon, Lord Lyveden, xi 329

—— Southwood, and social questions, xii 750

—— Colonel Spencer, English agent at Strassburg, ix 28; 30

—— Sydney, *Noodle's Oration*, ix 686; and *Edinburgh Review*, 687; epigrams of, x 665; 673; 679

—— Sir Thomas, English statesman and scholar, i 580 sq.; ii 484, 495; Somerset and, 496; ambassador to France, iii 8, 16–17, 748; iv 735; and Virginia Company, 748

—— William, Liberal M.P., viii 302

—— William, palaeontologist, xii 771

—— William Farrar, American general and engineer, vii 511

—— William Henry, Leader of House of Commons, xii 46 sq.; death of, 48; Irish Secretary, 84

—— William Robertson, Semitic studies of, xii 846

—— Sir William Sidney, British admiral, viii 609 sqq., 615, 617, 629; with squadron in Tagus, ix 303–4; 382; and Congress of Vienna, 662; x 547

—— Canadian Chief Justice, protest of, ix 743

—— American Secretary of Interior, resigns (1896), vii 673

Smith Sound, exploration from, xii 815

Smolensk, annexed to Russia, v 479 sqq.; 493; retained by Poland, 504; restored to Russia (1667), 505; 531; Catharine II and, vi 694; siege of (1812), ix 492 sqq.; French retreat to, 498 sqq.

Smolenski, Colonel, Greek officer, xii 421 sq.

Smolka, František, Polish politician, xi 660

—— Stanislas, Polish historian, xi 660

Smollett, Tobias George, vi 79; x 718

Smolna, school at, vi 692

Smorgonie, Charles XII at, v 597 sq.; Napoleon at, ix 504

Smyrna, burnt by Venetians, i 80; Anglo-Dutch convoy from, v 262; British and French fleets at, x 195; xii 37; 402

Smyth, Sir Jeremy, English naval officer, v 183; 186

—— American general, invades Canada (1812), vii 338

Snell, Willebrod, geometrician, v 715

Snellman, Finnish writer, x 434

Sniadecki, Jan, Rector of University of Vilna, x 459

Soanen, Jean, Bishop of Senez. *See* Senez

Sobat river, Marchand on, xii 813

Sobdar Khan, xi 736

Sobieski, James, and Polish Crown, v 370, vi 191
—— John. *See* John III, King of Poland
—— Maria Clementina, marries Prince James Stewart (the Old Pretender), vi 37, 105
Soboleff, Russian general, in Bulgaria, xii 405
Sobor, The, Muscovite assembly under Ivan IV, v 492 sq.; 497; 501 sqq.
Sobraon, Sir Harry Smith at, xi 739
Sochi, rising in, xii 363
Social movements, Vol. xii, Chap. xxiii, 730–65
Socialism, growth of modern movement of, xii 758 sqq.; in Belgium, from 1896, 253 sqq.; Danish, 292; and French Revolution, viii 790; in France, in late 19th century, xii 126 sqq.: in Germany, Social-democratic party and Bismarck, 152 sqq.: in Holland, 248: in Italy, in late 19th century, 231 sq.: Polish, from Limanowski (1868), 337; Russian, xi 627 sq.; repression of, xii 296 sq.; sociological individualism of Mikhailovsky, 302 sqq.; and Karl Marx, 329 sqq.; action of, in 1905, 350; 353; in Universities, 358; Finnish, 377; in Spain, government action towards, 267: Swedish, gains a footing in Diet, 276
Société des Amis de la Presse, x 61
—— *des Droits de l'Homme*, x 489; 491
Society for commemorating the Revolution, vi 477
—— for Constitutional Information, vi 477
—— for the Propagation of the Gospel, founded in 1701, vii 57; attacks on, in Massachusetts (1763), 144
—— Islands, France and, xii 666 sq.
—— of the Bill of Rights, vii 477
Society of United Irishmen, founded, viii 771
Socinians, origin of, in Poland, ii 637 sq.
Socinus. *See* Sozzini, Fausto *and* Lelio
Socorro, revolt in (1780), x 275
Sodalitas Staupitiana, at Nürnberg, i 683
Soddy, Frederick, and radio-activity, xii 790
Soderini, Cardinal Francesco, i 150; ii 22
—— Paol' Antonio, i 156, 160, 169
Söderköping, Swedish Estates at (1595), iv 171
Södermanland, assigned to Charles (IX), iv 160
Soest, occupied by Spanish garrison, iv 10
Sötern, Philip Christopher von. *See* Trier
Sofia, Solyman II at, iii 125; xii 384; captured, 389; 407; revolution in, 408 sq.; 409 sq.; Macedonian Committee at, 425
Sohr, Prussian victory at, vi 242
Soiron, Alexander von, Baden politician, xi 163; 165; 221
Soissons, allotted to Mayenne, iii 668; Congress of, vi 147
—— Charles de Bourbon, Count of, iii 674

Soissons, Louis de Bourbon, Count of, iv 131; at Sedan, 150; death of, 151
Sokalnitz, Russian attack on, ix 260
Sokolli, Mohammad, commands the Turkish army against Ferdinand I, iii 122; becomes Grand Vezir (1565), 125, 128, 130–3, 136–9; death of, 139
Sokolowski, Archbishop of Lemberg. *See* Lemberg
Sokoto, xii 659; explorers at, 807
Solano, José, Spanish admiral, vi 377; 453
Solari, Pietro Antonio, Milanese architect, v 482
"Solemn League and Covenant," iv 506
Solferino, battle of (1796), viii 575, xi 383 sq., 403, xii 176
Solignac, Jean-Baptiste, French general, at Oporto, x 331 sq.; 488
Solimões river, Jesuits on, vi 390
Solingen, Clauberg born at, iv 789
Solis, Juan Diaz de, reaches the Plate River (1515), i 36
Sollicitudo omnium ecclesiarum, Pius VII's Bull, x 6
Sollogub, Count Vladimir, xi 625
Solms, Count Albert von, at Prague, iv 24
—— Amalia von. *See* Orange
—— Count Ernest of, iii 628
—— Count Philip Reinhard of, envoy of Gustavus at the Saxon Court, iv 213
—— Count Victor Friedrich of, Prussian diplomat, vi 732
Solms-Braunfels, Count Heinrich Maastricht of, v 315
Solomon Islands, xii 666; Germany and, 667; 668
Solothurn, and Neuchâtel, v 449; canton of, vi 612; 625; xi 234; government of, 235; reaction in, 238; 240; joins *Siebnerkonkordat*, 242; 246
Solovetski monastery, v 509, 511
Solovieff, Sergyei Mikhailovich, Russian historian, xii 842
Solovyéff, A., attempts to shoot Tsar Alexander II, xii 306
Soltikoff, Nicolai Ivanovitch, Prince, x 8
—— Count Peter, Russian commander-in-chief, vi 291 sqq.; 297; 323; at Kunersdorf, 324; 325; superseded, 326
Solway Moss, battle of (1542), ii 456
Solyman, Sulayman, Suleiman. *See* Suleymán
Somaglia, Giulio Maria della, Cardinal, x 139; 152
Somaliland, xii 3; 241; Indian troops in, 493; 659 sq.; division of, 664; exploration in, 813
Somers, Sir George, in Virginia, vii 5
—— Henry, American statesman, vii 234
—— John, Lord, and Revolution settlement, v 249 sq.; 253; 255; and currency, 269; 271; Lord Keeper, 274; impeachment of, 275, 397; 277; Lord President of Council, 465; 466 sq.; 469; Earl of Oxford and, 470, 474

Somerset, "Bloody Assizes" in, v 232
—— Anne Stanhope, Duchess of, liberated by Mary, II 521
—— Charles Seymour, 6th Duke of, v 476
—— Lord Charles, Governor of Cape Colony, XI 780
—— Edward Seymour, Earl of Hertford and Duke of, II 82; invades Scotland, 459 sq.; 474; becomes Protector, 476; character of, 476 sq.; foreign policy of, 486 sq.; agrarian policy of, 489–92; negotiation of, with Charles V, 493; plots against, 494; fall of, 495 sq.; release of, 504; alleged plot of, 505; trial and death of, 506 sq.; Scottish policy of, 556; III 262
—— Lord Fitzroy. *See* Raglan, 1st Lord
—— Frances (Countess of Essex), Countess of, III 559–60
—— Robert Carr, Earl of, III 559; Lord Chamberlain, 560 sq., 566
—— Lord Robert Edward Henry, with Horse Guards at Waterloo, IX 635
Somerville College, Oxford, XII 762
Sommario della Santa Scrittura, II 386
Sommariva, Giovanni Battista, and Cis-alpine Republic, IX 84
Somnath, the (spurious) gates of, XI 735
Somosierra, Pass of, forced by Napoleon (1808), IX 444
Son of the Fatherland, Russian journal, XII 347
Sonderbund, The Swiss, XI 237; 248 sqq.
Sondrio, capital of the *Terzero di Sotto*, IV 35; 37; 39; 41; Rusca archpriest of, 49; 58; Rohan at, 63
Sonino (Sonnino), a stronghold of robbers, x 139
Sonnenfels, Joseph von, VI 635; VIII 776
Sonnenstein, fortress of, v 594
Sonnino, Baron Sidney, Italian statesman, XII 221; Ministry of, 227 sq.; 232; 238
Sonora, Joseph de Galvez, Marquis de, Spanish general, VI 382
Sonoy, Stadholder of West Friesland (the North Quarter), III 621–3
Sontai, taken by French, XII 525
Soochow, opened to trade, XII 512
Sophia, Tsarevna, Regent of Russia, v 518 sqq.; and conspiracy against Peter the Great, 522; 523; 525
—— Tsaritsa (Zoe, daughter of Constantine Palaiologus), v 482 sq.
—— Archduchess of Austria, XI 154; 171; and *Camarilla*, 175, 182; 190; 398; and Alexander Bach, 401
—— Electress of Hanover. *See* Hanover
—— Queen of the Netherlands, consort of William III, XII 244
—— Charlotte, Queen of Prussia (Electress of Brandenburg), 2nd consort of Frederick I, v 662 sq.; 665; 670 sq.; death of, 667; 741; VI 2; 8; 205
—— Dorothea, wife of George I, King of England, VI 3

Sophia, Dorothea, Queen of Prussia, consort of Frederick William I, VI 2 sq.; 210
—— Magdalena, Queen of Denmark, consort of Christian VI, VI 738 sq.
—— Magdalena, Queen of Sweden, consort of Gustavus III, VI 741
Sopoto, ceded to Turks, III 137
Soranzo, Giacomo, Venetian ambassador in England, II 513, 529, 544
—— Vittorio. *See* Bergamo, Bishop of
Sorbonne, The, condemns Luther's writings, II 283; attacks Calvin's *Institutio*, 288; issues *Index Expurgatorius*, 288; III 46, 447, 657; submits to Henry IV, 663; v 78; Turgot at, VIII 83
Sorel, Albert, French historian, XII 833 sq.
Soriano, Antonio, II 26
Sosnofski, Colonel, in Central Asia, XII 799, 802 sq.
Sostegno, Alfieri di. *See* Alfieri
Sotin de la Coindière, Pierre-J.-M., Minister of Police, VIII 508
Soto, Hernan de, Governor of Cuba, expedition to Florida of, I 54
—— Juan de, secretary of Don John of Austria, III 497
—— Fray Pedro de (confessor of Charles V), II 250; 402, 526; Professor of Hebrew at Oxford, 541
Sotomayor, Duke of, Spanish statesman, XI 555
Soubirous, Bernadette, of Lourdes, XI 714
Soubise, Benjamin de Rohan, Seigneur de, IV 127 sq.; defeated off La Rochelle, 130
—— Charles de Rohan, Prince de, Marshal of France, VI 263 sqq.; 269 sqq.; at Rossbach, 272, 341; 274; 426
—— Michelle de Saubonne, Madame de, II 384
Souches, Ludwig Raduit de, Austrian field-marshal, v 347
Souham, Comte Joseph, French general, VIII 435; succeeds Clausel in command, IX 474; combines with Soult, 475; at Versailles, 558
Soulier, French officer, IX 144
Soult, Nicolas-Jean-de-Dieu, Duc de Dalmatia, Marshal of France, VIII 661; IX 58; receives Dalmatia, 111; 252; crosses Rhine, 253; invests Ulm, 254; 257, 260; at Baireuth, 274; pursues Hohenlohe, 277; pursues Blücher, 280; 284; guards Warsaw, 285; at Allenstein, 285; at Eylau, 286; 335; sent to Leon, 444; on the Carrion river, 445; pursues Moore, 447; and French invasion of Portugal, 449 sqq.; marches on Plasencia, 453; 456; besieges Cadiz, 457–8; takes Badajoz, 462 sqq.; 466; at Albuera, 467; at Badajoz, 468; unable to quit Andalusia, 469; Napoleon's directions to, 471; in Andalusia, 473; his force at Valencia, 474; summoned to Germany, 475; sent to reorganise army in Spain, 478; resumes

offensive, 479; repulsed at San Marcial, 480; foiled at Saint Pierre, 481; retreat of, 482; Minister of War, 571; dismissed, 574; and Belgian campaign, 625, 634; Ministry of, x 489; 494, 510 sqq.; and Algiers, 503; and Turko-Egyptian Question, 562, 565; 570

Soumet, Alexandre, x 88

Sound Dues, The, Swedish exemption from, vi 37; abolished, xi 687; 693

Soupire, de, French commander in southern India, vi 547

Sourdis, Charles d'Escoubleau, Marquis de, commands reserve force at Langres, iv 251

—— Henri d'Escoubleau de. *See* Bordeaux, Archbishop of

Sousa, Francisco de, Portuguese ambassador at the Hague, iv 401

—— Martim Affonso de, Viceroy of Portuguese India, i 49

Sousa Coutinho, Francisco de, Portuguese diplomat, vi 375

South African Republic, xii 245

Southampton, Spanish vessels at, iii 493; Treaty of (1625), iv 262, 739; and South America, xii 684

—— Henry Wriothesley, 3rd Earl of, iii 572; and the London Company, vii 6

—— Thomas Wriothesley, 1st Earl of (2nd cr.), ii 475 sq., 488; plots against Somerset, 494 sq.; Warwick and, 497 sq.

—— Thomas Wriothesley, 4th Earl of, v 93; 106

—— William Fitzwilliam, Earl of (1st cr.), Lord High Admiral of England, ii 472

South Beveland, General Hope takes island of (1809), ix 358

"South Carolina Exposition," The, vii 380

Southesk, James Carnegie, 5th Earl of, vi 98; 103

Southey, Robert, writings of, vi 832, 836, x 708 sq., 720; undergraduate at Oxford, viii 764, 766 sqq.; and child labour question, x 659; career of, 708 sq.; 722

South Island, New Zealand, xi 795 sq.; 799

Southland, province of, xi 799

South Pole, expeditions to the, xii 815

—— Sea Company (British), v 445; vi 39; 41; 45; 61; Spain and, 64 sqq.; 146; 151; 157; origin and history of, 177 sqq.; 363; 530; and the slave trade, x 260

—— Sea Company (Swedish), iv 759

—— Seas, German trade in, xii 160

Southwark, Jacobite trials at, vi 117

Southwell, Wolsey at, ii 434; Charles I at, iv 339, 507

—— Sir Richard, ii 497

—— Sir Robert, English envoy in Portugal, v 105, 109

—— Lady, iii 361

Southwold Bay, English victory at (battle of Lowestoft, 1665), v 110, 181; Dutch victory at (1672), 43, 158, 192 sq.

Soutzo, Alexander, Greek poet, xi 278

Sovana, annexed by Cosimo de' Medici, iii 386

Soyejima, Japanese Foreign Minister, xii 557

Sozh river, Lithuanian boundary, v 481

Sozzini, Fausto (Socinus), in Transylvania, ii 393; founder of Unitarians in Transylvania, 637 sq.; iii 80, 390

—— Lelio (Socinus), Italian Reformer, ii 393, 637, 716; iii 390

Spa, death of Parma at, iii 627

—— Fields riot (1816), x 577 sq.

Spada, Bernardino, Cardinal, iv 686

Spaen, Baron van, Dutch plenipotentiary at Congress of Vienna, ix 586

Spaight, Richard D., deputy for North Carolina at the Constitutional Convention (1787), vii 246

Spain

i	i	The Age of Discovery, *passim*, 7–36
	ii	The New World, *passim*, 37–66
	xi	The Catholic Kings, 347–83 [*See also* xv, Economic change, *especially* 518 sqq., xviii, Catholic Europe, *and* xix, The Eve of the Reformation, *passim*]
ii	ii	Habsburg and Valois (I), *passim*, 36–65
	iii	Habsburg and Valois (II), *passim*, 66–103
	xii	The Catholic South, *especially* 399–411
	xviii	The Church and Reform, *passim*, 639–89
iii	vi	The Revolt of the Netherlands, *passim*, 182–220
	vii	William the Silent, *passim*, 221–59
	ix	The Elizabethan Naval War with Spain, *passim*, 294–327
	xv	Spain under Philip II, 475–525
	xvi	Spain under Philip III, 526–47
	xvii	Britain under James I, *passim*, 549–78
iv	ii	The Valtelline (1603–39), *passim*, 35–63
	iii	The Protestant Collapse, (1) the Palatinate War (1620–3), 77 sqq.
	iv	Richelieu, *passim*, 118–57
	xiv	The Peace of Westphalia, *passim*, 395–433
	xxi	Mazarin, *passim*, 592–622
	xxii	Spain and Spanish Italy under Philip III and IV, 623–65
	xxiii	Papal policy (1590–1648), *passim*, 666–88
	xxv	The transference of Colonial Power to the United Provinces and England, *passim*, 728–59
v	ii	The foreign policy of Louis XIV (1661–97), *passim*, 32–63

Spain (*contd.*)

v   xiii   The Treaties of Partition and the Spanish Succession, 372–400

      xiv   The War of the Spanish Succession, 401–59

      xxii   The Colonies and India (I), *passim*, 673–94

vi   iv   The Bourbon governments in France and Spain, I (1714–26), 120–44

      v   The Bourbon governments in France and Spain, II (1727–46), 145–67

      vi   Financial experiments and Colonial development, *passim*, 168–90

      viii   The War of the Austrian Succession, *passim*, 201–50

      xi   The reversal of alliances and the Family Compact, 329–60

      xii   Spain and Portugal (1746–94) (1) Spain under Ferdinand VI and Charles III, 361–84

      xvi   Italy and the Papacy, *passim*, 586–610

vii   ix   The struggle [of the United States] for commercial independence (1783–1812), 305–34

      xi   The growth of the nation [United States] (1815–28), *passim*, 349–77

      xxi   The United States as a World-Power (1885–1902), 674–86

ix   viii   The command of the sea (1803–15), *passim*, 208–43

      xv   The Peninsular War (1808–14), 428–82

      xix   The Congress of Vienna, I (1814–5), *passim*, 576–615

      xxi   The Congress of Vienna, II (1815), *passim*, 646–71

x   v   The Papacy and the Catholic Church, *passim*, 131–68

      vii   Spain (1815–45), 205–43

      viii   The Spanish Dominions in America, 244–79

      ix   The establishment of independence in Spanish America, 280–309

      xxiii   Economic Change, *passim*, 727–62

xi   xx   The course of revolution in Spain and Portugal (1845–71), 550–75

      xxv   Rome and the Vatican Council, *passim*, 703–23

xii   x   The Iberian Peninsula, 257–69

      xx   The European Colonies, *passim*, 607–71

      xxi   The Republics of Latin America, *passim*, 672–702

Spalatinus. *See* Burkhardt, George, of Spelt

Spandau, secured by Gustavus, IV 201, 203; surrender of (1806), IX 278; 514

Spangenberg, August Gottlieb, Moravian Bishop, v 762

Spanheim, Ezechiel, Brandenburg ambassador at Paris, v 654

Spanish America, Spanish Colonies. *See* America, Spanish

"**Spanish Fury, The,**" at Antwerp (1576), III 246

Spanish Netherlands. *See* Netherlands, Spanish

—— Succession. *See* Spain, *and especially* Vol. v, Chaps. XIII and XIV

Spark (*Iskra*), Russian journal, XII 331 sq.

Sparre, Aage. *See* Lund, Archbishops of

—— Erik, Swedish noble, IV 165; constitution drawn up by, 167; 168 sq.; flight and execution of, 172 sq.

—— Ernest George, Imperialist general, at Nürnberg, IV 218; Saxony and, 225

—— Baron, Swedish Minister in Paris, VI 104

Sparta, excavation in, XII 845

Spaventa, Silvio, Neapolitan politician, XI 379

Speckbacher, Tyrolese leader, IX 355

Specx, Jacob, Dutch Governor-General of the Indies, IV 711

Spee, Friedrich von, Jesuit, IV 425; v 758

Speenhamland, meeting of Berkshire justices at, IX 691

Speier, Congress of Cities at (1523), II 153; Council of (1524), 173; Diet of (1526), 196; recess of this Diet, *ib.*, 203 sq.; Diet of (1529), 61, 203 sq., 206, 330; (1542), 242; (1544), 77, 244, 661; secret understanding of Lutheran princes at (1529), 204, 206; Diet of (1570), III 173, 177; *Deputationstag* at, 718; under French protection, IV 597; bishopric of, 407; v 56; occupied by the French, 435; captured (1792), VIII 299, 413; evacuated (1793), 415; Soult crosses the Rhine at, IX 253; Baden and the bishopric of, X 361

—— George von Schwalbach, Bishop of, I 573

—— Philip Christopher, Bishop of. *See* Trier

Speke, John Hanning, in Africa, XII 439; 809

Spence, James, Confederate foreign agent, VII 611

—— Thomas, VIII 761; *The End of Oppression*, 769; x 684; 576

Spencer, George John Spencer, 2nd Earl, VI 478; and the Whig party, IX 673; accepts Privy Seal, 674; Secretary for Home Department, 685; 698–9

—— Herbert, VI 821; XII 300; 772 sq.; 776

—— John Charles (Viscount Althorp), 3rd Earl, x 593; 603; and the Reform Bills, 609 sqq.; 614; 655; 657; emancipates the Crown slaves, 659; and the Factory Act, 660; and the house-tax, *ib.*;

and the Poor Law, 662; resigns, 663 sq.; takes office in the Melbourne Ministry, 664; succeeds to the earldom, 665; and municipal reform, 670; 673; 676 sqq.; XI 3

Spencer, J. Poyntz Spencer, 5th Earl, Lord-Lieutenant of Ireland, XII 40; 43; 81 sq.

—— Governor of Bengal, VI 558

Spencer's Gulf, settlement of, XI 792

Spener, Philipp Jacob, founder of the Pietists, V 671; 759 sq.; 762; VI 226; XI 710

Speng, Jakob, II 403 sq.

Spengler (German Reformer), II 138

Spens, Sir James, at Stockholm, IV 89 sq.

Spenser, Edmund, III 299, 366, 370, 600; VI 829 sq.

Speranski, Count Michael, Russian states-man, character of, IX 484; fall of, 487; Secretary of State, X 413; 417; 419; and Russian serfdom, 427; and the December rising, 441; 443; XI 264

Speratus, Paul, Reformer, II 160

Sperlette, John, Professor at Halle, IV 791

Speroni, Sperone, III 466; *Canace*, 467, 472

Spes, Gerau de, III 492-3

Speult, van, Dutch Governor of Amboina, the "massacre" and, IV 739

Speyerbach, French victory at (1703), V 408

Speziale, Pietro, of Cittadella, *De Gratia Dei*, II 380; 394

Spezzia, island stronghold of, X 196

Sphakianákes, Dr, in Crete, XII 423

Spicheren, battle of, XI 586 sq., 589

Spiegel, Lorenz Pieter van de, Grand Pen-sionary of Holland, VIII 288

Spieghel, Hendrik Laurenszoon, IV 718

Spielberg, castle of, X 118; 127, XI 75

Spielhagen, Friedrich, German novelist, XI 417; 419 sq.

Spielmann, Baron Anton, Austrian envoy to Prussia, VIII 333, 536

Spiera, Francesco, Italian Reformer, II 394 sq.

Spilbergen, George van, voyages of, IV 713

Spina, Cardinal, Archbishop of Corinth, Papal diplomatist, IX 181-3; 195, 198; at Laibach and Verona, X 150

Spinalonga, retained by Venice, V 349; French occupation of, XII 423

Spinola, Ambrogio de, Marquis of, succeeds to the Marquisate, III 535, 537, 539, 569, 636-8, 640, 643, 655, 722, 733; IV 3; 32; 66 sq.; recalled to Low Countries, 78; 81; captures Breda, 88, 642, 691, 698; 105; in Milan, 136, 679; and Palatinate, 34, 641, 673; death of, 138, 644

—— Federigo, Marquis of, killed at sea, III 535

—— Papal Legate in Romagna (1838-43), X 156

Spinoza, Baruch (*called also* Benedict), II 691, 708 sq.; IV 722; 789; V 744; 754 sq.

Spion Kop, British forces at, XII 642

Spiridónova, assassinates Luzhenovsky, XII 363

Spiring family, Great Elector and the, V 641

Spiritual Exercises, Ignatius Loyola's, II 657 sq.

Spithead, French fleet at, V 177; mutiny at (1797), VIII 476 sqq.

Spittler, Baron Ludwig Timotheus von, German historian, XII 817; 846

Spitzbergen, fishery disputes at, III 644; discovery of, XII 795

Spizza, fortress of, XII 387; 390; 392; ceded to Austria, 396 sq.; 428

Spoleto, Mastai-Ferretti (Pius IX) at, XI 72

Sponneck, Count Wilhelm Karl Eppingen von, Danish Minister of Finance, XI 225

Sporades, The, acquired by Venice, I 255

Sporck, Johann, Count von, Bavarian officer, IV 391

Spotswood, Alexander, Lieutenant-Governor of Virginia, VII 10

Spotsylvania, battle of (1864), VII 517 sq.

Spottiswoode, John, Archbishop of St Andrews, IV 487; 489; Lord Chancellor, 493; flight of, to England, 497; Charles I and, 503, 512

—— Sir Robert, IV 501

Spragg, Sir Edward, Admiral, V 189; 192 sq.; and Prince Rupert, 194, 197; 195 sq.

Sprat, Thomas, Bishop of Rochester, V 126; 132 sq.; 234

Spree district, acquired by Brandenburg, V 620

Spremberg, Hadik's troops near, VI 292

Sprenger, Jacob, *Malleus Maleficarum*, I 642

Sprengporten, Russian general (1800), IX 42

Sprengtporten, Baron Jakob Magnus, Colonel of the Nyland Dragoons (1772), VI 770

Spring Hill, battle at (1864), VII 524

Springfield (Illinois), growth of, VII 444; Lincoln buried at, 546

—— (Mass.), battle at (1787), VII 313

—— (Missouri), Lyon at, VII 460

Spuj, acquired by Montenegro, XII 396

Spuller, Eugène, French politician, XII 119

Spynie, Alexander Lindsay, 2nd Baron, at Stralsund, IV 107

"Squatter sovereignty," VII 427 sq., 430

Squillaci, Marquis of, Spanish statesman, VI 367; 370 sq.

Staaff, K., Swedish statesman, XII 278

Stackelberg, Count Ernest, Russian chief of Finance Ministry (1857), XI 618

—— Count, Russian Minister at Stock-holm, IX 38; at Vienna, 586

—— Russian general, in Russo-Japanese War, XII 587 sqq., 593

Stade, English Merchant Adventurers at, IV 8; captured by Danes (1712), V 582, 607; Danish occupation of, VI 23; 24; 263; 266; 272

Stadion, Count Francis von, Austrian states-
man, xi 156; 171; and Galicia, 174, 178;
187; Minister of Interior, 190, 398; re-
tirement of, 216; 403
—— Johann Kaspar, Baron von, iv 238
—— Johann Philipp Karl Joseph, Count
von, ix 259; replaces Cobenzl, 262; policy
of, 288; advice of, 316; 341–3, 359;
retirement of, 360
Stadt en Landen, iii 627
Stadtlohn, battle of (1623), iv 86, 91
Stäfa, agitation at, vi 625
Stägemann, Friedrich August, Prussian
statesman, at Congress of Vienna, ix 585
Staël, Madame de. *See* Staël-Holstein
Staël [-Holstein], Anne-Louise-Germaine *née*
Necker, Baroness of, vi 836; viii 220,
507; ix 21 sqq.; 130–2; society assembled
by, 427; and Constitutionalists, 569;
571, 575; x 40; 41; 52; 53; 100; 102;
De l'Allemagne, 401; 514; xi 507; 519
—— Baron Eric Magnus de, Swedish
ambassador in Paris, viii 789
Stämpfli, Jakob, Swiss politician, xi 256
Stafford, Cumberland's army at, vi 114;
496
—— Edward, iii 34
—— Sir Edward William, in New Zealand,
xi 799
—— Granville Leveson-Gower, 1st Marquis
of (2nd Earl Gower), vi 424; President of
Council, 439, 468; 450; 457; 464; and
Pitt Administration, 467
—— George Granville Leveson-Gower, 2nd
Marquis of (3rd Earl Gower), recalled
from Paris, vi 477
—— Thomas, rebellion of, against Mary,
ii 546
—— William Howard, Viscount, v 220;
execution of, 227; 231
Staffordshire, condition of miners in, xi 1
Stageführ, Dr, Cologne Reformer, ii 613
Stahl, Friedrich Julius, Prussian Conserva-
tive leader, xi 223; 395 sqq.; xii 826
—— George Ernest, physician, v 732;
734; xii 768
Stair, Sir James Dalrymple, Viscount,
President of Court of Session, v 287
—— Sir John Dalrymple, 1st Earl of,
Lord Advocate, v 292; 294 sq.
—— John Dalrymple, 2nd Earl of, vi 38;
70; 237
Stakhóvich, Russian politician, xii 365 sq.
Stålarm, General, in Finland, iv 172; 174
Stallupönen, Russians at, vi 264
Stalmann, agent of Christian William of
Brandenburg, in Magdeburg, iv 195
Stambul, vi 305; peace negotiations at, 308
Stambuloff, Stepan, Bulgarian Minister, xii
342; 406; 409 sqq.
Stamp Act, the American impost, of 1765,
vi 433 sqq., vii 148 sqq., 159 sq., 184
sqq., 194, 204 sq.
—— Acts, English, proposal to reduce
(1834–5), x 673

Stampalia, surrendered by Venice to the
Turks, iii 116
Stancari, Francisco, leader of the Polish
Unitarians, ii 637
Stańczyki, in Galicia, xii 337
Standen, Anthony, iii 18
Standish, Henry, Bishop of St Asaph, ii
431
Stang, Emil, Norwegian statesman, xii
285 sq.
Stångebro, Sigismund defeated at (1598),
iv 172
Stanhope, Alexander, English envoy to
Madrid, v 374 sq.; 380; 384
—— Charles Stanhope, 3rd Earl (Viscount
Mahon), vi 467
—— Charles, and the South Sea Company,
vi 41, 181
—— Lady Hester L., ix 685
—— James, 1st Earl Stanhope, in Spain,
v 376; captures Minorca, 426, 444; 466;
vi 13; 21; Secretary of State for Foreign
Affairs, 22; mission of, to Vienna, 23;
26 sq.; 29 sq.; and Quadruple Alliance,
31; 35; and Spain, 33, 38 sq.; 41; 104;
207
—— Philip Henry Stanhope, 5th Earl,
xii 840
—— William. *See* Harrington, Earl of
Stanislaus (I) Leszczynski, King of Poland,
v 593; 595 sqq.; and Mazepa, 600; 601;
603; 605; recognised by Great Britain,
608; recognised by Prussia, 667; vi 143;
152; 155 sq.; 192; and Polish Succession,
193 sqq.; re-elected King, 195; abdicates,
197; at Nancy, 199; 303; 310
—— (II) Augustus Poniatowski, King of
Poland, vi 200; 354; 628; election of,
666 sqq.; 671; 729 sq.; 765; viii 308,
Chap. xvii *passim*; ix 36
Stankar, Francis, iii 80
Stanley Pool, explorer at, xii 812
—— Arthur Penrhyn, Dean of Westminster,
xii 774
—— Hans, British envoy at Paris, vi 343;
345; 418; 420
—— Sir Henry Morton, xii 159; 167;
256; 658; finds Livingstone, 809; 810
sqq.
—— Owen, Captain, at Banks' Peninsula,
xi 793
—— Sir William, assists Warbeck and is
executed, i 468 sq.
—— Sir William, adventurer, iii 622
—— *See* Derby, Earls of
Stanton, Edwin McMasters, American Secre-
tary of War, vii 472, 572, 624, 630, 653
Stanyhurst, Richard, iii 369
Stanz, Swiss defeated at (1798), viii 640 sq.
Stanza della Segnatura, wall-paintings of
Raffaelle in the, ii 14
Staphylus (Stapellage), of Osnabrück, iii
161
Stapleton, Colonel, Governor of the Lee-
ward Islands, v 690

Staps, Friedrich, attempts to assassinate Napoleon, IX 139

Star Chamber, Court of, I 465; under Elizabeth, III 292, 342 sqq.; under James I, 561, 567, 571; and Laud, IV 278 sqq.; abolished, 291; suggested revival of, V 98

Stara Serbia, Austria and, XII 396

—— Zagora, Russian defeat at, XII 388

Stargard, taken by Gustavus Adolphus (1630), IV 196; Wittgenstein at (1813), IX 511

Starhemberg, Count George Adam, VI 140; Imperial ambassador at Paris, 252, 254, 335; and Treaty of Versailles, 337 sqq.; 341 sq.; 400

—— Count Guidobald von, Austrian field-marshal, V 408; in Spain, 426, 428; 434; 435; 446

—— Gundacker, Austrian Minister of Finance, VI 204

—— Prince Ludwig Joseph Max, Austrian envoy, in Antwerp, VIII 429; in London, 643; recalled (1808), IX 309; returns (1809), 344, 357

—— Count Rüdiger, Governor of Vienna, V 361

Staring, Antoni, Dutch writer, XI 676

Stark, John, guerrilla leader, VII 127

Starke, John, American general, VII 215

Starkey, Thomas, on agrarian reform, II 490

Stary-Borissoff, Partouneaux at, IX 503

Stasyulévich, Russian journalist, XII 298

Staszic, Stanislas, X 432; 449

—— Xavier Stanislas, Polish writer, VI 671

States of the Church. *See* Rome *and* Legations

—— General, of France, at Tours (1484), I 399; at Orleans (1439), 411, (1561), II 674; at Blois (1576), III 31, 44–5; at Paris (1593), 52; meeting of 1614, IV 120 sq.; of 1789, VIII 66, 87; meeting of, demanded by *Parlement*, 73, 97, 106; 108, 110, 113; meeting of, summoned, 114 sqq.; elections to, 118, Chap. V, 119–44; meeting of (1789), Chap. VI, 145 sqq.; Third Estate of, becomes the National Assembly, 153; finance of, 689 sqq. *See* National Assembly

—— —— The, of the Netherlands, II 74, 102

Statius, Achilles (Achille Estaço), Portuguese scholar, I 578

Stauffenberg, Franz von, Liberal leader in Germany, XII 146

Staunton, Federal advance on, VII 530; Sheridan at, 537

—— Francis, French officer, repulses the Peshwa's army, XI 726

Staupitz, Johann von, I 460; Luther and, 682; works of, 683; Vicar-General of Augustinians, II 115–8, 168

Stavuchanak, battle of, VI 307 sq.

Stayner, Sir Richard, Admiral, destroys Spanish Plate fleet, IV 484, 660; V 372

Stazio, lays foundation for Bibliotheca Vallicelliana, III 444

Steczyc, Diet of, III 91–2

Steelboy rising in Ireland, VI 491

Steele, Sir Richard, V 128; 467; 474

—— Thomas, X 227

Steen, Johannes Vilhelm Christian, Norwegian statesman, XII 285 sq.

Steenwyk, siege of (1592), III 626

Stefanóvich, Russian revolutionary, XII 307

Steffens, Henry, philosopher, VIII 788; professor of physics at Breslau, IX 327–8; philosophy of, XI 697 sq.

Stegeborg, Sigismund victorious at (1598), IV 172

Steigentesch, Baron, IX 352

Steiger, Jakob Robert, Swiss statesman, XI 247

Stein, Albrecht von, of Bern, II 315

—— Heinrich Friedrich Karl, Freiherr vom und zum, Prussian statesman, VI 728; VIII 773; IX 272; 282; intercepted letter of, 317; 328; life of, 329–35; favours Austrian alliance, 344; adviser of the Tsar, 513; schemes of, for Germany, 580; at Congress of Vienna, 586–8, 592, 598, 601, 609 sqq., 653; X 135; and German unity, 340, 345; 348 sqq.; retirement of, 352; excluded from Nassau Diet, 362; 365; 370; XII 820; 823

—— Heynlin von, opponent of Lutheran reforms, II 168

—— Marc Aurel, in Central Asia, XII 803

Steinau, Prussian force at, VI 230

Steiner, Jakob, mathematician, XI 260

Steinheil, Baron Thaddaeus, Governor-General of Finland, X 435

Steinkirke, battle of (1692), V 60, 261, 263

Steinmetz, Karl Friedrich von, Prussian general, XI 580; 585 sq.; at Spicheren, 587; at Gravelotte, 593 sq.; 606

Steinsiedel, fighting at (1813), IX 517

Steinwich, burgomaster of Stralsund, IV 106

Stellaland, established by Boers, XII 638

Stellenbosch, surrender of district of, IX 749; XI 778

Stelvio Pass, XI 243

Stenay, IV 612 sq.; Condé and, 615, 619; ceded to France, V 33; German occupation of, XI 596 sq.

Stenbock, Count Magnus, Swedish general, V 581 sq.; 603; 608 sq.

Stendhal. *See* Beyle, Marie-Henri

Stensen, Nicolaus, V 729; 731 sqq.; 738 sqq.

Stenzel, Gustav Adolf H., German historian, XII 824

Stephen, Archduke of Austria, Palatine of Hungary, XI 155; 181 sqq.

—— (the Great), Prince of Moldavia, and the Turks, I 83 sq.

—— Báthory, Prince of Transylvania, King of Poland, encouragement of Socinians by, II 638; III 91, 94; election and reign of, 97–103, 170; 180; and the Pope, 450; death of, 698; IV 167; V 344; 494; 498; 504

Stephen Bocskai, King of Hungary and Voivod of Transylvania, III 700; x 421
—— Crnoiević. *See* Crnoiević
—— Dushan, Tsar of Servia, XII 401
—— Thomas, King of Bosnia, I 71 sqq.
—— Tomasević, King of Bosnia, I 72 sq.
Stephen, James, Master in Chancery, and the abolition of slavery, x 659
Stephens, Alexander Hamilton, Confederate Vice-President, VII 522, 536, 576, 581, 603 sq.; opposes Confederate policy, 608 sq.
—— James, Fenian leader, XI 343
—— Joseph Rayner, x 659; 682 sq.
Stephenson, Robert, engineer, in Egypt, XII 430
Stepney, George, envoy to Brandenburg, v 662; VI 8
Stepniak, Sergius. *See* Kravchinsky
Sterbini, Pietro, Roman revolutionary, XI 91; 93
Sternbald, Franz, x 403
Sternhold, Thomas, composes metrical version of the Psalms, II 482
Steterburg, battle at (1553), II 275
Stettin, Peace of (1570), IV 166; and Sweden, 194, 196, 199, 203, 404, 427, 432; and Brandenburg, 430; restored to Sweden, v 45, 652; siege of (1676-7), 569 sq., 652; the "sequestration" of, 609; 610 sq.; VI 24; 36; 39; acquired by Prussia, 206 sq., 209, v 615; VI 218; 266; 298; shipbuilding at, 718; Hohenlohe retreats to, IX 277; capitulation of (1806), 279; negotiations concerning, 318; 514
Steuart, Sir James, *Principles of Political Oeconomy*, x 770
Steudner, Hermann, African explorer, XII 811
Stevens, Alfred, IX 416
—— Thaddeus, American statesman, VII 624 sq., 628, 653
—— Thomas, English Jesuit, IV 729
Stevenson, William, III 372
Stevinus, Simon, mathematician, v 709 sq.; 712
Stewart, Alexander, Earl of Moray. *See* Moray
—— Lady Arabella, III 358, 534
—— Archibald, Provost of Edinburgh, VI 112 sq.
—— Charles Edward, the Young Pretender. *See* Charles Edward
—— Charles William (Vane), Lord. *See* Londonderry, 3rd Marquess of
—— Sir Donald Martin, Field-Marshal, in Afghánistán, XII 470 sq.; 475
—— Dugald, VIII 770
—— Esmé, Lord of Aubigny, Duke of Lennox. *See* Lennox
—— Henry. *See* Methven
—— Henry Benedict, second son of the Chevalier St George, Cardinal of York, VI 113; 117; x 132
—— Sir Herbert, General, and the Gordon relief expedition, XII 442 sq.

Stewart, James (Prince of Wales), the Old Pretender. *See* James Francis Edward
—— James, Earl of Arran. *See* Arran
—— Lord James. *See* Moray, Earl of
—— John, Jacobite, VI 109
—— Colonel O. H., in Egypt, XII 440 sq.; murder of, 442
—— Sir Robert, defeats O'Neill, IV 526
—— William, Viscount Mountjoy. *See* Mountjoy
—— of Ardshiel, VI 111 sq.
Steyer, armistice at (1800), IX 68
Stiernhielm, George, Swedish man of science, IV 575
Stiernhöök, Swedish man of science, IV 575
Stillingfleet, Edward, Bishop of Worcester, v 749
Stirbey, Barbe, Hospodar of Wallachia, XI 284; 643
Stirling, and English Liturgy, IV 497; VI 92; Jacobite advance on, 99 sq.; 102; Gardiner's Horse at, 112; 115
—— Sir James, Captain, Governor of Western Australia, XI 791
—— Sir William Alexander, Earl of, poet, grant of Nova Scotia to, VII 75, 110 sqq.
Stirlingshire, Jacobitism in, VI 93
Stith, William, VII 60
Stoakes, Captain John, IV 485
Stockach, battle of (1799), VIII 655 sq.; engagement at (1800), IX 58
Stockdale, John Joseph, publisher, x 680
Stockhausen, August Wilhelm Ernst von, Prussian Minister of War, XI 229
Stockholm, marriage of Gustavus Adolphus at, IV 68; 89; 161; Estates at (1563), 162; 164 sq.; Diet at (1582), 167; 170 sq.; and Charles IX, 172, 174 sq.; Christian IV at, 179; 195; 209; Descartes dies at, 779; 787; bank of, v 268; 566; Estates at (1680), 573; Diet at (1682), 576; *Riksdag* at, 585; Patkul at, 586; 591; VI 36; Hat party at, 308; Prince Henry of Prussia at, 668; 740; 760 sq.; 765 sq.; conspiracy at, 771; 775; 778 sq.; 780; Gustavus III assassinated at, 784; Golovkin sent to, IX 36; Reuterholm returns to, 37; Stackelberg at, 38; Gustavus IV at, 322-4; agitation in, XI 684; 685; University of, XII 280
—— Truce of (1641), v 641; Treaty of (1719), 814 sq., VI 106, (1720), v 614 sq., (1724), 542
Stockholms Blodbad (1520), II 604
Stockmar, Christian Friedrich von, Baron, and Queen Victoria, x 674 sq.; XI 160; 166; Frederick William IV and, 191; 192
Stockton, Robert Field, in California, VII 395 sq.
Stoczek, fight at (1831), x 469
Stoddart, Charles, in Afghánistán, XII 800; 801
Stöcker, German Court-Preacher, XII 155

Stoessel, Russian general, in the Russo-Japanese War, xii 583; 585 sq.; 589; surrenders Port Arthur, 595 sq.

Stofflet, Nicolas, Vendean leader, viii 266, 355, 382; executed, 395

Stoianoff, Unionist leader in Eastern Rumelia, xii 406

Stoiloff, Bulgarian Minister, xii 411

Stokes, Sir George Gabriel, xii 782

Stokesley, John, Bishop of London, ii 433

Stoke-upon-Trent, battle of (1487), i 466 sq.

Stolberg, Count Anton, xi 51

—— Count Friedrich L. von, German poet, viii 773 sq.; 776; x 160

—— Juliana von, iii 190

Stolbova, Peace of (1617), iv 181 sq., v 503, 610

Stoletoff, General, Russian envoy to Kabul, xii 469 sq.

Stolhofen, Lewis of Baden at, v 407 sq.; taken by the French, 418

Stolpen, camp of, vi 288; 289

Stolýpin, Peter, Russian Minister of the Interior, xii 366 sq.; Prime Minister, 368; policy of, 369 sqq.; and the third Duma, 375 sq.; 377

Stommelin, Christine de, correspondence of, i 626

Stone, Andrew, Under-Secretary of State, vi 488

—— George, Archbishop of Armagh (brother of above), vi 488 sq.

—— William, Governor of Maryland, vii 33

—— Captain, killed by Indians, vii 19

—— Miss, captured by brigands, xii 425

Stony Point, captured by Wayne (1779), vii 220

Storch, Nicholas, Anabaptist, ii 166 sq.

Storkyro, battle of the (1714), v 609

Storm, Lambertus Dominicus, Dutch politician, xi 663

—— Theodor Waldsen, German writer, x 405; xi 412; 414; 417 sq.; 420

Stormberg, taken by the Boers, xii 642

Stormont, Viscount. *See* Mansfield, David Murray, 2nd Earl of

Stornoway, Jacobites at, vi 105

Story, Dr John, ii 474, 585

Stosch, Albrecht von, Prussian general, xi 456

Stourdza, Alexander, Russian diplomatist and writer, x 21; pamphlet of, circulated by the Tsar, 364 sq.

—— Michael, Hospodar of Moldavia, xi 282 sqq.

Stowe, Harriet Elizabeth Beecher, *Uncle Tom's Cabin*, vii 440, 746

Stowell, Sir William Scott, Lord, ix 45; xii 713 sqq.

Strachan, Captain Sir Richard, ix 234; 239; and the British expedition to the Scheldt, 358

Strachey, Henry, at Lake Manasarowar, xii 798

Strachey, Sir John, xii 460; 462; and Indian famine, 472; and Indian finance, 473, 476

—— Sir Richard, General, xii 462; and the Indian Famine Commission, 472; 798

Strachwitz, Count Moritz von, German poet, xi 413 sq.

Strada, Famianus, iii 213

Stradella, Prince Eugene at, v 415

—— Pass, seized by Sardinians, vi 245

Strängnäs. *See* Strengnaes

Straeten, van der, Belgian writer, prosecution of, x 530

Strafford, Frederick Thomas Wentworth, Earl of, viii 294

—— Thomas Wentworth, 1st Earl of, iii 610, 737; early career of, iv 263 sqq.; home policy of, 269 sq.; 272; 276 sq.; Lord Deputy of Ireland, 278; 283 sq.; impeachment and trial of, 287 sqq.; death of, 290 sqq.; 295 sq.; 303; 316; 318; Irish policy of, 517 sq.; "Graces" and, 519; 520 sq.; vi 786

—— Thomas Wentworth, 3rd Earl of (Lord Raby), v 431 sq.; 438 sq.

Straits Convention, xi 30

—— Settlements, Crown colony of, xii 532

Stralen, Antony van, iii 216, 225

Stralsund, iv 105 sq.; siege of (1628), 106 sqq.; Sweden and, 186, 191 sqq.; 195; 219; restored to Sweden, v 45; besieged (1676), 569; 603; (1712), 582, 607; 608; Charles XII at, 610 sq.; lost by Swedes (1678), 652; vi 24; fall of (1715), 25; 37; 276; blockade of, 277; 279; Russian troops at, ix 251, 263; siege of (1807), 288–9, 295, 300, 368, 396; Clinton at, 297; 337; falls into Schill's hands (1809), 357

Strange, Lord. *See* Derby

Strangford, Percy Clinton Sidney Smythe, 6th Viscount, at Lisbon, ix 301

Straparola, Gianfrancesco of Caravaggio, iii 468

Strassburg, ii 87; Swiss religious influence on, 160; 205; rejection of Schwabach articles by, 210; the *Tetrapolitana* and, 212; surrenders to Charles V (1547), 258; 328 sq.; joins Schmalkaldic League, 336; Calvin at, 363; withdrawal of Archbishop Gebhard to, iii 708; schism of, 709; ecclesiastical difficulty in, 712, 715, 717, 718; Protestant Union joined by, 725; troops levied in, 731; Spanish in, iv 129; French in (1633), 144; 209; 368; 405; 407; occupied by French (1681), v 48, 50, 63, 230, 357, 364; 422; and the Peace of Utrecht, 436, 450; Villars at, 435, 452; 653; University of, 628; vi 123; Austria and, 141; 144; 238; and the States General, viii 125; Duc d'Enghien at, ix 30; 57; Lutheran consistory at, 204; magazine formed at, 252; Napoleon at (1805), 253; Berthier

at (1809), 347; Jews of, 588; Rapp in (1815), 645; bishopric of, x 361; xi 31; political demonstrations at, 137; 243; 464; 576; 580; siege of, 588; fall of, 600, 604; and insurance against unemployment, xii 755

Strassburg, Erasmus, Bishop of (1541), iii 158

—— John zu Manderscheid, Bishop of, iii 158

Stratford de Redcliffe, Stratford Canning, 1st Viscount, at Congress of Vienna, ix 585; 600; at St Petersburg, x 189 sq.; 191; at Constantinople, 549; 551; in Turkey, xi 275 sqq.; 306; and causes of Crimean War, 313 sq., 316; 320; and Suez Canal, 638

Strathallan, James Drummond, 5th Viscount, vi 117

Strathcona, Donald Alexander Smith, Lord, xi 774

Strathnairn, Hugh Henry Rose, Lord, at Constantinople, xi 313; in India, 749

Stratimirović, George, Serb leader, xi 180

Stratton, victory of Hopton at (1643), iv 313

Straubing, French army at, vi 236 sq.

Straudenz, Prussian army at, vi 242

Strauss, David Friedrich, theologian, ii 697; x 382; xi 246

—— Jacob, Reformer, ii 160, 183

Strawberry Hill, xi 355

Strengnaes, Diet of (1523), ii 622; free school of, iv 187

—— Bothvid, Bishop of, ii 629

—— Matthias Gregory, Bishop of, killed in Stockholm Blood Bath, ii 604

—— heretic Bishop of, crowns Sigismund, iv 171

Strickland, Francis, Jacobite, vi 111

—— Walter, at the Hague, v 138

Strieltsy, Russian arquebusiers, v 484; 578 sq.; at Azoff (1695), 521; revolt of the (1698), 523 sqq.

Strindberg, August, Swedish writer, xii 280

Strobach, Anton, Vice-President of the Austrian *Reichstag*, xi 178

Strode, William, iv 281; impeached, 297

Stroganoff, Gregory, Russian colonist, v 494

—— Count Paul, Russian Minister, viii 784, 786; ix 306; influence of, 483

Stromboli, naval battle off (1676), v 44, 162

Stroppiana, Langosco di, iii 401

Strousberg, Bethel Henry, German banker, xi 646

Strozzi, Carlo, member of Florentine *Pratica*, i 176

—— Filippo (Giambattista), of Florence, ii 26; 72

—— Filippo (grandson of above), French general, ordered to raid Spanish coasts, iii 16; refused entrance by Rochelle, 20; sent to treat with La Noue, 24, 300, 303, 387, 501

Strozzi, Francesco, the *Thucydides*, iii 471

—— Piero, ii 77 sq., 88

Struensee, Charles Augustus, vi 747

—— John Frederick, Count, Danish statesman, vi 735; 744; 746 sqq.; execution of, 750; 751; 756

Strutt, Robert John, and radio-activity, xii 790

Struve, Gustav von, Baden politician, xi 61 sq.; 145; 163 sq.; imprisoned, 192

—— Russian Liberal, xii 330; 333; 375; 378

Stryeshneff, Peter, uncle of Peter the Great, v 521

Strzygowski, Josef, xii 845

Stuart, Sir Charles, Colonel, vii 230

—— James Ewell Brown, Confederate general, vii 478; killed (1864), 519

—— Sir John, in Calabria, ix 270; in Sicily, 382; victory of, at Maida, 404

—— John MacDouall, Australian explorer, xi 798

—— Villiers, elected for Waterford, x 644

—— Colonel, in Ceylon, ix 733

—— de Rothesay, Sir Charles Stuart, Baron, x 98; and Portuguese affairs, 312, 319 sqq.

Stubbs, William, Bishop of Oxford, xi 363; historical works of, xii 835, 839, 850

Studer, Bernhard, Swiss geologist, xi 260

Studianka, French cross the Berezina at, ix 502

Stübner, Marcus, Anabaptist, ii 166 sq.

Stühlingen, beginning of Peasants' Rising at (1524), ii 177 sq.

Stuhlweissenburg, coronation of Ferdinand I at, i 97; Zápolya crowned at, ii 198; Ferdinand I crowned at, 199; deputation from Diet of Poland to Báthory at, iii 97; siege of (1543), 118

Stuhm, Swedes at, iv 187, 192

Stuhmsdorf, negotiations at (1635), iv 365 sq., 577, v 638

Stukeley, Sir Thomas, iii 286, 597

Stuñiga, Diego Lopez de. *See* Zuñiga

—— or Zuñiga, Lope de, Spanish poet, i 379

Stupan, Domenic, iv 52

Sture, Erik, murder of, iv 164

—— Nils, stabbed in prison by Erik XIV, iv 164

—— Sten (the younger), ii 601, 603 sq., 621

—— Svante, administrator of Sweden (d. 1512), ii 603

—— Count Svante, murder of, iv 164

Sturm, Beata, Pietist, v 762

—— Jacob, German Reformer, ii 204, 258

—— John, Professor at Paris, ii 286

Sturt, Charles, Captain, Australian explorer, xi 792; 795

Sturzl, Dr Jacob, ii 329

Stuttgart, siege of (1525), by Ulrich of Würtemberg, ii 181; meeting of Protestant Princes at (1607), iii 724; (1609),

730; Prince Eugene at, v 452; 762; Ney at (1805), ix 253; Napoleon confiscates stores at, 373; disturbances in, xi 61; Russian Liberal journal published at, xii 333

Stuve, Johann Karl Bertram, Hanoverian statesman, xi 148; 220

Stuyvesant, Peter, Governor of New Netherlands, vii 22; 39 sq.

Styfel, M., German Reformer, ii 160

Styria, transferred to Ferdinand I, ii 150; overrun by Turkish horsemen, iii 107; Protestantism in, 702; Estates of, 728; Austria and, vi 204; 628; revolutionary movement in, xi 155; and German unity, 173; 179; 184; and Hungary, 202; 399

Styrum, Hermann Otto, Count of Limburg-Styrum, Imperial field-marshal, v 407 sq.

Suakin, assigned to Egypt, xii 439; 440 sqq.; Indian garrison at, 447; 806; 811

Suard, J.-B.-Antoine, viii 512, 515

Suarez, Franciscus, iii 744, 746; statements in, 757, 765, 767; xii 708

—— Prussian Privy Councillor, vi 728

Submission of the Clergy in England, The (1532), ii 438

Suboff, Plato, and Catharine II, vi 696

Suchet, Louis Gabriel, Duc d'Albufera, ix 61; receives Albufera, 111; defeats Blake before Saragossa, 454; repulsed at Valencia, 457; cooperates with Macdonald, 464; besieges Tortosa, 465; 470; directions of Napoleon to, 471; at Valencia, 473 sqq.; Soult joins, 482; 624, 645

Suchow, captured by "Taipings," xi 821; xii 793; travellers at, 799, 802

Suchtelen, Count Jan Pieter, Russian Minister in Stockholm, xi 679

Suckling, Sir John, plot of, iv 289; v 745; 747

Sucre, revolutionary leader and President of Bolivia, x 295 sqq.

Suczawa, seized by Solyman II, iii 117

Suda, fortress of, retained by Venice, v 349

—— Bay, Ibrahim Pasha at, x 189; xii 420; Turkish fort in, 423

Sudan, the Egyptian (1841–1907), Vol. xii, Chap. xv; 3; Great Britain and, 40 sq.; 55; France and, 129; 132; 240; 343; 658 sq.; rivalry of the Powers in, 660; 662; 664; 812 sq.

Sudéikin, Russian Chief of Detective Department, xii 306; 311

Sudermania, Duke Charles of. *See* Charles XIII of Sweden

Sudzha, protest by agricultural committee in, xii 329

Sue, Eugène, French novelist, xi 131; 427

Suet river, Marchand on, xii 813

Suez, Turkish fleet leaves, for India (1538), iii 117; Isthmus of, viii 597; Napoleon at, 607; xi 346

—— Canal, xi 637 sq., 788; Disraeli and, xii 32; 390; 430 sqq.; opening of, 433;

and Egyptian question, 445; and Indian trade, 463; 499

Suez Canal Convention, xii 456

Suffolk, Charles Brandon, Duke of, i 484; ii 47; invades France, 421 sq., 425, 446, 560; iii 360

—— Henry Grey, Marquis of Dorset, created Duke of, ii 505; 510, 516 sq.; 518–28

—— Edmund de la Pole, Earl of, i 452, 474 sq., 481

—— Richard de la Pole, titular Duke of. *See* Pole, de la

—— Henry Howard, Earl of, vi 443 sq.; 450

—— Thomas Howard, Earl of, iii 323; 559 sq.; 567; 571

—— (Mass.), significant political meeting at (1774), vii 161, 163

Suffren de Saint-Tropez, Pierre-André de, French admiral, vi 454; 469; 577

Sugiyama, Japanese *attaché* at Peking, xii 520 sq.

Suhm, Peter Friderik af, Danish historian, vi 750

Suiva river, Russian fleet built on, v 591

Sujah, *or* Shuja, Shah, Amir of Afghánistán, ix 732; xi 731 sq.; 734; 736

Sukhúm, rising in, xii 363

Suleymán (Solyman), the Magnificent, Ottoman Sultan, i 92 sq.; Hungary invaded by (1521), 93, 96 sq., 337; capture of Rhodes by (1522), 93 sq.; Francis I and, 94 sq.; victory of, at Mohács, 96 sqq.; invades Hungary (1529), ii 206; (1532), 67, 218 sq.; (1538), 242; (1543), 77; Vol. iii, Chap. iv *passim*; at Bagdad (1535), 113; resolves on war with Venice (1537), 114, 115–6; takes field against tributary Prince of Moldavia (1538), 117; campaigns of, in Hungary, 118–9; keeps his conquests at Peace of 1547, 120; begins new campaign against Persia (1548), 120; confers lordship of Transylvania upon Zápolya's widowed Queen, 122; peace with Ferdinand (1562), 123; the maritime struggle with Spain, 124; despatches a fleet to Malta (1565), 125; death of (1566), in camp before Szigeth, 126; the re-organisation of Ottoman State, 127–30, 169–70; v 341; 347; vi 507; x 171

—— (Solyman) II, Ottoman Sultan, v 367; death of, 369

—— Pasha, Governor of Rumelia, i 80 sq.

—— Pasha. *See* Sèves

—— Pasha, xii 388 sq.

—— son of Zobeir Pasha, xii 439; 441

Sulkovski, Prince, at Diet of Posen, x 463

Sullivan's Island, bombardment of (1776), vii 173

Sully, Maximilien de Béthune, Baron de Rosny, Duke of, i 525 sq., iii 12, 41, 398, 536, 664–5, 671, 673, 677–8, 681–2; financial administration of, 693 sqq.;

and Turks, IV 8 sq.; retires to Bastille, 118; 122; religious freedom and, 624; 625

Sully-Prudhomme, René-François-Armand, XI 515

Sulpicians, French order of the, V 79

Sulz, Alvig von, in Engadine, IV 56

—— Count Rudolf von, II 329

Sulzbach, and Landshut War, I 315

—— House of, VI 231

—— Count Palatine Augustus of, at Dresden, IV 215 sq.

—— Charles Theodore, Count Palatine of. *See* Palatinate (Electors Palatine)

—— Philip of, in Fünen, IV 589

Sumatra, Dutch trade in, IV 711, 740; Great Britain and, VI 429; Dutch supremacy in, XI 667; Dutch War in, XII 243; 669

Summa Doctrinae Christianae, by Canisius, II 682

Sumner, Charles, American statesman, VII 429, 624 sq., 628, 636 sq.; and reaction, 640; 653; 744; XII 21

—— Edwin Vose, American general, VII 476

Sumter, Thomas, American general, VII 225 sq.

Sumter, Confederate man-of-war, XII 17

Sumy, peasant rising in, XII 361

Sunda, Rájah of, and the Portuguese, IX 718

Sunderland, Charles Spencer, 3rd Earl of, V 461; Secretary of State, 465; 466; 469; VI 40 sq.; 70; 181

—— Robert Spencer, 2nd Earl of, Secretary of State, V 224; 226; 230; and James II, 231; 233 sqq.; and William of Orange, 243; dismissal of, 245; 255; 271; 273; and William III, 274; 307; 461

Sundgau, French claims to the, IV 602

Sungari river, navigation of, XI 273

Sunnenvæder, Peter (Jakobsson), II 623

Sunnites, struggle between the Shiites and the, I 90

Suok, caravan route to, XII 793; 798

Superior, Lake, navigation of, XII 612

Supernae dispositionis arbitrio, Bull, II 31

Supremacy, Act of (1559), III 284

Surat, the English and Dutch at, IV 741 sqq.; the Dutch in district of, V 697; 698; 703; regained by France, VI 464; 521; Treaty of, 575; Mornington's policy in, IX 724

Suresnes, Conference at, III 52; Truce of, 417

Surhud, English traveller at, XII 800

Surian, Michiel, II 373, 547

Surinam, English colony at, IV 755; the Dutch in, V 110, 151, 161, 688; 154; 189; exchanged for New York, VII 80; taken by British (1799), VIII 484; reduced (1804), IX 240, 750

Surji Arjangáon, Treaty of, IX 726

Surlet de Chokier, Baron, Regent of Belgium, X 539 sq.

Surman, embassy of, to Delhi, V 701; VI 559

Surraino, Michele, III 169, 188

Surrey, Henry Howard, Earl of (by courtesy), III 365, 367; executed, II 462

—— Thomas Howard, 1st Earl of. *See* Norfolk, 2nd Duke of

—— Thomas Howard, 2nd Earl of. *See* Norfolk, 3rd Duke of

Susa (Turin), acquired by France, IV 134 sq.; Treaty of (1629), 275

—— (Susiana), archaeological discoveries at, XII 846

Suso, Heinrich, mystic, V 758

Sussex, Sir Thomas Radcliffe, 3rd Earl of, Lord Deputy of Ireland, III 278-9, 282, 588, 590

Sussy, Collin de, IX 142

Sutherland, John Gordon, 15th *or* 16th Earl of, VI 99 sqq.

—— 1st Duke of. *See* Gower, G. G. Leveson-Gower, Lord

Sutlej river, boundary of Sikh kingdom, XI 731; 735; 738; 740; exploration on, XII 798

Sutter, John Augustus, Californian settler, VII 400

Sutter's Fort, built, VII 400

Sutton, Charles Manners-. *See* Canterbury, Viscount

—— Thomas Manners-. *See* Manners

—— Sir Robert, and the Peace of Passarowitz, VI 32; at Paris, 38

Sutzo, Michael, X 179

Suvórin, the *Novoë Vremya*, XII 314

Suvóroff, Alexander Vasilievich, Russian field-marshal, VI 697; VIII 316, 326, 336; in Poland, 546 sq.; arbitrarily disgraced, 646; commands Austro-Russian force (1799), 654, 656 sq., 659 sqq.; IX 41; 49, 57; Turks defeated by, 385; X 431

Suys, Baron de, Wallenstein and, IV 237

Suzannet, *Chouan* leader, IX 2; 14

Svane, Hans, Bishop of Zealand. *See* Zealand

Sveaborg, Finnish fortress, VI 770; 775; 779; Swedish fleet shut up in, VIII 325; armed rising at, XII 369; 377

Svenskund, battle of, VI 782

Sverdrup, Johan, Norwegian statesman, XII 283 sqq.

Svoboda, Václav, Čech writer, XI 654

Svyatopolk-Mirsky, Prince, XII 346 sq.; 350

Svyesti Krest, evacuated by Russia, VI 304

Swabia, Bernard in, IV 216; Gustavus and, 219; ravaged in the War, 418; French invasion of, V 418; 622; Austria and, VI 204; 238; and the Congress of Vienna, IX 588

—— Frederick (of Hohenstaufen), Duke of, V 630

Swabian League, The, Knights of St George in, I 292, 296; Swiss refuse to join, 307, 321; II 41, 146; joins in crushing Franconian Knights (1524), 156 sq., 178, 181, 220, 224

Swallow Islands, annexation of, xii 667
Swammerdam, Jan, iv 722; v 727; 737
Swan river, exploration on, xi 791
Swatis, The, attack British posts, xii 488
Swaziland, the Transvaal and, xii 640
Sweating Sickness, The (1485), i 488
Sweden
  ii   xvii   The Scandinavian North (III), 599–602, 621–33
  iv   v   The Vasa in Sweden and Poland (1560–1630), 158–89
        vi   Gustavus Adolphus (1630–2), 190–222
        vii Wallenstein and Bernard of Weimar (1632–5), *passim,* 223–55
        xiii The later years of the Thirty Years' War (1635–48), *passim,* 364–94
        xiv The Peace of Westphalia, *passim,* 395–433
        xx   The Scandinavian North (1559–1660), 560–91
  v   ii   The foreign policy of Louis XIV (1661–97), *passim,* 32–63
        xviii The Scandinavian Kingdoms, 558–83
        xix Charles XII and the Great Northern War, 584–615
        xxi The Great Elector and the first Prussian King, *passim,* 639–72
  vi   ix   The Seven Years' War, *passim,* 251–300
        x   Russia under Anne and Elizabeth, *passim,* 301–28
        xxi Denmark under the Bernstorffs and Struensee, *passim,* 735–57
        xxii The Hats and Caps under Gustavus III (1721–92), 758–84
  viii xi   The European Powers and the Eastern Question, *passim,* 306–37
  ix   ii   The Armed Neutrality (1780–1801), *passim,* 34–54
        xi   The Napoleonic Empire at its height (1807–9), *passim,* 294–340
        xiii The Continental System (1809–14), *passim,* 361–89
      xix and xxi The Congress of Vienna, I and II (1814–5), *passim,* 576–602, 646–71
  xi   xxiv Scandinavia (1815–70) (1) Sweden and Norway, 677–90
  xii xi   Scandinavia (1872–1909), 273–90
Sweelinck, Dirk, iv 720
Swellendam, surrender of, ix 749
Swieten, Geraard van, vi 635; x 159
—— van, Dutch general, xii 243
Swiętochowski, Polish publicist, xii 337 sq.

Swift, Jonathan, v 70; 458; 467; 469; 471; *Drapier's Letters,* vi 485
Swinburne, Algernon Charles, xi 357 sq.; 365
Swiss Leagues, The, and Pope Julius II, i 135 sq., 137; and France (1516), 142; 293, 295; 307 sq.; ii 306, 320, 324, 341; mercenaries of, in French and Imperial armies, 44 sq.; treaty of, with France (1522), 62; and Neuchâtel, v 449. *See also* Switzerland and the various Cantons, etc.
Switzerland
  ii   x   The Helvetic Reformation, 305–41
        xi   Calvin and the Reformed Church, *passim,* 342–76
  vi   xvii Switzerland from the Treaty of Aarau to the French Revolution, 611–25
  viii xxi The Second Coalition, *passim,* 633–64
  ix   iv   France and her tributaries (1801–3), *passim,* 81–106
        xiv The French Dependencies, and Switzerland, 390–427
      xix and xxi The Congress of Vienna, I and II (1814–5), *passim,* 576–615, 646–71
  x   x   Economic Change, *passim,* 727–62
  xi viii The achievement of Swiss Federal Unity, 234–61
  xii xxiii Social Movements, *passim,* 730–65
        [*See also* Swiss Leagues, Helvetic Republic, Grisons and the several Cantons]
Sword, Order of the, iii 73, 82; v 630
Sybel, Heinrich von, German historian, xi 231; xii 146; 827 sq.
Sydenham, Charles Edward Poulett Thomson, Lord, Governor-General of Canada, xi 758 sqq.; 766 sq.
—— Col. William, expelled from Parliament, iv 548
Sydney (New South Wales), colony established at, ix 737; xi 790; and Victoria, 792; 794 sq.; industries of, xii 623; University of, 627; 628; Federal Convention at, 631; 634; 666
—— (Ontario), xii 612
—— Henry, Earl of Romney. *See* Romney
—— Thomas Townshend, 1st Viscount, vi 462; 468; and New South Wales, ix 736
Sykes, Molesworth, in Persia, xii 801
Syllabus, The Papal, published (1864), xi 539; 712 sqq.
Sylvester II (Gerbert), Pope, i 536
Sylvius (de La Boé), Francis, physiologist, v 730 sqq.; 734
Symonds, John Addington, *Renaissance in Italy,* xii 849

Syracuse, citadel of, vi 153

Syria, Ottoman conquest of, i 91; Spanish, etc. factories in, 496; the Osmanli Sultans and, vi 507; Napoleon's expedition against, viii 607 sqq.; Mehemet Ali and, x 512; invaded by Ibrahim Pasha, 547, 549 sq.; 553; 559 sqq.; 566; 569; 571; xi 276; Napoleon III and, 476; 634; France and, 636; Turkey and, xii 4

Syrokorenie, Ney crosses the Dnieper at, ix 501

Szabács, on the Save, captured by Corvinus (1476), i 81; taken by Solyman the Magnificent (1521), 93

Szakmáry, George. *See* Pécs, Bishop of

Szalankemen, battle of (1691), v 61, 369

Szalay, Ladislas, Hungarian historian, xi 431

Szápáry, Count Julius, Hungarian statesman, xii 199

Szász, Charles, Hungarian writer, xi 430

Szatmar, annexed by John Sigismund Zápolya, iii 125

Szczaniecki, Ludovic, Polish colonel, x 453

Széchenyi, Count Stephen, Hungarian patriot, viii 777; x 371; xi 155; 172; 183; 205; *Survey*, 400 sq.; writings of, 425 sqq., 431

Szech'uan, xii 502; disturbances in, 515; 793; travellers in, 796 sq.; 805

Szécsen, Count Anton, Hungarian statesman, xi 404; xii 177

Szegedin, Diet of (1458), i 72; Ferdinand defeated at (1552), iii 123; xi 210; fight at (1849), 211

Széklers, The, and Hungary, xi 202

Széll, Koloman, Hungarian statesman, xii 191; 204 sq.

Szemere, Bartholomew, President of Hungarian Ministry, xi 207; 210; 212 sq.

Szent Tomasch, Hungarian repulse at, xi 182

Szerenes, Diet at (1605), iii 701

Szigeth, besieged by Solyman, iii 126; taken by the Turks (1566), 130, 170

Szigligeti, Ede, Hungarian dramatist, xi 427

Szilágyi, Alexander, Hungarian historian, xi 431

—— D., Hungarian Minister of Justice, xii 199

Szimanski, Polish socialist, xii 337

Szlachta, Polish gentry, elevation to power of, iii 76 sqq.

Szön, Peace of, iv 192

Szöreg, battle of, xi 211

Szony, engagement at, xi 206

Szujski, Józef, Polish historian, xi 660

Taaffe, Count Eduard von, Austrian statesman, xii 186 sq.; 192; Ministry of, 193 sqq.; 199 sq.

—— Theobald, Earl of Carlingford. *See* Carlingford

Taaffe, Count, Governor of Galicia, x 462

Table Bay, Dutch East India Company and, iv 713

Tablet, Catholic newspaper, xii 69

Tabley, de, John Byrne Leicester Warren, Lord, English poet, xi 353

Tabor, Austrian army in, vi 233

Taborberg, Austrian force on, vi 257

Taborites, Hussite sect, ii 186

Taboureau Desréaux, Louis-Gabriel, French financier, viii 89

Tabriz, arrival of Turkish army at (1534), iii 112; taken by Solyman II, 120; Morier at, xii 800

Tachard, Father, Jesuit missionary in Siam, xii 534

Tachau, General Bellegarde's army at, ix 347

Taché, Sir Étienne Pascal, Premier of Canada, xi 769; 775

Tachenius, Otto, chemist, v 731

Ta-chien-lu, travellers at, xii 797, 803

Tacitus, works of, published by Beroaldus, ii 16

Tadcaster, Catholic Earls at, iii 281

Tafel, Julius, German chemist, xii 770

Tafilet, French explorer at, xii 808

Tafna, Treaty of the (1837), x 504

Taft, William Howard, Governor of the Philippines, xii 531

Taganrog, founded, v 522; 527; 605; razed by Peter the Great, 606; ix 47; death of Alexander I at, x 190, 439

Tagliamento river, French advance on (1800), ix 68; Archduke Charles at, 258; Austrian advance on, xi 86

Tagus river, Santa Cruz's fleet in, iii 504; British force in, ix 303–4; Russian squadron in, 367; Spaniards rally behind (1809), 448, 450; Soult marches on, 453; Wellington fortifies mouth of, 459; Masséna withdraws to, 462; Marmont in the valley of, 468 sq.; boat-bridge on, destroyed, 472; Portuguese royal family sails from, x 310; 317; French fleet in (1831), 325 sq.; defence of, 328; Portuguese fleet sails from, 333; Napier enters (1833), 334; French men-of-war in, xi 574

Tahiti, xi 16; 35; annexed by French, 793; xii 668

Tahmasp, Shah. *See* Tamasp

Taille, French hearth-tax, account of, i 406; iv 120, 152 sq.; at opening of the Fronde, 606; 621; v 8 sq.; on eve of the Revolution, viii 67

Taine, Hippolyte-Adolphe, historian, viii 53, 64, 78; xi 523 sq.; 527; xii 93; 114; 831; 833 sq.

"Taiping" Rebellion, xi 820 sq.; xii 502

T'aitsung, Emperor of China, xii 509

Taitzu-ho river, xii 591; fighting on, 592; 593; 597

T'aiwên Kun. *See* Tai Won Kun

Tai Won Kun (T'aiwên Kun), The, father of King of Korea, xii 509; 567; 570 sq.

Takadzukasa, Japanese noble, XI 834;
837 sqq.
Takasugi, Chōshiu leader, XI 852
Taku, projected railway to, XII 505; 514;
518 sq.; 521; Japanese force at, 575;
796
—— forts, capture of, XI 812; 817 sq.
Takushan, Japanese troops land at, XII 585
Tak van Poortvliet, J. P., Dutch statesman,
XII 244; 246 sq.
Talabot, Paulin, French politician, XI 298
Talamone, retained by Philip, III 385
Talana Hill, Boers repulsed at, XII 642
Talavera, Synod of (1498), I 651; Vendôme
at, V 428; IX 443; Victor's headquarters
at, 451; campaign of (1809), 452 sqq.
—— Ferdinand Mendoza de, Archbishop
of Granada (d. 1507). *See* Granada
Talbot, Charles, Duke of Shrewsbury. *See*
Shrewsbury
—— Sir Gilbert, envoy to Denmark, V 109
—— Peter, titular Archbishop of Dublin,
V 305
—— Richard, Earl of Tyrconnel. *See*
Tyrconnel
—— Thomas, X 691
—— William, Bishop of Salisbury, VI 43
—— William Henry Fox, and photo-
graphy, XII 783
Talienwan, Japanese occupation of, XII 511;
589
—— Bay, European force at, XI 818
Ta-li-fu, XII 500; caravan route to, 793;
796 sq.
Tallard, Camille d'Hostun, Comte de,
Marshal of France, ambassador in
London, V 382, 385 sqq., 430; in cam-
paign against the Allies, 407 sqq.
Talleyrand-Périgord, Charles Maurice de,
Prince of Benevento, VII 321, 324; VIII
102, 159, 178; and Constitution of 1791,
183; 191, 198; and Church property, 195,
694; and diplomatic relations of, with
Great Britain (1792), 296, 298; Minister
of Foreign Affairs, 493 sq., 508; 507, 596,
667 sq.; and Napoleon, 675, 680; IX 1;
4; eludes Napoleon's domination, 10; 30,
47, 65, 75–6, 101; leader of a peace party,
103; 107; Vice-Grand Elector, 110; 136;
Grand Chamberlain, 111; receives Benevento, *ib.*; 138, 194, 268–9; and Concordats, 180–4, 189; 194; retirement of,
195; 252, 259, 262; and Prussia, 265–6;
268–9; policy of, towards England, 270;
288, 296 sqq., 320, 342; and *Bibliothèque britannique*, 427; concerned in
intrigues at Paris, 445; interview with
Alexander, 556; 558; and Bourbons,
559 sqq.; and Ministry of Louis XVIII,
565; advice of, 567; and Duc d'Orléans,
573; services of, 575; and First Peace
of Paris, 576; and Congress of Vienna,
579, 584, 647, 652–3, 667; and slave
trade, 662; and the peace negotiations,
664; X 4; doctrine of Legitimacy of, 5;

retirement of, 13; 41; recalled to office,
44; 45; resigns, 46 sq.; opposes compensation for the *émigrés*, 83; and
Algerian expedition (1830), 98; and
negotiations with the Papacy, 140; and
revolution of 1830, 477; French ambassador in London, 482 sq.; and Belgian
question, 483 sqq.; 487; and Thiers,
495; and Algiers, 502
Tallien, Jean Lambert, VIII 234, 249, 265;
and fall of Robespierre, 366; 369 sq.;
at Bordeaux, 372; on *Comité de Salut
Public* (1794), 375, 377 sq., 392; joins
the *Montagnards*, 397; 515
Talmash, Thomas, lieutenant-general, V 246
Talon, Jean, Canadian *Intendant*, VII 72,
80 sq.
—— Omer, IV 621
Talsy, interview between Condé and Catha-
rine de' Medici at, III 2
Tamai, battle of, XII 441
Tamames, skirmish at (1809), IX 455
Tamarit, Catalan chief, and Louis XIII,
IV 649
Tamasese, King of Samoa, VII 662
Tamasp, Shah of Persia, III 124; VI 507;
511 sq.
Tamaulipas, Mexican State, VII 394
Tambóff, XII 327; 329; action against
Liberals in, 349; 363
Tamburlaine, Marlowe's, III 374
Tamerlane. *See* Timur
Tammany Hall, VII 639, 645
Tanaro, the Allies on the, V 408
Tanchelin, Flemish sectary (c. 1100), I 626
Tandy, Napper, Irish patriot, VIII 772
Taney, Roger Brooke, American jurist, VII
383, 435, 575
Taneytown, Meade at, VII 488
Tanezruft, explorers in, XII 808
Tanganyika, Lake, XII 661 sqq.; discovered,
809; 810
Tangier, V 61; ceded to England (1661),
105, 106 sq.; 113; 178; bombarded by
French, XI 35; Emperor William II at,
XII 132; 133
Tan-ho river, fighting on, XII 591
Tanjore, Mornington's policy in, IX 724;
disputed succession in, VI 538; 540 sq.;
bombardment of, 547; 548
—— Sarboji, Rájah of, IX 724
Tanlongo, Director of Banca Romana, XII
218
Tann, Baron Ludwig von der, Bavarian
general, XI 602 sq.
Tannenberg, Polish victory at (1410), V 633
Tantia Topi, Brahman officer, XI 738 sq.
Tanucci, Bernardo, Marquis di, Neapolitan
statesman, VI 592 sq.; and Papacy, 594;
597; 599; VIII 778
Tao, Chinese general, XII 511
Tao Kwang, father of Prince Ch'un, XII
501
Taormina, capture of, XI 92
Tapanuli, ceded to Great Britain, VI 429

Taranaki, xi 793; native troubles at, 799; 800

Taranto, threatened by Barbarossa, iii 112; ceded to France (1801), ix 69; evacuated (1802), 77; French occupation of, 245

Tarapacá, province of, ceded to Chili, xii 679

Tarbagatai mountains, xii 793; exploration in, 799

Tarbé, Louis Hardouin, Minister of Finance to Louis XVI, viii 216, 222

Tarbes, Gabriel Grammont, Bishop of, ii 427 sq.

Target, Gui-J.-B., French politician, viii 132, 154, 183, 691, 715; ix 175

—— Paul-Léon, French politician, xii 108

Targowice, Confederation of (1792), viii 531 sq., 536 sq., 540

Tarifa, Spanish force sent to (1810), ix 464; 469

"Tariff of Abominations," vii 377

Tariffs, Colbert's, v 10 sqq.; in the U.S.A., the demand for Protection and its introduction, vii 355 sq.; struggle and revision of tariffs, 375 sqq.; 382; after Civil War, 635; 650 sqq.; Chap. xxi (1885–1902) *passim*; and economic development, 698 sqq., 722; English, Walpole's policy in regard to, vi 49 sq.; the Trianon (1810), ix 372 sq.; influence of, in Europe, in the early 19th century, x 752; later English, Huskisson and, 588 sq.; Mr Chamberlain and, xii 54; Canadian, 606; Chap. xx, European Colonies, *passim*, 602–71; the German, of 1879, Bismarck's later policy in regard to, 154 sqq., *see also Zollverein*; Russian, of Witte, 325; Swedish, in the late 19th century, 277

Tarim river, exploration on, xii 802

Tarleton, Sir Banastre, General, vii 224 sq., 227

Tarlo, Adam, Palatine of Lublin, vi 194; 197

Tarnopol, acquired by Russia (1809), x 413; restored to Austria (1815), 445, 461

Tarnov, ecclesiastical seminary of, x 462

Tarnowski, Jan, Castellan of Cracow, iii 79

—— Count Stanislaus, Polish writer, xi 660

Tarragona, and Catalan revolt, iv 648 sq.; Reding's army in, ix 448; besieged by Suchet (1811), 465; taken, 470; abandoned (1813), 479

Tartars, Russia and, v 477 sqq., 484; invade Lithuania, 481; vi 305; 674; rising of, 681; in China, xi 803; in the Caucasus, xii 342; 343

Tartary, Crimean, vi 634

—— Gulf of, xi 272, 819

Tarutino, Russian retreat to (1812), ix 497–8

Tarvis, Austrians cross Italian frontier at, ix 355

Ta-shih-chiao, battle of, xii 589

Tashkent, captured by Russians, xi 631; railway at, xii 343; 344

Tasman, Abel, voyages of, iv 713

Tasmania, discovery of, iv 713; Bass's exploration of, ix 740; transportation to, xi 784, 794 sq.; separated from New South Wales, 789; 790 sq.; population of, 796, 799; 797; xii 619; 621; 624 sq.; political development of, 626 sq.; University of, founded, 627; 630; and federation, 631

Tassino, favourite at Court of Milan, i 106

Tassis, Juan de, Count of Villamediana, iii 536

Tasso, Bernardo, iii 471–2

—— Torquato, iii 434, 455, 457, 466–7, 471–4

Tassoni, Alessandro, iii 461

—— (il Vecchio), evidence of, concerning Reformation in Italy, ii 386

Tast, Hermann, Danish Reformer, ii 160, 611

Tata, acquired by Solyman II, iii 124; attacked by Maximilian's troops, 125

—— Giovanni, Orphanage of, xi 72

Tataraimaka, the Maori and, xi 799 sq.

Tatar-Bazardjik, insurrection at, xii 384

Tatarsk, Charles XII at, v 598

Tate, Nahum, English dramatist, v 134

—— Colonel, American in the French Service, viii 475

Tati, discovery of gold at, xi 787

Tatistcheff, Dmitri Pavlovitch, Russian ambassador to Spain, vii 366; x 21, 209, 211 sq.

Tattenbach, Count Hanns Erasmus von, and Hungarian conspiracy, v 351 sq.

Tauenzien, Bogislav F. E., Count von Wittenberg, Prussian general and Minister, viii 548 sq., 551; retreats before Bernadotte, ix 275; at Jena, 276; 525 sqq.

Tauler, Johann, German mystic, i 434; v 755

Taunton, during Civil War, iv 313, 328 sq., 331

Tauria, acquired by Russia, vi 675

Taurida, Catharine II visits, viii 315

Tauroggen, Convention of (1812), ix 505

Tausen, Hans, "the Danish Luther." *See* Ribe, Bishops of

Tausenau, Karl, Austrian Radical, xi 185

Tavannes, Gaspard de Saulx de, Marshal of France, iii 10 sqq., 19, 21

—— Jean de Saulx, Vicomte de, Marshal of France, iii 672

—— de Saulx, Comte de, in Burgundy, iv 612 sq.; in command of Condé regiments (1650), 614 sqq.

Tavanti, Tuscan Minister of Finance, vi 602

Tavières, and battle of Ramillies, v 415

Tavira, occupied by Napier (1833), x 333

Tavora, Marquis of, vi 386

—— Marchioness of, vi 386

Tayasu, Japanese noble, xi 825

Tayler (*or* Taylor), John, English ambassador in France, ii 427

Taylor, Annie, traveller, in Tibet, xii 804

Taylor, Brook, mathematician, v 717; 722
—— Brooke, British Minister at Copenhagen, ix 297
—— Sir Henry, dramas of, xi 352 sq.
—— Sir Herbert, secretary to William IV, x 615
—— Jeremy, Bishop of Down and Connor, v 119; 304; 321; 326; 328; *Liberty of Prophesying,* 329, 332; 748 sq.
—— John, hymn-writer, viii 764
—— Richard, Confederate general, vii 524; surrender of, 543
—— Rowland, Protestant Reformer, ii 539
—— Tom, dramatist, xi 352
—— William, man of letters, viii 764
—— Zachary, commands army in Texas (1845), vii 394 sqq., 399; President of United States, 400; death of (1850), 404; 416
Tazzoli, Enrico, Italian priest, xi 376 sq.
Tchernitcheff, Russian general, and Napoleon, ix 487; crosses the Oder, 514; at Lüneburg, 515
Tchesmé, vi 355; 633; battle of, 673
Tchitchagoff, Paul Vasilievitch, Russian admiral and general, commands Army of the Danube, ix 489; defeats Schwarzenberg, 499; marches to Berezina, 501 sqq.; joins Wittgenstein, 511; at Bromberg, 512
Tebaldeo, Antonio, of Ferrara, iii 458
Tecklenburg, countship of, v 668, ix 410
Tecpanecs, The (Mexican tribe), i 39
Tecumthe, Shawnee chief, vii 337, 341, 345
Teelinck, Wilhelm, Dutch mystic, v 754
Tegerrie, British explorers at, xii 807
Teglio, Valtelline district, iv 35; 37; massacre in, 49
Tegnér, Esaias, Swedish poet, xi 686 sq.
Teheran, French officers sent to, ix 289; French ambassador at, 308; British representative at, xii 492; 793; Morier at, 800
Tehuantepec, and Panama Canal, xii 686
Teignmouth, burnt by French (1690), v 261
Teisserenc de Bort, Pierre-Edmond, French politician, xii 99
Teixeira, Gaspar, Portuguese general, x 329 sq.
Tej Sing, commander of Khalsa troops, xi 738 sq.
Teleki, Michael, leader of Hungarian rebels, v 353; 355; 358
—— Samuel, African traveller, xii 813
Tel-el-Amarna tablets, xii 846
Tel-el-Kebir, battle of, xii 40, 437 sq.; 441
Telesio, Bernardino, ii 706
Telford, Thomas, engineer, x 738 sq.; 744 sq.; xi 684
Telissu, battle of, xii 587
Tell, William, the legend of, xi 261
Telles-Jordão, Portuguese general, x 334
Tellnitz, Russian attack on (1805), ix 260
Tello, archaeological discoveries at, xii 846

Temesvár, besieged by Mohammad Sokolli, iii 122; captured (1552), 123, 124; congress at, v 346; 370 sq.; Banat of, vi 626; Austrian retreat from (1788), viii 325; evacuated by Turks, *ib.*; xi 184; battle of, 211
Tempest, The, and Shakespeare's progressive quality, iii 378
Templars, Order of the, v 630 sq.
Temple, George Nugent-Temple-Grenville, Earl. *See* Buckingham, Marquis of
—— Sir John, iv 534
—— Sir Richard, xii 460; 462; and Indian famine, 472
—— Richard Temple Grenville, Earl, vi 419; 424; resigns, 426; 430 sq.; dismissed, 432; 434 sqq.; and the *Letters of Junius,* 441; 442
—— Sir Thomas, vii 75, 111
—— Sir William, and Triple Alliance, v 119 sq., 153, 191; 201; and Prince of Orange, 213; 224; 265
Temporal Power of the Papacy. *See* Rome, the ecclesiastical state
Temps, Le, French journal, xi 487; xii 97
Ten, Council of. *See* Council of Ten
Ten Articles, The (1536), ii 446
Tenant-Right League, in Ireland, xii 69
Tenasserim, capture of, xi 728; lost by Burma, xii 479
Tencin, Pierre Guérin de, Cardinal, vi 110; 239
Tenczyn, Count of, iii 90
Tenczynski, Jan, Palatine of Belz, iii 96, 99
Tenda, purchased by Savoy, iii 407
Tendilla, Inigo Hurtado de Mendoza, 2nd Count of, Captain-General of Granada, i 360 sq.
Tenedos, lost by Venice (1381), i 264; temporarily recovered, v 342
Teneriffe, Nelson repulsed at, viii 464
Tenison, Thomas, Archbishop of Canterbury, v 753
Tennessee, settlers in, vii 221; enters Union (1796), 357, 413; population of, 359, 689; in Civil War, 462, 471, 581; campaign in (1864), 523 sqq.; peace in, 544; emancipation in, 587, 598; new government set up in, 625
—— East, Confederates in, vii 463, 500; Burnside in, 508
—— river, settlers on, vii 357; operations on (1861-2), 463, 494, 496 sq., (1863), 508 sqq.
Tennhart, Johann, Pietist, v 761
Tennyson, Alfred, Lord Tennyson, poems of, xi 350 sq.; and Browning, 352; 353; 364 sq.; 701
Tenos, island of, devastated by Turks (1570), iii 134
Ténot, Eugène, *Paris in December 1851,* xi 488
Teplitz, Austrian magazine at, vi 257; flight of Louis Bonaparte to (1810), ix 371; retreat of Allies to (1813), 527;

Treaty of (1813), 579; meeting at (1819), x 366 sq.; Conference at (1831), 376; meeting of the Emperor of Austria and the King of Prussia at, xi 224

Te Rauparaha, Maori chief, xi 793; 795

Terceira, island of, Spanish defeat of French fleets off, iii 294, 299, 302, 501; reception of Don Antonio at, 501; Constitutionalists in, x 323 sq.; Villa Flôr in, 326; Dom Pedro at (1832), 328

—— Antonio José de Sousa Manuel, Duke of, Count of Villa Flôr, x 322; 324; at Terceira, 326 sq.; in Portugal, 328 sq.; created Duke, 330; 332 sq.; captures Lisbon, 334; 336; Minister of Maria II, 338; insurrection by, 339; Ministry of, *ib.*

Terdshan, victory of Turks at (1473), i 82

Teresa, St, accused of heresy, ii 409

Te Rewi, Maori chief, xi 799 sqq.

Tergoes, taken by Spaniards (1572), iii 234

Termes, Maréchal de, ii 93

Ternate, Dutch trade at, iii 638, iv 733, 742

Ternay, Admiral, vi 453

Terni, Neapolitan defeat at (1798), viii 652

Térouanne, capture of, by English (1513), i 140, 481; captured by Charles V (1533), ii 89, 274; restored to France (1558), 94

Terracina, Concordat concluded at (1818), x 143

Terranova, Duke of, iii 252-3

Terray, Joseph-Marie, French statesman, vi 356 sq.; 359; viii 25, 74, 82, 99

Territories, The. *See* Delaware, State of

"Terror," The, Vol. viii, Chap. xii, 338-71, *also* Chap. xiii *passim*; the so-called "White," 387

Terry, Alfred Howe, American general, vii 529, 557

Terserus, Professor, Swedish finances and, iv 575

Tertre, Jean Baptiste du. *See* Du Tertre

Tertullian, early printed editions of, i 616

Teschen, Treaty of (1779), vi 632 sq., 677, 707, viii 309 sqq., ix 39; 93

Tessé, Mans-Jean-Baptiste-René de Froulay, Comte de, Marshal of France, v 402; 416; 419; ambassador in Spain, vi 137; 140; 165

Tesselschade, Maria. *See* Vischer

Tessin, and Congress of Vienna, ix 587

—— Count Carl Gustav, Swedish statesman, vi 759 sqq.

—— Nicodemus, Swedish architect, vi 759

Test Act, The, passed, v 210; James II and, 232 sqq., 239 sq.; 333 sq.; Lord John Russell procures the repeal of (1828), x 593

Teste, Charles, x 485; 491

—— Jean-Baptiste, French statesman, xi 39

Testi, Fulvio, Count, Italian poet, v 69

Tetrapolitana, The (Confession of the four Cities), ii 212; drawn up by Bucer and Capito (1530), 335 sq.; League of Schmalkalden joined by the four Cities, 215 sq.

Tetschen, the Preliminaries of Breslau and, vi 235

Tettenborn, Russian general, crosses the Oder, ix 514; enters Hamburg, 515

Tetuan, occupied by the Spaniards, xi 564

—— Duke of. *See* O'Donnell, Enrique

Tetzel, John, ii 121, 130, 134, 204

Teusin, Peace of (1595), iv 171

Teutonic Order of Knights. *See* German Order

Tewfik (Tawfik) Pasha, Khedive of Egypt, xii 40; accession of, 435; 436 sqq.; Turkey and, 444; death of, 454

Texas, French and Spanish claims in, vii 362; annexation of, 390 sqq.; becomes an independent State (1836), 392, 406; admitted to Union (1845), 394, 413; 397 sq.; boundary of, disputed, 403 sqq.; and secession, 446; joins Confederacy, 453, 457; blockade-running in, 620; slavery abolished in, 626; reconstruction in, 632 sq.; becomes Democratic (1874), 642; population of, 696, 711

Texel, action off (1653), iv 436, 476, 478; v 181; battle off (1673), 195 sq.; Dutch fleet captured at, viii 436; blockaded (1797), 481; captured (1799), 483; 662; Allied force at, ix 219

Tezcucans, The (Mexican tribe), i 39

Thacher, American lawyer, vii 179, 185

Thackeray, William Makepeace, x 724; xi 358 sq.

Thackwell, Sir Joseph, lieutenant-general in India, xi 741

Thames, The, de Ruyter's fleet in, v 37, 113; Dutch fleet off, 182, 189; the Great Seal recovered from, 247

—— (Ontario), battle of the (1813), vii 341, 389

Thana, Danglia imprisoned at, xi 725

Theatines, origin of Order of the, ii 23, 379, 648

Theden, Johann Christian Anton, Prussian surgeon-general, vi 725

Theiss river, war on, xi 204 sq., 210 sq.

Theisz, French politician, xi 502

Thelwall, John, Reformer, viii 761

Themptander, O. R., Swedish statesman, xii 277

Theodore, Emperor of Abyssinia, xi 752 sq.; xii 664

—— King of Corsica. *See* Neuhof

—— I (Ivanovich), Tsar, v 495 sq.; death of, 497; 514

—— III *or* II (Romanoff), Tsar, v 486; 516 sqq.; death of, 519; 524; 741

—— Godunoff, Tsarevich, v 499

—— of Tarsus, Archbishop of Canterbury, i 535, 598

Theodosia, daughter of Theodore I, Tsar, v 496

Theophilanthropists, French religious sect, under the Directory, VIII 501

Theophrastus, and sexuality in plants, V 736

Théot, Catharine, arrest of, VIII 366, 370

Theotókes, Greek statesman, XII 422

Therisso, insurgents at, XII 423

Thesaurus Linguae Graecae, by Guarino di Favera, II 17

Theses, Luther's, II 123, 128–32; Zwingli's, 321; theses of Zwingli, Haller and Roll, 327

Thessaly, insurrection in (1821), X 180; Greek invasion of, XI 639 sq.; and the Greek frontier, XII 37, 403; insurrection in (1877–8), 391; 392; war in, 421; Turkish evacuation of, 422; 428

Theux de Meyland, Barthélemi Theodore, Belgian statesman, XI 669 sq.

Thevenot, Melchisedec, traveller, V 740

Thiard, Comte Henri-Charles de, VIII 112

Thibaudeau, Comte Antoine-Claire de, VIII 386, 397, 488, 507, 515; IX 151–2

Thibault, *curé* of Souppes (Nemours), VIII 179

Thibaut, Anton Friedrich Justus, jurist, XII 819

Thibaw, King of Burma, XII 479

Thibet. *See* Tibet

Thiébault, Paul-C.-F.-A.-H.-D., French general, VIII 653

Thielmann, J. A., General, and the Belgian campaign, IX 631; at Waterloo, 637 sqq.

Thiene, Count Gaetano da (founder of the Oratory of Divine Love), II 23, 379, 640, 648

Thierry, Amédée-S.-D., French historian, XII 830

—— Baron Charles de, in New Zealand, XI 793

—— Jacques-Nicolas-Augustin, X 102; 514; XI 523; XII 830 sq.

Thiers, Louis-Adolphe, X 95 sq.; Spanish policy of, 237; 379; and the revolution of 1830, 477; supports Casimir Périer, 487; Minister of Interior, 489 sq.; 492; 494; foreign policy of, 495 sq.; and Algeria, 503 sq.; 505; and opposition to Molé, 507 sqq.; Ministry of, 513; and Turko-Egyptian Question, 566 sqq.; resignation of, 570; (1840–8), Vol. XI, Chap. II *passim*; 16; 96; Ministry of (1848), 98 sq.; elected to Constituent Assembly, 110; 114; 119; President of Education Commission, 120; 128; 131; opposes Louis-Napoleon, 133; arrested, 136; 467; in opposition, 475, 477; 479 sqq.; opposes declaration of war, 495; mission of, to European Courts, 497, 611; 498; and peace negotiations, 500, 612; 501; and Paris Commune, 503 sqq.; 506; XII 91 sqq.; 95; President of French Republic, 103; 104 sqq.; and Monarchists, 107; succeeded by MacMahon,

108; 110; death of, 111; 114; 135; 140; and Ranke, 825; writings of, X 514, XI 524, 832 sqq.

Thijssen, Vice-Admiral Martin, IV 707 sq.

Thile, Ludwig Gustav von, Prussian general and statesman, XI 51

Thionville, captured by Guise (1558), II 93, 361; restored by France (1559), 93; siege of (1643), IV 595; ceded to Germany, XII 95

Thirlby, Thomas, Bishop of Norwich and Ely, II 475; First Prayer-Book and, 484; 502, 513, 543

Thirlwall, Connop, Bishop of St David's, XII 836

Thirty Years' War, The, III 181, 395; character of, 568; 696; *see* Vol. IV, *especially* Chap. I, The Outbreak, 1–34; Chap. II, The Valtelline (1603–39), *passim*, 35–63; Chap. III, The Protestant Collapse (1620–30), 64–117; Chap. IV, Richelieu, *passim*, 129–50; Chap. VI, Gustavus Adolphus (1630–2), 190–222; Chap. VII, Wallenstein and Bernard of Weimar, 223–55; Chap. XIII, The later years of the War, 364–94; Chap. XIV, The Peace of Westphalia, 395–433; *also* Chaps. XXI and XXIII *passim*; V 339; 341; 348; 372; 637 sq.; 645; 657

Thirty-Nine Articles, The (1563), II 587; III 740; and the Westminster Assembly, IV 358–9. *See also* Prayer Book

Thistlewood, Arthur, X 576 sq.; 582

Tholen, defeat of John of Nassau near (1631), IV 695

Thomar, oath of allegiance of Portuguese Cortes to Philip at (1581), III 500

—— Costa Cabral, Count of, Portuguese statesman, X 339; XI 572; takes refuge in Spain, 573; 574

Thomas, Charles, editor of the *National*, X 499

—— Clément, French general, XI 109; 501

—— George Henry, VII 463, 495; at Chickamauga, 509 sq., 523; succeeds Rosecrans, 510; and campaign in west (1864), 520; and the campaign in Tennessee, 523 sqq., 528

—— Jean-Jacques, French deputy, VIII 247

—— Pierre-Émile, French politician, XI 111

—— William, execution of, II 528

Thomasius, Christian, philosopher, V 758; 760

Thomé, Thomas, grenadier, VIII 687

Thomond, Donough O'Brien, 4th Earl of, III 604

—— Murrough O'Brien, 1st Earl of, Baron Inchiquin, III 583 sq., 587

Thompson, David, New England settler, VII 21

—— Jacob, VII 447

—— Joseph, African traveller, XII 658; 812

Thompson, Perronet, and working classes of Bolton, XII 730

—— William, economic theories of, X 780 sq.

Thomsen, Vilhelm, Danish philologist, XII 292

Thomson, James, poet, VI 77; 823; 827 sq.; 830; X 698; 724

—— Sir Joseph John, physicist, XII 788; 790

Thorbecke, Johan Rudolf, Dutch statesman, XI 662 sq.; Ministry of, 664 sq.; returns to office, 666 sq.; death of, 667; 668; XII 243

Thoré, William de Montmorency, Seigneur de, III 22 sq., 26, 28, 32

Thoreau, Henry David, VII 739, 745 sq.

Thorild, Thomas, Swedish poet, VIII 789

Thorkildssön, Olaf. *See* Bergen, Bishop of

Thorn, Peace of (1411), V 633; the Second Peace of (1466), I 293, V 634; capitulates to Charles X (1655), IV 428; Treaty of (1709), V 602, 604; 538; siege of (1703), 592; Prussian League and, 634; "Charitable Conference" at (1645), 743; captured by Russia, VI 196; 291; 669; 671; Prussia and, 708 sq.; 734; Prussia's designs on, VIII 293, 330, 333, 523 sqq.; ceded to Prussia (1793), 535, 551; Ney and Bernadotte at, IX 284; French base at (1807), 287; Archduke Ferdinand and, 354; fortress of, 511; ceded to Prussia (1815), 598, 655, X 463

Thorndike, Herbert, of Cambridge, MSS by, I 616; V 331

Thornton, Sir William, lieutenant-general, VII 346

"Thorough," breakdown of Charles and Wentworth's policy of, IV 285; Bolingbroke's policy of, V 474

Thorpe, Benjamin, historian, XII 835

Thorwaldsen, Albert Bertel, sculptor, and Pius VII, X 151; XI 692

Thou, François-Auguste de, executed, IV 151; 155

—— Jacques-Auguste de (Thuanus), III 64

Thouars, customs of, V 13; captured by the Vendeans, VIII 340

Thouret, Jacques-Guillaume, French politician, VIII 183

Thouvenel, Édouard-Antoine, French Foreign Minister, XI 387; 474; 534; XII 19

Thouvenot, Pierre, French general, VIII 417, 419

Thrace, conquered by Turks, I 67; XII 381; 393; Treaty of Berlin and, 398; 428

Three Rivers, trading-post at, VII 76 sq., 94

Throckmorton, Francis, III 290; 301

—— Sir Nicholas, plot of, against Mary, II 544; ambassador in France, 573, 576; III 2, 264, 276

Throgmorton. *See* Throckmorton

Thucydides, Hobbes' translation of, VI 792

Thüngen, General, at Speyerbach, V 408

Thugut, Baron Franz Maria, Austrian statesman, VI 634; VIII 419, 429, 536, 544; and Partition of Poland, 548 sqq.; and Great Britain, 559, 583, 642 sq.; 634, 643, 645; and Second Coalition, 660 sq., 664; attitude of, towards reform, 777; IX 56; 65; Foreign Minister, 248; 315, 591

Thumery, Marquis de, IX 30

Thun, military school at, XI 239

Thunberg, Daniel af, Swedish architect, VI 775

Thun-Hohenstein, Count Francis, Austrian statesman, XII 202 sq.

—— Count Leo, XI 177 sq.; Austrian Minister of Education, 401; 656; XII 176

Thurgau, The, disputed jurisdiction in, I 308; added to Swiss Confederation, II 306; canton of, VI 613; XI 236; 240; joins *Siebnerkonkordat*, 242; 243; and Articles of Baden, 246

Thuringia, Banér in, IV 366 sq., 372, 383; Guébriant in, 385 sq.; Prussian army in, VI 264, 268; 269; 274 sq.; revolutionary movement in, XI 149 sq.

Thuringian States, and Customs' Union, X 372 sq., 378; support Hanoverian opposition, 380

Thuriot de la Rosière, Jacques Alexis, VIII 213, 343, 350; on the *Comité de Salut Public*, 375

Thurloe, John, Secretary of State, letters of, IV 443, 448; Bill of, 449; 451; V 146

Thurlow, Edward Thurlow, Lord, Lord Chancellor, VI 443 sq.; 450; 457 sq.; 462; 464; and India Bill, 467; 468; and Regency Bill, 474; and Libel Bill, IX 672; X 625

Thurman, Allen Granbery, American statesman, VII 653

Thurn, Count Francis, III 93

—— Georg von, Austrian general, XI 86

—— Count Matthias, III 734; and the Bohemian succession, IV 15 sqq., 19 sqq.; commands forces of Bohemia, 21 sqq.; and Imperial election, 28; and Bethlen Gabor, 31; 65 sq.; 70 sq.; in Danish service, 102; in Stockholm, 195; 206 sq.; 209; at Nürnberg, 218; Swedish commissioner in Silesia, 224, 233; and Wallenstein, 213, 234 sqq.; imprisoned and liberated, 237

—— and Taxis, Prince Maximilian Charles I (d. 1831), at Diet of Posen (1827), X 463

—— and Taxis, Maximilian Charles II, Prince of, general (1850), XI 230 sq.

—— and Taxis, Prince of, hereditary postal administration of, XI 460

Thurot, François, French naval commander, VI 489

Thusis, IV 37; 41; *Strafgericht* at, 46 sqq.; 51 sq.; 55

Tiagya, Seraskier, defends Ochakoff, VI 307

Tian Shan mountains, xii 793; 804

Tibaldi, Paolo, xi 304

Tibesti mountains, exploration in, xii 811

Tibet, China and, xi 802; xii 4; 34; Great Britain and, 56, 490 sq.; 485; 492; exploration in, 792 sq., 797 sqq., 802 sqq.

Tichborne, Sir Henry, iv 531

Tichelaer, Willem, and the murder of the brothers de Witt, v 159

Ticino, canton of, xi 236; 239 sq.; 244; Radical agitation in, 246; 251

—— river, crossed by Piedmontese troops, xi 82; 89

Ticknor, George, vii 745

Ticonderoga, French at, vii 125, 127, 129; Abercrombie attacks (1758), 132, 134 sq.; Amherst attacks (1759), 137; captured by colonists (1775), 165; evacuated (1777), 214

Tidikelt, French occupation of, xii 129

Tidone, battle on the, viii 657

Tidor, Dutch trade with, iii 638; attacked by the Dutch (1605), iv 733; xii 669

Tieck, Ludwig, German poet, x 398 sq.; and Romantic School, 401 sqq.; 405; 407 sq.; xi 411; 417; xii 818

Tiedge, Christoph August, German poet, x 394

Tiefenbach, Field-Marshal von, iv 199; 209

Tieken de Terhove, de, Belgian general, x 541 sq.

Tielemans, editor of *Le Belge*, x 532

Tieling, occupied by Japanese, xii 598

Tienhoven, Cornelis van, Dutch statesman, xii 246

Tientsin, massacre at, xi 804, 814; 812; 817; occupied by Allies, 818; 819 sq.; railway at, xii 505 sq.; 509; 515; foreign settlements at, besieged, 519; 520; 526; 567; Boxer movement at, 575

—— Treaty of (1858), xi 807, 817, xii 485, 500, 523, 796; (1884), 131; (1885), 132

Tiepolo, Bajamonte, conspiracy of, i 261, 273

—— Giovanni-Battista, Venetian artist, i 284

—— Jacopo, Doge of Venice, i 269

Tierney, George, leads opposition, ix 676, 681, x 574; 580; joins Canning, 591

Tierra del Fuego, boundary question in, xii 679

Tietzen, General von, enters Cassel, xi 230

Tifernas, Gregory, Greek lecturer in Paris, i 575

Tiflis, Russia and, x 175

Tigri, Italy and, xii 241

Tilburg, death of William II of Holland at, xi 664

Tilbury, camp ordered at, iii 530

Tilden, Samuel Jones, Governor of New York, vii 645

Tilley, Canadian politician, xi 775

Tillot, Guillaume Léon du, Marquis de Felino, Minister at Parma, viii 778

Tillotson, John, Archbishop of Canterbury, v 332; 334; 752 sq.

Tilly, Count Claude van, v 159

—— Count John Tzerklaes von, iii 573; enters Upper Austria, iv 34; and the battle of Prague, 65 sq.; 71; 78 sq.; victories of, at Wimpfen and Höchst, 80 sq.; takes Heidelberg, 82; 85 sq.; remaining campaigns of, 91–102, 115, 214; besieges and takes Magdeburg, 201 sqq.; Imperial plenipotentiary at Lübeck, 108 sq.; 208; driven into Bavaria, 213; death of, 214; 642

Tilsit, Peace of (1807), ix 195, 235, 292–9, 304, 329, 340; secret articles of, 304 sqq.; Turkey and, 308, 311, 385, 485; Prussia and, 327, 508; Poland and, 337; and Continental System, 364, 366, 379, 428; return of Napoleon from, 136, 237; Russian army crosses Niemen at, 291; Queen Louisa of Prussia at, 292, 308, 336; Conference at, 388

Timásheff, A., Russian Minister of the Interior, xii 298; 300

Timbuktu, the English and, iv 759; xii 3; French occupation of, 129, 659; 805 sqq.; Alexander Laing at, 808; Barth at, 810; 812

Times, The, x 365; opposes Poor Law Bill, 662; 666 sqq.; and Parnell, xii 86

Timiryázeff, Russian Minister of Commerce, xii 380

Timmerman, Franz, in Russia, v 520

Timok river, and the frontier question, xii 407

Timotheevich, Ermak, Cossack chief, v 495

Timur (Tamerlane), Mongol conqueror, v 479; vi 506; 509

Ting, Chinese admiral, xii 512

Tinné, Alexine, African traveller, xii 811

Tinta, Indian revolt in (1780), x 266

Tintoretto (Jacopo Robusti), i 284

Tippecanoe, Indians defeated at (1811), vii 389

Tipperary, "undertakers" in, iii 599; Catholic demonstrations in, x 648 sq.

Tipu, Sultan of Mysore, vi 469; 475; 577; viii 608; ix 363; relations of, with the Nizám, 710; 714 sqq.; with Sindhia, 720; power of, 720 sqq.; death of, 723

Tirah valley, campaign in, xii 488 sq.

Tirano, iv 35 sq.; strategical importance of, 39; 41; massacre in, 49; 50 sq.; 58; Rohan at, 61

Tirard, Pierre-Emmanuel, French statesman, xii 119

Tiris, Spain and, xii 660

Tirlemont, engagement near (1705), v 414; Austrians repulsed at (1793), viii 420

Tirso de Molina (Gabriel Tellez), iv 662

Tiryns, excavations in, xii 845

Tissot, Pierre-François, excluded from College of France, x 73

Tisza, Koloman, Hungarian statesman, xii 190 sq.; Ministry of, 197 sqq.; 203 sq.

Tisza, Count Stephen, Hungarian states-man, xii 204 sq.; 207
Titelman, Peter, iii 194
Titian (Tiziano Vecellio) of Cadore, i 284
Titicaca, Lake, Peruvian settlements round, i 45
Tiumen, founded by Cossacks, xii 794
Tizin, Afghans defeated at, xi 735
Tkachéff, Russian revolutionary, xii 303
Tlaxcallan (settlement of the Nahuatlacâ), i 39, 41 sq.
Tlaxcaltecs, The, join Cortes as allies, i 42
Tobago, the Earl of Warwick and, iv 758; captured by English (1665), v 110; Dutch in, 151, 687; captured by French (1677), 688; vi 185 sq.; 322; assigned to Great Britain, 428; reduced by de Grasse (1781), 453; restored to France (1783), 464, ix 748; proposed cession of, to Great Britain, viii 297; captured by British (1793), 484, ix 749; again reduced (1803), 484; retained by Great Britain, 564, 576, 755; government of, xii 656 sq.
Tobolsk, v 494; iron mines of, 533; founded by Cossacks, xii 794
Tocco, Neapolitan family of (rulers of Cephalonia, etc.), i 81
Tochi valley, rising in, xii 488 sq.; 490
Tocqueville, Alexis-Charles-Henri Clérel de, quoted, viii 8, 21, 41, 46; writings of, x 514; xi 96; 112; 115; 125 sqq.; and Louis-Napoleon, 133 sq.; 524; xii 833
Todd, Elliott D'Arcy, British Resident at Herat, xi 733
Todleben, Franz Eduard Ivanovich, Russian general at Sevastopol, xi 318
Todtleben, Russian general (1760), vi 326
Tökölyi, Count Emeric, leader of the Hungarian revolt, v 35; 352; 355 sqq.; marriage of, 358; revolt by, *ib.*; 359; attacks Pressburg, 361; 363; visits Sultan Mohammad IV, 364; in Transylvania, 369; defeat of, 366; 371
—— Stephen, v 351 sq.
Tönning, v 580; captured by Danes (1714), 582; Stenbock in, *ib.*, 609
Töpffer, Rodolphe, Swiss writer, xi 261
Töplitz. *See* Teplitz
Török, Valentine, Hungarian Lutheran, i 340
Törring, Count Ignaz Felix von, Bavarian general, vi 233
Toggenburg, the Empire and, vi 613 sqq.
—— House of, iv 36; 55
Togo, Heihachiro, Japanese admiral, xii 522; at Port Arthur, 580 sq., 585 sq.; 589 sq.; 595 sq.; defeats Rozhdestvensky, 599; 600 sq.
Togoland, Germany and, xii 3, 160, 659 sq.
Toiras, Jean de Saint-Bonnet, Seigneur de, Marshal of France, at Ré, iv 132
Tokar, capitulates, xii 441; 443
Tokat, Armenian massacres at, xii 418

Tokay, attacked by Maximilian's troops, iii 125; submits to Emperor Leopold I, v 366
Tōkiō (*see also* Yedo), xi 862 sqq.; Kim-ok Kiun at, xii 510; 543; 545; National Council at, 547; 548; 560; 563
Tokmash, Shah of Persia, v 544
Tokugawa dynasty, in Japan, xii 538
—— family, xi 825
Tolain, Henri-Louis, French politician, xii 94
Toland, John, in Hanover, vi 8
Tolbooth, Town Council of Edinburgh confined in, iii 268
Toldy, Francis, Hungarian writer, xi 426; 431
Toledo, Parliament in, iii 485; depopulation of, v 376; 381; French troops in (1808), ix 435; re-occupied by French (1812), 475; evacuated (1813), 477; 478
Toledo, Archbishops of:—
—— Archduke Albert, iii 699
—— Alfonso Carillo d' Acuña, i 355, 651
—— Bartolomé Carranza, ii 377, 404; the Inquisition and, 409 sq.; iii 426; 480
—— Alonso Fonseca, ii 401
—— Loaysa, iii 526
—— Juan Martinez Siliceo, i 657
—— *See also* Ximenes, Cardinal, *and* Mendoza, Pedro Gonzalez de, Cardinal
Toledo, Eleanora de, Duchess of Florence, ii 72
—— Fadrique de, at Bahia, iv 704 sq.
—— Francisco, Viceroy of Peru, x 244; and the *mita* of Potosí, 264
—— Frederick of, iii 18, 215, 231, 234–7, 520
—— Garcia de, Viceroy of Sicily, iii 125, 489
—— Juan de, Cardinal, ii 85
—— Pedro de (d. 1553). *See* Villafranca, Marquis of
—— Pedro de, Governor of Milan. *See* Ferandina
—— Father, iii 445, 448
Tolentino, Treaty of (1797), viii 581, 637, ix 603, x 132; battle of (1815), ix 621
Toleration, influence of discovery of New World upon, i 47 sqq.; in pre-Reformation period, of free discussion, etc., 624 sqq.; and the *Politiques*, iii 7 sq., Chap. i, The Religious Wars in France, 1–52 *passim*; and the Religious Peace of Augsburg (1555), 140 sqq., 754 sq.; Bacon's plea for, 347; the Vaudois question and, 403 sqq.; William of Orange an advocate of, 238, 244; rejected by both parties in the revolt of the Netherlands, 251; attitude of Dutch Church parties towards, 646 sqq.; and Edict of Nantes, 675 sqq.; as conceived by Henry IV, 692; character of English Toleration Act, 754; in 16th century political thought generally, *see* Chap. xxii, *passim, especially* 740, 753 sqq.; in the Empire, no real or integral part of

the Treaty of Westphalia, IV 410 sqq.; in England, and Cromwell, and Instrument of Government, etc., 453 sqq.; in France, under Richelieu, 156–7; in Brandenburg, under Great Elector, V 648; in 17th century England, Chap. XI, Religious Toleration in England [*see* England]; *also ib.* 96, 98 sqq.; Charles II and, 201 sq.; 209; James II and, 234 sq., 237; Act of 1689, 259, 336 sq.; William III and, 277; changed feeling in France in regard to (1655–85), 21 sqq.; in Hungary, 357; in Russia, under Peter the Great, 529; in Scotland, VI 94 sqq.; the Act of 1712, 95; in early 18th century, 79 sqq.; in Prussia, under Frederick William I, 226; and Roman Catholic relief, 454 sq.; and Protestant dissent, 455; in Ireland, in late 18th century, 489; in Austria, Joseph II's views in regard to, 628; Patent of Tolerance, 635 sq.; in Belgium, Joseph II's Patent of Tolerance (1781), 649; in Russia, Catharine II and, 693; Locke on, 813 sq.; of 18th century France, VIII 56; French law in regard to heretics in age of Revolution, 727 sq., 732 sqq.; of Irish Catholics and the Union, IX 678 sqq., 693 sqq., *but see* Chap. XXII *passim*; in Great Britain, Catholic Relief Bill passed, X 593; *see* Chap. XIX, 620–54

Toll, Johan Kristoffer, Swedish statesman, VI 770; 776 sqq.

—— General von, advice of, IX 492; 497, 499

Tollens, Hendrik, Dutch poet, XI 676

Tolosa, captured by French (1794), VIII 440

Tolstoi, General A. I. *See* Ostermann-Tolstoi

—— Count Fiodor, X 427

—— Count Lyof, Russian writer, XI 650 sqq.; XII 13; 317

—— Count Peter Alexandrovich, Russian ambassador, IX 308-9; 316, 320

—— Count Peter Andryevich, and Tsarevich Alexis, V 539 sq.; 549; 552 sq.; at Stambul, 593; 603 sq.; 612; VI 302

Tolstói, Count Dmitry, Russian Minister of Public Instruction, XII 295; 298 sq.; dismissed, 309; Minister of Interior, 313 sqq.; and peasant administration, 318 sq.; 320; 376

Toltecs, The (Mexican tribe), I 40

Tomasević, Stephen. *See* Stephen Tomasević, King of Bosnia

Tomkins, Thomas, chaplain to Archbishop Sheldon, V 331

Tommaseo, Niccolò, X 126; XI 76; release of, 82; 83; writings of, 545

Tomory, Paul, Archbishop of Kalocsa, defence of Hungary against Turks by, I 96 sq., 339

Tompa, Michael, Hungarian poet, XI 428; 430

Tomsk, emigration to, XI 273; post-road through, XII 792; 794

Tone, Theobald Wolfe, VIII 475 sq., 498, 771 sq.; pamphlet of, IX 694; 697; death of, 702; founder of United Irishmen, X 628; 631

Tonga, British protectorate over, XII 667 sq.

Tong-Haks, The, Korean rebels, XII 510

Tong Kingsing, and Chinese railways, XII 505

Tonk State, The, XI 725

Tonkin, France and, XII 131 sq., 503, 506, 523 sqq.; rivers of, explored, 797; 803

Tonnage and Poundage, levy of, under Charles I, IV 266, 271, 281; Bill for regulating, 291

Tonnay-Charente, taken by Mayenne, III 32

Tooke, John Horne (John Horne), VI 441; 444; VIII 755; trial of, 761; 765; member for Old Sarum, IX 681

—— Thomas, and free trade, X 771; career and writings of, 783

Toombs, Robert, VII 603; Confederate Secretary of State, 604

Topchibásheff, Russian Mussulman, XII 344

Topete, Juan Bautista, Spanish admiral, XI 569 sq.

Torbay, William of Orange lands at, V 246

Torcello, Domenico di Domenichi, Bishop of, I 647, 674

Torcy, Jean-Baptiste Colbert, Marquis de, French Secretary of State, V 394; and the peace negotiations, 417, 422 sq., 427, 430, 440; 472; VI 98

Tordenskiold, Peter, Danish admiral, V 583

Tordesillas, Treaty of, VI 390

Torell, Otto, Swedish man of science, XII 280

Torelli, Giuseppe (Ciro d'Arco), Italian writer, XI 65

—— Lelio, III 388

Toreno, José Maria Queipo de Llano, Conde de, Spanish statesman, X 219; 221; 234; 236 sq.

Torfou-Tiffauges, battle of, VIII 353

Torgau, Philip of Hesse and Elector of Saxony at, II 195; *Formula*, III 179; conference at (1576), 704; alliance of, 712–3; John George and, IV 204; 211; Banér at, 373 sq.; 390; VI 265; 267 sq.; 273; battle of, 296; surrender of (1813), IX 518; ceded to Prussia (1815), 598

Tormassoff, Russian general, commands reserve (1812), IX 489; at Lutsk, 490; commands main army, 497; 501 sqq.

Tormes river, British army on, IX 475

Tornabuoni, Lorenzo, Medicean partisan, I 175 sq.

Toro, battle of (1476), I 352

Toronto, captured by Americans (1813), VII 341; failure of Mackenzie's march on, X 692; University of, XI 778; industries of, XII 612

Torquemada, John of, *De Potestate Papae*, III 736 sq., 744

Torquemada, Tomas de, Grand Inquisitor in Spain, I 359 sq., 649; II 650

Torre, Count da, at Pernambuco, IV 708

—— Giulio della. *See* Della Torre

Torrecusa, Marquis of, at Monjuich, IV 649

Torrens, Sir Robert Richard, XI 797

Torres, Lozano de, Spanish Secretary of Justice, X 212

—— Vedras, lines of, IX 456, 459; Masséna at, 460; rebels defeated at, XI 572

Torresano, Andrea, of Asola, Venetian printer, I 284

Torricelli, Evangelista, experiments of, IV 794; V 715

Torrigiani, Cardinal, Minister of Clement XIII, VI 592

Torrington, Arthur Herbert, Earl of, Admiral, V 242 sq.; 245; 261

—— George Byng, Viscount, in Baltic, VI 28; annihilates Spanish fleet, 32 sq., 104; 93

Torstensson, Lennart, Count of Ortala, Swedish general, IV 366; at Kyritz, 367; at Wittstock, 372; in command, 386; invades Denmark, 387; 388 sqq.; Oxenstierna and, 569; 571; Charles X and, 576, 582; 584 sq.; V 609

Torti, Giovanni, X 126

Tortona, occupied by French (1499), I 121; VI 155; Maillebois' forces at, 245; occupied by French (1796), VIII 567

Tortosa, captured by Philip IV (1650), IV 661; Franco-Spanish capture of (1708), V 426; French attack upon (1810–1), IX 464–5

Tosa, *daimiō* and clan of, Vol. XI, Chap. XXVIII (2) *passim*; XII 562

Toscanelli, Paul del Pozzo, Colombo and, I 20 sq.

Toski, dervishes defeated at, XII 443

Tóth, Kálmán, Hungarian poet, XI 430

Totleben, Governor-General of Odessa (1879), XII 307

Tott, Baron François de, in Turkey, VI 355

—— Swedish general, at Rostock, IV 207; 220

Touaregs, The, attack French outposts, XII 129

Touat, French occupation of, XII 129

Touchet, Marie, III 14

Toul, occupied by Henry II (1552), II 87, 144; bishopric of, and France, IV 404, 602 † XI 592; captured by the Germans, 600

Toulon, Christian slaves sold at, II 77; Rupert and Maurice at, IV 465; development of, V 14; Tourville at, 61 sq.; 183; Marlborough's designs on, 412, 414; 413; attacked by Prince Eugene (1707), 419; 426; the plague at, VI 128; 160; 236 sq.; 239; fortifications at, 350; French fleet intercepted at, VII 132; riot at, VIII 192; 448; surrenders to English (1793), 348, 431, 437, 457 sq.; recaptured, 352 sq.,

458; "White Terror" at, 387; blockaded, 460; French and Spanish fleets at, 461; Napoleon sails from (1798), 597, 620; Russian expedition fitted out at, IX 40; French fleet at, 53; 210, 212; British blockade of 1803, 211, 214 sq.; Nelson and, 216; French ships at, 219; Allemand at, 237; British at (1809), 238–9; Murat escapes to, 622; Lowe at, 760; XI 117; 137; French expedition leaves for Greece, 313; 485; Russian fleet at, XII 9, 98

Toulouse, *bourse* started at, II 65; Edicts of (1538–42), 288; University of, 95; *Parlement* of, III 6, V 4, VIII 47; the League and, III 661, 664, 668; battle of (1814), IX 482; royalists in (1815), 617; Commune at, XI 503

—— Louis-Alexandre de Bourbon (son of Louis XIV and Mme Montespan), Count of, VI 129 sq.

—— Countess of, VI 164

—— Archbishop of. *See* Loménie de Brienne

Touraine, customs of, V 13

Tournay, surrendered to England (1513), I 481, 483; captured by English (1521), II 44, by Imperialists (1521), 102, 419; *Parlement* of, V 4; 48; taken by French (1667), 199; captured by Allies (1709), 424 sq.; 428; 434; Barrier Treaties and, 457 sqq.; fall of (1745), VI 242

Tournebus. *See* Turnebus

Tournebut, royalist sympathy at, IX 136

Tournon, François de, Cardinal, Minister of Francis I, II 97, 288, 290, 293

Tours, Synod of French clergy at (1510), I 135, II 29; Estates of (1484), I 387, 399, 403; silk trade of, 414; Henry IV withdraws to, III 48; *Parlement* of, 659, 663; tax collectors imprisoned in, V 8; XI 498; army corps organised at, 602

Tourville, Anne-Hilarion de Costentin, Comte de, French admiral, V 58 sq.; 61 sq.; 261; 412 sq.

Toussain, Jacques, III 53

Toussaint, Anna Louise Gertrude, Dutch novelist, XI 676

Toutsch, Bonaventura, IV 52; death of, 55

Tovar, de, Governor of La Goleta, III 114

Towerson, Gabriel, IV 739

Townley, Francis, Jacobite, VI 114

Towns, the Flemish, decline of, in 15th century, and its causes, I 428 sqq.; German, development of, under Maximilian I, 327; and modern trade routes, 502; and capitalists, 506; and development of mining in Germany, 506 sq.; the Italian, and modern economic changes, Chap. XV, Economic Change, *passim, and especially* 515 sq.; reasons for decline of certain great cities of the Middle Ages, 529 sq.; Congress of cities at Speier, II 152 sq.; decay of German, 279. *See* Hanseatic League, *Rheinbund*, etc., *and*

individual place names, but also for later modern conditions, Vol. xii, Chap. xxiii, Social Movements, *passim*, 730–65

Townshend, Charles Townshend, 2nd Viscount, v 422 sq.; signs first Barrier Treaty, 424; 427; 432; and Whig party, 466; vi 16; 18; Secretary of State for Foreign Affairs, 22; dismissed, 27; 39; 41; 57; and Gibraltar, 58; forms Hanover Alliance, 59; dismissed, 60; 61; and Jacobite rising, 102; 417; vii 147

—— Charles, vi 430; 435; Chancellor of the Exchequer, 436; 437; death of (1767), 438; vii 152, 154

—— George Townshend, 4th Viscount and 1st Marquis, vi 438; 440; 464; Lord-Lieutenant of Ireland, 492 sqq.; vii 137, 141

—— Thomas, Viscount Sydney. *See* Sydney

Tractarian movement, x 657; xi 5 sq.; reflected in literature, 348 sq.; 354; results of, 709 sqq.

Tracton, stormed by Fitzmaurice (1569), iii 595

Tracy, Alexandre de Prouville, Marquis de, vii 80 sq.

—— Antoine-Louis-Claude Destutt, Comte de, ix 132

Trade and Industry, Arabian, the Asiatic trade, i 27 sqq.

—— Austro-Hungarian, recent arrangements in regard to, xii 204

—— the Baltic commerce, vi 24

—— Belgian, effect of English use of machinery on, xi 670; in recent years, xii 255 sq.

—— in Brandenburg, under the Great Elector, v 646 sq.

—— Chinese, i 27 sqq.; Vol. xi, Chap. xxviii, 802–23 *passim*; Vol. xii, Chap. xvii, 500–22 *passim*

—— Danish, under Christian VI, vi 738 sq.; under Struensee, 748; 752; in the late 19th century, xii 291 sq.

—— Dutch, first in the world at close of the great war with Spain, iii 630 sqq.; in 1652, iv 467 sq.; colonial, in the earlier half of 17th century, 703 sqq.; of recent years, xii 249

—— in the Empire, in the early 17th century, iv 7 sq.; after the Thirty Years' War, 417 sqq.

—— English, extension of, in the New World, i 33 sq., *see* Chap. ii; for the break-up of the medieval systems of, *see* Chap. xv, Economic Change, *passim*, *but especially* 521 sqq.; and the dissolution of the monasteries, ii 468 sq.; in the time of Edward VI, 489 sqq.; under Elizabeth, iii 355 sqq.; trading voyages under Henry VIII and Elizabeth, 294 sqq.; commerce and colonisation under James I, 562; growth of, as shown in revenue, 567; 569 sq.; 1652, iv 467 sq.; colonial,

English and Dutch especially, Chap. xxv *passim*, The transference of Colonial Power to the United Provinces and England, 728–59; Council of Trade formed (1660), v 107; commercial negotiations with Portugal, *ib.*; and the Revolution of 1689, 263 sqq.; Board of Trade constituted with permanent staff, 264; under Walpole, vi 44 sqq.; in the English colonies in America, vii 56, 67 sq.; trade regulations in, 104 sqq.; external trade and English regulation, 182 sqq., 204; treaty with France (1786), viii 284 sqq.; factory legislation and distress in (1802–12), ix 691 sq.; in India, under Wellesley, 729; after Wars of the Revolution, x 575 sqq.; with colonies in the early 19th century, 586 sqq.; in general, 588 sqq., *see also* Colonies; Chap. xxiii *passim*, 727–62; Chap. xxiv, The British Economists, *passim*, 763–84; Vol. xi, Chap. i, Great Britain and Free Trade (1841–52), 1–21; and Gladstone's financial policy, 311; Cobden's commercial treaty with France, 333 sq.; colonial, 762 sqq., 776, 787 sq., 795 sqq.; with China and Japan, *see* Chap. xxviii *passim*; Employers' Liability Acts, Unemployed Workmen's Act, etc., xii 61; growth of trade in recent years, 63; in Malay States, 533; with Siam, 535; the principle of cooperation in, 739 sqq.; with her colonies, Chap. xx, 602–71

Trade and Industry, European in general, world-wide extension of, in Africa, the East, and to America, by Genoese, Portuguese, Spanish, English, and French, Vol. i, Chap. i, The Age of Discovery, 1–36, *and* Chap. ii, The New World, 37–66; from the 14th to the 16th centuries, Chap. xv, Economic Change, 493–531; and the colonisation of the chief European nations, *see* Vol. v, Chap. xxii *passim*; Vol. x, Chap. xxiii *passim*, 727–62; and China and Japan (1815–72), *see* Vol. xi, Chap. xxviii *passim*; xii 12 sq.; Chap. xvii, The Far East, 500–33; Colonial in general, Chap. xx *passim*, 602–71

—— Flemish, decline of, in the 15th century, i 429

—— Florentine and Tuscan, under Cosimo de' Medici, iii 392 sq.; under Ferdinand de' Medici, 398 sq.

—— French, extension of, in the New World, Vol. i, Chap. ii; revival in, after English Wars, 414; for the break-up of the medieval systems of, *see* Chap. xv, Economic Change, *passim*, *but especially* 503 sqq., 525 sqq.; under Henry IV, iii 694; under Richelieu, iv 153; under Colbert, v 10 sqq.; French Canadian, vi 85 sqq., 90 sqq.; trade regulations, 104 sqq.; under Choiseul, 350 sq.; treaty with England (1786), viii 284 sqq.; Napoleon's economic policy, ix 120 sqq.; 142 sq.; 375 sqq.; *see also* Continental System;

from 1830, x 493; under Napoleon III, xi 299 sqq.; and Cobden Treaty, 470 sq.; of recent years, xii 100 sqq.; with Siam, 536

Trade and Industry, German, and new imperial taxation (1522), ii 152 sq.; struggle for commercial supremacy in Baltic, 227 sqq.; and Bismarck, xii 152 sqq.; since 1870, 168 sqq. *See also Zollverein*

—— Indian, internal trade (1717–62), vi 559 sq. *See also* East India Company

—— Irish, iii 579; for the "land" question, plantations, etc., Chap. xviii *passim*; linen industry ruined by English legislation, v 264 sq.; Irish woollen industry likewise crippled, 322 sq.; effects of the destruction of the woollen industry, vi 482 sqq.; linen industry, *ib.*; distress of 1776, 495; proposals to meet it and indignation in England, 496 sq.; withdrawal of opposition, 498; trade distress, 502 sq.; Pitt's project of Commercial Union, 503 sq.

—— Italian in general, Vol. i, Chap. xv, Economic Change, *passim*, *but especially* 515 sqq.; under Cavour's administration, xi 371; and the Minghetti Ministry, 538; of recent years, xii 235 sqq.

—— Japanese, Vol. xi, Chap. xxviii, 823–65 *passim*

—— in Netherlands generally, at close of the Middle Ages, i 420; from 14th to 16th centuries, *see* Chap. xv, Economic Change, *passim*, *but especially* 507 sqq., 521

—— Norwegian, in late 19th century, xii 280 sq.; and Swedish, the freeing of, xi 688

—— in the Papal States, under Consalvi, x 136 sq.

—— Polish, in 16th century, i 346; after 1815, x 449

—— Portuguese, enormous extension of, in Africa and America, *see* Vol. i, Chaps. i *and* ii, The Age of Discovery *and* The New World; *see also* Chap. xv, Economic Change, *passim*; since 1871, xii 269

—— Prussian, under Frederick William I, vi 224 sqq.; under Frederick the Great, 715, 719 sqq.; legal reforms affecting, ix 330 sq.

—— Russian, under Peter the Great, v 533 sq., 543 sq., 549, 555; under Catharine II, vi 691 sq.; in 19th century, xi 269 sqq.; from 1858, xii 301; from 1880, 319 sqq.; in Siberia, 345; England and, 380

—— Savoyard, at the accession of Emmanuel Philibert, iii 400; under his policy, 409 sq.

—— Spanish, enormous extension of, especially in the New World, *see* Vol. i, Chaps. i, The Age of Discovery *and* ii, The New World; home products and home and foreign trade at the close of the 15th century, 356 sqq.; Saracen industry in Spain,

383; *see also* Chap. xv, Economic Change, *passim*, *but especially* 518 sqq.; under Charles V, ii 100 sq.; in New World, suffers from English seamen under Henry VIII and Elizabeth, iii 294 sqq.; under Philip II, 481 sq.; English and French smuggling in Spanish America, 492 sq.; effects of Philip's policy on, 495 sq.; 519; under Philip III, 528, 537; and expulsion of the Moriscos, 543 sq.; and the *alcabala*, iv 627; under Philip IV and Olivares, 655 sq.; in 17th century, v 376; commercial intercourse with England and Holland, 378 sq.; Spanish American, from 16th century onward, x 254 sqq.; growth of, in late 18th century, 275; of recent years, xii 267 sq.

Trade and Industry, Swedish, under Gustavus Adolphus, iv 187 sq.; under Charles XI, v 577; xi 688; xii 278 sq.

—— Tuscan, under Peter Leopold, vi 603

—— of the United States, Vol. vii, Chap. ix, the struggle after the Revolution for commercial independence, 305–34; after Peace of Ghent (1814), 350 sqq.; 375; Chap. xii *passim*; 567; crisis after Civil War (1873), 642 sq.; recovery, 647; Chap. xxii *passim*, 687–722

—— Venetian, Vol. i, Chap. viii *passim*, *especially* 277 sq., 283 sq.; *see also* Chap. xv, Economic Change, *passim*; decay of, vi 606

Trade Unionism, English, development of, xii 748 sqq.

Tradition and Scripture, authority of, discussed at Council of Trent, ii 665 sq.

Trafalgar, battle of (1805), ix 193, 210, 230 sqq.; significance of, 243

—— Square, demonstration in, xii 43, 47

Trágala, Spanish patriotic song, x 218

Traherne, Thomas, poet, iv 771

Traietto, Duchess of. *See* Gonzaga, Julia

Traité de l'homme, iv 790

—— *simulé*, drafted (1670), v 204 sq.; 212. *See also* Dover

Tranent, Cope at, vi 113

Tranquebar, Danish fort at, iv 746

Tranquillo, Andronico, iii 118–9

Translations and Translators. *See* Literature *and the* Renaissance

Transvaal, The, xi 781 sq.; Republic of, 785 sq.; discovery of gold in, 787; and Delagoa Bay, 789; (1877–1906), xii 635 sqq.; 35; War in (1880–1), 39; Jameson Raid in, 53; annexed by Great Britain, 54; Holland and, 245; and Union question, 646

Transylvania, the Unitarians of, ii 393; Stephen Báthory, Prince of, iii 91 sqq.; Christopher Báthory, Vice-Regent of, 97; 100; John Zápolya's widowed Queen banished to, 118; under Zápolya's Queen and Martinuzzi, 122; claimed by Ferdinand I,

123; adjudged by Solyman to Zápolya's son, *ib.*; Reformation in, 147; Archduke Matthias empowered to act in, 720; and Turkey, v 36, 40, 344 sqq.; and the Habsburgs, 63, 339 sq.; precarious independence of, 339; 352; Duke Charles IV of Lorraine in, 367; Tökölyi in, 369; 371; German Order in, 630; 744; Estates of, x 356; 382; xi 173; Hungary and, 180, 202; Bem in, 204 sqq.; 207; 209; Austro-Russian forces in, 211; 213; 215; reaction in, 217; 399; 538; xii 180; reincorporated into Hungary, 190; 198 sq.

Transylvania, Princes of:—
—— Michael Apaffy, v 345 sq.; 348; and Hungarian conspiracy, 351; 353; treaty of, with France, 354; 355; 367; death of, 368
—— Achatius Barczai, v 345
—— Gabriel Báthory, iv 10
—— Stephen Báthory, Prince of, and King of Poland. *See* Stephen Báthory
—— Stephen Bocskai, and King of Hungary. *See* Stephen Bocskai
—— Bethlen Gabor, Turkish designs concerning, iv 10; established in Transylvania, 11; 24; 26; and Hungary, 28 sqq.; advance into Hungary and retreat of, 30 sq.; elected King at Pressburg, 64; 66; 68; 71; makes peace with Emperor, 75; 85; 86; in Moravia, 87; 88; marriage of, 91; 96 sqq.; and Sigismund III, 189; death of, 194; and Bohemian throne, 233; v 339; xi 421
—— John Keményi, v 345 sq.
—— Francis Rákóczy II, v 351 sq.; 358; 596; vi 31; 197; xi 421
—— George Rákóczy I, iv 387; 389; Mazarin and, 602; v 339; 344
—— George Rákóczy II, repulsed by Hatzfeldt, iv 429; Charles X and, 580, 583; v 339; 344 sq.; 351
—— Francis Redei, named and deposed, v 344
—— John Zápolya, King of Hungary. *See* John Zápolya, King of Hungary
—— John Sigismund Zápolya, King of Hungary. *See* John Sigismund Zápolya

Trant, Sir Nicholas, brigadier-general in Portuguese army, occupies Coimbra, ix 461

Trapani, Charles V at, iii 111; citadel of, vi 153

—— Count of, xi 553 sq.

Trapezuntius, Georgius (George of Trebizond), translator of Eusebius, i 542, 558, 595, 601

Traquair, Charles Stewart, 4th Earl of, v 290
—— Charles Stewart, 5th Earl of (succ. 1741), vi 109; 111
—— Sir John Stewart, 1st Earl of, Charles I and, iv 498; royal commissioner, 503

Trarbach, captured by Marlborough (1704), v 411

Tras-os-Montes, Wellington sends troops to, ix 476; risings in (1823), x 316, (1826), 321

Traun, Count Otto Ferdinand, Austrian general, vi 153; 237; on Rhine, 240; 241

Trautmannsdorff, Prince Ferdinand von, Minister Plenipotentiary in Austrian Netherlands, vi 651; viii 320, 329
—— Count Maximilian von, sent to Wallenstein, iv 238 sqq.; at Pirna, 252; Imperial plenipotentiary at Münster, 400, 412

Travail, Le, French journal, xi 486

Travancore, vi 475 sq.; attacked by Tipu (1789), ix 714, 717

Traventhal, Peace of (1700), v 581, 588

Travers, Walter, iii 757

Traversari, Ambrogio (d. 1438), i 586; translations by, from Greek, 595, 601

Trczka, Count Adam Erdmann, Bohemian politician, and Wallenstein, iv 213, 234; dismissal of, 240 sqq.; murdered at Eger, 242

Treason Act, English (1549), ii 496 sq.; of 1795, ix 675

Treatise of Civil Power, The, iv 543

Trebbia river, battle on (1799), viii 657

Trebizond, fall of (1461), i 78, 103; surrendered to the Turks, 285; ix 385; xii 392 sq.; Armenians massacred at, 417

Treiden, Benigna von, Duchess of Courland. *See* Courland

Treilhard, Comte Jean-Baptiste, viii 196 sq., 249, 269; on *Comité de Salut Public*, 375; Director, 517; at Rastatt, 641, 669; ix 163 sqq.

Treitschke, Heinrich, German historian and politician, xi 448; xii 8; 146; 828

Treitzsaurwein, Max, *Weisskunig*, i 326

Trélat, Ulysse, x 485; 492; 501; Minister of Public Works, xi 111 sq.

Trelawny, Charles, major-general, v 243

Trélazé, insurrection at, xi 304

Tremaine, secret agent between France and Elizabeth, ii 576 sq.

Tremblay, François du. *See* Joseph, Père

Tremellius, John Emmanuel, Italian Protestant refugee in England, ii 391, 477

Trémouille, Louis de La *See* La Trémouille

Trĕnggánu, Great Britain and, xii 536

Trenholm, George A., Confederate Secretary of Treasury, vii 604, 613

Trent, Vendôme at, v 407 sq.; French army at (1800), ix 68; Austria receives bishopric of (1803), 94; Bishop of, deported, 202; regained by Austria (1815), 660
—— Council of (1545–63), i 235, 621, 625, 652, 691; ii 33, 77–87; Indulgences and, 127; 168; 251; removed to Bologna, 260; Queen Elizabeth and, 583, 586 sq.; 661–84; procedure of, 664; Spanish Bishops at, 665; iii 6 sq.; Catholic reaction in Poland and, 81, 83; 126, 145,

159; significance of, for Catholicism, 162
sqq.; 198 sq., 271, 390; decrees of, 389,
404, 466; v 742; ix 193
Trent, British Mail Steamer, xi 335 sq.
Trent, Bishops of:—
—— Christoforo Madruzzo, Cardinal-
Bishop of. *See* Madruzzo
—— Ludovico Madruzzo, ii 676, 684
Trenton, captured by Washington (1777),
vii 213
Trépoff, Dmitry, General, xii 295; 305;
Chief Police-Master of Moscow, 331;
Governor-General of St Petersburg, 350;
and Moscow Congress, 355 sq.; 358;
dismissed, 359; 362; 368
Tresckow, Hans Ludwig Udo von, German
general, xi 604
Trescorre, Garibaldi at, xi 533
Treslong, William de Blois of. *See* Blois
Treuenbrietzen, and the False Waldemar,
v 621; Imperial army in, vi 296
Trevelyan, Sir George Otto, Secretary for
Ireland, xii 40; 43 sq.; 46; *Early Life
of Charles James Fox*, 841
Trèves. *See* Trier
Trevett, John, and the Force Act, vii 313
Treviso, armistice at (1801), ix 68; xi 86;
captured by the Austrians, 87
—— Marshal Édouard-A.-C.-J. Mortier,
Duc de. *See* Mortier
Trevor, Sir John, diplomatist, v 153
—— *See* Hampden, J. Hampden Trevor
Treworgie, John, Commissioner of New-
foundland, vii 52
Trézel, Camille-Alphonse, French general,
x 503 sq.
Trianon, The, Tariff of (August 5, 1810),
ix 372; 375; Napoleon at, 373; Louis
XVIII at, 572
Tribune, La, French journal, xi 487
Trichinopoly, vi 540; besieged, 541; 542
Tricou, French Minister at Shanghai, xii
526
Tridon, French politician, xi 502
Triebel, Werth at, iv 392
Triennial Act, repealed (1664), v 98; passed
(1694), 273
—— Bill (1640–1), iv 290
Trier, Diet of (1512), i 320; siege of (1522),
ii 155; and Religious Peace, iii 142;
Reformation in, 155; lost by France
(1675), v 44; occupied by Marlborough
(1704), 411; cessions to Prussia in, ix
657; the "holy coat" of, xi 52
Trier, Electors of:—
—— Clement Wenceslas, Prince of Poland,
viii 220 sq.; x 158
—— Francis George von Schönborn, vi
231
—— Francis Lewis, Palatine of Neuburg,
vi 202
—— Jacob of Baden, i 316
—— Jakob von Eltz, iii 155
—— John of Baden, i 316
—— John of Isenburg, ii 671

Trier, Electors of (*contd.*):—
—— John von der Leyen, iii 142; 155;
176, 178; appointed to Commission at
Aachen, 706
—— John of Metzenhausen, ii 220
—— John Hugo von Orsbeck, v 403
—— Philip Christopher von Sötern,
iv 84; accepts French Protection, 141
sq.; 144; 210; secures "neutrality,"
215; appeal of, to France, 226, 230;
246; carried off by Spaniards, 251; re-
instated at Peace of Westphalia, 409
—— Richard of Greifenklau, war of, with
Sickingen, ii 155 sq.
Trier, Wilhelm Arnoldi, nineteenth century
Bishop of, xi 52
Trieste, vi 153; and Mediterranean trade,
606; 639; retained by Austria (1805),
ix 261; port of, annexed by France
(1809), 418; regained by Austria (1815),
660; Sardinian squadron at, xi 87; 394
Trikoúpes, Charilaos, Greek statesman, xii
403; 408; 420; 422
Trimbakji Danglia, Poona Minister, xi 725
Trincomali, captured by Dutch (1673), v
696; vi 454; taken by French, 469
Trinidad, founding of, iv 758; the Spaniards
in, v 687; cocoa plantations of, vi 186;
taken by British (1797), viii 484, ix 750;
viii 498; Nelson moves on, ix 225; retained by Great Britain, 75, 77, 752; x
276; Miranda starts from, 281; xii 653
sq.; government of, 656 sq.
Trinity College, Dublin, foundation of University of, iii 611
Trinomali, Haidar Ali defeated at, vi 567
Triple Alliance, The (May 20, 1571), of
Spain, the Pope and Venice against Turks,
iii 134; of 1668, formation of, v 38 sqq.;
ephemeral character of, 153 sq.; and
Holland, 200 sq.; of 1717, vi 27; of
1788, and its results, viii 288 sq.; 324;
of 1815, ix 597; of 1872, xi 634; of 1882,
between Germany, Austria, and Italy, xii
240; renewed (1887), 341; renewed (1902),
242
Triploe Heath, army at, iv 343
Tripoli, given to Knights of St John, ii 60,
68; Turkish capture of (1551), 86, 268;
captured by Barbary corsairs, iii 486;
Spain and, vi 381; Denmark and, 756;
Ganteaume off coast of, ix 53; xii 4;
Italy and, 241; 428; exploration from,
806 sqq.; 810 sq.
Tripolitza, storming of (1821), x 180
Trissino, Giovan (Gian) Giorgio, Italian
Reformer, ii 395; iii 469, 471
Tristam, Nuño, Portuguese explorer of
African coast, i 13
Tristany, Benito, Spanish priest, xi 556
Trithemius, Johannes (von Trittenheim), i
323, 325, 611; ii 29
Triumphus, Augustinus, iii 744, 753
Triumvirate, The French so-called (of
1561), ii 300

Trivulzio, Agostino, II 16
—— Gian Giacomo, I 114, 118; Governor of Milan, 121 sqq.; 135 sq., 198, 249
—— Teodoro, II 57
Trnovo, XII 404 sq.; captured, 388; 410; 427
Trochu, Louis-Jules, General, Military Governor of Paris, XI 497 sqq.; 600; 605 sq.; 608; 611
Troestra, van, Dutch socialist, XII 248
Troezen, Greek National Assembly at, XI 277
Trogoff, Comte Jean-Honoré de, French admiral, VIII 457
Troia, Carlo, Neapolitan statesman, XI 85; 90
Troibreze, Colonel, at Ratisbon, IV 231
Troitsa monastery, V 501, 508
Trolle, Erik, Administrator of Sweden, II 603
—— Gustaf. *See* Upsala, Archbishops of
—— Henrik af, Swedish admiral, VI 775
Trollope, Anthony, novelist, XI 360 sq.
Tromp, Cornelis, Dutch admiral, V 161; victory of, at Öland, 162; in the Four Days' Battle, 183 sq.; 186 sq.; 190; 195 sq.
—— Lieut.-admiral Martin Harpertzoon, naval victories of, IV 147; 311; action off Folkestone and, 471; 472 sq.; victory of, off Dungeness, 474; defeat of, off Portland, 475; 476 sqq.; Resolutions of (1652), 479; at Dunkirk, 598, 703; 646; at the battle of the Downs, 700; engagement of, with Blake, V 139; 140
Tronchet, François-Denis, VIII 183, 257, 488, 742, 746; IX 150
Tronçon-Ducoudray. *See* Tronson du Coudray
Trondhjem, Treaty of Roeskilde and, IV 586; restored to Denmark (1660), 591; Charles XIV in, XI 681
—— Olaf Engelbrektsson, Archbishop of, II 618 sqq.
Tronson du Coudray, Guillaume-Alexandre, French politician, VIII 507, 512
Troplong, Raymond-Théodore, French statesman, XI 140
Troppau, the Preliminaries of Breslau and, VI 235; Conference of (1820), VII 368, X 12, 27–9; 69; 113; the Papacy and, 150 sq.; attitude of Great Britain at, 186; 194; and Spanish revolution, 223; Protocol, 28 sq., 39
Trotter, Paymaster-General, under Melville, IX 684
Troubridge, Sir Thomas, Admiral, VIII 454; at Cape St Vincent, 462; at Naples, 657 sq.
Trouvé, Baron Charles-Joseph, Commissary at Milan, VIII 518
Troy, excavations in, XII 845
Troya, Carlo, the "Neo-Guelf," X 128; XII 842
Troyes, peace with England concluded at

(1564), III 7; taxation remitted at, 666; nuns in, VIII 53; stormed by Napoleon (1814), IX 549
Troyon, Constant, painter, XI 528
Trubetskoi (Trubetskóy), Prince Eugene, XII 360
—— Prince Nikita, VI 312
—— Prince Sergius, XII 354; 357
—— Prince Sergius, Russian colonel, X 441
—— Prince, and Ivan IV, V 491
Truchsess von Waldburg. *See* Waldburg
Trudaine de Montigny, Jean-C.-P., VIII 22, 24
True Law of Free Monarchy, III 751
Truguet, Comte L.-J.-F., French admiral, VIII 456; Minister of Navy, 490, 507 sq.; in command of Brest squadron, IX 212; dismissed, 216
Trumbull, Lyman, Republican leader, VII 628, 640
Trutvetter, Dr Jodocus, censor of the Press, I 685
—— John, "the Erfurt Doctor," II 112
Truxillo, destroyed by Dutch, IV 751
Try, member of French Commission on Civil Procedure (1802), IX 166
Tryon, William, Governor of North Carolina, VII 145
Tsailan, Prince, sentenced to death, XII 521
Tsana, Lake, in Abyssinia, XII 805; 808
Tsarskoe Selo, church of, VI 322; Tsar at, IX 34; railway to, XI 266
Tschernembl, Baron Erasmus von, Protestant leader in Austria, III 721, 726; IV 16; 21
Tsêng, Marquis, Chinese ambassador in London, XII 503 sq.; 507
Tseng Kuotsuan, Chinese general, XI 821
Tsinan Fu, railway to, XII 513
Tsingtao, German occupation of, XII 513
Tsungli Yamên, The, XII 500 sqq.; 504; and Great Britain, 508; and war loan, 513; and orphanages, 515; 516; and Boxer movement, 518, 520; 521; 525; 527
Tsushima, Japanese port, XI 841; 843; battle of, XII 354, 599 sq.
Tsuyama, *daimiō* of, XI 832
Tsze-Kwang-Ko, Chinese reception pavilion, XII 504
Tuam, Cathedral of, III 593
Tuan, Prince, and Boxer agitation, XII 518; 521
Tuckie, James, on the Congo, XII 807
Tuckney, Anthony, and Whichcote, V 750
Tucumán, administration of, X 249; insurrection in, 267; junta in, 269; 286 sq.
Tudela, Spanish defeat at (1808), IX 443–4
Tübingen, University of, III 723; opposed to Heidelberg, IV 5; Spener at, V 762; theological faculty of, and dogma of Immaculate Conception, XI 713; historical study at, XII 847
Türkenglocke, The, III 700
Tugela river, Sir Redvers Buller at, XII 642

Tugendbund, formed at Königsberg, IX 328; x 135

Tuileries, The, the mob in (June 20), VIII 228 sqq.; defence of, 235 sq.; meetings at, IX 9; new Court formed at, 23; marriage of Napoleon at, 140; welcome to Louis XVIII at, 562; proposed assault on (1815), 572; tricolour hoisted on, 575; Napoleon at, *ib.*, 616; Louis XVIII returns to, 645

Tula, revolutionaries at, v 500; iron-works at, 533; province of, famine in, XII 315

Tulchan Bishops, III 550

Tulczyn, secret society in, x 432

Tullibardine, William Murray, Marquis of, VI 98; 103; 105 sq.; 111

Tullin, Christian B., Norwegian writer, XI 700

Tuln, allied army at (1683), v 361, 362

Tulsk, battle of, III 604

Tumanbeg, Sultan of Egypt, I 91

Tumen river, Russian activity on, XII 576

T'ung-Chih, Emperor of China, XII 501 sq.; 504; 518; 557

T'ungchow, XII 505; evacuated by the Chinese, 520

Tung Fuhsiang, Chinese general, XII 518; 520

Tunis, European factories in, I 496; sack of, by Charles V (1535), II 69, III 105, 111; seized by Barbarossa, 110; offered by Charles V to Barbarossa, 114; retaken by the Turks (1574), 136; captured by Don John (1573), 497; assault upon, 541; dealings of Blake with, IV 483; French expedition against, VI 350; Spain and, 381; Venice and, 606; French occupation of, XII 3; 9; 158; 217; Italy and, 239; France and, 129; 132

Tunisia, XII 98; a French protectorate, 428

Tunstall, Cuthbert, Bishop of Durham, II 148, 432, 448, 471, 482, 484, 501; deprivation of, 507; restored by Mary, 521; Elizabeth and, 563; 571

Tupa Catari (Julian Apasa), x 267

Tupac Amaru (José Gabriel Condorcanqui), VI 381; x 267 sq.; 275; 299

Tupi-Guarani, The, of Brazil, I 38, 44, 59

Tupper, Sir Charles, Prime Minister of Nova Scotia, and Canada, XI xi; 769 sq.; 774 sq.

Tura river, Cossacks settle on, XII 794

Turati, Filippo, Italian socialist, XII 225 sq.; 231

Turberville, George, writer of verse, III 367

Turcoing, French victory at, VIII 435

Turco-Venetian treaty (1540), III 116–7

Turenne, Henri Vicomte de. *See* Bouillon, Henri de la Tour-d'Auvergne, Duke of
—— Henri de la Tour d'Auvergne, Vicomte de, Marshal of France (Marshal Turenne), trained in wars of Louis XIII, IV 149; 368; wounded at Zabern, 370; 376 sq.; on the Rhine, 388 sqq.; 392 sq.; and James II, 540; account of, 595;

597 sqq.; and the Bernardines, 595, 610; joins first French rebellion (1649), 611 sqq.; concludes treaty with Spain, 613; 615 sqq.; 659; conversion of, v 22; 43 sq.; Bossuet and, 86; 160; 199; death of, 217; 232; 340; 372; 651; Napoleon's recollection of, IX 93

Turfan, explorers at, XII 802

Turgenieff, Ivan, Russian writer, XI 614; 650; XII 297
—— Nicholas, Russian Councillor of State, x 432

Turgot, Anne-Robert-Jacques, Baron de l'Aulne, VI 830; VIII 3, 14, 17, 24 sq.; Comptroller-General, 37, 44, 66, 74, 77, 82; administration of, 83 sqq.; dismissed, 88; x 729; *Réflexions*, 770; *Discourse at the Sorbonne*, XII 817

Turin, II 70 sqq.; retained by France (1559), 94, III 400; Henry III at, 25; ceded to Savoy, 406–7; fortification of, 410; printing in, 412; v 408; siege of (1705), 414 sq.; 668; VIII 567; French troops in (1798), 644, 654; Allies enter (1799), 656; *émigrés* in, 780; Melas marches on (1800), IX 61; to be gallicised, 397; Victor Emmanuel I in (1814), x 13, 108; the Spanish Constitution proclaimed at, 116; appointment of a Nuncio at, refused, 142; XI 41; 78; death of Kossuth at, 215; 366; attacks on clerical party in, 368; 373; patriotic monument in, 374; 381; meeting of parliament at, 390; 535; massacres in, 539; strikes at, XII 224 sq.
—— Peace of (1381), I 264, (1601), III 419, (1703), v 448; Treaty of (1733), VI 152 sqq., (1860), XI 388, 469
—— Girolamo della Rovere, Archbishop of, III 404
—— Luigi Franzoni, Archbishop of, XI 368 sq.

Turini, Baldassare, da Pescia, II 13, 16

Turkestan, Russia and, XI 631; XII 95; exploration in, 792; 796
—— Afghan, rebellion in, XII 482
—— Chinese, XI 819; XII 4, 792; 794; exploration in, 799 sq., 802, 804
—— Russian, XII 801

Turkey
I   iii   The Ottoman Conquest, 67–103
              [For early struggles with Venice, see Chap. viii *passim*, 253–87]
III iv   The height of the Ottoman power, 104–39
              [For struggles with Spain, *see also* Chap. xv, 475–520 *passim*, and for Turkish relations with Rudolf II, 700 sq.]
v   ii   The foreign policy of Louis XIV (1661–97), *passim*, 32–63
     xii   Austria, Poland, and Turkey, 338–71
     xix   Charles XII and the Great Northern War (1709–13), *passim*, 603 sqq.

Turkey (*contd.*)

VI   x   Russia under Anne and Elizabeth, *passim*, 301-28

xi   The reversal of Alliances and the Family Compact, *passim*, 329-60

[*See also* Chaps. xviii and xix *passim*]

VIII xi   The European Powers and the Eastern Question, 306-37

IX   xi   The Napoleonic Empire at its height, *passim*, 294-340

x   vi   Greece and the Balkan Peninsula, *passim*, 169-204

xvii Mehemet Ali, *passim*, 545-72

XI   ix   [Russia and] the Levant, *passim*, 275-85

xi   Great Britain and the Crimean War (1852-6), *passim*, 309-24

xxii Russia and the Levant after the Crimean War, *passim*, 633-47

XII   xiv The Ottoman Empire and the Balkan Peninsula, 381-428

xv   Egypt and the Egyptian Sudan (1841-1907), *passim*, 429-56

Turkey Company, complaints of, against Dutch, v 108

Turkheim, fight at (1675), v 651

Turkmanchay, Treaty of (1828), x 444, xi 273

Turnebus (Adrien Turnèbe), French Hellenist, I 576 sq., 613; III 53

Turner, Sir James, in Scotland, v 284
—— Joseph M. W., artist, xi 356
—— Samuel, visits Tibet, xii 798

Turnham Green, Charles checked at (1642), IV 308 sq.

Turnhout, fight of (1597), III 629; Austrian defeat at (1789), vi 652, viii 329; canal at, xi 670

Túroczi, Benedictus, Minister of Matthias Corvinus, I 343

Turreau de Linières, Baron Louis-Marie, Commissioner, viii 562; General, 379, 439; ix 61

Turriani, Giovacchino, General of the Dominicans, I 183

Turton, Thomas A., xi 766

Tusanus. *See* Toussain, Jacques

Tuscany, Elba and Piombino occupied by, II 84; 94; Siena acquired by, 88; 396 sq.; under Cosimo, Francis, and Ferdinand de' Medici [q.v.], Grand Dukes of, Vol. III, Chap. xii, Tuscany and Savoy, 383-99; 415, 423, 430, 436, 438, 451-3, 666 sq., 674, 683; Habsburg influence over, 689; and Spain, iv 666; and War of the Barberini, 686 sq.; and the Spanish Succession, v 384, 389; vi 29; Spain and, 60; Elisabeth Farnese and, 122; 124; 126; Don Carlos and, 138, 150; 139; 152; 155; succession in, 158; 167; Treaty of Seville and, 202; clerical domination in, 590; 597; under Grand Duke Leopold, 600 sq.; 655; France

makes peace with (1795), viii 381; government of, 778; ix 57; Austrians in, 63; French in, 68-9; condition of, 87; French annexation of, 114; 398 sqq.; grand duchy of, given to Élise Bonaparte, 399; and Congress of Vienna, 602; x 105; under Ferdinand III, 107 sq.; literary and scientific movement in, 127 sqq.; relations of Papacy with, 142 sq.; road-making in, 729; xi 68 sqq.; national movement in, 75; a Constitution proclaimed in, 80; and the Italian Revolution, 83 sq.; the situation in (1848), 89 sqq.; Constituent Assembly in, 91; restoration of Leopold II, 94; 259; reaction in, 377 sq.; and War with Austria, 383; 385 sqq.; 468; 531; disorder in (1898), xii 220; 842

Tuscany, Grand Dukes of:—
—— Cosimo I (Medici), II 72, 81 sqq.; III 384-91; 399; economic policy of, 392 sq.; patron of art, 394; character of rule of, 395; death of, 396; and literature, 466, 470; v 739; vi 138; 152
—— Cosimo II (Medici), iv 81
—— Ferdinand I (Medici), Cardinal, III 390; 394; accession of, 396, 450; policy of, 397 sqq.; 419; and Sixtus V, 430; attitude of, towards Spain, iv 666
—— Ferdinand II (Medici), neutrality of, iv 600; v 740
—— Ferdinand III (Habsburg), viii 554; ix 92; 94, 602; and the Final Act of the Congress of Vienna, 660; x 128
—— Francis I (Medici), III 395-6, 399, 427, 430, 432, 450
—— Francis II (Habsburg). *See* Francis I, Emperor
—— Giovanni Gastone de' Medici, vi 138; 147; 156
—— Leopold I. *See* Leopold II, Emperor
—— Leopold II (Habsburg), x 128; and the Scientific Congress at Pisa, 128-9; xi 68 sq.; 78 sqq.; and War with Austria, 83 sq.; and Italian Federation, 89; retires to Gaeta, 91, 379; 93; restoration of, 94 sq., 377 sq.; 383; revokes Statute of 1848, 706

Tuscany, Élise, Grand Duchess of. *See* Bonaparte, Elise
—— Prince Leopold of, brother of Grand Duke Ferdinand II, Cardinal, v 740
—— Maria Louisa, Grand Duchess of, vi 601

Tuscarora Indians, The, vii 37 sq.

Tuscumbia, Hood at, vii 524

Tushino, Russian Pretender at, v 500

Tutbury, Mary Stewart at, iii 281

Tuttlingen, victory of Imperialists at (1643), iv 388

Tutuila, acquired by United States (1899), vii 663, xii 667

Tuyl, Baron de, Russian Minister to United States, vii 371

Tver, annexed by Ivan the Great, v 479; address to Tsar Alexander II from, xII 306, 322; 327

Tweeddale, John Hay, 2nd Marquis of, v 298

Twelve Years' Truce, The (1609), III 641–2, 728–9

Twiggs, David Emanuel, American general, vII 455

Two Sicilies, The. *See* Sicily *and* Naples 203 Metre Hill, xII 594 sq.

Tyard, Pontus de, III 55

Tyler, John, vII 388 sq.; President of United States, 390, 392 sqq.

—— Wat, II 175

Tyndale, William, translates Bible, II 464–5; the *Obedience of a Christian Man* (1528), III 752

Typaldos, Greek naval officer, xII 422

Tyrconnel, Rory O'Donnell, 1st Earl of, III 611 sq.

—— Richard Talbot, Earl of, v 233 sq.; 305; Viceroy of Ireland, 306 sq.; and James II, 308; 310 sqq.; and siege of Limerick, 315 sq.; visits France, 316; death of, 318

Tyrconnell, invaded by O'Neill, III 591; Sir Niall Garv claims lordship of, 613

Tyre, capture of, by Crusaders, I 254

Tyrell, James, *Patriarcha non Monarcha*, vI 803

Tyrnau, Peace of (1615), IV 11

Tyrol, acquired by Frederick III, I 296; II 150; Peasants' Revolt in, 182; loyal to Ferdinand, IV 23; under Archduke Leopold, 26; 35; 39; Planta's possessions in, 46; Austrian power in, 54; 61 sq.; v 401 sq.; Elector of Bavaria in, 407; the French in, 408; 414; Austria and, vI 204; 243; rising in (1797), vIII 583; French army on frontiers of (1800), IX 64; French conquests in, 68; plan of Allies in (1805), 250; Ney sent to, 256; ceded to Bavaria, 262; patriotic rising in (1808–9), 341, 355 sqq.; Austrian campaign in, *ib.*; acquisition of, by Austria (1815), 658; Church government in, x 145; lost by Bavaria, 146; Lombard volunteers in, xI 85; Estates of, 178; 457

Tyrone, invaded, III 591; plantation of, 614; resists English allotment, 615

—— Con Bacach O'Neill, 1st Earl of, III 584–90

—— Hugh O'Neill, 2nd Baron of Dungannon, 2nd Earl of, III 521, 529, 531 sqq., 590, 601 sqq., 611 sq.

—— John O'Neill, titular Earl of, death of, IV 522, 649

—— Shane O'Neill, Lord of, III 589 sqq.; death of (1567), 592 sq.; 610

Tzarevo-Zaimische, Barclay at (1812), IX 494

Tzschirner, Samuel Erdmann, Saxon politician, xI 219

Tz'ŭ An, Chinese Empress, xII 501 sq.; death of, 503

—— Hsi, Empress Dowager of China, xII 14; 501 sqq.; and currency, 506; 507; resumes power, 517; 518; flight of, 520; 526; death of, 522

Ubaghs, Gérard Casimir, philosopher, xI 712

Ubanghi river, xII 130; exploration of, 811 sq.

Uceda, Cristoval Gomez de Sandoval y Rojas, Duke of, at Court, IV 628 sq.; at Burgos, 630; 631 sqq.; Olivares and, 635 sq.

Uchanski, J., Primate of Poland. *See* Gnesen

Uckermark, Swedish troops in the, vI 280, 287, 294, 296

Udaipur, State of, xI 726

—— Rána of, joins Sindhia, IX 719; condition of, 730

Udall, John, III 345

—— Nicholas, editor of Erasmus' *Paraphrase*, II 481

Uddevalla, Convention at, vI 780

Udine, Austrian army at, xI 84

—— Giovanni da, artist, II 13

Überlingen, placed in Swedish hands, IV 391

Uffizi gallery, Cosimo's collections the nucleus of the, III 394

Uganda, British protectorate in, xII 49; Germany and, 167; settlement of frontier of, 449; 661 sq.; explorers in, 809; missionaries in, 810; 812

Ugarte, Antonio, x 208 sq.

Uglich, Tsarevich Dmitri sent to, v 496

Uhland, Johann Ludwig, German poet, x 361, 405 sq.; xI 164; 195; 413 sq.

Uhlich, Leberecht, German theologian, xI 51

Uhrich, Jean-Jacques-Alexis, French general, xI 588

Uitenhage, district of, xI 778

Uj-Besce, Jellačić at, xI 211

Ujiji, Livingstone and Stanley at, xII 809

Ujlaky, Lawrence, supporter of John Zápolya, I 336 sq.

Ukhtomsky, Prince, xII 315; 345

Ukraine, swept by Tartar horde (1575), III 92; and Treaty of Oliva, IV 591; v 349; Turks in, 353; 355; abandoned by Turkey, 358; revolt in (1648), 504 sqq.; 596 sq.; Swedish army in, 598, 600; Mazepa and, 599 sq.; partisans of Stanislaus in, vI 197; 302; lines of, 305 sqq.; 324; Catharine II and, 695

Ukraintseff, Emelyan, Russian plenipotentiary in Turkey, v 527

Uleaborg, occupied by Russia (1808), IX 314

Ulema, in Ottoman State under Mohammad II, I 101; in time of Solyman the Magnificent, III 127 sq., 132

Ulfeld, Korfits, Christian IV and, IV 572; at the Hague, 573 sq.; 584 sq.; Treaty of Roeskilde and, 586; v 558, 560

Ulfeld, Leonora Christina, marriage of, IV 573

Uliassutai, caravan route to, XII 793; 798

Uliungar, Russian explorers in, XII 799

Ulloa, Antonio de (Spanish explorer and scientist), economics of, VI 157; Governor of Louisiana; secret report of, X 250, 273

—— Don Osorio de, III 242

Ulm, Protestantism in, II 161, 205; rejects Schwabach articles, 210; submits to Charles V, 258; religious disturbance in, III 724; Protestant Union joined by, 725; Union at, IV 34; Treaty of (1620), 125; 209; 214; 220; Truce of (1647), 391; capture of (1702), V 406; 407; 409; Kray shelters in, IX 58; besieged by Moreau (1800), 64; surrender of, demanded by Napoleon, 65; magazine formed at, 252; capitulation of (1805), 254-5, 258; fortifications at, XI 50

Ulric of Denmark. *See* Schwerin

Ulrica Eleonora, Queen of Sweden, consort of Charles XI, V 571 sq.; 595; 614

—— Eleonora, Queen of Sweden (sister of Charles XII), VI 28; 761

Ulrich of Würtemberg. *See* Würtemberg

Ulster, disaffection in, III 529; O'Neill in, 589-91, 611; plantation of, 614, 616, IV 513; Calvinism in, III 616; IV 520; rebellion in, 522 sq.; 524 sqq.; 531 sq.; Cromwell's campaign in, 534; restoration of Episcopacy in, V 304; VI 482; Presbyterians of, 483, IX 696; disturbances in, VI 490; 491; 495; Volunteers of, 499; Orange Society of, IX 700; and rebellion (1798), 702; and the Union, 707-8; land tenure in, XII 70

Ultramontanism, as opposed to Gallicanism, Vol. V, Chap. IV *passim*, 72-91; origin of modern, X 157 sqq.; spread of, in early 19th century, 159 sqq.; great writers of, 161 sqq.; in Prussian Rhine Province, XI 53; Chap. XXV, Rome and the Vatican Council, *passim*, 703-23; French, of the 19th century, and de Maistre, 707; development of, in general, 716 sqq.; in France, and decrees of 1870, XII 92 sq.; after 1871, opponents of, 93; defeat of, in 1879, 116 sq.; and "Dreyfus affair," 121; Catholic historical scholarship and, 848

Ulundi, Zulus defeated at, XII 35, 636

Umbria, rising in (1798), VIII 638; revolutionary movements in (1830-1), X 120, 155; national movement in, XI 384; 387; 390; invasion of, 469; 530; annexed to Italy, 709

Uminski, General, and Polish Patriotic Society, X 453

Unam Sanctam, Bull of Boniface VIII, confirmed, II 31; III 757

Undertakers, the Irish, of Archbishop Boulter, VI 487 sqq.

Ungaba, district of, XI 776

Ungebauer, General, X 553

Uniformity. *See* Act of Uniformity

Unigenitus, Bull (1713), V 90 sq.; VI 131; 163; promulgated by Clement XI, and its results, 588 sqq.; Benedict XIV and, 591; 637; results of, in France, VIII 9

Union, of the British Islands, attempts of Henry VIII in relation to Wales and Ireland, II 470 sqq.; of England and Scotland, Somerset's scheme for, 487; mooted by James I, III 556 sqq.; final accomplishment of, V 297 sqq.; the Act itself, and Jacobitism, Vol. VI, Chap. III, 90-119; between England and Ireland, the 18th century preparation therefor, Chap. XIV *passim*; IX 702 sqq.; Chap. XXII *passim*. *See also* Act of Union

—— of Evangelical Estates (German Protestant), III 687 sq.; Congress of, at Schwäbisch Hall, 689 sq.; rise of, 725 sqq.; and outbreak of the Thirty Years' War, Vol. IV, Chap. I *passim*; dissolution of, 69

Union, La, French newspaper, XI 292

—— *Libérale, La*, French newspaper, XI 123; 127

Unions, Micoud de, work at Liége of, IX 416

Unità Cattolica, Italian journal, XI 714

Unitarians, in England, and growth of toleration, V 327; in Transylvania, *see* Sozzini, Fausto

United Irish League, XII 89

United Irishman, newspaper, XI 13

"United Irishmen," Society of, started by Wolfe Tone, VIII 771 sq.; X 628 sq.

United Kingdom of Great Britain and Ireland. *For affairs in common, see* England

—— Provinces of the Netherlands. *See* Netherlands, United Provinces of the

United States of America, The
VII   i   The first century of English colonisation (1607-1700), 1-52
       ii   The English Colonies (1700-63), 53-69
       iii The French in America (1608-1744), 70-113
       iv   The Conquest of Canada (1744-1761), *passim*, 114-43
       v   The quarrel with Great Britain (1761-76), 144-74
       vi   The Declaration of Independence (1761-76), 175-208
       vii The War of Independence (1776-83), 209-34
       viii The Constitution (1776-89), 235-304
       ix   The Struggle for Commercial Independence (1783-1812), 305-34
       x   The War of 1812-5, 335-48
       xi   The Growth of the Nation (1815-28), 349-77

United States of America, The (*contd.*)

VII   xii   Commerce, expansion and slavery (1828–50), 378–404

    xiii   State Rights (1850–60), 405–42

    xiv   The Civil War, I (1861), 443–71

    xv   The Civil War, II (1862–3), 472–513

    xvi   The Civil War, III (1864–5), 514–48

    xvii   Naval operations of the Civil War (1861–5), 549–67

    xviii   The North during the War (1861–5), 568–602

    xix   The South during the War (1861–5), 603–21

    xx   Political Reconstruction (1865–85), 622–54

    xxi   The United States as a World-Power (1885–1902), 655–86

    xxii   Economic Development of the United States, 687–722

    xxiii   The American Intellect, 723–51

XI   xii   Great Britain (1856–68), *passim*, 325–46

    xxvii   Great Britain and her Colonies (1840–70), (ii) The Federation of Canada, *passim*, 766–78

    xxviii   The Far East (1815–71), *passim*, 802–65

XII   ii   Foreign relations of the United States during the Civil War, 16–22

    xx   The European Colonies, *passim*, 602–71

    xxi   The Republics of Latin America, *passim*, 672–702

    [*See also* Chaps. xxii and xxiii *passim*]

Univers, Le, French journal, political work of, x 500; xi 27; 292; 296; suppressed, 469; 707 sq.; 721

Universities, in Australia and New Zealand, xii 627: Canadian, *Laval, McGill, Kingston, Toronto,* xi 778: Danish, *Copenhagen* becomes important under Christian II, ii 605, 617; refounded by Christian VI, vi 739: in Empire, Maximilian I and those of *Vienna, Freiburg in the Breisgau,* etc., i 325; in 17th century, iv 424 sq.; xi 169 sq.; *Prague,* xii 195: English, *Oxford* and *Cambridge* and Renaissance, i 579 sq.; in 1542–8, ii 468; James II's attack on, v 237 sq.; in 18th century, viii 763 sq.; *see also* Oxford *and* Cambridge; the modern, *London,* x 668, *Manchester, Liverpool,* etc., xii 763: French, *Nîmes,* ii 291; *Paris,* i 635 sq.; 667; and the Renaissance, 575 sq.; *Paris, Poitiers,* etc. and Holy See, 635 sq., 667; *Paris,* condemns Luther, ii 283; state of, in 1523, 350; Nicolas Cop's rectorial address to, 285, 354; xi 67, 297, xii 762; *Poitiers,* iv 778; *Toulouse,* legists at, ii 95; the *Imperial*

University of France (with *Paris* as its centre), founded by Napoleon, ix 127 sqq.; under Louis XVIII, x 73; xi 67; under Napoleon III, 297; and education of women, xii 762; *see also* Paris: German (including Prussian), and the Renaissance, i 574; and the Holy See, 636; great growth of, in the pre-Reformation period, 637 sq.; *Berlin,* ix 327, xii 820 sq.; *Breslau,* ix 327 sq., x 355; *Duisburg,* iv 789; *Erfurt,* in Luther's days, ii 110 sqq.; *Frankfort-on-Oder,* v 624, ix 327, x 355; *Herborn,* iv 789, 791; *Ingolstadt,* i 622; *Jena,* ix 325, x 364, 375, xi 150; *Kiel,* vi 753; *Königsberg,* iii 74, 78, ix 327; *Leipzig,* v 760; *Wittenberg,* in Luther's days, ii 116 sqq.; and the progress of Reform, 165; *see also* Wittenberg; foundation of *Marburg,* 201; ix 411; German in general, agitation in, after 1815, x 363: in India, and Lord Curzon, xii 494: Irish, in 19th century, 29; 71 sq.; *Dublin,* ix 696, xi 9; *Trinity College,* iii 611, xi 9; Italian, *Bologna,* iii 447; xi 86; x 137; *Perugia,* ix 402; *Pisa,* under Cosimo de' Medici, iii 392; *Rome,* founded (1513), ii 16 sq.; *see also* Rome: in Netherlands, *Groningen,* ix 417; *Louvain,* i 419; and its studies, 436; 636; theological seminary established in, by Joseph II, vi 649 sq.; viii 318; ix 415; *Leyden* and Renaissance, i 579; iv 717; 789; v 753; ix 417: Polish, *Cracow,* in 16th century, iii 77 sq.; and neglect of education in Poland, *ib.*; Stephen Báthory and, 102 sq.; foundation of *Warsaw,* x 449, xi 629: Russian, from 1804, x 430 sq.; in 19th century, xi 267; under Alexander II, 624, 627; and Count Dmitry Tolstoi, xii 298 sq.; reformed (1863), 294 sq.; revolutionary character of, 303 sq.; protests of, against government repression, 315 sq.; *Dorpat,* 336; closing of (1905), 350; claim of self-government for, 353; political action of, 357 sq.: Spanish, *Alcalá,* i 380; fostered by Ximenes, 400; and Renaissance, 578: Swedish, xii 280, 273: Swiss, *Geneva,* prospers under Calvin, ii 372 sq.; *Bern,* xi 241; *Zurich,* 241, xii 303, 762; in 19th century, xi 260 sq.: in the United States, *Harvard,* vii 744. *See also under names of cities*

Unkiar Skelessi, Treaty of (1833), x 494, 505, 512; Austria and, 546; significance of, 555 sqq., 562; 564; 572

Untereyk, Theodor, Pietist, v 757

Unterwalden, canton of, vi 613; revolt in (1798), viii 640; xi 242; 245; and Aargau monasteries, 247; 251

Upper Peru. *See* Bolivia

Upsala, battle of (1520), ii 603; Constitution (1562), iv 161 sq.; 164; Resolution of, 170, 175; 171 sq.; 184; University of, 187, 578; consultation at (1629), 193; 207; 787; Estates at (1675), v 568

Upsala, Archbishops of:—
—— Gustaf Trolle, II 603 sq., 614 sq., 622 sq.
—— Joannes Magni (Johan Magnusson), II 622–7
—— Laurentius Petri (Lars Petersson), II 624; translator of Bible, 625; 628, 630
—— Laurentius Petri Gothus, II 630 sq.
Upsala-möte, The (1593), Swedish religious settlement at, II 632 sq.
Upshur, Abel Parker, American Secretary of State, VII 391 sqq.
Uraga, American expedition at, XI 824, 828 sq.
Urals, iron industries of, XI 618
Urana, surrendered by Venice to the Turks, III 116
Urban II (Eudes de Chastillon), Pope, II 126
—— IV (J. Pantaleon), Pope, III 464
—— VIII (Maffeo Barberini), Pope, and Valtelline, IV 57 sq., 129 sq.; and Treaty of Monzon, 60, 675; 74 sq.; 84; and House of Habsburg, 88, 365; and Edict of Restitution, 113; espouses cause of Nevers, 115, 678 sq.; 143; and Richelieu, 156; 211; 367; 373; and Treaty of Westphalia, 396 sqq.; 668; 674; 676; Galileo and, 677; European policy of, 680 sqq.; internal government of, 684 sq.; war of the Barberini and, 686; 687 sq.; XI 713
Urbino, Cesare Borgia and, I 194, 240; Papacy and State of, III 385; brigandage in, 430; Habsburg influence over, 689; Court of, under Guidobaldo of Montefeltro, 462, 471; duchy of, Urban VIII and, IV 684, 686; duchy of, incorporated in Italian kingdom (1808), IX 400
—— Elizabeth di Gonzaga, Duchess of (d. 1526), culture of the court of, III 462
—— Federigo di Montefeltro, Duke of (d. 1482), library of, I 553
—— Francesco Maria I della Rovere, Duke of, general for Julius II, I 136, 138; attacked by Leo X, II 14; general for Clement VII, 53 sq., 56, 58; attacked by Paul III, 69
—— Francesco Maria II, Duke of, dependent on Spain, IV 666
—— Guidobaldo da Montefeltro, Duke of (restored, 1503–8), I 244 sq.; culture of Court of, III 462
Urbiztondo, Antonio de, Spanish Minister of War, XI 563
Urga, XII 792; trade route from, 795 sq.; Prjevalsky at, 798 sq.; 804
Urgel, La Seo de, seized by insurgents (1822), X 225
Uri, canton of, VI 613; rising against, 625; revolt in (1798), VIII 640; XI 237; 239; 242; and Aargau monasteries, 247; 251
Uriu, Sotokichi, Japanese admiral, XII 522; 580
Urne, Lage. *See* Roskilde, Bishops of

Urquiza, Juste José de, President of Argentine Confederation, XII 682 sq.
Ursek Ujvar. *See* Neuhäusel
Ursel, Duc d', Belgian statesman, X 525; 536
Ursins, Princesse des. *See* Orsini
Ursinus, Zacharias (Beer), German theologian, III 154
Urslivenus, German theologian, XI 51
Uruguay. *See* Banda Oriental
Urumtsi, Mark Bell at, XII 802
Urúsoff, Prince, Russian Minister, XII 360; 363; resigns, 364; 367
Usbegs, VI 508 sq.; besiege Kabul, 517; 518; 525
Usedom, Gustavus Adolphus lands on, IV 191, 193, 197
—— Baron Karl G. L. G. von, Prussian diplomatist, XI 163; 165 sq.
Uskoks, in Carniola, Croatia, and Dalmatia, IV 11; 40; and Archduke Ferdinand, 45
Uskub, Servia and, XII 424; 426
Usora, battle at (1415), I 71
Uspensky Cathedral, V 604
—— Russian monk, XII 343
Usselincx, Willem, III 633; and Dutch West India Company, IV 703, 750; Gustavus and, 759
Ussher, James, Archbishop of Armagh, V 238; 745
Usson, de, French officer, in Ireland, V 316 sqq.
Ussuri river, Russian advances on, XI 273; 819; XII 792; ceded to Russia, 796
Ustariz, Jerome, Spanish economist, VI 157
Uster, great political meeting at, XI 240
Usteri, Martin, IX 427
—— Paulus, Swiss politician, XI 239
Usupoff, General, and Empress Anne, V 557
Utah, ceded to United States (1848), VII 397; admission of, to Union, 403 sq., 417; slavery in, 416; and currency question, 673; women's franchise in, XII 763
Utenhove, Charles, Protestant refugee in England, II 477, 592
Utopia, Sir Thomas More's, II 183, 490
Utraquists, in Bohemia, spread of Lutheran doctrines among, III 147 sq.
Utrecht, Burgundian power in, I 423; annexed to Netherlands (1527–8), II 102, 144; see of, secularised by Charles V, 212; transferred to Burgundian circle, 263; William of Orange at, III 211–2; refuses to pay Alva's tax, 226; *Gueux de Mer* seize, 229–30, 233, 248; Union of (1579), 251–2, 646, 704; province of, 618, 650; democratic party at, 620–1; Deventer at, 623; Remonstrants in, 647; Commission sent to, 651; province of, ravaged, IV 693; negotiations at Münster and, 715; Academy founded at, 717; Union of (1579), 723, V 448; invaded by French (1672), 43, 157; and Eternal

Edict, 155; 161; 458; Gisbert Voet at, 753; favours Stadholder, VIII 287; French *lycée* at, IX 417; proposed archbishopric at, XI 665

Utrecht, Peace (or Treaty) of (1713), Vol. V, Chap. XIV (2); 30; 399; 431; 432 sqq.; Brandenburg and, 658; Prussia and, 668; and Brazil, 679; and Spanish America, 684; and West Indies, 688; 693; Bothmer and, VI 13; Handel and, 19; and Dunkirk, 23, 464; 49; 58; 60; 63 sq.; and Old Pretender, 96; 97; 104; 121 sq.; Ripperdá, of service in, 139; and Spain, 151, 167, 249; 153; 159; 178; 181; France and, 194; 313; 331; 391; and America, 411; 428; and Papacy, 587; and Venice, 605; confirms English claim to Newfoundland, VII 52; and New France, 70; VIII 281; X 2; 31

—— David, Bishop of, I 423; 435; 437; 445; 460

—— Engelbert of Cleves, Bishop of, I 445

—— (Transvaal), district of, XI 785

Uttenheim, Christopher von. *See* Basel, Bishop of

Uwajima, *daimiō* of, XI 825; 836 sq.; 851 sq.; 856

Uxbridge, negotiations at (1645), IV 327 sq.; 343

—— Sir H. W. Paget, 2nd Earl of. *See* Anglesey, Marquis of

Uyeno, fight at, XI 859

Uyesugi, Japanese noble, XI 850

Uyttenbogaert, Johannes, III 646–8, 652

Uzès, H.-B.-J. de Béthizy de Mézières, Bishop of, VIII 179

Uzés, Duke of, III 26

Vaal Kranz, British forces at, XII 643

Vacherot, Étienne, French philosopher, XII 99

Vachott, Alexander, Hungarian writer, XI 426

Vacquerie, Auguste, French journalist, XII 94

Vadian (von Watt), of St Gallen, Zwinglian, II 315

Vadier, Marc-G.-A., French deputy, VIII 380, 384

Vadstena, IV 165; constitution promulgated at, 167; 169; 172

Värälä, Peace of, VI 676, 782, VIII 295, 336, IX 37

Västerås. *See* Vesterås

Västergötland, and Danes, IV 180

Vaillant, Édouard, French politician, XI 502 sq.

—— Jean-Baptiste-Philibert, Comte, Marshal of France, XI 125; 322

Valais, The, Alliance of, with Savoy, III 405–6, 411, 421; French army enters (1800), IX 59; proposed separation of, 98; 99; excluded from Federation, 104; French annexation of (1810), 141; Republic of, 374; formal absorption of, 424;

forms Swiss canton (1814), 601; XI 234; 236; Jesuits in, 239; 244; and Aargau monasteries, 247; civil war in, *ib.*; 251

Valazé, Charles-Eléonore Dufriche de, French deputy, VIII 214, 254, 357

Valckenier, Gillis, opposes de Witt, V 154, 156; 164; death of, 165

Valdemar. *See* Waldemar

Valdés, Alfonso de, Spanish follower of Erasmus, II 388

—— Diego Flores de, Spanish admiral, III 307

—— Fernando de. *See* Seville, Archbishop of

—— Francisco de, besieges Leyden, III 239

—— Juan de, Spanish Reformer in Naples, II 387–90; writings of, 388 sq.; 410; scholar, III 466

—— Pedro de, Spanish commander, III 307, 312

—— Spanish colonel, X 230

Val de Travers, Republican movement in, XI 253

Val di Noce, bay of, XII 402

Valdivia, and Peru, X 248; capture of (1820), 292

Valdore, Lally at, VI 549

Valecilla, Portuguese vice-admiral, IV 708

Valée, Comte Silvain-Charles, Marshal of France, X 504

Valeggio, Imperial victory at (1630), IV 679

Valençay, Ferdinand VII imprisoned in, IX 433; released, 482; Treaty of (1813), X 205

Valence, Pius VI removed to, VIII 638

—— Jean de Montluc, Bishop of, II 297 sq., 300, 303

—— Comte Cyrus M. A. de Timbrune de, commands Army of the Ardennes, VIII 416, 419; deserts to Austria, 422; 429

Valencia, condition of, in Middle Ages, I 352; revolt of the *Germania* in, 376 sq.; expulsion of Moriscos from, III 541 sqq.; Cortes of, IV 628, 643; the Allies in, V 416; lost (1707), 419; 426; liberties of, VI 136; rising in (1808), IX 434; 435; Moncey fails to capture, 436; Suchet defeated at (1810), 457; surrender of Blake in (1812), 470; French at, 473 sqq.; Ferdinand VII at, X 205; risings in (1822), 224; Carlist forces in province of, 239 sq.; Moderate Ministry appointed in, 241; military plot at, XI 568; clerical influence in, XII 258; 259; 263

—— the Cardinal of. *See* Borgia, Cesare

—— Duke of. *See* Narváez

—— de Alcantara, taken by British troops, VI 426

Valenciennes, captured from the Spaniards (1572), III 17, 230–1; siege of (1567), 212; Turenne defeated at (1656), IV 619, 659 sq.; taken by French (1677), V 44; 45; 422; and Barrier Treaties, 457 sq.; and

States General, VIII 125; Coburg captures
(1793), 347, 429 sq.; claimed by Austria,
430; recaptured by France (1794), 436;
Treaty of (1794), 555
Valengin, Prussia and, V 449, 669
Valentin, Marie-Edmond, French Re-
publican, XI 136
Valentine, Basil, alchemist, V 730 sq.
—— Benjamin, imprisonment of, IV 281
Valentino, Bonifacio, Modenese Reformer,
II 387
—— Filippo, Modenese Reformer, II 387
Valentinois, Duke of. *See* Borgia, Cesare
Valenza, occupied by the French (1499), I
121; taken by the Allies (1705), V 416
Valenzuela, Fernando de, Spanish states-
man, V 35; 45
Valer, Rodrigo de, Spanish Reformer, II 404
Valera, Cipriano de, Spanish Reformer, II
406, 411
Valeriano, Giampetro Bolzani, *De Litera-
torum Infelicitate*, I 567, II 15; I 612
Valetta, VIII 596; surrenders to French
(1798), 598, 645
Valiant, Thomas, Brigadier, at Karachi,
XI 736
Valla, Lorenzo, *De Elegantiis Latinae
Linguae*, I 545; criticisms of, on Dona-
tion of Constantine, 546, 602, 608, 664;
565; and on Dionysius the Areopagite,
602; *Voluptas*, II 3; *De Donatione Con-
stantini Magni*, and its influence on the
Reformers, 694; III 456
Valladolid, the Reformation in, II 399, 404,
407 sq.; *auto de fé* at, III 480, 482; V
220; rising in, 376; 428; advance of
Dupont to (1808), IX 430; Moore and,
444; Masséna and, 457; rising at (1854),
XI 560
Vallandigham, Clement Laird, American
politician, VII 573 sqq., 579 sq.
Valle, Andrea della. *See* Della Valle
—— Joseph de, Spanish general, VI 381
Vallé, French soldier executed for con-
spiracy, X 76
Vallès, Jules, French political writer, XI
486
Valley, Count von. *See* Kurtz, Baron
—— Forge, Washington at, VII 217
Valls, Reding defeated at (1809), IX 448
Valmy, battle of, VIII 251, 299, 410 sq.
Valois, House of, III 18. *See also* Henry II,
Francis II, Charles IX, Henry III, etc.
—— Adrien de, III 61, 63
—— Charlotte-Aglae de. *See* Modena,
Duchess of
—— Francis of. *See* Anjou, Duke of
Valona, Italy and, XII 242
Valori, Francesco, Savonarolist, I 169 sq.,
172; death of, 181; 183
—— Count de, French ambassador at
Berlin, VI 338
Valparaiso, bombardment of, XI 567; XII
678
—— Count of, VI 364

Valromey, ceded to France, III 419, 677
Valtelline, The, gained by Grisons, II 309;
closed to Spain, III 684; Vol. IV, Chap. II;
Richelieu and, 123, 141, 148, 642; 129
sq.; 136; Philip III and, 634 sq.; 640
sq.; Protestant massacre in, 672 sq.;
Gregory XV and, 674; Urban VIII and,
675; seized by Rohan, 683; annexed to
Cisalpine Republic (1797), VIII 589, 592;
annexed by Austria (1814), IX 601,
660
Valutina-Gora, fight at (1812), IX 493
Valúyeff, Russian Minister of the Interior,
XII 295; 298 sq.; 308
Vámbéry, Arminius, XI 431; in Central
Asia, XII 801
Van, surrendered to the Turks, III 120;
Armenian massacres in, XII 417, 419
—— member of Congress (1775), VII 166
Vanbrugh, Sir John, V 128; 130 sq.
Van Buren, Martin, President of United
States, VII 385, 388 sq.; and annexation
of Texas, 392 sq.; 399
Vance, Zebulon Baird, Governor of N.
Carolina, VII 605, 609
Vancouver, British possession, VII 398;
united to Canada, XI 776; 777
—— George, explorer, voyage of, IX 748
Vandal, Albert, French historian, XII 834
Vandamme, Dominique-René, Comte d'Une-
bourg, French general, VIII 435; IX 260;
commands in Bremen, 515; at Pirna,
526-7; at Priesten, 528; and the Belgian
campaign, 625; 627
Vandeleur, Sir John Ormesby, General,
cavalry brigade of, at Waterloo, IX 639-40
Van den Peereboom, J., Belgian statesman,
XII 254
Van der Helst, Bartholomaeus. *See* Helst
Vandervelde, Emile, Belgian socialist, XII
253
Van Diemen, Anthoni. *See* Diemen
Van Diemen's Land. *See* Tasmania
Vane, Sir Henry, the elder, at Mainz, IV
209; 220; witnesses against Strafford,
289; abolition of Episcopacy and, 292
—— Sir Henry, the younger, at Leith, IV
317; 322; and Cromwell, 448; 451;
foreign policy and, 541 sq.; and re-
ligious toleration, 543; Committee of
Safety and, 546; expelled from Parlia-
ment, 548; execution of, V 94; Governor
of Massachusetts, VII 17 sq.
—— Sir Walter, at Berlin, V 109
Vanini, Cesare, IV 777
Vannes, A. F. X. Mayneaud de, Bishop of,
IX 188-9
—— Peter (Pietro Vanni), English ambas-
sador, in Venice, II 513, 526
Vannicelli, Cardinal, X 156
Vannucci, Atto, X 109
Van Rensselaer, Solomon, American general,
VII 338
Vansittart, Henry, Governor of Bengal, VI
558 sqq.

Vansittart, Nicholas (Lord Bexley), Chancellor of the Exchequer, x 574 sq.; 587 sq.

Vanstabel, Pierre-J., French admiral, VIII 466

Varanger Fiord, Russia and, XI 687

Varax, Spanish general, III 629

Varberg, capture of (1565), IV 163; recovered, 166

Varchi, Benedetto, III 394, 472

Varennes, the flight to, VI 477, 783, VIII 200, 215

—— French *chargé d'affaires* at Constantinople, x 551

Varesini, Alexander Dominic. *See* Sassari, Bishop of

Vargas, Alonso de, III 516

—— Francisco, Minister of Charles V, at Council of Trent, II 264

—— Juan de, III 216 sqq.

—— Fray Martino de, Reformer of Spanish Cistercians, II 399

—— Dr, Spanish Reformer, II 267, 405

Varignano, Garibaldi at, XI 534

Varignon, Peter, mathematician, v 718

Varlet, C.-Z.-J., French deputy, VIII 342

Varlin, Eugène, French politician, XI 492; 502

Varna, French and English forces at, XI 317 sq.; harbour of, XII 395

Varnbüler, John Conrad, Protestant plenipotentiary at Congress (1645–8), IV 401; 409

Varoux, attacked by French, VI 247

Varzin, Bismarck's negotiations at, XII 152

Vasa, House of, *see* Vol. IV, Chap. v

—— *See* Gustavus, King of Sweden

Vasaborg, Count Gustaf Gustafsson, IV 408

Vasari, Giorgio, III 394, 457; *Lives of the Painters*, 473–4

Vasconcellos, Miguel, rule of, in Portugal, IV 650 sq.; killed, 652; 654

Vasilchikoff, Illarion, Prince, Russian general, x 439

Vasili (Wasilei) III, Tsar, I 343; v 479; 481; reign of, 487

—— —— IV, Tsar, election of, v 499; alliance with Charles IX of Sweden, IV 176; reign of, v 500 sq.

Vasily Island, Peter II at, v 554

Vasquez, Mateo, III 514–5

—— Rodrigo, III 518

Vassian, pupil of Nil Sorski, v 508

Vássos, Colonel, Greek officer, XII 420; 422

Vassy, massacre of, II 584, III 1

Vasto, Alfonso d'Avalos, Count del, II 53, 55, 72, 77

Vasvar, Truce of (1664), v 40, 348, 350, 358

Vatable, François, French Hebraist, II 282

Vaterlandsvereine, German political club, XI 149

Vatican, The, Codex B of, I 595; library of, founded by Nicholas V, 595 sq.; III

444 sq.; Catalogue of MSS begun, VI 589; museum of, I 547; palace of, enlarged and decorated by Julius II, II 5, 12; guaranteed to the Pope, XII 229

Vatican Council, The, and the Lanza Ministry, XI 543; Chap. XXV, Rome and the Vatican Council, *especially* 717 sqq.; XII 92 sq.; Germany and, 147 sq.; Döllinger and, 848

Vatimesnil, Antoine-F.-H. Lefebvre de, x 92

Vatke, Wilhelm, Semitic studies of, XII 846

Vattel, Emeric de, XII 714

Vauban, Sébastien le Prestre, Seigneur de, Marshal of France, v 15; 25; 29 sq.; 429; VII 113; VIII 8; *Dîme Royale*, 15; x 47

Vaublanc, Comte Vincent-M.-Viénot de, French politician, VIII 213; Minister of the Interior, x 47; electoral proposals of, 49–50; retires, 50; and policy of Villèle, 80

Vaubois, Claude-Henri Belgrand, Comte de, French commander, VIII 578

Vaucelles, Treaty of (1556), II 89–92, 544 sq., III 184; rupture of, II 92

Vauchamp, Napoleon attacks Blücher at (1814), IX 548

Vaucoulleur, French economist, VI 599

Vaud, Davel and, VI 625; risings in, IX 95, 100; and Congress of Vienna, 587; 600; XI 234; 236; 240; 244; anti-Jesuit rising in, 247; 259

Vaudémont, Louis, Count of, II 55

—— Louise de, becomes Queen of Henry III (1575), III 26

—— René de. *See* Lorraine, Dukes of

Vaudois, The, heresy among, III 400, 402; rebellion of, against Savoy, 403, 417; persecution of, IV 439

Vaudoncourt, French refugee in Spain, x 221; 224

Vaudreuil, Philippe de Rigaud, Marquis de, Governor of Canada (1703–25), VII 90

Vaudreuil-Cavagnal (son of above), Pierre François de Rigaud, Marquis de, Governor of Canada (1755–60), VII 125, 129, 138, 143

Vaugelas, Claude Favre de, IV 156

Vaughan, Henry, religious attitude of, IV 766; and nature, 770; 772; 774

—— Richard, Earl of Carbery. *See* Carbery

Vaulabelle, Achille Tenaille de, French statesman, XI 115

Vaulgrenant, French ambassador in Spain, VI 156

Vaulx, Seigneur de. *See* Passano

Vauquelin, Louis-Nicolas, excluded from the Sorbonne, x 78

Vauréal, Louis Guido Guérapin de. *See* Rennes, Bishop of

Vaux, Lawrence, III 284

—— Noël de Jourda, Comte de, Marshal of France, reduces Corsica, VI 350; at Grenoble, VIII 113

Vavasour, Sir Charles, iv 526

Vay, Baron, Hungarian Conservative, xi 184

Vazerol, *Bund* of 1471 at, iv 36

Vecchio, Geronimo, iv 789

Veche, popular assembly of Novgorod the Great and of Pskoff, v 479, 484

Vedel, French general, sent to secure the Despeña Perros, ix 437; conduct of, 438

Vega, Garcilasso della, Spanish secretary at Rome, seized by Paul IV, ii 91

Veiga, Alves, Portuguese Republican leader, xii 271

Veit, Philipp, artist, x 151

Vela, Pedro Nuñez, Spanish Reformer, ii 404

Velabrum, The, iii 443–4

Velarde, Spanish officer, killed in riot at Madrid, ix 434

Velasco, Don Luis, Spanish officer, vi 369
—— Martino, agent of Charles V at the Council of Trent, ii 264

Velasquez, Diego, Governor of Cuba, i 41

Velasquez de Silva, Diego Rodriguez, portraits by, iv 637, 658, 687; Philip IV and, 664

Veldencze, fight at, xi 184, 203

Velestino, battle at, xii 422

Velez, Pedro Fajardo de los, 3rd Marquis, iii 494

Velez Malaga, naval fight off (1704), v 413

Velichevo, French at, ix 499

Velletri, and War of Austrian Succession, vi 241; 596; Cardinal Mattei at, x 139

Vellingk, Count, Swedish Governor of Bremen, vi 28

Vellore, mutiny at, ix 731

Velly, Paul-François, French historian, xii 829

Veltwyck, joint ambassador of Charles V and Ferdinand I to Poland, iii 120

Venables, General Robert, expedition of, to West Indies, iv 481 sq.; in Ulster, 534

Venaissin, v 449; united to France (1791), viii 217; Pius VII and, x 144

Vence, French admiral, viii 471

Vendée, The, insurrection in (1793), viii 265 sqq., 270, 340 sq., 345 sqq., 353 sqq., 379, 381; renewed hostility in (1795), 391; end of struggle in, 395, 497, 500; insurrections in (1814–5), ix 564, 617, 624

Venden, the Russians overthrown at (1578), iv 167

Vendôme, French retreat to, xi 607
—— Antoine, Duke of, invades Artois (1542), ii 76
—— César, Duke of, iii 675; iv 119; expedition against, 120; 124; 126; imprisoned, 131; family of, 609; 617
—— Charles de, Cardinal (from 1590 known as the young Cardinal de Bourbon). *See* Bourbon
—— Louis, Duke of, *and* Duke of Mercœur, supports Mazarin, iv 609, 612, 618

Vendôme, Louis-Joseph, Duke of, Marshal of France, captures Barcelona, v 62; in Italy, 405 sqq.; 414; replaces Villeroi in Netherlands, 416; 418; 420; defeated at Oudenarde, 421; 422; in Spain, 428
—— Philippe de, Grand Prior of France, v 414

Vendramin, Lorenzo, translations by, from Cicero, iii 471

Venegas, Spanish general, ordered against Madrid, ix 452; defeated at Almonacid, 454–5

Venero, Antonio de, iii 255

Venetia, and Austria, ix 247; ceded to Italy (1805), 261, 267; creation of duchies in, 268, 400; and Italian Concordat, 401; Austrian designs on, 591; Austrian rule in, x 104 sqq.; 109; conspiracies in (1820–1), 117; Church government in, 145 sq.; hostility to Austria in, xi 75 sq.; 78; 81; and union with Piedmont, 84, 86, 90; 87 sq.; and negotiations with Austria, 92; 448; 479; ceded to Italy, 480, 540 sq.; King Victor Emmanuel and, 531. *See also* Venice

Venetz, Ignace, Swiss man of science, xi 260

Venezuela, dispute between Great Britain and the United States over, vii 670 sqq.; trade of, x 257; government of (1731), 274; 276; 288; invaded by Bolívar, 289; 290; struggle in (1816–30), 293 sqq.; separates from Colombia, 296; under Paez, *ib.*; and Bolívar's scheme of federation, 297; municipalities suppressed in, 298; royalists in, 306; seeks British aid, 307; dispute of, with Great Britain, xii 52, 56, 687 sq., 721; 655; 672 sq.; 690; 692; naval demonstration against, 695, 701; 696

Venice, the Turks and, i 68; wars of (1463), 76, 285 sqq., (1470), 79, (1499), 87; loss of Negroponte by, 79 sq.; Peace of, with Turks (1479), 81, 286, (1503), 88; league against France joined by (1494–5), 118, 362; attacks Julius II (1503), 244; designs against, and League of Cambray, 130 sq., 246; War of the League, 132–4, 246; peace, 134, 247; Chap. viii *passim*; trade of, in 14th century, 494; manufacture of glass and silk at, 496, 512; library of San Giorgio founded at, 552; Aldine press, 562; *Neacademia*, 561, 563; disputes between the Papacy and, 657 sq., 660 sq., 662; ii 60; the Mediterranean War and, 72; desire for reform in, 378; the Reformation, 381–4; iii 48; joint embassy to, of Charles V and Ferdinand I, 115 sq.; and the Peace of 1540, 116; and Peace with the Porte (1547), 120 sq.; War of, with Selim II, 130 sqq.; battle of Lepanto and the Peace, 135 sqq.; 390, 395, 406, 415, 423 sqq., 430 sqq., 450 sq., 465, 494; 497; trade of, with East Indies, 499; 541; relations of Holland with, 645;

allied with Grisons, 684; and France, 686; Henry IV fails to win, 688; significance of struggle of, with the Pope, 744; and Styria, iv 11, 123; and Bohemia, 23; and Valtelline, Chap. ii *passim*; the Emperor's campaign against, 73; 75; and Peace of Monzon, 88; 95; 98; 119; league of, with France, 130; 134 sq.; action of Seigniory of, 396, 398; and Savoy, 626, 631; conspiracy against, 632 sq.; 639; 643; 666; Paul V and, 669 sqq.; 673; Treaty of Monzon and, 675; Treaty between France, Sweden and, 679; roused to rebellion, 686 sq.; and Turks, v 40, 342, 359, 368; bank of, 266, 268, 270; and the Peace of Carlowitz, 371; joins Holy League, 364; 365; 402; and Russia, 482; Galileo at, 713; Brunswick-Lüneburg Dukes and, vi 5; 30; 124; 149; John Law in, 177; and Austrian Succession, 228; and Clement XI, 587; and Benedict XIV, 590; Clement XIV and, 594; 605; decline of, 606 sq.; 675; 796; 812; Austro-Russian designs on (1795), viii 441, 508, 550; government of, 555, 778; and Peace of Leoben, 583 sqq.; fall of, 587; ceded to Austria (1797), 590 sqq.; government of Republic of, 778; surrendered (at Campo Formio), ix 82; commercial decline of, 87; 396; and the kingdom of Italy, 386; Austrian dominion over, 599; x 105; the *Gazette* of, 106; Consalvi at, 132; Germanic Confederation and, 343; xi 70; scientific congress in, 76; 81; the Revolution (1848) in, 82 sq.; and Salasco armistice, 89; and union with Piedmont, 90; fall of (1849), 95; disturbances at, 152; 374; 377; 384; 449; Napoleon III and, 450; ceded by Austria, 453 sq.; 457; Garibaldi and, 533; strike at, xii 225; 227; 829. *See also* Venetia

Venier, Sebastian, iii 135

Venizélos, Cretan politician, xii 423

Venloo, falls into Parma's hands, iii 620; surrender of William of Cleves at (1543), ii 244; besieged by Marlborough (1702), v 406; ceded to the United Provinces, 459

Venner, Thomas, Fifth Monarchy preacher, v 100; 113; 329

Venosta, The, Valtelline noble family, iv 48

Ventura, Gioacchino, Italian priest, xi 122; 712

Vera Cruz, trade of, v 684, vii 327, x 254, 256, 274; captured by Scott (1847), vii 396; English captives at (1567), x 253; and slave trade, 260; sacked (1683), 272; English trade to, 273; riot at (1808), 303; General Prim lands at, xi 565; French squadron at, xii 676

Verböczy, Stephen, Hungarian statesman, i 337, 339

Vercelli, claimed by Spain, iii 400–1; fortifications abandoned at, 410; Savoy defeated at, iv 626

Verchni Udinsk, founded by Cossacks, xii 794

Verden, iv 390; bishopric of, claimed by Sweden at Osnabrück, 403 sq.; duchy of, included in Hildesheim Alliance, 425; 432; 584; Sweden and, v 562; 613; Hanover and, 550, 611, 615; Swedes expelled from (1676), 569, 652; occupied by the Danes (1712), 582, 607, 610; vi 21; annexed to Hanover, 23 sq., 36; 28; 34; 39; Sweden and, 104

—— Bishop of. *See* Frederick III, King of Denmark, *also* Wartenberg

Verdi, Giuseppe, music of, x 130; xi 546; 549

Verdier, French general, and Aragon, ix 438–9

Verdugo, Spanish commander, iii 520; 626; death of, 628

—— Count, Imperialist officer, iv 66

Verdun, occupied by Henry II (1552), ii 87; 144; bishopric of, ceded to France, iv 404; 602; capitulates (1792), viii 242, 409; French retreat to, xi 589; Napoleon III at, 590; 591

—— Aymard-C.-F.-M. de Nicolay, Bishop of, vi 356

Vere, capitulates to British (1809), ix 358

—— Sir Francis, iii 531, 568, 626, 635–6

—— Sir Horace, Baron Vere of Tilbury, leader of English volunteers for Germany, iv 34; 77 sq.; 82; killed, 693

Vereeniging, peace negotiations at, xii 643

Verelst, Harry, Governor of Bengal, vi 557 sq.; 566

Verevkin, Colonel, xi 630

Vergara, agreement between Espartero and Maroto at, x 240 sq.

—— Juan de, ii 400 sq.

Vergennes, Charles Gravier, Count of, French ambassador in Constantinople, vi 355; in Sweden, 358, 768; 379 sq.; and American Peace, 461 sq.; 644; vii 210; French Minister for Foreign Affairs, viii 82, 87, 281, 283 sq.; on the Council of Finance, 96 sqq., 101; death of, 102, 314, 323; policy of, in East, 310; in United Provinces, 321, 323; ix 362

Vergerio, Pietro Paolo. *See* Capo d'Istria, Bishop of

Vergerius, Pietro Paolo (the elder), *De Ingenuis Moribus*, i 556

Vergil, Polydore, imprisoned by Wolsey, i 489

Vergilius Maro, Publius, xi 422

Vergniaud, Pierre-Victurnien, viii 214, 223, 228, 237; in National Convention, 242, 249, 251; at King Louis XVI's trial, 258 sq.; 271, 274; trial and execution of, 357

Verhoeff, Hendrik, and murder of the de Witts, v 159

Verino, Ugolino, Florentine humanist, i 188

Vermigli, Pietro Martire (Peter Martyr), at the Colloquy of Poissy, II 302; 390, 391 sq., 393; in England, 477; 502, 508, 563, 589

Vermont, jurisdiction of, VII 300; 337; encouragement of manufactures in, 354; 356; upholds Tariff, 381; abolition in, 388

Vermorel, Auguste-Jean-Marie, French journalist, XI 486; 502

Vernadsky, Russian politician, XII 348

Vernet, Horace, IX 135

Verneuil, Marquise de. *See* Entragues

Verney, Sir Edmund, IV 304

Verni, fort at, XI 273

Vernier, Comte Théodore, President of the National Assembly, VIII 388

Verninac Saint-Maur, Raimond, IX 99

Vernon, Sir Edward, Admiral, VI 72; 454; X 273

Véron, François, Sieur de Forbonnais, French writer, VIII 70, 73

—— Jean, Protestant refugee in England, II 477

Verona, restored to Venice (1516), I 487; surrender of, by Maximilian I, II 39; revolt in (1797), VIII 583 sqq.; French occupation of (1800), IX 68; Masséna at (1805), 258; XI 82; and War of Independence, 85; 86; Radetzky at, 88; 384

—— Congress of (1822), VII 369; X 31, 33–7; 79; Papacy and, 150 sq.; 184; 186; and Spanish Question, 225 sq.; and Spanish America, 308; XI 239, 682

Verona, Bishops of:—

—— Giammateo Giberti, II 23, 33, 60, 398; Oratory of Divine Love and, 399; 640 sqq.; church reform and, 643 sqq.; 660; III 457, 459

—— Lippomanno, Luigi, and the Society of Divine Love, II 379; papal representative at the Council of Trent, 671

—— Bernardo Navagero. *See* Navagero, Cardinal

Verona, Guarino. *See* Guarino

Veronese, Paolo, Venetian painter, I 284

Verrazzano, Giovanni da, exploration of coast of N. America by, I 36, 43 sq., 50

Verri, Count Pietro, Milanese economist, VIII 777 sqq.

Versailles, V 15; 17; James II at, 316; Louis XV at, VI 132, 164; *lit de justice* at (1787), VIII 106, (1788), 110; States General at (1789), 145 sqq.; attack on (Oct. 1789), 184 sq.; cavalry school at, 446; Museum of, X 494, 509; XI 498; National Assembly at, 501 sqq., XII 91; Germans at, XI 606, 609; 611; proclamation of German Emperor at, 466, 612

—— first Treaty of (1756), VI 251 sqq., 320 sq., 336, 345, 400 sq., VIII 314; second Treaty of (1757), VI 262, 339, VIII 308; third Treaty of (1783), VI 342, 549, 577, 597, XI 776; (1870), XII 134

Versen, Major von, mission of, to Spain, XI 571

Vershoor, Jacob, and Spinoza, V 754

Vertus, Holy Alliance announced at, X 9

Vervins, Peace of (1598), III 418, 420, 523 sq., 534, 540, 629, 674, 678, 682

Vesalius, Andreas, Belgian anatomist, III 394; V 723 sqq.

Vesc, Étienne de, French printer, I 109, 117

Vesoul, German force at, XI 609

Vespasiano da Bisticci, Florentine dealer in MSS (1421–98), I 551 sqq.

Vespucci, Amerigo, I 24, 34 sq., 57

—— Guidantonio, Florentine lawyer, I 169, 176, 222

Vesselényi, Francis, Palatine of Hungary, V 351 sq.

Vesterås, Diet of (1527), II 625; Recess of (1527), 626; Ordinances of (*Vesterås ordinantie*), *ib.*; free school of, IV 187

—— Peter Magnusson, Bishop of, II 623

"Vestiarian Controversy," II 490

Vesuvius, eruptions of, VI 600, XII 228

Vetkoopers, The, Frisian party, I 421

Vetter, Anton, Hungarian commander-in-chief, XI 205

Vettori, Francesco, Florentine historian, I 200; II 22 sq., 26

Veuillot, Louis, editor of *L'Univers*, XI 27; 34; 121; 286; 296; opposes Napoleon III, 469; 526; 707; 714; and the Syllabus, 716

Vial, Honoré, French general, VIII 601 sq.

Viale-Prela, Michele, Papal Nuncio in Vienna, XI 77

Viana, Manoel Nunes, leader of *Forasteiros*, V 679

Vianna, Nunez, Brazilian rebel leader, VI 390

Viasemski (Viazemsky), Prince, Russian statesman (1764), VI 682; 687; 693 sq.; 697

—— Prince Paul, censor, XI 625

—— Prince Peter, Russian poet, X 431; 438 sq.

Viatka, annexed by Ivan the Great, V 479; improvements in, XII 327; 376

Viau, Théophile de, French poet, IV 777

Viazma, Napoleon at, IX 499–500

Vibera, Leonor de, Spanish Reformer, II 407 sq.

Viborg, Russo-Swedish Alliance at (1609), IV 176; captured by Russians (1710), V 603; 614; ceded to Russia, 615; province of, added to Finland (1811), X 433 sq.; meeting of ex-members of Duma at, XII 368; 374

Viborg, Bishops of:—

—— Jörgen Friis, II 610, 613

—— Paulus Juusten (Ordinary), II 629

Viborg, Jens, Lutheran preacher in Norway, II 618

Vic, Dominique de, sent to Cambray (1595), III 669

—— Méry de, envoy to Grisons, IV 41 sq.

Vicálvaro, fight at, xi 560
Vicente, Gil, Spanish writer, i 380
Vicenza, siege of, by Carrara (1402), i 266; taken by Austrians, xi 86 sq.
Vichy, Huguenot forces at, iii 29
Vicksburg, surrender of (1863), vii 490, 505, 616; Farragut attacks (1862), 499 sq.; campaign of (1862–3), 501 sqq.; 551; naval operations against, 559 sq.
Vico, Giovanni Battista, iv 791; viii 777; xii 817
Victor, Claude Perrin, Duc de Belluna, ix 62; receives Belluna, 111; sent to Spain, 441; defeats Blake at Espinosa, 443; and French invasion of Portugal, 449 sqq.; at Cadiz, 456 sqq.; 464; and Russian campaign, 488 sqq.; at Laon, 551; adheres to Bourbons, 621; x 74; 80
Victor Amadeus. *See* Savoy, Dukes of
—— Emmanuel I, King of Sardinia, relations of Austria with, ix 599; resignation of territory by, 601; x 13; restoration of, 108; and revolt in Piedmont, 114; abdication of, 116; 117; relations of Papacy with, 142; and Spanish revolutionaries, 213
—— Emmanuel II, King of Italy, accession of, xi 93; and peace negotiations (1849), 366 sq.; and Cavour, 369; 371; and the clericals, 373; visits Paris and London, *ib.*; 374; alliance of, with Napoleon III, 381, 478; and War with Austria, 383 sq.; and peace negotiations (1859), 384 sq.; 386; and cession of Nice and Savoy, 387; 388; in Naples, 389 sq.; King of Italy, 390; 446; and Venice, 531; calls Rattazzi to office, 532; and Garibaldi, 533; schemes of, against Austria, 537 sq.; 539; and War with Austria (1866), 540; 541; 544; 571; marriage of daughter of, 574; 705; 708 sq.; xii 14; and France, 116; at Berlin, 139; 213 sq.; and Pius IX, 229; death of, 216
—— Emmanuel III, King of Italy, xii 122; accession of, 223; 225; and the Papacy, 229; 414; 722
Victoria, colony of, created, xi 16; exploration of, 792; gold in, 796, 798; 797; population of, 799; development of, xii 620 sq.; 623 sq.; and immigration, 625; 626 sq.; labour parties in, 629; social reforms in, 630 sq.; 747; 751
—— (South Africa), fort at, xii 639
—— Falls (Zambesi river), discovered, xii 808
—— Lake, John Wood at, xii 801
—— Land, discovery of, xii 815
—— Nyanza Lake, discovery of, xii 439; 661 sq.; 809 sq.; 812
—— Empress of Germany, consort of Frederick I, xii 163; 341
—— Queen of Great Britain and Ireland, accession of, x 674; and Lord Melbourne, 675; and Sir Robert Peel, 678, 681;

marriage of, *ib.*; xi 10; and Spanish marriages, 17, 33, 553; and Palmerston, 18, 320, 331; at Eu, 33, 37, 553; King Frederick William IV and, 143; 214; and Danish succession question, 226; and Napoleon III, 308; and Lord Aberdeen, 309; sends for Lord Derby, 328; and death of Prince Consort, 336; and Schleswig-Holstein, 338; 340; and Moldo-Wallachia, 644; and Leopold I, 673; 787; xii 14; proclaimed Empress of India, 32, 466, 474; 36; and electoral reform, 42; Jubilee of, 46 sq.; and France, 97; and relations with Germany, 141; 266; 393; and King John of Abyssinia, 444; 503; and Siam, 535; death of, 53
Victoria, Queen of Spain, consort of Alfonso XIII, xii 266
—— Princess of Schaumburg-Lippe, xii 163
Victorius, Petrus (Pietro Victorio), *Variae Lectiones*, i 567; 615
Victory, Nelson's flagship, at Trafalgar, ix 229 sqq.
Vida, Marco, *Poetica*, i 564; ii 15
Vidal, François, French politician, xi 131
—— Portuguese leader in Brazil, revolt of, against Dutch, iv 714
Vidin, xii 388; siege of, 390, 407
Vieira, Antonio, Jesuit, in Brazil, vi 390
—— Fernandes, leader of the Portuguese revolt in Brazil, iv 714; 753; v 674 sq.
Vielhorski, Count Joseph, Polish general, x 451
Vielopolski, Alexander, Marquis, Polish statesman, xi 628 sq.; 658 sqq.; xii 311
Vien, Joseph Marie, ix 135
Vienna, Hungarians expelled from (1490), i 296; 314; University of, 325; captured by Matthias Corvinus (1485), 335; Congress of (1515), 344; besieged by Turks (1529), 97 sq., ii 61, 207; threatened by Solyman the Magnificent (1532), 67, (1543), 77; Polish embassies to, iii 97–8; cause and results of Solyman's siege of, 104–6; Turkish agent at, 108; Digby sent to, 572; Fynes Moryson at, 696; meeting of Archdukes at, 720, 735; embassy from Union to, 726; Catholic party in, iv 11; 22; Thurn at, 25, 27 sqq.; 31; march of Bohemian army on, 64; 71; Caraffa at, 73; University of, 77; 92; 94; 98; 100; 108; 114; Richel's correspondence and, 238; 240 sq.; in danger from the Swedes, 389; 391; 427 sq.; Imperial succession and Court of, 429; 678; Cabinet of, and Urban VIII, 681; besieged by Turks (1683), v 41, 49, 340 sq., 360 sqq., 366, vi 4; v 347; 358; Prince Eugene at, 370, 414; threatened by Villars, 407 sqq.; 411; 417; the plague at, 451; flight of the Tsarevich Alexis to, 539; 653; scientific societies at, 741; vi 30; Ripperdá's

mission to, 139 sq.; 151; and War of Austrian Succession, 231 sqq.; 240; 276; 315 sq.; Pius VI at, 636; 637; Allies meet at (1822), VII 368 sq.; approach of Moreau to (1800), IX 68; Napoleon's advance on (1805), 256–8; 269, 275, 317; convention with Prussia concluded in (Jan. 1809), 344; attacked by Napoleon (May, 1809), 350; Turkish embassy at, 386; centre of government for Lombardy and Venetia, x 106; Count Confalonieri at, 118; Dom Miguel at, 317, 321; ministerial conferences at (1834), 378; Galician students at, 462; death of Duke of Reichstadt at, 488; Bank of, IX 415, X 746, XI 181 sq.; Liberal movement in, 45; revolution (1848) in, 81, 88, 93, 151 sqq.; situation in, 169 sqq.; 178 sq.; insurrection in, 185 sq.; investment of, 187 sq.; capture of, by Windischgrätz, 189; 192; 206; 208; the Court at, 215; 284; 314; 316; peace conference at, 321; Imperial Council at, 404; Burgtheater at, 416; King William I of Prussia and, 455 sq.; Austro-Italian peace signed at, 541; financial crisis in, XII 189; 202; 824

Vienna, Preliminaries of, VI 146 sq., 155; Treaty of (1606), III 720 sq., 726; (1719), VI 33; (1725), 57 sq., 141, 150, 202; (1731), 60, 149, 202; (1805), IX 262 sq., 265 sq.; (1815), V 620, X 9, 11, 16, 17, 203, XI 674; (1864), 442; Peace of (1738), V 437; (1809), *see* Schönbrunn

—— Congress of, proposed, IX 564; Chaps. XIX and XXI *passim*; position in Europe after, X 1 sqq.; slave trade condemned by, 19; 44; effect of, upon Italy, 104, 111, 130; Consalvi at, 134 sq., 141; and ecclesiastical affairs in Germany, 145; and Bavaria, 146; and Eastern question, 175; and Spain, 211; and Germanic Confederation, 343 sq.; 369; and Poland, 445 sq., 457, 473 sq.; and republic of Cracow, 460; and Galicia, 461; and grand duchy of Warsaw, 463 sq.; and Netherlands, 524; XI 236 sq., 244, 691

—— Conference (1819–20) of, Final Act (1820), X 22; 366 sqq., 372

—— Anton, Bishop of, Wallenstein and, IV 238; 240

—— Melchior Klesl, Bishop of Neustadt and. *See* Klesl

—— (near Washington), Federals fired on, at (1861), VII 464

Vienne, Council of (1311), I 537, (1313), V 631

Vienne, Archbishops of:—

—— J.-G. Lefranc de Pompignan, VIII 116, 156, 186

—— Charles de Marillac, II 297 sq.

—— Pierre Palmier, II 411

Vierklosterstreit, The, III 718

Vierkönigsbündniss, The, XI 223

Viervoet, fight at, XI 784

Vierzehnheiligen, French occupation of (1806), IX 276

Vieta, Francis, mathematician, V 709 sq.

Vieusseux, Pietro, at Florence, X 128; and scientific congress at Pisa, *ib.*

Vigarny, Philip de, Spanish sculptor, I 382

Vigevano, armistice concluded at, XI 89

Viglius, President of Privy Council of Netherlands, III 188, 191–2, 198–9, 226

Vignale, conference at, XI 366

Vignerte, French republican, X 491

Vignier, Nicolas, French historian, III 63

Vignola, Giacomo Barozzio da, one of the architects of St Peter's, III 441

Vigny, Alfred de, French poet, VI 832; X 101 sq.; 514 sq.; influence of Byron and Scott upon, 725 sq.; XI 508; character and poetry of, 512; 514 sq.; 519; historical novels of, XII 831

Vigo, French fleet destroyed at (1702), V 412; capture of, VI 35; 125; Allemand puts into, IX 225; Villeneuve retires to, 226, 251; French ship taken at, 238

Vigodet, Gaspar, Captain-general of Madrid, X 222

Világos, Hungarian surrender at, XI 213

Vilain, Adrian, Lord of Rasenghien, I 447

Vilate, Joachim, French political agent, VIII 367

Villach in Carinthia, Charles V in, II 87, 272

Villadarias, Marquis of, at Gibraltar, V 413

Villa-de-Conde, Dom Pedro's fleet at, X 328

Villa Flôr. *See* Terceira, Duke of

Villafranca, Philip II's power in, III 400; Emmanuel Philibert surprised at, 410; Treaty of, XI 331 sq.; 384 sq., 468

—— Pedro de Toledo, Marquis of, Viceroy of Naples, II 70 sq., 81, 88

Villa Gandolfo, Papacy and, XII 229

Villalar, rout of the *Comuneros* at (1521), I 375, II 42

Villanova d' Asti, retained by France, II 94, III 400

Villanueva, Joaquin L., X 219 sq.

Villanuova, retained by France (1559), II 94

Villarejo de Salvanés, General Prim at, XI 567

Villaret, J. Chrysostom de. *See* Casal, Bishop of

Villaret-Joyeuse, Comte Louis-Thomas, French admiral, VIII 391, 466 sqq.; and invasion of England, 473; at Martinique, IX 221

Villari, Pasquale, Italian historian, XII 217; 232; 842

Villarias, Marquis of, Spanish statesman, VI 65 sqq.; 156; 159; Elisabeth Farnese and, 166; 361

Villars, Claude-Louis-Hector, Duke of, Marshal of France, V 26; 52; 57; threatens Vienna, 407 sq.; recall of, 408; 414; 416; captures Stolhofen, 418; 423 sq.; defeated at Malplaquet, 425 sq.; 428; success of Marlborough against,

431; at Denain, 433 sq.; on the Rhine, 435; and Peace of Rastatt, 435, 451 sq.; vi 146; 152 sqq.

Villars, League commander, defends Rouen (1591–2), iii 51; Governor of Rouen, 663, 669, 675

Villa Ruffi, political arrests at, xii 214

Villastellona, Prince Eugene at, v 415

Villavelha, capture of, vi 426

Villa Viciosa, besieged (1665), v 34; battle at (1706), 428; Godoy prisoner at, ix 431

Villebon, Governor of Acadia, vii 111

Villedeuil, Laurent de, French Comptroller-General, viii 104; resigns, 107

Villegagnon. *See* Durand

Villèle, Jean-Baptiste-G.-M.-S.-J., Comte de, x 31; 35; 47; electoral proposal of, 49 sqq.; 54; 56 sqq.; attacks Decazes Ministry, 60; 61 sq.; and new electoral scheme, 64; 67 sq.; succeeds Richelieu, 70, 74; 73; policy of, 75; Ministry of (1821–7), 75–91; financial schemes of, 82 sq., 85 sq.; resignation of, 91; and Martignac, 92; 94; and elections of 1827, 95; 96 sq.; and Spanish affairs, 224 sqq.

Villemain, Abel-François, French politician, x 59, 89, 93, 102 sq.; and revolution of 1830, 476 sq.; 508; 511; writings of, 514; 516; xi 34 sq.; succeeded by Salvandy, 86; 525

Villeneuve, Pierre-C.-J.-B.-Silvestre de, French admiral, viii 480; in command of Toulon squadron, ix 218; sails for West Indies, 219; captures Nelson's despatches, 220; sails for Cartagena, 220; ordered to attack India, 222; ordered to Martinique, *ib.*; sails for West Indies, 225; returns to Ferrol, 225; retires to Corunna, 226–7; concentrates at Cadiz, *ib.*; 228; ordered to Channel, *ib.*; 229; at Trafalgar, 230 sqq.; retires to Vigo, 251

—— Marquis de, French ambassador in Turkey, vi 304

Villeneuve-Saint-Georges, Turenne at, iv 617

Villeneuve-sur-Lot, rising at, xi 137

Villequier, member of Henry III's Council, iii 26

Villeroi (Villeroy), François de Neufville, Duke of, Marshal of France, v 262; in Italy, 402 sq.; in Netherlands, 408; joins Tallard in Alsace, 410; 411; opposed by Marlborough, 414; at Ramillies, 415 sq.; vi 131; 144

—— Nicolas de Neufville, Seigneur de, French Secretary of State, iii 43, 52, 661–5; 691; iv 45; 118; superseded, 122

—— Nicholas de Neufville, Seigneur de, ambassador in England, i 489

Villers-Cotterets, Edict of (1539), ii 96, ix 164; 169

Villersexel, engagement at, xi 609

Villetard, Comte Alexandre-E.-P., viii 677

—— Secretary to Embassy at Venice, viii 586

Villiers, Charles Pelham, and Corn Laws, xi 9; 21

—— Christopher, iii 570

—— Edward, Earl of Jersey. *See* Jersey

—— Sir Edward, iii 570

—— Elizabeth, Countess of Orkney. *See* Orkney

—— George, Duke of Buckingham. *See* Buckingham

—— Hyde, x 660; 680

—— du Terrage, R. E. de, viii 605

Villingen, v 407; attacked by Tallard, 410

Villon, François, i 415

Vilmanstrand, Swedish defeat at, vi 310, 760; 314

Vilna, Jesuits established in diocese and town of, iii 83, 102; Palatine of, 88; capital of Lithuania, v 480; Russians expelled from (1794), viii 542; reoccupied, 546; captured by French (1812), ix 490; Napoleon at, 491; Murat at, 509; proposed appointment of Metropolitan at, x 141; University of, 430 sq., 459, xi 267; x 440; Patriotic Society in, 454; Russian administration of, 459 sq.; 468; xii 336; strike in, 350; 373

—— Constantine Brzostowski, Bishop of, vi 192

Vilvoorde, taken by Parma, iii 618; Prince Frederick at, x 585 sq.

Vimiero, British attacked by French at (1808), ix 440–1

Vináver, Russian politician, xii 341

Vincennes, plot at, iii 23–4; escape of Beaufort from, iv 609; rebel Princes imprisoned at, 612; Castle of, Duc d'Enghien at, ix 31; xi 100; revolutionaries imprisoned at, 110

—— (Indiana), captured by Hamilton (1777–8), vii 222; recaptured by Clarke (1778), *ib.*; 356

Vincent, François-Nicolas, revolutionary agent, viii 360, 362, 424

—— Henry, political agitator, x 682 sq.

—— Freiherr Karl von, Austrian general, ambassador at Paris, ix 320; at Brussels, x 520

—— Colonel, sent to Paris by Toussaint L'Ouverture, ix 421

Vincent de Paul, Saint, iv 156; 621; v 78; 80

Vinci, Leonardo da, ii 13 sq.; v 724; 738 sq.

Vinciguerra, Antonio, iii 459

Vincke, Georg von, Prussian statesman, xi 58; 158; 165; 195; and Frankfort Constitution, 218; 397

—— Ludwig, Baron von, x 353

Vindiciæ contra Tyrannos (probably by Duplessis-Mornay), iii 760–4, 769

Vinegar Hill, captured by Lake (1798), ix 702

"Vineland," discovered by Northmen, I 19 sqq., 33, 50

Vinet, Alexandre Rodolphe, Swiss critic (d. 1847), XI 261; 525; XII 114

Vinius, Andrei, v 525

Vinje, Aasmund, Norwegian poet, XI 702

Vinkovo, Murat defeated at (1812), IX 498

Vinográdoff, Paul, Russian historian, XII 315; 333; 850

Vinoy, Joseph, French general, XI 499; 597; 600

Vintimille, Pauline-Félicité, Marquise de, and Louis XV, VI 164; 330

Vinuesa, parish priest of Tamajón, the murder of, X 223

Vio, Tommaso de (Cajetan), Cardinal, II 16, 20, 28, 30, 132, 138, 641; III 737

Viollet, Paul, French jurist, XII 850

Vionville. *See* Mars-la-Tour

Virág, Benedict, Hungarian writer, XI 422

Virarajendra Wodiyar, Rájah of Coorg, XI 730

Viret, Pierre, II 293, 368

Virginia, named in compliment to Queen Elizabeth, III 333; attempt to colonise, 562; province of, IV 747; Dutch forbidden to trade in, 470; Charles II and, V 101; VI 52; 187; trade of, 447; VII 2–10, 11; 53 sq.; economic conditions in, 55 sq.; religious conditions in, 58, 145; taxation in, 66 sq.; 68; and Boston, 160; disaffection in, 164, 169, 730; writs of assistance in, 181; charter of, 198 sq.; British raid into (1779), 220; Constitution of, 237 sqq.; and Annapolis Convention (1786), 244; and Constitutional Convention, 246 sq., 249, 251 sq., 255, 263 sq., 275, 278, 281 sqq., 286, 298 sqq., 302; opposition to the Constitution in, 303; representation of, 306; cessions in, 308; trade regulations in, 311 sq.; encouragement of manufactures in, 354; and Tariff, 381; slavery in, 386 sq., 401 sq., 439, 587; statesmen of, 407; white population of (1860), 415; and secession, 453 sqq., 581, 603; McClellan in (1862), 472 sqq.; emancipation in, 595; contraband trade in, 620; reconstruction in, 625, 632 sq.; Army of, 477

—— West, State of, admitted to Union (1863), VII 456; Federal conquest of (1861), 457, 470; and emancipation, 593 sqq.; becomes Democratic, 642

—— Company, IV 748, VII 12 sqq., 73. *See also* London Company *and* Plymouth Company

Virginian Convention (1775), The, VII 164

Virués, Fray Alonso, Spanish Reformer, II 401

Viry, Count of, Sardinian envoy to England, VI 424

Visch, ex-Procurator, hanged at Ghent, III 251

Vischer, Peter, Maximilian I's tomb at Innsbruck and, I 326

Visconti, Dukes of Milan. *See* Milan, Dukes of

—— Bernabò, murder of, IV 35

—— Bianca, married to Francesco Sforza, I 281

—— Carlo, at Council of Trent, II 679

—— Ennio Quirino, Italian archaeologist, XII 842

—— Giammastino, and the Valtelline, IV 35

—— Giullo, Viceroy of Naples, VI 153

—— Valentina. *See* Orleans, Duchess of

—— Milanese advocate, one of Cisalpine Triumvirate, IX 84

Visconti-Venosta, Emilio, Marquis, Italian Foreign Minister, XI 543; XII 215

Vishnegradsky, Russian Minister of Finance, XII 320; 323

Vishnyakoff, Russian resident at Stambul, VI 306

Visions of Philander, IV 425

Visitatsbog, The, by Peder Plade, II 616

Visotsk, military colony in, X 416

Visscher, Anna, IV 718; 720; poetry of, 721

—— Maria (Tesselschade), IV 718; correspondence of Hooft with, 720; poetry of, 721

—— Roemer, and Dutch letters, IV 718

Vistula river, bridged at Warsaw, III 86; V 597; meeting of Tsar Peter I and Augustus II on, 602; 629; 631; 634; VI 196; French reverses on, 197; 304; 322; 326; 328; fortifications on, 729; 732 sq.

Vitebsk, district of, VI 669; Bagration at, IX 491; 498; Russians capture (1812), 500; Russian administration of, X 459; 469; XII 339; disorder in, 354

Vitelli, Alessandro, Imperial general, III 387

—— Paolo, *condottiere*, I 192

—— Vitellozzo, Cesare Borgia and, I 193, 195, 673

Viterbo, rising at, X 156

Vitovt, Prince of Lithuania, I 345

Vitrier, Jean, heretical preacher at Tournay, I 681

Vitrolles, Eugène-François-Auguste d'Arnaud, Baron de, French royalist emissary to Tsar, IX 555; 560–1; advice of, 574; besieged in Toulouse, 617; X 47; 56; 65; 476

Vitry, Napoleon at, IX 554

—— Nicolas-Marie de l'Hospital, Marquis de, French envoy in Poland, V 359 sq.

Vittoria, occupied by French (1795), VIII 441; Joseph Bonaparte at, IX 477; battle of (1813), 478, 521

Vittorino da Feltre, humanist and educator, I 543, 556 sqq.

Vittsjö, Gustavus surprised near (1612), IV 179

Vivarais, revolt in, V 9

Vivarino, Luigi, Giovanni Antonio, and Bartolommeo, Venetian painters, ı 284

Vives, Luis, Spanish humanist, ı 379

Vivian, Sir Richard Hussey, 1st Baron, lieutenant-general, cavalry brigade of, at Waterloo, ıx 739–40

Viviani, French socialist, xıı 127 sq.

Vivien, Alexandre-François-Auguste, French politician, xı 115

—— Nicolaas, Pensionary of Dort, v 145; 155

Vivier, Nicolas-Joseph, French Communist, vııı 371

Viviers, C. de la Font de Savine, Bishop of, vııı 198

Vizille, irregular assembly of Estates of Dauphiné at, vııı 113, 116

Vizthum, Count, chamberlain to Augustus II, v 602

Vlacich, Mattia. *See* Illyricus, M. Flacius

Vlad IV, Prince of Wallachia, resists the Turks, ı 82 sq.

Vladímir, trade depression in, xıı 319

Vladimir I (the Saint), Tsar, v 477; 483 sq.

—— II Monomakhos, Tsar, v 484

Vladivostók, founded, xıı 344; 362; railway to, 507, 521; 577 sq.; Russian ships at, 579; 582 sq.; 589 sq.; 596; 599 sq.; postroad to, 792, 794; ceded to Russia, 796

Vlie, Dutch vessels destroyed in the (1666), v 187

Vlytingen, British force at, vı 248

Vodzicki, President of the Republic of Cracow, x 460

Vörösmarty, Michael, Hungarian poet, xı 425; 427; 430 sq.

Voet, Gisbert (Voetius), theologian, ıv 788; v 82; 753 sqq.; 757

Vogel, Eduard, travels of, in Africa, xıı 810 sq.

Vogelsberger, Sigismund, ıı 268

Vogorides, Alexander (Aleko Pasha), Governor-General of Eastern Rumelia, xıı 405

Vogt, Karl, German zoologist and politician, xı 200; 260

Vogüé, Vicomte E. M. de, xıı 119

Voice, The, journal, xıı 309; 312; 338 sq.

Voigt, Johannes, German historian, xıı 824

Voigtland, The, raided by Holk, ıv 235

Voigts-Rhetz, Constantin Bernard von, German general, xı 590

Voirol, French general, in Algeria, x 503

Voisin, Daniel-François, Chancellor of France, vı 121

Voiture, Vincent, ıv 156; v 70

Volga river, Bashkir rising on (1707), v 597; peasant settlements on, vı 690; navigation of, xıı 491; 793

Volhynia, Swedish army in, v 594; vı 198; Austria and, 630; Grand Priory of Knights of St John at, ıx 39; Russian army in (1812), 490; Patriotic Society in, x 453 sq.; Russian administration of, 459 sq.; 469; Polish raid in, 471

Volkovisk, Russian army at, ıx 490

Volmar, Isaac, ıv 400

Volney, Constantin François Chasseboeuf, Comte de, ıx 132

Vologda, military centre at, v 500

Volta, Count Alessandro, xıı 786

Voltaire, François-Marie Arouet de, v 69 sq.; vı 79; and Fleury, 162; 165; and Frederick the Great, 267, 298; 416; 589; and Catharine II, 657, 664, 678, 686, 698; 724; and Rousseau, 825 sq.; 833; vııı 4, 7; *Letters on the English*, 9 sq.; *Dictionary*, 11; 12 sqq., 25, 28, 32, 35; in exile, 56; 71; pamphlet of, in favour of Turgot, 87; and Penal Code, 743 sq.; ıx 169; xı 421; 424; historical works of, 523; 524; 526; xıı 767; 817; 849

Volterra, Pius IX educated at, xı 72

Voltri, French brigade sent to, vııı 565

Volturno, battle of, xı 536

Voluinsky, Artamon, Russian Minister at Ispahan, v 544

Volunteers, the Irish, rise of, vı 496 sqq.; English movement which founded the, xı 332 sq.

Vonck, Francis, Belgian politician, vı 652 sq.; vııı 786

Vondel, Joost van den, dramatic works of, ıv 718 sq.; 720 sq.; xı 676

Voniza, Ali of Janina captures, x 176; meeting at, xı 641

Vonkassowitch. *See* Vukassovich

Voorstonden, van, Dutch plenipotentiary at the Congress of Vienna, ıx 586

Vorarlberg, Kray tries to reach, ıx 58; Moreau and, 64; Allies in (1804), 250; retreat of Jellachich to, 255; ceded to Bavaria (1805), 262; Austrian acquisition of (1815), 658

Voronezh, fleet built at, v 521 sq.; 600; xıı 327; 329; disorder in, 354; 362

Voronicz, John-Paul. *See* Warsaw, Archbishop of

Vorontsoff, Elizabeth, mistress of Peter III, vı 660 sq.

—— Count Michael, Grand Chancellor of Russia, vı 311; 322; 327

Vorontzóff-Dashkoff, Count, Viceroy of the Caucasus, xıı 353

Vorpommern. *See* Pomerania, Western

Vorstius (Everard van Voorst), ıv 717

Vos, Jan, Dutch dramatist, ıv 720

Vosges mountains, evacuated by Prussians (1794), vııı 437; xı 580; 582; 585; 604; xıı 159; and German frontier, 136; 159

Voss, Johann Heinrich, vııı 773; poetry of, x 387; 396

Vossem, Peace of (1673), v 650

Vossius (Gerard John Vos), Dutch humanist, ı 579; ıı 718; ıv 717; 720

Vota, Charles Maurice, Italian Jesuit, v 663

Vougiers, German army at, xı 597

Voysey, John, Bishop of Exeter, ıı 501

Voysin, Daniel-François, French Secretary of State, v 2

Vranya, Servian victory at, xii 390; 396

Vries, Gerrit de, Dutch statesman, xii 243

Vrioni, Omar, x 185

Vronchenko, Russian Minister of Finance, xi 266

Vuchidol, Turks defeated at, xii 387

Vucovics, Sabbas, Hungarian Minister of Justice, xi 212

Vukassovich, Baron Joseph Philip von, Austrian commander, viii 566; ix 61

Vukčić, Stephen, *Voivod* of Herzegovina, i 71 sq.

Vulgate, Trent publication of, by Sixtus V, iii 445

Vulliemin, Louis, Swiss historian, xi 261

Vulpius, Grisons leader, escape of, iv 55

Vuyst, Dutch Governor of Ceylon, v 696

Vylezynski, Thaddaeus, Polish colonel, x 467; 469

Vysocki, Peter, Polish officer, x 464; 466

Waag river, Imperial fortress on, v 348, 350; Hungarian force on, xi 210

Waardgelders, Dutch troops raised in 1616, iii 649, 650-2

Wachau, Napoleon at, ix 535

Wachtmeister, Hans, Swedish statesman and officer, v 573 sq.; 578; 582

Wackenroder, Wilhelm Heinrich, x 398 sq.; 401; 403; 407

Wadai, xii 130; Vogel in, 810

Waddington, William Henry, French statesman, supports Thiers, xii 107; 113; 239; Foreign Minister, 394; at the Berlin Congress, 398

Wade, Benjamin Franklin, American statesman, vii 429, 469, 624, 653

—— George, Field-Marshal, vi 107; 114; 240

—— Sir Thomas Francis, ambassador to Peking, xii 501 sq.

Wadi Halfa, defence of, xii 447; 448

Wadi-Ras, fighting at, xi 564

Waerdenburgh, Colonel Diederik van, iv 707

Wagener, Hermann, editor of *Neue Preussische (Kreuz-) Zeitung*, xi 192; 396

Wager, Sir Charles, British admiral, v 551; vi 60; 145; 147; 150

Waghäusel, engagement at, xi 221

Waghorn, Thomas, and the overland route to India, xii 430; 439

Wagner, Adolf, German economist, xii 155

—— Gabriel, iv 791

—— Heinrich Leopold, x 386

—— Richard, operas of, xi 415; xii 14

Wagram, battle of (1809), ix 239, 353 sq.; "grand battery" of, 345; conduct of Austrians at, 346; Archduke John and, 355; 359

Wahabi, State of, regains independence, xii 429

Wahabites, ix 385; successes of, 387

Wahlkapitulation, iii 143, 180

Waiblinger, Wilhelm Friedrich, German poet, x 406

Waidhaus, Mansfeld dislodged from, iv 78

Waikato district, the Maori in, xi 799

Wairau valley, xi 793

Waitangi, Treaty of, xi 793, 800

Waitara, the Maori and, xi 799 sq.

Waite, Sir Nicholas, at Bombay, v 700 sq.

Waitz, Georg, German historian, xi 164; xii 827; 850

Waitzen, occupied by Ferdinand's troops, iii 118; Hungarian army at, xi 204; 206

Wake, William, Archbishop of Canterbury, vi 78

Wakefield, Captain Arthur, in New Zealand, xi 793

—— Edward Gibbon, colonial statesman, xi 16; 765 sq.

—— Gilbert, viii 764 sq.; letters of Grey to, ix 676

—— William Hayward, in New Zealand, xi 793

Wakeman, Sir George, physician, v 220; 224 sq.

—— John, Bishop of Gloucester, ii 467

Walachs. *See* Roumans

Walaeus, Dutch preacher, iii 654

Walcheren, Calvinist attempt on, iii 211; captured by Sea Beggars, 230, 498; communication with, cut off, 242; the Treaty of Dover and, v 154, 204; British expedition to (1809), ix 139, 238-9, 343, 357 sqq., 369, 688; annexed by Napoleon (1810), 370

Waldburg, George Truchsess von, invades Würtemberg, ii 181; suppresses Peasants' Rising, 182, 189 sq.

—— Otto Truchsess von, Cardinal Bishop of Augsburg. *See* Augsburg

Waldeck, revolutionary movement in, xi 150

—— Benedikt Franz Leo, Prussian politician, xi 193

—— Count Franz von. *See* Münster, Bishop of

—— Prince George Frederick of, and Frederick William of Brandenburg, iv 426 sqq., 430; passes into service of Sweden, 429; v 59; 151; 160; 167; and Brandenburg, 642 sq., 655; 661; vi 4

Waldeck - Rousseau, Pierre - Marie - René, French statesman, xii 113; 121; 127

Waldegrave, James Waldegrave, 1st Earl, vi 63; 162

—— Maria, Countess Dowager, married to the Duke of Gloucester, vi 445

Waldemar II, King of Denmark, v 620

—— III (Atterdag), King of Denmark, ii 600

—— the Victorious, King of Denmark (1204-41), ii 599

—— (the False). *See* Brandenburg

—— Prince, of Denmark, xii 409

Waldenses, massacre of (1545), ii 289 sq.

Waldkirch, Provost of, ii 203

Waldmann, Hans, Swiss statesman, II 311 sq.

Waldmünchen, Austrians in, VI 240

Waldorfer, Venetian printer, I 284

Waldshut, Peasants' Rising at, II 178, 190; the Christian Union established at, 330

Wales, Royalist rising in North, IV 540; rising in South (1648), 348 sq.; agriculture in, X 740; Liberalism in, XII 31; and disestablishment, 49, 51; University of, 763

Walewski, Alexandre-Florian-Joseph Colonna, Comte, French Foreign Minister, XI 327 sq.; dismissal of, 387; and Napoleon's Italian policy, 468; 482; mission of, to Buenos Ayres, XII 681

Walfart und Strasse zu Sant Jacob, pilgrims' guide-book, II 106

Walfisch Bay, British occupation of, XII 638; 659

Walke, Henry, American admiral, VII 497

Walker, David, writes *Walker's Appeal*, VII 386 sq.

—— Francis Amasa, American statistician, VII 703

Wall, Richard, Spanish Minister of Foreign Affairs, VI 344; 364 sq.; 367; retires, 370

Wallace, Alfred Russel, XII 772

—— Sir Donald Mackenzie, XI 274; 617

—— Lewis, American general, VII 531

—— Thomas, Baron Wallace, Vice-President of Board of Trade, X 586

Wallachia, and Turkish struggle, I 82 sqq.; Transylvania and, V 339, 344; VI 630; Turkey and, 634; 648; 672; 674; Joseph II and, VIII 324; Russian annexation of, IX 308, (1808), 320, 485; hospodars of, 386; and Treaty of Bucharest, X 169; suppression of the revolt in, 179; 188; occupied by Russia (1829), 444; rising in, XI 206; 276; 281 sqq.; Napoleon III and, 306; 321; independence of, 323; Russian occupation of (1853), 314, 316 sq., 401; union of, with Moldavia, 633, 643 sq. *See also* Danubian Principalities

—— Hospodar of (1709), V 601

—— and Moldavia, Prince of. *See* Couza

Wallenstein (Waldstein), Albrecht, Graf von (*afterwards* Duke of Mecklenburg and Prince of Friedland), IV 26 sq.; 71 sqq.; 81; 87; 92; Prince of Friedland, 93; in Lower Saxony, 94; at Dessau Bridge, 95 sqq.; sends an agent to Brunswick (1625), 96; 98 sqq.; at height of his power, 103; Duke of Mecklenburg, 104; 105 sq.; besieges and fails before Stralsund, 107 sqq.; and Peace of Lübeck, 109 sq.; and Edict of Restitution, 111 sqq.; dismissal of, 114 sqq.; character of, 117; return of, 141; 195 sq.; 198; army of, 200; 203 sq.; negotiations between Gustavus Adolphus and, 192, 206; 207; 209 sqq.; 212; takes possession of Prague,

213; 214 sqq.; campaign before Nürnberg of, 217 sq.; 219 sq.; at battle of Lützen, 221; 222; end of, *see* Chap. VII; 277; 364; 372; would-be arbiter of peace in Empire, 395; 400; 680; murder of, 143, 276, 683; V 338; 372; 638

Wallenstein, Maximilian von, IV 242

Waller, Edmund, Royalist plot of, IV 314; 343; poetry of, V 70, 132; 210

—— Sir Hardress, in Ireland, IV 547

—— Sir William, IV 304; at Portsmouth, 305; 312; defeated at Roundway Down, 313; 314 sq.; member of Committee of Both Kingdoms, 320; victory of, at Cheriton, 322; invests Oxford, 323; 324 sq.; at Taunton, 328; imprisonment of, 447

Wallhof, Swedish victory of (1626), IV 182, 185

Wallingford, William Knollys, Viscount (*afterwards* Earl of Banbury), III 567

Wallis, canton of. *See* Valais

—— John, mathematician, V 710 sq.; 713

—— Count Olivier, Austrian commander, VIII 444 sq.

Wallmerode, Count, and Wallenstein, IV 241

Wallon, Henri-Alexandre, French politician, XII 110

Wallop, Sir John, II 457

Wallqvist, Olaf. *See* Wexiö, Bishop of

Walmer, Melville at, IX 682, 684

Walmoden-Gimborn, Count Johann Ludwig von, Field-Marshal, VIII 431

—— L. G. T., Count von, abandons Hamburg, IX 520; in Hanover, 530

Walpole, Horace, Earl of Orford. *See* Orford

—— Sir Robert, Earl of Orford. *See* Orford

—— Sir Spencer, historian, XII 841

—— Spencer Horatio, Home Secretary, XI 331

—— of Wolterton, Horace, 1st Baron, English ambassador at Paris, V 555; VI 27; 54; 148; 308

Walsh, Anthony, Jacobite, VI 111

—— Peter, Irish Franciscan, V 304

—— William J., Roman Catholic Archbishop of Dublin, XII 85

Walsingham, Sir Francis, III 15–17, 20, 34, 291, 331, 500, 502

—— William de Grey, Lord, Attorney-General, VI 437; 441

Waltensburg, Grey Leaguers of, IV 36

Walter (à Water), John, of Cork, supporter of Warbeck, I 470, 473

—— Sir John, suspension of, IV 281

Walters, Lucy, V 226

Walton, Colonel Valentine, army and, IV 545, 547

Walzmüller, Martin, of St Dié in Lorraine, printer (1507), I 35

Wana, included in the frontier province, XII 490

Wandesforde, Sir Christopher, Strafford's deputy, IV 521; death of, *ib.*

Wandiwash, battle of, VI 548

Wangenheim, Freiherr Karl August von, Würtemberg statesman, X 343; 360 sq.; 362; opposes Metternich, 368; 369
—— Baron von, Hanoverian Minister, XI 220

Wangting, Great Britain and, XII 508

Wapowski, Castellan of Przemysl, III 89

"War of the Three Henrys," III 40 sqq.

Wara, Vogel murdered at, XII 810

Warbeck, Perkin (the pretended Duke of York), I 451 sq., 468 sqq., 472 sq.; III 579

Warburton, William, Bishop of Gloucester, VI 78; 431

Ward, Artemas, American general, VII 168
—— John ("Captain Ward"), pirate, III 541
—— William George, theologian, and the Oxford Movement, XI 349; 716
—— United States Minister in China, XI 817; 821

Warde, Luke, III 309

Warden, Major, repulsed by the Basutos, XI 784

Wardle, Gwyllym Lloyd, and the army commissions scandal, IX 688

Wardship, finally abolished as a feudal incident, V 94

Ware, Sir James, historian, VI 800

Wargaon, Convention of, VI 576

Warham, William, Archbishop of Canterbury, I 491, 612, 644; II 428, 436, 439

Wark Castle, siege of (1523), II 422

Warkworth, the Old Pretender proclaimed at, VI 98

Warmia (Ermeland), III 83; and Gustavus Adolphus, IV 186; and Treaty of Königsberg, 428; bishopric of, V 634, VI 669; Prussia and, V 667; VI 730 sq.
—— (Ermeland), Andrew Chrysostom, Bishop of, V 663

Warnemünde, Peter the Great and, V 611

Warner, Thomas, at St Kitts, IV 758; VII 74

Warneton, ceded to France, V 45; and Barrier Treaties, 459

Warnsfeld, death of Sidney at, III 622

Waroux, The, faction in Liége, I 422

Warrego river, exploration of, XI 795

Warren, Sir Charles, General, in South Africa, XII 638
—— Gouverneur Kemble, American general, VII 538
—— James, of Boston, VII 146, 151, 161
—— Sir John, IX 234
—— Sir John Borlase, commodore, VIII 472, 476; IX 234
—— Sir Peter, Vice-Admiral, VI 248; VII 115 sq.

Warrington, Royalists at, IV 540

Warsaw, rivals Cracow, III 76; Edict of (1557), 80; national convention at (1573), 84; Compact of, 85–7; Stephen Báthory enters, 99; banished Nuncio returns to, 100; battle of (1656), IV 428; Swedish expedition to (1655), 581 sqq.; seized by Sweden, V 505; Charles XII at, 592; seized by Augustus (1704), 593 sq.; VI 152; Stanislaus in, 195; 196; Russian agents in, 667; 670; Russians evacuate (1794), VIII 542; Prussians attack, 546; Russians capture, 547; Louis XVIII at (1803), IX 28; Davout advances on, 281; Bennigsen occupies (1806), 283; Napoleon at, 284–5; French troops in, 315–6; Archduke Ferdinand occupies (1809), 354; Decree of Napoleon from (1807), 366; duchy of, formed, 293–4, 336–40; frontier of, 325; Austrian designs on, 346–7, 353–4, 486; suggested abolition of, 521; partition of, 579, 591 sqq.; grand duchy of, X 353, 413, 430, 445 sqq.; primacy of, established, 424; Zalucki library removed from, 431; 439; taken by Russia (1831), 444, 473; city improvements in, 449; Archbishopric of, *ib.*; University of, *ib.*; Nicholas I in, 458 sq.; Land Bank in, 462; secret association in, 464; 465; rising (1830) in, 466 sqq.; Russian government in, 474; meeting of the Emperors at, XI 210; 229; 266; insurrection in, 434, 475; Council of State at, 628; University of, 629; 659; growth of, XII 337; Nicholas II at, 338; 360
—— Diets at (1556), III 80, (1573), 86 sqq., (1574), 90 sq., (1577), 101, (1733), VI 194, (1736), 197, (1788), VIII 524 sqq., (1812), IX 491, (1818), X 428, 450, (1825), 435, 455, (1830), 458
—— John Paul Voronicz, Archbishop of, X 449; 452; at coronation of Nicholas I, 458

Wartburg, Luther at the, II 141, 163; festival, the (1817), X 364

Wartenberg, Count Francis William von, Bishop of Osnabrück, etc., Cardinal, IV 96; 112; representative of Electoral College (1645–8), 400 sq.; expelled from bishopric of Verden, 404
—— Johann Casimir Kolbe, Count von, V 664 sq.; 671

Wartenburg, Bertrand retreats from (1813), IX 531, 532

Wartensleben, Count, Danish envoy, IV 233

Warthe river, and the New Mark, V 618; VI 279; Cossacks on, 281; 283; 291; 717

Warton, Joseph, X 698; 710
—— Thomas, writings of, VI 830, X 698; 710

Warwick, disturbances at, XI 2
—— Ambrose Dudley, Earl of (6th cr.), evacuates Havre, II 518, 584; III 3, 6
—— John Dudley, Earl of. *See* Northumberland, Duke of

Warwick, John Dudley, Lord Lisle and Earl of (eldest son of Duke of Northumberland), II 504, 518
—— Edward Plantagenet, Earl of, I 465, 473
—— Richard Neville, Earl of (the Kingmaker), I 464
—— Sir Robert Rich, 2nd Earl of (7th cr.), Admiral of the fleet for Parliament, IV 301, 326, 351, 460; and Trinidad, 758
—— Sir Philip, IV 307
Warwyck, Admiral, III 638
Washington, City of, planned, VII 316; chosen as seat of government, 325; captured (1814), 344, 348, 352; Boundary Treaty concluded at, 367; peace convention at (1861), 448; Federal concentration at (1861), 464, 470 sq., 473; Early threatens (1864), 531 sq.; Treaty of (1871), 658 sq., XI 776, XII 22, 28, 617, 717, 720 sq.; Arbitration Treaty signed at (1897), VII 672; XII 12; Venezuelan Commission at, 695; Panamerican Congress at, 700
—— George, VII 120, 123 sqq., 136, 146; commander-in-chief, 167, 172; evacuates New York (1776), 212; captures Trenton (1777), 213; 216 sq.; at Yorktown, 230 sq.; becomes President (1789), 303, 315 sqq., 322, 328; resigns (1796), 372; 407; and Francisco Miranda, X 280
Wasilei Ivanovič, Tsar of Russia. *See* Vasili III
Wassenaer, Jacob, Baron van (of Obdam), Dutch admiral, V 146 sq.; death of (1665), 181
—— Jacob van (of Obdam), Dutch general, V 382; 407
—— Twickel, Carel Georg, Count of (son of following), Dutch ambassador to Vienna (1782-5), VIII 281
—— Unico Willem, Count of, Dutch envoy to Paris (1746), VI 246
Waterboer, Andries, Griqua leader, XI 783; 787
Waterford, trade in, III 579; "undertakers" in, 599; meeting of clergy at, IV 530; 534; and the Act of Satisfaction, 536; captured by William III (1690), V 315; election at, X 643 sq.
—— Henry de la Poer Beresford, 2nd Marquess of, X 643 sq.
Waterloo, battle of (1815), IX 632 sqq.; Napoleon's account of, 761
Waterston, physicist, XII 785
Watken, Privy-Councillor, at Congress of Vienna, IX 583
Watson, Charles, Rear-Admiral, in India, VI 531; 552; and Clive, 553; 554; 556
—— James (the elder and younger), agitators, X 577; 579
—— Joshua, and elementary education, IX 692
—— Richard, Bishop of Llandaff, VIII 763; X 704

Watson, Thomas, II 501
—— Thomas, poet, III 376
—— William, conspirator, III 554
Watt, James, VIII 765; inventions of, IX 372, X 733 sq.
Watteau, Jean-Antoine, painter, XI 528
Watteville, de, Swiss Landammann, letter to Napoleon of, IX 424
Wattignies, battle of, VIII 351, 432
Wattli, Melchior, II 316
Watts, Isaac, X 699
—— Resident at Murshidábád, VI 554; 556
Wauthier, major-general, City Commandant of Brussels, X 534
Wavre, Prussian retreat to (1815), IX 628, 630; advance from, 637; Grouchy marches on, 641
Waxhaws, Buford annihilated at (1780), VII 224
Wayne, Anthony, American general, VII 220, 357
Wealth of Russia, journal, XII 313
Weaver, James B., Populist candidate for President, VII 665
Webb, Daniel, Colonel, VII 126, 129 sq.
—— John Richmond, General, V 422
Weber, Wilhelm, X 379
Webster, Augusta, poetess, XI 353
—— Daniel, and nullification debate, VII 381, 412 sqq.; 390 sqq.; "Seventh of March" speech of, 403; 404; death of, 418; oratory of, 743 sq.
—— John, III 381; V 126
Webster-Ashburton Treaty (1842), VII 391, XI 17
Wedderburn, Alexander. *See* Loughborough
Wedel-Jarlsberg, Count Hermann, XI 680 sq.
Wedell, Carl Heinrich von, Prussian general, VI 287; 292; 324
Wedgwood, Josiah, VIII 765; X 736
—— Thomas (son of above), influence of Godwin on, VIII 768
Weeden, Newport butcher, and U.S. money of 1786, VII 313
Weekly Political Register, The, X 577
Weert, de, Vice-Admiral, III 638
Wegscheider, J. A. L., X 382
Wehe, Jacob, leader in Peasants' Rising, II 181 sq.
Wehlau, Treaty of (1657), IV 429, 585
Weichselmünde, port of Danzig, VI 197
Weigant, leader of Peasants' Rising, II 184
Weigel, Valentin, theologian, V 759
Wei-Hai-Wei, XII 52; 132; Chinese man-of-war at, 510; captured by the Japanese, 512; leased to Great Britain, 514
Weil, Gustav, German historian, XII 846
Weiland, Ludwig, at Jena, X 364
Weimar, league between Hesse and Saxony at (1528), II 202; VI 267; Frederick the Great at, 263; Murat at, IX 276; Prussian retreat on (1806), 277; Napoleon at, 278; admitted to Confederation of the Rhine, 279; Lord Morpeth at, 282; rising at, XI 150; historical research at, XII 825

Weimar, Karl August, Duke of, IX 277; 280; in Netherlands, 550; at Congress of Vienna, 583; 594

Weingarten, Abbey of, given to Prince of Orange (1801), IX 90

Weinsberg, massacre of, by peasants, II 187

Weishaupt, Adam, German author, VIII 772

Weisse Berg, at Prague, Frederick the Great at the, VI 257; 259

Weissembourg. *See* Weissenburg

Weissenburg, captured by French (1705), V 414; King of Poland at, VI 143; defences of, VIII 423; French retreat to, 425 sq.; fighting at, 428; armistice signed at (1795), 443; French reverse at, XI 583 sq.

Weissenfels, headquarters of Imperialists, IV 220

Weissenstein, taken by Ivan (1573), IV 166; 174

Weiszäcker, Carl von, German historian, XII 847

Weitzel, Godfrey, American general, VII 539, 544

Wekerle, Alexander, Hungarian statesman, XII 198 sq.; 206 sq.; 210

Welcker, Friedrich Gottlieb, German scholar, XII 822

—— K. T., Professor, and Frankfort plot, X 377; XI 61; 63; 164; 198

Welden, Baron Franz Ludwig von, Austrian general, XI 89; 207

Welhaven, Johan Sebastian, Norwegian poet, XI 701

Welland Canal, XI 763

Wellby, Montagu Sinclair, in Tibet, XII 803

Welle river, discovered, XII 811

Welles, Gideon, American Secretary of Navy, VII 450, 589

Wellesley, province of, XII 532 sq.

—— Sir Arthur. *See* Wellington, Duke of

—— Henry. *See* Cowley, Henry Wellesley, 1st Baron

—— Richard Colley Wellesley, Earl of Mornington, Marquis, work of, as Governor-General of India, IX 721 sqq.; conquest of Mysore, 722 sq.; policy of, 724 sqq.; annexes Gwalior, 727; recall of, 728 sq.; Foreign Secretary (1808), 689; Viceroy of Ireland, X 637; and the Coercion Bill, 663; 668; XI 724; 730

Wellhausen, Julius, Semitic studies of, XII 846

Wellington, XI 793; 796; 799; capital of New Zealand, 800

—— Arthur Wellesley, 1st Duke of, in Peninsular War, Vol. IX, Chap. XV *passim*; lands in Portugal, 235; complains of navy, 239; effect of victories of, 369; 370, 384, 440; commander-in-chief, 441; in Portugal, 449 sqq.; Junta and, 455; prepares for defence of Portugal, 456 sqq.; Torres Vedras, 459 sq.; 463; besieges Almeida, 465; losses of, at Fuentes d'Oñoro and Almeida, 466; in Estremadura, 467; fails at Badajoz and Ciudad Rodrigo, 468; offers battle at Sabugal, *ib.*; takes Ciudad Rodrigo and Badajoz, 470-1; wins battle of Salamanca, 472; enters Madrid, 473; at Burgos, 474 sqq.; wins battle of Vittoria, 477; before Pampeluna, 480; at Bayonne, 481; wins battle of Toulouse, 482; in France, 542-3; at Orthez and Bordeaux, 550; opinion of Louis XVIII of, 562; 566; succeeds Castlereagh at Congress of Vienna, 585; 602; Belgian campaign of, 622 sqq.; at Quatre-Bras, 626 sqq.; at Waterloo, 631 sqq.; marches on Paris, 643; opposes diminution of French territory at Congress of Vienna, 653; and First Peace of Paris, 664; called to Canning's post, 689; resigns, 690; commands in India (1803), 726 sq.; victories of, at Assaye and Argáon, 726; and Napoleon's captivity, 759; at Conference of Aix-la-Chapelle, X 14 sq.; 18; at Congress of Verona, 33 sqq.; attitude of, on Spanish Question, 35 sq.; and second Restoration in France, 44; 50; and evacuation of France, 56; 181; mission of, to St Petersburg (1826), 191 sq.; and Turkish Question, 193 sq.; succeeds Canning as Premier, 198; policy of, towards Greek Question, 199 sqq.; and Treaty of Adrianople, 203; and Spanish affairs, 207, 225 sq.; 281; 290; at Verona, 308; and Portuguese affairs, 322 sq.; and Prussia, 349; and Orleans Monarchy, 482; and Eastern Question, 557; 573; and Canning, 591; and the Corn Law, 591 sq.; Ministry of, 592 sqq.; and parliamentary reform, 601, 603; fails to form a Ministry (1832), 615; and opposition to Reform Bill, 615 sq.; and Catholic emancipation in Ireland, 645, 650 sqq.; supports Irish Church Bill, 657; supports Poor Law Bill, 662; 666; Minister for Foreign Affairs, 667; 674; 678; and Peel's Ministry (1841), XI 2; 10; 340; and Lord Ellenborough, 734; 736; 758; 795 sq.; and relations with China, 805 sq.

Wells, Horace, dentist, XII 779

Wels, death of Maximilian I at (1519), I 322

Welsers, The, of Augsburg, financiers, I 506 sq., 518

Welsh Copper Company, VI 179

Welti, Emil, Swiss statesman, XI 257

Wemyss, meeting of Mary Queen of Scots and Darnley at, III 269

Wenceslas of Luxemburg (1356), I 419; marries Joan of Brabant, 421

—— II, King of the Romans and Emperor, I 105; deposed (1399), 292; 294; 421

Wênchow, opened to foreign trade, XII 502

Wends, subjugation of, V 617; 618 sq.

Wentworth, Peter, III 358

—— Thomas, Baron, II 499

Wentworth, Thomas, Earl of Strafford.
See Strafford
—— William Charles, Australian explorer,
xi 790 sq.
Wenyon, Charles, Asiatic traveller, xii 793
Weraroa, capture of, xi 800
Werben, Gustavus Adolphus at, iv 203 sq.;
Banér at, 366, 372
Werden, claimed by Murat, ix 272
Werdenberg, rising in, vi 625
—— Count Felix von, ii 190
Werder, Count August von, German general,
xi 588; 604; at Dijon, 606; 609
Werelä. *See* Värälä
Werff, van der, iii 240
Wergeland, Henrik, Norwegian writer, xi
700 sq.
Werklein, Baron, rule of, in Parma,
x 107
Werkmeister, Benedict, ix 201
Wernburg, Charles XII at, v 588
Werneck, Austrian general, ix 254; sur-
render of, 255
Werner, Friedrich Ludwig Zacharias, Ger-
man dramatic poet, x 402
Werth, Johann von, iv 223; at Ratisbon,
231; 244; at Nördlingen, 245; at Heidel-
berg, 246, 248 sq.; takes Speier, 250; in
Picardy, 371; 374 sqq.; 388 sqq.; havoc
wrought by, 621
Wertheimer, Eduard, German historian,
xii 829
Wertingen, engagement at (1805), ix 254
Wesel, taken by Spaniards (1598), iii
634, 717; centre of Dutch immigration,
705; occupied by Spinola (1614), 733;
captured by Dieden (1629), iv 693; Dutch
troops at, ix 274; ceded to France (1808),
410
—— Johann (John Rucherath of Ober-
wesel), German humanist (d. 1481), i 626,
652, 680
Wesembeke, Jacques de, iii 227, 231
Weser river, closed to English trade, ix
374; and Heligoland, xii 167
Wesley, Charles, v 759 sq.; vi 82; 87; 89;
in Georgia, vii 63; x 698 sq.
—— John, v 759 sq.; vi 40; 77; 80 sqq.;
in Ireland, 489; death of, 86; in Georgia,
vii 63
Wessel, Johan Herman, Norwegian writer,
xi 700
—— (Wesselus Gansfortius) of Goesevort
and Groningen, Johann, German humanist (d. 1489), i 437, 460, 624, 626, 636 sq.,
652, 680; ii 111
Wessenberg, Bishop Ignatius Henry Charles
von, at Congress of Vienna, ix 587–8;
and Germanic Constitution, 649; x 6;
and ecclesiastical affairs in Germany,
145 sq.; 148; 362; and German Catholic
Church, 380
—— Baron John von, at Congress of
Vienna, ix 580 sqq.; 648 sq.; and
Second Peace of Paris, 665

Wessenberg - Ampringen, Baron Johann
Philipp, Austrian Foreign Minister, xi 88;
92; 176; 183; 186 sq.
Wessprim, taken by Turks (1552), iii 123;
attacked by troops of Maximilian II, 125
West, Nicholas, Bishop of Ely, i 482
Westermann, François - Joseph, French
general, viii 232, 237, 353 sqq.; trial and
execution of, 363 sq.; 412
Western Port, convict settlement at, xi 790
West India Company (Dutch), iv 694;
formed (1621), 703; at San Salvador, 703
sqq.; 706; Pernambuco taken by, 707;
709 sq.; Peace of Münster and, 716; 728;
American coast and, 749; in Brazil, 750
sq.; Joan Maurice of Nassau and, 752 sq.;
in South America, 755; and Providence
Island, 758; v 146, 674 sq., 691; vi 389;
vii 22, 39 sq., 86
—— India Company (French), reconstituted, iv 759; v 692
—— India and Guinea Company (Danish),
vi 738
—— Indies, Prince Rupert in, iv 465;
the French in, v 12 sq.; 104 sq.;
English, French, and Dutch in, 110,
112, 149; Peace of Breda and, 151; 179;
English and French in, 189, 442; 378 sq.;
the Grand Alliance (1701) and, 398; 679
sq.; decline of Spanish power in, 684;
English policy in, 686; European com-
petition in, 687 sqq.; English government
in, 690; piracy in, 691; 694; slave trade
in, vi 25; and British trade, 52; 60 sq.;
65; smuggling in, 152; 158; 177; 183;
economic conditions in, 184; European
Powers in, 185 sq.; 189; 236; 248;
France and, 327, 346 sq.; 350; Choiseul's
schemes in, 351; Spanish losses in, 369;
Franco-Spanish expedition to, 379; Pitt
and, 414 sq.; 449; 451; Franco-British
war in, 452 sqq.; Denmark and, 756;
Spain, England and, iv 439; vii 70;
settlements in, 74, 78 sq.; Colbert's
policy in, 85 sq.; 91; prosperity of, 95
sqq.; Rodney in, 231; French fleet in,
233; trade in, 309, 316, 318 sqq., 358,
363, 688; French ships captured by
American squadron in, 322; American
trade with, 350; French trade with, viii
60; and the Revolution, 193; mutiny in
(1797), 480; operations in (1793–1800),
484 sq.; French fleet in (1803), ix 209;
French designs on, 217 sqq.; British fleet
in, 219; French invasion of (1805), 219–
23; Nelson sails for, 224; insurance of
merchantmen for, 242; affairs in (1793–
1807), 748 sqq.; Spanish trade in, x 276;
Spanish troops in, 306 sq.; pirates in,
308; trade with, 658, 761; xi 16; trade
of, with Canada, 777; xii 21; affairs in,
after 1815, 652 sqq.; 670. *See also under*
Indies
—— (Danish), American annexation
of, vii 637, 673

Westland, province of, xi 799
—— Whigs, Scottish recusants in south-west, v 283, 287 sq.
Westmeath, Richard Nugent, 2nd Earl of, iv 535
Westminster, conference concerning Mary Stewart at (1568), iii 278; and the franchise, x 605
—— Assembly, iii 758; Vol. iv, Chap. xii
—— Treaty of (1527), ii 56 sq.; the Colloquy of (1559), 568; Treaty of (1655), iv 619, v 162; (1674), vii 41; (1677-8), vi 449; (1716), 25, 29 sq., 104; (1756), 251 sq., 254, 320, 334, 399 sqq., 403, 407
Westmoreland, John Fane, 10th Earl of (2nd cr.), and Catholic emancipation, ix 678-81; Viceroy of Ireland, 693; and the Catholics, 695 sqq.
—— Charles Neville, Earl of (1568), iii 278, 281
Weston, Richard (*afterwards* 1st Earl of Portland), Wentworth and, iv 272; character of, 278; 281 sq.
—— Robert, Irish Lord Chancellor, a Lord Justice in Ireland, iii 594
Westphal, Joachim, ii 588
Westphalen, Ferdinand O. W. H. von, Prussian Minister of Interior, xi 395
Westphalia, invaded by Maurice, iii 673; condition of towns of, iv 420 sq.; and the Old Mark (Brandenburg), v 619; iron industry in, vi 719; Prussian gains in (1803), ix 94; Napoleon's designs on, 278; kingdom of, 293-4, 336, 408 sqq.; Stein and, 335; Müller in, 335; insurrection in (1809), 357; Prussian accessions in (1814), 592; 596; acquired by Prussia (1815), 657-8; Church affairs in, x 147 sq.; and Hesse-Cassel, 346; Vincke's administration in, 353; 355; religious question in, 380; agriculture in, 731; roads in, 745; industries in, 756 sq.; revolutionary movement in, xi 157; the Catholic party in, xii 146
—— Peace of (1648), due to Richelieu, iv 141, 157; and events in England, 352; *see* Chap. xiv; 421; triumph of Mazarin's policy, 602; 603; 607; 620; 688; 702; v 46 sqq., 338, 373, 450, 453 sq., 577; Brandenburg and, 641, 643 sq.; 652; 659; 743; vi 2; 252; 273; and Switzerland, 612, 614, 622
West Point (New York), surrender of (1780), vii 226; 474, 476
Westport, Parnell at, xii 76
West river (China), trade on, xii 506
Wetstein, John Rudolf, burgomaster of Basel, at Congress of Münster, iv 401
Wette, W. M. L. de, x 870
Wetter, family of, vi 625
Wetterau, The, and the War, iv 418; and Congress of Vienna, ix 588
—— the Counts of, iii 704, 715
Wettin, House of, v 660; vi 704; ix 593. *See also* Saxony

Wetzlar, *Kammergericht* fixed at, i 317; acquired by Prussia (1815), ix 657
Wexford, captured by Cromwell, iv 435; plantation of North, 513; 525; sack of (1649), 534; and Act of Satisfaction, 536; captured by William III (1690), v 315; rebellion in (1798), ix 701 sq.
Wexiö, Olaf Wallqvist, Bishop of, vi 777 sq.; 780
Weyer, Silvain van de, Belgian politician, x 532; 536 sq.; 540; xi 670
Weyler, Valeriano, Spanish general, vii 675; xii 266
Weymouth, parliamentary representation of, x 613
—— 3rd Viscount. *See* Bath, 1st Marquis of
Weyrother, Franz von, Austrian officer, viii 575; ix 259; 260
Whalley, Edward, major-general and regicide, iv 329; vii 25
Whampoa, opium smuggling at, xi 806; 815
Wharncliffe, J. A. Stuart-Wortley-Mackenzie, Lord, x 610
Wharton, Philip, Lord Wharton, v 218
—— Philip Wharton, Duke of, vi 142
—— Sir Thomas, ii 455 sq., 515
—— Thomas, 1st Marquis of Wharton, v 243; 274; 466
—— Thomas, physician, v 729; 731
Whately, Richard, Archbishop of Dublin, x 676; xi 794
Wheatstone, Sir Charles, and telegraphy, xii 786
Wheeler, Sir Hugh Massy, Major-general, at Cawnpore, xi 747
Wheeling, trade of, vii 360; Convention at (1861), 455
Wheelwright, John, preacher in Massachusetts, vii 17 sq.
Whetham, Nathaniel, iv 547
Whewell, William, xii 711
Whichcote, Benjamin, and Cambridge Platonists, v 750
Whig Examiner, The, v 469
Whish, Sir William Sampson, Commander of the Multan field force, xi 741
Whitbread, Samuel, politician, protests against war, ix 618; resolutions of, 684; and the Whig party, 687-91
Whitby, captain of the *Leander,* vii 328
White, Sir George Stuart, General, at Ladysmith, xii 642
—— John, Bishop of Lincoln, ii 531
—— John, settles in Virginia, vii 3
—— John, incumbent of Dorchester, vii 15
—— Sir William, xii 393
Whiteboy disturbances in Ireland, vi 484, 490
Whitefield, George, Methodist, vi 81 sqq.; vii 57, 737
Whitehall, Elizabeth at, iii 357
White Hill, battle on the, iii 569

White Lake, monastery of the, v 507

Whitelock, Bulstrode, and Cromwell's office, IV 443; and Richard Cromwell, 448; 450; 548

Whitelocke, James, III 564

—— John, lieutenant-general, in La Plata, IX 753, x 281

White Sea, v 512; visited by Peter the Great, 520; 552; Richard Chancellor at, XII 793; 795

Whitgift, John, Archbishop of Canterbury, II 161, 592, 597; III 341-8, 554

Whiting, Richard, the last Abbot of Glastonbury, II 450

Whitman, Walt, VII 747

Whitmore, Edward, General, VII 132

Whitney, Eli, inventor of the cotton-gin, VII 351, 374, 688

Whitshed, Irish Chief Justice, VI 485

Whittier, John Greenleaf, VII 746

Whit-Wednesday (The Terrible), revolt in Flanders (1438), I 427

Whitworth, Charles Whitworth, Baron, VI 28; 35

—— Sir Charles, Earl, British ambassador at St Petersburg, VIII 646 sqq., 654; IX 28, 37, 39; sent to Copenhagen, 45; 102 sqq.; and Napoleon, 208; 209

—— Sir Joseph, x 734

Wiapoc river, France and, v 679

Wicklow Hills, Emmet escapes to, IX 707

Wiclif, John, II 175; the *De Ecclesia*, 313; the Bible of, 464; v 633

Wicquefort, Abraham de, XII 710

Widdin, destroyed by Hunyady (1454), I 69; captured by Turks (1690), v 61, 369; 368; IX 385; Hungarian refugees at, XI 215

Widdrington, William Widdrington, 4th Lord, VI 101; 103

Widmanstetter, Johann Albrecht, Syriac New Testament of, I 604

Wied, Count Frederick von, III 156, 172

—— Hermann von. *See* Cologne, Archbishop-Elector of

Wieland, Christopher Martin, VIII 774; Napoleon's interview with, IX 319; 335; x 385; 387 sq.; XI 411; 423

Wielicz, ceded to Poland (1582), III 101

Wielun, Edict of (1424), III 74

Wiesbaden, revolutionary movement at, XI 147

Wieselgren, Peter, Canon, XI 688

Wiesensteig, Saxony and, VI 632

Wiesloch, Mansfeld at, IV 80

Wieuwerd, the Labadists at, v 756

Wigan, Government force at, VI 101

Wiggens, Joseph, navigator, XII 795

Wight, Isle of, Spaniards reported in, III 531; Charles I in, IV 346, 507; Dutch fleet at, v 206; threatened invasion of, VI 376

Wightman, Joseph, major-general, VI 106

Wigtownshire, recusants in, v 283

Wiju, XII 583; Japanese force at, 584

Wilamowitz-Möllendorff, Ulrich von, historian, XII 845

Wilberforce, Samuel, Bishop of Oxford, XI 326

—— William, and the abolition of slavery, IX 614; VI 188; 472; 475; VIII 763; supports censure of Melville, IX 684; and India, 733; x 658; XII 806

Wilchingen, revolt at, VI 625

Wildenberg, Planta's fortress at, IV 46 sq.

Wildenbruch, Major von, XI 162

Wilderness, The (Virginia), battle of (1864), VII 516 sqq.

Wildhaus, Zwingli born at, II 306

Wildman, Sir John, and Rye House plot, v 229

Wilford, Ralph, pretended Earl of Warwick, I 473

Wilhelm, Karl, German composer, XI 412

Wilhelmina, Queen of Holland, XII 245; 247 sq.

—— Princess of Prussia. *See* Brandenburg-Baireuth, Margravine of

Wilhelmstein, military school at, IX 332

Wilhelmsthal, battle of, VI 426

"*Wilhelmus van Nassouwen*" (patriotic warsong), III 231

Wiliczka, salt mines of, assigned to Austria, IX 655

Wilken, Friedrich, German historian, XII 823

Wilkersdorf, Prussian army at, VI 282; 286

Wilkes, Charles, American admiral, captures Mason and Slidell, VII 470; XI 335 sq.; XII 18 sq.

—— John, and the *North Briton*, VI 429 sqq.; returns to England, 440; 441 sq.; 444; takes his seat in Parliament, 446; 460; and Reform, 465; x 599

—— Sir Thomas, diplomatist, III 26

Wilkins, John, Bishop of Chester, v 332 sqq.

Wilkinson, James, American general, VII 341, 343

Willach-Laibach, Austrian invasion of Italy from, IX 347; Archduke John retires to (1809), 355

Willaumez, Comte Jean-Baptiste-Philibert, French rear-admiral, attacks British merchantmen, IX 234; sails from Brest, 238; replaced by Allemand, *ib.*

Willcocks, W., and irrigation in Egypt, XII 446

Willebroek, conference at (1567), III 213

Willekens, Jacob, takes San Salvador, IV 750

Willems, Jan Frans, Flemish writer, XI 673; 676

William III, King of England, Scotland, and Ireland, and Prince of Orange: (1) *Prince of Orange*: birth of, IV 701, 727; 720; proclaimed Stadholder of Holland and Zeeland, v 43, 157; 44; at battle of St Denys, 45; 46; and French siege of Luxemburg, 48 sq.; alliance of,

with the Great Elector, 52; 53 sq.; guardianship of, 107, 148, 151; Act of Seclusion and, 141 sqq.; 153; character of, 154 sq., 166 sq.; and States of Zeeland, 155 sq.; 157; policy of, 158, 162; and downfall of de Witt, 159 sq.; successes of, against French, 160 sq.; increased power of, 161; at Seneff, *ib.*; relations of, with England, 162 sq.; marriage of, 163, 213 sq., 219; relieves Mons, 164 sq.; opposition to, 165; forms an alliance against France, 166; and Queen Mary, 167, 258; 197 sq.; and Treaty of Dover, 204; 208; and Charles II, 230; and Duke of Monmouth, 232; and James II, 235, 238 sqq.; attitude of, towards England (1687–8), 241; and invitation from England, 242 sq.; attitude of the Powers to, 244; sails for England, 55, 245; landing of, 246; 247; and flight of James II, 248; opposition of, to Louis XIV, 349; and Austria, 359. (2) *King of England, Scotland, and Ireland*: accession of, 56 sq.; coronation of, 167; recognised by Emperor Leopold I, 58; 59; and the Revolution settlement, 249 sq.; proclaimed King, 251; 252 sq.; cautious policy of, 255; character and aims of, 256 sqq.; Parliament and, 259; and the Act of Grace, 260; at Steinkirke, 60; at Neerwinden, 61, 262; and France, 62 sq.; in Ireland, 260 sq.; plot to assassinate, 262; and War with France, 262 sq.; and English attitude towards the war, 263; 264 sqq.; and currency, 269 sq.; and executive government, 272 sq.; and legislature, 273; and the Whigs, 274; 275 sq.; political action of, in England, 276 sq.; influence of, upon European polity, 277; and Scotland, 290 sqq.; and Tyrconnel, 307; and Louis XIV, 308; 399; and Grand Alliance, 311, 398 sq.; 403; in Ireland, 313 sqq.; and capture of Athlone, 317; and Ireland, 320 sqq.; and religious toleration, 336 sq.; 340; and the Emperor Leopold I, 368 sq.; and Spain, 374, 437; and Spanish Succession, 379, 381 sqq.; difficulties of, in England, 386 sq.; and accession of Philip V of Spain, 395 sqq.; supported in England, 397, 400; and Partition Treaties, 384, 389 sq.; and Philip V, 401; and Marlborough, 405; and Mediterranean, 411; 429; foreign policy of, 440; 449; 461; sends fleet to Baltic, 588; and Sweden, 591; 654; and the Elector Frederick III, 660 sqq.; 688; and colonial affairs, 691; and East India Companies, 701; death of, 276, 668, vi 9; 4; 6; and succession, 7 sq.; 31; 586; 808; 815; and New England Colonies, vii 30; viii 321

William IV, King of Great Britain, and Hanover, x 374, 379; 482; 557; Lord High Admiral, 591; succeeds to throne, 593; and Reform Bills, 609 sq., 614 sq.;

dissolves Parliament, 610 sq.; calls Lord Melbourne to office (1834), 664; and Brougham, 665; dismisses the Melbourne Ministry, 666; and Peel Ministry, 666 sqq.; and second Melbourne Ministry, 669 sq.; and Orange Lodges, 672; death of, 674

William I, German Emperor (Prince of Prussia to 1861), xi 56; 158 sq.; and German National Constitution, 163; 199; in command of Baden expedition, 221; 229; 231; opposes the Government, 396; policy of, as Regent, 406; accession of, *ib.*; and Austria, 407 sq.; and army reform, 408 sq., 432; struggle with Parliament, 410; founds Schiller prize, 416; and Tsar, 434; and the Frankfort assembly of princes, 435; and Schleswig-Holstein, 440, 445; 442; and the war with Austria, 448, 451, 455 sq.; President of North German Confederation, 459; and Spanish succession, 462 sq.; at Ems, 463, 578; proclaimed Emperor, 465 sq., 612; and Luxemburg, 483; and peace negotiations, 495, 498; 540; 578 sq.; and Franco-German War, 580; and Papacy, 708; 777; xii 28; 97; 116; and Bismarck, 137, 162; 138 sqq.; 141; and Russo-Turkish War, 142; 143; and Austro-German Alliance, 144; 152; attempts on life of, 153; death of, 163

—— II, German Emperor, xii 14; 55; at Tangier, 132; accession of, 165; policy of, 166 sqq.; 379; and Greece, 421

—— I, King of the Netherlands, at Erfurt, ix 277; (Prince of Orange) deprived of his German possessions, 278; Prussian envoy in Austria, 352; enters the Hague, 550; King of the Netherlands, 654; at Congress of Vienna, 586, 605, 667; engagement of, to Princess Charlotte, 690; and Belgium, x 376, 480, 488 sq., 505 sq.; accepts sovereignty of Holland (1813), 517; character of, *ib.*; 518; and union of Holland and Belgium, 519 sqq.; enters Brussels, 524; territories of, *ib.*; and Catholic clergy, 526 sq.; and a national language, 527; and national finances, 528; policy of, towards Belgium, 529 sqq.; and the Belgian revolution, 535 sqq.; and the Powers, 538 sqq.; and the settlement with Belgium, 543 sq.; xi 661; abdication of, 662; death of, *ib.*; 673; and Luxemburg, 674

—— II, King of the Netherlands, x 521; in Brussels (1830), 535; 537; invades Belgium, 541 sq.; accession of, xi 662; and constitutional reform, 663; 668; and Luxemburg, 674; and Japan, 823; death of, 664

—— III, King of the Netherlands, accession of, xi 664; 665; 667; and Luxemburg, 674 sq.; xii 244 sq.; death of, 246

William I, King of Würtemberg, x 36; 361; and Metternich, 368; and Frankfort plot, 377; xi 61; 148; and Frankfort Assembly, 200; 223; and Hesse-Cassel, 229
—— Prince (of Denmark). *See* George I, King of Greece
—— the Silent. *See* Orange, William (the Silent) of Nassau, Prince of
—— Prince of Orange (son of William III, King of the Netherlands), xii 244
—— of Gap, Abbot of St Denis, brings books from Constantinople, i 588
—— of Malmesbury, i 598
Williams, Sir Charles Hanbury, British ambassador in Russia, vi 200; 334
—— David, and the Theophilanthropists, viii 501
—— Helen Maria, ix 24
—— John (Baron Williams of Thame), ii 496
—— John, Archbishop of York, Dean of Westminster, iii 560; Bishop of Lincoln, 573; Lord Keeper, iv 258; persecution and, 260; before Star Chamber, 280; Episcopacy and, 292; impeached, 297; 356
—— Roger, tract of, iv 320; minister of Salem (Mass.), vii 17, 19, 25; sent to England, 24
—— Thomas, American general, vii 502
Williamsburg, British victory at (1813), vii 341; battle of (1862), 474 sq.
Williamson, Hugh, deputy for N. Carolina at Constitutional Convention (1787), vii 246, 255, 267, 287, 290
—— Sir Joseph, Secretary of State, v 210
Willinger, Achatius, iv 76
Willis, Sir Richard, iv 540
—— Thomas, physician, v 733 sq.
Willisen, Baron Wilhelm von, Prussian general, xi 164; 225; 227
Willock, John, "Superintendent" of Glasgow, ii 591
Willot, Comte Amédée de, on the *Conseil des Cinq-Cents*, viii 509, 512
Willoughby, Sir Hugh, search for North-East passage by, i 53, v 512, xii 793 sq.
—— of Parham, Charles Willoughby, 2nd Baron, iii 48
—— of Parham, Francis Willoughby, 5th Baron, at Gainsborough, iv 314; 321; in the Downs, 350; at Surinam, 755; Governor of Barbados, v 189; 688
—— of Parham, William Willoughby, 6th Baron, Governor of Barbados, v 690
Wills, Sir Charles, General, vi 101
—— William John, Australian explorer, xi 798
Willughby, Francis, naturalist, v 736 sq.
Wilmington (N. Carolina), loyalist attempt on (1776), vii 173; Cornwallis at, 229; captured by Federals (1865), 534; railway communication with, 551; importance of, 552, 556 sq.; blockade-running at, 620

Wilmington, Spencer Compton, Earl of, vi 71; 73
Wilmot, David, American politician, vii 397
"Wilmot Proviso," vii 397, 399, 403 sq.
Wilna. *See* Vilna
Wilson, Andrew, smuggler, vi 108
—— Sir Archdale, General, at Delhi, xi 746 sq.
—— Sir Charles Rivers, and Egyptian Finance, xii 434
—— Sir Charles William, General, and the Gordon relief expedition, xii 443
—— Henry, of Massachusetts, vii 399
—— James, Pennsylvanian deputy at Constitutional Convention (1787), Vol. vii, Chap. viii *passim*
—— James H., American general, vii 680
—— James, financial member of Council of India, xi 752
—— John, playwright, v 130
—— John ("Christopher North"), xi 362
—— Sir Robert Thomas, General, at St Petersburg, ix 305; British commissioner in Russia, 499; and Spanish foreign legion, x 227
—— William Lyne, American statesman, vii 669
—— Dr, trial of, ii 443 sq.
Wilson Bill, The, vii 669
Wilson-Gorman Bill, The, vii 669
Wilson's Creek, battle of (1861), vii 460
Wilton, Lord Grey de. *See* Grey de Wilton
Wiltshire, Thomas Boleyn, Earl of, ii 429, 433 sq., 445
—— William Paulet, Lord St John, Earl of. *See* Winchester, Marquis of
Wimbledon, Sir Edward Cecil, Viscount, attack of, upon Cadiz, iv 642
Wimpfen, battle of (1622), iv 80 sq.
Wimpffen, Emmanuel-Félix de, French general, xi 597 sq.
Wimpheling, Jacob, scholar, career of, i 634 sq.; 690; the *Gravamina Germanicae Nationis*, ii 29; 32, 160
Wimpina, Conrad, answers Luther's Theses, ii 130
Winceby, fight at (1643), iv 315
Winchelsea, D. Finch, Earl of. *See* Nottingham
Winchester, James I's audience to Lerma at, iii 536
—— Charles Paulet, 7th Marquis of (*and* 2nd Duke of Bolton), v 321
—— John Paulet, 5th Marquis of, iv 315
—— William Paulet, Lord St John, Earl of Wiltshire and Marquis of, ii 495, 499, 505, 517, 570
—— James, American general, vii 339
—— (Virginia), General J. E. Johnston at, vii 465, 467; Early at, 531; Early driven from, 532
Winckelmann, Johann Joachim, x 385; 390; 396; xii 817
Windau, port of, vi 666

Windebank, Sir Francis, Panzani and, IV 280; flight of, 287

Windelin of Speier, printer at Venice (1469), I 284

Winder, William H., American general, VII 344

Windesem Congregations, in the Netherlands, I 435

Windham, William, statesman, Secretary to Viceroy of Ireland, VI 464; 478; VIII 759; and Whig party, IX 673; Secretary for War, 674; 685, 698; and recall of Fitzwilliam, 699

Windischgrätz, Alfred, Prince von, Austrian field-marshal, XI 154; 170 sq.; 176; quells Prague insurrection, 177 sq.; 182; besieges Vienna, 187 sqq.; 190; in Hungary, 202 sqq.; recall of, 206; 208 sq.; 501

Windsheim, one of the fourteen Protestant cities, II 205

Windsor, Treaty at, between Charles V and Henry VIII (1522), II 45, 419; IV 348; Charles I at, 354; Charles II at, V 225; 227

Windthorst, Ludwig, German politician, XII 147; 149

Windward Coast, Portuguese on, VI 187
— Islands, V 687 sq.; government of, 690; English and French in, VI 184 sqq.; French in, VII 96; XII 653 sq.; government of, 656 sq.; annexed by France, 666

Wingate, Alfred Woodrow Stanley, in China, XII 796
— Sir Francis Reginald, Sirdar of Egyptian army, XII 448 sq.

Wingfield, Sir Anthony, II 496, 499
— Sir Richard, English ambassador, I 486
— Marshal, III 613

Winnington Bridge, Booth defeated at (1659), IV 541

Winnipeg, La Verendrye at, VII 94; XII 608; industries of, 612

Wins, Baron Joseph de, Austrian general, VIII 444, 558

Winslow, Edward, and the Pilgrim Fathers, VII 13
— John, in New England, VII 30

Winter, John William van, Count of Huessen, Dutch admiral, VIII 481 sqq.
— William. *See* Wynter, Sir William

Winterfeldt, Johann Carl von, Prussian general, VI 256 sq.; 264

Winterthur, industries of, XI 259

Winther, Christian, Danish writer, XI 699

Winthrop, John, Governor of Massachusetts, VII 15 sq., 21
— John (son of above), Governor of Connecticut, VII 18; in England, 26

Wintoun, George Seton, 5th Earl of, VI 101; 103

Wintzingerode, Baron Ferdinand von, Russian general, IX 250; marches on Dresden, 514; in Holland, 550

Wintzingerode, Heinrich Karl F. Levin, Count, IX 609; X 36; 369

Winwood, Sir Ralph, Secretary of State (1614–6), III 560

Wirsberg, F. von. *See* Würzburg, Bishop of
— Janko and Livin von, German sectaries (1466), I 623

Wirsung, Johann Georg, German anatomist, V 729

Wirth, J. G. A., German journalist, X 375

Wisbech Castle, leaders of the English mission in, III 353

Wischau, French outposts driven from, IX 260

Wischegrad, occupied by Ferdinand's troops, III 118; taken again by Turks, 119

Wisconsin, enters the Union (1848), VII 421; and the slavery question, 424; negro suffrage in, 629; population of, 695, 702

Wishart, George, II 461; burning of, 556; III 262
— Sir James, English admiral, V 446

Wisin, Russian dramatist, VI 698

Wismar, Gustavus and, IV 191; 204; claimed by Sweden at Osnabrück, 403 sq.; 407; commercial prosperity of, 420; Treaty of (1636), 370, 373; taken by Danes (1675), V 569; 579; 603; Swedish army at, 608; Hanover and, 610; Russia and, 611; capitulates (1716), 612

Wisniowiecki, Michael Korybut. *See* Michael, King of Poland

Wissenberg, city of, joins Protestants (1529), II 205

Wissmann, Hermann von, African explorer, XII 811

Withers, George, English Puritan exile, at Heidelberg, II 596
— Major-general, at Malplaquet, V 425

Witsen, Nicolaes, opposes Prince of Orange, V 165

Witt, John de, statesmanship of, IV 727; V 110; Pensionary of Dort, 138; Grand Pensionary of Holland, 36 sq., 139; and the negotiations with England, 113, 140 sqq.; marriage of, 144 sq.; financial reforms by, 145; and Portugal, 146, 148; and struggle in Baltic, 146 sq.; and restoration of Charles II, 148; and the young Prince of Orange, *ib.*; 149; and War with England, 150; and Peace of Breda, 151; forms a coalition against France, 152 sq.; and Peace of Aachen, 153 sq.; opposition to, 154, 156; simplicity of life of, 155; and Eternal Edict, 155 sq.; and designs of Louis XIV, 156 sq.; popular hatred of, 158; resigns the office of Grand Pensionary, 159; 179 sq.; 185; and the war with England, 187 sqq., 191 sq.; 197; and Triple Alliance, 200 sq.; 206; murder of, 43, 159, 208
— Cornelis de, V 138; 145; 158; murder of, 43, 159, 208

Witt, Jacob de, imprisonment of, IV 726; V 137 sq.; 145

Witte, Count Sergius Julievich de, Russian Minister of Finance, XII 323 sqq.; agricultural committees of, 328 sq.; 330; and reform, 348; 350; 358; administration of, 359 sqq.; dismissed, 365; 376; 379; negotiates peace with Japan, 600 sq.

—— de With, Vice-Admiral Witte Corneliszoon de, succeeds Van Tromp, IV 473; in the Texel, 476; 478; Christian IV and, 572; at the battle of the Downs, 700; 703; 726; defeat of, at the Reciff, 753; V 147

Wittelsbach, the House of, the anti-national policy of, I 296; disputes between branches of, 315; V 621; IX 582. See also Bavaria and the Palatinate

Wittenberg, Luther in, II 117–23, 167; "Wittenberg Concord" (1536), 234, 339; "Wittenberg Reformation," 250; surrender of (1547), 261; University of, founded (1502), 117; V 624, 670, X 355; Stanislaus Orzechowski at University of, III 67; Poles at, 78, 723; IV 201; Swedes advance to, 204; VI 265; 273; Frederick II and, 704; Napoleon's decree from (1806), IX 278; Schill at, 357; Eugene at, 514

—— Arvid, marches towards Warsaw, IV 581 sq.

Wittenweier, battle of (1638), IV 376 sq.

Wittgenstein, Louis Adolph, Prince of Sayn, Russian field-marshal, IX 501; pursues Grand Army, 511 sqq.; at Gross-Görschen, 517; at Bautzen, 518; replaced by Barclay, 520; at Liebertwolkwitz, 534

—— Wilhelm Ludwig Georg, Prince of Sayn, Prussian statesman, X 350; 352; 366; 377

Witthoft, Russian admiral, at Port Arthur, XII 588 sqq.

Wittstock, victory of Banér at (1636), IV 372, 374

Witu, Germany and, XII 167; 661

Witwatersrand, mines of, XII 639

Witzleben, Job von, Prussian general, V 350; X 350

Wladislav. See Ladislaus

Wobersnow, General von, VI 291

Wodehouse, Lord. See Kimberley, Earl of

Wodzicki, Count Ludwik, Polish writer, XI 660

Wöhler, Friedrich, German chemist, XII 770

Wölflin, Heinrich (Lupulus), Swiss humanist, II 307

Wöllner, Johann Christoph von, Prussian statesman, VI 726 sq.

Woerden, attack on (1672), V 160

Wörth, Allies at (1793), VIII 425; evacuated, 427 sq.; battle of, XI 584 sq., 587, 595

Wohlau, principality of, V 652; 659; duchy of, VI 229

Wohlgemuth, Baron Ludwig von, Austrian general, XI 206; defeats Görgei, 210; in Transylvania, 215, 217

Wolf, Frederick Augustus, German philologer, influence of, IX 326; 327; XII 819 sqq.; 823

—— Rudolf, Swiss astronomer, XI 260

Wolfe, David, Irish Jesuit, II 583; III 592; arrives at Cork, 593

—— James, General, VI 342b (in Vol. XIII); VII 132 sq., 137

Wolfenbüttel, defence of, against the Schmalkaldic League, II 243; IV 70; Christian IV at, 96 sq.; 102; Imperialists at, 385 sq. See also Brunswick-Wolfenbüttel

Wolff, Christian, expelled from Halle, V 760; VIII 772; X 384; 410

—— Sir Henry Drummond, British Minister at Teheran, XII 45, 492; in Egypt, 445

—— Joseph, at Bokhara, XII 801

—— Julius, German poet, XI 413

—— Father, Jesuit (Baron F. von Lüdinghausen), V 663; 665; 671

Wolfgang of Bavaria. See Bavaria-Munich

Wolgast, V 611; the Great Elector at, 639

Wollaston, William Hyde, man of science, XII 782

Wollemborg, Leone, and Casse Rurali, XII 237

Wollstonecraft (Godwin), Mary, VIII 758, 765, 790; Vindication of the Rights of Women, XII 762

Wolmar, Melchior, Lutheran, II 291, 351, 352

Wolowski, Louis - François - Michel - Raymond, French politician, XI 109; 111

Wolseley, Garnet Joseph Wolseley, Viscount, in Canada, XI 777; in Egypt, XII 40, 437, 442; 441

—— William, Brigadier-general, V 313

Wolsey, Thomas, Cardinal and Archbishop of York, I 323 sq., 336; Chap. XIV, ii passim, 645 sq.; II 22, 42–5, 147, 416–35; fall of, 432; death and character of, 435; 490; III 737

Wolverhampton, Henry H. Fowler, Viscount, XII 493

Wongrowa, Polish malcontents at, VI 195

Wood, Anthony, antiquary, VI 797

—— Benjamin, IV 729

—— Sir Charles. See Halifax, Viscount

—— Fernando, American politician, VII 576

—— Sir Henry Evelyn, Sirdar of the Egyptian army, XII 440; 447

—— John, Asiatic traveller, XII 800 sq.

—— Robert, Under-Secretary of State, VI 432

—— William, Survey of Trade, V 378

—— William, and Irish coinage, VI 47; 80; 484 sq.

Woodfall, Henry Sampson, printer of Letters of Junius, VI 441

Woodford, General, U.S. Minister to Spain, VII 677 sq.

Woodville, Lord. *See* Scales, Lord, *and* Rivers, Lord

Woodward, John, geologist, v 738

Wool, John Ellis, American general, VII 396, 455; occupies Norfolk (Virginia), 474

Wooler, Government force at, VI 101

—— Thomas J., political writer, x 579

Woolwich, defence of, v 189

Woosung, capture of, XI 809

Worcester, occupied by Essex, IV 307; King at, 323; 331 sq.; 335; victory of Cromwell at (1651), 436, 510

Worden, John Lorimer, American admiral, VII 561 sq.

Wordsworth, William, VI 824 sqq.; 833 sq.; 836 sq.; VIII 641, 765 sq., 768; x 703 sqq.; 713 sq.; Keats and, 720 sq.; 722 sqq.; XI 347 sqq.

Working Man's Association, x 682 sq.

Worms, Diet of (1495), I 303 sqq., (1497), 306 sq.; Edict of, 305 sq.; Diet of (1521), II 42, Luther at the, 139 sq., 146 sq., reforms instituted at the, 149, 151 sq., the Edict of, 158; Vergerio's oration at (1540), 394; (1545), 80, 250, 662; printing press established in, 139; statue of Luther at, 208; Conference at (1540), 239, 645; Colloquy of (1557), 568, III 162-3; *Deputationstag* at, 704; forces of Union at, IV 66 sq.; 84; Convention (1635), 249; Oxenstierna at, 251; captured by Turenne, 389; 597; sacked (1689), v 56; Pragmatic army at, VI 238; Treaty of (1743), 239; 608; occupied by the French (1792), VIII 414; evacuated (1793), 415; Brunswick evacuates, 428

Woronzoff, Count Michael, Russian ambassador, VIII 283

—— Count Simon, Russian diplomatist, IX 256; 270

Wotton, Sir Henry, v 118

—— Dr Nicholas, secretary to Northumberland, II 496; 513, 518, 526, 530, 571, 580

Wrangel, Count Friedrich von, Prussian general, XI 162; 167; 188; occupies Berlin, 193; in Schleswig-Holstein, 440

—— Hermann, Swedish Marshal, in Prussia, IV 186; invades Brandenburg, 372 sqq.

—— Karl Gustaf, Count of Sylfnitzburg, Swedish general, IV 386; carries on Danish War, 388; succeeds in Swedish command, 390 sqq.; at Kolberg Heath, 571; captures Bornholm, 572; 580; in Denmark, 584 sqq.; 591; v 147; 568

—— Swedish general (1740), VI 760

—— Island, discovered, XII 795

Wratislaw, Count Johann Wenzel, Austrian ambassador at the Hague, v 398; 432

Wrede, Karl Philipp, Prince von, Bavarian field-marshal, IX 355; near Hanau, 540;

besieges Hüningen, 544; at La Rothière, 545; at Congress of Vienna, 587, 597, 609 sqq.; unpopularity of, 658; x 146; 343

Wrede, Karl Theodor, Prince, XI 146

Wren, Sir Christopher, v 713

—— Matthew, VI 797

Wrexham, Royalists at, IV 540

Wright, Abraham, VI 798

—— Horatio Gouverneur, American general, VII 531, 538

—— Captain John Wesley, IX 29; death of (1804), 761

Wriothesley, Thomas, Earl of Southampton. *See* Southampton

Wrisberg, Christopher von, II 251, 261

Wuchang, captured by the "Taipings," XI 820

Würgen, Charles XII at, v 592

Würtemberg, Habsburgs driven out of (1534), II 68; religious disturbances in, III 723 sq.; IV 4; depopulation of, 418; agricultural conditions in, 419; government of, 424; French invasion of (1707), v 418; 762; and Austrian Succession, VI 228; and Treaty of Füssen, 242; 246; and Diet of Ratisbon (1803), IX 94; the Church in, 201; joins France (1805), 253; 262; proposals of Metternich to, 507; and Congress of Vienna, 587; 609 sqq., 649, 651; appeals to the Tsar Alexander I, x 22; relations of Papacy with, 148; and German unity, 342 sq.; and the Germanic Confederation, 344, XI 222 sq.; and the Liberals, x 347, 358; constitutional concessions in, 360; reactionary policy of William I in, 361; and Conference at Vienna (1819), 368; and the *Triasidee*, 369; and the Congresses, *ib.*; and the customs treaties, 372 sq., XI 462; x 374; supports Hanoverian opposition, 380; literature in, 406; XI 60 sq.; revolutionary movement in, 148, 152; and Frankfort Constitution, 218; 221; and Austro-Prussian War, 457; and North German Confederation, 460, 464 sq.; and Franco-German War, 464; and Papacy, 708

—— House of, III 704; and Peace of Westphalia, IV 409

—— Christopher, Duke of, II 220, 266, 276, 587 sq.; III 154, 158-9, 162, 164, 167-8, 173, 210

—— Duke Eberhard of, at Strassburg, IV 245; and the Peace of Prague, 254

—— Duke Eugene of, IX 50; 275; 277; at Priesten, 528; at Leipzig, 535-6

—— Duke Ferdinand William of, in Ireland, v 314, 316

—— Frederick I, Duke of, III 714, 725

—— Frederick II, Duke of (Elector since 1803), recognised as King (Frederick I, 1806), IX 262

—— Duke John Frederick of, IV 67; agrees to abandon Frederick of Bohemia, 69; 80

Würtemberg, Duke Magnus of, with Margrave George Frederick of Baden, IV 80
—— Sophia of. *See* Maria Feodorovna
—— Ulric VI, Duke of, I 321 sq.; evicted, II 41; attempts to recover his duchy, 146, 181; 169, 177; Peasants' Rising and, 220; restoration of, 221; 234, 241; surrenders to Charles V (1547), 258, 323–35
—— Duke Ulric of, march of, on Paris (1652), IV 617
—— Ferdinand, Prince of (1815), X 462
—— William, Crown Prince of, at Montereau, IX 549; at Sainte-Croix, 553; affianced to Grand Duchess Catharine of Russia, 581; patriotism of, 582; at Congress of Vienna, 610
Würzburg, surrender of (1525), II 190; the see of, III 709; Catholic League at (1610), 729, IV 32, 100; Tilly repulsed at, 208; civil administration of, 208; Horn at, 213; capitulation of, 245; Jourdan captures, VIII 497; Jourdan repulsed at, *ib.*; magazine at, IX 252; Elector of Bavaria at, 253; Bernadotte marches to (1805), *ib.*; feudal rights in, relinquished by Austria, 262; acquisition of, by Bavaria (1815), 658
Würzburg, Bishops of:—
—— Conrad III von Thuenguen, attacked by peasants, II 188
—— Frederick von Wirsberg, III 161
—— Julius Echter von Mespelbronn, III 176, 709, 729
—— Melchior von Zobel, III 151
—— Philipp Adolf von Ehrenberg, IV 210, 423; V 758
—— Rudolf von Scherenburg, I 675
Wuhu, opened to foreign trade, XII 502
Wulffen, Luben von, and peasant tenures in Prussia, V 670
Wullenwever, Jürgen, of Lübeck, II 228–31, 614 sq.
Wurmb, Prussian Privy Councillor, VI 721
Wurmser, Count Dagobert Sigmund von, Austrian field-marshal, VIII 415, 419, 423 sqq., 428, 442 sq.; in Italy (1796), 572 sqq., 578 sq.
Wurzach, defeat of peasants at (1525), II 182
Wusung river, Japanese vessels on, XII 512
Wyatt, Sir Thomas (the elder), ambassador in Spain, II 449; III 365
—— Sir Thomas (the younger), II 518; heads insurrection against Mary, 527; execution of, 528
Wyburd, Lieutenant, at Bokhara, XII 801
Wych, Sir Cyril, English Minister at St Petersburg, VI 315
Wycherley, William, dramatist, V 128; 130
Wyel, Alard, of Cologne, editor of the *Magna Bibliotheca*, I 618
Wyke, Sir Charles Lennox, British envoy in Mexico, XI 565

Wylie, James, physician to the Tsar, at Tilsit, IX 298; X 439
Wyndham, George, Secretary for Ireland, XII 61; 90
—— Sir William, V 475; VI 71
Wynendael, French defeated at (1708), V 422
Wynn, Charles Watkin Williams, X 574
Wyoming, part of, ceded to the United States, VII 397; women's franchise in, XII 763
—— valley, punitive expedition to, VII 220
Wynter, Edward, III 301
—— Sir William, English admiral, in the Forth, II 576; III 265; 298; and the Armada, 309, 313
Wyse, Bonaparte, and the Panama Canal, XII 698
—— Thomas, of Waterford, X 627
Wysocki, Joseph, Polish general, XI 207
Wyttenbach, Thomas, Swiss Reformer, II 307, 327

"X, Y, Z despatches," The, VII 321
Xanten, Treaty of (1614), III 643, 733, IV 10, 13, V 637
Xavier, Candido José, X 327; 330
—— Francis. *See* Francis Xavier (Saint)
Ximenez, Francisco Ximenez de Cisneros, Cardinal Archbishop of Toledo, I 355; 860 sqq., 380, 578, 625, 650 sq.; ecclesiastical reforms of, II 399 sq., 646; as Inquisitor, 650

Y, estuary of the, XII 249
Yadkin, Greene crosses the, VII 228
Yaguzhinsky, Paul Ivanovich, Russian Procurator-General, V 546; 549; 556; Russian ambassador at Berlin, VI 302
Yahuarpampa, victory of Peruvians at, I 45
Yakub Khan, Amir of Afghánistán, XII 465; 470 sq.; 502 sq.
Yakushkin, Ivan, Russian officer, X 432; 442
Yakutsk, XII 794; explorers at, 795
Yale College, VII 741
Yalu river, XII 510; Chinese retreat across, 511; 522; 576 sq.; Russo-Japanese War on, 580 sq., 583 sqq.
Yamagata, Chōshiu leader, XI 852; 865
Yamaguchi, fortress of, XI 852
Yamassee Indians, The, VII 38
Yamuish, Lake, Russian expedition to, V 544
Yanaon, France and, VI 347
Yancey, William Lowndes, Confederate senator, VII 605
Yandabu, Treaty of, XI 728
Yangtsun, Boxers at, XII 519 sq.
Yang-tsze-kiang river, XI 809; XII 505; 512; Great Britain and, 514; 517; 596; exploration of, 797 sqq.; 803
Yanza river, hospital on, V 531

Yar Mohammad, intrigues with Persia, xi 733

Yara, rising at, xii 264

Yarkand, caravan route to, xii 793; travellers at, 800 sq.

Yarmouth, troops at, v 194 sqq.; mutiny at (1797), viii 479; English fleet at, ix 51; Gambier sails from, 236

—— Amalie Sophie Marianne Wallmoden, Countess of, vi 42; 76; 403

—— Lord. *See* Hertford, Francis Charles Seymour-Conway, 3rd Marquis of

Yates, Robert, New York deputy at Constitutional Convention, vii 246, 264

Yavorsky, Stephen, Archbishop of Ryazán. *See* Ryazán

Yaytse (Jajce), captured by Turks (1463), i 73; retained by Hungary (1464), *ib.*; captured by Turks (1528), 97; captured by Austrians, xii 400

Yeardley, George, Governor of Virginia, vii 6

Yedo, Vol. xi, Chap. xxviii (2) *passim*

Yeh, Commissioner at Canton, xi 815 sq.

—— Chinese general, xii 511

Yeh-ho-na-la, Chinese Empress, xii 504

Yellow Sea, engagement in, xii 580

Yelverton, Barry. *See* Avonmore, Viscount

Yemen, accepts Solyman's overlordship, iii 117

Yenikale, Russia and, vi 634, 674

Yenisei river, xii 794; exploration on, 795

Yeniseisk, founded by Cossacks, xii 794

Yenishehr, victory of Selim I over Ahmad at (1513), i 90

Yeo, Sir James Lucas, British naval captain, vii 341

Yermoloff, Alexis Petrowitch, Russian general, at Borodino, ix 495; attacks French, 503; x 441

Yermóloff, Russian Minister of Agriculture, xii 351

Yezd, English travellers at, xii 800

Yezo, island of, seized by rebels, xi 860; Russia and, xii 574 sq.

Yilgarn, gold discovered at, xii 619

Yingkow, xii 511; 586 sq.; secured by the Japanese, 589 sq.; 596

Ymuiden, harbour of, xi 666

Yokohama, American expedition at, xi 829; 833; opened to trade, 840 sq.; 842; 845; 848; port of, 850 sq., 859; foreign residents in, xii 542; the *Maria Luz* at, 554

Yola, Barth at, xii 810

Yonézawa clan, xi 859

Yonge, Charlotte Mary, novelist, xi 360

—— Sir George, in Cape Colony, ix 750

Yonne, Paul Bert elected for, xii 105

Yoritomo, xi 826

York, conference on Mary Stewart's case at (1568), iii 278; Council of Peers at (1640), iv 285; 301; 311; Newcastle at, 308, 315, 321; v 229; taken by Earl of

Danby (1688), 246; Jacobite trials at, vi 117

York, Anne Hyde, Duchess of, v 211

—— Frederick, Duke of. *See* Frederick Augustus, Duke of York and Albany

—— James, Duke of. *See* James II, King of England

—— Richard Plantagenet, Duke of, i 465

—— Cardinal of. *See* Stewart, Henry Benedict

—— Governor of Zutphen (1586), iii 622

—— von Wartenburg, Hans David Ludwig, Count, Prussian field-marshal, ix 332; concludes Convention of Tauroggen, 505; commander of Prussian corps, 510 sqq.; Governor-General of East and West Prussia, 513; marches on Magdeburg, 514; at Bautzen, 518; relations of, with Blücher, 524; at Möckern, 537; at Leipzig, 539; harasses French retreat, 540; at Châlons, 547; at Laon, 551

—— (Maine), settlement at, vii 22

Yorke, Charles, Lord Chancellor, vi 435 sqq.; 443

—— Sir Joseph (Lord Dover), major-general, vi 278; British Minister at the Hague, 343, vii 234

Yorkshire, conspiracy in (1541), ii 452; Charles I in, iv 305; attitude of, towards Civil War, 308; 313 sq.; 320 sqq.; 332; Royalist risings in, 441, 548; General Wade in, vi 114; Reform meetings in, 455; 504; spinning and weaving in, x 735 sq.

Yorktown (Virginia), capitulation of (1781), vi 456, vii 230 sq., viii 92; capture of (1862), vii 474 sq.

Yoshimuné, Prince of Kishiu, xi 825

Youghal, duty on wines unshipped at, iii 594; sacked by Desmond (1579), 597

Young, Arthur, observations of, in France, viii 21, 40, 53, 57, 60, 62 sq., 170; *Travels*, 756; 762; and English food supply, ix 691; and Irish Union, 702; the writings of, x 782 sq.

—— Edward, poet, vi 828; x 697 sq.; xi 422

—— Sir John. *See* Lisgar, Lord

—— Thomas, and the theory of light, xii 782

—— Thomas, Egyptologist, xii 845

Young Italy, aims and methods of the union of, x 121-2; journal, 127

Younghusband, Sir Francis Edward, mission of, to Tibet, xii 490; in Central Asia, 798, 802 sqq.

Youri, explorers at, xii 807 sq.

Youssouf Izz-ed-din, xi 637

Ypres, growth of industrial importance of, i 425; Calvinists at, iii 205; iconoclastic riot at (1566), 208; ceded to France, v 45; 63; captured by French (1678), 164, 219; Barrier Treaties and, 457 sqq.; taken by Marshal Saxe, vi 240; 339; capture of (1794), viii 435

Ypres, Bishop of, III 219 sq.
Ypsilanti, Prince Alexander, IX 581; relations of, with Alexander I, 654; invades Moldavia, X 30; rising and defeat of, 178 sq.
—— Demetrios, X 181
Yssel river, abolition of tolls on, XI 664
Ystad, Danish force lands at, V 569
Yuan Shikai, Chinese commander, XII 523
Yucatan, reached by Spaniards, I 41, 43; peninsula of, V 687; administration of, X 248
Yukon district, XI 633, 776
Yunnan, opened to French traders, XII 132; Mussulman rebellion in, 500, 502; 506; French exploration in, 524; 526; 536; caravan route through, 793; travellers in, 796 sq., 803
Yuriev. *See* Dorpat
Yuste, Charles V retires to, II 90
Yverdun, Pestalozzi's school at, IX 326, 427

Zaandam, first saw-mill erected at (1596), III 631
Zabala, Juan de, Marquis of Sierra Bullones, Spanish general, XI 569
Zabergrund, ravine of, VI 283 sqq.
Zabern, captured by peasants (1525), II 182; occupied by French, IV 144; Gallas in, 368; siege of (1636), 370
Zablat, Mansfeld routed at (1619), IV 27
Zaccaria, Antonio, founder of Barnabites, II 648
Zachariä von Lingenthal, Carl Eduard, XII 845
Zacharias, Pope (741–52), MSS of, in Vatican Library, I 552
Zagréb. *See* Agram
Zaikonnospasky monastery, V 519
Zaïmes, Cretan High Commissioner, XII 424
Zaisan lake, explorers at, XII 799
Zajechar, Servian check at, XII 386
Zakrevski, Arsenij, Governor-General of Finland, X 435
Zalaszowska, Catharine, III 74
Zaluski, Andrew Chrysostom, Bishop of Warmia. *See* Warmia
—— Joseph, Bishop of Kijow, and Andreas, Bishop of Cracow, library of, X 431, 449
Zamán Shah, leader of Afghans, IX 724
Zambesi river, Portugal and, XII 3; 663 sq.; Livingstone on, 808
Zambolim, acquisition of, by Portuguese, IX 718
Zamboni, Luigi, leader of Jacobin plot in Bologna, VIII 557
Zambra. *See* Prevost
Zamora, Alonzo Osorio de Acuña, Bishop of, leads revolt of *Comuneros*, I 374
—— Alfonso de, Hebraist, II 400
Zamorin, The, of Calicut, Da Gama and, I 26, 29 sq.

Zamosz, stormed by Poniatowski (1809), IX 354; surrender of fortress of (1831), X 473
Zamoyski *or* Zamoiski, Count Andrzej (Andrew), XI 628; writings of, 657, 659
—— Jan, Chancellor of Poland, III 85 sqq., 99, 101; arrests Samuel Zborowski, 102, 698; election of Sigismund and, IV 168; 174; conquers Moldavia, 188; death of, 175, 189
Zanardelli, Joseph, Italian Minister of Public Works, XII 214; 222 sq.; 225
Zancani, Andrea, Venetian envoy to Turks, I 87
Zanchi, Girolamo, Italian Reformer, II 391, 716
Zanella, Giacomo, Italian poet, XI 547
Zanivki, Napoleon at, IX 503
Zante, returned to Venice by the Turks (1485), I 81
Zanzibar, XII 47; annexed by Great Britain, 130; Germany and, 166; Great Britain and, 658; 660; partition of, 661; 662; explorers in, 809; 812
Zapata, Francesco, III 586
Zapoli, negotiations between Muscovy and Poland at (1581–2), III 101
Zápolya, John. *See* John Zápolya, King of Hungary
—— John Sigismund. *See* John Sigismund Zápolya
—— Stephen, I 336
Zaporogia, Russia and, V 506
Zara, recovery of, by Venetians, I 255
Zariategui, Juan Antonio, Carlist general, X 239
Zarubeieff, Russian general, defeated at Ta-shih-chiao, XII 589
Zarutski, Cossack leader, V 502
Zasius, Ulrich, German jurist, I 637
Zastrow, Heinrich Adolf von, German general, XI 587
—— Prussian general, IX 281–2, 287, 289
Zasúlich, Vera, attacks General Trépoff, XII 305
Zasulich, lieutenant-general, in Russo-Japanese War, XII 583 sqq., 587
Zayonch, Joseph, general, Viceroy of Poland, X 448
Zbaski, Abraham, III 74
Zborowski, House of, opposes Stephen Báthory, III 101 sq.
—— Christopher, banished (1586), III 102
—— Peter, Castellan of Sandomir, III 84
—— Samuel, III 89; tried and executed (1584), 103
—— Marshal, III 102
Zealand, Torstensson in, IV 387; 561; struggle between Danes and Swedes in, 584 sq., 587, 589; Charles XII invades (1700), V 581; Russo-Danish army in (1716), 612; British operations in (1807), IX 236, 299–300

Zealand, Hans Svane, Bishop of, v 559
Zeehan, silver discovered at, xii 619
Zeeland, growth of towns of, i 420; revolt in, iii 230, 242; Act of Union between Holland and (1576), 243; Countship of, accepted by Orange (1584), 617; Province of, 618; wealth of, 620; freed from Spaniards, 629; condition of, 630–1; trading companies of, 632–3; 642, 644; represented at Münster, iv 401, 715; 473; 691; 694; naval enthusiasm of, 700; William II of Orange and, 724; French force defeated in (1672), v 43; 148; and Eternal Edict, 155 sq.; William III of Orange and States of, 156 sq.; vi 247; serfdom in, 736; Province of, proposes separation, viii 286
Zehdenick, French army at, ix 279
Zehngerichten, iv 35 sq.; votes for the Venetian alliance, 42; 55
Zeissberg, Heinrich, Ritter von, German historian, xii 829
Zeitz, Austrians in, vi 297; Miloradovitch at, ix 518
Zekki Pasha, and the Armenian massacres, xii 416
Zekko, Mollah, Albanian leader, xii 425
Zelanti, The, in Conclave of 1740, vi 589; attacks Napoleon's Concordat (1814), x 139 sq.
Zell, Matthew, German Reformer, ii 160, 162
Zeller, Christopher, iv 76
—— Eduard, German historian, xii 845
—— disciple of Pestalozzi, starts school in Königsberg, ix 326
Zellweger, family of, vi 625
Zelo domus Dei, Innocent X's Bull, iv 415; 688
Zemshchina, Russian administrative sphere instituted by Ivan IV, v 490 sq.
Zemstva, Russian County Councils, created (1864), xii 295; begin work, 299; Conference of 1878, 306; 311; *see* Chaps. xii and xiii *passim,* 294–380
Zemstvo, Russian journal, xii 309
Zenete, Marquis of, suppresses revolt in Valencia, i 377
Zeno, Antonio, Venetian commander in Greece, v 365
—— Carlo, Venetian admiral, i 259
—— Renier, iv 40
Zenta, battle of (1697), v 61, 370
Zentner, Freiherr G. F. von, Bavarian Minister, x 359; opposes Metternich, 368; 370
Zerafshan, ceded to Russia, xi 631
Zerbold, Gerard, of Zutphen, Dutch mystic, i 627; ii 657
Zerboni di Sposetti, Joseph, Governor of Posen, x 463 sq.
Zernez, the Preachers at, iv 46; 58
Zerotin *or* Zierotin, Karl von, iii 721, 726; moderate policy of, iv 22; debt of Habsburgs to, 28; 74

Zeta valley, Turkish reverse in, xii 389
Zeuss, Johann Caspar, German philologer, xii 822
Zevenbergen, Maximilian von, Minister of Charles V, ii 145 sq.
Zhelyáboff, Russian revolutionary, xii 307 sq.; 310 sq.
Zhukovsky, Vasili, tutor to Tsar Alexander II, xi 613
Zicher, Russians at, vi 284
Zichy-Vásonykeö, Count Ferdinand, Military Commandant at Venice, xi 82; 203
Ziegler, Jakob, Lutheran scholar, ii 380
—— Swiss Federal officer, xi 251
Zierickzee, siege of, by Mondragon (1575–6), iii 242, 244; retaken from the Spaniards (1577), 247; capitulates to the British (1809), ix 358
Ziethen, Hans Joachim von, Prussian general, vi 261; 296
—— Count Hans Ernst Karl von, general, retreat of, ix 625–6; 631; at Waterloo, 638, 640
Zinzendorf, Count Nicolas Ludwig von, v 762
Zips, The, vi 630; Austria and, 669 sq.; 730
Ziska, John, leader of the Hussites, i 331; ii 175
Ziskaberg, Austrian force on, vi 257
Zittau, Austrian force at, vi 262
Zittel, Karl, Baden politician, xi 60
Znaim, Wallenstein at, iv 212 sq.; Austrian army in, vi 233 sq.; retreat of Kutusoff to (1805), ix 257; fighting at (1809), 353; armistice of, 354; 356–7
Zobeir Pasha, xii 439; Gordon and, 441 sq.
Zobel, Melchior von, Bishop of Würzburg. *See* Würzburg
Zodiacus Vitae, by Angelo Manzioli, ii 384
Zöllner, Prussian Court Chaplain, vi 727
Zola, Émile-E.-C.-A., xii 120; 126
Zolkievski, Polish commander, iv 176; expels Cossacks from the Ukraine, 188; death of, 189
Zollern, Counts of, v 622
Zollicoffer, Felix Kirk, vii 462 sq., 495
Zollverein, The (German Customs' Union), beginnings of, x 372 sq.; transformation of, from Prussian into German, 378 sq.; 752; and trade with Great Britain, xi 15; 28; 47; accession of Luxemburg and Brunswick to, 53 sq.; in Saxony, 59; 63; progress of, after 1848, 393 sqq.; 443; renewed (1864), 444; and Italy, 447; North German Confederation and, 461 sq.; and China, 819
Zorbás, Colonel, and Greek "Military League," xii 422
Zorndorf, vi 281 sq.; battle of, 283 sqq., 290, 292, 295, 322
Zornosa, battle of (1808), ix 443
Zorrilla, José, x 241
—— Ruiz, Spanish statesman, xii 259 sq.
Zoutman, Admiral, in North Sea, vi 452

Zoutpansberg, Boers at, xi 781; 785; 787

Zrinyi, Countess Helen, marriage of, v 351, 358; 367

—— Nicholas, defends Szigeth (1566), iii 126

—— Count Niklas, Ban of Croatia, v 347; 351

—— Count Peter, and Hungarian conspiracy, v 351 sqq.

Zschinsky, Ferdinand von, Saxon statesman, xi 219

Zschokke, Johann Heinrich Daniel, ix 427; xi 239

Zsitva-Torok, Peace of (1606), iii 701, 720 sq., 726, iv 8, 11, v 342

Zubátoff, Moscow police official, xii 331; 349

Zubiaur, Spanish vice-admiral, iii 532-3

Zuboff, Nicholas, ix 35, 49 sq.

—— Platon, ix 34-5, 49-50

Züllichau, Prussian army at, vi 291 sq.

Zug, canton of, vi 613; town of, 625; xi 234; 244; and the Aargau monasteries, 247; 251

—— Lake, French routed at (1798), viii 640

Zuiderzee, The, Spaniards in, iii 626; trade of, 631; department of, ix 417

Zulfikar, Abdurrahman and, xii 478

Zululand, xii 636; Boers in, 638; 640; annexed to Natal, 645

Zulus, xi 781; defeated by Boers, 782; war of, with Great Britain, xii 35, 636

Zumalacarregui, Tomás, Carlist general, x 234 sq.

Zumel, Dr, proctor of Burgos, leader of Cortes, i 370, 374

Zuñiga, Baltazar de, at Linz, iv 11; and Madrid negotiations (1620), 53; 637 sq.

—— Caspar de, Cardinal Archbishop of Seville, iii 283

—— Don Diego de, ambassador to France (1572), iii 20

—— Diego Lopez de, theologian, attacks Erasmus, ii 400 sq.; 699

Zurara, Gomez Eaunes de, Portuguese chronicler, i 15 sq.

Zurawna, Treaty of (1676), v 41, 45, 355 sq.

Zurbano, Martin, Customs Inspector at Barcelona, x 242

Zurbaran, Francisco, art of, iv 664

Zurich, the Peasants' Rising and, ii 179; Chap. x *passim*; Reformation in, 313; First Disputation at (1523), 317; Second (1523), 319; Conference of Reformers at, 359; heresy in, iii 402, 405; 408; and Spanish Alliance, iv 45; appeal of the *Bund* to, 50; 52; canton of, vi 613 sqq., 619, 622; town of, 625; battle of (1799), viii 661, 663, 674, ix 96; Federation of, 100; Fichte at, 325; dissatisfaction in (1804), 424; manufactures of, 425; Diet at (1813), 426; Society of Public Utility founded at, 427; and Congress

of Vienna, 600-1; xi 234; Federal Pact confirmed at, 236; 237; reaction in, 238; 240; joins *Siebnerkonkordat*, 242; University of, 241, xii 303, 762; xi 242; Federal Diet at, 243 sq.; Protestant rising in, 246; 247; and the *Sonderbund*, 248; 254; 257; industries of, 259; 260; Treaty of (1859), iv 63, xi 385

Zurlauben, family of, vi 625

Zurleder, Bernese deputy at Congress of Vienna, ix 600

Zurlo, Giuseppe, President of Neapolitan Feudal Commission, ix 406

Zusmarshausen, death of Melander at, iv 393

Zutphen, acquired by Charles the Bold, i 390; cession of the county of, to Charles V, ii 77; sack of (1572), iii 234-5; Parma at, 257; surrender of, 622; siege of (1591), 626

Zuylen van Nyevelt, Baron Jacobus Petrus van, Dutch statesman, xi 666

Zweibrücken, House of, Charles X heir of, iv 578

—— Adolphus John, Count Palatine of. *See* Adolphus John

—— Charles (II) Duke of (of Birkenfeld), vi 631; 633; and exchange of Bavaria, 647; 703; viii 300; 539

—— John I, Count Palatine and Duke of, iii 687, 712, 714, 716

—— John II, Count Palatine and Duke of, claimant for Jülich-Cleves succession, iii 725, 730, 734

—— John Casimir I, Count Palatine of (d. 1592), iii 10, 26, 29 sqq., 173 sqq., 249 sq., 703-4, 707-8, 710-2; death of, 713

—— John Casimir II, Count Palatine of, iv 182; at Stockholm, 191; 568; 575 sq.; Oxenstierna and, 577

—— Magdalena, Countess Palatine and Duchess of, iii 716

—— Wolfgang, Count Palatine and Duke of, iii 12

Zwettel, taken by Thurn, iv 25

Zwilling, Gabriel, Reformer, ii 161, 165, 167

Zwingli, Bartholomew, ii 307

—— Huldreich, ii 160, 179, 216, 306; at Conference of Marburg, 207-10, 333 sq.; statement of belief by, 212; education of, 307 sq.; poems of, 309; visits Italy, 309; comparison of, with Erasmus and Luther, 309 sq.; at Zurich, 310-5; *Archeteles*, 316; other writings of, 318 sq., 320 sq.; difficulties of, with Anabaptists, 322 sq.; at Disputation of Bern, 327; 332-40; *Fidei Ratio*, 335; contrast between Luther and, 345 sq.; 715; death of, at Kappel, 216, 337; iv 36; vi 619

Zwinglians, Vol. ii, Chap. x, The Helvetic Reformation, *passim*, 305-41; distribution of, in modern Switzerland, xi 234. *See also* Zwingli

CAMBRIDGE: PRINTED BY
W. LEWIS, M.A.
AT THE UNIVERSITY PRESS